THE OXFORD HANDBOOK OF

LANGUAGE

CONTACT

Edited by

ANTHONY P. GRANT

OXFORD

UNIVERSITY PRESS

OXFORD
UNIVERSITY PRESS

Oxford University Press is a department of the University of Oxford. It furthers
the University's objective of excellence in research, scholarship, and education
by publishing worldwide. Oxford is a registered trade mark of Oxford University
Press in the UK and certain other countries.

Published in the United States of America by Oxford University Press
198 Madison Avenue, New York, NY 10016, United States of America.

Library of Congress Cataloging-in-Publication Data
Names: Grant, Anthony, 1962– editor.
Title: The Oxford handbook of language contact / edited by Anthony Grant.
Description: New York, NY : Oxford University Press, [2019] | Includes bibliographical references and index.
Identifiers: LCCN 2018033666 (print) | LCCN 2018042700 (ebook)
| ISBN 9780199984015 (online content) | ISBN 9780199945108 (updf) | ISBN 9780190876906 (epub)
| ISBN 9780199945092 | ISBN 9780199945092(cloth :alk. paper)
Subjects: LCSH: Languages in contact. | Language and languages–Variation. | Linguistic change.
Classification: LCC P130.5 (ebook) | LCC P130.5 .O94 2019 (print) | DDC 306.44/6–dc23
LC record available at https://lccn.loc.gov/2018033666

1 3 5 7 9 8 6 4 2

Printed by Sheridan Books, Inc., United States of America

Contents

PART I LANGUAGE CONTACT AND LINGUISTIC THEORY

PART II LANGUAGE CONTACT IN SEVERAL LANGUAGES

LIST OF FIGURES

LIST OF MAPS

LIST OF TABLES

ABBREVIATIONS

1	first person
2	second person
3	third person
3P	third person plural
3S	third person singular
ABLl	ablative
ABS	absolutive
ACC	accusative
ADVZ	adverbializer
ALL	allative
ANAPH	anaphora
ANIM	animate
AOR	aorist
Arab., Arb.	Arabic
Aram.	Aramaic
ART	article
ASRT	assertive
ASSOC	associative
ASSOC.PL	associative plural
AUG	augmented number
AUX	auxiliary
Azer.	Azerbaijani
c.	common
C	Christian
CAUS	causative
CM	class marker
COLL	collective
COM, COMIT	comitative

COMP	complementizer
COND	conditional
CONJ	conjunction
CONS	consequence clause
CS	change of state
CV	circumstantial voice
DAT	dative
DEF	definite
DEM	demonstrative
DIM	diminutive
DIR	directional marker
DIS	discourse marker
DIST	distal
DOM	differential object marking
DU	dual
EMPH	emphasis
Eng.	English
EPEN	epenthetic
ERG	ergative
EXCL	exclusive
EZ	Ezafe
F	feminine
FOC	focus
FUT	future
GEN	genitive
GENR	general tense/aspect/mood marker
Hb.	Hebrew
HORT	hortative
HYP	hypothetical
I	independent pronoun
I.	Iraqi
IMPF	imperfect
INANIM	inanimate
INCHO	inchoative

INCL	inclusive
INCP	inceptive
IND	indicative
INDF	indefinite
INTERR	interrogative
IPFV	imperfective
IRR	irrealis
J.	Jewish
Kurm.	Kurmanji
LNK	linker
LOC	locative
LOG.SP	speaker logophoric
LVM	loan verb marker
M	masculine
Mal.	Malayalam,
Mar.	Marathi
MIN	minimal number
N	noun
NEG	negative, negation
NMLZ	nominalizer
NOM	nominative
NPST	nonpast
NSP	non-specific
O	object pronoun
OBJ	object
OBLIG	obligative
OBL.PRO	oblique pro-form PAST.REM remote past
PERF	perfective
Per., Pers.	Persian
PERS	personal marker
PFV	perfective
PHR.TRM	phrase terminal
PL	plural
PLD	primary linguistic data

POSS	possessive
PRES	present
PREST	presentative
PRF	perfect
PROGR	progressive
PROX	proximal
PST	past
PUR	purpose
PVB	preverb
Q	Quadriradical
REDUP	reduplication
RFL	reflexive
S	subject pronoun
SBJV	subjunctive
SEQ	sequential
SG	singular
Skt.	Sanskrit
Sor.	Sorani
SP	specific
SPEC	specific article
STG	something
SUB	subordinative
SUBJ	subject
Syr.	Classical Syriac
TOP	topic
TRANS	transitive
TRR	transitivizer
Turk.	Turkish
UV	undergoer voice
USIT	usitative
VOC	vocative
VSO	verb-subject-object

Acknowledgments

I am very grateful to Brian Hurley of Oxford University Press for approaching me to undertake this project and for his assistance in the early stages of its development, to Hallie Stebbins, who continued support of this work so enthusiastically, and to Hannah Doyle and Meredith Keffer who kept it going. I am very grateful to the contributors themselves. I also wish to thank my wife Dr. Margaret A. Taylor for her encouragement, Sophie Ferguson for bibliographic assistance, Kumar Anbazhagan and Dorothy Bauhoff for help with production, Dr. Sarah Irving for invaluable assistance with obtaining research materials, and also to remember the late Martin French, who gave so much encouragement to the project.

Ormskirk and London, May 2018

Contributors

Robert Adam is Director of Continuing Professional Development at the Deafness Cognition and Language Research Centre, University College London. His research interests include sociolinguistics, bilingualism, and Deaf interpreters; his doctoral studies focused on language contact between two sign languages.

Alexandra Y. Aikhenvald is Australian Laureate Fellow, Distinguished Professor, and Director of the Language and Culture Research Centre in the College of Art, Society and Education and the Cairns Institute, James Cook University, Australia. She is an expert on languages and cultures of Amazonia and the Sepik region of Papua New Guinea, in addition to linguistic typology, general linguistics, and a few other areas. Her major publications include grammars of Bare (1995), Warekena (1998), plus *A Grammar of Tariana, from Northwest Amazonia* (Cambridge University Press, 2003), in addition to essays on various typological and areal features of South American languages. Her other major publications, with Oxford University Press, include *Classifiers: A Typology of Noun Categorization Devices* (2000), *Language Contact in Amazonia* (2002), *Evidentiality* (2004), *The Manambu Language from East Sepik, Papua New Guinea,* (2008), *Imperatives and Commands* (2010), *Languages of the Amazon* (2012), *The Art of Grammar* (2015), and *How Gender Shapes the World* (2016). She is the editor of numerous books, among them *The Oxford Handbook of Evidentiality* (Oxford University Press, forthcoming) and co-editor, with R. M. W. Dixon, of *The Cambridge Handbook of Linguistic Typology* (Cambridge University Press).

Ad Backus is Full Professor in the Faculty of Humanities at Tilburg University, Netherlands. He has worked extensively on code-switching and immigrant Turkish, and his major publications include: *Colloquial Turkish* (with Jeroen Aarssen, 1992) and *Two in One: Bilingual Speech of Turkish Immigrants in the Netherlands* (Tilburg University Press, 1996).

Marlyse Baptista has a doctoral degree from Harvard University and is currently a professor of Linguistics in the Linguistics Department and the Department of Afroamerican and African Studies at the University of Michigan. Her works include *The Syntax of Cape Verdean Creole: The Sotavento Varieties* (John Benjamins, 2002) and *Noun Phrases in Creole Languages: A Multi-faceted Approach*, co-edited with Jacqueline Guéron (The Creole Language Library, John Benjamins, 2007).

Joan C. Beal is Professor Emerita at the University of Sheffield and was formerly Director of the National Centre for English Cultural Tradition at the University of Sheffield. Her books include *An Introduction to Regional Englishes* (Edinburgh University Press, 2010) and *English in Modern Times 1700–1945* (Hooder Arnold, 2004).

Oleg Belyaev is a lecturer in the Department of Theoretical and Applied Linguistics, Lomonosov State University, Moscow, and a Research Fellow in the Sector of Typology in the Institute of Linguistics at the Russian Academy of Sciences, and works on Ossetic and Nakh-Dagestanian languages.

Carlos M. Benítez-Torres is finishing his PhD on Tagdal at the University of Leiden. A native of Ponce, Puerto Rico, long resident in Miami, and a member of the Summer Institute of Linguistics, he is currently teaching at Payap University, Chiang Mai, Thailand.

Anna Berge received her PhD in 1997 from the University of California at Berkeley; she then did a Postdoctoral Fellowship at the Institut for Eskimologi in Copenhagen in 1999–2000 and has been working at the Alaska Native Language Center since 2001. She has worked especially with Baffin Island Inuktitut (Inuit Eskimo) and West Greenlandic (Inuit Eskimo) from 1991 to 2002 and with Aleut from 2002 to the present. Since 2005, she has been increasingly interested in comparative studies of the Eskimo-Aleut language family. Her specialties include the interface of syntax and discourse, language documentation and description, and most recently, the prehistory of Aleut and language contact.

Adam A. H. Blaxter Paliwala was born in Port Moresby shortly after Papua New Guinean Independence and grew up in the United Kingdom. After reading English Literature and Social and Political Science at Cambridge University, Adam won a Northcote Graduate Scholarship to continue work on the relationship between Tok Pisin and English in Papua New Guinea at the University of Sydney. Adam lives in London and continues to publish.

Miriam Bouzouita is Professor of Hispanic Linguistics at the Linguistics Department of Ghent University. She has also taught at the University of Cambridge and Queen Mary, University of London. She is active in several research areas, such as Hispanic philology, historical linguistics, dialectology and formal linguistics (Dynamic Syntax). She has published on the development of clitic pronouns, left periphery phenomena, the Latin influence in Biblical translations, and spatial adverbial expressions.

Eleanor Coghill studied Assyriology, Arabic, and Hebrew at the University of Cambridge, before specializing in the study of the endangered dialects of Neo-Aramaic, spoken in Iraq, Turkey, Iran, and Syria. Following a PhD and Junior Research Fellowship, also at Cambridge, she worked on the Cambridge North-Eastern Neo-Aramaic Project, documenting some of the huge dialectal diversity of the language. She has also investigated aspects of change in Aramaic, both short and long term. Between

2010 and 2015 she was at the Zukunftskolleg and Department of Linguistics at the University of Konstanz, leading a project funded by the German Research Council on how the grammar of Neo-Aramaic dialects has been affected by contact with neighboring languages. This was followed by a research position on the Language and Space project at the University of Zürich. As of 2016 she is Professor of Semitic Languages at Uppsala University.

Eva Duran Eppler teaches at Roehampton University and researches in language, code-switching, and power. Her publications include *Language, Society and Power: A Reader* (with Annabelle Mooney, Routledge, 2011), *Emigrants: The Syntax of German-English Code-Switching* (2010, Braumüller) and *English Words and Sentences* (with Gabriel Ozón, 2012, Cambridge University Press).

Mark Faulkner is Ussher Assistant Professor of Mediaeval Studies at Trinity College Dublin, whither he came in 2016 after previous appointments at University College Cork and the University of Sheffield. He has published extensively on Old and Middle English.

Francesco Gardani, PhD in Linguistics (2009), University of Vienna, is currently appointed as a senior postdoctoral researcher in the Department of Linguistics at the University of Zurich. His main areas of research and publication include morphology, contact linguistics, historical linguistics, Romance linguistics, and linguistic typology.

Jorge Gómez Rendón lectures at the Pontificia Universidad Católica de Ecuador. His research focuses on the linguistic and social outcomes of contact between Amerindian languages and Spanish, in particular the emergence of mixed varieties such as Media Lengua and Jopará. In recent years he has been active in the documentation of indigenous languages in Ecuador and the study of pre-Inca languages in the Northern Andes.

Anthony P. Grant has been Professor of Historical Linguistics and Language Contact at Edge Hill University, UK since 2008. A native of Bradford, UK, he studied at the Universities of York and Bradford, where he gained his PhD ("Agglutinated Nominal in Creole French: Synchronic and Diachronic Aspects") in 1995. He has published extensively on Native North American languages, Romani, Austronesian languages, pidgins and creoles and English.

Clive G. Grey recently retired from Edge Hill University, having studied at the University of Bangor and subsequently at Fitzwilliam College, Cambridge, where he completed a PhD on Welsh phonology. His publications include *The Mersey Sound: Liverpool's Language, People and Places* (2007), with Anthony Grant.

John Haiman is Professor Emeritus of Linguistics at Macalester College. A typologist and descriptive linguist, his works include *Hua: A Papuan Language of the Eastern Highlands of New Guinea* (John Benjamins, 1980), *Hua-English Dictionary: With an English-Hua Index* (John Benjamins, 1991), and *Cambodian: Khmer* (John Benjamins, 2011).

Birgit Hellwig has been Lichtenberg Professor of Linguistics at the University of Cologne since 2014. She has worked and published extensively on West Chadic, Kordofanian, and Nubian languages in Africa, and is currently investigating child language among the Qaqet Baining people of New Britain, Papua New Guinea.

Raymond Hickey is Professor of Linguistics at the University of Duisburg-Essen, and has written extensively on language contact and world Englishes, especially Irish Englishes. He is editor of the forthcoming *Cambridge Handbook of Areal Linguistics.*

David Kaufman received his PhD on the Lower Mississippi as a Sprachbund at the University of Kansas in 2015. He has worked with the Kaw Tribe of Oklahoma on reviving their Siouan language, which is often known as Kanza, and has re-edited data on the extinct Siouan language Biloxi, originally collected by James Owen Dorsey in the late nineteenth century.

The late **Thomas B. Klein** (1964–2014) was Professor of Linguistics at the Department of Writing and Linguistics, Georgia Southern University, Statesboro, Georgia, where he founded the program in linguistics. A phonologist with a PhD from the University of Delaware, he conducted extensive fieldwork on Chamorro in Guam and Saipan, and on Gullah/Geechee in the Sea Islands, South Carolina, and Georgia. His publications include *"Umlaut" in Optimality Theory: A Comparative Analysis of German and Chamorro* (Tübingen: Niemeyer, 2000).

Natalia J. Laso is a Serra Hunter fellow in English Linguistics at the University of Barcelona. She holds a PhD in English Philology from the University of Barcelona and is also a member of the GRELIC-Lexicology and Corpus Linguistics Research Group. Her research is focused on two main areas: a) science writing and the main challenges that NNES writers face when writing their research in English; and b) the use of corpora in the linguistics classroom. She has co-edited the volume *Biomedical English: a corpus-based approach* (by Isabel Verdaguer, Natalia J. Laso & Danica Salazar. Eds.), published by John Benjamins Publishing.

Lígia Maria Herbert Duarte Lopes Robalo has a Bachelor's degree in Modern Languages and Literatures from the University of Lisbon and a Master's degree in Creolistics and the Cape Verdean language from the University of Cape Verde. She is the President of the Portuguese Language Olympiads and a Counselor in Pedagogical Training at the University of Cape Verde. She is affiliated with the Ministry of Education and the Escola Secundária Cónego Jacinto Peregrino da Costa in Cape Verde.

John McWhorter completed his PhD under John R. Rickford at Stanford University (1995) and has taught at Columbia University. The author of over a dozen books and dozens of articles, which have been highly influential in Creolistics, he works for the Manhattan Institute, New York. *Defining Creole* (Oxford University Press, 2004) and

Linguistic Simplicity and Complexity: Why Do Languages Undress? (De Gruyter, 2011) contain some of his most important articles.

Brian Mott is "Professor Honorífic" of the University of Barcelona, from which he retired in 2016. He taught phonetics and phonology, semantics, translation, composition and grammar from 1972 after three years at the University of Saragossa. From 2004 to 2010 he tutored on the Summer Course in English Phonetics at University College London directed by Professor John Wells. He has an MA in Spanish Studies (Aberdeen, 1969) and a PhD in Aragonese Dialectology (Barcelona, 1978). He has also studied the Mirandese dialect spoken in North East Portugal, and has published many books and articles covering all the above areas.

Åshild Næss is Professor of Linguistics at the University of Oslo, Norway. After studying in Norway she took her PhD at Radboud University Nijmegen. She has worked extensively on syntactic and semantic typology, on language contact, and on documenting the languages of the Reef Islands in the Temotu Province of the Solomon Islands, and understanding of whose history is crucial to a full picture of the dispersal of the Oceanic languages throughout the Pacific.

E-Ching Ng teaches English linguistics at the National University of Singapore. She received her PhD from Yale University in 2015. Her dissertation, "The Phonology of Contact: Creole Sound Change in Context," identifies phonetic biases in different types of language contact. Her other research includes stress and tone in Colloquial Singaporean English and its substrates.

Carmel O'Shannessy is Associate Professor of Linguistics at the University of Michigan. She completed her PhD in Linguistics at the University of Sydney (Australia) and the Max Planck Institute for Psycholinguistics (The Netherlands) in 2007. Within the areas of language contact, endangered languages, and language acquisition, her research focuses on the genesis and development of Light Warlpiri, a newly emerged mixed language in north Australia, and documentation of children's bilingual acquisition of Light Warlpiri and Warlpiri. She also works on the documentation of traditional Warlpiri songs. She has been involved with languages in remote Indigenous communities in Australia since 1996, in the areas of bilingual education and her current research.

Gabriel Ozón lectures in Linguistics at the University of Sheffield, having studied at the Universidad de Buenos Aires and University College London, where he gained his PhD. His publications include *English Grammar: Words and Sentences* (with Eva Duran Eppler, Oxford University Press, 2011).

Mikael Parkvall teaches linguistics at the University of Stockholm, where he defended his doctoral dissertation in 2000, which was published as *Out of Africa: African Influences in Atlantic Creoles* (Battlebridge, 2000). He has written widely on general linguistics (most notably *Limits of Language: What You Didn't Know You Didn't Know about Languages* (Battlebridge, 2007) and on pidgins and creole languages.

David Quinto-Pozos is an Associate Professor in the Department of Linguistics at the University of Texas at Austin. He has conducted research on American Sign Language (ASL) and Mexican Sign Language (LSM). His current work includes projects on the interaction of language and gesture, trilingual (Spanish-English-ASL) interpreting, and developmental signed language disorders. David has also studied signed language contact and signed language interpretation.

Malcolm Ross is an Emeritus Professor of Linguistics at the Australian National University. He taught and researched at the ANU from 1986 to 2007. Before that he taught for ten years in Papua New Guinea. He has published a number of articles and chapters on contact-induced change, especially on its effects on morphosyntax. His areal interest is in languages of New Guinea and the Pacific, and he is a co-author of *The Oceanic Languages* (Curzon, 2002) and of *The Lexicon of Proto Oceanic* (Pacific Linguistics 1998, 2003, 2008, 2011). He has held visiting positions at Frankfurt and Oxford Universities, Academia Sinica (Taipei), Max Planck Institutes in Leipzig and Jena, and was Collitz Professor of Historical Linguistics at the Linguistic Society of America's Summer Institute at University of California, Berkeley, in 2009.

Norval Smith taught phonology and general linguistics for over three decades at the University of Amsterdam, where he was a Reader, and published and presented voluminously. He is now attached to the University of Vienna.

Sérgio Soares da Costa, has a Bachelor's degree in Portuguese Language and Applied Foreign Languages from the Portuguese Catholic University (Portugal), in addition to a Master's in Creolistics and the Cape Verdean language, from the University of Cape Verde (Cape Verde islands). He is currently the parliamentary editor for the National Assembly of Cape Verde.

Ho-min Sohn is Professor of Korean Linguistics at the University of Hawaii at Manoa (UHM) and President of the Korean Language Education & Research Centre. He is a past Chair of the Department of East Asian Languages and Literatures and a past Director of the Centre for Korean Studies at UHM and a past President of both the International Circle of Korean Linguistics and the American Association of Teachers of Korean. His numerous publications include *Essentials of Korean Culture* (2014), *Topics in Korean Language and Linguistics* (2013), *Korean Language in Culture and Society* (2006), *The Korean Language* (1999), *Korean* (1994), *Linguistic Expeditions* (1986), *Woleaian-English Dictionary* (1996), *Woleaian Reference Grammar* (1975), and *A Ulithian Grammar* (1973).

Lameen Souag (PhD, SOAS 2010) studied Mathematics at the University of Cambridge and completed his PhD on contact effects of Arabic on Siwi and Korandje in 2010. Part of this was published as *Berber and Arabic in Siwa (Egypt)* (Rüdiger Köppe, 2014). He works at CNRS-LACITO in Paris, where he is completing an in-depth study of Korandje.

P. Sreekumar teaches at Dravidian University, Trivandrum, India, and has worked extensively on the major Dravidian languages, including his native language, Malayalam.

Graham Thurgood (PhD Berkeley 1976) is Professor of Linguistics at California State University at Chico, and a specialist in language contact, Tibeto-Burman and Chamic. His publications include *From Ancient Cham to Modern Dialects: Two Thousand Years of Language Contact and Change* (University of Hawai'i Press, 1999) and *A Grammatical Sketch of Hainan Cham: History, Contact and Phonology* (with Ela Thurgood and Fengxiang Li, De Gruyter, 2015).

Manuel Veiga has a doctoral degree in Applied General Linguistics from the University of Aix-en-Provence (France). He is a Professor of Linguistics and Director of the Master's Program in Creolistics and the Cape Verdean language offered by the University of Cape Verde. He has held multiple governmental positions in Cape Verde, including that of Minister of Culture. He has also authored several novels in Cape Verdean Creole and Portuguese, in addition to a Cape-Verdean Portuguese dictionary.

Donald Winford received his undergraduate degree at King's College, University of London in 1968, graduating with First Class Honors in English. He completed his D. Phil. (Linguistics) at the University of York, England, in 1972. He is currently Professor of Linguistics at the Ohio State University. His teaching and research interests are in creole linguistics, variationist sociolinguistics, contact linguistics, and African-American English, and he has published widely in those areas. He is the author of *Predication in Caribbean English Creoles* (1993), and *An Introduction to Contact Linguistics* (2003). He served as President of the Society for Caribbean Linguistics from 1998 to 2000, is currently President of the Society for Pidgin and Creole Linguistics, and has been editor of the *Journal of Pidgin and Creole Languages* since August 2001.

....

CHAPTER 1

CONTACT-INDUCED LINGUISTIC CHANGE

An Introduction

....

ANTHONY P. GRANT

1.1 INTRODUCTION

....

LANGUAGE contact—the results of the contact of different linguistic communities—has been a major field of investigation since World War II, and has attracted hundreds of books and monographs, and two international and highly esteemed journals (*Journal of Pidgin and Creole Languages* [1986–] and *Journal of Language Contact* [2007–]) in English alone. The literature on the topic and its subtopics is immense, as befitting a topic that has affected the linguistic behavior of most if not all users of language, now and in past centuries.

Languages as abstractions or idealizations or systems do not do things; people do things with languages, or rather, they do things with linguistic systems. That being the case, there has probably never been, nor is, nor ever will be, a linguistic system that has not been modified in some way by the incorporation of elements from at least one other linguistic system. If we cannot find any such transfers in our data on a language, a uniformitarian approach suggests that (1) the availability of more data would make such transfers manifest, and/or (2) there are transferred elements, but we do not yet have enough apposite linguistic knowledge to recognize them.

The term *language contact* is somewhat misleading, as it generally refers to an outcome (namely the changes wrought upon a language system as the result of its speakers coming into contact with users of another language system—we may call this contact-induced linguistic change, or CILC)—rather than to the process(es) by which this outcome occurs. Speakers of one language may not have sufficient contact with speakers of a neighboring language to absorb elements from this neighboring language. Or the interaction between the groups may indicate contempt, enmity, or fear, either in one direction or mutually between the groups. These are factors that would discourage the transfer or replication of much or even any linguistic material from one group to another.

Quite often the interaction between the groups is socially unequal, and this is reflected in the fact that in many cases borrowing of words or constructions goes mostly or entirely in one direction, from the more powerful or prestigious group to the less favored one. The languages of socially subordinated groups may from quite an early period of contact provide terminology for realia or practices with which speakers of the more powerful group were previously unfamiliar, but the effects of contact in that direction may not progress any further than this. In some cases, as with the Dharug language of Sydney, Australia, the source of some of the earliest loans from Indigenous Australian languages into English, the fate of the language system that provided such terms (in this case, including the etyma of *boomerang* and *wombat*) is extinction after the obliteration of many of its speakers. The remainder shifted to varieties of English, the language of the people who had slain their kinfolk. In other cases, both languages survive with fluent speakers; in some cases, neither does (as in the case of Latin and its loan source Etruscan).

The degree of the effects of contact-induced linguistic change varies from one language to another, and the strength of contact varies between pairs of languages in which CILC can be diagnosed. Typological and genealogical factors, such as the depth of historical closeness of the languages, play a huge role. So do the length of the period of contact, the intensity of contact in terms of the comparative size of the speech communities, and the consistency of dominance of one speech community over another (sometimes the donor language assumes the role of recipient language when political circumstances change).

We can think of such linguistic systems that have been most strongly influenced by other languages as *heavy-borrowing languages*. (This is of course a gradient.) On the whole, these (and not only languages such as these) are characterized by the replacement of a considerable amount of their preexisting lexical and/or structural material with items that have been absorbed from other linguistic systems: this is *intimate language contact*, much like Bloomfield's *intimate borrowing* (Bloomfield 1933). If we look at the proportion of loans in the general lexicon of a language, we can get a very crude picture of the effects of "borrowing" (Haspelmath and Tadmor eds. 2009 gives an interesting range of languages for which this is done), and sometimes this is still the most information that we have.

Measuring the impact of CILC upon a language involves two sets of elements. On the one hand, we count the totality of morphemic forms that are transferred or copied into a linguistic system. On the other hand, we must also count the totality of structural patterns of all types (including instances of lexical and other kinds of semantic patterning) that can be shown to have been absorbed by a linguistic system rather than being transmitted from earlier stages of that language.

Not all languages have had their contact histories thoroughly explored. That of English is especially well known (see Miller 2012 for an exploration of the facts about contact in Old and Middle English, and Laker 2013 for a critique of this). But even so, there are questions about the contact history of English that remain unanswered because of a dearth of data from English in the later Norman, Angevin, and early Plantagenet period (ca. 1100–1250): most of the writing from England and Southern Scotland that has been preserved from that time is in Latin or Norman French. The contact history of many other languages (and indeed the major features of their historical linguistic developments) are often much less well explored. There are some languages, for example the Algonquian language Blackfoot, about which both the contact history and the rest of the pattern of historical development are still uncertain, even though there is no dearth of data in Blackfoot (Proulx 1989; Berman 2006).

In this regard, we should note that there is an increasing amount of research on the effects of CILC in the languages of areas, such as Australia and the Americas, which had previously not received much attention (examples are Mithun 2006; Heggarty and Beresford Jones eds. 2012; McConvell 2012; Berez-Kroeker and Walker et al. 2016). Even so, the contact history of some heavy-borrowing languages, such as Lake Miwok of northern California (Callaghan 1964), which has absorbed many loans from Patwin, Wappo, and Southeastern Pomo, and also from Spanish and latterly English (and which has absorbed new consonants from all of these), is known to be extensive. Callaghan (2014) has documented this in greater detail from the available printed and (rather extensive) unpublished resources on the language and has placed it in a greater genealogical and areal context.

Campbell's paper (1989) on proposed constraints in borrowing (referencing Moravcsik 1978's claims that verbs cannot be borrowed) shows that laying down hard and fast rules about what is impermissible in borrowing is not always possible, as exceptions can be found. Yet we should not assume that all languages have been equally strongly shaped by the effects of CILC, which after all is just one set of processes or features among the many that shape the history of a language. CILC (or its effects) explains less of the history and development of German than it does that of English; it tells us less about the history of Italian than that of Romanian; it probably reveals less of the history of Sasak than that of Chamorro, and so on. As a result, there are some languages whose degree of CILC is so great that they immediately lend themselves to students of language contact as being interesting as a matter of course.

Several of them are discussed in this book, and in many cases the authors of the chapters have provided textual illustrations that highlight the effects of CILC on the language being discussed. The languages chosen for discussion in this book are ones in which CILC at various levels and in various structural areas has been important (in different ways in different languages) and where it shows its effects clearly. Grant (2012) looked at data from over a dozen languages from around the world in an attempt to analyze and compare the degree of borrowing of basic and less basic vocabulary, and of morphology. If the data for a range of languages had been more plentiful or had been available, yet other languages would have been included in that study—or indeed in this book.

Detailed data on heavy-borrowing languages continue to become available as the decades roll on, and in some cases the results of the effects of other languages upon these are both widespread and profound. Over the past few years, extensive and high-quality data have become available for Berber languages such as Siwi (Souag 2014) and Ghomara (Mourigh 2015), and for other non-Berber heavy borrowers such as Tsat or Hainan Cham from near Sanya City in Hainan, China (Thurgood 2015), and from the Near East, Domari (Matras 2012 and sources cited therein). All that links this set of heavy-borrowing languages is that their speakers practise varieties of Sunni Islam; despite this, the impact of Arabic on Tsat is minimal, comprising a few loanwords, though it is profound in the case of the other languages named. We may combine and compare these languages with linguistic data from Chamorro (Salas Palomo 2009), the Mexicanero variety of Western Nahuatl spoken in Durango, Mexico (Canger 2001), and Garifuna of Central America (Taylor 1977; Cayetano 1993; Sabio and Ordóñez 2005). We can add Kalderash Romani, originating as a distinct Romani variety in Transylvania and spreading throughout the world (Gjerdman and Ljungberg 1963 and Boretzky 1992 are especially valuable sources here because they provide etymological information, but note also Lee 2010, 2011). Such a comparative study shows that the range of features that have been transmitted from one language to another is very extensive and truly startling—more so if we added data from another form of Romani, namely Dolenjska Romani of Slovenia (Cech 2006). This matter is explored in greater depth in section 1.6 in this chapter.

Contact-induced linguistic change is most easily exemplified from data from spoken languages, but data from written languages exemplifies its effects as well, sometimes in ways that are not also reflected in the corresponding spoken language modality. The use of symbols that represented words of the extinct isolate Sumerian, which were incorporated into texts written in the Indo-European language Hittite in Anatolia in the second millennium BC (using a cuneiform system that also employed elements of Peripheral Akkadian cuneiform writing, employed in writing an East Semitic language), is one such instance.

From the same part of the world, a more recent yet still striking example of this is what happened in records of the Semitic language Syriac, a form of Western Aramaic, after about 1000 CE. Syriac was written in a consonantal script in which vowels (especially short vowels) were not usually indicated. For many centuries a large proportion of writers of Syriac were also able to read (and maybe speak) Greek. As writers of Syriac felt that it was increasingly important to indicate vowels, Greek alphabetic vowel letters were taken over and were written in small characters within Syriac words. This is despite the fact that the Syriac and Greek scripts are of different types (consonantal vs. alphabetic) and even though Syriac words containing such vowels continued to be written from right to left, whereas Greek script at that time was consistently written from left to right (Daniels 1995). Aramaic is also discussed by Eleanor Coghill in Chapter 22 in this *Handbook*.

Sometimes the effects of one language system upon another are subtle and less easy to detect. We may think, for instance, of the use of a retroflex post-alveolar sibilant in Quapaw, formerly spoken in Oklahoma, rather than the post-alveolar sibilant that other Dhegiha Siouan languages use (Rankin 1987). This is part of the evidence of Quapaw being influenced by Muskogean and other languages of the Lower Mississippi

Sprachbund, a grouping that is discussed by David Kaufman in Chapter 30 in this *Handbook*, but one to which Quapaw does not itself belong. Another example of subtlety in the transfer of a feature is from a form of South Siberian Turkic, languages that have in the past couple of centuries been strongly influenced by Russian, which is now replacing them. Gregory Anderson noted that in his fieldwork he found speakers of the Khakas language who had been born in the 1970s. In their speech they used the genitive (rather than the traditional Turkic ablative) with their verb 'to fear,' on the model of Russian *bojat'sja* (Anderson 2005: 180–181). Other features of verb argumentation can be transferred from one language to another: an example is the form for 'to play,' in German *spielen*, but in standard Yiddish *zikh shpiln*, the verb being made reflexive on the lines of co-territorial Polish *bawić się* (Lockwood 1965: 244).

Furthermore, as Chapter 31 by David Quinto-Pozos and Robert Adam in this collection shows, CILC is not confined to spoken languages and their written manifestations, but can also be found in other modalities; Quinto-Pozos and Adam exemplify this with data from a signed language, American Sign Language (ASL). ASL has been able to take over elements developed in a spoken language and to make them its own in a different modality; for instance, the past-tense marker represented by the symbols *e-x* is a carryover from English *ex-*, itself a derivational prefix that has been taken from Latin (Carol Neidle, personal communication 2004).

There are several good accounts of the general kinds of CILC that have been noted. Hickey (2011) summarizes the issues and incidentally, in doing so, presents a nice primer on many aspects of Irish-English and Irish-Anglonorman CILC. One of the most striking accounts is that by Matisoff (1996), a work that had not been intended for publication, which draws heavily upon Matisoff's experience working on languages of Southeast Asia that have been massively impinged upon by Chinese and in many cases also by Indic languages. Good summaries of the major concepts and mechanisms of CILC can be found in other sources as part of their theoretical backdrop; we can find this, for instance, in the relevant chapters in Stapert (2011), a discussion of CILC in Dolgan, a Turkic language of Siberia, which has borrowed greatly from Mongolic and latterly Russian.

A picture of the kinds of influences that can occur in CILC can be seen in Figure 1.1. This framework is extensive, flexible, and logically rooted, but it is not complete—for

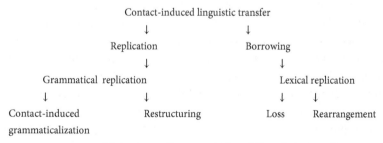

FIGURE 1.1 Main types of contact-induced linguistic transfer.

Source: After Heine and Kuteva (2008: 59).

example, it does not cover instances of phonetic or phonological borrowing except by default (as they occur in instances of restructuring, or as part of the consequences of lexical borrowing). But within its terms of reference, it is insightful and brings a degree of welcome order and logical hierarchy to the field.

There are many distinctions that we can make when we attempt to classify and scrutinize the kinds of contact-induced linguistic changes that one finds in linguistic systems. We can distinguish between those which make a system more complex, and those which simplify it (Trudgill 2011). Aikhenvald (2002) took a similar but slightly differently oriented approach, examining changes that occurred in some languages in Amazonia, and asking whether they helped to preserve the features of a linguistic system or whether they changed it. There again, we may distinguish mechanisms of change that are gained slowly over generations of speakers, versus those gained at once or very quickly. Another distinction that can usefully be made is between those changes that need bilingualism among speakers of the recipient language and those that do not.

It should go without saying that the effects of borrowing vary whether the donor language is Arabic, Chinese, Russian, Spanish, or indeed English (which in general had not been much of a donor language, except to languages spoken in early colonized areas such as Kuna of Panama or Yahgan of Chile, until the beginning of the nineteenth century). Different languages are inclined to borrow different kinds of items. Certain items, such as acculturational lexicon, higher cardinal and ordinal numerals, or subordinating and coordinating conjunctions, are often transferred. Others, such as basic prepositions, are more often transferred from Chinese into other languages (for instance, into Hmong-Mien and Kra-Dai languages; see, for instance, Moskalev 1978 on a Hmong-Mien case) than from the others listed in the preceding. Similarly cliticized pronominals following prepositions or adverbs are found borrowed into some languages influenced by Arabic, for instance Tamazight (Abdel-Massih 1971), but not (say) in languages influenced by Spanish.

1.2 CILC, Social and Other Considerations

Linguistic complexity seems to have developed millennia ago and not to be a new development (Wray and Grace 2007), and the same is the case with CILC. Speakers of all languages seem to borrow or absorb new elements into their languages, and often do this in order to find ways of naming previously unfamiliar concepts or expressing previously unlabeled concepts. In other cases, the elements that are borrowed supplement, replicate, or replace (wholly or partly) elements that were previously in use. The motivation for material from one language exerting influence upon another is tied in with issues of **power** and **prestige**. Prestige here refers to high cultural status, which is either **overt,** when it reflects the linguistic usage of people holding power, or in some cases **covert,** when it reflects the linguistic usage of people who do not have power but who may have social cachet, often because their activities run counter to those endorsed by the power-holders in society). Thomason and Kaufman (1988) argue for the centrality and indeed supremacy of sociolinguistic (rather than merely structural) factors in the operation of CILC. Milroy (1997) supports this; see also the later discussion of Field (2001). Bayley, Cameron, and Lucas (2013) is a solid account of modern thought in sociolinguistics, which takes into account the effects of contact-induced change.

In the framework presented by Frans van Coetsem (especially van Coetsem 2000), these relate to issues of **borrowing**, already a familiar term. But there are also cases of CILC that are the result of van Coetsem's other mechanism, **imposition**. If a language is acquired by a large number of people who learn it as the language of the colonizers, then it may absorb features of the languages of those who were colonized. This is probably the case with Old English, as it was acquired by speakers of British Celtic who underwent language shift (see the discussion in Beal and Faulkner, Chapter 16 in this volume).

The role and history of borrowing (itself a loaded and inaccurate term, of course) is not always recognized in the literature on a language, though. In many cases, the contact history of a language is underexplored in linguistic scholarship, and only when the scholarship becomes richer can we see the extent to which the effects of such contact have pervaded the language. In some cases it is largely a question of us metaphorically polishing the spectacles through which we look at the language in question, and of jettisoning a priori assumptions that are not as watertight as we might once have believed.

It is not the case that all heavy-borrowing languages borrow the same kinds of features. Some languages absorb plenty of lexicon without causing great adjustments to their morphosyntactic patterns; they may even accommodate all or most borrowed items to their preexisting phonological categories in respect to the phonemes and syllabic templates available for incorporating borrowed items. (This is especially, but not always, the case if such a language already has a rich segmental and templatic phonological inventory.)

Some languages undergo sweeping syntactic change but do so without borrowing large amounts of lexicon or phonological elements. The Oceanic and therefore Austronesian language Takia (Ross 1996, 2009) remodeled much of its morphosyntactic structure on nearby Papuan languages such as Waskia, performing what Ross called *metatypy*, but Takia borrowed very little lexically and took nothing morphologically from them. Nonetheless, it was not averse to absorbing new lexicon. It did borrow from the non-Austronesian language Bargam (more so than from Waskia), and also from Takia's close relative Gedaged, from German (the colonial language in the area from the 1880s until 1918), and latterly from Tok Pisin and nowadays increasingly English. In some instances, the kinds of change on the recipient language are subtler. Carvalho (2018) discusses loans from Tupi-Guarani languages into Teréna and Kadiwéu, which has resulted in the creation of a new class of vowel-initial nouns; previously, nouns could not be vowel-initial.

We may suggest that the typical pattern of borrowing starts with cultural borrowing, the borrowing of the names of previously unfamiliar acculturational items, and ends in the taking over and productive use of items of inflectional morphology. One may typify most languages as **core-periphery languages**, in which all or the bulk of the roster of affixes plus the most frequent, polyvalent, and additionally the most readily grammaticalized content and function words derive from the ancestral language, while items that have been acquired from other language systems are peripheral to this. In this case, the question is how thick the core is, and where the periphery starts. This model roughly or snugly fits most languages, even massively heavy borrowers such as Nihali of India, with between 25% and 30% of items on the longer Swadesh list being borrowed (Nagaraja 2015), but there are exceptions.

The picture sketched in the preceding is an idealization of what happens in CILC. There are some unusual patterns of very basic borrowing between languages, wherein large sets of borrowed material are not matched by similar sets of shared inflectional morphology, and therefore we cannot demonstrate that the languages are descendants of one proto-language. This is the case, for instance, with Quechuan and Aymaran of Andean South America, which share about a fifth of their core vocabularies (including some, but not all, of the lower numerals) but none of their inflectional morphology. There is a huge literature on the relationship (whether it is genealogical or otherwise) between Quechuan and Aymaran/Jaqi languages (a situation most recently highlighted in Emlen 2017). This has been obscured by the fact that Cuzco Quechua, the most frequently studied form of Quechua outside the Andean area, has been heavily influenced by Aymaran languages in a second wave of influence, which is easy to identify. Conversely, the Aymaran language Jaqaru has been strongly influenced by Central Quechuan varieties (Cerrón-Palomino 2000a, 2000b).

Another but differently anomalous case is the relationship between Miskitu and Northern Sumu (already clear from Lehmann 1920, and set in contrast with Southern Sumu or Ulwa), which share the forms of their personal pronouns and many basic adjectives (whose morphological structure is transparent in Northern Sumu but opaque in Miskitu) but few other items. Even so, Miskitu, which had more social prestige than Sumuan languages, has provided these languages with borrowings over the past centuries, and all of them also have numerous loans from Creole English and latterly from Spanish (themselves transmitted via Miskitu).

Yet another pattern characterizes the Kari'na Pidgin element in Garifuna of Central America (and formerly the Lesser Antilles); the elements here are the relics of a by now evanescent genderlect distinguishing men's from women's speech in this Arawakan language. If we assume that all referents in the language of the Island Caribs, who gave rise to the earlier form of Garifuna, had both Kari'na and Arawakan (Igneri) equivalents at some point in the past, this was true of about a third of the referents by the mid-seventeenth century (Taylor 1977). Nowadays, about 17% of the items on the long form of the Swadesh list derive from Kari'na Pidgin. This is true of rather less of the vocabulary as a whole, which contains a greater proportion of elements from Spanish, French—both creolized and non-creole—and (mostly creolized) English, all of which figure, though more slightly, on the Garifuna Swadesh list.

A more mainstream but nonetheless striking instance of a very thin core and a dense periphery is true of a small family of languages that have been built out of elements or two or more preexisting languages, namely the Northern Songhay languages of Mali, Niger, and Algeria. These languages, Tagdal, Tadaksahak (Christiansen-Bolli 2010), Tasawaq, the extinct Emghedeshie, and Korandje of Algeria, combine Berber (not merely Tuareg) and Songhay elements. Songhay elements, including inflectional morphs and function words, account for about 300 elements in these languages, while forms of Berber origin are far more numerous and account for almost half the Swadesh list (other forms derive from local African languages such as Fulfulde and Dogon, from Arabic, and latterly from French). Berber also provides such elements as the mechanisms of causative morphology in most of these languages.

Issues respecting the relationship of core and peripheral elements within a language are less easy when much of the morphemic material has no known etymology. In the Algonquian language Blackfoot, for instance, the morphology is clearly Algonquian but most of the lexicon (basic and less basic) has no cognates in other Algonquian languages, and essentially none of this has etyma in any other known language (Bakker 2000; Proulx 1989).

We cannot always divine the answers to these or many other questions. Ethnolinguistic considerations (including the speakers' own ideas about what language is and what belongs in their language and what doesn't) are crucial, and these can affect borrowing patterns even within the confines of the Swadesh list. To take a single example, the use of nouns rather than pronouns for the self-designation of people in a number of East Asian languages has resulted in the absorption of some high-frequency borrowed elements that were originally taken over as words meaning 'slave' or 'subject.' This is the case in Japanese and Malay-Indonesian, for example (Schmidt 2009: 570; Tadmor 2009: 711). This is also the case with the names of celestial bodies such as 'sun' and 'moon' in languages of greater India, which are often taken over as loans from Sanskrit because of the roles of these bodies in Hinduism (this can be seen in Sridhar 1990 for Kannada).

What unifies cases of heavy borrowing is the fact of prestige and power exerted by the linguistic behavior of some representatives of the donor language community upon those of the recipient language community. A considerable degree of what Bloomfield (1933) described as **intimate borrowing**—the transfer of elements that already had equivalents or exponents in the recipient language—takes place. This is what Clark (1982), not without caution, termed "unnecessary borrowing."

If the evidence of CILC suggests a degree of social contact between two or more societies—even though such contact need not result in any transfer of linguistic material from one group to another—the reverse is also true. Just because certain groups have dwelt in isolation for hundreds of years does not mean that their languages cannot show the impact of other languages. Some communities believed that they were the only people in the world: this is true of both the Polar Inuit and the Angmassallik Inuit on what they had assumed was their first contact with outsiders in the nineteenth century—two groups speaking Eskimo languages who were unaware of each other's existence and that of other groups (van der Voort 1996). Even nowadays, reports of previously uncontacted groups occasionally reach news agencies from the Amazon or from New Guinea.

Sometimes a single word from another language is the best evidence that a speech community was in contact with another one from far away. Frachtenberg (1920) lists a form that we can phonemicize as *t'aw'ay'u*[1] as the word for 'horse' in the now dormant Alsea language of northern coastal Oregon. It is clearly Spanish *caballo*, very probably taken over as a result of Alseas coming into contact with the Spanish expedition in the Pacific led by the Basque military leader Bruno de Heceta in 1775, since the Alseas lived a couple of hundred miles north of the start of the California Franciscan mission belt, where Spanish was dominant. It is also the only Spanish loan recorded in Alsea.

Some populations, of course, purposely separate themselves from all others and remain inward facing. The few hundred people who live on North Sentinel Island, in the Andamans, have been isolated from other populations almost completely since first records of contact with them in the early nineteenth century. All that is known of their language is that it did not seem to be comprehensible to speakers of the southern Andamanese language Önge on the rare occasions when these latter people encountered them. This does not mean that the Önge and North Sentinelese languages cannot be related in the way in which Önge and the Jarawa language are related; we simply have no evidence for the nature and structure of the latter language (Anhava 2013 gives good insights into this and other cases).

Many languages—known as isolates—have no known or at least no surviving relatives. Nonetheless, we know that some are actually the last remnants of previously larger families (Basque, with its scantily attested relative Aquitanian, is one such example; Trask 1997). Such languages are not immune to borrowing: more than half the Basque vocabulary derives from Latin or Romance languages, as Trask pointed out, and this includes almost 10% of the longer Swadesh list.

Speakers of some languages know that to function fully in society one needs to command two or more linguistic systems. One of these systems is used more frequently in written (but not in impromptu spoken) form than the other, which is the spoken language used every day and which is the first to be acquired by members of this speech community. Ferguson (1959) described situations where this division occurred, designating the more formal version H ('high') and the less formal one L ('low'). He presented four case studies, from Egypt, Greece, German-speaking Switzerland, and Haiti. H languages were as follows: for Egypt, Modern Standard Arabic (*fuṣha*), deriving from Classical Arabic; for Greece, Katharev(o)usa (an artificially archaizing literary Greek); for Switzerland, High German; and for Haiti, French. The L-languages were as follows: Egyptian Arabic varieties; Dhimotiki; Swiss German; and Haitian Creole. Political and social situations have changed much since the 1950s, and though Modern Standard Arabic and High German still dominate in written media in Egypt and Switzerland, Haitian Creole has spread massively as a written medium. Meanwhile, Katharevousa has largely fallen into disuse, while Dhimotiki dominates in written

---

[1] I wish to thank Gene Buckley for supplying me with this form. The term was also taken over into the dormant language Siuslaw to the south of Alsea, as a form to be phonemicized as *tauwayu* (Frachtenberg 1914: 116).

Greek in Greece (and also in Cyprus, where it is considerably removed from spoken Cypriot Greek). Even in those areas where forms of diglossia remain, it is still the case that H elements can and do enter the L language, even if speakers of L actively command little or none of the H language. This is the case, for instance, in the major South Dravidian languages but not so in Malayalam, as Sreekumar's Chapter 23 in this volume demonstrates.

We may also discuss instances of semanteme-specific bilingualism of the kind illustrated by the compulsory use of Spanish numerals for certain purposes in Christian Philippine languages. Speakers of major languages such as Tagalog, Cebuano, Ilocano, and of minor Philippine languages such as Ibanag—and of dozens of other languages— may not be able to name simple objects in Spanish or conduct simple conversations in Spanish. But they routinely tell the time and count money using Spanish numerals, while otherwise using the numerals of their indigenous languages for many other kinds of counting and expression of quantities (Rubino 2002 provides information on this for Tagalog). This is part of the ethnolinguistic knowledge of such speakers.

Ethnolinguistic considerations of another type are mentioned in Alexandra Aikhenvald's Chapter 10 in this volume. Linguistic exogamy in the Vaupés area of northern Amazonia has been a staple in the literature since Arthur Sorensen's account of it in the 1960s (Sorensen 1967). One of the features of this is **linguistic purism**: speakers do not intentionally take over words from the languages of their neighbors and indeed take steps to avoid what they see as borrowings. Purism in language has characterized many societies and many eras throughout the world; Katharevousa in modern Greece was characterized in part by an attempt at avoiding loanwords from Turkish, Italian, French, and English. And although purism is about the avoidance of the effects of contact, it is still something that needs to be discussed in studies of CILC as a countervailing (and generally futile) social force. Purism can operate even in cases of extreme language shift: Sala (1970) described the deleterious effects of purism on the Judezmo (Judaeo-Spanish) spoken in Bucharest in the late twentieth century, where speakers tried to avoid Judezmo words that had similar shapes and meanings to those in the coterritorial language Romanian. Another case is that of the last speakers of Natchez in Mississippi, members of a tribe who were defeated militarily by the French in 1729 and then dispersed widely (some into slavery in the West Indies). Despite the fact that all of the last few speakers of Natchez, the last of whom died in the 1950s, were multilingual (in Natchez, Creek, Cherokee, and latterly English), lexical items from other languages account for less than 1% of the recorded vocabulary of about 4,000 items.[2] (Kimball 2003 describes Natchez structure.)

Borrowing itself is a pervasive yet pernicious and vain term because the item is neither returned to the donor nor lost from the donor's use—contact-induced linguistic change, or CILC, is better. One advantage of this term is that it locates language

---

[2] There are a number of calques, however: Natchez ʔayaM means both 'bedbug' and 'axe' on the model of Cherokee *galuysdi*. (Natchez data are from Mary Haas's fieldnotes, now housed in the American Philosophical Society, Philadelphia; Cherokee form is from Feeling and Pulte 1975.)

contact and borrowing firmly within the endless stream of linguistic change. For many languages (if we may anthropomorphize them thus), CILC is the major kind of linguistic change that they have undergone at one or more period of their existence. For others, CILC is just one of several kinds of change that have modified the language over centuries or millennia.

1.3 Notes on the Historiography of CILC: Documents and Findings

People describing languages and cultures have long recognized that one language may contain elements of another, be they the remarks about the speech of the Sauromatae in Book IV of Herodotus's *Histories*, or the list of 329 Hungarian words of Slavonic origin listed in Vrančić (1595), who apart from compiling the first Croatian dictionary also invented the parachute. The development of theory in CILC in its various forms has a long historiography, from the work of creolists and historical linguistics such as Hugo Schuchardt (e.g., Schuchardt 1884, 1914) and the American philologist William Dwight Whitney (e.g., Whitney 1881). The classics on linguistics by Sapir (1921) and Bloomfield (1933) both contain chapters on the effects that one language system can have upon another (and Bloomfield's tripartite division between *cultural, intimate,* and *dialect borrowing* is still valuable).

The theory of contact-induced linguistic change becomes more deeply developed and more nuanced and complex after World War II, and a large number of works have pieces to contribute to the picture, and employ techniques that help us to understand the minutiae of the methods and results of CILC. Articles such as Haugen (1950), and the monograph by Weinreich (1953), which is still consulted today (see Joseph 2016 for a discussion of André Martinet's preface to this work), develop their theories from narrower (Haugen) or wider (Weinreich) collections of data on various types of CILC, including borrowing, loan translation, pidginization, and creolization. We may note some less renowned but meritorious work on CILC from that era, notably the paper by Vogt (1956) and the book on linguistic borrowings by Deroy (1956).

The 1960s and 1970s saw the production of much work on creolistics, the study of creole and pidgin languages. In this regard the single most important collection is Hymes (ed. 1971), which explores these issues and many more, including some cases of heavy borrowing and some work on what became mixed languages. The potency of this work and its dense sectional introductions is far from being exhausted half a century after the papers were presented at the University of the West Indies, Mona, Jamaica, in April 1968.

The 1970s saw work by Jeffrey Heath, examining some cases of profound borrowing and diffusion in Arnhem Land, northern Australia, and the work on this (Heath 1978; the promised lexical appendix never appeared) draws inferences from the contact histories of English and Romanian to add to our understanding of CILC. Heath conducted his own fieldwork on Arnhem Land languages, many of which were isolates, and some of which were down to their last speaker or two (and none was widely spoken). He has continued to work on CILC and on documenting the languages of the Sahel, themselves often very rich in contact phenomena; Heath (1984) introduced the term *pattern transfer*, which led Grant (1999, 2002, 2004) to develop the complementary (**not** opposing) term *transfer of fabric* to refer to the replication of morphs (including lexicon) from one language to another.

The careful book of lectures on language contact written by Ilse Lehiste (Lehiste 1987) draws strongly on her experience as a polyglot brought up in interwar Estonia. The following year saw the work by Thomason and Kaufman (1988), probably the most influential book in the field after Uriel Weinreich's monograph, and this brought to wider attention a five-level borrowing scale, and the idea that creole languages resulted from abrupt transmission of lexical and other material. Thomason (ed. 1997) is an important descriptive work on a range of contact languages, while Thomason (2001) is a state-of-the-art report on language contact theory with plentiful examples, not least from her own fieldwork. The highly productive creolist Pieter Muysken (a former pupil of Thomason at Yale) produced a cross-linguistic study of code-switching, which covers much more than its title suggests (Muysken 2000; see also van Hout and Muysken 1994 on modeling lexical borrowability). Important works were produced by the Romanian-Argentinian scholar Marius Sala, drawing plentifully on data from Spanish, Judezmo, and Romanian varieties (Sala 1988). In the previous year some detailed work on CILC and language creation in New Britain, furnished with plentiful data, was presented in Thurston (1987). One notes his ideas about endogenous and exogenous language creation and the relative permeability of the "endolexicon" and its outer carapace the "exolexicon," and the emblematic nature of language systems that are not usually acquired by outsiders but that coexist in bilingual relationships with more widespread linguistic systems. Wray and Grace (2005) also look at the role of inward-facing rather than outward-facing speech communities. What is more, Hickey (2012: 18) talks of a distinction between supportive transfer, which reinforces a feature that the linguistic system already had, and innovative transfer, which introduces a new structural feature into the linguistic system.

In the following year was published the major work by Frans van Coetsem (van Coetsem 2000; see also van Coetsem 1989). This was a cognitively oriented approach in which he developed to the fullest his ideas about the primacy of the distinction between borrowing and imposition, and his concepts of source languages and recipient languages, which are gaining further appreciation (see Winford's Chapter 2 in this volume, and also the discussions of CILC in Lucas 2012, 2014). Another cognitive approach to CILC, concentrating especially on paradigmatic change and positing three levels at which this can operate, is Gast (2016).

Matras (2009) and Hickey (ed. 2012) are accounts of modern thinking on CILC. The former follows a functionalist approach, with accounts of a number of important topics such as lexical borrowing, in addition to several early chapters providing plentiful material on a case of Hebrew-German-English trilingual acquisition by a boy named

Ben, and what Ben's output illustrates about processes of contact-induced change. Matras's four mechanisms, which are cognitively and functionally oriented, and which he uses to account for what is found in CILC, are categorical fusion, selective replication, lexical reorientation, and convergence. Meanwhile, Hickey's book follows the approach of a compendium, with chapters on various general linguistic topics by experts in the field. There are also a number of studies of the effects of particular languages (for instance, Spanish) on other languages. There is also plentiful information there on convergence in both major linguistic senses. The term *convergence* can mean the interaction of language system-internal factors with external factors in the development of a new linguistic structure, but it can also refer to the processes by which one linguistic system becomes typologically more similar to a neighboring one.

The period since 2005 has seen the publication of numerous edited volumes on aspects of CILC, combining theoretical position papers with data-driven studies of aspects of CILC in particular languages. These include Stolz, Bakker, and Salas Palomo (eds. 2008) on general topics; Muysken (ed. 2008) on linguistic areas; Vanhove, Stolz, and Urdze (ed. 2012) on morphologies in contact; and Johanson and Robbeets (eds. 2012) and Gardani (ed. 2015) on borrowed morphology. There are also Matras and Sakel (eds. 2007), Chamoreau and Leglise (eds. 2012), and Wiemer, Wälchli, and Hansen (eds. 2012) on issues in grammatical borrowing more widely construed, and Haspelmath and Tadmor (eds. 2009) on loanwords in a selection of the world's languages. (Several authors helpfully have chapters on different aspects of contact in the same language in both the Matras/Sakel and Haspelmath/Tadmor collections.) The most recent contribution to this field is Hickey (ed. 2017) on areal linguistics, a topic previously explored in Matras, McMahon, and Vincent (eds. 2004), a volume with chapters on linguistic areas provided by experts in individual fields.

Investigations of CILC involving certain languages bring to light new patterns of CILC that have not been documented in other languages. For instance, the investigation of CILC in some languages of the Near East (especially when they are donors rather than receptors) has brought to light the issue of *parallel system borrowing* (as so named in Kossmann 2010). In this, borrowed verbs retain some or most of the conjugational systems of their source languages, while inherited verbs follow the paradigms of their source language. This is the case, for instance, with verbs of Turkish origin in some Romani varieties (Gilliat-Smith 1915–1916; Igla 1996), and most verbs of Arabic origin in some Berber varieties (for instance, Mourigh 2016). Parallel system borrowing is also found with verbs of Romance origin in Maltese (Mifsud 1995). It also has been noted for the Even dialect of Sebjan-Küöl, a Tungusic language of Siberia, which has borrowed some paradigms from the locally dominant Turkic language Sakha (Pakendorf 2009).

In terms of important studies of CILC focusing on a single situation of language contact, one should also mention Haase (1992), an exemplary study of the effects of French and Gascon on a variety of Basque in southwestern France, and Souag (2014), which examines the structural impact of varieties of Arabic on the Berber language of the Siwa oasis in western Egypt. Both these studies show that there is more to CILC studies than simply long lists of loanwords; another superb study, King (2000), not only presents plentiful detail on English loans into Nova Scotian Acadian French, but also describes and illustrates morphosyntactic influences.

Though not focusing on a single language, Aikhenvald (2002) is an important study of aspects of CILC among some languages in Amazonia, in which the author presents copious data from her fieldwork on a number of languages, including Tariana and Baniwa, in addition to her theory of CILC and her valuable concept of "system-changing" and "system-preserving" features. Descriptive studies of languages that have absorbed heavily from other languages are numerous (though we may wish for more), and some of these descriptions focus throughout on CILC and its effects. Two important titles that are especially comprehensive in their treatment of contact are Nurse (2000), describing two Bantu languages, Daiso and Ilwana, which have been heavily influenced by non-Bantu languages, and Thurgood (2015), which documents Hainan Cham, an Austronesian language that has been influenced by a number of languages, including Mon-Khmer languages, Hlai, and more than one form of Chinese.

Another work partly created by Derek Nurse, namely Nurse and Hinnebusch (1993), on the history of Swahili, includes an immense amount of data on language contact and various forms of the Sabaki group. It includes a lot of material showing the effect that Northern Swahili varieties (especially Kiamu, the dialect of the island of Lamu and an early literary language) had upon the Southern Swahili variety KiUnguja, the Zanzibari variety that underpins modern literary Swahili. Of works that are article-length rather than book-length, one of the best attempts to describe CILC is Sasse (1992) on Greek influence upon Arvanitika, the diasporic Tosk Albanian dialects of Greece.

A number of individual articles have also contributed to theoretical advances in aspects of CILC, and to new ways of examining the topic. The ideal reader in CILC would also include work such as Jill Brody's papers (Brody 1987, 1995) on the borrowing of discourse markers in Mayan languages, Malcolm Ross's (1995) paper on metatypy in some languages of New Guinea, and Maarten Kossmann's (2010) work on parallel system borrowing of morphology in Kormakiti Arabic and certain Berber languages. The paper by Matras (1998) on utterance modifiers and borrowing has enjoyed popularity. A rather less well-known but certainly powerful and fertile approach, and one that, like Matras's approach, recognizes the importance of pragmatics in CILC, is the work on ERIC, an approach to CILC that is "Essentially Rooted In Conversation." This is a discourse-driven account of CILC devised by Victor A. Friedman and Brian D. Joseph, and named after their former teacher, Eric P. Hamp of the University of Chicago (himself a keen contactician among a mastery of many linguistic subfields: Hamp 1989, for instance). This draws inspiration from CILC in languages of the Balkans and suggests a hierarchy of items, such as greetings, imprecations, and numerals (and I would add ethnonyms) that are most likely to be borrowed early in interchange or unidirectional borrowing between speech communities. Friedman and Joseph (2011) is a presentation on this approach.

What we have learned from this literature is vast, and the following summary, concentrating on the possibilities of CILC, is perforce highly selective; there may yet be much more to discover. Any kind of phenomenon can notionally be borrowed (or indeed, any kind of phenomenon can be lost through the effects of borrowing). Lexicon as a whole seems to be the stratum that is borrowed or shared with the greatest ease. All kinds of vocabulary can be borrowed in the form of what we call loanwords, and Thomason and Kaufman (1988: 74–76) demonstrate this in their highly regarded five-point borrowing scale. (This scale, which is based on the findings of more than fifty case studies of contact-induced change that the authors examined from primary documentation, is reduced to four points in Thomason 2001). No item on that standard diagnostic instrument of lexical stability, the Swadesh 100-item list, or its longer companions (one of which is presented in Swadesh 1955), is immune to borrowing, and the same is true of the later production, the Leipzig-Jakarta list (Haspelmath and Tadmor 2009, while the proof of this is in Grant to appear). Any item on either of these lists can be shown to have been borrowed in at least one language (an example of this extreme borrowing can be seen in the South Siberian Turkic language Tuvan, which has borrowed its word for 'what,' čüü, from Mongolic; Harrison and Anderson 2006). Verbs are anecdotally regarded as being hard, if not impossible, to borrow, but this is not the case, as Jan Wohlgemuth's superb study (Wohlgemuth 2009) indicates, with plentiful exemplification. Thomason and Everett (2000) is a crisp paper on the issue of borrowing personal pronouns, another group of words that are often assumed to be borrowing-proof. It is not always easy to find reasons on a case-by-case basis why the replacement of one item in a language by a borrowed item takes place. Indeed, the solution often eludes us—but exploring such cases of *intimate language contact* should enable us to dig more deeply into the kinds of linguistic features that are most readily borrowed.

New sounds and new kinds of sounds can be transferred, and this is usually carried out through the transmission of loanwords, even when this requires the adoption of new distinctive features, or indeed the use of previously unemployed airstream mechanisms, into the recipient language's phonological system. (Maddieson 1989, with its richness of detail, is a useful first pass at analyzing this issue; see also Grant, Klein, and Ng's Chapter 3 in this *Handbook*.) Especially interesting evidence of this comes from the Bantu Nguni languages of South Africa, especially Xhosa, which has absorbed hundreds of words from the Khoe language !Ora, or Korana. Many of these have come into Xhosa with an admittedly somewhat reduced but nonetheless still impressive range of the ingressive and velaric consonants that they had in their source language. (However, Korana permits word-final consonants, which Xhosa does not.) These sounds at least partly entered the Nguni languages through their employment in the *hlonipha* speech-avoidance style in which wives were not supposed to utter the syllables that comprised their husbands' names, and were to substitute other syllables (Lanham 1962; Louw 1986; Ownby 1985; Herbert 1991). For instance, Korana /awa 'to gather together' is taken into Xhosa as i-/áwa, written as <i-cawa> 'church; Sunday.' The semantics of this form and its secondary meaning of 'Sunday' resemble those of Zulu *i-sonto* 'church; Sunday,' which is also a loan, but this time from Afrikaans *sondag* 'Sunday.'

Morphological borrowing and the integration of borrowed morphs into a language's structure are far from being unknown: Frank Seifart's website *AfBo* (Seifart 2014) collects instances, collected from over a hundred languages from all around the world, of productively borrowed elements of affixal morphology. Seifart has also conducted primary research on the Colombian Arawakan language Resígaro, which has absorbed many inflectional morphemes from the unrelated Bora language, including a whole set of noun-class markers, but has borrowed very little lexicon from Bora or, for that matter, from Spanish (see Seifart 2012).

There are doubtless hundreds of other productive examples of this kind of borrowing in languages across the world. Sometimes even whole classes of new kinds of elements are transferred from one language to another, as Seifart's works show. Furthermore, evidence from languages such as Pearl Lagoon Basin Miskitu of eastern Nicaragua, which has absorbed and integrated the completive marker *don* from Caribbean Creole English, reveals that elements of free inflectional morphology (such as tense-aspect-mode particles in certain languages) can also be borrowed. Examination of trends in borrowing across the world's languages suggests that (in very general terms) items of derivational morphology can be borrowed more readily than items of inflectional morphology, although there are exceptions, and even some heavy-borrowing languages, for example Chamorro, have eschewed borrowing derivational morphology productively.

But it remains the case that some kinds of phenomena are more amenable to what is often styled as borrowing than others are, and even if aprioristic hierarchies (rather than the a posteriori hierarchy presented in Thomason and Kaufman 1988) prove to be too restrictive, it is clear that tendencies and preferred kinds of borrowing do exist. The book by Fredric Field (2002), informed strongly as it is by an analysis of the effects of fusional Spanish upon a variety of agglutinative Nahuatl in terms of form-meaning sets in the two languages, casts light on this: Field offers two principles, the *principle of system compatibility* and its corollary, the *principle of system incompatibility*. These invite the reader to examine possibilities and constraints (or indeed embargoes) on borrowability through the comparison of the morphosyntactic typology of the donor and recipient languages. Genealogical considerations in this case are less important than the existence of a high degree of isomorphism (similarity in the patterns of organization of form-meaning sets) between the languages involved. A good recent collection of papers on this approach is Besters-Dilger, Dermarkar, and Pfänder (eds. 2014).

Similarities in typology between donor and recipient language are often the case because the languages involved are genealogically related, sometimes very closely. This should not surprise speakers of English, influenced as it was by its Germanic relatives Norse and Dutch. Indeed, some languages (given the caveat in the first paragraph of this piece) have been most strongly influenced by linguistic systems that are either closely related to them at various degrees of separation (Swedish by Middle Low German [Walshe 1964] and North Frisian by Danish [Hoekstra 2017] are two of many cases). In other cases, they are heavily influenced (by means of back-borrowings from that language) by the language from which they themselves have developed. The impact of Latin as a source of transfer material on its descendants (Spanish, French, Italian, etc.) is huge. (In contrast, the amount of back-borrowing from Old English into Modern English is minimal: *witangemot*, *scramaseax*, and a few more.)

A third state of affairs involves languages that combine elements of more than one language, specifically of two languages that are genealogically related, which descend from a single proto-language, and which have given rise to a language that cannot be safely assigned to the taxon to which either of these languages belongs. Stedsk or Town Frisian, blending West Frisian and Dutch (van Bree 1994, 2001a, 2001b), is one such case. Another is the Mayan language Tojolab'al (Law 2016), which blends Tzeltalan and Chujean elements, items from two branches of the Mayan language family. Some cases of heavy intra-familial borrowing are well described: Costa (2013) is a splendid account of the way in which Potawatomi, a Great Lakes Algonquian language that is most closely related to Ojibwe, has absorbed a huge number of loans form Fox-Sauk-Kickapoo, which is also Algonquian but less closely related to Ojibwe than Potawatomi is. Other cases need more description, though the raw data are abundant. For instance, the effect of Georgian upon Mingrelian, which is also Kartvelian but which belongs to a different branch of that family, deserves closer examination. The discussion of mixed languages later in this chapter is also germane here.

Meanwhile, though, it is easier for a feature to pass into one language from another if the two are typologically similar (whether or not they are genealogically related to one another) than it is if they are very different typologically (even if they can be shown to descend from the same proto-language). Typological change, and furthermore any syntactic change, is not always the result of CILC, though the wide-ranging paper by Campbell, Bubenik, and Saxon (1988) presents some robust examples of typological syntactic change through CILC, occurring in several members of families such as Iranian or Ethiosemitic, or in individual languages such as Cappadocian Greek. Anyone who thinks that the typological patterning of structures within a language family is always uniform should bear the following in mind. No fewer than seven of the seventeen actually attested orders that combine various exponents of subject-verb-object, genitive-noun, noun-adjective, and preposition/postposition out of the twenty-four theoretically possible ones discussed in Greenberg (1963), which were reviewed by Campbell, Bubenik, and Saxon (1988), can be found among members of the Indo-European language family. Meanwhile, even a casual comparison of the typological profiles of English and Hindi, at phonological, morphological, syntactic, and semantic levels, will show how much two languages that ultimately derive from the same proto-language can diverge in the space of a few millennia.

The bigger the language family is, the greater the potential for typological diversity. (This potential need not be realized, of course.) Thurgood's Chapter 7 in this collection, though it focuses on sociocultural rather than purely typological considerations, shows how this is just as true of Tsat or Hainan Cham, a fully tonal language that developed from a non-tonal language (Proto-Chamic), which is closely related to and closely resembled non-tonal Malay, in less than a millennium. About two thousand or so years ago, Chamic and Malay were closely related branches of the same sub-branch of Western Malayo-Polynesian.

Replacement of preexisting items by words from another language is a form of *relexification*, a process that is often extensive, though always partial, as no language ever relinquishes all its lexicon. Relexification contrasts with cultural borrowing (*adlexification*) insofar as relexification refers to the replacement of a preexisting label for a concept that the speech community had already recognized and labeled. *Supralexification* (coined in Hancock 1971: 288) also involves the complication of preexisting semantic fields through borrowing terms that add to the complexity of the post-borrowing system. Welsh Romani (Sampson 1926) inherited words for BLACK, WHITE, and RED from Indic and used a pan-Romani loan from South Slavic for GREEN. It did not preserve the widespread Romani form of South Slavic origin for YELLOW, replacing this with the Welsh loan *melanō* (Welsh *melyn*). It added a word for BLUE, *blūa*, from English (no pan-Romani forms for BLUE are attested, although some borrowed forms for BLUE are widespread in Romani varieties). Similarly, Welsh *gwyrdd* (from Latin *viridis*) 'green' provided a fresh label for a color whose territory had hitherto been subsumed between *glas* 'blue, grey' and *llwyd* 'grey, brown' (Palmer 1976).

1.4 A CASE IN POINT: GLIMPSES OF CILC IN MODERN ENGLISH

The case of English (discussed also in Chapter 16 by Beal and Faulkner) is one that demonstrates that CILC does not explain everything about the later history of a language. Modern English is so much more than simply Old English or "Anglo-Saxon" plus CILC. As a Western Germanic language, Old English had absorbed loans directly or sometimes via intermediaries from Latin, Greek, Aramaic, and unknown languages before a speaker of what became Old English ever set foot on English shores. It became adopted by a population that had switched from a somewhat latinized British Celtic, which served as a substratum to Old English. Later, Old English was adopted as a second but everyday language by the Vikings. These were speakers of Old Danish and Old Norwegian. A couple of centuries later, it was adopted by speakers of Norman French (themselves also descendants of Vikings, but who had been christianized and Gallicized and who now spoke a form of French with some Norse borrowings: Norman French, and later its English offshoot, Anglo-Norman). The cultural prestige language in this environment was Latin, which also exerted a strong influence on English, directly but also indirectly via its descendant French, and which also served as a conduit for numerous elements from Greek, which had long since been absorbed into Latin. But it is doubtful whether we can safely attribute the changes that modified English morphology so much (notably the reduction of most final-syllable vowels to schwa in later Old English) directly to the effect of any of these languages.

CILC is essential to the history of English, but it is far from being the whole story. The second paragraph of this introduction contains forty-eight words or tokens, and thirty-nine types or different words (related forms of the same word are included within the same type). Eleven of these types are from other languages loaned into English; another (*never*) combines an Old English negator with an adverbial form that is exclusive to English and that is of unknown etymology (forms of unknown origin in languages abound, and though their history perforce remains mysterious, we should not ignore them). The use, though not the etymon, of auxiliary 'do' looks like a strong candidate for loan-translation (calquing) from the British Celtic substrate; the relative pronoun 'which' shows us using what was originally an interrogative pronouns as a relative pronoun, as French, Latin, and occasionally Norse did, but Old English did not. 'Not' itself has shifted from its original meaning of 'nothing' (OE *nāwiht*). But the syntagm that places it after 'do' and before the main or lexical verb is something that developed in the late Middle Ages and spread rapidly in Early Modern English, while the construction 'that being the case' echoed the Latin ablative absolute, itself an adjunctive echo of the Greek genitive absolute. Cases of true grammaticalization of items taken over through CILC are hard to find, though they occur frequently in English. For instance, *want*, borrowed from Old Norse as a lexical verb meaning 'to be in need of, to be missing' (and resembling the neuter form of the cognate adjective meaning 'lacking') has gained a new lease on life as an auxiliary or catenative verb, while its predecessor in its current slot, namely *will*, now indicates futurity.

As Grant (2002) has pointed out, any kind of CILC in any language can be expressed as being *transfer of fabric* (this denotes the borrowing of morphemes, including lexemes) or *transfer of pattern* (the borrowing of ways of using morphemes), and the two kinds of transfer are certainly not mutually exclusive within the same construction. They may and often do co-occur. Furthermore, both kinds of transfer can result in words or constructions that then take on linguistic lives of their own, undergoing changes quite independent of the source material or source languages. Once a word or a construction has been taken over from one linguistic system into another, its subsequent adventures and changes are part of the history of that new linguistic system, and these developments may not be replicated or paralleled or preempted in the language from which the term was originally taken. The history of the English verb STOP, which ultimately derives from a Greek word referring to the substance 'tow,' is a glorious example of this (OED Online, s.v. STOP1).

Indeed we may ask of any potential instance of CILC the following questions: *Does this instance involve transfer of fabric? Does this instance involve transfer of pattern?* If the answer to either or both of these is "yes," then we are dealing with a case of CILC.

1.5 CILC IN ANTIQUITY: SOME CASES

Has there always been borrowing between languages? All the evidence available to us from the earliest stages of recorded human language (which are preserved in written form) suggests a positive answer to this question; we may assert that a uniformitarian approach, by which the ways in which languages interacted five thousand years ago are still valid today, is supported by plentiful evidence. Even so, most studies concentrate on, or are simply limited to, the examination of the borrowing of cultural lexicon into the languages in question, rather than examining the absorption of structural and other features from one language to another.

There has been some amount of study of loan strata in the world's earliest written language that can be read, namely the Mesopotamian isolate Sumerian, for which our earliest records date from about 3000 BC. These include some cultural loan material that we can identify as coming from Akkadian, and other items that we assume came into Sumerian from what are otherwise unknown languages (Rubio 1999). An account of this is provided in Michailowski (2004), while in a study that looks beyond the transfer of lexicon into Sumerian, Edzard (2003) discusses Akkadian syntactic influence on later stages of Sumerian, including the borrowing into Late Sumerian of the Akkadian *ū* 'and,' a coordinating conjunction with relatives in other Semitic languages. Sumerian influence upon Akkadian is the earliest instance of CILC about which we have information.

There is also evidence of borrowing from other languages into another Mesopotamian isolate, Elamite (Stolper 2004), and there are discussions of borrowings into Hurrian (Wilhelm 2004a), and its close relative Urartian, or Urartaean (one possible loan into Urartian from Akkadian, *kubša* 'helmet,' is mentioned in Wilhelm 2004b, this being the only loan identified so far in our sparse Urartaean material). None of these languages has left descendants, but we have evidence for borrowing from other sources in a variety of languages, some of which do have living relatives: Semitic Akkadian (Huehnergard and Woods 2004; loans from Sumerian). Another Semitic language, Hebrew (McCarter 2004), shows borrowings from Greek, Persian, Akkadian, Aramaic, Hittite, Sumerian, and Egyptian), and its sister Afro-Asiatic language Egyptian (Loprieno 2004 indicates the presence of loans from Semitic and possibly other sources). Hebrew, in the revived form that Zuckermann (2003) has called Israeli, has speakers to this day.

There are also cases of borrowing in ancient Indo-European languages, for instance, in Hittite (Watkins 2004 mentions loans from Semitic, and also from Hurrian, the extinct isolate Hattic and elsewhere). Sanskrit (Burrow 1955; Burrow 1973 discusses loans from Latin, Greek, and Old Persian, in addition to the ones from Dravidian and to a lesser extent Austroasiatic, which had already been discussed in Burrow 1955), Classical Greek (Woodard 2004), and Latin (Clackson 2004) all show the evidence of borrowings from other languages—in the case of Greek and Latin, there has been very considerable borrowing between them, especially from the first into the second, a process of transfer that continues apace after the Classical Latin period ends. Latin also contains loans from Oscan and Sabellian (also Italic languages), Etruscan, and Phoenician, while a large amount of the Ancient Greek lexicon originates in a language or languages unrelated to Greek, whose names we do not know. Additionally, there is evidence of borrowing into the Sino-Tibetan language Ancient Chinese (Peyraube 2004, discussing loans from Austroasiatic and Hmong-Mien languages into the language). In addition, we can find evidence for borrowings from Mixe-Zoquean languages into early hieroglyphic records of various Mayan languages of ancient Mexico and Guatemala (Bricker 2004). Woodard (ed. 2004), a collection of descriptive articles written by experts on each language surveyed, is obviously a major resource here, and most of the chapters give a number of examples of borrowed items in the languages in question.

The loan history of Hebrew is especially well covered in this regard. In addition to Horovitz's and Kutscher's works (Horovitz 1960; Kutscher 1984) on loans into earlier and later Hebrew in general, we may also note specific shorter studies, such as those of Lambdin (Lambdin 1953) and Stephen Kaufman (Kaufman 1974), which focus on Egyptian and Akkadian elements in Biblical Hebrew, respectively. (The latter comprises more than 1% of the recorded Old Testament Hebrew wordstock, which is itself surely a small fragment of the actual vocabulary known to a speaker of Hebrew in Biblical times; Akkadian provided some 80 or so elements from about 7,450 separate types attested in the Hebrew Bible.) Meanwhile, Horowitz and Kutscher both additionally discuss borrowings from Greek, Latin, medieval European languages, Yiddish, Palestinian Arabic, and modern European languages into Mishnaic (for Latin only), Medieval, and later stages of Hebrew. Also worthy of mention for semiticists interested in language contact is Zammit (1994) on loans from Persian, Nabataean (a variety of Aramaic), Greek, and other languages into the seventh-century Arabic of the Qur'an.

These works are all specialist studies concentrating on a single language; in a more general account, Thomason (2004) discusses borrowings into ancient languages (including some proto-languages) in general, but especially borrowings into certain languages of the Middle East, including those listed in the preceding.

1.6 A COMPARISON OF TRANSFERRED FEATURES AMONG HEAVY-BORROWING LANGUAGES

It may be naively assumed that the proportion of borrowed non-lexical linguistic features in a language, especially one that has borrowed heavily, is directly or closely equal to the proportion of borrowed basic or non-basic vocabulary in that language. Whether this is the case is something that can be submitted to analysis using available data, though in some cases the quantity of relevant data is not as great as might be hoped. Such an investigation also enables us to test and verify hypotheses.

Table 1.1 presents data from a number of languages, chosen in the first instances for their high scores in borrowed vocabulary on the Swadesh 225-item list. The structural and other categories that could be analyzed are numerous; drawing on a detailed case study, the categories that I have selected for cross-linguistic examination are those specified in the analysis of Indic and Arabic elements in Southern Domari in Matras (2003), with a

Table 1.1 Inherited and Borrowed Linguistic Features in a Selection of Heavy-Borrowing Languages

	Kalderash	Domari	Siwi	Ghomara	Hainan Cham	Chamorro	Garifuna	Mexicanero
Swadesh 225 list loans, in %	28	22 (n = 155)	26	35 (n = 155)	25 (n = 173)*	33.5	22	25
Numerals 1–5	—	—	B, A	B (1), A 2–5	H	S	Aw; K, F	N
10, 100		—	A	A	H	S	F	S
Other numbers above 5	I = 6, 20; Others Gk	A	A	A	H	S	F	S
Bound case markers	—	—	—	—	—	—	K	N
Indefinite article	—	—	—	—	H	S	—	N
'What/who/where?'	Inn	A	B	A	H	—	Aw/K	N
'How much?'	—	—	A	A	Ch	—	Aw	N
Person concord	—	—	B	B	—	—	Aw	N
Possessive markers	I, (Gk)	I, A	B	B	H, Ch	—	Aw	S
Bound plural markers	Rom	—	B	B	—	—	Aw	N
Adjectival comparison and superlation	—	A (via suppletion)	A (suppletion)	A (suppletion)	—	S	Aw	S
Bound tense markers	—	—	B	B	—	—	Aw	N
Bound aspect markers	—	—	B	B	—	—	Aw	N
Bound modality markers	—	—	B	B	—	—	Aw	N
Bound converb markers	Ir	—	—	—	—	—	Aw	N
Lexical verb negation	—	Ir	A	B	Ch	Chm	Aw	—
Nonverbal predication marker	I?/Ir	—	—	B	Unk, Ch	—	—	N
'can'	—	—	B	B	Ch	Chm	Aw	N
'can' inflection and negation	Gk ,Slv	A	BA	B	Ch	Chm	Aw	SN
Other modals	I (Ir negation)	A	A	B, A	Ch	S	Aw, F	N
Other modal inflection and negation	—	A	A	B, A	Ch	Chm, S	Aw	N
Aspectual auxiliaries	—	A	—	—	—	—	Aw	—
Aux inflection	—	A	B	B	Ch	—	—	—
Aux negation	—	A	A	B	Ch	—	Aw	—
Existential present	—	—	—	—	Ch	S	—, S	N
Neg of existential present	—	—	—	—	Ch	—	Aw	N

(continued)

Table 1.1 Continued

	Kalderash	Domari	Siwi	Ghomara	Hainan Cham	Chamorro	Garifuna	Mexicanero
Existential past/subjunctive	—	A, I	A	—	Ch	S	—	N
Neg of existential past	—	I, A	A	—	Ch	—	—	N
Personal pronouns	—	—	B	B	H	Chm	Aw (K)	N
Demonstratives	Inn	A	B	B	H	S, Chm	Aw	N
Relative pronoun	—	A	A	A	Ch	Chm	—	N, S
Resumptive pronoun	—	A	—	—	—	—	—	—
Resumptive pronoun agreement	—	A	—	—	—	—	—	—
Bound adpositions	—	—	BA	A	—	—	—	—
Unbound adpositions	I (R)	A	B	B A	H, Ch	Chm, S	Aw	SN
Coordinating conjunctions	I, R	A	B, A	A	H, Ch	Chm, S	F, E	S (N)
Subordinating adverbial conjunctions	I, R	A	A	A	Ch	(Chm), S	Aw (F)	S
Complementizer	—	A	A	—	—	—	—	S
Complementizer agreement	—	A	—	—	—	—	—	S
Phasal adverbs	—	A	B, A	B, A	H	S	Aw	S
Focus particles	—	A	B	B	H	Chm	Aw	N

Key: A = Arabic; Aw = Arawakan; B = Berber; C = Chamic; Ch = Chinese; Chm = Chamorro; F = French; Gk = Greek; H = Hainan Cham inherited; HCh = Hainan Cham; I = Indic; Ka = Kari'na; Inn = Innovation; Ir = Iranian; MK = Mon-Khmer; N = Nahua/Nawa; R = Romanian; S = Spanish; Slv = South Slavonic; Unk = Unknown origin; — = the feature in question is absent from the language; ? = data regarding the feature are not available.

Sources: Southern Domari (Matras 2003: 161; Matras 2012); Kalderash Romani (Boretzky 1993); Siwi (Souag 2010); Ghomara (Mourigh 2016); Hainan Cham/Tsat (Thurgood 2014); Chamorro (Topping and Ogo 1973; Topping, Ogo, and Dungca 1975); Garifuna (Taylor 1977; Sabio and Ordóñez 2005; Larsen-Haurholm 2016); Mexicanero (Canger 2001).

few additions of my own. The contact history of this particular language is well known, and our ability to distinguish inherited from loan elements is assured here. It was decided to preserve the categories investigated in the original study (not all are universal) and add a few more. However, we recognize that not all languages have overt exponents of all the categories listed in the leftmost column. Domari is somewhat distantly related to Kalderash Romani, as both are Indic languages that have undergone some influence from Iranian languages. For the past several centuries, and probably for a millennium, Domari has been influenced extensively by Arabic (and also Kurdish in the case of Domari only), as has Ghomara Berber of northern Morocco, and so has Siwi Berber in Egypt. Again, the contact histories of these languages are well known, and we can compare the potentially differential impact of Arabic on two Berber languages.

Kalderash shared many of the influences that all other forms of Romani have undergone since around 1000 CE, namely Iranian, Armenian, Greek, and South Slavic. Kalderash was also exposed to several centuries of influence from Romanian and (in Transylvania) also Hungarian and Transylvanian Saxon, and latterly from the co-territorial languages that the Roma encountered after their liberation from servitude in Wallachia and Moldavia in 1861.

Hainan Cham and Chamorro are both Austronesian languages, but are probably more distantly related to one another than either of the two preceding pairs of languages is. Hainan Cham has been influenced by the Kra-Dai language Hlai, from maybe a millennium ago, and later (from an unknown date, but especially since 1949) from varieties of Chinese. As a Chamic language, Hainan Cham also has been influenced by Mon-Khmer languages from the early centuries of the Common Era, and shows some of the internal lexical and other innovations that help distinguish Chamic languages from their nearest Malayic relatives. Its development of tones predates Chinese influence, which has nonetheless been stupendous. Chamorro was extensively influenced by Spanish from the 1660s to 1898 (and for a shorter period in the 1520s) but had previously been influenced by an unknown Philippine language (or languages) for a period of time that has yet to be determined.

Finally, Garifuna is an Arawakan language and Mexicanero is Uto-Aztecan, so that neither is related to any other language on the table. Both Garifuna and Mexicanero have been influenced by Spanish (as has Chamorro, and also Ghomara Berber) since at least the seventeenth century, or a century earlier in the case of Mexicanero. But Garifuna shows evidence of strong influence from other languages, too, namely French and Antillean Creole French (both of these seem to have made contributions from the seventeenth century onward), and later from Creole English and maybe non-Creole English, and—earlier than these (maybe from the fifteenth century or earlier)—from Kari'na Pidgin.

In the HCh material there are numerous forms that have Chinese and non-Chinese exponents (including all numerals, for instance), in addition to several forms for which the only item used in HCh derives from Chinese. Additionally, a high proportion (ca. 20%) of HCh Swadesh list forms are without etymology, and a couple of other forms are compounds that use items that have already been found in use elsewhere on the list.

The matrix of features that are examined in Table 1.1 are relevant most clearly for languages that have been influenced by systems, such as Arabic, which have resumptive pronouns, person-marking on prepositions and agreement on complementizers. Most languages lack these features either through inheritance, innovation, or borrowing. The fact that these typologically unusual features are transferrable into languages that previously had no such features, and that had no features which resembled them, is striking: the effects of CILC include typological change at micro- and macro-levels.

Nonetheless, our overall findings are somewhat surprising. Our published Swadesh-list lexical data for Domari and Ghomara are seriously incomplete (and the 155 forms listed for the Swadesh list in each language are for different Swadesh-list items in each case). Even so, we can observe that Ghomara seems to have borrowed twice as much non-Berber vocabulary as Domari has taken from non-Indic sources (Northern Kurdish in addition to Arabic). This is so even though both have been in contact with Arabic for several centuries and the speakers of both languages are (and have long been) bilingual in Arabic. Not all heavy-borrowing languages take over the same kinds of features from the language systems that influenced them. The length of time in which two languages have been in contact and the degree of disparity in prestige or power that the donor language has over the recipient are both important factors. But quantifying them and developing a formula that will allow us to gauge the depth of contact is not easy to draw up; the degree of bilingualism, its duration, and the degree to which it is reciprocal are also important considerations.

We should also discuss Dolenjska Romani of Slovenia and northern Italy (for instance, Cech 2006). Dolenjska Romani in its several varieties has borrowed massively from Slovene (in addition to possessing several Slovene-Romani lexical pairings). Once again, we have sub-adequate records for the long and short Swadesh list, on the lines of about 175 forms for the full list, of which at least 55 concepts are solely expressed by loans from Slovene, with a handful more coexisting with original Romani equivalents (themselves of various origins), and conjunctions are here also taken wholesale from Slovene. The paucity of Greek loans in the language has been commented upon; the reason for this (which is obvious when one examines the lexical evidence) is that the referents which are labeled in other Romani languages by Greek loans have names in Dolenjska Romani that generally come from Slovene. Some interesting cases of grammaticalization can be found, not least the construction of the comparison of adjectives using pre-posed *hede*, a grammaticalization of *feder* 'better,' itself an old borrowing from Ossetic. What does mark Dolenjska Romani out from other varieties is that it has taken a few verbal inflectional endings from Greek (such as the 3SG.PRES.INDIC –*i*, found also in Slovene) and has employed them productively on verb stems of all origins, with just a few older monosyllabic verbs preserving original Romani 3SG.PRES.INDIC –*el*/-*al*. In the world's languages, verbal morphology tends to be replaced (through extension in use of prior forms, grammaticalization of what were previously lexical items, etc.) rather than through borrowing. But it is far from immune from change. Incidentally, Herrity (1996: 233 on *i*-stem verbs in Slovene) shows that –*i* is the regular ending for such verbs, and this may well have bolstered the use of Greek-origin –*i* as the 3SG present indicative ending in Dolenjska Romani.

The preceding features concern lexicon and inflectional morphology, and Table 1.1 suggests that some features (e.g., adjectival comparison) are more amenable to replacement through borrowing than others (e.g., finite verbal inflection), and that with more features and more languages available, a scale of borrowing might be able to be assembled. It would be possible to construct a similar table for various features of derivational morphology, such as agentive affixes, markers of causativity, and so on (and here Kalderash, with its fully integrated abstract noun marker –*mo* taken from Greek and the like would score highly). Yet here the kinds of features that have overt exponents in a subset of languages may be even more diverse than those in Table 1.1.

The greater the number of case studies of pairs of linguistic systems in contact, the greater the range of kinds of CILC one can exemplify, and the greater the number of features that can be identified as open to borrowing. The sheer weight of evidence from these examples shows that there are apparently no restrictions on what can be borrowed, especially within cases of Bloomfieldian *dialect borrowing* (and secondly, that rigorous hierarchies of borrowing are rather difficult to set up). Indeed, identifying what has been borrowed in these languages can often only be clearly identified once the source language for these borrowings is out of the sociolinguistic picture. The closer the languages are, the greater is the possibility for copying and transfer, but this does not mean that there will certainly be a greater degree of borrowing: sociolinguistic factors, including the access to the target donor language, are crucial, and they can stymie the transfer of plentiful forms. Some kinds of borrowing seem to be especially widely found within certain kinds of languages. Typology and isomorphism are crucial, too, but (*pace* Field and Meillet, and Sapir before Meillet) their absence does not present a barrier to transfer. Nor can what is to be borrowed be predicted, just understood ex post facto. What can be borrowed is constrained by the features that the donor language has to offer, and despite our wealth of knowledge there may yet be much to discover about the ways in which one linguistic system may reshape other ones.

1.7 PIDGINS, CREOLES, KOINES, LINGUA FRANCAS, MIXED LANGUAGES, AND LINGUISTIC AREAS

CILC can help to create new languages, or as Smith (1999) referred to them, **younger languages**. Linguistic systems that develop because of the need for people without a common linguistic background to communicate with one another for trade, politics, or other purposes are known as **pidgins**. These have been attested everywhere from the Arctic to Tierra del Fuego, and new pidgins are being noted (or exhumed from earlier records) all the time. Pidgins are characterized by sparse morphology, a stronger dependence upon word order to clarify relations within the clause, and small lexica. Some of these lexica may be **macaronic** (composed of elements from two or more different languages) but this is not always the case.

Pidgins that become the dominant or sole language of a speech community are known as **creoles**. Creoles develop from pidgins; this view is controversial, but the immense amount of linguistic evidence to support this opinion brooks no dissent. As such, their structural capacities and lexica expand considerably, so that they can be used for all the purposes that other first languages can be. Their structures may echo features of the structure of their **chief lexifier** (or **superstrate**)—the language that provided the bulk of the everyday vocabulary—but they do not continue the actual morphological systems of these languages. These often mirror many of the typological (but rarely the actual morphological) features of the **substrate** languages spoken as native or dominant languages by the people who helped to creolize pidgins, generally in oppressive social circumstances. Some languages that are thought of as pidgins are used as first languages by a minority of their speakers and as the major everyday language (but not their only language) by the remainder, and these are nowadays known as **pidgin/creoles**.

Creole languages are often further modified by interaction with languages that play important social or political roles in creolophone societies, and these are known as **adstrate** languages. The literature on and in creole languages is massive; much attention has been paid to the ultimate origins of creoles (namely, whether or not they derive from prior pidgins). The fact that they do so derive is reinforced by computational studies, notably the collection of studies assembled in a project conducted at the University of Aarhus and edited by Peter Bakker (Bakker et al. 2017), which use phylogenetic methods to demonstrate the interrelatedness of various groups of creole languages and their descent from prior pidgins. For deeper and wider reading, Holm (1988–1989, 2000), Holm and Patrick (eds. 2007), Velupillai (2015), Michaelis et al. (2013) and Bakker and Daval-Markussen (2017) are essential reading, but do not by any means exhaust even the list of languages that fall under these categories (see also Chapter 11 by Parkvall and Chapter 12 by McWhorter in this volume).

The term **koine** or **koiné** (from Greek *hē koinē dialektos* 'the common dialect,' referring to the kind of Attic Greek in which the New Testament was first presented) refers to a variety of language that represents a leveling or compromise among several closely related varieties. It is generally based upon one socially dominant variety that has absorbed some features of other varieties (Siegel 1985), and which may have undergone some structural simplification (McWhorter 2007). A koine may be slightly simplified structurally, and may serve as a **lingua franca**, the common language between people who lack a shared first language. Lingua francas (the term is Italian but is usually pluralized as if it were English) may have undergone some structural simplification, but this too is not necessarily so. Pidgins, creoles, and mixed languages may all serve as lingua francas in the right social circumstances. Koineization is a kind of **new dialect formation** (Trudgill 2004), a linguistic process that has received much attention of late, not least in Anglophone areas such as New Zealand, where varieties of

English English, Scottish English, and Irish English came together against the backdrop of New Zealand Māori, and developed into a distinctive set of national varieties. The rise of New Zealand English was investigated by a team led by Elizabeth Gordon in the ONZE (Older New Zealand English) Project. New towns, such as the English new town Milton Keynes, also have been investigated with regard to the formation of new dialects (Kerswill and Williams 2005). An important process assisting in new dialect formation is **dialect leveling** (Hinskens 1998).

Over the past few decades a great amount of attention has been paid to **mixed languages,** for which the coverage was more diffuse in previous decades (and indeed, some of them were regarded initially as pidgins or creoles, from both of which categories they are certainly structurally distinct). These are sometimes the dominant language of a speech community, and because they have achieved a high degree of stability (which is to say that they show a limited degree of internal variation between the sources of their various components), they are known as **stable mixed languages.** Some of these show a primary division between nominal elements (both lexical and morphological) and verbal elements (again both lexical and morphological), which come from different languages that may be closely related, distantly related, or completely unrelated genealogically, while some others divide their components between taking lexicon from one source and bound morphology from another. Velupillai (2012) treats these in her book, which also covers pidgins and creoles, and Bakker and Mous (eds. 1994) and Thomason (ed. 1997) provide some crucial basic reading on several of them, while Bakker (2017) is a superb introduction to the subject, with snippets from a wide range of mixed languages. Versteegh (2017) casts doubt upon the existence of mixed languages (see also Chapter 13 by Smith and Grant in this volume).

Ever since the pioneering work of Jernej Kopitar on structural similarities among some of the languages in the Balkans (Kopitar 1829), linguists have been interested in bundles of structural and/or lexical phenomena that cross genealogical boundaries within a particular geographical or cultural area. These features are held to be shared among some languages that belong to more than one family (or which may be isolates), yet which do not characterize all the languages in all the genealogical groups that exhibit these features. Such collections of shared features are known as **linguistic areas** or **Sprachbünde.** Linguistic areas are dynamic rather than static; they can change over time, and some linguists (notably Campbell 2017) have observed that it can be difficult to define them satisfactorily. Matras, McMahon, and Vincent (eds. 2004) and especially Hickey (ed. 2017) are valuable introductions to this subject and contain numerous case studies of linguistic areas from around the world.

Recent decades have seen an interest in the rise and development of urban (multi) ethnolects, which are used as in-group languages and which combine lexical and sometimes other elements from a wide range of languages. Kiessling and Mous (2004) explore some urban youth languages of this kind from sub-Saharan Africa, while Cheshire, Nortier, and Adger (2015) discuss emerging multiethnolects in Europe. This is further evidence of CILC as a dynamic field. This can also be seen in the recent paper by Frank Jablonka (Jablonka 2017) on the rise of new mixed ethnolects as a fresh result of language contact. A converse view, which shows that controversy remains alive in the field, can be seen in the paper by Kees Versteegh (2017) on what he perceives as the myth of the mixed language.

The interaction of various factors which shape the effects of CILC is complex and multifarious. Table 1.2, whose findings are based on my four decades of studying this topic, indicates something of the degrees to which various kinds of factors, and the circumstances governing their propagation and continuation, may interact within a linguistic system. The overall impression is one of conditioning factors being important but not essential for certain kinds of CILC to occur.

1.8 THE CONTENT OF THIS VOLUME

After the present chapter, which constitutes the introduction, the content of this book falls into two main divisions. A series of thematic chapters examining the interaction of CILC with various levels of language structure or language use discusses phonology (Grant, Klein, and Ng, Chapter 3), morphology (Gardani, Chapter 4), syntax (Ross, Chapter 5) and lexis and semantics (Mott and Laso, Chapter 6). In addition, it includes an account of theories of CILC (Winford, Chapter 2), CILC and its relations with endangered languages (Aikhenvald, Chapter 10), and the role of code-mixing and code-switching in the instigation of CILC (Backus, Chapter 8), in addition to issues linking CILC and first- and second-language acquisition (Chapter 9). There are also chapters on CILC and pidgins (Parkvall, Chapter 11), creoles (McWhorter, Chapter 12) and stable mixed languages (Smith, Chapter 13). Sociolinguistic aspects are exemplified in a chapter that looks at a series of related case studies of CILC in the Sinosphere (Thurgood, Chapter 7).

This collection is followed by chapters that discuss the impact of CILC upon a range of languages throughout the world. Most are originally spoken languages that have often later been reduced to writing, although we have included an examination of language contact effects upon American Sign Language (Quinto-Pozos and Adam, Chapter 31). All continents are represented in this selection, and although the collection includes five Indo-European languages, there is also exemplification of case studies from several other families and from Korean (Sohn, Chapter 24), which is often regarded as an isolate, and which may or may not be related to Japanese—although it is certain that Korean has borrowed material from Japanese. Meanwhile the genealogical affinities of Äiwoo of the Santa Cruz Islands, Solomon Islands (Næss, Chapter 28), were uncertain until recently, when it was established that it is indeed Oceanic and therefore Austronesian, although it has been profoundly influenced by non-Austronesian languages. Emphasis has been given to depicting the situation of CILC in languages where the effects of contact-induced change are especially strong, varied in nature, or simply pervasive. In several cases, short texts have been presented, and in these the

Table 1.2 Features and characteristics of CILC compared according to causes and effects, and set in tabular form

Feature	Changes internal structure of subsystem?	Simplifies system?	Compli-cates subsys-tem?	Bilingualism by some required to actuate this?	Transfer occurs between consecutive generations?	Transfer occurs through gradual language shift?	Transfer occurs through childhood transmission?	Transfer occurs through adult trans mission?	Involves transfer of pattern?	Involves transfer of fabric?
Lexical borrowing	1	1	2	2	1	1	1	1	2	4
Partial relexification	1	1	1	2	3	3	3	3	2	4
Full relexification	1	2	3	4	4	3	1	3	1	4
Van Coetsem feature imposition	3	2	2	4	4	4	4	4	4	1
Change in templatic phonology	3	2	3	3-4	3	1	1	3	4	3-4
Addition of phonological segments	3	1	3	3-4	3	2	1	4	3-4	4
Grammaticalisation of items from lexicon to morphology	4	1	3	2-3	3	3	2	2-4	4	3
Metatypy	4	1	2	3	4	3	0	4	4	3
Calquing	0	1	1	4	2-3	2	2	4	4	0-1
Simplification	4	4	0	4	3	2	2	4	2	2
Complexification	4	0	4	3	4	3	1	3	3	3
Core-periphery changes	2	2	3	3	4	3	1	4	2	4
Interdialectal borrowing within a language	2	2	2	4	2	3	1	4	1	4
Calquing	1	3	2	4	2	2	0	4	4	2
Koineisation	3	4	1	4	2	2	0	4	1	4
Pidginisation	4	4	0	4	1	0	0	3	1	2
creolisation	4	3	1	2	4	1	4	2-4	3	3

0 = never occurs, 1- rarely, 2 = sometimes, 3 = usually; 4 = always the case. NA – not applicable.

multifarious effects of CILC on the relevant language have been illustrated, in order to show readers what the effects of CILC can look like. Individual studies of the effects of CILC upon a pidgin (Blaxter Paliwala, Chapter 27), a creole (Baptista et al., Chapter 33), a stable mixed language (Benítez-Torres, Chapter 18), and a linguistic area or Sprachbund (Kaufman, Chapter 30) have been presented. There is also the discussion of the effects of CILC on pre-modern varieties of a small language family, namely Celtic (Hickey, Chapter 14). It had been hoped that we could include accounts of the effects of CILC upon a number of other languages upon which CILC has wrought especially strong changes, but space, time commitments, and the inability to obtain chapters from suitably qualified authors meant that this was not always possible. For this we crave the reader's indulgence.

In this volume no single ideological or theoretical viewpoint has been imposed upon the authors as a kind of "party line," and the authors have been given a free hand to take whatever theoretical positions they choose, on the understanding that such positions are not a prioristic assumptions but are empirically supported and can be substantiated with bodies of evidence.

The volume falls into Parts I and II, comprising general chapters and case studies, respectively. After this introductory chapter, Part I commences with Chapter 2 by **Donald Winford**, who presents theories of contact-induced linguistic change. Work on the topic has been extensive since around 1950, and especially since the publication of Thomason and Kaufman (1988). Winford gives particular attention to the theories of Frans van Coetsem, who posited two transfer types: borrowing as generally understood, and imposition, in which features (rather than elements) of a language that was spoken by a dominated population shaped the language of the invaders. That language may have prevailed but was thus modified as a result of contact with the substrate language.

Chapter 3, by **Anthony Grant**, the late **Thomas Klein,** and **E-Ching Ng**, examines CILC and phonology. The levels at which speakers of one language can modify the language of another group are legion. While one of the commonest levels is for a language to absorb new phonemes from another language, or to promote previous allophones to phonemes because they now create minimal pairs, other features such as new intonational or word-stress patterns, new syllabic canons, and the introduction (or even loss) of processes of vowel harmony or tonogenesis have been attested.

Morphology, both inflectional and derivational, is closely entwined with the rest of the basic structure of a language, and Chapter 4, by **Francesco Gardani**, documents and discusses a wide number of cases of borrowing, especially in the realm of inflectional morphology.

Malcolm Ross discusses the effects of CILC on several aspects of clausal and sentential syntax in Chapter 5. His theory of metatypy, in which a language gradually changes its syntactic typology as a result of borrowing features from a more powerful language (from which it need not also borrow morphemes) is discussed here, with important attention being paid to its effects on some Slavic languages in contact with one another and with German.

The effects of CILC on several branches of semantics are illustrated by **Brian Mott** and **Natalia Laso**, who demonstrate in Chapter 6 that this extends way beyond the extension of the meanings of preexisting words in order to accommodate new concepts that had not previously been lexicalized. Lexicology is examined, too, so that issues such as lexical borrowing and loanblends are illustrated, as are subtler cases in which, for example, verbs that governed one case in a language change their case-government in order to align with that found in a more dominant language.

The preceding chapters deal with what are sometimes described as microlinguistic matters. Introducing the macrolinguistic dimension is Chapter 8 on code-switching by **Ad Backus**. Code-switching (CS) and code-mixing have long been seen by many scholars (though by no means all of them) as engines of CILC, and Backus discusses the theories and illustrates the effects of CS, often with examples from his own research involving Dutch and Turkish.

First and second-language acquisition (also known as *L1 and L2 acquisition*) and their interaction with CILC constitute the subject of Chapter 9 by **Gabriel Ozón and Eva Duran Eppler**. These modes of language acquisition have also often been seen as the means by which CILC occurs in languages, and this chapter examines the evidence for the separate roles of these modes of acquisition in shaping and affecting language change.

Language acquisition is at the heart of Chapter 7 by **Graham Thurgood**, who examines the effects of the processes of acquisition (especially L1) on some members of the Chamic languages. These comprise a group of Austronesian languages on mainland Southeast Asia that have been profoundly affected by Mon-Khmer languages, not all of which can be identified. This state of affairs has continued into modern times, with some Chamic languages being influenced by Khmer and many more by Vietnamese, while Hainan Cham has been latterly massively influenced by Chinese, and this influence continues.

Alexandra Aikhenvald in Chapter 10 discusses the effects of CILC on languages that are in a state of endangerment. Thousands of languages are in danger of being abandoned by their speakers in favor of other languages that confer more prestige and power (however limited) on their speakers, and speakers of these languages have developed a number of responses to this effect, including overt or covert resistance to the influence of these languages. Aikhenvald draws upon her extensive fieldwork on languages in Papua New Guinea and the Vaupés (Amazonia) to illustrate these issues.

Exploring attestations and sources from around the world, **Mikael Parkvall** in Chapter 11 presents an innovative account of pidgins, demonstrating their general structural and social characteristics, and presenting examples in the form of sentences and textlets from a range of pidgins, some of which have barely been discussed in the literature before now.

Not all linguists are as yet convinced of the truth that pidgins underlie the development of creoles, but this is made clear in Chapter 12 by **John H. McWhorter**, who draws upon data from "radical" creoles such as Saramaccan to demonstrate the innate connection between pidgins and creoles. In this way, one may elucidate the relationship between the substrate (the languages spoken by the people whose pidgin gave rise to many typological properties of the creole), superstrate (the source of the lexicon), and adstrate (a later and secondary source of lexicon and other features) in creoles.

Norval Smith and **Anthony Grant** in Chapter 13 discuss mixed languages, linguistic systems (sometimes the only one used by a speech community, at other times one of many deployed within a single speech community) that have often been lumped together with pidgins and creoles, but which do not demonstrate the kinds of structural simplification that typify pidgins.

Part II of this book explores the effects of CILC on a number of languages, and for this reason they are often furnished with illustrative texts that highlight such contact effects. These works all draw upon the authors' fieldwork and specialist knowledge, and in some cases (Sreekumar, Sohn, Adam, Baptista, Veiga, Soares, and Lopes Robalo, and indeed Beal and Faulkner) the authors are themselves L1 users of the languages that they describe.

Raymond Hickey discusses in Chapter 14 how early Celtic languages, and furthermore Irish in its various stages, have been affected by a number of languages. For Irish, these include Latin, British Celtic, Norse, Norman French, and English. But there has also been influence by a language or languages whose identity is as yet unknown, but which may have been spoken in northwestern Europe before Celtic languages reached the area in the first millennium BC. This linguistic influence has been passed on from a time before Celtic languages were written down, and can be seen in modern Celtic languages.

In Chapter 15, **Clive Grey** examines the effects upon Welsh of other languages. The focus here is on English as the major source of influence, and this influence continues apace, although the impact of other languages (notably Latin at various stages) is also highly significant, while Norse, Irish, French, and indirectly Flemish (via Pembrokeshire English) have also made contributions.

Joan C. Beal and **Mark Faulkner** in Chapter 16 present a crisp account of influence upon English, a language whose history is probably the most intensely and copiously described of all. CILC has affected English greatly, and although our records of documented English have gaps (especially during the Norman period, 1066–1204) it is clear that the five centuries beginning in 1000 CE are the ones when the influence was strongest. We should not lose sight of the facts that the languages which affected the everyday vocabulary of English the most included Norse and Dutch/Low German, both of them closely related to English, while Latin (and to a lesser extent its descendants, especially various forms of French) has been a source of influence from Old English times onward. Nor should we neglect the effect of British Celtic on Old English, which has been a matter of discussion for decades but which is still underplayed by some because of the dearth of British loanwords into English.

Miriam Bouzouita in Chapter 17 examines CILC in Spanish, itself a language that has exerted great influence on many other languages (as Jorge Gómez-Rendón's Chapter 32 on Guaraní indicates). Like English, Spanish is a language that has been massively influenced by languages to which it is closely related (especially French, but also Italian) or from which it is descended (in this case, Latin). Arabic's impact on Spanish is well known and richly documented, and the impact of Basque has been slight, but because we know little of Celtic in Roman Iberia (Celtiberian and also Tartessian) and even less of Iberian and its assumed relatives, we cannot say how deeply these under-documented languages shaped Iberian Latin. Meanwhile, English exerts an ever greater influence, not just in the places (such as the US) where it has de facto official status, de jure or de facto.

In Chapter 18, **Carlos M. Benítez-Torres** describes the genesis and composition of Tagdal, one of a small group of Berber-Songhay mixed languages (so-called Northern Songhay languages), which are spoken in the Azawagh Valley in Mali and Niger (with an outlier, Korandje, being spoken in the village of Tabelbala in western Algeria). The basic morphology and a few hundred words of the high-frequency lexicon of these languages derive from Songhay languages, while some less frequent structural features and the bulk of the everyday lexicon derive from Berber (Amazigh) languages, not merely from the co-territorial Tuareg varieties, with further lexical strata from Fulfulde, French, and especially Arabic. These are *core-periphery* mixed languages, with a core of morphemes deriving from one source and a larger body of material from another. What distinguishes these from other languages that have borrowed heavily (such as English) is the thinness of the core.

The subject of Chapter 19 by **Birgit Hellwig** is Goemai, a Chadic language of northeastern Nigeria, which shows influence from unrelated Niger-Congo languages in addition to considerable (and continuing) lexical and structural influence from Goemai's distant relative Hausa.

Lameen Souag in Chapter 20 gives an account of CILC in Berber varieties—for it is of course a language family, not a single language. Berber is a donor language (or language family) as well as a recipient. Latin, Punic, and Ancient Egyptian have made contributions in ancient times, while Western European languages, such as Spanish and especially French, have influenced Berber lexicon. But the overwhelming source of influence on Berber languages is Arabic in its diachronic and diatopic varieties, and in the case of some forms, such as Siwi (Egypt) and Ghomara (northern Morocco), this influence has been immense and is continuing. Meanwhile, Berber languages have played a strong part in shaping Maghrebi Arabic, and especially varieties spoken in Morocco.

Oleg Belyaev has examined in Chapter 21 a wide range of the structural and lexical effects of CILC from many sources upon Ossetic (especially the Iron dialects). An Iranian language, Ossetic contains some elements originating in Turkic and also in Arabic and Ossetic's relative Persian/Farsi, but as most Ossetes did not adopt Islam, these effects are minor. More important has been the influence of languages of the Caucasus, both Nakh-Dagestanian languages such as Chechen, and the dominant Kartvelian language Georgian, while later influences upon Ossetic have come from Russian. Indeed, certain features that Ossetic has preserved from Proto-Iranian and which its sister-languages have lost (often as the result of Arabic influence) suggests that we should claim that some features of Ossetic have been preserved through contact-induced conservatism.

Eleanor Coghill in Chapter 22 describes contact effects of many languages upon Neo-Aramaic, specifically the North-Eastern Neo-Aramaic on which she did fieldwork and which malign geopolitical forces have kept in a state of peril for more than a century. Various forms of Aramaic were once lingua francas throughout the Near East, and having themselves absorbed elements from Akkadian (some of these being from Sumerian) and Persian, later absorbed elements of Greek and Latin. (Absorption of Greek influence occurred to the extent that some alphabets used for writing the Western Aramaic variety known as Syriac used minuscule Greek alphabetic letters in their consonantal semi-alphabetic script, blending styles of letters and directions of writing; Morag 1961). Translated materials written in Syriac served as the conduit for the perpetuation of many Greek scientific texts, which were later translated into Arabic and which had a profound effect in the history of science, and the impact of Aramaic on Qur'anic and most spoken forms of Arabic is considerable. Now Neo-Aramaic is severely endangered, its speakers perforce at least bilingual, in Kurdish (in the case of the varieties that Coghill has described), in Hebrew (in Israel), in Turkish, in Georgian, in Farsi—and in the diaspora of the Western world, in European languages such as English. In some places, Kurdish-Neo-Aramaic bilingualism has been in place for centuries, and while both are minority languages when opposed to Arabic or Turkish, Kurdish is nonetheless the dominant partner: few if any Kurds would nowadays learn Neo-Aramaic.

P. Sreekumar's discussion of Malayalam and its contact history in Chapter 23 illustrates that, as the language of the Malabar Coast, it has been influenced by languages brought by traders from afar, speaking Arabic, Portuguese, and later English. This is in addition to influence from Hebrew and Syriac, both of which were brought by members of religious minorities (Cochin Jews and St. Thomas Syro-Malabar Christians, respectively). Influence from Indic languages, especially Sanskrit, is massive, prolonged, and evident at every level, from segmental phonology to word formation.

Ho-min Sohn in Chapter 24 shows the history of Korean and the waves of influence it has undergone from other language. Here, as is the case with many languages surveyed in this book, one language has been dominant; in this case it is Chinese, which has influenced Korean for over a millennium. Even the strokes that comprise the characters of Han'gul, the system used for writing Korean, are modeled on those used in Chinese characters, as is the arrangement of these alphabetic symbols into syllables that resemble Chinese characters in shape. Other languages have influenced Korean, too: English is the major source of influence at least in South Korea, while Japanese, Dutch, Portuguese, and (at an earlier stage) Mongolian have also made lexical contribution.

In Chapter 25, **John Haiman** exemplifies the effects of language contact in Khmer. Nowadays the major sources of CILC are French and English, but the major impact on Khmer was from Sanskrit and Pali, to the extent that some important means of derivational morphology were taken over from these languages, and since then also have been used with stems of Khmer origin. Khmer has had a complex contact relationship with Thai and with Khmer's distant relative Mon (which itself has influenced Thai), and these have also served as conduits for the absorption of elements from Chinese. Khmer therefore bridges the Indosphere and the Sinosphere, the two great spheres of linguistic and cultural influence in East Asia.

Australian Aboriginal languages have had long histories of CILC, much of which has only recently been discovered, while some other instances involve the interaction of Aboriginal languages with English and the creolized varieties known generically as Kriol, and have been investigated in full only within the last decade or so. Chapter 26 by **Carmel O'Shannessy** touches on both these topics. She explores Warlpiri, a Ngumpin-Yapa language of the Northern Territory that has undergone influence from the Western Desert language, which like Warlpiri is a Pama-Nyungan language (and thus a member of the widely ramified family that covers seven-eighths of indigenous Australia) but which belongs to a different branch from the Ngumpin-Yapa languages. In the mouths of younger generations, Traditional Warlpiri has interacted with Kriol and English to give rise to Light Warlpiri, which like Tagdal is a mixed language.

Adam Blaxter Paliwala in Chapter 27 discusses modern influences upon Tok Pisin, an English-lexifier pidgin/creole closely related to Solomons Pijin, Bislama, and Torres Straits Broken. Separate from those, it also contains elements from German, Malay, and Oceanic languages of Papua New Guinea, but which has never lost touch with its chief lexifier, by which it continues to be reshaped (see also G. P. Smith 2008), and with which it shares official status in Papua New Guinea.

Contact of a very different kind is documented by **Åshild Næss** in her account in Chapter 28 of Reef Island languages of Temotu province, in the Solomon Islands. These languages puzzled scholars for decades with respect to their affinities, because they seemed to combine Austronesian and non-Austronesian elements in a very non-Austronesian way. This was complicated by the fact that there were no non-Austronesian languages spoken in Temotu, while the Austronesian—and specifically Oceanic—element in the language was very small. Næss examines this small family of strikingly disparate languages and describes the ways in which the elements combine.

In Chapter 29, **Anna Berge** studies the impact of CILC on Eskimo-Aleut languages, giving an especially detailed account of the effects of other languages upon Aleut. Berge provides lexical and textual data from Pribilof Aleut, which has been sparsely represented in previous documentation. Aleut's major source of influence is Russian, as it has been since the eighteenth century (and most Aleuts to this day are Russian Orthodox), and influence from English came much later.

David Kaufman explores the structure and defining features of a Sprachbund, the Lower Mississippi linguistic area, in Chapter 30. The languages in this Sprachbund, which borders Louisiana, Texas, Oklahoma, and Arkansas, are Native American ones (including the pidgin language Mobilian Jargon), many of them isolates (that is, languages without identifiable genealogical affiliation) and most of them are no longer spoken, having lost their last remaining speakers in the first half of the twentieth century. Work on this Sprachbund is therefore largely philological and is constrained by the nature of the data collected on them (not all of which have been published). It is also dependent upon the kinds of investigation conducted by the researchers (which in the case of one investigator,

James Owen Dorsey, proved fatal; we know practically all we have of Biloxi from his work conducted in the months before he died of typhoid in Louisiana). Probable causes of the areal features and their spread are discussed and illustrated.

David Quinto-Pozos and **Robert Adam** in Chapter 31 provide us with an illustrated account of CILC in American Sign Language: language contact is not confined to languages transmitted by the oral modality. The authors discuss a series of forms of CILC, including fingerspelling, mouthings (oral movements made in conjunction with signs, with or without vocalization), and code-switching between spoken English and ASL, and between ASL and other sign languages. The fact that these do not exhaust the possibilities for creativity in language contact in sign languages can be illustrated by the fact that some ASL users employ fingerspelled "E-X-" as a means of representing past tense.

Turning to Latin America, **Jorge Gómez Rendón** describes in Chapter 32 the multiple effects of contact-induced change in Paraguayan Guaraní, which shows profound influence from regional Spanish (and which in its turn has influenced Paraguayan Spanish). A mixed-Guaraní-Spanish language *Jopará* (named after a dish mixing meat and vegetables) has developed and is widely used, not least in urban areas. Purism is common in Guaraní as a reaction against the influence of Spanish, and to this end we have seen the rise of a cardinal numerical system stretching into the millions and using native elements, even though traditional Guaraní did not provide for numerals above '5.'

The final chapter (Chapter 33) in this section is by **Marlyse Baptista, Sérgio Soares da Costa, Manuel Monteiro da Veiga**, and **Lígia Maria Herbert Duarte Lopes Robalo**. They examine Kabuverdianu or Cape Verdean Creole, a creole language group that was structurally and lexically shaped by Atlantic languages such as Balanta and Mandinka (which the ancestors of the speakers of Kabuverdianu had originally spoken), and its centuries of relations with its major lexifier, Portuguese. Each island has its own variety, and these can be divided into Barlavento and Sotavento varieties, the latter being more clearly removed from Portuguese, though speakers in both groups are constantly in contact with Portuguese. Many speakers of Kabuverdianu live in areas, such as New England or Amsterdam, where Portuguese has no official status, and the impact of English or Dutch on diasporic Kabuverdianu will provide fruitful material for present and future researchers on language contact, for here as elsewhere there is still much to discover.

References

Abdel-Massih, Ernest T. 1971. *A Computerized Lexicon of Tamazight*. Ann Arbor: University of Michigan, Center for Near Eastern Studies.

Aikhenvald, Alexandra Yur'yevna. 2002. *Language Contact in Amazonia*. Oxford: Oxford University Press.

Anderson, Gregory D. 2005. *Language Contact in South Central Siberia*. Berlin: Harrassowitz.

Anhava, Jaakko. 2013. In search of hidden languages. *Studia Orientalia Electronica* 113: 1–6.

Bakker, Peter. 1997. *A Language of Our Own: The Genesis of Michif, the Mixed Cree-French Language of the Canadian Metis*. New York: Oxford University Press.

Bakker, Peter. 2000. Rapid language change: Creolization, intertwining, convergence. In *Time Depth in Historical Linguistics*, edited by Larry Trask, Colin Renfrew, and April McMahon, 585–620. Papers in the Prehistory of Languages. Cambridge: McDonald Institute for Archaeological Research.

Bakker, Peter, Finn Borchsenius, Carsten Levisen, and Eeva Sippola (eds.). 2017. *Creole Genesis: Phylogenetic Approaches*. Philadelphia; Amsterdam: John Benjamins.

Bakker, Peter, and Aymeric Daval-Markussen. 2017. Typology of Creole languages. In *Cambridge Handbook of Language Typology*, edited by Alexandra Y. Aikhenvald, 254–286. Cambridge: Cambridge University Press.

Bakker, Peter, and Maarten Mous (eds.). 1994. *Mixed Languages: 15 Case Studies in Language Intertwining*. Amsterdam: IFOTT.

Bayley, Richard, R. Cameron, and Ceil Lucas (eds.). 2013. *The Oxford Handbook of Sociolinguistics*. Oxford: Oxford University Press.

Berez-Kroeker, Andrea L., Diane Hintz, and Carmen Jany (eds.). 2016. *Language Contact and Change in the Americas: Studies in Honor of Marianne Mithun*. Amsterdam; Philadelphia: John Benjamins.

Berman, Howard. 2006. Studies in Blackfoot prehistory. *International Journal of American Linguistics* 72(2): 264–284.

Besters-Dilger, Juliane, C. Dermarkar, S. Pfänder, and A. Rabus (eds.). 2014. *Congruence in Contact-Induced Language Change: Language* Families, *Typological Resemblance, and Perceived Similarity*. Berlin: Walter de Gruyter.

Bloomfield, Leonard. 1933. *Language*. New York: Henry Holt.

Boretzky, Norbert. 1992. Zum Erbwortschatz des Romani. *STUF-Language Typology and Universals* 45(1–4): 227–251.

Boretzky, Norbert. 1993. *Bugurdži: Deskriptiver und historischer Abriss eines Romani-Dialekts*, Vol. 21. Wiesbaden: Otto Harrassowitz Verlag.

Bricker, Victoria R. 2004. Mayan. *Cambridge Encyclopaedia* of the *World's Ancient Languages*, edited by Roger Woodard, 1041–1070. Cambridge: Cambridge University Press.

Brody, Jill. 1987. Particles borrowed from Spanish as discourse markers in Mayan languages. *Anthropological Linguistics* 29: 507–521.

Brody, Jill. 1995. Lending the "Unborrowable": Spanish discourse markers in indigenous American languages. *Spanish in Four Continents: Studies in Language Contact and Bilingualism*, edited by Carmen Silva-Corvalán, 132–147. Washington, DC: Georgetown University Press.

Burrow, Thomas. 1955. *The Sanskrit Language*. London: Faber and Faber.

Burrow, Thomas. 1973. *The Sanskrit Language*. 3rd edition. London: Faber and Faber.

Callaghan, Catherine. 1964. *A Grammar of the Lake Miwok Language*. PhD dissertation, University of California at Berkeley.

Callaghan, Catherine. 2014. *Proto Utian Grammar and Dictionary: With Notes on Yokuts*. Berlin: Walter de Gruyter.

Campbell, Lyle. 1993. On some proposed universals of borrowing. In *Historical Linguistics 1989: Papers from the 9th International Conference on Historical Linguistics, New Brunswick, 14–18 August 1989*, edited by Henk Aertsen and Robert J. Jeffers, 91–109. Amsterdam: John Benjamins.

Campbell, Lyle. 2017. Why is it so hard to define a linguistic area? The Cambridge Handbook of Areal Linguistics, edited by Raymond Hickey, 19–39. London: Cambridge.

Campbell, Lyle, Vit Bubenik, and Leslie Saxon. 1988. Word order universals: Refinements and clarifications. *Canadian Journal of Linguistics/Revue canadienne de linguistique* 33: 209–230.

Canger, Una. 2001. *Mexicanero de la sierra madre occidental*. Mexico City : El Colegio de México.

Carvalho, Fernando. 2018. Arawakan-Guaicuruan language contact in the South American chaco. *International Journal of American Linguistics* 84: 243–263.

Cayetano, E. Roy (ed.). 1993. *The People's Garifuna Dictionary*. Dangriga, Belize: The National Garifuna Council of Belize.

Cech, Petra, 2006. Dolenjska Romani: the dialect of the Dolenjski Roma of Novo Mesto and Bela Krajina, Slovenia. Munich: Lincom Europa.

Cerrón-Palomino, Rodolfo. 2000a. *Lingüística aimara*. Lima: Centro de Estudios Regionales Andinos "Bartolomé de Las Casas."

Cerrón-Palomino, Rodolfo. 2000b. El origen centroandino del aimara. *Boletín de Arqueología PUCP*, 131–142.

Chamoreau, Claudine, and Isabelle Léglise (eds.). 2012. *Dynamics of Contact-Induced Language Change*. Berlin: Walter de Gruyter.

Cheshire, Jenny, Jacomine Nortier, and David Adger. 2015. *Emerging Multiethnolects in Europe*. London: Queen Mary's Occasional Papers Advancing Linguistics 33.

Christiansen-Bolli, Regula. 2010, *A Grammar of Tadaksahak, a Northern Songhay Language of Mali*. Köln: Rüdiger Köppe.

Clackson, James P. T. 2004. Latin. In *Cambridge Encyclopedia of the World's Ancient Languages*, edited by Roger Woodard, 789–811. Cambridge: Cambridge University Press.

Clark, Ross. 1982. Necessary and unnecessary borrowing. In *Papers from the Third International Conference on Austronesian Linguistics*, edited by Amran Halim, Vol. 3: *Accent on Variety*, l37–l43. Canberra: Pacific Linguistics.

Costa, David J. 2013. Borrowing in Southern Great Lakes Algonquian and the History of Potawatomi. *Anthropological Linguistics* 55: 195–233.

Daniels, Peter T., and William Bright. 1995. *The World's Writing Systems*. Oxford: Oxford University Press.

Deroy, Louis 1956. *L'emprunt linguistique*. Paris: Les belles lettres.

Edzard, Dietz Otto. 2003. *Sumerian Grammar*. Leiden: Brill.

Emlen, Nicholas Q. 2017. Perspectives on the Quechua–Aymara contact relationship and the lexicon and phonology of Pre-Proto-Aymara. *International Journal of American Linguistics* 83: 307–340.

Ferguson, Charles Albert. 1959. Diglossia. *Word* 15: 325–340.

Field, Fredric. W. 2002. *Linguistic Borrowing in Bilingual Contexts*. Amsterdam: John Benjamins.

Frachtenberg, Leo Joachim. 1914. *Lower Umpqua Texts: And Notes on the Kusan Dialects*. New York: Columbia University Press.

Frachtenberg, Leo Joachim. 1920. *Alsea Texts and Myths*. Bureau of American Ethnology 67. Washington, DC: US Government Printing Office.

Friedman, Victor A. 2014. Some lessons from Judezmo regarding the Balkan Sprachbund and contact linguistics. *International Journal of the Sociology of Language* 226: 3–23.

Friedman, Victor A., and Brian D. Joseph. 2013. Expanding the typology of loanwords: The role of conversational interaction. Paper presented at the Societas Linguistica Europeae, Split, Croatia, September 19, 2013.

Gardani, Francesco, Peter Arkadiev, and Nino Amiridze. 2015. Borrowed morphology: An overview. In *Borrowed Morphology*, edited by Francesco Gardani, Peter Arkadiev, and Nino Amiridze, 1–23. Berlin: De Gruyter.

Gast, Volker. 2016. Paradigm change and language contact: A framework of analysis and some speculation about the underlying cognitive processes. JournaLIPP 5: 49–70.

Gilliat-Smith, Bernard (writing as Petulengro). 1915–1916. Report on the Gypsy tribes of north-east Bulgaria. *Journal of the Gypsy Lore Society* (new series) 9(1): 1–109.

Gjerdman, Olof, and Erik Ljungberg. 1963. *The Language of the Swedish Coppersmith Gipsy Johan Dimitri Taikon: Grammar, Texts, Vocabulary and English Word-Index.* Stockholm: Lundequistska bokhndel.

Grant, Anthony P. 1999. *Mixed Languages: A Conspectus.* April 1999. Manuscript, University of Southampton.

Grant, Anthony P. 2002. Fabric, pattern, shift and diffusion: What changes in Oregon Penutian languages can tell historical linguistics. In *Proceedings of the Meeting of the Hokan-Penutian Workshop, June 17–18, 2000, University of California at Berkeley,* edited by Laura Buszard-Welcher, 33–56. Berkeley: Survey of California and Other Indian Languages 2002.

Grant, Anthony P. 2003. Review of King (2000). *Word* 54: 251–256.

Grant, Anthony P. 2012. Bound morphology in English (and beyond): Copy or cognate? *Copies and Cognates in Bound Morphology,* edited by Lars Johanson and Martine Robbeets, 93–122. Leiden: Brill.

Grant, Anthony P., Greenberg, J. H. 1963. Some universals of grammar with particular reference to the order of meaningful elements. *Universals of Language,* Vol. 2, edited by Joseph H. Greenberg, 73–113. New York: Academic Press.

Haase, Martin. 1992. *Sprachkontakt und Sprachwandel im Baskenland: die Einflüsse des Gaskognischen und Französischen auf das Baskische.* Hamburg: Buske.

Hamp, Eric P. 1989. On signs of health and death. In *Investigating Obsolescence: Studies in Language Contraction and Death,* edited by Nancy Dorian, 197–210. Cambridge: Cambridge University Press.

Hancock, Ian F. 1971 A provisional comparison of the English-derived Atlantic Creoles. In *Pidginization and Creolization of Languages,* edited by Dell Hymes, 287–292. Cambridge: Cambridge University Press.

Harrison, K. David, and Gregory Anderson. 2006. *Tyvan Dictionary.* Munich: Lincom Europa.

Haspelmath, M., and U. Tadmor. 2009. *Loanwords in the World's Languages: A Comparative Handbook.* Berlin: Mouton de Gruyter.

Haugen, Einar. 1950. The analysis of linguistic borrowing. *Language* 26: 210–231.

Heath, Jeffrey. 1978a. *Linguistic Diffusion in Arnhem Land.* Canberra: Australian Institute for Aboriginal Studies.

Heath, Jeffrey. 1978b. *Ngandi Texts and Dictionary.* Canberra: Australian Institute of Aboriginal Studies.

Heath, Jeffrey. 1984. Language contact and language change. *Annual Review of Anthropology* 13: 367–384.

Heggarty, Paul, and David Beresford-Jones. 2012. *Archaeology and Language in the Andes.* Proceedings of the British Academy. Oxford: Oxford University Press.

Heine, Bernd, and Tania Kuteva. 2008. Constraints on contact-induced linguistic change. *Journal of Language Contact* 1(2): 57–90.

Herbert, Robert K. 1990a. The relative markedness of click sounds: Evidence from language change, acquisition and avoidance. *Anthropological Linguistics* 34: 295–315.

Herbert, Robert K. 1990b. The sociohistory of clicks in Southern Bantu. *Anthropological Linguistics* 34: 295–315.

Herrity, Paul. 1996. *Slovene: A Reference Grammar*. Columbus: Slavica.

Hickey, Raymond. (ed.). 2012. *Blackwell Handbook of Language Contact*. London: Wiley-Blackwell.

Hickey, Raymond. 2012. Introduction. In *Blackwell Handbook of Language Contact*, edited by Raymond Hickey, 1–26. London: Wiley-Blackwell.

Hickey, Raymond. (ed.). 2017. *The Cambridge Handbook of Areal Linguistics*. Cambridge, UK: Cambridge University Press.

Hinskens, Frans. 1998. Dialect levelling: A two-dimensional process. *Folia Linguistica* 32(1–2): 35–52.

Hoekstra, Jarich. 2017. On the fringe between West and North Germanic: The Danish substrate in North Frisian. Paper presented at Language Shift and Substratum Interference in (Pre)history," July 11–12, 2017, Max Planck-Institute for the Study of Human History, Jena, Germany.

Holm, John A. 1988–1989. *Pidgins and Creoles*, Vol. 2: *Reference Survey*. Cambridge, UK: Cambridge University Press.

Holm, John A. 2000. *An Introduction to Pidgins and Creoles*. Cambridge, UK: Cambridge University Press.

Holm, John, and Peter L. Patrick (eds.). 2007. *Comparative Creole Syntax*. London: Battlebridge.

Horowitz, Edward. 1960. *How the Hebrew Language Grew*. New York: Ktav.

Hout, Roeland. van, and Pieter Muysken. 1992. Modeling lexical borrowability. *Language Variation and Change* 6: 39–62.

Huehnergard, John, and Christopher Woods. 2004. "Akkadian and Eblaite." In *The Cambridge Encyclopedia of the World's Ancient Languages*, edited by Roger D. Woodward, 218–287. Cambridge, UK: Cambridge University Press.

Hymes, Dell (ed.). 1971. *Pidginization and Creolization of Languages*. Cambridge, UK: Cambridge University Press.

Igla, Birgit. 1996. *Das Romani von* Ajia Varvara: *deskriptive und historisch-vergleichende Darstellung eines Zigeunerdialekts*. Wiesbaden: Harrassowitz.

Jablonka, Frank. 2017. Contacts de langues sans limites? Vers une nouvelle typologie des contacts de langues. *Zeitschrift für Romanische Philologie* 133: 650–672.

Joseph, John Earl. 2016. Divided allegiance. *Historiographia Linguistica* 43: 343–362.

Kaufman, Stephen A. 1974. *The Akkadian Loanwords in Aramaic*. Chicago: University of Chicago Press.

Kerswill, Paul, and Ann Williams. 2005. New towns and koineization: Linguistic and social correlates. *Linguistics* 43(5): 1023–1048.

Kiessling, Roland, and Maarten Mous. 2004. Urban youth languages in Africa. *Anthropological Linguistics* 46(3): 303–341.

Kimball, Geoffrey. 2005. Natchez. In *Native Languages of the Southeastern United States*, edited by Heather Hardy and Janine Scancarelli, 385–453. Lincoln: University of Nebraska Press.

King, Ruth. 2000. *The Lexical Basis of Grammatical Borrowing: A Prince Edward Island Case Study*. Amsterdam: John Benjamins.

Kopitar, Jernej. 1829. Albanische, walachische und bulgarische Sprache. *Jahrbücher der Literatur* (Wien) 46: 59–106.

Kossmann, Maarten. 2010. Parallel system borrowing: Parallel morphological systems due to the borrowing of paradigms. *Diachronica* 27(3): 459–488.

Kutscher, Edward Yechezkiel. 1984. *A History of the Hebrew Language*. Jerusalem: Magnes.

Laker, Stephen. 2013. Review of Miller, D. Gary. 2012. *External Influences on English: From Its Beginnings to the Renaissance*. *Lingua* 133: 73–83.

Lambdin, Thomas. 1953. Egyptian loanwords in the Old Testament. *Journal of the American Oriental Society* 73(3): 145–155.

Lanham, Leonard W. 1962. The proliferation and extension of Bantu phonemic systems influenced by Bushman and Hottentot. In *Proceedings of the Ninth International Congress of Linguistics, Cambridge, Mass., August 27–31, 1962*, edited by Horace G. Lunt, 382–391. Janua Linguarum, Series Maior 12. The Hague: Mouton.

Larsen-Haurholm, Steffen. 2016. *A Grammar of Garifuna*. PhD dissertation, University of Bern.

Law, Danny. 2017. Language mixing and genetic similarity: The case of Tojol-ab'al. *Diachronica* 34: 40–76.

Lee, Ronald. 2010. *Romani Dictionary: Kalderash-English*. Toronto: Magoria Books.

Lee, Ronald. 2011. *Romani Dictionary: English-Kalderash*. Toronto: Magoria Books.

Lehiste, Ilse. 1987. *Lectures on Language Contact*. Cambridge, MA: MIT Press.

Lehmann, Walter. 1920. *Zentral-Amerika*. Berlin: Dietrich Reimer.

Lockwood, William Burley. 1965. *An Informal History of the German Language*. London: Heffer.

Loprieno, Antonio. 2004. Ancient Egyprian and Coptic. In *The Cambridge Encyclopedia of the World's Ancient Languages*, edited by Roger Woodard, 160–217. Cambridge, UK: Cambridge University Press.

Louw, Johan A., 1986. Some linguistic influence of Khoi and San in the prehistory of the Nguni. In *Contemporary Studies on Khoisan,* edited by Rainer Voßen and Klaus Keuthmann, Vol. 2, 141–168. Quellen zur Khoisan- Forschung 5. Hamburg: Helmut Buske.

Lucas, Christopher. 2012. Contact-induced grammatical change: Towards an explicit account. *Diachronica* 29: 275–300.

Lucas, Christopher. 2014. Contact-induced language change. In *The Routledge Handbook of Historical Linguistics*, edited by Claire Bowern and Bethwyn Evans, Bethwyn, 519–536. London: Routledge.

Maddieson, Ian. 1986. Borrowed sounds. In *The Fergusonian Impact*, edited by Joshua A. Fishman et al., Vol. 1, 1–16. The Hague: Mouton.

Matisoff, James Alan. 1996. Contact-induced change, genetic relationship, and scales of comparison. In *The Fourth International Symposium on Language and Linguistics, Thailand*, edited by Suwilai Premsrirat, Vol. 5: *1591–1612*. Bangkok: Institute of Language and Culture for Rural Development, Mahidol University.

Matras, Yaron. 1998. Utterance modifiers and universals of grammatical borrowing. *Linguistics* 25 (20: 281–333.

Matras, Yaron. 2003. Mixed languages: Re-examining the structural prototype. *The Mixed Language Debate*, edited by Y. Matras and P. Bakker, 151–176. Berlin: De Gruyter.

Matras, Yaron. 2009. *Language Contact*. Cambridge, UK: Cambridge University Press.

Matras, Yaron. 2012. *A Grammar of Domari*. Berlin: Mouton de Gruyter.

Matras, Yaron, and Sakel, Jeanette. (eds.). 2007. *Grammatical Borrowing in Cross-Linguistic Perspective*. Berlin: Mouton de Gruyter.

Matras, Yaron, April M. S. McMahon, and Nigel Vincent (eds.). 2004. *Linguistic Areas: Convergence in Historical and Typological Perspective*. New York: Palgrave Macmillan.

Maurer, Philippe, S. M. Michaelis, Magnus Huber, and Martin Haspelmath. 2013. Directional serial verb constructions with 'come' and 'go.' In *The Atlas of Pidgin and Creole Language*

Structures, edited by P. Maurer, S. M. Michaelis, M. Huber and M. Haspelmath, 334–337. Oxford: Oxford University Press.

McCarter, P. Kyle. 2004. Hebrew. *The Cambridge Encyclopaedia of the World's Ancient Languages*, edited by Roger Woodard, 319–364. Cambridge: Cambridge University Press.

McConvell, Patrick. 2010. Contact and indigenous languages in Australia. In *The Handbook of Language Contact*, edited by Raymond Hickey, 770–794. New York: Wiley-Blackwell.

McWhorter, John Hamilton. 2007. *Language interrupted*. Oxford: Oxford University Press.

Michalowski, Piotr. 2004. Sumerian. In *The Cambridge Encyclopaedia of the World's Ancient Languages*, edited by Roger Woodard, 19–59. Cambridge: Cambridge University Press.

Mifsud, Manwel. 1995. *Loan Verbs in Maltese: A Descriptive and Comparative Study*. Leiden: Brill.

Miller, D. Gary. 2012. *External Influences on English: From Its Beginnings to the Renaissance*. Oxford: Oxford University Press.

Milroy, James. 1997. Internal vs. external motivations for linguistic change. *Multilingua* 16: 311–323.

Mithun, Marianne. 2005. Ergativity and Language Contact on the Oregon Coast: Alsea, Siuslaw, and Coos: *Proceedings of the Berkeley Linguistics Society* 24: 77–95, edited by Andrew K. Simpson. Berkeley: University of California.

Morag, Shlomo. 1961. Notes on the Vowel System of Babylonian Aramaic as Preserved in the Yemenite Tradition. *Phonetica* 7(4): 217–239.

Moravcsik, Edith A. 1978. Language contact. In *Universals of Human Language*, edited by Joseph H. Greenberg, Charles A. Ferguson, and Edith A, Moravcsik, Vol. 1, 93–123. New York: Academic Press.

Moskalev, A. A. 1978. *Jazyk duan'skix jao (jazyk nu)*. Moscow: Nauka.

Nagaraja, K. S. 2015. *The Nihali Language: Grammar, Texts and Vocabulary*. Mysore: Central Institute of Indian Languages.

Mourigh, Khalid, 2015. *A Grammar of Ghomara Berber*. PhD dissertation, Leiden University Centre for Linguistics (LUCL), Faculty of the Humanities, Leiden University.

Mourigh, Khalid. 2016. *A Grammar of Ghomara Berber*. Köln: Rüdiger Köppe.

Muysken, Pieter, 2000. *Bilingual Speech: A Typology of Code-Mixing*, Vol. 11. Cambridge: Cambridge University Press.

Muysken, Pieter, 2008. *Functional Categories*. Cambridge: Cambridge University Press.

Nurse, Derek. 2000. *Inheritance, Contact and Change in Two East African Languages (Language Contact in Africa)*. Köln: Rüdiger Köppe.

Nurse, Derek, and Thomas J. Hinnebusch. 1993. *Swahili and Sabaki: A Linguistic History*. University of California Publications in Linguistics 121. Berkeley; Los Angeles: University of California Press.

OED online. http://en.oxforddictionaries.com. Last accessed August 16, 2019.

Ordóñez, Celia Karina, and Fernando Sabio. 2005. *Hererun wagüchagu*. Tegucigalpa: Ceiba.

Ownby, Carolan Postma. 1985. *Early Nguni History: The Linguistic Evidence and Its Correlation with Archaeology and Oral Tradition*. PhD dissertation, University of California, Los Angeles.

Pakendorf, Brigitte 2009. Intensive contact and the copying of paradigms: An Éven dialect in contact with Sakha (Yakut). *Journal of Language Contact* 2(2): 85–110.

Palmer, Frank R. 1976. *Semantics*. Cambridge: Cambridge University Press.

Peyraube, Alain. 2004. Ancient Chinese. In *The Cambridge Encyclopaedia of the World's Ancient Languages*, edited by Roger Woodard, 988–1014. Cambridge: Cambridge University Press.

Proulx, Paul. 1989. A sketch of Blackfoot historical phonology. *International Journal of American Linguistics* 55: 43–82.

Robbeets, Martine. 2013. Genealogically motivated grammaticalization. In *Shared Grammaticalization with Special Focus on the Transeurasian Languages*, edited by Martine Robbeets and Hubert Cuyckens, 147–175. Amsterdam: Benjamins.

Ross, Malcolm. 1996. Is Yapese Oceanic? In *Reconstruction, Classification, Description: Festschrift in Honor of Isidore Dyen*, edited by Bernd Nothofer, 121–164. Hamburg: Abera.

Ross, Malcolm. 1996. Contact-induced change and the comparative method. In *The Comparative Method Reviewed*, edited by Mark Durie and Malcolm Ross, 180–217. Oxford: Oxford University Press.

Ross, Malcolm. 2005. Pronouns as a preliminary diagnostic for grouping Papuan languages. In *Papuan Pasts: Cultural, Linguistic and Biological Histories of Papuan-Speaking Peoples*, edited by Andrew Pawley, Robert Attenborough, Jack Golson, and Robin Hide, 15–65. Canberra: Pacific Linguistics.

Ross, Malcolm. 2007. Calquing and metatypy. *Journal of Language Contact* 1(1): 116–143.

Ross, Malcolm. 2009. Loanwords in Takia. In *Loanwords in the World's Languages: A Comparative Handbook*, edited by Martin Haspelmath and Uri Tadmor, 744–770. Berlin: Mouton de Gruyter.

Rubino, Carl Ralph Galvez. 2002. *Tagalog-English English-Tagalog Standard Dictionary*. New York: Hippocrene.

Rubio, Gonzalo 1999. On the alleged "Pre-Sumerian Substratum." *Journal of Cuneiform Studies* 51: 1–16.

Sabio, Fernando, and Celia Karina Ordóñez, 2005. *Hererun wagüchagu*. Tegucigalpa: Ceiba.

Sala, Marius. 1970. *Estudios sobre el judeoespañol de Bucarest*. Flora Botton-Burlá (trans.). México: Universidad Nacional Autónoma de México.

Sala, Marius. 1971. *Phonétique et phonologie du judéo-espagnol de Bucarest*. The Hague: Mouton.

Sala, Marius. 1988. *El problema de las lenguas en contacto*. Mexico City: UNAM.

Salas Palomo, Rosa. 2009. Pro or contra hispanisms: Attitudes of speakers of modern Chamoru. In *Hispanisation: The Impact of Spanish on the Lexicon and Grammar of the Indigenous Languages of Austronesia and the Americas*, edited by Thomas Stolz, Dik Bakker, and Rosa Salas Palomo, 237–268. Berlin: Mouton de Gruyter.

Sapir, Edward. 1921. *Language: An Introduction to the Study of Speech*. New York: Harcourt, Brace.

Sasse, Hans-Jurgen. 1992. Language decay and contact-induced change: Similarities and differences. In *Language Death: Factual and Theoretical Explorations with Special Reference to East Africa*, edited by Matthias Brenzinger, 59–80. Berlin: Mouton de Gruyter.

Schmidt, Christopher J. 2009. Loanwords in Japanese. In *Loanwords in the World's Languages: A Comparative Handbook*, edited by Martin Haspelmath and Uri Tadmor, 545–574. Berlin: De Gruyter.

Schuchardt, Hugo. 1884. *Slawo-deutsches und Slawo-italienisches*. Graz: Leuschner & Lubensky.

Schuchardt, Hugo. 1914. *Die Sprache der Saramakka-Neger in Suriname*. Amsterdam: Johannes Muller.

Seifart, Frank. 2012. The principle of morphosyntactic subsystem integrity in language contact: evidence from morphological borrowing in Resígaro (Arawakan). *Diachronica* 24: 371–504.

Seifart, Frank. 2014. *AfBo: Affix Borrowing*. Online: frankseifart.info/

Siegel, Jeff. 1985. Koines and koineization. *Language in Society* 14: 357–378.

Smith, Geoff P. 2008. Tok Pisin in Papua New Guinea: Phonology. In *Varieties of English*, Vol. 3: *Pacific and Australasia*, edited by Bernt Kortmann and Edgar W. Schneider, 188–210. Berlin: Walter de Gruyter.

Smith, Norval S. H. 1999. Younger languages: Genetically modified? Paper given at the Second International Workshop on Mixed Languages, University of Aarhus, May 1999.

Sorensen, Arthur. 1967. Multilingualism in the Northwest Amazon. *American Anthropologist* 69: 670–684.

Souag, Lameen, 2010. *Grammatical Contact in the Sahara: Arabic, Berber, and Songhay in Tabelbala and Siwa.* PhD dissertation, SOAS, University of London.

Souag, Lameen, 2014. Siwi addressee agreement and demonstrative typology. *STUF-Language Typology and Universals* 67(1): 35–45.

Sridhar, S. N. 1990. *Kannada*. London: Routledge.

Stapert, Eugénie. 2011. *Contact-Induced Change in Dolgan: An Investigation into the Role of Linguistic Data for the Reconstruction of a People's (Pre)history.* PhD dissertation, University of Leiden, Utrecht.

Stolper, Matthew W. 2004. Elamite. In *The Cambridge Encyclopedia of the World's Ancient Languages*, edited by Roger Woodard, 60–94. Cambridge: Cambridge University Press.

Stolz, Thomas, D. Bakker, and R. S. Palomo (eds.). 2008a. *Aspects of Language Contact: New Theoretical, Methodological and Empirical Findings with Special Focus on Romancisation Processes.* Berlin: Walter de Gruyter.

Stolz, T., Dik Bakker, and Rosa Salas Palomo (eds.). 2008b. *Hispanisation: The Impact of Spanish on the Lexicon and Grammar of the Indigenous Languages of Austronesia and the Americas.* Berlin: Walter de Gruyter.

Swadesh, Morris. 1955. Towards greater accuracy in lexicostatistic dating. *International Journal of American Linguistics* 21: 121–137.

Tadmor, Uri. 2009. Loanwords in Indonesian. In *Loanwords in the World's Languages: A Comparative Handbook*, edited by Martin Haspelmath and Uri Tadmor, 686–716. Berlin: De Gruyter.

Taylor, Douglas. 1977. *Languages of the West Indies*. Baltimore, MD: Johns Hopkins Press.

Thomason, Sarah Grey (ed.). 1997. *Contact Languages: A Wider Perspective*. Amsterdam: John Benjamins.

Thomason, Sarah Grey. 2001. *Language Contact: An Introduction*. Edinburgh: Edinburgh University Press.

Thomason, Sarah Grey. 2004. Determining language contact effects in ancient contact situations. In *Lenguas en Contacto: El testimonio escrito*, edited by Pedro Bádenas de la Peña, Sofía Torallas Tovar, Eugenio R. Luján, and María Ángeles Gallego, 1–14. Madrid: Consejo Superior de Investigaciones Científicas,

Thomason, Sarah Grey, and Daniel Leonard, Everett. 2000. Pronoun borrowing. In *Annual Meeting of the Berkeley Linguistics Society*, Vol. 27, 301–316. Berkeley: Berkeley Linguistic Society.

Thomason, Sarah Grey, and Terrence Kaufman. 1988. *Language Contact, Creolization and Genetic Linguistics.* Berkeley, Los Angeles: University of California Press.

Thurgood, Graham. 2015. *A Grammatical Sketch of Hainan Cham: History, Contact and Phonology.* Berlin: De Gruyter Mouton.

Thurston, William R. 1987. *Processes of Change in the Languages of North-Western New Britain.* Pacific Linguistics B: 99. Canberra: Australian National University.

Topping, Donald Medley, with B. C. Dungca. 1973. *Chamorro Reference Grammar*. Honolulu: PALI.

Topping, Donald M., Pedro M. Ogo, and Bernadita C. Dungca. 1975. *Chamorro-English Dictionary*. Honolulu: University of Hawai'i Press.

Trask, Robert Laurence. 1997. *The History of Basque*. London: Routledge.

Trudgill, Peter. 2004. *New-Dialect Formation: The Inevitability of Colonial Englishes*. Edinburgh: Edinburgh University Press.

Trudgill, Peter. 2011. *Sociolinguistic Typology: Social Determinants of Linguistic Complexity*. Oxford: Oxford University Press.

Van Bree, Cor. 1994. The development of so-called Town Frisian. *Mixed Languages* 15: 69–82.

Van Bree, C. 2001a, b. De morfologie van het Stadtfries. *Tijdschrift voor Nederlandse Taal- en Letterkunde* 117: 41–58, 133–148.

Van Coetsem, Frans, 1989. *Loan Phonology and the Two Transfer Types*. Amsterdam: Story Scientia.

Van Coetsem, Frans. 2000. *A General and Unified Theory of the Transmission Process in Language Contact*. Heidelberg: Carl Winter.

Van der Voort, Hein. 1996. Eskimo pidgin in West Greenland. In *Language Contact in the Arctic: Northern Pidgins and Contact Languages*, edited by Ernst Håkon Jahr and Ingvild Broch, 157–258. Berlin, New York: Mouton de Gruyter.

Vanhove, Martine, Thomas Stolz, Aina Urdze, et al. (eds.). 2012. *Morphologies in Contact*. Berlin, Boston: Akademie Verlag.

Velupillai, Viveka. 2012. *An Introduction to Linguistic Typology*. Amsterdam: John Benjamins.

Versteegh, Kees. 2017. On the nonexistence of mixed languages. *Advances in Maltese Linguistics*, edited by Benjamin Saade and Mauro Tosco, 217–238. Berlin, New York: Mouton de Gruyter.

Vogt, Hans. 1954. Language contacts. *Word* 10: 365–374.

Vrančić, Faust. 1595. *Dictionarium quinque nobilissimarum linguarum Latinae, Italicae, Germanicae, Dalmaticae, et Ungaricae*. Venice: Niccolò Moreto.

Walshe, M. O'C. 1964. *Introduction to the Scandinavian Languages*. London: André Deutsch.

Watkins, Calvert. 2004. Hittite. In *Cambridge Encyclopaedia* of the *World's Ancient Languages*, edited by Roger Woodard, 551–575. Cambridge: Cambridge University Press.

Weinreich, Uriel. 1953. *Languages in Contact: Findings and Problems*. The Hague: Mouton.

Wiemer, Bjoern, B. Wälchli, and Bjoern, Hansen (eds.). 2012. *Grammatical Replication and Borrowability in Language Contact*. Berlin: Walter de Gruyter.

Wilhelm, Gernot. 2004a. Hurrian. In *The Cambridge Encyclopedia of the World's Ancient Languages*, edited by Roger Woodard, 95–118. Cambridge: Cambridge University Press.

Wilhelm, Gernot. 2004b. Urartian. In *The Cambridge Encyclopedia of the World's Ancient Languages*, edited by Roger Woodard, 119–137. Cambridge: Cambridge University Press.

Whitney, William Dwight. 1881. On mixture in language. *Transactions of the American Philological Association* 12: 5–26.

Wohlgemuth, Jan. 2009. *A Typology of Verbal Borrowings*. Berlin: Walter de Gruyter.

Woodard, Roger D. (ed.). 2004. *Cambridge Encyclopaedia* of the *World's Ancient Languages*. Cambridge: Cambridge University Press.

Wray, Alison M., and George W. Grace. 2007. The consequences of talking to strangers: Evolutionary corollaries of socio-cultural influences on linguistic form. *Lingua* 117: 543–576.

Zammit, Martin. 1994. *A Comparative Lexical Study of Qur'anic Arabic*. Leiden: Brill.

Zuckermann, Ghil'ad. 2003. *Language Contact and Lexical Enrichment in Israeli Hebrew*. London: Palgrave Macmillan.

PART I

LANGUAGE CONTACT AND LINGUISTIC THEORY

CHAPTER 2

....

THEORIES OF LANGUAGE CONTACT

....

DONALD WINFORD

2.1 INTRODUCTION

....

THE field of contact linguistics has progressed very rapidly, particularly since Weinreich's (1953) pioneering attempt to formulate a unified interdisciplinary approach to the study of language contact. The roots of the field go back to nineteenth-century studies of various kinds of contact situations and their outcomes, including the foundational work of Hesseling (1899, 1905), Schuchardt (1882, 1883), and others on creoles, and the early attention to linguistic areas such as the Balkan Sprachbund (Kopitar 1829; Schuchardt 1884). Further foundations of the field were laid in early twentieth-century studies of processes of pidgin formation (Broch 1927); contact phenomena such as code-switching (Braun 1937), language maintenance and shift (Kloss 1927); immigrant languages (Herzog 1941, Reed 1948, etc.), and so on.

All of these various lines of approach, some primarily linguistic, others primarily sociological or anthropological, contributed to the emergence of the new field now known as contact linguistics. The field has always been conceived of as a multidisciplinary area of study, built around linguistic, sociolinguistic, and psycholinguistic approaches. Weinreich (1953) was the first to propose a systematized and integrated framework within which language contact could be investigated. In particular, he emphasizes that the components of an explanatory framework must include "purely structural considerations . . . psychological reasons . . . and socio-cultural factors" (1953: 44). These three components—the linguistic, the psycholinguistic, and the sociolinguistic—remain central to the study of language contact. The challenge facing the field is to integrate them into a unified theoretical framework.

A unified theory of language contact must address, first, the nature of the processes underlying contact-induced change, that is, both the actuation and the implementation of change (Weinreich et al. 1980), which relate, respectively, to the roles played by the individual and the community in the origin and spread of change. It is generally agreed that the locus of an innovation is the individual; hence the mechanisms or processes of change have to be explained in terms of how linguistic systems or inputs interact in the individual mind (i.e., in psycholinguistic terms). At the same time, if the locus of the propagation of change is the set of networks that link individual to individual, and each to the broader social structure, then this aspect of change must be explained in sociolinguistic terms (Bachus 2009). Meanwhile, the task of linguistic approaches is to describe the kinds of changes that occur, explain their structural characteristics, and identify the principles and processes they involve. Achieving a unified account of these various aspects of contact-induced change is of course an extremely difficult task, so my main goal here is to outline the dimensions of the challenge, by evaluating the contributions made by existing frameworks, and suggesting ways in which they have contributed toward the goal of a unified theory. In section 2.2, I discuss the contributions of sociolinguistic approaches to our understanding of the ways in which social contexts and social factors influence the outcomes of language contact. In section 2.3, I evaluate various frameworks that have been proposed for describing the linguistic outcomes of language contact, the mechanisms involved, and the classification of contact phenomena. I argue that van Coetsem's (1988, 2000) model of language contact offers a more consistent, accurate, and principled explanation of the processes of change associated with different types of contact. In section 2.4, I show how a wide variety of contact phenomena can be accounted for in terms of just two universal mechanisms of change—borrowing and imposition. Section 2.5 discusses ways in which psycholinguistic models of language production can contribute to our understanding of these mechanisms of contact-induced change.

2.2 SOCIAL FACTORS AND LANGUAGE CONTACT

The centrality of social factors to the understanding of contact-induced change was well recognized by Weinreich.

> To predict typical forms of interference from the sociolinguistic description of a bilingual community and a structural description of its languages is the ultimate goal of interference studies. (Weinreich 1953: 86)

Similarly, Thomason and Kaufman (1988) assign primary importance to the role played by social factors in shaping the consequences of contact, declaring that "[i]t is the sociolinguistic history of the speakers, and not the structure of their language, that is the primary determinant of the linguistic outcome of language contact" (1988: 35). What this suggests, first, is that we need to distinguish among the various social contexts of language contact if we are to understand the nature and direction of cross-linguistic influence. Second, it is necessary to examine, where possible, the actual speech behavior of individuals in each contact situation in order to uncover the factors that motivate them to change their language in one way or another. Weinreich's insight also led him to distinguish the non-structural factors that operate on both the macro (societal) level, and those that operate on the micro (individual level).

The first challenge for a sociolinguistic approach is to determine how the overall organization of the speech community affects the outcomes of language contact. The issue here is whether differences in the configuration of social groups and their languages correlate with differences in the types of contact-induced change. Scholars have proposed different taxonomies of speech communities in this regard. For instance, Loveday (1996: 16) has suggested that communities might be categorized according to the degree of bi- or multilingualism within them. He suggests that there are six "archetypal contact settings," each characterized by different arrays of contact phenomena, which form a continuum from relatively monolingual to highly multilingual. At one end of the spectrum we find relatively homogeneous communities of monolinguals, most of whom have little or no direct contact with speakers of other languages. Such "distant" contact typically results in lexical borrowing alone. In the middle, there are situations involving varying degrees of bi- or multilingualism within the community. These include communities with minority language groups that are either relatively isolated (e.g., Gaelic in Scotland), or in which different ethnic groups vie for equal status in the same territory, each preserving its own language, but also learning the other (e.g., French and English in Montréal). Then there are communities characterized by "diglossia," a situation in which two languages, one (H)igh and the other (L)ow, fulfill complementary functions in the community (e.g., Standard German and Schwyzertüütsch in Switzerland). Many situations in the middle of the spectrum are characterized by ongoing language shift, particularly among minority groups subject to strong cultural pressure from a dominant group. At the other extreme of the continuum, we find highly heterogeneous communities characterized by high degrees of individual multilingualism, such as the village of Kupwar in India, described by Gumperz and Wilson (1971).

Other contact situations involve different speech communities that engage in constant interaction, and the fluidity of their social boundaries is matched by the fluidity of their linguistic practices. The Aboriginal groups of Arnem Land, Australia (Heath 1978) and the villages of Northwest New Britain in Papua/New Guinea (Thurston 1987, 1994) are examples of this type. All of these settings offer a rich range of possibilities for contact-induced changes of one type or another. There may be borrowing across languages, code-switching behaviors, substratum influence on varieties acquired as second languages, various types of convergence, and the creation of entirely new contact languages. The particular outcomes have to do with a range of social factors, some favoring the preservation of language boundaries, others favoring different degrees of language mixture, switching, and convergence, yet others promoting language shift.

Finally, there are the social contexts that lead to the formation of new contact languages, including pidgins, creoles, "indigenized varieties," and bilingual mixed languages. Each of these outcomes involves a different constellation of social groups, interactional settings, and social relationships. The contexts in which they arise have been well documented, so there is no need to repeat them here. An interesting approach, which attempts a unified account of how macro-level social factors shape the creation of creoles and indigenized varieties, is Mufwene's (2001, 2008) Ecology of Language (EL) framework. Mufwene argues that different colonization types, and the kinds of economic systems they engendered, led to differences in population structures, which directly affected the evolution of English and other European languages in their colonial settings. Thus, in general, colonies established mostly for trade purposes in places like Africa and the Pacific produced pidgins, while "exploitation" colonies in the same regions produced "Indigenized" varieties such as Nigerian, Indian, and Singapore English. By contrast, "settlement" colonies such as those in the United States, Australia, New Zealand, and so on, produced outcomes that were closely related to their European sources, while "plantation" colonies produced creoles. Mufwene and Vigouroux (2013: 111ff) identify a number of macro-level social factors that influenced language evolution in these colonial settings, including the following:

- Differences in economic systems (which influence population structure);
- Population structures (which determine who interacts with whom);
- Demographic strengths of populations.

The proposed taxonomy has much in common with those proposed by scholars like Gupta (1997) and Schneider (2010). Mintz (1971: 48) proposes a similar model of the three broad social conditions that shaped the emergence of creole languages in the New World:

- The demographic makeup of each colony, including population ratios between the groups, and their places of origin;
- The types and patterns of contact among the groups, which were generally determined by the codes of social interaction governing their relative statuses and relationships;
- The nature of the community settings in which the groups interacted.

These macro-level factors figure in most frameworks for investigating how contact languages emerged.

Though these taxonomies are quite useful, it is clear that there is no consistent correspondence between the type of community and the pattern of contact-induced change within it. Bilingual communities, for instance, may be characterized by stable maintenance in some cases, language shift in others, or by both. Long-term stability can translate into rapid shift, given the right circumstances. Each contact situation has its own set of social contexts and forces at work, which determine whether individuals or groups are more or less proficient in one or the other language, whether they maintain their ancestral languages or shift toward a second language, or whether they maintain a kind of balanced bilingualism. Each of these sociolinguistic configurations can have profoundly different effects on how the languages in contact influence each other, since they determine not just the social dominance relationships between the languages, but also their linguistic dominance relationships within individual members of the community.

The second major task of sociolinguistic approaches is to explain the processes by which innovations spread, or competition between alternative features is resolved at the level of the community. This calls for closer examination of the social factors that operate at the micro-level of individual language use and choices, which in turn involve the patterns of interaction that individuals engage in. Mufwene's EL framework attaches central importance to such micro-level factors in regulating the spread of changes across idiolects. In this approach, the propagation of changes at group or community level involves a process of selection from among competing variants—a process that is subject to various external constraints, pertaining to both social and linguistic influences. This model of competition and selection at both individual and group level lends itself quite readily to an explanation of change in sociolinguistic terms. The approach is by no means new, and has been explored in numerous ways in the literature. In particular, sociolinguists have investigated the propagation of change within and across social networks (Milroy and Milroy 1985; Eckert 2000; Labov 2001); the role of "leaders" of change (Eckert 2000; Labov 2001); and the role of accommodation or divergence in promoting or inhibiting change (Giles et al. 1991). Weinreich once more anticipated this approach in stressing that the individual speaker's "specialization in the use of each language by topics and interlocutors" was an important factor in contact-induced change. In addition, he identified the following factors (1953: 3–4):

- The speaker's facility of verbal expression in general and his or her ability to keep two languages apart;
- Relative proficiency in each language;
- Manner of learning each language;
- Attitudes toward each language, and whether idiosyncratic or stereotyped.

As we will see in section 2.5, the first three of these factors are quite relevant to understanding the psycholinguistic mechanisms underlying contact-induced change.

We are still a long way from fully understanding the ways in which micro-level social factors interact with others in regulating the outcomes of language contact. This represents a promising area for future research (see the papers in Leglise and Chamoreau 2013 for a step in this direction).

2.3 CLASSIFICATIONS OF CONTACT PHENOMENA, AND MECHANISMS OF CHANGE

One of the major obstacles to a unified theory of language contact has been the failure of linguists to achieve consensus on two broad issues: the definition and classification of contact phenomena, and the processes and principles underlying different types of contact-induced change. With regard to the former, most frameworks follow

Weinreich's distinction between contact-induced changes due to borrowing, and those due to what Weinreich called "interference." For instance, Thomason and Kaufman (1988: 37) classified contact-induced changes into two broad types—those due to borrowing, and those due to interference through shift (1988: 37). Other scholars have adopted different terminology. Thus Johanson (2000, 2002) distinguishes between "adoption" (a term that he prefers to "borrowing") and "imposition," which corresponds closely to interference through shift (see further discussion later in the chapter). Unfortunately, there are various problems with these classifications. In the first place, there is by no means any agreement on what terms like "borrowing" and "interference" refer to. For instance, Aikhenvald (2002), following Trask (2000: 44), defines borrowing as "the transfer of features of any kind from one language to another as the result of contact." For Aikhenvald, apparently, borrowing covers a broad range of phenomena, including cases of "direct diffusion," that is, the transfer of overt forms, as well as "indirect diffusion," the transfer of categories and patterns (Aikhenvald 2002: 4). Similarly, some scholars use the term "interference" to refer to any type of cross-linguistic influence, including borrowing, while others use "transfer" in the same broad sense. Andersen (1983: 7) discusses the "long and confusing history" of these terms.

To complicate matters further, some scholars employ classifications that are based primarily on the nature of the linguistic features that are transferred. For instance, Heath (1984: 367) distinguishes between "direct transfer of forms from the other language," and "structural convergence (using native morphological material)." Croft (2003: 51) distinguishes between "borrowing" and "convergence," describing the former as the transfer of "substance linguemes" (i.e., actual forms with their meanings), and the latter as the transfer of "schematic linguemes" (i.e., grammatical elements which are made up of form only or meaning only, but not the combination of the two). Matras and Sakel (2007: 829) distinguish between "replication of linguistic matter" or MAT (i.e., morphemes and phonological shapes from a source language), and "replication of patterns" or PAT (i.e., patterns of distribution of grammatical and semantic meaning, and formal-syntactic arrangement). Heine and Kuteva distinguish between borrowing, which they define as "contact-induced transfer involving phonetic substance of some kind or other" (2005: 6), and the transfer of meanings (including grammatical meanings or functions) and of syntactic relations (i.e., the order of meaningful elements) (2005: 2). Finally, Johanson distinguishes between "global copying" (the total transfer of a linguistic element, including its form and functions) and "selective copying" (the copying of selected structural properties without the material forms of the elements in question) (2002: 291).

All of the preceding classifications are problematic because they refer primarily to the results of contact-induced change, not to their underlying mechanisms or psycho-linguistic processes. Van Coetsem identifies the problem precisely when he notes that the terms "borrowing" and "transfer," as they are traditionally used, "do not indicate the direction of the influence, and thus fail to bring out the agent of the action" (van Coetsem 1988: 2). Van Coetsem proposes a classification that is based precisely on this notion of agentivity, which I discuss more fully in the following subsection, as a prelude to evaluating other current frameworks.

2.3.1 Van Coetsem's Framework

Like other researchers, van Coetsem makes a broad distinction between two broad mechanisms of contact-induced change, which he calls "borrowing" and "imposition," but his main contribution was to refine and clarify the traditional distinction between the two mechanisms by making more explicit the types of agency that they involve. In both types of transfer, there is a source language and a recipient language. The direction of transfer is always from the source language to the recipient language, but the agent of the transfer can be either the recipient language speaker or the source language speaker. In the former case we have borrowing (recipient language agentivity); in the latter, imposition (source language agentivity). The distinction between these two types of transfer is based, crucially, on the psycholinguistic notion of language dominance. This refers roughly to the degrees of proficiency that the speaker has in each language, though it allows for the fact that a speaker may have different degrees of proficiency in different areas of a language. Generally, however, a speaker is linguistically dominant in the language in which he is more proficient or fluent—which is usually, but not necessarily, his first or native language (van Coetsem 1988: 13). van Coetsem (1988: 3) defines borrowing as follows:

> If the recipient language speaker is the agent, as in the case of an English speaker using French words while speaking English, the transfer of material (and this naturally includes structure) from the source language to the recipient language is *borrowing (recipient language agentivity).*   (italics in original)

Imposition, on the other hand, is a process by which the speaker transfers features of her linguistically dominant language (as SL) into her version of the recipient language (RL). In this case, "the source language speaker is the agent, as in the case of a French speaker using his French articulatory habits while speaking English" (van Coetsem 1988: 3). There are several aspects of van Coetsem's framework that are crucial to our understanding of the processes underlying contact-induced change. One is the assertion that contact-induced changes originate as innovations in individual speakers' language use. This reflects a common understanding among contact linguists, which is reflected in Weinreich's (1953: 6) observation that "the individual is the ultimate locus of contact." A second major premise of van Coetsem's model is that such changes are introduced in the course of language production, that is, in "the speech behavior of bilingual individuals" (Weinreich 1953: 4). But the most important of van Coetsem's claims is that it is the nature of the linguistic dominance relations between the languages in contact that decides the agency and type of contact-induced changes. This is a radical departure from other approaches that assigned primary importance to the social dominance relationship between the languages in contact. It must therefore be emphasized that linguistic dominance is an individual psycholinguistic phenomenon, while social dominance is a sociopolitical concept, based on the power or prestige standing of one of the languages. Only the former is relevant to the agency of contact-induced change and its underlying processes and mechanisms. It must be noted also that the socially dominant language may or may not be the linguistically dominant language of the speaker as agent of change. In addition, both linguistic and social dominance relationships may change over time, in individual speakers and in the community at large. Such reversals of dominance relationships also play a crucial role in determining the outcomes of language contact, but they have largely been ignored in the literature, as we will see. It is precisely these insights of van Coetsem's framework that are lacking in other approaches to contact-induced change, which we now turn to.

2.3.2 Competing Frameworks for the Study of Contact-Induced Change

One of the most important contributions to our understanding of contact-induced language change was Thomason and Kaufman's (1988) study, which provided a highly innovative historical linguistic perspective on language contact and its outcomes, and established the foundation for future work in the field. They emphasized the interaction of linguistic and social factors, and the key role played by the sociolinguistic history of the community, in determining the nature and degree of contact-induced change. Their classification of contact-induced changes is based on a distinction between "borrowing" and "interference via shift." However, the framework is highly problematic in some respects, primarily because of vagueness or inaccuracy in their definitions of the two key mechanisms of change.

Thomason and Kaufman (1988: 37) define borrowing as "the incorporation of foreign features into a group's native language by speakers of that language: the native language is maintained but is changed by the addition of the incorporated features." The other mechanism—"interference via shift"—refers to the transfer of features of learners' first languages into a second language that they are in process of acquiring. While this distinction is helpful in identifying a wide variety of contact-induced changes, it suffers from serious flaws when applied to certain situations of language contact. The chief weakness in Thomason and Kaufman's approach is their assumption that borrowing is inextricably linked to language maintenance, and that "interference" is exclusively a product of shift that produces "imperfect" second-language acquisition. In fact, there is no one-to-one relationship between any mechanism of change and the type of language situation that is involved. This is because both situations of maintenance and situations of language shift can involve differences in dominance relationships between the languages in contact. Hence there is potential for both borrowing and imposition to come into play in both situations. Moreover, linguistic dominance relations vary from individual to individual, and from community to community. This makes it impossible for us to treat all cases of language maintenance or shift as if they were the same, or could produce predictable results.

Among the situations that pose particularly difficult problems for Thomason and Kaufman are those in which a community maintains its ancestral language while becoming bilingual, and increasingly more proficient, in a socially dominant language. Such a situation existed in the immigrant Dutch community of Iowa, as described in Smits (1998), where English had become the linguistically dominant language for most speakers, though Dutch was still maintained. As a consequence, many speakers are no longer very proficient or fluent in their ancestral language. The linguistic consequences include the following:

- Lexical influence from English is highly marginal;
- The Dutch inflectional system has been seriously affected both by internal processes of reduction and external influence from English;
- There is a great deal of phonological and syntactic interference from English.

Smits concludes from this that the changes in Iowa Dutch are clearly the result of imposition, that is, transfer from the linguistically dominant language, English, into the less dominant one, Dutch, under the agency of English-dominant bilinguals. Indeed, these changes are precisely what van Coetsem's model would predict. Yet, under Thomason and Kaufman's approach, such changes would have to be ascribed to borrowing. Not surprisingly, then, Smits criticizes Thomason and Kaufman's approach for including under the umbrella of borrowing both changes that are due to RL agentivity, and others that are due to SL agentivity or imposition. She notes that, in their approach,

> [. . .] borrowing not only entails interference from a linguistically non-dominant language into a maintained *linguistically dominant* RL . . . but also entails interference from a linguistically dominant SL into a *linguistically non-dominant* RL.
> (1998: 387; italics in original)

As a consequence, Thomason and Kaufman's notion of borrowing "refers to two fundamentally different contact situations, yielding fundamentally different linguistic effects" (Smits 1998: 387).

For these reasons, Thomason and Kaufman's interpretation of "borrowing" leads to mischaracterization of a broad range of contact-induced changes that occur in situations of language maintenance, where a community maintains its ancestral language while shifting to a second language. When such speakers attain greater proficiency or even dominance in their second language, they tend to transfer features from it to their original language. Such changes fall under the ambit of imposition via SL agentivity. These are the kinds of changes that have been mistakenly characterized as cases of structural borrowing in the work of Thomason and Kaufman as well as others. A well-known case in point is that of Asia Minor Greek, which changed drastically at all levels of structure under the influence of Turkish. Thomason and Kaufman (1988: 218) treat this as a case of structural borrowing, arguing that "if Turks did not shift to Greek, all of the interference must be due to borrowing." Winford (2005: 408) notes that "this overlooks the strong possibility that bilinguals, especially those that were Turkish-dominant, played a key role in introducing these changes." This is in keeping with van Coetsem's observation that "the linguistic dominance relation between the RL and the SL [. . .] determines whether RL or SL agentivity will result from the contact" (1988: 83).

Thomason (2003: 692) revises her distinction between borrowing and shift-induced interference, arguing that "the crucial sociolinguistic factor is not whether or not shift takes place, but whether or not there is imperfect learning by a group of people." This leads her to redefine borrowing as transfer into a language spoken fluently, and "shift-induced interference" as transfer into a language that is learned imperfectly. But, as Smits (1998: 386) notes, the reformulation still mischaracterizes as "borrowing" changes that are introduced into a maintained language by speakers who have become dominant in a second language—changes which, as we have seen, are due to imposition.

Another framework that has gained currency in recent times is that of Johanson (2002), who makes a clear distinction between the results of contact-induced change and the mechanisms underlying them. He uses the term "code copying" to refer to the resulting contact phenomena, which he classified into two broad categories—global and selective code copying (2002: 291). The former refers to the copying of both the form and functions of some linguistic element, while the latter type refers to copying of structural features, and "is traditionally known as 'loan phonology,' 'loan semantics,' 'loan syntax,' etc." (2002: 292). According to Johanson, code copying is the result of two mechanisms, which he labels "adoption" and "imposition." Adoption refers essentially to the mechanism that others refer to as borrowing—a term that Johanson rejects as being "based on a deceptive metaphor" (2002: 288). By contrast, Johanson's concept of "imposition" is fundamentally different from van Coetsem's. This is because Johanason defines both borrowing and imposition in terms of the social dominance relationship between the languages in contact, not in terms of linguistic dominance, as in van Coetsem's framework:

> In the case of adoption, speakers of a sociolinguistically-dominated code A insert copies from a sociolinguistically-dominant code B. In the case of imposition, speakers of the sociolinguistically-dominated code A insert copies from it into their own variety of the sociolinguistically-dominant code B.   (2002: 290)

This strict equation of transfer type with a particular social dominance configuration of course runs completely counter to the psycholinguistically based association of a transfer type with a particular linguistic dominance configuration, as in van Coetsem's model. For Johanson, any form of transfer from a socially dominant to a subordinate language must be borrowing, while any form of transfer in the opposite direction must be imposition. This means that, like Thomason and Kaufman, his classification of contact-induced changes is flawed, and leads to inaccurate predictions for many cases of language contact. For instance, he cites Jones's (2002) description of changes in Guernésiais (Guernsey French) under English influence as instances of "adoption" (borrowing, in our sense). Examples provided by Jones include the following:

- The tendency to prepose adjectives;
- Copying of the syntax of passive constructions;
- Use of a single preposition 'with' for both comitative and instrumental meanings;
- Change of meanings and connotations of Guernésiais verbs due to formal similarities to English verbs.

Again, such cases of transfer can be better explained in terms of the growing dominance of English among speakers of Guernésiais, leading to imposition (in our sense) of the same sort that Smits describes for Iowa Dutch.

Johanson himself has nothing to say about linguistic dominance relationships and the role they play in contact-induced change. In fact, he specifically eschews any attempt to explain contact phenomena in psycholinguistic terms:

> [...] changes due to code-copying will be discussed exclusively in terms of observable linguistic structures. It will not be claimed that copies are psycholinguistically produced or processed in the steps discussed.   (2002: 287).

Such an approach is unfortunate, since it incorrectly assigns many instances of contact-induced change to the wrong category of "adoption" (i.e., borrowing), rather than recognizing them as cases of imposition, in van Coetsem's sense of the term. The implications are far-reaching, since imposition can occur in any situation of bi- or multilingualism where the dominance relationship between the languages changes. As we will see in section 2.4.2, contemporary bilingual situations provide rich and abundant illustrations of these patterns of change.

None of the preceding criticism is meant to deny the importance of social dominance relationships between languages as an important factor in contact-induced change. Rather, it is meant to remind us that such relationships are often trumped by the nature of the linguistic dominance relationship between the languages in contact among the speakers who are the agents of change. Moreover, since it is based on how linguistic dominance shapes the agency of speakers, van Coetsem's framework is compatible with psycholinguistic approaches to language contact (see section 2.5). His emphasis on the cognitive processes involved in the creation of contact languages is an important complement to other approaches that are more concerned with sociohistorical and sociolinguistic aspects of contact. In addition, van Coetsem's model has the distinct advantage of uniting a wide variety of apparently disparate contact phenomena under the umbrella of each of the major mechanisms of change. This is discussed in the following section.

2.4. On the Unity of Contact Phenomena

Each of the major mechanisms of contact-induced change, borrowing and imposition, is associated with a wide variety of contact phenomena that have been treated independently of one another in the literature. We will first discuss those that can be unified under the umbrella of borrowing.

2.4.1 Outcomes of Borrowing

To recap, *borrowing* is defined as the transfer of linguistic materials from a source language into a recipient language via the agency of speakers for whom the latter is the linguistically dominant language, in other words, via RL agentivity. Essentially, it refers to a psycholinguistic mechanism by which speakers introduce materials from an external language into a language in which they are (more) proficient. In doing so, they tend to preserve the more stable (i.e., structural) domains of the recipient language. This is not to say that borrowing never involves structural elements or abstract grammatical features, only that such structural borrowing occurs only under specific circumstances, which will be discussed further later. It follows that most borrowings tend to be lexical, and it is not surprising that the bulk of the literature has been devoted to these. Such borrowing does not lead to simple copying of source language materials, since various creative processes of adaptation and integration come into play as part of the mechanism. Thus the results of lexical borrowing are quite varied, ranging from close imitations of SL items (e.g., *rendezvous* borrowed from French into English), to drastic adaptations such as Japanese *pokemon* (<English *pocket monster*), to imitation of compounding patterns (Spanish *rascacielos* modeled on *skyscraper*), to completely new creations based on native materials (Zapotec *éxxuwí* 'fig' < *exxu* 'avocado' + *wí* 'guava'), and so on. The various processes of imitation and adaptation exemplified here demonstrate that borrowing involves complex patterns of lexical change that create new lexical entries or modify existing ones. In all cases, borrowed items are manipulated so that they conform to the structural and semantic rules of the recipient language. This is the definitive mark of borrowing under recipient language agentivity.

In addition, lexical borrowing often acts as the conduit for the introduction of new structural features, both phonological and morphological, into a recipient language. For instance, distinctions between /s/ and /z/, /f/ and /v/, and /ʃ/ and /ʒ/ emerged in Middle English as a result of the heavy borrowing of French words containing the voiced members of the respective pairs (Thomason and Kaufman 1988: 124, 308). But see Laker (2009) for an alternative explanation. At the morphological level, free functional elements such as conjunctions, prepositions, pronouns, and even complementizers can be borrowed directly. On the other hand, bound derivational morphemes tend to be introduced to a recipient language along with lexical borrowings, and can become productive if the borrowed words are numerous. For example, French borrowings into Middle English, such as *conspir-acie*, *charit-able*, and others, yielded suffixes like *–acy* and *–able*, while *en-rich*, *dis-connect*, and others yielded new prefixes (Dalton-Puffer 1996). Direct borrowing of overt inflectional morphology appears to be very limited; again, however, lexical borrowing can be the channel for such transfer, as exemplified in the introduction of the plural inflection *–im* into Yiddish via borrowed Hebrew pairs such as *mín/miním* 'sort' (Thomason and Kaufman 1988: 21).

2.4.1.1 *Lexical Borrowing Compared with Other Contact Phenomena*

The view of borrowing as a process that involves recipient language agentivity allows us to link phenomena that have been interpreted in very different ways in the literature.

Among them are classic code-switching,[1] relexification, and the creation of bilingual mixed languages. In classic insertional code-switching, a speaker retains the morpho-syntactic frame of his dominant language (as the RL), and imports single content morphemes or phrases from an external source language, as in the following example of French/Arabic switching (Bentahila and Davies 1983: 319).

(1) C'est une pauvre *bint*.
     'She is a poor girl.'

Myers-Scotton (1993, 2002) has shown that, in these cases, one language, the RL in our terms, acts as the matrix language, that is, provides the morphosyntactic frame for the utterance. Moreover, the items incorporated from the embedded or source language consist mainly of open-class content morphemes, which are inflected according to the rules of the recipient language. For this reason, it seems reasonable to treat insertional code switches and lexical borrowings as manifestations of the more general phenomenon of borrowing under recipient language agentivity (Winford 2009). While the results may differ in some ways, the underlying mechanism is the same. Understanding borrowing in terms of processes rather than results also helps us to explain how certain kinds of contact language were created in the past. In some contact situations, the process of incorporating content morphemes into a recipient language can be taken to an extreme, resulting in new languages that derive their morphosyntactic frame from one language, and their lexicon from another. These creations are referred to as intertwined languages, or "Lexicon-Grammar mixed languages" (Bakker 2003). Perhaps the best-known example is Media Lengua, a language spoken in central Ecuador, in which almost the entire grammatical frame is Quechua, but practically all content morphemes or lexemes derive from Spanish. The following example illustrates (Spanish items in italics):

(2) Media L: *Unu fabur*-ta   *pidi*-nga-bu   *bini*-xu-ni   (Muysken 1997: 365)
               one   favor-ACC   ask-NOM-BEN   come-PROG-1
               'I come to ask a favor.'
     Quechua: Shuk fabur-da   maña-nga-bu   shamu-xu-ni
     Span: Vengo para pedir un favor.

The process of incorporating and integrating Spanish stems into a Quechua morphosyntactic frame is identical to what we saw earlier in the cases of classic code-switching. Muysken described this process as "relexification... the process of vocabulary substitution in which the only information adopted from the target language [source language – DW] in the lexical entry is the phonological representation" (Muysken 1981: 61). It seems clear that the process of lexical incorporation that Muysken describes is in essence the same as that which occurs in lexical borrowing

---

[1] Myers-Scotton (2002) uses this term to refer to the insertion of embedded language morphemes into the morphosyntactic frame of a matrix language.

and classic code-switching. In all cases, source language lexical forms are imported and integrated into the unchanged structural frame of a recipient language, via RL agentivity. Further discussion of the psycholinguistic aspects of this process can be found in section 2.5.

2.4.2 Contact Phenomena United under the Umbrella of Imposition

The mechanism of imposition offers a more consistent, accurate, and principled explanation for various types of grammatical replication associated with different scenarios of language contact, including second-language acquisition (SLA), creole formation, language attrition, and others. I use "grammatical replication" (Heine and Kuteva 2005: 6) as a cover term for a wide range of labels that have been used in the literature, including pattern replication, indirect diffusion, functional transfer, selective copying, substratum transfer, convergence, and so on. Labels like these seldom speak to the actual psycholinguistic processes that initiate change as a result of the contact between competing linguistic systems in the minds of individual speakers who are the agents of change. All of the instances of grammatical replication mentioned in the preceding involve transfer from a linguistically dominant first language into a non-dominant second language, so they are clear cases of imposition or SL agentivity. They fall into two broad types. First, there are cases that involve the replication of some L1 grammatical pattern, meaning, or function in a language acquired as an L2; Liu et al. (1992: 451) refer to this as "forward transfer." Second, there are cases that involve transfer of patterns from an L2 in which the speaker has become dominant, into an original L1 that is undergoing attrition; Liu et al. (1992: 451) refer to this as "backward transfer," that is, "the use of L2 processing strategies in L1, a possible symptom of language loss."

2.4.2.1 *Imposition from L1 to L2*

The vast majority of the literature is concerned with transfer from L1 to L2, which covers situations involving tutored and natural SLA, as well as (expanded) pidgin and creole formation. There is a huge literature on these kinds of change, so I will provide only a few examples here, from situations of natural SLA and creole formation. An example of the former type of situation is Andean Spanish. Odlin (1990) reports that, in this contact variety, the SVO order of general Spanish is often replaced by an SOV pattern, under the influence of Quechua, as in the following example (Odlin 1990: 103):

(3)   Y mi hermano aquí otro paloma hembra había chapado
       'And my brother here another dove female had caught.'

Similarly, Sanchez (2006) discusses the Andean Spanish use of the Spanish verb *querer* 'to want' to convey the sense of an imminent action, on the model of the Quechua affix

–*naya*–, which expresses both a desiderative sense, and the imminent nature of a verbal action. The following examples from Sanchez (2006: 289), produced by the same bilingual child, illustrate:

(4) And. Span. *Y   el   perrole (e)sta queriendo morder a   ese   sapo*
                  And   the   dog   is   wanting   to.bite P   that toad
                  'And the dog wants to/is about to bite the toad'

(5) Quechua *Achku   miku-naya-yka-n*
              Dog   eat-DES-PROG-3
              'The dog wants to/ is about to bite.'

Similar kinds of impostion are found in creole formation. For example, Caribbean creole languages have a wide range of serial verb constructions that replicate similar structures in the West African substrate languages. For instance, Migge (1998) demonstrates that Ndjuka, a Surinamese creole, employs a range of SVCs with "give" as the V2, where 'give' introduces a range of thematic roles (recipient, benefactive, substitutive, etc.) that are also found in Gbe and other languages that were the principal substrates for the Surinamese creoles.

(6) Ndjuka *Mi   seli   a   osu   gi   en*   (Migge 1998:236)
              1sg   sell   DET house SV   3sg
              'I sold the house to him/her'

(7) Ewegbe *ye   dʒra   maʃina-a   ne   amba*
              3pl   sell   machine-the SV   Amba
              'They sold the computer to Amba'

2.4.2.2 *Imposition from L2 to L1*

Unlike cases of transfer from L1 to L2, transfer in the other direction has been largely neglected in the contact linguistics literature, even though there is evidence that it is quite common. Such "backward" transfer is particularly common among bilinguals for whom the L2 has become the primary and dominant language, and whose L1 is undergoing attrition. Clyne (2003) discusses various examples of how Dutch and German immigrants in Australia, who have become dominant in English, introduce English syntactic patterns into their declining ancestral languages.

(8) a. Aus. German *Wir   haben   gegangen zu   Schule in   Tarrington*
                     We   have   gone   to   school in   Tarrington
     b. St. German   *Wir   sind   in   Tarrington zur   Schule gegangen*
                     we   Aux.be in   Tarrington to   school gone
                     'We went to school in Tarrington.'   (Clyne 2003: 80)

(9) a. Aus. Dutch *je heb te look voor een ander job*

b. St. Dutch | *je* | *moet* | *een* | *andere* | *baan* | *gaan* | *zoeken* |
|---|---|---|---|---|---|---|
| you | must | an | other | job | go | seek |

'You have to look for another job.'   (Clyne 2003: 178)

Other examples of this kind of "backward" transfer include the cases of Guernsey French and Iowa Dutch, which were discussed earlier. Silva-Corvalán (1998) also describes changes in the Spanish of third-generation Hispanic immigrants in Los Angeles, which are due to influence from their more dominant language, English.

This brief summary shows that grammatical replication via imposition is an extremely common phenomenon in various contact situations in which one language dominates the other in bilinguals' competence and production. It manifests itself in cases of language shift, where L1 features are imposed on a developing L2, as well as in cases of L1 attrition, where features from a now dominant L2 are imposed on the declining L1. In the following section, I discuss how psycholinguistic models of language production can shed light on the nature of borrowing and imposition as the two major mechanisms of contact-induced change.

2.5 Pyscholinguistic Insights into Contact-Induced Change

Psycholinguistic approaches to language contact view contact phenomena as arising from the different contributions made by the languages in contact during the course of language production. Most approaches are based on Levelt's (1989) model of monolingual language production, which has been modified by de Bot (2000) and others to account for bilingual production. The full details of the model need not concern us here (see Bock and Levelt 1994 for further details). It is generally agreed that three types of mental processes are involved: conceptualization processes that specify which concepts are to be expressed verbally; formulation processes that select appropriate lexical items and construct the syntactic and phonological structure of the utterance; and articulation processes that realize the latter as overt speech (Roelofs 1993: 108). The general outline of the model is shown in Figure 2.1 (Bierwisch and Schreuder 1993: 25).

Our main concern here is with the level of the Formulator, which is concerned with grammatical processing or encoding. This in turn involves lexical selection, which "involves identifying the lexical concepts and LEMMAS suitable for conveying the message" (Bock and Levelt 1994: 947), the building of constituent structures via assignment of functions to selected lexical items, and fixing the order of these items, among other procedures.

De Bot (2001) has suggested various ways in which Levelt's model of monolingual production can be adapted to account for bilingual speech, particularly code-switching.

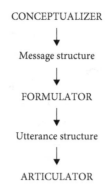

CONCEPTUALIZER

↓

Message structure

↓

FORMULATOR

↓

Utterance structure

↓

ARTICULATOR

FIGURE 2.1 A simplified model of language production.

Source: Levelt (1989).

As he points out, the model must not only account for cross-linguistic influences of various types, but also "deal with the fact that the speaker does not master both language systems to the same extent" (2001: 425). Hence, such a model must be able to account for the following aspects of bilingual language production (De Bot 2001: 425):

- The two language systems involved can be used independently of each other, or they may be mixed in various ways (as in code-switching, for example);
- The two systems may influence each other;
- The bilingual speaker may have different degrees of proficiency in each system;
- Interactions can take place between languages that are typologically similar or dissimilar.

De Bot accepts Green's (1986) suggestion that there may be three levels of activation involved in plurilingual language production. First, there is a selected language that controls the speech output; second, there is an active language that plays some role in ongoing processing and works parallel to the selected language; and third, there may be a dormant language that plays no role in processing. According to this hypothesis, one language is always selected, but more than one language may be active or latent. Moreover, the active language may do everything the selected language does, such as retrieve lexical items, form sentences, generate surface structures, and even make a phonetic plan (Green 1986). It follows that differences in the roles played by each language in the production process can lead to different kinds of contact phenomena or language mixture. Crucially for our purposes, the nature of these roles will depend on which language is dominant in the speaker's competence, and in the production process.

Let us first consider how this would apply to cases of borrowing and code-switching, that is, recipient language (RL) agentivity. Pyscholinguistic approaches view dominance relations between languages in code-switching in terms of which language is more activated in the production of code-mixed utterances. Myers-Scotton's (2002) notion of "matrix language" (ML) is in fact specifically defined as the language whose grammatical encoding procedures are more activated in the production of mixed speech. The ML is equivalent to the RL in van Coetsem's framework. In both lexical borrowing and classic insertional code-switching, speakers employ the morphosyntactic procedures of the RL as the dominant language, and selectively introduce source language (SL) lexical items, or more accurately lexemes, which are associated with lemmas belonging to RL lexical entries. This is basically the same procedure that creators of intertwined languages employed in fashioning languages such as Media Lengua and Angloromani, which Muysken's relexification model attempts to capture. What it suggests is that bilinguals can in fact attach the source language lexeme to the RL lemma as an alternative phonological shape that replaces the equivalent RL lexeme (de Bot 2001: 441). In terms of van Coetsem's framework, then, direct lexical borrowing, insertional codeswitching, and the across-the-board insertion of SL lexemes found in intertwined languages are all the result of the same linguistic mechanism that we have defined as borrowing via RL agentivity.

Insights from psycholinguistic models can also shed light on how the mechanism of imposition operates to produce various kinds of grammatical replication resulting from both "forward" and "backward" transfer. From the psycholinguistic perspective, imposition can be described as the use of the formulation procedures of the SL in producing utterances in the RL. We can illustrate this with two examples of grammatical replication. Recall that a key part of grammatical encoding involves lexical selection, that is, identifying the lexical concepts and lemmas that are suitable for conveying the message. As we saw earlier, one of the assumptions of language production models is that lemmas activate or trigger syntactic procedures that correspond to their syntactic specifications. Thus, a verb will trigger construction of a VP, a noun the construction of an NP, a preposition the construction of a PP, and so on. The argument structure and syntactic subcategorization properties of verbs, in particular, are crucial to appropriate assignment of functions to the constituents of a sentential structure. There is evidence from the SLA literature that many cases of transfer from L1 to L2 involve the assignment of an L1 lemma to an L2 verb form or lexeme, which results in production of L2 utterances that have the grammatical pattern of the L1. For instance, Nemser (1991) provides the following examples of L2 English, produced by L1 German learners in Austria.

(10)   L2 English   *Explain me something*
      German   *Erklär mir was*

(11)   L2 English   *You just finished to eat*
      German   *Du hast gerade aufgehört zu essen*

In these cases, the L2 English verbs assume the subcategorization properties of their semantically equivalent German counterparts, resulting in utterances that employ English lexical items, organized according to German constituent structure.

Similar processes can be observed in cases of "backward transfer." For example, Silva-Corvalán (1998: 233) has documented examples of Spanish utterances like the following, produced by Spanish-English bilinguals in Los Angeles, for whom English has become the dominant language.

(12) a. LA Spanish. *Yo   gusto   eso*
      I   like-1s   that

   b. Gen. Span. *A   mi   me   gusta   eso*
      To   me   pro   please-3s   that
      "I like that."

In this case, the argument structure of English *like* is substituted for that of Spanish *gustar*. In General Spanish, the theme of *gustar* is mapped onto the subject function, while the Experiencer role is mapped onto an indirect object. However, the speaker producing the English-inflenced variety of LA Spanish has activated the lemma associated with English *like*, and imposed it on the Spanish lexeme *gustar,* producing an English-like structure in which the Experiencer role is mapped onto the subject function and the Theme role onto the object function. This procedure is motivated by the speaker's perception of a semantic equivalence between *like* and *gustar*—a classic trigger for imposition.

2.6 OTHER APPROACHES TO GRAMMATICAL REPLICATION

Treating cases of grammatical replication in terms of imposition seems intuitively more economical than other approaches that appeal to different mechanisms of change, such as "pivot matching" (Matras and Sakel 2007) or "contact-induced grammaticalization" (Heine and Kuteva 2005). Matras and Sakel suggest that pivot matching "involves identifying a structure that plays a pivotal role in the model construction and matching it with a structure in the replica language, to which a similar, pivotal role is assigned in a new replica construction" (2007: 830). However, this implies that speakers can match entire constructions and then replace one with the other, and it also assumes far greater metalinguistic awareness on the part of speakers who have low proficiency in one of the languages than they actually have. Moreover, Matras and Sakel claim that "pattern transfer" is often excluded when there is no available structure in the replica language that can assume the role of the "pivotal feature" of the model construction (2007: 847). However, this makes little sense for most cases of grammatical replication, particularly those involving learners who attempt to use an L2 with which they are not familiar. In such cases, learners clearly have no knowledge of the grammatical encoding procedures of the L2, far less any knowledge of L2 "structures" that might be equivalent to those of their L1. Yet they manage to replicate quite complex L1 grammatical patterns in their version of the L2, particularly in cases of natural SLA and creole formation. The concept of imposition, that is, the use of the language-production procedures of the dominant language in producing the less dominant one, offers a compelling account of how such replication takes place.

Another concept that can be explained in terms of imposition is that of "contact-induced grammaticalization"—a term introduced by Heine and Kuteva to explain the replication of grammatical functions and categories in cases of language contact. Of particular interest is the notion of "replica grammaticalization," in which "the model language provides a model for both a category and the way that category is replicated" (Heine and Kuteva 2005: 80). An example of this is the reanalysis of the verb *kaba* (< Portuguese *acabar* 'finish') as a marker of Completive aspect in the Surinamese creoles.

(13)   Sranan   A   kownu   doro   kaba
                DET   king   arrive   COMPL
                'The king has arrived.'

Winford and Migge (2007: 84) demonstrate that the category is closely modeled on the Completive aspect category found in Gbe languages, as illustrated in the following example.

(14)   Ajagbe   àxɔsu   lɔ   à,   e   vá   lɔ́   vɔ̀
                King   DET   TOP   he   come   arrive COMPL
                'As for the king, he has already arrived.'

Once more, such kinds of reanalysis, which are abundant in both creoles and other contact languages, can be explained in terms of imposition. In this case, learners established an interlingual identification between the lexical item *kaba* and its Gbe counterpart *vɔ̀*, on the basis of their semantic similarity. Then they extended the aspectual function of the substrate lexical item to its superstrate counterpart, by simply transferring the lemma of the former to the latter. Other approaches have explained this process in terms of "relexification" and "reanalysis" (Lefebvre 1998), or "functional transfer" (Siegel 2008). Such explanations are quite compatible with the notion of imposition as described here, but the notion of imposition captures the psycholinguistic process involved in these types of grammaticalization more clearly by linking it more directly to the language-production procedure.

Van Coetsem's framework provides a sound basis on which to integrate psycholinguistic approaches to language contact more fully with linguistic approaches, since it is compatible with psycholinguistic models of language production. These links are already well established in Levelt's language production mode, which draws on lexicalist approaches to syntax such as Lexical Functional Grammar (Bresnan 1982). This is in keeping with Levelt's view that "the lexicon is an essential mediator between conceptualization and grammatical encoding" (1989: 51). But in principle the approach is also compatible with other linguistic frameworks. A task for future research is to pursue the connections between linguistic and psycholinguistic approaches to language contact.

2.7 CONCLUSION

The unified theory of language contact that we are seeking must integrate the sociolinguistic, the linguistic, and the psycholinguistic aspects of change. First, it must be able to describe and classify both the processes and outcomes of contact-induced change in accurate linguistic terms. Second, it must account for the mechanisms involved in the origins of innovations in individual idiolects—a fundamental aspect of the actuation question that can only be understood in psycholinguistic terms. Third, it must account for the role of macro-level social factors in contact-induced change, as well as the social processes by which change is propagated through social networks, leading to conventionalization of community grammars. It is only by combining these approaches that we will achieve the kind of interdisciplinary model that Weinreich conceived of.

REFERENCES

Aikhenvald, A. 2002. *Language Contact in Amazonia*. Oxford: Oxford University Press.

Andersen, Roger W. 1983. Transfer to somewhere. In *Language Transfer in Language Learning*, edited by S. Gass and L. Selinker, 177–201. Rowley, MA: Newbury House.

Bachus, Ad. 2009. Code switching as one piece of the puzzle of linguistic change: The case of Turkish *yakmak*. In *Multidisciplinary Approaches to Code Switching*, edited by Ludmila Isurin, Donald Winford, and Kees de Bot, 307–336. Amsterdam: John Benjamins.

Bakker, Peter. 2003. Mixed languages as autonomous systems. In *The Mixed Language Debate: Theoretical and Empirical Advances*, edited by Yaron Matras and Peter Bakker, 107–150. Berlin; New York: Mouton de Gruyter.

Bentahila, Abdelâli, and Eirlys E. Davies. 1992. Code-switching and language dominance. In *Cognitive Processing in Bilinguals*, edited by R. J. Harris, 443–458. Amsterdam; New York: Elsevier Science.

Bierwisch, M. and R. Schreuder. 1993. From concepts to lexical items. In *Lexical Access in Speech Production*, edited by W. J. Levelt, 23–60. Oxford: Blackwell.

Bock, K., and W. Levelt. 1994. Language production: Grammatical encoding. *Handbook of Psycholinguistics*, edited by M. A. Gernsbacher, 945–984. New York: Academic Press.

Braun, Maximilian. 1939. Beobachtungen zur Frage der Mehrsprachigkeit. *Göttingsche Gelehrte Anzeigen* 199: 116–130.

Bresnan, J. (ed.). 1982. *The Mental Representation of Grammatical Relations*. Cambridge: MA: MIT Press.

Broch, Olaf. 1927. Russenorsk. *Archiv für slavische Philologie* 41: 209–267.

Clyne, M. 2003. *Dynamics of Language Contact*. Cambridge: Cambridge University Press.

Croft, W. 2003. Mixed languages and acts of identity: An evolutionary approach. In *The Mixed Language Debate: Theoretical and Empirical Advances*, edited by Y. Matras and P. Bakker, 41–72. Berlin; New York: Mouton de Gruyter.

Dalton-Puffer, Christiane.1996. *The French Influence on Middle English Morphology*. Berlin; New York: Mouton de Gruyter.

De Bot, K. 2001. A bilingual production model: Levelt's 'speaking' model adapted. In *The Bilingualism Reader*, edited by Li Wei, 420–441. London: Routledge.

Eckert, Penelope. 2000. *Language Variation as Social Practice*. Oxford: Blackwell.

Giles, Howard, Nikolas Coupland, and Justine Coupland. 1991. Accommodation theory: Communication, context and consequence. In *Contexts of Accommodation: Developments in Applied Sociolinguistics*, edited by Howard Giles, Justine Coupland, and Nikolas Coupland, 1–68. Cambridge: Cambridge University Press.

Green, D. W. 1986. Control, activation, and resource: A framework and a model for the control of speech in bilinguals. *Brain and Language* 27: 210–223.

Gumperz, John J., and Robert Wilson. 1971. Convergence and creolization: A case from the Indo-Aryan/Dravidian border in India. In *Pidginization and Creolization of Languages*, edited by Dell Hymes, 151–167. Cambridge: Cambridge University Press.

Gupta, Anthea F. 1997. Colonisation, migration, and functions of English. *Englishes around the World*, Vol. 1: *General Studies, British Isles, North America*, edited by Edgar W. Schneider, 47–58. Amsterdam: John Benjamins.

Heath, Jeffrey. 1978. *Linguistic Diffusion in Arnhem Land*. Australian Aboriginal Studies: Research and Regional Studies No. 13. Canberra: Australian Institute of Aboriginal Studies.

Heath, Jeffrey. 1984. Language contact and language change. *Annual Review of Anthropology* 13: 367–384.

Heine, B., and T. Kuteva. 2005. *Language Contact and Grammatical Change*, Cambridge: Cambridge University Press.

Herzog, George. 1941. Culture change and language: Shifts in the Pima vocabulary. In *Language, Culture and Personality. Essays in Memory of Edward Sapir*, edited by Leslie Spier, A. Irving Hallowell, and Stanley S. Newman, 66–74. Menasha, WI: Sapir Memorial Publication Fund.

Hesseling, Dirk Christiaan. 1899. *Het Afrikaansch: Bijdrage tot de geschiedenis der Nederlandsche taal in Zuid-Afrika*. Leiden: Brill.

Hesseling, Dirk Christiaan. 1905. *Het Negerhollands der Deense Antillen: Bijdrage tot de geschiedenis der Nederlandsche taal in Amerika*. Leiden: Sijthoff.

Johanson, L. 2000. Linguistic convergence in the Volga area. In *Languages in Contact*, edited by D. Gilbers, J. Nerbonne, and J. Schaeken, 165–178. Amsterdam; Atlanta GA: Rodopi.

Johanson, L. 2002. Contact-induced change in a code-copying framework. In *Language Change: The Interplay of Internal, External and Extra-linguistic Factors*, edited by Mari C. Jones and Edith Esch, 285–313. Berlin: Mouton de Gruyter.

Jones, M., 2002. Mette a haout dauve la grippe des Anglais: Convergence on the Island of Guernsey. In *Language Change: The Interplay of Internal, External and Extra-Linguistic Factors*, edited by Mari C. Jones and Edith Esch, 143–168. Berlin: Mouton de Gruyter.

Kloss, Heinz. 1927. Spracherhaltung. *Archiv für Politik und Geschichte* 5(4): 456–462.

Kopitar, Jernej. 1829. Albanische, walachische und bulgarische Sprache. *Jahbücher der Literatur* 46: 59–106.

Labov, William. 2001. *Principles of Linguistic Change: Social Factors*. Malden, MA: Blackwell.

Lefebvre, Claire. 1998. *Creole Genesis and the Acquisition of Grammar: The Case of Haitian Creole*. Cambridge: Cambridge University Press.

Léglise, Isabelle, and Claudine Chamoreau (eds.). 2013. *The Interplay of Variation and Change in Contact Settings*. Amsterdam: John Benjamins.

Levelt, W. 1989. *Speaking: From Intention to Articulation*. Cambridge, MA: MIT Press.

Liu, H., Bates, E., and Li, P. 1992. Sentence processing in bilingual speakers of English and Chinese. *Applied Psycholinguistics* 13: 451–484.

Loveday, Leo J. 1996. *Language Contact in Japan: A Socio-linguistic History*. Oxford: Clarendon Press.

Matras, Y., and J. Sakel. 2007. Investigating the mechanisms of pattern replication in language convergence. *Studies in Language* 31: 829–865.

Migge, B. 1998. Substrate influence in creole formation: The origin of *give*-type serial verb constructions in the Surinamese Plantation Creole. *Journal of Pidgin and Creole Languages* 13(2): 215–265.

Milroy, James, and Lesley Milroy. 1985. Linguistic, social network, and speaker innovation. *Journal of Linguistics* 21: 339–384.

Mintz, Sidney W. 1971. The socio-historical background to pidginization and creolization. In *Pidginization and Creolization of Languages*, edited by Dell Hymes, 481–496. Cambridge: Cambridge University Press.

Mufwene, Salikoko. 2001. *The Ecology of Language Evolution*. Cambridge: Cambridge University Press.

Mufwene, Salikoko. 2008. *Language Evolution: Contact, Competition, and Change*. London: Continuum.

Mufwene, Salikoko, and Cécile B. Vigouroux. 2013. Individuals, populations, and timespace: Perspectives on the ecology of language. *Construction des connaises sociolinguistiques: Du terrain au positionnement théretique*, edited by Françoise Gadet, 111–137. Brussels: EME & Intercommunications.

Muysken, Pieter. 1981. Halfway between Quechua and Spanish: The case for relexification. In *Historicity and Variation in Creole Studies*, edited by Arnold Highfield and Albert Valdman, 52–78. Ann Arbor, MI: Karoma.

Muysken, Pieter. 1997. Media lengua. In *Contact Languages: A Wider Perspective*, edited by Sarah G. Thomason, 365–426. Amsterdam: John Benjamins.

Myers-Scotton, Carol. 1993. *Dueling Languages: Grammatical Structure in Code-Switching*. Oxford: Clarendon Press.

Myers-Scotton, Carol. 2002. *Contact Linguistics: Bilingual Encounters and Grammatical Outcomes*. Oxford: Oxford University Press.

Nemser, W., 1991. Language contact and foreign language acquisition. In *Languages in Contact and Contrast: Essays in Contact Linguistics*, edited by V. Ivir and D. Kalagjera, 345–364. Berlin: Mouton de Gruyter.

Odlin, T. 1990. Word order transfer, metalinguistic awareness, and constraints on foreign language learning. In *Second Language Acquisition/Foreign Language Learning*, edited by B. van Patten and J. F. Lee, 95–117. Philadelphia: Multilingual Matters.

Reed, Carroll E. 1948. The adaptation of English to Pennsylvania German morphology. *American Speech* 23: 239–244.

Roelofs, A. 1993. A spreading-activation theory of lemma retrieval in speaking. *Lexical Access in Speech Production*, edited by Wim Levelt, 107–142. Cambridge, MA; Oxford: Blackwell.

Sanchez, L. 2006. Bilingual grammars and creoles: Similarities between functional convergence and morphological elaboration. In *L2 Acquisition and Creole Genesis*, edited by C. Lefebvre, L. White, and C. Jourdan, 277–294. Amsterdam: John Benjamins.

Schneider, Edgar W. 2010. Developmental patterns of English: similar or different? In *The Routledge Handbook of World Englishes*, edited by Andy Kirkpatrick, 372–384. London; New York: Routledge.

Schuchardt, Hugo. 1882. Kreolische Studien I. Ueber das Negerportugiesische von S. Thomé (Westafrika). *Sitzungsberichte der kaiserlichen Akademie der Wissenschaften zu Wien* 101(2): 889–917.

Schuchardt, Hugo. 1883. Kreolische Studien V. Ueber das Melaneso-englische. *Sitzungsberichte der kaiserlichen Akademie der Wissenschaften zu Wien* 105(1): 151–161. Reprinted in

English in Schuchardt, 1979, *The Ethnography of Variation: Selected Writings on Pidgins and Creoles*, edited and translated by Thomas L. Markey, 18–25. Ann Arbor: Karoma.

Schuchardt, Hugo. 1884. *Slawo-deutsches und Slawo-italienisches*. Graz: Leuschner & Lubensky.

Siegel, Jeff. 2008. *The Emergence of Pidgin and Creole Languages*. Oxford; New York: Oxford University Press.

Silva-Corvalán, C., 1998. On borrowing as a mechanism of syntactic change. *Romance Linguistics: Theoretical Perspectives*, edited by A. Schwegler, B. Tranel, and M. Uribe-Etxebarria, 225–246. Amsterdam: Benjamins.

Smits, C. 1998. Two models for the study of language contact: A psycho-linguistic perspective versus a socio-cultural perspective. In *Historical Linguistics 1997*, edited by M. Schmid, J. Austin, and D. Stein, 377–391. Amsterdam: John Benjamins.

Thomason, S. G. 2003. Contact as a source of language change. In *The Handbook of Historical Linguistics*, edited by B. D. Joseph and R. D. Janda, 687–712. Oxford: Blackwell.

Thomason, S. G., and T. Kaufman. 1988. *Language Contact, Creolization and Genetic Linguistics*. Berkeley: University of California Press.

Thurston, William R. 1987. *Processes of Change in the Languages of Northwest New Britain*. Pacific Linguistics Series B, No. 99. Canberra: Department of Linguistics, Australian National University.

Thurston, William R. 1994. Renovation and innovation in the languages of Northwestern New Britain. *Language Contact and Change in the Austronesian World*, edited by Tom Dutton and Darrell Tryon, 573–609. Berlin; New York: Mouton de Gruyter.

Trask, Lawrence. 2000. *The Dictionary of Historical and Comparative Linguistics*. Edinburgh: Edinburgh University Press.

van Coetsem, Frans. 1988. *Loan Phonology and the Two Transfer Types in Language Contact*. Dordrecht: Foris.

van Coetsem, Frans. 2000. *A General and Unified Theory of the Transmission Process in Language Contact*. Heidelberg: Universitätsverlag, C. Winter.

Weinreich, U. 1953. *Languages in Contact: Findings and Problems*. New York: Linguistic Circle of New York. Reprinted 1986, The Hague: Mouton.

Weinreich, Uriel, William Labov, and Marvin I. Herzog. 1980. Empirical foundations for a theory of change. In *Directions for Historical Linguistics: A Symposium*, edited by W. P. Lehman and Yakov Malkiel, 95–188. Austin: University of Texas Press.

Winford, D. 2005. Contact-induced changes: Classification and types of processes. *Diachronica* 22(2): 373–427.

Winford, D. 2009. On the unity of contact phenomena and their underlying mechanisms: The case of borrowing. In *Multidisciplinary Approaches to Code Switching*, edited by Ludmila Isurin, Donald Winford, and Kees de Bot, 279–305. Amsterdam: John Benjamins.

Winford, D., and B. Migge. 2007. Substrate influence on the emergence of the TMA systems of the Surinamese creoles. *Journal of Pidgin and Creole Languages* 22(1): 73–99.

CHAPTER 3

....

CONTACT-INDUCED CHANGE AND PHONOLOGY

....

ANTHONY P. GRANT, THOMAS B. KLEIN†,
AND E-CHING NG

3.1 INTRODUCTION
....

ONE of the clearest areas of language where the effects of contact-induced change can often be seen is in the phonological system of the affected language, and the forms that this change can take are extremely varied.[1] Allophones can become phonemes; pre-existing phonemes can merge or become zero; new phonemes can be added, and the minimal pairs that are used to justify these phonemes can be added to the lexicon of the language. Constraints on occurrences of features in the structure of onset, nucleus, and coda can be taken over from one language to another and can even be implemented in non-borrowed lexical items. Stress and intonational patterns can be added to or simplified. Tonogenesis and the loss of tone can both take place.

Kang (2011) is a recent and partly diachronic review of the literature on loanword adaptation, and her paper provides a typology of adaptation strategies and a summary of current theoretical challenges. Maddieson (1988) is another important cross-linguistic study that concentrates on the borrowing of sounds to help fill preexisting gaps within a language's phonological system; much of the work on this topic has been carried out as part of more broadly conceived studies of contact-induced change in individual languages.

---

[1] Prof. Thomas Benno Klein, an imaginative and inspiring scholar, teacher, and musician, died in November 2014, and his co-authors dedicate this paper to his memory.

Not only can sounds from new words from other languages be incorporated as allophones or even phonemes into the recipient language, or can lead prior allophones to be promoted to phonemic status (as can be said to have happened with /v ð z/ in Middle English; in addition, kinds of syllabic templates can also be transferred. Furthermore, phonological rules or restrictions can be taken over from one language system to another. Transfer of features can transcend the adoption of segments and syllabic or other phonological templates; suprasegmental features can be borrowed. For example, many languages that were previously non-tonal have developed partial or full lexical tone systems as a result of contact with speech communities where these are in use. Thurgood (1999) demonstrates this for the originally non-tonal Chamic language Tsat, which has been strongly influenced by Hlai (Kra-Dai) and Hainanese Chinese (Sino-Tibetan), both of which are robustly tonal.

This last development shows that the influence of one language upon another is not confined to the transmission of material that is added to the store of another language. Callaghan (2014) shows that some borrowed phones, from Hill Patwin (Wintun), Wappo (possibly Yukian or else an isolate), Eastern Pomo (Pomoan), and later on Spanish, which together have doubled the size of the consonantal inventory of Lake Miwok in central California (and which have added some distinctive features to the language's phonology), have begun to be used in words that have derived from Proto-Miwok. A similar state of affairs is reported by Ozanne-Rivierre (1994) for Fagauvea of Uvea, New Caledonia, a Polynesian Outlier that has absorbed many vocalic and especially consonantal sounds from the more prestigious neighboring Oceanic but non-Polynesian language Iaai, some of which have passed into the most high-frequency morphemes in the language.

It should also be recognized that although linguistic systems will be altered by contact-induced change, this change may take the form not of addition of an element, but of the deletion or loss of an element, in order to increase the degree of isomorphism between the phonological system of the donor language and that of the less dominant recipient language. Again, Lake Miwok is relevant here; other Miwokan languages have two central vowels /ə, ɨ/ but Lake Miwok has only /ə/; the Californian languages that helped shape it and which provided it with a lot of loan lexicon (Hill Patwin, Eastern Pomo, Southeastern Pomo, and Wappo) have five-vowel phonemic systems /i, e, a, o, u/, and Lake Miwok has all these, too (Callaghan 2014).

Similarly, Garifuna, one of the languages in the small sample for the case study in the next section, has modified its previous three-series stop system (which, for instance, contrasted /tʰ t d/) by merging aspirated and unaspirated voiceless stops, since these kinds of stops are not distinguished phonemically in Kari'na, Spanish, English, and Antillean Creole French, the languages that have shaped Garifuna so much. Maltese, as a North African Arabic variety, once had a series of emphatic coronal consonants that contrasted phonemically with non-emphatic equivalents, as they still do in other Arabic varieties, but this distinction was resolved in favor of the non-emphatic coronals as a result of massive borrowing from Sicilian and Italian (Borg and Azzopardi-Alexander 1997).

3.2 A SMALL CROSSLINGUISTIC EXAMINATION OF BORROWED SOUNDS AND TEMPLATES

It is clear that some languages have absorbed and assimilated a greater number of borrowed features of different kinds than others have, and that there is at best a weak correlation between the amount of borrowing of basic lexicon and the amount of structural influence on the same language. As with many other instances of contact-induced change, the features of borrowing are best examined by discussing (however briefly or telegraphically) the results of interactions between speakers of pairs of languages, in terms of the transfer of features from an individual donor language or from an individual recipient language. Most contact-induced changes are examples of the addition of rules or features to a preexisting phonological system.

In terms of the bipartite view of contact-induced language change being pursued in this book, we may state that "phonological borrowing" of this sort is in each case an instance of *transfer of pattern* being brought about in a recipient language as a result of *transfer of fabric*. It is rather unusual for a borrowed sound or a borrowed phonological pattern to permeate words in a donor language that have not been borrowed, though such sounds or templates may of course be available to words from subsequent languages entering a donor language. (Prosody may be an exception: examples of surface tone and intonation transfer are discussed later, and similarly, Maghrebi Arabic has absorbed Berber syllabic templates; see Heath 1997 for a discussion of Moroccan Arabic phonology.) Chapters in Kaye and Daniels (eds. 1997) discuss the phonological features (especially segmental ones) of Hindi-Urdu, Berber varieties, and Swahili.

The paper by Maddieson (1986), which discusses borrowed sounds in a range of over three dozen languages from around the world, uses a version of (or draws insights from) distinctive feature theory in order to enable us to categorize the depth and extremity of borrowing of each sound from the donor to the recipient language. The study is confined to consonantal sounds, but there is no reason why this approach cannot also be applied to vowel sounds, and we have done this here. Maddieson recognizes six increasingly intense (one might say, increasingly system-altering) degrees of borrowing of sounds into a recipient language. He takes examples from over forty languages from throughout the world, belonging to a wide range of language families (with some isolates), in order to demonstrate his ideas of the relative ease (or increasing and incremental difficulty) of borrowing sounds. Three of these languages are included in our sample, namely English, Hindi-Urdu (Maddieson concentrates especially on the latter variety), and Standard Swahili. The other languages sampled are Siwi Berber, Tagalog, Acehnese of Sumatra (a sister-language of Tsat), Yapese, Ifira-Mele of Vanuatu, Ngandi of northeastern Arnhem Land, Australia, Pipil of El Salvador, Garifuna of Belize, and Cuzco Quechua. In section 3.3 of this chapter we

Table 3.1 Borrowed Sounds in Sample Languages, Arranged According to Maddieson's Classes

Language	#1	#2	#3	#4	#5	#6	Total	New Templates
English	ʒ ɔɪ		v z ð				8	–
Kalderash	f z ʒ dʒ			h ï ə			16	CCC-
Hindi–Urdu		f ṣ ŋ è ò		x ɣ q		'	37	CC-, -CC
Acehnese	Z	e o f					7	CC-
Tagalog	e o	f ts ~ c		r			10	CC-
Chamorro	b d k	e o w		r			13	CC-
Yapese	dʒ			h			5	V-, -V
Ifira–Mele			mʷ pʷ j	l w			17	CC-, -C#
Ngandi	nh lh (lamino dental)						2	–
Pipil	o	b d g f		r			17	CC-
Garifuna	p o						2	(CC)
Cuzco Quechua		ph th ch kh qh p' t' c' k' q' b d g					26	CC-
Berber varieties	sˁ dˁ x (p v)			ħ q '			15–17	–
KiUnguja		x ɣ θ ð		r			12	CC-

Notes: CC- indicates a complex onset with two initial consonants, CCC- one with three. (CC) means that very few instances of CC- occur in the language; -C# is a coda-final consonant.

examine data from Chamorro, like Yapese, Ifira-Mele, Acehnese and Tagalog an Austronesian language, and one very strongly influenced by Spanish. Chamorro has also been included in larger studies of which this illustration is part, and is included in Table 3.1. All these languages have borrowed at least 10% of their Swadesh list vocabulary (and a much greater proportion of other kinds of vocabulary) from other languages. This sample is discussed further in Grant (2013).

Maddieson scores each borrowed sound in each recipient language separately, according to which of the six categories of borrowing it belongs. The six classes that Maddieson describes in his paper are broadly incremental or hierarchical in nature, such that a Class 2 sound represents a greater change from the status quo than a Class 1 sound does, and the details are given in the following. In Maddieson's paper the concepts of place and manner of articulation are especially important.

In Class 1 we see that the borrowed sound already has a counterpart in the recipient language in regard to place of articulation and that it already has another sound as counterpart with regard to the manner of articulation. Thus a language that already possesses /v/ and /s/ will be open, ceteris paribus, to the borrowing of /z/ because both its place and manner of articulation are already represented and employed in the recipient language. This would account, for example, for the (late) borrowing of /p/ into Kabyle via loans from French, as Kabyle already had /b/ and /f/ at its disposal.

In Class 2 we can see that the borrowed sound introduces a new manner of articulation to the phonological system of the language. For example, a language with only voiceless stops plus voiced nasals may also borrow voiced stops, as is the case in Cuzco Quechua, which has done this feat of borrowing of manners of articulation of stops for three such manners. In Class 3 it is found that the sound in question is promoted within the language from being an allophone to a full-fledged phoneme. This is so with the voiced fricatives /v z ð/ in Middle and Modern English, which were promoted to phonemic status from an allophonic status in Old English.

Maddieson classified the first three groups as affecting "close segments"; in his view, the remaining three groups of sounds, Classes 4 to 6, involve the adoption of what he calls "remote segments" (which are segments that are new to the language systems in question). In Class 4 we may note that the sounds in this class involve the borrowing of new manners of articulation (for instance, voiced stops), which may not have preexisting voiced nasals at every stop. In this regard it differs from the kind of sound borrowing that counts as Class 2, but Maddieson makes it clear that on occasion the same borrowed sound can belong to more than one class.

In Class 5 we find that the borrowed sound has introduced a new place of articulation to the phonological system of the language. Indeed, Maddieson cites the borrowing of the (voiceless) post-alveolar sibilant into Hindi and Urdu as an example of this, as the post-alveolar place of articulation was not previously used in the language.

Finally, and most dramatically, in the case of Class 6 the kind of borrowing that is involved is one in which the borrowed segment introduces both a manner and a place of articulation that was hitherto not used in the language. Maddieson points out that the borrowing of the glottal stop from Arabic into Hindi-Urdu is an example of a borrowing within Class 6. (Maddieson also refers to the use in Hindi-Urdu of a voiced uvular approximant, a sound about which my sources on the language, however, are silent, so I have not discussed it here, though the sounds represented as /x ɣ/ are often articulated as uvular rather than as velar sounds and thereby align with the borrowed uvular stop /q/ rather than with the inherited voiceless unaspirated velar stop /k/.)

It is apparent that the number of examples of borrowed segments grows fewer and fewer when one moves from Class 1 onward through to Class 6. Table 3.1 indicates the number of sounds in each language in each of the six classes (these are marked as #1 to #6; each sound is counted only once, and if poised to belong to more than one class, it is assigned to the class with the lowest number). Given the increasing remoteness of the six classes, we may notionally award points on a system that scores each Class 1 sound with one point, each Class 2 sound with two, and so on. For what (if anything) they are worth, we provide the total number of points in the penultimate column.

The overall position of the borrowed sounds in the phonological systems of the languages being surveyed is one of marginal status in these systems, and of these sounds being characteristic of loans in the languages in question. With the exception of the case of the "promotion to phonemic status" of the voiced English fricatives, which falls under Class 3, few of them have permeated the outer core of borrowings deeply enough for them now to be used as phones in inherited words in the languages observed. (Even so, some of these sounds may be available for use in borrowed words deriving from loan strata that entered the language subsequent to those which provided the borrowed sounds.) These are sounds that are still preeminently found in the borrowed words which introduced them into the respective language systems, and that is where in general they have stayed.

3.3 LOAN PHONOLOGY AND DISTINCTIVE FEATURE THEORY

In this regard it is worth examining the extent to which new distinctive phonological features (of the kind discussed, for example, in Jakobson, Fant, and Halle 1961 or Ladefoged 1886) have been added to the roster of a language's features as a result of borrowing morphs. Jakobson set up some two dozen such features. Although some languages in the sample have not borrowed any fresh distinctive features (this seems to be the case with English, Ngandi, and Garifuna, though all three have borrowed individual sounds), a number of such phonological features can be shown to have been borrowed or transferred in some of the languages in the sample. By contrast, several of the more frequent distinctive features, such as [+ anterior], [+ continuant], [+ nasal], if not universal linguistically, are nonetheless found in all the languages in the sample and in many others besides.

Pipil may have borrowed certain classes of sounds, such as rhotics, but it has not borrowed new distinctive features per se. Some speakers of Tagalog have borrowed [del rel] by acquiring č from Hokkien, English, and Spanish words. Ifira-Mele has (re)acquired the feature [+ lateral]; its ancestor, Proto-Polynesian, used both *l and *r, which merged as /r/ in Ifira-Mele. Although plosive sounds containing [+ constricted glottis] (that is, ejectives) and [+ spread glottis] (in other words, aspirated plosives) both appear to be sets of borrowed segments in Cuzco Quechua, only the former can be regarded as a borrowed distinctive feature, since /h/ occurs in native Quechua words such as *hatun* 'big' but /ʔ/ does not occur in Cuzco Quechua at all. The feature [+ constricted glottis] is also borrowed into Acehnese and Urdu, in both cases via loans from Arabic, though in neither is it frequent. In contrast with Cuzco Quechua, Kalderash contains many inherited words that feature voiceless aspirated plosives containing [+ spread glottis] but the sound *h* on its own seems to be almost completely confined to borrowed words. Urdu also borrowed [+ uvular] via loans from Arabic, as have the various forms of Berber that have been examined here, though the latter already possessed continuant pharyngealized sounds. One can say that [+ spread glottis] has also entered Yapese through loans from Japanese and English. KiUnguja originally acquired [+ rhotic] from Southern Cushitic languages (-*zuri* 'good') and has added massively to its frequency by borrowing many words containing it, especially from Arabic and European languages.

The vocalic feature [+ mid] is probably borrowed from Mon-Khmer languages into Acehnese, whence it spreads via sound change into inherited words, while it entered Tagalog through loans from Spanish (and later English), with perhaps some impetus from Kapampangan, which developed *e* and *o* from earlier *ay* and *aw* (as entries in Forman 1973 show when compared with their cognates in Tagalog). It may also have been borrowed from Spanish into Chamorro, as mid-vowels are now phonemic in Chamorro.

Hindi-Urdu has reacquired the feature [+ distributive] because of the borrowing or rather re-borrowing of voiceless (and, very marginally, also voiced) post-alveolar sibilants in words from Sanskrit, Arabic, Persian, and English. This feature probably existed in Hindi's Indic forebear, but it was lost when the three voiceless sibilants of Sanskrit were merged into one sibilant in later forms of Indic languages, usually as /s/.

3.3.1 A Note on Borrowed Templates

The number and variety of templates in a language can also be increased by borrowing, and often is. The preceding data set provides several examples of these, and even a few in which "borrowed" templates leach slightly into native lexicon, and in most cases we can probably find examples of consonant clusters (onsets and or codas) that add to the set of consonantal clusters already available in the language, but not to the range of types of new template. English, Ngandi, and Berber varieties do not instantiate any examples of borrowed templates, unsurprisingly given the range of templates (and especially the range of complex codas) that were already available in the inherited lexicon.

The type of template most frequently borrowed is that of the complex consonantal onset involving the borrowing of CC- or occasionally CCC- onsets. This is most marginal in Garifuna, occurring only in recent loans from English and Spanish, and in Acehnese this kind of cluster, born out of the loss of medial vowels in CVC- onsets, is inspired by Mon-Khmer syllabic structure, but is also found in inherited words (Thurgood 1999), since Mon-Khmer languages with complex onsets, sesquisyllabic structures, and rich vowels systems that include several centralized vowels came into contact with a Malayo-Chamic variety which had four vowels and a restricted range of templates (V, VC, CV, CVC). Kalderash CCC- syllables are from European loans (*strefjal* 'lightning is flashing' from Greek). CC- and -CC in syllables in Hindi-Urdu are found in loans from Sanskrit (this is true of both onset and codas, though Sanskrit did not have complex codas; in Hindi they occur in sanskritisms that have been denuded of their inflectional endings) and English, while -CC codas are also found in Persian and Arabic loans. CC- onsets, from Arabic (*starehe* 'watch out!') but also found in English loans, are rather rare in KiUnguja Swahili, while in Ifira-Mele they typify loans from South Efate or Bislama or its major lexifiers, French and English, while geminate initial consonants are also found as a secondary development in Ifira-Mele as the result of the deletion of vowels in CVC- sequences in which both consonants are identical. CC- clusters in Tagalog, Chamorro, Pipil, and Cuzco Quechua have come in with loans from Spanish, and few Spanish loans into these languages have their clusters broken up with svarabhakti vowels.

Vowel-initial and vowel-final words in Yapese were previously confined to a small number of function words, and borrowed items in Yapese that were vowel-initial in their source languages were furnished with word-initial and word-final glottal stops (written <q>). This is true of loans from Palauan, Trukic, Polynesian, Spanish, Latin, and German, and some loans from Japanese and English, but later loans from Japanese and English can now begin with vowels.

3.4 CONTACT-INDUCED CHANGE AND SUPRASEGMENTALS

Several suprasegmental patterns have attracted considerable attention in the language contact literature; see Salmons (1992) for an overview. The most striking of these is *tonogenesis*, the set of processes by which a language that previously lacked lexical tone develops a tonal system. Tone must be treated with extreme caution in linguistic reconstruction, because it is said to diffuse easily across families, as well as emerging in isolation (Campbell 1997: 347; Matisoff 2001). Suprasegmentals also appear to be a notable exception to the general rule that the transfer of phonological patterns is the result of transferring lexical material; numerous contact-induced suprasegmental changes are found in the near-absence of loanwords. There are even changes that appear to be contact-induced but cannot easily be classified as transfers, because they do not reproduce patterns found in any of the source languages.

An example of borrowing suprasegmental features without borrowing more than a few loans from one language to the other can be found in varieties of English spoken in Wales. Features such as the lengthening of many medial consonants before vowels (and sometimes before consonants also) in Welsh English echoes a subphonemic feature that is found in Welsh (which only has /nn/ and /rr/ as true geminate consonants opposed by /n/ and /r/) and which has been carried over into varieties of English that are often spoken by people who know no Welsh and who have lived in areas that have been monoglot in English for many decades (Penhallurick 2004 gives details).

As with other contact-induced sound changes, loanwords are, nonetheless, an important vehicle for prosodic transfer. Fixed initial stress became the rule in Czech due to intense contact with German, but was lost in English due to heavy borrowing from French and Latin (Berger 2016; more examples in Salmons 1992: 43). A combination of internal and external factors was probably responsible for the development of lexical tone in Southeast Asian and Hainan Chamic languages (Thurgood 1999: 232; cf. Kingston 2011: 2317). Conversely, tone has been lost in Wutun (a hybrid of Lingxia Chinese, Tibetan, and Bao'an Mongolian) even in the Chinese vocabulary (Li 1986; Lee-Smith and Wurm 1996). Tone borrowing and loss are also reported in Africa (Salmons 1992: 26–33)—ChiTumbuka of Malawi and most significantly KiSwahili in East Africa would be cases of tone loss—though some of these cases have been questioned (e.g., Nicolaï in press).

Among the Atlantic creoles, perhaps the most extreme example of tonal borrowing is Saramaccan, an English creole spoken in Surinam. This language gives the auditory impression of tone, but unpredictable tonal patterns occur only in vocabulary of African origin, while vocabulary of European origin is more economically analyzed as pitch-accent (Good 2004). A mix of tone and accent occurs in Nigerian Pidgin English and Krio, with some contrastive pairs such as NPE ['mɔdà] 'mother' and ['mɔdá] 'school marm' (Faraclas 1984; Finney 2004). There is a recurring (though not straightforward) tendency to associate high tone and etymological stress as a result of contact, not only in the Atlantic creoles, but also English varieties with Chinese substrates (Hong Kong English: Cheung 2008; Chinese Pidgin English: Li, Matthews, and Smith 2005; Stephen Matthews, personal communication, April 23, 2013; cf. Devonish 2002; De Lacy 2006), albeit with some exceptions (Jamaica: Gooden 2003; Trinidad: Drayton 2006; Singapore: Ng 2012). Syllable timing and adjacent stresses are also reported in these varieties, possibly conflating the same phonetic phenomenon (timing: Wells 1982: 572; Mesthrie 2008: 317; stress: Brousseau 2003; Bao 2006).

In addition to word-level prosody, intonation can also be transferred as a result of contact. In some cases, these intonation patterns can be traced to an L1 source with relative confidence. In the Spanish of Buenos Aires and Montevideo, final stressed syllables have a pitch rise followed by a long fall; this pattern has been connected with a strong Italian presence, but is not limited to speakers of Italian origin (Colantoni and Gurlekian 2004; Lipski 2010b: 560). Similar claims are made for Yiddish influence on the intonation of some American English speakers (Weinreich 1956). In India, the high density of pitch accents (especially L*+H) by Indian English speakers has been compared to Gujarati and Tamil intonation (Wiltshire and Harnsberger 2006), though Sangaja (2009: 84) suggests that similar claims with respect to syllable timing have yet to be verified. In Germany, Turkish-German bilinguals use two pragmatically distinct types of rising intonation in both languages, one originating in German (L*HH%) and the other (L%H%) in Turkish (Queen 2001).

In many cases, contact-induced prosodic changes cannot be classified as transfer, because they do not reproduce patterns found in any source language. For instance, the word-final high tone in Colloquial Singaporean English (e.g., àmāzíng) appears to be a compromise between Southern Min Chinese word-final tone sandhi, Malay phrase-final rising intonation, and Indian English foot-final rising intonation (Ng 2012). In Equatorial Guinea, surface high and low tones are said to be assigned with little regard for stress (Lipski 2010a: 563), whereas Palenquero has been characterized as requiring pitch polarity (Lipski 2010b). Tone can even interact with morphosyntax, as with

Papiamentu participles and Saramaccan quantifiers (Rivera-Castillo and Pickering 2004; Kramer 2007).

3.5 DETAILED CASE STUDY: CHAMORRO

The endangered Austronesian language Chamorro (also *CHamoru*), spoken indige-nously on Guam and the Northern Mariana Islands (Saipan, Rota/Luta, Tinian) borrowed a massive number of lexical items, including basic words, during its extensive contact with Spanish between first contact in 1521, the establishment of the first Jesuit mission in 1668, and the end of the Spanish American War in 1898. Counts of the percentage of Spanish loans in the total Chamorro lexicon (55%, Rodríguez-Ponga 1995) differ considerably from connected speech or text (20+%, Pagel 2010: 56; ca. 28%, Stolz 1998, 2003). This case study briefly examines phonological adaptation of the Spanish loans and hispanization in the phonology of Chamorro. Blust (2000) points out that /b d/ and onset-initial /k/ also mark borrowed words, as does the very rare /w/ (found only in *wahu* 'wahoo, kind of fish'), as Chamorro contains layers of loans from (as yet mostly unidentified) Maustronesian languages that influenced Chamorro before the arrival of the Spanish, and also items form Tagalog.

Modern Chamorro has the phonemic six-vowel system /i, u, e, o, a, ɑ/. The literature has stated that Chamorro had the four-vowel system /i, u, a, ɑ/ before Spanish contact (Topping 1973: 23). Blust (2000: 86) wrote:

> In native Chamorro forms, the high vowels *i, u,* and their midvowel counterparts *e, o* are *essentially* in complementary distribution, the former occurring in open, and the latter in closed syllables. This distribution was disrupted by the introduction of hundreds of Spanish loanwords, so that it now is more economical to treat *e* and *o* as phonemes. (our emphasis)

We have emphasized the word *essentially* in the preceding to highlight that there are a handful of items of non-Hispanic stock that feature mid vowels in stressed open syllables in Chamorro. In the following, all Chamorro data are taken from Aguon (2009) or Topping, Ogo, and Dungca (1975). The Chamorro orthography follows Aguon (2009).

(1)   Non-Hispanic items with mid vowels in stressed open syllables
/ˈdeʔun/ *de'on* 'to pinch'
/ˈke-/ *ke-* (stress-attracting prefix) 'to try'
/ˈcocu/ *chocho* 'to eat'
/ˈboʔan/ *bo'an* '(to) foam'

Given data such as the items in (1), it appears that Spanish did not introduce stressed mid vowels in open syllables *de novo*. Instead, it seems more plausible that the massive number of loans from Spanish merely increased the frequency of mid vowels in

Chamorro. Chamorro vowels are limited to /i, u, a/ in unstressed position. This vowel reduction applies to native Chamorro words and Spanish loans, as is evident in (1) and in many forms in the following. The vowel fronting/*umlaut* alternation fronts initial (stressed) back vowels adjacent to certain particles including the definite article *i* 'the' (Chung 1983; Klein 2000). However, not all Spanish roots participate.

(2)   (Non-) participation of Spanish loans in Chamorro *umlaut*
       (a) /'fogːun/ *foggon* 'stove' < *Sp. fogón*
            /i 'fegːun/ i feggon 'the stove'

       (b) /'goma/ *goma* 'rubber' < *Sp. goma*
            /i 'goma/ i goma 'the rubber'

Spanish loans are usually fully integrated into Chamorro morphophonology. They participate in reduplication and infixation, for example, but not always in *umlaut*, as the date in (2) (a) versus (2) (b) show.

Topping (1973: 67) advances the generalization that when "Spanish words were borrowed, the pronunciation of them was usually changed to conform to the sound system of Chamorro." This expresses a pre-theoretical view of "nativization." Topping (1973) does not always clearly distinguish between pronunciations and spelling; for example, he examines "the Spanish sound -*ll*-." For phonological purposes, this must be understood as "the Spanish sounds [ʎ] or [j] represented by the grapheme <ll>." We also need to keep in mind not just modern Spanish, but also the historical varieties of Spanish that the Chamorro population can be assumed to have been exposed to at the time of initial contact and in the extended period thereafter. This method can affect the understanding of the claims made in Topping (1973).

For example, he posits that the "Spanish [s]ound z (in all positions) [changed to the] Chamorro [s]ound s" (Topping 1973). According to Hualde (2005), all Medieval Spanish sibilants had evolved to /s/ in Andalusia and Latin America, that is, in the varieties with which colonial Chamorro would have been in contact. For example, *brazo* 'arm' evolved from /bɾátso/ to /bɾáso/ (Hualde 2005: 159). Given Chamorro *bråsu* /'bɾɑsu/ 'arm,' there is no change in sibilant phonetics to be observed, in contrast to the expectation raised by Topping's (1973) statement. This form would also indicate that we must indeed look at (Early) Modern, not Medieval, Spanish to make the appropriate comparison with Chamorro. If Chamorro speakers had been exposed to Medieval Spanish, we would expect the affricate /t͡s/ to appear as its closest equivalent /c/ <ch>. Yet, */bɾɑcu/ *<brachu> is unattested in Chamorro. This is unsurprising, since the dominance of the Spanish in the Marianas began in the late 1660s, in the Early Modern Spanish period and continued until 1898, although Spanish-Chamorro contacts had occurred sporadically since 1521.

When we systematically investigate the question of how Spanish roots changed when they came into Chamorro, we note an uneasy fit with the notion of "nativization." Instead, we find four of the puzzling patterns of adaptation identified in Kang's (2011) survey of loanword phonology: *the too-many-solutions problem, divergent repair, unnecessary repair*, and *differential importation*.

The grapheme <ll> corresponds to [ʎ] or [j] in Early Modern and Modern varieties of Spanish (Hualde 2005: 180). Chamorro possessed neither the palatal labial nor the palatal semiconsonant; the palatal affricate /ɟ/ appears instead.

(3)   Fortition of Chamorro /ɟ/ < Spanish [ʎ]/[j]
      /kabaɟu/ *kabâyu* 'horse' < *Sp. caballo*
      /siɟa/ *siya* 'chair' < *Sp. silla*
      /ɟabi/ *yâbi* 'key' < *Sp. llave*
      /ɟanu/ *yâno* 'level' < *Sp. llano*

The choice of /ɟ/ over other potential candidates in sound adaptation can be used to illustrate what Steriade (2001) calls *the too-many-solutions problem.* The substituted sound /ɟ/ preserves voicing and palatality of the original ʎ/j, but the question is why other available sounds were not used. In particular, the palatal nasal /ɲ/ would have maintained voicing, palatality, and sonorancy, whereas alveolar /l/ would also have preserved voicing and sonorancy and in cases of Spanish input [ʎ] laterality as well.

As far as adjacent vocoids are concerned, only the diphthongs *au* and *ai* occur in native Chamorro words (the word *hagoe* 'lagoon' is of unknown origin). Other sequences, including /ia/ and /ea/, have been added from not only Spanish, but also English. On occasion the new sequences are broken up by /h/ (Topping 1973: 68) to supply a syllable onset.

(4)   Variable vowel hiatus avoidance in loan words
      /dia/, /diha/ *dia, diha* 'day' < *Sp. dia*
      /ispia/, /ispiha/ *espia, espiha* 'to seek' < *Sp. espiar*
      /fia/, /fiha/ *fia, fiha* 'to trust' < *Sp. fiar*
      /gia/, /giha/ *gia, giha* 'gear' < *E. gear*

The strategy to optionally insert /h/ to avoid vowel hiatus is not available in the native lexical stock in Chamorro. The glottal stop /ʔ/ must be employed here, as shown in the following for the prefixes *mi-* and *ke-*.

(5)   Vowel hiatus avoidance in native words
      /acuʔ/ *âcho'* 'rock'   /miʔacuʔ/ *mi'âcho'* 'rocky'
      /unai/ *unai* 'sand'   /miʔunai/ *mi'unai* 'sandy'
      /aca/ *acha* 'to hammer'   /keʔaca/ *ke'acha* 'try to hammer'

The contrast between the data in (4) and (5) reveals a fresh case of what Kenstowicz (2005) called *divergent repair.* The hiatus avoidance through /h/-insertion is available only in loanwords, but not in native words.

The insertion of /h/ observed in the preceding is complemented by a process of /h/-deletion to create vowel hiatus in Spanish loans.

(6)   Variable vowel hiatus creation in loan words
      /rikohi/, /rikoi/ *rikohi, rikoi* 'to gather' < *Sp. recoger*
      /tiheras/, /tieras/ *tiheras, tieras* 'scissors' < *Sp. tijeras*
      /maneha/, /manea/ *maneha, manea* 'to manage' < *Sp. manejar*

The data in (4) and (6) show that we are dealing with an *h/Ø*-alternation in Spanish
loans overall. Vowel hiatus is tolerated or can be avoided through the insertion of /h/,
regardless of whether /h/ or vowel hiatus was present in the foreign etymon. However,
this intervocalic *h/Ø*-alternation is observed only with loans, not with native vocabulary
items in Chamorro.

   Whereas Spanish has /a/ as the only low vowel phoneme, Chamorro has front /a/
and the more common back /ɑ/ in stressed position. Thus, we might not expect
Spanish /a/ to undergo any change in Chamorro since it appears phonetically (near-)
identical to Chamorro /a/. However, Spanish /a/ is regularly backed to Chamorro /ɑ/.

(7)   Low vowel shift of Spanish /a/ to Chamorro /ɑ/
      /ˈbrɑsu/ *bråsu* 'arm' < *Sp.* /ˈbraso/ *brazo*
      /ˈdɑɲu/ *dåñu* 'damage' < *Sp. daño*
      /ˈlana/ *låna* 'wool' < *Sp. lana*
      /ˈtɑca/ *tåcha* 'to criticize, blame' < *Sp. tacha*

The preceding examples show stressed low back /ɑ/ surrounded by coronal consonants
in Chamorro. This excludes the potential for a coarticulatory effect to favor /ɑ/. The
Chamorro adaptations clearly have gone beyond what was given in the Spanish speech
signal. Peperkamp (2004) has called this *unnecessary adaptation*. The observed substitution does not replace some sound that the recipient language lacks. Instead, a sound
present in both languages appears as a neighboring phoneme in the borrowing language.

   Non-geminate syllable codas in Chamorro are restricted to voiceless obstruents and
the nasals /m/, /n/, and /ŋ/. Geminates can license voiced obstruents in the Chamorro
coda. These coda conditions had a profound effect on Spanish loans.

(8)   Desonorization of Spanish coda liquids
      (a) /matkadot/ *matkadot* 'engraver' < *Sp. marcador*
           /betdi/ *betde* 'green' < *Sp. verde*
           /lugɑt/ *lugåt* 'place' < *Sp. lugar*

      (b) /satmon/ *satmon* 'salmon' < *Sp. salmón*
           /asut/ *asut* 'blue' < *Sp. azul*
           /atkahot/ *atkahot* 'alcohol' < *Sp. alcohol*

The items in (8) (a) and (8) (b), respectively, show that Chamorro did not tolerate
Spanish *r* or *l* in syllable-final position and that it regularly transformed both into
t (Topping 1973: 67f.), preserving only coronality. This fact, which also is found in
Chamorro loans into Carolinian (Jackson and Marck 1991), is sharply distinct from the

sound's behavior in syllable-initial position. Syllable-initial *l* could appear natively, so its preservation in Spanish loans was predictable. Blust (2000) claimed that *r* did not occur anywhere in native Chamorro (*sirek* 'to masturbate,' a verb that may be an Oceanic loan, cf. Woleaian *siir* 'to drip,' and which has also been borrowed into Yapese, may be an exception). Yet *r* was accepted into Chamorro in syllable onsets, but not in syllable codas.

(9) Spanish liquids in onsets
     (a) /rumot/ *rumot* 'rumor' < *Sp. rumor*
         /rubetbit/ *rubetbet* 'revolver' < *Sp. Revolver* < English
         /riat/ *riåt* 'real' < *Sp. real*

     (b) /luna/ *luna* 'moon' < *Sp. luna*
         /labius/ *låbios* 'lip(s)' < *Sp. labio(s)*
         /licera/ *lechera* 'dairy cow' < *Sp. vaca lechera*

The data in (9) (a) and (9) (b), respectively, show that Chamorro included /r/ and /l/ from Spanish in singleton syllable onsets. Remarkably, complex onsets involving liquids from Spanish also appear in Chamorro, even though the native vocabulary does not allow them (Topping 1973: 36f.; Blust 2000; Pagel 2010: 63).

(10) Consonant-liquid clusters in Chamorro
     (a) /bruha/ *bruha* 'witch' < *Sp. bruja*; contrast Tagalog *buruha* 'witch'
         /troŋku/ *trongko* 'trunk' < *Sp. tronco*
         /primu/ *primu* 'cousin' *Sp. primo*

     (b) /planu/ *plånu* 'plan' < *Sp. plano*
         /floris/ *flores* 'flower' < *Sp. flor(es)*
         /klaba/ *klåba* 'to nail' < *Sp. clavo* 'nail'

The Spanish input contained three types of novel structures involving liquids: liquids in coda position, rhotics as syllable onsets, and consonant+liquid clusters in onset position. They were dealt with in markedly different ways in Chamorro. Whereas the coda liquids were subjected to native Chamorro coda restrictions, the syllable-initial rhotic and the consonant+liquid clusters were accepted into the borrowing language. This is a case of *differential importation* (Kang 2011). The restriction against *r* was relaxed in onset position. Cl/r clusters were absorbed without change into the heritage CV(C) syllable template, even though liquids would not appear in syllable codas.

We encounter a number of expected adaptation processes affecting Spanish roots including variable *umlaut*, consonant fortition, and desonorization in syllable codas. Vowel hiatus avoidance or creation through *h/Ø*-alternation is puzzling because it diverges from the native model. Low vowel shift is unexpected because there is no phonological necessity for it. Chamorro phonology changed measurably through borrowing from Spanish, including the full set of liquids in syllable onsets, the addition of initial consonant+liquid clusters, the enlargement of possible vocoid sequences, and the increase in the rate of occurrence of mid vowels.

3.6 The Possibilities of Contact-Induced Phonological Change: The Case of Tsat

The impact of Spanish and other languages upon Chamorro is striking, but some cases are even more dramatic. Tsat (whose phonological history is documented in Thurgood 1999) is spoken in one village near Sanya City in the far south of Hainan Island by a few thousand Sunni Muslims who are largely endogamous and largely bilingual in Minnan Chinese and also often in Cantonese and increasingly Mandarin/ Putonghua. Earlier inhabitants of this area spoke Li/Hlai languages, which belong to the Tai-Kadai family and which are still spoken by hundreds of thousands of people in Hainan. These exerted some slight influence on Tsat, which is a migrant language. Tsat is Austronesian, and more specifically a Chamic language, related to Acehnese, Cham, and several other languages of Vietnam, and a little less closely related to Malay (as part of an originally rather conservative Malayo-Chamic branch of Malayo-Polynesian, which a phonology not unlike that of pre-Spanish Chamorro). Speakers of Tsat left northern Vietnam and came to Hainan about 1000 CE. Its closest relative is probably Northern Roglai.

Malay phonology is non-tonal; words are generally disyllabic or longer and use six vowels, of which the mid-vowels are of rather restricted occurrence. The language that underlay Proto-Chamic had a similar system until it came into contact with Mon-Khmer languages in mainland Southeast Asia. The results of this contact (apart from a huge tranche of loanwords, many of which replaced preexisting forms of Malayo-Polynesian origin) included an increase in the number of vowel qualities, especially among mid-level and centralized vowels, increasing use of diphthongs, the concomitant contraction of many disyllables into monosyllables, increasing use of glottal stop as an onset, and the absorption of implosive consonants at labial, dental/alveolar, and often also palatal points of articulation, which contrast with preexisting voiced and voiceless stops. The use of palatal voiceless stops and nasals, embargoed in Malay but widespread in Mon-Khmer, is also permitted in Chamic, as is the use of monosyllabic content words.

Hlai and the Chinese languages are monosyllabic and fully tonal. Malay and most Chamic languages are non-tonal, though some Chamic languages have begun to develop a tonal system (Jarai has low tone on the vowel preceding a final glottal stop) and some others, such as Phan Rang Cham of Vietnam (Brunelle 2012), have gone further than this (Brunelle 2006). In this and other regards Tsat has squeezed itself into the corset of Min Chinese phonology, having already absorbed phonological properties (and much lexicon) from Mon-Khmer languages (and Tsat, like other Chamic languages, contains many other words, many of them both pan-Chamic and monosyllabic, of unknown etymology). Tsat is fully tonal—all its syllables are

Table 3.2 Some Cardinal Numerals in Austronesian Languages

Malay	Acehnese	Tsat	English
satu	Sa	sa33	'one'
dua	Duwa	thua11	'two'
empat	puɘt	pa:ʔ24	'four'
lima	limʌŋ	ma33	'five'
tujuh	Tujoh	su55	'seven'
sembilan	sikurwaŋ	thua11 pa:nʔ42	'nine'

tone-bearing—and many of its contentives are monosyllabic, though there are many disyllables and trisyllables as well.

The tonology of Tsat has clearly developed in stages much like those of Phan Rang Cham, in which the lowering properties of breathy voice are important for developing a low tone. The features of Tsat tonology resemble those of Hlai and Minnan but are not identical with either system. Thurgood construes Tsat tones as always being double, comprising two notes drawn from one of five pitch levels. Three tones are level (55 high, 33 mid, and 11 low) and two are mobile, one rising (24) and one falling (42).

There have also been changes in consonantal onsets, in order to accommodate the Tsat words more closely to southern Chinese phonology. The onsets, rhymes, and codas of Tsat are very largely those permitted by Minnan phonology, for instance the use of both aspirated and unaspirated stops in onset position. Other changes have taken place, too; for instance, earlier *j becomes /s/. Stress is a primary consideration in Tsat historical phonology: the numerous monosyllabic forms in Tsat derive their shapes from the primary stressed syllable in Proto-Chamic words, while unstressed syllables often drop away completely.

Changes wrought on Tsat phonology can be seen by comparing some lower cardinal numerals in Tsat, Acehnese, Malay, and English (see Table 3.2; from Thurgood 1999: 38).

3.7 General Conclusions

The overall conclusions that we may come to when we have examined the borrowed phones or phonemes insofar as they are manifested in loanwords in the languages under investigation are threefold:

(1) Borrowed sounds in the various languages rarely penetrate into items in the lexical layers in the recipient language that had existed before the donor language(s) had provided the words through which the recipient language had absorbed its new

sounds. Exceptions to this principle include the spread of centralized vowels (and also of Slavic-style palatalized consonants) into inherited words and older loans in Kalderash Romani (Boretzky 1991).

(2) The corollary is not also true: many languages have resisted the spread of non-indigenous sounds into their language even though they occur in source-language forms of non-indigenous words. We cannot assume that "foreign" sounds are going to be preserved intact in "foreign" words that are borrowed into a given language, even if a large number of words (including relexificational vocabulary items) are taken into the language from that source. Among the languages presented in the sample, this is especially the case with borrowed Kari'na and European words in Garifuna, which have long been very thoroughly assimilated to the original Garifuna phonology, at both segmental and templatic levels. We should not be surprised when phonological borrowing of that kind takes place, but we must not assume that it is going to happen as a matter of course, even if the recipient language contains a great deal of borrowed morphemic material.

(3) There is no particularly sharp correlation between (say) the degree of bilingualism or period of bilingualism in a particular language and the number of borrowed sounds that it has absorbed, and the same is true of the amount of basic vocabulary that the language has replaced by borrowings when contrasted with the number and nature of borrowed sounds. At one extreme Hindi-Urdu has absorbed the greatest number of sounds, and this includes the addition of new places of articulation to its repertoire, while at the other extreme Ngandi has barely taken any borrowed sounds over (and those it has taken are very rare), and the same is true of Garifuna, English, and Yapese. The degree and intensity of contact between these languages also needs to be gauged against the pre-contact typological similarity or otherwise of the languages whose speakers have come into contact. Tagalog and Kapampangan are genealogically related languages and also have very similar phonological systems, so that there was very little scope for the absorption into Tagalog of unfamiliar sounds in Kapampangan words. (However, the sound systems are not identical: the Kapampangan phonemic schwa found no parallel in Tagalog, so that words from Kapampangan containing schwa, written <e> in Kapampangan orthography, such as *pawes* 'sweat,' were absorbed in Tagalog with /i/: Tagalog *pawis* 'ditto.': Zorc 1993: 205) Those languages that have borrowed the greatest number of sounds have absorbed a great deal of lexicon from languages with very different phonemic inventories from those of the recipient languages.

(4) There are other kinds of phonological feature borrowing that are not attested in the languages in the first data set in the preceding but which are certainly found elsewhere, not least in cases such as Tsat. Two such types of borrowing from donor or source language to recipient language are the beginning of the transmission of patterns of vowel harmony, such as happened in some varieties of Cappadocian Greek that were especially strongly influenced by Turkish (Dawkins 1916), which passed from Turkish-derived forms to being used in inherited Greek forms, and, as previously noted, the development of lexically defined and distinctive pitch tone systems in languages previously lacking them.

In short, here as elsewhere in language, we cannot assume that there will be perfect correlations between the degree of borrowing of core (or non-core) vocabulary from one language to another and the degree of borrowing of unfamiliar sounds in a particular language or across languages.

REFERENCES

Aguon, K. (ed.). 2009. *The Official Chamorro-English Dictionary/ Ufisiåt na Diksionårion Chamorro-Engles*. Hagåtña, Guam: Department of Chamorro Affairs.

Bao, Zhiming. 2006. Clash avoidance and metrical opacity in Singapore English. *Sprachtypologie und Universalienforschung: STUF* 59(2): 133–147.

Berger, Tilman. 2014. The convergence between Czech and German between the years 900 and 1500. In *Family Effects in Language Contact: Modeling Congruence as a Factor in Contact Induced Change*, edited by J. Besters-Dilger, C. Dermarkar, S. Pfänder, and A. Rabus, 184–198. Berlin: De Gruyter.

Blust, R. 2000. Chamorro historical phonology. *Oceanic Linguistics* 38(1): 83–122.

Boretzky, Norbert. 1991. Contact-induced sound change. *Diachronica* 8: 1–15.

Borg, Albert, and Marie Azzopardi-Alexander. 1997. *Maltese*. London: Routledge.

Brousseau, Anne-Marie. 2003. The accentual system of Haitian Creole: The role of transfer and markedness values. In *Phonology and Morphology of Creole Languages*, edited by Ingo Plag, 123–145. Linguistische Arbeiten. Tübingen: Max Niemeyer.

Brunelle, Marc. 2006. A phonetic study of Eastern Cham register. In *Chamic and Beyond: Studies In Mainland Austronesian Languages*, edited by A. Grant and P. Sidwell, 1–36. Canberra: Pacific Linguistics 569.

Brunelle, Marc. 2012. Dialect experience and perceptual integrality in phonological registers: Fundamental frequency, voice quality and the first formant in Cham. *Journal of the Acoustical Society of America* 131(4): 3088–3102.

Callaghan, Catherine A. 2014. *Proto-Utian Grammar and Dictionary: With Notes on Yokuts*. Berlin: De Gruyter Mouton.

Campbell, Lyle. 1997. Amerindian personal pronouns: A second opinion. *Language* 73: 339–351.

Cardona, George, and Dhanesh Jain (eds.). 2002. *The Indo-Aryan Languages*. London: Curzon.

Cheung, Winnie H. Y. 2008. Span of high tones in Hong Kong English. *HKBU Papers in Applied Language Studies* 12: 19–46.

Chung, Sandra. 1983. Transderivational relationships in Chamorro phonology. *Language* 59: 35–64.

Colantoni, Laura, and Jorge Gurlekian. 2004. Convergence and intonation: Historical evidence from Buenos Aires Spanish. *Bilingualism: Language and Cognition* 7(2): 107–119.

de Lacy, Paul. 2006. *Markedness: Reduction and Preservation in Phonology*. Cambridge, UK: Cambridge University Press.

Drayton, Kathy-Ann. 2006. *Word-Level Prosody in Trinidadian English Creole: A Phonetic Analysis*. Unpublished PhD seminar paper, University of the West Indies: St. Augustine.

Dwyer, Arienne M. 2008. Tonogenesis in Southeastern Monguor. In *Lessons from Documented Endangered Languages*, edited by K. David Harrison, David Rood, and Arienne Dwyer, 111–128. Typological Studies in Language 78. Amsterdam; Philadelphia: John Benjamins.

Faraclas, Nicholas. 1984. Rivers Pidgin English: Tone, stress, or pitch-accent language? *Studies in the Linguistic Sciences* 14(2): 67–76.

Finney, Malcolm Awadajin. 2004. Tone assignment on lexical items of English and African origin in Krio. In *Creoles, Contact and Language Change: Linguistics and Social Implications*, edited by Genevieve Escure and Armin Schwegler, 221–236. Amsterdam; Philadelphia: John Benjamins.

Forman, Michael. 1973. *Kapampangan Dictionary*. Honolulu: University of Hawai'i Press.

Good, Jeff. 2004. Tone and accent in Saramaccan: Charting a deep split in the phonology of a language. *Lingua* 114: 575–619.

Gooden, Shelome. 2003. *The Phonology and Phonetics of Jamaican Creole Reduplication*. PhD thesis, Ohio State University.

Grant, Anthony P. 2013. *The Boundaries of Borrowing*. Unpublished manuscript.

Heath, Jeffrey. 1997. Moroccan Arabic phonology. In *Phonologies of Asia and Africa (including the Caucasus)*, edited by Alan S. Kaye and Peter T. Daniels, 205–217. Winona Lake, IN: Eisenbrauns.

Hualde, J. I. 2005. *The Sounds of Spanish*, Cambridge, UK: Cambridge University Press.

Jakobson, Roman, Gunnar Fant, and Morris Halle. 1961. *Preliminaries to Speech Analysis: The Distinctive Features and Their Correlates*. Cambridge, MA: MIT Press.

Kang, Y. 2011. Loanword phonology. In *Blackwell Companion to Phonology*, edited by Marc van Oostendorp, Colin Ewen, Elizabeth Hume, and Keren Rice, 2258–2282. Malden, MA: Wiley-Blackwell.

Kaye, Alan S., and Peter T. Daniels (eds.). 1997. *Phonologies of Asia and Africa (including the Caucasus)*. Winona Lake, IN: Eisenbrauns.

Kenstowicz, Michael. 2005 The phonetics and phonology of Korean loanword adaptation. In *Proceedings of the 1st European Conference on Korean Linguistics (ECKL 1)*, edited by S.-J. Rhee, 17–32. Seoul: Hankookmunhwasa.

Kingston, John. 2011. Tonogenesis. In *The Blackwell Companion to Phonology*, Vol. IV: *Phonological Interfaces*, edited by Colin J. Ewen, Elizabeth Hume, Marc van Oostendorp, and Keren Rice, 2304–2333. Malden, MA: Wiley-Blackwell.

Kramer, Marvin. 2007. Tone on quantifiers in Saramaccan as a transferred feature from Kikongo. *Synchronic and Diachronic Perspectives on Contact Languages*, edited by Magnus Huber and Viveka Velupillai, 43–66. Amsterdam; Philadelphia: John Benjamins.

Klein, Thomas B. 2000. *Umlaut in Optimality Theory*. Tübingen: Niemeyer.

Ladefoged, Peter. 1996. *The Sounds of the World's Languages*. Oxford: Blackwell.

Lee-Smith, Mei W., and Stephen A. Wurm. 1996. The Wutun language. *Atlas of Languages of Intercultural Communication in the Pacific, Asia, and the Americas*, edited by Stephen A. Wurm, Peter Mühlhäusler, and Darrell T. Tryon, 883–898. Berlin; New York: Mouton de Gruyter.

Li, Charles N. 1986. The rise and fall of tones through diffusion. *Berkeley Linguistics Society* 12: 173–185.

Li, Michelle, Stephen Matthews, and Geoff Smith. 2005. Pidgin English texts from the Chinese English Instructor. *Hong Kong Journal of Applied Linguistics* 8: 79–167.

Lipski, John. 2005. *A History of Afro-Hispanic language: Five Centuries and Five Continents*. Cambridge, UK: Cambridge University Press.

Lipski, John M. 2010a. Pitch polarity in Palenquero: A possible locus of H tone. In *Romance Linguistics 2009: Selected Papers from the 39th Linguistic Symposium on Romance Languages (LSRL), Tucson, Arizona, March 2009*, edited by Sonia Colina, Antxon Olarrea, and Ana Maria Carvalho, 111–127. Amsterdam: John Benjamins.

Lipski, John M. 2010b. Spanish and Portuguese in contact. In *The Handbook of Language Contact*, edited by Raymond Hickey, 550–580, London: Blackwell.

Maddieson, Ian. 1986. Borrowed sounds. In *The Fergusonian Impact: Papers for Charles A. Ferguson in Honor of his 65th birthday*, edited by Joshua A. Fishman, A. Tabouret- Keller, M. Clyne, B. Krishnamurti, and M. Abdulaziz, 1–16. Berlin; New York: Mouton de Gruyter.

Matisoff, James A. 2001. Genetic versus contact relationship: Prosodic diffusibility in South-East Asian languages. In *Areal Diffusion and Genetic Inheritance: Problems in Comparative Linguistics*, edited by Alexandra Y. Aikhenvald and R. M. W. Dixon, 291–327. Oxford: Oxford University Press.

Mesthrie, Rajend. 2008. Synopsis: The phonology of English in Africa and South and Southeast Asia. In *Varieties of English*, Vol. 4: *Africa, South and Southeast Asia*, edited by Rajend Mesthrie, 307–339. Berlin; New York: Mouton de Gruyter.

Ng, E-Ching. 2012. Chinese meets Malay meets English: Origins of the Singaporean English word-final high tone. *International Journal of Bilingualism* 16(1): 83–100.

Nicolaï, Robert. 2006. A Songhay-Mande convergence area? Facts, questions, frames. *Annual Publication in African Linguistics* 4: 5–30.

Ozanne-Rivierre, Françoise. 1994. Iaai loanwords and phonemic changes in Fagauvea. In *Language Contact and Change in the Austronesian World*, edited by Thomas E. Dutton and Darrell T. Tryon, 523–549. Berlin; New York: Trends in Linguistics, Studies & Monographs 77.

Pagel, Steve. 2010. *Spanisch in Asien und Ozeanien*. Frankfurt am Main: Peter Lang.

Penhallurick, Robert A. 2004. Welsh English: Phonology. In *Handbook of the Varieties of English*, Vol. 1: *Phonology*, edited by Bernd Kortmann and Edgar Werner Schneider, 98–112. Berlin: De Gruyter.

Peperkamp, S. 2004. A psycholinguistic theory of loanword adaptation. In *Proceedings of the Annual Meeting, Berkeley Linguistics Society*, edited by M. Ettlinger, N. Fleisher, and Mischa Park-Doob, 30, 341–352. Berkeley: Berkeley Linguistics Society.

Queen, Robin. 2001. Bilingual intonation patterns: Evidence of language change from Turkish-German bilingual children. *Language in Society* 30(1): 55–80.

Rivera-Castillo, Yolanda, and Lucy Pickering. 2004. Phonetic correlates of stress and tone in a mixed system. *Journal of Pidgin and Creole Languages* 19(2): 261–284.

Rodríguez-Ponga y Salamanca, Rafael. 1995. *El elemento español en la lengua chamorra (Islas Marianas)*. PhD thesis, Universidad Complutense de Madrid.

Salmons, Joseph. 1992. *Accentual Change and Language Contact: Comparative Survey and a Case Study of Early Northern Europe*. Stanford: Stanford University Press.

Sampson, John. 1926. *The Dialect of the Gypsies of Wales*. Oxford: Clarendon Press.

Sangaja, P. 2009 *Indian English*. Edinburgh: Edinburgh University Press.

Steriade, Donca. 2001. Directional asymmetries in place assimilation: A perceptual account. In *The Role of Speech Perception in Phonology*, edited by Elizabeth Hume and Keith Johnson, 219–250. San Diego: Academic Press.

Stolz, Thomas. 1998. Die Hispanität des Chamorro als sprachwissenschaftliches Problem. *Iberoamericana* 70(2): 5–38.

Stolz, Thomas. 2003. Not quite the right mixture: Chamorro and Malti as candidates for the status of mixed language. In *The Mixed Language Debate: Theoretical and Empirical Advances*, edited by Y. Matras and P. Bakker, 271–315. Berlin: Mouton de Gruyter.

Thurgood, Graham. 1999. *From Ancient Cham to Modern Dialects: Two Thousand Years of Language Contact and Change*. Oceanic Linguistics Special Publications 29.

Topping, Donald M. 1973. *Chamorro Reference Grammar*. Honolulu: University of Hawaii Press.

Topping, D., P. M. Ogo, and B. C. Dungca. 1975. *Chamorro-English Dictionary*. Honolulu: University of Hawaii Press.

Weinreich, Uriel. 1956. Notes on the rise-fall intonation contour. In *For Roman Jakobson*, edited by Morris Halle, 633–643. The Hague: Mouton.

Wells, J. C. 1982. *Accents of English*, Vol. 3: *Beyond the British Isles*. Cambridge, UK: Cambridge University Press.

Wiltshire, Caroline R., and James D. Harnsberger. 2006. The influence of Gujarati and Tamil L1s on Indian English: A preliminary study. *World Englishes* 25(1): 91–104.

Zorc, R. David Paul. 1993. "The Prehistory and Origin of the Tagalog People." In *Language - a doorway between human cultures: tributes to Dr. Otto Chr. Dahl on his ninetieth birthday*, edited by Oyvind Dahl, 201–211. Oslo: Novus.

CHAPTER 4

···

MORPHOLOGY AND CONTACT-INDUCED LANGUAGE CHANGE

···

FRANCESCO GARDANI

4.1 INTRODUCTION

···

RECENT years have seen a flourishing interest in the effects of language contact on morphology, as reflected by titles such as *Copies versus Cognates in Bound Morphology* (Johanson and Robbeets 2012), *Morphologies in Contact* (Vanhove et al. 2012), and *Borrowed Morphology* (Gardani et al. 2015). Contact-induced morphological change has initially attracted the attention of historical linguists, and later, of scholars of language contact and also morphologists. The general interest of historical linguists in this field of research is due to the prominent role that borrowing—though not necessarily morphological borrowing—has played in language change, of which it has traditionally been considered one of the principal sources, along with sound change and analogy. Still, contact phenomena occurring in the area of morphology have long been quite ignored because they are less frequent than others, for example, lexical borrowings.

As early as the second half of the nineteenth century, it was acknowledged that morphology is more resistant to borrowing than other areas of grammar are, to the extent that many students of language denied that bound morphology could be borrowed. In this respect, an exception to the then-prevailing retentionist positions was Hugo Schuchardt, who claimed that there are no completely unmixed languages (Schuchardt 1884: 5). Schuchardt's interest was devoted not only to pidgins and creoles, but to all forms of contact-induced language change, including the borrowing of bound morphemes; in his *Brevier* (Schuchardt 1928: 195), he fleetingly mentions purported cases, such as the Caucasian -*k'* in the Armenian plural, the Latin -*eta* in the Basque plural, and the Armenian -iw in the Georgian instrumental (see also Weinreich 2011: 50).[1] While Schuchardt was a forerunner, the turning point came in 1953, with Weinreich, who claimed that derivational affixes are more easily transferable than highly bound inflectional affixes, but attested also some instances of transfer of highly bound morphemes (Weinreich 1953: 31–33).[2]

The fact that (bound) morphology is more resistant to change than other areas of grammar has led scholars of language contact to view the borrowing of morphology as a reflex of very strong pressure that one language, the source language (SL), exerts over another, the recipient language (RL). This has motivated linguists to design a number of borrowing scales (or scales of borrowability), most prominently Moravcsik (1978), Thomason and Kaufman (1988), Field (2002), in all of which morphology ranks quite high when it comes to the intensity of contact, which is deemed necessary for morphological borrowing to occur (see Matras 2009: 153–165 and Wohlgemuth 2009: 11–17, for good overviews). However, acknowledging this does not amount to saying that morphology is an insurmountable block of marble, in two respects: first, we know that morphology is borrowed; second, the concept of morphology covers a rather wide range of phenomena, from compounding to inflection, which have to be distinguished in terms of the place they occupy in grammar; different areas of morphology have been claimed to have different degrees of borrowability. As we will see in sections 4.3 and 4.7, the frequency of morphological borrowing correlates with the type of morphology that is borrowed, in terms of the distinction between word formation and inflection, and even within the subgroup of inflection.

In recent times, progresses in both language description and linguistic typology, and to a lesser extent, morphological research, have promoted a research branch that combines the study of language contact with theories of morphology (the necessity of a rapprochement between contact linguistics and general theoretical morphology has been pointed to by Wilkins 1996: 116). First and foremost, the compilation of comprehensive grammars of previously undescribed languages, including endangered languages, has extended the database and has increased our knowledge of the contact history of more languages. Second, studies based on large cross-linguistic data have allowed for comparative analyses and insights in terms of (universal) tendencies (e.g., Matras and Sakel 2007; Wohlgemuth 2009). Third, language contact has increasingly been acknowledged as a source of evidence for the theory of morphology, in terms of

---

[1] Most of these purported instances either have been rejected or are not supported by convincing evidence.

[2] On a terminological note, the term "transfer" is often used as a general heading (e.g., in van Coetsem 1988) for phenomena that other scholars (e.g., Thomason and Kaufman 1988) have contrasted, such as borrowing and interference through shift. Johanson (1999, 2008) has introduced the term "copying," in order to raise the awareness that the copies are the output of a creative process and are never identical to their inputs. Although "copying" and "borrowing" basically mean the same, the term "borrowing" is more anchored in the terminological tradition. Singh (2010) is a critical voice about the characterization of borrowing as "morphological."

generalizations about the so-called architecture of grammar (see Myers-Scotton 2002; Gardani 2008, 2012; Meakins 2011a).

Also, the study of morphological transfer has proved a useful heuristic tool in investigations of the genealogical relatedness of languages or language groups (see Robbeets 2012, 2015, for a fruitful example with respect to the Transeurasian hypothesis; Whaley 2012, for a study of genealogical relatedness, based on evidence from derivational morphology; as well as Bowern 2013; Epps 2013; Mithun 2013; Law 2013, for morphological change induced by contact between genealogically related languages).[3]

The present chapter has two main goals: first, to provide an overview of the main tenets of contact-induced language change; and second, to detail the most recent developments in research on morphological borrowing (though without any claim to exhaustiveness).

After this brief introduction, in the next three sections, I propose an analysis of contact-induced morphological change, captured in terms of a gradient ranging from the morphological (i.e., inflectional) integration of loanwords, to the borrowing of morphological material (and structure) from a source language into a recipient language, to, eventually, extreme language mixture. In particular, section 4.2 surveys the continuum between morphological integration and morphological borrowing, including different degrees of integration, non-integration (indeclinability and maintenance of original markers), and borrowing. Section 4.3 is devoted to different types of borrowing, in particular the distinctions between PAT(TERN) borrowing and MAT(TER) borrowing, and between DER(IVATIONAL) borrowing and INFL(ECTIONAL) borrowing. As different situations of language contact can give rise to different linguistic results and processes, some of which go beyond borrowing, section 4.4 treats the topics of extreme borrowing and language mixture. In section 4.5, three major types of mechanisms leading to morphological borrowing are introduced. Section 4.6 discusses intra-linguistic and extra-linguistic factors that have been claimed to possibly favor morphological borrowing; and finally, section 4.7 offers a concluding lesson for the theory of morphology.

4.2 SCALE OF MORPHOLOGICAL INTEGRATION

It is well known that when two (or more) languages are in contact, the transfer of lexical material is very common, even when the level of bilingualism in the contact situation is low. When lexical matter has entered a recipient language, two main

---

[3] As a word of warning, the methods of contact linguistics and historical linguistics not only should be applied soundly but also complement each other. The long-held belief that morphology is the most reliable basis for genealogical classification of languages (the so-called *Ludolf's rule*) may induce to wrong analyses, for example, if borrowings are not recognized as such (see Grant 2008: 166).

options are at hand: either it is integrated or it is not. Besides phonological integration ("accommodation"), in non-isolating recipient languages, borrowed lexemes can be integrated morphologically, in terms of the realization of language-specific morpho-syntactic features. However, this need not be the case, that is, borrowed forms can stay unchanged without any drawback for the recipient language's syntax. Between these extremes, several types and degrees of morphological integration are possible, as I will show in the following subsections.

4.2.1 Inflectional Integration

Morphological integration is a matter of degree, and at least four degrees can be observed along a decreasing hierarchical scale, ranging from full integration to non-integration.

Full integration[4] occurs when loan nouns and verbs are realized as forms that conform to the inflectional subsystems of the recipient language, by means of productive native rules. Consider, for example, the integration of the Ancient Greek noun *lampás* (gen. *lampádos*) into the Latin inflectional class *rosa* (gen. *rosae*), as *lampada* (gen. *lampadae*). The integration into a non-isomorphic paradigm is due to the full productivity, thus the force of attraction, of the recipient class (Gardani 2013: 48).

(1)

	SG		PL	
	Latin	Greek	Latin	Greek
nom	*lampada*	*lampás*	*lampadae*	*lampádes*
gen	*lampadae*	*lampádos*	*lampadarum*	*lampadón*
dat	*lampadae*	*lampádi*	*lampadis*	*lampási(n)*
acc	*lampadam*	*lampáda*	*lampadas*	*lampádes*
voc	*lampada*	*lampás*	*lampadae*	*lampádes*
abl	*lampada*	—	*lampadis*	—

Less intensely, *partial integration* occurs when loan nouns and verbs maintain part of their original inflections in the recipient language. For example, in Latin, some Greek-origin loan nouns have less integrated, Graecizing inflections, such as the nominative, accusative, and vocative forms of the singular paradigm of *idolatres -ae* 'idolater,' borrowed from the Ancient Greek *eidolátres -ou*, in (2) (compare the corresponding fully integrated inflections, in example (1)) (Gardani 2013: 173).[5]

---

[4] This has been termed "paradigm insertion" by Wohlgemuth (2009: 87), with respect to loan verbs. The same term would perfectly apply to loan nouns, too. In this chapter, I use the term "full integration," instead, because it is more adequate to label a level of the integration scale.

[5] Note that some nouns have variants, such as *poeta -ae* and *poetes -ae* 'playwright,' from the Ancient Greek *poietés -oŭ*.

(2)		Latin	Greek
	nom	*idolatres*	*eidolátres*
	gen	*idolatrae*	*eidolátrou*
	dat	*idolatra*	*eidolátre*
	acc	*idolatren*	*eidolátren*
	voc	*idolatres*	*eidolátres*
	abl	*idolatra*	—

A different kind of partial integration is *incomplete paradigmatic integration* with resulting defectiveness. It occurs when loan nouns or loan verbs, once they have entered the recipient language, are not realized for all morphosyntactic values. In the following example from Portuguese, *abolir* 'abolish,' not directly inherited but borrowed from Classical Latin ABOLĒRE (or perhaps via French or Italian), is defective in the whole present subjunctive paradigm, as well as in the singular and third person forms of the present indicative (Maiden and O'Neill 2010: 104–107).

(3)	prs.ind		prs.sbjv	
	Portuguese	Latin	Portuguese	Latin
	—	*aboleō*	—	*aboleam*
	—	*abolēs*	—	*aboleās*
	—	*abolet*	—	*aboleat*
	abolimos	*abolēmus*	—	*aboleāmus*
	abolis	*abolētis*	—	*aboleātis*
	—	*abolent*	—	*aboleant*

Occasionally, nouns are borrowed in their plural forms and additionally marked for plural via native formatives, resulting in a *native-foreign-mix*, a mixture of native and non-native affixes. Consider the following instance from Yaqui (Uto-Aztecan), which shows the simultaneous occurrence of the Spanish plural suffix *-s* and of the Yaqui plural formative *-im*, on the Spanish-borrowed noun *vaca* 'cow' (data in (4a) from Estrada Fernández and Guerrero 2007: 421).[6]

(4) Yaqui
    a. *waka-s-im*   b. *wakas-im*
       cow-PL-PL   cow-PL
       'cows'   'cows'

A similar, but somehow more drastic, change involves suffixation, via the Romance formative *-i*, of a native Semitic broken plural form, in Maltese. In the following example the form *cnieg* (5b) correctly realizes the plural value of the noun *cinga*

---

[6] Estrada Fernández and Guerrero (2007: 421) explain this case in terms of semantic bleaching of the Spanish plural suffix, which can be best captured by the analysis in (4b). See Gómez-Rendón (2007: 488) for parallel cases in Imbabura Quichua.

'strap,' borrowed from the Sicilian *cinga*, following a Semitic CCV:C pattern. The peculiarity of this case is the combination of the Romance concatenative affix -*i* with the Semitic templatic morphology, in the form *cnieg-i* (5a) (Maris Camilleri, personal communication, October 30, 2012).

(5)   Maltese
    a. *cnieg-i*   b. *cnieg*
      strap.PL-PL   strap.PL
      'straps'   'straps'

4.2.2 Non-Integration

Morphological integration does not occur when loanwords, especially loan nouns,[7] are not assigned any paradigmatic pattern; they are indeclinable.[8] In Standard Italian, for example, the Japanese-borrowed noun *kimono* has a constant paradigm, that is, there is invariance in the realization of the singular and plural cells:

(6)   Italian
    (*il*) *kimono*   (*i*) *kimono*
    '(the) kimono' '(the) kimonos'

Coming down to the lowest step of the integration scale, the highest degree of non-integration is maintenance of original formatives, in the form of frozen morphology. The following two examples illustrate different types of this case.

In the Neo-Aramaic language of Tūrōyo (which was spoken, as of 1965, in the village Mīdin, Turkey, by 920 speakers), the Kurdish adjectival feminine ending -*e* has remained confined to one Kurdish-borrowed adjective, *rāṣṭ* 'right' (data from Jastrow 1985: 238).

(7)   Tūrōyo Aramaic
    ʾídi ʾí-rāṣṭe
    'my right hand'

Another kind of non-integration is the overall transfer of paradigms. The stock example is English *alumnus-alumni*, a singular-plural pair borrowed *tout court* from Latin, by retaining the (relevant) Latin inflections. Kossmann (2010) has labeled this phenomenon *Parallel System Borrowing* (PSB), has shown that is more diffused than is generally assumed, and has provided a brilliant analysis thereof, in terms of etymon-related compartmentalization. Accordingly, PSB is a transfer process by which loan-words retain their original paradigms, thus coming to establish themselves as

---

[7] Data collected in a cross-linguistic study confirm the long-held generalization that nouns are more borrowable than verbs (31% vs. 14% of total loanwords) (Tadmor 2009: 61).

[8] With respect to loan verbs, Wohlgemuth (2009: 94) terms this strategy "direct insertion."

systems parallel to the native paradigms of the host language. (As a matter of fact, transferred inflections can engage in competition with native inflections, such as the English *fungus*, which has both a learnèd plural form *fungi* and a nativized word-based plural form *funguses*.[9]) In languages with elaborated paradigms, PSB is more prominent, as shown in the following example from the Northern Berber language of Ghomara, northwestern Morocco, where the paradigms of the native Berber verb *kšəm* 'enter' (8a), and of the Arabic-borrowed verb *ṭlaqa* 'meet' (8b, c), coexist as parallel systems (data from Kossmann 2010).[10]

(8)   Ghomara Berber

	a. Native paradigm	b. Loan paradigm (ipfv)	c. Loan paradigm (pfv)
1SG	kəšm-əx	n-ṭlaqa	ṭlaqi-t
2SG	t-kəšm-ət	t-ṭlaqa	ṭlaqi-t
3SG.m	i-kšəm	i-ṭlaqa	ṭlaqa
3SG.f	t-əkšəm	t-ṭlaqa	ṭlaqa-θ
1PL	n-əkšəm	n-ṭlaqa-w	ṭlaqi-na
2PL	t-kəšm-əm	t-ṭlaqa-w	ṭlaqi-θum (?)
3PL	kəšm-ən	i-ṭlaqa-w	ṭlaqa-w

The attentive reader may wonder why I treat PSB under "integration," and not under "borrowing." The question is legitimate, for some authors do not make the notion of borrowing depend on whether or not loan formatives apply to native lexemes of the recipient language. In my view, however, borrowing occurs when loan formatives are extended so that they apply to native lexemes of the recipient language (see later discussion). In PSB, however, new inflections are transferred into the recipient language, but are not extended to native words; in our specific example, Arabic paradigms, thus, in more abstract terms, new inflectional classes are introduced into Berber, but do not apply to native lexemes (see also the case of Korlai Indo-Portuguese, discussed in Clements and Luís 2015). Thus, PSB is a borderline phenomenon, situated in the context of the boundaries between non-integration and borrowing.

A question that is worth discussing in this context is whether or not a terminological and theoretical limit between PSB and borrowing can be established, and whether this would match a psycholinguistic difference. My answer to the question is that it *is*

---

[9] In the case of English *impetus-impetuses*, nativization via plural suffixation in *-es* is virtually compulsory, because the original Latin plural form *impetūs* wouldn't be able to convey any number value opposition in English.

[10] While Berber conveys aspectual and modal distinctions by stem allomorphy, Arabic-borrowed verbs have two paradigms, one for perfective inflection and one for imperfective inflection (for more details, see Kossmann 2010: 473 and Kossmann 2013: 270–271; but note that Kossmann mistakenly labels perfective the imperfective paradigm and vice versa; I owe thanks to Skye Anderson for pointing that out to me, July 9, 2015). Note that the striking similarity between the Berber prefixes and the Arabic prefixes of the perfective paradigm, in the 2SG, 3SG.m, 3SG.f, 1PL, and 2PL, is either due to chance or Afro-Asiatic heritage (Maarten Kossmann, personal communication, Febraury 9, 2014).

possible to distinguish between inflectional classes that have been introduced into the recipient language but remain limited to loan vocabulary, from inflectional classes that extend to native (or nativized) lexemes of the recipient language. What is beyond this line is "borrowing proper."

At the end, if borrowed formatives become productive in the recipient language, there will be a coincidence of borrowing with the initial stage of the integration scale, namely, full integration via productivity.

4.3 Beyond Integration: Borrowing

In section 4.2, we have seen that inflections can cross the boundaries between two languages in contact, but often do not apply to native vocabulary items.[11] However, cases are attested in which native lexemes of a recipient language inflect by means of borrowed formatives (or new lexemes are formed through borrowed derivational morphemes). I term these cases "borrowing proper," on the basis of the following constraint:

> Morphological borrowing occurs when formatives apply to native lexemes of the recipient language.[12]

However, not all borrowed formatives necessarily become fully productive in a recipient language. In fact, borrowing is rather a matter of stabilization, than of full nativization. Stabilization is the very criterion discerning between the phenomenon of borrowing and the phenomenon of code-switching (see Gardner-Chloros 2009). Code-switching is "a kind of contact-induced speech behavior" (Haspelmath 2009: 40), whereas borrowing "refers to a completed language change, a diachronic process that once started as an individual innovation but has been propagated throughout the speech community" (Haspelmath 2009: 38). (At the same time, code-switching is a mechanism that can lead to borrowing, as we will see in section 4.6.)

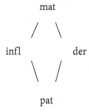

FIGURE 4.1 Types of morphological borrowing.

---

[11] The same observation is valid for derivational morphemes, as well.

[12] A weaker version of this constraint would include extension to loanwords from other source languages, too. This usually happens in languages that have different strata of lexical borrowings (cf. example (17)).

In the next subsections, I will detail two fundamental distinctions in relation to borrowing, in terms both of borrowing matter as opposed to borrowing pattern (4.3.1), and of borrowing inflection as opposed to borrowing derivation (4.3.2). Figure 4.1 shows that MAT borrowing and PAT borrowing can regard both inflection and derivation (and vice versa).

4.3.1 MAT Borrowing Versus PAT Borrowing

A first fundamental distinction concerns the type of the borrowed entity, in terms of its being an actual morpheme or an abstract pattern. This distinction is not new: the first type has traditionally been referred to not only as "borrowing," but also as "direct transfer," "direct diffusion," and "transfer of fabric"; the second type has often been called "replication," "indirect transfer," "indirect diffusion," "loan-formation," "calque," and so forth (to my knowledge, there is no terminological survey in the literature, to which the reader could be referred). More recently, Sakel (2007) has introduced the term pair "MAT borrowing" and "PAT borrowing." This is inspired by the work of Grant (2002, 2004, 2017) involving the distinction of "transfer of fabric" and "transfer of pattern," which has successfully been adapted and has neutralized the terminological proliferation that had gripped the field. In this chapter, I adopt these terms, MAT borrowing and PAT borrowing, too.

The following example shows a case of MAT borrowing that occurred in Turkish. In (9a), the adjectivizer *-vari*, borrowed from Persian (cf. (9b)), applies to the Turkish noun *yengeç* 'crab' (data from Seifart 2013).

(9)   Turkish   Persian
        a. *yengeç-vari*   b. *pishrow-var*
        'crab-like'   'leader-like'

In morphology, PAT borrowing implies that a recipient language rearranges its own inherited morphological structure in such a way that it becomes structurally closer to the source language and that structural convergence results. A straightforward instance of PAT borrowing is found in Selice Romani, which replicates a Hungarian pattern according to which nouns denoting humans have an associative plural, in addition to the canonical plural form. In the following example, I contrast the Selice Romani forms (associative plural in (10a), neutral plural in (10b)), with the corresponding model forms in Hungarian, for the noun *kĕmivĕši* 'bricklayer' and its Hungarian source *kőműves* (Elšik 2007: 266–267). (Note that the Hungarian grapheme <é> renders [eː], while <e> renders [ɛ].)

(10)   Selice Romani   Hungarian
        a. *kĕmivĕš-ingere*   a′. *kőműves-ék*
           bricklayer-assoc.PL
           'bricklayer and his work team'

b. *kĕmivëšš-ë* b'. *kŏmŭves-ek*
bricklayer-PL
'bricklayers'

A case of PAT borrowing at the level of morphosyntax is described by Adamou (2013) for Oaxaca Romani, a variety of Romani spoken in Mexico, under the influence of Spanish. Oaxaca Romani has replicated the uses of the Spanish *estar*—specifically, in attributive, locative, and participle constructions—by recycling the nearly obsolete Romani subject clitic pronoun *lo* (which Matras 2002: 106–107 reconstructs from **ata*). The data in (11a) (from Adamou 2013: 1075) is contrasted with the use of the copula *si* 'is' in Thrace Romani in (11b) (fieldwork data from Evangelia Adamou, personal communication, February 11, 2014).

(11)   a. Oaxaca Romani
          o   raklo=lo   felis
          def.m boy=3SG.m   happy
          (Cf. Spanish: *El nino está feliz*.)

       b. Thrace Romani
          o   muruʃ   si   sevintʃli
          def.m man   be.3SG happy
          'The man is happy.'

Wohlgemuth (2009: 224) has claimed that languages borrow not only accommodation formatives but also accommodation patterns, referring to cases similar to those described by Breu (1991) for Bulgarian, Macedonian, and other languages of the Balkan Sprachbund. The formative *-s-*, originally borrowed from the Greek verbalizer *-iz-* (cf. *alat-íz-o* 'to salt' from *aláti* 'salt'), was later isolated and came to be productively used as an integrating element that has become the general integration suffix throughout the Balkan Sprachbund. In Bulgarian, for example, the Turkish verb *boya-mak* 'to color' has been integrated as a composite stem *bojadi-s-*, to which the inflections apply (data from Breu 1991: 45).

(12)   Bulgarian
       bojadi-s-vam
       color:lvm-lvm-1SG
       'I color'

However, an analysis of the Bulgarian example, just as of the examples quoted by Wohlgemuth (2009: 224–241), shows that the borrowing of an abstract accommodation pattern (in the sense of PAT borrowing) has not occurred. Rather, it is the matter, namely the Greek verbalizer *-iz-*, and not an abstract pattern, that has been borrowed and refunctionalized as a loan verb marker.

Other data show a combination of MAT borrowing with PAT borrowing. For instance, in Modern Persian some native Indo-European nouns have broken plural forms, according to a Semitic non-concatenative pattern. Compare, in the following example, the plural form of the native Persian noun *farmān* 'order' (cf. Old Persian *framāna-* 'order'), with the plural of the Arabic *ṣandūq* 'box,' which is instantiated by the same pattern CaCa:Ci:C (data from Jensen 1931: 45; see also Mumm 2007: 41) (cf. also example (20)).

(13)   Modern Persian   Arabic
      a. *farmān* 'order'   b. *ṣandūq* 'box'
          farāmīn 'orders'   *ṣanādīq* 'boxes'

Here, not only has the abstract Semitic root-and-pattern structure been taken over, but also the concrete actualization of the pattern CaCa:Ci:C, for plural formation, which applies to quadrilateral nouns with a long second vowel, namely singular CVCCV:C.

4.3.2 Borrowability of Morphology

As I have mentioned in the introduction and shown in several examples so far, morphology is as subject to borrowing as other parts of grammars are, even though to a different extent. Also, different areas of morphology seem to differ in the extent to which they are borrowed. It is widely assumed that derivation is borrowed more frequently than inflection (cf. Thomason and Kaufman 1988: 74–75).

In virtue of the fact that different components of morphology have different degrees of borrowability, we have to draw a further distinction, between the borrowing of derivation (DER borrowing) and the borrowing of inflection (INFL borrowing).[13] (As Figure 4.1 illustrates, the split in derivational borrowing and inflectional borrowing can apply both to MAT borrowing (see example 9) and to PAT borrowing (cf. examples 10 and 11). For reasons of space, in the following subsections, I present only cases of MAT borrowing.

4.3.2.1 *DER borrowing*

As of today, no survey of the great amount of borrowed derivation in the languages of the world has been produced—such work is indeed an urgent desideratum. In fact, while everybody agrees on the fact that derivational borrowing occurs, and not infrequently, we do not have an exact idea of the global size of the phenomenon. The scarcity of interest in a comprehensive cross-linguistic coverage is possibly due to two reasons: first, the impressionistic observation that derivational borrowing isn't

---

[13] There is no disguising the fact that the distinction between inflection and derivation is neither obvious nor uncontroversial. Born out in linguistic studies focusing on Indo-European languages, the distinction between inflection and derivation has proved "particularly elusive" to capture (Laca 2001: 1215). Some scholars (e.g., Bybee 1985; Dressler 1989; Plank 1994) have advocated a non-discrete, gradual distinction along a continuum which matches that ranging from the syntax to the lexicon, whereas others (e.g., Behrens 1996; Haspelmath 2013) challenge the validity of this distinction as a universally applicable comparative concept (see Laca 2001: 1215–1218, for an insightful discussion).

infrequent (probably due to the prominent presence of derivational borrowings in (Middle) English from French, combined with the overall disproportionate concern of linguists with the English language) may have silenced the linguists' conscience and prevented scholars from investigating other languages more properly, in this respect; second, the entrenched belief that the diffusion of derivational categories has no true impact on the recipient language and "is hardly different in kind from the mere borrowing of words" (Sapir 1921: 216) has undoubtedly made derivational borrowing a less coveted topic. However, the papers in Matras and Sakel (2007) and, in particular, Seifart's (2013) *AfBo* database, collect quite a many instances of DER borrowing, in terms of MAT borrowing, and thus can be considered a good basis to promote work in this direction.

Among the categories of derivation, agentive nominalization and diminutive meanings have often been argued to be borrowed more frequently, perhaps because they carry out more "concrete" meanings. The *AfBo* figures confirm that adjectivizers, diminutives, and nominalizers (especially to form agents) rank highest among the MAT-borrowed derivational affixes (see the role of *semantic fullness* in borrowing, in section 4.6.1). To exemplify this, in addition to the Bulgarian case in (12), I present a case from Tetun Dili, an Austronesian language spoken in East Timor. Tetun Dili has borrowed the agentive suffix *-dór* (14a) from Portuguese (14b). (In Tetun Dili, the suffix has received a secondary pejorative connotation.) The loan suffix applies to native roots, as in the following example from Hajek (2007: 172), where the native root *hemu* 'to drink' is used.

(14)   Tetun Dili   Portuguese
    a. *hemu-dór*   b. *trabalha-dor*
     'someone who likes to drink'   'laborer'

4.3.2.2 *INFL borrowing*

As we have seen in section 4.1, Weinreich (1953: 44) argues in support of the hypothesis that "the transfer of individual morphemes of all types is definitely possible." This claim has been confirmed by different scholars, most prominently Thomason and Kaufman (1988), based on a large corpus of evidence. Inspired by this work, Gardani (2008) has provided a monographic study of the borrowing of inflectional morphemes in language contact, insisting on the constraint of nativization ("spread to native bases") to discern the status of INFL borrowing (see section 4.3).

As a first example, in Arnhem Land (Australia), Ritharrngu (Pama-Nyungan) has borrowed from Ngandi (Gunwinyguan) a suffix *-ʔmayʔ*, which inflectionally realizes negation on verbs or other non-verbal constituents, replacing the previously used independent particle *yaka*. Compare the Ritharrngu form in (15a) with a Ngandi form bearing the source negative suffix in (15b) (data from Heath 1980: 101 and Heath 1978: 108).

(15)   Ritharrngu   Ngandi
    a. *waːn-i-ʔmayʔ-ni:*   b. *gu-ḍawal-ʔmayʔ*
     go-fut-neg-you   cm-place-neg
     'You will not go!'   'not at place'

Negation is a feature of polarity that can be characterized in terms of inherent inflection, according to the famous distinction between inherent and contextual inflection introduced by Booij (1994, 1996).[14] Based on a cross-linguistic survey of the then-known cases of INFL borrowing, Gardani (2008, 2012) has offered a principled analysis of the variance in the degree of borrowability (in the sense of frequency, not of ease) of different inflectional formatives, in terms of Booij's dichotomy, and has shown that formatives that realize inherent inflection are borrowed more frequently than those realizing contextual inflection.

An example of a borrowed formative that realizes contextual inflection is found in Megleno-Romanian, a Balkan-Romance language spoken in southeastern Macedonia and northern Greece. In the Megleno-Romanian varieties spoken in the villages of Nǎnti, Ošinj, Lundzinj, and Kupǎ, some first-conjugation verbs ending in the consonant cluster *muta cum liquida* display the formative *-m*, for the 1SG of the indicative present, which is added to the corresponding native Romance formative *-u* on inherited Romance bases (*a afla* 'to find out' < Latin AFFLARE 'blow, breathe') (data from Capidan 1925: 159 and Atanasov 1990: 213–214).[15] The formative *-m* has been borrowed from the neighboring southeastern Macedonian dialects. In (16), the verb form with borrowed formative (16a) is contrasted with the corresponding form both of the same verb in the standard variety of Megleno-Romanian (16b) and of the Macedonian verb *nosi* 'to carry' (16c).

(16)	Megleno-Romanian			Macedonian
	a. *aflu-m*	b. *afl-u*	c. *nos-am*
	find.1SG-1.SG	find-1SG	carry-1SG
	'I find out'	'I find out'	'I carry'

According to a weaker version of the nativization constraint formulated in section 4.3, foreign formatives must apply at least to loanwords, in order for them to be rated as INFL borrowings. This applies, for example, to the Romanian-borrowed plural suffix *-ur(j)a*[16] in Kalderash Romani, which is extended to bases of Greek origin, such as the loan noun *foro(s)* 'town' (cf. Greek *phoros* 'market'). Example (17) compares the plural of the loan noun *foro(s)* (a) with that of the native Romance noun *ochi* 'eye' (b) (data in (17a) from Sakel and Matras 2008: 78).

---

[14] Inherent inflection is context-free, that is, it depends on the free speech intention of the speaker. Features of inherent inflection include number, gender, inherent cases, and negation, in the NP; degree, in the AP; tense (except *consecutio temporum*), aspect, negation, and mood, in the VP. Contextual inflection is context-sensitive, that is, it occurs when particular forms of a word are required by the syntactic context. Features of contextual inflection include structural cases and cases governed by VP, PP, in the NP; number, gender, and case, in the AP; person, number, and gender, in the VP.

[15] While an explanation of the phenomenon in terms of an internal Romance development is conceivable, too, nonetheless the explanation in terms of the influence of Macedonian on the Megleno-Romanian dialects cannot be ruled out completely (see Friedman 2012: 324–328).

[16] The form *-urja* is a contamination of the Romanian-borrowed plural formative *-uri* with the inherited (Indo-Aryan) plural marker *-a* (Matras 2002: 85).

(17) Kalderash Romani
    a. *foro(s)*   b. *ochi*
      'town'   'eye'
      for-urja   *ochi-uri*
      'towns'   'eyes'

The last example shows borrowing of plural formatives. Gardani (2012) has demonstrated that the value of plural on NPs has a higher-than-average borrowing rating, and explained this from the fact that plural in the NP is a prototypical category of inherent morphology, thus closer to derivation (and the lexicon) than contextual inflection, and as such is characterized by a higher semantic load (cf. the discussion in section 4.7).

4.4 Extreme Borrowing and Mixed Languages

Different language contact situations can give rise to different linguistic processes and results. Based on the structural effects induced by language contact, Thomason (2001: 60) proposes a threefold classification, which includes contact-induced language change, extreme language mixture, and language death. To be sure, this outline hardly covers the complexity of contact-induced language change, but is nevertheless a meaningful approximation of the contact-linguistic facts. With respect to morphological borrowing, some scholars (e.g., Thomason and Kaufman 1988) treat ordinary contact-induced change and mixed languages as separate phenomena, based on the argument that languages which have undergone contact-induced change, but are clearly traceable back to one ancestor of which they are the descendants, cannot be treated on a par with new languages that emerged from the mixture of two or more source languages, under specific social circumstances. Other scholars (e.g., Matras and Sakel 2007 and papers therein) simply do not differentiate, and label borrowing as both cases of borrowing originated via ordinary contact-induced language change, and occurrences of SL-derived formatives in a mixed language. I adhere to the first school of thought and hold the view that the difference between the outcome of processes of ordinary contact-induced language change and the outcome of processes of mixed-language genesis is a matter of degree and not of kind—an opinion, by the way, already expressed by Thomason (2003: 26). As a case in point, I will discuss the issue of the transfer of entire inflectional paradigms in language contact, in the remainder of this section.

    The transfer of entire inflectional paradigms has long been regarded as the last challenge to morphological borrowability. Weinreich (1953: 44) had observed that the adoption of a full set of morphemes "has apparently never been recorded." The later-reported case of the Russian-derived finite verbal paradigm in (the meanwhile nearly extinct) Mednyi Aleut (spoken east of Kamchatka, Russia) has been dealt with as a case of borrowing of entire inflectional paradigms (Menovščikov 1969; Golovko and

Vakhtin 1990; Thomason 1997). But considering this a case of borrowing is not uncontroversial for the very fact that Mednyi Aleut is a mixed language. In recent works, however, there have been reported cases that do count as instances of paradigm borrowing, for example, in Lamunkhin Ėven. This endangered Western dialect of Ėven (Northern Tungusic), spoken in the village of Sebjan-Küöl in the Republic of Sakha (Yakutia, Siberia), has heavily borrowed from the Turkic language of Sakha (Yakut): Two paradigms, the necessitative and the assertive, are established borrowings; two paradigms, the indicative present tense and the hypothetical paradigm, are potentially ongoing borrowings (see Pakendorf 2009). The following example contrasts the Lamunkhin Ėven necessitative paradigm of the verb *haː-* 'to know' (18a), with the Sakha necessitative paradigm of the verb *bar-* 'to go' (18b) (data from Pakendorf 2014: 293).

(18)		Lamunkhin Ėven		Sakha
1SG	a.	*haː-jaktaːkpịn*	b.	*bar-ịaχtaːχ-pïn*
2SG		*haː-jaktaːkkịn*		*bar-ịaχtaːχ-χïn*
3SG		*haː-jaktaːk*		*bar-ịaχtaːχ*
1PL		*haː-jaktaːkpịt*		*bar-ịaχtaːχ-pït*
2PL		*haː-jaktaːkkịhnan //*		*bar-ịaχtaːχ-χït*
		haː-jaktaːkkịt		
3PL		*haː-jaktaːk-a-l*		*bar-ịaχtaːχ-tar*

As has repeatedly been remarked (see Meakins 2013: 212, for an overview), it is of paramount importance to take into account the chronology, as well as, whenever available, synchronic historical data, in order to provide sober analyses of mixed languages. Whereas Mednyi Aleut was already acknowledged as a mixed language at the time of its investigation, in the case of Lamunkhin Ėven (which looks like a mixed language in the making), we don't know, in fact, whether or not it is on the way to becoming a mixed language (although it is currently still being passed on to children, it is spoken by approximately 300 people only, in an environment in which the dominant language is Sakha; see Pakendorf 2015: 161–162) The issue is very interesting, but also complex, and the space here is too limited to discuss it in depth.

The case of Gurindji Kriol (northern Australia) is of particular relevance in this respect, since it is, as of today, the only mixed language to have been documented diachronically, from the mid-1970s to the present day (McConvell 1988; McConvell and Meakins 2005; Meakins 2011b), although with serious lacunae in the 1980–1990s, which is the period in which code-switching started becoming stable, giving rise to the mixed language (Meakins 2011a: 145). Meakins has shown that in Gurindji Kriol the complete paradigms of the ergative and dative case are Gurindji-derived. In the following example, (19a) shows a Kriol-derived noun (cf. English *pussycat*) to which the Gurindji-derived ergative suffix applies (Meakins 2011a: 68), while (19b) shows a noun marked by the same source formative, in Gurindji (Meakins 2011b: 14).

(19)   Gurindji Kriol   Gurindji
     a. *pujikat-tu-ma*   b. *ngakparn-tu*
        cat-erg-top   frog-erg

4.5 MECHANISMS OF MORPHOLOGICAL BORROWING

In this section, I propose to classify three major kinds of mechanisms involved in contact-induced morphological change: *macro-mechanisms*, *meso-mechanisms*, and *micro-mechanisms*.

The first kind is macro-mechanisms. They are general psycholinguistic mechanisms of transfer conceived in terms of agentivity. Van Coetsem (1988, 2000) distinguishes two fundamental types of transfer in terms of either SL agentivity or RL agentivity, which is based on the notion of linguistic dominance. While the direction of transfer is always from an SL to an RL, the agents of change can be speakers of either language. Thus borrowing occurs when the agents are dominant in the language *into* which they transfer (RL agentivity), and imposition occurs when agents are dominant in the language *from* which they transfer (SL agentivity). While this view resembles the distinction between borrowing and (interference through) shift proposed by Thomason and Kaufman (1988), it is, in fact, more sophisticated, for it contemplates a third scenario, in which the distinction between the two transfer types is neutralized. That is, RL agentivity and SL agentivity can be complementary, as occurs in many contact situations. According to Winford (2005: 408), for example, in the well-informed case of Asia Minor Greek described by Dawkins (1916), both Greek-dominant bilinguals implemented RL agentivity and Turkish-dominant bilinguals implemented SL agentivity. Moreover, "some bilinguals may have implemented both types simultaneously" (see van Coetsem 1990: 261–264, for a discussion of the two approaches and for examples).

The second kind is meso-mechanisms. By this term, I mean less general mechanisms, (conscious and unconscious) techniques that are responsible for contact-induced language change. They can be captured in terms of the ways in which formatives are transferred. According to Thomason (2001: 129–152), there are seven mechanisms: code-switching, code alternation, passive familiarity, "negotiation," second-language acquisition strategies, bilingual first-language acquisition, and change by deliberate decision. The limited space of this chapter cannot do justice to the multifacetedness of the topic. I will only point to the idea of "Trojan horse," which has been introduced by Meakins (2011a), in the context of code-switching. Analyzing the transfer of the Gurindji case paradigm into Gurindji Kriol, Meakins has shown that, originally, case-marking was present only on Gurindji nominal adjuncts. She has labeled "these nominals *Trojan horse structures* because they aided the transfer of case-marking into the Kriol matrix language without the conscious decision of speakers, as often occurs in borrowing or code-switching" (Meakins 2011a: 60). At a later stage of development, case formatives were extended to Kriol-derived nouns (cf. (19a)). Meakins's metaphor of the "Trojan horse" has soon been taken over and applied, for example, by Roseano (2014) to Friulian data of INFL borrowing from Italian and other languages.

The third kind of mechanisms involved in contact-induced morphological change is micro-mechanisms. These are local, concrete mechanisms, mostly at the level of lexical borrowing, which can, however, effect structural borrowing, too. (They mainly concern MAT borrowing.) To this kind belongs, for example, reborrowing, which—to my knowledge—has never been discussed in the literature, in this context. As I have already mentioned, in New Persian, some lexemes of Persian ancestry display broken plural forms, for example *būstān* 'fruit garden,' which follows the same pattern as (13) (data from Jensen 1931: 45). Compare the singular and plural form of *būstān* (20a) with both that of the Persian *bāḡ* 'garden' (20b) and that of the Arabic *miftāh* 'key' (20c).

(20)   New Persian   Arabic
   a. *būstān*   b. *bāḡ*   c. *miftāh*
      'fruit garden'   'garden'   'key'
      basātīn   *bāḡ-hā*   *mafātīh*
      'fruit gardens'   'gardens'   'keys'

Given that the contact between Persian and Arabic was long-lasting and intensive, a Persian lexeme may have been first loaned into Arabic, there Arabized, and finally reborrowed into Persian *tout court*, along with the Arabic non-concatenative morphology (Peter-Arnold Mumm, personal communication, September 20, 2009). In fact, however, we don't know how exactly such plural forms arose, whether it was through direct borrowing, or through extension of borrowed patterns that became productive, or via reborrowing. In any case, reborrowing is a viable path.[17]

Another micro-mechanism is reanalysis. Reanalysis is based on superficial similarities between native and non-native formatives (termed "lookalikes" by Aikhenvald 2007: 33). These lookalikes trigger morphological borrowing. A clear example is found in Arvanítika, a variety of Tosk Albanian spoken in Greece and (The Former Yugoslav Republic of) Macedonia for more than four centuries, which has been involved in intense language contact with Greek. In Arvanítika, when Greek nouns ending in [a] are borrowed, this ending is replaced by [ə]. This replacement is triggered by the speakers' perceiving that [a] as the Albanian postposed definite feminine article. Therefore, this segment is reanalyzed and reintroduced as a definitive marker, as in the following example (from Tsitsipis 1998: 22). Here, the Arvanítika noun for 'needle' is shown in both the reference form and the definitive singular form (21a), and compared with its Albanian counterparts (21b).

---

[17] If reborrowing would be at hand here, the data in (13) and (20) should be considered instances of lexical borrowing, for broken plural patterns have seemingly not become productive in New Persian (Mumm 2007: 40).

(21)   Arvanítika   Albanian
    a. *velónë*   b. *gjilpërë*
        'needle'   'needle'
        velón-a   *gjilpër-a*
        'the needle'   ·   'the needle'

4.6 Factors Favoring Borrowing

In language-contact literature, there is a widespread belief that structural similarity between source and recipient language favors the borrowing of affixes (see Weinreich 1953: 44; Field 2002: 42; Winford 2005: 387). On the other hand, there is also a consensus that structural properties do not suffice to explain morphological transfer, but that social circumstances are at least as favoring a factor (see Weinreich 1953: 3). Thomason (2008) has gone so far as to explicitly argue that social factors are more reliable predictors of contact-induced change than structural factors. Nevertheless, the "myth" of structural similarity as a factor favoring affix borrowing is still in vogue.

As a matter of fact, sound analyses of contact-induced morphological change must be built on a holistic approach, which views the phenomenon from different angles and combines sociological and structural facts.

4.6.1 Intra-Linguistic Factors

The first set of factors related to the study of morphological borrowing has to do with linguistic properties of the languages involved in a contact situation. I will first briefly discuss the previously mentioned factor of *structural similarity* between a source language and a recipient language.

As a case in point, let us consider the borrowing of the diminutive suffixes *-ito* and *-ita* from Spanish in Mesoamerican languages. Chamoreau (2012) shows that, while Mesoamerican languages that lack grammatical gender distinction use only *-ito* to realize diminutivization, Yucatec Maya, which has a weak grammatical gender distinction,[18] accepts both markers and uses them also on native roots. In the following example, the suffix *-ita* occurs on an adjective that agrees in gender with a noun denoting a female human being (Chamoreau 2012: 84).

---

[18] In Yucatec Maya, gender distinction is expressed by prefixes, for examples, in semi-pairs, such as *j-meenwaaj* 'baker(m)' and *x-meenjanal* 'cook(f)' (Chamoreau 2012: 78).

(22)   Yucatec Maya
       bek'ech-ita   *u*   *y-íits'in*
       thin-dim   erg:3SG   pos-younger.sister
       'His younger sister is slender.'

Thus, in Yucatec Maya, the preexistence of a grammatical gender distinction, though weak, is supportive of the MAT borrowing from Spanish. However, Thomason and Kaufman (1988: 53) have provided solid evidence that structural similarity (or "typological proximity," as they call it) is irrelevant when language contact is strong and pressing, since in moderate and heavy structural borrowing, features are transferred regardless of the typological congruence between source and recipient language (for even stronger claims about the unsuitability of structural similarity as a factor favoring borrowing, see Babel and Pfänder 2014: 254; Seifart 2015).

Other intra-linguistic predictors that have been claimed to boost morphological, and particularly inflectional, borrowing, include structural, functional, and semantic types (see Gardani 2008: 45–47, for an overview). Structural factors are *reinforcement*, that is, the replacement of zero-morphemes, shorter and phonetically weaker forms, through stronger forms (according to Weinreich 1953: 33, reinforcement is due to the bilingual speaker's "need to express some categories of one system no less strongly than in the other"); *sharpness of boundaries* (or morphotactic transparency), which is based on the idea formulated by Heath (1978: 106) that clear morphological contours between the morphological exponents are better segmentable, thus more recognizable, and easier to process than, for example, paradigmatically organized inflections or processes involving umlaut; and *categorical clarity*, which is a morpheme's property of being functionally independent from the broader morphosyntactic environment. Functional factors chiefly include *filling of functional gaps*, that is, the idea that the lack of shared structural similarity triggers borrowing. Finally, semantic factors include *monofunctionality*, that is, a morpheme's property to realize only one main function (i.e., relational invariance between signified and signifier); and *semantic fullness*, that is, the idea that concrete derivational morphemes or inflectional formatives realizing inherent inflection are more borrowable than formatives that realize slots generated in the syntax.

While sharpness of boundaries, categorical independence, monofunctionality, and semantic fullness have been recognized to favor inflectional borrowing, the idea that borrowing can exercise a therapeutic function, in that it fills functional gaps, has proven wrong (see Gardani 2008: 88; Thomason 2015: 42).

4.6.2 Extralinguistic Factors

Extralinguistic factors include social, cultural, economic, and ethno-historical circumstances, which, in a multilingual context, can affect a linguistic group, with possible consequences on the internal structure of that group's language. I summarize the most relevant extra-linguistic factors in the following short overview (Weinreich 1953: 83–110 is still the most detailed reference).[19]

The intensity of contact is a primary matter. It involves both the *degree of multilingualism*: the higher that the level of multilingual proficiency in a contact setting is, the more likely it is that not only vocabulary, but also structure, is borrowed; and the *duration of the contact*: if extensive multilingualism persists over a long period of time, the borrowability of matter is more probable.

Other extra-linguistic predictors discussed in the literature as possibly favoring morphological borrowing are the *socioeconomic dominance* of one group over another group: a dominant groups may impose its language on a subordinate population that lives within its sphere of dominance; the *prestige and status of the involved languages*: a language invested with a higher prestige is likely to affect a less prestigious language with which it is in contact, and to be less subject to foreign influence, and vice versa; *language loyalty*, which is reflected in the attitude of the speakers' community to explicitly resist changes in either the functions or in the linguistic subsystems of its language; the *size of the groups involved in the contact*: given a demographic asymmetry between communities in contact, the smaller group is more likely to borrow from the more numerous one; and *exogamy*: the bilingual family can be envisaged as the primary source of multilinguistic transmission. Whenever information was available, these factors have all been shown to play a supporting part in the process of inflectional borrowing (Gardani 2008: 85–88).

4.7 Conclusion: A Lesson for the Theory of Morphology

The question of which kinds of morphemes are borrowed more frequently is not simply a matter of statistics or of bet among contact linguists and historical linguists. It is much more than that, since it contributes important insights into models that try to describe the so-called architecture of grammar, or, more specifically, of morphology.

According to Sapir (1921: 204), morphemic diffusion is typically confined to derivational concrete categories that have no true impact on the recipient language; for example, he argues that the influence exerted by French on English, in terms of derivational morphology, hardly makes "more difference to the essential build of the language than did the mere fact that it incorporated a given number of words" (Sapir 1921: 216). This claim is true. But it is shortsighted, because it is not embedded in a theoretical understanding of morphology including its demarcations.

---

[19] Further factors, such as the attitudes of the receiving language's speakers toward the source language, may also play an important role (see Weinreich 1953: 3–4; Thomason 2001: 77–85). Unfortunately, these factors can hardly be detected for diachronic studies.

In section 4.3.2 and subsections, we have seen that the frequency of borrowing types correlates with the type of morphology that is borrowed, in terms of the distinction between derivation and inflection. Generally, derivation is more frequently borrowed than inflection. As yet, however, there are no monographic studies on the cross-linguistic borrowing of derivational matters or patterns, which would possibly point at differences in the degree of borrowing of different derivational types. Based on the distinction between prototypical and non-prototypical inflection, on the one hand, and between prototypical and non-prototypical derivation, on the other hand, as formulated in Dressler (1989, 1997) (see also Bauer 2004), I hypothesize that affixes or categories of prototypical derivation, such as deverbal result nouns, denominal adjectives, and de-adjectival nouns, are more prone to borrowing than those of non-prototypical derivation, such as agent noun formation, action noun formation, and diminutives. Still, all this has to be tested on a large and accurate database.

As concerns inflection, we have seen that inherent inflection is more frequently borrowed than contextual inflection. This can be explained by assuming that inherent inflection is more similar to prototypical derivation than contextual inflection, for at least four reasons (see Haspelmath and Sims 2010: 100–102). First, inherent inflection may not apply universally (in English, collective nouns may not have a dedicated plural form, e.g., *informations*); second, formatives that realize categories of inherent inflection can be lexicalized and have an unpredictable meaning (by Dutch *oud-er*, one would expect the meaning of 'older,' but in fact, it means 'parent'); third, inherent inflection is more frequently comes along with base allomorphy than contextual inflection (cf. English *sing/sings* (agreement) vs. *sing/sang* (tense)); fourth, the rare cases in which an inflectional affix is closer to the base/stem/root than a derivational affix (e.g., German *Kind-er-chen*, 'child-pl-dim'), or in which an inflectional affix occurs on the first member of a compound (e.g., English *acquisition-s editor*), commonly involve morphemes that realize inherent inflection. All these characteristics are also proper of prototypical derivation.

Based on the distinction between contextual and inherent inflection, Gardani (2012) shows that formatives that realize nominal plural, which is a prototypical category of inherent morphology, have a higher-than-average borrowing rating.[20] This claim is also supported by evidence found in code-switching research. In the *4-M model*, Myers-Scotton (2002: 16–18, 2006: 267–270) maintains that plural morphemes are "early system morphemes," which are activated immediately after content morphemes and before late system morphemes, such as the English formative -s for the third person singular indicative present. Early system morphemes are more susceptible to various kinds of change than late system morphemes, and in code-switching, sometimes they come along with their embedded language (i.e., the source language). Thus, the borrowing of plurals is in line with the maintenance of plural inflection observed in bilinguals during code-switching (see Myers-Scotton 2002: 91–93).

---

[20] Gardani (2012) shows also that the properties of morphotactic transparency and bi-uniqueness play a fostering role in the process of INFL borrowing.

In conclusion, the data and analyses of morphological borrowing, in terms of different grades of resistance, or conversely, proneness, to borrowing, are supportive of a view of morphology as a gradient module of grammar, along a continuum between prototypical derivation and prototypical inflection (i.e., contextual inflection). However, they do not allow, at present, to make generalizations about prototypical and non-prototypical derivation. More data will have to be made available, both on DER borrowing and INFL borrowing, and more scholars will have to pursue the investigation of contact-induced morphological change from the perspective of the theory of morphology.

References

Adamou, Evangelia. 2013. Replicating Spanish *estar* in Mexican Romani. *Linguistics* 51(6): 1075–1105.

Aikhenvald, Alexandra Y. 2007. Grammars in contact: A cross-linguistic perspective. In *Grammars in Contact: A Cross-Linguistic Typology*, edited by Alexandra Y. Aikhenvald and Robert M. W. Dixon, 1–66. Oxford: Oxford University Press.

Atanasov, Petar. 1990. *Le mégléno-roumain de nos jours: Une approche linguistique*. Balkan-Archiv, Beheft 7. Hamburg: Buske.

Babel, Anna, and Stefan Pfänder. 2014. Doing copying: Why typology doesn't matter to language speakers. In *Congruence in Contact-Induced Language Change: Language Families, Typological Resemblance, and Perceived Similarity*, edited by Juliane Besters-Dilger, Cynthia Dermarkar, Stefan Pfänder, and Achim Rabus, 239–257. Linguae and Litterae 27. Berlin: De Gruyter.

Bauer, Laurie. 2004. The function of word-formation and the inflection-derivation distinction. In *Words in Their Places: A Festschrift for J. Lachlan Mackenzie*, edited by Henk Aertsen, Mike Hannay, and Rod Lyall, 283–292. Amsterdam: Vrije Universiteit.

Behrens, Leila. 1996. Lexical rules cross-cutting inflection and derivation. *Acta Linguistica Hungarica* 43: 33–65.

Booij, Geert E. 1994. Against split morphology. In *Yearbook of Morphology 1993*, edited by Geert E. Booij and Jaap van Marle, 27–50. Dordrecht: Kluwer.

Booij, Geert E. 1996. Inherent versus contextual inflection and the split morphology hypothesis. In *Yearbook of Morphology 1995*, edited by Geert E. Booij and Jaap van Marle, 1–16. Dordrecht: Kluwer.

Boretzky, Norbert, and Birgit Igla. 1999. Balkanische (südosteuropäische) Einflüsse im Romani. In *Handbuch der Südosteuropa-Linguistik*, edited by Uwe Hinrichs, 709–731. Wiesbaden: Harrassowitz.

Bowern, Claire. 2013. Relatedness as a factor in language contact. *Journal of Language Contact* 6(2): 411–432.

Breu, Walter. 1991. Abweichungen vom phonetischen Prinzip bei der Integration von Lehnwörtern. In *Slavistische Linguistik 1990: Referate des XVI. Konstanzer Slavistischen Arbeitstreffens Bochum/Löllinghausen 19.–21.9.1990* (Slavistische Beiträge 274), edited by Klaus Hartenstein and Helmut Jachnow, 36–69. München: Otto Sagner.

Bybee, Joan L. 1985. *Morphology: A Study of the Relation between Meaning and Form*. Typological Studies in Language 9. Amsterdam; Philadelphia: John Benjamins.

Chamoreau, Claudine. 2012. Spanish diminutive markers *-ito/-ita* in Mesoamerican languages: A challenge for acceptance of gender distinction. In *Morphologies in Contact*, edited by Martine Vanhove, Thomas Stolz, Aina Urdze, and Hitomi Otsuka, 71–90. Berlin: Akademie Verlag.

Clements, J. C., and Ana R. Luís. 2015. Contact intensity and the borrowing of bound morphology in Korlai Indo-Portuguese. In *Borrowed Morphology* edited by Francesco Gardani, Peter Arkadiev, and Nino Amiridze, 219–240. Language Contact and Bilingualism 8. Boston; Berlin: De Gruyter Mouton.

Dawkins, R. M. 1916. *Modern Greek in Asia Minor: A Study of the Dialects of Sílli, Cappadocia and Phárasa with Grammar, Texts, Translations and Glossary*. Cambridge: Cambridge University Press.

Dressler, Wolfgang U. 1989. Prototypical differences between inflection and derivation. *Zeitschrift für Phonetik, Sprachwissenschaft und Kommunikationsforschung* 42(1): 3–10.

Dressler, Wolfgang U. 1997. Universals, typology, and modularity in natural morphology. In *Language History and Linguistic Modelling: A Festschrift for Jacek Fisiak on his 60th Birthday*, Vol. 2: *Language History and Linguistic Modelling*, edited by Raymond Hickey and Stanisław Puppel, 399–1421. Berlin; New York: Mouton de Gruyter.

Elšik, Viktor. 2007. Grammatical borrowing in Hungarian Rumungro. In *Grammatical Borrowing in Cross-Linguistic Perspective*, edited by Yaron Matras and Jeanette Sakel, 261–282. Berlin; New York: Mouton de Gruyter.

Epps, Patience. 2013. Inheritance, calquing, or independent innovation? Reconstructing morphological complexity in Amazonian numerals. *Journal of Language Contact* 6(2): 329–357.

Estrada Fernández, Zarina, and Lilián Guerrero. 2007. Grammatical borrowing in Yaqui. In *Grammatical Borrowing in Cross-Linguistic Perspective*, edited by Yaron Matras and Jeanette Sakel, 419–433. Berlin; New York: Mouton de Gruyter.

Field, Fredric W. 2002. *Linguistic Borrowing in Bilingual Contexts*. Studies in Language Companion Series 62. Amsterdam; Philadelphia: John Benjamins.

Friedman, Victor A. 2012. Copying and cognates in the Balkan Sprachbund. In *Copies versus Cognates in Bound Morphology*, edited by Lars Joanson and Martine I. Robbeets, 323–336. Leiden; Boston: Brill.

Gardani, Francesco. 2008. *Borrowing of Inflectional Morphemes in Language Contact*. Frankfurt am Main: Peter Lang.

Gardani, Francesco. 2012. Plural across inflection and derivation, fusion and agglutination. In *Copies versus Cognates in Bound Morphology*, edited by Lars Johanson and Martine I. Robbeets, 71–97. Leiden; Boston: Brill.

Gardani, Francesco. 2013. *Dynamics of Morphological Productivity: The Evolution of Noun Classes from Latin to Italian*. Empirical Approaches to Linguistic Theory 4. Leiden; Boston: Brill.

Gardani, Francesco, Peter Arkadiev, and Nino Amiridze (eds.). 2015. *Borrowed Morphology*. Language Contact and Bilingualism 8. Boston; Berlin: De Gruyter Mouton.

Gardner-Chloros, Penelope. 2009. *Code-Switching*. Cambridge: Cambridge University Press.

Golovko, Evgenij V., and Nikolai B. Vakhtin. 1990. Aleut in contact: The CIA enigma. *Acta linguistica Hafniensia* 22: 97–125.

Gómez-Rendón, Jorge. 2007. Grammatical borrowing in Imbabura Quichua. In *Grammatical Borrowing in Cross-Linguistic Perspective*, edited by Yaron Matras and Jeanette Sakel, 481–521. Berlin; New York: Mouton de Gruyter.

Grant, Anthony. 2002. Fabric, pattern, shift and diffusion: What change in Oregon Penutian languages can tell historical linguists. In *Proceedings of the Meeting of the Hokan-Penutian Workshop, June 17–18, 2000, U. of California at Berkeley. Report 11, Survey of California and Other Indian Languages*, edited by Laura Buszard-Welcher, 33–56. Berkeley: Department of Linguistics, University of California at Berkeley.

Grant, Anthony. 2004. Review of Ruth King, *The Lexical Basis of Grammatical Borrowing: A Prince Edward Island Case Study* (Amsterdam: Benjamins, 2000). *Word* 54: 251–256.

Grant, Anthony. 2008. Contact-induced change and the openness of 'closed' morphological systems: Some cases from Native America. *Journal of Language Contact* 2(1): 165–186.

Grant, Anthony. 2017. The Western Micronesian Sprachbund. In *The Cambridge Handbook of Areal Linguistics*, edited by Raymond Hickey, 852–877. Cambridge: Cambridge University Press.

Hajek, John. 2007. Language contact and convergence in East Timor: The case of Tetun Dili. In *Grammars in Contact: A Cross-Linguistic Typology*, edited by Alexandra Y. Aikhenvald and Robert M. W. Dixon, 163–178. Oxford: Oxford University Press.

Haspelmath, Martin. 2009. Lexical borrowing: Concepts and issues. In *Loanwords in the World's Languages: A Comparative Handbook*, edited by Martin Haspelmath and Uri Tadmor, 35–54. Berlin: De Gruyter Mouton.

Haspelmath, Martin. 2013. An inflection/derivation distinction on the other side of the globe? http://dlc.hypotheses.org/388.

Haspelmath, Martin, and Andrea D. Sims. 2010. *Understanding Morphology*, 2nd edition. London: Hodder Education.

Heath, Jeffrey. 1978. *Ngandi Grammar, Texts, and Dictionary*. Canberra: Australian Institute of Aboriginal Studies.

Heath, Jeffrey. 1980. *Basic Materials in Ritharngu: Grammar, Texts and Dictionary*. Pacific Linguistics, Series B, Monographs 62. Canberra: Australian National University.

Jastrow, Otto. 1985. *Laut- und Formenlehre des neuaramäischen Dialekts von Mīdin im Ṭūr 'Abdīn*. 3rd edition. Wiesbaden: Harrassowitz.

Jensen, Hans. 1931. *Neupersische Grammatik: Mit Berücksichtigung der historischen Entwicklung*. Indogermanische Bibliothek / 1 / 1 22. Heidelberg: Winter.

Johanson, Lars. 1999. The dynamics of code-copying in language encounters. In *Language Encounters across Time and Space: Studies in Language Contact*, edited by Bernt Brendemoen, Elizabeth Lanza, and Else Ryen, 37–62. Oslo: Novus forlag.

Johanson, Lars. 2008. Remodeling grammar: Copying, conventionalization, grammaticalization. In *Language Contact and Contact Languages*, edited by Peter Siemund and Noemi Kintana, 61–79. Hamburg Studies on Multilingualism 7. Amsterdam; Philadelphia: John Benjamins.

Johanson, Lars, and Martine I. Robbeets (eds.). 2012. *Copies versus Cognates in Bound Morphology*. Leiden; Boston: Brill.

Kossmann, Maarten. 2010. Parallel System Borrowing: Parallel morphological systems due to the borrowing of paradigms. *Diachronica* 27(3): 459–487.

Kossmann, Maarten. 2013. *The Arabic Influence on Northern Berber*. Studies in Semitic Languages and Linguistics 67. Leiden; Boston: Brill.

Laca, Brenda. 2001. Derivation. In *Language Typology and Language Universals*, Vol. 1, edited by Martin Haspelmath, Ekkehard König, Wulf Oesterreicher, and Wolfgang Raible, 1214–1227. Handbücher zur Sprach- und Kommunikationswissenschaft 20. Berlin; New York: De Gruyter.

Law, Danny. 2013. Inherited similarity and contact-induced change in Mayan Languages. *Journal of Language Contact* 6(2): 271–299.

Maiden, Martin, and Paul O'Neill. 2010. On morphomic defectiveness: Evidence from the Romance languages of the Iberian Peninsula. In *Defective Paradigms: Missing Forms and What They Tell Us*, edited by Matthew Baerman, Greville G. Corbett, and Dunstan Brown, 103–124. Proceedings of the British Academy 163. Oxford; New York: Published for the British Academy by Oxford University Press.

Matras, Yaron. 2002. *Romani: A Linguistic Introduction*. Cambridge: Cambridge University Press.

Matras, Yaron. 2009. *Language Contact*. Cambridge Textbooks in Linguistics. Cambridge: Cambridge University Press.

Matras, Yaron, and Jeanette Sakel (eds.). 2007. *Grammatical Borrowing in Cross-Linguistic Perspective*. Berlin; New York: Mouton de Gruyter.

McConvell, Patrick. 1988. MIX-IM-UP: Aboriginal code-switching, old and new. In *Code-switching: Anthropological and Sociolinguistic Perspectives*, edited by Monica Heller, 97–150. Contributions to the Sociology of Language 48. Berlin: Mouton de Gruyter.

McConvell, Patrick, and Felicity Meakins. 2005. Gurindji Kriol: A mixed language emerges from code-switching. *Australian Journal of Linguistics* 25(1): 9–30.

Meakins, Felicity. 2011a. Borrowing contextual inflection: Evidence from northern Australia. *Morphology* 21(1): 57–87.

Meakins, Felicity. 2011b. *Case-Marking in Contact: The Development and Function of Case Morphology in Gurindji Kriol*. Creole Language Library 39. Amsterdam; Philadelphia: John Benjamins.

Meakins, Felicity. 2013. Mixed languages. In *Contact Languages: A Comprehensive Guide*, edited by Yaron Matras and Peter Bakker, 159–228. Language Contact and Bilingualism 6. Boston; Berlin: De Gruyter Mouton.

Menovshchikov, G. A. 1968. Aleutskij jazyk. In *Jazyki narodov SSSR*, Vol. 5: *Mongol'skie, tunguso-man'chzhurskie i paleoaziatskie jazyki*, edited by P. J. Skorik, 386–406. Leningrad: Nauka.

Mithun, Marianne. 2013. Challenges and benefits of contact among relatives: Morphological copying. *Journal of Language Contact* 6(2): 243–270.

Moravcsik, Edith A. 1978. Language contact. In *Universals of Human Language: Method and Theory*, edited by Joseph H. Greenberg, Charles A. Ferguson, and Edith A. Moravcsik, 93–122. Stanford, CA: Stanford University Press.

Mumm, Peter-Arnold. 2007. *Strukturkurs Neupersisch*. Universität München.

Myers-Scotton, Carol. 2002. *Contact Linguistics: Bilingual Encounters and Grammatical Outcomes*. Oxford, New York: Oxford University Press.

Myers-Scotton, Carol. 2006. *Multiple Voices: An Introduction to Bilingualism*. Malden, MA: Blackwell.

Pakendorf, Brigitte. 2009. Intensive contact and the copying of paradigms: An Èven dialect in contact with Sakha (Yakut). *Journal of Language Contact* 2(2): 85–110.

Pakendorf, Brigitte. 2014. Paradigm copying in Tungusic: The Lamunkhin dialect of Èven and beyond. In *Paradigm Change: In the Transeurasian Languages and Beyond*, edited by Martine I. Robbeets and Walter Bisang, 287–310. Studies in Language Companion Series 161. Amsterdam; Philadelphia: John Benjamins.

Pakendorf, Brigitte. 2015. A comparison of copied morphemes in Sakha (Yakut) and Èven. In *Borrowed Morphology*, edited by Francesco Gardani, Peter Arkadiev, and Nino Amiridze, 157–188. Language Contact and Bilingualism 8. Boston; Berlin: De Gruyter Mouton.

Plank, Frans. 1994. Inflection and derivation. In *The Encyclopedia of Language and Linguistics*, Vol. 3, 1st edition, edited by R. E. Asher, 1671–1678. Oxford: Pergamon Press.

Robbeets, Martine. 2012. Shared verb morphology in the Transeurasian languages: Copy or cognate? In *Copies versus Cognates in Bound Morphology*, edited by Lars Johanson and Martine I. Robbeets, 427–446. Leiden; Boston: Brill.

Robbeets, Martine. 2015. Common denominal verbalizers in the Transeurasian languages: Borrowed or inherited? In *Borrowed Morphology* edited by Francesco Gardani, Peter Arkadiev, and Nino Amiridze, 137–154. Language Contact and Bilingualism 8. Boston and Berlin: De Gruyter Mouton.

Roseano, Paolo. 2014. Can morphological borrowing be an effect of codeswitching? Evidence from the inflectional morphology of borrowed nouns in Friulian. *Probus* 26(1): 1–57.

Sakel, Jeanette. 2007. Types of loan: Matter and pattern. In *Grammatical Borrowing in Cross-Linguistic Perspective*, edited by Yaron Matras and Jeanette Sakel, 15–29. Berlin; New York: Mouton de Gruyter.

Sakel, Jeanette, and Yaron Matras. 2008. Modelling contact-induced change in grammar. In *Aspects of Language Contact: New Theoretical, Methodological and Empirical Findings with Special Focus on Romancisation Processes*, edited by Thomas Stolz, Dik Bakker, and Rosa S. Palomo, 63–87. Berlin: Mouton de Gruyter.

Sapir, Edward. 1921. *Language: An Introduction to the Study of Speech*. New York: Harcourt, Brace.

Schuchardt, Hugo. 1884. *Dem Herrn Franz von Miklosich zum 20. Nov. 1883. Slawo-Deutsches und Slawo-Italienisches*. Graz: Leuschner & Lubensky.

Schuchardt, Hugo. 1928. *Hugo Schuchardt-Brevier*. 2nd edition. Halle: Niemeyer.

Seifart, Frank. 2013. *AfBo: A World-Wide Survey of Affix Borrowing*. Leipzig: Max Planck Institute for Evolutionary Anthropology. http://afbo.info.

Seifart, Frank. 2015. Does structural-typological similarity affect borrowability? A quantitative study on affix borrowing. *Language Dynamics and Change* 5(1): 92–113.

Singh, Rajendra. 2010. Multilingualism, sociolinguistics and theories of linguistic form: Some unfinished reflections. *Language Sciences* 32(6): 624–637.

Tadmor, Uri. 2009. Loanwords in the world's languages: Findings and results. In *Loanwords in the World's Languages: A Comparative Handbook*, edited by Martin Haspelmath and Uri Tadmor, 55–75. Berlin: De Gruyter Mouton.

Thomason, Sarah. 2008. Social and linguistic factors as predictors of contact-induced change. *Journal of Language Contact* 2(1): 42–56.

Thomason, Sarah G. 1997. Mednyj Aleut. In *Contact Languages: A Wider Perspective*, edited by Sarah G. Thomason, 449–468. Creole Language Library 17. Amsterdam; Philadelphia: John Benjamins.

Thomason, Sarah G. 2001. *Language Contact: An Introduction*. Edinburgh; Washington, DC: Edinburgh University Press and Georgetown University Press.

Thomason, Sarah G. 2003. Social factors and linguistic processes in the emergence of stable mixed languages. In *The Mixed Language Debate: Theoretical and Empirical Advances*, edited by Yaron Matras and Peter Bakker, 21–39. Trends in Linguistics. Studies and Monographs 145. Berlin; New York: Mouton de Gruyter.

Thomason, Sarah G. 2015. When is the diffusion of inflectional morphology not dispreferred? In *Borrowed Morphology*, edited by Francesco Gardani, Peter Arkadiev, and Nino Amiridze, 27–46. Language Contact and Bilingualism 8. Boston; Berlin: De Gruyter Mouton.

Thomason, Sarah G., and Terrence Kaufman. 1988. *Language Contact, Creolization, and Genetic Linguistics*. Berkeley: University of California Press.

Tsitsipis, Lukas D. 1998. *A Linguistic Anthropology of Praxis and Language Shift: Arvanítika (Albanian) and Greek in Contact*. Oxford Studies in Language Contact. Oxford; New York: Clarendon Press; Oxford University Press.

van Coetsem, Frans. 1988. *Loan Phonology and the Two Transfer Types in Language Contact*. Publications in Language Sciences 27. Dordrecht; Providence, RI: Foris Publications.

van Coetsem, Frans. 1990. Review of Thomason and Kaufman (1988); Lehiste (1988); Wardhaugh (1987). *Language in Society* 19(2): 260–268.

van Coetsem, Frans. 2000. *A General and Unified Theory of the Transmission Process in Language Contact*. Monographien zur Sprachwissenschaft 19. Heidelberg: Winter.

Vanhove, Martine, Thomas Stolz, Aina Urdze, and Hitomi Otsuka (eds.). 2012. *Morphologies in Contact*. Berlin: Akademie Verlag.

Weinreich, Uriel. 1953. *Languages in Contact, Findings and Problems*. New York: Linguistic Circle of New York.

Weinreich, Uriel. 2011. *Languages in Contact: French, German and Romansch in Twentieth-Century Switzerland*. Based on Weinreich's 1951 dissertation at Columbia University. Amsterdam; Philadelphia: John Benjamins.

Whaley, Lindsay. 2012. Deriving insights about Tungusic classification from derivational morphology. In *Copies versus Cognates in Bound Morphology*, edited by Lars Johanson and Martine I. Robbeets, 395–409. Leiden; Boston: Brill.

Wilkins, David P. 1996. Morphology. In *Kontaktlinguistik: Ein internationales Handbuch zeitgenössischer Forschung. Halbband 1*, edited by Hans Goebl, Peter H. Nelde, Zdeněk Starý, and Wolfgang Wölck, 109–117. Handbücher zur Sprach- und Kommunikationswissenschaft 12.1. Berlin; New York: Walter de Gruyter.

Winford, Donald. 2005. Contact-induced changes: Classification and processes. *Diachronica* 22(2): 373–427.

Wohlgemuth, Jan. 2009. *A Typology of Verbal Borrowings*. Trends in Linguistics. Studies and Monographs 211. Berlin; New York: Mouton de Gruyter.

CHAPTER 5

SYNTAX AND CONTACT-INDUCED LANGUAGE CHANGE

MALCOLM ROSS

5.1 INTRODUCTION

THE topic of this chapter is contact-induced syntactic change or, from the perspective adopted here, contact-induced change in grammatical constructions, whether this change has occurred as a result of speakers' bilingualism or of rapid adult language shift.

One can investigate contact-induced change at two levels. The first is external to the linguistic system: What happens to the changing language sociolinguistically and psycholinguistically? The second is the linguistic system itself: What happens to the grammar of a language when its speakers copy constructions from another languages? This chapter is concerned with the second question. For example, a rural Irish English speaker might say *They are after doing the work*, where a British English speaker might say *They have done the work* or *They have finished the work* (Hickey 2010: 156). The Irish English construction reflects a construction in Irish Gaelic, which, like many languages, lacks a construction that corresponds straightforwardly to the English present perfect (Hickey 2013: 102).

In this chapter the term *copying language* (CL) is used for the language that copies a construction (Irish English in the preceding example) and the term *model language* (ML) for the language on which the copy is modeled, here Irish Gaelic. Other terms commonly used in literature on contact are *source language* and *donor language*, but neither is satisfactory, as they imply, respectively, that a construction is taken from the source language, or given by a donor language and inserted into the recipient language. These are not appropriate metaphors for contact-induced constructional change (henceforth CICC). The copying metaphor is preferable, as a copy can be imperfect or incomplete (Johanson 2002b). This point is made in an important paper on a construction copied from a Slavic language into Yiddish by Prince (1998). She showed that grammatical copying is rarely a complete copy. Instead, it is an adaptation of a CL construction to imitate the structure and function of an ML construction.

Since Weinreich (1963: 38) referred briefly to CICC, there has been a plentiful supply of case studies, but CICC has yet to find its place as a distinct topic in contact textbooks (e.g. Thomason 2001; Matras 2009). The reason for this is that research on the typology of CICC has been decidedly limited, although Aikhenvald (2007), Matras (2007), and Matras and Sakel (2007a, 2007b) represent first steps in this direction.

Many case studies have tended to focus on a single construction (or group of related constructions). This is true of some of the earliest (e.g., Nadkarni 1975 on relative clauses in Indo-Aryan Konkani, copied from Dravidian Kannada) and also of some of the most recent (e.g., Lucas and Lash 2010 on Coptic influence on Arabic negation). Although single-construction case studies are very useful if they are careful and detailed (as the named examples are), there has been a growing understanding among contact linguists that it is not enough to look at copied constructions singly. It is important to understand how the copied construction affects and fits into the grammar of the CL as a whole. This realization has led to a number of case studies, mostly chapters in edited volumes (Aikhenvald and Dixon 2007; Sakel and Matras 2008), and a few of book-length (Haase 1992; King 2000; Aikhenvald 2002).

For this reason, most of the examples in this chapter are drawn from just two languages, unusual though this is in a contribution to a handbook. Examples of bilingually induced constructional change are from Colloquial Upper Sorbian, whose speakers have long been bilingual in German. Examples of shift-induced constructional change are from rural Irish English, the outcome of rapid shift to English by speakers of Irish Gaelic.

The reader may wonder why two Indo-European languages, each in contact with another Indo-European language, have been chosen as illustrations. The reason is that in order to make real progress in contact linguistics, we need to examine cases where we have a good understanding of the changes that have occurred in the CL (i.e., of its structure both before and after copying) and a good understanding of the ML at the time that copying took place. We also need reliable information about the sociolinguistic circumstances of contact—information that is independent of the linguistic data.

There are not many documented cases that satisfy these conditions. For example, the author has written on CICC in Takia, an Oceanic Austronesian language spoken on an island off the north coast of New Guinea (Ross 1996, 2001, 2003, 2007, 2009). Although conclusions about its history are well supported by the linguistic data, that history is inferred from comparisons of present-day Takia with related Oceanic Austronesian languages (Ross 2008) and with neighboring Papuan languages, which have apparently been the models for Takia's many copied constructions. The inferences here are many, and independent information about sociolinguistic prehistory is almost nil. There is a danger—often encountered in contact studies—that one infers sociolinguistic prehistory from linguistic data alone, and then makes sociolinguistic generalizations based on a number of inferentially based case studies. This is risky at best, and at worst unscholarly.

For this reason it is useful to search the literature for cases of CICC where we have good knowledge of both the CL and the ML, as well as independent sociolinguistic evidence, and no obvious additional complications that render the vase unfit as a control example. Several well-described cases of CICC do not quite meet these criteria. Old Amish Pennsylvania German (Raith 1982; Louden 1992; Louden and Page 2005; Fitch 2011) comes close, but is so closely related to its ML, American English, that it is difficult to separate out contact from independent parallel development. The sociolinguistic circumstances of Cappadocian Greek contact with Turkish (Dawkins 1916) varied considerably across dialects and are hard to disentangle (Hovdhaugen 1976; Brendemoen 1999, discussed by Johanson 2002a). Several cases of CICC shade into the rather different phenomena of language death. These include the Albanian dialects of central Greece, eventually displaced by Greek (Sasse 1985); Northwest (Lithuanian) Karaim, a Turkic language influenced by Russian (Csató and Johanson 1995, Csató 1996, 2000, 2001, 2002, 2008); and apparently Prince Edward Island French, influenced by Canadian English (King 2000).

Cases of bilingually induced constructional change that apparently do satisfy the preceding criteria are Molise Croatian, spoken in central Italy and influenced by the local Italian dialect (Breu 1992, 1999, 2003b, 2003c, 2004b, 2009a, 2009b, 2011; Marra 2012); Mixe Basque, a dialect influenced by Gascon and French (Haase 1992); and Colloquial Upper Sorbian, of which more later. Case studies of shift-induced constructional change that even potentially satisfy the criteria are much thinner. One is Taiwan Mandarin, resulting from the rapid shift of Taiwan Southern Min speakers to Mandarin after the Kuomintang assumed government in 1949 (Kubler 1985a, 1985b).

Another is South African Indian English, a complicated case because the MLs are from two language families, Indo-Aryan and Dravidian (Mesthrie 1992). A third is rural Irish English. Examining these cases and others, a preliminary typology of CICC can be built based on the degree to which a construction is altered as a result of copying. The four degrees are listed in (1).

(1)   As a result of contact, an existing construction
    a. is used more frequently;
    b. is used for a new function;
    c. is formally modified (i.e., constructional calquing occurs);
    d. is structurally altered to more closely match a corresponding ML construction (i.e. metatypy occurs).

This brief typology of additive CICCs forms the framework for much of the rest of the chapter. Note, though, that an additive change often entails a simultaneous subtractive change, whereby an existing construction is used less frequently, loses one of its functions, or disappears entirely in favor of another construction.

The term *construction* is ubiquitous in this chapter. It is used in the sense of Croft (2001: 15–28), where constructions range in schematicity from morphosyntactic units composed of specific words and morphemes to units composed entirely of schematic components.[1] A construction is a pairing of form and meaning/function. At the specific-word end of the schematicity range, constructions are simultaneously complex lexical items. An advantage of this perspective is that it allows us to generalize about processes of change that are not restricted to distinct parts of the grammars of languages in contact.[2] Other scholars writing about contact-induced grammatical change use rather different terminologies, but these are readily conceptualized in constructional terms. Heine and Kuteva (2003, 2005) write about contact-induced grammaticalization. As Himmelmann (1997: 33; 2004) points out, the locus of grammatical change is the construction, and what is grammaticalized is not just a morpheme, but the construction in which that morpheme occurs.[3] Conceptualizing grammaticization in terms of constructions is thus fairly straightforward.

Aikhenvald (2007) approaches grammatical change in terms of systems, and asks whether a system is preserved, perhaps with the addition of a category member, or changed through the creation of a new category. Linguistic categories are defined by the constructions in which they occur (Croft 2001: 45–53), so the creation of a new category entails the creation of a new construction, typically by calquing (section 5.2.4, section 5.3.4).

The remainder of this chapter falls into four sections. Section 5.2 concerns bilingually induced change, section 5.3 shift-induced change. Section 5.4 looks briefly at the processes of change, and section 5.5 at similarities and difference between bilingually induced and shift-induced change.

Nothing has been said thus far about pidgins and creoles, because the process entailed in pidgin formation seems to me to be a different one from the two contact processes outlined in the preceding. In bilingually induced change, speakers already command two (or more) languages. In shift-induced change, they command (at least) one and are endeavoring to master another. In pidgin formation, speakers of different languages set out to communicate with each other with whatever linguistic resources are at their disposal. Despite the use in the literature of the term *target language*, speakers in such a situation are intent upon linguistic interaction, not on learning another language (Parkvall 2013). This process tends to create constructions rather than to copy them.

5.2 BILINGUALLY INDUCED CONSTRUCTIONAL CHANGE

I turn now to examples of bilingually induced constructional change in Colloquial Upper Sorbian, which has copied constructions from German as a result of

---

[1] Constructions are also ranged along a complexity dimension, but this does not impinge on the discussion here.

[2] On constructional change in general, see Fried (2013) and Trousdale (2013).

[3] One or two authors, e.g., Fried (2013), use the term "constructionalization" for the grammaticalization of a construction, but if this is the only grammaticalization there is, the term is redundant.

Sorbian/German bilingualism. Scholze (2007), a revision of which was published as Scholze (2008), provides ample information, and there is also work by Breu (2000, 2003a, 2004a, 2005, 2012), Lötzsch (1996), Michałk (1962), Schaarschmidt (1997), Toops (1992a, 1992b, 1998, 2001, 2006), and Scholze herself (Breu and Scholze 2006; Kaiser and Scholze 2009; Scholze 2012).

5.2.1 Colloquial Upper Sorbian

The Sorbs are descended from speakers of common Slavic or common West Slavic who settled the eastern region of present-day Germany in the fifth and sixth centuries of the Christian era. As the language diversified, the language of the northern part of the region became Polabian (which became extinct in the early eighteenth century), the southern Sorbian. Map 5.1 gives an approximate picture of the situation perhaps 250 years before the Holy Roman Emperor Lothar III invaded Slav-speaking regions in the second half of the twelfth century and progressive Germanization began, with German spoken in the towns, Sorbian elsewhere. Interaction between town and country, together with the spread of education, brought about widespread Sobian–German

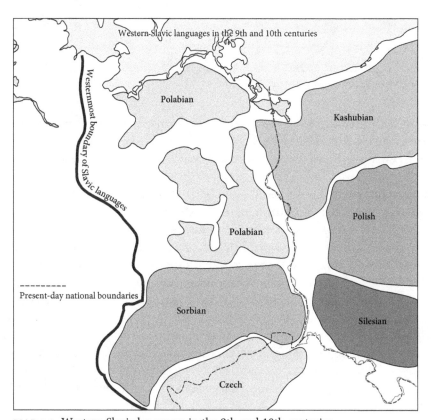

MAP 5.1 Western Slavic languages in the 9th and 10th centuries.

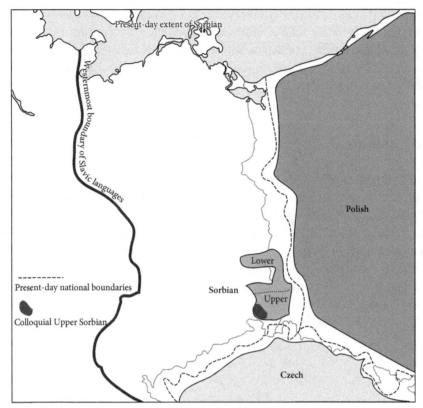

MAP 5.2 Present-day extent of Sorbian.

bilingualism. The area where Sorbian was spoken shrank progressively until it reached is present extent (Schaarschmidt 1984, Stone 1993), shown in Map 5.2. At some point, it split into the Lower and Upper Sorbian languages (which are still joined by a small band of transitional dialects).

In the second half of the nineteenth century the "Sorbian national rebirth" movement set out to purify Sorbian of German influences (Michałk 1962: 232). The leaders of this movement did much of their work at the *Sorbski seminar* (Sorbian institute) in Prague (Toops 2006). The result is that written Upper Sorbian tends to be less Germanized than Colloquial Upper Sorbian (CUS) and syntactically somewhat more like Czech. The label "Colloquial Upper Sorbian" applies to the dialect described by Scholze (2007, 2008), spoken in Catholic villages in the southwestern part of the Upper Sorbian–speaking area, which can be regarded as the core of present-day Upper Sorbian. To identify changes that have occurred in the CL, we need to have an idea what the language was like *before* CICC took place. The earliest Sorbian documents date from the sixteenth century, and a number of distinctive Sorbian changes had already occurred. Since Sorbian is closely related to Polish and Czech and was contiguous with Czech until the twelfth century and with Polish until the early seventeenth century (Schaarschmidt 1997: 440), where Polish and Czech (and other Slavic languages) agree, we can take this as a proxy for the pre-contact structure of Sorbian.

In the following I will look in turn at each of the four degrees of additive constructional change in (1) as they are manifested in rather simple examples in CUS. Uncomplicated examples have been chosen deliberately in order to illustrate the typology. The literature on CICC in CUS includes a wealth of more complex examples.

5.2.2 More Frequent Use

The first degree of CICC in (1) is where contact causes an existing CL construction to be used more frequently, matching the use of a ML construction. Ideally we need a corpus-based statistical investigation to detect increase in frequency, but to my knowledge no CUS corpus is generally available.

There is a CUS case, though, of a less used construction displacing a more frequent one. It concerns the presentative use of CUS *jen*, which serves both as numeral 'one' and as an indefinite article:[4]

(2)	SUS	*Ø*	*běše*	*jemo*	*Ø*	*stara*	*žona*
	CUS	*To*	*běše*	*jemo*	**jena**	*stara*	*žona*
		it.NOM	be.3sIPF	once	a.NOM	old.NOM	woman.NOM
	German	*Es*	*war*	*einmal*	**eine**	*alte*	*Frau*
		it.NOM	be.3sPST	once	a.NOM	old.NOM	woman.NOM
		'There was once an old woman.' (Breu 2012: 281)						

In (2) ('purified') Standard Upper Sorbian (SUS) reflects the most frequent Slavic situation, in which there is no indefinite article in a presentative construction. In CUS, however, its presence is obligatory, on the model of the German indefinite article *ein* 'a, one.' According to Breu (2012), other Slavic languages sometimes use the numeral 'one' in this construction, so it appears that the less used variant of the construction with 'one' has displaced the variant without 'one' (i.e., it has increased in frequency).

A number of instances of the increased use of a construction are reported in the contact literature. Fortescue (1993) surveys a text corpus from Eskimo languages and shows that where speakers are bilingual in English, this has nudged the languages' otherwise flexible constituent order in an English-like direction. McAnallen (2011, 2012) shows that apparent calques of predicative possession constructions in Russian and Czech are not in fact calques (section 5.2.4). Bilingual speakers have selected from among existing constructions the one that most closely matches the predicative possession construction in their other (non-Slavic) language, its use increasing until the alternative constructions vanished from use. Matras and Tufan (2007) discuss increased use of various constructions in Gostivar Turkish of Macedonia.

---

[4] Glosses follow the Leipzig Glossing Rules. Features irrelevant to the discussion (e.g., gender) are omitted. Lower-case 's' and 'p' without a preceding full stop mark singular and plural.

5.2.3 New Function

In the second degree of CICC in (1), an existing CL construction is used in a new function in order to imitate a construction/function pairing in the ML. Since a construction is a form–function pairing, this creates a new construction in which an existing structure is used with a new function. Example (2) also illustrates this. Standard Upper Sorbian has no clause-initial pronoun and begins simply with a form of the verb 'be,' whereas CUS uses *to* 'it' + the verb 'be' here, imitating German *es* 'it' + the verb 'be.' CUS *to* is the neuter singular form of the neutral demonstrative. This looks straightforward, but there is a story here. CUS has another *to* 'it' + 'be' construction with a nominal complement (either definite or indefinite), which is also found in Czech and Polish and thus apparently dates from the pre-contact period. This construction is used to introduce or to classify something, so *to* here is referential, even though it is marked for neither number nor gender of referents:

(3) CUS   *To*   *jo*   *te*   *blido.*
             it.NOM   be.3sPRS   the.NOMs   table.NOMs

     German *Das*   *ist*   *der*   *Tisch.*
             that.NOM be.3sPRS   the.NOMs   table.NOMs
             'That is the table.' (Scholze 2007:167)

     Czech   *To*   *je*   *student.*
             it.NOM   be.3sPRS   student.NOM
             'That's a student.'

     Polish *To*   *jest*   *mój*   *brat.*
             it.NOM   be.3sPRS   my.NOM   brother.NOM
             'That's my brother.'

In the construction that CUS has copied, in (2), CUS *to* and German *es* are non-referential dummies. Thus use of the preexisting CUS *to* 'it' + 'be' construction in (3), where *to* is referential, has been extended to the presentational function, where to becomes non-referential. This is a new function for the CUS *to* 'it' + 'be' construction.

Reports of the use of an existing construction for a new function are fairly rare in the contact literature, but Csató (2002: 318–321) describes how several Turkic possessor constructions have been redeployed in Northwest Karaim.

5.2.4 Formal Modification: Constructional Calquing

The third degree of CICC in (1) is the formal modification of an existing CL construction to render it more congruent with a ML construction. The extension of *to* to a non-referential function presented in section 5.2.3 is not the only such extension in CUS. We also find non-referential *to* matching German *es* in the impersonal weather construction in (4) and in a time construction in (5). These are evidently formal modifications of earlier constructions, as *to* does not occur in the corresponding constructions in Czech or Polish.

(4) CUS   *To*   *so*   *hrimoce.*
              it.NOM   REFL.ACC   thunder.3sPRS

     German   *Es*   *donnert.*
              it.NOM   thunder.3sPRS
              'It is thundering.' (Scholze 2007: 322)

     Czech   *Prší.*
              rain.3sPRS
              'It is raining.'

     Polish   *Pada*   *śnieg.*
              fall.3sPRS snow.NOM
              'It's snowing.'

(5) CUS   *To*   *jo*   *dźěwećich.*
              it.NOM   be.3sPRS   nine.o'.clock

     German   *Es*   *ist*   *neun*   *Uhr.*
              it.NOM   be.3sPRS   nine   o'.clock
              'It is nine o'clock.' (Scholze 2007: 322)

     Czech   *Je*   *děvet   hodin.*
              be.3sPRS   nine   o'.clock
              'It is nine o'clock.'

     Polish   *Jest*   *godzina piątą.*
              be.3sPRS   o'.clock five
              'It is five o'clock.'

To is also found as an expletive. German uses *es* 'it' similarly to English *it* in the construction in (6), postposing the infinitive phrase *nicht hinzugehen* from the sentence *Nicht hinzugehen wäre feige* 'Not to go there would be cowardly' and inserting *es* as a placeholder. This postposing has been copied into CUS, where the placeholder is *to* 'it.' The fact that there is no expletive in Czech or Polish supports the inference that this is a copy from German.[5]

(6) CUS *To*   *bu*   *fajge*   *bóło,*   *nic*   *hin-hić.*
           it.NOM AUX.3sSBJV   cowardly   be.PTCP.sN   NEG   DEIC-go.INF

---

[5] In (6) and subsequent examples, CUS 'be' employed as an auxiliary is glossed AUX.

German	*Es*	*wäre*	*feige,*	*nicht*	*hin-zu-gehen.*
	it.NOM	be.3sIPF.SBJV	cowardly	NEG	DEIC-to-go.INF

'It would be cowardly not to go there.' (Scholze 2007: 323)

Czech	*Je*	*možno*	*to*	*změnit.*
	be.3sPRS	possible	it.ACC	change.INF

'It is possible to change it.'

Polish	*Szkoda*	*mówić.*
	pointless	talk.INF

'It's pointless to discuss it.'

Even in these relatively simple examples, we see an important feature of CICC. Language in use consists of intersecting constructions, and contact may affect just one construction represented in a given clause or sentence without affecting others. In (4), CUS has copied the impersonal construction with *es* + weather verb from German, but it retains the argument structure construction of the verb 'thunder', which in CUS is an impersonal reflexive. In (6) and subsequent examples, CUS 'be,' employed as an auxiliary, is glossed AUX.

In the Czech and Polish constructions with referential *to* in (3), *to* is always sentence-initial. Significantly, in the constructions in (2), (4), (5), and (6), where CUS has extended the use of *to* on the model of German *es*, *to* only occurs clause-initially. If an adverb or a conjunction assumes clause-initial position, as in as in (7) and (8), German *es* occurs postverbally, but CUS *to* does not appear.

(7)
CUS	*Čora*	*jo*	*so* Ø	*hrimotało.*
	yesterday	be.3sPRS	REFL.ACC	thunder.PTCP

German	*Gestern*	*hat*	*es*	*gedonnert.*
	yesterday	have.3sPRS	it.NOM	thunder.PTCP

'Yesterday it thundered.' (Scholze 2007:323)

(8)
CUS	*dókejš*	Ø *jo*	*zno*	*swětło* . . .
	because	be.3sPRS	already	bright

German	*weil*	*es*	*schon*	*hell*	*ist* . . .
	because	it.NOM	already	daylight	be.3sPRS

'because it is already daylight . . .' (Scholze 2007: 323)

Note that the clause structures of the CUS and German adverbial clause constructions with 'because' do not match. This is a topic I return to in section 5.2.5.

The absence of CUS *to* from (7) and (8) illustrates the point made by Prince (1998). Constructional copying is rarely pure copying, but the modification of an existing construction in the CL to match a ML construction. CUS speakers have extended the construction with preexisting clause-initial *to* in (3) to the constructions in (2), (4), (5). and (6), but they have not copied the use of German *es* in clause-medial position in (7) and (8), as there was no preexisting CUS construction with clause-medial *to*.

The case of clause-initial *to* illustrates yet one further point. We might expect that the German phrase *Es geht mir gut* meaning 'I am well' (lit. 'It goes me well'), which begins with the nonreferential dummy *es*, would have a CUS equivalent with *to*, but (9) shows that it does not. The CUS expression is very probably a translation of the German, as it uses impersonal 'go' (Czech and Polish use impersonal 'have') and a dative experiencer, but the impersonal feature represented by German *es* is encoded Slavic-style in CUS by a reflexive pronoun.

(9) German *Es   geht   mir   gut.*
               it.NOM   go.3sPRS   me.DAT   well
               'I am well' (lit. 'It goes to-me well.')

     CUS   *Mi   so   dere   dźo.*   **To so mi dere dźo.*
               me.DAT   REFL.ACC   well   go.3sPRS
               'I am well' (lit. 'It goes itself to-me well.') (Scholze 2007: 322)

     Czech   *Jak   se   máš?*
     Polish   *Jak   się   masz?*
               how   REFL.ACC   have.2sPRS
               'How are you?'

Despite being a translation, the CUS phrase has not been affected by the extension of the *to* construction. The reason is almost certainly that the idiom is very frequently used, and frequently used items are less susceptible to change (Bybee 2007).[6]

The grammatical conservatism of the CUS expression resembles the preservation of the British English greeting *How do you do?* The rise of progressive aspect forms in English had made *How do you do?* grammatically anomalous, but it took a long time for it to start being replaced by *How are you doing?* (Tottie 1991).

A rather different instance of the formal modification of a CUS construction is found in the expression of the future-in-the-past in CUS. Czech and Polish have no sequence of tenses in indirect speech:

(10) Czech *Karel   řek-l,   že   přijde   zítra.*
               Karel   say-PTCPs   that   come.3sFUT   tomorrow
               'Karel said that he would come tomorrow.' (lit. 'will come tomorrow')

German uses the imperfect subjunctive form of the future auxiliary verb *werden* to form future-in-the past. CUS speakers imitate German by using the perfect subjunctive for the future-in-the-past (Toops 2006), producing the un-Slavic sequence of tenses in (11).

---

[6] This analysis implies, incidentally, that translation with 'go' took place earlier, and extension of the *to* construction followed later.

(11)   CUS   *Aleksej překladowaše kajku   rólu   by   hra-ł*
               Aleksej consider.3sIPF which.ACC role.ACC be.3sSBJC play-PTCP

       German   *Aleksej überlegte,   welche Rolle er spiel-en würde.*
               Aleksej consider.3sPST which role   he play-INF AUX.3sPST.SBJC
               'Aleksej considered which role he would play.' (Toops 2006: 151)

Where do CUS speakers get this usage from? The source of the copy is clear. In German the imperfect subjunctive of the future auxiliary is used both as future-in-the-past, as in (11), and in the hypothetical condition construction in (12). By analogy with German, CUS speakers have equated the future-in-the-past verb with the hypothetical condition verb, and thus use the CUS perfect subjunctive form for future-in-the-past as well.

(12)   CUS   *Ja   bu   to   sóbučini-ł,*
               I   be.3sSBJC   it   join.in-PTCPs
               hdyž   bu   ja   jene   ordentlich skater mě-ł.
               if   be.3sSBJC   I   one.PL   decent   skates have-PTCPs

       German   *Ich   würde   das   mitmach-en,*
               I   become.1sPST.SBJC   it   join.in-INF
               wenn   ich   ordentliche   Skater   hab-en   würde.
               when   I   decent   skates   have-INF   AUX.1sPST.SBJC
               'I would join in it if I had decent skates.' (Scholze 2007: 120, 148)

This inference presupposes that the CUS hypothetical condition construction is older than the future-in-the-past, and the presupposition is borne out by the Czech hypothetical condition in (13).

(13)   Czech   *Kdy=bych   mě-l   čas,*
               if=be.1sCOND   have-PTCPs time
               še-l=bych   do   kina.
               go-PTCPs=be.1sCOND   to   cinema.GEN
               'If I had time, I would go to the cinema.'

In this section, two examples of CUS constructional calquing (i.e., the formal modification of an existing construction to imitate a German construction, namely non-referential *to* and future-in-the past) have been presented. Constructional calquing is by far the most commonly mentioned in the contact literature out of the four degrees of constructional change. It is hard to know whether these frequent reports reflect frequent occurrence, or whether calquing is frequently mentioned because it is more readily recognized than either increase in use or use in a new function. Nadkarni (1975) describes how the Kamataka Saraswat Brahmin dialect of (Indo-Aryan) Konkani has copied a participial relative clause construction from (Dravidian) Kannada, in addition to an existing correlative construction that survives in one context, thus adding to the language's complexity. Haase (1992: 96–102) describes how, among other calques, Mixe Basque has modified a resultative construction to create a passive in imitation of Gascon. Prince (1998) analyzes Eastern Yiddish calquing of a Slavic cleft construction. Turkic Northwest Karaim has calqued the Russian use of the instrumental case with a predicate nominal in the classifying construction ('she is a teacher'), as well as the predicative possession construction and the polar interrogative construction (Csató 2000, 2001, 2002). Aikhenvald (2003) and Epps (2007a, 2007b) record a number of Tariana and Hup constructional calques, including calques from East Tucanoan languages of constructions that encode evidentiality.

5.2.5 Altered Structure: Metatypy

The fourth degree of CICC, which I have labeled *metatypy* (Ross 1996, 2006, 2007), is much less frequent than constructional calquing. In metatypy, an existing CL construction is structurally altered to more closely match a corresponding ML construction. The term *metatypy* was coined as a label for the changes that have happened in Oceanic Austronesian languages of Papua New Guinea, where, among other changes, SVO has become SOV, prepositional phrases have been replaced by postpositional phrases, possessum + possessor order has become possessor + possessum order, and in some languages parataxis has been replaced by clause-chaining. Metatypy has evidently taken place in the order of clause constituents in CUS, but the details of the process have remained obscure. An attempt is made in the following to clarify them. In the terms used by Vallduví (1992), a Czech or Polish clause ends with the focus (new information) and begins with the link (alias 'topic,' telling the hearer where the new information belongs in his or her knowledge store). The default order is usually claimed to be SVO.

(14)   Czech   *[Pavel]LINK*   *zabil*   *[Petra]FOCUS*
                Pavel.NOM   killed   Petr.ACC
                'Pavel killed Petr.'

                [Petra]LINK   *zabil*   *[Pavel]FOCUS*
                Petr.ACC   killed   Pavel.NOM
                'Petr was killed by Pavel.'/'It was Pavel who killed Petr.'

                [Pavel]LINK   *Petra*   *[zabil]FOCUS*
                Pavel.NOM   Petr.ACC   killed
                'Pavel **killed** Petr."/'Killed was what Petr did to Pavel.'

There is a complication in Czech, however: auxiliaries are second-position (Wackernagel) clitics.

(15)   Czech   *My* *jsme*   *se*   *uči-li.*
        we   AUX.1pPRS   REFL.ACC   study-PTCPp
        'We studied/were studying.'
        Uči-la   *se-s?*   (se-s < jse se)
        study-PTCP.f   AUX.PRS-REFL.ACC
        'Were you studying?'

The history of auxiliary cliticization in Polish is somewhat complicated, but it is likely that Czech is more conservative in this regard (Borsley and Rivero 1994; Migdalski 2004). Presumably CUS clause structure was once similar to Czech and Polish, particularly to Czech.

However, CUS clause constructions are today rather different from those of other Slavic languages. By default, a clause is verb-final.

(16)   CUS   *To*   *ja* *z*   *ruku*   *šo*   *wólpokwem.*
        that.ACC   I   with   hand.INS   all   wash.up
        'I'll wash all that up by hand.' (Scholze 2007: 329)

(17)   CUS   . . . *zo*   *tam*   *jen*   *pólcaj*   *prede*   *towo*
              that   there   a.NOM   policeman   in.front.of   the.GEN
        awta   *stój.*
        car.GEN   stand.3sPST
        '(he saw) that a policeman was standing there in front of the car.'
        (Scholze 2007: 329)

An auxiliary is in second position, as in Czech, but its dependent lexical verb remains in final position, as in (7) and (12), repeated here as (18):

(18)   CUS   *Ja*   *bu*   *to*   *sóbučini-ł,*
        I   be.3sSBJC   it   join.in-PTCPs
        hdyž   *bu*   *ja* *jene*   *ordentlich*   *skater*   *mě-ł.*
        if   be.3sSBJC   I   one.PL   decent   skates   have-PTCPs
        'I would join in it if I had decent skates.'

The CUS constructions bear some resemblance to their German equivalents, but also differ from them considerably. First, German has different structures in main and subordinate clauses. Main clauses are verb-second (V2).

(19)   German   *Gestern*   *sah*   *ich*   *einen*   *Mann*   *im*   *Park.*
             yesterday   saw.1sPST   I.NOM   a.ACC   man   in.the.sDAT   park
             'Yesterday I saw a man in the park.'

If there is an auxiliary, it is V2 and its dependent lexical verb is clause-final.

(20) German *Gestern*   **habe**   *ich einen Mann   im*   *Park*
          yesterday have.1sPRS I   a.ACC   man   in.the.DAT park
          gesehen.
          see.PTCP
          'Yesterday I saw a man in the park.'

Subordinate clauses are verb-final.

(21) German *Der*   *Mann, den*   *ich gestern   im*   *Park*
          the.NOM   man   REL.ACC   I   yesterday in.the.DAT park
          sah . . .
          saw.1sPST
          'The man I saw in the park yesterday . . .'

If there is an auxiliary, it occupies verb-final position and usually follows its dependent lexical verb

(22) German *Der*   *Mann, den*   *ich gestern   im*   *Park*
          the.NOM   man   REL.ACC   I   yesterday in.the.DAT park
          gesehen   habe . . .
          see.PTCP   have.1sPRS
          'The man I saw in the park yesterday . . .'

   If we compare the structures of CUS and German (treating German as SVO, its default order, rather than V2, which does not affect the comparison), we see that CUS SOV matches a German subordinate clause construction, and CUS SAuxOv matches a German main clause construction.

(23) CUS   **SOV**   or   **SAuxOV**
      German Main: SVO   or   **SAuxOV**
      German Subord: **SOV**   or   SOVAux

This has caused some controversy among scholars of CUS as to whether the CUS order is the result of German influence or not. Perhaps the majority believes that it must be (Michałk 1962; Stone 1993: 652–654; Breu and Scholze 2006), and I agree with them, but not always with their reasoning. Breu and Scholze (2006: 52–53) propose that at some level, CUS speakers recognized that German was underlyingly verb-final and shifted to that pattern. But there is no evidence I know of to suggest that bilingual speakers recognize and adopt 'underlying' patterns that are not manifest on the surface.

On the other hand, much has been made of the fact that both CUS and German SAuxOV clauses form a *Satzklammer*, a clausal bracket construction whereby the auxiliary is in second position and the dependent lexical verb at the end, and these constituents bracket the rest of the clause, except for the constituent before the second-position auxiliary. However, there is a difference between the two languages: the CUS auxiliary is a second-position clitic, whereas second position in German is the position of the main verb. We have already seen that the Sorbian auxiliary has not moved, as its ancestral position was second position.

The crucial question, then, is how did the Sorbian lexical verb come to be positioned at the end of the clause, in clauses both with and without an auxiliary? The answer is a little complex. The change from the information-structurally based order of Czech or Polish to fairly consistent verb-final order is unlikely to have occurred spontaneously and more likely to be the result of contact. Such a change in constituent order does not occur spontaneously (Dunn et al. 2011). The only known contact language was German, and contact has been intense, so German is almost certainly the ML here, as elsewhere. On grounds of saliency, it is more likely that Sorbian copied a German main clause construction than a subordinate clause construction. It follows from (23) that this was the German SAuxOV main-clause construction, its auxiliary position matching that of Sorbian. But as the Sorbian auxiliary was a fixed-position clitic, Sorbian SAuxOV was (and still is) simply a variant of SOV, which became the default constituent order.

We should, of course, ask whether German constituent order at the time was similar to modern German. Pre-medieval German did not have such a fixed order as German has today, but the literature suggests that the dominant patterns of OHG (750–1100) were moving toward those of modern German (Axel 2007). It thus looks as if CUS verb-final order is the result of very early contact, after which each language—CUS and German—followed its own grammaticization path. There is a tendency in modern CUS for more verbs to be recruited to the clitic position. Originally it was occupied by forms of the auxiliary verb *bóć* 'be,' but forms of *měć* 'have,' *hić* 'go,' *cyć* 'want to,' and various modals also tend to occur there, and there are signs that this is spreading to other verbs, too. The data are not clear, but if this is a change in process, it is surely the result of contact with German.

Heine (2008) claims that metatypy, as I describe it here, does not occur. On his interpretation, what we find is increased use of one of a language's several available constituent orders (i.e., the first degree of constructional change) until it becomes a new default. Since Sorbian pre-contact clause order was apparently flexible like Czech and Polish, and SOV was one of several possible orders, as in (14), under this rubric CUS does not reflect metatypy, but simply the increased use of one of several available orders. However, the process was more complicated than this. The Czech clauses in (14) illustrate a single information structure construction, crudely

(24)   LINK < X < FOCUS (where '<' means 'precedes')

but this construction intersects with the Czech transitive clause construction S, V, O (where commas indicate that the constituents are unordered) to give the three Czech constructions illustrated in (14):[7]

(25)   S < V < O
        O < V < S
        S < O < V

Each of these is a form–function pairing, and so Czech S < O < V inherits from (24) the facts that the subject is the LINK and the verb is the FOCUS. This, however, is not the CUS form–function pairing, as (24) is not a CUS construction. Instead, SOV is the default CUS transitive clause construction. If the default pre-contact construction was SVO, then metatypy has occurred.

In any case, instances can be found where a copied structure does not reflect the (functional) expansion of an existing structure. Numerous Oceanic Austronesian languages of New Guinea have right-headed syntax on the model of neighboring Papuan languages, entailing orders that did not occur in their left-headed ancestor. The head-marking languages Tariana and Hup have developed dependent-marking constructions by copying from East Tucanoan languages (Aikhenvald 2003; Epps 2007: 273). Other cases of metatypy are reported in the literature (for example, Harris and Campbell 1995: 137 provide a list of possible cases and briefly mention a number of case studies [142– 147]), but careful examination of their histories—which may or may not be accessible—is needed in order to be certain that they are cases of metatypy rather than of the expansion of one or more existing constructions at the expense of others.

5.3 SHIFT-INDUCED CONSTRUCTIONAL CHANGE

Shift-induced change refers here to rapid shift that entails imperfect adult language learning. Such cases are relatively rare. Far more frequent is shift that occurs over a number of generations, during which children learn the new language natively. Shift then occurs when children no longer acquire the heritage language and only learn the "new" language. This, however, typically causes no constructional change.

---

[7] This is an instance of multiple inheritance in a constructional network: see Croft (2001: 53–57) and Trousdale (2013).

5.3.1 Rural Irish English

English entered Ireland with the Anglo-Norman invasion of 1169, but few of the population learned it in the ensuing centuries. The language of the vast majority continued to be Irish Gaelic, a Celtic language. But plantation settlements after the British occupation of 1603 brought a considerable growth in the number of English speakers. Even then, the spread of English among people of Irish descent was slow, and only took off around 1750. By then the British had taken over most of the land and were economically and politically dominant, so English became attractive to Irish Gaelic speakers. Bilingualism in Irish Gaelic and English first became established in and around the towns of Belfast and Dublin and spread outward from them, leading to language shift over the period 1750–1900 (McCafferty 2004). The greatest blow to Irish Gaelic during this period was the Great Famine of the 1840s, which by death and emigration reduced the number of speakers by two million within a decade. It led to a need for Irish Gaelic speakers to know English in order to emigrate or to survive in a changed society (Hickey 2010: 152–153). Thus there is no doubt about the rapidity of the shift.[8] The Irish English from which I draw examples of the degrees of CICC listed in (1) is the English spoken in the countryside, especially by earlier generations. Sources are Filppula (1986, 1999), Harris (1991), and Hickey (2010, 2013).

5.3.2 More Frequent Use

Wald (1996) and Sankoff (2002) show that shifting speakers select the second-language constructions that are perceived as most congruent with those of their first language. In other words, they use an existing construction in their second language more frequently than might native speakers of that language.

An example comes from Filppula's (1986) corpus-based study of Irish English (summarized by Harris 1991). British English uses two constructions for contrastive focus. The default is to use intonation with a high falling tone on the focus constituent:

(26)   BrEn   *John* *went to Derry yesterday.* (i.e., not David, etc.)

An alternative is to use a cleft in which the extracted constituent is in contrastive focus:

(27)   BrEn   *It's* *John* *who went to Derry yesterday.* (i.e., not David, etc.)

        IrGa   *Is   é   Seán   a   chuaigh   go   Doire   inné*
                  is   him   John   REL   go.PAST   to   Derry   yesterday
                  'It's John who went to Derry yesterday.' (Harris 1991: 197)

---

[8] Today there are just three West Coast pockets of Irish Gaelic, now heavily influenced by English.

Irish Gaelic uses clefts as the default, and this has led to a higher incidence of clefts in rural Irish English than in British English (Harris 1991: 198).

5.3.3 New Function

Irish English clefts differ from Standard English clefts both functionally and syntactically, on the model of Irish Gaelic. Here we are concerned with an added function. In Irish Gaelic, clefting is used not only for contrastive focus. It is also used for sentence focus, where all the information is new.

This function has been added to subject clefts in Irish English (Harris 1991: 198). In (28) a father asks his son, 'What has happened to you?' The son answers,

(28) IrEn   *It was Mícheál Rua who gave me a beating.* (Filppula 1986, cited by Harris 1991: 198–199)

This is the translation equivalent of the Irish Gaelic response, which is syntactically a cleft.

(29) IrGa *Mícheál   Rua   a   bhuail   mé*
             Mícheál   Rua   REL   beat   me
             'Mícheál Rua beat me.' (lit. '[it was] Mícheál Rua who beat me')

In British English this is pragmatically infelicitous, as it presupposes that there has already been mention of the son receiving a beating.

Prince (2001) discusses a similar case in the English of New York Yiddish–English bilinguals, namely so-called Yiddish movement. One of her examples is (30).

(30) *In less than a week it's Rosh Hashan* [Jewish New Year] *and he thinks I should take a vacation.*
       Ten people *I'm having. What do you think, a chicken cleans itself?* (Prince 2001: 347)

The standard English focus fronting construction (as in *He's buying a Saab—No, a Volvo he wants*) has a narrowly constrained function: the proposition is hearer-old and the fronted item is a hearer-new member of a hearer-old set (in this case, of makes of cars: *Saabs, Volvos, Fords, Chryslers*, etc.). In Yiddish movement, however, focus fronting assumes a broader function, and the fronted item is simply hearer-new.

5.3.4 Formal Modification: Constructional Calquing

Irish Gaelic clefting also exemplifies the formal modification of a construction in the CL, in this case English, on the model of Irish Gaelic, the ML. In Standard English the elements that may be extracted as focal constituents in clefts are limited to subject NP, object NP, complement of preposition, and certain types of adjunct (Harris 1991). Verbs, subject complements, and manner adverbs cannot be extracted. In Irish Gaelic, on the other hand, one can also place a non-finite VP, a subject complement or a manner adverb in focal position, and these possibilities have been copied into Irish English, giving rise to constructions that standard British English speakers can usually understand but would not use. The extracted element is in focus, but not necessarily contrastive focus.

Irish English examples are found where the extracted element in the cleft is a non-finite VP:

(31)   IrEn   *It's doing his lessons that Tim is.* (Harris 1991: 197)

IrGa   *Is   ag   déanamh   a   chuid   ceachtannaí   atá   Tadhg.*
is   at   doing   his   portion   lessons   REL.be   Tim
'Tim is doing his **lessons**'/'What Tim is doing is his lessons.'

And where it is a subject complement:

(32)   IrEn   *It's drunk he is.* (Harris 1991: 198)

IrGa   *Is   caochta   atá   sé*
is   drunk   REL.be   he
'He's **drunk**.'/'What he is is **drunk**.'

And where it is a manner adverb:

(33)   IrEn   *It's not well he saw them.* (Harris 1991: 198)

IrGa   *Níg   o=maith   a   chonaic   sé   iad*
is.not   well   REL   see.PST   he   them
'He didn't see them **well**.'

Notice that these are constructional calques—loan translations. They entail formal modification of the existing English cleft construction, but they are not examples of metatypy, as metatypy entails matching the sequence of constructional elements to those of the ML. Metatypy does not happen in Irish English. Irish Gaelic is VSO. IrEn remains SVO.

A second example of the formal modification of an English construction in Irish English arises from the fact that Irish Gaelic has no verb form directly corresponding to the English perfect. Given the complex and unusual semantics of the English perfect, this is not surprising. Harris (1991: 201–205) points out that Irish English has at least four constructions that replace the use of the English perfect. One of these is very well known and fairly well studied, the so-called *after* perfect. There is general agreement among scholars that it is a translation equivalent of the Irish Gaelic immediate perfect structure with 'after' (which corresponds structurally to the 'at' progressive construction in (31). In the examples, the brackets indicate the nominalized VP that functions as the object of the preposition 'after.'

(34) IrEn *They are after doing the work.* (Hickey 2010: 156; 2013: 95)

    IrGa *Tá   siad   tar éis   [an   obair   a   dhéanamh]*

            bePRS   they   after   the   work   COMP   do$_{\text{VERBAL NOUN}}$

            'They have done the work.'   (McCafferty 2004:114)

(35) IrEn *She's after selling the boat.*

    IrGa *Tá   sí   tréis   [an   bád   a   dhíol]*

            bePRS   she   after   the   boat   COMP   sell

            'She has just sold the boat.' (Harris 1991: 205)

Pietsch (2008) asks whether the *after* construction could reflect an English construction from the period in which shift occurred. He checks Van Bergen and Denison's (2003) corpus of seventeenth- and eighteenth-century English to see whether there was an English template for such a construction in the period when shift was occurring. He finds constructions with *for,* expressing intention, and *about,* expressing imminence (i.e., *about* V-*ing* where modern English uses *about to* V)

(36) BrEn . . . *he is not **for** seling any coales* [1788]

          'He does not intend to sell any coal.'

His conclusion is that these constructions provided a template for the Irish English *after* V-*ing* construction, but that the *after* construction nonetheless has its origin in copying from Irish Gaelic. A number of other instances of constructional calquing in language shift can be found in the literature. Lucas and Lash (2010) argue that the presence of bipartite negation in Egyptian Arabic and right across North Africa can be attributed to the shift to Arabic by a majority Coptic-speaking population.

    Matthews and Yip (2009: 368) comment that Taiwan Mandarin has grammaticized *shuō* 'say' as a complementiser on the model of Taiwan Southern Min *kóng* 'say,' an innovation that has not occurred in standard mainland Mandarin.

5.3.5 Altered Structure: Metatypy

The fourth degree of CICC is metatypy—the alteration of a construction's structure to more closely match a corresponding ML construction. I have found no cases of metatypy in Irish English, nor in any other independently attested instances of shift. In any case, it seems unlikely that metatypy would occur in the context of rapid adult language shift. Metatypy happens in bilingually induced change when bilingual speakers reduce their processing burden by aligning the structures of one of their two languages with the other. Shifting speakers, on the other hand, are trying to learn their "new" language as fully as they are able and are unlikely to alter its constituent orders.

5.4 How Does CICC Occur?

King (2000) has suggested that all CICC occurs as a result of lexical copying. She considers that the copying of English phrasal verbs (variously verb + preposition, verb + particle, verb + adjunct) in Prince Edward Island French has led to the latter's copying of the English preposition-stranding construction. But the evidence for this association is not compelling, and the presence of preposition stranding in Prince Edward Island French appears to be directly due to constructional calquing.

Cases where lexical calquing leads to the adoption of a construction do sometimes occur, however. Haase (1992: 80) lists instances where Mixe Basque has copied Gascon "complex locative prepositions," collocations derived from a complex prepositional phrase with the structure PREPOSITION1 + RELATIONAL NOUN + PREPOSITION2 + NP. The calqued construction in Mixe is NP–CASE-MARKER2 + RELATIONAL NOUN–CASE-MARKER1, in accordance with Basque constituent order.

The sequences in (37) show near translation equivalence. Gascon *au* 'to the' is translated as the Mixe locative case-marker*[e]an* . Gascon *de* 'of' is translated as the Mixe genitive case-marker, and Gascon dative/allative *a* as the Mixe dative or allative case-marker.

(37)		Gascon	Mixe Basque
	'behind, at back of'	*au darrèr de*	GEN *gibel-ean*
	'in front of'	*au davant de*	GEN *aintzin-ean*
	'between'	*entermiei de*	GEN *arte-an*
	'toward, in the direction of'	*[de] cap a*	DAT/ALL *bu[r]uz*
	'as far as'	*dinc a*	[ALL] *artio*
	'near, beside'	*acostat a*	DAT *hurbil*

The process of translation equivalence has evidently been going on for a long time. The form in (38a) is common Basque, and the case-marked form in (38b) is also ancient. However, the form in (38c), with a dative, occurs only in Mixe Basque, and evidently represents the most recent stage of calquing, whereby a postpositional phrase construction has arisen.

(38) a. *eliza   aintzin-ean*
         church   front-LOC
         'in front of the church'

b. *eliza-[r]en*   *aintzin-ean*
   church-GEN   front-LOC
   'in front of the church'

c. *eliza-ri*   *hurbil*
   church-DAT near
   'near the church' (Haase 1992: 79–80)

The Mixe case differs from the Prince Edward Island French case. The former entails calquing of complex lexical items (or, depending on one's theoretical predilections, of lexical items with their associated phrase structure). Where several items of the same ML structure are copied, generalization across these items gives birth to a new CL construction. What happens in Prince Edward Island French is different. The preposition stranding construction is not itself part of the copied lexical items, that is, the English prepositions (and occurs in this dialect with French prepositions), and appears to reflect constructional copying, like the Sorbian *to* constructions or the Irish English clefts. These represent attempts to copy the morphosyntactic organization of one language into another. Whether CICC takes place or not depends on speakers being able to equate the constructions of their two languages in such a way that they can copy them. This in turn is determined by two interacting factors (Muysken 2013).

The first is the typological distance between the languages in contact and whether they manifest "easily recognizable, straightforward relationships between content and expression" with metaphorical transparency, low allomorphy, and constituent structure that reflects semantic structure (i.e., modifiers and complements remain with their heads) (Johanson 2002a: 44–47; see also Haig 2001: 210–217). Where languages are closely enough related for their speakers to be aware of the relationship, the possibility of copying is greatly increased (François 2011; Epps, Huehnergard, and Pat-El 2013).

However, typological distance alone does not determine whether copying takes place (Harris and Campbell 1995: 122–128). Crucial is speakers' recognition of congruence between their two languages. This recognition is only partly determined by typological distance; it is ultimately subjective and belongs to the speech community's social knowledge (Sebba 1998). It depends on social factors: generally, the more frequent the use of both languages and the longer the community has been bilingual, the more congruence is recognized by bilingual speakers. Moreover, whether a copied construction continues into the next generation depends on its adoption by a sufficient proportion of the speech community, and this in turn depends on factors like community size and norm enforcement.

The reader who is familiar with surveys of contact-induced change will note a near-absence of comment in this chapter about the sequence(s) in which various kinds of change occur in a contact-affected language. Implicational statements about change are often along the lines of "syntactic copying does not take place unless lexical copying has occurred," and lie outside the chapter's scope.

But statements have sometimes been made (by the present author, among others) about the sequence in which contact-induced changes occur within the morphosyntax of a language. Such claims need to be related to cause and effect. For example, as shown in the preceding, calquing of complex lexical items from Gascon has given rise to a new postpositional phrase construction in Mixe Basque. A similar but more radical change has occurred in Pipil, where calquing from Spanish has for the first time created adpositions (Campbell 1987; Harris and Campbell 1995: 126–127). In such a case, we can say that calquing has caused structural change. However, chronological sequence does not necessarily reflect causation. Lexical and grammatical calquing usually precede metatypy (Ross 2006, 2007), but it is not clear that calquing causes metatypy. Rather, the chronological relationship between them is due to the fact that metatypy only takes place where bilingualism is well established and constant, and this is likely already to have led to calquing. The implicational relationship between them is thus chronological, not causal, and only probabilistic.

It is sometimes claimed that, among CICCs, changes that affect the marking of coordination and subordination occur early (Aikhenvald 2002: 27). This may well be generally true, as bilingual speakers display a preference for organizing discourse in a similar way in both their languages (Matras 1998). But this is not always the case. Takia employs complex clause-final enclitics to encode interclausal relationships, and these cannot have developed until after some ancestor of Takia had shifted to SOV clause order (Ross 2008). Thus attempts to formulate sequences of changes need to take cause into account, acknowledging that causal factors specific to a given language may upset generalisations about chronological sequence.

5.5 SIMILARITIES AND POSSIBLE DIFFERENCES BETWEEN BILINGUALLY INDUCED AND SHIFT-INDUCED CONSTRUCTIONAL CHANGE

In bilingually induced constructional change, bilingual speakers copy constructions through a natural tendency to ease the processing burden caused by speaking two languages rather than one. Sasse (1985: 84) remarks pithily in his account of the hellenization of the Albanian dialects of central Greece, "gemeinsamen Denken folgt gemeinsames Ausdrucksbedürfnis" (from shared thinking comes a shared expressive need). A similar point has been made by others (Ross 1996: 204–205; Matras 2000; Sakel and Matras 2008: 66).

Shifting speakers, on the other hand, struggle to express in their "new" language functions for which they have a construction in their "old" language. In the process, they may seize upon a construction in the "new" language and copy onto it morphosyntactic features and the function of a construction perceived as similar in the "old" language. This difference in process is perhaps reflected in differences in constructional copying. Metatypy is apparently a component of bilingually induced change, but not of shift-induced change (section 3.5). It is possible that there is also a difference when a construction undergoes formal modification. Both the Irish English cleft construction and the Irish English *after* V-*ing* construction introduce formal changes in an existing construction, and also use the changed construction in a new function, because a construction in the CL (the "new" language) has been equated with a functionally different construction in the ML (the "old" language). Thus the English cleft is used for contrastive focus, but the Irish English cleft adds non-contrastive focus and sentence focus. The English preposition + V-*ing* construction is used in Irish English with *after* as an immediate perfect construction, a function it never serves in British English. However, the formally changed Sorbian constructions we examined earlier, the *to* constructions and the future-in-the-past construction, are used for the function the construction had before the formal change, not for a new function.

The implication here is that in bilingually induced change a formally altered construction does not serve a new function, but in shift-induced change it may. This putative distinction requires further research, however. If it should prove to be a generalization, then we can probably attribute it to speakers' differing motivations in the two kinds of CICC. Despite these possible differences between bilingually induced and shift-induced change, it will probably be only occasionally feasible to use them to diagnose the different histories of languages.

First, it is only the presence of metatypy that is diagnostic (of bilingually induced change). Because of its rarity, its absence tells us nothing. Second, we need detailed diachronic information to determine whether a formally altered construction is serving an old or a new function. Where we have it, we usually don't need diagnostic evidence!

Otherwise, the outcomes of bilingually induced and shift-induced constructional change look remarkably similar, and there is a reason for this, namely the mediating role that pre-adolescent children play in language change (Ross 2013). The first generation to make constructional changes will do so in a haphazard and irregular manner. It is kids who conventionalize and regularize the messy linguistic input from their parents, caregivers (who may only be a few years older), and other kids in their interactions with each other. Children know nothing of the history of the language they are learning, and the process by which they conventionalize the input is the same, regardless of how constructional change has entered that input. This being so, constructional changes made within the two contact processes do not differ formally.

REFERENCES

Aikhenvald, Alexandra Y. 2002. *Language Contact in Amazonia*. Oxford: Oxford University Press.

Aikhenvald, Alexandra Y. 2003. Mechanisms of change in areal diffusion: New morphology and language contact. *Journal of Linguistics* 39: 1–29.

Aikhenvald, Alexandra Y. 2007. Grammars in contact: A cross-linguistic perspective. In *Grammars in Contact: A Cross-Linguistic Typology*, edited by A. Aikhenvald and R. M. W. Dixon, 1–66. Oxford: Oxford University Press.

Aikhenvald, Alexandra Y., and R. M. W. Dixon (eds.). 2007. *Grammars in Contact: A Cross-Linguistic Typology*. Oxford: Oxford University Press.

Axel, Katrin, 2007. *Studies on Old High German syntax: Left Sentence Periphery, Verb Placement and Verb-Second*. Amsterdam: John Benjamins.

Borsley, Robert D., and María Luisa Rivero. 1994. Clitic auxiliaries and incorporation in Polish. *Natural Language & Linguistic Theory* 12: 373–422.

Brendemoen, Bernt, 1999. Greek and Turkish language encounters in Anatolia. In *Language Encounters across Time and Space*, edited by Bernt Brendemoen, Elizabeth Lanza, and Else Ryen, 353–378. Oslo: Novis forlag.

Breu, Walter. 1992. Das italokroatische Verbsystem zwischen slavischem Erbe und kontakt-bedingter Entwicklung. In *Slavistische Linguistik 1991*, edited by Tilmann Reuther, 93–122. München: Otto Sagner.

Breu, Walter. 1998. Romanisches Adstrat im Moliseslavischen. *Die Welt der Slaven* 43: 339–354.

Breu, Walter. 1999a. Der Konditional im Moliseslavischen. Ein Beitrag zur Kontaktlinguistik. In *Ars Philologica: Festschrift für Baldur Panzer zum 65. Geburtstag*, edited by Karsten Grünberg and Wilfried Potthoff, 243–253. Heidelberg: Peter Lang.

Breu, Walter. 1999b. Die Komparation im Moliseslavischen. In *Des racines et des ailes: Théories, modèles, expériences en linguistique et didactique: Mélanges en l'honneur de Jean Petit pour son soixante-dixième anniversaire*, edited by René Métrich, Albert Hudlett, and Heinz-Helmut Lüger, 37–63. Nancy: Association des Nouveaux cahiers d'allemand.

Breu, Walter. 2000. Der Verbalaspekt in der obersorbischen Umgangssprache im Rahmen des ILA-Modells. In *Slavistische Linguistik 1999: Referate des XXIV. Konstanzer Slavistischen Arbeitstreffens, Konstanz, 7.–10.9.1999*, edited by Walter Breu, 37–75. München: Otto Sagner.

Breu, Walter. 2003a. Der indefinite Artikel in slavischen Mikrosprachen: Grammatikalisierung im totalen Sprachkontakt. In *Der indefinite Artikel in slavischen Mikrosprachen: Grammatikalisierung im totalen Sprachkontakt*, edited by Holger Kuße, 27–68. München: Otto Sagner.

Breu, Walter. 2003b. Impersonales Neutrum im Moliseslavischen. *Rusistika—Slavistika—Lingvistika: Festschrift für Werner Lehfeldt zum 60. Geburtstag*, edited by S. Kempgen, U. Schweier, and T. Berger, 57–71. Die Welt der Slaven, Sammelbände Bd. 19. München: Otto Sagner.

Breu, Walter. 2003c. Bilingualism and linguistic interference in the Slavic-Romance contact area of Molise (Southern Italy). In *Words in Time: Diachronic Semantics from Different Points of View*, edited by R. Eckardt, K. von Heusinger, and C. Schwarze, 351–373. Berlin: Mouton de Gruyter.

Breu, Walter. 2004a. Der definite Artikel in der obersorbischen Umgangssprache. In *Der definite Artikel in der obersorbischen Umgangssprache*, edited by Christian Sappok and Marion Krause, 9–57. München: Otto Sagner.

Breu, Walter. 2004b. Die Genuskategorie im Moliseslavischen. In *Germano-Slavistische Beiträge*, edited by Miloš Okuka and Ulrich Schweier, 29–43. München: Otto Sagner.

Breu, Walter. 2005. Verbalaspekt und Sprachkontakt: Ein Vergleich der Systeme zweier slavischer Minderheitensprachen (SWR/MSL). In *Slavistische Linguistik 2003*, edited by Sebastian Kempgen, 37–95. München: Otto Sagner.

Breu, Walter. 2008. Der slavische Lokativ im Sprachkontakt.]: Ein Beitrag zur Binnendifferenzierung des Moliseslavischen. In *Slavistische Linguistik 2006/2007*, edited by Peter Kosta and Daniel Weiss, 59–102. München: Otto Sagner.

Breu, Walter. 2009. Situationsgeflechte: Zum Ausdruck der Taxis im Moliseslavischen. *Von grammatischen Kategorien und sprachlichen Weltbildern—Die Slavia von der Sprachgeschichte bis zur Politsprache: Festschrift für Daniel Weiss zum 60. Geburtstag*, edited by Tilman Berger, Markus Giger, Imke Mendoza, and Sibylle Kurt, 83–108. München: Otto Sagner. (Wiener Slawistischer Almanach Sonderband 73)

Breu, Walter. 2011. Il verbo slavomolisano in confronto con altre lingue minoritarie: mutamento contattodipendente, resistenza e sviluppo autonomo. In *L'influsso dell'italiano sul sutema del verbu delle lingue minoritarie: Resistenza e mutamento nella morfologia e nella sintassi. Atti del 2° Convegno Internazionale, Costanza, 10–13 dicembre 2008*, edited by Walter Breu, 149–184. Bochum: Brockmeyer.

Breu, Walter. 2012. Aspect forms and functions in Sorbian varieties. *Sprachtypologie und Universalienforschung* 65: 246–266.

Breu, Walter. 2012. The grammaticalization of an indefinite article in Slavic micro-languages. In *Grammatical Replication and Borrowability in Language Contact*, edited by Björn Hansen, Bernhard Wälchli, and Björn Wiemer, 275–322. Berlin: De Gruyter Mouton.

Breu, Walter, and Lenka Scholze. 2006. Sprachkontakt und Syntax. Zur Position des Verbs im modernen Obersorbischen. In *Slavistische Linguistik 2004/2005*, edited by Tilman Berger, Jochen Raecke, and Tilman Reuther, 41–88. München: Otto Sagner.

Bybee, Joan. 2007. *Frequency of Use and the Organisation of Language*. Oxford: Oxford University Press.

Campbell, Lyle. 1987. Syntactic change in Pipil. *International Journal of American Linguistics* 53: 253–280.

Croft, William. 2001. *Radical Construction Grammar: Syntactic Theory in Typological Perspective*. Oxford: Oxford University Press.

Csató, Éva A. 1996. Some typological properties of North-Western Karaim in areal perspectives. In *Areale. Kontakte. Dialekte. Sprache und ihre Dynamik in mehrsprachigen Situationen*, edited by Norbert Boretzky, Werner Enninger, and Thomas Stolz, 68–83. Bochum-Essener Beitrage zur Sprachwandelforschung 24. Bochum: Brockmeyer.

Csató, Éva A. 2000. Contact-induced phenomena in Karaim. *Berkeley Linguistics Society* 25: 54–62.

Csató, Éva A. 2001. Syntactic code-copying in Karaim. In *Circum-Baltic Languages*, Vol. 1: *Past and Present*, edited by Östen Dahl and Maria Koptjevskaja-Tamm, 271–283. Amsterdam: John Benjamins.

Csató, Éva A. 2002. Karaim: A high-copying language. In *Language Change: The Interplay of Internal, External and Extra-Linguistic Factors*, edited by Mari C. Jones and Edith Esch, 315–327. Berlin: Mouton de Gruyter.

Csató, Éva A. 2008. Some typological features of the viewpoint and tense system in spoken North-Western Karaim. In *Tense and Aspect in the Languages of Europe*, edited by Östen Dahl, 725–751. Berlin: Mouton de Gruyter.

Csató, Éva A., and Lars Johanson. 1995. Zur Silbenharmonie des Nordwest-Karaimischen. *Acta Orientalia Academiae Scientarum Hungaricae* 3: 329–337.

Dawkins, R. M. 1916. *Modern Greek in Asia Minor: A Study of the Dialects of Sílli, Cappadocia, and Phárasa*. Cambridge: Cambridge University Press.

Dunn, Michael, Simon J. Greenhill, Stephen C. Levinson, and Russell D. Gray. 2011. Evolved structure of language shows lineage-specific trends in word-order "universals." *Nature* 473 (May 5): 79–82.

Epps, Patience. 2007a. The Vaupés melting pot: Tucanoan influence on Hup. In *Grammars in Contact: A Cross-Linguistic Typology*, edited by A. Aikhenvald and R. M. W. Dixon, 267–289. Oxford: Oxford University Press.

Epps, Patience. 2007b. Grammatical borrowing in Hup. In *Grammatical Borrowing in Cross-Linguistic Perspective*, edited by Y. Matras and J. Sakel, 551–565. Berlin: Mouton de Gruyter.

Epps, Patience, John Huehnergard, and Na'ama Pat-El. 2013. Introduction: Contact among genetically related languages. *Journal of Language Contact* 6: 209–219.

Fitch, Gesche Westphal. 2011. Changes in frequency as a measure of language change: Extraposition in Pennsylvania German. In *Studies on German Language Islands*, edited by Michael T. Putnam, 371–384. Amsterdam: John Benjamins.

Filppula, Markku. 1986. *Some Aspects of Hiberno-English in a Functional Sentence Perspective*. University of Joensuu Publications in the Humanities 7. Joensuu: University of Joensuu.

Filppula, Markku. 1999. *The Grammar of Irish English: Language in Hibernian Style*. London: Routledge.

Fortescue, Michael. 1993. Eskimo word order variation and its contact-induced perturbation. *Journal of Linguistics* 29: 267–289.

François, Alexandre. 2011. Social ecology and language history in the northern Vanuatu linkage: A tale of divergence and convergence. *Journal of Historical Linguistics* 1: 175–246.

Fried, Mirjam. 2013. Principles of constructional change. In *The Oxford Handbook of Construction Grammar*, edited by Thomas Hoffmann and Graeme Trousdale, 419–437. Oxford: Oxford University Press.

Haase, Martin. 1992. *Sprachkontakt und Sprachwandel im Baskenland: Einflusse des Gaskognischen und Franzosischen auf das Baskische*. Hamburg: Buske.

Haig, Geoffrey. 2001. Linguistic diffusion in present-day East Anatolia: From top to bottom. In *Areal Diffusion and Genetic Inheritance: Problems in Comparative Linguistics*, edited by Alexandra Y. Aikhenvald and R. M. W. Dixon, 195–224. Oxford: Oxford University Press.

Harkins, William E. 1953. *A Modern Czech Grammar*. New York: Kings Crown Press, Columbia University.

Harris, Alice C., and Lyle Campbell. 1995. *Historical Syntax in Cross-Linguistic Perspective*. Cambridge: Cambridge University Press.

Harris, John. 1991. Conservatism versus substratal transfer in Irish English. In *Dialects of English: Studies in Grammatical Variation*, edited by Peter Trudgill and J. K. Chambers. London: Longman.

Heine, Bernd. 2008. Contact-induced word order change without word order change. In *Language Contact and Contact Languages*, edited by Peter Siemund and Noemi Kintana, 33–60. Hamburg Studies on Multilingualism 7. Amsterdam: John Benjamins.

Heine, Bernd, and Tania Kuteva. 2003. On contact-induced grammaticalization. *Studies in Language* 27: 529–572.

Heine, Bernd, and Tania Kuteva. 2005. *Language Contact and Grammatical Change*. Cambridge: Cambridge University Press.

Hickey, Raymond. 2010. Contact and language shift. In *The Handbook of Language Contact*, edited by Raymond Hickey, 151–169. Oxford: Wiley-Blackwell.

Hickey, Raymond. 2013. English as a contact language in Ireland and Scotland. In *English as a Contact Language*, edited by Daniel Schreier and Marianne Hundt, 88–105. Cambridge: Cambridge University Press.

Himmelmann, Nikolaus P. 1997. *Deiktikon, Artikel, Nominalphrase: Zur Emergenz syntaktischer Struktur*. Tubingen: Niemeyer.

Himmelmann, Nikolaus. 2004. Lexicalisation and grammaticalization: Opposite or orthogonal? In *What Makes Grammaticalization? A Look from Its Fringes and Its Components*, edited by Walter Bisang, Nikolaus P. Himmelmann, and Björn Wiemer, 21–44. Berlin: Moutin de Gruyter.

Hovdhaugen, Even. 1976. Some aspects of language contact in Anatolia. *Working Papers in Linguistics from the University of Oslo* 7: 142–160.

Janda, Laura A., and Charles E. Townsend. 2000. *Czech*. München: Lincom Europa.

Johanson, Lars. 2002a. *Structural Factors in Turkic Language Contact*. Richmond, Surrey: Curzon.

Johanson, Lars. 2002b. Contact-induced change in a code-copying framework. *Language Change: The Interplay of Internal, External and Extralinguistic Factors*, edited by Mari C. Jones and Edith Esch, 285–313. Berlin: Mouton de Gruyter.

Kaiser, Georg A., and Lenka Scholze. 2009. Verbstellung im Sprachkontakt—das Obersorbische und Bündnerromanische im Kontakt mit dem Deutschen. In *Veränderung bei Pygmäen und Giganten: Festschrift für Walter Breu zu seinem 60. Geburtstag*, edited by Lenka Scholze and Björn Wiemer, 305–330. Bochum: Brockmeyer.

King, Ruth. 2000. *The Lexical Basis of Grammatical Borrowing: A Prince Edward Island French Case Study*. Amsterdam: John Benjamins.

Kubler, Cornelius C. 1985a. *The Development of Mandarin in Taiwan: A Case Study of Language Contact*. Taipei: Student Book.

Kubler, Cornelius C. 1985b. The influence of Southern Min on the Mandarin of Taiwan. *Anthropological Linguistics* 27: 156–176.

Labov, William. 1971. The notion of 'system' in creole studies. In Hymes 1971: 447–472.

Lötzsch, Ronald. 1996. Interferenzbedingte grammatische Konvergenzen und Divergenzen zwischen Sorbisch und Jiddisch. In *Sprachtypologie und Universalienforschung* 49: 50–59.

Louden, Mark. 1992. Old Order Amish verbal behavior as a reflection of cultural convergence. In *Diachronic Studies on the Language of the Anabaptists*, edited by Kate Burridge and Werner Enninger, 264–278. Bochum: Brockmeyer.

Louden, Mark, and B. Richard Page. 2005. Stable bilingualism and phonological (non) convergence in Pennsylvania German. In *ISB4: Proceedings of the 4th International Symposium on Bilingualism*, edited by Kellie Rolstad James Cohen, Kara T. McAlister, and Jeff MacSwan, 1384–1392. Somerville, MA: Cascadilla Press.

Lucas, Christopher. 2007. Jespersen's cycle in Arabic and Berber. *Transactions of the Philological Society* 105: 398–431.

Lucas, Christopher. 2012. Contact-induced grammatical change: Towards an explicit account. *Diachronica* 29: 275–300.

Lucas, Christopher, and Elliott Lash. 2010. Contact as catalyst: The case for Coptic influence in the development of Arabic negation. *Journal of Linguistics* 46: 379–413.

Marra, Antonietta, 2012. Contact phenomena in the Slavic of Molise: Some remarks about nouns and prepositional phrases. In *Morphologies in Contact*, edited by Martine Vanhove, Thomas Stolz, Aina Urdze, and Hitomi Otsuka, 265–282. Berlin: Akademie Verlag.

Matras, Yaron. 1998. Utterance modifiers and universals of grammatical borrowing. *Linguistics* 36: 281–331.

Matras, Yaron. 2000. Fusion and the cognitive basis for bilingual discourse markers. *International Journal of Bilingualism* 4: 505–528.

Matras, Yaron. 2009. *Language Contact*. Cambridge: Cambridge University Press.

Matras, Yaron, and Jeanette Sakel, eds. 2007. *Grammatical Borrowing in Cross-Linguistic Perspective*. Berlin: Mouton de Gruyter.

Matras, Yaron, and Şirin Tufan. 2007. Grammatical borrowing in Macedonian Turkish. In *Grammatical Borrowing in Cross-Linguistic Perspective*, edited by Y. Matras and J. Sakel, 215–227. Berlin: Mouton de Gruyter.

McAnallen, Julia. 2010. Developments in predicative possession in the history of Slavic. In *Diachronic Slavic Syntax: Gradual Changes in Focus*, edited by Björn Hansen and Jasmina Grković-Mejdžor, 131–142. Munich: Institut für Slavische Philologie, Universität München. (Wiener slawistischer Almanach, Sonderband 74)

McAnallen, Julia. 2011. *The History of Predicative Possession in Slavic: Internal Development vs. Language Contact*. PhD dissertation, University of California, Berkeley.

McCafferty, Kevin. 2004. Innovation in language contact: Be after V-ing as a future gram in Irish English, 1670 to the present. *Diachronica* 21: 113–160.

Mesthrie, Rajend. 1992. *English in Language Shift: The History, Structure and Sociolinguistics of South African Indian English*. Cambridge: Cambridge University Press.

Michałk, Frido. 1962. Der Einfluß des Deutschen auf die Stellung des Verbum finitum im sorbischen Satz. *Zeitschrift für Slawistik* 7: 232–262.

Migdalski, Krzysztof Marek. 2006. *The Syntax of Compound Tenses in Slavic*. PhD dissertation, Universiteit van Tilburg.

Muysken, Pieter. 2013. Language contact outcomes as the result of bilingual optimization strategies. *Bilingualism: Language and Cognition* 16: 709–730.

Nadkarni, Mangesh V. 1975. Bilingualism and syntactic change in Konkani. *Language* 51: 672–683.

Naughton, James. 2005. *Czech: An Essential Grammar*. London: Routledge.

Nomachi, Motoki, and Bernd Heine. 2011. On predicting contact-induced grammatical change: Evidence from Slavic languages. *Journal of Historical Linguistics* 1: 48–76.

Parkvall, Mikael. 2013. Motivation (or the lack thereof) in pidginization/creolization. Talk at the first Workshop on Intentional Language Change (WILC), Leiden University, September 27–28, 2013.

Pietsch, Lukas. 2008. Prepositional aspect constructions in Hiberno-English. *Language Contact and Contact Languages*, edited by Peter Siemund and Noemi Kintana, 213–236. Hamburg Studies on Multilingualism 7. Amsterdam: John Benjamins.

Prince, Ellen F. 1998. The borrowing of meaning as a cause of internal syntactic change. In *Historical linguistics 1997: Selected Papers from the 13th International Conference on Historical Linguistics, Düsseldorf, 10–17 August 1997*, edited by Monika S. Schmid, Jennifer R. Austin, and Dieter Stein, 339–362. Amsterdam: John Benjamins.

Prince, Ellen F. 2001. Yiddish as a contact language. In *Creolization and Contact*, edited by Norval Smith and Tonjes Veenstra, 263–290. Amsterdam: John Benjamins.

Raith, Joachim. 1982. *Sprachgemeinschaftstyp, Sprachkontakt, Sprachgebrauch: eine Untersuchung des Bilingualismus der anabaptistischen Gruppen deutscher Abstammung in Lancaster County, Pennsylvania*. Zeitschrift für Dialektologie und Linguistik. Beihefte 36. Wiesbaden: Franz Steiner Verlag.

Ross, Malcolm. 1996. Contact-induced change and the comparative method: Cases from Papua New Guinea. *The Comparative Method Reviewed: Regularity and Irregularity in Language Change*, edited by Mark Durie and Malcolm Ross, 180–217. New York: Oxford University Press.

Ross, Malcolm. 2001. Contact-induced change in Oceanic languages in north-west Melanesia. In *Areal Diffusion and Genetic Inheritance: Problems in Comparative Linguistics*, edited by R. M. W. Dixon and Alexandra Y. Aikhenvald, 134–166. Oxford: Oxford University Press.

Ross, Malcolm. 2003. Diagnosing prehistoric language contact. In *Motives for Language Change*, edited by Raymond Hickey, 174–198. Cambridge: Cambridge University Press.

Ross, Malcolm. 2006. Metatypy. In *Encyclopedia of Language and Linguistics*, edited by Keith Brown, Vol. 8, 95–99. 2nd edition. Oxford: Elsevier.

Ross, Malcolm. 2007. Calquing and metatypy. *Journal of Language Contact: Thema* 1: 116–143.

Ross, Malcolm. 2008. A history of metatypy in the Bel languages. *Journal of Language Contact: Thema*: 149–164.

Ross, Malcolm. 2009. Loanwords in Takia, an Oceanic language of Papua New Guinea. In *Loanwords in the World's Languages: A Comparative Handbook*, edited by Martin Haspelmath and Uri Tadmor, 747–770. Berlin: De Gruyter Mouton.

Ross, Malcolm. 2013. Diagnosing contact processes from their outcomes: The importance of life stages. *Journal of Language Contact* 6: 5–47.

Sakel, Jeanette, and Yaron Matras. 2008. Modelling contact-induced change in grammar. In *Aspects of Language Contact: New Theoretical, Methodological and Empirical Findings with Special Focus on Romancisation Processes*, edited by Thomas Stolz, Dik Bakker, and Rosa Salas Palomo, 63–87. Berlin: Mouton de Gruyter.

Sankoff, Gillian. 2002. Linguistic outcomes of language contact. In *Handbook of Language Variation and Change*, edited by Jack K. Chambers, Peter Trudgill, and N. Schilling-Estes, 638–668. Oxford: Blackwell.

Sasse, Hans-Jürgen. 1985. Sprachkontakt und Sprachwandel: die Gräzisierung deralbanischen Mundarten Griechenlands. *Papiere zur Linguistik* 32: 37–95.

Schaarschmidt, Gunter. 1984. Theme-rheme structure and the article in Sorbian. *Working Papers of the Linguistics Circle, University of Victoria (Canada)* 4: 75–90.

Schaarschmidt, Gunter. 1997. Rule convergence in language contact situations: The case of Sorbian and German. *Canadian Slavonic Papers* 39: 439.

Scholze, Lenka. 2007. *Das grammatische System der obersorbischen Umgangssprache unter besonderer Berücksichtigung des Sprachkontakts*. PhD dissertation, Universität Konstanz.

Scholze, Lenka. 2008. *Das grammatische System der obersorbischen Umgangssprache im Sprachkontakt*. Bautzen: Domowina-Verlag.

Scholze, Lenka. 2012. On the grammaticalization of the definite article in Colloquial Upper Sorbian (CUS). In *Grammatical Replication and Borrowability in Language Contact*, edited by Björn Hansen, Bernhard Wälchli, and Björn Wiemer, 323–353. Berlin: De Gruyter Mouton.

Sebba, Mark. 1998. A congruence approach to the syntax of codeswitching. *International Journal of Bilingualism* 2: 1–19.

Stone, Gerald. 1993. Sorbian (Upper and Lower). In *The Slavonic Languages*, edited by Bernard Comrie and Greville G. Corbett, 593–685. London: Routledge.

Thomason, Sarah Grey. 2001. *Language Contact: An Introduction*. Edinburgh: Edinburgh University Press.

Toops, Gary H. 1992a. Upper Sorbian prefixal derivatives and the question of German loan translations. *The Slavic and East European Journal* 36: 17–35.

Toops, Gary H. 1992b. Lexicalization of Upper Sorbian preverbs: Temporal-aspectual rami-
fications and the delimitation of German influence. *Germano-Slavica* 7: 3–22.

Toops, Gary H. 1998. On the functional status of derived imperfectives in contemporary
upper Sorbian. *The Slavic and East European Journal* 42: 283–297.

Toops, Gary H. 2001. The grammar of "paraphrastic imperfectives" in Latvian and Upper
Sorbian. *The Slavic and East European Journal* 45: 96–113.

Toops, Gary H. 2006. A contrastive perspective on several morphosyntactic features of Upper
Sorbian. *Canadian Slavonic Papers* 48: 137–155.

Tottie, Gunnel. 1991. Lexical diffusion in syntactic change: Frequency as a determinant of
linguistic conservatism in the development of negation in English. In *Lexical Diffusion in
Syntactic Change: Frequency as a Determinant of Linguistic Conservatism in the Development of Negation in English*, edited by Dieter Kastovsky, 439–467. Berlin: Mouton de
Gruyter.

Trousdale, Graeme. 2013. Multiple inheritance and constructional change. *Studies in Language* 37: 491–514.

Vallduví, Enric. 1992. *The Informational Component*. New York: Garland.

Van Bergen, Linda, and David Denison, 2003. *Corpus of Late 18th Century Prose*. University of
Manchester/Oxford Text Archive.

Wald, Benji. 1996. Substratal effects on the evolution of modals in East Los Angeles.
In *Sociolinguistic Variation: Data, Theory, and Analysis: Selected Papers from NWAV 23
at Stanford*, edited by Jennifer Arnold, Renee Blake, Brad Davidson, Scott Schwenter, and
Julie Solomon, 515–530. Stanford, CA: CSLI Publications.

Weinreich, Uriel. 1963. *Languages in Contact: Findings and Problems*. The Hague: Mouton.

CHAPTER 6

SEMANTIC BORROWING IN LANGUAGE CONTACT

BRIAN MOTT AND NATALIA J. LASO

6.1 INTRODUCTION

ALL languages take advantage of the possibility of borrowing elements from other languages to a greater or lesser degree. English is the obvious example of a language that has borrowed extensively from other languages, while Icelandic, through its isolation from the outside world, has barely borrowed at all, except in recent times, when there has been an influx from American English of both spoken and written forms. Romanian, like English, is a heavy-borrowing language—among the top five, in fact, out of a worldwide sample of forty-one languages (Tadmor 2009: 56)—having borrowed extensively from the Slavonic languages, but also French, German, Hungarian, Greek, Turkish, and Albanian. Any contact situation will inevitably lead to linguistic interference of some kind. Thus Russian has naturally left its mark on the Baltic languages: a study by Tölgyesi (2012), for example, claims that Lithuanian has acquired numerous lexical borrowings from Russian via Internet forums. For many other examples, see Grant (2015).

Borrowing may be phonological, grammatical and syntactic, morphological or lexical. In the first case, particular sounds may be imported, which happens very often if they fill a gap in the phonological system of the host language, as is the case in English of the voiced post-alveolar fricative /ʒ/, which joined the unvoiced post-alveolar fricative /ʃ/ (as in *sheep* /ʃiːp/, *fish* /fɪʃ/ and *washer* /ˈwɒʃə/) through assimilation of /z/ + /j/ intervocalically in words like *vision* /ˈvɪʒən/ and *measure* /ˈmeʒə/ in the seventeenth century (Barber 1997: 125), but was subsequently extended to initial and final position through imported French words, like *genre* /ˈʒɒ^{n}rə/, *beige* /beɪʒ/ and *camouflage* /ˈkæməflɑːʒ/ (C19–20). Another example is the marginal use in English of the unvoiced velar fricative /x/ in *loch* 'lake,' inherited from Gaelic (and ultimately Old Irish), which many speakers, however, render as /lɒk/. A good example of phonotactic accommodation can be found in Finnish, which does not permit initial clusters in native words, but allows them in foreign words, like *krokotiili* 'crocodile,' *kruunu* 'crown,' *presidentti* 'president,' and *smaragdi* 'emerald' (from Swedish *smaragd*) (Campbell 2013: 60).

Second, a particular grammatical structure may be adopted from another language variety. For example, Romanian uses finite subordinate clauses introduced by *să* instead of infinitival clauses even when the subject of the main clause and the subordinate clause is identical (*Vreau să învaț română* 'I want to learn Romanian'; cf. Serbian, *Hoću da učim srpski* 'I want to learn Serbian'), a structure generally attributed to the merger of the infinitive and subjunctive in Greek (cf. Greek *Thelo na matho Ellinika* 'I want to learn Greek'), subsequently spreading across the Balkan Peninsula (Schulte 2009: 249). Or a syntactic order may gain in popularity, like the adjective + noun order of English used in certain Catalan expressions, such as *Catalunya exprés* 'Catalan express train' and *boixos nois*, literally 'boxwood boys,' but generally mistranslated as 'mad boys' (in which case the adjective would be spelled *bojos*), referring to a group of extremists who support Barcelona Football Club. Note also that the Catalan savings bank *Caixa Catalunya* became *CatalunyaCaixa* several years ago, before merging with BBVA in 2016. This same patterning is reflected once again in Spanish *ciencia ficción* and *cineclub*, probably based on English *science fiction* and *film society*, respectively, though the Spanish versions could also be interpreted as two juxtaposed nouns in a coordinative relationship, rather than noun + noun sequences with the first noun adopting an adjectival function. On the morphological level, we might also mention the rise of the Anglo-Saxon genitive in Spanish names, like *Pepe's Bar* or *Pepes Bar*, and the increasing use of *-ing* forms in Spanish, such as *balconing* 'jumping from a hotel balcony into a swimming-pool,' *puenting* 'bungee-jumping,' *Vueling*® (Mott 2015a: 180) (see also subsection 6.2.2.1.2).

Examples of lexical borrowing, that is, the transfer of a name for a concept from a donor language to a host language, are fairly numerous and can be subcategorized as in Figure 6.1.

6.2 CONTACT PHENOMENA

6.2.1 Loan Creations

We will exemplify loan creations first, as they are a category apart. As can be seen from Figure 6.1, the distinction made by Betz (1949) between *Lehnwort* (loanword) and *Lehnprägung* (loan coinage or creation) still holds good and is basic to current descriptions of loan phenomena (Winford 2003: 42).

A loan creation is a new coinage fabricated out of donor materials; in other words, the receiving language takes certain borrowed elements and puts them together to

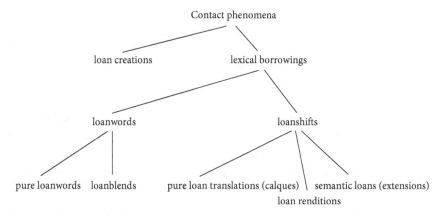

FIGURE 6.1 Contact relations in tree form.

Source: Based on data from Winford 2003, 42–46 (in turn based on Haugen 1950a, 1950b, 1953).

produce a novel expression. Japanese provides good examples of this sort of invention: *wan-man-ka* 'bus without a conductor' from English *one+man+car* (Winford 2003: 42); *goo-sutoppu* 'traffic lights,' with innovative compounding of English *go + stop* (Winford 2003: 33).

6.2.2 Lexical Borrowings

6.2.2.1 *Loanwords*

Words that are borrowed from the donor language into the host language can be grouped into two kinds: (a) those that are adopted wholesale, with minimal changes in pronunciation and morphology (**pure loanwords**), and (b) those that are adopted only partially (**loanblends**).

6.2.2.1.1 PURE LOANWORDS

When pure loanwords are adopted, no conscious effort is made to adapt them to the phonology or morphology of the receiving language. Thus Modern English *wine* is an early borrowing of Latin vīnum into Old English at a date when <v> was still pronounced as /w/ in Latin, whereas *vine*, acquired from Old French, shows the later pronunciation shift in Latin of /w/ to /v/. However, certain adjustments in pronunciation will be inevitable, so that such forms as German *Kindergarten* and Spanish *macho* have been given a pronunciation more attuned to the phonetics of English. The final <o> of *macho*, for example, will be diphthongized in southern British accents, which do not have short vowels in word-final open syllables. In the case of French *rendezvous*, few English speakers will use a uvular fricative for the first segment and nasalize the first vowel properly, even though they will omit the final consonant of this word, just as they will drop that of *gourmet*, as is the norm in French. French *restaurant* may be given a nasalized final syllable and be pronounced with a quasi-French accent. But words like this often acquire a nativized pronunciation and are then fully integrated into the new system and eventually are no longer considered as loans. This is the case for the many speakers of English who pronounce *restaurant* as /ˈrestrɒnt/ or /ˈrestrənt/ instead of /ˈrestrɒ̃/. It is also true of Italian *firma* 'signature,' which was borrowed into commercial vocabulary in early English as *firm* and by a process of metonymy came to mean 'the whole enterprise represented by that signature.' The word no longer looks foreign in Modern English, perhaps partly due to its coexistence with the adjective *firm*, to which it is ultimately related (Sihler 2000: 125).

Adaptation to native phonology can in fact render the original form totally opaque; witness the Spanish football term *orsay* < English *offside*, in which the Spanish aversion to obstruents and preference for nasals and liquids in syllable codas, or no coda consonant, can be clearly seen.

6.2.2.1.2 LOANBLENDS

Loanblends involve the borrowing of only a part of a lexical item, so a loanblend is a word containing mixed morphology (i.e., a mixture of native and imported morphemes). Thus, Pennsylvanian German has *esix-jug*, from German *Essig* 'vinegar' + English *jug* (Winford 2003: 43). Likewise, while many -*ing* forms in Spanish are direct borrowings from English with no morphological change (e.g., *catering, ranking*), there are examples of inventions with a Spanish stem + the bound inflectional morpheme -*ing*, like *balconing* (< *balcón* 'balcony,' *puenting* < *puente* 'bridge,' and *Vueling*® (< *vuelo* 'flight') (see section 6.1).

Recent incorporations into Spanish of lexical items from the semantic field of new technologies also illustrate morphological adaptation. English terms like *google* and *blog* (< *web log* 'a kind of online diary') have undergone a process of derivational affixation by having the Spanish verbal suffix -*ear* attached to them, and have given rise to new verb forms, such as *googlear* 'to search the Internet using the Google search engine' and *bloguear* 'to write a post for a blog.'

6.2.2.2 *Loanshifts*

Loanshifts are the result of another type of lexical borrowing, which, broadly speaking, consists of extending a word's meaning to accommodate a new concept or sense acquired from a donor language. Loan shifts have also been referred to in the literature (e.g., Smith 1989: 125; Matras 2009: 31) as semantic extension.

6.2.2.2.1 PURE LOAN TRANSLATIONS (CALQUES)

Loanshifts imply that new meaning is amalgamated with preexisting native morphology. Obvious examples of this are **pure loan translations** or **calques**, such as English *honeymoon*, rendered in Spanish as *luna de miel*, Portuguese as *lua de mel*, French as *lune de miel*, Italian as *luna di miele*, and in Romanian as *lună de miere* (see also section 6.2.2.2.2). Spanish also has *rascacielos*, with morphemic reordering of the English elements in *skyscraper*. Similarly, Spanish *guerra fría* is based on English *cold war*, and *ataque al corazón* (sometimes *ataque de corazón*) 'heart attack' is often found instead of *infarto*. *Glass ceiling* is rendered in Spanish by the *Gran Diccionario Oxford* (2003) as *techo de cristal*, *tope*, but, somewhat more cautiously, *Larousse* (2004) gives *barreras laborales o profesionales*, and *Collins* (2009) gives *barrera, tope invisible*. At the pragmatic level, we have translations of English formulae like *Don't hesitate to contact us*, rendered in German as *Zögern Sie nicht uns zu kontaktieren* (see also section 6.2.2.5).

English *power politics* owes its existence to German *Machtpolitik*. Conversely, German *Wochenende* and *Kettenraucher* are modeled on English *weekend* and *chain smoker*, respectively. German *Umwelt* (*Um-welt* 'around world,' i.e., 'world around us') was coined to render French *milieu* (*mi-lieu* 'mid-place') 'environment'; French *presqu'île* (*presque* 'almost' + *île* 'island') was calqued from Latin PAEN-INSULA 'peninsula' (Haspelmath 2009: 39–40); Old English *godspell* / *gōdspel* 'gospel,' composed of *gōd* 'good' + *spell* / *spel* 'message,' is probably a translation of Latin BONA ADNUNTIĀTIO, itself a translation of Greek *euangélion* 'evangel' (Barnhart and Steinmetz 1988: 443). In the same class of loan, Romanian has *sfârşit de săptămână*, *universitate deschisă*, and *navă spaţială*, based on English *weekend, open university*, and *spaceship*, respectively. And perhaps Lithuanian *apsieiti be* is modeled on Russian *obojtis bez* 'to do without' (according to Ian Press, personal communication).

The type of loanshifts we have described are particularly common in German. Instead of adopting the Greek morphemes for 'acid' and 'material,' as English did in *oxygen*, German translated them as *Sauerstoff* (*sauer* 'sour, sharp, acid' + *Stoff* 'substance'); similarly, *Wasserstoff* (*Wasser* = 'water') for 'hydrogen' and *Fernsprecher* (*fern* 'distant, far away' + *Sprecher* 'speaker') for 'television,' and so on (Lehmann 1992: 264). The Yiddish compound *mitkind* (*mit* 'with' + *kind* 'child') 'fellow child' is calqued on English *sibling*, German *Geschwister*, and the like (Winford 2003: 44, from Weinreich 1953: 51).

Vendryès (1979: 237) speaks of "creación de palabras por imitación" (imitative creation of words), whereby languages express a concept through the same metaphor (though see the first paragraph of section 6.2.2.2.4 and the reference to Coseriu). For example, the word for 'weasel' (*Mustela*) in various languages is based on a stem meaning 'pretty,' no doubt a term of appeasement for a fearsome animal: French *belette*, German *Schöntierle* (standard *Wiesel*), Breton *kaerell*, Basque *andereder* (literally 'pretty woman' < *andere* 'woman' + *eder* 'pretty').

6.2.2.2.2 LOAN RENDITIONS

If **calques** in general are a kind of halfway house between straightforward adoption of a foreign word and the borrowing of meaning (see section 6.2.2.2.3), **loan renditions** are a more dynamic and imaginative kind of calque in which the translation of the foreign word is less than literal. Such is the case of German *Wolkenkratzer*, literally 'cloud-scraper,' as an adaptation of English *skyscraper* (cf. the French calque *gratte-ciel*), and

Catalan *cap de setmana* 'weekend' perhaps fits this category, too, since the basic meaning of *cap* < CAPUT is 'head', and *fi* < FĪNE might have provided a more literal rendering of *end*. For 'honeymoon,' Hungarian has *mézeshetek* 'honey weeks' and Welsh uses *mis mêl* 'honey month,' like Russian *medóvij més'ats*, Ukrainian *medóvij mís'ats*, Polish *miodówy miésąc*, Lithuanian *medaus mėnuo*, and Hebrew *yeraj dvash* (the first element in Hebrew means both 'moon' and 'month'). The first reference in English is not to a period of one month at all, but an ironic allusion to sweet affection dwindling, like the waning moon (Barnhart and Steinmetz 1988: 489).

One might well ask why the Germans invented *Wolkenkratzer* for 'skyscraper' instead of using the more literal calque **Himmelkratzer*. The fact is that, as German does not make a distinction between the concepts of 'heaven' and 'sky,' then the latter choice might have been interpreted as 'heaven scraper,' thus invoking unfortunate associations with the Tower of Babel (Hock and Joseph 1996: 265).

6.2.2.2.3 SEMANTIC LOANS (EXTENSIONS, SEMANTIC CALQUES)

In semantic borrowing, a foreign concept is borrowed without its corresponding linguistic form, and a native word accommodates the meaning. The standard example might be considered to be Polish and Czech *zamek*, meaning initially 'lock,' but subsequently also 'castle' through the influence of German *Schloss*, which has both meanings. This is presumably a clear-cut case of polysemy in German deriving from metonymic extension of the 'lock' meaning to the sense 'place which can be locked up,' though Ullmann (1972: 180) treats it as homonymy. Russian distinguishes the two meanings through contrastive word stress: *zámok* 'castle' versus *zamók* 'lock.' Russian itself has left its mark on other languages, like the Baltic language Lithuanian, which may have added the meaning 'satellite' to its existing word *palydovas* 'fellow traveler' through influence of Russian *sputnik* 'traveling companion, satellite' (I thank Ian Press for this information).

Sala (1988: 172ff.) recognizes three scenarios related to the borrowing of meaning. First of all, a new sense usually coexists with the old, as in the case of Romanian *verde*, which has the meaning 'green,' but also 'bold, robust' from Old Slavonic *zelenŭ*, with both meanings. This is also the case of Romanian *vână*, which denotes both 'vein' and 'nerve' through Slavonic influence (Bulgarian, Serbian, and Croatian *žila* means both).

Judaeo-Spanish *ora*, like Romanian *ceas*, means both 'hour' and 'clock,' perhaps through influence of Turkish *saat* with the same meanings (Wagner 1954: 269–281), while Romanian *carte* 'book' has calqued other meanings from French, like 'business card' and 'postcard' (Sala 1988: 174).

Hock (1986: 398) furnishes us with examples of a subtler sort of semantic borrowing in which a deep, drastic cultural change in a society has a long-lasting impact on the existing vocabulary. With the introduction of Christianity to England, older Germanic religious terms extended their range of meaning, so that Old English *heofon* 'sky, abode of the gods and warriors fallen in battle,' *hel* 'abode of the dead who have not fallen in battle (below the earth),' and *god* 'heathen god' all extended their meanings to embrace the concepts of 'Christian heaven,' 'abode of all the dead (below the earth),' and

'Christian god,' respectively, through influence of the Latin terms CAELUM, INFERNUS, and DEUS.

There are many other instances of outside influence on Old English. Very frequently, cognates or apparent cognates transfer meanings. For example, *drēam*, which meant 'joy' in Old English, acquired its modern sense from Old Norse *draumr*; *eorl* 'warrior, noble,' later *earl*, came to be applied to a particular rank through Old Norse *jarl*; *dwellan* 'to lead/go astray, linger' takes on the meaning 'to live' from Old Norse *dvelja*, and *brēad* 'morsel' has its modern meaning from Old Norse *brauð* (Waldron 1967: 125; Burnley 1992: 491; Kastovsky 1992: 491; Lehmann 1992: 264). By the twelfth century, Old English *rīce* 'powerful' had begun to take on the sense of French *riche*, and it seems likely that, in the case of Old English *blǣw*, which meant 'blue' or 'hue,' French *bleu* reinforced the 'blue' sense (Burnley 1992: 490; Kastovsky 1992: 490).

After the Old English period, semantic loans rose in English through the influence of French and, in the Renaissance, Latin. Waldron (1967: 125–128) gives several interesting accounts of English words making additions to their acceptations, among which is *chew*, whose sense 'ruminate' may have been an imitation of Latin RŪMINĀRE 'to chew the cud, ruminate.' A relatively recent semantic borrowing from French is the use of *arrive* in the sense of 'attain success'; *to intrigue* meaning 'to interest' also comes into this category (and the older *intrigue* meaning 'to plot' is also a Gallicism).

In the nineteenth century, German exerted its influence in the sphere of philology, so that words such as *fracture*, *mutation*, and *gradation* owe their linguistic senses to German *Brechung*, *Umlaut*, and *Ablaut*, respectively (Waldron 1967: 127), and there is little need to emphasize the legacy of German in the field of psychoanalysis through the influence of Freud and Jung.

However, newly acquired senses may be lost (Sala 1988: 175): Romanian *lemn* 'wood' acquired the additional sense of 'tree' from Old Slavonic *drěvo*, but no longer retains this older acceptation. Similarly, Romanian *limbă* 'language' once meant 'people,' too, through influence of Old Slavonic *jezykŭ*, which had the two senses.

In the second scenario described by Sala, the primary sense of a word is lost or eclipsed. For example, Modern Romanian *vită* 'cattle, beast' < VĪTA 'life' now only has the meaning 'animal, ox, cow,' which it probably acquired from Slavonic *životŭ* 'animal, life.' The lost meaning 'life' is now expressed through *viață* (Rosetti 1978: 326; Sala 1988: 174) (< *VIVITIA < VIVUS 'live, alive, living' [*DEX* 1975]). Similarly, Romanian *lume* 'people' < LŪMEN once meant only 'light,' a meaning now invested in the word *lumină*, originally the plural of Latin LŪMEN. Then it came under the influence of Old Slavonic *světŭ* 'light, world, people,' took on the additional meanings, and lost its original reference (Rosetti 1978: 325; Sala 1988: 174). This is probably also true of Hungarian *világ*, which added the 'world' meaning to the original one, 'light' (Ullmann 1962: 180). The sense 'light' is now expressed in Hungarian through *világos*.

Sometimes, meanings may be "shared out" among words in the same semasiological field. Thus Southern Slavonic (Bulgarian, Macedonian, Serbian, and Croatian) merges 'time' and 'weather' in one lexical unit, but Romanian has two words, *timp* (< Latin TEMPUS) and *vreme* (< Slavic *vrěmen*). These two words were both used to express the two different concepts, but at some stage *vreme* increasingly took on the 'weather' meaning (Schulte 2009: 244), though it is still used to mean 'period, epoch': *pe vremea lui Ceauşescu* 'in Ceauşescu's time.' In Modern Romanian, *lună* means both 'moon' and 'month,' the second sense having been taken from Southern Slavonic, but Arumanian and Megleno-Romanian still preserve the original distinction between LUNA and *mes* < MENSE (Sala 1988: 186).

The third scenario that Sala (1988: 175) refers to is the very common one in which a foreign word is formally similar to one already existing in a language, so that it may spread its meaning(s) to the host language. For instance, English *engine* influenced Brazilian Portuguese *engenho* 'ingenuity,' so that it came to mean 'locomotive' as well (Weinreich 1968: 667). In recent times in Spain, Spanish *relevante* has adopted the meaning of English *relevant* (i.e., 'directly related to the matter in hand'), traditionally Spanish *pertinente, que viene al caso*, though *DRAE* (2001) still does not record this sense, clinging stubbornly to the acceptations 'outstanding, important' and, among the principal bilingual Spanish-English dictionaries we have consulted for this chapter, it seems that only Collins (2009) gives it any credence.

English, of course, has influenced many genealogically related languages with words like *realize* and *introduce* (Sala 1988: 175). The meaning 'understand' has been transferred, for example, to Italian *realizzare* and German *realisieren* 'carry out,' a meaning traditionally conveyed in Italian by *accorgersi* and in German by *erkennen*. This is also true of French *réaliser*, though it is strongly resisted by purists (Ullmann 1972: 171). As for *introduce*, it has bequeathed the meaning 'acquaint two or more people with each other' to Canadian French *introduire*, Brazilian Portuguese *introduzir*, Italian *introdurre*, and Latin American Spanish *introducir*.

A comparison of *DRAE* (1992) and *DRAE* (2001) brings to light many other examples of the influence of English on Spanish as far as the borrowing of meaning is concerned and provides us with a rough idea of when additional meanings were considered to be of sufficient currency to merit inclusion in works of reference. One such, found in *DRAE* (2001), is the use in computer language of the meaning 'program' for *aplicación*, also recorded in Moliner (1998), and, of course, the metaphorical use of *mouse* as a device for moving the cursor on a computer screen must have been diffused to most languages, which acquired the term either in its original form as a bona fide loanword (e.g., Italian/Romanian *mouse* [cf. *topo* and *şoarece*, respectively, for the rodent]) or as a semantic loan added to the existing word for the animal mouse (Spanish *ratón*, Catalan *ratolí*, French *souris*, Serbian *miš*, etc.). Likewise, *DRAE* (2001) adds to *evidencia* the meaning 'prueba determinante en un proceso' ('decisive piece of evidence in a trial'), also transferred to Italian *evidenza* (Furiassi 2010: 58, note 64), a sense corroborated but criticized in Seco (1987: 191) as an Anglicism of improper use, and gives *emergencia*, traditionally 'act of emerging,' the additional meaning of English *emergency*.

Such "contaminated" forms abound in newspapers and news broadcasts, where the text reproduced may in fact be a translation of an English version composed by an agency (see also section 6.2.2.2.4). Thus we find Spanish *asumir*, usually meaning 'take on,' with the added meaning 'suppose' (like Italian *assumere* [Furiassi 2010: 58, note 64]), and *admitir*, usually meaning 'allow in,' with the additional meaning of English *admit* 'confess' in the following examples:

Indonesia asume que el avión de la AirAsia está "en el fondo del mar". *(El Periódico,* December 30, 2014) (Indonesia assumes that the AirAsia plane is on the seabed)

El gobierno francés admite deficiencias en seguridad. *(El Periódico,* January 11, 2015) (The French government admits to loopholes in security)

Surely, there is no implication in this last example that the French government is willing to accept flaws in its system of security.

In *DRAE* (1992) one finds *colapso* with the principal medical sense in first place; in *DRAE* (2001) this has been relegated to fourth place. The sense that currently seems to be taken as primary in dictionaries is 'destruction of a system' or that of 'financial collapse.'

A particularly good source of Anglicisms in Spanish, with detailed discussion of them in some cases, is a series of collections of articles by Ramón Carnicer (1969, 1972, 1977, 1983), which were originally published in *La Vanguardia.* Carnicer (1969: 25–70) comments on semantic influence from the English cognates of the Spanish words *discutir, interesar, impacto, honesto, responsable* (now used as a noun as well as an adjective), and *establecer* (English *discuss, interest, impact, honest, responsible,* and *establish*) (for more examples, see section 6.2.2.2.4). *Interesar* shows the influence of English syntax on Spanish semantics, so that a structure like *Las damas se interesan por la costura* is now used as an equivalent of *A las damas les interesa la costura* ([The] ladies are interested in sewing), and *Fulano está interesado en esto* is now used as an alternative to *A Fulano le interesa esto* or *Fulano tiene interés en esto* (So-and-so is interested in this). The pronominal verb form *interesarse por* is traditionally used in Spanish to mean 'to ask after somebody' (Carnicer 1969: 55).

Carnicer (1972: 34–36) claims that *oportunidad* is now being used where *ocasión* was more usual through influence of English *opportunity, funeral* has broadened its semantic range in Spanish, and *tópico* through pressure from English *topic* now shares the meaning of *tema* or *asunto*; *deteriorado* is no longer used only in the physical sense but is also applied to relationships, like English *deteriorated* (Spanish *agriarse, enfriarse, malearse*) (Carnicer 1972: 118), and *educación* now has the sense of English *education* (Spanish *cultura*) (Carnicer 1972: 124–126) and is used in many expressions like *educación sexual* 'sexual education.' There have also been shifts in the meaning of Spanish *romance, balance* (*balance del poder* < English *balance of power*), *memorial,* and *individual,* due to their English counterparts, and *entrenar* can now be used intransitively, like English *to train* (Carnicer 1972: 232–235).

Carnicer (1977: 201–204) devotes some space to the recent proliferation of the verb *contemplar* in Spanish, which the author sees as originating in English *to contemplate* with the meaning 'to consider' (e.g., *contemplate suicide/resigning,* etc.), which is the second sense given in Alfaro's *Diccionario de anglicismos* (1970). He also discusses a few of the numerous Mexican Spanish words that show the impact of American English, such as *ordenar* 'order food' < AmE *to order* (Spanish *pedir*) (Carnicer 1977: 111–112).

Carnicer (1983) returns to words dealt with in previous volumes (*asumir* [63], *honesto* [91], *responsible* [111]), but also looks at others, such as *década* 'series or group of ten' (109), now with the meaning of English *decade* (Spanish *decenio*).

Naturally, many of these English semantic loans are also to be found in other European languages, apart from Spanish, with similar transparent cognates. Some meanings are propagated extensively, both within Europe and beyond. We have already mentioned one or two items from computer technology. Pulcini, Furiassi, and Rodríguez González (2012: 8) offer other examples of meanings added to existing words, like Danish *åbning* 'opening,' now also 'opportunity'; French *papillon* 'butterfly,' now also 'swimming style'; Italian *rovescio* 'backhand,' now also 'tennis shot'; Norwegian *het* 'hot,' now also 'trendy'; Swedish *huvudvärk* 'headache,' now also 'problem,' and so on.

One very widespread example is the extended use of words meaning 'star, heavenly body' to refer to famous entertainers or film stars: Spanish *estrella (de cine)*, Portuguese *estrela (de cinema)*, Romanian *stea (de cinema) / star*, Croatian *(filmska) zvjezda*, Icelandic *(mydin) stjörnu*, Norwegian *(film)stjerne*, Dutch *(film)ster*, Russian *(kino) zvezdá*, Ukrainian *(kino)zirká*, Czech *(filmová) hvězda*, Polish *gwiazda (filmova)*, Lithuanian *(kino) žvaigžde*, Hebrew *kojav kolnoa* (the first element by itself only means 'star in the sky'), and Vietnamese *(ngôi) sao (màn bạc)*.

It is not just lexical words, notably nouns, that can extend their range of application, but also grammatical words and morphemes. One such case in Spanish is the use of the adverbs *solamente* and *únicamente* to express reservation, just like English *only* meaning 'but': *Únicamente, de momento se pospone* 'Only, for the moment, it's postponed' (Spanish TV, December 29, 2014). Nevalainen (1992: 383–384) explains how *sub-*, increasingly used as a nominal prefix with personal nouns in sixteenth- and seventeenth-century English (*sub-agent*, *sub-commissioner*), extended its application to non-personal nouns (*subsection*, *subspecies*) and, after 1600, was added to adjectives, like *subspinal* and *submarine*, while *super-* shifted from exclusively locative contexts (*superimposition*, *superstructure*) to take on an intensifying function, as in *superserviceable* and *supersensual*. These additional meanings were presumably borrowed from uses of the prefixes in Latin.

Verbs, too, can have their semantic specifications modified by contact-induced change. For instance, in some Siberian Turkic languages, such as Khakas, the verb 'to fear' does not take the genitive case as it does in other Turkic languages, but the dative, as with Russian *bojat'sja* 'to fear' (Anderson 2005: 179).

Polysemy from sense borrowing arises any time a language comes under the influence of another. Chaucer resorts to the loanwords *declination* and *hemisphere* only as astronomical terms, while a number of their modern senses do not appear until the sixteenth century, although, admittedly, such developments could have taken place language-internally (Nevalainen 1992: 362).

6.2.2.2.4 CAUSES OF SEMANTIC BORROWING

We begin this section with a caveat: languages very often display similar polysemy. For example, English *taste*, French *goût*, Spanish / Italian *gusto*, and German *Geschmack* all display a similar range of meanings, which include 'flavor,' 'aesthetic sense or taste,' 'judgment,' and 'decorum,' but there is no evidence for all of these senses being calqued among these languages. Hope (1971: 644) says that Italian *gusto* and German *Geschmack* apparently acquired the meaning 'aesthetic taste' from French *goût* in the early eighteenth century, and the metaphor may ultimately be a Hispanicism in French, but in many such cases we are dealing with the consequences of parallel linguistic development, a product of human cognition, as is the case of analogous, collateral metaphor.

Metaphors may be borrowed, like English *wave of violence* > Spanish *ola de violencia*, but by and large, if they are the same in different languages, this may be simply because they result from the same way of visualizing the world. Ullmann (1972: 225) remarks that "[i]n many languages, for example, verbs meaning 'to catch' or 'to grasp' are used figuratively in the sense of 'to understand': English *catch*, *grasp*; French *comprendre* (from *prendre* 'to take'), *saisir*; Italian *capire*, from Latin CAPERE 'to catch'; German *begreifen*, from *greifen* 'to grasp'; and there are similar forms in Russian, Finnish, Hungarian and Turkish." There may have been some degree of interlingual interference in such cases, but it is not necessarily so. Unrelated, geographically separated languages that have had little or no mutual contact have been found to generate the same metaphors (Ullmann 1972: 226). The English metaphor *eye of a needle* has exact parallels in Eskimo and Chuvash, a Turkic language spoken in Russia. In more than thirty languages belonging to diverse groups, the apple of the eye is called 'little girl' or, more rarely, 'little boy.' And examples can be found for metonymy, too: the word for the organ that we call *tongue* in English also denotes 'language' in many languages. On the subject of the polygenesis of metaphor, Coseriu (1961: 17–18) showed that a number of semantic developments in Spanish attributed to Arabic, like *ojo de manantial* 'spring of water,' have also been found in other Romance languages.

The most obvious trigger for semantic borrowing in many cases must be formal similarity of cognates. Thus in a contact situation such as that involving second-language acquisition where two or more genealogically related languages are involved, one can expect interference among words of similar form, even though many false friends exist (e.g., Spanish *corpulento* 'well-built,' but English *corpulent* 'fat'; for further details, see section 6.2.2.3.

In an article entitled "Anglicismos," Ramón Carnicer (1969: 205–209), while recognizing a reluctance toward the overuse of foreign words in the Spanish of his time, admits to extensive semantic borrowing in many Spanish words, which he attributes to automatic translations of books, film dubbing, and international news from agencies and correspondents who use words of Latin origin. The English words he examines are *assume*, *serious* and *severe*, *generous*, *informal* and *experience*, all of which have appended senses to Spanish *asumir*, *serio* and *severo*, *generoso*, *informal* and *experiencia*, respectively.

Apart from the role of the media in the diffusion of meanings alien to native words, we must also bear in mind the part played by immigration. Manoliu (1994: 105–107) reports on the "American Romanian" spoken by Romanian immigrants in North America. For example, *comoditate* means 'comfortableness' or 'indolence,' but has adopted the meaning of English *commodity*; *a sucede* means 'to follow (succeed)', but is also used to express the commoner meaning of English *to succeed*, 'to be successful.'

The long-standing contact between Greek and Roman culture brought about significant influence of Greek vocabulary on Latin forms (Sihler 2000: 129). Very often, Latin words acquired additional meanings from Greek words in the same field, not least in the area of traditional grammar, since the Roman grammars largely derived from their Greek predecessors. Thus Latin CĀSUS 'fall' (supine of the verb CADERE) took on the meaning 'grammatical case' from Greek *ptôsis*, which had both senses (since oblique cases, like the accusative and genitive, represent a "falling away" from the nominative). The Romans also took to using the word MUNDUS 'world, universe' in the sense of 'facial make-up, ladies' toilet,' as Greek *kósmos*, basically 'order, arrangement,' was used to refer both to the physical universe (i.e., the natural order of things) and by extension to ornamentation (i.e., anything added to this natural order). Another similar example is provided by Latin NĀVIS, meaning 'ship' but also 'temple' (homonymy in pre-Greek times; for the full story, see Sihler 2000: 131). Eventually the meaning 'nave' was grafted onto German *Schiff* 'ship' and Hungarian *(templom) hajója* '(church) ship' (Sihler 2000: 129–130).

As regards the type of loans produced depending on the relative status of the language varieties involved, it can be said that adstratal relationships (e.g., English and Norse in early England) are most conducive to the borrowing of everyday and basic vocabulary. If the donor language is a superstratum (e.g., Norman French influence on Anglo-Saxon), then the loans and their connotations tend to be of a more prestigious type. If the donor language is a substratum, loans tend to be limited to cases of necessity (such as new place names) and to have derogatory connotations (Hock and Joseph 1996: 274). For example, the low prestige of the Celts in Anglo-Saxon times must be the reason why very few Celtic words were borrowed into Anglo-Saxon. In fact, many of the place names appear to have come into Anglo-Saxon in Latinized form, reflecting the greater prestige of the earlier Roman culture (Hock and Joseph 1996: 272). Probably, the Celts took CASTRA 'military camp' into their language and passed it on to the Anglo-Saxons. Place names with the element *caster, cester, chester* abound in England (e.g., *Doncaster*, on the River Don; *Gloucester*, in which the first element is Celtic and means 'bright'; *Colchester*, on the River Colne).

6.2.2.3 *Influence of L1 in Second-Language Acquisition*

That L1 influences L2 in second-language acquisition has been recognized for a very long time. Weinreich (1953) referred to this influence as "interference," a term more or less equivalent in Weinreich's usage to the present-day concept of "transfer." In any case, when L2 learners retain features of the L1 to compensate for their lack of knowledge of the target language (TL), one can expect such phenomena to be eventually ironed out and replaced by more covert, less obvious "mistakes" derived from the semantics of similar L1 forms. Nemser (1991: 352–353) found that beginner and intermediate German-speaking Austrian students of English used the word *brills* for English *glasses* (German *Brille*). More advanced students conferred the meaning 'thin' on *meager* (German *mager*) and 'valid' on *guilty* (German *gültig*). Many similar pairs of false friends can be obtained by comparing French and English lexis: French *demander* 'to ask' versus English *demand*, French *ignorer* 'not to know' versus English *ignore*. This so-called negative transfer can occur in either direction. For Spanish, note the examples from Carnicer discussed earlier.

Sometimes the learner assumes complete overlap between the meanings of the L1 and L2 words. For instance, German speakers may use *carry* in the sense of 'wear (clothes)' through the influence of *tragen*, which has both meanings. Spanish speakers do the same with *llevar*: *Farmer Jones is wearing cabbages, carrots, and onions* makes it sound as if he is dressed in some kind of carnival attire, rather than transporting vegetables from one place to another.

The kind of semantic transfer we have here is similar to the process of borrowing, except that the direction of the change is the opposite (i.e., the new meaning is temporarily imposed on the TL term).

6.2.2.4 *Influence of the Standard Language on Dialect*

As dialects often share a great deal of the lexis of the standard languages with which they coexist, or the two varieties possess very similar forms, there will naturally be numerous occasions on which the standard transfers meanings to dialect forms, and sometimes vice versa. Einar Haugen (1950b: 220) makes the important point that lexical congruence may actually make it almost impossible to detect any kind of borrowing at all.

It is sometimes the case that speakers of a dialect are not simultaneously speakers of the standard through isolation or lack of educational opportunity, but, even then, as the standard gradually encroaches on the dialect, thus leading to eventual death of the local speech variety, dialectalisms will approximate more to the standard in phonology, morphology, and meaning, and may over time fall into disuse and disappear.

Several centuries of contact between Aragonese and Castilian, together with the circumstance of their having a common origin, have created a common lexical hoard: *saber* 'to know,' *vaca* 'cow,' *zapato* 'shoe,' *coche* 'car,' *edificio* 'building,' and *rincón* 'corner' are all words known to both Castilian and Aragonese speakers. Meanwhile, *hablar* 'to talk,' *gente* 'people,' *hermano* 'brother,' and *ajo* 'garlic' are borrowings from Castilian that are now part of the core vocabulary of some Aragonese varieties, like the recessive Chistabino dialect, spoken in Gistaín (Huesca, Spain), older dialectal terms having been displaced by these (Mott 2015b: 5).

As for semantic borrowing, Castilian acceptations are bound to be added to formally identical or similar expressions. In present-day Chistabino, *aprés* (< *a exprés*) 'conveniently' is sometimes used with the meaning 'on purpose' through influence of the Spanish adverb *expresamente*, which has this meaning. Similarly, Chistabino *a veces* 'by chance' has naturally added the Castilian meaning 'sometimes' to this phrase (Mott 2015b: 45, 166).

Another consequence of contact between a dialect and the standard is that, rather than meanings from the lexis of the standard being grafted onto dialectal words (which may or may not be cognates with similar morphological structure), two or more different word forms may come to exist side by side with different functions. In Gistaín, *lixiva* < (AQUA) LIXĪVA means 'mixture of water and ashes formerly used to wash clothes,' but Castilian *lejía* is the bleach that you now buy in plastic bottles; *sarra* < SERRA means 'saw,' but Castilian *sierra* is used in Chistabino for 'mountain range' (Mott 2015: 2, 5).

6.2.2.5 *Pragmatic Borrowing*

Most research on linguistic borrowing is predominantly concerned with lexis. However, the notion of pragmatic borrowing—that is, the transfer of discourse and pragmatic features from a source language to a recipient language—is also intimately bound up with semantic borrowing and is therefore worth exploring, too. The globalization of Anglo-American culture has exerted numerous influences on the languages of the world. Such is the case of the farewell wish *Have a nice day!*, which has its roots in the United States, but has now transferred its illocutionary force to syntactically similar phrases in other languages, for example, German *Haben Sie noch einen schönen Tag!* and Danish *Kan du have en god dag!* Likewise, it has become common to end phone calls to close friends and relatives in English with *Love you*, and this expression of a routine goodbye has now been implanted on parallel utterances in other languages, such as German *Ich liebe dich* or *Ich hab' dich Lieb* and Danish *Jeg elsker dig*.

Certain English uses of *please* and *thank you* as politeness markers have been transferred to other languages, not least Spanish, which traditionally did not use the equivalents of these English words, *por favor* and *gracias*, to make routine requests and acknowledge everyday acts of service. *Póngame una cerveza* has always meant 'Could I have a beer, please?' while *Póngame una cerveza, por favor* can make the service sound like a special favor, although it is increasingly becoming common as a hedging device, as in English, that mitigates the illocutionary force of what the speaker is requesting in directives of this kind.

Agustín Llach (2006: 97) comments on an increasing use of *por favor* in Spanish when handing something to someone, which she assumes has been transferred from German *bitte*. But it should be mentioned that other languages have equivalent expressions, though not necessarily with their everyday words for 'please': Italian performs the same act with *prego* (cf. *per favore*) and Romanian uses *poftiți* (cf. *vă rog / te rog*).

Such pragmatic uses of phrases are hard to distinguish from **loan translations** or **calques** (see section 6.2.2.2). For example, Serbian *Da li mogu da vam pomognem?* would appear to be a calque of the English expression *Can I help you?* as used in service, though its prior existence as an offer of help outside business transactions is undeniable. So are we dealing with a translation of the English expression or a transposition of meaning onto an already existing expression in Serbian, which has now acquired the pragmatic force of traditional *Izvolite?* Similar examples, culled from a talk given by Biljana Mišić Ilić at the European Society for the Study of English (ESSE) Conference in Košice in 2014 for the pragmatic borrowing panel, are *Ne želiš* *da znaš* with the force of English *You don't want to know* (said when you want to warn somebody not to get involved in something), *Čuvaj se!* 'Take care!' instead of the more usual *Pazi!* or simply *Zdravo!* 'Goodbye,' and *Moj ime je* 'My name is,' often used nowadays for *Zovem se*, literally 'I am called.' Poor or literal translations often become perpetuated as a productive model, so Serbians often say *Ja dolazim iz . . .* , literally 'I come from . . .' rather than *Ja sam iz . . .* , literally 'I am from . . .' on the basis of the English form.

The motivation behind pragmatic borrowing is particularly complex and may involve economic, technological, sociocultural, and political factors, as well as the question of linguistic prestige, which is obviously at play in the case of direct borrowings into Serbian of English words like *pliz* 'please' and *sori* 'sorry' (*Još jednom sori* 'Sorry once again'). English is always believed to express technological concepts better than other languages, and is fashionable and considered a superior cultural reference for the young. Overt expression of gratitude in Anglo-Saxon culture has also promoted the spread of equivalents of English *please* in Hispanic culture (see earlier discussion), and is no doubt responsible also for the pragmatic extension of the words *exacto* and *correcto*, now used as exclamations of agreement, but formerly used in Spanish only to confirm the precision of an idea or result (Carnicer 1969: 116–117).

6.3 CONCLUSIONS

The type of analogical sense-loans that we have attempted to describe in this chapter are due to a variety of causes, which may be linguistic, material, or social. It is tempting to see semantic borrowing in language contact situations as an extension of the "one form, one meaning" principle, also called Humboldt's Universal and the Principle of Isomorphism (Campbell 2013: 267), so perhaps there is a "one form, one range of meanings" principle whereby cognates are coerced into semantic conformity by a dominant language. Increased global communication is obviously making language contact much commoner, and this is reinforcing the influence of English, a primary example of a dominant language, on many other languages.

However, as Hope (1971: 646–647) says, when attempting to determine whether meaning has been calqued from one language onto another, or whether we are dealing with parallel semantic development, we need to reconstruct in detail the history of the lexical items in question and apply all criteria that offer reliable information.

Moreover, although cognates are obviously prime targets for semantic borrowing, words that are related in meaning but not form also receive one-way or mutual influence. Analogical influence on meaning in other languages is in no way exceptional or new. The spread of the learning of schools of thought and the advances made in science and technology always involve the dissemination of new vocabulary and the modification and adaptation of the meaning of existing words.

References

Agustín Llach, M. Pilar. 2006. La competencia pragmática y los errores pragmático-léxicos en la classe de ELE. In *Actas del XVI Congreso Internacional de ASELE*, edited by Alfredo Álvarez et al., 96–102. Oviedo: Universidad de Oviedo. Servicio de Publicaciones.

Alfaro, Ricardo Joaquín. 1970. *Diccionario de anglicismos*. 3rd ed. Madrid: Gredos.

Anderson, Gregory D. S. 2005. *Language Contact in South Central Siberia*. Wiesbaden: Harrassowitz.

Barber, Charles. 1997 [1976]. *Early Modern English*. Edinburgh: Edinburgh University Press.

Barnhart, Robert K., and Steinmetz, Sol (eds.). 1988. *Chambers Dictionary of Etymology*. London: Chambers.

Betz, Werner. 1949. Lehnwörter und Lehnprägungen in Vor- und Frühdeutschen. In *Deutsche Wortgeschichte*, Vol. I, edited by F. Maurer and F. Stroh, 127–147. Berlin: De Gruyter.

Burnley, D. 1992. Lexis and semantics. In *The Cambridge History of the English Language*, Vol. II: *1066–1476*, edited by Norman Blake, 409–499. Cambridge: Cambridge University Press.

Campbell, Lyle. 2013. *Historical Linguistics*. 3rd ed. Edinburgh: Edinburgh University Press.

Carnicer, Ramón. 1969. *Sobre el lenguaje de hoy*. Madrid: Editorial Prensa Española.

Carnicer, Ramón. 1972. *Nuevas reflexiones sobre el lenguaje*. Madrid: Editorial Prensa Española.

Carnicer, Ramón. 1977. *Tradición y evolución en el lenguaje actual*. Madrid: Editorial Prensa Española.

Carnicer, Ramón. 1983. *Desidia y otras lacras en el lenguaje de hoy*. Barcelona: Planeta.

Collins. 2009. *Diccionario bilingüe español-inglés, English-Spanish*. 9th ed. Glasgow: HarperCollins.

Coseriu, Eugenio. 1961. ¿Arabismos o romanismos? *Nueva Revista de Filología Hispánica* 15: 4–22.

DEX (*Dicţionaril Explicativ al Limbii Române*). 1975. Bucureşti: Editura Academiei Republicii Socialiste România. Institutul de Lingvistică din Bucureşti.

DRAE. Real Academia Española. Diccionario de la Lengua Española. 1992. 21st ed. Madrid: Espasa-Calpe.

DRAE. Real Academia Española. Diccionario de la Lengua Española. 2001. 22nd ed. Madrid: Espasa-Calpe.

Furiassi, Cristiano. 2010. *False Anglicisms in Italian*. Monza (Milano): Polimetrica International Scientific (*Lexicography Worldwide: Theoretical, Descriptive and Applied Perspectives*, 8).

Grant, Anthony. 2015. Lexical borrowing. In *Oxford Handbook of the Word*, edited by John R. Taylor, 431–444. New York: Oxford University Press.

Haspelmath, Martin. 2009. Lexical borrowing: Concepts and issues. In *Loanwords in the World's Languages: A Comparative Study*, edited by Martin Haspelmath and Uri Tadmor, 35–54. Berlin: Mouton de Gruyter.

Haspelmath, Martin, and Uri Tadmor (eds.). 2009. *Loanwords in the World's Languages: A Comparative Study*. Berlin: Mouton de Gruyter.

Haugen, Einar. 1950a. Problems of bilingualism. *Lingua* 2: 271–290.

Haugen, Einar. 1950b. The analysis of linguistic borrowing. *Language* 26: 210–231.

Haugen, Einar. 1953. *The Norwegian Language in America: A Study in Bilingual Behaviour*, Vol. I: *The Bilingual Community*; Vol. II: *The American Dialects of Norwegian*. Bloomington: Indiana University Press. (Reprinted 1969).

Hock, Hans Henrich. 1986. *Principles of Historical Linguistics*. Berlin: Mouton de Gruyter.

Hock, Hans Henrich, and Brian D. Joseph. 1996. *Language History, Language Change, and Language Relationship*. Berlin: Mouton de Gruyter.

Hope, T. E. 1971. *Lexical Borrowing in the Romance Languages*. New York: New York University Press.

Kastovsky, Dieter. 1992. Semantics and vocabulary. In *The Cambridge History of the English Language*, Vol. I: *The Beginnings to 1066*, edited by Richard M. Hogg, 290–408. Cambridge: Cambridge University Press.

Larousse. 2004. *Gran Diccionario English-Spanish; Español-Inglés*. Barcelona: Larousse.

Lehmann, Winfred P. 1992. *Historical Linguistics*. 3rd ed. London: Routledge.

Manoliu, Maria M. 1994. Language standardization and political rejection: The Romanian case. In *The Changing Voices of Europe*, edited by Mair Parry, Winifred Davies, and Rosalind Temple, 95–108. Cardiff: University of Wales Press in conjunction with the Modern Humanities Research Association.

Matras, Yaron. 2009. *Language Contact*. Cambridge: Cambridge University Press.

Moliner, María. 1998. *Diccionario de uso del español*. 2 vols. 2nd ed. Madrid: Gredos.

Mott, Brian. 2015a. The rise of the English *-ing* form in Modern Spanish: A source of pseudo-Anglicisms. In *Pseudo-English: Studies on False Anglicisms in Europe*, edited by Cristiano Furiassi and Henrik Gottlieb, 175–196. Berlin: DeGruyter Mouton.

Mott, Brian. 2015b. *Nuevo diccionario chistabino-castellano*. Berlin: Logos Verlag.

Nevalainen, Terrtu. 1992. Early Modern English lexis and semantics. In *The Cambridge History of the English Language*, Vol. III: *1476–1776*, edited by Roger Lass, 332–458. Cambridge: Cambridge University Press.

Oxford. 2003. *Gran Diccionario Oxford Español-Inglés, Inglés-Español*. 3rd ed. Oxford: Oxford University Press.

Pulcini, Virginia, Cristiano Furiassi, and Félix Rodríguez González. 2012. The lexical influence of English on European languages: From words to phraseology. In *The Anglicization of European* Lexis, edited by Virginia Pulcini, Cristiano Furiassi, and Félix Rodríguez González, 1–24. Amsterdam; Philadelphia: John Benjamins.

Rosetti, Al. 1978. *Istoria limbii române*. 2nd ed. Bucureşti: Editura şfiinţifică şi Enciclopedică.

Sala, Marius. 1988. *El problema de las lenguas en contacto*. Mexico: Universidad Nacional Autónoma de México.

Schulte, Kim. 2009. Loanwords in Romanian. In *Loanwords in the World's Languages: A Comparative Study*, edited by Martin Haspelmath and Uri Tadmor, 230–259. Berlin: Mouton de Gruyter.

Seco, Manuel. 1987. *Diccionario de dudas y dificultades de la lengua española*. 9th ed. Madrid: Espasa Calpe.

Sihler, Andrew L. 2000. *Language History: An Introduction*. Amsterdam: John Benjamins.

Smith, Colin. 1989. The anglicism: No longer a problem for Spanish? In *Actas del XIII Congreso Nacional de la Asociación Española de Estudios Anglo-Norteamericanos (AEDEAN), Tarragona, 18–20 de diciembre de 1989*, 119–136. Barcelona: Promociones y Publicaciones Universitarias.

Tadmor, Uri. 2009. Loanwords in the world's languages: Findings and Results. In *Loanwords in the World's Languages: A Comparative Study*, edited by Martin Haspelmath and Uri Tadmor, 35–75. Berlin: Mouton de Gruyter.

Tölgyesi, Beatrix. 2012. Lexikai russzicizmusok a litván internetes fórumok nyelvében (Lexical Russianisms in the Language of Lithuanian Internet Forums). Budapest: Hungarian Semiotic Society, 54–58. (www.academia.edu/10698416)

Ullmann, Stephen. 1972. *Semantics: An Introduction to the Science of Meaning*. Oxford: Blackwell.

Vendryès, Joseph. 1979. *El lenguaje: Introducción lingüística a la historia*. México: Unión Tipográfica Editorial Hispano-Americana.

Wagner, Max Leopold. 1954. Calcos lingüísticos en el habla de los sefarditas de Levante. In *Homenaje a Fritz Krüger*, Vol. II, edited by Antonio Alatorre, Margit Frenk, and Juan M. Lope Blanch, 269–281. Mendoza: Universidad Nacional de Cuyo.

Waldron, R. A. 1967. *Sense and Sense Development*. London: Andre Deutsch.

Weinreich, Uriel. 1953. *Languages in Contact: Findings and Problems*. The Hague: Mouton.

Weinreich, Uriel. 1968. Unilinguisme et bilinguisme. In *Encyclopédie de la Pléiade: Le Langage*, edited by André Martinet, 647–684. Paris: Éditions Gallimard.

Winford, Donald. 2003. *An Introduction to Contact Linguistics*. Oxford: Blackwell.

CHAPTER 7

SOCIOLINGUISTIC, SOCIOLOGICAL, AND SOCIOCULTURAL APPROACHES TO CONTACT-INDUCED LANGUAGE CHANGE

Identifying Chamic Child Bilingualism in Contact-Based Language Change

GRAHAM THURGOOD

7.1 INTRODUCTION

SOCIOLINGUISTIC considerations of various types shape profoundly the effects of contact-induced change upon a language. This chapter is an exploratory attempt to identify these, and specifically the remnants of early child bilingualism in the Chamic languages, focusing on the characteristics of the restructuring of several Chamic languages, a subgroup of Austronesian found along the coast (Phan Rang Cham and its archaic written counterpart Written Cham) and in the highlands of Vietnam (including Jarai, Rade, and Haroi), on Hainan Island just off mainland China (Hainan Cham or Tsat), in Cambodia (Western Cham), and at the northern tip of Sumatra (Acehnese; see the papers in Grant and Sidwell eds. 2007 for more information). We focus on three of these languages, in which we argue that the linguistic record shows evidence of child bilingualism: Proto-Chamic [PC], Haroi in the highlands, and Hainan Cham on Hainan Island. For these languages, non-linguistic evidence for the existence of prior child bilingualism is provided by our understanding of the history of the area, and, for PC, by the evidence of molecular evolution.

Historically, Champa itself was a group of Chamic speaking, loosely affiliated political entities that functioned as part of Austronesian trade patterns (Hall 1955, 1981, 1985; Higham 1989, 2002; Thurgood 1999; Southworth 2004; Bellwood 2007; Solheim et al. 2007). Although strong disagreement exists about the details of Austronesian trade patterns, from the Chamic perspective, little doubt exists that the earliest traders were Austronesian-speaking males. It also follows that these traders formed households with Mon-Khmer [MK] speaking females, raising children bilingual in Chamic and a MK language.

The scenario of male Austronesian-speaking traders marrying MK-speaking females is given support by the molecular evolution work by Peng et al. (2010). Examination of the mitochondrial DNA (mtDNA)—the matrilineal line—of 168 Cham speakers and 139 Kinh speakers (Vietnamese) led to the conclusion that (2010: 2417) "the Chams had a closer affinity with the Mon–Khmer populations in MSEA [Mainland South-East-Asia] than with the Austronesian populations from Island Southeast Asia (ISEA)." They further concluded that "the origin of the Cham was likely a process of assimilation of massive local Mon–Khmer populations." Local populations would have adopted Chamic as their language.

Although the study states that it is only the matrillineal line that was analyzed, Peng et al. (2010: 2427) bring up the possibility of an "asymmetric sexual gene flow" on the paternal side, an analysis consistent with a historical scenario in which male Cham-speaking traders married MK-speaking local women.

7.1.1 Child versus Adult Language Learners

The most basic division in language acquisition is between child first-language acquisition and adult second-language acquisition. Unless there are extenuating circumstances, children by far out-perform adults, attaining a significantly higher degree of language mastery; in contrast, adults, although often they may often achieve some degree of success, fall noticeably short of mastery. Updating Thurgood (2000), what this chapter suggests is that a similar continuum can be found in language contact: specifically, child bilinguals often incorporate material from one of their languages into another, and that they do so not only with far greater faithfulness and speed than adults do, but may also far more faithfully transfer the sound system from one language into the other. Children also transfer grammatical structures from one language to another with similar faithfulness (see also Ozón and Eppler, Chapter 9 in this volume).

7.1.2 The Linguistic Evidence

When it exists, the transfer of marked aspects of phonological system of one language to another contact strongly suggests that child bilingualism was involved. The evidence is particularly salient in cases where two typologically distinct phonological systems come into contact. Other evidence may include widespread lexical borrowing, particularly of basic vocabulary. Additional evidence exists in the form of faithful borrowing of constructions, along with the morphemes that mark these structures.

As a caveat, however, it must be borne in mind that in the cases including those discussed here, the child bilingualism of the initial contact was followed by a subsequent period in which this contact was at least supplemented by contact with less accomplished adult learners. Thus, it is necessary to attempt to sort out the layers of child bilingualism from borrowing involving adult bilingualism.

7.2 The Proto-Chamic Linguistic Record

The reconstruction of PC reveals phonological, lexical, and grammatical evidence of the child bilingualism implicit in the DNA evidence in Peng et al. (2010).

7.2.1 Phonological Restructuring

The change of Proto-Malayo-Chamic phonological system to PC reflects a major restructuring in the direction of MK. The originally Proto-Malayo-Chamic roots were originally disyllabic with penultimate stress in all roots (except for forms having a schwa in the initial syllable); these became finally stressed, accompanied by a strong tendency toward reduction of the initial syllable. The four inherited vowels in the now unstressed initial syllable remained, but the vowel inventory in the stressed final syllable expanded. All four of the inherited simple vowels were retained, with the two inherited PC high vowels *i and *u splitting into *-i-, *-$əy$ and *-u-, *-$əw$, respectively. Several new vowels were added through borrowing: *$ɛ$, *$ə$, and *$ɔ$ (both long and short). For several syllable-final vowels, a vowel length distinction was added. The incorporation of length was frequently through the accurate borrowing of words with a length distinction into a language that otherwise lacked such a distinction. The three PMC diphthongs were likewise retained; to these were added several other diphthongs, and at least one triphthong. Finally, two glottalized consonants, *$ɓ$- and *$ɗ$, have been added (Greenberg 1970). In short, the phonological system was made significantly more complex: the morphemes were restructured, new vowels and consonants were added, vowel length was added, and marked consonants, some internally developed and others borrowed, have been added.

If one views these changes from the viewpoint of the changes in Malayo-Chamic as it became Chamic, the phonology has become far more complex and far more marked—not what is usually expected in language contact. If it had been largely adult learners incorporating these MK features into their Chamic, one would expect simplification, not faithful incorporation. Thus, much of this transfer must have been done by children, not adults. For the children of bilingual households, these features were already part of their linguistic repertoire; they only needed to transfer these features from their MK to their Cham. (For a Chamic example of language contact initiating phonological change in other directions, see Blood 1962, where it is shown that the impact of Vietnamese upon earlier Phan Rang Cham phonology has pushed Cham phonology in the direction of Vietnamese. Blood further shows that phonological conservatism, which includes the preservation of some sounds, such as /-l/ rather than its merger with preexisting /-in/, is something which equates with gender, age, and educational variables: people who keep /-l/ distinct from /-n/ when Blood was doing his research in the 1950s were generally male, literate in the old style of Written Cham, which uses an Indic script, and were in the older age brackets.)

7.2.2 Lexical Borrowing

Another type of evidence, supportive but not as compelling, is the presence of extensive borrowing of basic vocabulary. PC is replete with MK loans, including pronouns, kinship terms, and basic vocabulary. Roughly twenty-three of the sixty body-part terms in my PC database are MK borrowings, including words for *yawn, penis, finger, waist, loins, buttocks, cheek, jaw, meat, lungs, dead skin, neck, vomit, excrement, heel, head, lips, gums, stomach, large intestine, back, right (side), left (side)*, and so on. Such borrowing is associated here and elsewhere with bilingual households; P. J. Mistry (personal communication, 1999) said this kind of borrowing is not uncommon in places in India.

7.2.3 Grammatical Borrowing and Restructuring

Without grammatical reconstructions of both Chamic and Bahnaric, there are serious limitations on the database. However, although all the evidence is still not in, PC borrowed at least some of its grammatical morphemes and structures from its MK donor.

The widely used reciprocal -$k^haw?^{43}$ 'mutual, reciprocal (RECP)' < PC #*gəps 'group' is from MK. In all examples, the reciprocal refers back to subjects, as is not typologically unexpected (Maslova and Nedjalko 2011). The *-ən- 'instrumental infix,' as Blust (2000: 441) writes, "almost certainly is MK, not An" (contra Thurgood 1999). Blust (2000: 442) also notes that "the presence of *-an- 'nominalizer' and *pa- 'causativizer' in Chamic languages is more likely due to borrowing from MK languages than the reverse." In addition to these examples, the imperatives #*bɛ? and #*juəy, the interrogative #*hagɛt -f 'why, what,' and the preposition #*məŋ 'from,' with the possible exception of #*hagɛ-f, appear to be very early MK incorporations into PC.

7.3 THE HAROI LINGUISTIC RECORD

Haroi is another member of the Chamic subgroup of Austronesian, whose speakers are found in the highlands of Vietnam. Haroi has radically restructured its phonological system under the influence of intimate contact with a MK register system, probably Hrê (or, Proto-Hrê), all North Bahnaric (MK) register languages. Smith's map (1972: iv) suggests that Haroi is no longer in contact with any of these register systems.

7.3.1 Phonological Restructuring

Comparison of PC with the modern Haroi data reveals a language that has undergone far more dramatic vocalic restructuring than its Chamic sister languages. Although Southern Roglai (Lee 1977: 92) and Western Cham also have registers (Edmondson and Gregerson 1993), these are less robust. Haroi has what Huffman (1976) termed a *restructured register system*. In terms of Haroi, certain classes of PC initials led to distinctive phonation differences: (1) PC voiceless obstruents led to tense register on the following vowels; (2) PC voiced obstruents led to breathy voice, and the remaining initials remained modal. Then, (3) these voice-quality distinctions produced differences in the vowels, that is, led to a register system with voice-quality differences associated with differences in vowel quality. Finally, the voice-quality distinctions that originally conditioned the vowel splits disappeared, leaving behind a large number of now redistributed vowels and often new vowel contrasts.

Lee (1977: 87, 92) recognized the components of an earlier Pre-Haroi register system in a set of what would be otherwise unrelated changes from PC to Haroi. One characteristic change is development of most PC voiced obstruents into aspirated voiceless stops (*dlay > Haroi thiai 'forest') or, in the case of certain medials, into a voiceless unaspirated obstruent (PC *bra:s > Haroi priah 'husked rice'). In either instance, the following vowel behaved as if, at some point, it had breathy voice. Following former PC voiced obstruents, the former breathy voiced vowels developed an -i- onset on the mid vowel *a (PC *kabaw > Haroi kəphiaw 'water buffalo'). The *-a- > *-ia change is not found elsewhere in Chamic, but is common in North Bahnaric. The mid vowels *ɛ, *ə, *ɔ raised to ı, i, and ʊ, respectively; the PC diphthong *-əy raised its onset, becoming Haroi -ii. Following former PC voiceless obstruents (> tense voice), the high vowels (PC *tujuh > Haroi cəsuh 'seven'; PC phun > Haroi phon 'plant') and the onsets of diphthongs beginning with high vowels lowered (PC *jahit > pre-Haroi siiʔ > Haroi seiʔ 'sew'). Following glottalized obstruents, voiced aspirates, and sonorants (> modal voice), the vowels remained unchanged.

These changes, combined with initials correlated vowel splits, were, as Lee noted, all features that had their common origin in an earlier register system. In addition, many of these vowel changes are associated with breathy voiced vowels not just in Hrê (Phillips 1973: 63), a MK language, and Haroi, an Austronesian language, but in various languages of the world (Thurgood 2002: 346–347).

7.3.2 Lexical Borrowing

In addition to the pervasive phonological restructuring Haroi has undergone, there is evidence of intense contact in the borrowings. Tegenfeldt-Mundhenk and Goschnick

(1977: 2) write that Haroi has more Bahnaric borrowings than either Rade or Jarai have, an observation that holds up under my own rough counts. They also note that some have referred to Haroi as Bahnar Cham, but Tegenfeldt-Mundhenk and Goschnick leave open the precise question of which Bahnaric language it had contact with.

It is not possible yet, if it ever will be, to differentiate between MK basic vocabulary (e.g., body parts), which has been borrowed into PC and then inherited in Haroi from MK loans at the later Haroi stage.

7.3.3 Grammatical Borrowing and Restructuring

It would also be instructive to compare the syntax of Haroi and potential linguistic contacts, but not enough has been done on the grammars of Hrê and Haroi, specifically, and on Chamic in general to determine what sort of grammatical borrowings and restructuring exists in Haroi.

7.4 THE HAINAN CHAM LINGUISTIC RECORD

Hainan Cham ([tsã:ʔ], etymologically *cam* 'Cham,' sometimes anglicized as Tsat) is spoken on the outskirts of Sanya on the coast of Hainan Island, a Chinese island just off the mainland. The speakers are the last remaining remnants of the Champa traders once found distributed around the island in coastal settlements, where they came into contact with various local groups including Hlai (Li) speakers, but most prominently with speakers of a dialect of Southwestern Mandarin (Thurgood, Thurgood, and Li 2014), which we have termed Sanya Chinese. Although the Hainan Cham now live in their own villages and typically marry within the Muslim community, the linguistic evidence suggests that at some point most of the traders took Southwestern Mandarin–speaking wives.

The evidence is overwhelming that, despite the existence of a small number of loans from other Sinitic languages (Chinese dialects), it was a Southwestern Mandarin (SW Mandarin) dialect, Sanya Chinese, that had the original pervasive influence on Hainan Cham. Our only recorded Sanya Chinese, a word list of about 200 Sanya Chinese words, is found in the back of Zheng's book (1997). Some of these Sanya Chinese words also occur in Hainan Cham, and when they do, these words are often identical or nearly identical with the Hainan Cham, and regular sound–meaning correspondences can be established. Although the Sanya Chinese base is limited, direct comparisons with Mandarin as well as comparisons with Baxter's *A Handbook of Old Chinese Phonology* (1992) both reveal correspondence patterns regular enough to establish that most of the Hainan Chinese loans are from Mandarin. For the Chinese constructions borrowed into Hainan Cham, lacking any Sanya Chinese data, direct comparisons with Mandarin were made; for the Hainan Cham and the Mandarin, constructions are so close that no doubt exists but that Sanya Chinese was extremely close to modern Mandarin.

7.4.1 Phonological Restructuring

This Hainan Cham stage began roughly a thousand years ago with the arrival of a large group of Chamic speakers in Hainan, supplementing what was a more modest number of traders already on the island. Primarily under the influence of the dialect of Southwestern Mandarin spoken near Sanya City and under more modest contact with Hlai languages, Hainan Cham has undergone complete phonological restructuring (e.g., Thurgood 1999), going from disyllabic and sesquisyllabic to monosyllabic, and from atonal to tonal, while incorporating a handful of new sounds. Some of the earlier PC vowel length distinctions were lost, but the consonant and vowel inventory increased. Most strikingly, Hainan Cham became fully tonal, displaying five distinct lexical tones.

7.4.2 Lexical and Construction Borrowings

Mandarin loans pervade the lexicon. The early ones are mainly from Sanya Chinese and the more recent ones mainly from the regional variety of the national language. Scattered among these are a handful of loans from other Chinese sources. Our word counts, similar to those of Zheng (1997: 54), show that roughly a quarter of the nouns (230 of 891), verbs (152 of 620), and adjectives (61 of 259) are Mandarin in origin.

The linguistic record does not show much Mandarin basic vocabulary borrowed into Hainan Cham, but this is not particularly expected. While the earliest Hainan Cham speakers must have married Mandarin-speaking wives, for some time now the Hainan Cham have lived largely separated from Chinese speakers, now only learning Mandarin as they approach their teen years and spend significant time outside the two villages.

7.4.3 Recent or Undateable Constructions

Here, as elsewhere, many borrowed morphemes are better described as borrowed constructions, with accompanying grammatical constraints on word order being borrowed along with the morphemes. This first set of lexical constructions show Mandarin contact, but without any evidence that allows us to narrow the incorporations to the period of child bilingualism. Some, like the development of a benefactive from 'give,' are difficult to evaluate not only because they occur so frequently cross-linguistically that it is hard to rule out independent but parallel innovation, but also because of the lack of in-depth syntactic analyses for most Chamic languages. For example, the resultative construction seems to have developed out of a serial verb construction with the use of 'get' as a marker of the resultative segment, evolving under the influence of the Mandarin *dé* 'get,' but its origins are hard to pin down without more data.

7.4.4 Intensifiers

For emphatics we use the term *intensifiers* instead of König and Siemund's *emphatics* (2007). Intensifiers are marked either by (1) the native *kiə³³kiə³³* or (2) the Mandarin borrowing *tsi³³ki²¹* < Mandarin *zìjǐ*; the Mandarin *tsi³³ki²¹* is a more recent borrowing (3), still restricted to the more sinicized texts. An etymology for *kiə³³kiə³³* would be welcome.

(1) | *ha³³* | *ŋan³³* | *tʰay²¹may²¹* | *na:wʔ³³* | *ʔa²¹ti²¹* | *kiə³³kiə³³* | *na:wʔ³³*? |
|---|---|---|---|---|---|---|
| 2P | with | younger.sister | go | or | EMPH | go |
| *nǐ* | *hé* | *mèimei* | *qù* | *háishì* | *zìjǐ* | *qù* |
| 你 | 和 | 妹妹 | 去 | 还是 | 自己 | 去 |

你和妹妹去还是自己去?   (Zheng 1997: 85)

'Are you going with younger sister or going by yourself?'

(2) | *kiə³³kiə³³* | *tsu⁵⁵va³³* |
|---|---|
| EMPH | heave.sigh |
| *zìjǐ* | *tànqì* |
| 自己 | 叹气 |

自己叹气,

'(I) myself heaved a sigh . . .'

In the more sinicized texts, as in (3), *tsi³³ki²¹* 'EMPH' < zìjǐ 自己 is sometimes found. As indicated by the underlining, all four components in this phrase are Mandarin borrowings.

(3) | *tsiʔ⁴³* | *kuanʔ⁴³* | *tsi³³ki²¹* | *pʰat²⁴sa:y²¹*, (Text 2.7d) |
|---|---|---|---|
| only | care.about | EMPH | get.rich |
| *zhǐ* | *guǎn* | *zìjǐ* | *fācái* |
| 只 | 管 | 自己 | 发财 |

因为国民党的官员只顾自己发财,

'because (they) only care about themselves getting rich . . .'

7.4.5 Classifiers

There is no reason not to assume that PC inherited its classifier system from Malayo-Chamic. However, in contact with Mandarin, numerous classifiers were borrowing into Hainan Cham. Roughly 20% of the classifiers are Mandarin (51 of 231). Of the mensural classifiers, 13 of the 16 are Mandarin; trade is carried on in Mandarin. With the sortals, which mainly track entities in discourse, a simple count shows show some 30 borrowed forms, but in actual usage, 85% (143 of 173) of the time the classifier used is either se^{55}/se^{21} 'CLF, people, animals, birds; general classifier (for animates)' < PC *$drəy$ 'body' or p^ho^{21}/p^ho^{55} 'round object classifier, piece; general classifier (for inanimates)' < PC *$bɔh$ > 'fruit, round object CLF.' Most classifiers occur but once in our data.

7.4.6 Kinship Terms

Two kinship terms, $ʔa^{21}ko^{33}$ 'older brother' and $ʔa^{21}tsiə^{33}$ 'older sister,' are distinguished. The second syllable of older brother -ko^{33} seems related to Mandarin $gēge$, and the second syllable of $ʔa^{21}tsiə^{33}$ look to be of a Chinese but not Mandarin origin. The extensions of both are critical to interacting with non-Chamic speaking neighbors. Other kinship terms seem inherited.

7.4.7 Negation

The most prominent negation marker, pu^{33}, comes from Sanya Chinese, although a distinct but related word is found throughout the region. The same pu^{33} occurs in three other borrowed Mandarin negatives: $pu^{33}maʔ^{43}$ 'not have,' $pu^{33}zien^{21}$ 'not so, or else,' and $pu^{33}da:nʔ^{33} \dots ʔə^{21}se^{21}$ 'not only . . . but also.'

7.4.8 Aspect

Mandarin has also contributed the three variant perfective particles lo^{33}, lo^{21}, and $lə^{33}$, $lə^{21}$, the third with tonal *variation*.

7.4.9 Numbers

The higher order numbers for ten thousand, myriad, 100,000, and zero have been borrowed. The ti^{33} marking ordinals is borrowed. Hainan Cham uses Mandarin numbers for days, months, and years.

7.4.10 Prepositions

The widely used prepositions $hioŋʔ^{33}$ 'to, toward; direction' and $suŋ^{21}$ 'from' are borrowed. There are another four prepositions borrowed from Mandarin, but their restriction so far to sinicized material indicates that these are recent incorporations into Hainan Cham, only partially nativized.

7.4.11 Superlatives

The two superlatives, both borrowed from Mandarin, are $tsuy^{33}$ 'most,' *zuì* before the adjective (4), or $ken\textipa{P}^{33}kia^{33}$ '(even) more' (< Mandarin *gèngjiā*). The $ken\textipa{P}^{33}kia^{33}$ '(even) more,' of course, is a comparative in its source language.

(4) se^{33} $\textit{d}oy\textipa{P}^{43}$ <u>$tsuy^{33}$</u> sia^{55} (Zheng 1997: 76)
     horse   run   most   fast
     'The horse runs the fastest.'

7.4.12 Quantifiers

The quantifiers 'each' kok^{43}, 'every' may^{21}, 'all' $\textit{d}aw^{33}$, and 'only' tsi^{21} are Mandarin in origin and in the available data follow Mandarin word order (5).

(5)   <u>$kok^{43}za$:$\eta\textipa{P}^{33}$</u>   <u>$may^{21}zay^{33}$</u> $ta^{21}p^hi^{55}$ <u>$\textit{d}aw^{33}$</u>
     <u>each</u> person   <u>every</u>day   everyone   <u>all</u>
     各人   每   天大家   都
     gèrén   *měitiān*   *dàjiā*   *dōu*
     'each person'   'every day'   'everyone'

7.4.13 Adverbial Classifiers

Mandarin is the source for at least most of the adverbial classifiers, a construction that is functionally adverbial but structurally a classifier (that is, a numeral + a classifier). All of the nine adverbial classifiers follow Mandarin word order, and seven of the nine have Mandarin classifiers. (The classifier in $ta^{21}\textbeta a$:$\eta\textipa{P}^{21}$ 'an instance' (6) is a MK borrowing into Chamic.) Sometimes the number is Mandarin in origin ($zit^{24}ku\eta^{33}$ 'altogether' and $zi^{21}ki\eta^{33}$ 'already'); sometimes the number is Chamic ($ta^{21}tan^{33}$ 'once,' $ta^{21}p^ha$(:)$n\textipa{P}^{33}$ 'a portion').

(6) ha^{33} sa^{33} $va^{55}ka$:n^{33} se^{33} p^ha^{33} kaw^{33} ηuy^{33} $ta^{21}\textbeta a$:$\eta\textipa{P}^{33}$!
     2P   NOM   fishing-pole   borrow   give   1P   use   one-CLF
     nǐ   *de*   *diàoyú gān*   <u>*jiè*</u>   *gěi*   *wǒ*   *yòng*   *yǐxià*
     你   的   钓鱼竿   借   给   我   用   以下
     你的钓鱼竿 借 给 我 用以下吧!
                      (Zheng 1997: 105)
     'Your fishing pole that you lent to me I used one time!'

Despite the construction itself being Mandarin, there is no strong evidence that adverbial classifiers developed specifically under the influence of child learners.

7.4.14 Conjunctions

Contact has led to Hainan Cham borrowing Mandarin conjunctions. The conjunctions $hok^{24}tsak^{43}$ 'or' and $ziu^{33}\ldots ziu^{33}$ 'both...and...' are from Mandarin. Among the coordinate clause conjunctions, four are borrowed: $Pa^{21}ti^{21}$ 'or,' $\dot{d}a{:}nP^{33}(si^{21})$ 'but', $ta{:}n^{33}$ 'but,' and the correlative $pu^{33}\dot{d}a{:}nP^{33}\ldots Pə^{21}se^{21}\ldots$ 'not only...but also...'. Ten of the eleven clausal conjunctions we found were also Mandarin borrowings: $sawP^{43}$ 'then,' $zi^{21}ko^{21}$ 'if,' $so^{21}zi^{21}$ 'therefore,' $suy^{33}zien^{21}$ 'although,' $pu^{33}zien^{21}$ 'not so, or else,' $ziu^{21}zi^{21}$ 'due to,' $lien^{21}$ 'even (including),' $say^{33}zien^{21}$ 'since,' $ko^{43}zien^{21}$ 'sure enough,' and $zin^{33}vuy^{21}$ 'because'; the form $Pa{:}nP^{33}tuy^{33}$ lacks an etymology so far.

A caveat is in order here: despite the pervasive Mandarin influence, one cannot argue that this is residue from child bilingualism since conjunctions are so freely borrowed, particularly into languages with only a modest set of clausal conjunctions.

7.4.15 Indefinite Constructions

Indefinite or approximate numbers are indicated one of two ways: The first is to add a phrase meaning 'around, about.' The inherited phrase is $tsun^{33}\eta u^{24}$ [down up] 'approximately'; the unrelated Mandarin counterpart would be *shàngxià* [up down] 'about; more or less.' Borrowed from Mandarin are $tso^{33}ziu^{33}$ 'about; around; nearby' (< Mandarin *zuǒ* 'left' + *yòu* 'right') and $ta^{33}zok^{24}$ < Mandarin *dàyuē* 'about.' The borrowings follow Mandarin word order. The other way to show indefinite numbers is to use two sequenced numbers in a row, such as 'three, four' or 'sixty, seventy.'

7.4.16 Constructions Suggesting Child Bilingualism

There is widespread syntactic restructuring in Hainan Cham, which involves the transfer of constructions from Mandarin to Hainan Cham, sometimes with a morpheme borrowed from Mandarin serving as the focus of the construction and often with associated word order change. It can be argued that this set of constructions was acquired by bilingual children.

Particularly strong evidence that the donor was Mandarin, not some other Sinitic language, and that child bilingualism was involved is provided by typological constructions such as the rare comparative with the preposition pi^{21} and the adversative agentive passive pi^{33}, which, as Chappell (2001: 350–351) notes, are also specifically

Mandarin. For the latter, Chappell writes that when this does occur in Southern Chinese, it is a formal register borrowing from Mandarin.

7.4.17 Word Order Change

There is widespread word order change, which mainly consists of movement from the older posthead nominal modification to the more Mandarin-like prehead modification. Much of the word order change was mediated through the sa^{33} construction developed under the influence of the *de* constructions of Mandarin, which has counterparts throughout Southeast Asia, but has not been previously recognized in Chamic.

In our analysis, the sa^{33} constructions consist of two sets of patterns: one with the pattern *X* sa^{33} *NP*, and the other the juxtaposition of a nominalized constituent to an Nh and *X* sa^{33}, marking a constituent as nominalized. The *X* sa^{33} *NP* pattern, calqued on Mandarin, was the path by which Hainan Cham developed various prehead modifying constructions. This has resulted in many Hainan Cham grammatical constructions being paired, having both a posthead inherited pattern and a Mandarin-influenced prehead pattern. Among these paired entities are prehead and posthead genitives, adjectives, demonstratives, comparatives, and relative clauses (see Table 7.1).

In inherited material, the typical pattern of noun phrase modification is overwhelmingly posthead modification: head nouns are followed by predicates (both stative and non-stative), genitive pronouns, prepositional phrases/quantifiers (order indeterminate) and demonstratives, in that order. This prehead modification is losing ground to a prehead pattern calqued on SW Mandarin: modifier $+sa^{33}+$head (see Table 7.1). In some of the more sinicized constructions the sa^{33} has been replaced by ti^{33}, which is borrowed from Mandarin *de*.

Table 7.1 Word Order: Inherited versus Borrowed

Structure:	Inherited Head Modifier	>	SW Mandarin Modifier (sa^{33}) Head
Genitives:			
Full NPs:	Nh NP	>	NP sa^{33} Nh
Pronouns:	Nh GENPr	>	Pr sa^{33} Nh
Adjectives:	Nh Adj NP	>	Adj sa^{33} Nh
Demonstratives:	Nh Dem NP	>	Dem sa^{33} Nh
Relative clauses:	Nh RCl NP	>	RCl sa^{33} Nh
NN compounds:	Nh N	>	N Nh
Comparatives:	Adj Standard	>	Standard Adjective Marker-Standard-Adjective

Key: Nh = head noun, Pr = pronoun, GEN = genitive, Adj = adjective, RCl = relative clause, Dem = demonstrative

7.4.18 Relative Clauses

Hainan Cham relative clauses provide an example of word order restructuring. The post-head relative clauses are inherited. They are formed through the deletion of the co-referential subject noun phrase in the relative clause (Andrews 2007: 206–236; Schachter and Shopen 2007: 30) and occur in two positions in the matrix sentence, modifying the sentence-final noun phrase carrying the focused information in the presentative construction, see (7), and as a modifier of the subject noun phrase of the matrix clause (8).

(7) t^ha^{21} $za:\eta^{33}$ [Ø le^{24} sia^{43} ha^{33}]!   (Zheng 1997: 91)
     have   person   Ø   fall.in   sea   !
     yǒu   rén   Ø   luò   hǎi   la
     有   人   Ø   落   海   啦
     有人[Ø掉下海啦]。
     'There was somebody who fell into the sea.'

(8) [za:ŋ^{33} [Ø li^{55} $ʔan^{33}$]] $za:yʔ^{33}$ p^hi^{55} (OZ 1983a: 38)
     person   Ø   sell   vegetables   come   CMPL
     rén   Ø   mài   cài   lái   le
     人   Ø   卖   菜   来   了
     卖菜的来了。
     'The person selling vegetables came.'

The prehead relative clauses with their construction-marking relative clause-final sa^{33} have evolved under the influence of Mandarin. These occur as a modifier of the subject noun phrase of the matrix clause (9), (10).

(9) [[Ø li^{55} $ʔan^{33}$ sa^{33}] $za:\eta^{33}$] $za:yʔ^{33}$ p^hi^{55} (OZ 1983a: 38)
     Ø   sell   vegetables   NOM   person   come   CMPL
     Ø   mài   cài   de   rén   lái   le
     Ø   卖   菜   的   人   来   了
     卖菜的来了。
     '(The person) who sells vegetables came.'

(10) [[Ø $dî^{55}$ nan^{33} sa^{33}] mo^{33}] si^{21} may^{33} sa^{33}
     Ø   lie.down   that   NOM   cow   be   female   NOM
     Ø   tǎng   nà   de   huángniú   shì   mǔ   de
     Ø   躺   那   的   黄牛   是   母   的
     躺着的那头黄牛是母的。
                                                         (Zheng 1997: 73)
     'The yellow cow lying down is female.'

This construction was incorporated into Hainan Cham from Mandarin. As Dryer (1992: 86) notes about his sample of relative clauses in VO languages, NRel relative clauses outnumber RelN by sixty to one, with the lone exception being the RelN relative clause of Mandarin. Hainan Cham is, like Mandarin, an SVO language. Here, we have a construction with a highly marked configuration being borrowed into a language where it is just as highly marked. The highly marked nature of the borrowed construction at least suggests that the corporation involved bilingual children.

7.4.19 Comparative Constructions

Hainan Cham comparatives show two patterns: one an inherited construction, and another construction from SW Mandarin. The inherited comparative marker *la:wʔ³³* developed out of the verb *la:wʔ³³* 'pass; exceed' (11); following Heine (1997: 114), we term this the *surpass comparative*. Its adjective-standard word order is expected for VO languages.

(11) *naw³³*   *maʔ⁴³*   *la:wʔ³³*   *ha³³*   (Zheng 1997: 75)
      3P   fat   CM   2P
      ADJ   ST
      'He is fatter than you.'

Ansaldo (2010: 919) notes that surpass comparatives are widely distributed both in Southern Mandarin and in other non-Sinitic languages of the area.

The borrowed construction involves the preposition *pi²¹* from SW Mandarin (12), (13) and the word order standard-adjective. The Chinese is the translation of the Hainan Cham into Mandarin; the Mandarin and the Hainan Cham match morpheme-for-morpheme.

(12) *kaw³³*   *pi²¹*   *ha³³*   *tsat²⁴tso³³*   *kiə³³*   *sun³³*   (Zheng 1997: 75)
      1P   CM   2P   short   three inch
      我   比   你   矮   三   寸。
      wǒ   *bǐ*   *nǐ*   *ǎi*   *sān* *cùn*
            bǐ   ST   ADJ
      'I am three inches shorter than you.'

(13) *naw³³*   *pi²¹*   *kaw³³*   *kʰioŋ²¹*   *piay³³ta:ŋʔ³³*   (Zheng 1997: 97)
      3P   CM   1P   tall   a.lot
      他   比   我   高   许多。
      tā   *bǐ*   *wǒ*   *gāo*   *xǔduō*
            bǐ   ST   ADJ
      'He is a lot taller than I am.'

It is not just the morpheme-to-morpheme match that makes these data interesting; it is also the typological parallelism: for VO languages, the standard-adjective word order is highly marked. In fact, Dryer (1992: 91–92) writes that, among VO languages in his sample, the order standard-adjective is found only in Chinese (that is, Mandarin), to which Hainan Cham now needs to be added.

Chappell (2011) asks whether this typologically rare comparative configuration for SVO languages is the norm for Sinitic languages or is restricted to Northern Chinese (Mandarin). The answer seems to be, as Ansaldo (2010: 919) writes, except for instances that appear to be recent borrowings from Mandarin, the typologically marked, prepositional comparative is restricted to Mandarin dialects. This makes its borrowing into Hainan Cham, a VO language, even more marked.

7.4.20 The Adversative Agentive *pi³³* Passive

The Hainan passive is both agentive and adversative, like its Mandarin source *bèi*. It begins with a sentence-initial object followed by a *pi³³*+subject phrase, which marks the subject as agentive, and distinguishes the construction. The examples in the database denote something negative happening to the undergoer, including typhoons, the sun, and the like, marking the passive adversative as well (Li and Thompson 1981: 492–508; Shibitani 1994; Keenan and Dryer 2007: 341) (14, 15, 16, 17).

(14) *na²¹ku⁵⁵* *[pi³³* *miaw³³]* *maʔ²⁴* *pʰi⁵⁵*.   (Zheng 1997: 93)
mouse PASS cat grasp CMPL
lǎoshǔ *bèi* *māo* *zhuō* *le*
老鼠 被 猫 捉 了
老鼠[被猫]捉住了。
'The mouse, by the cat was caught.'

(15) *ʔa:w²¹* *kaw³³* *[pi³³* *sa:n²¹]* *sio²¹ ha³³!*   (Zheng 1997: 105)
clothes 1P PASS rain drench !
yīfú *wǒ* *bèi* *yǔ* *lín* *la*
衣 我 被 雨 淋 啦
我的衣服[被雨]淋了。
'The rain drenched my clothes.'

(16) *zəʔ²⁴* *pi³³* *loŋ²¹zay³³* *tsu⁵⁵* *ta:yʔ³³* *ʔa³³*   (Zheng 1997: 90)
grass PASS sun burn die DECL
cǎo *bèi* *tàiyáng* *shāo* *sǐ* *a*
草 被 太阳 烧 死 啊
草[被太阳]烧死了。
'The grass was burned to death by the sun.'

(17) *na²¹nuk²⁴* *pi³³* *miao³³* *kʰiayʔ³³* *baŋ³³* *pʰi*   (OZ 1983a: 39)
chicken PASS cat wild eat CMPL
jī *bèi* *māo* *yě* *chī* *le*
鸡 被 猫 野 吃 了
鸡[被野猫]吃了。
'The chicken was eaten by the wild cat.'

Chappell (2001: 350–351) notes that being both adversative and passive is a characteristic of Sinitic. However, the pi^{33} is Mandarin (Northern Chinese) in origin; when it occurs in Southern Chinese, it is apparently a borrowing from Mandarin. Matisoff (1991: 449, fn. 19) mentions what looks like the same entity in Vietnamese, its adversative passive *bị*, which he notes looks like the Mandarin adversative passive *bèi*, but as with the Hainan Cham passive, this must be a specifically Mandarin borrowing.

7.4.21 An Apparent "Disposal" Construction

Hainan Cham has what appears to be a disposal construction, with parallels to the *bǎ* construction of Mandarin (Li and Thompson 1981: 464–483). Structurally, the construction has the following configuration: subject + $tu\imath^{24}$ + direct object + verb, with the possibility that a readily recoverable subject has been omitted.

Semantically, the following three examples, (18), (19), and (20), all illustrate the construction. The $tu\imath^{24}$ marks the definite direct object, an affected entity, and thus occurs preverbally. In the examples, the underline indicates where the object would normally be found.

(18) [$tu\imath^{24}$ non^{33}] $pa:t^{24}$ ____$na:y\imath^{33}$ (Zheng 1997: 89)
      take   carrying.pole   take   ____good
      bǎ   *biǎndān*   *ná*   ____*hǎo*
      把   扁担   拿   ____好
      [把扁担]___拿好。
      'The pole, take <u>it</u> carefully.'

(19) [$tu\imath^{24}$ $\Omega a:w^{21}$] p^ha^{33} kaw^{33} _____   (Zheng 1997: 90)
      take   clothes   give   1P   ____
      bǎ   *yīfú*   *gěi*   *wǒ*   _____
      把   衣服   给   我   ____
      [把衣服]给我。
      'The clothes, give me <u>them</u>.'

(20) $zay^{33}ni^{33}$ nan^{21} [$tu\imath^{24}$ ma^{33}] Ωua^{33} p^hi^{55},   . . .
      today   can   take   field   plow   CMPL,   . . .
      tiānzhè   *néng*   *bǎ*   *tián*   *lí*   *wán*,   . . .
      天这   能   把   田   梨   完,   . . .
      今天能把田梨完, . . . 。   (Zheng 1997: 103)
      'Today the field gets plowed, . . .'

There is a close match in both the syntax and the semantics between the Hainan Cham and the Mandarin, but not so obviously datable to child bilingualism.

7.5 CONCLUSIONS

Although they have in no sense been immune to the effects of other sociolinguistic processes, including those in which gender and age are indexical of linguistic variation, PC, Haroi, and Hainan Cham all contain linguistic evidence that is arguably the product of earlier child bilingualism. For PC, the most robust indicator of child bilingualism is the pervasive restructuring of the sound system from a largely unmarked Austronesian system with penultimate stress and disyllabic roots to a MK-like system with final stress, a plethora of final syllable vowels, and a scattering of marked sounds (implosive consonants, etc.). The morphological evidence includes the borrowing of a number of MK constructions. Further evidence is found in existence of numerous MK-derived names for body parts and basic vocabulary.

For Haroi, the bulk of the evidence is in the complete reworking of the phonological system from one without any obvious marked phonation to a restructured register system. That is, it is one in which there were vowel register distinctions dependent upon register distinctions; the subsequent loss of the phonation distinctions made the previously phonetic vowel distinctions phonemic. The Haroi restructured register system is not just strikingly similar to the register system of MK Hrê, but the two languages have undergone some of the same phonological changes (Thurgood 2003).

For Hainan Cham, we have multiple indications of child bilingualism. Perhaps the strongest is the restructuring of an atonal language into a language with a five-way tonal system. For the tonal system, we have a short but accurate word list recording the tones in Sanya Chinese, the donor language; comparison shows that the tones have been rendered quite faithfully. This accurate tonal rendering alone would suggest it was the input of bilingual children.

Comparison of Hainan Cham directly with Mandarin (due to the lack of Sanya Mandarin Chinese grammatical data) shows that numerous highly marked, quite sophisticated Mandarin constructions, often with a construction marking borrowed grammatical morpheme, have been faithfully rendered (the Mandarin constructions turn out to be so similar that the lack of Sanya Chinese materials makes no difference). In addition, Hainan Cham has developed a rich system that has prehead modification under the influence of Mandarin to complement the inherited posthead system.

Comparisons with other languages under contact that is known to have included a significant period of child bilingualism should be a fruitful undertaking. Such a study should reveal not just support for the categories found here—radical restructuring of sounds systems, significant borrowing of core vocabulary, and the borrowing of constructions along with their morphological marker—but other categories as well.

Acknowledgments

My analysis has benefited enormously from feedback from Bob Blust, Malcolm Ross, and Marc Brunelle. The Chinese has benefited from generous help from William Baxter.

References

Andrews, Avery D. 2007. Relative clauses. In *Clause Structure, Language Typology and Syntactic Description*, Vol. II, edited by Timothy Shopen, 209–236. 2nd edition. Cambridge: Cambridge University Press.

Ansaldo, Umberto. 2010. Surpass comparatives in Sinitic and beyond: Typology and grammaticalization. *Linguistics* 48(4): 919–950.

Baxter, William. 1992. *A Handbook of Old Chinese Phonology*. Mouton deGruyter: Berlin.

Bellwood, Peter. 2007. Prehistory of the Indo-Malaysian Archipelago. Canberra: ANU Press.

Blood, David L. 1962. A problem in Cham sonorants. *Zeitschrift für Phonetik* 15: 111–114.

Blust, Robert A. 2000. Review of *From Ancient Cham to Modern Dialects: Two Thousand Years of Language Contact and Change*. *Oceanic Linguistics* 39(2): 435–455.

Chappell, Hilary. 2001. Language contact and areal diffusion in Sinitic languages: Problems for typology and genetic affiliation. In *Areal Diffusion and Genetic Inheritance: Problems in Comparative Linguistics*, edited by Alexandra Aikhenvald and R. M. W. Dixon, 328–357. Oxford: Oxford University Press.

Chappell, Hilary. 2011. Word order disharmony in sinitic comparatives. Online. Last modified July 25, 2011.

Dryer, Matthew. 1992. The Greenbergian word order correlations. *Language* 68: 81–138.

Edmondson, Jerold A., and Kenneth J. Gregerson. 1993. Western Cham as a register language. In *Tonality in Austronesian Languages*, edited by Jerry Edmondson and Ken Gregerson, 61–74. Oceanic Linguistics Special Publication No. 24. Honolulu: University of Hawai'i Press.

Grant, Anthony, and Paul Sidwell (eds.). 2007. *Chamic and Beyond: Studies in Mainland Austronesian Languages*. Canberra: Pacific Linguistics 569.

Greenberg, Joseph H. 1970. Some generalizations regarding glottalic consonants, especially implosives. *International Journal of American Linguistics* 36: 123–145.

Hall, Daniel George Edward. 1955, 1981. *A History of South-East Asia*. 1st edition; 4th edition. New York: St. Martin's Press.

Hall, Kenneth R. 1985. *Maritime Trade and State Development in Early Southeast Asia*. Honolulu: University of Hawai'i Press.

Heine, Bernd. 1997. *Cognitive Foundations of Grammar*. Oxford: Oxford University Press.

Higham, C. 2002. *Early Cultures of Mainland Southeast Asia*. Bangkok, Thailand: River Books.

Higham, C. 1989. *The archaeology of mainland Southeast Asia: From 10,000 BC to the fall of Angkor*. Cambridge: Cambridge University Press.

Huffman, Franklin E. 1976. The register problem in fifteen Mon-Khmer languages. In *Austroasiatic Studies*, edited by Philip N. Jenner, Laurence C. Thompson, and Stanley Starosta, Vol. I, 575–590. Special publication of Oceanic Linguistics no. 13. 2 vols. Honolulu: University of Hawai'i Press.

Keenan, Edward L., and Matthew S. Dryer. 2007. Speech act distinctions in grammar. *Clause Structure, Language Typology and Syntactic Description*, Vol. 1, edited by Timothy Shopen, 276–324. Cambridge: Cambridge University Press.

Lee, Ernest Wilson. 1977. Devoicing, aspiration, and vowel split in Haroi: Evidence for register (contrastive tongue-root position). In *Papers in South East Asian Linguistics No. 4: Chamic Studies*, edited by David Thomas, Ernest W. Lee, and Nguyen Dang Liem, 87–104. Canberra: Pacific Linguistics Series A 48.

Li, Charles N., and Sandra A. Thompson. 1981. *Mandarin Chinese: A Functional Reference Grammar*. Berkeley: University of California Press.

Maslova, Elena, and Vladimir P. Nedjalko. 2011. Reciprocal constructions. In *The World Atlas of Language Structures Online*, edited by Bernard Comrie, David Gil, Matthew S. Dryer, and Martin Haspelmath, Chapter 106. Munich: Max Planck Digital Library. http://wals.info/chapter/1. Accessed on July 19, 2011.

Matisoff, James A. 1991. Areal and universal dimensions of grammatization in Lahu. In *Approaches to Grammaticalization*, Vol. 2, edited by Elizabeth Closs Traugott and Bernd Heine, 383–453. Amsterdam: John Benjamins.

Ouyang, Jueya, and Zheng Yiqing. 1983. The Huihui speech (Hainan Cham) of the Hui nationality in Ya County, Hainan. *Minzu Yuwen* 1: 30–40. [OZ]

Peng, Min-Sheng, Huy Ho Quang, Khoa Pham Dang, An Vu Trieu, Hua-Wei Wang, Yong-Gang Yao, Qing-Peng Kong, and Ya-Ping Zhang. 2010. Tracing the Austronesian footprint in mainland Southeast Asia: A perspective from mitochondrial DNA. *Molecular Biology and Evolution* 27(10): 2417–2430.

Phillips, Richard L. 1973. Vowel distribution in Hrê. *Mon-Khmer Studies* III: 63–68.

Schachter, Paul, and Timothy Shopen. 2007. Parts-of-speech systems. In *Typology and Syntactic Description*, Vol. 1., edited by Timothy Shopen, 1–60. 2nd edition. Cambridge, UK: Cambridge University Press.

Shibatani, M. 1994. An integrated approach to possessor raising, ethical datives, and adversative passives. *Proceedings of the 20th Annual Meeting of the Berkeley Linguistics Society*: 461–486.

Smith, Kenneth D. 1972. *A Phonological Reconstruction of Proto-North-Bahnaric*. Language Data, Asian-Pacific Series, no. 2. Santa Ana, CA: SIL.

Solheim, William G., D. Bulbeck, and A. Flavel. 2007. *Archaeology and Culture in Southeast Asia: Unraveling the Nusantao*. Quezon City: University of the Philippines Press.

Southworth, W. A. 2004. The coastal states of Champa. In *Southeast Asia: From Prehistory to History*, edited by I. Glover and Peter Bellwood, 209–233. London: Routledge.

Stassen, Leon. 2011. Comparative constructions. In *The World Atlas of Language Structures Online*, edited by Verbard Comrie, David Gil, Matthew S. Dryer, and Martin Haspelmath, Chapter 121. Munich: Max Planck Digital Library. Available online at http://wals.info/chapter/121. Accessed on August 8, 2013.

Tegenfeldt-Mundhenk, Alice, and Hella Goschnick. 1977. Haroi phonemes. In *Papers in South East Asian Linguistics No. 4: Chamic Studies*, edited by David Thomas, Ernest W. Lee, and Nguyen Dang Liem, 1–15. Pacific Linguistics Series A 48.

Thurgood, Graham. 1999. *From Ancient Cham to Modern Dialects: Two Thousand Years of Language Contact and Change*. Oceanic Linguistics Special Publication No. 28. Honolulu: University of Hawai'i Press.

Thurgood, Graham. 2000. Learnability and the direction of convergence in Cham: The effects of long-term contact on linguistic structures. In *Proceedings of the Western Conference on Linguistics, WECOL 2000*, edited by Vida Samiian, 507–527. California State University, Fresno.

Thurgood, Graham. 2002. Vietnamese and tonogenesis: Revising the model and the analysis. *Diachronica* 19(2): 333–363.

Thurgood, Graham. 2003. Hrê contact and the origins of the Haroi restructured register system: A case of shared sound changes. In *Papers from the Seventh Annual Meeting of the Southeast Asian Linguistics Society*, edited by K. L. Adams, 199–207. Tempe: Arizona State University, Program for Southeast Asian Studies.

Thurgood, Graham, Ela Thurgood, and Li Fengxiang. 2014. *A Grammatical Sketch of Hainan Cham: History, Contact, and Phonology*. Berlin: De Gruyter Mouton.

Zheng, Yiqing. 1997. *Huihui Yu Yanjiu* [A Study of Cham]. Shanghai: Yuandong Chuban She [Shanghai Far East Publishers]. [Zheng]

CHAPTER 8

CODE-SWITCHING AS A REFLECTION OF CONTACT-INDUCED CHANGE

AD BACKUS

8.1 INTRODUCTION

Two of the most robust distinctions that linguistics has made throughout the existence of the discipline are those between synchrony and diachrony and between lexicon and syntax (or between words and grammatical rules). While these distinctions are obviously important for any theory of language, I will argue in this chapter that we should reconsider how we make them if we want to develop an integrated account of language contact phenomena. Specifically, I will argue two things. First, the synchronic and diachronic planes are tightly interconnected, and recognizing that helps integrate the studies of code-switching and contact-induced change. Second, lexicon and syntax do not have to be strictly separated, as is done in many linguistic theories; recognizing *that* helps integrate the studies of code-switching and of grammatical interference. Together, these arguments should help integrate the field of contact linguistics, which is characterized by a disconnect between an essentially synchronic perspective on code-switching, focusing on lexical matters, and an essentially diachronic perspective on contact-induced change, focusing on grammar.

Sections 8.2 and 8.3 will review these different phenomena, discuss how they are generally studied and accounted for, and suggest a solution for the problems I identify. The first subsection is about synchrony and diachrony; the second one about lexicon and syntax. I will make the point that not integrating these perspectives under a general theoretical framework comes with a cost. This is accompanied by a suggestion for a way out: adopting a usage-based approach as a general theoretical framework. The chapter will finish by sketching what a usage-based account of the different contact phenomena looks like, illustrating this with samples of work on Dutch Turkish.

8.2 Synchrony and Diachrony

Pretty much everybody who takes a basic class on linguistics soon hears about the difference between synchronic and diachronic description. For most of us, the distinction is linked to Ferdinand de Saussure, as he introduced the idea that we need to separate the synchronic and diachronic dimensions. When we study the mental knowledge of the speakers of a particular language, we cannot make reference to historical developments in that language, since speakers don't have access to that kind of knowledge. The description of mental representation, therefore, has to be strictly synchronic. Diachronic questions are the province of historical linguistics. Throughout the twentieth century, theoretical linguistics has gradually come to be equated with the synchronic perspective. This has made language change somewhat of a tricky subject: if theoretical linguistics is the core of linguistics, and its aim is to study mental representation, and mental representation is assumed to be stable throughout a person's lifetime, then language change is not a rewarding topic for linguistic research.

This, now, has changed in recent years. Gradually, an alternative view on mental representation has been developing, under the heading of *usage-based linguistics*. Starting off as the basic approach underlying a number of theories, identified as *cognitive linguistics*, that were developed as an alternative to the generative paradigm, slowly but surely this approach has become firmly established as a serious and promising hypothesis about how humans learn, use, and develop their linguistic knowledge. The interesting thing from the perspective of the current chapter is that a usage-based account necessitates taking a diachronic perspective on board while describing a speaker's synchronic mental representation.

8.2.1 The Usage-Based Approach

A usage-based view on linguistic competence entails that each person builds his or her linguistic knowledge, or mental representation, on the basis of his or her language use, which includes both active use as a speaker and passive exposure as a hearer or bystander (e.g., when listening to the radio). Since building this mental representation is a cognitive activity, the linguistic input (*usage*) passes the filter of the cognitive skills we use to process all this linguistic experience. We store better, for example, what we often hear, we store patterns once we detect them as recurrent in language use, we note similarities between different usage events and form abstract categories on that basis, and we store information about how particular units are used and by what kinds of people in what kinds of situation. Now if competence is based on usage in this way, it follows that competence must be forever changing, since no day is like the next. Every communicative situation is unique, so even if you say the same utterance twice, the way it was used and the context-specific meaning it had may still be different. In addition, if things get stored better the more they are used, it follows that the degree to which they are stored, their degree of *entrenchment*, is in constant flux.

Important for our present concerns is that this entails that mental representation changes through time (i.e., it is built up diachronically on the basis of synchronic usage events). Therefore, a usage-based account has no choice but to study synchronic and diachronic phenomena simultaneously, since both dimensions are forever interacting. At the moment of writing this chapter, for example, I am also involved in an effort by the department in which I work to overhaul the bachelor and master's degree programs that we teach. As a result, I have been inundated with Dutch terms from the domain of educational management that until recently I hardly ever used, such as *curriculumschema* 'curriculum matrix,' *bestuurlijk traject* 'administrative path,' *naburige opleidingen* 'neighboring programs,' *opleidingsdirecteur* 'program director,' and *ESG-tekst* 'text for the Electronic Study Guide [describing the content and organization of a course].' I knew them, so they were "in" my lexicon, but I feel I know them much better now. I have a better idea of what they mean exactly, I am better able to connect them to related jargon terms, and I am probably more fluent in using them correctly (i.e., in the right context, with the right meaning, and in tune with what my interlocutors understand the term to mean). In the parlance of the usage-based approach, they are better *entrenched* in my idiolect now than they were a month ago. For lexical items, this is not a revolutionary portrayal of lexical knowledge, but that is only because linguistic knowledge has generally been equated with syntactic knowledge, the lexicon having been characterized as a relatively unstructured "bag of words" that are learned, like many other things, through experience. However, since usage-based linguistics doesn't make as strict a distinction between lexicon and syntax, as we will see, we will have to consider the preceding description of what knowledge entails, how it is acquired, and how it evolves, as also applying to syntactic knowledge.

Evidence for the central usage-based hypothesis has come from observed correlations between frequency data and experimental measures of entrenchment. Word combinations, for example, that are shown to be frequent in corpora tend to trigger faster responses in lexical decision tasks or other psycholinguistic tasks that yield relevant data. Also, studies of language acquisition have amassed evidence that children closely follow input in their linguistic development, producing earliest what they hear the most. While this is not the place to go into the finer points of the debate between usage-based linguistics and its rival, generative linguistics, about who is right and what data are admissible, the usage-based enterprise has been successful enough to warrant taking its implications for other domains, such as language contact, seriously. I have explored the nexus between these two fields in other writings (Backus 2014a, 2014b); here, I wish to focus on the two oppositions introduced in the introduction—synchrony versus diachrony, and lexicon versus syntax—as these have interesting implications for long-standing problems in the contact linguistic literature. At least one perennial question that is asked about code-switching is seen in a different light once we illuminate it from the perspective of a usage-based approach. This is the alleged difference between code-switching and borrowing, to be discussed in the next subsection.

8.2.2 Code-Switching versus Lexical Borrowing

Lexical borrowing is the most commonly discussed type of cross-linguistic influence, though it is often not presented as *contact-induced change*. The reason is probably that the influence is superficial, only concerning lexical change, and the conceptually simplest form of it at that. Loanwords can be seen as the diachronic reflex of the use of single-word code-switches in bilingual speech. Single word insertions are by far the most studied type of code-switching. It concerns the use of a word from Language B in a sentence otherwise framed in Language A, with Language A grammar and mostly Language A lexicon (though there may be more than one single-word insertion in the same sentence). A word from Language B that is *often* inserted into clauses framed by Language A becomes a loanword in Language A. This simple fact has been theorized surprisingly little. Perhaps that's because it's so obvious, but another reason is that code-switching is generally not studied for its diachronic implications. Instead, the literature on code-switching is filled with discussions about how to *distinguish* insertional code-switches from lexical borrowings in *synchronic* speech. I will now argue that this distinction is misguided, since code-switching is a synchronic phenomenon and borrowing a diachronic one. In addition, they are closely linked: they are the synchronic and diachronic manifestation of the same phenomenon.

A particular foreign word may be used often or almost never. In the first case, it makes sense to say that the word is an established loanword in the base language as spoken by the bilingual community; in the second case, it makes equal sense to say that it is not. In either case, whenever the word appears in the base language, it is a case of insertional code-switching. If one wishes to claim that the frequent word, when used in a base language utterance, is not a code-switch while the non-frequent word is, then one needs an independently established cutoff point: When is a word used too frequently to be called a code-switch? There are no objective criteria for establishing this frequency cutoff point. Poplack and Dion (2012) use a different way of making the distinction: if the word is treated morphosyntactically and distributionally like a base language word, then it's a borrowing ("established" if it's frequent; "nonce" if it's rare), and it is not a code-switch. This turns virtually all single-word insertions into loanwords, though.

More important, while it upholds the distinction between established loanwords and non-established loanwords, it does not get us any closer to how to make the distinction between code-switching and borrowing. Dutch Turks, for example, are observed to use the Dutch word *winkelen* 'to shop' regularly. In our recorded data, for example, we encountered the example *dün winkelen yaptık* (yesterday to.shop we.did: 'we went shopping yesterday'), in which the word in question in inserted into a Turkish clause. The insertion follows the pattern familiar from other studies of Turkish in contact with other languages: the foreign word is used in its infinitival form and co-occurs with the auxiliary verb *yap-* 'do', which bears the tense and person inflection. Do speakers use it often enough for it to be called an established loanword in Dutch Turkish? And is it widespread enough in the sense that many people in the community use it? Is it used whenever the concept comes up, or is it in competition with other, Turkish words for the same concept? If so, what is the distribution of these 'synonyms'? Answers to these questions would provide us with a solid basis for answering the larger question of whether it is an established loanword or not. There are no data, however, on which we could base our answers. Loanword status, in this perspective at least, is a matter of entrenchment (at the level of the competence of an individual speaker) and conventionalization (at the cumulative level of entrenchment in a big enough cross-section of individual speakers in the community). About neither of these levels do we have the right kind of data.

An additional complication is that we are dealing with bilingual competence here. Speakers of Dutch Turkish are also speakers of Dutch. Asking the question of whether a particular word is an established loanword in Turkish requires separating the bilingual competence of the speaker into a Dutch and a Turkish competence. However, it is not at all clear whether that is an accurate characterization of psycholinguistic reality. To be sure, it *must* be true to the extent that most speakers are perfectly able to stay in a monolingual mode. This is needed, for example, when talking to monolinguals in Turkey, or to non-Turkish people in Holland. In both cases, the interlocutor is not expected to know both languages. Since speakers can do this, they must know for every word whether it's Turkish or Dutch. It should not surprise us that they have this ability, given the almost total allocation of life domains to particular languages, sometimes to Turkish and mostly to Dutch, a state of affairs supported by two important facts. One is that there is an asymmetry in status that is typical for immigrant languages: they do not compete with the majority language for use in the public domain (e.g., work, school, national media, non-ethnic shopping, bureaucracy, etc.). Second, Dutch Turks tend to have extensive contacts with friends and family in Turkey, who share much of their background except that they don't speak Dutch. Any Dutch word would cause communication problems. As a result, Dutch Turks know which words are Turkish and which are Dutch.

Looking at the bilingual competence holistically, we see a huge collection of vocabulary items, and part of the represented meaning of every item is from which language it comes. In some psycholinguistic models of bilingualism in the past, this was formalized through a 'language index'; here I suggest it is just part of the meaning. A rich theory of meaning associates a given form not just with a denotational, dictionary-like semantic meaning, but also with pragmatic and sociolinguistic information about how the word is normally or often used. Just as we know of some words that they belong to a high or formal register and therefore are not to be used in informal communication with family members (recall the Dutch educational terms introduced earlier), so Dutch Turks know that some words are Dutch and therefore not to be used in Turkey, and that some words are Turkish and therefore not to be used in conversation with Dutch people. This adds another twist to the question of whether a particular Dutch word is an established loanword in Dutch Turkish or not. The word *winkelen* 'to shop' is for sure part of the lexical inventory of any Dutch Turkish speaker, by virtue of this speaker also being a speaker of Dutch (and *winkelen* being a normal everyday word). Therefore, it is an established lexical unit in the mental representation of this speaker. Since part of its meaning is that it is Dutch, the speaker knows not to use it in Turkey, but that it is fine to use when interacting with Dutch speakers. Since he also knows that speakers of Dutch Turkish know the word, and that it is perfectly all right to mix vocabulary from both languages when talking to one another, he knows he can use it when speaking Dutch Turkish, or the mixed lect. However, this holds for *any* Dutch word. They may not all be established loanwords in Dutch Turkish, but they are established words in the mental representation of the speaker. The question about established loanword status now reduces to the following: Is the word in common use as an insertion into otherwise Turkish clauses (i.e., as a code-switch)?

Note that the linguistic ecology is much simpler in cases where there is no real bilingualism, as is the case in the settings in which the spread of Anglicisms around the world is often investigated. If we want to know, for example, whether two given English words, say *crowdfunding* and *celebrity*, differ in the degree to which they are established loanwords in a particular language spoken by people who have some knowledge of English but don't use it together with their other language in everyday settings, say, Austrian German, all we have to do is find a way of checking the frequency with which these two words are used in the speech of a random sample of Austrians. When they use these words in their German, they are using words that they expect their inter-locutors to know and accept. The crucial difference with the Dutch Turks is that Austrians will only use English words that are more or less acceptable, for example because they fill a lexical gap or are generally known to be in widespread use. Any deviation from this principle will most likely be an act of willful creativity and may well be metalinguistically flagged. Dutch Turks, on the other hand, can use any Dutch word, by virtue of fellow Dutch Turks knowing all Dutch words. For this reason, it is conceptually easier to ask whether *crowdfunding* and *celebrity* are established loan-words in Austrian German than whether *winkelen* is an established loanword in Dutch Turkish.

Nevertheless, we need to engage with the question if we want to clarify the relation-ship between code-switching and borrowing. The only way the question seems to make sense is to look at bilingual speech and to see how often a particular Dutch word is used in a grammatically Turkish context. However, even then at least two problems remain. One is empirical: Data are not always neatly separable into Dutch clauses and Turkish clauses. Recordings of spontaneous conversation in a community in which rapid back-and-forth switching has become the in-group norm (i.e., where "CS is the unmarked choice"; Myers-Scotton 1993) contain numerous passages in which clauses are not clearly in Turkish or in Dutch. In the preceding characterization of relevant data, relatively few data points would remain in our Dutch Turkish corpus. Most code-switching is alternational, and even insertional code-switching from a Turkish base is often more complicated than simply the insertion of a Dutch content word into a Turkish grammatical frame. In the following two examples (from Demirçay and Backus 2014), it is not so easy to say in what language the utterances are framed.

(1)   *Of* düdüklü-de yap-ıyo *of gewoon pan.*
      or pressure cooker-LOC do-PRES.3SG *or regular pot*
      'She *either* does it in a pressure cooker *or a regular pot.*'

(2)   *Dus echt* düğün yap-mı-yo-lar?
      so real wedding do-NEG-PRES-3PL
      '*So* they are not having a *real* wedding?'

In (1), both conjunctions are uttered in Dutch. However, apart from the conjunction *of* ('either'), the first part of the correlative conjunctive phrase is in Turkish. The agreement between verb and subject is achieved in Turkish. The second part of the phrase, which is entirely in Dutch, is missing the preposition "in," which suggests that even the spatial meaning is achieved through the locative suffix *–de* in the Turkish part of the phrase. It is difficult to draw the line between a matrix language and an embedded language here. Example (2) is another utterance that starts with a Dutch conjunction. There is an alternation to Turkish midway in the sentence. However, the noun phrase meaning 'real wedding' is made up of the Dutch adjective *echt* ('real') and the Turkish noun *düğün* ('wedding'). It is possible that *düğün* is an insertion from Turkish and that the morphosyntactic frame of the first part of the utterance is in Dutch. However, the utterance continues in Turkish and ends with the Turkish finite verb inflection probably triggered by the object noun *düğün*. According to the common definition, this would make Turkish the matrix language.

It is possible that the switch into Turkish for *düğün* is pragmatically motivated, as it relates to a predominantly Turkish domain. Most of the speakers we recorded happened to talk about wedding-related subjects. Mostly this topic was discussed using Turkish, very rarely in Dutch. The fact that the noun phrase starts with a Dutch adjective that continues the language in which the clause was started and is followed by a finite verb that continues the language in which the object noun phrase ends points toward the intricate mixing type labeled "congruent lexicalization" in Muysken (2000). It is even possible that the bilingual phrase *echt düğün* ('real wedding') is a conventional lexical unit for these speakers. In any case, it is not prototypical insertion and not prototypical alternation.

The other problem is methodological: corpora are never going to give us *enough* data to answer the question. Individual content words are not particularly frequent, especially not the types of words that are caught up in cross-linguistic borrowing processes, as they tend to be semantically specific, rather than basic. Corpus linguistics is often able to circumvent this problem by making use of corpora of enormous size, running into billions of words. This, however, is only possible with written corpora, as texts can be thrown together relatively easily. In the debate about how to distinguish code-switching and borrowing, on the other hand, the most relevant data come from informal spoken conversation, and it is impossible to collect really large corpora for this register, as recorded spoken conversation requires transcription. Perhaps we could use the written corpora regardless, on the assumption that the differences between written and spoken language are negligible. If the corpus is big enough, and if it contains enough material from informal genres such as chat sites, perhaps the problem is manageable. Indeed, in the type of Anglicism research illustrated earlier with the hypothetical Austrian German example, such work has recently been pioneered (Zenner 2012), but recall the important differences between this kind of context and the contexts of "real" bilingualism with which we are concerned in the current chapter.

As a promising alternative, one could elicit other kinds of data. In the usage-based literature, many studies have employed experimental tasks and judgment tasks, partly to circumvent the problem of insufficiently large corpora, but mostly to see whether evidence would converge if we collect evidence from different sources. In our own work on Dutch Turkish, we have used judgment tasks and experimental studies regarding the conventionality of instances of structural borrowing (see the next section), and this could also be done with lexical items.

8.2.3 Interference versus Structural Borrowing

Language contact also typically gives rise to structural changes in one or both of the affected languages. The most common approach has been to describe synchronically which of the structures presently found in the language ultimately go back to foreign influence. For example, Haase (1992) is a presumably fairly complete inventory of grammatical aspects of Gascon Basque that have arisen because of influence from French or Gascon. Similar overviews exist for other languages (e.g., Dorian 1981 on East Sutherland Gaelic or Aikhenvald 2002 on Tariana). While these descriptions are technically synchronic, they are written with a diachronic perspective in mind: the whole reason why these studies are undertaken is to investigate how the language has changed over the years (or centuries), that is, diachronically. Where available, diachronic data are often used in addition, showing for instance through analysis of historical documents at what point a given structure was first attested in the language. In this sense, the prototypical study of contact-induced change is the opposite of the prototypical study of code-switching: while both make use of largely or exclusively synchronic data, one has a synchronic perspective and the other a diachronic one.

The main question for much of the literature on contact-induced change is whether it can indeed be proven that the change is contact-induced, a hypothesis that is notoriously hard to prove (Thomason and Kaufman 1988). Interesting as that question is, it has put so much emphasis on the origin issue that there is relatively little on how the change has subsequently propagated. In that sense, contact-induced change could be studied in a more diachronic way than has hitherto been done.

Young contact settings, such as the Dutch Turkish one, generally have no structures for which the change has run its course, and this means that propagation can be studied in real time. Borrowing the methodology of quantitative variational sociolinguistics, some work has been done on this issue, though it's generally not couched in terms of propagation. However, if the second generation is found to use a particular grammatical feature more often than the first generation and that feature is suspected to be the result of foreign influence, and if the third generation uses it even more, then the likely explanation is that the change is propagating. In work like Silva-Corvalán (1994), usage of the new variant is carefully investigated to see whether it correlates with both linguistic and extra-linguistic factors (i.e., with lexico-grammatical environments and with types of speaker and communicative setting), and this provides a pretty good picture of how the change is unfolding.

Yet here, too, we run up against the limitations of corpus analysis if the only data we can use are corpora of spontaneously recorded mixed speech. The number of speakers we can record and analyze is necessarily limited, considering the manpower needed to transcribe it all. Consequently, it is always difficult to know to what extent findings can be generalized to the community at large, and to other genres of conversation than the ones sampled in the corpus (which are usually informal talk among friends and/or interviews with the researcher). For that reason, we have combined such analyses with judgment and experimental tasks.

In one typical case, we have studied the fate of subordination in Dutch Turkish (Onar Valk and Backus 2013). Immigrant Turkish seems to be changing its way of making subordinate clauses. While Turkish as spoken in Turkey mostly has non-finite clauses that precede the matrix verb (as in example 4), NL-Turkish speakers show a preference for finite clauses that follow the matrix verb (see example 3). The non-finite subordinated verb in (4) uses a nominalization marker and a possessive marker to turn 'love' into a non-finite form which means something like 'your loving'; as this functions as the direct object of 'see,' it is also marked with accusative case.

(3) gör-üyo-m   [siz   birbiriniz-i   çok   sev-iyo-ruz]
     see-PROG-1SG   [you   each other-ACC   very   love-PROG-2PL]
     '. . . I see [that you love each other a lot] . . .'

(4) [siz   birbiriniz-i   çok   sev-diği-niz-i]   gör-üyo-m
     [you   each other-ACC   very   love-NMNL-2PL-ACC]   see-PROG-1SG
     '. . . I see [that you love each other a lot] . . .'

Onar Valk (2014) reports experimental evidence that confirms the corpus data. These data include the responses to an experimental task in which subordinate clauses were elicited, and to a judgment task in which various types of subordinate clauses were judged for the degree to which they sounded 'normal.'

In elicited imitation data, in which speakers had to repeat a sequence of three or four sentences immediately after hearing them, NL-Turkish speakers significantly more often preserved finite subordinate clauses and verb-medial structures present in a stimulus item than did TR-Turkish speakers, who instead tended to change such items to non-finite and verb-final structures. About a fourth of the time, NL-Turkish speakers even produced the Dutch-like structures if the stimulus item had contained the TR-Turkish structure, something TR-Turkish speakers never did. Similarly, when asked to rate the conventionality of stimulus items containing the various subordination structures in a judgment task, NL-Turkish speakers once again consistently gave higher conventionality ratings for finite subordination and verb-initial structures like the one in (3) than TR-Turkish speakers did. However, they also gave high ratings for the conventional non-finite and verb-final structures as exemplified in (4). A usage-based interpretation of these findings is that the finite and verb-initial structures are more entrenched for NL-Turkish speakers, and this is presumably because Dutch structures in general are more entrenched for them (i.e., they are Dutch-dominant), and that this often causes sentence planning in Turkish to go through Dutch as it were (Slobin 1996). Abundant use of finite and verb-medial structures increases their frequency, and thus their entrenchment in the competence of individual speakers.

It is encouraging that the three kinds of evidence converged. It means that the impression we would have formed about the propagation of the change only on the basis of recorded conversations would actually have been largely accurate.

In conclusion, while synchronically we can distinguish between relatively lexical and relatively syntactic contact phenomena, the process by which they become entrenched, by which they propagate toward the possible status of established contact-induced change, is the same for all subtypes, since the interconnection between synchronic use and diachronic use holds for all types of linguistic elements. This was illustrated for code-switching and lexical borrowing, and for grammatical interference and structural borrowing. If the interplay between synchronic variation and diachronic change is the same regardless of the type of linguistic element we are looking at, it makes sense to see to what degree we can merge theories of lexical and of structural change into a general theory of contact-induced change. For that, we need to engage further with the distinction between lexicon and syntax. This we will do in the next section.

8.3 LEXICON AND SYNTAX

At least as familiar for any student of linguistics as the distinction between synchrony and diachrony, and certainly more so for laypeople, is the basic distinction between words and grammar. Obviously, there is a real difference between the two: words have phonological content and generally have a fairly clear meaning, while grammar consists of phonologically empty (i.e., schematic) patterns that seem to be without a meaning of their own. These differences are so pervasive and clear that we separate vocabulary and grammar in our approach to language teaching and that linguistics works with the two separate modules of lexicon and syntax. Theories usually apply to one or the other, and links between the two are only made at the most abstract level (i.e., they are both part of language and interact in some way). Given the intuitively natural distinction between a meaning-based lexicon and a form-based syntax, this may seem indeed like it's the right way to look at words and grammar.

However, there are a number of empirical phenomena that make a strict dichotomous distinction between lexicon and syntax problematic. Most of these have been at the center of attention in usage-based linguistics, as they gave rise to this approach getting off the ground in the first place.

8.3.1 Lexicon and Syntax in the Usage-Based Approach

There are a number of reasons to be wary of the distinction between meaningful words and meaningless patterns. First, not all form-meaning units stored as a whole are single words. Multiword units such as *red wine, trick or treat, beyond the pale, score a goal,* and *I think that* clearly instantiate productive syntactic patterns (adjective + noun, verb *or* verb, preposition + noun phrase, verb + object noun phrase, and subject + verb + complementizer, respectively) but just as clearly are fixed units. Including them in the lexicon would require opening it up to more than just simple words, but the conventionality of such examples seems to make that an inescapable move. Second, not all grammatical elements are without meaning. The well documented process of grammaticalization shows that if an element was once a full lexical item and is now a grammatical morpheme, some of that older meaning still shines through in current usage, as in the auxiliary-like uses of 'threaten,' for example, in many European languages (Heine and Miyashita 2008). Positing a sudden jump from one module to the other is not the most intuitively attractive option for theorizing about this process. At the very least, it requires some kind of link between lexicon and syntax, and aspects of grammaticalization suggest that the border is at least fluid, and probably represents a transitional area on a continuum.

In addition, even grammatical patterns without any phonological content can have meaning. Turkish word order, for example, allows SVO order in addition to the canonical SOV, and hearers who encounter an utterance with SVO order will interpret the object as backgrounded, as that's what the post-verbal position 'means.' While all this doesn't necessarily obviate the need for a difference between lexicon and syntax, it does call into question that the difference resides in the lexicon's role as carrying meaning, with syntax only providing form. Third, there has been an explosion of studies into expressions that instantiate the type of common constructions that is sort of halfway between lexicon and syntax, as they are not quite multiword units and not quite fully compositional creations using an empty syntactic frame.

Perhaps the best known of such constructions is the so-called *way* construction, instantiated in such utterances as *he talked his way out of trouble.* Such constructions are productive, but also contain fixed elements (including, in this example, the word *way*, a possessive pronoun that agrees with the subject and with which it forms a noun phrase, a verb preceding that noun phrase, and a prepositional phrase indicating some kind of metaphorical path). This means that such constructions mix lexical and syntactic characteristics. Fourth, psycholinguistic studies pretty consistently report processing differences that correlate with items' frequencies of occurrence in corpora. For example, lexical decision tasks often show quicker reaction times for words that are frequent. This suggests that lexical knowledge involves more than just whether or not someone's inventory includes a particular word. Interestingly, this effect also extends to multiword forms: frequent combinations are accessed holistically. Arnon and Snider (2010), for instance, found that in a phrasal version of a lexical decision task, participants were quicker to recognize four-word phrases that occurred with high frequency than equally long phrases that occurred with low frequency; for example, *don't have to worry* was processed faster than *don't have to wait*: both phrases are encountered in everyday speech, but the first one is much more frequent. This suggests that these frequent phrases are stored holistically, as 'big words' (Dabrowska 2004; Wray 2008), so to speak. Holistic storage facilitates holistic access during production, meaning that the syntactic structure that underlies such phrases is bypassed.

Combined, these findings cast doubt on the psychological accuracy of a strict division between lexicon and syntax (Langacker 2008). At the very least, the definition of lexical item should be flexible enough to allow multiword units, make reference to degree of entrenchment, allow for relatively schematic or abstract meaning, and perhaps also allow for partially schematic and completely schematic forms to be included as a subtype of *lexical item*. However, once a linguistic theory embarks on this road, sooner or later it will face the question of whether there really is any syntax (see Goldberg 2009). The consensus that seems to be forming in usage-based linguistics is that lexicon and syntax are regions on a continuum going from phonologically fully specific to fully empty units, in which every unit is a combination of a form and a meaning. The degree of phonological specificity determines how close the unit is to the traditional notion of *lexical item*. Words remain the prototypical lexical item, and fully schematic patterns such as the word order pattern of a pragmatically neutral declarative transitive clause are prototypical syntactic items. It is likely that there is a correlation between having a specific form and having a relatively specific meaning, and between having a relatively schematic form and a more abstract meaning. It is furthermore an open question to what extent syntactic constructions are actively used when a speaker produces expressions that instantiate them.

While including multiword expressions and idioms can still support a relatively strict boundary between lexicon and syntax, requiring only the stipulation that a lexical unit can be of any size, the distinction really becomes problematic if partially schematic constructions are indeed seen as "big words." Dutch has borrowed the English expression *to go for something* and Dutch people can be heard to say things like the following.

(5) ik ga ervoor
     I go there.for
     'I'm gonna go for it'

(6) ik ga voor de steak
     I go for the steak
     'I'll go for the steak'

(7) hij ging voor een wereldrecord
     he went for a world.record
     'He went for the world record'

The most natural way of describing what must have happened is that Dutch has borrowed the construction [*go for X*], in which all the words and morphemes are realized in Dutch, the word order follows Dutch patterns, 'go' can be inflected for any person and tense combination, and X can be anything that fits the semantics of the construction. What has been borrowed by Dutch is partially lexical (a form of 'go' and the preposition 'for') and partially syntactic (the construction and its meaning). Since to use the construction one has to insert the right words, put them in the right order, and inflect them in the right way, it involves more than just the insertion of a borrowed lexical item.

Given these examples, the classic characterization of utterance production as consisting of the insertion of lexical items into a prepared grammatical structure seems untenable. Rather, speaking seems to be a matter of overlapping templates that sometimes do and sometimes don't include specific lexical or morphological material. I will argue in the following that this calls for some rethinking of the basic concepts that are used in code-switching research, such as insertion and alternation.

8.3.2 Lexicon and Syntax in Contact Linguistics

Like the rest of linguistics, contact linguistics also makes a principled distinction between words and structure. The very division between code-switching and structural borrowing, not just as phenomena but also as research traditions studying them, analyzed in the preceding as differing in having a synchronic versus diachronic outlook, rests on whether the foreign element being borrowed is lexical or structural. Code-switching by definition deals with overt (i.e., lexical) material from the other language; similarly structural borrowing is defined as the importation of foreign grammar.

The most recent incarnation of the distinction between words and structure in contact linguistics is the distinction between Matter (MAT) and Pattern (PAT) loans. MAT loans are basically borrowed words; PAT loans are borrowed structure. Before that, Johanson (2002) introduced the Code Copying Model, in which foreign material that gets incorporated into a base language is either globally or selectively copied. Global copies are actual words (or longer stretches), while selective copies are structural. It can be a shade of meaning (giving rise to semantic extension), a co-occurrence pattern (giving rise to loan translations), or simply an increase in frequency (giving rise to higher prominence of a structure that used to be more marginal, usually a structure that is superficially similar to a more unmarked structure in the other language).

Both models take an important step by combining lexical and structural phenomena in the same overall model, forcing the analyst to relate them to each other. In a way, they follow in the footsteps of Weinreich (1964), who also made a point of looking at lexical and structural cross-linguistic influence at the same time.

What I will argue for is that it will improve our analysis of contact phenomena if we examine both lexical and structural aspects of *each* phenomenon. Specifically, MAT loans may contain some aspects of PAT borrowing, and PAT borrowing may sometimes be more 'lexical' than it seems, even when no actual MAT loan is implicated. In Johanson (2002), there is a category called 'mixed copying' that does combine the two kinds of borrowing, but what I have in mind goes beyond that. In the previous section, I have made the argument that code-switching and lexical borrowing are essentially the same thing, though they describe different aspects of the phenomenon, one from a synchronic perspective and the other from a diachronic one. Following that, I argued that other contact phenomena should be interpreted the same way, giving rise to the pair of interference and structural borrowing. The ultimate conclusion was that the studies of code-switching and of contact-induced language change should be drawn closer together. The current section will now attempt to show that giving up the strict demarcation between lexical and structural borrowing calls for the same step.

There are many contact phenomena that have a lexical and a structural side. Sometimes borrowed words seem to take some borrowed structure along. If what is taken along is best characterized as lexical combinability (i.e., the sort of words with which the borrowed word co-occurs in the source language), this is what Johanson (2002) refers to as "mixed copies" (see Verschik 2008 for detailed analysis). Borrowed functional elements almost by definition "come with" structure attached, but borrowed content words often come with baggage, too. They may, for example, introduce a new way of conceptualizing a scene, a nuance lost if we only focus on the fact that a foreign word form is inserted.

"Mixed copies" (Johanson 2002) combine characteristics of loan translations and lexical borrowing. In ordinary loan translation, all morphemes are from the native language: it's the way in which they are combined that is taken from the foreign source. In mixed copies, at least one of the actual words or morphemes is borrowed. For example, all over the Western European Turkish immigrant diaspora, the verb *almak* 'to take' is used in combination with object nouns that denote some type of vehicle, such as trains, taxis or, in the following example, the subway. In this particular example, the actual object noun that is used is from German. Using the verb 'to take' to go with 'subway' reveals influence from German, since German uses its equivalent verb *nehmen* in these environments. The whole sequence functions as a mixed copy because it involves lexical borrowing (global copying, MAT borrowing: the German word) as well as loan translation (selective copying, PAT borrowing: the new combination the verb *almak* enters into).

Here is an example from German Turkish:

(8) *U-bahn*   almak (German noun and Turkish verb)
     subway   take
     'take the subway'
     TR-Turkish: *U-bahn*-a binmek ('get on the subway', **with dative and different verb**)

Note that it is not obvious whether speakers of Immigrant Turkish now have a "syntactic" construction [*VEHICLE almak*] or just a bunch of "lexical" expressions that happen to share the verb and the fact that the nouns all refer to some kind of vehicle. The fact that as linguists we see certain similarities and are able to construct the superordinate category does not mean that speakers do this as well. There is currently a lot of debate about the cognitive reality of schemas (i.e., syntactic patterns), and at which level of granularity they are cognitively real (e.g., Boas 2008; Perek 2012).

Structural effects of MAT loans are more directly in evidence when the borrowed morpheme is a functional element. Conjunctions and prepositions are defined partly by their associated structure, as implied by their names, and often this associated structure is borrowed along with the word (see, for example, the overview in Stolz and Stolz 1996 of borrowed Spanish conjunctions and discourse markers into Amerindian languages, including the grammatical implications for clause structures in these languages). In many cases, of course, the borrowing language already had the same structure, making any borrowing outcome invisible. This holds even more strongly for elements that are further down the cline of grammaticalization, such as case markers. It is probably not coincidental that such grammatical markers are rarely borrowed unless the languages involved are closely related. Nevertheless, in the gray area between lexicon and grammar, borrowing functional elements is relatively common, as it is between languages with little typological overlap.

Finally, there may be evidence of joint lexical and structural influence even if no overt foreign morpheme is being used. The following example illustrates what could be referred to as a loan translation involving a function word, in this case a Dutch preposition. The preposition *met* 'with' isn't used at all in this utterance, but its ghost is all over the unconventional use of its Turkish equivalent, the postposition *ile*, here realized in its suffixal form *–le*. Once more, what is borrowed is partly lexical (a particular use of the comitative postposition, i.e., a particular shade of meaning) and partly structural (its inclusion as an adjunct in the existential construction).

(9) Hiç fark-ı   yok   İngiliz-le
     No   difference-poss.3SG exist.not English-with
     'There is no difference with the English.'

     Dutch: helemaal geen verschil   met   Engels-en
             absolutely no   difference with English-PL

     TR-Turkish: hiç fark-ı   yok   ingiliz-den
                  No   difference-poss.3SG exist.not English-abl

What this section has argued is that if lexicon and syntax are regions on a continuum, and contact settings produce lexical and syntactic contact effects, we should be able to put these contact effects on a continuum as well. Exploring this is a major aim of the present chapter.

8.3.2.1 *Overt versus Covert Lexical Borrowing*

A particular kind of MAT-PAT opposition is the distinction between overt foreign words (i.e., insertional code-switches) and covert types of lexical influence. On this dimension, single- and multiple-word code-switching are opposed to semantic extension and loan translation and to structural interference if the foreign-influenced use concerns native functional elements.

The first comparison is between single-word code-switching and what is most often called *semantic extension*. As it bears some similarity to loan translation, Backus and

Dorleijn (2009) refer to it as "one-word loan translation." An example is the use of the word *kalabalık* 'crowded' in Dutch Turkish. An analysis that only focuses on overt lexical borrowing would miss the attested example (10a), and would only pay attention if instead the Dutch word *druk* had been used, as in the constructed example (10b). In the case of semantic extension, the influence of the Dutch word takes the form of changed usage of an existing Turkish word. The word takes over the shades of meaning that its Dutch translation equivalent has. The word acts as a pivot (Matras 2009) in this case of PAT borrowing.

(10) çocuk-lar   bugün   çok   kalabalık   [attested]
      child-PL   today   very   crowded
      'The children are very noisy today'

      Origin: Dutch *druk* 'busy,' 'noisy,' 'crowded'; Tr-Tu: kalabalık 'crowded'
      çocuk-lar   bugün   çok   druk   [constructed]
      child-PL   today   very   crowded
      'The children are very noisy today'

The same difference between overt and covert lexical borrowing is also in evidence when we compare multiple-word code-switching and loan translation. Code-switching data generally show frequent insertion of verb-object collocations, as in the following Dutch-Turkish example.

(11) Bu sene dört *college volg-en* yapı-yor-uz   [attested]
      This year four *class follow-INF* do-PROG-1pl
      'This year we're *taking* four *classes*'

At the same time, data also yield many examples of unconventional combinations of Turkish verbs and object nouns that together form the literal translation of a Dutch collocation. In (12), the Dutch combination of 'give' and 'guilt' is at the basis of the Turkish combination of the same words, to convey the meaning 'to blame.' TR-Turkish doesn't make use of this combination, and uses a verbalized form of the noun 'guilt' instead. Also given is the hypothetically possible version with the Dutch collocation inserted along the same pattern, as exemplified in (11).

(12) suç-u   bana   ver-di   [attested]
      guilt-ACC   to.me   give-PAST.3SG
      'he accused me'
      Dutch: de schuld geven; 'give the guilt';
      Turkish suçlamak 'accuse': (suç-la-mak 'guilt-VERBALIZER-INF')
      Or
      schuld-u   bana   *geven*   yap-tı   [constructed]
      guilt-ACC   to.me   *give*   do-PAST.3SG

In the traditional definition, a loan translation is strictly lexical: the new form is limited to a specific 'pivot' (be it a word, as in semantic extension, or a multiword sequence, as in loan translation). However, sometimes we get groups of similar loan translations, not unlike Heine and Kuteva's (2005) "minor use patterns" and the "partially schematic constructions" of cognitive linguists (Langacker 1991). The question is the same as the one illustrated earlier for usage-based linguistics in general: What level of specificity is cognitively real? The next subsection explores this issue a little further.

8.3.2.2 *Constructional Borrowing*

In Dutch Turkish (and presumably other immigrant varieties of this language), the verb *yapmak* 'to do' co-occurs with a host of object nouns that refer to a school type or to a school subject. The resulting expressions refer to classes one has taken, or a school type one has gone to. Some relevant examples are given in (13). Similarly, the verb *oynamak* ('to play') is used with the names of musical instruments (see 14). In both cases, the expressions betray Dutch influence, as Dutch uses the respective translation equivalents in these contexts, while TR-Turkish doesn't. These can be analyzed as individual cases of loan translation that happen to make use of the same verb, but more attractive is the generalization that the use of these verbs has changed, so that what has been changed are the partially schematic construction N + *yapmak* and N + *oynamak*. Since both instantiate the same structure, one could even entertain the hypothesis that both are instantiations of a changing N + light verb construction (i.e., of a maximally schematic construction).

(13)   NL-Turkish collocations with *yap-*
    a. Fransızca yap-   do French
    b. ilkokul yap-   do elementary school
    c. *wiskunde* yap-   do math
    d. *universiteit* yap-   study at university

(14)   NL-Turkish collocations with oyna-
    a. piyano oyna-   play the piano
    b. gitar oyna-   play guitar
    c. *trommels* oyna- play drums
    d. *trompet* oyna-   play trumpet

Finally, and probably more contentiously, we could also contemplate a lexical analysis of much larger units. Some types of code-switching appear to be cases of inter-clausal switching, but at the same time involve conventional chunks. In (15), the Dutch "main clause" that co-occurs with an "embedded" Turkish clause could also be analyzed as a Dutch discourse marker that conventionally introduces a reported speech clause that conveys the speaker's inner thought at a particular moment of time. This kind of code-switching is very common and accounts for a sizable portion of alternational cases. It co-occurs, though, with the increase in subordination structures that directly parallel the canonical Dutch structure discussed in section 8.2.3, with a postposed finite subordinate clause rather than the pre-posed non-finite structure that is more common in TR-Turkish (Onar Valk and Backus 2013).

(15)   *ik vind* kültürle, kültürle dini karıştırıyorlar . . .   [attested]
       '*I think* they are mixing up culture and religion . . .'

With the last example, one could say we have definitely entered the realm of grammatical interference. If Dutch Turkish changes its way of making subordinate clauses to be more in line with how Dutch does it, that's a case of contact-induced structural change (i.e., a textbook case of PAT borrowing). However, the example also showed that responsible for this change in at least some cases may be lexical influence, in the form of the insertion of a Dutch chunk that happens to play a crucial role in the associated grammatical structure. At other times the chunk may be loan translated, with the Turkish equivalent of *ik vind*, *düşünüyorum*, in the same position. Structural borrowing, I suggest, may at times involve the loan translation of a particular lexical multiword expression and its associated grammatical structure.

This perspective can also be explored for other types of grammatical borrowing. The following example is a textbook case of grammatical interference: non-conventional case marking. Could this also be seen as a kind of "loan translation" (i.e., does it have aspects that are "lexical")?

(16)   NL-Turkish: Türk müziğ-i   çok   sev-iyor-um.
                     Turkish music-poss.3SG   a.lot like-prog-1SG.
                     'I like Turkish music a lot'

       NL: Ik hou van Turkse muziek.
                     I like   Turkish music.
                     'I like Turkish music'

       TR-Turkish: Türk müziğ-i-ni   çok   sev-iyor-um.
                     Turkish music-poss.3SG-acc   a.lot like-prog-1SG.
                     'I like Turkish music a lot'

In TR-Turkish, this construction requires accusative marking of the direct object. Turkish direct objects are case-marked if they are definite and/or specific, and a convention of the language is that compound nouns always count as definite, as far as accusative marking is concerned. This is because compounds are marked with the third person possessive marker, and direct objects that end in the possessive marker are counted as inherently definite. In other words, the possessive triggers the accusative. However, in the actually attested Dutch Turkish example, the accusative is not used. The rule that the possessive must be followed by the accusative in a direct object is apparently relaxed. The speaker treats the direct object as the generic object that it (also) is, and generic direct objects normally do not call for the accusative.

Dutch influence is likely, but the question is how to characterize it. Is it importation of the Dutch habit of marking direct object status solely through word order (i.e., is the model that VN order 'means' that the noun phrase following the verb is a direct object, a model then adapted to Turkish NV order)? Or is it a copy of the Dutch zero marking of the direct object (i.e., is the model V N-ə, adapted to N-ə V)? Or is it a translation of an entire Dutch expression, making the lack of accusative marking merely a byproduct (i.e., the model is *Ik hou erg van Turkse muziek*, adapted to 'Türk müziği çok seviyorum')? In the latter case, it would be suitable to use the term *loan translation* for the entire utterance. The first two explanations are syntactic; the third, lexical.

Different as all these examples may seem to be, they all share that something from the other language has been translated into the borrowing language. If the model is semantically rich, we talk of loan translation or semantic extension; if it is semantically general, we talk about grammatical interference, or structural borrowing. Conceptualizing the underlying dimension as the degree of semantic detail entails that these different kinds of cross-linguistic influence differ only in degree, not in kind.

This, I think, is the ultimate consequence if one adopts the usage-based definition of *lexical unit*: a form-meaning combination of any size or complexity.

8.4 PROPAGATION

A final point of attention to be touched upon only briefly will be the nature of the evidence we can use to assess how far advanced a change is in diachronic terms and to what degree a change is lexical or structural. Section 8.2 sketched a usage-based approach in which data on synchronic use are used to extrapolate hypotheses about diachronic processes. It is clear that synchronic data cannot be direct evidence for change. The evidence is circumstantial: if we see a particular phenomenon being used now, and it was not part of the language before contact, while it does show similarities with a structure in another language that the speakers also know, we can surmise with some confidence that contact has led to structural borrowing. However, that doesn't mean we know how far the change has progressed. Exceptions notwithstanding, phenomena tend to be described at the level of the language, which operates on the assumption that all or most speakers of the language use the feature under investigation. Whenever variation within a speech community is a topic of interest, we often see differences between subgroups in the community in the degree to which they use particular contact-induced features. Code-switching patterns, for example, often differ across generations, correlating with differences in proficiency distributions.

If it is true that the contact effects we find occur in the speech of all or most members of a community, then we can safely say that conventions have been changed, or are in the process of changing. However, in general we lack the requisite data to back up the implicit assumption that these changes are widespread if all we have is one-off recordings of natural conversations. The situation is a lot easier, of course, in settings in which the change has run its course. Many indigenous minority languages have gone through centuries of contact with a locally dominant language, and often this has produced structures that once were lacking in the language but by now have been established as the sole convention. A descriptive grammar of Sorbian, for example, will contain many structures that are the result of German influence. Often, there will be no variation between an inherited structure and a borrowed structure, since only the borrowed structure is still in use. Backus, Heine, and Doğruöz (2011) make an explicit comparison between Sorbian and NL-Turkish, and find that the Dutch-influenced changes that are ongoing in NL-Turkish, as evidenced by occasional use of an innovative borrowed structure and overwhelming use of the inherited TR-Turkish equivalent, are matched by categorically occurring (i.e., established) grammatical patterns in Sorbian that find their origin in German.

One way of assessing the degree of propagation is to ask the judgments of community members regarding the degree to which a particular phenomenon is used a lot in the community. This was illustrated in Section 8.2 for the domain of subordinate clauses in NL-Turkish. Sahin (2015) asked 135 Dutch Turkish bilinguals whether they "liked" selected stimulus items, which were given to them embedded in sentences. The target items were loan translations from Dutch we had also attested in natural conversations. In addition, they rated many stimulus items that followed TR-Turkish conventions. Bilinguals rated some loan translations higher than their TR-Turkish conventional equivalents, especially those that instantiated the construction [Musical Instrument + 'play'], as in (14). They even 'corrected' the TR-Turkish forms in these cases. For most items, however, NL-Turkish loan translations and TR-Turkish conventions were rated equally high. This was a surprising result, as the TR-Turkish forms were never used in the recorded conversations. This resembles the result we found for subordinate clauses (Onar Valk 2014), suggesting a common pattern.

Data such as these put us on safer footing if we want to claim that a change has been propagated to a point where we can really talk of "change" in the normal non-technical sense of the word, as, in this case, a way of speaking Turkish that is qualitatively different, and consistently so, from how it is spoken in Turkey. The critical mass of speakers shown to be partaking in the change that is needed to say a new variety has come into existence cannot easily be reached if we are dependent on recorded conversations. In addition, judgment and experimental data also provide *different kinds* of evidence, so that the conclusions are more robust, providing that the evidence from corpora, judgments, and experiments actually converges.

References

Aikhenvald, Alexandra. 2002. *Language Contact in Amazonia*. Oxford: Oxford University Press.
Arnon, Inbal, and Neil Snider. 2010. More than words: Frequency effects for multi-word phrases. *Journal of Memory and Language* 62: 67–82.

Backus, Ad. 2014a. A usage-based approach to borrowability. In *New Perspectives on Lexical Borrowing: Onomasiological, Methodological and Phraseological Innovations*, edited by E. Zenner and G. Kristiansen, 19–40. Berlin: Mouton de Gruyter.

Backus, Ad. 2014b. Towards a usage-based account of language change: Implications of contact linguistics for linguistic theory. In *Questioning Language Contact: Limits of Contact, Contact at Its Limits*, edited by R. Nicolaï, 91–118. Leiden; Boston: Brill.

Backus, Ad, and Margreet Dorleijn. 2009. Loan translations versus code-switching. In *The Cambridge Handbook of Linguistic Code-Switching*, edited by B. Bullock and A. J. Toribio, 75–93. Cambridge: Cambridge University Press.

Backus, Ad, A. Seza Doğruöz, and Bernd Heine. 2011. Salient stages in contact-induced grammatical change: Evidence from synchronic vs. diachronic contact situations. *Language Sciences* 33: 738–752.

Boas, Hans. 2008. Determining the structure of lexical entries and grammatical constructions in construction grammar. *Annual Review of Cognitive Linguistics* 6: 113–144.

Dąbrowska, Ewa. 2004. Rules or schemas? Evidence from Polish. *Language and Cognitive Processes* 19: 225–271.

Demirçay, Derya, and Ad Backus. 2014. Bilingual constructions: Reassessing the typology of code-switching. *Dutch Journal of Applied Linguistics* 3(1): 30–44.

Dorian, Nancy. 1981. *Language Death: The Life Cycle of a Scottish Gaelic Dialect*. Philadelphia: University of Pennsylvania Press.

Goldberg, Adele E. 2009. The nature of generalization in language. *Cognitive Linguistics* 20(1): 93–127.

Haase, Martin. 1992. *Sprachkontakt und Sprachwandel im Baskenland: Die Einflüsse des Gaskognischen und Französischen auf das Baskische*. Buske Verlag, Hamburg.

Heine, Bernd, and Tania Kuteva. 2005. *Language Contact and Grammatical Change*. Cambridge, UK: Cambridge University Press.

Heine, Bernd, and Hiroyuki Miyashita. 2008. Accounting for a functional category: German *drohen* 'to threaten.' *Language Sciences* 30: 53–101.

Johanson, Lars. 2002. *Structural Factors in Turkic Language Contacts*. London: Curzon.

Langacker, Ronald W. 2008. *Cognitive Grammar: A Basic Introduction*. Oxford: Oxford University Press.

Matras, Yaron. 2009. *Language Contact*. Cambridge: Cambridge University Press.

Matras, Yaron, and Jeannette Sakel. 2007. Investigating the mechanisms of pattern replication in language convergence. *Studies in Language* 31: 829–865.

Muysken, Pieter. 2000. *Bilingual Speech: A Typology of Codemixing*. Cambridge, UK: Cambridge University Press.

Myers-Scotton, Carol. 1993. *Social Motivations for Codeswitching: Evidence from Africa*. Oxford and New York: Oxford University Press.

Onar Valk, Pelin. 2014. Convergent developments on Dutch Turkish word order: A comparative study using 'elicited production' and 'judgment' data: Converging evidence? *Applied Linguistics Review* 5(2): 351–372.

Onar Valk, Pelin, and Ad Backus. 2013. Syntactic change in an immigrant language: From nonfinite to finite subordinate clauses in Turkish. *Journal of Estonian and Finno-Ugric Linguistics* 4(2): 7–29.

Perek, Florent. 2012. *Verbs, Constructions, Alternations: Usage-Based Perspectives on Argument Realization*. Unpublished PhD dissertation, Université Lille III, Charles de Gaulle; Albert-Ludwigs Universität Freiburg.

Poplack, Shana, and Nathalie Dion 2012. Myths and facts about loanword development. *Language Variation and Change* 24(3): 279–315.

Sahin, Hülya. 2015. Cross-linguistic influences: Dutch in contact with Papiamento and Turkish. PhD dissertation Radboud University Nijmegen. Utrecht: LOT.

Silva-Corvalán, Carmen. 1994. *Language Contact and Change: Spanish in Los Angeles*. Oxford: Clarendon Press.

Slobin, Dan. 1996. From "thought and language" to "thinking for speaking." *Rethinking Linguistic Relativity*, edited by John J. Gumperz and Stephen C. Levinson, 70–96. Cambridge, UK: Cambridge University Press.

Stolz, Christel, and Thomas Stolz. 1996. Funktionswordentlehnung in Mesoamerika: Spanisch-amerindischer Sprachkontakt (Hispanoindiana II). *Sprachtypologie und Universalienforschung* 49: 86–123.

Thomason, Sarah Grey, and Terrence Kaufman. 1988. *Language Contact, Creolization, and Genetic Linguistics*. Berkeley; Los Angeles; London: University of California Press.

Verschik, Anna. 2008. *Emerging Bilingual Speech: From Monolingualism to Code-Copying*. London: Continuum.

Weinreich, Uriel. 1964 [1953]. *Languages in Contact: Finding and Problems*. Mouton, The Hague.

Wray, Alison. 2008. *Formulaic Language: Pushing the Boundaries*. Oxford: Oxford University Press.

Zenner, Eline. 2013. *Cognitive Contact Linguistics. The Macro, Meso and Micro Influence of English on Dutch*. PhD dissertation, KU Leuven, Faculty of Arts.

CHAPTER 9

....

FIRST- AND SECOND-LANGUAGE ACQUISITION AND CILC

....

GABRIEL OZÓN AND
EVA DURAN EPPLER

9.1 INTRODUCTION

....

THE aim of this chapter is to discuss whether first-language acquisition (L1A) or second-language acquisition (L2A) significantly contribute to contact-induced language change (CILC). This issue is far from settled, and vigorous debate is ongoing. Consider, for instance, the following quotes:

> [T]he ultimate source of [...] linguistic change [...] is the process of language acquisition.   (Andersen 1978: 21)

> The belief that children initiate change was a hopeful guess made by linguists to whom the whole process of change was mysterious. In fact, similarities between child language [acquisition] and language change are largely illusory. Children are unlikely to *initiate* change, since change is *spread* by social groups, and babies do not have sufficient group influence to persuade other people to imitate them.
> (Aitchison 1991: 179, our italics)

> Language change and language acquisition are distinct processes and while they interact, the second doesn't cause the first.   (Bybee 2009: 345)

These differences of opinion exist without taking the third variable of language contact into consideration in the explanation of change. In other words, even disregarding contact scenarios, linguists are not agreed on what and/or who causes and drives change. The reasons behind existing discrepancies can be attributed mainly to a combination of three factors: (1) field of research; (2) theoretical approach; and (3) methodological limitations/advances.

(1) The first factor refers to the subdiscipline of linguistics that informs the research: (diachronic/synchronic) language change, language acquisition, or language contact. We focus mainly on the second as the more relevant to this chapter, and bring insights from the other two whenever necessary.

Despite some early attempts (e.g., Schumann 1978; Bickerton 1981; Andersen 1983; DeGraff 1999) at bringing language acquisition research and the study of language contact together, the potential synergies between these disciplines have only recently started to emerge (Yip and Matthews 2007; Meisel 2011; Thomason 2013).

Within the field of language acquisition, change has alternatively been attributed to children acquiring their first language in a monolingual environment (L1A), children acquiring two languages simultaneously (bilingual first-language acquisition, BFLA), children learning one language after acquiring another (child L2A), and adult L2 speakers (either as a source of input or as agents of change themselves).

(2) The discipline within which an explanation of language change is pursued also determines —in part— the type of assumptions made by the researcher. These in turn condition the theoretical approach employed. The assumptions we are talking about are mainly to do with the *locus* of change (e.g., the individual child or adult, the speech community), the possible *causes* of grammatical change (e.g., changing frequencies in usage patterns, structural ambiguity in the input, language contact), and the actual *processes* involved in change (e.g., reanalysis, version 1). These assumptions tend to cluster and give rise to two main approaches, generativist and non-generativist.

Within the generativist framework, the child is assumed to have innate abstract linguistic knowledge (UG principles). Language acquisition involves the setting of a range of parameters on the basis of limited input and within a certain time frame (Lightfoot and Westergaard 2007; Meisel et al. 2013). This approach provides cross-linguistically valid, theory-internal explanations for the success, speed, and uniformity of first-language acquisition.

In this approach, language change results from the language-learning child constructing a grammar that is different from that of his or her caregivers based on the available linguistic input (e.g., because it is structurally ambiguous). On these assumptions, language change is assumed to happen abruptly and to take place at the level of the individual.

On the other hand, within non-generativist frameworks,[1] it is general cognitive and communicative processes (e.g., intention reading, analogy making) that are thought to explain the acquisition of abstract grammatical categories and constructions. In emergentist/constructivist approaches, language acquisition is not about the setting of

---

[1] We use *non-generativist* only for convenience, as there is no term that covers the different labels (e.g., *emergentist/ constructivist/ probabilistic*, etc.) used for these approaches in various subdisciplines. This does not mean that we think these approaches need to define themselves in opposition to a generativist outlook.

parameters; rather, the language-learning child is assumed to employ general cognitive learning mechanisms (such as inductive generalization) to extract statistical regularities from experience.

Language change is accounted for by the learners' response to a variable linguistic environment, to speakers' variable behavior, and to properties of the linguistic community. On these assumptions, language change is taken to be gradual, and to occur at the community level, not the individual level.

A fundamental difference between the two approaches is that for generativists only qualitative changes in the underlying language system count as language change; for non-generativists, on the other hand, quantitative changes in usage patterns (frequency) can lead to changes in the underlying language system.

(3) We should also note methodological limitations/advances. The type of information available to language change and language acquisition researchers also contributes to the different opinions illustrated by the quotes at the start of this chapter. Briefly, historical linguists have access to outcomes of language change over time, but not to the processes that brought them about. Language acquisition researchers and synchronic linguists, on the other hand, are able to observe ongoing developments, but so far have not been able to successfully predict their outcomes.

Despite all these differences between (contact-induced) language change and language acquisition, there are at least two things they have in common: (1) as Aitchison (1991) notes (cited earlier), isolated individuals cannot accomplish one or the other (even under a generative individualist view, exposure to primary linguistic data produced by other speakers is required); (2) methodologically, they have to be studied through natural language data, which contain a high degree of variation.

In the remainder of this chapter, a number of key terms and concepts are employed; a brief discussion and definitions are given in the following.

Language acquisition refers to the acquisition of a language or languages the child encounters in his or her immediate environment. In the case of just one language, we talk about monolingual first-language acquisition (L1A). In the case of two (or more) languages learned early in childhood, we talk about bilingual first-language acquisition (BFLA). Second-language acquisition (L2A) refers to the learning of additional languages at a secondary stage, that is, after at least one language has already been acquired. In this chapter, we use the prevalent cutoff point of three years (see Genesee, Paradis, and Crago 2004) to separate L1A/BFLA from L2A.

Language variation is the variable use of different linguistic forms from (more than) one language. It either refers to variability across varieties of a language (*dialect variation, intersystemic variation*) or to *inherent*, quantitative variation (*intrasystemic variation*). This pertains to variation in any relevant language component: phonetics/phonology, morphology, syntax, semantics, and pragmatics. The relationship between language variation and change is best summarized as "not all variability and heterogeneity in language structure involves change; but all change involves variability and heterogeneity" (Weinreich, Labov, and Herzog 1968: 187).

Language change: history has shown us that, over time, no language remains unchanged. Like variation, change can affect every level of a language. Language change can have both internal and external motivations. Internal change involves changes to the system of a language that are not triggered by external factors. External motivations for change, on the other hand, involve factors independent of the language system itself (e.g., borrowing in contact scenarios). Language change is seen as comprising two distinct processes: an innovation, and the spread of that innovation through a speech community (cf. Aitchison 1991; and see Croft 2000; Thomason 2013; and others). In this light, language change is concerned with how an individual behaves when surrounded by variation and how this behavior in turn affects the rest of the population (Zuraw 2006).

Broadly speaking, *language contact* refers to "the use of more than one language in the same place at the same time" (Thomason 2001: 1). Language contact happens both at the level of the individual and at the level of the community. At the individual level, language contact can manifest in various different phenomena (borrowing, code-switching, calquing, etc.). Community languages can be in contact in one or several domains or related social situations, including family, religion, education, employment, and friendship. These factors influence the potential outcomes of language contact (e.g., language change, shift, death).

Contact-induced language change (CILC) normally refers to structural influences of one language upon another. Thomason (2001: 62) defines CILC as "any linguistic change that would have been less likely to occur outside a particular contact situation." In order to attribute a particular language change to CILC, certain conditions must be met: contact must be established for a particular time period; the languages in contact must share independent features in several structural subsystems; the feature in question can be shown to be old in the proposed source language and innovative in the proposed receiving language (Thomason 2001: 91–95).[2] The point of these conditions is first, to ensure that the language change has actually occurred, and second, that this is a product of contact and not an internally motivated change.

In what follows, we discuss the role of L1A and L2A in CILC. We examine different language-acquisition scenarios and their potential for leading to contact-induced language change. In order to do this, we first present main facts about L1A, BFLA, and L2A. We then use the different language-acquisition types as testing grounds for the motivations behind (i.e., causes for and triggers of) language change. In the following two sections we first give an overview of the main mechanisms involved in the acquisition of phonetic, phonological, lexical, and morphosyntactic knowledge,

---

[2] Poplack and Levey (2010: 398) suggest more rigorous variationist sociolinguistic methods to rule out (unchanging) synchronic variation and other possible explanations for the phenomena under consideration: "A candidate for contact-induced change in a contact variety is present in the presumed source variety and either (1) absent in the pre-contact or non-contact variety, or (2) if present (e.g., through interlingual coincidence) is not conditioned in the same way as in the source, and (3) can also be shown to parallel in some non-trivial way the behavior of a counterpart feature in the source."

before considering their potential for being involved in processes of change (e.g., reanalysis, cross-linguistic influence, fusion of linguistic systems). Section 9.2 looks at monolingual and bilingual first-language acquisition, section 9.3 looks at (child and adult) second-language acquisition, and section 9.4 considers which of the language-acquisition scenarios is more likely to play a role in CILC, and why.

9.2 First-Language Acquisition (L1A) and Bilingual First-Language Acquisition (BFLA)

In this section, we evaluate whether young children can initiate language change in the process of acquiring one (or more) first languages (cf. quotes from Andersen 1978 and Aitchison 1991 in the introduction to this chapter). We look at monolingual and bilingual first-language acquisition, the (pre)conditions for change they provide, and which processes can be operative in both language acquisition and language change.

9.2.1 L1A (Monolingual Settings)

Children learn the language(s) they hear around them. If they hear one, they learn this one; if they hear more than one, they will learn them. We start by looking at monolingual first-language acquisition because it is the least complex scenario, and can thus function as a baseline for the other two scenarios (BFLA and SLA/L2A).

L1A researchers agree that there are striking parallels in the rate and stages of language development in children that are largely independent of language type, modality (spoken or signed), and sociocultural setting. There is also considerable variability, both in the input and in the output. The question is whether this variability in language acquisition leads to change or not (cf. Weinreich, Labov, and Herzog 1968 quote in the previous section). To be able to evaluate this question, we need to consider the basic facts about monolingual first-language acquisition.

Infants' perceptual systems are at first quite open (i.e., able to discriminate sounds produced in the languages of the world). Between 6 and 18 months, the system is tuned to the phonological categories of the exposure language.[3] Roughly at the same time, children start segmenting the speech stream into meaningful units (e.g., words, formulaic expressions, phrases, etc.) and become sensitive to the ordering of these units. These are necessary prerequisites for matching linguistics forms to meaning (i.e., learning words).

---

[3] Kuhl et al. (2003) showed that it takes only 12 sessions of interpersonal interaction in a different language to reverse this decline in foreign-language phonetic perception.

The time when children produce their first recognizable words is generally between 10 and 18 months. Early words tend to be nouns, but the distribution of lexical items in terms of word classes not only varies among children, but also cross-linguistically. Between ages two and six, children learn approximately 9–10 words per day.

Morphological and syntactic development progress in parallel, and general patterns hold up across languages. There is no apparent preference for any morphosyntactic types (e.g., isolating, agglutinating, etc.), nor for any type of semantic or other organization (see Slobin 2006: 300). Children learning highly inflected languages produce words with inflectional marking from the beginning, usually accurately, with occasional errors of omission (e.g., *walk* instead of *walk-ed*) and later of commission (e.g., *ran-ed*).

When they have 50–60 words in their active vocabulary (14–24 months), children start combining words. Some of these multiword utterances may be rote-learned as a whole, others may be slot-and-frame patterns, and most of them are missing features that are provided in the input (such as functional categories). There is disagreement in accounts of how children learn the basic morphosyntax of the language they are exposed to between ages two and four. According to generativist accounts, children are endowed with a biological system that grows in children's minds/brains in the first few years of life (I-language) if exposed to ambient E-language. According to emergentist accounts, on the other hand, children learn from the sequential probabilities of strings on the surface of the input and work out the structure, function, and meaning of novel complex constructions (from existing structures and form-meaning mapping). Regardless of how it is done, basic grammatical elements and structures are learned during the first four years, but language development is not over then: fine-tuning of linguistic structures continues through childhood. How rapidly these skills develop and how far children get with them are related to the complexity of the language they hear at home and at school (including literacy).

In generativist work on language change (e.g., Lightfoot 1999, 2006; Weerman 1993, 2011; Meisel 2011; Westergaard 2008), the fact that each new generation of children acquires a language is ultimately held responsible for the fact that languages change in the course of time. Children are assumed to set the parameters of the language they are acquiring on the basis of the Primary Linguistic Data they are exposed to.

Under the generative view, this creates the "logical problem of language change" (Niyogi and Berwick 1995; Brandner and Ferraresi 1996): if children set parameters on the basis of the previous generation's E-language, languages should not change but remain constant. It is therefore assumed that children "grow" a new I-language on the basis of exposure to significantly different E-language (defined as aggregate I-languages of many individuals; see Figure 9.1).

The prime triggers for language change in L1A are considered to be (1) changes in the *frequency* of use in particular constructions, and (2) *structural ambiguity* of constructions (Lightfoot 1991). Researchers working within the generative paradigm generally assume that parameters can be set on minimal input, but it is unclear what the triggering threshold for parameter setting is (Lightfoot [1997: 179] suggests "somewhere between 17 and 30%"). Conflicting evidence provided by two languages/varieties in

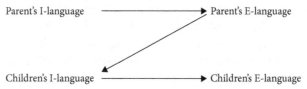

FIGURE 9.1 The dynamics of language acquisition and language change.

Source: Chomsky (1986).

situations of language or dialect contact is a special case of (2), in that it also involves structurally ambiguous input; we return to this point under BFLA and L2A.

The generative position on whether monolingual first-language acquisition can account for language change is brought to a point by Weerman (2011: 149) who states that "[w]hat was and is one of the starting points of the generative enterprise (why is it that children are so good at learning their L1?) makes it difficult to consider them as agents of change" (see 9.6 in this chapter).

Constructionists accept both changing frequency of use and structural ambiguity as causes/triggers of change, which do not pose a theoretical obstacle for linking language change to language acquisition.

9.2.2 BFLA (Multilingual Settings)

This section addresses the question of whether bilingual first-language acquisition (i.e., the simultaneous acquisition of two languages from birth until the age of three)[4] can cause language change. If researchers such as Meisel (2007) are right in claiming that simultaneous acquisition of two or more languages can indeed be classified as an instance of multiple first-language acquisition, then both mono- and bilingual first-language acquisition should play similar roles in CILC (i.e., none). We begin with an evaluation of Meisel's claim by looking at similarities and differences between first-language acquisition in mono- and multi-lingual environments.

We adopt a cross-linguistic comparative approach because this method is important for historical theories of language evolution and change (Slobin 2006: 229), and because it is applicable both to the study of individual differences between children learning a particular language as well as to individual differences in a cross-linguistic context. This approach is also useful for revealing the mix of factors that influence acquisition and their potential to trigger/contribute to change.

Research has shown that both monolingual and bilingual infants use the same perceptual biases (e.g., rhythm) to discriminate their two native languages from each

---

[4] The distinction between *simultaneous* and *successive* bilingual language acquisition is generally set at this age (see Paradis et al. 2011; Unsworth 2013); some researchers have set more rigid criteria, e.g., De Houwer (1990).

other and from unfamiliar languages (Ramus, Hauser, Miller, Morris, and Mehler 2000; Byers-Henlein, Burns, and Werker 2010). There is some evidence for a temporary delay in the perception of specific vowel contrasts (Bosch and Sebastián-Gallés 2003; but see also Albareda-Castellot, Pons, and Sebastián-Gallés 2011), but not for consonants. Similar patterns have been found for the development of phonological production (Gildersleeve-Neumann and Wright 2010). Generally, the sparse evidence for cross-linguistic phonological influence in BFLA is limited to small contrasts (e.g., transfer of final devoicing and de-aspiration of stops).

Vocabulary is the area where significant and persistent bilingual-monolingual differences have been observed. When BFLA learners' languages are considered separately, their vocabulary in each language is smaller than that of monolingual children of a similar age (Pearson, Fernandez, Lewedag, and Oller 1997). If both languages are considered, their rate of vocabulary acquisition generally falls within the range reported for same-age monolinguals. The distribution of lexical categories is similar to that observed in monolingual children (Nicoladis 2001). The relative amount of time spent in each language and the contexts in which the languages are used can affect the domain-specific relative vocabulary size in a multilingual context (see Montanari 2010, cited earlier; and Bialystok, Luk, Peets, and Yang 2010; Oller, Pearsons, and Cobo-Lewis 2007).

One reason for this difference is that the *mutual exclusivity constraint* (the assumption that each object category must have a different label) is not as prominent in BFLA as it is in L1A (Houston-Price, Caloghiris, and Raviglione 2010). Mutual exclusivity seems to be learned (Deuchar and Quay 2000), and the clear violation of this constraint in multilinguals suggests that (at least from the age of 1;5) bilingual children may have two distinct (i.e., separate) lexical systems. Depending on how much morphosyntactic information one assumes to be stored in the lexicon, distinct lexical systems would not predispose bilingual children to become major players in CILC.

Studies that address the relationship between lexical and grammatical development in bilingual children (Marchman, Martinez-Sussman, and Dale 2004; Conboy and Thal 2006) have shown that the within-language connection between the lexis and grammar of one language (lexis A and grammar A) is stronger than the across-language connections (between lexis A-lexis B and/or grammar A-grammar B). This again can curtail the potential role BFLA has to play in CILC.

This preliminary summary of bilingual language acquisition has shown that Meisel (2007) appears to be right: bilingual children are able to differentiate between the two languages from early on (Genesee 1989; De Houwer 1990; Genesee, Nicolaidis, and Paradis 1995).

The development of separate grammars in bilingual children, however, does not preclude cross-linguistic influence. What is at issue is (1) the nature of the influence (whether quantitative, Yip and Matthews 2007; qualitative, see Thomason 2001; transfer or other forms of CLI, see Döpke 2000; Hulk and Müller 2000); (2) whether it is temporary or has long-lasting effects; (3) whether it affects competence or performance; and (4) whether such individual-level effects can become one mechanism by which structural influence takes hold on a community level (Thomason 2001; Yip and Matthews 2007).

Opinions on the role of BFLA in an account of diachronic change are about as divided as opinions about the role of monolingual language acquisition (see quotes in the introductory section). Yip and Matthews (2007: 37), for example, consider that "[s]tudies of grammatical interaction in bilingual children [. . .] suggest that child bilingualism is a potential mechanism for contact-induced change." Meisel, on the other hand, believes that "simultaneous acquisition of bilingualism is no more likely to lead to grammatical reanalysis [which can then lead to change] than monolingual L1 development" (2011: 139, our brackets). The issue remains to be settled.

To summarize, the main idea behind most accounts of diachronic change contingent on acquisition is that, in a bilingual setting, children are exposed to two (or more) language systems that contain conflicting evidence. Language-learning children deal with this conflicting evidence in the input data by incorporating elements (e.g., features, words, structures/parameter values) of one grammar into another. The evidence from BFLA reviewed earlier shows that children are capable of differentiating the linguistic systems they are exposed to early on, and thus speaks against the idea that language contact will result in grammatical blending/creolization. Cross-linguistic influence, however, does happen in both BFLA and L2A, and this is dealt with in the next section.

Language contact is mainly attributed to three main factors: frequency changes, structural ambiguity, and language contact. There is widespread agreement that some form of language contact tends to provide the necessary trigger for grammatical change (Thomason and Kaufman 1988). For generativists, these mechanisms needed to apply during L1A (because within this framework, core properties of grammar cannot be altered in adulthood). Recent generative work (Meisel et al. 2013), however, suggests that change is only likely to happen when L2 learning is involved. This is where we move on to next.

9.2.3 L2 Acquisition

The study of how a second language is learned presents researchers with a different set of challenges from L1A/BFLA. This section discusses what happens when someone learns a second language, and its potential for leading to CILC.

There is widespread agreement about typical characteristics of L2A (Ozón 2016), for example:

- L2A is slower than L1A.
- Motivational factors play a major role determining proficiency.
- L2 learners can rely on more metalinguistic (L1) knowledge, and more developed cognitive skills.
- Formal instruction is helpful or necessary.
- Fossilization of specific non-target-like linguistic features, i.e., features that are non-existent in L1 speakers' of the L2, is common.

- Whereas all L1 learners attain full competence, this is not necessarily the case for most L2 learners.
- At the same time, most L2 learners will make mistakes attributable to L1 influence (*cross-linguistic influence*).

Since every L2 learner is already equipped with an existing L1, one strand of language learning research concerns itself with the question of how similar/different L1A and L2A are.

Some research, largely that produced by non-generative researchers, suggests that both types of language learning (L1A and L2A) are systematic, and that both L1 and L2 learners proceed through invariant (if not identical) sequences in their acquisition of morphosyntactic properties of target languages (Dulay and Burt 1974). Potential answers to how this could be the case (called the *developmental problem*) are starting to emerge in the form of an implicational hierarchy of processing procedures that govern both L1A and L2A. Processability Theory (Pienemann 1998, 2005), for example, deals quite successfully with simplification phenomena (e.g., scarcity/lack of inflection, unmarked syntactic structures such as basic word order, question formation, and negation). This research suggests that L2 errors may be developmental in origin, rather than attributable to the interaction between L1 and L2. In sum, there is evidence to support the claim that L1 and L2 share acquisition patterns.

Another group of researchers, on the other hand, assume that L1A and L2A are fundamentally different (Fundamental Difference Hypothesis, FDH; Bley-Vroman 1990). The FDH claims that language-acquisition mechanisms (Language Acquisition Device, LAD; Language Making Capacity, LMC) employed in early childhood become unavailable after the Critical Period (a particular time span during which L1 can be most easily acquired; Lenneberg 1967), and thus cannot be used for L2A. L2A therefore has to rely on domain-general problem-solving skills. The FDH is able to explain most typical characteristics of L2A mentioned earlier. Researchers adhering to the FDH (Stewart 2003; Montrul 2009) generally acknowledge that there are similarities between L2 learners and unbalanced early bilinguals, but suggest that the differential performance by the two groups may have different roots—namely, insufficient input in early bilinguals, but inefficient learning mechanisms in L2 learners.

As for BFLA and L2A, researchers have also looked for similarities and recurrent patterns between them, given that both involve the learning of two languages. However, since (1) BFLA children differentiate from early on the linguistic systems of the languages to which they are exposed, (2) proceed through the same developmental phases as the respective monolinguals (see Paradis and Genesee 1996; Meisel 2007), and (3) are able to attain native competence in each of their languages (Meisel 2001, 2004), it is generally agreed that BFLA is an instance of simultaneous L1A, and thus more like L1A than L2A.

A distinction is furthermore made in the acquisition literature between child L2A and adult L2A, that is, L2A at different ages of onset of acquisition (generally assumed to be at either side of the CPH). The earlier the onset of acquisition for child L2A, the more similarities it will have with L1A: after age seven, child L2 learners increasingly resemble adult L2 learners. The similarities between adult and child

L2A, however, outweigh any differences: both (1) manifest L1 transfer and presence of functional categories (Unsworth 2004), (2) show similar behaviors in areas of inflectional morphology, and (3) offer considerable evidence of cross-individual and intra-individual variation in their use of L2 knowledge (Meisel 2011). These characteristics set both child and adult L2A apart from BFLA.

Without doubt, a language learner's first language(s) exert an influence on both the process and the result of SLA (see Eckman 2004), with L2 learners gradually developing a system that shows features of both the L1 and L2 in question. This *cross-linguistic influence* affects elements on different language levels. Despite terminological variation (*interference, L1 influence, interlanguage, transfer, cross-linguistic influence*, and others), there is widespread agreement in what the terms denote, that is, "the transfer of linguistic features (with or without actual morpheme transfer) from one language to another" (Thomason 2013). We employ *cross-linguistic influence* (CLI) as a superordinate term because it highlights the fact that language influence can be mutual (see Verhoeven 1991, 1994).

The interplay between the different features (and/or rules) of an L1 and an L2 has been shown be able to have a visible effect on the lexicon (borrowings, loans), on morphosyntax (production of mixed structures), on semantics (conceptual transfers), as well as on avoidance/preference patterns in language production (see, e.g., Gass 1996 for an overview). All language levels appear to be susceptible to CLI (see Gut 2011 for a summary). We discuss some of these manifestations of CLI in the following.

9.2.3.1 *Phonology*

The influence of the L1 is highly apparent in L2 phonology (Paradis 2008). The starting point for L2 speech development is the L1 phonetic categories (Flege 1999). In other words, L2 learners rely on their L1 phonological system to pronounce words. This is seen in, for example:

- phone substitution, splits, and mergers (due to differences in phonemic inventories; see Winford 2003; Archibald 2011);
- difficulties in acquiring new features (when contrasts are not available in the L1);
- changes in phonotactics (Winford 2003; Bybee 2009), e.g., L2 syllabification (modifying an L2 word so that it fits the L1 syllable structure);
- over-generation of L1 stress patterns applied to L2.

9.2.3.2 *Lexicon*

L2 lexical learning differs from L1 in that the child "has an existing lexicon in their L1 to draw upon for insight into conceptual–lexical mappings" (Paradis 2008: 390), which, in theory, allows L2 learners to build their lexicon at a faster rate than monolingual speakers. CLI manifests itself in more visible ways; learners may:

- employ loans (including overt lexical items) from the L1; this includes set phrases and constructions;

- reinterpret L2 words in terms of the semantics of similar L1 forms (e.g., false cognates);
- assume complete semantic overlap between certain forms in their L1 and their L2;
- create loan translations employing L2 forms combined according to an L1 pattern (Winford 2003).

9.2.3.3 *Morphology*

Unlike at the phonological and lexical level, it is traditionally claimed that there is no (direct) transfer of L1 morphology in L2A (Winford 2003; Muysken 2006). That is, L1 affixes never appear on L2 lexical items, but rather they are reduced or eliminated (which in the case of these affixes being inflectional, may in turn lead to grammaticalization), and resort is made to periphrasis. On the rare occasions when morphemes are borrowed, they form part of an unanalyzed whole, with bound morphemes being borrowed along with a lexical item. Countervidence to these claims is, however, available from L2 learning situations that result in mixed codes (e.g., *ge-bother-ed*, an English lexical item with inflectional German circumfix; see Duran Eppler 2010).

9.2.3.4 *Syntax*

CLI in syntax is most noticeable and widespread in word order, with learners frequently resorting to L1 word order in attempting to produce L2 utterances (Winford 2003). Other cases include:

- null pronouns: increase/decrease of subject pronouns in L2 as a consequence of CLI from neighboring varieties with differing PRO-drop settings (Lipski 1996; Holm 1978; O'Neil 1993; Muysken 2006);
- overextension of correlative patterns, e.g. to form new relative clause structures (Appel and Muysken 1987; Muysken 2006);
- V-raising (see Lightfoot 1999, 2006);
- Changes in valency patterns (Green and Ozón 2019).

A related manifestation of recurrent CLI effects on different languages/L2 structures is *simplification*, which may be regulated by universal principles (Winford 2003). There seems to be a need to achieve "maximum regularity and transparency in the grammar," (Winford 2003: 220) as evidenced in, for example, reduction of L2 structures (bound morphology, reduction in phonemic inventory) and rule regularization (analogical leveling, overgeneralization).

Processes (and effects) found in typical L2A have also been found in contact scenarios:

- *addition of linguistic features* (lexical, phonological, morphological, syntactic);
- *replacement* (lexical, morphological, syntactic; less clear in phonology);
- *feature loss* (lexical, phonological, morphological, syntactic) (Thomason 2001).

Different theoretical approaches account for data that reflect these processes and effects in different ways. Generativists assume that language is a fairly autonomous system and that children are equipped with a specific innate language-learning mechanism, the LAD. The role the LAD might play in L2 acquisition is, however, quite controversial: is it available to L2 learners at all (Corder 1967)? If UG is inaccessible to L2 learners, then parameters cannot be (re)set in L2 acquisition. This means that while there are similarities in L1 and L2 output, these are only superficial, and not evidence of grammatical knowledge/competence. If this assumption is true, the lack of uniformity in L2 attainment would also follow from this impossibility of new parameter settings in L2. In this light, L2 knowledge would be a hybrid system (Meisel 2011: 193), comprising (1) an approximate/incomplete version of the target grammar, (2) learned linguistic knowledge that is not fully constrained by UG principles, and (3) knowledge derived from domain-general cognitive operations.

Emergentists, on the other hand, view language as part of the cognitive system and argue that in learning a language, humans employ domain-general sociocognitive skills (not any specialized and innate cognitive system like the LAD). Research within this framework focuses on how linguistic units are derived from patterns of language use; *frequency* information (i.e., statistical properties of the input) therefore plays a major explanatory role. Emergentist accounts of the similarities between L2A and contact data assume that L2 learners are blinded to certain aspects of the L2 sample by their "L1-tuned expectations and selective attention" (Ellis 2006; Ellis and Sagarra 2010), which lead to limited attainment.

Following this overview of L2A, we can now start addressing the connection between L2A and CILC by discussing relevant aspects of language change.

An emergentist/usage-based perspective assumes that the frequency, form, and function of constructions between languages interact as learners acquire another language: L2 learner language manifests transfer effects as a result of L1 entrenchment (MacWhinney 2008). In parallel, language interactions can preserve language stability (by replicating linguistic conventions), bring about innovation (by *altered replication;* (Keller 1994), e.g., the Great Vowel Shift, the grammaticalization of *going to*) and give rise to propagation due to the "differential selection of certain kinds of features by language users in a sociocultural context" (Evans and Green 2006: 128), resulting in the establishment of new conventions. These new conventions are ultimately seen as instances of language change.

If we go with generative theory and accept the assumption that core features of a language system do not change in the course of adult life (CPH), the main locus of change has to be the language-learning child. However, it has been shown that L1A and BFLA do not lead to transmission failure (which could in turn lead to morphosyntactic change)[5]: (1) in L1A, the LAD is assumed to be robust enough to ensure a smooth

---

[5] See also Lightfoot's (2014) critique of Meisel et al. (2013), which asserts that there cannot be any transmission failure because in fact "NOTHING is transmitted: I-languages grow afresh in each individual on exposure to ambient E-language" (Lightfoot 2014: 759).

acquisition process, regardless of changing frequencies or ambiguous constructions in the input (Meisel et al. 2013: 171); (2) there is evidence that children learning two languages simultaneously separate their systems early on in the acquisition process (Paradis and Genesee 1996). If (1) turns out to be true, then the most likely locus for incomplete acquisition (and ensuing diachronic change) lies in successive acquisition (i.e., L2A). Meisel et al. (2013) claim that it is *both* children and adult L2 learners who are potential prime agents of language change. Changes do not just emerge when children reanalyze input: rather, "the speech of L2 learners which serves as input for L1 learners contains the triggers necessary for reanalysis, possibly because L2 learners transfer parameter settings from their L1 onto their L2" (Meisel et al. 2013: 156). In other words, L2A can be involved in language change in two ways: first, adult L2 speakers provide input that may lead to change; and second, language-learning children exposed to L2 input may change language.

The previous sections have discussed different acquisition scenarios and their potential for diachronic change; this is, whether change is deemed possible in individual instances of L1A, BFLA, and L2A. However, while a particular linguistic innovation starts with the individual, it becomes more visible and less transient in proportion to the degree to which it is spread and adopted into the language of the community. The spread of an innovation involves considering social aspects, including (sociolinguistic) ecologies in mono- and multilingual settings. We turn to this in the next section.

9.3 LANGUAGE ACQUISITION AND CILC

Language change consists of two parts: innovation (which is largely individual) and propagation (which involves the spread of the innovation through the community). We start by looking at different accounts of propagation, and move on to a discussion of CILC, which leads us into prototypical cases where such changes are most evident: pidgin and creole languages.

Previous sections addressed the different loci for change. L1A is considered to be the main locus of innovation within the generative paradigm. If children, however, grow exact copies of the language they are exposed to, languages should not change (cf. "logical problem of language change"; see, e.g., Niyogi and Berwick 1995; Brandner and Ferraresi 1996). BFLA was also considered as a potential locus of innovation, but while it is acknowledged that CLI between languages does exist, children exposed to two languages simultaneously and in roughly equal quality/quantity tend to become competent in both languages (and not change either). The proposed locus of language change has therefore shifted to L2A for several prominent authors in the field (e.g., Weerman 2011; Meisel et al. 2013), and here a distinction is made between child L2A and adult L2A. While this view goes against the grain of generative theory (no parameter resetting after the Critical Period), it nonetheless attempts to bring L2A in line with generative tenets, inasmuch as children who have been exposed to an L2 in early life (i.e., closer to the Critical Period) are considered to be more instrumental in bringing about language change than adults. Recent work, however, considers adult L2 learners to be equally instrumental in language change, in their dual role as providers of input to language-learning children as well as learners themselves (Meisel et al. 2013). Language acquisition and CILC research are thus picking up a point long made by contact linguistics, that is, "the ability of second-language speakers to drastically restructure their grammar" (Mühlhäusler 1986: 182; see also Hellinger 1985; Holm 1988). This can lead to change only if a group of adult L2 learners radically restructure their L2 in the same direction.

The diffusion of change across individuals (propagation) within a linguistic community poses a different challenge: why would a large group of individuals manifest identical linguistic innovations?

In the generativist paradigm, innovations are normally assumed to take place in the process of L1A by individual children (e.g., Halle 1962; Andersen 1973; Lightfoot 1979, 1999, 2002, 2006), but little is said about how innovations spread from the individual to the community. Generativist have tended to focus on innovations, and only recently (Yang 2000) have started to model language change. In Yang's model, it is not transmission failure that accounts for change; rather, LA is viewed as a variational process in which the distribution of grammars (see Kroch 1989) changes as an adaptive response to the linguistic evidence in the environment. Non-generativist studies (e.g., Bybee 2009), on the other hand, allow for innovation to be triggered by changing frequencies in language use, and to take place throughout the life span of individuals.

A plausible explanation for the spread of innovations over a linguistic community can be found in cases when individuals are exposed to identical input/triggering experiences (i.e., where innovations appear in the input). For those who believe that L1A is the locus of innovation, the LAD will smooth out variation in the input, with no changes happening. However, for those working under the hypothesis that L2A (especially child L2A) is the locus of innovation, exposure to changing/imperfect input (provided mostly by L2 learners) could explain the emergence as well as the spread of an innovation. This would, however, require a favorable sociolinguistic context for an influential role of L2 speakers in terms both of their numbers and of their social role. Specific conditions involve the following: the group of L2 learners should be substantial enough relative to L1 speakers, and L2 learners have only limited access to L1 speakers (i.e., most of their PLD will be provided by adult L2 learners, which is imperfect), thus L2 learners are not likely to acquire the majority language with full competence. For example, the change from OV to VO in English (but not, e.g., in Dutch or German), is accounted for by Weerman (1993) by the presence of powerful outsiders (Vikings, Normans), scenarios which fit both of the preceding conditions.

Language change can only take root when a community (wholly or in part) acquires or shifts to an L2 (Meisel 2001; Meisel et al. 2013): very often, this situation would result in a contact language significantly different from the original L2 (e.g., Singlish, pidgin and creole languages). Studies on contact linguistics (Thomason and Kaufman 1988; Kroch and Taylor 1997) also agree that L2 acquisition can only lead to grammatical change in similar sociolinguistic settings. Favorable scenarios for this type of contact are as follows:

- Community-wide language shift: adults transmitting what is for them a second language to the children (e.g., in nineteenth-century Ireland);
- Second-generation migrants: children of immigrants growing up acquiring the host-community language, alongside or even replacing the parental variety;
- Systematic contact between child speakers of different dialects: emerging koiné formation (e.g., Høyanger and New Zealand) (Kerswill et al. 2013: 265).

While the linguistic outcome of the first scenario may involve CLI on the emerging L1, there is enough diachronic evidence on the second scenario (from, e.g., Turkish migrant groups in Germany and Holland) showing that CLI effects may remain visible in the speech of second-generation migrants throughout their life, but tend to disappear in subsequent generations. There is no conclusive evidence that this type of contact scenario leads to change in the host-community language. The linguistic outcome of the final scenario may be a new mixed variety, with features from contributing dialects (as well as some simplification, particularly in morphology).

The literature in this field is huge; in addition to works mentioned in the text, one can profitably read Aboh and Ansaldo (2006), Hickey (2010), Kouwenberg and Singler (2008), Lefebvre, White, and Jourdan (2006), Mitchell and Myles (2013), Mufwene (2001), Mukherjee and Hundt (2011), Odlin (1989), Ritchie and Bhatia (1996), Romaine (1994), Schneider (2013), Selinker, Swain, and Dumas (1975), Volterra and Taeschner (1978), and Zobl (1983).

9.4 CONTACT-INDUCED LANGUAGE CHANGE

Contact has been broadly considered to be a crucial if not necessary factor causing change (e.g., Weerman 1993), with CLI as one of its main mechanisms. For innovations to take hold in individuals as well as in community, it may be crucial where within individuals the change establishes itself, in language use/performance and/or competence. Uriel Weinreich used a memorable simile to capture this difference: "In speech, interference is like sand carried by a stream; in language, it is the sediment deposited on the bottom of a lake" (1966 [1953]: 11). Weinreich implies that occasional CLI can be washed out in use; it is when CLI starts laying foundations in the language system/competence that it can become the basis for change. This is yet another controversial issue between generativists and non-generativists. For generativists, only changes in the linguistic system count; for non-generativists, on the other hand, changes in usage can lead to changes in the underlying system.

There is widespread agreement that processes by which changes are often introduced into a linguistic system in contact situations operate (singly or in combinations) largely in L2A/BFLA scenarios and affect all levels of the linguistic system (Thomason 2001). The core mechanism that brings about CILC is assumed to be *CLI* (broadly defined as the transfer of linguistic features from one language to another, i.e., Weinreich's *interference*; see Thomason 2013). CLI is active in BFLA as well as in L2A, but possibly to different degrees and with different results. In BFLA, CLI is often subtle and affects largely non-salient linguistic elements, often taking more nuanced (quantitative) forms than in L1A (e.g., frequency of null objects, see Yip and Matthews 2007; frequency of V2 word-order patterns, see De Houwer and Meisel 1996). Other mechanisms of CILC potentially include borrowing, code-switching, and SLA strategies (Thomason 2001). As far as borrowing and *code-switching* (the use of linguistic units and/or structures from more than one language within one sentence) are concerned, there is little evidence to date of how exactly they contribute to CILC (Heine and Kuteva 2005). One of the reasons may be that this would require longitudinal studies, which are still rare in code-switching (but see Demircay and Backus 2014). (A separate chapter [see Backus, Chapter 8 in this volume] is dedicated to code-mixing/-switching in CILC.) *SLA strategies*, on the other hand, include negotiation, gap-filling, and the projection of L1 distinctions into L2 (see Thomason 2001 for an overview, and evidence of how they have led to change).

Some recent work, however, expresses skepticism about the role of contact in bringing about diachronic change, for example claiming that CILC is not an inevitable outcome of language contact (Poplack and Levey 2010: 412), and that it should best be regarded as a necessary but not sufficient condition for the emergence of grammatical change (Meisel et al. 2013: 175).

9.5 Pidgin and Creole Languages

Different language-acquisition types, and the mechanisms involved in each, have been used to account for the genesis of extreme cases of language contact, such as pidgin and creole (P/C) languages. These contact languages involving bilingual or multilingual language acquisition are particularly interesting for investigating language change, especially if we see that as involving reorganization of grammars. We provide a brief overview, but see Chapter 11 by Parkvall, Chapter 12 by McWhorter, and Chapter 13 by Smith in this volume.

CLI and other L2A mechanisms, mainly structural *simplification* and *transfer* (e.g., presence of substrate features), figure largely in accounts of P/C genesis (Siegel 2008b: 189).[6] It has

---

[6] We use *simplicity* as a comparative, formal (as opposed to psycholinguistic) notion. Pidgin and creole languages are "simpler" than either of the languages involved in their formation, in terms of, e.g., "a smaller phonemic inventory, fewer word classes, fewer bound morphemes, fewer exceptions" (Siegel 2008b: 189).

been pointed out that the (synchronic) boundary between CLI and CILC (especially in morphosyntax) is hard to draw (e.g., Muysken 2006).

The essential claim is that processes found in typical L2A (e.g., simplification and transfer) are also found in P/C formation, and it has even been claimed that "[L2A] and individual pidginization are really the same phenomenon viewed from different perspectives" (Andersen 1980: 274). This is the context in which Bickerton's well-known claim that "pidginization is second-language learning with restricted input, and creolization is first-language learning with restricted input" (1977: 49) is to be understood. Language change emerges when the outcomes of these processes become the norm via increased use. P/C languages thus provide researchers with the most obvious manifestations of CILC.

CLI (specifically, transfer) is not assumed to play a significant role in pidgin formation (with simplification playing a major role). On the other hand, it does play a much more significant role in creole formation, where (along with bilingualism, see Siegel 2008b) it can account for the presence of substrate features in creoles that were lacking in their pidgins. This provides an indication of the much more complex role CILC has to play in creolization. There is no consensus about the exact role that CLI (simplification and transfer) plays in the formation of P/C languages, or about how and when they apply (Siegel 2008b).

Inasmuch as pidgin genesis involves situations in which imperfect learning is a significant factor (adult L2A), pidgin languages provide evidence for adults as the primary agents of CILC. In the formation of creole languages, on the other hand, children are the primary agents of change. In these situations, children are L1 learners who rely on input from L2/pidgin speakers, which contains necessary evidence on which they can grow a new (creole) grammar (see cascade model in DeGraff 2003).

9.6 CHILDREN AND ADULTS

Children and adult learners make different contributions to CILC. Children (1) first borrow non-basic vocabulary, and later structural features and basic lexical items (Thomason 2013), (2) are mainly responsible for morphosyntactic changes, (3) target more abstract and less salient structural features (e.g., object omission, see Müller and Hulk 2001; intonation, see Queen 2001). Innovations by children make the existing system more complex (*complexification*), particularly through the addition of new linguistic categories (see, e.g., Trudgill 2010). An extreme example of this is the creolization of Nicaraguan Sign Language (Morgan and Kegl 2006).

On the other hand, adult learners are mostly responsible for the spread of innovations, while they can also (1) introduce borrowings from written sources, and (2) manifest CLI effects mainly in phonological and syntactic features (lexical and morphological CLI are also possible, Thomason 2013). Simplification seems to be predominantly an adult phenomenon, involving loss of morphological categories and an increase in morphological transparency. When confronted with another language in a contact situation, adult L2 learners thus show a tendency to establish one-to-one correspondences between particular linguistic forms and their functions (cf. Uniqueness Principle, Winford 2003), which is also a main process in code-switching (see Backus, Chapter 8 in this volume).

In sum, both children and adults are responsible for CILC; their respective contributions to contact-induced language change reflect what each are good at in terms of language learning (cf. Kerswill 2013).

This section has discussed different acquisition types (L1A, BFLA, L2A) and their interfaces with CILC. We noted that learning processes that are shared between BFLA and L2A (e.g., transfer/CLI) are also more likely to contribute to CILC, and thus play a significant part in the genesis of pidgin and creole languages. We also considered processes of innovation and propagation, and touched upon the different roles that children and adults perform in contact scenarios as agents of change. We conclude that children are better at generating new productive structures, while adults play a more significant role in spreading these innovations, because of their double role as input providers to language-learning children and major participants in social networks.

9.7 CLOSING REMARKS

The interrelation between language acquisition, language change, and contact linguistics is an exciting area of research, with a growing number of recent studies bringing these three fields together (Adone and Plag 1994; Wekker 1996; Bybee 2003; Montrul 2004; Sánchez 2004; Toribio 2004; Yip and Matthews 2007; Meisel et al. 2013). The preceding sections have looked at different acquisition types (L1A, BFLA, L2A) and have examined their potential for CILC. We discussed similarities and differences among them, and identified some promising avenues for understanding the driving forces, causes, and processes behind language acquisition and CILC.

We would now like to turn the question with which we started this chapter on its head, and answer the question "Can languages change without the involvement of (1) language acquisition, and (2) contact?" The answer depends on the *field* of research, the *theoretical* approach, and the available *data*.

Many researchers working in diachronic linguistics have little to say about the role of language acquisition in change, because they are mainly concerned with the mechanisms of change, their results, and how these spread. Language acquisition researchers naturally assume that acquisition is the key to change, whereas language contact researchers favor contact as an explanation of change, but generally do not rule out some involvement of acquisition. Language change, however, needs to be studied from both a synchronic and a diachronic perspective, because innovation occurs at a specific point in time, but spread takes place over a period of time.

The answer to the question of whether languages can change without the involvement of language acquisition and contact also depends on the *theoretical* framework adopted. For generativists, language change is not possible without the involvement of language acquisition; and contact is frequently invoked as a contributing factor. This chapter may seem biased toward a generative account of language acquisition and CILC. We would like to stress that this is not because of the authors' theoretical commitments, but due to historical, theoretical, and empirical reasons. First, for thirty years (1960s–1990s), virtually all research in language acquisition has been conducted within the generative framework. Second, generative approaches are based on assumptions that provide a clear benchmark and strong predictions, especially for language acquisition but also for language change. These predictions encourage and facilitate empirical testing. Non-generativist approaches are considerably younger, and while they achieve a good level of descriptive adequacy, there is currently no comprehensive emergentist theory of language or its acquisition (O'Grady 2011). Despite various emergentist-inspired research programs, there is as yet no cohesive theory underpinning these approaches. Predictions emerging from these are so far not as constrained, which makes them more difficult to evaluate.

Finally, the answer to the question of whether languages can change without the involvement of language acquisition and contact is likely to depend on the availability of *data*. Language acquisition data have been collected for over a century now, but still, tracking linguistics changes from the original innovation to potential community spread remains an unachievable task (Thomason 2001). When diachronic evidence on language acquisition data becomes available/usable, the answer to the question of whether languages can change without the involvement of language acquisition and/or contact will become more empirically approachable.

To return to the quotes in our introduction, Anderson's view that language acquisition is the ultimate source of linguistic change seems too exclusive (to the detriment of contact); Aitchison's conflates innovation and propagation. We go with Bybee's position (2009: 350) that language acquisition plays a role in the emergence and propagation of change, but that the role of children must be carefully assessed and not just assumed.

References

Aboh, E., and U. Ansaldo. 2006. The role of typology in language creation. *Deconstructing creole*, edited by U. Ansaldo, S. Matthews, and L. Lim, 39–66. Amsterdam: Benjamins, 39–66.

Adone, D., and I. Plag (eds.). 1994. *Creolization and Language Change*. Tübingen: Niemeyer.

Aitchison, J. 1991. *Language Change: Progress or Decay?* Cambridge: Cambridge University Press.

Albareda-Castellot, B., F. Pons, and N. Sebastián-Gallés. 2011. The acquisition of phonetic categories in bilingual infants: New data from an anticipatory eye movement paradigm. *Developmental Science* 14: 395–401.

Andersen, H. 1973. Abductive and deductive change. *Language* 49: 765–793.

Andersen, H. 1978. Perceptual and conceptual factors in abductive innovations. In *Recent Developments in Historical Phonology*, edited by J. Fisiak, 1–22. The Hague: Mouton.

Andersen, R. 1980. Creolization as the acquisition of a second language as a first language. In *Theoretical Orientations in Creole Studies*, edited by A. Valdman and A. Highfield, 125–133. New York: Academic Press.

Andersen, R. W. (ed.). 1983. *Pidginization and Creolization as Language Acquisition*. Rowley, MA: Newbury House.

Appel, R., and P. Muysken. 1987. *Language Contact and Bilingualism*. London; Baltimore, MD: Edward Arnold.

Archibald, J. 2011. Second language acquisition. In *Contemporary Linguistics*, edited by William O'Grady, John Archibald, and Francis Katamba, 394–427. London: Pearson.

Bialystok, E., G. Luk, K. F. Peets, and S. Yang. 2010. Receptive vocabulary differences in monolingual and bilingual children. *Bilingualism: Language and Cognition* 13: 525–531.

Bickerton, D. 1977. Pidginization and creolization: Language acquisition and language universals. In *Pidgin and Creole linguistics*, edited by Albert Valdman, 49–69. Bloomington: Indiana University Press.

Bickerton, D. 1981. *Roots of Language*. Ann Arbor, MI: Karoma.

Bley-Vroman. R. 1990. The logical problem of foreign language learning. *Linguistic Analysis* 20: 3–49.

Bosch, L., and N. Sebastián-Gallés. 2003. Simultaneous bilingualism and the perception of a language-specific vowel contrast in the first year of life. *Language and Speech* 46: 217–243.

Brandner, E., and G. Ferraresi. 1996. Language change and generative grammar. *Language* 75: 624–625.

Bybee, J. 2003. Cognitive processes in grammaticalization. In *The New Psychology of Language*, edited by Michael Tomasello, 145–167. Mahwah, NJ: Lawrence Erlbaum.

Bybee, J. 2009. Grammaticization: Implications for a theory of language. In *Crosslinguistic Approaches to the Psychology of Language*, edited by J. Guo, E. Lieven, N. Budwig, S. Ervin-Tripp, K. Nakamura, and Seyda Özçalişkan, 345–356. New York; Hove: Psychology Press.

Byers-Heinlein, K., T. C. Burns, and J. F. Werker. 2010. The roots of bilingualism in newborns. *Psychological Science* 21: 343–348.

Chomsky, N. 1986. *Knowledge of Language: Its Nature, Origin, and Use*. New York: Praeger.

Conboy, B. T., and D. Thal. 2006. Ties between the lexicon and grammar: Cross-sectional and longitudinal studies of bilingual toddlers. *Child Development* 77(3): 712–735.

Corder, S. P. 1967. The significance of learner's errors. *International Review of Applied Linguistics in Language Teaching* 5(4): 161–170.

Croft, W. 2000. *Explaining Language Change: An Evolutionary Approach*. London: Longman.

DeGraff, M. 1999. Creolization, language change, and language acquisition: A prolegomenon. In *Language Creation and Language Change: Creolization, Diachrony, and Development*, edited by Michel DeGraff, 1–46. Cambridge, MA: MIT Press.

DeGraff, M. 2003. 'Creolization' is acquisition. Paper presented at the Society for Pidgin and Creole Linguistics, University of Hawai'i at Manoa.

De Houwer, A., and J. M. Meisel. 1996. Analyzing the relationship between two developing languages in bilingual first language acquisition: Methodology, data, findings. Paper presented at the Workshop on Language Contact: Linking Different Levels of Analysis. Wassenaar: Netherlands Institute for Advanced Study.

De Houwer, A. 1990. *The Acquisition of Two Languages from Birth: A Case Study*. Cambridge: Cambridge University Press.

Demirçay, D., and Ad Backus. 2014. Bringing disparate languages closer together through intense code-switching: The next generation's Turkish-Dutch mixing. Paper presented at the 47th Annual Meeting of the Societas Linguistica Europaea, Adam Mickiewicz University, Poland.

Deuchar, Margaret, and Suzanne Quay. 2000. *Bilingual Acquisition: Theoretical Implications of a Case Study*. Oxford: Oxford University Press.

Döpke, S. 2000. *Cross-Linguistic Structures in Simultaneous Bilingualism*. Amsterdam; Philadelphia: John Benjamins.

Dulay, H., and M. Burt. 1974. Natural sequences in child second language acquisition. *Language Learning* 24: 37–53.

Duran Eppler, Eva. 2010. *Emigranto*. Vienna: Braumüller.

Eckman, F. 2004. From phonemic differences to constraint rankings. *Studies in Second Language Acquisition* 26: 513–549.

Ellis, N. C. 2006. Selective attention and transfer phenomena in L2 acquisition: Contingency, cue competition, salience, interference, overshadowing, blocking, and perceptual learning. *Applied Linguistics* 27(2): 164–194.

Ellis, N. C., and N. Sagarra. 2010. The bounds of adult language acquisition: Blocking and learned attention. *Studies in Second Language Acquisition* 32(4): 553–580.

Evans, V., and M. Green. 2006. *Cognitive Linguistics*. Edinburgh: Edinburgh University Press.

Flege, J. 1999. Age of learning and second language speech. In *Second Language Acquisition and the Critical Period Hypothesis*, edited by David Birdsong, 101–132. Mahwah, NJ: Lawrence Erlbaum.

Gass, S. 1996. Second language acquisition and linguistic theory: The role of language transfer. In *The Handbook of Bilingualism*, edited by T. K. Bhatia and W. C. Ritchie, 317–345. Oxford: Blackwell.

Genesee, F. 1989. Early bilingual development, one language or two? *Journal of Child Language* 16: 161–179.

Genesee, F., J. Paradis, and M. Crago. 2004. *Dual Language Learning and Disorder: A Handbook on Bilingualism and Second Language Learning*. Baltimore, MD: Brookes.

Genesee, F., E. Nicolaidis, and J. Paradis. 1995. Language differentiation in early bilingual development. *Journal of Child Language* 6: 161–179.

Gildersleeve-Neumann, C. E., and K. L. Wright. 2010. English speech acquisition in 3- to 5-year-old children learning Russian and English. *Language, Speech, and Hearing Sciences in Schools* 41: 429–444.

Green, M., and G. Ozón. (2019). Valency and transitivity in contact: Evidence from Cameroon Pidgin English. *Journal of Language Contact* 12 (1): 52–88.

Gut, U. 2011. Studying structural innovations in New English varieties. In *Exploring Second-Language Varieties of English and Learner Englishes: Bridging a Paradigm Gap*, edited by J. Mukherjee and M. Hundt, 101–124. Amsterdam: John Benjamins.

Halle, M. 1962. Phonology in a generative grammar. *Word* 18: 54–71.

Heine, B., and T. Kuteva. 2005. *Language Contact and Grammatical Change*. Cambridge: Cambridge University Press.

Hellinger, M. 1985. *Englisch-orientierte Pidgin- und Kreolsprachen Entstehung, Geschichte und sprachlicher Wandel*. Darmstadt: Wissenschaftliche Buchgesellschaft.

Hickey, R. (ed.). 2010. *The Handbook of Language Contact*. Oxford: Wiley-Blackwell.

Holm, J. A. 1978. *The Creole English of Nicaragua's Miskito Coast: Its Sociolinguistic History and a Comparative Study of Its Syntax and Lexicon*. PhD dissertation, University of London.

Holm, J. A. 1988. *Pidgins and Creoles*, Vol. 1: *Theory and Structure*. Cambridge: Cambridge University Press.

Houston-Price, C., Z. Caloghiris, and E. Raviglione. 2010. Language experience shapes the development of the mutual exclusivity bias. *Infancy* 15: 125–150.

Hulk, A., and N. Müller. 2000. Bilingual first language acquisition at the interface between syntax and pragmatics. *Bilingualism: Language and Cognition* 3: 227–244.

Keller, R. 1994. *On Language Change: The Invisible Hand in Language*. London: Routledge.

Kerswill, P., J. Cheshire, S. Fox, and E. Torgersen. 2013. English as a contact language: The role of children and adolescents. In *English as a Contact Language*, edited by D. Schreier and M. Hundt, 258–282. Cambridge: Cambridge University Press.

Kouwenberg, S., and J. V. Singler (eds.). 2008. *The Handbook of Pidgin and Creole Studies*. Oxford: Blackwell.

Kroch, A. 1989. Reflexes of grammar in patterns of language change. *Language Variation and Change* 1: 199–244.

Kroch, A., and A. Taylor. 1997. Verb movement in Old and Middle English: Dialect variation and language contact. In *Parameters and Morphosyntactic Change*, edited by Ans van Kemenade and Nigel Vincent, 297–325. Cambridge: Cambridge University Press.

Kuhl, P. K., F.-M. Tsao, and H.-M. Liu. 2003. Foreign-language experience in infancy: Effects of short-term exposure and social interaction on phonetic learning. *Proceedings of the National Academy of Sciences* 100: 9096–9101.

Lefebvre, L., C. White, and C. Jourdan. 2006. *L2 Acquisition and Creole Genesis: Dialogues*. Amsterdam: John Benjamins.

Lenneberg, Eric 1967. *Biological Foundations of Language*. New York: John Wiley.

Lightfoot, D. 1979. *Principles of Diachronic Syntax*. Cambridge: Cambridge University Press.

Lightfoot, D. 1991. *How to Set Parameters: Arguments from Language Change*. Cambridge, MA: MIT Press.

Lightfoot, D. 1999. *The Development of Language: Acquisition, Change, and Evolution*. Oxford: Blackwell.

Lightfoot, D. 2002. Myths and the prehistory of grammar. *Journal of Linguistics* 38: 113–136.

Lightfoot, D. 2006. *How New Languages Emerge*. New York: Cambridge University Press.

Lightfoot, D. 2014. Review of *Meisel et al. (2013)*. *Journal of Linguistics* 50: 757–761.

Lightfoot, D., and M. Westergaard. 2007. Language acquisition and language change: Inter-relationships. *Language and Linguistics Compass* 1(5): 396–415.

Lipski, J. M. 1996. Los dialectos vestigiales del español en los Estados Unidos: estado de la cuestión. *Signo y Seña* 6: 459–489.

MacWhinney, B. 2008. A unified model. In *Handbook of Cognitive Linguistics and Second Language Acquisition*, edited by P. Robinson and N. C. Ellis, 341–371. New York; London: Routledge.

Marchman, V., C. Martinez-Sussman, and P. S. Dale. 2004. The language-specific nature of grammatical development: Evidence from bilingual language learners. *Developmental Science* 7: 212–224.

Meisel, J. M. 2001. The simultaneous acquisition of two first languages: Early differentiation and subsequent development of grammars. In *Trends in Bilingual Acquisition*, edited by J. Cenoz and F. Genesee, 11–42. Amsterdam: Benjamins.

Meisel, J. M. 2004. The bilingual child. In *The Handbook of Bilingualism*, edited by T. K. Bhatia and W. C. Ritchie, 91–113. Oxford: Blackwell.

Meisel, J. M. 2007. On autonomous syntactic development in multiple first language acquisition. In *Proceedings of the 31st Boston University Conference on Language Development*, edited by H. Caunt-Nulton, S. Kulatilake, and I.-H. Woo, 26–45. Somerville: Cascadilla Press.

Meisel, J. M. 2011. Bilingual language acquisition and theories of diachronic change: Bilingualism as cause and effect of grammatical change. *Bilingualism: Language and Cognition* 14: 121–145.

Meisel, J. M., M. Elsig, and E. Rinke. 2013. *Language Acquisition and Change: A Morphosyntactic Perspective*. Edinburgh: Edinburgh University Press.

Mitchell, R., and F. Myles. 2013. *Second Language Learning Theories*. London: Routledge.

Montanari, S. 2010. Translation equivalents and the emergence of multiple lexicons in early trilingual development. *First Language* 30: 102–125.

Montrul, S. 2004. *The Acquisition of Spanish: Morphosyntactic Development in Monolingual and Bilingual L1 Acquisition and in Adult L2 Acquisition*. Amsterdam: Benjamins.

Montrul, S. 2009. Reexamining the Fundamental Difference Hypothesis: What can early bilinguals tell us? *Studies in Second Language Acquisition* 31(2): 225–257.

Morgan, G., and J. Kegl. 2006. Nicaraguan Sign Language and Theory of Mind: The issue of critical periods and abilities. *Journal of Child Psychology and Psychiatry* 47(8): 811–819.

Mufwene, S. 2001. *The Ecology of Language Evolution*. Cambridge: Cambridge University Press.

Mühlhäusler, P. 1986. *Pidgin and Creole Linguistics*. Oxford: Blackwell.

Mukherjee, J., and M. Hundt (eds.). 2011. *Exploring Second-Language Varieties of English and Learner Englishes*. Amsterdam: Benjamins

Müller, N., and A. Hulk. 2001. Crosslinguistic influence in bilingual language acquisition: Italian and French as recipient languages. *Bilingualism: Language and Cognition* 4: 1–21.

Muysken, P. C. 2006. Mixed codes. In *Multilingual Communication*, edited by Peter Auer and Li Wei, 303–328. Berlin: Mouton de Gruyter.

Nicoladis, E. 2001. Finding first words in the input. In *Trends in Bilingual Acquisition*, edited by J. Cenoz and Fred Genesee, 131–147. Amsterdam: Benjamins.

Niyogi, P., and R. C. Berwick. 1995. The logical problem of language change. Massachusetts Institute of Technology, Center for Biological and Computational Learning: AI Memo No.1516/C.B.C.L. Paper No. 115.

O'Neil, W. 1993. Nicaraguan English in History. In *Historical Linguistics: Problems and Perspectives*, edited by Charles Jones, 279–318. London: Longman.

Odlin, T. 1989. *Language Transfer*. Cambridge: Cambridge University Press.

Oller, D. K., B. Z. Pearson, and A. B. Cobo-Lewis. 2007. Profile effects in early bilingual language and literacy. *Applied Psycholinguistics* 28: 191–230.

Ozón, G. 2016. European Englishes. In *Investigating English in Europe—Contexts and Agendas*, edited by Andrew Linn, 72–78. Berlin: Mouton de Gruyter.

Paradis, J. 2008. Second language acquisition in childhood. In *Blackwell Handbook of Language Development*, edited by E. Hoff and M. Shatz, 387–405. Oxford: Blackwell.

Paradis, J., and F. Genesee. 1996. Syntactic acquisition in bilingual children: Autonomous or independent? *Studies in Second Language Acquisition* 18: 1–15.

Paradis, J., E. Nicoladis, M. Crago, and F. Genesee. 2011. Bilingual children's acquisition of past tense: A usage-based approach. *Journal of Child Language* 38: 554–578.

Pearson, B. Z., S. C. Fernández, V. Lewedag, and D. K. Oller. 1997. The relation of input factors to lexical learning by bilingual infants (ages 10 to 30 months). *Applied Psycholinguistics* 18: 41–58.

Pienemann, M. 1998. *Language Processing and Second Language Development: Processability Theory.* Amsterdam: John Benjamins.

Pienemann, M. (ed.). 2005. *Cross-Linguistic Aspects of Processability Theory.* Amsterdam: Benjamins.

Poplack, S., and S. Levey. 2010. Contact-induced grammatical change: A cautionary tale. In *An International Handbook of Linguistic Variation,* edited by Peter Auer and J. Schmidt, 391–418. Berlin: Mouton.

Queen, R. 2001. Bilingual intonation patterns: Evidence from language change from Turkish-German bilingual children. *Language in Society* 30: 55–80.

Ramus, F., M. D. Hauser, C. Miller, D. Morris, and J. Mehler. 2000. Language discrimination by human newborns and by cotton-top tamarin monkeys. *Science* 288: 349–351.

Ritchie, W., and T. Bhatia (eds.). 1996. *Handbook of Second Language Acquisition.* San Diego, CA: Academic Press.

Romaine, S. 1994. *Bilingualism.* Oxford: Blackwell.

Sánchez, L. 2004. Functional convergence in the tense, evidentiality and aspectual systems of Quechua Spanish bilinguals. *Bilingualism: Language and Cognition* 7: 147–162.

Schneider, E. W. 2013. English as a contact language: The "New Englishes." In *English as a Contact Language,* edited by Daniel Schreier and Marianne Hundt, 131–148. Cambridge: Cambridge University Press.

Schumann, J. 1978. *The Pidginization Process: A Model for Second Language Acquisition.* Rowley: Newbury House.

Selinker, L., M. Swain, and G. Dumas. 1975. The interlanguage hypothesis extended to children. *Language Learning* 25: 139–152.

Siegel, J. 2008a. *The Emergence of Pidgin and Creole Languages.* Oxford: Oxford University Press.

Siegel, J. 2008b. *Pidgins/Creoles and Second Language Acquisition: The Handbook of Pidgin and Creole Studies,* edited by Silvia Kouwenberg and John Victor Singler, 189–218. Oxford: Blackwell.

Slobin, Dan. 2006. Cross-linguistic comparative approaches to language acquisition. In *Encyclopedia of Language and Linguistics,* edited by Keith Brown, 299–301. Oxford: Elsevier.

Stewart, J. M. 2003. Is there a fundamental difference? The availability of universal grammar in child versus adult second language acquisition. In *Proceedings of the 6th Generative Approaches to Second Language Acquisition Conference,* edited by J. M. Liceras et al., 308–314. Somerville: Cascadilla.

Thomason, S. G., and T. Kaufman. 1988. *Language Contact, Creolization, and Genetic Linguistics.* Berkeley: University of California Press.

Thomason, S. G. 2001. *Language Contact.* Edinburgh: Edinburgh University Press.

Thomason, S. G. 2013. Innovation and contact: The role of adults. *English as a Contact Language,* edited by Daniel Schreier and Marianne Hundt, 283–297. Cambridge: Cambridge University Press.

Toribio, A. J. 2004. Convergence as an optimization strategy in bilingual speech: Evidence from code-switching. *Bilingualism: Language and Cognition* 2: 165–173.

Trudgill, P. 2010. Contact and sociolinguistic typology. In *The Handbook of Language Contact,* edited by Raymond Hickey, 299–319. Oxford: Wiley-Blackwell.

Unsworth, S. 2004. On the syntax-semantics interface in Dutch: Adult and child L2 acquisition compared. *International Review of Applied Linguistics* 42: 173–187.

Unsworth, Sharon. 2013. Current issues in multilingual first language acquisition. *Annual Review of Applied Linguistics* 33: 21–50.

Verhoeven, L. T. 1991. Acquisition of biliteracy. In *Reading in Two Languages*, edited by J. H. Hulsijn and J. F. Matter, 61–74. Amsterdam: AILA.

Verhoeven, L. T. 1994. Transfer in bilingual development: The linguistic interdependent hypothesis revisited. *Language Learning* 44: 381–415.

Volterra, V., and T. Taeschner. 1978. The acquisition and development of language by bilingual children. *Journal of Child Language* 5: 311–326.

Weerman, F. 1993. The diachronic consequences of first and second language acquisition: The change from OV to VO. *Linguistics* 31: 901–931.

Weerman, F. 2011. Diachronic change: Early versus late acquisition. *Bilingualism: Language and Cognition* 14(2): 149–151.

Weinreich, U. 1966 [1953]. *Languages in Contact*. The Hague: Mouton.

Weinreich, U., W. Labov, and M. I. Herzog. 1968. Empirical foundations for a theory of language change. In *Directions for Historical Linguistics: A Symposium*, edited by Winfred P. Lehmann, 95–195. Austin: University of Texas Press.

Wekker, H. (ed.). 1996. *Creole Languages and Language Acquisition*. Berlin: Mouton de Gruyter.

Westergaard, M. 2008. Acquisition and change: On the robustness of the triggering experience for word order cues. *Lingua* 118: 1841–1863.

Winford, D. 2003. *An Introduction to Contact Linguistics*. Oxford: Blackwell.

Yang, C. D. 2000. Internal and external forces in language change. *Language Variation and Change* 12: 231–250.

Yip, V., and S. Matthews. 2007. *The Bilingual Child: Early Development and Language Contact*. Cambridge: Cambridge University Press.

Zobl, H. 1983. Contact-induced language change, learner language and the potentials of a modified contrastive analysis. In *Second Language Acquisition Studies*, edited by M. Bailey, M. Long, and S. Beck, 104–112. Rowley: Newbury House.

Zuraw, Kie. 2006. Language change, probabilistic models of. In *The Encyclopedia of Language and Linguistics*, edited by Keith Brown, 349–357. Oxford: Elsevier.

CHAPTER 10

....

LANGUAGE CONTACT AND ENDANGERED LANGUAGES

....

ALEXANDRA Y. AIKHENVALD

10.1 LANGUAGE ENDANGERMENT AND LANGUAGE OBSOLESCENCE

....

LINGUISTIC minorities all over the world are losing ground to dominant and more prestigious languages. If one group aggressively imposes its language on another group, the language of the latter is threatened. The minority language may lose its own features (especially those absent from the dominant language). Speakers of an endangered language will gradually lose the capacity to fully communicate in the language and fully understand it. As a consequence, an endangered language—under threat and pressure from the dominant one—will gradually become obsolescent. The process of language obsolescence ultimately leads to language shift and language loss.

This is a classic scenario known as the "gradual death" of an endangered language (see Campbell and Muntzel 1989: 182–186, for further examples and definitions). Alternatively, a language can suffer "sudden death," if all, or almost all, of its speakers suddenly die or are killed (as was the case for Tasmanian languages). A third alternative is "radical language death." This implies rapid language loss due to genocide or political repression. This is what happened to Manao, an Arawak language formerly spoken in northwestern Amazonia. Instances of "gradual death" allow us to trace the impact of change, both externally and internally motivated. This chapter focuses on such instances.

An obsolescent language may be known just to a handful of last fluent speakers. This is the case for Ingrian Finnish in Estonia (Riionheimo 2002), Bare in Brazil and Venezuela (Aikhenvald 2012a), and Dyirbal and Yidiny in northern Australia (Dixon 1991a, 1991b), and Mawayana in Brazil, Guyana, and Suriname (Carlin 2006). This is known as "global" language obsolescence.

Language obsolescence may affect individuals or groups of individuals living away from the language community. This is often the case with speakers of immigrant languages, spoken by groups of varied size whose major language is the dominant language of the country. These varieties are sometimes referred to as "Heritage" languages (see Klintborg 1999; Milani 1996). This is "localized" language obsolescence.

Localized language obsolescence may occur within a broader context of global obsolescence of a language. Paumarí, an Arawá language from southern Amazonia, is gradually falling out of use, and more rapidly so in the communities on the River Ituxí than those on the River Purús. As a result, speakers from the Ituxí communities display more signs of language obsolescence (Chapman and Derbyshire 1991; Aikhenvald 2010). Processes of language obsolescence appear to be similar in the contexts of global and of localized obsolescence.

In the instances of localized language obsolescence, a student of language change can compare the obsolescent, or "Heritage" language, with the variety still actively spoken in the homeland. In the case of global obsolescence, we are sometimes fortunate to have access to a description of a pre-obsolescent variety of a language. Krejnovich's work gives us access to Nivkh as it used to be before the language ceased to be transmitted to the next generation (see Gruzdeva 2002, 2007, and references there). Numerous descriptions of Ingrian Finnish allow us to trace and to understand the processes of obsolescence of this language in Estonia (Riionheimo 2002). The grammar of traditional Paumarí by Chapman and Derbyshire (1991) helps us trace the nature of obsolescence in the present-day language. The obsolescent Dyirbal (Schmidt 1985; Dixon 1991a) can be contrasted and compared with the language described by Dixon (1972) when it was still actively spoken within communities. The Tariana language spoken by traditional representatives of the older generation (only a few of them still living) can be contrasted with the speech of younger people who are gradually relinquishing their ancestral language.

10.2 LANGUAGE CHANGE IN ENDANGERED LANGUAGES

Language endangerment is primarily caused by social factors. A primary reason is intensive contact with another group whose language—or linguistic variety—has gained, or is gaining, greater political, social, and economic prestige and advantages (see Lüpke and Storch 2013: 270–339 for an up-to-date summary of language endangerment criteria and their applicability). The loss of a language is frequently a gradual process due to a shift to the dominant language of the country, or of an area. Fewer and fewer children learn the endangered language, and the absolute numbers of speakers dwindle. Traditional speech genres and styles tend to be forgotten. An obsolescent language will no longer be actively used, nor is it being transmitted to the next generation.

An endangered language typically undergoes reduction of forms and loss of categories (called *morphological reduction* and *syntactic reduction*: see Hill and Hill 1977, 1986; Anderson 1982; Campbell and Muntzel 1989; and Maher 1991). This includes the regularization of paradigms and a reduction in the number of allomorphs. Synthetic forms tend to be replaced with analytic ones.

Speakers of an endangered language gradually lose the knowledge of traditional speech styles, including origins myths and songs. Special forms employed in storytelling may no longer be remembered. For instance, the dialogical style of telling origin myths among the Shokleng, a Jê-speaking group in southern Brazil, is no longer remembered. The formulaic ritual Wayamo language style traditionally employed during feasts and rites—and in shamanic chants—by Yanomami men is falling into disuse (Aikhenvald 2012b: 366–369). This is known as *stylistic shrinkage*.

An endangered language tends to become structurally similar to the dominant one. A bilingual speaker typically maintains the categories and distinctions found in both the healthy dominant language and the endangered language; that is, shared features are enhanced by language contact. Categories and distinctions not found in the dominant language tend to be lost. This is known as *negative borrowing*. The likelihood of loss of unmatched structures in endangered languages and the enhancement of the ones present in both languages can be explained by potentially greater efficiency for the bilingual brain to work with identical structures (see Andersen 1982: 97). The process of enhancement is well attested in many language-contact situations, and so is negative borrowing (see a summary in Aikhenvald 2006: 22–23).

Contact-induced changes can roughly be divided into three groups in terms of their stability. Following Tsitsipis (1998: 34), changes can be *completed, ongoing* (or *continuous*), and *discontinuous*. Completed changes cover those aspects of the language that do not show any synchronic variation and which go beyond speakers' awareness (see, for instance, the discussion of a Spanish-influenced passive in Purépecha by Chamoreau 2005). Ongoing, or continuous, changes are those in progress; here the degree of influence of the other language depends on the speaker's competence and possibly other, sociolinguistic, variables (such as age or degree of participation in community life). Discontinuous changes are one-off deviations characteristic of individual speakers. These deviations often differentiate fluent speakers of an obsolescent language from less proficient ones (Dorian 1977). The effects of contact-induced change on obsolescent languages are discontinuous in nature.

Speakers of endangered languages tend to vary in their proficiency in the language, depending on their age, socioeconomic status, and the degree of exposure to the language. Fluent speakers of East Sutherland Gaelic, between seventy and eighty years of age, constituted the minority of those who had command of the language (Dorian 1977, 1978). People between the age of forty-five and sixty-five in one village, and between thirty-five and forty-five in another one, could make themselves understood in Gaelic: these "semi-speakers" displayed lack of fluency and more grammatical reduction than older and more traditional ones. In the Dyirbal-speaking community of Jambun, only those over thirty-five spoke the traditional language in the early 1980s; fifteen- to thirty-five-year-olds spoke "Young People's Dyirbal," that is, an "imperfect" variety which bore an impact from English (younger people had no fluency in the language: Schmidt 1985: 22–23).

In a situation of language endangerment and impending language obsolescence, one often encounters a multiplicity of sporadic changes that would be considered to be mistakes by fluent speakers (if they existed). A further feature of endangered and obsolescent languages is a high degree of individual variation. Obligatory grammatical rules fail to apply in the speech of individual people due to the attrition of linguistic community, and loss of the previously existing norm (see Klintborg 1999 on American Swedish; Campbell and Muntzel 1989: 189 on American Finnish). The extent of impact of a dominant language may vary depending on the individual proficiency (see Dorian 2010: 283–285).

Speakers of several obsolescent dialects of the same language tend to merge the dialectal forms and lose the original distinctions. This is what happened with some of the last fluent speakers of Traditional Dyirbal (Dixon 1991a: 195–199). Similar processes may happen if the dominant language is closely related to the obsolescent one. Creation of mixed dialects and mixed, or "blended" languages is a further consequence of language obsolescence.

Mechanisms of contact-induced change in endangered and obsolescent languages are essentially the same as in languages whose vitality is beyond doubt. A high degree of individual variation between speakers and disintegration of language communities results in the lack of continuity and stability of linguistic change. The "transient" and ephemeral nature of contact-induced change is especially characteristic of languages at the advanced stages of language obsolescence (cf. Klintborg 1999; Aikhenvald 2014).

A further difference between contact-induced language change in "healthy" and in endangered or obsolescent languages often lies not in the sorts of change, which tend to be the same. It tends to lie in the quantity of change, and in the speed with which the obsolescent language changes (Campbell and Muntzel 1989; Aikhenvald 2006: 43–44, 2012a; Campbell and Palosaari 2011). In her seminal study of Young People's Dyirbal, Schmidt (1985: 213) pointed out that "one distinguishing feature of the Dyirbal death situation is that vast amounts of change are compressed into a short time span of about 25 years" (see also Aikhenvald 2002: 243–264, for similar examples).[1]

Contact and linguistic pressure from the dominant language do not explain all the changes in language obsolescence. Terminal speakers of Arvanitika Albanian in Greece sporadically lose gender and number agreement. Their entire system of tense-aspect-mood categories is disintegrating—imperfective past forms are not used at all, and the marking of grammatical person is "morphologically distorted" (Tsitsitpis 1998: 44–62).

---

[1] See Maandi (1989). Similar correlations between the age and language proficiency have been described for many other areas: see, for instance, Li Fengxiang (2005), Lau Chun Fat (2005), and papers in Dorian (1989), and Vakhtin (2007). Specific instances of structural changes accompanying language obsolescence have been addressed in Campbell and Muntzel (1989); Chamoreau (2000); Dorian (1977, 1978); Grenoble and Whaley (1998); Aikhenvald (2002: 243–259) and Dixon (1991a, 1991b). The role of men and women in promoting the dominant language and maintaining the endangered one depends on the community: in some, men are more likely to lead in the process of language shift, while in others, women more actively promote shift to the dominant language (as is the case for the Reindeer Sámi in Finnish Lapland: Aikio 1992).

This "agrammatism" cannot be explained by *negative borrowing*, that is, loss of categories not present in the dominant language, Greek, since Greek possesses all these categories, which are now lost in the obsolescent Arvanitika (Sasse 1992: 69–70). The loss of categories is due to general simplification of the language structure as it falls into disuse.

Changes in endangered and in obsolescent languages may also be due to language-internal processes in conjunction with the influence of a major language. For example, the loss of the distinction between partitive and genitive case to mark objects in immigrant Estonian, especially among second-generation speakers, is partly due to the influence of Swedish. This process could have been enhanced by dialectal influence (since the same process has occurred in some dialects spoken in Estonia), and by a general tendency toward simplification of the case system.[2]

The impact of the increasingly dominant language onto the receding, obsolescent language, which is gradually falling into disuse, tends to involve a massive influx of non-native forms from the dominant language. This may result in cross-linguistically unusual phenomena, including borrowed bound morphemes.

10.3 BORROWED FORMS IN ENDANGERED LANGUAGES

Direct diffusion, or borrowing forms, is a frequent outcome of language contact. Once a language becomes endangered, we often witness the increase in sheer number of free forms from the dominant language. In Haugen's (1989: 67) words, "the adoption of English loans" was the "first great step in the direction of English" for immigrant speakers of Norwegian.

Speakers of Tlaxcalan Nahuatl, a highly endangered Uto-Aztecan language of Mexico, use an impressive number of Spanish words in their conversations. These include kinship terms (*padres* 'fathers, parents'), terms for animals (*burro* 'donkey'), plants (*abas* 'broad beans,' *trigo* 'wheat'), verbs (*leer* 'read,' *condenaroa* 'condemn'), conjunctions and discourse markers *entonces* 'so, then,' *cuando* 'when,' *porque* 'because,' *pero* 'but'), and preposition *para* 'for' (Hill and Hill 1977).

The lexicon of Evenki, an endangered Tungusic language, is heavily affected by borrowings from the dominant Russian in many fields, including reindeer husbandry and daily life (e.g., Evenki *stada* 'herd' from Russian *stado* 'herd,' replacing Evenki *aβdu*). Along similar lines, speakers of Nivkh, a highly endangered Paleo-Siberian isolate of the Sakhalin and Amur regions, use more and more Russian terms, instead of Nivkh forms (e.g., *boʈ'ka* 'barrel,' from Russian *bochka* 'barrel,' instead of the Nivkh *sidux*). Younger speakers of Hakka in Hong Kong have limited competence in the

---

[2] Dixon (1991b) offers further examples of multiple motivation for changes in the obsolescent Yidiny.

language, which is being lost under encroaching pressure from Cantonese. As a result, they "are speaking Hakka with an overwhelming number of Cantonese words" (Fat 2005: 33). Speakers of Young People's Dyirbal "frequently depend on English words to bridge gaps in their Dyirbal communicative competence" (Schmidt 1985: 183); as a result, their Dyirbal is inundated with English forms.

Excessive code-switching is a further feature of language obsolescence (see the case study in Martin 2005). A further issue for the study of an obsolescent language no longer actively used concerns difficulties in distinguishing between code-switching and established borrowings. Code-switching refers to the use of elements of another language following specific conventions. Borrowings are an established part of the language. As a language becomes obsolescent, the existing linguistic norm disintegrates. Different speakers and semi-speakers vary in how many forms from the dominant language they use, and under what conditions. A speaker may insert a non-native form as an ad-hoc way of filling a lexical gap in a language one does not speak well any longer. Blurring the boundaries between borrowing and code-switching goes together with the inherently unstable character of languages on the path to extinction.

Conjunctions and discourse markers are highly susceptible to borrowing under any circumstances of language contact (Stolz and Stolz 1996; Aikhenvald 2006). Obsolescent languages are likely to borrow these. Traditional Gooniyandi and Warrwa, Australian languages of the Kimberleys in Australia, had no coordinating conjunctions. The remaining obsolescent speakers use English forms *nd* (from *and*) and O (from *or*). Traditional Nyulnyul did have a conjunction *agal* 'and.' The two remaining fluent speakers use the English form *nd* (McGregor 2002: 177).

Texts and conversations recorded from the last fluent speaker of Bare, a now extinct North Arawak language from Venezuela and Brazil, contain numerous instances of Spanish subordinating conjunctions *mientre ke* (from Spanish *mientras que*) 'while, whereas,' *purke* 'because' (from Spanish *porque*), and *pero* 'but' (from Spanish *pero* 'but'). These are absent from the earlier and healthier stages of the language (see further discussion in Aikhenvald 2012a).

Obsolescent languages may borrow grammatical forms, only occasionally borrowed in "healthy" language situations (further examples are in Aikhenvald 2012a). These include personal pronouns. Mawayana (Carlin 2006) is a highly endangered North Arawak language spoken by just two elderly people in a village where Trio and Waiwai, from the Carib family, are the dominant languages. The two remaining speakers of Mawayana have little opportunity to use the language.

Like most other Arawak languages, Mawayana originally had first, second, and third person, without distinguishing between first person plural inclusive (I and you) and exclusive (I and a third person, excluding you). In contrast, Waiwai and Trio have different forms for first person inclusive and for first person exclusive. As a result of influence from Waiwai and Trio as dominant languages with an obligatory distinction between inclusive and exclusive, the two remaining speakers of Mawayana consistently use the Waiwai pronoun *amna* to express the concept of first person plural exclusive, for example Waiwai *amna krapan* 'our (exclusive) bow.' The original first person plural prefix *wa-* in Mawayana has been reinterpreted as inclusive, as in Mawayana *amna saruuka* (our.exclusive fishtrap) 'our (exclusive) fishtrap' and *wa-saruuka* (1plural. POSSESSIVE=inclusive-fishtrap) 'our (inclusive) fishtrap.' The borrowed form *amna* does not occur in the previous records of the language, collected when the language was more actively spoken than it is at present. This suggests that borrowing a pronoun—something not unheard of, but rather unusual—could be the result of an influx of non-native forms characteristic of Mawayana as an obsolescent language.

Ingrian Finnish is spoken by a handful of elderly people scattered around Estonia. Estonian is their major language of communication. Estonian and Ingrian Finnish are closely related and structurally similar. The most striking foreign form recorded in the language of the few remaining speakers of Ingrian Finnish is the Estonian past tense marker *-si-* employed instead of the Ingrian Finnish *-i-* (Riionheimo 2002: 201–202). This past tense marker is highly productive in Estonian. Its appearance in Ingrian Finnish can thus be explained by the influence of the dominant language. This is an instance of a typologically unusual borrowing of a bound form. However, since the language is on its way out, the borrowing is a token of discontinuous unstable change.

10.4 DIFFUSION OF PATTERNS IN ENDANGERED LANGUAGES

An influx of forms from a dominant language is not a universal outcome of language obsolescence. Last speakers sometimes consciously avoid using recognizable loan forms. R. M. W. Dixon (1977: 29) reports that Dick Moses, one of the very last fluent speakers of Yidiny, made sure his language was free of English intrusions, in place of what had been established loanwords. For instance, instead of *mudaga* 'motor car' and *biligan* 'billy can' he used *dundalay* and *gunbu:l*, which he said came from the avoidance style for these items. Similar examples of purism have been documented for Arizona Tewa, a Tanoan language (Kroskrity 1993); Kiliwa, a Yuman language from Baja California (Mixco 1977); and Tariana, the only Arawak language in the multilingual area of the Vaupés River Basin (Aikhenvald 2002).

"People generally construe languages as being collections of words" (Thurston 1987: 93). Contact-induced structural similarities, and diffusion of patterns, are much harder to control: speakers are often not aware of a rapid expansion of grammatical and lexical calques and indirect diffusion of patterns from the dominant language into the one on its way out. Language endangerment and impending language shift may result in a massive calquing of structures from the dominant language and accelerated diffusion of patterns.

A phonological or a morphological distinction, constituent order or a syntactic construction may be replicated in an obsolescent language—see section 10.4.1. A morpheme that has a similar phonetic shape in both languages can change its meaning to fit in with that of the dominant language. This is known as *accommodation*—see section 10.4.2. Or a native category or construction can be reinterpreted to fit in with the pattern present in the dominant language—see section 10.5.2.

10.4.1 Replicating a Pattern

Manambu, from the Ndu family, is currently spoken by about two thousand people in five villages in the Sepik area of Papua New Guinea. During the last twenty years, its spheres of usage have been reduced with the obsolescence of traditional cultural practices and the expansion of Tok Pisin, the local lingua franca, and also Papua New Guinea English. The number of Tok Pisin and English forms in Manambu has drastically increased since the 1990s (when I first started fieldwork on the language). There is also a growing number of calques from Tok Pisin. For instance, the spatial preposition *kuker* 'at the back of, behind something' has recently started to be used with temporal meaning, 'after,' by analogy with Tok Pisin *bihain* 'behind, after.'

The meaning of a word may become extended, to match the pattern found in the dominant language. The Lakota verb *iNyaNk* originally meant 'to run,' that is, to describe 'the activity of moving fast on one's legs.' Nowadays, English is quickly becoming the dominant language in Lakota communities. And, as a result, in contemporary Lakota, this same verb is commonly used to mean 'to run for election, to function, operate, work' (e.g., a device or a machine) (Ullrich 2008: 775; similar examples can be found in Weinreich 1953).

Indirect diffusion may affect the phonology of an endangered language. Anong is a highly endangered Tibeto-Burman language spoken in Yunnan Province in China. Over the past four decades the language has become severely endangered. As a consequence of the large influx of loans from Chinese that contain nasalized vowels and diphthongs, the language has developed phonological diphthongs and nasalized vowels. Some of these now occur in native words (Sun and Liu 2009: 128).

Word order in phrases and order of constituents in clauses in an endangered language are often modified under the influence of a dominant one. In traditional Nivkh, number words used to follow the head noun (e.g., *pit ɣəŋ t'ogř* [book five] 'five books'). Under the influence of Russian, the head noun in the obsolescent Nivkh tends to follow the number word, especially if the noun is a borrowing, for example *t'ogř čas* (five[Nivkh] hour[Russian]) 'five hours' (Gruzdeva 2000: 124–125, 2007: 195–196). Within Evenki noun phrases, word order is changing from possessor-possessee to possessee-possessor, following the Russian model (Grenoble 2000: 107–109).

Constituent order in Nivkh used to follow a strict subject-object-verb pattern. Under the influence of Russian, which has free constituent order, it has become less rigid: nowadays, object-verb-subject and subject-verb-object orders are attested (Gruzdeva 2000: 125–127). In Evenki, a Tungusic language with originally strict subject-verb-object order, the order is becoming more relaxed, as the language becomes more obsolescent. This is also a consequence of contact with the dominant Russian (Grenoble 2000: 109).

Traditional Tariana used to have free constituent order determined by discourse-pragmatic factors. Younger and not very proficient speakers of Tariana are developing a strictly verb-final constituent order, mirroring the order in the dominant Tucano. An emergent cleft construction is evolving under the influence of Portuguese, another dominant language in the area (Aikhenvald 2002: 166–168).

An obsolescent language may develop an agreement system, mirroring the one in a dominant language. Traditional Nivkh had no number agreement in noun phrases with number words, for example *xerrit'uɣr t'ex* (match.SINGULAR.NOMINATIVE three) 'three matches.' Nowadays, plural forms are used with numbers, for example *ķan-gu meķř* (dog-PLURAL two) 'two dogs,' replicating the Russian plural number marking in a corresponding NP Russian *dve sobak-i* (two:FEMININE:NOMINATIVE dog-FEMININE: PLURAL:NOMINATIVE) (Gruzdeva 2000: 123).

Traditional Nivkh had singular, dual, and plural distinctions in its positive imperatives. The obsolescent language has lost dual forms and is now using plural imperative forms instead, under the influence of Russian (which does not have dual). Third person imperative forms in Nivkh are now accompanied by particles *p'eɣrdoy* and *hağ*aro* 'let.' Both combine with the corresponding form of the third person imperative. This replicates the Russian third person imperative, which consists of the particle *pustj* 'let' and a third person form of the verb. Under Russian influence, Nivkh is now using a second person plural imperative as a polite form (Gruzdeva 2000).

Clause-linking techniques in an endangered language are often affected by those in a dominant one. The obsolescent Nivkh is using conjunctions borrowed from Russian, replacing traditional coordination patterns with Russian-style coordination (Gruzdeva 2000: 124). Interrogative pronouns in modern Evenki are now used as markers of complement clauses (e.g., 'tell me where the book is'), paralleling a construction found in Russian (Grenoble 2000: 115–188).

Tariana is the only Arawak language spoken in the Vaupés basin in northwestern Amazonia (spanning adjacent areas of Brazil and Colombia). Its growing obsolescence and rapid replacement by the now dominant Tucano, an East Tucanoan language, is accompanied by an increasing number of calqued forms and constructions. Like many Arawak languages, Tariana employs prefixes for subject cross-referencing, while Tucanoan languages are predominantly suffixing. Younger speakers of obsolescent Tariana are developing a system of subject enclitics, mirroring the Tucanoan pattern. Such enclitics in Tucano combine information on person, number, and gender of the subject and tense and information source. The new enclitics in Tariana express only person, number, and gender. A speaker of obsolescent Tariana used the form *dy-uka-na=diha* (3singular.nonfeminine-arrive-REMOTE.PAST.VISUAL=3masculine.singular) 'he arrived.' Compare the corresponding Tucano form *etâ-wĩ*) (arrive-3masculine.singular. REMOTE.PAST.VISUAL) 'he arrived.' A fluent traditional speaker used the form *dy-uka-na* and commented that *=diha* should not appear there (see Aikhenvald 2012a).

The presence and the number of calques from the dominant language may differentiate less proficient speakers of endangered languages from more proficient ones. Younger speakers of Nez Perce, a highly endangered Sahaptian language in the

United States, may use calque translations from English instead of a Nez Perce term, for example *kakmám hí:semtuks* (full luminary) 'full moon' instead of *wiya:swalá:wit* used by older and more proficient speakers (Aoki 1971).

10.4.2 Accommodation

Words and grammatical morphemes in an endangered language may become similar without being directly borrowed. In a situation of traditional inhibition against borrowed forms, growing language obsolescence may go hand in hand with expansion of forms that have the same form in the obsolescent and in the dominant language. Obsolescent younger speakers are reinterpreting Tariana morphemes in accordance with the meaning their look-alikes have in Tucano. The Tariana clitic *-ya* 'emphatic' is increasingly used by obsolescent insecure speakers as a marker of immediate command, as in (1), mirroring the Tucano imperative *-ya* illustrated in (2):

(1)   pi-ñha-ya   Tariana
       2singular-eat-IMPERATIVE
       'Eat!'

(2)   ba'â-ya   Tucano
       eat-IMPERATIVE
       'Eat!'

The few traditional older speakers concur that commands like (1) are not 'proper Tariana' (see Aikhenvald 2002: 131). Another similar example is the increased use of nominalizations marked with *-ri* in Tariana commands with an overtone of a warning, for example *pi-ñha-ri*! (2singular-eat-NOMINALISATION) 'Eat!' (make sure you eat, lest you go hungry).

This usage is restricted to obsolescent younger speakers for whom Tucano is the main language of day-to-day communication. Tucano, just like most other East Tucanoan languages, has a suffix *-ri* used in commands with an overtone of warning, with the meaning of 'or else' (see Ramirez 1997: 146–147). The usage of nominalizations as commands in Tariana has in all likelihood been influenced by the *-ri* marked imperative in Tucano. This usage is rejected by traditional speakers as incorrect.

Semantic extensions based on phonetic similarity are a feature of the endangered American Norwegian. For instance, Norwegian *grøn* 'cereal food' was extended to mean 'grains,' and *brand* 'fire' acquired the meaning of 'bran' under English influence (Haugen 1969: 402–403). In Hinuq, an endangered Northeast Caucasian language of Daghestan, some words, for example *-iti* 'similar,' display a change, by younger speakers, from /i/ to /e/ as a consequence of their phonological accommodation to Tsez. The form in Hinuq is pronounced as *-ite*, just like in Tsez (Forker 2010: 15). The marker of possession *-pal* in Pipil, a highly endangered Uto-Aztecan language (Campbell and

Muntzel 1989: 195), was originally a relational noun and used to take prefixes, as in *nu-pal* 'mine,' *mu-pal* 'yours,' and so on. On the basis of similarity with Spanish *para* 'for, in order to,' this morpheme can now appear without any prefixes and has the meaning of 'in order to, so that' and is used to introduce a subordinate clause.

Instances of grammatical and lexical accommodation of look-alikes (whereby a native morpheme can be reinterpreted on the model of a phonetically similar morpheme in the source language) are not restricted to endangered languages (see Campbell and Muntzel 1989: 195; Aikhenvald 2006: 24). The difference between the impact of this process in a healthy and in an endangered language lies in the speed of change and its instability. The accommodations in an endangered language tend to be unstable, since they tend to be produced by those whose linguistic competence is dwindling. The presence or the absence of accommodations often differentiates proficient traditional speakers from less proficient younger ones.

10.5 Reinforcement of Shared Patterns, and Negative Borrowing

A further outcome of language contact on endangered languages may involve reinforcement of forms and patterns shared with the dominant language. The reverse involves loss of forms or patterns absent from the dominant language.

10.5.1 Reinforcement of Shared Patterns

An endangered language often tends to become structurally similar to the dominant one. Features shared by the two languages tend to be maintained. This is known as *reinforcement*, or *enhancement*.

Paumarí, an endangered Arawá language, has two noun classes whose assignment is based on shape properties of the noun. There is also an independent system of masculine and feminine genders whose choice is based on sex for animates, and is largely unpredictable for inanimates. The language is rapidly becoming obsolescent and is losing ground to Portuguese. The agreement in noun class is getting to be optional, especially for younger and less competent speakers. In contrast, the gender agreement continues to be stable and obligatory. Portuguese, the dominant language, has a system of two genders and a robust system of gender agreement. The maintenance of gender in Paumarí is at least in part due to similar agreement patterns in Portuguese. Portuguese has no equivalent to a shape-based noun class system, which is rapidly being lost in Paumarí (Aikhenvald 2010). Along similar lines, in Arvanitika, an endangered dialect spoken by Albanians who immigrated to Greece in the eleventh and fifteenth centuries, the three genders remain distinct. This may be due to the fact that the three-way gender distinctions in Arvanitika and Greek are structurally similar (Trudgill 1977: 35; Sasse 1985).

Enhancement of a phenomenon shared by an obsolescent language and the dominant one may result in its regularization. Traditional Nivkh had optional number agreement with the subject on the verb (Gruzdeva 2000: 123–124, 2007: 193–194). Under the influence of the dominant Russian, number agreement on the verb has become obligatory.

10.5.2 Negative Borrowing

Linguistic consequences of language obsolescence include simplification and reduction of grammar and lexicon. Categories absent from the dominant language are particularly endangered: over the course of time, or even in a span of a generation, linguistic features not shared by both languages are susceptible to loss by bilingual speakers (see an overview in Dorian 2006: 557–558).

In Hinuq, an endangered Northeast Caucasian language of Daghestan, the loss of the front rounded vowel is, in all likelihood, due to the influence of Tsez, a majority language in the area that does not have this vowel. The loss of contrast between velar and uvular consonants in Nivkh is likely to be due to the influence of Russian, which lacks this contrast (Gruzdeva 2002: 94). Anong is rapidly losing its consonant clusters, under the influence of Chinese, which has none (Sun and Liu 2009: 129–130). Most living Nambiquara languages of Brazil have a complex system of tones. Sabanê and Latundê/Lakondê, the Nambiquara languages on the brink of extinction, have lost their tonal distinctions, as the speakers have shifted to Portuguese (see Aikhenvald 2012b: 122).

The rich system of Korean numeral classifiers becomes reduced to just a few in Korean as it is spoken by young people in Canberra (Lee 1997) whose major language of communication is English. One of the features of the obsolescent Nivkh is drastic reduction of its numeral classifier system. Some obsolescent speakers do not use any classifiers (Gruzdeva 2002: 97–99). Mensural classifiers often refer to culture-specific arrangements and measures, and the obsolescence of cultural knowledge inevitably leads to their loss. This explains why they tend to suffer more dramatic reduction in the speech of younger and less fluent people than sortal classifiers (see Marnita 1996 for Minangkabau, and Lee 1997 for Korean).

Younger and less proficient speakers of Oroqen, an endangered Tungusic language spoken in northeastern China and Inner Mongolia, are no longer using nominalizing suffixes, reduplication, and subject-verb agreement found in the speech of older and more proficient speakers. None of these categories is found in the dominant Chinese. Along similar lines, the accusative case marker is used only sporadically. Younger speakers show a strong preference for analytic constructions over traditional synthetic ones, under the pressure from Chinese (Fengxiang 2005).

Evidentials (that is, obligatory markers of information source) become lost in language obsolescence if the dominant language does not have this category. Nivkh once had a visual versus non-visual opposition in the apprehensive (preventive) mood (Gruzdeva 2001). The visual versus non-visual opposition in apprehensives has been lost from the language. Traditional Sm'algyax (Tsimshian) had a reported enclitic -*gat* (Boas 1911: 348–349). Stebbins (1999), who worked with the remaining semi-speakers of the language in the 1990s, reports that this marker was considered archaic and did not feature in her data. Latundê/Lakondê has a number of grammatical evidentials reflecting the information source of the speaker. The few obsolescent speakers who still occasionally use the language prefer to use a lexical expression 'she left, I saw (it)/I didn't see it/ I heard it' and so on (Telles 2002: 290), just like they do when speaking Portuguese. Such instances of negative borrowing go together with a general morphological reduction characteristic of semi-speakers' competence.

Language attrition and language shift may result in a partial loss of a category, and its restructuring to fit in with the patterns in the dominant language. Traditional Dyirbal had four semantically assigned genders: class 1 including male referents; class 2 including feminine referents and those associated with water, fire, and fighting; class 3 for non-flesh food; and class 4, neuter, for the rest. Young People's Dyirbal has gradually simplified its noun class system so that it became similar to the way *he*, *she*, *it* are used in English. The noun class referring to 'non-flesh food' (which did not have a counterpart in English) was lost. The scope of noun class 2 was reduced and came to be reserved only for females (ceasing to include water, fire, and things associated with fighting). In the traditional language, some referents were assigned gender by mythical association: for instance, birds were believed to be the souls of dead women, and were consequently assigned to the feminine gender. This and other mythological associations were lost by younger speakers. The residue neuter gender was expanded, to include all inanimates (Schmidt 1985).

In the 1930s, Dorothy D. Lee (1959) described Wintu, an isolate from California, as a language with five evidentials: visual; non-visual sensory, inferential based on logic, inferential based on personal experience, and reported. In the 1950s, when Harvey Pitkin (1963: 105) worked on the language, he recorded an evidential system with just two choices—visual and reported. At the same time, the two evidentials developed strong epistemic overtones, of certainty versus uncertainty. The visual evidential became associated with full certainty, and the reported acquired overtones of uncertainty (absent from the traditional language). Thus, under the pressure from English, the system started shifting toward marking epistemic distinctions rather than evidentiality.

Negative borrowing, enhancement of matching structures, and convergence are not exclusive features of obsolescent languages (see also Dorian 2006). What makes them special is the drastic character of loss and the instability of the emergent systems.

10.6 MERGED DIALECTS AND BLENDED LANGUAGES

Language endangerment and impending language shift may result in dialect leveling, and creating new mixed or "blended" languages and new contact languages.

As a language becomes obsolescent, it is used less and less, and loses its ground in speech communities. Dialectal norms become endangered, as the numbers of speakers for each dialect dwindles. Speakers of Jirrbal and Girramay, the two mutually intelligible dialects of Dyirbal, each spoke their own dialect in the 1960s when the traditional language was still actively spoken. Twenty years later, the remaining traditional speakers effectively merged the two dialects, creating a new single dialect (Dixon 1991a: 195–197). This new merged dialect had predominantly Jirrbal grammar and lexicon, with just a few elements from Girramay. There are now only a handful of semi-speakers of this dialect left—as expected for a language on its way out. Dialect mergers in healthy languages may result in the creation of a koine, or a stable literary language. In the case of obsolescent languages, leveling dialect differences and no longer knowing which forms belongs to which dialect are a sign of demise.

Intense language contact on the border between communities who speak closely related languages may result in language "blends." Well-known examples of healthy language blends include Portunhol or Pourtuñol (a "mixture" of Portuguese and Spanish spoken on the border between Brazil and Argentina), Surzhyk (a mixture of Ukranian and Russian in Ukraine and adjacent areas of Russia), and a few more (see Auer 1999; Aikhenvald 2014). Speakers of blended languages tend to be well-balanced bilinguals who can, if required, differentiate between the two languages.

When an obsolescent language undergoes blending with a dominant one, speakers may no longer identify which form comes from which language. Kumandene Tariana is spoken by about 100 people in the village of Santa Terezinha on the Iauarí River in northwestern Amazonia (Brazil). The major language spoken in the village is Baniwa, closely related to Tariana (but not mutually intelligible). Baniwa is spoken by all members of the community on a day-to-day basis, while Tariana is a language of identity for many. Those who still speak Kumandene Tariana use numerous Baniwa forms and sounds, creating a curious Baniwa-Tariana language mixture. This mixture is characterized by a high degree of individual variation, depending on speakers' age and audience. Younger speakers mistake Baniwa forms for Tariana proper (details are in Aikhenvald 2014).

Ingrian Finnish, spoken by a handful of elderly people scattered around Estonia, is another case in point. Most speakers are undergoing a rapid shift to Estonian. The two languages are closely related and structurally similar; as a result, it is not always possible to distinguish Estonian and Finnish forms (Riionheimo 2002: 201–202).

Language endangerment and language shift may lead to the formation of new languages. These include pidgins, creoles, and bilingual mixed languages. When speakers of several different languages are brought together (for instance, in situations of slavery, trade, and colonial expansion), they need to communicate. Then, a contact language develops (see Winford 2003 for an in-depth analysis of pidgins as autonomous systems). This contact language is only used for limited communication with speakers of other languages. It typically has simpler morphology than source languages, and limited lexicon. A pidgin may stop being used once the situation in which it has developed ceases to exist, as was the case for Russenorsk, a Russian-Norwegian pidgin (Jahr 1996). Alternatively, a pidgin may be learned as a first language by the next generation, may expand in its complexity, and may be used to talk about anything.

It then becomes a creole. Development of a creole language may occur over several generations (see Winford 2003; O'Shannessy 2011: 84–85).

A creole develops as a primary language of communication by speakers of several language groups. As it becomes a first language, the languages that contributed to its creation may cease to be first languages of the creole-speaking generation. This is what has happened in many parts of New Guinea where Tok Pisin, an English-based creole, has become the first language for many groups. A new creole language can develop within one generation (see O'Shannessy 2011: 85 for examples from Northern Australia). A creole may become endangered, just like any language. In the case of contact with another dominant language, a creole may undergo de-creolization and gradually fall into disuse. This is happening to the urban Tok Pisin in Papua New Guinea, where it is being ousted by Papua New Guinea English.

A creole can participate in the creation of a bilingual mixed language, resulting from intense cultural pressure leading to partial loss of an indigenous language. Code-switching between the indigenous language and other languages spoken in the community, including a creole, may become conventionalized, creating a new bilingual mixed language. Light Warlpiri is spoken by young adults and children in one community. Its verbal system comes mostly from Kriol, an English-based creole language, and its nominal system is mostly from Warlpiri (O'Shannessy 2005, 2013). A similar bilingual mixed language has been documented for Gurinji-Kriol (McConvell and Meakins 2005). According to O'Shannessy (2011: 86), appearance of the newly emergent languages and their maintenance are signs of resistance to language shift and loss, and the establishment of a local identity within a wider indigenous-language speech community. These two new bilingual mixed languages are currently spoken by the first generation of speakers, all of them children and young adults. It is unclear whether children learn them as one of their primary languages. Whether these languages will be transmitted to further generations and whether they are likely to increase their functions and domains (for instance, in administration and education) are yet to be seen. The question about their stability in the context of impending loss of Australian indigenous languages remains open.

10.7 CONCLUDING REMARKS

A major reason for language endangerment is intensive language contact with a dominant language, ultimately leading to language loss and language shift.

Typical effects of language contact on obsolescent languages include influx of non-native forms and patterns, enhancement of those patterns that are shared with the dominant language, and loss of those patterns that are not. Intensive contact with a dominant language may result in a language blend that combines features of both languages. Or an obsolescent language in the last stages of its existence may tend to become a relexified variety of a dominant language.

The mechanisms and the effects of contact-induced change in endangered languages are essentially the same as in healthy languages. But any language change in endangered languages tends to be unstable. It is often the case that younger and less competent speakers display more pronounced effect of a dominant language than older and more traditional ones. The degree of contact-induced change may depend on the language proficiency of speakers (something that is irrelevant for a healthy language, where all speakers are equally competent in the language).

Speakers of endangered languages are often aware that their languages are "contaminated" with the impact of the dominant language, and lament this fact (see Hill 1998 on the ensuing "discourse of nostalgia"). The outcome of this awareness may be linguistic purism. However, borrowing forms is not a symptom of impending language loss. On the contrary: Hamp (1989) and Johanson (2002) have shown that allowing a certain number of loan forms by no means endangers a language. The more conservative one of the two varieties of Arvanitika Albanian in Greece is more endangered than the one more open to innovations and influence from the dominant Greek (Hamp 1989). Speakers of the Santa Rosa dialect of Tariana are highly puristic, and resist any recognizably borrowed forms from the dominant Tucanos. This dialect is no longer spoken by children. In contrast, the Periquitos dialect of the same language has a few borrowed forms of Tucanoan origin. This dialect is still learned by children and actively used by all generations. Survival of a language requires compromise (see Aikhenvald 2002: 261–264; see Dorian 1994 on the impact of language purism on endangered languages). An openness to accept some loans from a dominant language is likely to assist a language to survive.

Contact-induced change does not always result in language extinction. Language obsolescence may go together with structural changes that are impressive in their extent. Before passing into extinction, an obsolescent language may become a relexified variety of the dominant idiom. But since language change in language obsolescence is unstable and discontinuous, chances are that a new relexified variety, and a typologically unusual blend, will not survive beyond the life span of the last speakers.

ACKNOWLEDGMENTS

I am deeply grateful to the late Candelário da Silva, the last speaker of Bare, to the members of the Brito family who taught me their native Tariana, and my adopted family at Avatip who taught me their native Manambu. Special thanks go to R. M. W. Dixon, who provided invaluable comments on this chapter.

REFERENCES

Aikhenvald, Alexandra Y. 2002. *Language Contact in Amazonia*. Oxford: Oxford University Press.

Aikhenvald, Alexandra Y. 2006. Grammars in contact: A cross-linguistic perspective. In *Grammars in Contact: A Cross-Linguistic Typology*, edited by A. Y. Aikhenvald and R. M. W. Dixon, 1–66. Oxford: Oxford University Press.

Aikhenvald, Alexandra Y. 2010. Gender, noun class and language obsolescence: The case of Paumarí. In *Linguistics and Archeology in the Americas*, edited by E. B. Carlin and Simon van de Kerke, 236–252. Leiden: Brill.

Aikhenvald, Alexandra Y. 2012a. Language contact in language obsolescence. In *Dynamics of Contact-Induced Language Change*, edited by Claudine Chamoreau and Isabelle Léglise, 77–109. Berlin: Mouton de Gruyter.

Aikhenvald, Alexandra Y. 2012b. *The Languages of the Amazon*. Oxford: Oxford University Press.

Aikhenvald, Alexandra Y. 2014. Language contact, and language blend: Kumandene Tariana of north-west Amazonia. *International Journal of American Linguistics* 80: 323–70.

Aikhenvald, Alexandra Y., and R. M. W. Dixon (eds.). 2006. *Grammars in Contact: A Cross-Linguistic Typology*. Oxford: Oxford University Press.

Aikio, Marjut. 1992. Are women innovators in the shift to a second language? A case study of Reindeer Sámi women and men. *International Journal of the Sociology of Language* 94: 43–62.

Andersen, R. 1982. Determining the linguistic attributes of language attrition. In *The Loss of Language Skills*, edited by R. D. Lambert and B. F. Freed, 83–118. Rowley, MA: Newbury House.

Aoki, Haruo. 1971. A note on language change. In *Studies in American Indian languages*, edited by Jesse Sawyer, 1–9. Berkeley: University of California Publications in Linguistics 65.

Auer, Peter. 1999. From codeswitching via language mixing to fused lects: Toward a dynamic typology of bilingual speech. *International Journal of Bilingualism* 3: 309–332.

Austin, Peter K., and Julia M. Sallabank (eds.). 2011. *The Cambridge Handbook of Endangered Languages*. Cambridge: Cambridge University Press.

Boas, F. 1911. Tsimshian. In *Handbook of American Indian languages*, Part 1, edited by F. Boas, 223–422. Bureau of American Ethnology Bulletin 40. Washington, DC: Smithsonian Institution.

Campbell, Lyle, and Martha Muntzel. 1989. The structural consequences of language death. In *Investigating Obsolescence: Studies in Language Contraction and Death*, edited by N. Dorian, 181–196. Cambridge: Cambridge University Press.

Campbell, Lyle, and Naomi Paalosaari. 2011. Structural aspects of language endangerment. In *The Cambridge Handbook of Endangered Languages*, edited by P. K. Austin and J. M. Sallabank, 100–119. Cambridge: Cambridge University Press.

Carlin, Eithne. 2006. Feeling the need: The borrowing of Cariban functional categories into Mawayana (Arawak). In *Grammars in Contact: A Cross-Linguistic Typology*, edited by A. Aikhenvald and R. M. W. Dixon, 313–332. Oxford: Oxford University Press.

Chamoreau, Claudine. 2000. Chronique d'une mort annoncée: Un exemple de réduction en phurhépecha. In *Actes du XXIème Colloque International de la Société Internationale de Linguistique fonctionnelle (SILF)*. Iasi (Roumanie), 26 junio–2 julio 1996, 127–132.

Chamoreau, Claudine. 2005. Reorganición de la voz en purépecha: Una visión dinámica. In *Dinámica lingüística de las lenguas en contacto*, edited by Claudine Chamoreau and Yolanda Lastra, 67–86. Sonora: Universidad de Sonora

Chapman, Shirley, and Desmond C. Derbyshire. 1991. Paumarí. In *Handbook of Amazonian Languages*, Vol. 3, edited by Desmond C. Derbyshire and Geoffrey K. Pullum, 151–355. Berlin; New York: Mouton de Gruyter.

Dixon, R. M. W. 1972. *The Dyirbal Language of North Queensland*. Cambridge: Cambridge University Press.

Dixon, R. M. W. 1977. *A Grammar of Yidiny*. Cambridge: Cambridge University Press.

Dixon, R. M. W. 1991a. A changing language situation: The decline of Dyirbal, 1963–1989. *Language in Society* 20: 183–200.

Dixon, R. M. W. 1991b. Reassigning underlying forms in Yidiny: A change during language death. In *Language and History, Essays in Honour of Luise A. Hercus*, edited by P. Austin, R. M. W. Dixon, T. Dutton, and I. White, 89–99. Canberra: Pacific Linguistics.

Dorian, Nancy C. 1977. The problem of the semi-speakers in language death. *Linguistics* 191: 23–32.

Dorian, Nancy C. 1978. The fate of morphological complexity in language death. *Language* 54: 590–609.

Dorian, Nancy C. (ed.). 1989. *Investigating Obsolescence: Studies in Language Contraction and Death*. Cambridge: Cambridge University Press.

Dorian, Nancy C. 1994. Purism vs. compromise in language revitalisation and language revival. *Language in Society* 23: 479–494.

Dorian, Nancy C. 2006. Negative borrowing in an indigenous-language shift to the dominant national language. *Journal of Bilingual Education and Bilingualism* 9: 557–577.

Dorian, Nancy C. 2010. *Investigating Variation: The Effects of Social Organization and Social Setting*. Oxford: Oxford University Press.

Fat, Lau Chun. 2005. A dialect murders another dialect: The case of Hakka in Hong Kong. *International Journal of the Sociology of Language* 173: 23–35.

Fengxiang, Li. 2005. Contact, attrition, and structural shift: Evidence from Oroqen. *International Journal of the Sociology of Language* 173: 55–74.

Forker, Diana. 2010. *A Grammar of Hinuq*. PhD dissertation, University of Leipzig.

Grenoble, Lenore A. 2000. Morphosyntactic change: The impact of Russian on Evenki. In *Languages in Contact*, edited by D. G. Gilbers, J. Nerbonne, and J. Schaeken, 105–120. Amsterdam: Rodopi.

Grenoble, Lenore A., and L. J. Whaley. 1998. Towards a typology of language endangerment. In *Endangered languages*, edited by L. Grenoble and L. J. Whaley, 22–54. Cambridge: Cambridge University Press.

Gruzdeva, Ekaterina Yu. 2000. Aspects of Russian-Nivkh grammatical interference: The Nivkh imperative. In *Languages in Contact*, edited by D. G. Gilbers, J. Nerbonne, and J. Schaeken, 121–134. Amsterdam; Atlanta, GA: Rodopi.

Gruzdeva, Ekaterina Yu. 2001. Imperative sentences in Nivkh. In *Typology of Imperative Constructions*, edited by V. S. Xrakovskij, 59–77. Munich: Lincom Europa.

Gruzdeva, Ekaterina Yu. 2002. The linguistic consequences of Nivkh language attrition. *SKY Journal of Linguistics* 15: 85–103.

Gruzdeva, Ekaterina Yu. 2007. A comprehensive representation of language change in language shift (a case study of Nivkh) [Kompleksnoe predstavlenije jazykovykh izmenenih v uslovijakh jazykovogo sdviga]. In *Jazykovye izmenenija v uslovijakh jazykovogo sdviga* [Language changes in language shift], edited by N. B. Vakhtin, 188–212. St. Peterburg: Nestor.

Hamp, Eric. 1989. On signs of health and death. In *Investigating Obsolescence: Studies in Language Contraction and Death*, edited by N. Dorian, 197–210. Cambridge: Cambridge University Press.

Haugen, Einar. 1969. *The Norwegian Language in America*. Bloomington: Indiana University Press.

Haugen, Einar. 1989. The rise and fall of an immigrant language: Norwegian in America. In *Investigating Obsolescence: Studies in Language Contraction and Death*, edited by N. Dorian, 61–74. Cambridge: Cambridge University Press.

Hill, Jane H. 1998. "Today there is no respect": Nostalgia, "respect" and oppositional discourse in Mexicano (Nahuatl) language ideology. In *Language Ideologies: Practice and Theory*, edited by Bambi B. Schieffelin, Kathryn A. Woolard, and Paul V. Kroskrity, 68–86. New York: Oxford University Press.

Hill, Jane H., and Kenneth C. Hill. 1977. Language death and relexification in Tlaxcalan Nahuatl. *International Journal of the Sociology of Language* 12 (Special issue, *Language Death*, edited by Wolfgang Dressler and Ruth Wodak-Leodolter): 55–70.

Hill, Jane H., and Kenneth Hill. 1986. *Speaking Mexicano: Dynamics of Syncretic Language in Central Mexico*. Tucson: University of Arizona Press.

Jahr, E. H. 1996. On the pidgin status of Russenorsk. In *Language Contact in the Arctic: Northern Pidgins and Contact Languages*, edited by E. H. Jahr and I. Broch, 107–122. Berlin: Mouton de Gruyter.

Johanson, Lars. 2002. Do languages die of structuritis? On the role of code-copying in language endangerment. *Rivista Italiana di Linguistica* 14: 249–270.

Klintborg, S. 1999. *The Transience of American Swedish*. Lund: Lund University Press.

Kroskrity, Paul V. 1993. *Language, History and Identity: Ethnolinguistic Studies of the Arizona Tewa*. Tucson: University of Arizona Press.

Lee, Dorothy D. 1959. *Freedom and Culture*. Englewood Cliffs, NJ: Prentice-Hall.

Lee, Y. 1997. *Classifiers in Korean*. Honors thesis, Australian National University.

Lüpke, Friderike, and Anne Storch. 2013. *Repertoires and Choices in African Languages*. Berlin: De Gruyter Mouton.

Maandi, Katrin. 1989. Estonian among immigrants in Sweden. In *Investigating Obsolescence: Studies in Language Contraction and Death*, edited by N. Dorian, 227–241. Cambridge: Cambridge University Press.

Maher, Julianne. 1991. A crosslinguistic study of language contact and language attrition. In *First Language Attrition*, edited by H. Seliger and R. Vago, 67–84. Cambridge: Cambridge University Press.

Marnita, R. 1996. *Classifiers in Minangkabau*. MA thesis, Australian National University.

Martin, Peter. 2005. Language shift and code-mixing: A case study from Northern Borneo. *Australian Journal of Linguistics* 25: 109–126.

McConvell, Patrick, and Felicity Meakins. 2005. Gurindji Kriol: A mixed language emerges from code-switching. *Australian Journal of Linguistics* 25: 9–30.

McGregor, William. 2002. Structural changes in language obsolescence: A Kimberley (Australia) perspective. *SKY Journal of Linguistics* 15: 145–186.

Milani, C. 1996. Language contact among North-American people of Italian origin. In *Language Contact across the North Atlantic*, edited by P. S. Ureland and I. Clarkson. *Linguistische Arbeiten* 359: 479–501. Tübingen: University of Tübingen.

Mixco, M. 1977. The Kiliwa response to Hispanic culture. *Proceedings of the Third Annual Meeting of the Berkeley Linguistics Society* 3 (General session): 12–23.

O'Shannessy, Carmel. 2005. Light Warlpiri: A new language. *Australian Journal of Linguistics* 25: 31–59.

O'Shannessy, Carmel. 2011. Language contact and change in endangered languages. In *The Cambridge Handbook of Endangered Languages*, edited by P. K. Austin and J. M. Sallabank, 78–99. Cambridge: Cambridge University Press.

O'Shannessy, Carmel. 2013. The role of multiple sources in the formation of an innovative auxiliary category in Light Warlpiri, a new Australian mixed language. *Language* 89: 328–353.

Pitkin, Harvey. 1963. *Wintu grammar*. PhD dissertation, University of California.

Ramirez, Henri. 1997. *A fala Tukano dos Yepâ-masa*. Tomo 1. Gramática. Manaus: Inspetoria Salesiana.

Riionheimo, H. 2002. How to borrow a bound morpheme? Evaluating the status of structural interference in a contact between closely related languages. *SKY Journal of Linguistics* 15: 187–218.

Sasse, Hans-Jürgen. 1985. Sprachkontakt und Sprachwandel: Die Gräzisierung der albanischen Mundarten Griechenlands. *Papiere zur Linguistik* 32(1): 37–95.

Sasse, Hans-Jürgen. 1992. Language decay and contact-induced change: Similarities and differences. In *Language Death'. Factual and Theoretical Explorations with Special Reference to East Africa*, edited by Matthias Brenzinger, 58–79. Berlin: Mouton de Gruyter.

Schmidt, A. 1985. *Young People's Dyirbal: An Example of Language Death from Australia*. Cambridge: Cambridge University Press.

Stebbins, T. 1999. *Issues in Sm'algyax (Coast Tsimshian) Lexicography*. PhD dissertation, University of Melbourne.

Stolz, C., and T. Stolz. 1996. Funktionswortenentlehnung in Mesoamerika: Spanisch-amerindischer Sprachkontakt (Hispanoindiana II). *STUF* 49: 86–123.

Sun, Hongkai, and Guangkun Liu. 2009. *A Grammar of Anong: Language Death under Intense Contact*, translated, annotated, and supplemented by Fengxiang Li, Ela Thurgood, and Graham Thurgood. Leiden: Brill.

Telles, Stella. 2002. *Fonologia e gramática Latundê/Lakondê*. PhD dissertation, Free University of Amsterdam.

Thurston, W. R. 1987. *Processes of Change in the Languages of Northwestern Britain*. Canberra: Pacific Linguistics.

Trudgill, Peter. 1977. Creolization in reverse: Reduction and simplification in the Albanian dialects of Greece. *Transactions of the Philological Society* 32–50.

Tsitsipis, Lucas. D. 1998. *A Linguistic Anthropology of Praxis and Language Shift: Arvanítika (Albanian) and Greek in Contact*. Oxford: Clarendon Press.

Ullrich, Jan. 2008. *New Lakota Dictionary*. Bloomington, IN: Lakota Language Consortium.

Vakhtin, N. B. (ed.). 2007. *Jazykovye izmenenija v uslovijakh jazykovogo sdviga* [Language changes in language shift]. St. Peterburg: Nestor.

Weinreich, U. 1953. *Languages in Contact*. New York: Linguistic Circle of New York.

Winford, Donald. 2003. *An Introduction to Contact Linguistics*. Oxford: Blackwell.

CHAPTER 11

PIDGINS

MIKAEL PARKVALL

11.1 INTRODUCTION

IN the late nineteenth century, two European travelers described their overseas adventures.[1] One of them was the British journalist Edward Frederick Knight, who traveled in Albania (then still part of the Ottoman Empire). He was accompanied by a local guide with whom he shared no language:

> I now discovered that Marco's linguistic powers were very limited. Give him an order; he never confessed to his absolute ignorance of what you were talking about, but blithely came out with his perpetual *ça bonne, ça bonne*, as if that was all that was required of him. However, by degrees I discovered what words he knew of French, what of Italian, and what of English (for he had even picked up some words of our tongue when in the service of the commissioners). With the addition of a few words of Sclav and Albanian, I then manufactured a mongrel tongue, which was common to Marco and myself, and utter gibberish to any one else.   (Knight 1880: 165)

Slightly later, Frenchman Henri d'Orléans went to Vietnam. As it happened, the native guide supplied to him spoke no French (and d'Orléans knew no Vietnamese), but had learned some Latin at a mission school. Neither d'Orléans nor his Vietnamese guide was very proficifent in Latin, and neither had used it for a long time. Still, it provided the basis for an apparently relatively successful communication:

> At first, intercourse was not easy. Our oratorical attempts were hardly brilliant; there were even times when we were not in touch. By degrees, however, we gained fluency, and in a month had completely mastered each other's idiosyncrasies of expression. But what Latin! *Horresco referens*! Solecisms, barbarisms, neologisms, and all the "isms" invented might be applied to our jargon. Luckily, we had only ourselves for audience.   (Orléans 1898: 145)

---

[1] Thanks go to Päivi Juvonen for comments on a previous draft.

These two cases, I believe, are relatively good examples (although one would of course want more details!) of what happens in an intercultural encounter yielding a pidgin, and I think they also illustrate what indeed did happen when the first steps toward those we know today were taken. We shall return to our two globe-trotters in a while.

The existence of pidgin languages is well known to both linguists and laypersons. Nevertheless, it turns out that few people have a clearly defined understanding of what the concept denotes, and fewer still have manifested a serious interest in the language type. As so many others, I too once wondered why anyone would be interested in languages that lack so much of what drew most of us to linguistics in the first place. Since then, however, I realized that they constitute a fascinating species in themselves, and that they have implications for concepts such as *linguistic complexity* (e.g., Bickerton 1988; Muysken 1988; McWhorter 2001, 2005; Kusters 2003; Ansaldo and Matthews 2007; Givón 2009; Miestamo et al. 2008; Sampson, Gil, and Trudgill eds. 2009), a subject that has a clear connexion to any investigation of the human language faculty as such. .

11.1.1 What is a Pidgin?

In both lay discourse and academic writing, the term *pidgin* is used for a wide range of phenomena. Two of the most frequent uses include "an unstable learner variety" and "a language possessing more than a handful of loanwords." In my view, the extension of the label to such varieties is unfortunate, not least because there already are established terms which cover them: *interlanguage* or *basic variety* in the first case, and, well, *language* in the second.

Therefore, I would argue that *pidgin* is best restricted to a third among its current uses, and the one for which there is no other term: a lingua franca that is lexically and structurally very restricted, but which has an amount of norms and stability across its speakers. Its limited nature implies that it is not (normally) spoken as a first language.

Attempts at a strict definition of the phenomenon have been attempted by myself and others, but at the end of the day, the perfectly water-tight definition is difficult, if not impossible, to produce. As with terms such as *language* versus *dialect*, we are dealing with continuous phenomena, and there are bound to be intermediate cases. After all, how "reduced" is "reduced"? I myself am somewhat restrictive in preferring to include only varieties that are *very* reduced, rather than those which have experienced just a slight amount of downsizing, while many other observers are more liberal.

Most pidgins derive the lion's share of their lexicon from an existing language, which is therefore referred to as the *lexifier*. The other languages whose speakers were involved in pidgin genesis are termed *substrates*. While these terms are often taken to imply various things regarding their (and their speakers') relationship to one another and to the pidginization process, I am making no such claims, and am retaining the traditional terminology for convenience only.

11.2 THE AMOUNT OF DOCUMENTATION

Pidginization is considered central enough to the field of linguistics to merit mention in just about every introductory textbook, usually in connection with creolization. Given this, and the enormous body of literature on creoles, one might expect pidgins to be reasonably well studied, but they are not. There exist numerous descriptions of individual varieties, but very few cross-linguistic studies. The only monograph devoted to that subject is Bernd Heine's (1973) *Pidginsprachen im Bantu-Bereich*, which, as its title suggests, restricts its scope to Africa. Works with both "pidgin" and "creole" in their titles typically concentrate on creoles, and often include only a few token notes on pidginization.

For this reason, there is a belief that pidgins are better known than they actually are. Perhaps the best illustration of this is Bakker's (2003) study on reduplication. The literature is replete with statements assuring that reduplication is exceedingly common in pidgins. This seems to be based on the fact that it is indeed common in creoles, combined—I suspect—with a feeling that such an iconic process would be in line with the overall simplicity of pidgins. Bakker shows, however, that pidgins are, if anything, characterized by the *absence* of reduplication.[2] The nature of pidgins can thus not simply be guessed at (even if several features are rather predictable), but needs actual study.

11.3 WHAT PIDGINS LOOK LIKE

Before we proceed, it might be useful for the reader to have a couple of example sentences illustrating what the varieties under discussion may look like. Here follow some example sentences, chosen more or less at random:

(1) Chinese Pidgin English:
Spose my all same you sick my must wantee toomuch
ENG If 1SG as 2SG sick 1SG must want a.lot
chinchin that large Joss
worship that big God
'If I were as sick as you are, I would certainly pay much reverence to the Supreme God' (Shi 1991: 29)

(2) Yokohama Pidgin Japanese:
Nanny to hanash, watarkshee boto piggy
What and speak, 1sg boat remove
'Should any one enquire for me, say I've gone out in the boat for a spin around the bay' (Atkinson 1879: 21)

[2] In all fairness, though, the discrepacy is no doubt partly due to differing perceptions of the phenomenon; Bakker restricts himself to reduplication as a *morphological* device, rather than simple repetition as a syntactic or pragmatic one, which is presumably what many others had in mind.

(3)   Français Tirailleur
       Moi   content, moi   parler unpeu   pour moi
       1sg   like   1sg   speak   somewhat   for   me
       'I'm happy to get to speak to you a little'   (Sœur Victorien 1908: 339)

(4)   Chinook Jargon/Chinuk Wawa
       Naika tiki   xlwima   pipa
       1sg   want   different apper
       'I want a different newspaper'   (Robertson 2011: 419)

The most striking property here is perhaps the analyticity of the examples—there is basically a one-to-one correspondence between morph, morpheme, and word. As is well known, Japanese is agglutinative, and it should be borne in mind that Chinook was a highly agglutinative language. None of the morphological features of the languages that contributed the lexica are evident here, and indeed not much of their structural properties in general. One might also want to note certain lexical features, such as the monomorphemic (despite the etymologising spellings) *too much* 'a lot' and *un peu* 'a little.'

Parkvall and Bakker (2013) include an overview of linguistic features more or less typical of pidgins, and the reader is referred to that work for a slightly more detailed discussion of the summary presented here.[3]

11.3.1 Pidgin Lexica

A pidgin lexicon is indeed small in comparison to traditional languages. Of course, every linguist is aware of the impossibility of precisely assessing the size of the lexicon of any language, but it is equally well known that the lexical inventories of traditional languages are typically described as including tens of thousands of items. As for pidgins, the figures given are usually below 2,000, and not rarely half or one-fourth of that—so the range would seem to be between a couple of hundred and a couple of thousand words.

Quite predictably, this leads to an immense amount of polysemy and multifunctionality, where one and the same phonetic string doubles in (from the point of view of a traditional language) several syntactic roles and covers an impressively wide semantic array. From Chinook Jargon, one might cite *tilikam*, which, depending on the context, has been translated as 'man,' 'people,' 'person,' 'Indians,' 'natives,' 'relatives,' 'kindred,' 'non-chiefs,' 'same tribe,' 'same band,' 'friend.' Similarly, while 'heart' can be suspected to be the original meaning of *tumtum*, the word has since expanded to cover concepts such as 'mind,' 'stomach,' 'conscience,' 'soul,' 'to think,' 'will,' 'opinion,' (Johnson 1978: 222, 240–241). Making the same point, Eells (1894: 310) gives twenty-four English

---

[3] Whcn no specific work is explicitly cited in this section, an appropriate reference is found in Parkvall and Bakker (2013).

translations of the Chinook Jargon word *kaltas* 'bad,' and no less than eighty for *wawa* 'language; to speak.'

Compensatory strategies devised to get maximal mileage out of the limited lexical resources include compounds and circumlocutions (e.g., 'iron' + 'rope' = 'chain'; 'hand + boots' = 'gloves'; 'smoke' + 'eat' + 'thing' = 'pipe') and productive (analytic) use of negations to form inversives (e.g., NEG + 'good' = 'bad'; NEG + 'fast' = 'slow'). Also present (albeit less so than one might thnk) is the use of light verbs, a subject that is surveyed by Juvonen (in press).

A more unexpected pidgin tendency is the drift toward bisyllabic word structure that has been proposed by Heine (1979: 90) and Mühlhäusler (1997: 161; see also Stolz 1986 for a similar observation regarding creoles).

11.3.2 Morphology

Not only is the number of lexical morphemes very limited, but the same applies to grammatical ones. A prime example is the fact that quite a number of pidgins happily restrict themselves to one and only one adposition, which therefore carries meanings such as 'on,' 'in,' 'during,' 'for,' 'to,' and everything imaginable in-between these. This sole adposition is often derived from one of the more frequent corresponding items in the lexifier, but in Govorka, for example, it is derived from the Russian noun meaning 'place.'

The near-total lack of productive morphology (other than compounding) is possibly the most conspicuous trait of pidgins. There is no denying that some varieties frequently labeled "pidgins" do make use of a small number of bound morphemes, but for one thing, these languages tend to display fewer reductive traits in other areas as well (the moral being that morphological downsizing is not the only thing pidginization is about). Second, even these invariably display fewer morphological processes than their lexifiers, and for the most part also than their substrates.

As for the nature of the morphological processes, two related generalizations can be made: (1) if there is any morphology in the first place, it will be derivational rather than inflexional; and (2) it will be inherent rather than contextual (in the terminology of Booij 1994). In other words, to the extent that pidgins have any morphology at all, it is, unsurprisingly, not going to manifest itself as agreement marking or as grammatical gender, and will tend toward the less, rather than the more grammaticalized pole of the continuum.

Marking of categories such as definiteness, number, case, and tense/mood/aspect are normally, if at all present, not obligatory in pidgins. It is not rare to have weakly grammaticalized and optional markers for these categories, where, for instance, plurality is indicated by a word meaning 'many' or something similar, an object marker equaling a word most closely corresponding to English 'for,' and tense/mood/aspect morphemes whose literal translation would be, for instance, 'now,' 'finish,' 'later,' or 'before.' But again, these display—for the most part—neither obligatoriness, nor other indicators of going beyond incipient grammaticalization.

11.3.3 Phonology

Pidgin phonologies appear to be somewhat less spectacular. The inventories tend to be of an average size, and perhaps also to a greater extent (in comparison to other linguistic subsystems) predictable from the languages involved. Pidgin syllable structures have often been considered closer to a generic CV template than those of traditional languages, but it still has not been ascertained whether this is a general pidgin feature or simply a consequence of certain languages involved in the genesis of these contact languages.

Other suggested commonalities of pidgin phonological systems involve a (relative) lack of distinctions with regard to tone, length, allophony, and allomorphy, but it is difficult to avoid the formulaic "a lot more research is needed."

11.3.4 Syntax

Regarding word order, there seems to be a preference for SVO word order, but it is again not clear that this would reflect a tendency inherent in pidginization. To the extent that the preference exists, it can, in my view, be suspected to be an artifact of the fact that many of the documented pidgins share input languages (European and other) that happen to prefer this order.

The fixedness of the word order appears to be dependent on the developmental stage of the contact language—a jargon (or pre-pidgin) may not have an obviously preferred constituent order at all, while a "true" pidgin that has taken further steps toward stabilization may settle on a particular order. Still later in the development, an expanded pidgin, on its way to becoming a creole, may develop the options typical of traditional languages, where differing orders may be exploited for stylistic effect. Somewhat paradoxically, perhaps, a stable pidgin may then display a more fixed word order than either its predecessor or its offspring.

Coordination and subordination sometimes occur in a semantic/pragmatic sense, but rarely receives overt morphosyntactic marking.

11.3.5 Part-of-Speech Categories

The extent to which pidgins distinguish different parts of speech is difficult to assess, not least because of the multifunctionality referred to earlier—one and the same phonetic string may be used in roles that, at least from a Western perspetive, would correspond to a noun, a verb, or an adjective. Most pidgins, however, do seem to distinguish closed classes from open ones (e.g., a pronoun cannot normally function as anything else), and it is not rare for certain categories to have a characteristic ending, such as -*e* in verbs in French-lexicon pidgins, while verbs in Fanakalo and Russenorsk tend to end in -*a* and -*ɔm*, respectively.

The pronominal system of the average pidgin distinguishes three persons and two numbers, just as traditional languages most often do. In a few cases (presumably due to substratal influence), additional features, such as clusivity, are found, and in others, the pronominal system is more reduced in lacking a number distinction. The pronouns (especially in the first and second person) are in most cases taken directly from the lexifying language, though it is not rare for the third person forms to derive from demonstratives. The lexifier forms chosen are often oblique or tonic forms, rather than nominatives, and these typically serve in all roles. Pidgin pronouns thus rarely display case distinctions, neither in terms of marking objects in relation to subjects, nor in marking possession.

Characteristic of many a pidgin is the lack of overt copular elements where the lexifier would require this. The absence of such an element is by no means universal, however, although its (their) distribution may differ from that found in the lexifier. Where they do occur, copulas are not necessarily derived directly from the lexifier, but are not infrequently (semi-) grammaticalized from locative verbs, such as 'to sit' or 'to live.'

Information on pidgin pragmatics remains rather more anecdotal than scientifically investigated, but frequently recurring comments remark on a low speech tempo, brief utterances, recourse to gesturing, a lack of stylistic variation, and—more generally—a heavy reliance on context.

11.4 ARE PIDGINS MIXED LANGUAGES?

A common belief is that pidgins are characterized by a high degree of mixture, and this is sometimes even considered a defining trait. The reader should be aware that I belong to a minority of contact linguists here, but I would argue that such a statement fits the facts rather badly. It would of course be astonishing if there were not evidence of language mixing in varieties that, after all, emerged in a contact setting and even *because of* contact. But in order to justify emphasis on that aspect, it would require that pidgins are *more* mixed than traditional languages are, and this appears not to be the case. Even among professional linguists, one comes across the even stronger statement that pidginization consists in combining the lexicon of language A with the structure of language B, something that is belied by a mere cursory glance at just about any pidgin. There do exist languages that have arisen through a combination of elements along these lines (the best known are probably Michif and Media Lengua; Bakker 1997 and Muysken 1981, respectively), but in all their glorious complexity, they have little in common with pidgins.[4]

Pidgins are certainly "inspired" (for want of a better word) by the languages spoken by their creators and users, something that is only to be expected. But the most

---

[4] "Mixed" pidgins (to which Grant 2013, 2014, in particular, has devoted a good deal of attention) indeed exist, just as there are strikingly mixed non-pidgins. My point here is not to deny their existence, but rather to highlight their atypical nature.

common state of affairs is that their lexica are dominated by material from one language (the lexifier), and that their grammars ignore most of what was offered by *either* the lexifier or the other languages involved (the substrates). In addition to this, it can also be demonstrated that pidgins sometimes contain structural (but only rarely lexical) material that originates from none of the input languages.

For example Singaporean Bazaar Malay lacks clusivity, even though this is a feature of both Hokkien and Malay (Aye 2005: 241), and the same was true for early Plantation Pidgin Fijian (Siegel 1987: 106). Similarly, Arafundi-Enga Pidgin has two pronominal numbers, despite the fact that both of its contributing languages had four (Williams 1995: 173), and the pronouns of Tok Tanim and Pidgin Delaware did not exhibit any number distinctions at all, despite pronominal number being a feature of the pronominal systems of *all* their respective input languages (Goddard 1995: 140–142, 2000: 70; Williams 2000: 47).

In semantics, the same obtains for the merger of the concepts 'eat' and 'drink' in Ndyuka-Trio Pidgin (Huttar and Velantie 1996: 117), and examples from phonology include the loss of /ʃ/ in Russenorsk and /k/ in Herschel Island Pidgin Eskimo (Broch and Jahr 1984: 31; Stefánsson 1909), again developments seemingly unrelated to any of the input languages.

Among traits not related to reduction, one might mention the expansion of the definite article in Fanakalo, or the partly five-based numeral system of Herschel Island Pidgin Eskimo, the lack of pro-drop in Lingua Franca, negation in Kisisi, and some word order issues in Russenorsk, Mobilian, Icelandic pidgin Basque—in all of these cases, the pidgins display patterns that lack models in the input languages (Stefánsson 1909; Gilmore 1979; Broch and Jahr 1984: 42; Bakker 1987: 9; Drechsel 1993; Mesthrie 2007: 79).

A version of the "mixedness" claim is that the very analyticity of pidgins is dependent on the analyticity of the languages in contact (Sweet 1900: 87; Becker and Veenstra 2003: 236; Aboh and Ansaldo 2007: 56). However, this view cannot be upheld if more than a few pidgins are taken into account. Arabic, Chinook, and Yimas are but some of the highly inflected languages that have lexified pidgins which behave expectedly (i.e., are analytic). As it happens, in none of these cases has the substratal input been dominated by analytical languages.

In other words, pidgins are emphatically not compromises between the contributing languages, although they—quite predictably—share numerous properties (beyond the lexical realm) with their lexifiers and their substrates. What instead characterises them, apart from the small lexicon, is that the grammatical apparatus is of less overall complexity than in any of the "conceiving" languages.

11.5 PIDGINIZATION

Pidgins are sometimes classified according to the circumstances that gave birth to them. The perhaps most typical situation is one involving (seasonal or otherwise intermittent) trade and diplomacy, but we also find varieties owing their existence to multilingual workplaces. Via plantations and slavery, there is a continuum between this and settings involving indenturement and confinement. Some pidgins have been created or propagated by multilingual military and police forces, and many have come about in the wake of colonization, something that often involves many of the preceding activities, in addition to settlement.

It seems futile to spend too much time on making situational typologies of this sort, especially since the borders between the categories are bound to be rather fluid. What is more interesting to ponder is what the contexts have in common, as they all resulted in pidginization. After all, the majority of language encounters fail to deliver such a result. Apparently, people prefer to communicate across language borders in something other than a pidgin, if there is such an option, and apparently there usually is. Speakers of most languages have been in contact with their neighbors for an extended period of time, and long before the advent of scholastic language teaching and modern media, at least some members of most ethnic groups have had a competence in other languages of the area.

So we clearly need something exceptional in order to generate what the pidginist wishes for. In my experience, two things stand out, namely that of suddenness and that of social barriers. In other words, two or more groups either experience a sudden need to communicate with one another,[5] so sudden that there is no time to acquire the other's language, or else the contact is such that they are reluctant to become too intimate with one another. The use of a pidgin can be a way of holding the others "at arm's length," to use Reinecke's (1938: 111) words with regard to Chinese Pidgin English. A somewhat similar modern-day example could be that which generated Gulf Pidgin Arabic, where Bakir (2010: 203) hardly overstates things when talking about a "wide social distance."

Of course, we can easily imagine contexts where timing and reluctance of the sort just described are both present.

11.5.1 Choosing a Lexifier

I mentioned earlier that my take on the mixed nature of pidgins is not shared by most contact linguists. I also hold two views on pidgin genesis that I would like to mention, although the reader should be aware that these views are not accepted by all.[6]

---

[5] When traveling overland, early explorers speaking A often brought an interpreter knowing languages A+B, and picked up more people speaking B+C, C+D, D+E (etc.), as they went along. A classic example of this is Lewis and Clark's legendary expedition across the United States. When Europeans were crossing the Atlantic for the first time, or setting foot in Australia, however, such a technique was impossible, and it must in this sense have been more like voyaging to another planet would be today.

[6] In my defense, however, the few people who have devoted time to actually studying pidgins are considerably more inclined to accept these conclusions.

The first controversial point has to do with the choice of a lexifier. It is normally taken for granted that pidgin genesis involves one more and one (or several) less powerful groups. The following quotes are quite representative:

> ...all pidgin geneses are characterised by a power asymmetry where the super-strate language is also the mother tongue of the socioeconomically dominant group.
>
> (Næss 2008: 27)

> Pidgins will not result if an attempt is not made by at least one linguistic group to come in contact with another which is dominant, advanced or possessed of superior skills.
>
> (Singh 1983: 136)

Indeed, in a number of contexts, there is a difference in power among the groups involved—an extreme example would be Lagersprache, the German-lexicon pidgin used in the Nazi concentration and extermination camps.

In others, though, the power relations are less straightforward than most people seem to realize. In situations involving European overseas colonization, the Europeans are almost universally thought of as the "top dogs" who imposed their language (or at least their lexicon) on the conquered populations. However, this simplistic view ignores the fact that several pidgins used between European colonizers and subjugated non-Europeans have been lexically based on languages of the latter group. The best-known examples would include Mobilian (southeastern US), Chinook Jargon (northwestern US), Sango (Central African Republic), and several varieties of Pidgin Eskimo once used in the Arctic.

One might also question how the concept of power is assessed. It is a historical fact that English came to provide the lexicon of most pidgins in Oceania, and the fact that many of the territories wound up becoming British colonies would seem to confirm beyond doubt that it was the Europeans who had the upper hand. However, when we focus on the earliest stages of contact, we are dealing with, on the one hand, Aborigines who outnumbered the British, who could easily call for reinforcements in case of a conflict, who were on their home turf and knew how to exploit the local resources, and, on the other hand, a party of scurvy-ridden seafarers, exhausted after a voyage halfway around the globe. If I may put it bluntly, it is not obvious that the need for beads and liquor among the natives was immensely greater than the need for freshwater and provisions among the sailors. It is not even clear that the latter had military advantages, as their weaponry and tactics were developed for a completely different environment.

If we turn to prestige, rather than brute force, there are plenty of examples where pidgins have developed in situations where *both* parties have considered themselves superior to the others, and nevertheless, a pidgin has developed that draws its lexicon from one of the languages in contact. Two obvious cases would be Chinese Pidgin English and Yokoha-mese, where English was the lexifier for the first, but the main substrate of the latter.

A case often invoked to demonstrate the role of power and prestige is that of Russenorsk, a nineteenth-century pidgin used (primarily) between Russians and Nor-wegians on the shores of the Arctic Ocean. It has an unusually mixed lexicon, to which both Russian and Norwegian have contributed heavily, and surely, many seem to reason, this is because of a relatively egalitarian relationship. When looking closer at the argument, it appears, however, that the main indication of this is—the pidgin's mixed lexicon!

Now, if power is not the main (I am not suggesting that it plays no role whatsoever) factor behind the choice of a lexifier for a future pidgin, then what is? How did Australian Aborigines come to speak a pidgin whose lexicon was primarily derived from English? Power and prestige are certainly a prime suspect, and would at first glance seem to be guilty beyond reasonable doubt. However, if we take into account the cases where a European language has not become the lexifier, it seems reasonable to search for an alternative explanation. My suggestion (and credit should go to Philip Baker [e.g., Baker and Huber 2001: 192, 195] for mentioning this before I did) is that an important factor is mobility. If the British in Australia first met group A, then group B, and then group C (etc.), then the British would, on their part, have learned certain communication strategies, and certain aboriginal words that seemed to do the trick in previous encounters. Some of the groups A, B, and C (etc.), on the other hand, may not have been in contact with one another before European colonization disrupted the previous status quo. When European settlement and European diseases forced them to relocate, the only vocabulary they had in common was that of the colonizers—not necessarily because these were capable of imposing their will on the native populations by means of firearms, but because they were more mobile (after all, they had in this particular case literally traveled to the other side of the planet). In the case of Australia, there exists a good deal of evidence (again compiled by Philip Baker, but as of yet largely unpublished) to support this interpretation.

In this context, one should also mention that there do exist a few pidgins that lack a lexifier in the first place. The best known is undoubtedly the Plains Indian Sign langauge. In every sense of the word, Plains Indian Sign is a pidgin, even though it occupies (at best) a marginal place in pidgin discourse. It was (or "is," since it is still marginally used) a medium of interethnic communication, and it was certainly a restricted code. The only thing it lacked was a (known) lexifier.

The choice of a lexifier has clear implications on another subject, namely the connection between second-language acquisition (SLA) and pidginization, which brings us to my final controversial point. Most contact linguists (and linguists in general) take for granted that pidgin formation is the result of SLA with limited access to the target language, and that this is so obvious that it (for the most part) does not even merit arguing. To the extent that arguments are presented, they are usually limited to presenting a few similarities between inter-language varieties and pidgins (ignoring that there are also differences) and an appeal to common sense—how could people possibly wind up speaking something that includes a subset of the lexicon and grammar of a preexisting language unless they had made a (failed, obviously) attempt at learning it?

My position here is that pidgins typically develop in settings where all parties have an interest in communicating, and that this pressing need overrides any prescriptive urges. The cases I have studied suggest not a teacher/learner scenario, but rather a situation where everyone involved is clutching at straws. The goal would have been sucessful communication, regardless of whether this was achieved by means of an already existing variety or not. In a trial-and-error kind of manner, anything understood by the other party stood a chance of entering the pidgin. The reader should recall that apart from the lexicon, pidgins typically contain very little material from their lexifiers. In other words, if one accepts my earlier reasoning regarding the choice of a lexical source, there is hardly anything left to suggest that pidginizers were trying to acquire an existing language.

11.5.2 Jargonization and Stabilization

Pidgins are typically thought to develop via a *jargon*. The term *jargon* refers to the developmental stage that precedes a pidgin proper (of course, many jargons die out without ever generating a pidgin). A jargon typically consists of a small number of lexical items (believed to be) understood by all parties involved, but without much in terms of structure and stability. In Fox's (1983: 101) words, it is "as much a strategy as a language in the normal sense."

An example of what I consider representative of the jargon stage is the following sentence, uttered in the 1680s by a native interpreter in what is today Liberia to a representative of the Brandenburg Africa Company:

(5)   Liberian Jargon Dutch: König Peter mie   sege ick   juw   sege König
                              King   Peter 1SG   say   1SG   2SG   say   King
      Peter sege mi, sege König Piter, Dassie hebbe, mi sege kike Dassie
      Peter say 1SG say King Peter gifts have   1SG say have gifts.
      'King Peter tells me to ask you for the presents, let's see them'   (Jones 1985: 34)

Another could be this utterance in a Japanese variety of Bamboo English, which displays an exceptionally high degree of context dependency:

(6)   Sayonara. Metermeter daijobu: testo-testo- dammeydammey bye. Examine: very
      good.
      Goodbye! Inspect okay   analyse damn bye. Look out very good.
      Try out: no good.
      Try out: no good
      'Get out of here! It's fine to look at the girl, but don't try anything else'
                                                                      (Goodman 1967: 53)

These, just like the "pidgin" examples in Bickerton (1984: 174), appear to display what Bickerton described as "no recognizable syntax." Therefore, a jargon is not a pidgin (and, given the lack of structure, perhaps not even a language).

In time, however, the jargon may stabilize (most jargons presumably never do) and expand into what we would rather call a pidgin (i.e., a variety with grammatical rules, albeit in limited number). This stabilization may be characterized as "not well understood," but appears to go hand in hand with increased usage. Much of the development of new structures mirror grammaticalization paths familiar from traditional languages, although seemingly proceeding at an accelerated pace. As is well known, pidgins may also proceed further along this line, and eventually become creoles,[7] but that is outside the scope of this overview.

Jargonization (or pidginization) has not been observed *in vivo*, in the sense that a contact between different languages has been documented from the first contact to the existence of a common (and reduced) medium used by a large number of people. In general, pidgins do not (if at all) receive the attention of linguists until some stabilization has appeared, and more often than not, not until after the contact language in question has met its demise.

However, there are a few interesting cases, where some observations have been made virtually from day one. The prime case here is Kisisi, documented by Gilmore (1979, 1983, 2015), which was created by two boys during an intense sixteen-month period of contact.[8]

For two other examples, let us return to Edward Frederick Knight and Henri d'Orléans, whom the reader may remember from the introduction to this chapter. Box 11.1 provides a slow-motion recap of what these gentlemen and their local pathfinders actually did.

This must certainly happen a lot more often than available documentation allows us to assess, but let us remember that the scenario is somewhat unusual. Someone (an anthropologist, a shipwrecked, a missionary), arriving alone at a place where a foreign language is spoken, would in most cases try to acquire this. If they have the means and the power (an invader, an officially appointed administrator or schoolteacher, a person with attractive trade items), they might insist that the locals learn their language. In most cases (a tourist, a salesperson), there is either someone present who can act as an interpreter, or the visitor could turn to another person or another village, hoping for easier communicative conditions elsewhere, and in some others (a plundering pirate) they might choose to instead let physical actions speak for them.

---

[7] It is currently controversial within creolistics whether or not *all* creoles derive from pidgins, but there is no doubt that *some* do—the best-known case is probably Tok Pisin, the English-lexicon pidgin-turned-creole of Papua New Guinea.

[8] Despite being unusual in having been created by two children, there can be no doubt that Kisisi was a pidgin: it was developed to solve an interethnic communication problem, but was unintelligible to outsiders. It drew its lexicon primarily from Swahili, but with influences from the native langauges of its creators. The lexicon included plenty of polysemy and analytic periphrases, and left many structural core distinctions unmarked (e.g., tense/aspect, copulas, articles). Also noteworthy is the fact that certain features (e.g., preverbal invariable monomorphemic negation) were not obviously derived from any of the input languages, but instead were similar to what we find in pidgins in general. When a certain expression was lacking, outright negotiation occurred between the speakers, who manifested creativity rather than simply tapping the lexifier (or the substrates).

Box 11.1 Development of lingua francas, as described by Messrs Knight and d'Orléans

---

- Initially, little or no communication was possible at all:
- *"At first, intercourse was not easy"*

- Language contruction involves grasping at bits and pieces of linguistic material that just possibly might be understood by the other, regardless of the origin of the words:
- *"I discovered what words he knew"; "the addition of a few words of Sclav and Albanian"*

- Both parties are flexible, and adapt to the interlocutor's way of speaking:
- *"completely mastered each other's idiosyncrasies"*

- And by time, some conventions are established:
- *"common to Marco and myself"*

- The writers know that what they are speaking equals no existing language, or at least no socially accepted version of it:
- *"manufactured a mongrel tongue"; "our jargon"*

- They are aware that the new tongue would not meet with approval from prescriptivists:
- *"But what Latin!"; "barbarisms"; "mongrel tongue"; "Luckily, we had only ourselves for audience"*

- Indeed, the jargon might not even be comprehensible to any outsider:
- *"utter gibberish to any one else"*

- At first, little can be said in the new common medium:
- *"Our oratorical attempts were hardly brilliant"*

- But at the end of the day successful communication is achieved:
- *"we gained fluency"*

But in the nineteenth-century cases in the preceding box, no alternative course of action is available to the European globetrotters. And so far as their native companions are concerned, they could certainly opt to wander off, but presumably had an economic incentive to stay, which implies trying to establish a functioning medium of communication.

I believe that the experiences of d'Orléans and Knight relatively accurately reflect—though obviously on a micro-scale—what took place in pidginization in other cases all around the globe.

11.6 AN INVENTORY OF KNOWN PIDGINS

The number of pidgins that exist or have existed is unknown, and all we can be certain of is that far more than we have records of must have existed. That said, I insist that pidgin creation is a relatively rare phenomenon. In the vast majority of language-contact situations that we know something about, interethnic communication has been assured by other means—either because some or many of the people involved were (or became) bilingual in the other party's language, or by means of an existing lingua franca.

I have compiled a list (which I would happily share with anyone interested) of varieties that are, may be, or have been claimed or suspected to be pidgins. That list currently includes about 300 entries, but some of these are such that I disagree with their being classified as pidgins, whereas many others represent likely cases on which we simply have far too little data to make a reliable judgment.[9] While I would like to remind the reader that my use of the word "pidgin" is less liberal than that of most other writers, only slightly more than two dozen varieties are such that they both qualify as pidgins (in my view) and are (by pidgin standards) reasonably well documented. These are noted in Table 11.1.

The most common lexifiers in pidginization are the languages of European colonization, such as English, French, Spanish, Portuguese, and Russian, together with a few major non-European languages such as Arabic, Malay, Japanese, and Swahili. While European lexifiers dominate when individual languages are counted, pidgins with a non-European lexifier are in fact twice as common as those lexified by a European language.

11.7 PIDGINIZATION TODAY

Most of the examples mentioned thus far deal with pidgins that are no longer spoken. Therefore, the question naturally arises—does pidginization still occur?

It still does, but for a variety of reasons, we would expect it to be less common today than it once was. "The world is smaller today" may sound like a tired cliché, but it nevertheless is one that is relevant in this case. Yet, there are a few varieties that are emerging today, or which have done so during the past couple of decades (Table 11.2).

To these, one might add other possible, but undocumented cases. One such, which has not been mentioned in the literature before, may be labeled "European trucker's jargon", and is an example of potentially ongoing (or future) pidginization. After the fall of the Eastern Bloc, more and more of the road transport in the European Union has been performed by East European drivers. Purely aprioristically, this situation would seem to provide a fertile ground for pidginization: the truck drivers are typically not highly educated, but are extremely mobile and thereby come into contact with a large number of different languages. This language contact situation has not been

[9] In the list, I have graded both the amount of documentation and the "degree of pidginhood" on a scale from zero to five. The grading is impressionistic, but can hopefully still serve as a rough indicator to myself and others.

Table 11.1 Pidgin Languages

Variety	Status	Lexifier	Primary Substrate(s)	(Main) Area
Amerindian English Pidgin(s?)	extinct	English	various North American languages	US
Australian/Melanesian Pidgin Englishes	creolizing	English	various Australian and Melanesian languages	Australia and Melanesia
Bazaar Malay	living, but declining	Malay	various languages of Indonesia and Malaysia, Sinitic languages, English, Dutch	Malaysia, Indonesia
Cape Pidgin Dutch	extinct	Dutch	Nama, Malay, Papia Kristang	South Africa
Chinese Pidgin English	extinct	English	Cantonese	China
Chinook Jargon	dying	Chinook	various North American languages, English, French	US, Canada
Fanakalo	living, but declining	Zulu	various Bantu languages, Afrikaans, English	South Africa
Fijian Pidgin Hindustani	dying	Hindi	Cantonese, Dravidian languages, Fijian	Fiji
Français–Tirailleur	extinct	French	Wolof, Bambara, Moore	West Africa
Govorka (Taimyr Pidgin Russian)	dying	Russian	Nganasan, Nenets, Enets, Yakut, Evenki	Russia
Gulf Pidgin Arabic	developing	Arabic	languages of the Indian subcontinent and the Philippines	around the Persian Gulf
Hawaiian Pidgin English	creolized	English	Cantonese, Portuguese, Hawaiian	Hawaii
Hiri Motu	living, but declining	Motu	various New Guinean languages	Papua New Guinea
Juba Arabic	creolizing	Arabic	Bari and other languages of South Sudan	South Sudan
Lingua Franca	Extinct	(Romance)	Arabic, Turkish	Mediterranian area
Mobilian	extinct	Choctaw	various North American languages, English, French	US
Pidgin Delaware	extinct	Unami	Dutch, Swedish, English	US
Pidgin Fijian	dying	Fijian	Hindustani, Cantonese	Fiji
Pidgin Hawaiian	extinct	Hawaiian	English, Portuguese, Cantonese	Hawaii
Pidgin Madame	living	Arabic	Sinhala	Lebanon
Plains Indian Sign	dying	none!	various North American languages and English	US
Russenorsk	extinct	Norwegian+Russian	Norwegian+Russian	Norway, Russia
Sango	creolizing	Ngbandi	languages of the Central African Republic, Bantu languages, French	Central African Republic
Tay Boi	extinct	French	Vietnamese	Vietnam
West African Pidgin Portuguese	extinct	Portuguese	various African languages	West Africa
Yokohama Pidgin Japanese	extinlct	Japanese	English	Japan

Table 11.2 Recently Documented Pidgins

Variety	Source
Arabic-lexicon pidgins of the Middle East	Al-Azraqi (2011), Albakrawi (2012), Almoaily (2012), Avram (2010), Bakir (2010), Bizri (2009, 2010), Næss (2008), etc.
Kisisi	Gilmore (1979, 1983, 2015)
The Bauxite Language	Perexvalskaya (2012)
Corozal Pidgin Spanish	Murrieta (2002)
Roquetas Pidgin Spanish	Haselow (2004, 2009)

investigated, but the following five utterances were provided by a documentary broadcast on Swedish television:[10]

My baby, dos	'I have two children'
Martin finito	'My marriage is over'
Camion no life	'Truck driving is not a life'
Grand problem	'I have big problems'
Mangiore no	'bad food'

A mere five sentences is of course not enough to base a serious assessment on, but my impression is that we are not dealing with an actual pidgin, but quite likely a jargon, and therefore a possible future pidgin.

If I may be so bold as to make an attempt at predicting the future, this budding variety illustrates the narrow time window available for pidgins creation in general; before 1989, East European truck drivers would not have been employed in Western Europe in the first place, while in a possibly not too distant future, they may well have embraced English as the one and only medium of interethnic communication.

11.8 CONCLUDING REMARKS

This chapter is primarily intended to give the reader an introduction to what we know about pidgins and their birth. For the most part, the material presented should be uncontroversial, but instead of refraining from giving my own views, I have tried to flag when these conflict with those of other contact linguists, and readers are invited to

---

[10] *Uppdrag Granskning*, broadcast on March 20, 2013. The program in question dealt with the exploitation in Western Europe of underpaid Balkan drivers. The translations given here are those that were provided in the (Swedish) subtitling. I assume that contextual information known to the reporters contributed to their interpretation.

make up their own mind. Apart from my more more restricted use of the term *pidgin* (which could, after all, be seen as a matter of taste), these conflicts regard the mixed nature of pidgins, the issue of power and prestige, and role of second language acquisition versus an unprejudiced trial-and-error approach.

REFERENCES

Aboh, Enoch, and Umberto Ansaldo. 2007. The role of typology in language creation: A descriptive take. In *Deconstructing Creole*, edited by U. Ansaldo, S. Matthews, and L. Lim, 39–66. Amsterdam; Philadelphia: John Benjamins.

Al-Azraqi, Munira. 2011. Pidginisation in the eastern region of Saudi Arabia: Media presentation. In *Arabic and the Media*, edited by R. Bassioueny, 159–173. Leiden: Brill.

Albakrawi, Hussien. 2012. The linguistic effect of foreign Asian workers on the Arabic Pidgin in Saudi Arabia. *Research on Humanities and Social Sciences* 2(9): 127–133.

Almoaily, Mohammad. 2012. *Language Variation in Gulf Pidgin Arabic*. PhD dissertation, Newcastle University.

Ansaldo, Umberto, and Stephen Matthews. 2007. Deconstructing creole: The rationale. In *Deconstructing Creole*, edited by U. Ansaldo, S. Matthews, and L. Lim, 1–18. Amsterdam; Philadelphia: John Benjamins.

Ansaldo, Umberto, Stephen Matthews, and Lisa Lim (eds.). 2007. *Deconstructing Creole*. Amsterdam; Philadelphia: John Benjamins.

Atkinson, Hoffman. 1879. *Revised and Enlarged Edition of Exercises in the Yokohama Dialect*. Yokohama: Japan Gazette Office.

Avram, Andrei. 2010. An outline of Romanian pidgin Arabic. *Journal of Language Contact* 3: 20–38.

Aye, Daw Khin Khin. 2005. *Bazaar Malay: History, Grammar and Contact*. PhD dissertation, National University of Singapore.

Baker, Philip, and Magnus Huber. 2001. Atlantic, Pacific, and world-wide features in English-lexicon contact languages. *English World-Wide* 22(2): 157–208.

Bakir, Murtadha. 2010. Notes on the verbal system of Gulf Pidgin Arabic. *Journal of Pidgin and Creole Languages* 25(2): 201–228.

Bakker, Peter. 1997. *A Language of Our Own: The Genesis of Michif, the Mixed Cree-French Language of the Canadian Métis*. Oxford: Oxford University Press.

Bakker, Peter. 2003. The absence of reduplication in Pidgins. In *Twice as Meaningful*, edited by Silvia Kouwenberg, 37–46. London: Battlebridge.

Becker, Angelika, and Tonjes Veenstra. 2003. Creole prototypes as basic varieties and inflectional morphology. In *Information Structure and the Dynamics of Language Acquisition*, edited by Christine Dimroth, 235–264. Amsterdam; Philadelphia: John Benjamins.

Bickerton, Derek. 1984. The language bioprogram hypothesis. *The Behavioral and Brain Sciences* 7: 173–188.

Bickerton, Derek. 1988. Creole languages and the bioprogram. In *Linguistics: The Cambridge Survey 2: Linguistic Theory: Extensions and Implications*, edited by F. Newmeyer, 268–284. Cambridge: Cambridge University Press.

Bizri, Fida. 2009. Sinhala in contact with Arabic: The birth of a new pidgin in the Middle East. In *Annual Review of South Asian Languages and Linguistics 2009*, edited by Rajendra Singh, 135–149. Berlin; New York: Mouton de Gruyter.

Bizri, Fida. 2010. *Pidgin Madame: Une grammaire de la servitude.* Paris: Geuthner.

Booij, Geert. 1994. Against split morphology. In *Yearbook of Morphology 1993*, edited by Geert Booij and Jaap van Marle, 27–49. Dordrecht: Kluwer.

Broch, Ingvild, and Ernst Håkon Jahr. 1984. Russenorsk: A new look at the Russo-Norwegian pidgin in northern Norway. In *Scandinavian Language Contacts*, edited by P. Sture Ureland and Iain Clarkson, 21–65. Cambridge: Cambridge University Press.

Drechsel, Emanuel. 1993. Basic word order in Mobilian Jargon: Underlying SOV or OSV? In *American Indian linguistics and Ethnography in Honor of Laurence C. Thompson*, edited by Anthony Mattina and Timothy Montler, 343–367. Missoula: University of Montana.

Eells, Myron. 1894. The Chinook Jargon. *American Anthropologist* 7(3): 300–312.

Fox, James. 1983. Simplified input and negotiation in Russenorsk. In *Pidginization and Creolization as Language Acquisition*, edited by Roger Andersen, 94–108. Rowley: Newbury House.

Gilmore, Perry. 1979. A children's pidgin: The case of a spontaneous pidgin for two. *Sociolinguistic Working Paper* 64. Austin: Southwest Educational Development Lab.

Gilmore, Perry. 1983. Ethnographic approaches to the study of child language. *The Volta Review* 85(5): 29–43.

Gilmore, Perry. 2015. *Kisisi (Our Language): The Story of Colin and Sadiki.* Hoboken: Wiley-Blackwell.

Givón, Talmy. 2009. *The Genesis of Syntactic Complexity: Diachrony, Ontogeny, Neuro-Cognition, Evolution.* Amsterdam; Philadelphia: John Benjamins.

Goddard, Ives. 1995. The Delaware Jargon. In *New Sweden in America*, edited by Carol Hoffecker, Richard Waldron, Lorraine Williams, and Barbara Benson, 137–149. Newark: University of Delaware Press.

Goddard, Ives. 2000. The use of pidgins and jargons on the East Coast of North America. In *The Language Encounter in the Americas, 1492–1800*, edited by Edward Gray and Norman Fiering, 61–78. New York: Berghahn books.

Goodman, John Stuart. 1967. The development of a dialect of English-Japanese pidgin. *Anthropological Linguistics* 9(6): 43–55.

Grant, Anthony. 2013. Chinuk Wawa. In *Survey of Pidgin and Creole Language Structures*, edited by Susanne Maria Michaelis, Philippe Maurer, Magnus Huber, and Martin Haspelmath, Vol. III, 147–155. Oxford: Oxford University Press.

Grant, Anthony. 2014. The 'language of Tobi' as presented in Horace Holden's Narrative. In *Pidgins and Creoles beyond Africa-Europe Encounters*, edited by Isabelle Buchstaller, Anders Holmberg, and Mohammad Almoaily, 41–56. Amsterdam: John Benjamins.

Haselow, Alexander. 2004. Analogías, simplificaciones y la búsqueda del mínimo común múltiplo: Notas sobre el español de los inmigrantes de Roquetas de Mar (Almería). *Revista electrónica de estudios filológicos* 8.

Haselow, Alexander. 2009. Características del vocabulario del pidgin español en Almería (Andalucía). *Revista Española de Lingüística* 39(1): 61–76.

Heine, Bernd. 1973. *Pidgin-Sprachen im Bantu-Bereich.* Berlin: Dietrich Reimer.

Heine, Bernd. 1979. Some linguistic characteristics of African-based pidgins. In *Readings in Creole Studies*, edited by Ian Hancock, Edgar Polomé, Morris Goodman, and Bernd Heine, 89–98. Ghent: Story-Scientia.

Huttar, George, and Frank Velantie. 1996. Ndyuka-Trio Pidgin. In Thomason (ed.), 99–124.

Johnson, Samuel Victor. 1978. *Chinook Jargon: A Computer Assisted Analysis of Variation in an American Indian Pidgin.* PhD dissertation, University of Kansas.

Jones, Adam. 1985. *Brandenburg Sources for West African History 1680–1700*. Studien zur Kulturkunde 77. Wiesbaden: Franz Steiner Verlag.

Juvonen, Päivi. in press. Making do with minimal lexica: Light verb constructions with MAKE/DO in pidgin lexica. *Lexico-Typological Approaches to Semantic Shifts and Motivation Patterns in the Lexicon*, edited by Päivi Juvonen and Maria Koptjevskaja-Tamm. Berlin; New York: Mouton de Gruyter.

Knight, Edward Frederick. 1880. *Albania: A Narrative of Recent Travel*. London: S. Low, Marston, Searle, & Rivington.

Kusters, Wouter. 2003. *Linguistic Complexity: The Influence of Social Change on Verbal Inflection*. Uitrecht: LOT.

McWhorter, John. 2001. The world's simplest grammars are creole grammars. *Linguistic Typology* 5: 125–166.

McWhorter, John. 2005. *Defining Creole*. Oxford: Oxford University Press.

Mesthrie, Rajend. 2007. Differentiating pidgin from early interlanguage: A comparison of pidgin Nguni (Fanakalo) and interlanguage varieties of Xhosa and Zulu. *Southern African Linguistics and Applied Language Studies* 25(1): 75–89.

Miestamo, Matti, Kaius Sinnemäki, and Fred Karlsson (eds.). 2008. *Language Complexity*. Amsterdam; Philadelphia: John Benjamins.

Mühlhäusler, Peter. 1997. *Pidgin and Creole Linguistics: Expanded and Revised Edition*. London: University of Westminster Press.

Murrieta, Griselda. 2002. Impacto sociolingüístico de la Zona Libre de Corozal, México-Belice. In *Anuario de la división de estudios internacionales*. Chetumal, Mexico: Universidad de Quintana Roo.

Muysken, Pieter. 1981. Halfway between Quechua and Spanish: The case for relexification. *Historicity and Variation in Creole Studies*, edited by Arnold Highfield and Albert Valdman, 57–78. Ann Arbor: Karoma.

Muysken, Pieter. 1988. Are creoles a special type of language? In *Linguistics: The Cambridge Survey 2: Linguistic Theory: Extensions and Implications*, edited by F. Newmeyer, 285–301. Cambridge: Cambridge University Press.

Næss, Unn Gyda 2008. *"Gulf Pidgin Arabic": Individual Strategies or a Structured Variety? A Study of Some Features of the Linguistic Behaviour of Asian Migrants in the Gulf Countries*. MA thesis, Department of Culture Studies and Oriental Languages, University of Oslo.

Newmeyer, Frederick (ed.). 1988. *Linguistics: The Cambridge Survey 2: Linguistic Theory: Extensions and Implications*. Cambridge: Cambridge University Press.

Orléans, Henri Philippe d'. 1898. *From Tonkin to India by thesSources of the Irawadi, January '95–January '96*. London: Methuen.

Parkvall, Mikael, and Peter Bakker. 2013. Pidgins. In *Contact Languages*, edited by Yaron Matras and Peter Bakker, 15–64. Berlin: Mouton de Gruyter.

Perexvalskaya, Elena. 2012. *Русские пиджины*. St. Petersburg: Алетейя.

Reinecke, John. 1938. Trade jargons and creole dialects as marginal languages. *Social Forces* 17(1): 107–118.

Robertson, David. 2011. *Kamloops Chinúk Wawa, Chinuk Pipa, and the Vitality of Pidgins*. PhD dissertation, University of Victoria.

Sampson, Geoffrey, David Gil, and Peter Trudgill (eds.). 2009. *Language Complexity as an Evolving Variable*. Oxford: Oxford University Press.

Shi, Dingxu. 1991. Chinese Pidgin English: Its origin and linguistic features. *Journal of Chinese Linguistics* 19(1): 1–40.

Siegel, Jeff. 1987. *Language Contact in a Plantation Environment*. Cambridge: Cambridge University Press.

Singh, V. D. 1983. Bazaar varieties of Hindi. *Studies in the Linguistic Sciences* 13(2): 115–141.

Sœur Victorien. 1908. Dahomey. *Les Missions catholiques* 40: 339–340.

Stefánsson, Vilhjálmur. 1909. The Eskimo trade jargon of Heschel Island. *American Anthropologist* 11(2): 217–232.

Stolz, Thomas. 1986. *Gibt es das kreolische Sprachwandelsmodell?* Frankfurt: Peter Lang.

Sweet, Henry. 1900. *The History of Language*. New York: Macmillan.

Williams, Jeffrey. 1995. Tracing Iatmul foreigner talk. *Journal of Linguistic Anthropology* 5(1): 90–92.

Williams, Jeffrey. 2000. Yimas-Alamblak Tanim Tok: An indigenous trade pidgin of New Guinea. *Journal of Pidgin and Creole Languages* 15(1): 37–62.

CHAPTER 12

....

CREOLES

....

JOHN McWHORTER

12.1 INTRODUCTION

....

PERHAPS the most prominent meme about pidgins and creoles among informed outsiders is that adults create pidgins as makeshift, rudimentary tools, and that creoles result when children expand pidgins into full languages. In fact, that basic formulation is highly controversial within creole studies. Arguments in its favor tend to encounter resistance, and an ironic fact after over fifty years of the institutionalized existence of creole studies is that its practitioners have yet to concur on a definition of creole language.

DeCamp (1971: 14) dated the official beginning of creole studies to a moment at a foundational conference in Jamaica in 1959 "when Jack Berry suddenly remarked 'All of us are talking about the same thing!'" Yet in the 2010s, it is safe to say that most specialists in pidgins and creoles would consider this "same thing" a highly elusive proposition.

12.2 CREOLE: BASIC CHARACTERIZATION

....

Unequivocal is that the term *creole*—derived from a word initially used in sixteenth-century Portuguese colonies in reference to whites born there, eventually extended to slaves born in European colonies and the Euro-African languages they developed—has been traditionally applied to vernacular languages born in plantation colonies from the fifteenth through the nineteenth centuries amidst the European-driven slave trade and other geopolitical developments in its wake. These languages contrast with the European languages providing most of their words—traditionally referred to as the *superstrate* or *lexifier*—in lacking a significant amount of their grammatical machinery, most saliently inflectional affixes.

An example is Haitian Creole, here contrasted directly with French:

(1)   (a) French:

Ils n'ont   pas   de   ressources   qui   puissent   leur
3P NEG.have   NEG   PART   resource.PL   REL   can.SUJ.3P   3P.OBJ
permettre   de   résister.
allow   to   resist

(b) Haitian:

Yo   pa   gen   resous   ki   pou   pèmèt   yo   reziste.
3P   NEG   have   resource REL   can   allow   3P   resist

(Ludwig, Telchid, and Bruneau-Ludwig 2001: 164)

Haitian, like all creoles, exhibits the basic grammatical complexity of all natural languages. However, French's concordial marking of case, person, and number, marking of grammatical gender and the partitive (via *de* and its conditioning), heterogenous syntactic position of object clitic *leur*, and its allomorphies and irregularities are absent in the Haitian sentence. Creolists are united in deriving this trait from the fact that creoles emerged from non-native acquisition, although the nature and degree of this acquisition is a matter of debate.

Creoles also differ notably from their lexifiers in containing a significant contribution, usually on all levels of structure, from the languages their creators spoke natively (traditionally referred to as the *substrate*). For example, Saramaccan Creole English of Surinam has serial verb constructions, postposed nominals to indicate spatial relations, CV syllable structure, and certain tonal patterns (as well as some core lexical items) that directly reflect equivalent structures in the Kwa Niger-Congo language spoken by an influential number of its creators, Fongbe:

(2)   (a) Kobí   sáka   kaábu   butá   a   dí   táfa   líba.
          Kobi   put.down   crab   put   LOC   DEF   table top
          'Kobi put crab on the table.'   (Author's data)

(b) Kòkú   sɔ́   àsɔ́n   ɔ́   távò   jí.
    Koku   take   crab   put   table on
    'Koku put crab on the table.'   (Lefebvre and Brousseau 2002: 410)

However, the concept of *creole* cannot be associated definitionally with plantation colonies. Most of the world's creoles—numbering in the several dozens depending on definitions of language versus dialect, as well as the eternally elusive definition of *creole* itself—have European lexifiers. However, creole genesis, yielding languages contrasting in the same way with their lexifiers as Haitian and Saramaccan, has occurred in several other contexts. The creole Portugueses of India emerged at trade posts amidst indigenes exposed to Catholicism in Portuguese. The Portuguese creoles of the Gulf of Guinea began amidst Euro-African marriages, while Unserdeutsch

Creole German developed in an orphanage in New Guinea. Nor are creole languages definitionally derived from European languages, as demonstrated by Nubi Creole Arabic (which emerged among relocating soldiers), and nativized versions of Chinook Jargon (on one Native American reservation) and Sango (derived from the Niger-Congo language Ngbandi).

12.3 CREOLIZATION AS CLINAL

Creolization is also a matter of degree, conditioned by sociohistorical variables. Many creoles, most famously the English-lexifier ones of the Caribbean, consist of an array of dialects ranging from a basilect typical of the most socioeconomically isolated, an acrolect spoken by the most educated that differs from the lexifier mainly in phonology and indigenous lexicon, and a mesolect in between. Certain constructions allow quite fine-grained distinctions along the continuum, such that *I gave him* in Guyanese Creole English is expressed in fifteen different ways from basilect to acrolect:

(3)   mi bin gii am
      mi bin gii ii
      mi bin gi i
      mi di gii ii
      mi di gi hii
      a di gii ii
      a did gi ii
      a did giv ii
      a did giv hii
      a giv ii
      a giv im
      a giv him
      a geev ii
      a geev him
      I gave him   (Romaine 1988: 158–159)

In other cases, these lectal differences apply not within a context but between two different ones. The creole French of Mauritius is much further from French the variety spoken on nearby Réunion, which is close enough to the French to be parsable by someone familiar only with the latter:

      Réunnionais French Creole
(4)   Alor   mõ   papa   la   tuzur   di   amwẽ...
      then   my   father PAST always   say   to.me
                          (cf. French *Alors mon papa m'a toujours dit ...*)
      'Then my father always said to me...'   (Chaudenson 1974: 1165)

Mauritian French Creole

(5) Zot   burzua   in   fek   pey   zot.
     3PL   boss   COMP   just pat   3PL
     'Their boss just paid them.'   (Corne 1981)

This kind of difference is traceable to initial sociohistorical conditions, and is paralleled by Cape Verdean Creole Portuguese dialects, which differ in distance from Portuguese according to the sociohistorical factors. Baker and Corne (1982) reconstruct that in Réunion, whites and Malagasy slaves worked in roughly equal numbers on small coffee plantations for several decades, allowing the slaves to acquire something close to French itself, after which they passed this on to the larger numbers of Bantu slaves required later to cultivate sugar. Mauritius, on the other hand, was peopled with large numbers of Bantu slaves closer to its initial foundation as a plantation colony, disallowing a period during which blacks could learn anything close to French, and conditioning a creole to emerge.

For this reason, varieties like Réunionnais have been termed *semi-creoles*, most influentially by Holm (cf. 2004), along with Afrikaans, Popular Brazilian Portuguese, Black English, and the vernacular Latin American Spanish varieties spoken by descendants of African slaves. For example, it has been argued that the reason no creoles emerged on the Spanish-run islands of Cuba, Puerto Rico, and Hispaniola is that a Réunion-style phase of numerical parity between black and white lasted so long that only modestly restructured Spanishes resulted (Mintz 1971).

While semi-creoles, with only modest elision of lexifier grammatical machinery and modest substrate contribution, are especially close to their lexifiers, even most other creoles' distance from their lexifiers is analogous to that of the mesolectal lects of English-lexifier creole continua. For example, Haitian in (1b) lends itself to analysis as a "kind of French," and even the basilectal range of the English-lexifier continuum creoles is submissible to the same judgment, one commonly held by many of its speakers, for one. Basilectal Jamaican patois is an example: *Dat wuman bier tuu daataz bisaidz, nou di tri sistaz liviŋ gud* (LePage and DeCamp 1960).

Creoles like these motivate proposals such as DeGraff's (1999) that Haitian differs from French largely in the resetting of certain syntactic parameter settings, rather than because of a break in transmission such as pidginization. Mufwene, similarly criticizing the derivation of creoles from pidgins, has offered the especially radical proposal (e.g., 2001) that creoles are simply mixtures of features from lexifier and substrate languages, in the same fashion as other notably mixed languages like Romanian (cf. section 12.5.4).

However, other creoles lend themselves less gracefully to such frameworks, basilectal to a much starker degree. Saramaccan in (2) is an example, as is its sister creole Sranan of Surinam, based on English:

(6) Te   den   yonkuman   fu   wrokope   yere   na   tori   dis,
     when   the-PL   young man   for   workplace hear   LOC   story this

dan	den	e	lafu.	Dati	na	wan	bigiman	srefisrefi.
then	they	PROG	laugh	that	COP	a	big-man	self-self

"Whenever the boys at work heard this, they would burst out in laughter 'That's one hell of a guy.'"   (Adamson and Smith 1995: 231)

Here, both derivation and inflection from English are absent, and the creole contains only 650 English roots, from which a new language was created. Also, the imprint of West African languages is much stronger on Sranan than on Haitian (or basilectal Caribbean English varieties). Creoles like this are unique in having developed largely apart from their lexifiers; for example, the English traded Surinam for New Amsterdam (later New York) with the Dutch only sixteen years after settling it. Thus there was no possibility of the development of a Sranan-to-English continuum as there was in most English colonies, or ongoing adstratal influence from English in general, as there was from French for creoles like Haitian.

Many creolists see evidence here of a break in transmission, whereby English was pidginized or underwent extensive second-language acquisition (creolists disagree on which concept is more appropriate and what distinguishes them), and subsequently filled out with substrate features and grammar-internal developments into a new language. Creoles of this kind, then, also exemplified by the Portuguese-based creoles of the Gulf of Guinea, Negerhollands Creole Dutch, and Tok Pisin of New Guinea and its relative varieties, motivate assumptions that creoles develop from pidgins.

12.4 THE NATURE AND ROLE OF PIDGINS

12.4.1 Definition

The definition of *pidgin* has occasioned less controversy than that of *creole*. The word is derived from the Chinese Pidgin English pronunciation of *business* (Baker and Mühlhäusler 1990), and refers conventionally to varieties that are native to no one and in no way qualify as full languages. Foley's (1988: 165) is a representative characterization:

Smaller vocabulary, generic terms rather than specific;
Monomorphemic words, paraphrases of complex words;
No subordinate clauses, parataxis;
Invariable word order;
Absence of copula, pronouns, function words;
Heavily reduced or no inflections;
No allomorphy, invariant stems (e.g., full forms as opposed to contractions);
CV monosyllables and CVCV disyllabics.

An example would be Chinese Pidgin English, which developed in Canton in the seventeenth century, with about 700 words and rudimentary grammatical structure:

(7) My wanchee wun pay soo belly soon. Spose fookkee too muchee pigeon: no can maykee.
     'I want a pair of shoes soon. But I fear you are too busy to make them for me now.'

                                                                    (Bauer 1974: 154)

Such varieties occur worldwide when groups come into contact, and are perhaps the most-used strategy of communication between groups that do not share a language, such that many pidgins, unlike English-dominant Chinese Pidgin English, split their lexicon between two languages. Examples include Russenorsk between Russian and Norwegian, and a pidgin between speakers of Surinam's Ndjuka creole and the Native American language Tirio.

12.4.2 Role of Pidgins in Creole Genesis

The nature of pidgins motivated what textbooks have often termed the "baby talk" hypothesis of creole genesis (first outlined by Bloomfield 1933: 472–473), under which pidgins emerged via speakers deliberately simplifying their language for subordinates via what is more conventionally termed *foreigner talk* (cf. Ferguson and DeBose 1977). Evidence of this practice where pidgins developed is not difficult to find. How central it was to pidgin structures beyond the most elementary ones is a question, however. Pidgins can easily emerge without such deliberate simplification—the learner can barely help acquiring what he hears in simplified form whether the speaker produces it in such form or not. Besides, the light that the "baby talk" scenario sheds on matters shines little beyond what many would term the *jargon* stage (*jargon* used by some researchers to distinguish the stage at which there is barely anything that could be called grammatical structure, as opposed to the moderately rule-governed nature of a pidgin).

While it is controversial whether the plantation-born creoles of the New World and the Indian Ocean developed from pidgins, it is explicitly documented that several varieties did, and as such, they demonstrate the "pidgin-creole life cycle" now viewed in some quarters as having a narrower realm of application than once supposed. The most studied have been Tok Pisin of Papua New Guinea, Bislama of Vanuatu, and Solomon Islands Pijin, sister languages that developed from a pidgin English born first among Australian aboriginals in the eighteenth century after the English settled that continent, and subsequently used in maritime and plantation contexts in Melanesia.

A limited English lexicon was recruited to fashion a new one. In the absence of English itself, morphemic boundaries were often reinterpreted: *nambis* (< on the beach) 'beach';

tudir (< too dear) 'expensive' (Mühlhäusler 1997: 155). Overt and grammaticalized marking of various distinctions emerged step by step over time, such as Mühlhäusler's (1997: 171) charting of the emergence of causative marking in Tok Pisin by verb type:

Step 1. stative verbs: *slip* 'sleep' / *slipim* 'to make lie down';
Step 2. adjectives: *bikim* 'to make big';
Step 3. non-stative verbs: *sanap* 'stand' / *sanapim* 'to make stand up';
Step 4. transitive verbs: *dring* 'drink' / *dringim* 'to make drink.'

12.4.3 Terminological Problem: Creoles Referred to as Pidgins

Tok Pisin and its family exemplify a terminological infelicity in creole studies: these languages have traditionally been referred to as *pidgins* rather than *creoles*, out of a sense that only languages acquired as first languages by children are to be termed *creoles*. However, for one, Tok Pisin et al. have been regularly acquired by children now for several decades. Moreover, even before this, they exhibited fully structured grammars, and contrasted with their lexifier in exactly the same fashion as languages classically treated as creoles do. "I was going" in Sranan is *Mi ben e go*, while in Tok Pisin it is the equally un-English *Mi bin go i stap*, with tense and aspect encoded with particles, elimination of English's affixes, and almost all case distinctions such as in pronouns (*me* as subject), and so on.

Long-term usage by adults can fashion a pidgin into either a full language or something very close to one, such that the effect of child acquisition is largely that increased speech tempo deepens phonology and morphophonology somewhat (Sankoff and Laberge 1980; Romaine 1992). As such, Tok Pisin, Bislama, Solomon Islands Pijin, and the Australian aboriginal Kriol dialects are creoles rather than pidgins in the linguistic sense, as are the English-based varieties of the West African coast, Ghanaian, Nigerian, and Cameroonian "Pidgin" English.

Meanwhile, the English-based creole of Hawaii is referred to as "Pidgin" because that was the name when it began as an actual pidgin before it was transformed into a full language.

12.5 CREOLE GENESIS DEBATES I: AGAINST THE PIDGIN-CREOLE LIFE CYCLE

Today, the most potent debate in creole studies is over whether the languages traditionally known as creoles began as pidgins at all. Current proposals as to how these creoles formed can in fact be grouped according to their approach to this question.

12.5.1 The Monogenesis Hypothesis: An Archival Matter

One approach assuming pidgin origin was the monogenesis hypothesis, now defunct, although gesturally referred to in many textbooks. Into the 1980s, some creolists derived European language–based creoles from a common Portuguese pidgin ancestor, relexified by various languages around the world. The hypothesis was motivated in part by a certain few Portuguese lexical items in creoles of disparate lexical base and geographical location. Goodman (1987), however, exhaustively accounts for this presence on the basis of the wide-ranging migrations of Portuguese-speaking slaveholders throughout the Caribbean in the seventeenth century. Furthermore, widespread items such as *sabi* 'to know' and *pikin* 'small child' are attributable to the Portuguese having been the first to establish a trade pidgin on the West African coast, and items from this pidgin having diffused into pidgins based on other European languages established later in the same areas.

The monogenesis idea was also based on the structural similarity between so many creoles. However, these similarities can be attributed to other factors, such as universals of second-language acquisition, of Universal Grammar (cf. Bickerton 1981, 1984, discussed later in this chapter), and diachronic relationships between creoles of the same lexical base (cf. Hancock 1987; Baker 1999; McWhorter 2005: 199–224). As such, no serious analysis has been based on the monogenesis hypothesis in over thirty years at this writing.

12.5.2 Substratist Works Eschewing Pidginization

Various proposals about creole genesis investigate what has collectively been termed the *substratist* hypothesis, focusing on the features of creoles—in practice, mostly grammatical rather than lexical—traceable to the native languages of their creators. Generally, substratist arguments are made within a framework that also includes pidginization or some degree of simplification (summary examples include Keesing 1988 on Tok Pisin, Bislama, and Solomon Islands Pijin, and the seminal Holm 1988 [textbook] and 1989 [encyclopedia]). However, some proposals attribute the substrate a larger role in which pidginization plays no significant role.

In pioneering substratist work, Alleyne (1971, 1980) questioned the assumption that Caribbean creoles began as pidgins, or in any other kind of lastingly simplified variety, proposing that the creoles were better analyzed as varieties of their lexifiers with heavy influence from substrate languages, in the same way that Romance languages harbor substrate-derived features. While Alleyne did not emphasize his dissocation of creoles from imperfect acquisition in later work, his approach inaugurated the cataloguing of the West African inheritances in plantation creoles. Boretzky (1983) was an equally valuable treatise, with the advantage of more African language data than was available to Alleyne, although because it was written in German it had limited influence. Later, Parkvall (2000) contributed a signature monograph on substrate influence in Atlantic creoles on the basis of the richer sociohistorical, as well as linguistic, data available by the time he wrote.

Since the 1980s, Lefebvre (most summarily, 1998) has developed a theory analyzing Haitian Creole—and by implication, other creoles—as a relexification of Fongbe (also the main substrate language of Saramaccan), a framework under which pidginization also has no place. Lefebvre hypothesizes that Fongbe speakers relabeled lexical and grammatical items with French ones. Where Haitian does not parallel Fongbe structure, Lefebvre proposes that French did not offer a readily plausible source for relabeling, or that there was dialect leveling between Fongbe and other varieties, such as the closely related Ewegbe. In later work Lefebvre has extended this analysis to Saramaccan.

While almost no creolist denies that substrate influence is robust in most creoles, Lefebvre's conception of creoles as outright relexifications has not gained adherents. Evidence is lacking that Fongbe was prevalent among slaves when Haitian was created, and others have noted that Haitian does not parallel Fongbe as closely as Saramaccan does, and have raised questions of falsifiability (cf. McWhorter 2011: 149–181). However, Lefebvre's work, couched in formalist syntactic analysis and also on extensive fieldwork on Fongbe itself, solidly resists Bickerton's charge that substratist work is based on an unsystematic "cafeteria principle" (see section 12.6.2) ignorant of science. Her work has also vastly enriched the literature on Haitian Creole and on one of the West African languages central to the genesis of many creoles.

12.5.3 Superstratist Work

Meanwhile, Chaudenson (most summarily, 1992) contests creoles' pidgin origins from a lexifier-based perspective, often termed a *superstratist* hypothesis. Chaudenson stresses that commonly, plantation colonies began as *sociétés d'habitation* (homestead societies), small farms where whites and the enslaved lived in numerical parity under intimate conditions. Here, slaves would have acquired the lexifier relatively completely. Later, such colonies switched to sugar cultivation, requiring vastly more manpower. New slaves acquired the lexifier more from the first ones rather than from the whites themselves, thus creating an "approximation of an approximation" of the full language; subsequent waves of slaves acquired the lexifier on the basis of this approximation, such that the variety that stabilized among the slaves was the product of this gradual dissolution of lexifier structure, titled by Chaudenson *français zéro*, a stage that scholars of second-language acquisition (and creolists working from its traditions; cf. section 12.7.1) would recognize as the Basic Variety analyzed by Klein and Perdue (1997).

As such, Chaudenson sees the reconstruction of a pidgin stage as scientifically unnecessary, and also considers the effect of substrate languages on creole structure to be modest. Rather, Chaudenson calls attention to the source of many creole structures in regional vernacular dialects of European languages, certainly consulted too little by creolists before he wrote, in favor of the standard dialects. As such, a Mauritian sentence like *Zot ti pe ale* 'They were going' is essentially the regional French *Eux-autres étaient après aller* spoken rapidly, and with modest effects of second-language acquisition. This contradicts any sense of *ti* and *pe* as exotic "creole" reinterpretations. This observation is important; Hancock (1994) usefully seconded it on English-lexifier creoles in his discussion of the parallels between Cornwall English and New World creoles, such that Gullah's habitual marker *blant*, superficially so unlike English as typically known, traces directly to the *belong to* construction in Cornwall.

Mufwene has brought this superstratist focus to the attention of creolists beyond the Francophone school with his terminologization, the Founder Principle (1996). While often read in passing as an argument that the initial peoples in a creole genesis context had the strongest impact on the creole's structure—something few analysts would deny—Mufwene's intent with the Founder Principle term is more specific: much of what appears novel or substrate-driven in creoles is directly descended from little-known dialects of the lexifier.

Chaudenson's ideas are especially attractive from the perspective of the French creoles that he focuses on, given that there is no French creole as divergent from its lexifier as Saramaccan or Tok Pisin are from English. The attention he has called to superstrate contributions is also invaluable to creolist analysis. Problematic, however, is evidence that full-blown creoles existed during the *société d'habitation* stage, such as in Martinique (Carden, Goodman, Posner, and Stewart 1990) and elsewhere. Also, it is difficult to see the especially basilectal creoles such as the Surinam ones, or Tok Pisin and its relatives, as products of "approximations of approximations" of English, or as harboring only modest substrate influence. To be sure, under Chaudenson's analysis Tok Pisin et al. qualify as pidgins, born under different conditions than the New World plantation contact languages he treats. However, besides questions about that classification (cf. section 12.4.3), the Surinam creoles (and the Portuguese ones of the Gulf of Guinea) do fall under the same bailiwick as the French plantation creoles, and Chaudenson's analysis squares less gracefully with them.

12.5.4 The Population Genetics Model

Yet it is reasonable to surmise that the main reason Chaudenson's work has been less central to general creolist discussion than it has been is that he writes in French. Salikoko Mufwene's work, proceeding from Chaudenson's, has therefore been invaluable in situating much of Chaudenson's thought into Anglophone creolist debates.

Mufwene's Population Genetics model (2001 is a fascicle of relevant articles) in fact extends Chaudenson's ideas into a more radical proposal. Similarly noting the absence of documented evidence of creoles' birth in pidgins, Mufwene argues that creoles be treated simply as the result of languages' features coming together to create new languages. This, to Mufwene, is what the result of the "approximations of approximations" process was, such that even taxonomizing creoles as a type of language is a reflexive legacy of colonialist essentializations (Mufwene 1997). Along the lines of Chaudenson's focus on lexifier sources, Mufwene notes that these varieties can even be seen as the source of much of the analyticity traditionally seen as stemming from incomplete acquisition. For example, vernacular Englishes often allow zero-marking in the third person singular present, while spoken French is much less inflected than the written language.

For Mufwene (2001), then, there is even no scientifically valid taxonomic difference between the histories of American English, Black English, and Gullah Creole: all are the product of language mixture under different circumstances. He states that rather than creoles harboring signs of birth in pidginization, "the extent of morphological complexity (in terms of range of distinctions) retained by a 'contact language' largely reflects the morphological structures of the target language and the particular languages that it came in contact with" (Mufwene 2009: 386). Simplification in creole genesis, under Mufwene's analysis, is manifested mainly as an elision of what he terms "redundancy," such as of NP concord.

Mufwene's work ranges widely, and is perhaps cited most for broader aspects of his message, such as the Founder Principle. However, applications of the Population Genetics model itself (e.g., Aboh and Ansaldo 2007) have left as many questions as answers. Plag (2011) has argued that as of yet, Population Genetics adherents' stipulation of "reassemblage" and "recombination" are unsystematized, qualifying more as description than explanation, as in classifying plural marking's tendency to be lost or narrowed in creolization as due to plurality being "semantically vacuous."

Meanwhile, McWhorter (2012) notes that many creoles lack even features that their source languages share, which would therefore be expected under a population genetics model. For example, in Palenquero Creole Spanish, an encounter between Spanish and the Bantu language Kikongo, there is no nominal concord, regular plural marking, a perfect tense, Differential Object Marking, or other features, most of which do not qualify as redundancies:

Kikongo (Bentley 1887: 526) (C8P = noun class 8 plural):

(8) O   ma-tadi   ma-ma   ma-mpembe   ma-mpwena
     AUG   C8P-stone   C8P-DEM   C8P -white   C8P -big

     i   ma-u   ma-ma   tw-a-mw-ene.
     COP   C8P-that   C8P-DEM   we-them-see-PERF.

Spanish:

(9) Est-a-s   piedr-a-s   grand-e-s   y   blanc-a-s
     DEM-FEM-PL   stone-FEM-PL   big-FEM-PL   and   white-FEM-PL

     son   las   que   hemos   visto.
     COP.3P   DEF.FEM.PL   REL   have.1PL   see.PP

'These great white stones are those which we have seen.'

Palenquero:

(10) Ese   ma   piegra   blangko   grande   e'   ese   ke suto a   miná.
     That   PLUR   stone   white   big   is   that   REL 1PL PAST   see.

'Those great white stones are those which we have seen.'

(Armin Schwegler 2016 personal communication.)

12.5.5 Creolization and Parameter Setting

Meanwhile, DeGraff (1999, 2001) has also been a passionate advocate for discarding the idea that creoles emerged from pidgins, concurring with Mufwene that this classification is a legacy of superannuated notions of European superiority. Much of DeGraff's work, couched in Chomskyan syntactic frameworks, has explored a creolization model based on parameter settings, such that adult acquisition did not pidginize lexifier languages, but had the less disruptive effect of changing certain parameter settings to "weak," with multiple effects therefrom.

Under this analysis, for example, the difference between these two sentences for 'Jacques never says hello':

(11)   French: *Jacques ne dit jamais bonjour.*
       Haitian Creole: *Jak pa janm di bonjou.*

stems from Haitian's inflection parameter being "weak," which means that the verb does not have to move leftward to get tense, explaining why the negative elements (and in other examples, adverbs with sentential focus such as *often*) precede the verb rather than following it, as most of them do in French. Other authors have joined DeGraff in this parametrical approach, including Veenstra (1996, although cf. his later work at section 12.7.1), Deprez (1999) and Baptista (2000).

These creolists' work has been invaluable in normalizing state-of-the-art generative analysis in a field in which it was relatively novel before the 1990s (unlikely now, for example, would be an anthology title such as that of Pieter Muysken's *Generative Studies on Creole Languages* of 1981). The verdict on these scholars' findings will differ according to the evaluator's sense of the prognosis for Chomskyan Minimalist theory. However, even under the most sanguine prospects for that school of thought, the features traced to parameter settings are but a subset of what distinguishes creoles from their source languages. The question posed by sentences (8) through (10) remains.

12.6 CREOLE GENESIS DEBATES II: ARGUING FOR THE PIDGIN-CREOLE LIFE CYCLE

12.6.1 The Pacific School

The vast body of work on the Australian and Melanesian pidgin/creoles comprehensively charts the development of these languages from the stage of lightly structured jargons to full languages (awkwardly titled "pidgins," as discussed in section 12.4.3). For these languages, the expansion process took place mostly in the late nineteenth and early twentieth centuries, such that ample historical documentation of the languages, as well as the social circumstances they developed under, survives for consultation.

Partly because these scholars can work with concrete data, rather than reconstruction and intelligent guesswork as scholars of Atlantic creoles must, Pacific pidgin and creole studies is not characterized by distinct competing schools of thought on genesis issues, despite predictable disagreements between individual scholars on more specific questions. The "pidgin/creole life cycle" considered a controversial proposition elsewhere is, in the Pacific context, an ineluctable fact.

As such, under the view (not shared by all creolists) that nothing significant qualitatively distinguishes the difference between Tok Pisin's source in English to Sranan's, the Pacific work constitutes an invaluable body of data and analysis on how creoles form. Key sources include Mühlhäusler (1997), Crowley (1990), Keesing (1988), and Tryon and Charpentier (2004). However, for reasons geographical, institutional, and philosophical, the study of Atlantic creoles has taken place largely separate from those of the Pacific, and occasional calls for this to change have born little fruit, despite a few scholars who have worked in both realms, such as Philip Baker.

12.6.2 The Language Bioprogram Hypothesis

One pidgin-based creole genesis scenario can be said to have galvanized the discipline. Bickerton's (1981, 1984) Language Bioprogram Hypothesis proposed that plantation creoles were created as a strategy by children who grew up in multilingual environments affording inadequate input to any natural language. With their parents' native languages used only marginally because of the linguistic heterogeneity of the context, and only distant access to the dominant European language, Bickerton's idea is that the children's only recourse was to fashion European lexical items into a new language on the basis of Universal Grammar in its "default" state, this default characterized by the "off" settings of parameters according to Chomskyan syntactic theory in its pre-Minimalist period.

Thus Bickerton argued that children expanded a pidgin (or more precisely, jargon) of this kind

(11)   Gud, dis wan. Kaukau enikain dis wan. Pilipin ailaen no gud. No mo mani.
        'It's better here than in the Phillipines—here you can get all kinds of food—but over there theer isn't any money (to buy food with).'

into a natural language, Hawaiian Creole English (locally known as "Pidgin") with grammaticalized markers of tense, specificity, and a contrast between realized and unrealized complementation, all in bold in the following, in which the *go* marker indicates the realized:

(12)   Dei **wen** go ap dea in **da** mawning **go** plaen.
        they PAST go up there in the morning go plant
        'They went up there in the morning to plant (things).'   (Bickerton 1984: 185)

Bickerton argued that this process explained why creole languages worldwide have such similar structures, including Hawaiian Creole English, created by speakers of languages quite unlike the West African ones of most plantation contexts. The features of the bioprogram included articles marking NPs according to specificity; preverbal particles marking anterior tense, progressive aspect, and irrealis modality; a distinction between a realized and an unrealized complementizer (see later discussion); a relative pronoun and subject copy; *have* expressing the existential; a locative copula separate from the equational; stative verbs instead of predicate adjectives; multiple negation; focus encoded via movement; no subject-verb inversion; bimorphemic question words; and no overt passive.

A conclusion especially provocative was that these features were unconnected to creole creators' native languages, and were rooted solely in the innate predispositions of Universal Grammar. Bickerton influentially characterized previous claims of substrate influence as based on an unsystematic "cafeteria principle," appealing to features in African languages regardless of whether they were actually spoken by the creoles' creators.

While certainly the most rigorously argued creole genesis theory at the time, Bickerton's hypothesis attracted a great deal of criticism. Many objected that creoles are not as structurally similar as Bickerton implied (Singler 1990). Bickerton's dismissal of substrate influence has also not stood the test of time. Various studies, founded in more rigorous identification of the relevant substrate languages than was common in the past, have demonstrated a rich array of creole-substrate parallels too close to be accidental (cf. Migge 2003; Hagemeijer and Ogie 2010). Roberts (2000) has proven that, as would seem intuitive, children in Hawaii were raised speaking the native languages of their parents. In addition, the idea that Hawaiian Creole English was created from mere fragments of English input would seem invalidated by the fact that, as Roberts documents, the children were being schooled in English.

However, Bickerton's central claim, that children created Hawaiian Creole English, was itself also confirmed by Roberts (2000), invalidating earlier claims that the creole had been created by adults before this generation (e.g., Goodman 1985). Even though the students, exposed to schoolroom English daily, hardly encountered "insufficient" English input, documentation confirms that they did create a creolized English on the basis of the semi-structured pidgin variety that their parents of various origins spoke. That the creole was created as a badge of identity rather than as a response to a linguistic emergency does not belie that a language was born that did not exist before the 1890s. Hawaiian Creole English is, in fact, the only creole empirically documented to have been created by children. The generation who created the creole, as well as the one before them who spoke the pidgin variety, were still living in the 1970s, allowing Bickerton to elicit data from them. Most creoles emerged centuries too early for such interviews to be possible, while written records of them began after the creoles had formed, and were created outside of settings where newspaper accounts could give hints of the nature of their genesis, as was the case for Hawaiian Creole English.

Furthermore, while many of the features of Bickerton's bioprogram are predictable from second-language acquisition or language universals in a general sense, the cross-creole contrast between realized and unrealized complementation, indicated in (12) by *go* rather than the unrealized complementizer *fo*, has never been explained.

12.6.3 The Creole Prototype Hypothesis

McWhorter's Creole Prototype hypothesis (2005: 9–37, revised in 2011: 29–61) has been as controversial as Bickerton's, paralleling the latter in treating creoles as less accreted manifestations of the language faculty than older ones—a basic proposition that most creolists tend to resist.

McWhorter argues that if a language combines three features, it is a creole: (1) little or no inflectional affixation, (2) little or no use of tone to distinguish monosyllabic lexical items or grammatical distinctions, and (3) little or no opaque derivation-root combinations along the lines of English's *understand*. McWhorter argues that these features are predictable from full languages that emerged relatively recently from pidgins, having not existed for long enough a time to undergo the processes that create the three prototype features.

McWhorter proposes that the prototype is expressed to degrees, depending on the creole's exposure to source languages and how closely related the source languages were, but that the prototype is expressed most purely among creoles that developed in the absence of their lexifiers, thus expanding into full languages grammar-internally in the fashion that the Australian and Melanesian "pidgins" are documented to have done.

While some creolists have concurred with McWhorter that creoles constitute a synchronic class of language (e.g., Bakker, Daval-Markussen, Parkvall, and Plag 2011), McWhorter's hypothesis has occasioned considerable resistance (cf. Aboh and Smith 2009). Observations that some creoles have inflectional affixes (e.g., Berbice Creole Dutch), contrastive tone (e.g., Papiamentu Creole Spanish), or ample noncompositional derivation (e.g., Haitian) can be subsumed under the clinal aspect of the framework. However, many analysts suspect unfalsifiability, under which possibly any exception in a creole to the prototype ideal can be dismissed as static (although cf. McWhorter 2012b), while any other language argued to have the prototype's features can be classified itself as a creole (as McWhorter has done for colloquial Indonesian dialects). Common is a conclusion that while creoles' displaying the three "prototype" features is indeed connected to their social history, older languages may happen to settle upon those three features by chance as well.

Equally controversial has been McWhorter's corollary proposal that as languages born from pidgins, creoles qualify as the least grammatically complex languages (albeit in themselves, quite complex, as all languages are) (McWhorter 2005: 38–71). Plag (2003) is an especially wide-ranging collection charting the complexities in various creoles, a type of analysis especially common since the turn of the millennium.

The Prototype idea and the complexity claim together constitute what McWhorter terms a hypothesis of Creole Exceptionalism, a term coined by DeGraff (2003) and later adopted by McWhorter. While only some creolists wholeheartedly agree with McWhorter's claims, most would agree that the debate over them since the late 1990s has stimulated a welcome amount of grammatical analysis of creoles, which before then had focused more on a certain few features of interest to variationist studies of Anglophone Caribbean creole continua and Bickerton's bioprogram proposal, such as copulas, tense-mood-aspect markers, and serial verbs.

The study of creole phonology, in particular, has advanced considerably, in studies such as Nikiema and Bhatt (2003), Good (2004), and Klein (2011). One general conclusion from this work is that creoles' inventory of sounds, while never extremely large in the cross-linguistic sense, are also far from the world's smallest, given that various older languages (most notably the Polynesian) have far fewer phonemes than any known creole (Klein 2011). Also, creole phonology is not less complex overall than that of older languages, such that creoles could not be identified as a class on its basis.

12.7 THE STATE OF THE ART

12.7.1 Current Consensus

Current consensus on creole genesis among most scholars would seem to be that second-language acquisition by adults significantly impacts creole genesis, to a greater degree in morphology and syntax than phonology. Veenstra (2003) and Plag (2008a, 2008b) provide especially concentrated arguments on morphology and syntax with detailed reference to second-language acquisition literature. Especially relevant here and in other work such as Owens' (to appear) on Nubi Creole Arabic is Klein and Perdue's (1997) description of second-language learners' documented Basic Variety stage, characterized by (1) mainly lexical categories with few function words, (2) a small number of syntactic, semantic, and pragmatic constraints determining most of the arrangement of the utterance, and (3) little if any functional inflection.

Here, creole studies would seem to have returned to a focus on second-language acquisition that took hold briefly in the late 1970s and early 1980s (e.g., Anderson 1983) but lost attention in favor of the controversy over the Language Bioprogram Hypothesis. However, given how few schools of creole genesis have ever philosophically dismissed second-language acquisition as a key factor in creole genesis, it could be argued that the consensus on its role was less frayed than neglected, amidst discussion of more inherently provocative propositions.

Few if any working creolists doubt, also, that substrate transfer tended to be ample amidst the genesis process.

12.7.2 Diachronic Relationships

An issue often touched upon in creole studies with little conclusion is the diachronic relationships between creoles of like lexical base. Hancock (1986) was first to argue that the English-lexifier creoles of the Caribbean stem from a single West African pidgin ancestor. McWhorter (2005: 199–224) presented an alternative version of this scenario, relocating the origin of the ancestor and the sequence of diachronic relationships, while Baker (1999), tracing the original language to Barbados or St. Kitts, made a careful case with extensive lexical comparisons. Equivalent interpretations of French creole data were more common in the past than subsequently, by scholars such as Goodman (1964), Alleyne (1971), and Hull (1979), although McWhorter (2000: 146–194) concurred.

That this approach has never made lasting inroads in creole studies is due in part to the fact that the intersection between diachronic linguistics and creole studies has been thin, for contingent reasons of academic culture (it was less true before the 1970s). However, some have questioned how languages could travel across vast distances, usually with what appears to have been small numbers of people, and survived, especially in the face of vast new populations of slaves in the new colony (cf. Bickerton 1998). Also, a commitment to charting substrate influence, in light of Bickerton's notorious denial of the same, ultimately encourages a localist focus, given the effort involved in uncovering source languages in even one location, as opposed to several related ones.

However, such localist accounts are hardly incompatible with simultaneously charting direct lines of descent between idiosyncratically similar creoles such as the English-lexifier Caribbean ones and the West African coastal ones such as Krio and Nigerian "Pidgin." The question as to transportability is well taken, but various studies have shown that pidgins and even creoles can survive great distances and considerable sociohistorical disruptions. Schwegler's work (e.g., 1993) shows that Palenquero Creole Spanish harbors Portuguese-derived lexical and grammatical items that are unexplainable except as the result of some of the slaves who created the language speaking a Portuguese pidgin born on the West African coast. Meanwhile, Jacobs (2012) has confirmed that Papiamentu was born of the transportation of Upper Guinea Creole Portuguese to the New World.

REFERENCES

Aboh, Enoch O., and Umberto Ansaldo. 2007. The role of typology in language creation. In *Deconstructing Creole*, edited by Umberto Ansaldo, Stephen Matthews, and Lisa Lim, 39–66. Amsterdam: John Benjamins.

Aboh, Enoch O., Umberto Ansaldo, and Norval Smith (eds.). 2009. *Complex Processes in New Languages*. Amsterdam: John Benjamins.

Adamson, Lilian, and Norval Smith. 1995. *Pidgins and Creoles: An Introduction*, edited by Jacques Arends, Pieter Muysken, and Norval Smith, 219–32. Amsterdam: John Benjamins.

Alleyne, Mervyn. C. 1971. Acculturation and the cultural matrix of creolization. In *Pidginization and Creolization of Languages*, edited by Dell Hymes. Cambridge: Cambridge University Press.

Alleyne, Mervyn. C. 1980. *Comparative Afro-American*. Ann Arbor: Karoma.

Anderson, Roger, ed. 1983. *Pidginization and Creolization as Language Acquisition*. Rowley, MA: Newbury House.

Baker, Philip. 1999. Investigating the origin and diffusion of shared features among the Atlantic English creoles. In *St. Kitts and the Atlantic Creoles*, edited by Philip Baker and Adrienne Bruyn, 315–364. London: University of Westminster Press.

Baker, Philip, and Chris Corne. 1982. *Isle de France Creole: Affinities and Origins*. Ann Arbor, MI: Karoma.

Baker, Philip, and Pieter Mühlhäusler, 1990. From business to pidgin. *Journal of Asian Pacific Communication* 1: 87–115.

Bakker, Peter, Aymeric Daval-Markussen, Mikael Parkvall, and Ingo Plag. 2011. Creoles are typologically distinct from non-creoles. *Journal of Pidgin and Creole Languages* 26: 5–42.

Baptista, Marlyse. 2000. Verb movement in four creole languages: A comparative analysis. In *Language Change and Language Contact in Pidgins and Creoles*, edited by J. McWhorter, 1–33. Amsterdam: John Benjamins.

Bauer, A. 1974. *Das melanesische und chinesische Pidginenglisch*. Regensburg: Hans Carl.

Bentley, W. Holman. 1887. *Dictionary and Grammar of the Kikongo Language*. London: Trübner.

Bickerton, Derek. 1981. *Roots of Language*. Ann Arbor, MI: Karoma.

Bickerton, Derek. 1984. The Language Bioprogram Hypothesis. *Behavioral and Brain Sciences* 7: 173–188.

Bickerton, Derek. 1998. A sociohistoric examination of Afrogenesis. *Journal of Pidgin and Creole Languages* 13: 63–92.

Bloomfield, Leonard. 1933. *Language*. New York: Henry Holt.

Boretzky, Norbert. 1983. *Kreolsprachen, Substrate und Sprachwandel*. Wiesbaden: Harrassowitz.

Carden, Guy, Morris Goodman, Rebecca Posner, and William Stewart. 1990. A 1671 French Creole text from Martinique. Paper presented at the Society for Pidgin and Creole Linguistics meeting, New York.

Chaudenson, Robert. 1974. *Le lexique du parler créole de la Réunion*. Paris: Champion.

Chaudenson, Robert. 1992. *Des îles, des hommes, des langues*. Paris: L'Harmattan.

Corne, Chris. 1981. A re-evaluation of the predicate in Ile-de-France creole. In *Generative Studies on Creole Languages*, edited by Pieter Muysken, 103–124. Dordrecht: Foris.

Crowley, Terry. 1990. *From Beach-la-Mar to Bislama: The Emergence of a National Language in Vanuatu*. Oxford: Clarendon Press.

DeCamp, David. 1971. Introduction: The study of pidgin and creole languages. In *Pidginization and Creolization of Languages*, edited by D. Hymes, 13–39. Cambridge: Cambridge University Press.

DeGraff, Michel. 1994. To move or not to move? Placement of verbs and object pronouns in Haitian Creole and in French. *Papers from the 30th Meeting of the Chicago Linguistic Society*, edited by Katherine Beals et al., 141–155. University of Chicago: Chicago Linguistics Society.

DeGraff, Michel. 1999. Creolization, language change, and language acquisition: An epilogue. In *Language Creation and Language Change*, edited by Michel DeGraff, 473–543. Cambridge, MA: MIT Press.

DeGraff, Michel (ed.). 1999. *Language Creation and Language Change*. Cambridge, MA: MIT Press.

DeGraff, Michel. 2001. On the origin of creoles: A Cartesian critique of Neo-Darwinian linguistics. *Linguistic Typology* 5(2–3): 213–310.

DeGraff, Michel. 2003. Against creole exceptionalism. *Language* 79: 391–410.

Deprez, Viviane. 1999. The roots of negative concord in French and French-Lexicon creoles. In *Language Creation and Language Change*, edited by M. DeGraff, 375–427. Cambridge, MA: MIT Press.

Ferguson, Charles F., and Charles DeBose. 1977. Simplified registers, broken languages and pidginization. In *Pidgin and Creole Linguistics*, edited by Albert Valdman, 99–129. Bloomington: University of Indiana Press.

Foley, William A. 1988. Language birth: The processes of pidginization and creolization. In *Linguistics: The Cambridge Survey*, Vol. IV, edited by Frederick J. Newmeyere, 162–183. Cambridge: Cambridge University Press.

Gilbert, Glenn G. (ed.). 1987. *Pidgin and Creole Languages*. Honolulu: University of Hawaii Press.

Good, Jeff. 2004. Tone and accent in Saramaccan: Charting a deep split in the phonology of a language. *Lingua* 114: 575–619.

Goodman, Morris. F. 1964. *A Comparative Study of Creole French Dialects*. The Hague: Mouton.

Goodman, Morris F. 1985. Review of Bickerton (1981). *International Journal of American Linguistics* 51: 109–137.

Goodman, Morris F. 1987. The Portuguese element in the American creoles. In *Pidgin and Creole Languages*, edited by G. Gilbert, 361–405. Honolulu: University of Hawaii Press.

Hagemeijer, Tjerk, and Ota Ogie. 2010. Edo influence on Santome: Evidence from verb serialization and beyond. In *Creoles, Their Substrates, and Language Typology*, edited by Claire Lefebvre, 37–60. Amsterdam: John Benjamins.

Hancock, Ian. 1986. The domestic hypothesis, diffusion and componentiality: An account of Atlantic Anglophone creole origins. In *Substrata vs. Universals in Creole Genesis*, edited by Pieter Muysken and Norval Smith, 71–102. Amsterdam: John Benjamins.

Hancock, Ian F. 1987. A preliminary classification of the Anglophone Atlantic creoles with syntactic data from thirty-three representative dialects. In *Pidgin and Creole Languages*, edited by G. Gilbert, 264–333. Honolulu: University of Hawaii Press.

Hancock, Ian F. 1994. Componentiality and the creole matrix: The Southwest English contribution. In *The Crucible of Carolina: Essays in the Development of Gullah Language and Culture*, edited by Michael Montgomery, 95–114. Athens: University of Georgia Press

Holm, John. 1988. *Pidgins and Creoles*, Vol. I. Cambridge: Cambridge University Press.

Holm, John. 1989. *Pidgins and Creoles*, Vol. II. Cambridge: Cambridge University Press.

Holm, John. 2004. *Languages in Contact*. Cambridge: Cambridge University Press.

Hull, Alexander. 1979. On the origin and chronology of the French-based creoles. *Readings in Creole Studies*, edited by Ian F. Hancock, Edgar Polomé, Morris Goodman and Bernd Heine, 201–216. Ghent: E. Story-Scientia.

Hymes, Dell. 1971. *Pidginization and Creolization of Languages*. Cambridge: Cambridge University Press.

Jacobs, Bart. 2012. *The Origins of a Creole: The History of Papiamentu and Its African Ties*. Berlin: Mouton de Gruyter.

Keesing, Roger M. 1988. *Melanesian Pidgin and the Oceanic Substrate*. Palo Alto, CA: Stanford University Press.

Klein, Thomas. 2011. Typology of creole phonology. *Journal of Pidgin and Creole Languages* 26: 155–193.

Klein, Wolfgang, and Clive Perdue. 1997. The basic variety. *Second Language Research* 13: 301–347.

Koefoed, Geert, and Jacqueline Tarenskeen. 1996. The making of a language from a lexical point of view. In *Creole Languages and Language Acquisition*, edited by Herman Wekker, 119–138. Berlin: Mouton de Gruyter.

Lefebvre, Claire. 1998. *Creole Genesis and the Acquisition of Grammar*. Cambridge: Cambridge University Press.

Lefebvre, Claire, and Anne-Marie Brousseau. 2002. *A Grammar of Fongbe*. Berlin: Mouton de Gruyter.

LePage, Robert B., and David De Camp. 1960. *Jamaican Creole*. London: Macmillan.

Ludwig, Ralph, Sylviane Telchid, and Florence Bruneau-Ludwig (eds.). 2001. *Corpus créole*. Hamburg: Helmut Buske.

McWhorter, John H. 2000. *The Missing Spanish Creoles*. Berkeley: University of California Press.

McWhorter, John H. (ed.). 2000. *Language Change and Language Contact in Pidgins and Creoles*. Amsterdam: John Benjamins.

McWhorter, John H. 2005. *Defining creole*. New York: Oxford University Press.

McWhorter, John H. 2012a. Case closed? Testing the Feature Pool Hypothesis. *Journal of Pidgin and Creole Languages* 27: 171–182.

McWhorter, John H. 2012b. The nature of argument: Is the Creole Exceptionalism Hypothesis Dead? *Journal of Pidgin and Creole Languages* 27: 379–389.

Migge, Bettina M. 2003. *Creole Formation as Language Contact: The Case of the Surinamese Creoles*. Amsterdam: John Benjamins.

Mintz, Sidney W. 1971. The socio-historical background to pidginization and creolization. In *Pidginization and Creolization of Languages*, edited by D. Hymes, 481–498. Cambridge: Cambridge University Press.

Mufwene, Salikoko S. 1996. The Founder Principle in creole genesis. *Diachronica* 13: 83–134.

Mufwene, Salikoko S. 1997. Jargons, pidgins, creoles, and koines: What are they? *The Structure and Status of Pidgins and Creoles*, edited by Arthur K. Spears and Donald Winford, 35–70. Amsterdam: John Benjamins.

Mufwene, Salikoko S. 2001. *The Ecology of Language Evolution*. Cambridge: Cambridge University Press.

Mufwene, Salikoko S. 2009. Restructuring, hybridization, and complexity in language evolution. In *Complex Processes in New Languages*, edited by Enoch Aboh and Norval Smith, 367–400. Amsterdam: John Benjamins.

Mühlhäusler, Pieter. 1997. *Pidgin and Creole Linguistics*. London: University of Westminster Press.

Nikiema, Emmanuel, and Parth Bhatt. 2003. Two types of R deletion in Haitian Creole. In *Phonology and Morphology of Creole Languages*, edited by I. Plag. Tübingen: Niemeyer.

Owens, Jonathan. 2014. The morphologization of an Arabic creole. Journal of Pidgin and Creole Languages 29: 232–98.

Parkvall, Mikael. 2000. *Out of Africa: African Influences in Atlantic Creoles*. London: Battlebridge.

Plag, Ingo (ed.). 2003. *Phonology and Morphology of Creole Languages*. Tübingen: Niemeyer.

Plag, Ingo. 2008a. Creoles as interlanguages: Inflectional morphology. *Journal of Pidgin and Creole Languages* 23: 114–135.

Plag, Ingo. 2008b. Creoles as interlanguages: Syntactic structures. *Journal of Pidgin and Creole Languages* 23: 307–328.

Plag, Ingo. 2011. Creolization and admixture: Typology, feature pools, and second language acquisition. *Journal of Pidgin and Creole Languages* 24: 89–110.

Roberts, Sarah J. 2000. Nativization and the genesis of Hawaiian Creole. In *Language Change and Language Contact in Pidgins and Creoles*, edited by John H. McWhorter, 257–300. Amsterdam: John Benjamins.

Romaine, Suzanne. 1988. *Pidgin and Creole Languages*. London: Longman.

Romaine, Suzanne. 1992. *Language, Education and Development: Urban and Rural Tok Pisin in Papua New Guinea*. Oxford: Clarendon Press.

Sankoff, Gillian, and Suzanne Laberge. 1980. On the acquisition of native speakers by a language. In *The Social Life of Language*, edited by G. Sankoff, 195–209. Philadelphia: University of Pennsylvania Press.

Schwegler, Armin. 1993. Rasgos (afro-)portugueses en el criollo del Palenque de San Basilio (Colombia). In *Homenaje a José Perez Vidal*, edited by Carmen Díaz D. Alayón, 667–696. La Laguna, Tenerife: Litografía A. Romero S. A.

Schwegler, Armin. 1998. El palenquero. In *América negra: Panorámica actual de los estudios lingüísticos sobre variedades criollas y afrohispanas*, edited by Matthias Perl and Armin Schwegler, 219–291. Frankfurt: Vervuert.

Siegel, Jeff. 2008. *The Emergence of Pidgin and Creole Languages*. New York: Oxford University Press.

Singler, John V. 1990. *Pidgin and Creole Tense-Mood-Aspect Systems*. Amsterdam: John Benjamins.

Tryon, Darrell T., and Jean-Michel Charpentier (eds.). 2004. *Pacific Pidgins and Creoles: Origin, Growth and Development*. Berlin: Mouton de Gruyter.

Veenstra, Tonjes. 1996. *Serial Verbs in Saramaccan*. The Hague: Holland Academic Graphics.

Veenstra, Tonjes. 2003. What verbal morphology can tell us about creole genesis: The case of French-related creoles. In *Phonology and Morphology of Creole Languages*, edited by Ingo Plag, 293–313. Tübingen: Niemeyer.

CHAPTER 13

··

MIXED LANGUAGES, YOUNGER LANGUAGES, AND CONTACT-INDUCED LINGUISTIC CHANGE

··

NORVAL SMITH AND ANTHONY P. GRANT

13.1 INTRODUCTION: THE NATURE OF YOUNGER LANGUAGES

··

THIS chapter has three themes. First there is a consideration of various types of recently created language, including mixed languages. We follow this with an attempt at a classification of various types of mixed language. In the course of this chapter we will also address the question of mixed pidgins and mixed creoles.

We use the term *younger languages* to refer to those types of language that are commonly referred to by the names of *pidgins, creoles*, and last but not least, *mixed languages*.[1] (There are also mixed pidgins and mixed creoles.) By this we mean that their creation has been claimed to have taken place fairly abruptly at some moment in the "historical" past—and as such can be dated with some degree of precision. By "historical," note that we do not refer solely to the past as recorded by means of documentary evidence, and therefore interpretable by historians, but also the past insofar as it is reconstructible by other means, not least by the techniques of historical linguistics itself.

To start with a case with a clear *terminus non ante quem*, we can say that the Saramaccan language, a mixed English and Portuguese-lexifier creole spoken by one of the so-called Bush Negro or Maroon tribes in the South American country of Surinam,

··

[1] NSHS first suggested this name during the discussion at the 1996 Westminster Creolistics Workshop. We would like to thank Carlos Benítez-Torres for the provision of useful insights and data.

is a younger language which must have developed in the period after 1665, because the combination of linguistic and historical factors making this development possible only existed in Surinam after 1665 (cf. Price 1983; Smith 1987, 2000a, 2000b; McWhorter 1998).

The English component is to be explained by the fact that Surinam was an English colony from 1651 to 1667, when it came into the possession of the Dutch under the terms of the treaty of Breda. Most of the English inhabitants who did not leave Surinam upon the transference of ownership in 1668 left the country in 1671 or 1675. We claim that Sranan must have been creolized in the 1660s, since it forms one of the components of Saramaccan, which itself must have been creolized around 1680 (when it was known as *Dju-Tongo* in its non-maroon manifestation; Smith 1987), while the English language was for all effects and purposes physically removed from the scene by 1675 (see also McWhorter 1998 for a similar reasoning). An earlier date than 1665 is unlikely for reasons discussed in Smith (2000a). As for the Portuguese component, in 1665 a group of Sephardic Jews—presumably mostly refugees via Cayenne from Dutch-conquered Northeast Brazil, which had been reconquered by Portugal/Spain in 1655 (this point of view is defended in Smith 1999; but cf. Arends 1999; Ladhams 1999a, 1999b)—were admitted to Surinam, and bought plantations on the middle Suriname River, where they came to form a major component of the white population at the end of the seventeenth century (see also for additional supporting evidence Smith 2000a, 2000b).

We also know from Price's innovative historical reconstruction (Price 1983), based on the Saramaccan secret traditional knowledge of early maroon times,[2] that the senior clan of the Saramaccan tribe, the Matjáu clan, was formed as a result of a mass escape in 1690 from a plantation on the Suriname River belonging to a Portuguese Jew by the name of Imanuël Machado (see further Smith 2000b). The mixed nature of the creole reflects the mixed English and Portuguese linguistic environment in which it developed.

Compare this with the case of English (see Beal and Faulkner, Chapter 16 in this volume, and references therein; see also Baugh and Cable 2012). The historically sophisticated but linguistically unsophisticated member of the general public might well claim that English also came into being at a definite moment in time (i.e., in the mid-fifth century AD when the English traditionally arrived in what later became England. However, this is just the approximate moment of immigration of the members of a number of apparently related Germanic tribes into southeastern Britain. In fact, the name *English*, or *Anglisc*, was brought from the Angeln peninsula in Eastern Schleswig, in what is now northern Germany. However, the whole question of the name of the language—or of any language, for that matter—is just a chimera. The names of languages are virtually completely irrelevant as far as the languages themselves are concerned, though of course it does tell us something about the language community, and their perception of their own language. Many languages do not have any particular name anyway. Before English was called English it was no doubt known by some other name, and if politico-historical fate had decided otherwise, it might well have ended up being called Saxon or Jutish. This would not necessarily have affected

---

[2] And in this case, also based on the etymology of Saramaccan clan names.

the form of the language to any great degree, but it might have had some implications for the shape of the standard form.

English is one of the members of the Western branch of the Germanic language family. It is assumed in turn that all the West Germanic languages (Scots, West Frisian, North Frisian, East Frisian, Dutch, German, etc.) developed from a single parent language, termed Proto-West Germanic by historical linguists. In turn, Proto-West Germanic descended from Proto-Germanic, which in itself represents an outgrowth of a Proto-Indo-European parent language, spoken perhaps around 5000 BC, probably in what is now Southern Russia. Further than this, we cannot go with any certainty, at least in the present state of our knowledge, although from time to time claims are made regarding the wider relationships of the Indo-European language family, for instance that it might be related to the Uralic, or Afro-Asiatic families. None of these claims has been satisfactorily demonstrated as yet. English has been influenced by other West Germanic languages, notably Dutch-Flemish and also Low German, by North Germanic languages (specifically Old Norse), and by non-Germanic languages.

Younger languages such as Saramaccan then, have not, we can reasonably claim, developed by means of the same familiar slow processes of language change as languages like English. Those languages that have developed by means of such processes we may refer to as *elder*[3] languages—their moment of creation is not precisely datable, and may for all we know go back to the beginnings of human speech, which may reasonably be assumed to date from the emergence of Homo sapiens about 100,000 years ago. We can of course say little about this, because the normal techniques of historical linguistics do not allow us to trace relationships back beyond 5,000–10,000 years ago or so with any degree of confidence. Before this point, patterns of relationship end up submerged beneath the noise caused by various types of change—both internal changes, such as lexical replacement, phonological merger, and typological restructuring, and external changes due to language contact.

It is of course quite likely that many, or even very many, of the languages that we now have no reason to assume to belong to the class of younger languages may in fact belong to this class. However, the processes that formed them may well no longer be recoverable, simply because of the considerable interval of time that has passed subsequent to their formation. This means that we have no means of distinguishing such languages from members of the class of elder languages.

Note also that the present state of our knowledge concerning the internal linguistic historical relationships of the language families that are currently recognized or claimed to exist, and of the histories of their speakers, remains very spotty and imprecise for the majority of the languages known to be spoken or to have been spoken on our planet. In other words, we not only lack knowledge of the depth of language history, we also lack knowledge of the breadth. In the lack of such more precise

---

[3] Note that there is no suggestion of any difference in status, functionality, intrinsic value or quality by this use of the terms *younger* and *elder*. Age has no particular virtue when it comes to languages, and also has nothing to do with the length of time a language has been written.

knowledge we will often not (or at least not yet) be able to determine the exact status of an individual language with any confidence. However, in this case, as our knowledge of the "breadth" increases, we have at least the potential to identify additional languages whose development turns out to be linguistically aberrant in some sense. If the history of the group using the language in question can also be shown to involve unusual circumstances, then we have an additional, albeit circumstantial, piece of evidence for hypothesizing that the language is a *younger* language. Even if confirmatory historical evidence is lacking, we will place greater importance on the linguistic evidence, and assume that in such a case that we have a possible candidate for the status of *younger* language. We use the word *candidate* with reason—we cannot of course claim omniscience.

We know, as already stated, that in general the more normal processes of language change proceed gradually, and not instantaneously. The term *gradual change* implies a number of different things. Phonological change, for instance, seems usually to proceed in smallish steps, whether viewed in articulatory or acoustic terms, rather than in great leaps and bounds. Phonological change moreover does not affect every susceptible word at the same time—the more frequently occurring items in the lexicon are affected first, so that the effect induced by a change proceeds slowly through the lexicon (Wang 1969; Liao 1976). Also, not all members of a speech community will be simultaneously affected by such a change. So even apparently fairly "instantaneous" changes, such as neutralization of a phonological contrast, still proceed gradually in these other senses. Also involved in phonological change is the existence of significant optionality—old and new forms coexist for a period. This offers the potential for one of the options to be hijacked as a sociolinguistic marker. Morphological change and syntactic change also tend to operate in fairly subtle jumps, typically with competing forms, (native speaker) analyses, and constructions overlapping for periods of many years.

This seems not to have been the typical route followed by the changes that produced the languages and dialects dealt with here. In the cases we know more about, the transition to the new system seems rather to have been of an abrupt nature. Additionally, for those cases where we know anything of the sociohistorical circumstances of the group(s) involved, it appears that in most cases this abrupt linguistic transition has been accompanied by an abrupt change in social (and sociolinguistic) environment.

It is not our intention here to examine the processes by which pidgin and creole languages arise (see Parkvall, Chapter 11, and McWhorter, Chapter 12, in this volume). Although there is considerable disagreement about the processes by which creole languages come into existence, and a fair bit of disagreement about how pidgins get elaborated, the discussion about these two types has been quite extensive. In particular, the literature on creolization has grown immensely over the last twenty years.

Here we will restrict the further discussion to languages that are undisputedly mixed to a large and obvious degree. This will not exclude reference to mixed pidgins and creoles. In particular, the existence of two fairly well-known "mixed" creoles—Saramaccan (of Surinam) and Berbice Dutch (of Guyana)—will receive attention. These two mixed creoles are so different in character—from each other, as well as from other creoles—as to require explanation.

We start with a more general picture, Tables 13.1 and 13.2 provide information on a range of these languages. These tables cover Ma'á (Tanzania), Media Lengua (Ecuador), Mednyj Aleut (Siberia), Michif (Manitoba and North Dakota), Saramaccan, Berbice Dutch, an three Songhay-Berber mixed languages of the Azawagh valley in Mali: Tagdal, Tadaksahak, and Tasawaq. In the rows in Table 13.2 the component that has provided the most material is listed before those that have provided fewer examples of the phenomenon under investigation.

L2 speakers of creoles can manage in their own languages, but they remain pidgins because they lack native speakers, the factor that is a sine qua non of *creole languages* or *creole*s. (L1 speakers of creoles need not be monolingual in their creole, though, and earlier generations of creole-speakers probably contained a very high proportion of people who also spoke one or more of the languages that shaped the creoles, in addition to maybe other languages.)

The lexica of *creoles* may (but need not) be mixed and contain components from two or more languages, or they may be more uniform, but their structures echo many (but not all) the morphosyntactic, semantic, and pragmatic features of the languages that the ancestors of the creators of the creoles had spoken. In a mixed creole (MC) such as Saramaccan, most of the function words and morphemes with predominantly grammatical roles derive from English via Sranan, as does much of the rest of the basic vocabulary. But there is also a large amount of Portuguese basic and less basic vocabulary (some shared with Sranan), many words of Kikongo and Gbe origin (many but by no means all of them non-basic), and additional lexicon from Dutch (this mostly brought into Saramaccan together with elements from Sranan), which this time serves as an adstrate.

Mixed languages (Bakker and Muysken 1994; Meakins 2013) arise in general under conditions of bilingualism, when groups attempt to define, redefine, retain, or even regain their ethnic status. This often results in (a degree of) language mixture. In Bakker and Mous (1994), this is referred to as *language intertwining*. In mixed pidgins, mixed creoles, and mixed languages, we may also find a proportion of lexical elements of unknown origin.

It is clear that the "plain" mixed languages referred to in section 13.2.2.1 must have arisen under conditions of bilingualism, and must have been spoken next to unmixed languages. Common sense would suggest that all mixed languages arise in a situation of symbiosis, in coexistence with unmixed languages.

A living example of the kind of situation envisaged can be found in Mbugu of Tanzania (Mous 2003), where two languages are spoken side by side—one an unmixed Bantu language—Normal Mbugu (practically identical to Pare)—and the other a mixture of Bantu grammar and diverse but partly Cushitic lexical material—*Inner Mbugu* (also known as *Ma'á*). Mous now thinks that some of the Cushitic material is inherited from the former language of the Ma'á, while the rest is a more recent accretion (Mous 2003). He suggests that the Southern Cushitic language Gorwaa is the likeliest source of much of the Ma'á material, though components from other Cushitic languages, plus Digo and other Bantu languages, and from Nilo-Saharan

Table 13.1 Strata in Some Stable Mixed Languages and Mixed Creoles

	Ma'á	Media L	Mednyi A.	Michif	Berbice D.	Saramaccan	Tagdal	Tadak	Tasawaq
Overall lexicon	Mixed: Bantu, West Rift, Eastern Cushitic, Maasai	85%–90% Spanish; rest Ecuadorian Quechua	Predominantly Attuan Aleut; some Russian	French, Plains Cree, many English loans	Dutch, Eastern Ijo, Arawak and Guyanese	English, Portuguese, Dutch, Kikongo, Gbe	75% Berber, depend-ing on domain	75%–80% Berber, depending on domain	65% Song hay
Swad-list lexicon (223-item list)	West Rift Cushitic predominates; Bantu and Maasai elements	Predominantly Spanish	Almost all Aleut	52% Cree; 47% French, 1% English	60% Dutch, 35% Eastern Ijo	50% English, 35% Portuguese. 15% Gbe, Loango Bantu, Wayana, Dutch, other	47% Berber, 48% Songhay	49.5% Berber, 48% Songhay	61% Song, 34% Berber
Segmental phonology	Tanzanian Bantu with three "exotic" phonemes /x ɬ ʔ/	Quechua with some Spanish phones	Aleut plus Russian sound sin Russian words	Cree in Cree part, French in Fr. Part	Broadly Dutch	Gbe	Berber for Berber part, Songhay for Songhay	Berber for Berber component, Songhay for Songhay	Berber for Berber component, Songhay for Songhay component
syllabic phonology	Bantu; only open syllables	Hispanicized Quechua (CC-, etc)	Aleut and Russian elements Largely Intact	Cree and French parts intact	Dutch	Gbe	Berber, Songhay components intact	Berber and Songhay components intact	Berber and Songhay components intact
Nouns	Etymologically mixed	Mostly Spanish	Aleut (rare Russian nouns)	Overwhelmingly French	Various	Various	Mixed, depend-ing on domain	Mixed, depending on domain	Mostly Songhay, depending on domain
Noun morphology	Pare Bantu	Quechua	Aleut	French	Eastern Ijo	None	Berber, Songhay	Berber, Songhay	Berber, Songhay
Verbs	Etymologically mixed	Mostly Spanish	Aleut, some Russian	Cree	Various	Portuguese, English	Berber and Songhay	Both Berber and Songhay	Berber and Songhay
Finite Verbal morphology	Pare Bantu	Quechua	Russian	Cree	Eastern Ijo	English – free morphs	Songhay	Songhay	Songhay
Non-finite VM	Pare Bantu	Spanish	Aleut	Cree	None	None	NA	NA	NA
Adjectives – source; structure	Mixed; nominal	Mostly Spanish; verbal	Aleut' verbal	French; Cree stative verbs	Various; verbal	Various; verbal	Berber / Songhay; nominal	Berber/ Songhay; nominal	Mostly Songhay; nominal

Table 13.2 Sources of Some Non-Content Items in Stable Mixed Languages and Mixed Languages

		Ma'á	MdAl	ML	Michif	Saram	BerbD	Tag	Tad..	Tasaw
1a	Personal pronouns	Cush	Eu,Al	Sp(Q)	Cr	En;Gv	Du,El	S	S	S
1b	Possessive pronouns	Cush	(Al)	Sp	Fr(cr)	En;Gb	Du;El	S	S	S
1c	Possession: NP of NP	Cush	Ru	Q	F	En	Du	B	B	B
2	Numerals	Cush	Ru	Wp	Fr	En:Du	Du	s/b	s/b	s/b/a
3	Other prenominal quantifiers	Cush	Ru;Al	Q	Fr,Cr	En;Du	Du;El	0	0	0
4	Quantifier nouns	Cush	Al	Sp	Fr,Cr	En	Du	B	b	B
5	Relative pronouns	Ban?	Ru	Q	Fr.Cr	En	Du	S	S	S
6a	Reflexives	Ban?	Al	?	Cr	En	Du	B	B	0/s
6b	Reciprocals	?	Al	?	Cr	Du	Du	B	B	0s
6c	Indefinite pronouns	?	Ru	?	?	En	Du	0	0	0
7	Interrogative forms	Cush	Al	Sp	Cr	En;Gb	Du	B	B	S
8	Quantifying adverbs	?	Ru;Al	Sp;Q	Cr;Fr	En;Po	Du	0	0	0
9	Place adverbs	Unk	Al	Sp	Cr	Po	Du;El	B	B	B
10a	Time adverbs	Unk	Ru	Sp	Cr(Fr)	En	Du;El	B	B	B
10b	Phasal adverbs	Unk	Al	Sp	Cr	Po	Du	0	0	0
11a	Abstract adpositions	Ban	?	Q	Cr,Fr	En;Po	El;Du	S/B	S/B	S/B
11b	Place adpositions	Ban	Ru	Q(Sp)	Cr,Fr	En;Po	Du	S	S	S
11c	Time adpositions	Ban?	Ru	Q	Cr,Fr	En;Po	Du	S	S	S
12	Dative word	Ban?	Ru	Q	Cr,Fr	En	Du	S	S	S
13a	Instrumental word	Ban	Ru	Q	Fr	En	Du	S	S	S
13b	'and' linking NPs	Ban	Ru	Sp;Q	Fr	En	Du	S	S	S
14a	'and' linking VPs	Ban	Ru	Sp;Q	Cr.Fr	En	Du	S	S	S
14b	Or	Cush?	Ru	?	Fr	En	Du	S	S	S
14c	But	Cush	Ru	?	Cr	Du	Du	B	B	S
14d	Other coordinators	Ban	Ru	Sp;Q	Cr,Fr	En	Du	S/B	S/B	S/B
15a	Most complementisers	Ban?	Ru	Sp	Cr	En	El	?	?	?
15b	If	Cush	Ru;Al	Sp	Cr	En	Du	?	?	?
15c	Because	Ban	Ru	Sp;Q	Fr	En	Du	B	B	B
15d	In order to	?	Ru	?	Cr	En	Du;El	0	0	0
15e	When (temporal)	?	Ru	?	Cr	Du	Du	S	S	S
15f	Other subordinators	?	Ru	Sp	Cr.Fr	Du?	Du	S/B	S/B	S
16a	Copulas	Ban	Al	Q	Cr,Fr	En	Du	S	S	S
16b	To have	Cu+Ban	Al	Sp	Cr	En	Du	S	S	S
17a	INFL morphs	Ban	Ru	Q	Cr	0	Du;El	S	S	S
17b	Modal verbs	Ban?	Ru	?	Cr.Fr	Du	Du;El	0	0	0
18	Negative particles	Ban	Ru;Al	Sp;Q	Cr,Fr	En	Du;El	S	S	S

(continued)

Table 13.2 Continued

		Ma'á	MdAl	ML	Michif	Saram	BerbD	Tag	Tad..	Tasaw
19a	Definite article	0	0	0	Fr	En	Du	0	0	0
19b	Indefinite articles	0	0	Sp	Fr	En	Du	0	0	0
19c	demonstratives	Cush	Al(Ru)	Sp	Cr	En	Du	S	S	S
19d	Other determiners	Cush	Al	Sp	Cr,Fr	En	Du	0	0	0
20	Plural NP markers	Ban	Al	Q	Cr,Fr	0	El	B	B	S/B
21	Question particle	0	Ru	0	Cr<Fr	0	0	S/B	S/B	S/B
22	Deictic adverbs	Unk	Ru	Sp	Cr	Po	El+Du	?	?	?
23	Manner adverbs	Unk	Ru	Sp	Cr	En	El	B	B	?
24	Focus particle	?	Ru	Q	?	Gb	?	S	S	S

The numerically dominant component is listed first; hyphens indicate converged forms a compound form, and brackets mark alternatives for the same form.

Maasai can also be found. Furthermore, the language is being continuously influenced by Swahili, the dominant language in Tanzania.

13.2.1 Types of Mixed Language

Mixed languages (ML) can be classified in a number of ways. This chapter adopts a sociolinguistic approach, in which mixed languages are classified according to the social situation in which the linguistic components coexisted when the ML arose, and also whether this situation remained in force later: were speakers of the ML in touch with one component language later on, or with more than one, or with none?

Four types can be recognized on sociolinguistic grounds. *Plain mixed languages* are opposed by *symbiotic mixed languages*, which include three types: *U-turn mixed languages*, *neo-ethnic symbiotic mixed languages*, and *assimilatory symbiotic mixed languages/core-periphery languages*. Using other approaches (e.g., structural criteria), other divisions could be made. For instance, one could see whether the sources of verbal morphology are the same as those of nominal morphology, or whether verb stems and noun stems come from the same source, or whether a language is primordial or else is a development from a preexisting mixed language, or indeed whether it is endogenous (native to the area) or whether it has been brought in from another location. Meakins (2013), the most recent general account of mixed languages, takes a structural approach. She divides mixed languages into *lexicon-grammar languages* (such as Angloromani, Old Helsinki Slang with its Scandoromani component in Finnish, and others), *structural mixes* (for example, Michif, Ma'á, and Gurindji Kriol), and *converted languages*. These last languages have used the processes of metatypy (Ross 1996; see also Ross, Chapter 5 in this volume) to restructure the syntactic typology (and often other subfields) of one language so as to resemble more closely that of another, though not necessarily also borrowing much lexicon from that language.

Mixed languages are not a new phenomenon. Canaano-Akkadian, combining West Semitic Canaanite and East Semitic Akkadian, is attested from the fourteenth century BC (Izre'el 2005). Our records of Island Carib Men's Pidgin, a roster of Karin'a lexical items used in an Igneri (Arawakan) framework, dates from the seventeenth century (Hoff 1994). But most mixed languages have been attested in the twentieth and twenty-first centuries, and many of them must have arisen within the past two centuries. Van Gijn (2009) is a good introduction to issues in the phonologies of some mixed languages, while discussions of mixed languages include Thomason (ed. 1997), Bakker and Mous (eds. 1994), Grant (2001), Matras and Bakker (eds. 2003), Meakins (2013), and Velupillai (2015), and most recently Bakker (2017).

13.2.2.1 *Plain Mixed Languages (M)*

One type of mixed language encountered is that where the grammar of one of the languages originally spoken in the group in question is combined with the content-words of another language known to the group. The resultant language replaces the original ethnic language(s), and is in general the only language spoken. This type we will refer to as (plain) *mixed languages* (M).

Obviously creoles may also be mixed (MC), as in the case of Saramaccan, or Angolar (Maurer 1995). These are cases that, we would argue, involved first creolization, and then subsequent language-mixing, with a small component of item of unknown origin in both cases. Berbice Dutch of Guyana may also be a case of this, although it does not easily fit into such a typology—or indeed into any typology. One recently documented creole that is mixed, and which has been documented from more than one generation of speakers, is Yilan Creole, the Japanese lexifier creole with an important Atayal lexical component that is spoken in Yilan County, Taiwan (Chien and Sanada 2010; Qiu 2015), which is currently absorbing more lexicon from local Chinese languages and replacing some Japanese and Atayal forms with Chinese loans.

The question of how these languages have developed does not permit a unique answer. It has been claimed (Myers-Scotton 1993) that some of these languages result from code-mixing between two languages that became so extensive that children finally failed to realize that there were two target-languages involved, and began to apply language-learning strategies as if there were only a single language. Some of the more disastrous[4] anecdotes concerning children being brought up bilingually may derive from cases where the parents went in for a lot of code-shifting between their two mother-tongues, and the child learned what he or she thought was a real language, but which in fact was not. In such cases the child would be the only speaker of the newly created mixed language—hardly a viable linguistic community, of course!

---

[4] The disaster is only in the parents' perception, of course. The child goes on to learn one or both languages correctly anyway.

Despite the fact that such languages can only have arisen in conditions of symbiosis involving two languages, we will distinguish these cases where such languages no longer coexist in a language community with one or both of their parents, these plain mixed languages, from those where this is still the case. The latter we will refer to as *symbiotic mixed languages* and treat in the next section.

13.2.2.2 *Symbiotic Mixed Languages (MS)*

Situations where a mixed language coexists with one or both parents we will term *symbiotic mixed languages* (MS). This type combines the grammatical structure of one language, and a lexicon (or partial lexicon[5] of basic words) from another source. What distinguishes such languages from plain mixed languages is that they comprise a mixture of material from two linguistic sources, and that one or both of these parent languages are *still spoken*. These languages are in other words in a *symbiotic* relationship with the MS. Such languages represent in a very real sense the parents of the symbiotic mixed language.

One may argue with Thomason and Kaufman (1988: 10) in their characterization of this type of relationship as *non-genetic*. The difference from the normal linguistic genetic situation is that the normal situation involves *one* parent—here we have potentially *two*. So we can speak of one-parent languages—the normal situation—and two-parent languages. This symbiosis must, as we claimed earlier, have pertained originally in the case of all mixed languages, so that we can regard all plain mixed languages as deriving from symbiotic mixed languages, too. However, precisely because the language involves *two* parents, it will qualify as a type of younger language. This situation represents a radical break with the preceding linguistic situation, such that a speaker of only one of the two component parent languages would not be able to understand the mixed language. The development of the language cannot be explained in terms of one of its parents alone.

A typical early result of such language mixture is that two communities share some geographical area—one speaking the mixed language, and the other one of the two component languages. Sometimes the mixed language continues to coexist with both parents.

An MS is thus by definition never the only language of its speakers. Often an MS will have the function of a *secret language*. There is variation within the class of MSs as to the age at which the MS is acquired. In some cases, like those of Inner Mbugu and (English) Shelta, the secret in-group language of the Irish Travellers that derives part of its non-English lexicon from phonologically modified Irish words, the MS is acquired more or less simultaneously with the other language used by the group—Pare Mbugu and English, respectively, in the examples given. In other cases, such as in the case of Angloromani, this acquisition takes place at a later age—during childhood, at puberty or initiation, or even later still. In general there would seem to be some correlation

---

[5] The size of these partial lexica of basic words varies from dozens to at least several hundred in number.

between the age at which the MS is acquired and the size of the lexicon originally derived from the second language (or at least not derived from the first language). The earlier the acquisition of the MS, the larger the specific vocabulary associated with it seems to be. Media Lengua of Ecuador (Muysken 1997; Gómez Rendón 2008) falls into this category. But one can acquire a second complete language after puberty, as happened in Gaelic-speaking parts of Scotland where previously monolingual Gaelic-speaking boys went to Lowland farms in order to learn English.

It may be the case that an MS is used in the same range of domains as the first language of the speakers. This depends on the function of the MS, on which see the discussion later in this chapter. Depending on the size of the lexicon not derived from the second language, a greater or lesser use may have to be made of compounds and circumlocutions to be able to talk about the same topics the dominant language is capable of dealing with, within the domain of usage. In other cases, more or less free use is made of the lexical resources of the dominant language. We might distinguish between these two conditions as *closed* and *open*, respectively. Inner Mbugu could be described as closed, in that, in general, ordinary, unaltered Pare Mbugu words will not be employed. Modern forms of Shelta, on the other hand, could be described as open. Where the language lacks words, the other language in symbiosis (in the case of Shelta, normally some form of English) will be called upon to make good this lack. This has led to the claim that such open symbiotic mixed languages are not really *languages* but just *registers*. On this point, see Smith (2000c) and now Smith and Hinskens (forthcoming).

Note that what we have in cases of languages with two components in their basic vocabulary—*open mixed languages*—is rather different from the classic case of what we have termed the *plain mixed language* where one language is, as it were, responsible for the morphosyntax, while another supplies the lexicon. The variation in the proportion of the lexicon that is supplied by one of the two contributing languages might be explained, as we have suggested earlier, by the age at which the mixed language is acquired. Note that it must always be the case—at the moment of creation of the mixed language—that we have some sort of bilingual situation. Otherwise we would not be able to speak of "mixing" languages.

So a mixed language acquired simultaneously with the original language of the group will probably tend to have a clearer separation into a morphosyntactic component supplied by one language, and a lexical component supplied by another. Precisely, a language acquired early on would seem to have more potential of becoming the only language of the group. So in the case of "(Irish) Gaelic Shelta"—now probably no longer spoken—we hear of cases of individuals who preferred to use it as their only language wherever possible (Macalister 1937). In most cases it was used next to English (and sometimes also Irish). Shelta was acquired at an early age.

Angloromani, on the other hand, is acquired around the age of puberty, and has a smaller replacive lexicon (derived from the unmixed Romani language) of around 800 words (Acton and Kenrick 1984; see also Matras 2010). This rather has the sole function of a "secret" language. The normal primary language of the group is English. Note that in this case the sentence structures used are apparently less complex in Angloromani than in English (Acton and Kenrick 1984), although in both cases the grammatical structure utilized is that of English.

13.2.2.2.1 "NEO-ETHNIC" SYMBIOTIC MIXED LANGUAGES (MSN)

The sociolinguistic explanation for the creation of new languages does not always have to be the same. For instance, in the case of Media Lengua, which is spoken in at least two locations in Ecuador, and which is a mixture of Spanish and Quechua, the correct explanation for its creation may have been that the speakers of the Amerindian language sought a means of marking a perceived new ethnic, or neo-ethnic, identity. They had achieved a unique (from a local point of view) social identity, and had a need to find a means of marking this linguistically (Muysken 1997; Stewart 2012). In some cases, then, the particular social identity of the group might require that the members of the group acquire a linguistic code that can function as a group-marker, in that it is different from those used by other groups with whom they interact. Callahuaya of Bolivia (Muysken 1997a), with its Quechua structure and mixed Puquina-Aymara-Quechua-Spanish lexicon (also containing quite a few items of unidentified origin) is another example of this.

Other examples of mixed languages of this sort are Michif of Canada and North Dakota (Bakker 1997, which draws in some measure on sentences in Laverdure and Allard, ed. Crawford 1983; see also Rhodes 1977), which is incidentally the only one of these languages to have native speakers researching their own language, Mednyj Aleut of the Commander Islands, Siberia (Golovko and Vakhtin 1991), most of the languages surveyed in Bakker and Mous (1994), some more recently attested ones such as Light Warlpiri (O'Shannessy 2005, 2012), and a group of so-called Northern Songhay languages—including Tasawaq, Tadaksahak, Tagdal of Niger and Mali and Korandje of western Algeria (Christiansen-Bolli 2010; Souag 2015; Benítez-Torres and Grant 2017). Northern Songhay languages retain Songhay structures and basic lexicon, but the Songhay component in this lexicon may only amount to about 300 items. Languages of the Qinghai-Gansu Sprachbund (Janhunen 2007; Janhunen et al. 2008), often heavily Mongolicized or Tibetanized varierties of Mandarin Chinese, may also fall into this category.

This sociolinguistic type we will refer to as *neo-ethnic symbiotic mixed languages*. The MSN has essentially L_1 phonology and phonetics. Table 13.2 indicates the origins of elements of various form classes in several of these languages. They do not all conform to a single structural type. Accounts of Tagdal and Light Warlpiri are presented in this volume (Chapters 18 and 26).

In the following we illustrate the nature of the mixing of Quechua and Spanish elements in Media Lengua, using a framework that can handle the facts of change in prominence of one language or another within the various strata. I compare here three subsets of grammar—lexicon, syntax, and phonology. In more detail, *lexicon* comprises (a) the basic lexicon (BLEX)—the Swadesh 100- or 200-word lists; (b) primary lexicon (PLEX)—other non-specialized general vocabulary; (c) cultural lexicon (CLEX)—culturally specific vocabulary; and (d) derivational morphology

(DMOR)—the derivational processes used in the formation of new words. *Syntax* consists of (a) (free) function words (FWD); (b) inflectional morphology[6] (IMOR); and (c) syntax (SYNT). In *phonology* we find (a) phonological structures and phenomena (PHNG); (b) phonemic systems (PHNM); and (c) phonetics (i.e., allophones) (PHNT). The major component is in **bold**. The first language listed is L1, the second is L2.

As we can see in Table 13.3, Spanish influence is largely lexical, with some influence at the more lexical end of grammar (i.e., function words, in particular). Further, the main feature is the expansion of the phonemic system, which in fact is not a specific language-mixture phenomenon (as in Media Lengua), as an expansion of this system is found in many Amerindian languages, from Mexico through to South America, which have borrowed many Spanish lexical items. However, the Spanish vowels /e/, /o/ do not seem to appear in Ecuadorean Quechua, for example (Muysken and Stark 1978).

Meakins's category of "structural split" mixed languages (Meakins 2013) is important here, and it requires that we make a distinction that the Table 13.3 does not capture. Michif, Mednyj Aleut, and Gurindji Kriol derive their finite verbal morphology from one language (Plains Cree, Russian, and Northern Territory Kriol, respectively), and their nominal morephology from another (French, Attuan Aleut, and Gurindji, respectively). The origin of verbal stems aligns with morphology in the case of Michif, but less regularly so in the case of the others (though Gurindji Kriol has a great number of Kriol-Gurindji lexical synonyms, not least in its basic lexicon; Meakins 2011). Most Mednyj Aleut verbs derive from Aleut, as do most basic nouns.

Inflectional morphology has long been held to be the part of a language that is most immune to being borrowed. This is especially held to be the case with aspects of verbal inflectional morphology. Roughly speaking, in terms of the categories that are overtly expressed, the morphological (and semantic) typology of the mixed language verb group—and the set of categories encoded in this verb group—is often that of the language that provided the verbal morphology (Grant 2015). The fact that in many languages a verb (usually containing many morphemes) can constitute a one-word sentence, and that a sentence in such a language can be coextensive with a verb group, supports this likelihood. Thus Media Lengua marks evidentials because Quechua does. The categories marked in the Ma'á verb are those found in Pare. Mednyj Aleut uses Russian inflectional and other morphs (including a productive negative proclitic) in an agglutinative verbal structure which resembles that of Attuan Aleut (it is known that many of the people who constituted the original population of Copper Island were non-Aleuts who spoke Russian only as a second language; Golovko and Vakhtin 1990), and Michif marks inverse relations between persons and uses multiple medial stems where necessary in its verbal morphosyntax because Cree can and does.

---

[6] One assumes that inflectional morphology has more to do with grammatical/syntactic structure than with *lexical items* as such. This is in line with much modern thinking about inflectional morphology.

Table 13.3 Quechua and Spanish Elements in Media Lengua

Media Lengua			MSN Neo-ethnic Symbiotic Mixed Language	
BLEX	Quechua	>	Spanish	[Basic Lexicon]
PLEX	Quechua	>	Spanish	[Primary Lexicon]
CLEX	Quechua	>+	Spanish	[Cultural Lexicon]
DMOR	**Quechua**	>+	(Spanish)	[Derivational Morphology]
FWD	**Quechua**	>+	Spanish	[Function Words]
IMOR	**Quechua**			{Inflectional Morphology]
SYNT	**Quechua**			[Syntax]
PHNG	**Quechua**			[Phonological Structures/Rules]
PHNM	**Quechua**	>+	Spanish	[Phonemic System]
PHNT	**Quechua**			[Phonetics]

Notes: ">" indicates *total replacement*; ">+" indicates *partial replacement/accretions.*
The language names in bold type indicate the strands present in the mixed language.

13.2.2.2.2 "U-TURN" SYMBIOTIC MIXED LANGUAGES (MSU)

There is one problem with the relation between the mixed language and the assumed original language of the group concerned. In rare clear cases of MSNs such as Media Lengua, the original morphosyntax is basically preserved, while virtually the whole lexicon is replaced or "relexified" with items from the second, *intrusive* or *replacive*, language, which became known, possibly only imperfectly, to the group. In other cases, such as (Inner) Mbugu, however, the morphosyntax has been supplied by the intruding Bantu Pare. Similarly, in the case of Angloromani (Table 13.4), the morphosyntax is supplied by the intruding language (from the point of view of the Romani ethnic group), namely English. How is this to be explained?

The likeliest explanation that has been given so far for these cases where the only thing that is preserved from the original language is lexical items is that the group language was in the process of dying and was being replaced by the dominant language. The native morphosyntax was the first thing to go, and lexical items the last, but there was sufficient social reason for preserving a separate linguistic identity.

This situation resulted in the preservation (or lack of loss) of a complete or partial second (replacive) lexicon, which could then only be used in the context of the morphosyntax of the intruder-language. The original language morphosyntax had already been lost. The reason for this could of course be the same as that for creating a new mixed language—the ethnic identity of the group (here of course it is rather the preservation of an old identity in a changed environment), or the practical need for a secret language. This has been referred to as the "U-turn" by Thilo Schadeberg (Schadeberg 1994). This type we will therefore refer to as *U-turn symbiotic mixed languages*.

Table 13.4 Romani and English Elements in Angloromani

Angloromani			MSU	U-Turn Mixed Language
BLEX	Romani			
PLEX	Romani	>+	English	>+ uncertain
CLEX	Romani			
DMOR	Romani	>+	English	
FWD	Romani	>+	English	
IMOR	Romani	>	English	
SYN	Romani	>	English	
PHNG	Romani	>	English	
PHNM	Romani	>	English	
PHNT	Romani	>	English	

The MSU has essentially L2 phonology and phonetics. Angloromani is an example of this; beginning in the early nineteenth century, materials on Angloromani contain (in addition to Indic-derived Romani elements and old loans found among Northern Romani languages) a small number of 'cant' words of uncertain origin that are not normally part of modern everyday English. In terms of lexical depletion (including the retention of a small number of function words), Angloromani somewhat resembles Shelta, though the typically Shelta lexicon is not the result of direct transmision of a portion of vocabulary from a prior language now extinct.

13.2.2.2.3 "SECRETIVE" SYMBIOTIC MIXED LANGUAGES (MSS)

A third type of language appears to be illustrated by many secret languages used by particular castes and guilds—often nomadic, and frequently marginal in societal terms. These basically keep the morphosyntax native to the original ethnic language, and varying amounts of the original lexicon. There is a replacive element whose source is often difficult to identify. Lexical elements may be borrowed from other marginal groups, phonologically transformed from the original form, given a novel or specialized meaning, or constructed anew from the basic morphological building blocks available from the native language. This type we will call the *secretive symbiotic mixed language*. Here we do not so much have "mixing" of languages, but rather the "mixing" of a (replacive) lexical component with the native lexicon.

The primary requirement of such languages is to prevent the members of the larger society within which they function from understanding what the speakers say to each other. For instance, the *(Southwestern) Bargoens*[7] of Zeele in Belgium had 44% different

---

[7] *Bargoens* is the original secret language of Dutch "Travellers," usually referred to in Dutch as Woonwagenbewoners ('caravan-dwellers'). Non-Dutch lexical elements are usually of uncertain origin, though some forms of Bargoens may contain elements from Sinto (German Romani), Hebrew, and Yiddish.

Table 13.5 Non–Dutch and Dutch Elements in Bargoens

Bargoens (Tienen)		MSS Symbiotic Mixed Language	
BLEX	Dutch (Flemish)	>+	Bargoens
PLEX	Dutch (Flemish)	>+	Bargoens
CLEX	Dutch (Flemish)	>	Bargoens
DMOR	Dutch (Flemish)	>+	Bargoens
FWD	Dutch (Flemish)	>+	(Bargoens)
IMOR	Dutch (Flemish)		
SYN	Dutch (Flemish)		
PHNG	Dutch (Flemish)		
PHNM	Dutch (Flemish)		
PHNT	Dutch (Flemish)		

words as compared to Dutch in terms of the Swadesh 100-word list, while that of Roeselare had 25% different.[8] The apparent difference between these two cases may well be largely due to the variable quality of our sources—it is notoriously difficult to do "fieldwork" on the languages of such marginal groups, at least while they are living, functional systems. As we have indicated earlier, it is the fact that the *basic* vocabulary—which goes beyond the Swadesh list, of course—is different that makes these languages so difficult to understand, and qualifies them in fact for the status of *separate* languages. Details for Tienen Bargoens (Pottefertaal), together with a sample sentence, are presented in Table 13.5.

The threshold of separate language status for related "normal" languages has been generally considered to be around 80% in terms of the Swadesh 100-word list (i.e., about a 20% difference in basic vocabulary between the languages), while proportion of lexicon from another language can go up to 90% (http://papuaweb.org/dlib/bk/pl/B31/03.pdf). Certain more specialized portions of the lexicon will also be different, of course, but specialized technical vocabularies do not confer on their users a separate linguistic identity as such, as we have remarked earlier. Here the distinction between L1 and L2 does not strictly arise. The grammar can generally be regarded as L1, sometimes with minor differences. Grammatical structures used tend to be simpler, more regular, with less allomorphy.

The coexistent systems—those of the unmixed language and the MSS—are frequently referred to in such cases as different *registers* of a single language. We should regard this as an erroneous viewpoint in cases where there is no mutual intercomprehension of basic messages. While the term *register* is suitable for varieties of speech used within

---

[8] We derive the data for these counts from data supplied by Moormann (1932–1934).

one community under differing conditions of formality, or used by different subgroups within one community, whereby one subgroup utilizes a specialized technical/cultural vocabulary that may not be (completely) familiar to another subgroup, if simple utterances are obscure, then it is difficult to see the systems involved as representing the same language. This applies even in cases where much of the two systems utilized in the two languages is the same.

This variant of Bargoens, is like most, incompletely documented. Two major strands of the lexicon tend to be replaced—the most basic words and technical words to do with the Dutch Travellers' (former) way of life. The grammatical structure is largely, and the phonology is wholly, that of the local Dutch dialect.

The case of Shelta, the secret language of Irish Travellers, is of great interest. A historical examination of various recorded forms of Shelta reveals that the *secret* vocabulary element (some of which is Irish backslang, but much of which is of unknown origin) behaves as if it were a separate unit that is capable of changing its host-language. This is the kind of thing that has encouraged some authors to regard these languages as registers. In fact, all it means is that the main symbiotic language has ceased to be Irish and has become English. Obviously, the speakers themselves are aware of which elements belong to the Shelta lexicon, and which do not. In Irish Shelta the everyday lexicon is Shelta, while the morphology, syntax, function words, and phonology are Irish. In Scottish Gaelic Shelta these categories are furnished by Scottish Gaelic, and in the Shelta used in Britain and now also in Ireland, English provides these elements.

13.2.2.2.4 "ASSIMILATORY" SYMBIOTIC MIXED LANGUAGES (MSA)

A fourth type of MS arises when a language of lower status borrows so massively at so many levels from another language of higher status with which it is in intimate contact that a new language effectively comes into being. Basic, and not just peripheral, words are borrowed. Grammatical and semantic patterns are also transferred into these languages (Grant 2002, 2002a, 2004). The question might be asked whether these languages are not just the same as our neo-ethnic type of mixed language, or alternately whether this category doesn't just represent languages that are in the process of dying. This is a moot point, though a structural (rather than sociolinguistic) case could be made to keep the distinction. But symbiotic mixed languages may not always remain in symbiosis with any of their components.

Such situations seem to arise when a linguistic group with lower status wishes to reduce the distance to a socially higher-regarded linguistic group. But we cannot judge, for lack of information, whether assimilation is the prime mover in (for instance) the case of younger generations' use of Linxia Baonan/Bao'an, a Mongolic language of western China that has been profoundly influenced by Chinese (Buhe and Liu 1982). Yet in this case the borrowing does appear to be on an extreme scale. Importantly, the entire younger generation group seems to be involved, not just a socially distinct segment of the population. Only time will tell whether we in fact have here a delayed form of language death. For this fourth type, the term *assimilatory symbiotic mixed*

Table 13.6 Division of Elements in Baonan/Bao'an

(NEW) LINXIA BAONAN		MSA		
BLEX	Baonan	>+	Chinese	
PLEX	Baonan	>+	Chinese	
CLEX	Baonan?			
DMOR	Baonan			[Chinese hardly has DMOR]
FWD	Baonan	>+	Chinese	
IMOR	Baonan			[Chinese hardly has IMOR]
SYN	Baonan			
PHNG	Baonan	>+	Chinese	
PHNM	Baonan	>+	Chinese	
PHNT	Baonan	>+	Chinese	

language suggests itself, at least as a provisional label. This corresponds to Anthony Grant's "core-periphery" mixed languages (see Benítez-Torres and Grant 2017). The MSA will have L1 phonology and phonetics.

13.3 IDENTIFYING UNDETECTED MIXED LANGUAGES

The problem of identifying mixed languages that have previously gone unrecognized as mixed languages is not a simple one. The mere fact of a language or dialect having a large body of loanwords does not necessarily qualify it as a mixed language.

For instance, the English-lexifier creole Ndyuka, spoken in Surinam, has hundreds of lexical items deriving from African languages—in particular, Gbe and Kikongo (or Loango Bantu) languages (Huttar and Huttar 1994). We do not, however, classify this creole as being a mixed language. Why not? Because the African-derived lexical items represent, for the most part, concepts that are culturally specific—implements, religious concepts, cooking terms, some flora and fauna, and so on—for which colloquial English has no equivalent terms because they are not found in the areas where English developed. The most basic vocabulary is, however, overwhelmingly English.

English itself is another clear case. Scheler (1977) claimed that more than half the English vocabulary in the *Oxford Advanced Learners' Dictionary* (Hornby 1974) is either borrowed or constructed from non-native elements. Once again, however, the basic vocabulary is overwhelmingly of native origin, as is all the inflectional morphology, and furthermore in running speech the great majority of tokens belong to the inherited vocabulary, indicating that the commonest lexical items are also inherited ones.

Quite a different state of affairs is seen in a creole spoken in the neighboring country to Surinam, the former Dutch possession of Guyana. Berbice Dutch has a majority of basic vocabulary from Dutch, but around 30% is from Eastern Ijo, a language or group of languages spoken in the Niger Delta region in Nigeria. Eastern Ijo has also influenced the morphosyntax of Berbice Dutch in various ways. For this reason, its genesis must be explained as resulting from a mixture (Smith, Robertson, and Williamson 1987; Kouwenberg 1993) of Eastern Ijo and a Dutch source, possibly a Dutch-lexifier pidgin or creole, as some forms in BD, such as *maskono* 'to clean' < Dutch *maak schoon* 'make clean' suggest (Adrienne Bruyn to Anthony Grant, personal communicatin, 2000).

It should be possible, then, to identify languages as being mixed that have a significant "strange" (and as yet unetymologized) component in their basic vocabulary. Candidates for this status might be, for instance, some of the languages spoken by the so-called Negritos or now Black Filipinos of the Philippines (Reid 1994). These languages have between 17% and 35% of their total vocabulary that cannot be explained in terms of Proto-Austronesian or Proto-Malayo-Polynesian, although the percentages are much lower for basic vocabulary in this particular case. The speakers of these languages are also physically distinct from the mass of the Philippine population, and are assumed to represent the original population of the Philippines. The "non-Proto-Austronesian" element consists partly of Austronesian words with unexpected developments (remnants of an early pidgin phase?), and partly of non-Austronesian words. These are assumed by Reid to have belonged to creoles formerly spoken by the Negritos. Mixed languages would perhaps be more probable.

The problems of identifying mixed languages are compounded when the question of the internal structure of a large language family is only relatively poorly known. Things are made more complicated when there is also evidence of large-scale migration on the part of the speakers of some of the languages at various times in the past, creating numerous opportunities for language-contact phenomena to occur, not least the borrowing of lexical items. When this has taken place long enough ago, it may be virtually impossible to disentangle the various lexical layers.

There are probably many cases, mostly as yet undetected. One such relevant example might be the (presumed) Niger-Congo language Chamba Daka on the Nigeria-Cameroon borderlands, discussed in Boyd (1994). This is one of two languages used by various groups claiming to be ethnically Chamba. Despite the fact that Chamba Daka shares its largest lexical component with Chamba Leko, the other Chamba language, Africanists are now agreed that these two languages are not closely related at all. The shared ethnic consciousness is of comparatively recent date, resulting from migration by the Chamba Daka into the Chamba area. How this proceeded is only approximately known, but apparently each group adopted aspects of the other's ethnic identity. Chamba Leko has apparently borrowed extensively from Chamba Daka, but is clearly related to other languages spoken in the same area. Now, Chamba Daka is isolated in Niger-Congo terms. It has no obvious close relatives, and is situated near the geographical boundary between the Bantoid and Adamawa subgroups of Niger-Congo. Is Chamba Daka the only representative of a subgroup of Niger-Congo, much like Armenian is in Indo-European, as many of those involved in discussions of the structure of the Niger-Congo family seem to think, or is it in fact an old mixed language? In other words, is the fact that it has drawn words from two or more immediate linguistic sources the reason why its lexicon is statistically poorly relatable to any of the well-known subgroups of Niger-Congo? We should note that this problem applies in this case to the basic vocabulary.

Berbice Dutch, however, uses a subset of Eastern Ijo inflectional morphology—all the bound inflectional morphology that Berbice Dutch has—and much Ijo basic lexicon, to be found in all form-classes and in all semantic fields except the numerals. However, most of the basic lexicon and many features of the phonology derive from Zeeuws Dutch. Much of the cultural lexicon comes from Lokono/Arawak (the original language of many of the Bovianders, the Amerindian/African/European group who adopted Berbice Dutch), though much is Dutch, while further lexicon is taken from Dutch or from Guyanese Creole English, and there are a few dozen words of unknown origin. Much of the history of Berbice Dutch—but certainly not all of it—is documented within the language and probably nowhere else.

We may also note Kilen, a language of northern China, which, though not a creole as far as we know, blends elements from three Southern Tungusic languages (two of them Nanaic, the third Manchu; Hölzl 2017).

We may compare this with the analysis of levels of lexicon and structure in Saramaccan (McWhorter and Good 2012), a strongly mixed creole but not one in which there is a primary distinction between the sources of lexicon and morphosyntax. Although all the means of indicating grammatical subsystems, such as definiteness,

Table 13.7 Strata in Berbice Dutch

Berbice Dutch	P		as MC		later		
BLEX	E. Ijo	>+	Dutch				
PLEX	E. Ijo	>		>	compound/Dutch		
CLEX	E. Ijo	>+	Arawak?				
DMOR	E. Ijo	>		>	E. Ijo	>+	Guyanese
FWD	E. Ijo	>	few	>+	Dutch/E. Ijo	>+	Guyanese
IMOR	E. Ijo	>		>	E. Ijo		
SYN	E. Ijo	>		>	Universals/E. Ijo		
PHNG	E. Ijo						
PHNM	E. Ijo	>	reduced				
PHNT	E. Ijo						

Table 13.8 Strata in Saramaccan

Saramaccan			P		C	M
BLEX	African lgs.	>	English		>+Portuguese	
PLEX	African lgs.	>		>	compound	
CLEX	**African lgs.**			>+	Carib (Kari'nja and Tiriyo)	
DMOR	African lgs.			>	English [recon/Gbe]	
FWD	African lgs.	>	few	>	English[recon]; >+Portuguese/Gbe	
IMOR	African lgs.	>				
SYN	African lgs.	>		>	Universals >+	Gbe?
PHNG	**African lgs.**					
PHNM	**African lgs.**					
PHNT	**African lgs.**					

negation, and TAM, derive ultimately from English (via a kind of Proto-Sranan), the basic and other levels of lexicon are heavily mixed and there are Gbe elements even among grammical words (Smith 2015). Details are shown in Table 13.8.

13.4 CONCLUSION

The various categories of mixed and younger language can be encapsulated in Table 13.9.

This, though, is a generalization or a simplification. Pidgins, creoles, and mixed languages are all younger languages. Creoles largely create items of morphology through grammaticalization of elements from the chief lexifier. Mixed languages often take over the major or most frequently occurring morphological patterns of one language and use them with lexical items form another language, or languages. Not all pidgins or creoles are mixed languages, though all are younger languages. The lexicon of some mixed languages, such as Ma'á, is diverse or macaronic and may include a proportion of elements of unknown etymology; such languages can also innovate lexically and structurally. Both transfer of fabric and transfer of pattern can occur in the construction of mixed languages, and such languages may be open to influence from dominant later adstrate languages as well.

Several kinds of mixed languages can be identified on sociolinguistic grounds in the light of what is known about the evolution of the speech community for that language. These sociolinguistic types are, however, internally diverse in terms of the typology and nature of mixture of elements in the languages in each type. It is also possible that some languages that have been difficult to classify cladistically or genealogically may have started out as mixed languages in which the sources of structure and lexicon are

Table 13.9 Summative Table

	Parent of Grammar	Parent of Lexicon
Elder language	Language A	Language A
(Bickertonian) Creole	None	Language A (superstrate)
(Jargon) Pidgin	None	None
Mixed language	Language A	Language B

different. We know much about mixed languages, but only further investigation—and further documentation of mixed languages—will enable us to know more.

REFERENCES

Acton, Thomas, and Donald Kenrick. 1984. *Romani Rokkeripen to Divvus: The English Romani Dialect and Its Contemporary Social, Educational and Linguistic Standing.* London: Romanestan Publications.

Arends, Jacques, 1999. The origin of the Portuguese element in the Surinam creoles. In *Spreading the Word: Papers on the Issue of Diffusion of Atlantic Creoles,* edited by Magnus Huber and Mikael Parkvall, 195–208. London: University of Westminster Press.

Bakker, Peter. 1997. *'A Language of Our Own': The Genesis of Michif, the Cree-French Language of the Canadian Metis.* Oxford: Oxford University Press.

Bakker, Peter. 2013. Michif. In *Atlas and Survey of Pidgin and Creole Languages,* Vol. III: *Contact Languages Based on Languages from Africa, Asia, Australia, and the Americas,* edited by Susanne Maria Michaelis, Philippe Maurer, Martin Haspelmath, and Magnus Huber, 158–165. Oxford: Oxford University Press.

Bakker, Peter. 2017. Typology of mixed languages. In *Cambridge Handbook of Linguistic Typology,* edited by Alexandra Y. Aikhenvald, 217–253. Cambridge: CUP.

Bakker, Peter, and Maarten Mous. 1994. *Mixed Languages: 15 Case Studies in Language Intertwining.* Amsterdam: IFOTT.

Bakker, Peter, and Pieter Muysken. 1994. Mixed languages and language intertwining. In *Pidgins and Creoles: An Introduction,* edited by Jacques Arends, Pieter Muysken, and Norval Smith, 41–52. Amsterdam: John Benjamins.

Baugh, Albert C., and Thomas Cable. 2012. *A History of the English language.* 6th edition. London: Routledge.

Benítez-Torres, Carlos M., and Anthony Grant. 2017. On the origin of some Northern Songhay mixed languages. *Journal of Pidgin and Creole Languages* 32: 267–307.

Boyd, Raymond. 1994. *Historical Perspectives on Chamba Daka.* Cologne: Rüdiger Köppe.

Buhe and Liu Zhaoxiong (eds.). 1982. *Bao'anyu jianzhi.* Beijing: Renmin Chubanshe.

Chien Yuehchen and Sanada Shinji. 2010. Yilan Creole in Taiwan. *Journal of Pidgin and Creole Languages* 25: 350–357.

Chinuk Wawa Dictionary Project. 2012. *Chinuk Wawa: Kakwa nsayka ulman-tilixam łaska munk-kəmtəks nsayka / As Our Elders Teach Us to Speak It.* Seattle: University of Washington Press.

Christiansen-Bolli, Regula. 2010. *A Grammar of Tadaksahak, a Northern Songhay Language of Mali*. Köln: Rüdiger Köppe.

Golovko, Evgeni V., and Bikolai B. Vakhtin. 1990. Aleut in contact: The CIA enigma. *Acta Linguistica Hafniensia* 72: 97–125.

Gómez-Rendón, Jorge. 2008. *Mestizaje Lingüístico en los Andes. Génesis y Estrúctura de una lengua Mixta*. Quito: Abya-Yala.

Good, Jeff. 2009. Loanwords in Saramaccan, an English-based creole. In *Loanwords in the World's Languages: A Comparative Handbook*, edited by Martin Haspelmath and Uri Tadmor, 918–943. Berlin: De Gruyter.

Grant, Anthony. 2001. Language intertwining: Its depiction in recent literature and its implications for theories of creolization. In *Creolization and Contact*, edited by Norval Smith and Tonjes Veenstra, 81–111. Creole Language Library 23. Amsterdam: Benjamins.

Grant, Anthony. 2002. Fabric, pattern, shift and diffusion: what change in Oregon Penutian languages can tell historical linguists. In *Proceedings of the Meeting of the Hokan-Penutian Workshop, June 17–18, 2000, University of California at Berkeley. Report 11, Survey of California and Other Indian Languages*, edited by Laura Buszard-Welcher, 33–56. Berkeley: Department of Linguistics, University of California at Berkeley.

Grant, Anthony. 2002a. On the problems inherent in substantiating a linguistic area: The case of the Western Micronesian Sprachbund. Conference on Linguistic Areas, Convergence and Language Change, University of Manchester, November 22–23, 2002. *The Oxford Handbook of Areal Linguistics*, edited by Raymond Hickey.

Grant, Anthony. 2004. Review of Ruth King, *The Lexical Basis of Grammatical Borrowing: A Prince Edward Island Case Study* (Amsterdam: Benjamins, 2000). *Word* 54: 251–256.

Grant, Anthony. 2013. Chinuk Wawa. Atlas and Survey of Pidgin and Creole Structures, edited by Susanne Maria Michaelis, Martin Haspelmath, Magnus Huber and Philippe Maurer, Vol. 3: 149–157. Oxford: Oxford University Press.

Grant, Anthony. 2015. The selection of element sources in the verbal syntagms of some stable mixed languages. Paper presented at the MPI-EVA Department of Linguistics Closing Conference, May 1–3, 2015.

Hoff, Berend J. 1994. Island Carib, an Arawakan language which incorporated a lexical register of Cariban origin, used to address men. In *Mixed Languages: 15 Case Studies in Language Intertwining*, edited by P. Bakker and M. Mous, 161–168. Amsterdam: IFOTT.

Hölzl, Andreas 2017. Kilen: Synchronic and diachronic profile of a mixed language. Paper presented at Ludwig-Maximilians-Universität München, 24th LIPP Symposium, Munich, June 21–23, 2017, Language in Contact: Yesterday – Today – Tomorrow.

Hornby, Alfred Sidney. 1974. *Oxford Advanced Learners' Dictionary*. Oxford: OUP.

Huttar, George, and Mary Huttar. 1994. *Ndyuka*. London: Routledge.

Izre'el, Shlomo. 2005. *Canaano-Akkadian*. Munich: Lincom Europa.

Janhunen, Juha. 2007. Typological interaction in the Qinghai linguistic complex. *Studia Orientalia* 101: 85–102.

Janhunen, Juha, Marja Peltomaa, Erika Sandman, and Xiawudongzhuo. 2008. *Wutun*. Munich: Lincom Europa.

Kouwenberg, Silvia. 1993. *A Grammar of Berbice Creole Dutch*. Berlin; New York: Mouton de Gruyter.

Ladhams, John, 1999a. The Pernambuco connection? An examination of the nature and origin of the Portuguese elements in the Surinam creoles. In *Spreading the Word: Papers on the Issue of Diffusion of Atlantic Creoles*, edited by Magnus Huber and Mikael Parkvall, 209–240. London: University of Westminster Press.

Ladhams, John, 1999b. Response to Norval Smith. In *Spreading the Word: Papers on the Issue of Diffusion of Atlantic Creoles*, edited by Magnus Huber and Mikael Parkvall, 299–304. London: University of Westminster Press.

Lang, George, 2009. *Making Wawa*. First Nations Languages. Vancouver: University of British Columbia Press.

Laverdure, Patline, and Ida Rose Allard, edited by John C. Crawford. 1983. *The Michif Dictionary: Turtle Mountain Chippewa-Cree*. Winnipeg: Pemmican.

Liao, C.-C. 1976. *The Propagation of Sound Change: A Case Study in Chinese Dialects*. PhD dissertation, University of California, Berkeley.

Macalister, R. A. S. 1937. *The Secret Languages of Ireland: With Special Reference to the Origin and Nature of the Shelta Language, Partly Based upon Collections and Manuscripts of the late John Sampson*. Cambridge: Cambridge University Press.

Matras, Yaron. 2010. *Romani in Britain: The Afterlife of a Language*. Cambridge: Cambridge University Press.

Matras, Yaron. 2003. Mixed languages: Re-examining the structural prototype. In *The Mixed Language Debate*, edited by Peter Bakker and Yaron Matras, 151–176. Amsterdam: John Benjamins.

Maurer, Philippe. 1995. *L'angolar: Un créole afro-portugais parlé à São Tomé*. Hamburg: Buske.

McWhorter, John H. 1998. Identifying the creole prototype: Vindicating a typological class. *Language* 74: 788–818.

McWhorter, John H., and Jeff Good. 2012. *A Grammar of Saramaccan Creole*. Berlin: Mouton de Gruyter.

Meakins, Felicity. 2011. *Case-marking in Contact: The Development and Function of Case Morphology in Gurindji Kriol*. Amsterdam: John Benjamins.

Meakins, Felicity. 2013. Mixed languages. In *Contact Languages: A Comprehensive Guide*, edited by Y. Matras and P. Bakker, 159–228. Berlin: De Gruyter.

Meakins, Felicity, and Carmel O'Shannessy. 2012. Typological constraints on verb integrations in two Australian mixed languages. *Journal of Language Contact* 5: 216–246.

Moormann, Julianus Geoirg Maria. 1932–1934. *De geheimtalen*. Zutphen: Thema.

Mous, Maarten. 2003. *The Making of a Mixed Language: The Case of Ma'á/Mbugu*. Amsterdam: John Benjamins.

Muysken, Pieter. 1997. Media Lengua. In *Contact Languages: A Wider Perspective*, edited by Sarah Grey Thomason, 365–426. Amsterdam: John Benjamins.

Muysken, Pieter. 1997a. Callahuaya. In *Contact Languages: A Wider Perspective*, edited by Sarah Grey Thomason, 427–447. Amsterdam: Benjamins

Muysken, Pieter, and Louisa Stark. 1978. *Diccionario español-quichua, quichua-español*. Quito-Guayaquil: Museo del Banco Central.

Myers-Scotton, Carol. 1993. *Social Motivations for Codeswitching: Evidence from Africa*. Oxford: Oxford University Press.

O'Shannessy, Carmel. 2005. Light Warlpiri: A new language. *Australian Journal of Linguistics* 25: 31–57.

Pasch, Helma. 1997. Sango. In *Contact Languages: A Wider Perspective*, edited by Sarah G. Thomason, 209–270. Amsterdam: Benjamins.

Price, Richard. 1983. *First Time*. Baltimore, MD: The Johns Hopkins Press.

Qiu Peng. 2015. *A Preliminary Investigation of Yilan Creole in Taiwan: Discussing Predicate Position in Yilan Creole*. MA thesis, University of Alberta.

Reid, Lawrence A. 1994. Possible non-Austronesian lexical elements in Philippine Negrito languages. *Oceanic Linguistics* 33(1): 37–72.

Rhodes, Richard. 1977. French Cree: A case of borrowing. In *Actes du Huitième Congrès des Algonquinistes*, edited by William Cowan, 6–25. Ottawa: Carleton University.

Ross, Malcolm. 1996. Contact-induced change and the comparative method: Cases from Papua New Guinea. In *The Comparative Method Reviewed: Regularity and Irregularity in Language Change*, edited by Malcolm Ross and Mark Durie, 180–217. New York: Oxford University Press.

Schadeberg, Thilo C. 1994. KiMwani at the southern fringe of KiSwahili. In *Mixed Languages: 15 Case Studies in Language Intertwining*, edited by Peter Bakker and Maarten Mous, 239–244. Amsterdam: IFOTT.

Scheler, Manfred. 1977. *Der englische Wortschatz*. Tübingen: Narr.

Shnukal, Anna, and Lynell Marchese. 1983. Creolization of Nigerian Pidgin English: A progress report. *English World-Wide* 4: 17–26.

Smith, Norval S. H. 1987. *The Genesis of the Creole Languages of Surinam*. Unpublished D.Litt. dissertation, University of Amsterdam.

Smith, Norval S. H. 1999. Pernambuco to Surinam 1654–1665? The Jewish slave controversy. In *Spreading the Word: Papers on the Issue of Diffusion of Atlantic Creoles*, edited by Magnus Huber and Mikael Parkvall, 251–298. London: University of Westminster Press.

Smith, Norval S. H. 2000a. The linguistic effects of early marronnage. Paper presented at the Society for Caribbean Linguistics 13th Biennial Conference: Caribbean Linguistics: Past, Present and Future, University of the West Indies, Mona, Jamaica, August 16–20, 2000.

Smith, Norval S. H. 2000b. The creole languages of Suriname: Past and present. In *The Languages of Suriname*, Jacques Arends and Eithne Carlin. Leiden: KITLV Press.

Smith, Norval S. H. 2000c. Why caste languages are not registers. Unpublished manuscript.

Smith, Norval S. H. 2015. A preliminary list of probable Gbe lexical items in the Surinam creoles. In *Surviving the Middle Passage: The West Africa-Surinam Sprachbund*, edited by Pieter Muysken and Norval Smith, 463–475. Berlin: Mouton de Gruyter.

Smith, Norval S. H., and F. Hinskens. Forthcoming. Potteferstaal, Groenstraat Bargoens, and the development of "have" and "be" in the wider context of contact. To appear in a work edited by Norval Smith, Enoch Aboh, and Tonjes Veenstra.

Smith, Norval S. H., Ian Robertson, and Kay Williamson. 1987. The Ijo element in Berbice Dutch. *Language in Society* 16: 49–90.

Souag, Lameen. 2015. Explaining Korandje: Language contact, plantations and the trans-Saharan trade. *Journal of Pidgin and Creole Languages* 30: 189–224.

Stewart, Jesse. 2011. *A Brief Descriptive Grammar of Pijal Media Lengua and an Acoustic Vowel Space Analysis of Pijal Media Lengua and Imbabura Quichua*. MA thesis, University of Manitoba.

Thomason, Sarah Grey, ed. 1997. Contact Languages: a wider Perspective. Amsterdam/Philadelphia: John Benjamins.

Thomason, Sarah Grey, and Terrence Kaufman. 1988. Language Contact, Creolization and Genetic Linguistics. Berkeley and Los Angeles: University of California Press.

Van Gijn, Rik. 2009. The phonology of mixed languages. *Journal of Pidgin and Creole Languages* 24: 91–117.

Velupillai, Viveka 2015. *Pidgins, Creoles and Mixed Languages*. Amsterdam: John Benjamins.

Wang, William S.-Y., 1969. Competing sound changes as a cause of residue. *Language* 45: 9–25.

PART II

LANGUAGE CONTACT IN SEVERAL LANGUAGES

CHAPTER 14

LANGUAGE CONTACT IN CELTIC AND EARLY IRISH

RAYMOND HICKEY

14.1 THE CELTIC BACKGROUND

KNOWLEDGE of the Celts in prehistory is derived from (1) references to them in the works of classical authors (the earliest is Herodotus, fifth century BCE, from whom comes the term 'Celt': Greek *Keltoi* 'Celts', later Latin *Celtae*) and (2) archaeological remains (Laing 1979: 1–14; Schlette 1979: 13–43; Eska 2020).[1] There is an identifiable culture known after the location of Hallstatt in Austria. This was early Iron Age (ca. 800–450 BCE), while the late Iron Age is represented by the La Tène (ca. 450–100 BCE) stratum of Celtic culture, named after a site in Switzerland.

The coming of the Celts to Britain is difficult to date and can be placed in any period from a distant 1000 BCE when the Bronze Age Beaker Folk came to Britain to a more recent 600 BCE when the Iron Age people arrived in successive waves (Dillon and Chadwick 1967: 4). The last distinct wave of immigration is of the Belgae in the first century BCE (Caesar mentions that they crossed from northern Gaul to Britain). This gives the following picture for Celts and their coming to Britain.[2]

Pre-Iron Age settlers   ?
Hallstatt stratum   600 BCE →
La Tène stratum   300 BCE →
Invasions of the Belgae   100 BCE
Immigration from Gaul on Roman subjugation, 58–50 BCE

---

[1] On the recent influence of English on Irish, see Stenson (1993).
[2] For a good archaeological history of Celtic Britain, see Laing (1979), Chapters 2 and 3, on the stages up to the end of the Roman period.

The Celtic languages today comprise six languages with greater or lesser degrees of vitality. These fall into two main groups, traditionally known as *Brythonic* or *Brittonic* (P-Celtic in type) and *Goidelic* from the *Goídil*, modern *Gaels* (Q-Celtic in type).

P-Celtic　　　　　*Q-Celtic*
Welsh, Cornish, Breton　Irish, Scottish Gaelic, Manx

The distinction between P-Celtic and Q-Celtic is based on the realization of words with inherited IE /k(w)-/. In the Q-Celtic branch this is retained, whereas in the P-Celtic branch it is shifted to /p/.[3]

(1)　Irish　　Welsh
　　ceann　*pen*　　　　　'head'
　　mac　　*mab* (< /map/)　'son'
　　ceathair　*pedwar*　　'four' (IE *qetwar*)

Linguistic evidence for continental Celtic is scanty, but there is enough to realize that the language forms spoken on the mainland of Europe still retained much of the morphology that they had inherited from Indo-European.

(2)　Gaulish　　Old Irish　Welsh
　　uxellos　*uasal*　*uchel*　'high, noble'
　　vindos　*find*　*gwynn*　'fair, beautiful'
　　nertomaros　*nertmar*　*nerthfawr*　'strong, powerful'

14.1.1 The Earliest Celtic-Germanic Contact

The Celts occupied central Europe in the first millennium BCE, during which time the Germanic peoples came in contact with them when they moved southward into roughly the same area. Furthermore, the embryonic Italic group was initially north of the Alps and hence broadly speaking in the area of the Celts. These facts led older scholars to postulate clusters of these subgroups, the most notable of which are the following.

(i) Hans Krahe *Old European*
　　Celtic, Italic, Germanic, Baltic, Illyrian

(ii) Antoine Meillet *West Indo-European*
　　Celtic, Italic, Germanic

---

[3] In early stages of Celtic /p/ and /k(w)/ are mutually exclusive in the respective branches, which is why one has a shift to the velar with early loans in Irish such as Latin *planta* > *cland* 'children'; *Patricius* > *Cothrige* (later borrowed as *Pátraic*). This is an issue of chronology with the oldest Latin borrwings showing this shift (McManus 1983; Uhlich 2004). In the P-Celtic branch many instances of /p/ are in fact retentions, as with the number 'five,' for instance, cf. IE **pempe* 'five,' Welsh *pump* but Old Irish *cóic*.

(iii) Hans Kuhn *Nordwestblock*[4]
       Germanic and Celtic plus non-Germanic, non-Celtic Indo-European languages
       in northern Europe

Some scholars have also maintained that there was a developmental stage at which
Italic and Celtic formed a unity.[5] This opinion rests on a number of phonological and
morphological parallels, which tend nowadays not to be regarded as evidence for a
period of unity but, inasmuch as they represent innovations, to be at most the result of
contact while Italic was in roughly the same part of central Europe as Celtic (i.e., before
it spread south of the Alps).

Turning to Germanic, a major defining feature of it as a branch of Indo-European is
the initial stress accent that separates it from other more conservative subgroups of the
family such as Slavic or Baltic. The fixing of stress can be postulated to have occurred
by about 500 BCE at a time when both Celtic and Germanic which were spoken in
central Europe (Salmons 1984: 269–275; 1992: 87–97). Salmons notes that accent shift,
particularly a fixed, stress accent, is a common feature in language-contact situations
and postulates that this held for the Germanic-Celtic interface at this early stage and
assumes (1984: 274) that the Celtic group was dominant over the Germanic one.[6]

There are a small number of recognizable loans from Celtic in Germanic at this early
stage. The first is the stem seen in German names like *Friedrich*; *Heinrich* (the latter
element is related to *Reich* 'domain; empire') and which is cognate with Latin *rex* 'king.'
This word had the original meaning of 'prince' or 'ruler' (Gothic *reiks*) and was first
recognized by Hermann Osthoff in 1884 to be a loan from Celtic. The reasoning is as
follows. Latin *rex: rēgis*, Gallic *rix*, Old Irish *rí*, Sanskrit *raj* show that the IE word must
have contained a long e:. In Gothic this ē more or less remains, spelled *ei: qeins, qē:ns*
'wife, woman' (in some instances *i*). In West and North Germanic the vowel is lowered
to *ā*: Goth. *mēna*, OHG *māno*, Old Norse *máni* 'moon.' The high vowel in Germanic
*re:ks (Holder 1896: 1198) is taken as proof that it is not a continuation of an IE root
reg'- but a loan from Celtic, which has regular raising of IE *e:* to *ī*.

The second keyword (Elston 1934: 166–168) is *ambactus* (see also Holder 1896: 114).
This Gallo-Latin form corresponds to Gothic *andbahts* and still has a reflex in German
Amt 'office,' *Beamter* 'civil servant.' The etymology is Celtic **ambi-* 'around' and **actos*,
the past participle of IE **ag'-* 'drive,' and the meaning in Gothic is 'vassal' or 'servant.'
Note that there is some doubt as to whether the word came from Celtic directly: it could
have been a loan from Latin; the *ht* /xt/ sequence might have been an adaption of /kt/ to
the phonology of Gothic, a very common type of alteration, and not necessarily proof

---

[4] The term *North-West* is used by Theo Vennemann as well, see Vennemann (2010).

[5] See Baldi (1983: 47–50) for a precise overview of the relevant facts. Krahe (1954: 83–98) offers a
comprehensive overview and concludes that the shared features of both subgroups do not speak for a
Celtic-Italic unity but are relics of their common ancestry.

[6] Salmons (1984: 118) is inconclusive on the direction of influence (Celtic to Germanic or vice versa)
and just points to Celtic domination. On the latter notion, see the comprehensive discussion in Elston
(1934: 57–65). See also Lane (1933) and Dillon (1943).

that it was borrowed into Germanic before the first consonant shift. It is beyond doubt that the word was well established in Gothic at the time of Wulfila's Bible, as it has the noun and the verb *andbahtjan* 'to serve' along with the derivative noun *andbahti* 'office, service.' The first Latin attestation is from ca. 170 BCE in the writings of the poet Ennius, who uses it in the sense of 'Gallic slave' (Elston 1934: 168).

Another shared lexical item in Celtic and Germanic is that for 'iron,' which is Germanic **isarna* and Celtic **isarno* (Holder 1896: 75). This root is only attested in these two subgroups[7] of Indo-European (Kluge-Mitzka 1975: 160–161), as is the word for 'lead' (the metal), cf. German *Lot*, Irish *luaidhe*. As the proto-Indo-European population is taken to have been in the transition between stone and metals in the period immediately before dispersion, the knowledge of metallurgy is ascribed in particular to the Celtic and Germanic subgroups. Much has also been made of the fact that Latin *gladius* 'sword' (Old Irish *claideb*, Thurneysen 1946: 103) would appear to have been a Celtic loan (Holder 1896: 2023). However, there is archaeological evidence that the Celts in the Hallstatt period (middle of the first millenium BCE) gained their ability to forge iron from a previous Illyrian culture in the Middle Danube region (Elston 1934: 179–180; this idea was supported by Pokorny as well; see also Krahe 1954: 122–123).

In the opposite direction, there are Germanic loans in Celtic, for example the words for 'breeches': Gaulish *brac(c)a*, OHG *bruoh*; 'shirt': Old Irish *caimis*, OHG *hemidi*. A balanced summary of the arguments concerning the nature of the mutual influence is to be found in Elston (1934: 185–188). He sees the relation of the two groups as one defined first and foremost by trade rather than by any considerable bilingualism. He also sees no firm ground for assuming that the Celts dominated the Germanic tribes in the parts of Germany where there was extensive contact (along the Rhine valley).

Phonological parallels between Celtic and Germanic are accidental, if they occur at all. Specifically, there is no connection between the first consonant shift and lenition as this later developed in Celtic. The consonant shift is an unconditional change, whereas lenition is an external *sandhi* phenomena that arose between a grammatical and a lexical word. Salmons (1992: 118) quotes Schrodt (1986: 105) approvingly in his rejection of a possible parallelism between Celtic lenition and the Germanic sound shift.

14.1.2 Accent and Lenition in Celtic

Two matters need to be broached when viewing Celtic-Germanic contact and possible influence of the former on the latter. These are interconnected but will be considered separately to begin with. The first is the nature of accent, and the second the phonetic weakening (lenition) that is a characteristic of Celtic and which led to radical typological changes in all the Celtic languages. An examination of accent must consider two

---

[7] There are other words, like that for 'hostage,' which may be of cultural significance, cf. German *Geisel*, Irish *giall* (Kluge-Mitzka 1975: 242).

aspects: its place in the word and its nature. The standard assumption is that the accent in early Celtic was a pitch accent, that is, accented syllables were spoken with a noted increase in frequency, with the other two possible parameters, length and loudness (amplitude), not varying significantly.

14.1.2.1 *Accent in Continental Celtic*

The scholars who have concerned themselves with continental Celtic assume that the accent in common Celtic was of the pitch type. Dottin (1920: 103–104) refers to "un accent tonique"/"un accent de hauteur" and states that by the time of Gaulish this must have been "un accent d'intensité." But the position of the accent shows a certain freedom. The antepenult is the most common position, but there are stressed penults and some cases of initial stress.

More recently there has been extended consideration of the question of accent placement in early Celtic. Salmons (1992: 146–174) sees Celtic, along with Germanic and Italic, as having initial stress from a very early stage (first half of the first millenium BCE) and the source of this being a substrate, in his opinion western Finno-Ugric languages in the region of the Baltic. Vennemann (1994: 272) rejects this as the location, for the contact is too far in the east of Europe. He pleads for a language of the Old European language group, which he identifies as the forerunner of present-day Basque on the basis of his major re-evaluation of Krahe's Old European hydronymy. There is evidence that Basque had an initial accent previously, although the situation today is dialectally quite diverse (Vennemann 1994: 257–258).

Disregarding the question of origin for a moment, both authors see western forms of Celtic (Irish and Celtiberian) as more archaic, in keeping with their geographical peripherality, and as preserving an original initial accent that arose at a very early stage, possibly through contact. Old Basque, like Celtic, did not have *p*. Scholars such as Michelena (1977) believe that Old Basque did not have either /p/ or /m/ but that these arose through later phonetic developments such as assimilations, and Hualde (1991: 10–11) does not list /p/ in his "common consonant inventory" for Basque.

Vennemann's standpoint (1994: 246) is that the language of Old European hydronymy led to Italic, Celtic, and Germanic developing initial stress (with temporal staggering). What is indisputable is that unambiguous signs of initial stress are present in each language group from the very beginning: (1) syncope in the second syllable with variable word length; (2) syllables have greatest complexity in initial position, which points to this being accented; (3) at least in Germanic and Celtic, alliteration is found in the earliest verse, something that is indicative of initial stress.

Within the continental Celtic conglomerate, Gaulish must be given separate consideration. The standard work on comparative Celtic, Lewis and Pedersen (1937: 68–69), maintains that the accent in Gaulish was on the antepenult or the penult and that this "may represent a trace of the free IE accent"; cf. *Balódurum*: Fr. *Balleure*; *Cambóritum*: Fr. *Chambort*; *Eburóuices*: Fr. *Evreux*. They point out that those syllables that immediately precede or follow the stressed syllable are most prone to reduction and/or syncope. As with Jackson, Lewis and Pedersen are reticent about the accent in earlier forms of Celtic.

Later authors do not share this previous view. Again, Salmons in his treatment (1992: 152–159) of Gaulish and Brittonic accent assumes that Gaulish had initial accent. Dottin (1920: 103–105) notes expiratory accent but does not state where this was placed. Altheim (1951) notes that those names with evidence for initial accent in Gaulish (with syncope of second syllables) are found in regions that were Romanized last. Olmsted (1989) remarks on the high incidence of alliteration in the Gaulish inscription of Larzac (pointing to initial accent).

14.1.2.2 *Accent in British*

This is an unsettled matter, ultimately deriving from the uncertainty about Gaulish. Jackson (1953: 265–266) assumes that before the separation of Welsh and Cornish/Breton the accent fell on the then penultimate syllable, which became the ultimate shortly afterward with the loss of final unstressed syllables.[8] Jackson assumes that this was a stress accent given the reduction of weak syllables. He avoids any commitment on an older different accentual type and says that nothing is known about a Common Celtic accent (Pedersen 1913, I: 256; Lewis and Pedersen 1938: 68–69) and mentions that the Irish accent need not have any relevance for British (i.e., that the accent system of the former probably represents an older state of affairs with the Gaulish/British accent an innovation).

Thurneysen (1883–1885: 311) apparently believed earlier that the British accent was initial and that there was a secondary stress on the penult: "Vielmehr scheint mir die irische Betonung [which was initial—RH] *alt-* und *gemeinkeltisch*" [emphasis in original] "rather the Irish stress pattern seems to me to have been a feature of Old and Common Celtic." As Jackson points out, this worked well for quadrisyllables but not for trisyllables such as *trinitas* (Irish *trínóid* showing a long vowel in the originally penultimate syllable, which points to stress on this syllable). Thurneysen apparently changed his mind and later claimed that from the second to the fifth century the accent "tended to be on the penultimate" (Jackson 1953: 266).

14.1.2.3 *Lenition in Continental Celtic*

When talking of lenition in Celtic, one must distinguish between its existence as a phonetic phenomenon and its establishment and orthographical recognition as a morphological device. In this latter function, lenition appears in British quite late (there is a consensus that it is to be posited at around the fifth century CE; Jackson 1953: 695).

Phonetic lenition is a much older phenomenon, and evidence for its occurrence in Continental Celtic is not overwhelming given the scanty nature of the attestations;

---

[8] Modern Welsh and Modern Breton (except the dialect of Vannes with ultimate stress; Jackson 1967: 67) reveal a penultimate accent, much as in Polish or Italian. The conclusion here is that there was an accent shift back one syllable to retain penultimate stress after apocope. The Vannes dialect of Breton can be interpreted as retaining the original stress pattern (penultimate), which after the loss of endings was thereafter on the final syllable.

nonetheless, it is enough to be certain about its existence (see preceding examples). Some instances of lenition are recognizable due to "misspellings." Dottin (1920: 67) mentions the lenition of /b/ to /v/, which is seen occasionally in these misspellings and thus assumes that it was definitely a Continental Celtic phenomenon.[9] The lenition of labials links up with the morphological lenition in Modern Irish and Welsh, where these segments are subject to fricativization. Earlier it was assumed that the initial segment that resulted from lenition was also nasalized (i.e., [ṽ]). The lack of stop lenition in Continental Celtic is not positive evidence of its nonexistence, as it may well have been present but not indicated orthographically. Indeed this situation obtained even for Old Irish, where lenition of voiced stops was not usually indicated (Quin 1975: 8).

14.1.2.4 *The Position with Latin*

British Latin appeared to have been peripheral and conservative. Loanword evidence can be advanced to attest this. Starting probably in the first century and completed definitely by the third, Latin *v* and *b* collapsed as [ß] (Gratwick 1982: 17). However, this is not reflected in the loanwords from British Latin into British, as these show unshifted /b/, which is then subject to lenition after the fifth century CE (Jackson 1953: 413, 548). Gratwick (1982: 62–63) thinks that some Latin loans must have entered several centuries earlier and that once they had entered British they remained unchanged as fossilized traits of the phonology of the original language, irrespective of the number of later bilinguals in Roman Britain (Gratwick 1982: 70; J. N. Adams 2003).[10]

14.1.2.5 *Latin in Ireland*

According to established tradition (O'Rahilly 1942), Ireland was Christianized in the early fifth century by St. Patrick. As a result of this, the Latin language was introduced and used by monks in religious rites and the study of church documents. Manuscripts in Latin from Ireland date back to the seventh century. Latin continued to be used as the language of formal writing into the second millenium, especially by ecclesiastical writers. Indeed, an identifiable variety of the language—characterized by ornate and often artificial vocabulary—seems to have been used by Irish monks (beginning in the first millenium CE) and is often referred to as Hiberno-Latin (Lapidge and Sharpe 1985; Picard 2003). The linguistic affects of contact are referred to the following section.

---

[9] For Old Irish, Thurneysen (1946: 27) maintains that "stress is expiratory and very intense, as may be seen from the reduction of unstressed syllables." He does not speculate, however, on what stress was like in other forms of Insular Celtic or in Continental Celtic, nor does he express an opinion as to how the initial stress of Irish arose.

[10] In addition to borrowings into Celtic, there was also transfer into Latin from Continental Celtic; see Schmidt (1967) for details.

14.2 Early Irish

The period of early Irish for which documentation is available in the Roman alphabet begins after the Christianization of Ireland in the fifth century CE. The first documents are glosses and marginalia from the mid-eighth century contained in manuscripts found on the Continent in the missionary sites of the Irish (Thurneysen 1946; E. G. Quin 1975). These were in Germany (*Codex Paulinus* in Würzburg, glosses on the letters of St. Paul), Switzerland (*Codex Sangallensis* in St. Gall with the glossed version of Priscian's grammar), and northern Italy (*Codex Ambrosianus* in Milan, glosses on some psalms). This period lasted until the end of the ninth century CE. The single external event that was most responsible for the demise of Old Irish in Ireland was the coming of the Vikings in the late eighth century.

By considering Latin loanwords in Irish, one can see that part of the phonological makeup of the language was the word-internal lenition (voicing of voiceless stops and deletion of voiced ones), which had begun during the Ogham period (before 600), for example *lebor* /lʲevər/, later /lʲaur/, from *liber* 'book'; *sacart* /sagart/ from *sacerdos* 'priest'; *airgid* 'silver' from *argentum*. These developments continue well into the Middle Ages and are evident in the Old Norse and Anglo-Norman loanwords from the thirteenth and fourteenth centuries (see later discussion).

14.2.1 Non-Indo-European Vocabulary in Irish

A cursory look at the vocabulary of Irish reveals that there are often two words for closely related concepts, where one is clearly Indo-European in origin and the other from another source. *Cathair* 'city' is Indo-European, whereas *baile* 'settlement, village' is not. *Bean* 'woman' is Indo-European, but *annir* 'young woman' is not. *Muir* 'sea, ocean' is of Indo-European origin, but *farraige* 'sea' is not.[11] On a few occasions there are single basic vocabulary items that are not Indo-European, such as *uisce*[12] 'water,' which does not continue the Indo-European root seen in Germanic and Slavic, cf. English *water*, Russian *voda*. This situation has led some scholars to delve further into the possible source of such non-Indo-European words, especially those with initial /p-/

---

[11] For *baile*, Buck (1949: 830) notes "etym.?". For *ainnir* (Old Irish *ainder*), Quin (1990: 18) states that it is explained by the native glossators as deriving from the negative prefix *a(i)n-* + *der* 'girl' (poetic), given that one of its meanings is 'non-virgin, married woman,' but it also has the opposite meaning 'virgin, maiden.' For *farraige* (Old Irish *fairrge*), Quin (1990: 293) suggests that it might be related to *fairsing* 'wide' (but gives no etymology), Buck (1949: 30–31) says "etym. disputed." The later electronic version of the *Dictionary of the Irish Language* (accessible at http://www.dil.ie) does not offer any information on these words beyond what is contained in the printed edition of the dictionary.

[12] Vennemann (1994) sees the Basque root *is* 'water' as occurring widely among the river names of Europe and in the word for 'ice' in Germanic (Vennemann 1997). The Irish word *uisce* /ɪʃkʲe/ 'water' might also contain this root.

(Schrijver 2000, 2005)[13] and to consider possible etymologies. To date (2019), the only coherent framework offered for these extraneous items in Irish and other languages or groups, noticeably West Germanic, is that presented by Theo Vennemann, who sees the peoples present in Western Europe before the arrival of Indo-European groups as responsible for the words clearly borrowed into the Indo-European subgroups, Germanic and Celtic.[14] These pre-Indo-European peoples are taken to have belonged to a now practically extinct language family whose only surviving member is present-day Basque. The language family is termed Vasconic and is seen as the main source of non-Indo-European vocabulary in Germanic and Celtic.

14.2.1.1 *Basque-Irish Correspondences*

The possible influence of a Vasconic language on Irish in the initial stage of Celtic settlement in Ireland can be addressed via loanwords. Here there are a number of intriguing sound correspondences between Irish and Basque, the sole remaining Vasconic language and so the only one that can be used for comparison. Some of the correspondences seem fairly straightforward, such as Middle Irish *ainder* whose Vasconic origin is suggested by comparing it with present-day Basque *and(e)re* 'lady' (Bizkaian *andra* 'woman'). Other correspondences involve semantic shifts that require a degree of unraveling to establish an etymological link. An example of this is Old Irish *bos/ bas* (= 'palm of hand,' Modern Irish: *bualadh bos* [strike palm] 'applaud, clap'). Julius Pokorny (1930: 111) notes that this word is non Indo-European, that is, not part of the inherited lexical stock of Irish, and hence postulates that it could be from Basque *bost/ bortz* 'five' He further links it to Berber *a-fus* 'hand, five' and *fus-t* 'clutch, fistful,' quoting Trombetti and Schuchardt *Revue International des Études Basques* (7: 339) in support of this, and states unequivocally: "Ich bin jedenfalls der Meinung, daß die keltischen Formen auf ein hamitisch-iberisches Substrat zurückgeführt werden können" ("I am at any rate of the opinion that the Celtic forms can be traced back to an Hamitic-Iberian substrate"; translation mine, RH). While many scholars might follow Pokorny in tracing Irish *bos/bas* to Basque, the question of a link to Berber (Basset 1952) is more speculative.

14.2.1.2 *The Afro-Asiatic Hypothesis*

The view that demographic contacts occurred along the west coast of Europe and in North Africa is fairly widespread in relevant literature throughout the past century or so. Take, for instance, the following quotation from Morris Jones (1900), an early, very

---

[13] The first of these articles is concerned with the etymology of Old Irish *portán* 'crab,' which Schrijver sees as stemming from a non-Indo-European language that survived until at least 500 CE in Ireland (Schrijver 2000: 197–198). He does not speculate about what this language was or about possible relationships with known non-Indo-European languages in Europe.

[14] This view was also represented by Julius Pokorny in a number of shorter pieces published in the first half of the twentieth century, see Pokorny (1930, 1949). Somewhat later the Swiss scholar Heinrich Wagner reflected these views in a number of publications, see Wagner (1959) and (1982), as did the Irish dialectologist George Brendan Adams, see Adams (1975). For more general studies on language contact in Britain and Ireland, see Ureland and Broderick (eds. 1991).

clear statement on the origins of the pre-Celtic population of Britain: "These non-Celtic inhabitants of Britain are believed by anthropologists to be of the same race as the ancient Iberians, and to have migrated through France and Spain from North Africa, where the race is represented by the Berbers and the ancient Egyptians" (1900: 618). Such views are echoed later in the twentieth century by linguists who have sought to trace grammatical features[15] to contact between speakers of Celtic and pre-Celtic languages. For instance, Heinrich Wagner, in his treatment of the verb in the languages of the British Isles (Wagner 1959), is quite explicit in his claim that the specific verbal structures in these languages, notably their analytic character and the presence of a progressive form for all of them, is something that was developed in the British Isles (1959: 119). He further links up these developments with parallels in other languages of the Atlantic coast and North Africa, specifically with Basque and with Berber (1959: 182–198). Wagner's methodology consists of repeatedly pointing out typological parallels between the languages of the British Isles and those in North Africa (Wagner 1982), which together form his "Euroafrican" type, which contrasts with a "Ural-Altaic" type, and which he sees as having influenced Proto-Germanic (1959: 148). There are strengths and weaknesses in Wagner's approach. His forte lies in the broad typological perspective that he brings to his subject matter; the inherent weakness of his investigation is that it is almost ideologically committed to tracing structural similarity to contact and gives little consideration to language-internal arguments.[16]

Opinions are much divided on the Afro-Asiatic substratum theory for Insular Celtic, with Isaac (2007) categorically rejecting it. An objective assessment is provided in Hewitt (2007), who examines closely the number of typologically unusual features that are shared or not shared between Insular Celtic and Afro-Asiatic.

14.3 CONTACT WITH OLD NORSE

In the late eighth century CE the Scandinavians became expansionist and raided neighboring coasts in the North Sea area and the coastline of northeast England, Scotland, and Ireland. The earliest attacks were on Lindisfarne and Jarrow in 793–794, followed by similar events on the island of Iona, a center of Hiberno-Scottish culture. In the course of the ninth century the initial plundering yielded to more permanent settlements in the parts of the British Isles that the Scandinavians had been to in previous decades. This was a qualitative change and was to have lasting consequences for the peoples of the British Isles. From this point onward the Scandinavians are

---

[15] Grammatical features from Celtic as a result of intensive contact are attested in Old English, where some features of the latter, such as the internal possessor construction or the isomorphy of emphatics and reflexives, can be traced to Celtic influence (Hickey 2012).

[16] Apart from verbal syntax, the Afro-Asiatic substrate in Celtic has been linked to VSO word order in Celtic and even to the systemic contrast in secondary articulation, in Irish between palatal and non-palatal consonants, and in Arabic between emphatic and non-emphatic consonants.

known as Vikings, a term whose first syllable derives either from Frisian *wic* 'settlement' or Old Norse *vik* 'bay.'

In Ireland, Scandinavian influence is taken to have ended with the Battle of Clontarf (then near Dublin) in 1014. In both Ireland and England the Scandinavians were assimilated into the local population, but in many cases they retained their names, typically those ending in *-son* (e.g. *Johnson, Anderson, Peterson*). In Ireland and Scotland, Scandinavian ancestry is apparent in certain surnames, for example *Ó hUiginn* (English *Higgins*) 'Viking,' which corresponds to Scottish *Mac Lochlann* (English *McLoughlin*) 'son of Viking' from *Lochlannach* 'Viking' (i.e., inhabitant of a country of lakes).

14.3.1 Norse Placenames in Ireland

The Scandinavians are responsible for the founding of most Irish towns that are situated at the estuaries of major rivers. Dublin and Belfast are two exceptions; the former city predates the coming of the Vikings, and the latter is a new settlement from the beginning of the seventeenth century. In some instances the English names of towns are derived from the Norse names and are not related to the Irish form: *Loch Garman* 'Wexford'; *Port Láirge* 'Waterford'; *An tInbhear Mór* 'Arklow'; *Howth* < Norse *huvud* 'head'; *Leixlip* 'salmon leap' was translated literally into Irish as *Léim an Bhradáin* 'leap of the salmon.' The island of Dalkey (south side of Dublin) derives from Norse *dalkr* 'thorn' + *ey* 'island' which gives Irish *Deilginis* 'thorn island.' In some cases the Irish name is a rendering of a Norse original, for example *Sceirí* (English 'Skerries') meaning 'reef islands' (now a town north of Dublin), which is cognate with modern Swedish *skären*, which denotes the same.

A later lack of knowledge of Old Norse has meant that some place names are folk etymologies with different original meanings. For instance, the small island just north of Dublin, *Ireland's Eye* has a second element from Scandinavian *ey* meaning 'island'. *Waterford* is from Scandinavian *Vadrefjord* and refers to the point at the river estuary where *wethers* 'castrated rams' were shipped to other ports (the first element is unrelated to the Old Norse word for 'water,' *vatn*).

Three of the four provinces of Ireland have a second syllable from Norse *staðr* 'place' (or possibly from a combination of genitival *s* + Irish *tír* 'country'): *Munster, Leinster, Ulster*. The first syllable is derived from a name for the tribe that lived in the area designated, as is the entire form of the fourth province, *Connacht*.

14.3.2 Linguistic Influence

Because of the considerable structural distance between Old Irish and Old Norse (much greater than that with Old English), no borrowings in the area of grammar are apparent, even though the sociolinguistic situation in the later Viking period must have been similar to that in England with Irish and Vikings living side by side.

Nonetheless, there are lexical borrowings from Old Norse (Schulze-Thulin 1996), which often reflect the areas of contact with Vikings, for example *ancaire* 'anchor', *seol* (< Old Norse *segl*) 'sail.' Some borrowings are similar to those in English, for example *fuinneog* /finʲoːg/ from Old Norse *vindauga* corresponds to the same borrowing into late Old English which gave modern 'window.' Some Old Norse borrowings belong to the more peaceful later period and suggest a different type of contact with Vikings than in the earlier period of plundering, for example *margadh* (< Old Norse *markadr*) 'market'; *bróg* (< ON *brók*) 'shoe.' There is a comparable influence of Old Norse on Scottish Gaelic during the Viking period in Scotland (Stewart 2004).

14.4 CONTACT WITH ANGLO-NORMANS

When the Anglo-Normans and English arrived in Ireland in 1169 the linguistic situation was quite homogeneous given that the Scandinavians had been assimilated in the previous centuries, just as they had been in England and northern France. For the period of the initial invasion, the Anglo-Normans were the leaders among the new settlers. The English were mainly their servants, a fact that points to the relatively low status of the language at this time. As in England, the ruling classes and the higher positions in the clergy were occupied by Normans soon after the invasion. Their language was introduced with them and established itself in the towns. Evidence for this is offered by such works as *The Song of Dermot and the Earl* (Orpen 1892; Long 1975) and *The Entrenchment of New Ross* (Shields 1975–1976) in Anglo-Norman, as well as contemporary references to spoken Anglo-Norman in court proceedings from Kilkenny (Cahill 1938: 160–161). The large number of Anglo-Norman loanwords in Irish (Risk 1971: 586–589), which entered the language in the period after the invasion, testifies to the existence of Anglo-Norman and the robustness of its position from the mid-twelfth to the fourteenth century (Hickey 1997). In fact, as a language of law it was employed up to the fifteenth century, as evidenced by the Acts of Parliament of 1472, which were in Anglo-Norman.

14.4.1 The Status of Anglo-Norman

Anglo-Norman remained the language of the ruling landlords for at least two centuries after the initial invasion in 1169. The English rulers of the time were themselves French-speaking: Henry II, who came to Ireland in 1171 and issued the Charter of Dublin in the same year, could not speak English, according to Giraldus Cambriensis (Cahill 1938: 164).

The extent of the Norman impact on Ireland can be recognized in surnames that became established. Such names as *Butler, Power, Wallace, Durand, Nugent*, and all those beginning in *Fitz-* (e.g., *Fitzpatrick, Fitzgibbon*) testify to the strength of the Normans in Ireland long after such events as the loss of Normandy to England in 1204. Anglo-Norman influence on Irish is considerable in the field of loanwords, but the reverse influence is not attested, although official documents exist to almost the end of the fifteenth century that were written in Anglo-Norman or Latin (Cahill 1938: 160). The high number of everyday loans (see the following) would suggest close contact between Anglo-Norman speakers and the local Irish.

The Anglo-Norman landlords established bases in the countryside, as clearly attested by the castles they built. These Normans were granted land by the English king and in principle had to render service or pay scutage. In their turn, they had others on their land who would also have been of Norman or English stock, while the native Irish were on the level of serfs. Because of this organization there were clear lines of contact between the natives and the new settlers that account for the linguistic influence of Anglo-Norman on Irish.

14.4.2 Anglo-Norman Loanwords

The high number of everyday loanwords from Anglo-Norman in Irish (Risk 1971, 1974; Hickey 1997) suggests that the new settlers used Anglo-Norman words in their Irish and that these then diffused into Irish by this variety being "imposed" on the native Irish (Hickey 2010: 10–11).

(3)   Anglo-Norman   Irish
    a. *joignour*   >   *siúinéir*   'carpenter'
    b. *warde*   >   *barda*   'guard'
    c. *flour*   >   *plúr*   'flour'
    d. *chaumbre*   >   *seomra*   'room'
    e. *archer*   >   *airseóir*   'archer'
    f. *page*   >   *páiste*   'child'
    g. *college*   >   *coláiste*   'college'

A similar model has been suggested for the appearance of a large number of Old Norse words in Scottish Gaelic with initial /s/ + stop clusters. Here the Old Norse settlers are assumed to have imposed their variety of Gaelic—which would have included many Old Norse words, identifiable by characteristic initial clusters—on the general Scottish Gaelic-speaking population around them (see remarks in section 14.3.2).

The quantity of loans from Anglo-Norman into Irish and their phonological adaptation to the sound system of Irish (see Hickey 1997 for details) speak for both a socially important donor group (the Anglo-Normans) and at the same time for a large and stable group of substrate speakers. This latter fact would explain why the loans from Anglo-Norman are completely adapted to the sound system of Irish, for example the word *páiste* /pɑsʲtʲə/ 'child' shows obligatory metathesis and devoicing of the /dʒ/ in *page* to make it conform to Irish phonotactics. This adaption is evidence of the robust position of Irish at the time and contrasts strongly with that today, where English loans are entering the language in large numbers (Hickey 1982; Stenson 1993) and are not necessarily adapted phonologically, for example *seaicéad* /sʲakʲeːd/ 'jacket,' an older loan that has a modern equivalent /dʒakit/ where the voiced affricate is not devoiced and simplified as in the earlier case.

14.4.3 Anglo-Norman Names

Despite the fact that the Anglo-Normans were fully Gaelicized, they retained their names and these are still quite distinctive, for example those beginning in *Fitz-* 'son of' (e.g., *Fitzpatrick, Fitzgerald, Fitzmaurice*) which testify to the numbers of Normans in Ireland.

The number of Norman placenames is remarkably small, especially considering the large amount of Norman surnames that became established in Ireland and the many loanwords in Irish from the Norman invaders. One reason might be that the Normans did not found towns. Instead they built keeps (fortified towers) in the countryside and ruled from fortified castles. But even there, few if any Norman names are to be found. Perhaps it has to do with the acceptance by the Normans of the names that went with the territories occupied by the Irish. Occasionally, there are recognizable instances of Norman names, for example English *Brittas*, Irish *Briotás* (south of Dublin) < Old French *Bretesche* 'boarding, planking' or English *Pallas*, Irish *Pailís* 'stockade.' A further case is that of regions dominated by a particular Norman family. Because the Normans were concentrated in the south of Ireland, there are names that derive from the province of Munster and a point of the compass: *Ormond* < *Iarmumhan* 'east Munster,' *Thomond* < *Thiarmumhan* 'north Munster,' and *Desmond* < *Deasmumhan* 'south Munster,' the latter later forming a common first name in Ireland.

14.4.3.1 *Word Stress*

A prominent feature of southern Irish is that long vowels in non-initial syllables attract stress, for example *cailín* /kaˈlʲiːnʲ/ 'girl.' This may be the result of Anglo-Norman influence (in the southeast) after the twelfth century, as older authors like O'Rahilly seem to think (1932: 86–98), and it certainly applied to many French loanwords, for example *buidéal* /bəˈdʲeːl/ 'bottle' (see Hickey 1997 for further discussion). This late stress in a word may be responsible for the procope that led to the first name *William* appearing in Irish as *Liam*.

14.4.3.2 *Lenition*

Historically, there are instances of Anglo-Norman (and English) loanwords where the initial segment of the word was regarded as lenited and then "de-lenited" on borrowing. This applies in particular to /v-/ and /w-/, which appear as /b-/ on borrowing, for example *barántas* 'warranty,' *balla* 'wall,' *bigil* 'vigil,' *bís* 'vice.' Older examples have this as well, for example *seabhac* < *hawk* where the initial /h-/ was interpreted as a lenited form of /sʲ/ and then reversed in Irish. More recent loans may also show this kind of reversal, for example *giúmar* from *humour* where the initial /j-/ was 'de-lenited' to /gʲ-/.

Lenition may also appear as a word-internal phenomenon (i.e., an internal voiceless segment may result in a voiced segment in the loanword). Irish loans from Anglo-Norman from the thirteenth and fourteenth centuries can be cited as instances of this lenition, for example *bagún* from *bacun* 'bacon' or *buidéal* from *botel* 'bottle.'

14.5 ENGLISH IN MEDIEVAL IRELAND

The English language was taken to Ireland with the settlers from Britain who arrived in the late twelfth century. Since then the fate of English has been closely linked with that of the Irish language, which it came largely to replace in the late modern period. In addition, the interaction of existing forms of English with the Scots imported in the early seventeenth century into the north of the country led to a linguistic division arising between Ulster, the most northerly province, on the one hand, and the rest of the country to the south, on the other.

Early borrowings from English into Irish betray older stages of the former language. In particular, the vowel values of the borrowings into Irish have vowel values that stem from the period before the shift of English long vowels, which began toward the end of the Middle English period (1100–1500). These loans show ME /i:/ (= ModE /ai/), for example *faoitín* /fiːtʲiːnʲ/ 'whiting,' ME /a:/ (= ModE /e:/) and ME /u:/ (= ModE /au/), for example *bácús* /baːkuːs/ 'bakehouse,' as well as ME /au/ (= ModE /o:/), for example *seabhac* /sʲauk/ 'hawk.' Table 14.1 summarizes the findings above.

Table 14.1 Summary of Contact in Celtic and Early Irish

Contact in the History of Celtic

Source Language	Approximate Time Period
pre Indo-European	first appearance of Celts; demise of Continental
Vasconic?	Celtic (beginning of CE)
Germanic	first millennium BCE
Latin	last centuries BCE and beginning of CE

Contact in the History of Irish

Source Language	Approximate Time Period
pre Indo-European	coming of Celts in Ireland, ca. 500 BCE
Vasconic?	
Latin	early centuries CE
Old Norse	800–1000 CE
Anglo-Norman	late twelfth century to ca. 1400
English	late twelfth century to present

Notes: The demise of Celtic on the continent is difficult to date precisely, and if Breton in Brittany is partly derived from Celtic survivals in this part of later France, then Continental Celtic never completely died out.

14.6 CONCLUSION

The consideration of language contact in Celtic and early Irish provides much evidence for mutual linguistic influence with both other subgroups of Indo-European and with pre-Indo-European languages of northwestern Europe. The analysis of this influence is naturally on a firmer footing with those languages that are genetically related. But for those that are not, the attempt to find possible etymological relationships is laudable, and the neglect of this search reduces the knowledge that could be gained from an examination of language contact at a very considerable time depth. Furthermore, contact in the history of Celtic and Irish illustrates a number of different external situations that yielded different linguistic results. In particular, the contact with Scandinavians and Anglo-Normans in medieval Ireland shows how the absorption of outsiders led to an expansion of Irish vocabulary through borrowings that are still recognizable today.

For the modern Irish language contact with English is pervasive in all domains of life and on all levels of language. This influence from the dominant language has already affected the lexical profile and typological structure of Irish and will continue to do so in future, especially given the extent to which second-language users of Irish now outnumber the native speakers in the historically continuous areas along the Western seaboard of Ireland.

REFERENCES

Adams, George Brendan. 1975. Hamito-Semitic and the pre-Celtic substratum in Ireland and Britain. In *Hamito-Semitica*, edited by James Bynon and Theodora Bynon, 233–247. The Hague: Mouton.

Adams, James N. 2003. *Bilingualism and the Latin Language*. Cambridge: Cambridge University Press.

Altheim, Franz. 1951. *Geschichte der lateinischen Sprache*. Frankfurt: Klostermann.

Azkue, Resurrecion M. 1984. *Diccionario vasco-espanol-frances*. Bilbao: Euskaltzindia.

Baldi, Philip. 1983. *An Introduction to the Indo-European Languages*. Carbondale: Southern Illinois University Press.

Basset, André. 1952. *La langue berbère*. Oxford: Oxford University Press.

Brooks, Nicholas (ed.). 1982. *Latin and the Vernacular Languages of Early Medieval Britain*. Leicester: University Press.

Buck, Carl Darling. 1949. *A Dictionary of Selected Synonyms in the Principal Indo-European Languages*. Chicago: University of Chicago Press.

Cahill, Edward. 1938. Norman French and English languages in Ireland, 1170–1540. *Irish Ecclesiastical Record, 5th Series* 51: 160–173.

Curtis, Edmund. 1919. The spoken languages of medieval Ireland. *Studies* 8: 234–254.

Dillon, Myles. 1943. Germanic and Celtic. *Journal of English and Germanic Philology* 42: 492–498.

Dillon, Myles, and Nora Chadwick, 1972. *The Celtic Realms*. 2nd edition. London: Weidenfeld and Nicolson.

Dolan, Terence P. 1991. The literature of Norman Ireland. In *The Field Day Anthology of Irish Literature*, 3 Vols., edited by Seamus Deane, 141–170. Derry: Field Day Publications.

Dottin, Georges. 1980 [1920]. *La langue gauloise: Grammaire, textes et glossaire*. Genève: Slatkine Reprints.

Elston, C. S. 1934. *The Earliest Relations between Celts and Germans*. London: Methuen.

Eska, Joseph F. 2020. Contact and the Celtic languages. In *The Handbook of Language Contact*, Second. edition. Edited by Raymond Hickey. Malden, MA: Wiley-Blackwell.

Gratwick, Adrian S. 1982. Latinitas Britannica: Was British Latin archaic? In *Latin and the Vernacular Languages of Early Medieval Britain*, edited by N. Brooks, 1–79. Leicester: University Press.

Hewitt, Steve. 2007. Remarks on the Insular Celtic/Hamito-Semitic question. In *The Celtic World IV, Celtic Linguistics*, edited by Raimund Karl and David Stifter, 230–268. London: Routledge.

Hickey, Raymond. 1982. The phonology of English loan-words in Inis Meáin Irish. *Ériu* 33: 137–156.

Hickey, Raymond. 1995. Sound change and typological shift: Initial mutation in Celtic. In *Linguistic Typology and Reconstruction*, edited by Jacek Fisiak, 133–182. Berlin: Mouton.

Hickey, Raymond. 1997. Assessing the relative status of languages in medieval Ireland. In *Studies in Middle English*, edited by Jacek Fisiak, 181–205. Berlin: Mouton de Gruyter.

Hickey, Raymond. 2010. Language contact: Reassessment and reconsideration. In *The Handbook of Language Contact*, edited by R. Hickey, 1–28. Malden, MA: Wiley-Blackwell.

Hickey, Raymond (ed.). 2010. *The Handbook of Language Contact*. Malden, MA: Wiley-Blackwell.

Hickey, Raymond. 2012. Early English and the Celtic hypothesis. *The Oxford Handbook of the History of English*, edited by Terttu Nevalainen and Elizabeth Closs Traugott, 497–507. Oxford: Oxford University Press.

Holder, Alfred. 1896. *Alt-Celtischer Sprachschatz*. 2 Vols. Leipzig: Teubner.

Hualde, José Ignacio. 1991. *Basque phonology* London: Routledge.

Isaac, Graham R. 2007. Celtic and Afro-Asiatic. In *The Celtic Languages in Contact*, edited by Hildegard L. C. Tristram, 25–80. Potsdam: Potsdam University Press.

Jackson, Kenneth. 1953. *Language and History in Early Britain*. Edinburgh: University Press.

Jackson, Kenneth. 1967. *A Historical Phonology of Breton*. Dublin: Institute for Advanced Studies.

Jucquois, Guy. 1970. La théorie de la racine en indo-européen. *La linguistique* 6(2): 69–102.

Kluge, Friedrich, and Walther Mitzka. 1975. *Etymologisches Wörterbuch der deutschen Sprache*. Berlin: de Gruyter.

Kortlandt, Frederik. 1986. Proto-European tones? *Journal of Indo-European Studies* 14: 153–160.

Krahe, Hans. 1954. *Sprache und Vorzeit. Europäische Vorgeschichte nach dem Zeugnis der Sprache*. Heidelberg: Quelle und Meyer.

Laing, Lloyd. 1979. *Celtic Britain*. London: Routledge and Kegan Paul.

Lane, George S. 1933. The Germano-Celtic vocabulary. *Language* 9: 244–264.

Lapidge, Michael, and Richard Sharpe 1985. *A Bibliography of Celtic-Latin Literature 400–1200*. Dublin: Royal Irish Academy.

Lehmann, Winfred P. 1974. *Proto-Indo-European syntax*. Austin: University of Texas Press.

Lewis, Henry, and Holger Pedersen. 1937. *A Concise Comparative Celtic Grammar*. Göttingen: Vandenhoeck und Ruprecht.

McManus, Damian. 1983. A chronology of the Latin loan-words in early Irish. *Ériu* 34: 21–71.

Michelena, Luis. 1977. *Fonética histórica vasca*. San Sebastian: Diputación Foral de Gipuzkoa.

Morris Jones, J. 1900. Pre-Aryan syntax in Insular Celtic. Appendix B of *The Welsh People*, edited by John Rhŷs and David Brynmor-Jones, 617–641. London: T. Fisher Unwin. (Reprinted in 2007 in *The Celtic World* IV, *Celtic Linguistics*, edited by Raimiund Karl and David Stifter, 103–122. London: Routledge.)

O'Rahilly, Thomas Francis. 1926. Notes on Middle Irish pronunciation. *Hermathena* 44: 152–195.

O'Rahilly, Thomas Francis. 1932. *Irish Dialects Past and Present*. Dublin: Browne and Nolan.

O'Rahilly, Thomas Francis. 1942. *The Two Patricks: A Lecture on the History of Christianity in Fifth-Century Ireland*. Dublin: Institute for Advanced Studies.

Olmsted, Garrett. 1989. The meter of the Gaulish inscription from Larzac. *Journal of Indo-European Studies* 17(1–2): 155–164.

Pedersen, Holger. 1913. *Vergleichende Grammatik der keltischen Sprachen*. 3 Vols. Göttingen: Vandenhoeck und Ruprecht.

Picard, Jean-Michel. 2003. The Latin language in early medieval Ireland. In *Languages in Ireland*, edited by Michael Cronin and Cormac Ó Cuilleanáin, 44–56. Dublin: Four Courts Press.

Pokorny, Julius. 1930. Keltisch-Baskisch-Hamitisches. *Zeitschrift für Celtische Philologie* 30: 111.

Pokorny, Julius. 1949. Zum nicht-indogermanischen Substrat im Inselkeltischen. *Die Sprache* 1: 235–245.

Quin, E. Q. 1975. *Old-Irish Workbook*. Dublin: Royal Irish Academy.

Quin, E. G. (ed.). 1983. *Contributions to a Dictionary of the Irish Language*, compact edition. Dublin: Royal Irish Academy.

Risk, Henry. 1971. French loan-words in Irish (i). *Études Celtiques* 12: 585–655.

Risk, Henry. 1974. French loan-words in Irish (ii). *Études Celtiques* 14: 67–98.

Salmons, Joseph C. 1984. *The Extent of Language Contact Change: Germanic and Celtic*. PhD dissertation, University of Texas, Austin.

Salmons, Josephs C. 1992. *Accentual Change and Language Contact: Comparative Survey and a Case Study of Early Northern Europe*. Stanford, CA: University Press.

Schlette, Friedrich. 1979. *Kelten zwischen Alesia und Pergamon*. Berlin: Urania Verlag.

Schmidt, Karl-Horst. 1967. Keltisches Wortgut im Lateinischen. *Glotta* 44: 151–174.

Schrijver, Peter. 2000. Non-Indo-European surviving in Ireland in the first millennium AD. *Ériu* 51: 195–202.

Schrijver, Peter. 2005. More on non-Indo-European surviving in Ireland in the first millennium AD. *Ériu* 55: 137–144.

Schrodt, Richard. 1976. *Die germanische Lautverschiebung und ihre Stellung im Kreise der indogermanischen Sprachen*. 2nd edition. Wien: Halosar.

Schulze-Thulin, Britta. 1996. Old Norse in Ireland. In *Language Contact across the North Atlantic*, edited by P. Sture Ureland and Iain Clarkson, 83–113. Tübingen: Niemeyer.

Stanihurst, Richard. 1965 [1577]. The description of Ireland. In *Chronicles of England, Scotlande and Irelande*, edited by R. Holinshed. London. Reprinted by Ams Press.

Stenson, Nancy. 1993. English influence on Irish: The last 100 years. *Journal of Celtic Linguistics* 2: 107–128.

Stewart, Thomas W. 2004. Lexical imposition: Old Norse vocabulary in Scottish Gaelic. *Diachronica* 21(2): 393–428.

Thurneysen, Rudolf. 1883–1885. Zur irischen Accent- und Verslehre. *Revue Celtique* 6: 309–347.

Thurneysen, Rudolf. 1946. *A Grammar of Old Irish*. Translated Daniel A. Binchy and Osborn Bergin. Dublin: Institute for Advanced Studies.

Uhlich, Jürgen. 2004. Weiteres zur Chronologie der lateinischen Lehnwörter im Irischen. *Keltologie heute. Themen und Fragestellungen*, edited by Erich Poppe, 57–79. Münster: Nodus.

Ureland, P. Sture, and George Broderick (eds.). 1991. *Language Contact in the British Isles*. Tübingen: Niemeyer.

Vennemann, Theo. 1994. Linguistic reconstruction in the context of European prehistory. *Transactions of the Philological Society*. 92(2): 215–284.

Vennemann, Theo. 1997. Some West Indo-European words of uncertain origin. In *Language History and Linguistic Modelling: A Festschrift for Jacek Fisiak on his Sixtieth Birthday*, edited by Raymond Hickey and Stanislaw Puppel, 879–908. Berlin: Mouton-de Gruyter.

Vennemann, Theo. 2002. Semitic → Celtic → English: The transitivity of language contact. In *The Celtic Roots of English*, edited by Markku Filppula, Juhani Klemola, and Heli Pitkänen, 295–330. Joensuu: University of Joensuu.

Vennemann, Theo. 2010. Contact and prehistory: The Indo-European Northwest. In *The Handbook of Language Contact*, edited by R. Hickey, 380–405. Malden, MA: Wiley-Blackwell.

Wagner, Heinrich. 1959. *Das Verbum in den Sprachen der britischen Inseln* Tübingen: Niemeyer.

Wagner, Heinrich. 1982. Near Eastern and African connections with the Celtic world. In *The Celtic Consciousness*, edited by Robert O'Driscoll, 51–67. Mountrath, Co. Laois: Dolmen Press.

CHAPTER 15

....

ENGLISH AND WELSH IN CONTACT

....

CLIVE G. GREY

15.1 INTRODUCTION

....

ENGLISH and Welsh have been in contact for fifteen hundred years, but perhaps only closely in the last five hundred.[1] Welsh has also been exposed to other influences, for example Latin, Irish, Old Norse, and Flemish (this last in the Welsh of Pembrokeshire), but English is the language with which Welsh has been in contact most, although contact with Latin may have begun over fifteen hundred years ago.[2] The greatest cross-exposure between English and Welsh has taken place since about 1850 with industrialization, and, in the twentieth century, migration and tourism became significant factors in the social history of Wales, all leading to the current situation of widespread bilingualism, even in the once monoglot Welsh-speaking heartlands of the west and northwest. The history of this contact is well recorded.[3]

Recent work on contact phenomena involving Celtic and English is well illustrated by Filppula (1997),[4] Filppula, Klemola, and Pitkänen (2002), and Filppula, Klemola,

---

[1] For introductions to Celtic see Jackson (1971), Thomson, R. L. (1984), Ball and Fife (eds. 2003: 3–98), and Ó Néill (ed. 2005).

[2] For Latin, e.g. L. *labor* > W. *llafur*, see Lewis (1943) and Haarmann (1970); for Irish, see Lockwood (1975); O'Rahilly (1924). Windsor Lewis (1990: 109) argues that it is difficult to untangle Scandinavian and Flemish influence on Welsh in many cases; however, some words are probably ultimately Norse, e.g., *bap* 'kind of loaf,' *better*, 'recovered from illness,' *devilskin* 'naughty child,' and *up in years* 'elderly.' Probable Flemish loanwords in Pembrokeshire English include *reeve* 'gather (of fabric),' *culf* 'hunk (of bread).' The well-known expression of shock *ach-y-fi* might also be Flemish ultimately (Windsor Lewis 1980: 111). Placenames such as *Skomer*, *Skokholm*, *Fishguard*, and *Bardsey* are of Norse origin.

[3] For a history of Welsh, see Ball (2007: 237–253) and for specific effects of immigration see Jenkins (2000). On the English language in Wales, see e.g.; Bellin (1984); Penhallurick (2007: 152–170) and Walters (2001: 285–304).

[4] Filppula, M (1997: 192–199).

and Paulsato (2008).[5] Their considered assessment of what effects the Celtic languages may have exerted on the development of English is discussed at length in successive chapters of the latter volume. One feature that attracts particular interest is the curious difference between English and the other Germanic languages in having developed a progressive aspect, a feature familiar to students of Irish and Welsh. Other features are often commented upon, for example the vestigial Celtic system for counting still in use in the English of Cumbrian shepherds in the late 1980s. A study of lexical relationships between the daughter languages of British Celtic appeared as Elsie (1979), with subsequent work on lexicostatistics and British Celtic appearing in print soon after (Elsie 1983). Celtic influence on Britain in relation to archaeology as well as language is reported in a series of papers in Cunliffe and Koch (2012).

Place names and loanwords are an indication of the way in which the English language has made its presence felt in Welsh. Several words in Welsh clearly show borrowing in the Anglo-Saxon period, e.g. W. *hebog* < OE *hæbuc* 'hawk'; W. *ffanugl* < OE *finugol* 'fennel'.[6] Other words like Welsh *fridd* or *frith* 'mountain pasture' (OE *(ge)fyr(h)þ*), are probably not directly from OE, but come via ME.[7] In the other direction, English words with British Celtic origins appear to include *bannock* 'small piece,' *brock* 'badger,' and *hogg* 'pig.' Some early loanwords into Welsh show relics of medieval sounds changes in English, for example the West Midland Middle English (ME) change of /a/ to /o/ before a nasal consonant, for example W. *lôn* < ME *lan* 'lane,' W. *bonc* < ME *bank*, 'a low ridge,' and *plismon* 'policeman.' Place names too often indicate archaic long-lost pronunciations of English words, so that, for example, the village of Newborough on Anglesey is *Niwbwrch* in Welsh, showing the original final velar fricative /x/ of Old English (OE) *bur* /burx/ still intact, a feature also found in W. *dracht* < E. *draught*. Similarly W. *cnaf* 'rascal' derives from OE *cnaf* with the initial /k/ still intact in Welsh (as in *cnocio* 'knock' (v)) and the old long monophthong of ME.[8]

Other fossils of lost pronunciations of English words are illustrated by W. *banced* < ME *ban(c)ket* 'banquet', and W. *amrel* < ME *amyrayl* 'admiral,' though it may be that the Welsh word is actually directly borrowed from French and not via English; working out which loanwords came directly into Welsh from French is a complex issue in its own right. How French and Welsh coexisted linguistically in the fortified towns of Wales in the fourteenth century particularly needs careful scrutiny, but contact

[5] See especially the extensive discussion in the second chapter entitled "The Linguistic Outcomes of the Early Contacts."

[6] But possibly directly from Latin, *fenuclum*.

[7] Welsh *fridd* may not be a direct borrowing from Old English. The present metathesized form is only recorded in English after 1375, which suggests that the word came into Welsh only in the fourteenth century. The Welsh use reflects OED *frith* sense 2: 'a piece of land grown sparsely with trees or with underwood only. Also, a space between woods: unused pasture land.'

[8] Place names also reflect this: Newborough in Anglesey is *Niwbwrch* in Welsh with the Old English final fricative intact, and the mountain near Porthmadog in Gwynedd known as *Cnicht* preserves not only the original initial /kn/, but also the final /x/ and even the old short vowel of E. *knight* as in Chaucer's time /knixt/.

between the two undoubtedly happened. Evidence of medieval pronunciations of English reflecting the French of the time also come through in some loanwords into Welsh: the French vowels /ã/ and /õ/ regularly appear in modern Welsh as /au/ for example in *dawns* 'dance,' *aparawns* 'apparent,' *galawnt* 'gallant,' *blesawnt* 'blazon,' and *daimawnt* 'diamond.' In southern England the nasal vowel has ultimately become a long vowel, while in Wales the diphthong has remained.

Local lexical items from English dialects also drift into adjacent areas of Wales, too, and appear in Welsh, thus *rwdins* (< E. *rootings*) 'swedes' in large areas of north Wales.[9] Thomas (1973) shows how, for example, W. *ratlin* (< E. *ratling*) 'the smallest pig in a litter' occurs just in east Montgomeryshire.[10] Distribution of loanwords thus varies enormously. Some loanwords are widespread. The words for 'sweets' have a remarkable geographical distribution.[11] Most of the regional terms for 'sweets' in Welsh are ultimately English in origin. Some occur widely, for example W. *fferins* 'sweets' (< E. *fairings*) is found across the entire north of Wales, but nowhere south of Aberystwyth, while *minciag* < E. *mintcake* occurs only in eastern Snowdonia. In the south, *swîts* (<Eng. *sweets*) is the typical word across the southwest, while *taffi(n)s* (< Eng. *toffees*) is commonest in the southeast. Why certain loanwords are preferred over others in different parts of the country might reflect the availability of the type of sweet at the time of introduction to the area. There is also *candi* (< E. *candy*) (a word confined largely to Anglesey), *los(h)ins* (< E. *lozenges*) in south Wales, and *cacen* (< E. *cake*) in Montgomeryshire. In Anglesey in the far northwest, the native *petha(u) da* 'good things' competes with *candi* and indeed *fferins*, while in Denbighshire in the northeast the loan *fferins* competes with native *dada*, literally 'good-good.'

Not until the appearance of Parry-Williams (1923) did a clear picture emerge of the extent of lexical borrowing from English into Welsh over the centuries. Written at a time just as work was beginning on the *Geiriadur Prifysgol Cymru/University of Wales Dictionary*, it is still remarkable for its detailed observation and systematic coverage. Semantic shift sometimes becomes evident, too. The word for 'upstairs' in many parts of Wales is *llofft*, a word clearly derived from the English *loft*, which now means a place where things are stored, not necessarily a place where sleeping occurs. Fowkes (1945) represents a later contribution to the discussion of English influence on Welsh. Work on the English of Wales is not extensive, but notable contributions are Coupland (ed. 1990), the *Survey of Anglo-Welsh Dialects* (SAWD),[12] the Archive of Welsh English,[13] the BBC four-part radio series *The Way That You Say It*[14] and Crystal and Crystal (2013: 117–130).

---

[9] National Museum of Wales Archive of Recordings website, Llannerch-y-medd, Anglesey.

[10] Thomas (1973), Item 186, p. 261. Interestingly, LGW does not pick up the loanword *ffebrins* 'gooseberries' found in eastern Montgomeryshire from English *feaberries*, a word now rare in English dialect.

[11] Thomas (1973), Item 132, p. 205.

[12] See Parry (1977) and subsequent volumes of SAWD.

[13] Originally set up by David Parry, and added to by David Penhallurick: http://www.swan.ac.uk/crew/researchprojects/thearchiveofwelshenglish/

[14] *The Way That You Say It: English in Wales*. BBC Radio Wales. March 23–April 13, 2003.

In trying to measure lexical borrowing, lexicologists have to confront many theoretical issues that are often difficult to resolve. These include the problem of dating a loanword's first appearance in a language—a word may enter speech first, then writing later, or the other way around, or the text in which the word first appeared in writing might no longer exist. Speakers' attitudes toward loanwords themselves is another complex question. Some speakers and certainly many writers view English loanwords as not proper Welsh words and avoid using them, even though they have been in general circulation for some time. Some loanwords come into Welsh several times in different periods in different forms. Then there is also the issue of attempts to change the form of an existing loanword to make it look as if it has a rather different linguistic history than appears to be the case, an issue discussed later.

Contact phenomena consist of more than just lexical borrowing, of course. At the syntactic level, Thomas noted the possibility that the English periphrastic 'do' constructions could reflect substratum effects of Welsh (Thomas 1984; also Penhallurick 1996, 2004), but Tristram (1999) and Klemola (2002: 206) have argued that Welsh was in contact with southwestern dialects of English in the Middle Ages and the features spread not from Welsh but *into* it.[15] Periphrastic verb constructions involving copula plus verb-noun are, however, a distinctive and long-standing feature of other Celtic languages such as Irish. What is interesting is that Welsh verbs have no present tense conjugations, only future, conditional, and past ones. A choice regularly exists between using an inflected verb or a construction with either *gwneud* 'do' or in some areas the deponent verb *ddarfu* 'happened,' so, for example, to say 'he refused' there are up to three possibilities:

(1) *mi*   *wrthododd*   *o*
     Particle-PAST   refuse+PAST   he

(2) *mi*   *wnaeth*   *o*   *wrthod*
     Particle-PAST   do+PAST   he   refuse

(3) *mi*   *ddarfu*   *iddo fo*   *wrthod*
     Particle-PAST   happened   to him   refuse
     (1) in speech generally becomes '*Aru fo wrthod*'.

To possible substratum effects as a feature of contact can be added switching, mid-sentence, between languages.[16] Jones (1998: 252) identifies four kinds of linguistic change that are attributable to the dominant language, in our case English. The first is lexical borrowing, consisting of the subtypes borrowing proper, and calques. Second,

---

[15] See also Hickey (1995) and Tristram (2002).
[16] Fowkes (1945) is an early discussion of this contact feature.

there is grammatical interference, for example the use of the English pattern of using a plural noun after a numeral: *saith o ferched* 'seven girls,' rather than the native standard pattern of numeral plus singular noun: *saith merch.* Jones also notes among younger speakers the use of a plural noun directly after a numeral: *eich dau cathod* 'your two cats,' with the masculine form of the numeral being used with a feminine noun also, rather than the "conservative" *eich dwy gath.*

Jones's third kind of linguistic change is code-switching, common in casual conversation, where short stretches of English vocabulary are interpolated, possibly where the English word has a meaning or resonance that cannot be exactly conveyed by the Welsh word, for example the use of an English word *wrong* in Welsh as in *Ych chi'n rong, gyboi* 'You're wrong, good boy (mate).' The reverse also occurs. Phrases such as *Go to gwely* 'Go to bed' are common in English in some parts of south Wales and have attracted the attention of dialectologists who term this Wenglish,' particularly in the variety of English of valleys north of Cardiff (Edwards 2003; Lewis 2008).[17]

Even in areas where Welsh-speaking is solid, like Pwllheli on the northwestern Lleyn (Llŷn) peninsula, examples of code-switching were commonly reported in 1970s dialect research, where numbers trigger a switch into English mid-sentence:

(4) *Ddeuson'*   *i lawr i*   *hundred and fifty* *ac*   *oedd*   *bargen*
      came+PAST+we   down to   150   and   be+PAST   bargain
      wedi ei streicio
      after its striking
      'we came down to 150 and a bargain was struck'

(5) *ma'*   *'na*   *twenty two* *o*   *fedrwms*   *yn* *y*   *tŷ*   *i gyd*
      Be+PLURAL   there   22   of   bedrooms   in   the   house   whole
      'there are 22 bedrooms in the whole house'[18]

Phonological interference is the fourth type Jones identifies, discussed in the following. Differences have emerged between the degree of integration of some English elements that have entered Welsh very recently. Some forms, such as *disapirio* 'to disappear' in place of native *diflannu*, or *smocio* 'smoke' for *ysmygu*, can be regarded as "innovatory" loans as against other more established loans termed here "lexicalized" loans in that they may not appear in all the syntactic contexts that lexicalized loans do. On the other hand, the new term *cyfrifiadur* 'computer' is holding its ground against *compiwter*.[19]

---

[17] Awareness of the subtle humor that can arise from code-switching was also exploited when a popular Welsh rock band caused much amusement among young people by calling itself *Ffa Coffi I Bawb*, 'coffee beans for all,' but if interpreted as a blend of English and Welsh a far ruder phrase results.

[18] Roberts, 1972.

[19] See website of *Geiriadur Prifysgol Cymru*, and the separate website for the *Introduction to Second Edition*. See also Griffiths and Jones (1995).

Eventually, innovatory loans may well become lexicalized so that it can become difficult to decide to which type a recent loan belongs, especially when there is little indication of its general use among speakers. In such a way, borrowings accumulate to form a substantial element within the language, like the Latin or French element in English. It is often the case, however, that native speakers refuse to accept that these loanwords occur at all, especially those of the more "transparent" variety, such as *byhafio* 'behave' (W. *ymddwyn*) and *rŵm* 'room' (W. *ystafell*). Some native speakers might rebuke others for using some of the more recent loans with the words *Siarad Cymraeg!* 'Speak Welsh!' as if they had been speaking momentarily in English.

Bilingualism and contact also produce many doublets with slight differences in register: the native verb *gyrru* and the loaned *dreifio* both mean 'to drive,' but the first is more literary, the other more casual in register. Similarly, there are native *hoffi* and loaned *leicio* (*licio*) 'to like,' and in both cases the loaned verb can attach native suffixes:

(6)   *Leiciech chi gael cipolwg?* Would you like to have a look?

Some of the early Welsh dictionaries ignore the English element in Welsh for the most part, the exception being where the loanword is sufficiently opaque and when historical links are not immediately obvious (e.g., *deon* 'dean,' *bwrdais* 'burgess,' *cario* 'carry'). More recently compiled dictionaries have included more loanwords, but more loan translations have also been introduced to offset the trend toward borrowing from English for deriving new words for new objects and ideas. The 1970s publication *Geiriadur Termau* [Dictionary of Terms][20] was an early product of the movement toward providing Welsh users with official loan translations for common English terms.

In passing, one may note that contact phenomena have themselves given rise to identity markers in speech. At the phonetic level, for example, Northern Welsh has no /z/. This feature is very distinctive as a marker of someone's ability to speak Welsh in the English speech of North Wales where /z/ is regularly replaced by /s/. Features like this become significant. Work in the mid-1970s showed how English speakers were evaluated in terms of the apparent strength of their Welshness by their adoption or non-adoption of features of Welsh phonology, or their avoidance of features of Received Pronunciation that might make them otherwise sound too English.[21] Contact phenomena are thus not just accidental in some cases, but often are consciously adopted and used to convey an identity to other people locally.[22]

---

[20] The complete set of official Welsh terminology dictionaries are now only accessible online.
[21] See, e.g., Giles and Powesland (1975).
[22] See Coupland (2006).

15.2 A 1970s Study of Lexical Borrowing

Grey (1978) represented an attempt to update the loanword study of Parry-Williams at a time when linguistic corpora for Welsh were unavailable.[23] One of the conclusions drawn at the time was that lexical borrowing was happening at a much faster rate than ever before, but even at that time, measuring the extent of lexical borrowing proved difficult, practically and theoretically, simply because written and spoken texts could only be analyzed and assessed impressionistically at the time, in an age before the existence of computerized corpora. Still, the data collected suggested various interesting features, for example that native morphological and syntactic processes were changing to accommodating English features, and that speech was far more likely to show contact features than writing, especially in informal registers.

Grey worked with the notion of *cambrification*, a process whereby what were arguably words borrowed from English to Welsh were apparently being reworked into something that looked or sounded older and less English (e.g., the word *radio*). In Welsh the word has a short vowel. One would have expected it to have the English diphthong /ei/ since English is the likely source. In its written form, the Welsh and English words are identical, but the pronunciation is different. The adoption of the short vowel /a/ by Welsh speakers is either a product of Welsh speakers thinking that the diphthong would make the word sound too English, or a conscious awareness that the word ought really to reflect the classical source language like Latin or Greek, a process not at all unknown in early modern English (*dette > debt, ancor > anchor*). This substitution of /a/ for /ei/ seems distinctly common. Working out the etymology of many modern Welsh words with counterparts in English is unexpectedly complex, especially in their spoken form. The issue is addressed again later in the chapter.[24]

In theory it is possible to date English borrowings into Welsh by looking at the operation of English sound changes. One English sound change that seems to be relevant for dating borrowing into Welsh is the so-called great vowel shift, a phonetic change that occurred in the late Middle Ages and had profound effects on the subsequent pronunciation of English.

Essential to an understanding of this is English's great vowel shift. While the long vowels of Welsh have more or less stayed the same over time, in English vowel shifts

---

[23] With the digital age has come the establishment of several corpora of Welsh texts, notably the *Welsh Language Corpus*, coordinated by the University of Bangor, a million words of Welsh, and Cambridge University's *Historical Corpus of the Welsh Language 1500–1850*. The data used in the Grey (1978) study were taken from contemporary editions of *Spurrell's Welsh Dictionary* and *Y Geiriadur Newydd* with dates of first recorded usage deriving from entries in those *Geiriadur Prifysgol Cymru* fascicles that were available at the time.

[24] Since 1993, work on providing new words for Welsh is coordinated by the Centre for the Standardization of Welsh Terminology, e.g., SALT Cymru.

have been quite dramatic in changing the way English sounded before and after 1500. The great vowel shift (GVS) is a process involving the displacement of long vowels into the phonetic space of neighboring long vowels. One view has it that vowels were pushed out of the way by their phonetically more open neighbors in a cyclic pattern that forces vowels to become phonetically closer, while close vowels become diphthongs. Whether the vowels were pushed or in fact pulled out of position is another matter for debate. The actuation of the sound change and the geographical spread of it across English-speaking territory is not so relevant here, but is not uncontroversial.[25] What is relevant is the outcome for interpreting the date of borrowing into Welsh of new words after 1500. Since contact between the two languages was happening before and after the English GVS, the kind of vowels we get in the loanwords themselves might in principle indicate when the word first arrived in Welsh. The GVS can be understood, or at least presented as, a series of "rules" (see Table 15.1).

Baugh and Cable, and others, state that these changes in southern English would certainly have been complete by 1700 and probably earlier,[26] depending on geographical location. Sometimes words borrowed into Welsh show the effects of the application of the GVS, and sometimes not, so that occasionally doublets are found, one showing a pre-GVS vowel, one showing a post-GVS vowel. Table 15.2 presents some examples.

Table 15.1 Occurrence of Pre- and Post-Great Vowel Shift Vowels in Welsh Loanwords Database

The Great Vowel Shift
ME /a:/ > PE /eɪ/ (via /e:/) (PE = Present-day English)
ME /e:/ > PE /i:/
ME /o:/ > PE /u:/
ME /i:/ > PE /aɪ/
ME /u:/ > PE /aʊ/

Table 15.2 Welsh Analogues of Middle English Vowels

ME /a:/	crwsad and crwsed	'crusade'	
ME /e:/	crepian and cripian	'creep'	
ME /i:/	crocodil and crocodeil	'crocodile'	
ME /o:/	cocon and cocwn	'cocoon'	
ME /u:/	ffwl* and ffowl	'fowl'	(ffwl is now obsolete)

[25] For classic treatments of the great vowel shift, see e.g. Baugh and Cable (2002) §177. For criticism, see e.g. Stockwell and Minkova (1998), Johnston (1992), and Lass (ed. 1995). Ekwall does not use the term great vowel shift, but discusses the dating of the phonetic evidence in detail. On the specific shifting of ME long /a:/ see Ekwall (1975: 15–16).

[26] Baugh and Cable (2002: 238–239).

Table 15.3 Principal Links

	pre	post
ME /aː/	117	9
ME /eː/	61	40
ME /iː/	74	50
ME /oː/	5	24
ME /uː/	16	20

The table from the 1978 study (Table 15.3) shows the relative frequency of pre- and post-GVS vowels in the words examined that in Middle English have the long monophthong:

The results show that 117 words in the loanword database had a pre-GVS vowel, while nine did not.

The results were rather unexpected. There was clear preference for /aː/ (or in some instances /a/) over /eɪ/ where /aː/ was suggested in the orthography of the corresponding English word containing <a> (e.g., *crusâd* 'crusade'). The results for the reflexes of ME /eː/ and ME /iː/ appear to be of near equal frequency; /oː/ appears far less frequently as the reflex of ME long /oː/ than /uː/. The study suggested that the number of borrowings before 1500 was about one-third of all the total number of borrowings into the language and that there appeared to be a general trend to use vowels that are associated with dates before 1500, even for words that entered the language long after the GVS had finished its course.

One thing noted was that literary Welsh seemed more likely to evidence cambrification than spoken Welsh. In spontaneous spoken Welsh the post-GVS vowels were apparently far more likely in recent borrowings.

One especially common example of this is the treatment of modern English /eɪ/ where the orthography has <a> reflecting Middle English /aː/, in words like *cable*, *cake*, *vulgate*, *face*, *frame*, *gate*, *plane*, usually represented by the sequence <aCe>, C representing any consonant. If one were to date the Welsh forms of these words, one would be surprised at the variety of dates after 1500, the date by which most varieties of English would have completed the GVS, converting ME /aː/ to /eː/, later /eɪ/. The hypothesis that all words borrowed with orthographic <aCe> into written Welsh are pre-1500 borrowings is thus incorrect. Some, of course, are, but many are not. Of the twenty-five loans having the <a>, only seven or so could be traced by the first method of dating to before 1500. Even allowing a hundred years for the effects of the GVS to be felt, new loanwords were still being evidenced with "pre-vowel shift" vowels long after the sound change had finished, for example *becwedd* 'bequeath' (1757), *befer* 'beaver' (1740), *bêm* 'beam' (C20), *cabal* 'cable' (1728) *cansen* 'cane' (n.) (1770), *crepian* 'creep' (1794), *cwafer* 'quaver' (1833), *fwlgat* 'vulgate' (C20), *generadu* 'generate' (C20), and so on. It seems odd that these Welsh words with "medieval" English vowels are only recorded in the last three hundred years, long after the GVS had finished. Maybe they existed only in speech until quite late. But some words, clearly reflecting new inventions or ideas unknown before 1800, also have the "medieval" "pre-shifted" vowels: *laser* 'laser' (1967), *amnesia* (1878), and *radio* (1926). It seems like there is a consistent reworking of the vowel to give the word more classical origins.

Furthermore, only the GVS is sufficiently useful to date any large number of loans. Other sound changes of English tended to be attested erratically in loanwords into English, and are more problematic to work with. The great problem with using sound changes as reference points for the date of initial borrowing is that it is often difficult to distinguish borrowings due to modern substitution effects from those showing actual pre-sound change importation. One has first to note correspondences of forms, and then sort them into those that have been reworked by cambrification, and those that genuinely reflect pre-sound change conditions at the time of intro-duction. Another problem is the lack of any substantial number of sound changes affecting loanwords once they have come into Welsh. The GVS, while providing a whole host of anomalies, is thus the only real tool to work with to establish a general picture of when a word was borrowed into Welsh. First recorded usage in print is only a partial guide.[27]

Much of this discussion takes for granted that a word comes into a language from a source just once. This is a rather unrealistically static view of the process of borrowing. Languages are not things that are simply out there, divorced from the people who speak them. If lexical borrowing is considered a much more dynamic process, so that the same word comes repeatedly into a language again and again as new generations learn the language and borrow words from their linguistic neighbors, then we should expect loanwords to encounter competing pronunciations that have been absorbed into the language at different periods. We should expect English loanwords in Welsh to have pre- and post-GVS vowel variants. The curious thing is that the post-GVS variants seem far fewer in number than the pre-GVS variants. It seems that early variants of English loanwords become entrenched and resist the arrival of phonetically different later arrivals.[28]

Lexically the linguistic effects of contact between Welsh and English have almost entirely been one-way. Very few words have entered into English from Welsh, pre-sumably because Welsh words had little status or prestige among the English, unlike French or Italian or Spanish words. Even now, loanwords like *eisteddfod* still retain their Welsh provenance when used in English. At the level of pronunciation, on the

---

[27] In passing, one may note how medieval Welsh spelling is often used as valuable evidence of how English was pronounced in the aftermath of the GVS. The *Hymn to the Virgin* is a remarkable text showing Welsh spelling conventions applied to English. Dobson (1955) makes great use of this text to determine the nature of English vowels in early modern English, particularly in relation to the reflexes of ME /u:/ (as in /ku:/ 'cow') and /ou/ (as in /lou/ 'low') and how they were kept apart as ME /u:/ became the present-day vowel of Eng. *house* (/au/).

[28] The British pronunciations of *missile* and *fragile* have failed to oust American ones for the same reason, despite close contact between the two varieties for nearly three centuries now.

other hand, the Welsh language has clearly influenced spoken English in Wales, especially since there have been large numbers of Welsh speakers in the past. Evidence of a Welsh accent in English stretches back to at least as far as Shakespeare's characters of Fluellen (Llywelyn) in *Henry V* and Sir Hugh Evans in *Merry Wives of Windsor*, who display some very striking, even exaggerated Welsh features in their speech.

15.3 GRAMMATICAL ACCOMMODATION

At this point, attention must turn to some of the effects of linguistic contact in contemporary Welsh. In relation to contact phenomena beyond lexical borrowing, at the morphological level there are at least three areas of interest: gender assignment, suffixation, and pluralization.

15.3.1 Gender Assignment

Grammatical gender is not marked in present-day English nouns. In contrast, Welsh nouns *are* grammatically marked for gender. The question is then how English loanwords in Welsh acquire their grammatical gender. Are nouns automatically masculine? The issue was addressed in 1978, and it appeared that the phonetic shape of the base of the word did partly determine the grammatical gender.

1. Of the monosyllabic loans in the database, 28.6%were feminine, while 19.4% of polysyllables were feminine. There was thus a greater tendency for monosyllabic loans to be feminine than polysyllabic ones.
2. Monosyllabic loanwords with initial <f>, <ff>, and <w> seemed more likely to be feminine than masculine. Monosyllable loanwords with other initial consonants were more likely to be masculine.
3. For monosyllabic loans, probability of feminine gender increased over the range: initial nasals, voiceless stops, voiced stops, vowels, affricates, liquids, continuants, and fricatives. For polysyllabic loans the same trend appeared, but the percentage of feminine nouns overall was less, except for initial /ʃ/ and /m/, where feminine nouns seemed to be above the norm.

A second indication as to the process of accommodation of loanwords into the gender system was revealed by an analysis of the phonetic quality of internal stressed vowels. Some internal vowels seem to trigger feminine gender, particularly /o/. Monosyllabic loans with /i/ seem more likely to be masculine on balance. While the pattern is not so obvious with native words, the study suggested a distinct tendency for loanwords at least to be feminine when this vowel occurred.

15.3.2 Lenition

There is also the issue of how English loanwords fit the grammatical processes of lenition, so distinctive of Welsh (and other Celtic languages). Many initial consonants in Welsh change their quality under certain grammatical conditions. Standard textbooks on Welsh refer to (at least) four types of lenition or word-initial mutation: (a) soft mutation, (b) nasal mutation, (c) aspirate mutation, and (d) H-prefixation.[29]

(a) Soft Mutation (Treiglad Meddal): this happens, e.g., after certain prepositions such as *i* 'to, into' and *o* 'from,' or for example if it is an object of an inflected verb.
Initial /p/ > /b/; /t/ > /d/; /k/ > /g/; /m/ > /v/; /b/ > /v/; /d/ >/ð/; /g/>zero, where <f> = /v/ and <dd> = /ð/:
For example *mawr* 'big'; *Mae hi'n fawr* 'It is big'
Under certain, more restricted, syntactic conditions the voiceless fricative lateral /ɬ/ <ll> also mutates, becoming voiced, /l/, and the voiceless trill /r̥/ <rh> becomes voiced /r/:
Llandudno 'Llandudno' > *O Landudno* 'from Llandudno'
(b) Nasal mutation (Treiglad Trwynol): this happens in only a few contexts, after certain prepositions like *yn*, 'in,' or the preposition *fy* (or *yn*) 'my'
initial /p/>/mh/; /t/>/nh/; /k/>/ngh/; /b/>/m/; /d/>/n/; /g/>/ng/
For example *Trawsfynydd* 'Trawsfynydd' *yn Nhrawsfynydd* 'in Trawsfynydd'
(c) Aspirate mutation (Treiglad Llaes): this happens in just a few contexts, for example after the conjunction *a* 'and' or after *tri* 'three'
/p/ > /f/; /t/ > /θ/ ; /k/ > /x/
cath 'cat' > *ci a chath* 'dog and cat'
(d) H-prefixation: Although not technically a mutation in the traditional use of the term, this process adds an /h/ to an initial vowel of a word when, for example, *ei* 'her' or *ei* 'their' occurs:[30]
afal 'apple' > *ei hafal* 'her apple'

---

[29] On Welsh lenition, see Morgan (1952) and Williams (1959), who claims a fifth lenition type, hard or internal mutation (Treiglad Caled/Treiglad Mewnol), operating as in, e.g., *teg* 'fair,' *tecach* 'fairer,' but this is not word-initial mutation here. Suffixes like *–ach* might be best treated as /hax/ at a deeper level with the /h/ simply obscured by the orthography. Watkins (2002: 307) claims that in spontaneous colloquial language there is complete loss of nasal and aspirate mutation. King (2003: 80) claims that aspirate and nasal mutation are nowadays avoided by many speakers, claiming that some are using expressions like *plant fi* for *yn mhlant* 'my children,' which King claims is "widely regarded as sub-standard." For recent statistical treatment of some mutations, e.g., the treatment of *blynedd* 'year' after numerals, see Borsley et al. (2007: 164).

[30] Watkins (2002: 307) includes the H-prefixation process here as simply an aspect of aspirate mutation, as V>hV, but notes the very restricted conditions for H-prefixation.

Phonetically the vowel becomes voiceless, and in that sense the process does function as a mutation, changing the phonetic quality along a phonetic dimension, not voicing or fricativization here, but devoicing.[31] The consonant phoneme inventories of Welsh and English (taking Received Pronunciation here) are different in many respects, for example in native words Welsh has /x/, while RP and does not;[32] /ɬ/ and /r̥/ can occur in word-initial position in Welsh but not in RP, while /r/ and /l/ cannot occur in this position in Welsh, unless they are the outcome of lenition. Similarly, /ð/ cannot appear word-initially in Welsh, unless as an outcome of soft mutation.

As a consequence, if a word does occur in Welsh with initial /r/ or /l/ outside of a leniting context, it is certainly a loan from English, for example W. *ras* '(sport) race,' *lamp* 'lamp.'[33]

One would not expect loanwords from English to undergo lenition, since /r/ and /l/ do not occur in word-initial position in native Welsh words, and yet some loanwords actually do in some areas, notably early ones. Consider this:

Welsh *ei* /i/ 'her' triggers aspirate mutation:
/i da:d/   *ei dad*   'his father'
/i θa:d/   *ei thad*   'her father'

What occurs in some areas is an extension of lenition to initial radical /l/, /r/, and /w/, but since aspirate mutation cannot apply to initial /l/ and /r/, an alternative H-prefixation process occurs, beyond the normal phonetic context, extended to contexts not only involving words with initial vowels, but consonants also, this apparently in order to convey the gender of the pronoun more overtly, a mechanism for semantic disambiguation:

/i lamp/   *ei lamp*   'his lamp'
/i lhamp/   *ei lamp*   'her lamp'[34]

---

[31]   King (2003: 80) notes that this prefixing of /h/ to a word-initial vowel shows little consistency in the spoken language, and many speakers seem not to have it. If this is so, then a pronoun has to be inserted to make clear the gender: *ei afal hi* 'her apple.' Williams does not categorize H-prefixation as a mutation at all, yet it clearly functions as one, involving phonetic change in word-initial position under certain grammatical circumstances, like other mutations. Clearly the effect of H-prefixation is to de-voice a following vowel.
In any case, the interpretation of /h/ in Welsh as an independent phoneme in Welsh is arguable. A rather different picture of Welsh mutation emerges if a systemic contrast between voiced and voiceless vowels is adopted, rather than one employing /h/. For a prosodic treatment, see Thomas (1966: 114–122).
[32]   In Welsh /x/ cannot appear in word-initial position, unless it is the outcome of lenition; /xʷ/ can appear in this position, however. Loanwords that in early English had initial /hw/ (now /w/), such as *chwilber* 'wheelbarrow' and *chwipio* 'to whip,' continue to reflect the voicelessness of the original English consonant.
[33]   The case of *lolfa* 'lounge' (n.), which does not look like a loan at first, is probably explained as composed of a loaned base *lol* (English *loll*) with a native derivational suffix *-fa*.
[34]   Jones (1967, 182–184).

Textbooks often fail to notice these extensions of lenition processes to loanwords, and they form a very interesting example of contact phenomena at the phonetic level as part of integration of certain lexical items to the native system. What appears here is the extension of lenition rules to phonetic contexts beyond the native system.

Not all nouns show initial lenition either. Welsh Personal names never mutate (these days). No speaker would say *Owen a Thim* for *Owen a Tim* 'Owen and Tim'. Names as objects of inflected verbs do not mutate either: **Mi welais Ddafydd* 'I saw David.' Place nouns do mutate, however: *Manceinion* in Welsh, but *Manchester* in English. One can say *Mi es i Fanceinion* 'I went to Manchester,' but if the speaker chooses to use the English version *Manchester* instead of *Manceinion* when speaking Welsh, then it does not mutate: *Mi es i Manchester*, not **Mi es i Fanchester*.

In general, loanwords that resist mutation give away the recentness of their introduction—the resistance gives away their lack of integration into the language. The less they are integrated, the more "foreign" they seem, and the more uncertain their linguistic status. Some examples are afforded by the spoken Welsh of Pwllheli,[35] thus *hen bitsh* 'old bitch,' not *hen fitsh* (*hen* 'old' automatically triggers soft mutation of native words), and *oedd 'na bensh fawr* 'there was a large bench,' not the expected *oedd 'na fensh fawr*, (mutation of subject noun when an adverb intervenes between a verb and its subject); with *bensh* identified as a feminine noun in Welsh, we can note in passing, shown in the mutation of *mawr* to *fawr*. Some notable loanwords resist mutation of any sort, despite being well established, for example *bêl* 'bale,' *bocs* 'box,' *bonet* 'bonnet,' *botel* 'bottle,' *byldar* 'builder,' *cîn* 'keen,' *crwd* 'crude,' and *bylding* 'building.'

Third, the question of the **plural form** of words: English plurals are virtually all formed by the suffixation of <s> or <es>. In Welsh there are many more different plural suffixes, for example <-(i)au> *afal* 'apple,' *afalau* 'apples'; <-od> *cath* 'cat,' *cathod* 'cats'; <-aid>, <oedd>, <ydd>, and <(i)on>. Grey (1978) found that in the database of loanwords investigated, three-quarters of the loanwords from English appearing in written Welsh showed <au> or <iau> as the plural suffix, for example *cordiau* 'cords,' *planciau* 'planks,' *sbeciau* 'specks,' *ponciau* 'banks,' and *sbrigiau* 'sprigs.' For the distribution of suffixes in the loanword database, see Table 15.4.

The selection of suffixes is not arbitrary, though; for example <-od> tends to occur only with words for animals, women, babies, some vegetables, and some nationalities.

The suffix <s> was not originally a productive suffix in Welsh, and certainly not a native suffix, but over time it has become established as a productive suffix and has been used as a suffix for many English loanwords, for example *jobs* 'jobs,' *marblys* 'marbles,' *plwms* 'plums,' and *teils* 'tiles.'

Another feature of interest is the regular pattern of starting off with the plural form of the English loanword, and making a singular out of it by suffixation, so that, in a sense, the plural comes first, and the singular comes after:

---

[35] Roberts (1972).

Table 15.4 Plural Suffix Selection in Database of English Loanwords in Written Welsh

Plural Suffix	No. of Instances of Suffix	% of All Plural Nouns
'AU' /aɨ /	1094	53.2
'IAU' /jaɨ/	457	22.2
'OEDD' /oɨð /	29	1.4
'YDD' /ɨð/	21	1.0
'ON' /on/	17	0.8
'ION' /jon/	47	2.3
'I' /i/	154	7.5
'S' /s/	125	6.1
'OD' /od/	39	1.9
'AID' /aid/	123	6.0

Source: (Grey 1978)

English plural + <-yn>: *cwilsyn* 'a quill,' *sialotsyn* 'a shallot,' *winwsyn* 'an onion.'

English plural + <-en> e.g., *bricsen* 'a brick,' *bynsen* 'a bun,' *clocsen* 'a clog,' *cyrensen* 'a current,' *gwsbersen* 'a gooseberry,' *plwmsen* 'a plum.'

The regular formation of a plural suffix added to a singular base also occurs:

English singular + <-yn> for example *cordyn,* 'cord,' *certyn* 'cart,' *jobyn* 'job,' *postyn* 'a post,' *potyn* 'a pot,' *rhosyn* 'a rose.'

English singular + <-en> *disgen* 'a disk,' *peren* 'a pear,' *petrisen* 'a partridge.'

Sometimes the singular and the plural are both formed by suffixation with singular suffix <–yn> and plural suffix <–iau>: *cordiau* 'cords,' *planciau* 'planks,' *sbrigiau* 'sprigs.'

15.3.3 Verb Suffixes

In relation to loanwords from English coming into Welsh, a rather similar pattern has emerged with verbs. Welsh has many native verb suffixes, but one suffix <-(i)o> (and its northern version <-ian>) has become highly productive and is virtually the only productive suffix for loaned verbs from English: *scretsh* 'screech'(n) > *scretshian* 'screatch' (v).

Modern English does not have an infinitive suffix, but in earlier periods <-an> and <-en> occurred (<-an> is also attached to certain native Welsh stems, as in, e.g., *clebran* 'to chatter').[36] Old English had a verb suffix <-an> or <-ian>. This suffix appears on

[36] OED records a figurative use of *clapper* meaning 'human tongue' as a noun that could be the source of the W. verb *clebran*.

many verb loans in present-day Welsh, for example *hofran* 'to hover,' *hongian* 'to hang.' Again, it is paradoxical that, in a sense, this is another example of Welsh retaining a once-productive feature of English, long after its disappearance from the host language. The commonest verb-noun suffix in Welsh is <-io>, added to many native and non-native stems: *dinistrio* 'to destroy,' *testio* 'to test.'[37] The <-an> and <-en> suffixes are clearly unproductive now in English, so their existence in loanwords in Welsh shows the antiquity of the loan. Oddly enough, however, some loanwords with <-an> are not recorded in Welsh usage until the seventeenth century (e.g., *clwcian* 'cluck,' *cwrian* 'cower,' and *jocan* 'joke,' so either they only existed in speech until that date and were not recorded in writing, or the <-an> suffix enjoyed a revival in Welsh for a time (in some areas at least), long after its disappearance in English. Note too that forms in <-io> are more frequent in northern Welsh than in the south, where <-o> is more likely: NW *peintio* versus SW *peinto* 'to paint.' Pwllheli dialect in the north has *cowntio* 'to count,' *dawnsio* 'to dance,' *trimio* 'to trim,'[38] while Llansamlet, Swansea, has *cownto, dawnso,* and *trimo.*[39]

15.4 Geographical Distribution of Loanwords

Grey (1978) concluded with an analysis of loanword data collected for the *Linguistic Geography of Wales* (LGW), a major study of the regional Welsh of 175 locations in the early 1970s.[40] Despite the small number of English loanwords in Welsh recorded in the LGW database, about 131 surprisingly well-defined patterns of distribution and loan counts emerged. The highest counts were recorded in the midlands, the lowest, as one might expect, in the northwest and, unexpectedly, in the far southeast, possibly as a consequence of anti-borrowing sentiments among speakers of Welsh being strongest where they do not form a sizable minority in the community, but where cultural groups are very active. Clear patterns emerged in the spread of loanwords, and of the linguistic homogeneity, or lack of this, in certain areas, shown in Maps 15.1 and 15.2.

There was no single loanword in the LGW material that was distributed throughout the entirety of Wales. Many of the loanwords had a rather limited distribution. As a result, although the same loan count might be recorded for places in the northwest and southeast, the actual loanwords themselves were different ones in different places for the most part. The use of loanword counts as a measure of anglicization requires some

---

[37] For a more detailed consideration of the inter-relationship between suffixes like <-i> and <-o> see Grey (1982).
[38] Roberts (1972).   [39] Watkins (1951).   [40] Thomas (1973).

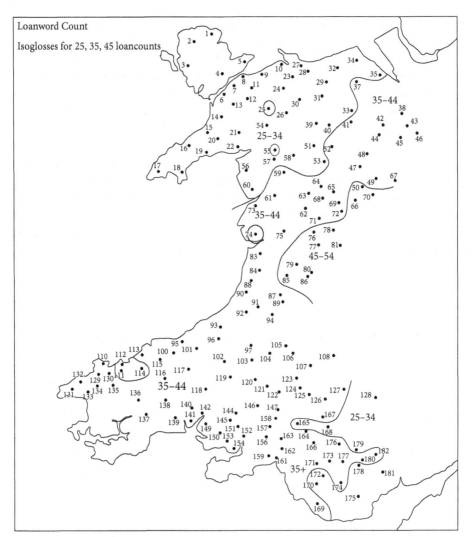

MAP 15.1 Loanword map 1.

care in interpretation; 23 loans occurred at fewer than 10 points of inquiry, and more significantly, 69, about half of the loans, occurred at fewer than a quarter (40) of the points. Just two loanwords in the survey occurred at more than 140 locations.

The study concluded that these patterns should not, however, be construed as indicating the general path of anglicization of Welsh, or indeed of Wales. Based as it was on the spread of 131 loanwords, the findings were suggestive of a wider process of language spread at the time. A larger study of loanwords and loan translations thirty-five years on might show patterns that confirm or, indeed, disconfirm this picture of the

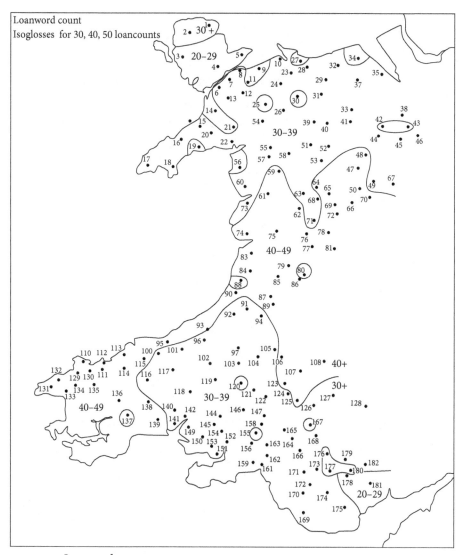

MAP 15.2 Loanword map 2.

spread of English vocabulary westward at the time.[41] A further feature of the study was to examine how loanwords grouped together locally. Looking at which loanwords were shared by neighboring points of inquiry in Map 15.3, a pattern emerged of how some communities of Welsh speakers bond together with neighboring ones, shown in Map 15.3, using the notion of *similarity networks*. The more solid the line, the greater

[41] See, however, the recent study by Parina (2010).

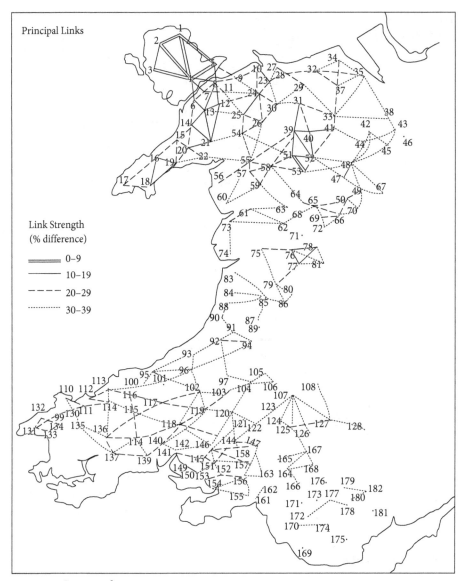

MAP 15.3 Loanword map 3.

the sharing of loanwords with a neighboring point of inquiry. The approach was taken up more extensively in Thomas (1980).

There are many more contact phenomena that could be reviewed here, but space does not permit it. The text that follows is designed to bring out some of the contact features discussed in the preceding.

15.5 AN ILLUSTRATIVE TEXT

15.5.1 Text

The informant is a female from Llannerch-y-Medd, Anglesey (no age given)

1. Padall huarn fawr fydda gin Mam, ar ben y pentan,'te . . . Pan
2. fydda hi'n mynd i dorri'riau, fydda blawd ar y *bord*, a ddaru'r
3. iau yn cal 'i roid yn fanno. A'i *sglisho* wedyn, a'i*dipio* fo'n y
4. blawd, cyn 'i *ffrio* fo, 'te. Wedyn mi fydda *nionod* yn cal 'u
5. ffrio, hefo'riau 'ma, yn ara' deg . . . Wedyn odd o'n cadw
6. yn *dendar neis*, ag yn boeth. Erbyn dôn ni o'r ysgol gyda'r
7. nos, ylwch. Ag amsar swpar, 'te, *chips* Nan Ŵan fydda hi,
8. *powlan,* am y *siop chips* NanŴan. O, odd Nan Ŵan yn gwerth . . .
9. Tydwi'm yn cofio neb yn gwneud *chips* ond NanŴan. Y hi odd . . .
10. yr *original.*[42]

15.5.2 Translation

'Mum had a large iron bowl over the fireplace, you know . . . When she came to chop the liver, there'd be flour sprinkled on the tabletop and the liver would be placed on it and sliced and then dipped in the flour before being fried. Then some onions would be fried with the liver, very slowly . . . Afterward it stayed nice and tender, and hot. By the time we came back from school at night, you see. And suppertime, it had to be chips, a bowl, from Nan Ŵan, the chip shop Nan Ŵan. Oh, Nan Ŵan sold . . . I don't remember anyone who made chips but Nan Ŵan. It was . . . the original one.'

15.5.3 Commentary

1. There are nine or so fairly obvious loanwords here, indicated in italics. *Swpa*r 'supper' is also from English, while *ysgol* 'school' is an old loan from Greek via Latin.
2. Some loanwords are clearly long established, given their plural suffix, for example *nionod* (3) 'onions' with the plural suffix -od.

---

[42] Source: National Library of Wales collection of recordings website. The translation is the contributor's own. I wish to thank Dr Beth Thomas, Keeper of History and Archaeology, St Fagans, National History Museum Cardiff, for permission to use this transscript.

3. *[S]glisio* 'slice' (3) is probably a loanword also: *slice* in English derives from ME *slice*, deriving ultimately from Old French, but the alternate ME form *sclice* is what appears in Welsh here. The pre-GVS vowel /i/ of the Welsh form confirms its early introduction. It is also entirely possible that the Welsh word comes directly from medieval French, the problem alluded to earlier.

4. Lenition of loanwords: *dendar* 'tender' (6) (soft mutation after predicative particle *yn*). The loan has been fully integrated into the native morphosyntactic system.

5. Modification: in the sequence N + N the second noun is plural in Welsh, but singular in English: *siop chips* 'chip shop' (8).

6. Gender attribution: *siop* 'shop' (8) in Welsh is feminine, a monosyllable containing an open back vowel with an initial fricative.

7. *[P]owlan* 'a bowl' (8) illustrates devoicing of the English initial /b/, and addition of the singular feminine suffix /-en/ (in this dialect /-an/), E. *bowl* being accommodated as a feminine noun in Welsh, twice over, with the /o/ and the suffix.

REFERENCES

Baugh, A. C., and T. Cable. 2002. *A History of the English Language.* 5th edition. London: Routledge.

Ball, M. 2007. Welsh. In *Language in the British Isles*, 2nd edition, edited by David Britain, 237–253. Cambridge: Cambridge University Press.

Ball, M., and J. Fife (eds.). 2003. *The Celtic Languages.* New York; London: Routledge.

Bellin, W. 1984. Welsh and English in Wales. In *Language in the British Isles*, 1st edition, edited by Peter Trudgill, 449–479. Cambridge: Cambridge University Press, 449–479.

Borsley, B., M. Tallerman, and D. Willis. 2007. *The Syntax of Welsh.* Cambridge: Cambridge University Press.

Coupland, N. (ed.). 1990. *English in Wales.* Clevedon, UK; Philadelphia: Multilingual Matters.

Coupland, N. 2006. The discursive framing of phonology in acts of identity: Welshness through English. In *English and Ethnicity*, 19–48, edited by C. E. Davies, J. Brutt-Griffler, and L. Pickering. London: Palgrave,

Crystal, D., and H. Crystal. 2013. *Wordsmiths and Warriors.* Oxford: Oxford University Press.

Cunliffe, B., and J. T. Koch (eds.). 2012. *Celtic from the West: Alternative Perspectives from Genetics, Language and Literature.* Oxford: Oxbow Books.

Dobson, E. J. 1955. The Hymn to the Virgin. In *The Transactions of the Honourable Society of Cymmrodorion* (Session 1954, 70–124). London: Honourable Society of Cymmrodorion.

Edwards, J. 2003. *Talk Tidy: The Art of Speaking Welsh English.* 2nd edition. Tidyprint Publications.

Ekwall, E. 1975. *A History of Modern English Sounds and Morphology.* Oxford: Basil Blackwell.

Elsie, R. W. 1979. *The Position of Brittonic: A Synchronic and Diachronic Analysis of Genetic Relations in the Basic Vocabulary of Brittonic Celtic.* Unpublished PhD dissertation, University of Bonn.

Elsie, R. W. 1983. Lexicostatistics and its application to Brittonic Celtic. *Studia Celtica* 18–19: 110–125.

Filppula, M. 1997. Grammatical parallels in "Celtic Englishes." In *Issues and Methods in Dialectology*, edited by A. R. Thomas, 192–199. Bangor: Department of Linguistics, University of Wales.

Filppula, M., J. Klemola, and H. Paulasto (eds.). 2008. *English and Celtic in Contact*. New York; London: Routledge.

Fowkes, R. A. 1945. English idiom in Modern Welsh. *Word* 1: 239–248.

Giles, H., and P. F. Powesland. 1975. *Speech Style and Social Evaluation*. New York: Academic Press.

Grey, C. G. 1978. *English Loanwords in Welsh*. Unpublished undergraduate dissertation, University of Wales, Bangor.

Grey, C. G. 1982. *The Word Phonology of Welsh*. Unpublished PhD dissertation, University of Cambridge.

Griffiths, B., and D. G. Jones (eds.). 1995. *The Welsh Academy English-Welsh Dictionary*. Cardiff: University of Wales Press.

Haarmann, H. 1970. *Der lateinsche Lehnwortschatz im Kymrischen*. Bonn: Romanisches Seminar der Universität Bonn, Romanistische Versuche und Vorarbeiten 36.

Hickey, R. 1995. Early contact and parallels between English and Celtic. *Vienna English Working Papers* 4: 87–119.

Jackson, K. H. 1971. *Language and History in Early Britain: A Chronological Survey of the Brittonic Languages 1st to 12th c. A.D.* Edinburgh: Edinburgh University Press.

Jenkins, G. H. (ed.). 2000. *The Welsh Language and Its Social Domains*. Cardiff: University of Wales Press.

Johnston, P. 1992. English vowel shifting: One great vowel shift or two small vowel shifts. *Diachronica* 9: 189–226.

Jones, D. 2000. The coming of the railways and language change in North Wales, 1850–1900. In *The Welsh Language and Its Social Domains*, edited by G. H. Jenkins, 131–149. Cardiff: University of Wales Press.

Jones, M. C. 1998. *Language Obsolescence and Revitalization: Linguistic Change in Two Sociolinguistically Contrasting Welsh Communities*. Oxford Studies in Language Contact. Oxford: Oxford University Press.

Jones, R. O. 1967. A structural phonological analysis of three Welsh dialects. Unpublished MA thesis, University of Wales.

Kastowsky, D., and G. Bauer (eds.). 1988. *Luick Revisited*. Tübingen: Max Niemeyer Verlag.

King, G. 2003. *Modern Welsh: A Comprehensive Grammar*. 2nd edition. London; New York: Routledge.

Klemola, J. 2002. Periphrastic DO in south-western dialects of British English. In *The Celtic Roots of English*, edited by M. Filppula, J. Klemola, and H. Pitkänen, 199–210. Studies in Languages 37. Joensuu, Finland: University of Joensuu, Faculty of Humanities.

Lass, R. (ed.). 1995. *Cambridge History of the English Language*, Vol. III: *1476–1776*. Cambridge: Cambridge University Press.

Lewis, H. 1943. *Yr Elfen Ladin yn yr Iaith Gymraeg* [The Latin Element in Welsh]. Cardiff: University of Wales Press.

Lewis, J. P. 1960. The Anglicisation of Glamorgan. *Morgannwg* 4: 28–49.

Lewis, R. 2008. *Wenglish: The Dialect of the South Wales Valleys*. Talybont, Ceredigion: Y Lolfa.

Lockwood, W. B. 1975. *Languages of the British Isles, Past and Present*. London: Deutsch.

Morgan, T. J. 1952. *Y Treigladau a'u Cystrawen* [The Mutations and their Syntax]. Cardiff: University of Wales Press.

Ó Néill, D. (ed.). 2005. *Rebuilding the Celtic Languages*. Talybont, Ceredigion: Y Lolfa.

O'Rahilly, Cecile. 1924. *Ireland and Wales: Their Historical and Literary Relations*. London: Longman, Green.

Parina, E. 2010. Loanwords in Welsh: Frequency analysis on the basis of *Cronfa Electroneg o Gymraeg* [Celts and Slavs in Central and South-eastern Europe]. In *Proceedings of the Third International Colloquium of the Societas Celto-Slavica, Dubrovnik, September 18–20, 2008*, edited by D. B. Rončević, M. Fomin, and R. Matasović, 183–194. Zagreb: Croatian Institute for Language and Linguistics.

Parry, D. 1977. *The Survey of Anglo-Welsh Dialects*, Vol. 1: *The South-East*. Swansea: Department of English Language and Literature, University College, Swansea.

Parry-Williams, T. H. 1923. *The English Element in Welsh* (Cymmrodorion Record Series, No. X)., London: Honourable Society of Cymmrodorion.

Penhallurick, R. 1996. The grammar of Northern Welsh English: Progressive verb phrases. In *Speech Past and Present: Studies in English Dialectology in Memory of Ossi Ihalainenen*, edited by M. Klemola, M. Kytö, and M. Rissanen, 308–342. Frankfurt am Main: Peter Lang.

Penhallurick, R. 2004. Welsh English: Morphology and syntax. In *A Handbook of Varieties of English*, Vol. 2: *Morphology and Syntax*, edited by B. Kortmann, K. Burridge, R. Mesthrie, and C. Upton, 102–113. Berlin: Mouton de Gruyter.

Penhallurick, R. 2007. English in Wales. In *Language in the British Isles*, 2nd edition, edited by David Britain, 152–170. Cambridge: Cambridge University Press.

Roberts, A. E. 1972. *Geirfa a Ffurfiau Cymraeg llafar Cylch Pwllheli* [The Vocabulary and Forms of Spoken Welsh of the Pwllheli District]. MA dissertation, University of Wales, Abersystwyth.

Stockwell, R. P., and D. Minkova. 1988. The English vowel shift: Problems of coherence and explanation. In *Luick Revisited*, edited by D. Kastowsky and G. Bauer, 355–394. Tübingen: Max Niemeyer Verlag.

Thomas, A. R. 1966. Systems in Welsh Phonology. *Studia Celtica* 1: 93–127.

Thomas, A. R. 1973. *The Linguistic Geography of Wales*. Cardiff: University of Wales Press.

Thomas, A. R. 1980. *Areal Analysis of Dialect Data by Computer*. Cardiff: University of Wales Press.

Thomas, A. R. 1984. Welsh English. In *Language in the British Isles*, 1st edition, edited by Peter Trudgill, 178–194. Cambridge: Cambridge University Press.

Thomson, R. L. 1984. The history of the Celtic languages in the British Isles. In *Language in the British Isles*, 1st edition, edited by Peter Trudsgill, 241–258. Cambridge: Cambridge University Press.

Tristram, H. L. C. 1999. "The Celtic Englishes": Zwei grammatische Beispiele zum Problem des Sprachkontaktes zwischen dem Englischen und den Keltischen Sprachen. In *Akten des Zweiten Deutschen Keltologen Symposiums* (Bonn 2–4 April, 1997), edited by S. Zimmer, R. Ködderitzsch, and A. Wigger, 254–276. Tübingen: Max Niemeyer.

Tristram, H. L. C. 2002. Attrition of inflections in English and Welsh. In *The Celtic Roots of English*, edited by M. Filppula, J. Klemola, and H. Pitkänen, 111–149. Studies in Languages 37. Joensuu, Finland: University of Joensuu, Faculty of Humumanities.

Walters, J. R. 2001. English in Wales and a 'Welsh Valleys' Accent'. In *World Englishes* 20, 3: 285–304.

Watkins, T. A. 1951. *Tafodiath Llansamlet* [The Dialect of Llansamlet]. MA dissertation, University of Wales, Aberystwyth.

Watkins, T. A. 2002. Welsh. In *The Celtic Languages*, edited by Martin Ball and James Fife, 289–348. London; New York: Routledge.

Williams, S. J. 1959. *Elfennau Gramadeg Cymraeg* [Elements of Welsh Grammar]. Cardiff: University of Wales Press.

Windsor Lewis, J. 1990. Syntax and lexis in Glamorgan English. In *English in Wales*, edited by Nikolas Coupland, 109–120. Clevedon, UK; Philadephia: Multilingual Matters/

Websites

Geiriadur Prifysgol Cymru:
  http://www.wales.ac.uk/dictionary/
Geiriadur Prifysgol Cymru. Introduction to Second Edition:
http://www.aber.ac.uk/geiriadur/gpc_pdfs.htm
Geiriaduron Termau [Terminology Dictionaries]
  http://termau.org/index.php/the-terminology-dicitionaries/?lang=en
Historical Corpus of the Welsh Language 1500–1850:
http://people.ds.cam.ac.uk/dwew2/hcwl/hafan.htm.
National Museum of Wales Archive of Recordings:
  http://www.amgueddfacymru.ac.uk/cy/rhagor/tafodiaith/llannerch-y-medd/es
Dialect collections
SALT Cymru:
  http://www.saltcymru.org/wordpress/?lang=en
Welsh Language Corpus:
  http://www.bangor.ac.uk/canolfanbedwyr/ceg.php.en

Websites accessed July 28, 2016.

CHAPTER 16

LANGUAGE CONTACT IN THE HISTORY OF ENGLISH

JOAN C. BEAL AND MARK FAULKNER

16.1 METHODOLOGICAL CHALLENGES

TRACING contact-induced language change in the history of English is a difficult undertaking. Only written evidence is available for the majority of its history, and we are therefore reliant on texts to provide evidence for changes that must generally have occurred first in spoken language. These texts survive very unevenly and are rare, or even nonexistent, for several key sites of contact, for example the fifth, sixth, and seventh centuries, and the North before 1350. Furthermore, particularly for the period to 1200, many of the surviving texts are written in a conservative orthography that repressed innovative forms developing in the spoken language. This means that several key linguistic changes are very difficult to date; hence the reduction of inflection has been variously attributed to pressure from Celtic (fifth to eighth centuries), Norse (eighth to eleventh centuries) or French (eleventh to thirteenth centuries). A further difficulty is that these contact languages are in general significantly less well attested than English: Welsh is not recorded extensively before the ninth century; Old Norse mostly survives only in manuscripts of the twelfth century or later; and there survives no pre-Conquest Norman French whatsoever (Peersman 2012).

Although a wider range of evidence is available for later periods of English, including recorded oral data after about 1850, British English had by this time become standardized and codified, so that contact on linguistic levels other than the lexical is largely confined to non-standard dialects, mainly in urban areas that had considerable in-migration during and after the Industrial Revolution. Evidence is patchy because dialectologists of the nineteenth century and the first half of the twentieth tended to concentrate their efforts on "pure" rural dialects, where contact was minimal. Some research indicates influence from Irish (possibly via Irish English) in urban areas where in-migration from Ireland was significant, most notably Liverpool (Crowley 2012), but also Newcastle (Beal and Corrigan 2009). In these cases the main methodological challenge is that of establishing what dialects of Irish and/or Irish English the migrants spoke, as well as the nature of their contact with the established English-speaking populations in these cities. Most recently, sociolinguistic research on the influence of post–World War II migration indicates that new contact varieties such as Multicultural London English are evolving in Britain's major cities (http://www.lancaster.ac.uk/fss/projects/linguistics/multicultural/index.htm).

16.2 CELTIC

Prior to the arrival of Germanic settlers in the fifth century, Britain was principally inhabited by speakers of Celtic languages. Traditional accounts of this migration describe a large invading army massacring the native population, but, in light of recent genetic studies that reveal the present-day population to be stubbornly Celtic, these accounts have been rejected in favor of seeing the immigrant Angles, Saxons, and Jutes as a relatively small group who achieved domination via cultural authority rather than military force (Higham 2007). In the face of this advance, the Celtic center of power was pushed inexorably westward into Wales and Cornwall. Yet many Britons remained; indeed, Gelling (1992) offers some evidence of Celtic continuing to be spoken in the West Midlands as late as the ninth century. They usually remained as a subordinated population, as the dual force of OE *wealh* (etymologically 'Briton' but subsequently also 'slave'; see Faull 1975) suggests. These Celts would have had a strong practical incentive to acquire English, a situation that makes contact-induced influence on English via language shift a priori plausible.

Textbook accounts of Celtic influence on English (e.g., Barber, Beal, and Shaw 2009: 105–107) typically suggest that such influence was limited, and focused principally on onomastics and lexis. A significant number of English placenames and especially river names are of Celtic origin, for example, Kent (< Br *Cantion*, 'corner land, edge of land') and Avon (< PrW *aβon* < Br *abona*, 'water'; cp. PDW *afon*). It is indicative of Celtic influence on naming practices that the man considered the first English vernacular poet, Cædmon, should have had a British name (<PrW *Caduann*). By contrast, widely diffused loanwords with unproblematic Celtic etymologies are rare, with even oft-mentioned examples like *dunn*, *brock*, and *tor* having been of limited currency in Old English (Kastovsky 1992: 317–320). However, an important article by Breeze (2002) suggested numerous new lines of inquiry, including prestige loans from early Irish missionaries (e.g., *dry*, 'magician' < I *druí*, 'druid, magician'), Anglo-Saxon adoption of Welsh military terminology (e.g., *syrce*, 'coat of mail' < W *seirch*, 'armor, trappings' < L *sarcio*, 'I patch') and Welsh loans in West Midlands Middle English (e.g., *baban*, 'baby').

In the early twenty-first century, however, scholars have begun to claim much more extensive, structural influence for Celtic, and this "Celtic Hypothesis" has become one of the most debated topics in English historical linguistics (Filppula, Klemola, and

Pitkänen 2002; Filppula, Klemola, and Paulasto 2008; Filppula and Klemola 2009). Structures as diverse as the internal possessor, the progressive, the it-cleft, the zero-relative, periphrastic *do*, and the Northern Subject Rule have all been attributed to Celtic influence. Since the majority of these structures do not often appear in English texts before the fourteenth century, and Old Welsh is itself only patchily attested, direct evidence for this influence is invariably wanting, and the case that a particular feature of English syntax developed from Celtic rests almost entirely on establishing typological agreement between (Middle) English and (Present-Day) Celtic against Common Germanic. Thus, while the sociocultural circumstances of early medieval Britain make Celtic substrate influence on early English extremely plausible, it is impossible to be certain what the specific linguistic consequences of that contact were.

Of course, contact between speakers of English and of Celtic languages has continued throughout the history of English. Later Celtic influence on Standard English is largely confined to a sprinkling of lexical items, such as *banshee* (1771), *ceilidh* (1875), and *fleadh* (1966) (all dates are those of first citations in the online *Oxford English Dictionary*). However, the influx of large numbers of migrants from Ireland to cities such as Glasgow, Liverpool, and Newcastle upon Tyne, particularly during and after the Great Famine (1845–1852), led to language contact that could well have contributed to the urban dialects developing in these cities. With regard to the dialect of Liverpool ("Scouse"), there has been some research into the influence of Irish and/or Irish English on phonology, most notably the lenition of voiceless stops and the "stopping" of TH. Hickey (2004: 101) argues that the "fricativisation of /p, t, k/ in weakening environments such as word-final position" in Scouse could be "a relic of a former situation in Irish English" and likewise indicates that stopping of TH in, for example, *thin, that* to /t, d/ in both Liverpool and Glasgow is "also associated with Anglo-Irish influence" (2004: 73). With regard to morphology, the occurrence of innovative second-person plural pronouns such as *yis, yees, yous(e)* in a number of urban dialects of England and Scotland has been attributed at least in part to Irish influence. Harris (1993: 139) states that "in some dialects, particularly those spoken in Ireland, as well as others with Irish connections, we find the vernacular form *youse*" and Hickey (2007: 242) likewise claims that this form "was transported to anglophone locations beyond Ireland where it was subsequently picked up and continued." Wright (1895–1905) has citations from Ireland, the United States, and Australia, but none from English or Scottish dialects. The spread of *yous(e)* forms to urban dialects such as those of Glasgow, Liverpool, and Newcastle (all cities with significant numbers of post-Famine Irish migrants) is not recorded in Wright, but this could be a reflection of the conservative nature of his sources. Cheshire, Edwards, and Whittle (1993) report that *yous(e)* forms had by the end of the twentieth century spread to other urban areas of Britain, notably inner-city Manchester. Of course, these forms fill a gap in the personal pronoun paradigm of English and, as such, are very likely to spread beyond the areas in which they may first have been adopted as Irish-English contact features (see Beal and Corrigan 2009 for further discussion).

16.3 LATIN

The influence of Latin on English differs fundamentally from the three other case studies discussed here, and its treatment under the rubric of language contact is itself non-trivial. This is because Latin influenced English primarily through the vector of written texts, not spoken interactions. However, the significance and longevity of Latin's influence means that it cannot be ignored, and there are good reasons why this influence should be seen as an example of language contact (Timofeeva 2010).

While some Latin speakers do seem to have remained in Britain after the Roman withdrawal (Schrijver 2007) and their ongoing presence is the most likely explanation for so-called second period Latin loanwords like *ceaster*, 'city' (< *castra*) and *wic*, 'village' (< *vicus*) (Kastovsky 1992: 304–305), Latin's major influence on medieval English came as a consequence of its prestige status as the language of religion after the conversion in the sixth and seventh centuries. This Latin was an acquired language, and—with a few exceptions, notably its use in the church liturgy—was used principally as a written register. A study of the second-language acquisition of Latin in medieval Britain is a desideratum; the extensive English code-switching in later medieval mixed-language business documents (on which see, e.g., Wright 2000) is suggestive that expression in Latin was heavily constrained.

The most vivid proof of Latin's overarching influence on the history of English is the Roman alphabet still used to write English. When Augustine and his colleagues arrived in Kent in 597, they brought with them the Latin manuscripts essential to the Christian religion (one of these books supposedly survives in the library of Corpus Christi College, Cambridge, and is used during the enthronement of new archbishops of Canterbury). Within ten years, the alphabet of these manuscripts, augmented with a few symbols from the epigraphical runic script, was used by King Æthelberht to record his laws in English in writing, and this alphabet has remained in use, with a few additions and subtractions, ever since (Scragg 1974: 1–14).

Latin also exercised significant influence on the syntax of written Old English, and some influence on its lexicon through semantic loans and lexical borrowings. Christianity required a vocabulary for concepts and rituals that Old English lacked, and this need was filled by both word and semantic borrowing, with, for example, *synn*, which originally meant 'hostility,' extended to cover the sense of Latin *peccatum*, 'sin' (Kastovsky 1992: 309). In the immediate post-conversion period, words like *abbod* (< VL *abbad-em* < L *abbat-em*) were typically adopted from spoken Latin, but particularly during the Benedictine Reform period of the late tenth century when the translation of Latin religious texts became common, loans like *declinian*, 'decline [a verb]' (< L *declinare*) came more often from written sources (Kastovsky 1992: 305–308). However, many of these later loans are likely to have been used only by monks in reformed religious houses—a very narrow domain—and are unlikely to have had much influence on contemporary spoken English. Latin syntactic influence has been suggested for appositive participles and accusative + infinitive constructions (Scheler 1961), but perhaps the best-known example of Latin syntactic influence is the dative absolute, for example *ut adryfenum þam deofle se dumba spræc*, 'when the demon was driven out, the mute man spoke,' which bears a considerable similarity to the Latin ablative absolute, which it was very often used to translate (Timofeeva 2008). While such constructions are unlikely to have been a feature of contemporary spoken English, and therefore have limited relevance to Present-Day English, they do show how some language users in a contact situation accommodated their usage to a more prestigious variety.

Much more important for the future history of English is the massive influx of mainly learned vocabulary from Latin in the Early Modern period. During this period, English was increasingly replacing Latin as the language of intellectual discourse. Since educated writers would have been virtually bilingual in English and Latin, and the latter was the medium through which grammar and rhetoric were taught in schools, authors aspiring to eloquence or high style would naturally import words and, to some extent, structures from Latin. This began with the "aureate diction" of fifteenth-century authors such as John Lydgate (Smith 2012: 152–153) and came to a head in the late sixteenth and early seventeenth centuries when the "inkhorn controversy" was at its height. Authors such as Ralph Lever and Thomas Wilson argued that the use of Latinate vocabulary defeated the object of writing in English by obscuring the meaning to those with little or no knowledge of classical languages. Lever advocated the coining of new words from English elements, but in most cases his recommendations, such as *backset* for *predicate*, were not successful. Indeed, the first extant monolingual dictionary of English, Robert Cawdrey's *A Table Alphabetical* (1604), describes itself on its title page as "conteyning and teaching the true writing and understanding of hard usuall English words, borrowed from the Hebrew, Greeke, Latine, or French &c." and intended "for the benefit & helpe of Ladies, Gentlewomen, or any other unskilful persons"—in other words, those without a classical education. Paula Blank argues that "the distinction between 'usual' and unusual words, between those in the know and those 'unlearned' in specialized languages, served to stratify the native tongue" and to "perpetuate the old class distinctions which were based, in part, on a privileged knowledge of classical languages" (2012: 277). This stratification of English vocabulary into "everyday" and "learned" words is the most enduring effect of language contact with Latin, but writers in the Early Modern period also introduced more elaborated syntactic patterns involving a greater use of subordination. Suzanne Romaine (1982) argues that the *wh-* relatives *who, whom, whose*, and *which* were introduced first into the most elaborated registers of English and still have not been fully integrated into informal spoken usage. Although *who, whom, whose*, and *which* are of Old English origin as interrogative markers, their use as relatives was almost certainly influenced by their being cognate with Latin *qui, quae, quod*, and so on.

16.4 NORSE

Early English contact with the Scandinavian languages came as a consequence of Viking raids, settlements, and later rule. One-off incursions are recorded from the late eighth century and include the famous sack of Lindisfarne in 793; settlement from 875 onward was focused in what came to be called the Danelaw (Hadley 2006). Here—an area covering East Anglia, Yorkshire, and the central and eastern Midlands—contact between speakers of Old English and Old Norse is likely to have been intense and prolonged. In the early to mid-eleventh century, with the rule of Cnut and his sons, England briefly became part of a Danish empire, but any possibility of a long-standing tie between the two kingdoms died with the failure of Harold Hardrada's claim to the throne in 1066. Old Norse and Old English are likely to have been sufficiently mutually intelligible to enable basic conversation (Townend 2002), but most Norse speakers eventually shifted to English. This process likely was slowest in the North, where epigraphical evidence suggests Norse continued to be used until at least 1100, but ongoing immigration likely kept Norse vital in other areas well into the eleventh century.

The most significant evidence for Old Norse influence on Present-Day English comes in the pronomial system, where the plural *th-* forms come from Norse. The earliest evidence for their use in English comes from twelfth-century Lincolnshire, a Danelaw county, but Chaucer still has some conservative *h-* forms in the late fourteenth century. It has been argued that their diffusion was due to the greater sign prominence of *th-* and a general linguistic preference for minimal ambivalence (Ritt 2003), but the low borrowability of pronouns cross-linguistically (Matras and Sakel 2007: 53–54) means that their borrowing remains remarkable. Old Norse lexical influence on Present-Day English is also considerable. The chronology for this influence is similar to that of the *th-* pronouns. Old English texts show a very limited range of borrowings, perhaps a hundred in total (including *husband, fellow,* and *outlaw*), and restricted to a limited range of semantic fields including law, ships and seafaring, and warfare (Pons-Sanz 2007, 2013), but such borrowings became much more common and varied in Middle English (Dance 2003), with numerous borrowings (e.g., *anger, cake, leg,* and *sky*) as well as semantic loans like *bread* (cf. OE *bread,* 'morsel') and *dream* (cf. OE *dream,* 'mirth, joy'). The fact that many of these borrowings are only attested a century or more after the end of the contact situation suggests that Old Norse–derived lexis was in general proscribed from Old English literary texts, despite its occasional strategic use by certain writers like Wulfstan the Homilist.

Numerous morphosyntactic features of Present-Day English have been attributed to Old English contact with Old Norse, including contact relatives, *shall* and *will* as future tense auxiliaries, prenominal and phrasal genitives, P-stranding, the use of the object pronoun after *to be*, the loss of V2 and the shift from OV to VO (Miller 2004). However, as with the Celtic hypothesis, such general claims are difficult to substantiate, and only more limited claims, like the Norse origin of completive *up* (compare twelfth-century

7 dide him gyuen up ðat abbotrice, 'and had him resign the abbacy,' with Old Norse *ef þú, kunungr, vilt gefa upp Búrisleifr konungi skatta*, 'if you, king, will give tribute to King Búrisleifr,' and cf. Old English *agifan, ofgifan*) can readily be sustained (Denison 1985).

How this influential period of the history of English fits within language-contact schemata is a matter of ongoing argument. While in some areas Norse-speakers would have been in the majority, the number of Norse settlers relative to the overall English-speaking population was small and, for most of the tenth century, these settlers were militarily on the back foot, meaning that Norse is best characterized as a substrate. However, as Lutz (2012: 509–510) has recently pointed out, the primacy of words relating to administration, law, and the military among eleventh-century loans is consistent with Norse becoming a superstrate during Cnut's reign. We should probably be unsurprised that a three-hundred-year contact situation shows considerable diachronic variation. A second issue is the role of abnormal transmission. The now-infamous suggestion that Middle English was a creole (Watts 2011: 83–113) most often rested on the claim that Old English had creolized with Old Norse. The sociolinguistically richest account (Poussa 1982) speculated that ninth-century Norse settlers in the Midlands intermarried with English women, raising children who grew up speaking a Norse-English creole and that this creole subsequently gained prestige as a supra-regional spoken koiné by Cnut and his court—prestige that eventually enabled it to influence written Middle English. While Middle English is clearly not a creole, creoles and creoloids must have formed as a consequence of Celtic and Norse contact, and arguably some evidence of them survives in aberrant features—like uninflected genitives (e.g., *on Eadread dagan*, 'in Eadred's days')—of the few early medieval texts like Gospatric's *Writ* and the *Kirkdale Inscription* that survive from Northern Britain. Alternative accounts (e.g., Thomason and Kaufman 1988: 275–304) strongly deny that anything other than normal transmission of English occurred, and explain Norse influence on English as a consequence of bilingualism and eventual language shift to the majority language.

16.5 FRENCH

Like its contact with Celtic and Norse, English contact with French began in earnest with a military event: the Norman Conquest of 1066, which made England part of a pan-European Norman empire until 1204, and French an important language of administration and law until well beyond the Renaissance (Kibbee 1991; Wogan-Browne 2009; Ingham 2010). While contacts with French predate the Conquest—influential tenth-century churchmen like Oswald studied on the continent; Edward the Confessor was raised in Normandy; and a few words (for example, *sot*, 'fool') seem to have been borrowed from French into Old English—the effect of the Conquest was dramatic. Within fifty years, the majority of the secular and religious elites had been replaced with immigrants who had French as their first language, and English had been rejected in favor of Latin as the language of royal administration (Clanchy 1993: 197–223). William the Conqueror reportedly tried to learn English, but failed.

Significantly more evidence is available for this contact situation than the earlier contacts with Celtic and Norse, and it is possible to build up a quite detailed understanding of who spoke which languages and in which domains (Richter 1979; O'Brien 2011: 69–121; Tyler 2011; Jefferson and Putter 2013; and for an important study of language acquisition, Ingham 2012). Contemporary responses to language contact ran the gamut from pragmatic cooperation (the compilation of the Domesday book has been described—perhaps incautiously—as "the most intensive scene of language contact in English history"; O'Brien 2011: 69) to misconceived violence (when, misunderstanding English cheers as the foment of rebellion, the Norman guards burned down Westminster Abbey in 1066). Among the elites, it is clear that some English learned French, and some French learned English, and that interpreters—*latimers*— were employed in certain circumstances to ease communicative difficulties. Some, like Samson, abbot of Bury St. Edmunds (the Ancient Monk of Carlyle's *Past and Present*), were trilingual in Latin, French, and English. The vast majority of the population is likely to have remained essentially monolingual (Short 2009).

As might be predicted from the superstrate status of French, its primary influence on English was lexical. French words—including *castle*, *chancellor*, and *procession*— appear with some frequency in English writings of the twelfth century (Skaffari 2009), but only become a flood in the fourteenth century (Dekeyser 1986; Coleman 1995), as part of the re-elaboration of English as a literary language by Chaucer and the Ricardian poets. The concomitant of this massive word borrowing was the attrition of the Old English word-hoard, a phenomenon that warrants detailed study. This word borrowing also led to the activation of French derivational suffixes like *marriage*, *amorous*, *Spaniard*, and *baptise* in English word formation (Dalton-Puffer 1996).

However, French influence on medieval English was not restricted to the lexical level. For example, contact with French was likely a significant factor in the phonemicization of /v/ and other fricatives in the twelfth or thirteenth century (Lass 1992: 58–59). In Old English, the distribution of the labiodental fricatives was allophonic—[f] occurred initially, in consonant clusters, and finally; [v] intervocalically—hence L *versus* was borrowed as *fers*. In Middle English, however, words like *victory* began to be borrowed from French without phonemic substitution, thus creating minimal pairs like *feel* and *veal*. There is also some tentative evidence for French phonemic interference in English, particularly with regard to [h]-dropping and [h]-adding (Milroy 1983; but cf. Crisma 2007; Lass and Laing 2010; etc.). Some twelfth-century scribes show considerable uncertainty about the use of <h> (writing, for example, *eui* for OE *hefig*, 'heavy,' or *halle* for OE *ealle*, 'all'), and, given that initial [h] was rarely pronounced in Anglo-Norman, it is tempting to infer that [h]-dropping was an attempt to sound French and [h]-adding was a hypercorrect attempt to avoid doing so.

Contact with French also influenced Middle English syntax, particularly at the phrase level (Prins 1952), with idioms like *have mercy on* (< *avoir mercy de*, cf. OE *(ge)miltsian*) and *take heed* (< *prendre garde*, cf. OE *gyman don*) entering the language at the expense of earlier alternatives. While some of these innovations doubtlessly originated in the spoken language, others (like the Old English dative absolute) likely originated as strategic calques in literary translation, and only thence achieved spoken currency. Evidence for French influence at the clause level is rarer, though Haeberli (2010) has suggested that the increase in VS word order with a pronominal subject between 1350 and 1500 derives from the imitation of written French. French-English biliteracy also affected English spelling, as Old English orthographical conventions like <s> for [ʃ] and <c> for [tʃ] were superseded by <sh> and <ch> (Scragg 1974: 38–51).

Although the most intense period of contact with French was that of Middle English, the prestige of French and its influence on English, at least at the lexical level, endures. In the eighteenth century, French was acknowledged to be the universal language of polite society, and, according to Robin Eagles, "still largely the language of polite society in England, and more so for written communication" (1995: 131), despite the fact that France and Britain were at war with each other throughout most of the century (Beal and Grant 2006; Beal 2012). Particularly in the fields of cuisine (*pressé* 1992) and fashion (*bustier* 1978), French lexical items continue to be introduced into English.

16.6 PASSAGE WITH COMMENTARY

KING EDWARD [*aside*]

> Her looks doth argue her replete with modesty,
> Her words doth show her wit incomparable;   85
> All her perfections challenge sovereignty:
> One way or other, she is for a king,
> And she shall be my love, or else my queen. —
> Say that King Edward take thee for his queen?

WIDOW

> 'Tis better said than done, my gracious lord: 90
> I am a subject fit to jest withal,
> But far unfit to be a sovereign.

KING EDWARD

> Sweet widow, by my state I swear to thee,
> I speak no more than what my soul intends,
> And that is to enjoy thee for my love.   95

WIDOW

> And that is more than I will yield unto.
> I know I am too mean to be your queen
> And yet too good to be your concubine.

> (*King Henry VI, Part III*, eds. J. D. Cox and
> E. Rasmussen [London: Routledge, 2001], 3.2.84–98)

Our commentary passage features Shakespeare's reimagining of Edward IV's attempts to coax the widowed Lady Elizabeth Gray into his bed in exchange for returning her dead husband's disputed lands, attempts that compelled Edward's marriage to her in 1464. The passage contains evidence for contact-induced change in orthography, phonology, syntax, and pragmatics, but, as is often the case, it is most overt at the lexical level. While the majority of the vocabulary is native English (e.g., *king, queen* [89] < OE *cyning, cwen*), there are numerous French borrowings, including *modesty* [84], *perfection* [86], and *incomparable* [85]. There is one Norse-derived word, *take* [89] (< *taka*), first attested in late Old English (Rynell 1948).

Shakespeare's English also shows clear evidence of contact-induced change in English syntax. The word order in the passage is generally SV, a tendency that derives from English's shift to an analytical structure, a change which is wrapped up in the loss of inflections, which itself—as we have seen—may have been partly catalyzed by contact with Celtic and Norse. Equally a consequence of this typological shift is the expression of the indirect object via a prepositional phrase where Old English would have used an accusative or dative (e.g., 'I swear to thee' [93]; cf. OE *he me aðas swor* and see also Fischer 1992: 379–380). The periphrastic do, used twice by King Edward in his aside ('doth argue ... doth show' [84–85]), is one of the most heavily discussed case studies of the Celtic Hypothesis (Filppula, Klemola, and Paulasto 2008: 49–59).

Evidence of historical contact-induced change in phonology comes from the reflexes of Old English /hC/ clusters in the passage ('lord' [90] < *hlaford*; 'what' [94] < *hwæt*). According to Schreier (2005), the reduction of /hn-/, /hr-/, and /hl-/ and their merger with /n/, /r/, and /l/ was catalyzed by contact with Anglo-Norman in the post-Conquest period. The spelling of [kw] as <qu> (e.g., *queen* [88 etc.]) also likely reflects external influence. Old English canonically had <cw> for [kw], but <qu> was adopted in Middle English. This has traditionally been explained as a French-derived practice (e.g., Scragg 1974: 8), but the influence of Latin writing was probably a more significant factor than Anglo-Norman, since Latin *qu-* was in that language generally represented as <k> (e.g., *ki* < L *qui*).

Stronger evidence for the influence of spoken French comes from a pragmatic feature of the passage: the widow's use of 'your' [97, 98] as a singular, polite pronoun. In Old English, the distinction between *þu* (singular) and *ge* (plural) was based exclusively on number, but, during the Middle English period, *thou* came to denote either intimacy or contempt, while *you* was neutral and polite. The first examples are from the second half of the thirteenth century, and probably occur under the influence of French (Blake 1992: 536–540).

Thus, while this short extract from *Henry VI* offers up considerable evidence of historical language change when the lines are compared with how they might have appeared in Old English, only some of this evidence can be made relevant to a discussion of contact-induced language change. This is probably the result of at least two factors: the recency of interest in contact-induced change in English historical linguistics, and the difficulty of proving the contact origins of particular features. But the pervasive French element in Shakespeare's lexis makes it clear that his English would have been very different without language contact.

References

Barber, Charles, Joan C. Beal, and Philip A. Shaw. 2009. *The English Language: A Historical Introduction.* 2nd edition. Cambridge: Cambridge University Press.

Beal, Joan C. 2012. A la mode de Paris: Linguistic patriotism and Francophobia in 18th-century Britain. In *The Languages of Nation: Attitudes and Norms,* edited by C. Percy and M.-C. Davidson, 141–154. Bristol: Multilingual Matters.

Beal, Joan C., and Karen P. Corrigan. 2009. The impact of nineteenth-century Celtic English migrations on contemporary Northern Englishes: Tyneside and Sheffield compared. In *Language Contacts Meet English Dialects: Studies in Honour of Markku Filppula,* edited by E. Penttilä and H. Paulasto, 231–258. Newcastle: Cambridge Scholars.

Beal, Joan C., and Anthony Grant. 2006. Make do and mend: An online investigation into processes of neologisation and the dearth of borrowing in newer English wartime vocabulary. In *Syntax, Style and Grammatical Norms: English from 1500–2000,* edited by Christiane Dalton-Puffer, Nikolaus Ritt, Herbert Schendl, and Dieter Kastovsky, 55–72. Frankfurt; Bern: Peter Lang.

Blake, Norman. 1992. The literary language. In *The Cambridge History of the English Language,* Vol. II: *1066–1476,* edited by Norman Blake, 500–541. Cambridge: Cambridge University Press.

Blank, Paula. 2012. The Babel of Renaissance English. In *The Oxford History of English,* 2nd edition, edited by Lynda Mugglestone, 262–297. Oxford: Oxford University Press.

Breeze, Andrew. 2002. Seven types of Celtic loanword. In *The Celtic Roots of English,* edited by Markku Filppula, Juhani Klemola, and Heli Pitkönen, 175–181. Joensuu: University of Joensuu, Faculty of Humanities.

Clanchy, M. T. 1993. *From Memory to Written Record: England 1066–1307.* 2nd edition. Oxford: Blackwell.

Coleman, Julie. 1995. The chronology of French and Latin loan words in English. *Transactions of the Philological Society* 93: 95–124.

Crisma, Paola. 2007. Were they "Dropping their Aitches"? A quantitative study of *h*-loss in Middle English. *English Language and Linguistics* 11: 51–80.

Crowley, Tony. 2012. *Scouse: A Social and Cultural History.* Liverpool: Liverpool University Press.

Dalton-Puffer, Christiane. 1996. *The French Influence on Middle English Morphology: A Corpus-Based Study of Derivation.* Berlin: Mouton de Gruyter.

Dance, Richard. 2003. *Words Derived from Old Norse in Early Middle English: Studies in the Vocabulary of the South-West Midland Texts.* Tempe: Arizona Center for Medieval and Renaissance Studies.

Dekeyser, Xavier. 1986. Romance loans in Middle English: A re-assessment. In *Linguistics across Historical and Geographical Boundaries,* edited by Dieter Kastovsky and Aleksander Szwedek, Vol. 1: 253–265. Berlin: Mouton de Gruyter.

Denison, David. 1985. The origins of the completive *up* in English. *Neuphilologische Mitteilungen* 86: 37–61.

Eagles, Robin. 1995. *Francophilia in English Society, 1748–1815.* Basingstoke: Macmillan.

Faull, Margaret Lindsay. 1975. The semantic development of Old English *wealh*. *Leeds Studies in English* n.s. 8: 20–44.

Filppula, Markku, and Juhani Klemola (eds.). 2009. Special Issue: *Re-evaluating the Celtic Hypothesis. English Language and Linguistics* 13(2).

Filppula, Markku, Juhani Klemola, and Heli Pitkänen (eds.). 2002. *The Celtic Roots of English.* Joensuu: University of Joensuu, Faculty of Humanities.

Filppula, Markku, Juhani Klemola, and Heli Paulasto. 2008. *English and Celtic in Contact*. London: Routledge.

Fischer, Olga. 1992. Syntax. In *The Cambridge History of the English Language*, Vol. II: *1066–1476*, edited by Norman Blake, 207–408. Cambridge: Cambridge University Press.

Fisiak, Jacek, and Magdalena Bator (eds.). 2011. *Foreign Influences on Medieval English*. Frankfurt-am-Main: Peter Lang.

Gelling, Margaret. 1992. *The West Midlands in the Early Middle Ages*. Leicester: Leicester University Press.

Hadley, Dawn M. 2006. *The Vikings in England: Settlement, Society and Culture*. Manchester: Manchester University Press.

Haeberli, Eric. 2010. Investigating Anglo-Norman influence on Late Middle English syntax. In *The Anglo-Norman Language and Its Contexts*, edited by Richard Ingham, 143–163. York: York Medieval Press.

Hickey, Raymond. 2004. *Legacies of Colonial English: Studies in Transported Dialects*. Cambridge: Cambridge University Press.

Higham, Nick (ed.). 2007. *Britons in Anglo-Saxon England*. Woodbridge: Boydell.

Ingham, Richard (ed.). 2010. *The Anglo-Norman Language and Its Contexts*. York: York Medieval Press.

Ingham, Richard. 2012. *The Transmission of Anglo-Norman: Language History and Language Acquisition*. Amsterdam: John Benjamins.

Kastovsky, Dieter. 1992. Semantics and vocabulary. In *The Cambridge History of the English Language*, Vol. I: *The Beginnings to 1066*, edited by Richard M. Hogg, 290–408. Cambridge: Cambridge University Press.

Kastovsky, Dieter, and Arthur Mettinger (eds.). 2003. *Language Contact in the History of English*. 2nd edition. Frankfurt-am-Main: Peter Lang.

Kibbee, Douglas A. 1991. *For to speke Frenche Treweley: The French Language in England, 1000–1600: Its Status, Description, and Instruction*. Amsterdam: John Benjamins.

Lass, Roger. 1992. Phonology and morphology. In *The Cambridge History of the English Language*, Vol. II: *1066–1476*, edited by Norman Blake, 23–155. Cambridge: Cambridge University Press.

Lass, Roger, and Margaret Laing. 2010. In celebration of Early Middle English "H." *Neuphilologische Mitteilungen* 111: 345–354.

Lutz, Angelika. 2012. Language contact in the Scandinavian period. In *The Oxford Handbook of the History of English*, edited by Terttu Nevalainen and Elizabeth Closs Traugott, 508–517. Oxford: Oxford University Press.

Matras, Yaron, and Jeanette Sakel. 2007. *Grammatical Borrowing in Cross-Linguistic Perspective*. Berlin: Mouton de Gruyter.

Miller, D. Gary. 2004. The morphosyntactic legacy of Scand-English Contact. In *For the Loue of Inglis Lede*, edited by Martin Krygier and Liliana Sikorska, 9–39. Frankfurt-am-Main: Peter Lang.

Miller, D. Gary. 2012. *External Influences on English: From Its Beginnings to the Renaissance*. Oxford: Oxford University Press.

Milroy, James. 1983. On the sociolinguistic history of /h/-dropping in English. In *Current Topics in English Historical Linguistics*, edited by Michael Davenport, Erik Hansen, and Hans Frede Nielsen, 37–54. Odense: Odense University Press.

O'Brien, Bruce. 2011. *Reversing Babel: Translation among the English during an Age of Conquests, c. 800 to c. 1200*. Newark: University of Delaware Press.

Peersman, Catharina. 2012. Written vernaculars in medieval and Renaissance times. In *The Handbook of Historical Sociolinguistics*, edited by Juan Manuel Hernández-Campoy and Juan Camilo Conde-Silvestre, 639–654. Oxford: Blackwell.

Pons-Sanz, Sara. 2007. *Norse-Derived Vocabulary in Late Old English: Wulfstan's Works, a Case Study*. Odense: University Press of Southern Denmark.

Pons-Sanz, Sara. 2013. *The Lexical Effects of Anglo-Scandinavian Linguistic Contact on Old English*. Turnhout: Brepols.

Poussa, Patricia. 1982. The evolution of Early Standard English: The Creolization Hypothesis. *Studia Anglica Posnaniensia* 14: 69–85.

Prins, A. A. 1952. *French Influence in English Phrasing*. Leiden: Leiden University Press.

Putter, Ad, and Judith Jefferson (eds.). 2013. *Multilingualism in Medieval Britain, c. 1066–1520: Sources and Analysis*. Turnhout: Brepols.

Richter, Michael. 1979. *Sprache und Gesellschaft im Mittelalter: Untersuchungen zur mündlichen Kommunikation in England von der Mitte des elften bis zum Beginn des Vierzehnten Jahrhunderts*. Stuttgart: Anton Hiersemann.

Ritt, Nikolaus. 2003. The spread of Scandinavian third person plural pronouns in English: Optimalisation, adaptation and evolutionary stability. In *Language Contact in the History of English*, 2nd edition, edited by Dieter Kastovsky and Arthur Mettinger, 279–304. Frankfurt-am-Main: Peter Lang.

Romaine, Suzanne. 1982. *Socio-Historical Linguistics: Its Status and Methodology*. Cambridge: Cambridge University Press.

Rynell, Alarik. 1948. *The Rivalry of Scandinavian and Native Synonyms in Middle English, Especially 'taken' and 'nimen': With an Excursus on 'nema' and 'taka' in Old Scandinavian*. Lund: Gleerup.

Scheler, Manfred. 1961. *Altenglische Lehnsyntax: die syntaktischen Latinismen im Altenglischen*. Berlin: Freien Universität.

Schendl, Herbert, and Laura Wright. 2011. *Codeswitching in Early English*. Berlin: Mouton de Gruyter.

Schreier, Daniel. 2005. On the loss of preaspiration in Early Middle English. *Transactions of the Philological Society* 103: 99–112.

Schreier, Daniel, and Marianne Hundt (eds.). 2013. *English as a Contact Language*. Cambridge: Cambridge University Press.

Schrijver, Peter. 2007. What Britons spoke around 400 AD. In *Britons in Anglo-Saxon England*, edited by Nick Higham, 165–171. Woodbridge: Boydell.

Scragg, D. G. 1974. *A History of English Spelling*. Manchester: Manchester University Press.

Short, Ian. 2009. *Anglici loqui nesciunt*: Monoglots in Anglo-Norman England. *Cultura Neolatina* 69: 245–262.

Skaffari, Janne. 2009. *Studies in Early Middle English Loanwords: Norse and French Influences*. Turku: University of Turku.

Smith, Jeremy J. 2012. From Middle to Early Modern English. In *The Oxford History of English*, 2nd edition, edited by Lynda Mugglestone, 147–179. Oxford: Oxford University Press.

Timofeeva, Olga. 2008. Translating the texts where *et ordo mysterium est*: Late Old English idiom vs. *ablativus absolutus*. *Journal of Medieval Latin* 18: 217–229.

Timofeeva, Olga. 2010. Anglo-Latin bilingualism before 1066: Prospects and limitations. In *Interfaces between Language and Culture in Medieval England: A Festschrift for Matti Kilpïo*, edited by Alaric Hall, Olga Timofeeva, and Ágnes Kiricsi, 1–36. Leiden: Brill.

Thomason, Sarah Grey, and Terrence Kaufman. 1988. *Language Contact, Creolization, and Genetic Linguistics*. Berkeley: University of California Press.

Townend, Matthew. 2002. *Language and History in Viking Age England: Linguistic Relations between Speakers of Old Norse and Old English*. Turnhout: Brepols.

Tyler, Elizabeth (ed.). 2011. *Conceptualizing Multilingualism in England, c. 800–c. 1250*. Turnhout: Brepols.

Watts, Richard. 2011. *Language Myths and the History of English*. Oxford: Oxford University Press.

Wogan-Browne, Jocelyn, et al. (eds.). 2009. *Language and Culture in Medieval Britain: The French of England c. 1100–c. 1500*. York: York Medieval Press.

Wright, Laura. 2000. Bills, accounts, inventories: Everyday trilingual activities in the business world of later medieval England. In *Multilingualism in Later Medieval Britain*, edited by David Trotter, 149–156. Cambridge: D. S. Brewer.

Websites

Multicultural London English
    http://www.lancaster.ac.uk/fss/projects/linguistics/multicultural/index.htm (accessed April 16, 2019).
Oxford English Dictionary
    www.oed.co.uk (accessed April 16, 2019).

CHAPTER 17

··

CONTACT-INDUCED LANGUAGE CHANGE IN SPANISH

··

MIRIAM BOUZOUITA

17.1 THE PRE-ROMAN LANGUAGES

··

THE oral varieties of Latin that the invading Roman troops spoke when arriving in the Iberian Peninsula in 218 BC can be considered the basis of the Spanish language. These Latin varieties entered into contact with the so-called pre-Roman languages, which include Iberian, Celtiberian, Lusitanian, Tartessian, and Basque, as well as two colonial languages, Greek and Phoenician. None of these has survived the ravages of time, except for Basque in the north of the Iberian Peninsula (for a linguistic characterization, see Correa Rodríguez 2008).

Although there is evidence for vernacular speakers learning Latin, indications of native Latin speakers learning any language other than Greek is virtually nonexistent (Adams 2003: 755). As such, the pressure to learn Latin was entirely on the subjugated populations, which ultimately gave rise to a language shift.[1] Another consequence of this contact situation is the presence of pre-Roman loanwords in the Spanish lexicon. Due to the military context in which contact between Latin and the pre-Roman languages took place, most pre-Roman loanwords are nouns that refer to concrete entities of the local fauna and flora, and not to abstract concepts, as illustrated by the following semantic fields: (1) geographical features (e.g., *arroyo* 'stream,' *barranco* 'ravine,' *barro* 'mud,' *charco* 'puddle,' *coto* 'enclosed land,' *vega* 'meadow'); (2) plants, tree names, and crops (e.g., *álamo* 'white poplar,' *arándano* 'cranberry,' *berro* 'cress'); (3) wild and domesticated animals (e.g., *ardilla* 'squirrel,' *becerro* 'calf,' *borrego* 'yearling

---

[1] For textual evidence of this language shift in progress and the changing linguistic identities of the local population, see Adams (2003: 279–283).

sheep,' *perro* 'dog,' *sapo* 'toad,' *zorro* 'fox'); (4) agricultural life and products (e.g., *cencerro* 'cow bell,' *serna* 'plowed field'); and (5) clothing and objects of daily life (e.g., *borracha* 'wine pouch,' *cama* 'bed,' *camino* 'road,' *gancho* 'hook,' *manteca* 'lard'). Among the few adjectives and verbs of pre-Roman origin, we find *izquierdo/-a* 'left,' *atollar* 'to get bogged down,' *mellar* 'to chip,' and *socorrar* 'to scorch' (Echenique Elizondo 2008: 75; Dworkin 2012: 18–40).

Importantly, not all Spanish loanwords of Celtic origin are due to direct contact: the intense Latin–Celtic contacts in Gaul and in the northern parts of Italy also resulted in lexical borrowings, which subsequently became part of spoken Imperial Latin and were then inherited by various Romance languages, for example *camisa* 'shirt,' *carro* 'cart,' and *cerveza* 'beer' (Dworkin 2012: 28). Similarly, considering that Basque is the only surviving pre-Roman language in the Peninsula and is thus both a substrate and an adstrate of Spanish, not all loanwords from this language have been borrowed in the same period: *zurdo/-a* 'left-handed; awkward, clumsy' and *zulo* 'hiding place, hideout, cache,' for instance, are said to have resulted from later contact (Echenique Elizondo 2008: 76; Dworkin 2012: 35).[2]

As concerns the borrowing of morphosyntactic features, suffixes of pre-Roman origin include *-(i)ego* (e.g., *gallego* 'Galician,' *veraniego* 'summery'); *-ieco* (e.g., *muñeca* 'doll'); *-itano* and *-etano* (e.g., *lusitano* 'Portuguese') (Pharies 2002: 317–319; Dworkin 2012: 40). The genesis of the suffixes/suffixoids *-arro/-arra*, *-orro/-orra*, *-urro/-urra*, as in *mocarro* 'snot,' *aldeorro* 'backward little place,' and *cazurro/-a* 'stubborn, sullen,' is attributed to the lexical borrowings from Basque (Pharies 2002: 108–109, 445–447, 537–538; Dworkin 2012: 40). Fernández-Ordóñez (1994, 2001, 2012a) attributes the origins of *leísmo*, that is, the use of the dative clitic *le* instead of its accusative counterpart *lo* for a direct object, particularly in cases with a male animate referent, to the contact with Basque (for an overview of the different hypotheses on the origins of *leísmo*, see Gómez Seibane 2013: 15–33; see also Camus Bergareche and Gómez Seibane forthcoming, and Gómez Seibane forthcoming).[3] Likewise, Rodríguez Molina (2010: 1951–1963) shows that the Romance-Basque contact in the North of the Peninsula could have been a contributing factor, one among others, to the loss of agreement between the past participle and the direct object in periphrastic perfect tense constructions, as is indicated by the geographical distribution of the loss of this morphosyntactic characteristic.

---

[2] The Basque language has also been said to have influenced the following phonological changes in Spanish: (i) the change from /f/ to /h/, (ii) the devoicing of the voiced sibilants, and (iii) the fusion of /b/ and /v/. For a summary of the discussion of the plausibility of the postulated contact-induced changes, I refer the reader to Klee and Lynch (2009: 28–31) and the references cited therein.

[3] Although *leísmo* is generally considered a dialectal feature, which can be found in both Peninsular and Latin American varieties of Spanish (e.g., Gómez Seibane 2012, 2013: 38–50, forthcoming), grammarians consider certain uses, such as personal *leísmo* with a male referent, to be part of standard Peninsular Spanish, whereas other instances, such as its use with a female referent, are deemed incorrect (e.g., Real Academia Española and Asociación de Academias de la Lengua Española 2009: section 16.5.1).

17.2 THE LATIN HERITAGE

As mentioned previously, Spanish arose from the oral Latin varieties introduced by the Roman troops in the Iberian Peninsula during the Second Punic War and is, as such, a continuation of Latin. Despite this mother–daughter relationship between Latin and Spanish, and more generally between Latin and Romance, the total of Latin words transmitted directly to its daughter languages is said to be relatively small (Stefenelli 2011: 568; see also Dworkin 2016).[4] Apart from the uninterrupted transmission of Latin elements, Spanish also underwent a thorough re-Latinization at different moments in its history through the massive influx of Latinisms, usually with minimal change, mainly from written sources (García Gallarín 2007: 391–399; Clavería 2008: 475–479; Dworkin 2008: 649–653, 2012: 157–181). Their presence has been so overwhelming that it has been claimed that "the number of Latinisms far exceeds the number of words inherited directly from spoken Latin" (Dworkin 2016: 587). Although the entry of Latinisms has been an ongoing process in the history of Spanish, there are periods in which their influx took place on a larger scale due to literary development in which translation from Latin or use of Latin literary models was frequent, such as in the thirteenth and fifteenth centuries: for example *bautizar* 'to baptize,' *medicina* 'medication,' *multiplicar* 'to multiply,' *manifestar* 'to demonstrate,' *veneno* 'poison' (Penny 2002: 258; Dworkin 2012: 159–167; see also Castillo Lluch and López Izquierdo 2010 and the studies cited therein, such as Barra Jover 2010).

This re-Latinization also affected other areas of the language, such as the morphology (e.g., García Gallarín 2007: 65–209; Verdonk 2008: 905–907; Azofra Sierra 2009) and the syntax, albeit only in certain registers and discourse traditions (e.g., García Gallarín 2007: 294–344). To illustrate, the derivational nominal suffixes *-ancia* and *-ción* are of learned Latin origin, for example, *infancia* 'infancy' and *vacunación* 'vaccination' (Pharies 2002: 70–71, 148–149). The same is true for the absolute superlative suffix *-ísimo*, which might have entered through contact with Italian (Dworkin 2012: 155; Pons Rodríguez 2012, 2015; for an alternative hypothesis, see Zieliński 2013). The accusative and infinitive construction discussed in Pountain (1998) is a case in point for the borrowing of learned syntax.[5] This structure, which contains a declarative verb

---

[4] According to Stefenelli (2011: 568), the retention rate for the total Latin-Romance lexicon amounts quantitatively barely to 15%. However, when highly frequent words of the "central lexicon" of (written) Latin are examined, the rate of lexical stability increases to 67% and 90%, depending on the size of the central lexemes list. See Dworkin (2016: section 32.1) for a discussion of the problems encountered when trying to determine the survival rate of inherited Latin lexicon in Romance.

[5] Cf. Bouzouita (2013, 2016) for future constructions; Castillo Lluch (2015) for preposed objects and participles; Cornillie and Octavio de Toledo y Huerta (2015) for the *amenazar* 'threaten' + infinitive construction; Del Rey Quesada (2017, 2019) and Romero Cambrón (2005–2006) for various (potential) syntactic Latinisms; Drinka (2016, 2017) for a discussion of the influence of Latin (as well as Arabic) on the grammaticalization of periphrastic perfects; Garachana (2016, 2017) for the influence of medieval Latin on the deontic periphrasis *ser tenudo/tenido Ø/a/de* + infinitive, which fell in disuse in the fifteenth century; and see Pons Rodríguez (2015) for an overview of Latinizing changes affecting fifteenth-century Spanish.

with a non-coreferential infinitive complement, has been described as "a constrained minority construction, [that] is attested in 15th-century authors of known Latinizing tendency [. . .] and is subsequently quite widely employed in the 16th century [. . .]" (Pountain 1998: 170). Today its use is restricted to very formal written registers.

17.3 GERMANIC INFLUENCES

The fifth century is marked by the invasion of the Iberian Peninsula by different Germanic tribes, such as the Suevi, Vandals, and, more importantly, the Visigoths, who established in Gallia Aquitania under Roman auspices a semi-autonomous kingdom. By circa 475 the Visigoths managed to take control of most of the Iberian territory, but only in 507 did they settle there in significant numbers, establishing Toledo as the new Visigothic capital. It is generally accepted that the Visigoths were partly Romanized before their entry into the Iberian Peninsula and spoke initially Latin alongside their Germanic vernacular (e.g., Kremer 2008: 137; Dworkin 2012: 66). It is thus not surprising that the influence of Gothic in Spanish is minimal and mainly limited to its lexicon, as in *agasajar* 'to lavish, honor,' *(a)gasajo* 'warm welcome,' and *ganso* 'goose' (Colón 2002: 32, 2007: 287; Kremer 2008: 139).

Some words of Germanic origin have been inherited from Latin, since they entered in contact with various Germanic languages in the frontier regions of its Empire: for example *yelmo* 'helmet' < *helm* (Colón 2007: 287; Kremer 2008: 139; Dworkin 2012: 69). Later borrowings from Gallo-Romance, in which the impact of Germanic was much greater, have also transmitted words with Germanic roots to Spanish, such as *albergue* 'hostel' (Colón 2002: 32, 2007: 287; Kremer 2008: 139; Dworkin 2012: 69).

Apart from the lexicon, the Germanic influence can also be observed in the morphology, in particular in the suffix *-engo*, which is used for relational adjectives, as in *abadengo* 'belonging to an abbey' and *realengo* 'belonging to the Crown' (Pharies 2002: 209–212; Kremer 2008: 137; Dworkin 2012: 77),[6] and possibly in the suffix *-ez, -oz*, found in surnames that used to be patronymic, for example *Rodríguez*, *Fernández*, and *Muñoz* (Penny 2002: 16).

17.4 THE ARABIC HERITAGE

In 711 the linguistic landscape of the Iberian Peninsula changed dramatically as a result of the Islamic Conquest, which brought the early Hispano-Romance vernaculars in contact with colloquial Arabic varieties, which gave rise to Andalusian Arabic in Al-Andalus. The contact with Andalusian Arabic had a considerable impact on the

---

[6] Dworkin (2012: 77) suggests that the Spanish suffix *-engo*, rather than being a direct borrowing of Germanic, might be a local adaptation of the Catalan/Provençal *-enc*.

Spanish lexicon, which various scholars have tried to quantify (e.g., Solà-Solé 1968: 276). Whatever the exact number may be, this contact influenced the makeup of the Spanish lexicon substantially, as Arabisms represent its second-largest component (Dworkin 2012: 83).

A high proportion of Arabisms are concrete nouns that designate material, techniques, and new cultural realities: (1) agricultural and irrigation techniques (e.g., *acequia* 'irrigation channel,' *alberca* 'reservoir,' *aljibe* 'cistern,' *noria* 'chain pump'); (2) commerce and trade (e.g., *aduana* 'customs,' *almacén* 'warehouse'); (3) architecture (e.g., *adobe* 'sun-dried brick,' *alcoba* 'bedroom,' *azotea* 'flat roof,' *azulejo* 'tile'); (4) weaponry and military (e.g., *atalaya* 'watchtower,' *adarga* 'shield'); (5) civil life (e.g., *aldea* 'village,' *alcalde* 'mayor,' *barrio* 'district of town'); (6) animals and plants (e.g., *alacrán* 'scorpion,' *albahaca* 'basil,' *aceituna* 'olive,' *algodón* 'cotton,' *arroz* 'rice,' *berenjena* 'aubergine,' *zanahoria* 'carrot'); and (7) sciences (e.g., *alambique* 'retort,' *álgebra* 'algebra,' *cifra* which originally meant 'zero' but now 'figure') (Steiger 1967: 131–141; Colón 2002: 34, 2007: 289–290; Dworkin 2012: 95).[7] A relatively small number of Arabisms are adjectives and verbs, such as *azul* 'blue,' *loco* 'mad, crazy,' *mezquino* 'mean, miserable,' *atamar* 'to finish,' and *halagar* 'to flatter.' Interestingly, the preposition *hasta* 'until, as far as' is also of Arabic origin (e.g., Steiger 1967: 108; Dworkin 2012: 100–103).

The only Arabic morpheme to have been incorporated into the Spanish morphology is the suffix *-í*, which is used to derive adjectives from nouns to express belonging: for example *baladí* 'of little importance, trivial,' *jabalí* 'wild boar,' and *marroquí* 'Moroccan' (Corriente 1999, 2008: 197; Pharies 2002: 289–290).

The earliest Arabisms have been attributed to contact with the Christians from Al-Andalus, the so-called Mozarabs, who were commercial agents or who emigrated to the northern Christian territories (Corriente 1992: 146, 2008: 189; García González 2007: 528–532; Dworkin 2012: 88–89). Recently, however, this view has been challenged: Oliver Pérez (2004: 1075–1080), for instance, has argued that the first Arabisms are due

---

[7] As can be seen from these examples, many Arabisms contain the agglutinated Arabic definite article *al-* or one of its variants. According to Solà-Solé (1968), 60% of Spanish Arabisms present this peculiarity, whereas in Portuguese 65% and in Catalan only 32%. Considering that Italian Arabisms do not exhibit this feature, this agglutination has been said to be due to the contact with Andalusian Arabic. Various hypotheses have been proposed for this agglutination (e.g., Steiger 1967: 109; Solà-Solé 1968: 280–281; Noll 2006; Winet 2006), one of which is the explanation by Lüdtke (1967: 467–471), upheld by Corriente (1999: 58–62). According to these linguists, as the mayority of the Islamic invaders were Berbers who had been Arabized only shortly before the Iberian Conquest, their knowledge of Arabic was likely superficial. Given that some Berber varieties do not possess definite articles, speakers are said to have reanalyzed this category as being part of the Arabic lexical item (for details on Arabic loanwords in Berber presenting this agglutinated article, see Kossmann 2009, 2013, and Souag, Chapter 20 in this volume). The Berbers who conquered the Italian regions of Magna Grecia, on the contrary, did not agglutinate the definite article, as they had been Arabized for a longer period. Winet (2006: 336), however, has demonstrated that for Arabisms which can be attested both with and without the agglutinated article, the forms without the agglutination tend to be documented earlier, refuting as such Lüdtke's hypothesis.

not only to the Mozarabs, but also to direct contact with Arabic in the North of the Peninsula. The Christian Reconquest (718–1492), which slowly moved southward, also caused the northern Hispano-Romance varieties to enter in direct contact with both Andalusian Arabic and Andalusi Romance in the twelfth and thirteenth centuries, causing a large contingent of Arabic-speakers to come under Christian control (e.g., García González 2007: 532–533, 2008a: 676).[8] At later times, however, the direct transmission of Andalusian Arabic words has been attributed to contact with the Mudejars (i.e., the Muslims of Al-Andalus who remained in Christian Iberia after the Reconquest) and the Moriscos, who were former Muslims who had been forced to convert to Christianity (Corriente 1992: 146, 2008: 189; Oliver Pérez 2004: 1085; García González 2007: 536, 2008a: 678; Dworkin 2012: 88–89). Widespread bilingualism in the Christian territories can thus not be regarded as the reason for the relatively heavy lexical borrowing from Andalusian Arabic. In fact, García González (2007: 545, 2008a: 682, 2008b: 276), using the scale of degrees of contact-induced language change developed by Thomason and Kaufman (1988), considers the medieval Spanish–Arabic contact situation to be a "category (1) case" of casual contact, in which "we expect only lexical borrowing, and then only in nonbasic vocabulary" (Thomason and Kaufman 1988: 77). However, the borrowing of the preposition *hasta* 'until, as far as' indicates that the contact process started entering the second phrase of the continuum, in which the borrowing of function words becomes more common. The significant borrowing is said to stem from two factors, to wit: (1) the need to name new concepts introduced into the Iberian Peninsula, and (2) the high prestige associated with the Arabic language in the early Middle Ages as it was "the vehicle of a culture which was consiberably more advanced than that of Christian Spain, and indeed than that of the rest of Christian Europe" (Penny 2002: 266).[9]

Although the vast majority of words with Arabic origins entered due to the contact with Andalusian Arabic, others were transferred via other European languages: for example *mafia* through Sicilian, *harén* 'harem' and *minarete* 'minaret, tower of a mosque' through French (Bustamante Costa 1998; Álvarez de Miranda 2008: 1055). Commercial and modern colonial contacts, for example during the Spanish Protectorate in Morocco, also gave rise to borrowings (e.g., *riesgo* 'risk' and *harca* 'armed group of Moroccan rebels'; Bustamante Costa 1998).

---

[8] Andalusi Romance, also infelicitously termed Mozarabic, is not an Arabic variety but a Romance one spoken in Al-Andalus, which is "the direct continuation of the Latin brought to Baetica by the Romans" (Dworkin 2012: 87). Loanwords of Andalusi Romance descent include *chícharo* 'pea, chickpea, bean' and *chocho* 'lupin' (Corriente 1999). The progressive 'Arabization' of the Andalusi Romance speakers is said to have contributed to the demise of their language (García González 2008a: 272).

[9] Nevertheless, the sociolinguistic nature of this contact situation is complex, and the attitude toward the Muslim world in medieval Spain was not always positive (see García González 2007, 2008a, 2008b).

17.5 CONTACT WITH GALLO-ROMANCE

Unlike the contact situations described in the previous sections, the contact between Spanish and Gallo-Romance has been uninterrupted owing to their geographical contiguity.[10] Consequently, Gallo-Romance loanwords have been entering the Spanish lexicon for over a thousand years.[11] Like Arabic, French has been the linguistic vehicle of a culture that has greatly influenced Spain. Additionally, there have been political, military, social, and religious contacts between Spain and France (Pottier 1967: 129–130; Dworkin 2012: 119).

We witness the borrowing of a whole range of Gallo-Romance nouns, verbs, and adjectives from various fields throughout the history of Spanish: (1) military terms (e.g., *aliar* 'to ally,' *botín* 'booty,' *flecha* 'arrow,' *galopar* 'to gallop,' and *malla* 'chainmail'); (2) religious terminology (e.g., *capellán* 'chaplain,' *fraile* 'monk,' and *hereje* 'heretic'); (3) feudal, chivalry, and lifestyle terms (e.g., *ardido* 'bold, daring,' *bailar* 'to dance,' *bello* 'handsome, beautiful,' *dama* 'lady,' *doncella* 'maiden,' *etiqueta* 'etiquette, label,' *jardín* 'garden,' *rima* 'rhyme,' and *trobador* 'poet, troubadour'); (4) words related to the household and food (e.g., *arenque* 'herring,' *botella* 'bottle,' *champaña* 'champagne,' *chimenea* 'chimney,' *croissan* 'croissant,' *flan* 'caramel custard,' *fresa* 'strawberry,' *hotel* 'hotel,' *jamón* 'ham,' *jaula* 'cage,' *manjar* 'food,' *marmita* 'cooking pot,' *servilleta* 'napkin,' *vianda* 'food'); (5) fauna and flora (e.g., *buganvilla* 'bougainvillea,' *laurel* 'laurel,' *faisán* 'pheasant,' *papagayo* 'parrot,' and *ruiseñor* 'nightingale'); (6) terms related to the financial and commercial world (e.g., *bolsa* 'stock exchange,' *finanzas* 'finances'); (7) technical terms (e.g., *avión* 'plane,' *garaje* 'garage'); (8) political terms (e.g., *comité* 'committee,' *debate* 'debate,' *parlamento* 'parlament,' and (9) words related to clothes and fashion (e.g., *chal* 'shawl,' *chaqueta* 'jacket,' *corbata* 'tie,' *corsé* 'corset,' *gris* 'grey,' *marrón* 'brown,' *maquillaje* 'makeup,' *moda* 'fashion,' etc.) (Colón 1967a: 165–192; Pottier 1967: 132–141; Penny 2002: 273–275; Álvarez de Miranda 2008: 1053; Clavería 2008: 481–482; Verdonk 2008: 901–902; Dworkin 2012: 120–135). Interestingly, the adjective *español* 'Spanish,' which in the Middle Ages was mostly used to refer to the inhabitants of the Iberian Peninsula and not the language, is also borrowed from Gallo-Romance (Penny 2002: 273; Dworkin 2012: 124). Additionally, a few Gallo-Romance function words can be found in the medieval Ibero-Romance varieties, such as the possessive *lur* 'their' (Pato 2010), the adverb/preposition *aprés* 'after; behind,' and the adverb *jamás* 'never,' the latter of which still exists in Spanish (Dworkin 2012: 125–126; see Octavio de Toledo y Huerta 2016: 86–89, 103–104 for more information on *aprés*, which was favored by the medieval oriental Ibero-Romance varieties).

---

[10] Following Dworkin (2012: Chapter 6), I will subsume under the term "Gallo-Romance" borrowings from both French and Occitan due to the difficulty to distinguish them caused by their shared linguistic ancestry.

[11] However, most Occitanisms entered in the medieval period (e.g., Colón 1967a: 158; Penny 2002: 272).

As concerns the morphology, due to the lexical borrowing of technical terms, such as *homenage* 'homage,' *lenguaje* 'language,' *viaje* 'trip,' speakers came to recognize -*aje*/-*age* as a derivational suffix and started using it to create denominal and deverbal derivations from existing lexical bases, as in *almacenaje* 'storage' (Pottier 1967: 128; Pharies 2002: 52–53; Dworkin 2012: 126–127).

All the previous leads Dworkin (2012: 138) to conclude that the linguistic contact between Spanish and Gallo-Romance can be classified on Thomason and Kaufman's (1988) borrowing scale as a category (3) case, considering that minor structural borrowing takes place (see also section 17.7).

17.6 THE ITALIAN COMPONENT

The linguistic contact with Italian arose largely due to the spread of Humanism and the Renaissance and to the military involvement of Spain in the Italian Peninsula. The apogee of its lexical influence on Peninsular Spanish took place in the sixteenth and seventeenth centuries (Dworkin 2012: 140–143).[12]

Although there are also verbs and adjectives, most Italianisms are nouns, the vast mayority of which belong to the semantic fields of the arts, military, commerce, and navigation. Within the arts, we find (1) literary and theater terms (e.g., *comedia* 'comedy,' *payaso* 'clown'); (2) plastic arts terminology (e.g., *acuarela* 'watercolor,' *diseñar* 'to design,' *esbelto* 'svelte'); (3) arquitectural words (e.g., *balcón* 'balcony,' *fachada* 'façade,' *planta* 'floor'); and (4) music vocabulary (e.g., *alto* 'alto,' *bajo* 'bass,' *ópera* 'opera,' and *soprano* 'soprano'). Military terms include *batallón* 'battalion,' *bombardear* 'to bomb,' *emboscar* 'to ambush,' *escopeta* 'shotgun,' and *tropa* 'troop(s).' *Bancarrota* 'bankruptcy,' *banco* 'bank,' *cambio* 'exchange,' and *crédito* 'credit' are a few of the Italian lexical borrowings related to commerce. Maritime vocabulary from Italian includes *brújula* 'compass,' *dársena* 'dock,' *fragata* 'frigate,' and *piloto* 'pilot' (Terlingen 1967: 266–304; Penny 2002: 281–284; Colón 2007: 292; Álvarez de Miranda 2008: 1053; Verdonk 2008: 897; Dworkin 2012: 151–154).

The Italian influence can also been found within Spanish morphology: Italianisms, such as *arabesco* 'arabesque,' *burlesco* 'burlesque,' and *grotesco* 'grotesque,' rendered the adjectival suffix -*esco* productive in neologisms, such as *cervantesco* 'Cervantine' (Pharies 2002: 236–237; Dworkin 2012: 154–155).

---

[12] Due to the massive influx of Italian immigrants in the nineteenth century and the beginning of the twentieth, certain Latin American varieties, most notably River Plate Spanish, have a more pronounced presence of Italianisms and present intonation patterns similar to those found in Neapolitan (e.g., Meo-Zilio 1965; Colantoni and Gurlekian 2004; Munteanu 2007; Klee and Lynch 2009: 185–191).

17.7 CONTACT WITH OTHER
IBERO-ROMANCE VARIETIES

As is the case for Gallo-Romance, Spanish has been in linguistic contact with its Ibero-Romance neighbor varieties throughout its history, especially considering their intertwined sociopolitical past.[13] Although some have claimed that the impact of Ibero-Romance varieties on standard Spanish is fairly reduced (e.g., Dworkin 2012: 198 for the lexicon), recent studies point out the need for more fine-grained historical research to determine the full extent of their (mutual) influence in the domain of morphosyntax, where the influence of the eastern Ibero-Romance languages, in particular (Navarro-) Aragonese, appears to have been underestimated. To illustrate, Rodríguez Molina's (2010: 1217–1226) remarkably detailed study demonstrates that the grammaticalization process of the periphrastic perfect advances from the northeastern Navarro-Aragonese territories to the South and the West of the Peninsula in Old Spanish. Octavio de Toledo y Huerta (in press) makes similar diatopic observations for the diachronic advancement of the use of the perfect subjunctive *haya* + past participle (cf. Marcet Rodríguez 2013 for an account of the periphrastic perfect in medieval Leonese).[14] It is further hypothesized that the Navarro-Aragonese varieties might have borrowed the periphrastic perfect from Gallo-Romance (Rodríguez Molina 2010: 1223; see also Drinka 2016, 2017: 193–216; see sections 17.1 and 17.2 in this chapter for the role of Basque and Latin, respectively, in the grammaticalization of verbal periphrases; see also Rosemeyer 2014).[15] A similar observation has been made for the grammaticalization of the future and conditional in Bouzouita (2016; see Primerano and Bouzouita in preparation and Bouzouita and Sentí in preparation for an account on Navarro-Aragonese and Catalan futures and conditionals, which display a higher use of synthetic futures in comparison to Castilian in the fourteenth century; cf. Garachana 2016, 2017). As such, these studies underline the importance of dialect and language contact in morphosyntactic language change and demonstrate the need for more research in this area.

As concerns the lexicon, most borrowings from Catalan in Spanish are nouns that reflect the Crown of Aragon's presence in commercial and maritime life in the

---

[13] Due to shared linguistic heritage, it is difficult to distinguish between Lusisms, Galicisms, and Leonisms, which explains why some linguists (e.g., Salvador 1967) subsume them under the term "Lusism" or "Occidentalism" (and their translational equivalents). A similar problem manifests itself when trying to differentiate between Aragonesisms, Catalanisms, and Occitanisms.

[14] Apart from the importance of the eastern Ibero-Romance varieties, Octavio de Toledo y Huerta (2017) also highlights the role of Latin syntax as a contributing factor in the grammaticalization process of the periphrastic perfect subjunctive, as it was readily imitated in the fifteenth century (see also section 17.2).

[15] See Fernández-Ordóñez (2011: 79, 2012b) for an overview of (potential) contact-induced changes that follow an East to West trajectory in the Iberian Peninsula; see del Barrio de la Rosa (2014) for a study of the importance of Navarro-Aragonese in the loss of gender distinction in the grammaticalization of the prenominal possessives, and Octavio de Toledo y Huerta (2016: 17–18, 227) for the spread of the adverbial constructions prefixed with the preposition *de*, as in *detrás de* 'behind' (cf. *encima* 'above, over,' which appears to have originated in western Ibero-Romance and spread from there to Castilian).

Mediterranean area in the fourteenth and fifteenth centuries. Among the lexical borrowings from Catalan we find (1) terms designating vessels (e.g., *buque* 'ship,' *bergatín* 'brigantine'); (2) vocabulary related to the construction of vessels, such as *remolcar* 'to tow'); (3) vessel parts (e.g., *velamen* 'sail'); (4) fishing material (e.g., *esparavel* 'net'); (5) terms referring to marine life (e.g., *calamar* 'squid,' *cigala* 'sea crayfish'); (6) meteorological terminology (e.g., *maestral* 'mistral'); and (7) commercial terms and products (e.g., *lonja* 'market,' *mercader* 'merchant,' *bonete* 'cap,' *frazada* 'blanket,' and *reloj* 'watch') (Colón 1967b; Prat Sabater 2005: 365–366; Dworkin 2012: 197). Another example of the influence of the eastern Ibero-Romance varieties on Spanish can be found in the use of the plural subject pronouns *nosotros* 'we' and *vosotros* 'you,' as suggested by Fernández-Ordóñez (2011: 76–79) and corroborated by Gomila Albal (2016). These pronouns result from the reinforcement of the personal pronouns *nós* and *vós* by a derived form of the Latin ALTEROS, a construction that over time lost its contrastive and emphatic value, as evidenced by the replacement of the original subject pronouns by these new lexicalized forms. While thirteenth- and fourteenth-century Occitan and Catalan already display reinforced pronouns without a contrastive or emphatic meaning, their use isn't widely disseminated in Castile until the fifteenth century. The fact that Aragonese texts of the end of the fourteenth century have proportionally a higher rate of use of the reinforced pronouns than Castilian documents and that their use trumps the simple subject pronouns also indicate that the spread of these lexicalized subject pronouns is due to dialect and language contact (Fernández-Ordóñez 2011: 77; see Gomila Albal 2016 for a quantitative study of this change).

It goes without saying that in the eastern varieties of Peninsular Spanish, Catalan's influence can be observed in all levels of the language of monolinguals and bilinguals in Catalonia (e.g., Sinner 2004; Blas Arroyo 2008, 2011, 2018; for a general overview of the characteristics of Spanish spoken in bilingual Peninsular areas, see Fernández-Ordóñez 2016: section 2; for commented fragments illustrating some of Catalan's influences in Spanish, see Enghels et al. 2015: 162–165 and also section 17.10).

With respect to borrowings from western Ibero-Romance, these appear to be limited largely to the lexicon, although here, too, more morphosyntactic research is needed.[16,17] Considering Portugal's historical reputation as a seafaring power, Portuguese lexical borrowings are mainly found in the maritime vocabulary, ranging from marine

---

[16] As pointed out by Fernández-Ordóñez (2011: 52, 68–69), although the loss of the non-deferential second-person plural subject pronoun *vosotros* in favor of *ustedes*, originally the deferential form, can be observed both in western Andalusian Spanish and the central and southern Portuguese varieties, the directionality of this potential morphosyntactic borrowing remains to be examined. Apart from western Andalusian (and Canarian) Spanish, this use of *ustedes* also forms part of the norm in Latin American Spanish, as is well known. For a discussion of remnants of the lost pronoun, see Dankel and Gutiérrez Maté in press.

[17] Structural borrowing from western Ibero-Romance is known to have taken place in the Middle Ages, as is for instance the case with interpolation, the phenomenon whereby one or more constituents can intervene between the preverbal weak/clitic pronoun and the following finite verb (Chenery 1905; Menéndez Pidal 1908; Castillo Lluch 1998; Bouzouita 2008).

life (e.g., *almeja* 'clam,' *mejillón* 'mussel,' and *ostra* 'oyster') to navigation terms (e.g., *carabela* 'caravel,' *marejada* 'ocean swell') and to weather-related terminology (e.g., *chubasco* 'rain shower' and *garúa* 'fine drizzle') (Salvador 1967: 244–250; Baez Montero 2006: 1279–1280; Colón 2007: 293; Dworkin 2012: 182–190; Venâncio 2017: 21, 26). As can be expected, the western varieties of Peninsular Spanish contain Lusisms that did not manage to penetrate into the standard language (e.g., Andalusian *apañar* 'to harvest olives') (e.g., Alvar López 1963: 313; Franco Figueroa 2017: 135–136; see also Clancy Clements et al. 2011), as do European and Latin American varieties that entered in contact with Portuguese or Galician during the colonial period and/or in later periods (e.g., Coll and Bertolotti 2017 for Uruguayan Spanish), as is exemplified by, for instance, *laja* 'slab,' found in Andalusia, the Canary Islands, Argentina, Bolivia, Chili, Honduras, Nicaragua, Panama, Puerto Rico, Uruguay, and Venezuela; Canarian and Dominican Spanish *callao* 'pebble' (e.g., Corbella 2016: 83; Frago 2017: footnote 23, 217–218, 225) or Dominican Spanish *picar* 'to wink' and *gaguear* 'to stammer' (e.g., Salvador 1967: 259–261; Pérez Guerra 2015; Rincón González 2017: 311; see Corbella and Fajardo 2017 and the studies cited therein).

Curiously, the indefinite pronoun *alguien* 'someone' has also been said to be a borrowing from Galician-Portuguese *alguém*, which displaced the use of Old Spanish *alguno* with human referents (Malkiel 1948). More recent studies, such as Pato (2009) and Fernández-Ordóñez (2011: 85), agree that this pronoun proceeds from the West of the Iberian Peninsula, but point to Asturian-Leonese as its source language, considering that its first attestations appear in Leonese texts from the thirteenth century, from which it appears to have spread to central Ibero-Romance varieties, but not the eastern ones (e.g., Catalan).

17.8 CONTACT WITH AMERINDIAN AND AFRICAN LANGUAGES

The arrival of the Spanish colonialists in the Americas brought their language in contact with a plethora of Amerindian languages. Despite the relatively profound linguistic consequences of these languages on Latin American Spanish varieties, especially those spoken by bilinguals (e.g., Lipski 2008a; Klee and Lynch 2009: 113–168; Escobar 2011, 2014; Gynan 2011; Palacios Alcaine 2013), their influence on European Spanish appears to be restricted to the lexicon (Dworkin 2012: 202).

During the first decades after the arrival of the Spanish in 1492, contact was limited to the indigenous languages of the Caribbean islands, such as Taíno, an Arawakan language. These provided the first Amerindian loanwords in Peninsular Spanish and subsequently in other European languages, such as *batata* 'sweet potato,' *caníbal* 'cannibal,' *canoa* 'canoe,' *huracán* 'hurricane,' and *maíz* 'corn' (Buesa 1967: 331–334; Dworkin 2012: 203). Further colonialist expansion resulted in lexical borrowings mainly from Nahuatl (e.g., *aguacate* 'avocado,' *cacahuete* 'peanut,' *chicle* 'chewing gum,' *chocolate, tomate* 'tomato') and Quechua (e.g., *alpaca, cancha* 'field,' *condór* 'condor,' *patata* 'potato,' and *puma* (Dworkin 2012: 203–204).[18]

The contact of Spanish with African languages, due to the exploitation of Africans as slaves, also resulted in a few loanwords, such as *marimba*. Here, too, the African influence is more noticeable in Latin American Spanish varieties, such as *banana, milonga* (e.g., in Uruguay: see Álvarez López and Coll 2012; in Bolivia: Lipski 2008b; for information on Afro-Hispanic varieties, see Lipski 2005, 2015; see also Klee and Lynch 2009: 78–112) than in Peninsular ones (see also Lipski 2014).

In the context of the Spanish colonialist expansion, we cannot forgo mentioning the existence of Spanish-based creoles, such as Chabacano and its various varieties spoken in different parts of the Phillipines (e.g., Grant 2002; Quilis and Casado-Fresnillo 2008; Sippola 2011; Sippola and Lesho In press) and Palenque(ro) spoken in Colombia (e.g., Schwegler 2011; Gutiérrez Maté 2012, 2016; see also Sessarego 2016).

17.9 CONTACT WITH ENGLISH

Most recently introduced loanwords in Spanish are Anglicisms. Although it is possible to find some dating from the eighteenth and nineteenth centuries, such as *stock, ponche* 'punch,' *mitin* 'meeting,' and *leader/líder, cheque*, the vast majority entered in the second half of the twentieth century through spoken and written transmission of American English, such as the media (Álvarez de Miranda 2008: 1054; Dworkin 2012: 228).

Lexical borrowings can be found in the semantic fields of (1) technology and science (e.g., *analgesia, best seller, casete, clip* 'paperclip, video clip,' *colesterol* 'cholesterol,' *show, tráiler*; (2) fashion and cosmetics (e.g., *champú* 'shampoo,' *loción* 'lotion,' *pijama* 'pyjama,' *rímel/rimmel* 'mascara,' *suéter/sweater* 'sweater'); (3) commerce and finance (e.g., *boom, deflación* 'deflation,' *devaluación* 'devaluation,' *manager*); (4) sporting language (e.g., *béisbol* 'baseball,' *fútbol* 'football,' *gol* 'goal,' *golf, boxear* 'to box') (5) drug culture (e.g., *join/yoin/joint* 'marijuana cigarette,' *chutarse* 'to shoot up,' *esnifar* 'to snort,' *flipar* 'to flip out') (6) the Internet (e.g., *bloguero/bloguera* 'blogger,' *chatear* 'to chat,' *internet*) (Lorenzo 1996; Penny 2002: 278–279; Dworkin 2012: 224–226; Detjen 2017: 174–237). Further, many Anglicisms take the form of semantic loans or calques, as can be observed in the following loan translations related to the Internet (e.g., *archivo adjunto* 'attached file, attachment,' *arrastrar* 'to drag,' *galleta* 'Internet cookie,' *página web* 'webpage,' *ratón* 'mouse') (Lorenzo 1996: 91; Dworkin 2012: 220–226). Some authors (e.g., Lorenzo 1996: 91; Rodríguez Medina 2002) have even suggested the existence of syntactic Anglicisms, in which existing Spanish constructions are being used more frequently: for example the increased use of (1) adverbs ending in *-mente*,

---

[18] See Enguita Utrilla (1996) for a comparative study on the Amerindian borrowings in Madrid, Mexico City, and Santiago de Chile.

instead of the use of verbal complements of the type *de manera/forma*+adjective, mimicking the English adverbs in *-ly*, or (2) passive constructions with *ser* 'to be' at the detriment of the passive with the clitic *se* (Rodríguez Medina 2002).[19]

Words of English origin have also entered the Spanish lexicon via other European languages, mostly French, as is the case for *biftec/bistec* 'beefsteak' and *club* (Álvarez de Miranda 2008: 1054). Apart from these, French also transmitted "pseudo-Anglicisms," which consist of "English words that are not used in the donor language the way that they are in French or Spanish, such as *autostop* 'hitchhiking,' *footing* 'jogging,' and *smoking* 'tuxedo'" (Dworkin 2012: 224; see also Lorenzo 1996).

17.10 TEXT FRAGMENT WITH COMMENTARY

In what follows we will discuss a fragment of a Spanish conversation to illustrate, albeit briefly, some of the influences from other languages that can be found in the linguistic makeup of Spanish.

- di-me J. ¿qué recuerdas   con más cariño   de tus   años en la escuela?
  tell-me J. what you-remember with more affection of your years in the school

de   cuando ibas   al   colegio   de   pequeño
from when   you-went to-the   secondary-school from   little

- [. . .] los niños estaban   en una parte y   las niñas estábamos a otra//   no
         the boys they-were in one part and the girls we-were   in another not

eran   como ahora que son   unisexos// entonces/ las chicas que les
they-were like   now   that they-are unisex.PL then   the girls   that to-them.CL

traían   a las maestras regalos   estaban   más   bien miradas// [. . .] pues
they-brought to the teachers presents they-were more well looked   well

no podíamos traer-le   una docena de huevos a la   maestra porque lo
not we-could bring-her.CL a   dozen of eggs   to the teacher because it.CL

necesitábamos para la casa// y   también pues: si podía me   escapaba y   me
we-needed   for the house and also   well if I-could me.CL I-escaped and me.CL

iba   a la parte de atrás   para no leer/ para no hacer las cosas/ porque
I-went to the part of behind to   not read to   not do   the things because

---

[19] For an overview of contact phenomena found in the Spanish varieties spoken in the United States, see, for instance, Klee and Lynch (2009: 193–262), Escobar and Potowski (2015: 113–155), and Otheguy (2011).

en el   fondo   me   sentía inferior/ [. . .] *entonces boicotear como ahora hacen   la-*
in the bottom me.CL I-felt inferior   then   boycott like now they-do the

en la   clase los niños// entonces no podías   porque te   castigaban/   te
in the class the boys   then   not you-could because you.CL they-punished you.CL

pegaban en la   mano con una regla// entonces te   tenían   dominada o te
they-hit in the hand with a   ruler then   you.CL they-had dominated or you.CL

llevaban   a casa   y   en casa pos era   una paliza   que también recibías
they-took to home and in home well it-was a   beating that also   you-received

In this fragment, taken from the corpus in Blas Arroyo et al. (2009: 382), most lexical items have been inherited from Latin: for example *recuerdas* (l.1), *años* (l.1), *escuela* (l.1), *ibas* (l.2), *chicas* (l.4), *maestra(s)* (l.5, 6), *docena* (l.6), *huevos* (l.6), *traer* (l.6), *escapaba* (l.7), *cosas* (l.8), *pegaban* (l.11), *regla* (l.11), *mano* (l.11), *llevar* (l.12), *recibías* (l.12), and so on.[20] Others, such as *colegio* (l.2), *necesitábamos* (l.7) and *dominada* (l.11), also proceed from Latin but were borrowed as learned words (DCECH; Dworkin 2012: 173). *Cariño* (l.1), first attested in the sixteenth century, has been considered by some scholars (e.g., Salvador 1967: 256) to be a Lusism, in which the diminutive suffix is combined with the adjective *caro* 'dear.' Others (e.g., DCECH), on the contrary, consider it a derivation of *cariñar* 'to miss a person or place,' found in Aragonese and as a Hispanism in Sardinian (Dworkin 2012: 184). *Regalos* (l.5) and *paliza* (l.12) are Gallo-Romance loanwords, the former a French one of Germanic origin and the latter probably an Occitanism (DCECH). This fragment also features two Anglicisms, *unisexos* (l.4) and *boicotear* (l.9), which have been adapted to Spanish morphology and orthography.

17.11 CONCLUDING REMARKS

Most contact-induced changes in standard Spanish are found in the lexicon: these tend to be lexical borrowings of nouns, verbs, and occasionally adjectives, though a few function words are also known to have been borrowed. Due to lexical borrowing, some derivational suffixes of foreign origin have also become productive in Spanish. These are mainly adjectival suffixes but there are also a few nominal ones. Spanish also underwent a few sporadic contact-induced morphosyntactic changes, such as *leísmo* and the loss of agreement in the past participle of perfects.

[20] Interestingly, this fragment also displays an example of syntactic inference from Catalan: the use of the preposition *a* 'in' (l.3) instead of *en*.

References

Adams, James N. 2003. *Bilingualism and the Latin Language*. Cambridge: Cambridge University Press.

Alvar López, Manuel. 1963. Portuguesismos en andaluz. In *Weltoffene Romanistik: Festschrift Alwin Kuhm zum 60. Geburtstag*, edited by Guntram Plangg and Eberhard Tiefenthaler, 309–324. Innsbruck: Sprachwissenschaftliche Institut der Leopold-Franzens-Universität.

Alvar, Manuel, Antonio Badía, Rafael de Balbín, and Luis Felipe Lindley Cintra (eds.). 1967. *Enciclopedia lingüística hispánica*, Vol. 2. Madrid: Consejo Superior de Investigaciones Científicas.

Álvarez de Miranda, Pedro. 2008. El léxico español, desde el siglo XVIII hasta hoy. In *Historia de la lengua española*, 2nd edition, edited by Rafael Cano Aguilar, 1037–1064. Barcelona: Ariel.

Álvarez López, Laura, and Magdalena Coll (eds.). 2012. *Una historia sin fronteras: Léxico de origen africano en Uruguay y Brasil*. Stockholm: Acta Universitatis Stockholmiensis.

Azofra Sierra, María Elena. 2009. Entre el préstamo léxico y el cultismo morfológico: La herencia del gerundivo latino en las lenguas romances. *Revista de Filología Románica* 26: 35–50.

Baez Montero, Inmaculada. 2006. Los lusismos en los diccionarios informatizados de la Academia. In *Actas del VI Congreso Internacional de Historia de la Lengua Española, Madrid, 29 de setiembre–3 de octubre de 2003*, edited by José Jesus de Bustos Tovar and José Luis Girón Alconchel, Vol. 2, 1269–1283. Madrid: Arco/Libros.

Barra Jover, Mario. 2010. Cómo vive una lengua "muerta": El peso del latín medieval en la evolución romance. In *Modelos latinos en la Castilla medieval*, edited by Mónica Castillo Lluch and Marta López Izquierdo, 63–79. Madrid/Frankfurt: Iberoamericana/Vervuert.

Blas Arroyo, José Luis. 2008. El español actual en las comunidades del ámbito lingüístico catalán. In *Historia de la lengua española*, 2nd edition, edited by Rafael Cano Aguilar, 1065–1086. Barcelona: Ariel.

Blas Arroyo, José Luis. 2011. Spanish in contact with Catalan. In *The Handbook of Hispanic Sociolinguistics*, edited by Manuel Díaz-Campos, 374–394. Oxford: Wiley-Blackwell.

Blas Arroyo, José Luis. 2018. The boundaries of linguistic convergence: Variation in presentational *haber/haver-hi*. A sociolinguistic comparative analysis of Spanish and Catalan grammars. *Languages in Contrast* 18(1): 35–68.

Blas Arroyo, José Luis, Beatriz Navarro Morales, and Juan Carlos Casañ Núñez. 2009. *Corpus sociolingüístico de Castellón de la Plana y su área metropolitana*. Castellón de la Plana: Universitat Jaume I.

Bouzouita, Miriam. 2008. At the syntax-pragmatics interface: Clitics in the history of Spanish', In: *Language in Flux: Dialogue Coordination, Language Variation, Change and Evolution*, edited by Robin Cooper, and Ruth Kempson, 221–263. London: College Publications.

Bouzouita, Miriam. 2013. La influencia latinizante en el uso del futuro en la traducción bíblica del códice Escorial I.i.6. In *Actes del 26é Congrés de Lingüística i Filologia Romàniques (València, 6–11 de setembre de 2010)*, edited by Emili Casanova Herrero and Cesáreo Calvo Rigual, Vol. 7, 353–364. Berlin: W. de Gruyter.

Bouzouita, Miriam. 2016. La posposición pronominal con futuros y condicionales en el códice escurialense I.i.6: Un examen de varias hipótesis morfosintácticas. In *Lingüística de corpus y lingüística histórica iberorrománica*, edited by Johannes Kabatek, 272–301. Berlin: W. de Gruyter.

Bouzouita, Miriam, Renata Enghels, and Clara Vanderschueren (eds.). forthcoming. *Convergence and Divergence: Case Studies from the Ibero-Romance World*.

Bouzouita, Miriam, and Andreu Sentí. In preparation. Tracing the grammaticalisation of the future in Ibero-Romance using parallel corpora: The case of Old Castilian and Old Catalan. Ghent University and University of Valencia. Ms.

Buesa, Tomás. 1967. Americanismos. In *Enciclopedia linguistica hispánica*, Vol. 2, edited by Manuel Alvar et al., 325–348. Madrid: Consejo Superior de Investigaciones Científicas.

Bustamante Costa, Joaquín. 1998. Algunos aspectos de las interferencias léxicas árabes en las lenguas de Europa. In *Estudios de la Universidad de Cádiz ofrecidos a la memoria del profesor Braulio Justel Calabozo*, edited by Antonio Javier Martín Castellanos, Fernando Nicolás Velázquez Basanta, and Joaquín Bustamante Costa, 13–24. Cádiz: Universidad de Cádiz.

Camus Bergareche, Bruno, and Sara Gómez Seibane. forthcoming. A contact-induced phenomenon in Spanish: The elimination of gender in accusative clitics in the Basque Country. In *Convergence and Divergence: Case Studies from the Ibero-Romance World*, edited by Miriam Bouzouita et al.

Cano Aguilar, Rafael (ed.). 2008. *Historia de la lengua española*. 2nd edition. Barcelona: Ariel.

Castillo Lluch, Mónica. 1998. La interpolación en español antiguo. In *Actas del IV Congreso Internacional de Historia de la Lengua Española: La Rioja, 1–5 de abril de 1997*, edited by Claudio García Turza, Fabián González Bachiller, and José Javier Mangado Martínez, Vol. 1, 409–422. Logroño: Asociación de Historia de la Lengua Española, Gobierno de La Rioja, Universidad de la Rioja.

Castillo Lluch, Mónica. 2015. El orden de palabras en los fueros castellanos del siglo XIII. In *El orden de palabras en la historia del español y otras lenguas iberorromances*, edited by Mónica Castillo Lluch and Marta López Izquierdo, 279–318. Madrid: Visor.

Castillo Lluch, Mónica, and Marta López Izquierdo (eds.). 2010. *Modelos latinos en la Castilla medieval*. Madrid/Frankfurt: Iberoamericana/Vervuert.

Chenery, Winthrop Holt. 1905. Object-pronouns in dependent clauses: A study in Old Spanish word-order. *Publications of the Modern Language Association of America* 20: 273–291.

Clancy Clements, J., Patrícia Amaral, and Ana R. Luís. 2011. Spanish in contact with Portuguese: The case of Barranquenho. In *The Handbook of Hispanic Sociolinguistics*, edited by Manuel Díaz-Campos, 395–417. Oxford: Wiley-Blackwell.

Clavería, Gloria. 2008. Los caracteres de la lengua en el siglo XIII: El léxico. In *Historia de la lengua española*, 2nd edition, edited by R. Cano Aguilar, 473–504. Barcelona: Ariel.

Colantoni, Laura, and Jorge Gurlekian. 2004. Convergence and intonation: Historical evidence from Buenos Aires Spanish. *Bilingualism: Language and Cognition* 7(2): 107–119.

Coll, Magdalena, and Viriginia Bertolotti. 2017. Voces de origen portugués en el español de Uruguay. In *Español y portugués en contacto: Préstamos léxicos e interferencias*, edited by Dolores Corbella and Alejandro Fajardo, 231–252. Berlin: W. de Gruyter.

Colón, Germà. 1967a. Occitanismos. In *Enciclopedia linguistica hispánica*, Vol. 2, edited by Manuel Alvar et al., 193–238. Madrid: Consejo Superior de Investigaciones Científicas.

Colón, Germà. 1967b. Catalanismos. In *Enciclopedia linguistica hispánica*, Vol. 2, edited by Manuel Alvar et al., 153–192. Madrid: Consejo Superior de Investigaciones Científicas .

Colón, Germà. 2002. *Para la historia del léxico español (I)*. Madrid: Arco/Libros.

Colón, Germà. 2007. Léxico. *Manual de lingüística románica*, edited by José Enrique Gargallo Gil and María Reina Bastardas, 275–295. Barcelona: Ariel.

Corbella, Dolores. 2016. Presencia del léxico gallego-portugués en el español atlántico: primeros testimonios. *Estudos de lingüística galega* 8: 69–87.

Corbella, Dolores, and Alejandro Fajardo (eds.). 2017. *Español y portugués en contacto. Préstamos léxicos e interferencias*. Berlin: W. de Gruyter.

Cornillie, Bert, and Álvaro S. Octavio de Toledo y Huerta. 2015. The diachrony of subjective *amenazar* 'threaten': On Latin-induced grammaticalization in Spanish. In *New Directions in Grammaticalization Research*, edited by Andrew D. M. Smith, Graeme Trousdale, and Richard Waltereit, 187–207. Amsterdam/Philadelphia: John Benjamins.

Corominas, Joan, and José A. Pascual. 2012. *Diccionario crítico etimológico castellano e hispánico* [DCECH]. Electronic edition. Madrid: Gredos.

Correa Rodríguez, José Antonio. 2008. Elementos no indoeuropeos e indoeuropeos en la historia lingüística hispánica. In *Historia de la lengua española*, 2nd edition, edited by Rafael Cano Aguilar, 35–57. Barcelona: Ariel.

Corriente, Federico. 1992. *Árabe andalusí y lenguas romances*. Madrid: MAPFRE.

Corriente, Federico. 1999. *Diccionario de arabismos y voces afines en iberorromance*. Madrid: Gredos.

Corriente, Federico. 2008. El elemento árabe en la historia lingüística peninsular: Actuación directa e indirecta. Los arabismos en los romances peninsulares (en especial, en castellano). In *Historia de la lengua española*, 2nd edition, edited by Rafael Cano Aguilar, 185–235. Barcelona: Ariel.

Dankel, Philipp, and Miguel Gutiérrez Maté. forthcoming. *Vuestra atención, por favor* ('your attention, please'): Some remarks on the usage and history of plural *vuestro/a* in Cusco Spanish (Peru). In *Forms of Address in Portuguese and Spanish: Studies in Diachrony and Diachronic Reconstruction*, edited by Martin Hummel and Célia dos Santos Lopes.

Del Barrio de la Rosa, Florencio. 2014. Factores externos y cambio lingüístico: La pérdida de la distinción genérica en los posesivos del espanol antiguo. *Revista de Historia de la Lengua Española* 9: 3–26.

Del Rey Quesada, Santiago. 2017. (Anti-)Latinate syntax in Renaissance dialogue. *Zeitschrift für romanische Philologie* 133(3): 673–708.

Del Rey Quesada, Santiago. 2019. Estructuras participiales y gerundiales en el castellano del s. XVI: caracterización sintáctica y estatuto variacional. *Revista de Filología Románica* 36: 179–199.

Detjen, Hendrik. 2017. *Anglizismen in Hispanoamerika*. Berlin: W. de Gruyter.

Díaz-Campos, Manuel (ed.). 2011. *The Handbook of Hispanic Sociolinguistics*. Oxford: Wiley-Blackwell.

Drinka, Bridget. 2016. Perfects in contact on the Iberian Peninsula: Ibero-Romance, Arabic, and the Charlemagne Sprachbund. In *En torno a* haber: *Construcciones, usos y variación desde el latín hasta la actualidad*, edited by Carlota de Benito Moreno and Álvaro S. Octavio de Toledo y Huerta, 281–326. Frankfurt: Peter Lang.

Drinka, Bridget. 2017. *Language Contact in Europe: The Periphrastic Perfect through History*. Cambridge: Cambridge University Press.

Dworkin, Steven N. 2008. La transición léxica en el español bajomedieval. In *Historia de la lengua española*, 2nd edition, edited by Rafael Cano Aguilar, 643–656. Barcelona: Ariel.

Dworkin, Steven N. 2012. *A History of the Spanish Lexicon*. Oxford: Oxford University Press.

Dworkin, Steven N. 2016. Lexical stability and shared lexicon. In *The Oxford Guide to the Romance Languages*, edited by Adam Ledgeway and Martin Maiden, 577–587. Oxford: Oxford University Press.

Echenique Elizondo, María Teresa. 2008. La lengua vasca en la historia lingüística hispánica. In *Historia de la lengua española*, 2nd edition, edited by Rafael Cano Aguilar, 59–80. Barcelona: Ariel.

Enghels, Renata, Clara Vanderschueren, and Miriam Bouzouita. 2015. Panorama de los corpus y textos del espanol peninsular contemporáneo. In *Manuel des anthologies, corpus et textes romans*, edited by Maria Iliescu and Eugeen Roegiest, 147–170. Berlin: W. de Gruyter.

Enguita Utrilla, José María. 1996. Indoamericanismos léxicos en el habla culta de Madrid: Coincidencias y divergencias respecto a otras ciudades hispánicas. In *Actas del III Congreso Internacional de Historia de la Lengua Española: Salamanca, 22–27 de noviembre de 1993*, edited by Alegría Alonso González, Ladislav Castro Ramos, Berta Gutiérrez Rodilla and José Antonio Pascual Rodríguez, Vol. 2, 1253–1266. Madrid: Arco/Libros.

Escobar, Anna María. 2011. Spanish in contact with Quechua. In *The Handbook of Hispanic Sociolinguistics*, edited by Manuel Díaz-Campos, 323–352. Oxford: Wiley-Blackwell.

Escobar, Anna María. 2014. Spanish in contact with Amerindian languages. In *The Handbook of Hispanic Linguistics*, edited by Ignacio Hualde, Antxon Olarrea, and Erin O'Rourke, 65–88. Oxford: Wiley-Blackwell.

Escobar, Anna Maria, and Kim Potowski. 2015. *El español en los Estados Unidos*. Cambridge: Cambridge University Press.

Fernández-Ordóñez, Inés. 1994. Isoglosas internas del castellano: El sistema referencial del pronombre átono de tercera persona. *Revista de Filología Española* 74: 71–125.

Fernández-Ordóñez, Inés. 2001. Hacia una dialectología histórica: Reflexiones sobre la historia del leísmo, el laísmo y el loísmo. *Boletín de la Real Academia Española* 81: 389–464.

Fernández-Ordóñez, Inés. 2011. *La lengua de Castilla y la formación del español*. Madrid: Real Academia Española.

Fernández-Ordóñez, Inés. 2012a. Dialect areas and linguistic change: Pronominal paradigms in Ibero-Romance dialects from a cross-linguistic and social typology perspective. In *The Dialect Laboratory: Dialects as a Testing Ground for Theories of Language Change*, edited by Gunther de Vogelaer and Guido Seiler, 73–106. Amsterdam/Philadelphia: John Benjamins.

Fernández-Ordóñez, Inés. 2012b. El norte peninsular y su papel en la historia de la lengua española. In *Estudios sobre tiempo y espacio en el español norteño*, edited by Sara Gómez Seibane and Carsten Sinner, 23–68. San Millán de la Cogolla: Cilengua.

Fernández-Ordóñez, Inés. 2016. Los dialectos del español peninsular. In *Enciclopedia lingüística hispánica*, edited by Javier Gutiérrez-Rexach, Vol. 2, 387–404. London/New York: Routledge.

Frago, Juan Antonio. 2017. Notas para el estudio del portuguesismo (y del occidentalismo) en el español de América. In *Español y portugués en contacto: Préstamos léxicos e interferencias*, edited by Dolores Corbella and Alejandro Fajardo, 201–230. Berlin: W. de Gruyter.

Franco Figueroa, Mariano 2017. Portuguesismos en andaluz. In *Español y portugués en contacto: Préstamos léxicos e interferencias*, edited by Dolores Corbella and Alejandro Fajardo, 129–150. Berlin: W. de Gruyter.

Garachana, Mar. 2016. La expresión de la obligación en la Edad Media: Influencias orientales y latinas en el empleo de *ser tenudo/tenido Ø/a/de + infinitivo*. In *El español a través del tiempo: Estudios ofrecidos a Rafael Cano Aguilar*, edited by Araceli López Serena, Antonio Narbona, and Santiago del Rey Quesada, 497–514. Seville: Universidad de Sevilla.

Garachana, Mar. 2017. Perífrasis formadas en torno a *tener* en español: *ser tenudo/tenido Ø/a/ de + infinitivo, tener a/de + infinitivo, tener que + infinitivo*. In *La gramática en diacronía. La evolución de las perífrasis verbales modales en español*, edited by Mar Garachana, 227–284. Madrid/Frankfurt: Iberoamericana/Vervuert.

García Gallarín, Consuelo. 2007. *El cultismo en la historia de la lengua española*. Madrid: Ediciones Parthenon.

García González, Javier. 2007. Una perspectiva sociolinguística de los arabismos en el espanol de la Alta Edad Media. In *De admiratione et amicitia: Homenaje a Ramón Santiago*, edited by Inmaculada Delgado and Alicia Puigvert, 523–548. Madrid: Ediciones Clásicas.

García González, Javier. 2008a. Viejos problemas desde nuevos enfoques: Los arabismos en el espanol medieval desde la perspectiva de la sociolingüística. In *Discurso y sociedad II: Nuevas contribuciones al estudio de la lengua en contexto social*, edited by José Luis Blas Arroyo, Manuela Casanova Avalos, Mónica Velando Casanova, and Javier Vellón Lahoz, 671–684. Castellón de la Plana: Universitat Jaume I.

García González, Javier. 2008b. Cuestiones pendientes en el estudio de los arabismos del español medieval: Una revisión crítica. In *Lenguas, reinos y dialectos en la Edad Media Ibérica: La construcción de la identidad. Homenaje a Juan Ramón Lodares*, edited by Javier Elvira, Inés Fernández-Ordóñez, Javier García González, and Ana Serradilla Castaño, 257–286. Madrid/Frankfurt: Iberoamericana/Vervuert.

Gómez Seibane, Sara. 2012. *Los pronombres átonos (le, la, lo) en el español*. Madrid: Arco/Libros.

Gómez Seibane, Sara. 2013. *Los pronombres átonos (le, la, lo) en el español: Aproximación histórica*. Madrid: Arco/Libros.

Gómez Seibane, Sara. Forthcoming. Exploring historical linguistic convergence between Basque and Spanish. In *Convergence and Divergence: Case Studies from the Ibero-Romance World*, edited by Miriam Bouzouita et al.

Gomila Albal, Marina. 2016. Sobre el origen y la difusión geográfica de las formas *nosotros* y *vosotros* en castellano. *Iberoromania* 83: 103–125.

Grant, Anthony. 2002. El chabacano zamboangueño: Una lengua mezclada. *Papia: Revista Brasileira de Estudos Crioulos* 12: 7–40.

Gutiérrez Maté, Miguel. 2012. Lengua afrohispánica, palenquero y español colombiano atlántico en el siglo XVII: Conciencia lingüística y testimonio directo en documentos de archivo. *Revista internacional de lingüística iberoamericana* 20(5): 83–103.

Gutiérrez Maté, Miguel. 2016. Reconstructing the linguistic history of "Palenques": On the nature and relevance of colonial documents. In *The Iberian Challenge: Creole Languages Beyond the Plantation Settings*, edited by Armin Schwegler, John McWhorter, and Liane Ströbel, 205–229. Madrid/Frankfurt: Iberoamericana/Vervuert.

Gutiérrez-Rexach, Javier (ed.). 2016. *Enciclopedia lingüística hispánica*. London; New York: Routledge.

Gynan, Shaw N. 2011. Spanish in contact with Guaraní. In *The Handbook of Hispanic Sociolinguistics*, edited by Manuel Díaz-Campos, 353–372. Oxford: Wiley-Blackwell.

Klee, Carol A., and Andrew Lynch. 2009. *El español en contacto con otras lenguas*. Washington, DC: Georgetown University Press.

Kossmann, Maarten. 2009. Loanwords in Tarifiyt, a Berber language of Morocco. In *Loanwords in the World's Languages: A Comparative Handbook*, edited by Martin Haspelmath and Uri Tadmor, 191–214. Berlin: W. de Gruyter.

Kossmann, Maarten. 2013. *The Arabic Influence on Northern Berber*. Leiden/Boston: Brill.

Kremer, Dieter. 2008. El elemento germánico y su influencia en la historia lingüística peninsular. In *Historia de la lengua española*, 2nd edition, edited by Rafael Cano Aguilar, 133–148. Barcelona: Ariel.

Lipski, John 2005. *A History of Afro-Hispanic Language: Five Centuries, Five Continents*. Cambridge: Cambridge University Press.

Lipski, John. 2008a. El español de América: Los contactos bilingües. In *Historia de la lengua española*, 2nd edition, edited by Rafael Cano Aguilar, 1117–1138. Barcelona: Ariel.

Lipski, John. 2008b. *Afro-Bolivian Spanish*. Madrid; Frankfurt: Iberoamericana/Vervuert.

Lipski, John. 2014. A historical perspective of Afro-Portuguese and Afro-Spanish varieties in the Iberia Peninsula. In *Portuguese–Spanish Interfaces: Diachrony, Synchrony, and Contact*, edited by Patrícia Amaral and Ana Maria Carvalho, 359–376. Amsterdam/Philadelphia: John Benjamins.

Lipski, John. 2015. La reconstrucción de los primeros contactos lingüísticos afrohispánicos: La importancia de las comunidades de habla contemporáneas. In *Dinâmicas Afro-Latinas: Língua(s) e História(s)*, edited by Juanito Ornelas de Avelar and Laura Álvarez López, 93–125. Frankfurt: Peter Lang.

Lorenzo, Emilio. 1996. *Anglicismos hispánicos*. Madrid: Gredos.

Lüdtke, Helmut. 1967. El *bereber* y la lingüística románica. In *XI Congreso Internacional de Lingüística y Filología Románicas: Actas*, edited by Antonio Quilis, Ramón B. Carril, and Margarita Cantarero, Vol. 2, 467–471. Madrid: Revista de Filología Española.

Malkiel, Yakov. 1948. *Hispanic* algu(i)en *and Related Formations: A Study of the Stratification of the Romance Lexicon in the Iberian Peninsula*. Berkeley, Los Angeles: University of California Press.

Marcet Rodríguez, Vicente. 2013. Los tiempos compuestos en el leonés medieval: *haber* + participio. *Iberoromania* 77: 47–71.

Menéndez Pidal, Ramón. 1908. *Cantar de Mio Cid: Texto, gramática y vocabulario*. Madrid: Espasa Calpe.

Meo-Zilio, Giovanni. 1965. Italianismos generales en el español rioplatense. *Thesaurus: Boletín del Instituto Caro y Cuervo* 20(1): 68–119.

Munteanu, Dan. 2007. Los italianismos léxicos en la norma culta de Salta (Argentina). *Zeitschrift für romanische Philologie* 123(2): 287–302.

Noll, Volker. 2006. La aglutinación del artículo árabe *al* en el léxico español. In *Cosmos léxico: Contribuciones a la lexicografía y a la lexicología hispánicas*, edited by Rafael Arnold and Jutta Langenbacher-Liebgott, 35–49. Frankfurt: Peter Lang.

Octavio de Toledo y Huerta, Álvaro S. 2016. *Los relacionantes locativos en la historia del español*. Berlin: W. de Gruyter.

Octavio de Toledo y Huerta, Álvaro S. 2017. El pretérito perfecto de subjuntivo en la Edad Media: Distribución dialectal, entornos sintácticos y tradicionalidad discursiva. *Moenia: Revista lucense de lingüística* 23: 317–366.

Oliver Pérez, Dolores. 2004. Los arabismos dentro de la historia del español: Estudio diacrónico de su incorporación. In *Escritos dedicados a José María Fernández Catón*, edited by Manuel Cecilio Díaz y Díaz, Mercedes Díaz de Bustamante, and Manuela Domínguez García, Vol. 2, 1073–1095. León: Centro de estudios e investigación "San Isidoro."

Otheguy, Ricardo. 2011. Functional adaptation and conceptual convergence in the analysis of language contact in the Spanish of bilingual communities in New York. In *The Handbook of Hispanic Sociolinguistics*, edited by Manuel Díaz-Campos, 504–529. Oxford: Wiley-Blackwell.

Palacios Alcaine, Azucena. 2013. Contact-induced change and internal evolution: Spanish in contact with Amerindian languages. In *The Interplay of Variation and Change in Contact Settings: Morphosyntactic Studies*, edited by Isabelle Léglise and Claudine Chamoreau, 165–198. Amsterdam/Philadelphia: John Benjamins.

Pato, Enrique. 2009. Notas aclaratorias sobre la historia del indefinido *alguien*: Una aplicación directa del uso de corpus diacrónicos. In *Diacronía de las lenguas iberorrománicas: Nuevas aportaciones desde la lingüística de corpus*, edited by Andrés Enrique-Arias, 401–416. Frankfurt/Madrid: Vervuert/Iberoamericana.

Pato, Enrique. 2010. Algo más sobre la historia del posesivo *lur*. *Archivo de Filología Aragonesa* 66: 13–32.

Penny, Ralph. 2002. *A History of the Spanish Language*. Cambridge: Cambridge University Press.

Pérez Guerra, Irene. 2015. Lusismos léxicos en el espanol domicano. Presentation held at *IV Jornadas de Lingüística Hispánica. Armonía y Contraste*. University of Lisbon.

Pharies, David A. 2002. *Diccionario etimológico de los sufijos españoles*. Madrid: Gredos.

Pons Rodríguez, Lola. 2012. La doble graduación *muy -ísimo* en la historia del español y su cambio variacional. In *Estudios de filología y lingüística españolas: Nuevas voces en la disciplina*, edited by Enrique Pato and Javier Rodríguez Molina, 93–133. Bern: Peter Lang.

Pons Rodríguez, Lola. 2015. La lengua del Cuatrocientos más allá de las Trescientas. In *Actas del IX Congreso Internacional de Historia de la Lengua Española (Cádiz, septiembre de 2012)*, edited by José María García Martín, Vol. 1, 393–433. Madrid/Frankfurt: Iberoamericana/Vervuert.

Pottier, Bernard. 1967. Galicismos. In *Enciclopedia linguistica hispánica*, Vol. 2, edited by Manuel Alvar et al., 127–151. Madrid: Consejo Superior de Investigaciones Científicas.

Pountain, Christopher J. 1998. Learnèd syntax and the Romance languages: The "accusative and infinitive" construction with declarative verbs in Castilian. *Transactions of the Philological Society* 96(2): 159–201.

Prat Sabater, Marta. 2005. La influència del català sobre el lèxic castellà: Visió diacrònica. *Llengua i literatura: Revista anual de la Societat Catalana de Llengua i literatura* 16: 363–388.

Primerano, Antoine, and Miriam Bouzouita. In preparation. La gramaticalización de los futuros y condicionales en navarroaragonés del siglo XIII y XIV: una comparación con el castellano medieval. Ghent University. Ms.

Quilis, Antonio, and Celia Casado-Fresnillo. 2008. *La lengua española en Filipinas: Historia, situación actual, el chabacano, antología de textos*. Madrid: Consejo Superior de Investigaciones Científicas.

Real Academia Española and Asociación de Academias de la Lengua Española. 2009. *Nueva gramática de la lengua española*. Madrid: Espasa Libros.

Rincón González, María José. 2017. Los portuguesismos en el español dominicano: Origen y pervivencia. In *Español y portugués en contacto: Préstamos léxicos e interferencias*, edited by Dolores Corbella and Alejandro Fajardo, 299–321. Berlin: W. de Gruyter.

Rodríguez Medina, María Jesús. 2002. Los anglicismos de frecuencia sintácticos en espanol: estudio empírico. *Revista española de lingüística aplicada* 15: 149–170.

Rodríguez Molina, Javier. 2010. *La gramaticalización de los tiempos compuestos en español antiguo: Cinco cambios diacrónicos*. PhD dissertation, Autonomous University of Madrid.

Romero Cambrón, Ángeles. 2005–2006. Latinismos sintácticos en la lengua herediana: A propósito de las *Historias contra los paganos* (ms. v-27). *Archivo de Filología Aragonesa* 61–62: 57–84.

Rosemeyer, Malte. 2014. *Auxiliary Selection in Spanish: Gradience, Gradualness, and Conservation*. Amsterdam/Philadelphia: John Benjamins.

Salvador, Gregorio. 1967. Lusismos. In *Enciclopedia linguistica hispánica*, Vol. 2, edited by Manuel Alvar et al., 239–261. Madrid: Consejo Superior de Investigaciones Científicas.

Schwegler, Armin. 2011. Palenque (Colombia): Multilingualism in an extraordinary social and historical context. In *The Handbook of Hispanic Sociolinguistics*, edited by Manuel Díaz-Campos, 446–472. Oxford: Wiley-Blackwell.

Sessarego, Sandro. 2016. Lenguas criollas del español. In *Enciclopedia lingüística hispánica*, edited by Javier Gutiérrez-Rexach, Vol. 2, 685–696. London/New York: Routledge.

Sinner, Carsten. 2004. *El castellano de Cataluña*. Tübingen: Max Niemeyer Verlag.

Sippola, Eeva. 2011. *Una gramática descriptiva del chabacano de Ternate*. PhD dissertation, University of Helsinki.

Sippola, Eeva, and Marivic Lesho. forthcoming [2020]. Contact-induced grammatical change and independent development in the Chabacano Creoles *Bulletin of Hispanic Studies*.

Souag, Lameen. XXX

Solà-Solé, Josep Maria. 1968. El artículo *al-* en los arabismos del iberorrománico. *Romance Philology* 21(3): 275–285.

Stefenelli, Arnulf. 2011. Lexical stability. In *The Cambridge History of the Romance Languages*, edited by Martin Maiden, John Charles Smith, and Adam Ledgeway, Vol. 1, 564–584. Cambridge: Cambridge University Press.

Steiger, Arnald. 1967. Arabismos. In *Enciclopedia linguistica hispánica*, edited by Manuel Alvar et al., 93–126. Madrid: Consejo Superior de Investigaciones Científicas.

Terlingen, Johannes H. 1967. Italianismos. In *Enciclopedia linguistica hispánica*, edited by Manuel Alvar et al., 263–305. Madrid: Consejo Superior de Investigaciones Científicas.

Thomason, Sarah G., and Terrence Kaufman. 1988. *Language Contact, Creolization, and Genetic Linguistics*. Berkeley, Los Angeles: University of California Press.

Venâncio, Fernando. 2017. Lusismos y galleguismos en uso en español: Una revisión crítica. In *Español y portugués en contacto: Préstamos léxicos e interferencias*, edited by Dolores Corbella and Alejandro Fajardo, 19–36. Berlin: W. de Gruyter.

Verdonk, Robert. 2008. Cambios en el léxico del español durante época los Austrias. In *Historia de la lengua española*, 2nd edition, edited by Rafael Cano Aguilar, 895–916. Barcelona: Ariel.

Winet, Monika. 2006. *El artículo árabe en las lenguas iberorrománicas (aspectos fonéticos, morfológicos, y semánticos de la transferencia léxica)*. Córdoba: Universidad de Córdoba.

Zieliński, Andrzej. 2013. Evolución semántico-sintáctica del sufijo superlativo *-ísimo* en castellano. *Romanica Cracoviensa* 13(1): 105–115. http://www.ejournals.eu/Romanica-Cracoviensia/Tom-13/Numer-1/art/1623 (last consulted on August 21, 2016).

CHAPTER 18

LANGUAGE CONTACT IN TAGDAL, A NORTHERN SONGHAY LANGUAGE OF NIGER

CARLOS M. BENÍTEZ-TORRES

18.1 INTRODUCTION: GENERAL INFORMATION

TAGDAL is a Northern Songhay language spoken in the modern-day Republic of Niger. Most speakers are semi-nomadic herders of Tuareg (Berber) descent, who range from the central to the northern regions of Niger, bordering the Sahara desert (see Map 18.1, based on Benítez-Torres and Grant 2017).

The main feature of all Northern Songhay languages is the interaction of Berber and Songhay features. Nicolaï (1979) divides Northern Songhay languages into a nomadic and a sedentary branch, a division that reflects grammatical, ethnic, and cultural levels, with the sedentary languages generally having fewer Berber features than the nomadic.[1] Kwarandzey (Souag 2010, 2012) presents a slightly different case, since it developed apart from the other three, in Algeria. Another Northern Songhay language, Emghedeshie (Lacroix 1975), was at one time the language of wider communication in the city of Agadez, but has been extinct since the early twentieth century.[2]

---

[1] For example, Tasawaq has tone and, unlike the nomadic varieties, the few Berber grammatical forms in Tasawaq tend not to be productive (Grant and Benítez-Torres 2017). Lacroix (1981) suggested that Tasawaq might actually be a heavily Berberised mainstream variety of the ancient vehicular Songhay spoken in modern-day northern Niger. In other words, if this were the case, then Tasawaq is actually mainstream, not Northern, Songhay.

[2] Lacroix (1981) considered Enghedeshie a vehicular variety of Tasawaq.

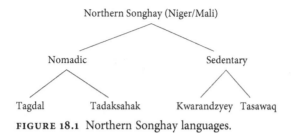

FIGURE 18.1 Northern Songhay languages.

18.1.1 Geographical Location

Map 18.1 (based on Benítez-Torres and Grant 2017) demonstrates the approximate locations of the most common Tagdal varieties spoken in the Republic of Niger.

Tagdal has three major varieties, which tend to differ mainly in their consonant inventories. Otherwise, the different Tagdal varieties are similar and are mutually intelligible. Rueck and Christiansen (1999) point out that speakers consider them "accents" of the same language.

The most common variety of Tagdal spoken in central Niger grasslands is Tarbun, spoken by the Tarbun and Kəl Amdid subgroups.[3] It ranges roughly from the town of Tahoua to the village of Aɣabrɣabr, some 200 kilometers south of Agadez, with some speakers reaching as far south as the outskirts of the town of Maradi near the Nigerian border and as far north as the outskirts of Agadez. Table 18.1 in section 18.3.1 describes the consonants in this variety.

A second common variety, is spoken by the Kəl Ilokkoḍ in roughly the same regions as the Tarbun variety and by the Abargan in Niger's northern regions, roughly from Aɣabrɣabr to the city of Agadez. Table 18.2 in section 18.3.1 describes the consonants found in this Tagdal variety.

Table 18.3 in section 18.3.1 gives the consonants present in Tabarog, spoken by the Ibarogan. The Ibarogan inhabit mainly the southern central regions of Niger, roughly between the towns of Tahoua and Maradi near the Nigerian border. Rueck and Christiansen (1999) found a high enough degree of intelligibility between Tabarog and other Tagdal varieties that they considered it Tagdal. For the most part, the Ibarogan seem to have different origins, yet they have maintained historical and linguistic ties to other Tagdal speakers.

Regardless, historic seasonal migration patterns, taking animals to different pasture-lands during different times of the year, have caused speakers of the diverse varieties of Tagdal to intermingle over hundreds of years. In addition, more recent disruptions of these traditional seasonal migration patterns, especially due to drought, have forced many formerly semi-nomadic Tagdal speakers to settle in towns and cities, such as Agadez or in the capital of Niamey, in order to look for work. This tends to lessen the

---

[3] It is often difficult to distinguish between Tagdal-speaking sub-groups, since speakers call them all *tawʃiten*, a term that could be used to describe tribe, ethnicity, or even animal or plant species.

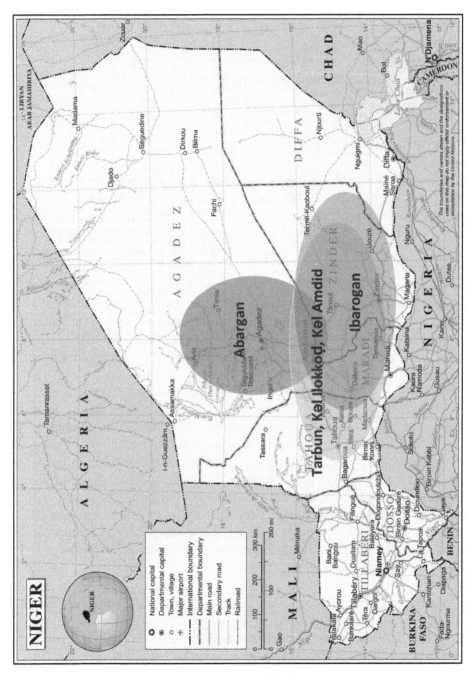

MAP 18.1 Tagdal location.

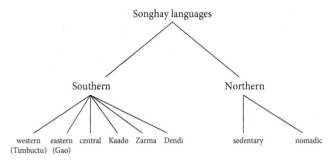

FIGURE 18.2 The Songhay language family, according to Nicolaï.

differences between the different Tagdal varieties, as well as to cause overall language shift in favor of major languages of wider communication such as Tamajaq (Berber) or Hausa.

18.1.2 Classification

Since Greenberg's (1963) landmark article, most linguists place Songhay languages in the Nilo-Saharan family.[4] Greenberg's classification has met with resistance from some researchers.[5] Nicolaï (1979: 14) suggested dividing the Songhay language family into a Northern and Southern branch, as Figure 18.2 demonstrates.

According to Nicolaï, Southern Songhay includes all of what could be considered "mainstream" Songhay languages, those with minimal or no Berber features. Northern Songhay (see Figure 18.1) is subdivided into a sedentary and nomadic branch. Souag (2009) questions the idea of Northern and Southern Songhay, suggesting instead a division of Western and Eastern, with the ancient vehicular Songhay from which Northern Songhay originated coming from one of these. Regardless, Northern Songhay languages, at least the nomadic varieties (Benítez-Torres and Grant 2017, form a distinct unit apart from mainstream Songhay languages (Kossmann 2011: 109).

18.2 Previous Literature on Northern Songhay Languages

Relatively little research exists on Northern Songhay languages. Christiansen and Christiansen (2002) and Christiansen-Bolli (2010) have written on grammatical and some phonological features of Tadaksahak, while Rueck and Christiansen (1999) and Heath

---

[4] For example, Bender (1996) and Ehret (2001).
[5] See, for example, Mukarovsky (1966), Creissels (1981), and Nicolaï's (2003) excellent critique of Bender and Ehret.

(2004) have produced basic vocabularies. Kossmann (2007a, 2007b, 2011) has described some grammatical features of Tasawaq, along with Alidou's MA thesis from the University of Niamey. Wolff and Alidou (2001) conclude that Tasawaq, as a contact language, does not have any genetic tie to other Songhay languages, something which, if true, could have serious implications for all Northern Songhay languages. Benítez-Torres (2009) explored known historical data from the region where Tagdal is spoken today in order to come to some tentative conclusions about its origin. Kwarandzey was described by Souag (2009, 2010). Nicolaï (1990a, 1990b, 2003, 2006a) has described various features of Songhay, including Northern Songhay, languages, coming to the conclusion (2006b, 2009) that Songhay languages originated from a possibly koineised, now extinct, Afro-Asiatic language, which over the centuries took on Mandé areal features.

18.3 PHONOLOGY

Because a number of very good descriptions of Tagdal phonology have already been produced,[6] I will not send much time on this subject here. Nevertheless, it should be mentioned that Tagdal has three main dialectal or variants, most often depending on speakers' geographical location.[7] The following is not meant to be an exhaustive list of all Tagdal varieties; rather, only of the most common ones.

18.3.1 Consonants

Perhaps the best-known variety of Tagdal is spoken principally by the Tarbun and Kəl Amdid in Niger's central regions, more or less between Tahoua to as far north as Aɣabrɣabr (see Map 18.1); it contains the consonants detailed in Table 18.1.[8]

The Abargan and Kəl Illokoḍ speak a variety of Tagdal whose consonant inventory is similar to that of Tadaksahak in Mali (Christiansen-Bolli 2010). The Abargan are the most numerous Tagdal-speaking group in northern Niger, located primarily between the central town of Aɣabrɣabr, as far north as the outskirts of Arlit, with the center of its geographical distribution in the area of the city of Agadez. The Kəl Ilokkoḍ, on the other hand, exist primarily in the south of Niger, in the same area inhabited by speakers of the Tarbun and Kəl Amdid dialects.

---

[6] See, for example, Nicolaï (1979, 1990a, 1990b) and Christiansen-Bolli's description of Tadaksahak phonology, which, as I mention in the following, is exactly the same as that of the Tagdal varieties spoken by the Abargan and Kəl Ilokkoḍ.

[7] A possible exception being the variety spoken by the Kəl Ilokkoḍ, which is spoken farther south in Niger, but has more similarities to Tagdal spoken farther north by the Abargan (Benítez-Torres and Grant 2017).

[8] See Nicolaï (1979) for a full comparison of all Northern Songhay languages' phonologies.

Table 18.1 Consonant chart, Tarbun, Kəl Amdid

	Labial	Alveolar	Pharyngealized	Palatal	Velar	Pharyngeal	Laryngeal
Stops	b	t d	ṭ ḍ		k g q		
Fricatives	f	s z	ṣ ẓ	ʃ ʒ	x ɣ	ħ ʕ	h
Glides	w			y			
Laterals		l	ḷ				
Taps		r	ṛ				
Nasals	m	n	ṇ		ŋ		

The main difference between these varieties and those spoken by the Tarbun and Kəl Amdid is the presence of *tʃ* and *dʒ*, contrastive with *ʃ* and *ʒ* (for example, *tʃin* 'say' and *ʃin* 'heavy'), whereas in the Tarbun variety in central Niger, *ʃin* 'say' and *ʃin* 'heavy' are pronounced the same way and context is needed to disambiguate. And *dʒe* 'only' in Abargan/Kəl Ilokkoḍ would be pronounced *ʒi* 'only' in Tarbun. Otherwise, Abargan/Kəl Ilokkoḍ is similar to other Tagdal varieties. Table 18.2 describes the consonants in Abargan/Kəl Ilokkoḍ Tagdal.

Table 18.2 Consonant chart, Abargan, Kəl Ilokkod

	Labial	Alveolar	Pharyngealised	Palatal	Velar	Pharyngeal	Laryngeal
Stops	b	t d	ṭ ḍ		k g q		
Affricates				tʃ dʒ			
Fricatives	f	s z	ṣ ẓ	ʃ ʒ	x ɣ	ħ ʕ	h
Glides	w			y			
Laterals		l	ḷ				
Taps		r	ṛ				
Nasals	m	n	ṇ		ŋ		

Tabarog, spoken by the Ibarogan, exists in the south of Niger, from Keita to as far south as the outskirts of Maradi. Rueck and Christiansen (1999) found a sufficiently high degree of intelligibility to consider Tabarog a variety of Tagdal. The main difference between Tabarog and Tagdal is the absence of *ʃ*, *ʒ*, *tʃ*, and *dʒ*. For example, *ʃin* 'say' or 'heavy' would be pronounced *sin* 'heavy,' and *ʒaɣʒi* 'day' would be pronounced *zaɣzi*. Otherwise, Tabarog is similar to other Tagdal varieties. Table 18.3 describes the consonants in Tabarog.

Table 18.3 Consonant chart, Tabarog

	Labial	Alveolar		Pharyngealised		Palatal	Velar		Pharyngeal		Laryngeal
Stops		b	t	d	ṭ	ḍ		k	g	q		
Fricatives	f		s	z	ṣ	ẓ		x	ɣ	ħ	ʕ	h
Glides		w					Y					
Laterals				l		ḷ						
Taps				r		ṛ						
Nasals		m		n		ṇ			ŋ			

18.4 VOWELS

All Tagdal varieties have a set of short vowels, as well as long vowels, the same as in Tadaksahak (Christiansen-Bolli 2010). Table 18.4 details the short vowels in Tagdal.

Table 18.4 Short vowels in Tagdal

	Front	Mid	Back
High	i		u
Mid-high	e	ə	O
Low		A	

Table 18.5 details the long vowels in Tagdal.

Table 18.5 Long vowels in Tagdal

	Front	Mid	Back
High	ii		uu
Mid-high	ee		Oo
Low		aa	

18.5 MORPHOLOGY

In this section, I will describe the noun structures in Tagdal, followed by the verb structures.

18.5.1 Nouns, Pronouns

First, I will describe the pronominal subsystem of Tagdal, which is exclusively of Songhay origin.[9] Then, I will describe its noun structures, first those of Berber origin, then those of Songhay origin. The subsection concludes with a few words concerning the pragmatics of when one would use Songhay versus Berber vocabulary.

18.5.2 Pronominal Subsystem

I will begin by describing the independent pronouns of Tagdal, then its proniminal clitics.

18.5.2.1 *Independent Pronouns*

Table 18.6 lists the independent pronouns in Tagdal.

Table 18.6 Independent pronouns

	Singular	Plural
First person	ɣaay	iiri
Second person	nin	anʒi
Third person	aŋga	iŋga / iŋgi

Note: *inga* is most common in the Tarbun and Kəl Amdid variety of Tagdal, while *ingi* tends to occur most often among the Abargan and Kəl Ilokkoḍ.

18.5.2.2 *Pronominal Clitics*

Table 18.7 lists the pronominal clitics in Tagdal. These are typically attached to the verb root, or to certain other morphemes when indicating the direct or indirect object.

Table 18.7 Pronominal clitics

	Singular	Plural
First person	ɣa-	iiri-
Second person	ni-/in-	anʒi-
Third person	a-	i-

Note: *ni-* and *-in* are allophones; *in-* occurs before the negation affixes sə- and nə-, as well as before the future tense affix tə-.

[9] Compare, for example, with the pronouns of Songhay from Timbuktu and Gao (Stauffer 1997; Heath 1999a, 1999b).

18.5.3 Nouns of Berber Origin

Typically, nouns of Berber origin can be distinguished rather easily because they typically begin with the normalizing prefix *a-* or *t-*. In addition, they tend to have, relatively speaking, rather more complex syllable patterns than those of Songhay origin (see later discussion). In Berber languages, nouns that begin with *a-* would be masculine and would typically require gender agreement at the phrase and verb levels.[10] Nevertheless, because Tagdal is essentially a Songhay language, it does not require any gender agreement. Table 18.8 demonstrates some typical nouns of Berber origin that begin with *a-* in Tagdal.

Table 18.8 Nouns of Berber origin that begin with *a-*

akasa	'vegetation'
agodrar	'dust'
amaxlak	'animal'
afarag	'garden'
atofan	'flood'

Typically, nouns of Berber origin that begin with *t-*[11] are feminine in Berber languages and would require gender agreement at the phrasal level and in the verb. However, as a Songhay language, Tagdal does not require this. Table 18.9 demonstrates some typical nouns of Berber origin in Tagdal that begin with *t-*.

Table 18.9 Nouns of Berber origin that begin with *t-*

takarakid	'shame'
tagarʃak	'evil eye'
tadaber	'dove'
təzori	'hyena'
tənfa	'profit, gain'

Though it is true that nouns that would otherwise be feminine in Berber languages do not require gender agree at the level of the grammar, sometimes the presence of the *t-* distinguishes whether the noun is feminine or diminutive, just as in Berber languages, as Table 18.10 demonstrates.

---

[10] See Kossmann (2011) for an example of typical Tuareg inflections.
[11] In nouns that end with a vowel, the *–t* will also be added (see Tables 18.12–18.14 for more).

Table 18.10 When _t-_ functions to indicate feminine or diminutive

aɣrəm	'town'	→	_taɣrəm_	'village'
barar[12]	'boy'	→	_tabarar_	'girl'
ahar	'lion'	→	_tahar_	'lioness'
akabar	'bowl'	→	_takabar_	'small bowl'

18.5.4 Nouns of Songhay Origin

Nouns of Songhay origin typically tend to begin with a consonant, typically other than _t-_,[13] and are usually recognizable due to their relatively simple syllable patterns. Table 18.11 shows some typical nouns of Songhay origin in Tagdal.

Table 18.11 Nouns of Songhay origin

boora	'person'
eeran	'water'
fiiʒi	'sheep'
haamu	'meat, flesh'
ganda	'land, country'

18.5.5 The Pragmatics of Berber and Songhay Vocabulary in Tagdal

No description of the noun in Tagdal would be complete without at least a mention of the pragmatics of Songhay and Berber vocabulary, though in a chapter of this length it would be impossible to give it a full treatment.[14] Nevertheless, it should be mentioned that often, when a discourse is started, a generic noun of Songhay origin is used. Then, as the discourse continues, the 'generic' Songhay noun is replaced with a more 'specific' one of Berber origin. Tables 18.12–18.14 demonstrate.

---

[12] Obviously, barar 'boy' is an exception to the rule that nouns of Berber origin typically begin with a- or t-.

[13] Two notable exceptions are _təguʒi_ 'tree', and tanɣɣaren 'lie,' both of Songhay origin.

[14] Especially since the entire phenomenon is so closely tied to the derivational subsystem, which includes Berber consonant roots along with their prefixes, suffixes, etc. (Benítez-Torres, forthcoming).

Table 18.12 Generic (Songhay) vs. Specific: 'goat'

	Songhay (generic)		Berber (specific)	
hinʃini	'goat'	→	*azolaɣ*	'large male goat'
			aynəs	'small goat' (male)
			taynəs	'small goat' (female)
			afeli	'newborn goat'

Table 18.13 Generic (Songhay) vs. Specific 'arm'

	Songhay (generic)		Berber (specific)	
kamba	'arm'	→	*aɣəl*	'right hand'
			taɣmur	'elbow'
			amansur	'forearm'
			aḍad	'finger'

Table 18.14 Generic (Songhay) vs. Specific 'child'

	Songhay (generic)		Berber (specific)	
ize	'child'	→	*barar*	'boy'
			tabarar	'girl'
			agugəl	'orphan'
			amaawa	'adolescent'
			tamaawat	'adolescent girl'
			awta	'youngest boy'
			tawtat	'youngest girl'

18.6 THE VERB

Here, I will describe the basic verb structures in Tagdal, including the inflectional prefixes and suffixes, of Songhay origin, as well as its derivational prefixes, of Berber origin.

18.6.1 Inflectional Morphology

Tagdal has a number of inflectional prefixes and clitics, which attach onto the verb root. These include a series of pronominal clitics (see earlier discussion), two negation particles, and the tense-aspect-mode (TAM) subsystem. Because the inflectional subsystem is of Songhay origin, this means that it is almsost impossible to produce a sentence in Tagdal without including some key Songhay element.

The incompletive negation sə- indicates that a particular action is not presently the case, or was not the case in the past. Example (1) demonstrates.

Example 1: incompletive negation
(1) *alwaq ayo kan, irisəbkoy lakol.*

alwaq	ayo	kan	iri=	sə-	b-	koy	lakol
time	DEM	in	1p	NEG	INC	go	school

'At that time, we didn't go to school.'

The second negation prefix indicates that the action was not completed at some fixed point in the past, or, in the case of stative verbs, that the action is not presently the case. Table 18.15 demonstrates.

Table 18.15 Completive negation

innəda-a?		*iŋga, inahossay.*		
in= nə- da =a		iŋga i= nə- hossay		
2s NEG do 3s		3pIND 3p NEG beautiful		
'You didn't do it?'		'Those (girls) are not pretty.'		

Now for the TAM subsystem. The completive aspect has no morpheme at all, and indicates that an action was completed at some fixed point in the past, or in the case of stative verbs, that something is the case, as Table 18.16 demonstrates.

Table 18.16 Completive aspect

iirida-a.		*iŋga, ihossay.*	
iiri= da -a		ina i= hossay	
1p do 3s		3pIND 3p beautiful	
'We did it.'		'Those (girls) are pretty.'	

The prefix *b-* marks the incompletive aspect, as material in Table 18.17 demonstrates.

Table 18.17 Incompletive aspect

abwa ha aayo.	*asəbwa ha aayo*
a= b- wa ha aayo	a= sə- b- wa ha aayo
3s INC eat eat DEM	3s NEG INC eat eat DEM
'He eats / is eating that.'	'He doesn't / didn't eat that.'

The prefix *m-* marks the irrealis mode, to indicate that something should (or should not, if a negation is present) be the case. The data in Table 18.18 show this.

Table 18.18 Modal

iirimkoy.	*iirimsəkooy-a.*[15]
iiri= m- koy	iiri= m- sə- koy =a
1p IRR koy	1p IRR NEG go 3s
'Let's go.'	'We shouldn't go there.'

Finally, the future tense indicates that the action will most likely happen, as in Table 18.19.

Table 18.19 Future tense

nin da, in tɘda ha kullu aayo nibaya!	*ʒaɣʒi aayo, ɣatakoy a-dayo.*
nin da in= tɘ- da ha kullu aayo ni= baya	ʒaɣʒi aayo ɣa- tɘ- koy a= dayo
	day DEM 1s FUT go 3s place
2s EMPH 2s FUT do thing all DEM 2s want	'Today, I'm going to his place.' (i.e., visit)
'(As for) you, you're going to do whatever (the heck) you want!'	

18.6.2 Derivational Morphology

As is the case with the noun in Tagdal, the verb root could be of either Songhay or Berber origin. The following items in Table 18.20 are sentences with verb roots of Berber origin.

---

[15] Normally, the negation would go before the TAM marker. However, in the case of *m-*, the negation follows.

Table 18.20 Verb roots, Berber origin

amətkəl an kamba.	anʒiyiɣlay-a.
a= m- ətkəl a= n kamba	anʒi= əɣlay =a
3s IRR raise 3s GEN hand	2p surround 3s
'He should raise his hand.' (i.e., swear an oath)	'You surrounded it.'

In Table 18.21, the verb roots are of Songhay origin.

Table 18.21 Verb roots, Songhay origin

ifur tonʒen.	iiribtuk ikaʃwaran kan.
i= fur tonʒen	iiri= b- tuk ikaʃwaran kan
3p throw rocks	1p INC hide mountains in
'They threw rocks.'	'We were hiding in the mountains.'

As we can see, the inflectional morphology does not change at all, regardless of whether the verb root is of Songhay or Berber origin. However, if the verb root is of Berber origin, a series of derivational prefixes attach themselves to the root. These change the verb's valence but do not affect the inflections in any way. The prefixes are the causative s-, the reflexive nəm- and the passive təw-. Table 18.22 demonstrates how these function.

18.6.3 Suppletion

Because the derivations can only affix onto verb roots of Berber origin, when the verb root is of Songhay and a derivation is required, an already derived Berber verb root suppletes any Songhay verb root. Table 18.23 demonstrates suppletion.

In forming sentences, it would only be necessary to add whatever inflectional prefixes—subject, negation (if necessary) TAM—might be necessary to the derived form.

18.7 SYNTAX

In the remainder of this chapter, I will concentrate briefly on Tagdal's canonical syntactic structure. In general, like many other Songhay languages (Nicolaï 1979: 26), Tagdal follows canonical SVO word order, as in Example 2.

Example 1: typical SVO word order in Tagdal

Table 18.22 Derivation of Berber verb roots

Verb root	Causative	Reflexive	Passive
ibaʈkəl in kamben. i= b- əʈkəl i- n kamben 3p INC raise 3p GEN hands 'They were raising their hands.'	*ibsaʈkəl in kamben.* i= b- s- əʈkəl i-n kamben 3pINCCAUS raise 3p GEN hands 'They were causing their hands to be raised.'	*ibnamaʈkəl in kamben.* i= b- nəm-əʈkəl i-n kamben 3p INC REC raise 3p GEN hands 'They were raising each others' hands.'	*In kamben ibtawaʈkəl.* i=n kamben i- b- təw- əʈkəl 3pGENhands 3p INC PASS raise 'Their hands were raised.'
way agəraz aro. way a= gəəraz aro woman 3s please man 'The woman pleased the man.'	*asəgraz aro.* a= sə- gəraz aro 3s CAUS please man 'She made him to be pleased.'	*inamagraz.* i= nəm- agraz 3p REC please 'They pleased each other.'	*Aro abtawagraz.* aro a= təw- agraz man 3s PASS please 'The man was pleased.'
iirimsarkab ʒifa. iiri= m- ərkəb ʒifa 1p IRR pull carcass 'We should pull the carcass.'	*iirimsarkab-a.* iiri= m- s- ərkəb =a 1p IRR CAUS pull 3s 'We should cause it to be pulled.'	*Hanʃen inamarkab ʒifa.* hanʃen i- nəm-ərkəb ʒifa dogs 3p REF pull carcass 'Dogs were pulling on the carcass.'	*ʒifa abtawarkab.* ʒifa a= b- t→w- ↔rkəb Carcass 3s INC PASS pull 'The carcass was being pulled.'

Table 18.23 Suppletion of Songhay verb roots

Songhay Verb Root		Causative	Reflexive	Passive
koy 'go'	→	səglu 'cause to go'	naməglu* 'make each other go'	tawaglu 'gone'
kəkay 'construct'	→	səkrəs 'cause to construct'	naməkrəs 'construct each other'	tawəkrəs 'constructed'
dab 'dress'	→	səlsa 'dress someone else'	naməlsa 'dress each other'	tawəlsa 'dressed'
nin 'drink'	→	ʃəʃəuw 'give someone a drink'	naməʃəuw* 'drink each other'	tawʃəuw 'drunk'
zumbu 'descend'	→	zəzəbət 'cause to come down'	naməzəbət* 'come down to each other'	tawazbət* 'having come down'
hanga 'hear'	→	sədərgən 'listen'	namədərgən 'hear each other'	tawadərgən* 'listened'
zay 'steal'	→	səbaydəg 'cause to steal'	nambaydəg 'steal from each other'	tawabaydəg 'stolen'
gora 'sit'	→	səqima 'force to sit'	naməqima 'force each other to sit'	tawaqima* 'having sat down'

Note: * indicates that, though the grammatical construction was correct, it was unacceptable to mother-tongue speakers, often causing a few laughs in the process.

(2) *aro afur təguʒi.*
     aro   a= fur   təguʒi
     man   3s throw   stick
     'The man threw the stick.'

In some cases, the direct object may be fronted in order to place focus upon the UNDERGOER, as in Example 3.

Example 26: alternate word order
(3) *təguʒi aro afur.*
     təguʒi   aro   a= fur
     stick   man   3s throw
     'It was a stick the man threw.'

This construction[16] has a very similar function to the passive voice. And, though technically it is not a passive voice—since verb valence does not change—it does underplay the importance of the AGENT and place the UNDERGOER in focus.

[16] Benítez-Torres (2009) and Grant and Benítez-Torres and Grant (2017), also point out other syntactic constructions with similar functions to the derivational affixes. However, these do not change the typical word order.

18.8 SHORT TEXT IN TAGDAL

Items underlined are of Berber origin, those in bold are from Arabic.

The fly, the clod of dirt, the toad and the blade of grass.

ɣabaɣa	sa	ɣatəda	anjisa	**arat**	**n**	**imayan**,
ɣaˈbaaɣa	sa	ɣatəˈda	ˈanjisa	arat	n	ˈimːaːjan

ɣa-	baɣa	sa	ɣa-	tə-	da	anji	-sa	arat	n	i-	eemay	-an
1s	want	that	1s	FUT	do	2p	BEN	small	GEN	PL	tale	PL

I want to tell you a little story

ablaɣ	wani	ənda	hamni	ənda	qora	ənda	subu.
ˈablaɣ	wani	ənda	ˈhamni	ənda	ˈqoːra	ənda	ˈsuubu
ablaɣ	wani	ənda	hamni	ənda	qora	ənda	suubu.
Clump of dirt	about	and	fly	and	toad	and	blade of grass

about the clump of dirt, the fly, the toad and the blade of grass.

Hamni	ənda	**ablaɣ**	ənda	qora	ənda	subu,	išikəl,	ihurru	hayni
ˈhamni	ənda	ˈablaɣ	ənda	ˈqoːra	ənda	ˈsuubu	i'ʃikəl,	ihuˈru	ˈhejni

Hamni	ənda	ablaɣ	ənda	qora	ənda	suubu,	i-	ʃikəl	i-	hurru
fly	and	clump of dirt	and	toad	and	blade of grass	3p	travel	3p	search

hayni
millet

The fly, the clump of dirt, the toad and the blade of grass were traveling to get some millet.

Ikoy	**agala**,	imay	farken.
Iˈkoj	ˈagːaːla,	i'mej	farˈken

i-	koy	agaala	i-	may	farka	-en
3p	go	south	3p	have	donkey	PL

They were going south with their donkeys.

Ikoy,	ibkoy	har	itenan	**agala**,	idaykat	hayni,	iyedkat.
Iˈkoy,	ibˈkoy	har	iˈteːnan	ˈagːaːla,	iˈdejkat	ˈhejni,	Iˈjedkat.

i-	koy	i-	b-	koy	har	i-	te	-nan	agaala	i-	day	-kat	hayni	i-	yed	-kat
3p	go	3p	INC	go	til	3p	arrive	ALL	south	3p	buy	ALL	millet	3p	return	VEN

They were going, they were going, until they arrived in the south. They bought millet and returned.

Sa	iyedkat,	**iyikla**	**asəwi**	fo	ga.
S	iˈyedkat,	iˈyɪkla	aˈsəwi	fo	ga.

sa	i-	yed	-kat	i	-yikla	asəwi	fo	ga
when	3p	return	VEN	3p	rest	forest	one	at

When they turned back, they took a rest in a forested area.

Sa **iyikla** jaɣji **n amas,** izumbu təguji **n šiday.**
S iˈyɪkla ˈʒaɣʒi n ˈamaas, izumˈbu təˈguːʒi n ʃiˈdej
sa i- yikla jaɣji n ammas i- zumbu təguji n šiday
when 3p rest day GEN middle 3p descend tree GEN shade
When they stopped to rest in the middle of the day, they got down under the shade
of a tree.

Izumbu ənda in kayatan, **təzar** išin **ablaɣ** sa amzərəg ənda farken.
Izumˈbu ənda in ˈkajːaatan təˈzar iˈʃin ˈablaɣ sa amˈzərəg ənda farˈken
i- zumbu ənda i- n kayaatan təzar i- šin ablaɣ sa a- m- zərəg ənda
3p descend with 3p GEN baggage then 3p say dirtclump BEN3s VOL water with
farka -en
donkey PL
They took down the loads, then they said to the clump of dirt that he should water
the donkeys.

Sa **ablaɣ** akoy, **təzar** ida **arat n aɣajira.**[17]
s ˈablaɣ aˈkoy təˈzar Iˈda ˈarat n aˈɣaʒːiira
sa ablaɣ a- koy təzar i- da arat n aɣajiira
when clump of dirt 3p go then 3p make little bit GEN aɣajiira
After the clump of dirt had left, they prepared some aɣajiira.

Sa ida **arat n aɣajira, tə'zar** inin-a.
s Iˈda ʿarat n aˈɣaʒiˀlra, təˈzar iˈniːn-a
sa i- da arat n aɣajiira təzar i- nin -a
when 3p make little bit GEN aɣajiira then 3p drink 3s
After preparing the aɣajiira, they drank it.

Təzar išin subu sa amfunus huru, imda **ašahi.**
təˈzar iˈʃin ˈsuubu sa amˈfuːnus ˈhuːru imˈda aˈʃahi
təzar i- šin suubu sa a- m- funus huuru i- m- da aššahi
then 3p say blade of grass BEN 3s VOL light fire 3p VOL make tea
Then they said to the blade of grass that he should light a fire so that they could
prepare some tea.

Hiyaw abfur. Subu akar ašana, təzar huru ajin akan, akurkur.
ˈhiyaw abˈfur ˈsuubu aˈkar aˈʃaana, təˈzar ˈhuːru aˈʒin ˈakan aˈkurkur
hiyaw a- b- fur suubu a- kar ašaana təzar huuru a- jin a- kan a- kurkur
wind 3s INC throw blade of grass 3s hit match then fire 3s grab 3s in 3s burn
The wind was blowing. The blade of grass struck the match, then the fire took him
and he burned.

---

[17] aɣajiira: drink made of curdled milk, sometimes with goat cheese, dates, and/or millet.

Təzar qora ašin hamni sa: "Kəma, tus nim me. Ablaɣ amsəte, amšin iirinin
təˈzar ˈqoːra aˈʃin ˈhamni sa kəˈma, tus nim me ˈablaɣ amsəˈte amˈʃin iiriˈnin
aˈɣaʒːiːra, irigiš-a."
aˈɣaʒira, iirigiiʃa

təzar	qora	a-šin	hamni	sa		kəma	tus	ni-	n	me	ablaɣ
then	toad	3s	sayfly	BEN	please	wipe	2s		GEN	mouth	clump dirt

a-	m-	sə-	te	a-	m-	šin	iiri-nin	aɣajiira	iiri-	giš	-a
3s	IRR	NEG	arrive	3s	IRR	say	1p	drink	aɣajiira	1p	leave	3s

Then the toad said to the fly "Wipe your mouth so that the clump of dirt won't come
back and say that we drank the aɣajiira and didn't leave him any."

Ablaɣ, sa atenan eran daɣo, ayiṭ kəlkat teɣar, ahurru sa atəinəz, aməṭ kəlkat eran.
ˈablaɣ s aˈteenan eeˈran daːˈyo aˈyıṭ kəlkat ˈteɣar ahuˈru sa atəˈinəz amˈəṭ kəl eeˈran

ablaɣ		sa	a- te-	nan	eeran	daɣo	a- əṭ kəl	-kat	teɣar,	a- hurru
clump dirt		when	3s	arrive	ALL	water	place	3s take	VEN	container	3s try

sa	a-tə-	inəz	a-	m-	əṭ kəl	-kat	eeran
that	3sFUT	bend	3s	VOL	take	VEN	water

When the clump of dirt arrived at the water place, he took the container and tried
to bend over to take up water.

Təzar ayirtək eran kan, təzar abun.
təˈzar aˈyirtək eeˈran kan, təˈzar aˈbun

əzar	a- ərtək	eeran	kan	əzar	a- bun
then	3s plop	water	in	then	3s die

Then he plopped into the water and died.

Hamni, sa qora ašin asa amtus am me, əzar atus-a.
ˈhamni, sa ˈqora a#ʃin ˈasa amˈtus am me, əˈzar aˈtuus-a

hamni	sa	qora	a- šin	a- sa	a- m-	tus	a- n	me	əzar	a- tus	-a
fly		when	toad	3s say	3s BEN	3s VOL	wipe	3s	GEN	mouth	ten	3s wipe	3s

When the toad told the fly to wipe his mouth, he wiped it.

Ašin asa, "Kəma, tus nim me wulen!"
Aˈʃin ˈas, kəˈma, tus nim me ˈwuleen

a- šin	a- sa	kəma	tus	ni-	n	me	wullen
3s say	3s BEN	please	wipe	2s		GEN	mouth	lots

He said, "Please, wipe your mouth a lot!"

Atus, əzar atus-a wulen ji. Hamni alafənjək, abun.
Aˈtus, əˈzar aˈtuus-a ˈwuleen ji. ˈhamni alaaˈfənjək, aˈbun

a-	tus	əzar	a- tus	-a	wullen	ji	hamni	a- əllafənjək	a- bun
3s	wipe	then	3s wipe	3s	lots	EMPH	fly	3s break apart	3s die

He wiped then he really, really wiped it hard, then the fly broke apart and died.

Sa hamni abun, **əzar** qora agora, abgargor ar **an šigəzal ifəqət.**
sa 'hamni a'bun, ə'zar 'qora agoo'ra ab'gargor ar ã 'ʃigəzaal I'fəqət
sa hamni a- bun əzar qora a- goora a- b- gargor ar a- n šigəzzal i- fəqət
when fly 3s die then toad 3s sit 3s INC laugh til 3s GEN entrails 3s exploded
When the fly died, the toad sat down laughing until his entrails exploded.

Tzar ikotayan ənda konda, ite, igora ibəʈkəl in hayni.
ə'zar I'kootayan ənda 'konda, I'te, igoo'ra ib'əʈkəl in 'hejni
əzar i- akootay -an ənda konda i- te i- goora i- b- əʈkəl i- n hayni
then PL mouse PL and ants 3s arrive 3s start 3s INC take 3s GEN millet
Then the mice and ants came and took their millet.

Wa ḥalas, azəbi ayiɣšad.
Wa ḥa'las a'zəbii a'yɪɣʃad
wa ḥalas azəbbi a- əɣšad
EMPH end voyage 3s ruin
That's all, the trip was ruined.

References

Alidou, Ousseina. 1988. *Tasawaq d'In-gall: équisse linguistique d'une langue dite "mixte."* MA thesis, University of Niamey.

Bender, M. Lionel. 1996. *The Nilo-Saharan Languages: A Comparative Essay.* München: LINCOM-Europa.

Benítez-Torres, Carlos M. Forthcoming. *Some Grammatical Features of Tagdal: A Northern Songhay language.* PhD dissertation, University of Leiden.

Benítez-Torres, Carlos, and Anthony Grant. 2017. On the origin of some Northern Songhay mixed languages. *Journal of Pidgin and Creole Languages* 32: 263–303.

Christiansen, Niels, and Regula Christiansen. 2002. Some verb morphology features of Tadaksahak: Berber or Songhay, this is the question. *SIL Electronic Working Papers 2002–005.* Dallas: SIL International. http://www.sil.org/silewp/2002/005/.

Christiansen-Bolli, Regula. 2010. *A Grammar of Tadaksahak: A Northern Songhay Language of Mali.* PhD dissertation, University of Leiden.

Creissels, D. 1981. De la possibilité de rapprochements entre le songhay et les langues Niger–Congo (en particulier Mandé). In *Nilo-Saharan: Proceedings of the First Nilo-Saharan Linguistics Colloquium, Leiden, September 8–10,* edited by Thilo Schadeberg and M. Lionel Bender, 185–199. Dordrecht: Foris Publications.

Ehret, Christopher. 2001. *A Comparative Reconstruction of Proto-Nilo-Saharan.* Cologne: Rüdiger Köppe Verlag.

Greenberg, Joseph, 1963. *The Languages of Africa* (International Journal of American Linguistics 29.1). Bloomington: Indiana University Press.

Heath, Jeffrey. 1999a. *A Grammar of Koyra Chiini: The Songhay of Timbuktu.* Berlin: Mouton de Gruyter.

Heath, Jeffrey. 1999b. *Grammar of Koyraboro (Koroboro) Senni, the Songhay of Gao.* Köln: Köppe.

Heath, J. 2004. Tadaksahak vocabulary. Unpublished manuscript. University of Michigan.

Kossmann, Maarten. 2007a. Grammatical borrowing in Tasawaq. In *Grammatical Borrowing in Cross-Linguistic Perspective*, edited by Yaron Matras and Jeanette Sakel, 75–90. Berlin; New York: Mouton de Gruyter.

Kossmann, Maarten. 2007b. The borrowing of aspect as lexical tone: y-initial Tuareg verbs in Tasawaq (Nothern Songhay). *Studies in African Linguistics* 36(2): 151–166.

Kossmann, Maarten. 2011. Adjectives in Northern Songhay. *Afrika und Übersee* 90: 109–132.

Mukarovsky, H. G. 1966. Zur Stellung der Mandesprachen. *Anthropos* 61: 679–688.

Nicolaï, Robert. 1979. *Les dialectes du songhay (Contribution à l'étude des changements linguistiques)*. PhD dissertation, University of Nice.

Nicolaï, Robert. 1990a. L'évolution 'problématique' du songhay septentrional (Analyse d'une situation de contact). In *Travaux du Cercle Linguistique de Nice 10–11*, 135–148. Presses universitaires de Nice.

Nicolaï, Robert. 1990b. *Parentés linguistiques (à propos du songhay)*. Paris. Éditions du CNRS.

Nicolaï, Robert. 2003. La force des choses ou l'épreuve 'nilo-saharienne': Questions sur les reconstructions archéologiques et l'évolution des langues. In *Sprache und Geschichte in Afrika* Beiheft 13. Cologne: Rüdiger Köpe.

Nicolaï, Robert. 2006a. Songhay-mande convergence area: Questions and frames. *Annual Publication in African Linguistics* 4: 5–30.

Nicolaï, Robert. 2006b. Aux marges de l'espace chamito-sémitique: Songhay et apparentements non-linéaires. In *Faits de langues, Les langues chamito-sémitiques (afro-asiatiques)*, edited by Amina Mettouchi and A. Lonnet, 245–277. Paris.

Nicolaï, Robert. 2009. Language contact, areality, and history: The Songhay question revisited. In *Sprache und Geschichte in Afrika* 19–20, edited by Wilhelm Möhlig, Frank Seidel, and Marc Seifert, 187–207. Cologne: Rüdiger Köppe.

Rueck, Michael, and Niels Christiansen. 1999. Northern Songhay speech varieties in Niger. *SIL Electronic Survey Reports 1999-008*. Dallas: SIL International. http://www.sil.org/silesr/1999/1999-008/silesr1999-008esr.pdf.

Souag, Lameen. 2012. The subclassification of Songhay and its historical implications. *Journal of African Languages and Linguistics* 33(2): 181–213.

Souag, Lameen. 2010. The Western Berber stratum in Kwarandzyey. In *Etudes berbères V, Essais sur des variations dialectales et autres articles*, edited by Harry Stroomer, Maarten Kossmann, Dymitr Ibriszimow, Rainer Vossen, and Rüdiger Köppe, 177–189. Cologne.

Stauffer, Daniel Ray. 1997. *Essential Elements of Songhai Grammar*. MA thesis, University of Texas at Arlington.

Wolff, H. Ekkehard, and Manou Ousseina Alidou. 2001. On the non-linear ancestry of Tasawaq (Niger). Or: how "mixed" can a language be? In *Historical Language Contact in Africa*, special volume of *Sprache und Geschichte in Afrika* 6/17, edited by Derek Nurse, 523–574. Köln: Rüdiger Köppe.

CHAPTER 19

LANGUAGE CONTACT IN THE WEST CHADIC LANGUAGE GOEMAI

BIRGIT HELLWIG

19.1 INTRODUCTION

GOEMAI is a West Chadic language that is spoken within the boundaries of the Jos Plateau Sprachbund of Central Nigeria. This Sprachbund comprises a large number of non-related Chadic and Benue-Congo languages. Its historical origin can be linked to the formation and expansion of the Jukun Empire of Kororofa (fourteenth to eighteenth centuries) and of several later emirates (nineteenth century) (Yearwood 1981; Isichei 1982). These states exercised control over the lowland societies and integrated them administratively, economically, and socially. At the same time, their rule triggered widespread migrations of small groups into the more inaccessible mountainous region of the Plateau. In both cases, speakers of different languages came into close contact with each other, and formed new political and ethnic groups. Goemai oral traditions, for example, give a Chadic origin for the Duut Goemai subgroup, but a Jukun (i.e., Benue-Congo) origin for the Dorok and K'wo Goemai. Linguistically, this intense contact has led to numerous structural convergences across the languages of this region. In the last century, the sociopolitical context that gave rise to this Sprachbund changed considerably, and the West Chadic language Hausa emerged as the lingua franca of this region. Its dominance led to the diffusion of many Hausa words and structures into the minority languages of the Plateau.

This chapter summarizes some salient linguistic traces of both types of language contact, and explores how they changed the Goemai language: the ancient contact with languages of the Jos Plateau (section 19.2), and the more recent contact with Hausa (section 19.3); section 19.4 offers concluding remarks.

19.2 GOEMAI AND THE JOS PLATEAU SPRACHBUND

The Jos Plateau Sprachbund is located within an area of great linguistic complexity (Greenberg 1956; Dalby 1970; Ballard 1971). It is home to languages from two language families (Chadic and Benue-Congo) whose linguistic structures show considerable convergences. At the same time, they lack many features that are considered typical for their respective language families. It is possible to note these similarities and differences, and to speculate on the potential diffusion of structures and on the circumstances that presumably led to the loss of inherited features. But it is very often no longer possible to determine the origins of a specific feature or to confidently trace the direction of borrowing. For this reason, Sprachbund situations are sometimes characterized as being "notoriously messy" (Thomason and Kaufman 1988: 95).

Goemai and its closely related languages of the Angas-Goemai group are Chadic languages: they share Chadic vocabulary and pronominal forms, and they retain remnants of Chadic morphology (Newman and Ma Newman 1966; Newman 1977a; Jungraithmayr and Ibriszimow 1994). But they also exhibit many atypical features, which prompted Jungraithmayr (1963) to entitle a paper "[o]n the ambiguous position of Angas." Subsequent research (e.g., Hoffmann 1970; Wolff and Gerhardt 1977; Jungraithmayr 1980, 1995; Gerhardt 1983; Frajzyngier and Koops 1989; Jungraithmayr and Leger 1993; Zima 2009; Storch et al. 2011; Hellwig 2012) added to his initial observations, showing that language contact shaped not only the Angas-Goemai group, but also all other languages of this region. There are lexical borrowings in both directions, but the most intriguing aspects of this Sprachbund are convergences in the areas of phonology and phonotactics (section 19.2.1), morphology (section 19.2.2), syntax (section 19.2.3), and semantics (section 19.2.4). The following sections illustrate each area as it applies to Goemai.

19.2.1 Phonology and Phonotactics

Wolff and Gerhardt (1977) were the first to report on areal convergences in phonology and phonotactics. There is evidence for the diffusion of sounds, as well as for the loss of typical Chadic features such as ejective consonants, geminate consonants, and contrastive vowel length. Interestingly, the Jos Plateau variety of the Chadic lingua franca Hausa has also lost these features (Pawlak 2002: 55–56, 62), presumably reflecting the phonological inventories of the indigenous languages. Most convergences, however, are in the area of phonotactics. Due to the erosion of word-final material, many languages have developed a preferred CV(V)C syllable structure and pose comparable restrictions on their coda consonants. Goemai conforms to this areal pattern, and this section outlines changes in its phoneme inventory (section 19.2.1.1) and syllable structure (section 19.2.1.2).

19.2.1.1 *Phoneme Inventories*

Goemai has lost some typical Chadic features (ejectives, geminates) and retains only a reduced system of contrastive vowel length (Hellwig 2011: 17–67). There is no clear evidence for the borrowing of sounds, but it is possible that the voiced obstruents and/or prenasalized consonants originated at least partly through language contact. This section traces the development of these sounds.

Goemai does not have ejective consonants: although earlier researchers noted a set of six ejectives that contrasted with plain obstruents (Greenberg 1958; Hoffmann 1975), the present-day language must have reanalyzed this contrast as a contrast between non-aspirated and aspirated obstruents (Tabain and Hellwig 2015). In any case, the former ejectives do not reflect Proto-Chadic ejectives. Rather, the ejective and plain obstruents developed from Proto-Chadic voiceless and voiced obstruents, respectively (Greenberg 1958; Newman and Ma Newman 1966: 226; Hoffmann 1975; Newman 1977a: 15; Jungraithmayr and Ibriszimow 1994: xx–xxix). Presumably, the voiceless sounds were realized aspirated at this stage. Ejective sounds, by contrast, do not occur aspirated: when they lost their laryngeal gesture for ejectivization, a phonemic contrast between aspirated and non-aspirated sounds was created. Table 19.1 visualizes the possible developments.[1]

An alternative scenario proposes that the Proto-Chadic voiceless and voiced obstruents merged in Goemai (Takács 2004: xxiii–xxiv): they were realized as voiceless aspirated obstruents, but had a non-aspirated allophone at the onset of unstressed syllables; this conditioned variation was later reanalyzed as a phonemic contrast. Further comparative research is needed to determine the likelihood of either scenario, but for the present discussion it is sufficient to note that both scenarios assume that Proto-Chadic voiced obstruents became voiceless. This means that the origins of Goemai's voiced obstruents /b, d, g; v, z, ʒ/ remain unaccounted for. Yalwa (1998) proposes that these entered the language through borrowings from Chadic Bole-Tangale languages, citing words such as Goemai *bái* 'return,' *bì* 'thing,' or *bél* 'pigeon' as evidence. His proposal argues against Greenberg (1958) and Jungraithmayr and Ibriszimow (1994: xx–xxix), who suggest that the voiced obstruents are reflexes of

Table 19.1 Proto–Chadic Obstruents and Their Goemai Reflexes

Proto-Chadic	Old Goemai	Present-day Goemai
p, t, c, k; f, s (voiceless)	p', t', c', k' ~ c'; f', s' (ejective)	p, t, k; f, s, ʃ (non-aspirated)
b, d, ɟ, g; v, z (voiced)	p, t, c, k ~ c; f, s (voiceless)	pʰ, tʰ, kʰ; fʰ, sʰ, ʃʰ (aspirated)

[1] With the exception of the IPA notations in Tables 19.1 and 19.2, this chapter uses an adapted version of the practical Goemai orthography developed by Sirlinger (1937). It includes the following symbols that are not self-explanatory: *p'*, *t'*, *k'*, *f'*, *s'*, *sh'* = non-aspirated obstruents; *b'*, *d'* = implosives; *oe* = [ə]; <u>u</u> = [ʉ]; <u>o</u> = [ɔ]. For other abbreviations, please see list of abbreviations in front matter of this volume.

prenasalized voiced obstruents. The evidence for the existence of prenasalized consonants in Proto-Chadic remains uncertain, however: the authors noted in the preceding reconstruct only prenasalized stops, and other authors do not reconstruct such sounds at all (Newman and Ma Newman 1966: 223–225; Newman 1977a: 11). It would therefore seem a promising line of inquiry to pursue Yalwa's (1998) proposal and to systematically search for potential sources of Goemai words containing voiced obstruents.

Present-day Goemai allows all consonants (not just the obstruents) to occur prenasalized, and this phenomenon cannot be traced back to Proto-Chadic. Some such words are even reconstructed without an initial nasal by authors who otherwise assume the existence of prenasalization for Proto-Chadic, for example, *m̀fèt* 'mosquito' (Proto-Chadic *br(t)*) (Jungraithmayr and Ibriszimow 1994: 121). Almost all such words are nouns, and they predominantly denote insects (e.g., *ǹgúm* 'beetle'), birds (e.g., *ǹténg* 'hoopoe') and other small animals (e.g., *ǹd'òòlk'úún* 'gecko'). A number of authors have argued that Chadic languages of the Jos Plateau have borrowed a Benue-Congo nasal noun class prefix (denoting a class of small animals) (Wolff and Gerhardt 1977; Frajzyngier and Koops 1989; Miehe 1991: 175–263). It is very likely that the prenasalized consonants in Goemai are remnants of this prefix: the prefix is no longer productive, but it surfaces in the phoneme inventory as a set of prenasalized consonants.

19.2.1.2 *Syllable Structures*

Goemai words are predominantly monomorphemic (see section 19.2.2), morphemes are predominantly monosyllabic, and syllables are predominantly CV(V)C. Only a limited number of consonants is allowed in syllable-final position, as illustrated with the help of near-minimal pairs in Table 19.2.

The attested syllable structures and the inventory of syllable-final consonants are characteristic of the whole Jos Plateau Sprachbund (Wolff and Gerhardt 1977). Their origins are unclear, though: reconstructions for Chadic and Benue-Congo posit mainly open syllables that ended in vowels. Jos Plateau languages of both families must have undergone parallel developments: losing the final vowels of polysyllabic words, re-syllabifying the remaining sounds, and imposing restrictions on the consonants now occurring in final position (see Storch 1999 for a careful study of this process among Jukunoid languages). In most languages, no voiced obstruents are allowed in final position at all, suggesting the presence of an areal devoicing rule.

Table 19.2 Syllable-Final Consonants in Goemai

p	t	k	s	m	n	ŋ	l	r	w	j
ɓáp	ɓát	ɓák	ɓàs	ɓàm	ká.ɓán	ɓáŋ	ɓál	há.ɓár	ɓòu	ⁿɓài.zʷám
mix	able	here	break off	stick	face down	red	hard	wrap	arrow	jackal

19.2.2 Morphology: Nominal and Verbal Number

One of the striking characteristics of Jos Plateau languages is their isolating nature. Jungraithmayr (1963) was the first to remark on the loss of Chadic plural morphology within the Angas-Goemai group. Subsequent research then showed that this loss or reduction of morphology extended to other areas of grammar as well, especially to verbal extensions (that change a verb's valency), and to (Chadic) gender and (Benue-Congo) noun classes. Pawlak (2002: 63, 78–82) reports similar changes to the variety of Hausa spoken on the Jos Plateau. Goemai is no exception to this areal pattern. It is a predominantly isolating language that has lost much of its inherited morphology: it does not generally mark nominal number, it does not have verbal extensions, and it has a reduced system of gender marking (only retained in 2SG and logophoric pronouns, i.e., in speech act contexts). Interestingly, though, there is one exception to this widespread areal loss of inherited morphology: the marking of verbal number. This section focuses on both nominal and verbal number.

Chadic languages often have elaborate systems of morphological plural marking on the noun (Frajzyngier 1977, 1997; Newman 1990). Jos Plateau languages, by contrast, either do not mark nominal number at all or rely on analytic means (Jungraithmayr 1963; Wolff and Gerhardt 1977). Goemai is such a case in point: it does not have any general and obligatory plural marking on the noun. Almost all nouns are compatible with both singular and plural reference (exemplified with *lwá* 'animal/meat' in (1a) and (1b) in the following example), many also with collective reference (as in (1c)), and some also with mass reference (as in (1d)). In all examples, disambiguation of number reference is left to other elements within the sentence (e.g., to the quantifier *díp* 'all' in (1a), to the plural diminutive morpheme *jàp* in (1b), or to number marking on the verb *twò* ~ *tù* 'kill' in (1b) and (1c)), as well as to pragmatic information. Morphological number marking is, in fact, restricted to eight nouns that have distinct singular and plural forms: some of them exhibit the inherited Chadic plural formative *-a-* (such as *k'én* (SG) ~ *k'án* (PL) 'mother's brother, sister's child'), while others use suppletive form (such as *là* (SG) ~ *jáp* (PL) 'child; DIM'). (Sources of sentence examples are given in small capitals.)

(1a) *Díp, bá ńdòe=lwá ń-s'ét gòepé nyáng*
all NEG SPEC=animal/meat LOC-bush THAT/WHEN hate(SG)
gòe kààt, bì bá.
SEQ greet thing NEG
'All (of them), there wasn't **a single animal** in the bush who refused to greet the thing.' (FOOJFUAN)

(1b) *Dé t'óng móe=twò ńdòe=jàp lwá*
SO.THAT IRR:CONS 1PL.S=kill(PL) SPEC=DIM(PL):GEN animal/meat
mén yì ń-ní.
1PL.POSS CONS COMIT-3SG.I
'So that we would kill our little **animals** with it.' (CO1FGHJARAM7)

(1c) *mùèp dók d'è ń-tù **lwá** à*
      3PL.S PAST.REM exist PROGR-kill(SG) animal/meat FOC
      góe mòe?
      COMIT what
      '[. . .] in the past, they used to kill **animal(s)** with what?' (C01FGHJARAM5)

(1d) *Gúlùk sh'ài tép, sh'ài **lwá** [. . .].*
      bat.type show.pride blackness show.pride animal/meat
      'The *guluk* bat shows pride in (its) black (color), (it) shows pride in (its) **flesh**
      [. . .].' (DOOJANIMAL8)

The preceding examples suggest that Goemai—like other Plateau languages—has lost
not only Chadic number-marking morphology, but the category of number itself. Such
an assessment would be misleading, though, because Goemai has developed other
means of indicating number: an invariant plural particle (section 19.2.2.1), number
marking on the verb (section 19.2.2.2), and an incipient system of marking number on
the noun (section 19.2.2.3). With the exception of verbal number, these strategies are
recent language-internal developments that follow standard patterns of grammaticalization. Nevertheless, it is striking that different languages have undergone parallel
structural developments: that is, the languages employ language-internal material to
compensate for the areal loss of number-marking morphology and to recreate this
morphology. The following sections illustrate each of the three possibilities in turn.

19.2.2.1 *Plural Particle* gwén

Goemai has an associative plural particle *gwén*, which denotes a person plus its
associates (as in (2a)). More recently, speakers have extended its use to express plurality
(as in (2b)): it is not obligatory in this context, and its presence implies that the
referents occur in different types. The existence of such an invariant particle is
reminiscent of the invariant plural particles found in other Jos Plateau languages
(Jungraithmayr 1963; Wolff and Gerhardt 1977), which can often be traced to a 3PL
pronoun. In Goemai, by contrast, it originated in the 2PL pronoun *gwĕn*. This form is
frequently used as a stylistic device in narrative genres, where a narrator directly
addresses the protagonist of a story or an audience by juxtaposing a second person
pronoun and a name (as in (2c)). In the course of grammaticalization, this pronoun
became integrated into the noun phrase. Even though many Jos Plateau languages use
invariant plural particles grammaticalized from personal pronouns, there is no evidence for any direct borrowing.

(2a) *lú mén tóe d'ì, lù **gwén** Shályén.*
      settlement 1PL.POSS EMPH LOC.ANAPH settlement:GEN ASSOC.PL <NAME>
      '[. . .] our compound (is) there, the compound of Shalyen and his people.'
      (DOOJROUTE)

(2b)   *Màng gwén, d'á gòe-t'wót d'i (. . .).*
       take ASSOC.PL calabash NMLZ-sit(PL) LOC.ANAPH
       '(He) took those kinds of calabashes that sat there [. . .].' (F99DLIIT)

(2c)   *Só hèn=b'òòl gwén dàsk'óóm [. . .].*
       so 1SG.S=beg/appeal 2PL.O elders(PL)
       'So I ask you, elders [. . .].' (DOONSPEAKING)

19.2.2.2 *Number Marking on the Verb*

Goemai marks number on the verb in two ways. First, there is a developing system of
subject agreement on the verb. Normally, the co-occurrence of both a subject noun phrase
and a subject pronoun is only employed to emphasize the subject. The main exception is a
3PL referent: here, speakers preferably use both a lexical noun and a cliticized pronoun,
which serves to unambiguously specify plural number (as in (3)). Again, it is likely that
this number-marking strategy constitutes a recent language-internal innovation.

(3)   *Gòemâi mu̱èp=yíl.*
       <ETHNIC.NAME> 3PL.S=write
       'The Goemai, they write (on it).' (CO1ANHAND)

And second, Goemai uses a mechanism that is well attested in this region: the marking
of verbal number. Number is marked morphologically on about 10% of Goemai's verbs.
Note that plural formation is not productive or predictable, but some formatives recur
and are of Chadic origin (Frajzyngier 1977, 1997; Newman 1990): the infix *-a-* (as in *lúút*
(SG) ~ *lwát* (PL) 'be afraid'), and possibly the suffixes *-k* (as in *dùm* (SG) ~ *dúk* (PL)
'become upside down') and *-t* (as in *twáám* (SG) ~ *twát* (PL) 'cause standing'). Some
common Chadic formatives such as *-n* and reduplication are absent. And other
formatives, including especially *-r-* and *-r* (as in *táp* (SG) ~ *táráp* (PL) 'snap'), are
assumed to have a Benue-Congo origin. In fact, it has long been noticed that Jos
Plateau languages not only mark verbal number, but even use similar formatives: the
category itself is likely to be of Chadic origin, but the morphological material comes
from both language families (Wolff and Gerhardt 1977; Gerhardt 1983). It is argued that
Benue-Congo languages have not only borrowed the category and the formatives from
Chadic, but also reanalyzed their inherited valency-changing morphology as plural
morphology. Following that, Chadic languages like Goemai must have borrowed some
of this reanalyzed morphology from Benue-Congo (presumably through borrowing
some of the verbs, although only very few borrowed items have been identified so far).
   In addition, Goemai has approximately twenty pairs that have no morphological
relationship between the singular and plural forms. Wolff and Gerhardt (1977) hypothesize that the existence of suppletive verbs is further evidence for language contact: the
speakers borrowed verbs that were semantically similar to preexisting verbs, and then
reinterpreted them as singulars or plurals of native verbs. This is a possible scenario,

but so far no suppletive Goemai verb has been traced to any Benue-Congo language. It is equally possible that such pairs result from language-internal developments. In present-day Goemai, there are a number of cases where two semantically similar verbs are becoming associated with a number distinction. For example, the two lexemes *dàp* 'slap' and *b'uát* 'beat repeatedly, flog, play a drum or string instrument' are increasingly used by speakers as a suppletive singular/plural pair.

Throughout the Jos Plateau, verbal number is used to mark event number (such as multiple or iterative actions) and participant number (especially the number of subject participants for intransitive verbs, or object participants for transitive verbs) (Frajzyngier 1977, 1997; Newman 1990; Corbett 2000: 243–264). Goemai exhibits an interesting idiosyncrasy here: only very few verbs (notably verbs that code a punctual change of state) can denote event number at all. This is illustrated in (4), where the event has a single subject participant (one dog) and a single object participant (one bone), but uses the plural verb to convey an iterative action (break repeatedly).

(4)   *P'yárám ués, k'áu k'áu k'áu.*
       break(PL) bone <QUOTE>
       '(He) broke the bone (iteratively), k'au k'au k'au.' (FOOCAAS)

Otherwise, however, verbs exclusively express participant number. Their distribution is partly determined by transitivity (intransitive verbs always mark number in their subject argument) and partly by semantic roles: transitive verbs with patient or theme direct objects mark the object argument (as in (5a) and (5b)), and transitive verbs with other semantic roles linked to their direct objects mark the subject argument (as in (6a) and (6b)). In all cases, it is ungrammatical to use the respective other verb: a singular verb denotes a singular participant, and a plural verb a plural participant—and this participant has to occur in the argument slot determined by the verb's transitivity and semantic roles. Such a pattern is not attested in other Jos Plateau languages (i.e., even though Goemai employs a common areal feature, it seems to use it in slightly different ways).

(5a)   *àkwái mòe-gòepé, muèp t'óng tù góe [. . .].*
       there.is/are NMLZ(PL)-THAT/WHEN 3PL.S IRR kill(SG) 2SGM.O
       '[. . .] there are those that will kill you [. . .].' (DOOJANIMAL7)

(5b)   *Tó, ní twó muèp díp.*
       okay 3SG.S kill(PL) 3PL.O all
       'Okay, he killed them all.' (DOOEWITCH4)

(6a)   *hèn=mì muép*
       1SG.S=be.related(SG) 3PL.O
       'I am related to them' (A-28/04/04)

(6b)   *muèp myá hèn*
       3PL.S be.related(PL) 1SG.O
       'they are related to me' (A-28/04/04)

19.2.2.3 *Marking Number Morphologically on the Noun*

Goemai uses the prefixes *gòe-* (SG) and *mòe-* (PL) to mark number agreement in some elements within the noun phrase (e.g., in the derived modifier in (7a)). Some speakers have started to extend these prefixes to overtly mark number on nouns themselves (as in (7b)).

(7a)   *Ńdòe=gùrùm **gòe-mìs** ná ń-d'é [. . .].*
        SPEC=person NMLZ(SG)-man(SG) PRES PRES-exist
        'See a male person is (there) [. . .].' (R01NSTAGE)

(7b)   *dé-gòe páár **gòe-gùrùm** [. . .].*
        PUR send NMLZ(SG)-person
        '[. . .] to send a person [. . .].' (TIEMSAN 1999: III)

The origins of these two prefixes are recoverable: *gòe-* (SG) was presumably grammaticalized from a spatial preposition, and *mòe-* (PL) is likely to be a reflex of the common Afro-Asiatic prefix **ma-* that originally derived nouns of agent (Greenberg 1966). This morphology does not have any parallels in other Jos Plateau languages.

19.2.3 Syntax

As discussed in section 19.2.2, Jos Plateau languages have lost much of their inherited morphology and have developed isolating structures instead, relying on syntactic and analytic means such as independent particles to mark categories such as tense, aspect, and mood (TAM), or developing serial verb constructions. While their isolating structures are a common areal pattern, the absence of shared forms makes it difficult to find clear evidence for language contact. Nevertheless, the languages also share syntactic structures that are typologically unusual, which makes it more likely that they originated in some form of language contact. One of these structures relates to the distribution and function of pronouns.

Wolff and Gerhardt (1977) already note the widespread areal occurrence of a so-called intransitive copy pronoun (ICP), that is, a pronoun that has the form and position of an object pronoun but occurs with intransitive verbs, "copying" the subject's number (and gender). There has been considerable research into this topic since, and a recent edited volume (Storch et al. 2011) shows that there are different types of copy pronouns: the classic ICP that occurs with intransitive verbs (not attested in Goemai), a copy pronoun that occurs in those TAM constructions that originated in multi-verb constructions (see section 19.2.3.1), and a copy pronoun that marks unexpected states-of-affairs (see section 19.2.3.2). The last two types are widespread in the southern part of the Jos Plateau Sprachbund, and are described in the following for Goemai.

19.2.3.1 *Subject Pronouns, Verb Serialization, and the Marking of TAM*

Many Chadic languages distinguish perfective from imperfective verb stems, and mark TAM categories morphologically on the verb or the pronoun (see, e.g., the discussions in Schuh 1976; Newman 1977b; Jungraithmayr 1979; Wolff 1979). Goemai, by contrast, exhibits none of these features: there is no evidence for a dichotomy between perfective and imperfective, and TAM is marked by free particles and discontinuous constructions. The forms show only little similarity to the forms attested in closely related languages, which makes it likely that they have only recently grammaticalized. In fact, most Goemai TAM constructions had their origins in multi-verb constructions, mostly in serial verb constructions. Evidence for this diachronic development comes from various sources (see Hellwig 2011: 323–373), and one of them is the unusual distribution of pronouns.

Goemai distinguishes two sets of pronouns: set 1 (1SG, 3SG, 3PL, addressee-logophoric pronouns) and set 2 (2SGM, 2SGF, 1PL, 2PL, speaker-logophoric pronouns). These two sets differ syntactically in a number of TAM and modal constructions: set 1 pronouns originated in nominal elements and behave like lexical nouns in that they occur once before the entire TAM or modal construction (e.g., preceding the verb in (8a)), while set 2 pronouns optionally occur before the first element (e.g., the verb) and obligatorily before the second (e.g., the TAM particle in (8b)).

(8a)   *ní wá kàm.*
       3SG.S return.home(SG) RESULT
       '[. . .] he has returned home' (NO1JTIME)

(8b)   *(dù)=yòk dù=kám.*
       (PL.LOG.SP.S)=return.home(PL) PL.LOG.SP.S=RESULT
       '(He1 said) they1 have returned home.' (R99DFROG)

This concordant marking of set 2 pronouns is observed in most TAM constructions (the four absolute tenses, the anterior and resultative particles, the irrealis particle, and the conditional, habitual, and progressive constructions) as well as with modal and phasal verbs (such as *b'óót* 'to be able to do something'). They all originated transparently in multi-verb constructions, usually in serial verb constructions. For example, the resultative construction in (8) grammaticalized from the serialized verb **kàm* 'stay.' Similarly, non-related languages of the southern part of the Jos Plateau Sprachbund, such as Jukun, are known to use copy pronouns in some of its modal and completive constructions, notably those that have a verbal origin (Storch et al. 2011).

Present-day Goemai still has serial verb constructions, and the distribution of pronouns is similar there: set 1 pronouns precede the first verb only (as in (9a)), and set 2 pronouns optionally precede the first verb and obligatorily all subsequent verbs (as in (9b)).

(9a)   *Muèp máng lyàk [. . .].*
       3PL.S take throw
       'They took (it and) threw (it) away [. . .].' (R01NSTAGE)

(9b) *(jì)=màng jì=wá ǹ-ní [. . .]*
     (SGM.LOG.SP.S)=take SGM.LOG.SP.S=return.home(SG) COMIT-3SG.I
     ǹ-lú=wà?
     LOC-settlement=INTERR
     '[. . .] does he take (it) (and) return with it home to the village?' (FO4ATAMTIS)

Verb serialization is very common in present-day Goemai: it is used extensively to express temporal relations among events (as in (9a) and (9b)), to change the lexical aspect of an expression (as in (10a), where stative *t'ó* 'lie' occurs in the inchoative serial verb construction to express inceptive 'lie down'), to give information on the deictic setting of an event (as in (10b), where the first instance of *dóe* 'come' expresses a simple motion event, but the second instance expresses the deictic setting of the following speech event), and to add participants to an event (as in (10c), where *póe* 'give' adds an addressee).

(10a) *yìtsáám máng k'úr mú? K'úr t'á t'ó.*
      sleep take tortoise INTERR tortoise fall(SG) lie(SG)
      'the tortoise became sleepy, right? The tortoise lay down.' (F99AKUR)

(10b) *dé gòe dóe yì dóe kùt kùt*
      SO.THAT OBLIG come CONS come talk talking
      'so that (he) should come (and) talk here (lit. come and come and talk)'
      (A- 13/06/01)

(10c) *mu̱èp t'át támtìs póe mu̱èp.*
      3PL.S propel/tell.folktale(SG) folktale give 3PL.O
      '[. . .] they tell them a folktale.' (DO1CLU)

In fact, serialization is characteristic of the entire region. It is mainly used to express TAM categories, grammaticalizing further into TAM morphemes (Gerhardt 1984), and to express complex motion events, grammaticalizing further into directional verbal extensions (Frajzyngier 1987a, 1987b, 1987c). Pawlak (2002: 66, 83–84) even observes the occurrence of serial verbs in the Jos Plateau variety of Hausa—bearing in mind that standard Hausa does not have verb serialization, and that serialization is not considered a typical feature of Chadic languages.

19.2.3.2 *Possessive Pronouns and the Marking of Unexpected States-of-Affairs*

Goemai has two sets of nominal possessive forms, and it uses both sets in adverbial function to describe an unexpected or surprising state-of-affairs (as in examples (11a) and (11b)). In (11a), the speaker expresses surprise that a story character is fat while the rest of his community is starving. And in (11b), the speaker expresses surprise at his own survival despite considerable hardships. This mirative use of pronouns is otherwise not attested in Chadic languages, but the possessive pronouns in Jukun languages are known to serve a comparable function (Storch et al. 2011).

(11a) *À ńd'àng mòe=ńd'è t'òng móe=rás yì,*
FOC how 1PL.S=exist PROGR 1PL.S=become.thin(PL) PROGR
gòe=làng mmàk t'òng góe=dóól yì?
2SGM.S=hang/move(SG) NMLZ.2SGM.POSS PROGR 2SGM.S=become.fat PROGR
'How (come) we are getting lean, (while) you keep on getting fat in your own way?' (FOOCFUAN)

(11b) *hén=láng bì=nóe muáán yì,*
1SG.S:CONS=hang/move(SG) thing=1SG.POSS go(SG):CONS CONS
hén gòemé.
1SG.I one
'[. . .] and so I am alive (lit. move) in my own way and walk around, I alone.'
(NO1JTIME)

19.2.4 Semantics

Most Chadic languages lexicalize property concepts in a small set of adjectives that share formal similarities with nouns. Goemai, by contrast, lexicalizes them mostly in state-change verbs. Example (12) illustrates the typical use of such a verb. Note that it would need to occur in a derived nominalized form in order to refer to the corresponding state of 'being red.'

(12) *Kàt là góe=ná lá-t'éng=hók b'áng ńt'ìt (. . .).*
maybe COND 2SGM.S=see child(SG):GEN-tree=DEF become.red well
'If you see (that) the fruit has become thoroughly red [. . .].' (POODCROPS)

There is evidence that this type of lexicalization is shared among the Chadic and Benue-Congo languages of the southern Jos Plateau (Hellwig 2012). Since Niger-Congo languages are known to have inchoative property verbs (Welmers 1973: 249–274, 336, 343–415; Stassen 1997: 470–485), it is likely that this lexicalization pattern originated with the Benue-Congo languages, and that Goemai and other Chadic languages have borrowed it.

There are a few cases where Goemai has borrowed verbs from Benue-Congo: for example, *b'áng* 'become red' in (12) was probably borrowed from a Jukun language—it has been reconstructed as **gban* 'red' for northern Central Jukunoid (Storch 1999). However, in the majority of cases, the forms are not similar (i.e., the convergences are due to shared patterns, not shared forms).

19.3 Hausa Words and Structures in Goemai

In the last century, the pattern of language contact on the Jos Plateau changed, and the Chadic language Hausa emerged as the dominant language of this region. This language has had considerable impact on the indigenous languages of the Plateau, including Goemai. Aside from integrating numerous lexical borrowings, Goemai has developed two new grammatical categories under its influence: auxiliary verbs (section 19.3.1) and conjunctions (section 19.3.2).

19.3.1 Auxiliary Verbs

Hausa has a category of aspectual or auxiliary verbs that require non-finite verb phrases as their complements (Newman 2000: 64–70, 288–292, 699–717). Goemai has borrowed many of these verbs, such as *fárà ~ párà* and *sómà* 'begin,' *gámà* 'finish,' *kárà* 'repeat,' *rígá* 'already,' or *táb'à* 'taste; have (n)ever done.' Older Goemai speakers rarely use these borrowed verbs, but they are attested with considerable frequency among younger speakers.

These speakers occasionally use them in a serial verb construction (13a), but mostly as auxiliary verbs followed by non-finite verbs (marked by the prefix combination *gòe-ǹ-*) (13b). They are even extending this auxiliary construction to native Goemai words (13c). The use of a serial verb construction is not surprising in this context (see section 19.2.3.1 for the extensive use of serialization). But the auxiliary construction constitutes an innovation. It has its origins in a nominalized participle, which occurs as a modifier within a noun phrase (13d). Younger speakers have then reanalyzed the syntax of this construction. Compare, for example, the position of the determiner =*hok*, which marks the end of a noun phrase: it follows the participle in (13d) (which forms part of the noun phrase), but precedes the complement in (13c) (which does not form part of the noun phrase). It is very likely that it was the borrowing of Hausa auxiliary verbs that necessitated this reanalysis and thus facilitated the introduction of a new grammatical category into Goemai.

(13a) *yì=pàrà yì=mán à ní.*
2SGF.S=begin 2SGF.S=know FOC 3SG.I
'[. . .] you began (and) knew him.' (= you started to know him) (N01JTIME)

(13b) *Mùèp sómà [shál]NP [gòe-ǹ-lyàk]COMPLEMENT*
3PL.S begin war NMLZ-ADVZ-throw
'They started waging the war [. . .].' (F99DPAAP)

(13c)   *Mụèp máng b'ít, b'ít gòepé muép t'óng **làngòedé***
3PL.S take day day THAT/WHEN 3PL.S:CONS IRR start
[gyà=hòk]NP [gòe-ǹ-màràp]COMPLEMENT.
performance=DEF NMLZ-ADVZ-step(PL)
'They picked a day, a day when they would start dancing the dance.'
(F99DPAAP)

(13d)   *sái gòe=nàk [ńdòe=háás gòe-ǹ-d'èk=hòk]NP (. . .).*
then/only 2SGM.S=fetch SPEC=flour NMLZ-ADVZ-move.up/down=DEF
'[. . .] then you fetch some of the winnowed flour [. . .].' (POODCROPS)

19.3.2 Conjunctions

Present-day Goemai has a fair number of phrasal and sentential conjunctions, but all of
them either constitute recent developments whose diachronic origins are still transparent, or are borrowings from Hausa. Like many Chadic languages (Frajzyngier 1996),
Goemai presumably used juxtaposition to express various logical relationships. This is
still a common strategy in the language, whereby the nature of the relationship is left
implicit: it includes conjoined (14a) and contrastive readings (14b), but also readings of
reason, purpose, or condition.

(14a)   *Mụèp s'óe bì, mụèp s'wá hààm, mụèp shín tàl.*
3PL.S eat thing 3PL.S drink water 3PL.S do greeting
'They eat things, (and) they drink water, (and) they perform greetings.'
(Ohikere and Tiemsan 1999: 2)

(14b)   *Bàkwá yóng yì, Démshìn, s'èm lú=hók*
<ETHNIC.NAME> call CONS <PLACE.NAME> name:GEN settlement=DEF
d'è bí=múk à Ngòòtlóng.
exist thing=3SG.POSS FOC <PLACE.NAME>
'And so the Hausa call (it) Demshin, (but) the name of the village is in its own
way Ngootlong.' (D04NLUDOROK)

Younger speakers, however, are increasingly using Hausa conjunctions to make such
relationships explicit. This includes especially the Hausa conjunctions *kó* 'or,' *àmmá*
'but' (as in (15)), *kàfín* 'before,' *sái* 'then/only,' *hár* 'until/even,' *sábò ńdòe* 'because of,'
and *kódàshíkè* 'even though.'

(15)   *ní góe mís, àmmá ní góe jáp bá.*
3SG.I COMIT man(SG) but 3SG.I COMIT children(PL) NEG
'[. . .] she has a husband, but she doesn't have children.' (DOOJFAMILY)

19.4 Summary and Conclusion

Although Goemai is a Chadic language, it is an atypical Chadic language: it does not have many of the expected Chadic features, and instead conforms more closely to patterns attested in related and non-related languages of the Jos Plateau. Convergences and contact-induced changes are attested in all areas of phonology and grammar, and this chapter has sketched the following phenomena:

- Phonology and phonotactics (section 19.2.1): Goemai has lost typical Chadic consonants (such as ejectives), while the presence of other phonemes can be attributed at least to some extent to language contact: the voiced obstruents (through the borrowing of words), and the prenasalized consonants (through the borrowing of a nasal noun class prefix, which is now unproductive). Furthermore, Goemai's syllable structure of CV(V)C and the distribution of syllable-final consonants both follow the general areal pattern.
- Morphology (section 19.2.2): Goemai has lost much of its inherited morphology to mark nominal number, gender, and valency. Interestingly, it has not lost the morphology to mark verbal number, and seems to even have borrowed Benue-Congo morphology to help express this category. Both the loss of morphology and the diffusion of verbal number are characteristic for Jos Plateau languages. Note, however, that the loss of morphology does not necessarily entail the loss of the corresponding category. For example, Goemai retained the category of nominal number and developed new strategies for marking it. Some of these strategies bear superficial similarities to those attested in other languages, but the evidence points to language-internal grammaticalization processes.
- Syntax (section 19.2.3): Goemai shares syntactic structures with other languages of the Jos Plateau, including verb serialization and the distribution and function of pronouns (in specific TAM and modal constructions, and to express unexpected states-of-affairs).
- Semantics (section 19.2.4): Goemai and other languages of the southern Plateau share the lexicalization of property concepts in state-change verbs.

All the preceding phenomena are suspected to have originated through language contact. They mostly constitute structural convergences, that is, the Jos Plateau languages have converged on similar patterns—rather than having borrowed forms. Of course, borrowing of lexical and morphological material is attested as well (see especially Hoffmann 1970; Wolff and Gerhardt 1977; Gerhardt 1983), but the Sprachbund overall is characterized by its shared patterns. Some of these patterns are typical for the Chadic or Benue-Congo language family, respectively. But most patterns are atypical for both families, that is, they must have developed in the contact situation itself, and it is no longer possible to trace their origins or directions of diffusion. In fact, since we are dealing with structural similarities, it is often not possible to prove conclusively that a structure is borrowed at all—it could alternatively constitute an independent, language-internal, development. This possibility was exemplified in section 19.2.2 with reference to the grammaticalization of nominal number. The languages have lost their inherited number-marking morphology, and many of them—including Goemai—currently re-create it by using forms and structures from within their languages (e.g., the development of plural particles from plural pronouns). Each such development can be explained language-internally by invoking typical grammaticalization trajectories. Yet it is striking to note that parallel developments take place in different languages. Possibly, such developments are instantiations of Sapir's drift, where genetically or areally related languages continue to use new material to re-create old categories (Sapir 1921; see also Givón 1975; LaPolla 1994).

The task of identifying borrowings is complicated by the fact that the structures of today's languages reflect an ancient contact situation that has ceased to exist 100 or more years ago. The original sociopolitical situation can no longer be witnessed and can only be reconstructed imperfectly. And enough time has passed for language-internal developments to take place and further obscure common structures. Today, we witness a very different type of language contact (discussed in section 19.3): the dominance of one single language, Hausa, and its lexical and structural influence on indigenous minority languages such as Goemai.

ACKNOWLEDGMENTS

I thank Trudel Schneider-Blum, Anthony Grant and an anonymous reviewer for their constructive feedback on earlier versions of this paper. My thanks also go to the many Goemai speakers who participated in this research, and especially to Louis Longpuan. I am furthermore very grateful to the Max Planck Institute for Psycholinguistic and to the Endangered Languages Documentation Programme for funding my research on Goemai.

REFERENCES

Ballard, J. A. 1971. Historical inferences from the linguistic geography of the Nigerian Middle Belt. *Africa* 41(4): 294–305.

Corbett, Greville. 2000. *Number*. Cambridge: Cambridge University Press.

Dalby, David. 1970. Reflections on the classification of African languages with special reference to the work of Sigismund Wilhelm Koelle and Malcolm Guthrie. *African Language Studies* 11: 147–171.

Frajzyngier, Zygmunt. 1977. The plural in Chadic. In *Papers in Chadic Linguistics*, edited by Paul Newman and Roxana Ma Newman, 37–56. Leiden: Afrika-Studiecentrum.

Frajzyngier, Zygmunt. 1987a. Encoding locative in Chadic. *Journal of West African Languages* 17(1): 81–97.

Frajzyngier, Zygmunt. 1987b. Ventive and centrifugal in Chadic. *Afrika und Übersee* 70: 31–47.

Frajzyngier, Zygmunt. 1987c. From verb to anaphora. *Lingua* 72: 155–168.

Frajzyngier, Zygmunt. 1996. *Grammaticalization of the Complex Sentence: A Case Study in Chadic*. Amsterdam; Philadelphia: John Benjamins.

Frajzyngier, Zygmunt. 1997. Grammaticalization of number: From demonstrative to nominal and verbal plural. *Linguistic Typology* 1: 193–242.

Frajzyngier, Zygmunt, and Robert Koops. 1989. Double epenthesis and N-class in Chadic. In *Current Progress in Chadic Linguistics*, edited by Zygmunt Frajzyngier, 233–250. Amsterdam; Philadelphia: John Benjamins.

Gerhardt, Ludwig. 1983. Lexical interferences in the Chadic/Benue-Congo border-area. In *Studies in Chadic and Afroasiatic Linguistics*, edited by Ekkehard Wolff and Hilke Meyer-Bahlburg, 301–310. Hamburg: Helmut Buske.

Gerhardt, Ludwig. 1984. More on the verbal system of Zarek (Northern Nigeria). *Afrika und Übersee* 67: 11–30.

Givón, Talmy. 1975. Serial verbs and syntactic change: Niger Congo. In *Word Order and Word Order Change*, edited by Charles Li, 49–111. Austin: University of Texas Press.

Greenberg, Joseph H. 1956. The measurement of linguistics diversity. *Language* 32(1): 109–115.

Greenberg, Joseph H. 1958. The labial consonants of Proto-Afro-Asiatic. *Word* 14: 295–302.

Greenberg, Joseph H. 1966. Afroasiatic. In *The Languages of Africa*, edited by Joseph H. Greenberg, 42–65. Bloomington: Indiana University Press.

Hellwig, Birgit. 2011. *A Grammar of Goemai*. Berlin; Boston: Mouton de Gruyter.

Hellwig, Birgit. 2012. Lexicalization of property concepts: Evidence for language contact on the southern Jos Plateau (Central Nigeria)? *Journal of African Languages and Linguistics*. 33(1): 67–95.

Hoffmann, Carl. 1970. Ancient Benue-Congo loans in Chadic? *Africana Marburgensia* 3(2): 3–23.

Hoffmann, Carl. 1975. Towards a comparative phonology of the languages of the Angas-Goemai group. Manuscript.

Isichei, Elizabeth (ed.). 1982. *Studies in the History of Plateau State, Nigeria*. London; Basingstoke: Macmillan.

Jungraithmayr, Herrmann. 1963. On the ambiguous position of Angas (N. Nigeria). *Journal of African Languages* 2(3): 272–278.

Jungraithmayr, Herrmann. 1979. Apophony and tone in the Afro-Asiatic/Niger-Congo frontier area. *Études Linguistiques* 1(1): 130–140.

Jungraithmayr, Herrmann. 1980. Kontakte zwischen Adamawa-Ubangi- und Tschad-Sprachen: Zur Übertragung grammatischer Systeme. *Zeitschrift der Deutschen Morgenländischen Gesellschaft* 130: 70–85.

Jungraithmayr, Herrmann. 1995. Was ist am Tangale noch tschadisch/hamitosemitisch? In *Sprachkulturelle und historische Forschungen in Afrika*, edited by A. Fleisch and D. Otten, 197–206. Köln: Rüdiger Köppe.

Jungraithmayr, Herrmann, and Dymitr Ibriszimow. 1994. *Chadic Lexical Roots*, Vol. 1: *Tentative Reconstruction, Grading, Distribution and Comments*. Berlin: Dietrich Reimer.

Jungraithmayr, Herrmann, and Rudolf Leger. 1993. The Benue-Gongola-Chad Basin: Zone of ethnic and linguistic compression. In *Berichte des Sonderforschungsbereichs 268*, Vol. 2, edited by G. Nagel, 161–172. Frankfurt: Goethe University.

LaPolla, Randy. 1994. Parallel grammaticalizations in Tibeto-Burman languages: Evidence of Sapir's drift. *Linguistics of the Tibeto-Burman Area* 17(1): 61–80.

Miehe, Gudrun. 1991. *Die Präfixnasale in Benue-Congo und in Kwa*. Berlin: Dietrich Reimer.

Newman, Paul. 1977a. Chadic classification and reconstructions. *Afroasiatic Linguistics* 5(1): 1–42.

Newman, Paul. 1977b. The formation of the imperfective verb stem in Chadic. *Afrika und Übersee* 60: 178–192.

Newman, Paul. 1990. *Nominal and Verbal Plurality in Chadic*. Dordrecht; Providence: Foris Publications.

Newman, Paul. 2000. *The Hausa Language: An Encyclopedic Reference Grammar*. New Haven, CT: Yale University Press.

Newman, Paul, and Roxana Ma Newman. 1966. Comparative Chadic: Phonology and lexicon. *Journal of African Languages* 5(3): 218–251.

Ohikere, Benjamin Jimoh, and Stephen Tiemsan. 1999. *Notes on the Reading and Writing of Goemai (Trial Edition)*. Jos: Goemai Literacy and Bible Translation Committee and Nigeria Bible Translation Trust.

Pawlak, Nina. 2002. *Hausa Outside the Mother Area: Plateau Variety*. Warsaw: Academic Publishing House DIALOG.

Sapir, Edward. 1921. *Language: An Introduction to the Study of Speech*. New York: Harcourt, Brace.

Schuh, Russel G. 1976. The Chadic verbal system and its Afroasiatic nature. *Afroasiatic Linguistics* 3(1): 1–14.

Sirlinger, Eugene. 1937. *Dictionary of the Goemai Language*. Manuscript.

Stassen, Leon. 1997. *Intransitive Predication*. Oxford: Clarendon Press.

Storch, Anne. 1999. *Das Hone und seine Stellung im Zentral-Jukunoid*. Köln: Rüdiger Köppe.

Storch, Anne, Gratien G. Atindogbé, and Roger Blench (eds.). 2011. *Copy Pronouns: Case Studies from African Languages*. Köln: Rüdiger Köppe.

Tabain, Marija, and Birgit Hellwig. 2015. Goemai: Illustration of the IPA. *Journal of the International Phonetic Association* 45(1): 81–104.

Takács, Gábor. 2004. *Comparative Dictionary of the Angas-Sura Languages*. Berlin: Dietrich Reimer.

Thomason, Sarah G., and Terrence Kaufman. 1988. *Language Contact, Creolization, and Genetic Linguistics*. Berkeley: University of California Press.

Tiemsan, Stephen. 1999. *Goemai: Moe t'at tamtis. Tamtis toetat-toetat (Goemai Fables and Stories). A Post-primer Reading Book in the Goemai Language of Plateau State*. Jos: Goemai Literacy and Bible Translation Committee and Nigeria Bible Translation Trust.

Welmers, William 1973. *African Language Structures*. Berkeley: University of California Press.

Wolff, Ekkehard. 1979. Grammatical categories of verb stems and the marking of mood, aktionsart, and aspect in Chadic. *Afroasiatic Linguistics* 6(5): 161–208.

Wolff, Ekkehard, and Ludwig Gerhardt. 1977. Interferenzen zwischen Benue-Kongo- und Tschad-Sprachen. *Zeitschrift der Deutschen Morgenländischen Gesellschaft* Supplement 3(2): 1518–1543.

Yalwa, Lawan 'Danladi. 1998. On 'articulatory evolution': The reconstruction of Hausa word initial consonants and those of its related proto-West Chadic-A languages. *Afrikanistische Arbeitspapiere* 56: 163–177.

Yearwood, Peter (ed.). 1981. *Jos Oral History and Literature Texts*, Vol. 1: *Mwahavul, Ngas, Mupun, Njak*. Jos: Department of History, University of Jos.

Zima, Petr (ed.) (2009). *The verb and related areal features in West Africa*. München: Lincom.

CHAPTER 20

....

LANGUAGE CONTACT IN BERBER

....

LAMEEN SOUAG

20.1 HISTORY

....

IN the east, proto-Berber speakers must have been in contact with Egyptian (spoken along the Nile) from an early period. Few Egyptian loans into Berber have been identified, even in eastern varieties; however, a couple of loans in the domain of date palms seem to date back to proto-Berber, notably *te-βǎyni 'date' (Kabyle *tiyni*), from Egyptian *bnj.t* (Vycichl 1951; Kossmann 2002). There is some reason to believe that contact with Semitic dates back to a similarly early period, although nothing certain can be said of its context. As suggested by van den Boogert (1997: 221), the proto-Berber numerals five through nine (Shilha *smmus, sdis, sa, tam, tza*) appear likely to derive from contact with Semitic (reconstructed *xamš-, šidθ-, šabʕ-, θmān-, tišʕ-*; Lipiński 1997: 290), rather than being a common Afro-Asiatic inheritance. However, while he attributes them to contact with Phoenician, they must reflect earlier contact; Berber *sdis* corresponds better to Proto-Semitic *šidθ- than to its reflexes in any Semitic languages of the Mediterranean by the time they are first attested in writing (Phoenician *šš*, Hebrew *šēš*, Aramaic *šitt*, Ugaritic *θθ*, Arabic *sitt* . . .).

Greek settlement in Cyrenaica began around the seventh century BC, presumably placing Greeks in contact with Berber speakers; Greek remained dominant there until the Islamic conquests. Nevertheless, Greek loans do not appear to be numerous even in eastern Berber; several comparisons have been proposed, more or less in passing (Schuchardt 1918; Colin 1926), but in most cases either the validity of the connection is questionable, or an indirect loan via Latin or Arabic cannot be ruled out. (For example, in the often-cited case of 'stork,' Kabyle *i-bəlliraj*, ultimately from Greek *pelargos*, the substitution of *j* for *g* suggests a borrowing via Arabic, and cognates are well attested throughout Maghrebi and Andalusi Arabic.) One striking Greek loan whose referent and limited distribution indicate a relatively late date is Siwi *a-səryen*, 'Bedouin Arab,' from *sarakēnos* 'Saracen' (Vycichl 2005).

Further west, a potential earliest identified loanword is *a-zrəf* 'silver,' which, like English 'silver,' may derive from the little-understood Iberian language of pre-Roman Spain (Boutkan and Kossmann 2001). However, the most important early influence in this region came from Phoenician, whose speakers began to settle the North African coast starting around the eighth century, establishing a powerful state centered on Carthage in modern Tunisia. While Carthage was famously destroyed by Rome in 146 BC, Punic—the North African descendant of Phoenician—continued to be spoken at least into the fifth century AD (Millar 1968), and probably continued to influence Berber. Punic provided early Berber with a number of words, of which a couple of dozen have survived. Punic influence (handily summarized in Vycichl 2005: 2–16; 1952) is especially prominent among the names of useful plants (e.g., Shawi *a-rmun* 'pomegranate' < **rimmūn*; Nefusi *dəffu* 'apple' < **tappūḥ*; Shilha *a-zalim* 'onion' < pl. **bəṣāl-īm*; Shilha and Kabyle *a-ɣanim* 'reeds' < **qān-īm*; Ouargla and Tuareg *ta-ɣəssim-t* 'cucumber, melon' < **qiššū-īm*; Kabyle *a-ḡusim* 'walnut' <**əguz-im*). A few forms also relate to technology: Tuareg *a-nəsmir* 'nail' < **masmēr*, *e-nir* 'lamp'< **nēr*. Punic loans are found well to the east of the regions where Punic was spoken, suggesting later influence from Northern Berber on these regions; thus at Awjila (in the hinterland of Greek-speaking Cyrenaica) we find *bẓalim* 'onion' and *kšaim* 'cucumber,' and in Siwa (in western Egypt) *a-rmun* 'pomegranate.'

Identifying Punic loanwords is made more difficult in principle by the possibility that later contact with Jews may have introduced Hebrew loans, virtually indistinguishable from their Punic counterparts; medieval historians such as Ibn Khaldūn report that some major Berber groups had converted to Judaism before Islam. In practice, however, this is unlikely to be a major confounding factor. Múrcia (2010: I.177) summarizes the handful of suggested Hebrew loans, of which the only widespread ones are the verbs *lmәd* 'learn' < √*lmd* (already attested in Berber by the tenth century, cf. Cohen 1972) and *ɣәr* 'call' < √*qr*, which may well be Punic after all; the other possibilities, such as Shilha *a-gar-muẓẓl* 'ill-fated' < Shilha *-gar-* 'bad' + Hebrew *mazzāl* 'constellation, luck,' have a much more restricted geographical distribution.

The Berber kingdoms that briefly profited from Carthage's fall were gradually forced into Rome's orbit, and by 40 AD the entire North African coast had been turned into Roman provinces. The Roman policy of settling veterans in conquered territories ensured the spread of Latin, which remained the official language of the region until after the Islamic conquests. Latin far outstrips Punic, Greek, or Egyptian as a source for known loanwords into Berber, as suggested by such studies as Vycichl (2005: 16–32), Colin (1926), and Schuchardt (1918). However, caution is required in evaluating such claims, not only because it is difficult to distinguish Latin loans from later Romance ones and because of Schuchardt's rather lax standards of comparison, but also because a few of the supposed loans may rather be loans into Latin, from Berber or from a common substratum (Boutkan and Kossmann 1999). The loans include common tools (e.g., Kabyle *a-tmun* 'plough tongue' < *tēmō(ne)*, Nefusi *tu-səbla* 'awl' < *sūbula*), and plants (Kabyle *ta-ḵtunya* 'quince' < *cydōnia*, *ulmu* 'elm' < *ulmus*), alongside some more surprising items such as Shilha *ta-ɣawsa* 'thing' < *causa*; since all Berber languages show the change **q > ɣ* (Kossmann 1999), the reflex of Latin *k* as ɣ in words like the latter demonstrates their antiquity within Berber. A handful of religious loans, such as Medieval Eastern Berber *ta-fəṣka* 'festival' < *pascha*, *anjlus-ən* 'angels' < *angelus*, *i-daymun-ən* 'devils' < *daemonium* (Brugnatelli forthcoming), make it clear that influence continued into the Christian period. The Vandal conquests of the fifth century had no known linguistic impact, and were reversed after a century by the Byzantines. More limited Latin influence probably continued for some time even after the Islamic conquest: a Romance language was still spoken in parts of North Africa as late as the twelfth century (Lewicki 1958).

Over a period of several decades starting from 642, the Arabic-speaking Caliphate gradually conquered the entirety of North Africa. During this period, the Berbers rapidly adopted Islam, and Arabic became the language of many major towns, and later of their hinterlands. Some Arabic loans related to religion, in particular the widespread forms *ẓall* 'pray' < *-ṣallī* and *ẓum* 'fast' < *-ṣūm-*, can plausibly be dated to the start of this period (Boogert and Kossmann 1997); *ṣ* became common in Berber thanks to later Arabic loanwords, but cannot be reconstructed for proto-Berber.

The decline of the Caliphate's power starting in the eighth century allowed North African kingdoms to claim independence, but did not seriously affect the status of Arabic, which remained the primary written language and the lingua franca of some of the most agriculturally productive regions.

Arabic loans, while much less numerous than today, are already moderately frequent in the handful of surviving Berber medieval texts, and already included verbs—for example, the twelfth-century eastern Berber fragments described by Lewicki (1934) contain such forms as *əd-din* 'religion' < *addīn*; *əl-mizan* 'scales' < *al-mīzān*; *tə-mlək* 'she married' < √*mlk* 'possess'; *wər nə-kniz* 'we have not amassed' < √*knz*. From an early period, Arabic influence also brought in indirect loans from languages further afield, for example Rif (Kossmann 2009): *a-fənžař* 'bowl' < Arabic *finjān*; 'cup' < Persian *ping-ān* 'clepsydra'; *ḍarrəz* 'to weave' < Arabic *darz* 'garment' < Middle Persian *darz* 'seam.'

In the mid-eleventh century, as the nomadic Sanhaja Berbers of Mauritania conquered Morocco and Spain, the nomadic Arab tribe of Banū Hilāl invaded Libya and Tunisia. The latter's arrival marks a turning point in the linguistic history of the region. Whereas prior waves of sedentary immigration had mainly focused on cities or rich farmland, the herding lifestyle of these newcomers encouraged them to remain highly mobile, putting Berbers far from any major towns in close contact with Arabic speakers. Over the following centuries, a combination of migration and language shift made Arabic the dominant language of the lowland pastures south of the Atlas, turning Berber from a dialect continuum into what it is today: a series of islands separated from one another by Arabic-speaking regions. The Arabic dialect of these nomads shows the reflex *g* for original Arabic *q*, making it often possible to distinguish loans from it; for example, Siwi *gaṣi* 'hard' < *-qāsī* can only have been borrowed from a Bedouin variety, whereas *a-tqil* 'heavy' < *θaqīl* almost certainly derives from a non-Bedouin one (Souag 2009). The far-reaching conquests of Almoravids, and their Almohad successors, must also have had an influence on Berber at this time, placing geographically far-flung varieties in greater contact with one another. However, intra-Berber contact effects are difficult to identify due to the family's relatively short time depth, and hardly any work has yet been done on this issue.

After the successor states of the Almohads had exhausted themselves in a series of internecine wars, exacerbated by Spanish attacks, most of North Africa apart from Morocco was loosely incorporated into the Ottoman Empire in the mid-sixteenth century. This produced a new elite in Algiers, Tunis, and Tripoli, highly diverse in origin but priding themselves on their command of the Turkish language. A number of Turkish borrowings reached Berber during this period, for example Shilha *a-ṭbji* 'gunner' < *topçu* (Boogert 1997: 225) or Kabyle *a-ḍəbṣi* 'dish' < *tepsi*, while refugees from post-Reconquista Spain, along with European visitors and captives, brought in new Romance loans, such as Kabyle *lfišṭa* '(secular) festival' < *fiesta* or Shilha *l-iččin* 'orange' < *china*. In both cases, however, these would usually reach Berber through the Arabic vernaculars of the coastal towns, rather than directly.

The large-scale Romance influence that would characterize the next period had not yet begun (Boogert 1997: 223). Although many Berber-speaking areas remained effectively ungoverned, the Ottoman policy of resettling outsiders in frontier areas had the effect of promoting the spread of Arabic during this period, and in regions such as Kabylie and the Mzab, the practice of young men traveling to find temporary work in major cities encouraged bilingualism. The extent of Arabic influence may be illustrated for the early eighteenth century by Shaw's (1758: 476–477) vocabulary of an Algerian variety which (though labeled "Showiah") appears to be Kabyle: among loans, he records not only nouns such as *a-bəhlul* 'fool' < *bahlūl*, or *l-qaʕa* 'earth [ground]' < *al-qāʕ*, but also the morphologically anomalous adjective *lʕali* 'good' < *al-ʕālī* 'the high,' the interrogative *qəddaš* 'how much?' < Maghrebi Arabic *qədd* 'size of,' *āš* 'what?' < *qadar* 'quantity' + *'ayy* 'which' + *šay'* 'thing,' and, already, all numerals greater than two. (Most Berber languages have borrowed all higher numbers from Arabic; Souag 2007.) By the early nineteenth century, Arabic loans were already found in virtually all semantic fields. The degree of borrowing varies; Kabyle has more Arabic borrowings than Shilha, which in turn has more than Tuareg; these are especially numerous among generic, intellectual, spiritual, and economic terms (Chaker 1984a). Frequently, inherited and Arabic synonyms for the same idea coexist, a situation sometimes exploited for rhetorical effect in poetry (Taïfi 2008).

The situation in the contemporary Sahel was quite different; no North African state succeeded in imposing more than, at best, nominal authority on the Tuareg- and Zenaga-speaking nomads of this region, and, after the fall of Songhay in 1591, West African states were equally unsuccessful in that task. While the continuing trans-Saharan trade exposed them to some North African influence, their contact history would be mainly determined by other factors. It was contact with Arab tribes coming in from the north that proved decisive for Zenaga: Mauritania took an irreversible turn toward Arabization after the war of Shar Bubba in the late seventeenth century, when Arab tribes became politically dominant, and the very word *aẓnāga* (Zenaga) came to mean 'tribute-paying tribes.' Zenaga held out longest in the southwest, but was already in decline by the colonial period, and is reportedly no longer spoken by children (Taine-Cheikh 2008). The Tuareg, by contrast, remained independent, and indeed, through slave-raiding and identity shift, incorporated many speakers of other languages into their society. As a result, Tuareg has far fewer Arabic loans than any other Berber variety, but has acquired a substantial number of loans from Sahelian languages: for example, *dăro* 'beer' from Bambara *dɔlɔ*, *băsaso* 'tamarind tree' from Songhay *bosso*, and *goḍəy* 'thank' from Hausa *gode* (Heath 2006; Souag 2008; Sudlow 2009). A few such loans made it further north, to Berber-speaking oases such as Timimoun and Ghadames (Souag 2013).

In a century-long process starting in 1830 with the French conquest of Algiers, all of North Africa and the Sahel came under European rule. French became the primary language of education, administration, and industry in most of the region, and European settlers were encouraged to immigrate to North Africa, often through the confiscation of natives' land. A small subaltern elite was given a European education. The concurrent introduction of a variety of new items and institutions absent from traditional society encouraged borrowing, particularly where European influence was strongest. For instance, in Olivier's (1878) dictionary of Kabyle, hardly a generation after the French conquest of Kabylie, we already find words referring to industrial materials such as *l-gaz* 'gas' < *gaz*, *s-siman* 'cement' < *ciment*; new products such as *l-gazuz* 'soft drink' < *gazeuse*, *l-gaziṭa* 'gazette'; new units such as *kilu* 'kilo,' *a-ṣantim* 'centime'; and colonial institutions, mainly military or governmental, such as *a-jadaṛmi* gendarme,' *ggaji* 'enlist' < engager, *jumitr* 'surveyor' < *géomètre*. The article *l-* on several of these betrays their passage via colloquial Arabic, as is usual for the period.

Over little more than a decade, from Libya's independence in 1951 to Algeria's in 1962, the entire region obtained independence. The new North African governments adopted Standard Arabic as an official language—although French often remained the working language of administration in practice—and introduced universal education for the first time. (In the Sahel, where national linguistic unity was obviously unachievable, French stayed official, but education remained far from universal.) This resulted in a few Standard Arabic loans, such as Kabyle *ta-wilay-t* 'wilaya (governorate)' < *wilāyah*, Rif *l-muʕallim* 'teacher' < *al-muʕallim*, and Siwi *əl-waḍʕ* 'situation' < *alwaḍʕ*, alongside the continuing stream of European ones—usually French, like Shilha *l-urdinatur* 'computer' < *l'ordinateur*, but in some regions Spanish, like Rif *kuku* 'coconut' < *coco* (Kossmann 2009). The impact of Standard Arabic, however, remained comparatively minor, as illustrated by Kossmann's (2009: 198) figures for Rif; he reports three times as many loans from French and Spanish as from Standard Arabic, and five times as many dialectal Arabic loans (many of which predate the colonial period) as loans from all three sources put together. Massive emigration from rural areas to non-Berber-speaking urban areas had a more serious impact, not only increasing colloquial borrowing but also encouraging language shift among emigrants. North African governments, which tended to see Berber as an obstacle to education and a threat to national unity, discouraged any efforts to preserve the language.

Activists (initially mainly Kabyle) responding by trying to develop Berber into a unified, literary, ultimately official language. One of their first priorities was to replace obvious loanwords with puristic neologisms—a huge task started by the Paris-based Académie Berbère in the late 1960s, and taken up more professionally by Mammeri (1976, 1980), followed by many others. This was variously accomplished by borrowing from other varieties (e.g., *a-zul* 'hello' < Zenaga *a-zol* 'peace' or Tamahaq *-ăhul* 'greet;' *a-šəngu* 'enemy' < Tamasheq *a-šăngo*), by repurposing existing words (e.g., *a-gdud* 'swarm' > '(the) people'), or by compounding (e.g., *ta-sn-iləs-t* 'linguistics' < *ssən* 'know,' *iləs* 'tongue'). The results could be quite difficult for ordinary speakers; Baamrani (2003: 3) confesses that "[s]ome may say: I do not understand much of the Tamazight in which he has written, and I am Amazigh!" In Algeria, after decades of protests, the state agreed in 1995 to teach Berber at school, providing a systematic means for neologisms to be spread. Morocco (2003) and Libya (2012) eventually followed step; indeed, in 2011 Morocco went further, making Tamazight co-official with Arabic. However, while some neologisms have enjoyed success, current circumstances make it unlikely that they will succeed in stemming the tide of French and Arabic loanwords. Monolingual Berber speakers, still common in many areas at independence, have become rare everywhere.

While Berber has been influenced by a wide variety of languages, by far the most intense contact, over the course of more than a millennium, has been with Arabic. Apart from a few local adoptions from Romance, such as French number/gender marking on recently borrowed French nouns in Kabyle (Kahlouche 1999), Arabic is the only well-documented source of external influence on Berber grammar. The remainder of this chapter will focus primarily on its impact; for a more detailed overview, see Kossmann (2013).

20.2 PHONOLOGY

The phonemic inventory of proto-Berber, as reconstructed by Kossmann (1999), lacked a number of consonants found in early Arabic: no pharyngeals (ʕ, ħ) or interdentals (θ, ð); no voiceless uvular fricative *x*; no emphatic *ṣ*; and no glottal *h*. There was no phonemic distinction between *q* and *ɣ* or between *d* and *ṭ*; in most varieties even now, morphologically motivated gemination of *ɣ*, *d* turns them into *qq*, *ṭṭ*, respectively; *š* was marginal at best, and the status of *ž* (the later Arabic reflex of *j*) is doubtful. Proto-Berber also had a few phonemes missing from Arabic: the voiced bilabial fricative *β*, the voiced emphatic alveolar fricative *ẓ*, and the voiceless palatal stop *c*. However, Proto-Berber predates contact with Arabic, and some changes need to be taken into account for comparison. Most extant varieties have lost *β*, and all have merged *c*, *j* with either *k*, *g*, or *š*, *ž*, probably starting before contact with Arabic. There are also indications that *x*, originally an allophone of *ɣ*, may have begun to behave as a separate marginal phoneme from a relatively early period. All varieties except Zenaga seem to have lost *ʔ* from an early period, and even in early Arabic this phoneme was subject to wide variation. Arabic changes also need to be taken into account; early Arabic *j* has become *j* or *ž* throughout Maghrebi Arabic (in certain contexts, also *d* or *g*), and the early Arabic interdentals (*θ*, *ð*) have been lost in many Maghrebi dialects through merger with *t*, *d*. Modern Arabic varieties of the region have also added phonemic *ṛ*, *ḷ* to their inventory, the former through phonemicization of previously allophonic contrasts due to short vowel mergers, the latter mainly stemming from the word *'aḷḷāh* 'God' and its derivatives.

In a few widespread loans, some of the originally missing Arabic consonants are adapted to Berber phonology: thus Siwi *nfu* 'benefit' < *-nfaʕ*, *zum* 'fast' < *-ṣūm*, and *ẓəll* 'pray' < *-ṣalli*. This is normally taken to be an indicator of their early date of entry. Berber phonology, however, everywhere changed under the pressure of the influx of loanwords. At present, all Berber languages seem to have developed phonemic *x*, *ṣ*, *h*, and a distinction between non-geminate *q* versus *ɣ* and *ṭ* versus *d*, and the new phonemes are common in loanwords: for example Shilha *a-xddam* 'worker' < *xaddām*, *l-hna* 'peace' < *al-hanā'*, *ḍhṛ* 'appear' < *-ḍhar*, and *samḥ* 'forgive' < *-sāmiḥ* (Destaing 1920).

Pharyngeal consonants entered somewhat less readily; some Shilha varieties still tend to realise *ʕ* as a lengthened *a* (Boogert 1997: 241), and most varieties of Tuareg still convert the pharyngeals *ħ*, *ʕ* into *x*, *ɣ* in loans, for example *ălxadd* 'Sunday' < *al-'aḥad* (Heath 2005: 24). Interdentals entered least readily of all, probably due to their cross-dialectal instability within Arabic itself and to their status as allophones of dental stops (transcribed *ṭ*, *ḍ*) in many Berber varieties. Even in the Sahara, where the dominant Arabic dialects today maintain interdentals, the available literature suggests that most Berber varieties merge them with *t*, *d*. However, in Siwi interdentals are optionally preserved (e.g., *a- θqil / a-tqil* 'heavy' < *θaqīl*). The glottal fricative *h* is lost sporadically, as in Kabyle *šaḅi* 'resemble' < *-šābih*; glottal stops, however, are almost always absent, except in a few loans usually influenced by Standard Arabic (e.g., Rif *l-ʔaṣnam* 'idol' < *al-ʔaṣnām*, Siwi *a-ʔəjjəṛ* 'to rent' < *ʔajjar*). More recently, Turkish and European influence has introduced new phonemes to regional Berber and Arabic alike; probably the most widely maintained of these is *p*, as in Rif *paɣa* 'wages' < *paga*, *ṭ-paḅu-ṭ* 'duck' < *pavo* (Kossmann 2009), or Kabyle *a-paki* < *paquet* (Chaker 1984b: 86).

The new phonemes are not restricted to loanwords. Northern Berber sometimes makes use of "expressive" formations, in which a consonant is added to or substituted in an existing root; this often results in non-etymological appearances of new phonemes in words based entirely on inherited material, for example Rif *a-ʕəddis* versus Figuig *ta-dis-t* 'belly' (Kossmann 2009: 204). In Siwi, the first person singular subject agreement morpheme has developed from -*ɣ*- to -*ʕ*- for many (but not all) speakers; since this change is still underway, and is not attested in the earliest sources on Siwi, we can assume that it postdates the introduction of *ʕ* from Arabic.

The effects of contact on Berber vowel systems, if any, are less clear-cut. Most Arabic varieties of Morocco and Algeria have the same minimal vowel system (*a, i, u, ə*) as most Berber varieties of those countries, but in both cases this system is innovative in merging all short/lax vowels to *ə*. Since variants of this system are attested in Berber varieties as far east as Siwa—whereas Arabic varieties in Tunisia and eastward retain a distinction between short/lax *ă* and *ə*—the innovation is likely to have begun in Northern Berber, but there is no direct evidence to prove this.

20.3 MORPHOLOGY

Nominal inflection has been significantly affected by Arabic; adjectival and prepositional inflection have been somewhat less open to influence, while verbal inflection remains unaffected in most varieties. Nevertheless—very unusually on a world scale as well as within the family—Ghomara Berber has borrowed even complete verbal paradigms from Arabic. A few derivational morphemes have also been borrowed. Borrowed morphemes are always initially used only with borrowed items, but in some cases have spread to inherited ones.

20.3.1 Nominal inflection

In Berber, all inherited nouns, except for a few irregular cases, take a prefix marking their gender and number—most commonly *a-* M.SG, *ta-* F.SG, *i-* M.PL, *ti-* F.PL. This prefix is normally also marked for case—typical allomorphs of the so-called construct state, used for postverbal subjects, possessors, and the objects of prepositions, respectively: *w-, t-, y-, t-*. Gender and number are also, additionally, typically marked on the stem, the commonest markers being: *-t* F.SG, *-ən* M.PL, *-in* F.PL; in addition to these plural suffixes, there are many "broken plurals" formed by imposing a particular vowel sequence on the stem.

Classical Arabic marks the feminine with *-at-* (prepausally *-ah*), and the plural either with suffixes (M *-īn*, F *-āt*) or through imposing a particular template on the stem. The article is an invariant prefix *al-* (the *l* assimilates to a directly following coronal consonant.) In Maghrebi Arabic, the feminine ending is *-a* (in the construct state *-ət*), and the suffixal plurals are *-in, -at* (vowel length is no longer phonemically relevant).

Many Arabic nouns—including, but not limited to, those thought to be the oldest— are borrowed as stems, to which Berber prefixes and often suffixes are added, and take Berber plural formations: thus 'mosque' (Table 20.1).

Many more, however, are borrowed as words, with the Arabic article as prefix, and retain their Arabic plural, for example 'pocket' (Table 20.2).

This results in the neutralization of case marking for these nouns, since case can only be marked on the Berber nominal prefix. In several eastern Berber varieties

Table 20.1 Berber 'Mosque'

	Shilha	Figuig	Arabic
SG	*ti-mzgida*	*ta-məzgida*	*masɟid*
SG C	*t-mzgida*	*t-məzgida*	–
PL	*ti-mzgad-iwin*	*ti-məzgid-awin*	*masāǰid*
PL C	*ti-mzgad-iwin*	*t-məzgid-awin*	–

Table 20.2 Berber 'Pocket'

	Shilha	Figuig	Arabic
SG	*l-žib*	*l-žib*	*al-ɟayb*
PL	*l-žyub*	*lə-žyub*	*al-ɟuyūb*

(Siwa, Sokna, Awjila, Nafusa, Ghadames), case marking has been lost entirely; the large number of Arabic loans may be one factor in this development, along with the fact that all spoken Arabic varieties have completely lost case marking.

In such cases, the treatment of feminine morphology varies. Somewhat unexpectedly, the Arabic feminine ending is usually replaced by -*ət*, contrasting with inherited -*t* by the presence of the schwa. While this is segmentally identical to the Maghrebi Arabic construct state feminine ending, the latter is not compatible with the definite article. In more recent loans, however, the normal Maghrebi Arabic feminine ending -*a* is often retained. Contrast, for example, Rif *ř-xədm-ət* 'work' < *al-xidm-ah* versus *ř-məħkam-a* 'court' < *al-maħkam-ah* (Kossmann 2009: 201–202). Less commonly, hybrid strategies may be observed. The singular may combine a Berber prefix with the Arabic one, as in Siwi *a-l-ħoš* 'date-drying yard' (*al-ħawš*), with an Arabic plural *lə-ħwaš*, (Souag 2010: sec. 2.3.1.2); or an originally Berber form may take an Arabic-style plural and, accordingly, an Arabic article, as in Siwi *a-gʷərzni* 'dog,' PL *lə-gʷrazən*. Occasionally, an originally Berber word is given an Arabic article even in the singular, as well as an Arabic-style plural, for example Figuig *r-ršəl* 'marriage,' PL *r-ršula* (Kossmann 1997: 81), which is not used in local Arabic. The article is occasionally left out; in particular, inalienable nouns are normally borrowed without the article. This set includes a number of family terms (e.g., Kabyle *xali* '[my] maternal uncle' < *xāl-ī* 'my maternal uncle'), in which the Arabic first person singular possessive suffix is reinterpreted as part of the stem (CP *xali-ḵ* 'your (M.SG) maternal uncle').

Both Arabic and Berber often have a three-way number opposition between a collective noun (morphologically masculine singular), and a pluralizable singulative (morphologically feminine). In Berber, the emergence of this distinction may be a result of Arabic influence (Kossmann 2008). In any case, the distinction in question is fairly often expressed using Arabic morphology, sometimes even for Berber words: thus Figuig colloquial *l-məlwi* (with the Arabic article), SG *ta-məlwi-t*, PL *timəlwi+ t-in* 'a type of bread' (Kossmann 1997: 84).

In addition to the singular and plural, Arabic has a dual number, marked with the suffix *-ayn*. In Standard Arabic its usage extends to all nouns, but in many North African varieties it is limited to a small set of nouns, mainly measures. Many Berber varieties have borrowed a few Arabic measure words together with their duals: for example (Kossmann 1997: 110), Figuig *šhəṛ* 'month' (Ar. *šahr*), DU *šəhṛ-ayən* (Ar. *šahr-ayn*), PL *šhuṛ* (Ar. *'ašhur*). In Kabyle, this has even been extended to at least one inherited measure word: *a-brid* 'road, time, way,' *berd-ayən* 'twice (two times),' *i-bərdan* 'roads, times, ways' (Dallet 1982: 42). Occasionally, the singular and/or plural are Berberized, while the dual retains Arabic morphology: thus Siwi *t-wagg-ət* 'oke,' DU *wagg-ət-en*, PL *ti-wəgg-a*.

20.3.2 Verbal Inflection

The domain of verbal inflection is far more resistant to Arabic influence than that of nominal inflection. Arabic verbs are almost always borrowed into Berber as stems, taking Berber agreement and aspect morphology (much of the latter being non-concatenative): contrast Siwi *bnu* 'build!' *bnu-x* 'I built,' *bənnu-x* 'I build,' or Kabyle *bnu* 'build!' *bni-ɣ* 'I built,' *bənnu-ɣ* 'I build,' with Arabic *ibni* 'build!' *banay-tu* 'I built,' *'a-bnī* 'I build.'

Only one variety is known to be an exception to the rule that inflectional morphology remains purely Berber. In Ghomara Berber, many Arabic verbs are consistently fully conjugated in Arabic: contrast *n-ṭlaqa* 'I meet with,' *ṭlaq-iṭ* 'I met with' (Maghrebi Arabic *n-tlaqa*, *tlaqi-t*) with inherited *kəččm-əx* 'I enter,' *kəšm-əx* 'I entered' (El Hannouche 2008; Kossmann 2010). A more indirect influence may be exemplified by the loss of gender distinctions in plural verbal agreement in Siwi. Most Berber varieties distinguish 2M.PL *-m* and 3M.PL *-n* from 2F.PL *-mt* and 3F.PL *-nt*; Siwi has reflexes only of the masculine plural forms, which are used irrespective of gender. This development, very unusual within Berber, is probably a calque of the similar loss of feminine plural in Egyptian (and wider sedentary) Arabic.

20.3.3 Adjectival Inflection

Most Berber varieties have two word subclasses typically used to express qualities: nominal adjectives (taking the same affixes as nouns, and agreeing in gender and number with their referents), and stative verbs (which, in conservative varieties, show a set of person/gender/number agreement suffixes distinct from those used by other verbs). In Arabic, adjectives are nominal, but usually have corresponding inchoative verbs. Arabic quality words are commonly borrowed from adjectives, and assigned to the nominal adjective class, for example Siwi: *a-ṭwil* 'tall' < *ṭawīl*, *a-šəbʕan* 'rich' < *šabʕān* 'full'. In other cases, they are borrowed as inchoative verbs, and assigned to the stative verb class, often with a new vowel pattern taken from Berber models, for example Kabyle: *ishil* 'be easy' < Maghrebi *sahəl* (or inchoative *shal*) < *sahl*, *məʕqul* 'be reasonable' < *maʕqūl*. In other instances, agreement may be partly or wholly dropped: for example, Kabyle *lʕali* 'good' < *al-ʕālī* 'the high' is invariant for number and gender.

In all these cases, adjectives are adapted to Berber morphology; thus Siwi *ləbkəm* 'mute' < *al-'abkam* marks agreement as follows:

	Siwi	Arabic
M.SG	*ləbkəm*	*al-'a-bkam*
F.SG	*t-ləbkəm-t*	*al-bakm-ā'*
M.PL	*lbəkm-ən*	*al-bukm*
F.PL	*tə-lbəkm-en*	*al-bukm*

However, in several of the smaller Berber varieties, adjectives may also sometimes be borrowed together with partial or full Arabic inflection; cp. 'missing' in Zuwara (Mitchell 2009: 82):

	Zuwara	Arabic
M.SG	*nákəz*	*nāqiṣ*
F.SG	*nákz-a*	*nāqiṣ-ah*
M.PL	*nakz-ín*	*nāqiṣ-īn*
F.PL	*nakz-aát*	*nāqiṣ-āt*

Most Berber languages have no special comparative/superlative morphology, instead using analytical structures. However, a few eastern Berber varieties have borrowed Arabic comparative forms, based on the template '*aCCaC*. In Siwi, these have even become productive for trilateral adjectives of Berber origin: thus inherited *a-zəggay* 'red' > *zgəy* 'redder,' just as borrowed *a-ṭwil* 'tall' > *ṭwəl* 'taller' (Arabic *ṭawīl*, comp. '*aṭwal*). The corresponding superlative is formed by adding the Arabic third person plural suffix *-hŭm*: *zgəy-hŭm* 'reddest.'

20.3.4 Prepositional and Adverbial Inflection

Throughout both Berber and Arabic, pronominal objects of prepositions are typically expressed through a suffix pronoun series, rather than through free pronouns. Both families also feature a few adverbs that agree with the subject of the predicate they modify. In many of the smaller Berber varieties, some borrowed prepositions/adverbs take Arabic rather than Berber pronominal suffixes: for example, Figuig *ʕəmməṛ-* 'ever' < Maghrebi *ʕəmməṛ-* < Arabic *ʕumr* 'life span,' which takes the Arabic pronominal suffixes (agreeing with the subject) 1SG *-ni*, 2SG *-ək*, 3M.SG *-u* / *-əh*, 3F.SG *-ha* ... (Kossmann 1997: 186); or Siwi *msabb* 'because of, for the sake of' < Arabic *min sabab* 'from the cause of,' which takes 1SG *-i*, 2M.SG *-ăk*, 2F.SG *-ki*, 3M.SG *-ăh*, 3F.SG *-ha*. ...

Native Berber prepositions may assign either case (free, or construct) to their objects; spoken Arabic has lost all case distinctions. In Berber, there seems to be a tendency for prepositions borrowed from Arabic to assign the free state alone, as in Figuig (Kossmann 1997: 229–231), which may reflect the lack of any such contrast in Arabic.

20.4 DERIVATION

Many Northern Berber varieties use *bu* < Arabic *'abū* 'father' and *m* < Arabic *'umm* 'mother' as heads to form compounds indicating the possessor of a certain characteristic: for example, Kabyle *bu t-ḥanuṭ-ṭ* 'shopkeeper' < *ṭa-ḥanuṭ-ṭ* 'shop,' *m u-qərru* 'stubborn woman' < *a-qərru* 'head' (Dallet 1982). The corresponding plurals are inherited from Berber, and based on the opposite metaphor: for example Kabyle *aṯ* (lit. 'sons of'), *suṯ* (lit. 'daughters of'). The *nisba* marker *-i / -awi*, forming adjectives from nouns, is widely borrowed, mainly as part of Arabic loans: for example Siwi *libya* 'Libya': *a-lib-i* 'Libyan' < Arabic *lībyā: līb-ī*, *maṣra* 'Egypt, Cairo' : *a-maṣr-i* '(urban) Egyptian, Cairene' < Arabic *miṣr: miṣr-ī*.

While Arabic inflectional verbal morphology is almost never borrowed, Arabic verbs often bring in derivational morphology with them, and where multiple members of the same word family are borrowed, this morphology may become analyzable in principle, even within the recipient language: for example Beni Snous *nəyyəl* 'dye (a cloth) indigo' : *ən-nil-əṭ* 'indigo' < Maghrebi *nəyyəl* : *ən-nil-a*; *sməḥ* 'forgive': *saməḥ* 'be forgiving' < Maghrebi *sməḥ* : *saməḥ* (Destaing 1914). Borrowed verbs often bring with them their original Arabic deverbal nouns, for example Kabyle *ləḇni* 'building' < *al-binā'*, *aḇənnay* 'builder' < Maghrebi *bənnay* < *bannā'*. Nonetheless, there are few if any cases of Arabic derivational verbal morphology becoming productive within Berber. In some varieties, the template *a-CəCCaC* is used to form professional nouns even from Berber roots (e.g., Siwi *a-diyyaz* 'poet, singer' < √*dyz*); this is probably a borrowing from Arabic, but may be a common Afro-Asiatic inheritance.

20.5 SYNTAX AND FUNCTION WORDS

Considerable convergence has taken place between Berber and Arabic negation in North Africa, sometimes making it difficult to determine its direction. The pattern of bipartite negation around the verb, with the second element dropped for emphasis or in the presence of a negated item such as 'ever' or 'anyone,' is an innovation shared by both Northern Berber and Maghrebi Arabic, as well as Arabic varieties further east, such as Egyptian or Palestinian; its history remains controversial, but Lucas (2007) argues that it ultimately derives from Coptic and reached Berber via Arabic. The preverbal negator (*ur/ul*, etc.) is almost always inherited; the postverbal negator is often based on inherited **căra* 'thing' (*ša, ara, ka, . . .*) but is sometimes reshaped based on the corresponding Arabic morpheme *šay'* (e.g., Figuig *šay*, eastern Rif *ši*), while the widespread vowel-less variants such as Shawi *-š*, corresponding precisely to regional Arabic, may equally well be derived from the Berber or Arabic forms. In emphatic negation with oaths, both Maghrebi Arabic and Northern Berber typically use a preverbal negator *ma* with no postverbal negator; in Berber, this is segmentally identical to the conditional 'if,' while in Arabic, it is segmentally identical to the normal negator derived from Classical Arabic (*mā*).

Ghomara, in keeping with its overall extreme level of Arabic influence, has completely borrowed Arabic negation, using preverbal *ma* and postverbal *ši* as in Arabic. This morphological borrowing has had syntactic effects; whereas (as elsewhere in Berber) inherited preverbal particles "attract" clitic object pronouns, leading them to appear preverbally rather than postverbally, *ma* leaves them postverbal (El Hannouche 2008: 138).

Siwi is a more difficult case (Souag 2010: sec. 7.6.1). It has no postverbal negator and no reflex of the normal Berber preverbal negator; the latter has been replaced by *la*. The most obvious source for *la* is Arabic *lā*, used in Classical Arabic to negate imperfectives and subjunctives but with a more restricted distribution in most colloquials. However, it is possible that the widespread Berber form *ula* '(not) even' also played a role in its development. Siwi clitic object pronouns remain postverbal in all circumstances, including negation; this development is very likely the result of Arabic influence, but cannot plausibly be attributed to the borrowing of *la*, since it also applies to the non-Arabic aorist marker *ga*, and also applies in neighboring Awjila, which has retained Berber negators.

In general, Berber handles subject relatives with a special form of the verb not conjugated for person and in some varieties lacking agreement altogether, the so-called participle; non-subject relatives are typically handled by gapping and/or "pied-piping," with any stranded preposition being raised to the start of the relative clause. The colloquial Arabic relative marker *əlli* is borrowed in many smaller varieties, from Ghomara (Morocco) to Tamezret (Tunisia) or El-Fogaha (Libya); this borrowing is generally accompanied by a restructuring of the relative clause along the lines of Arabic, which has no equivalent of the Berber "participle" and uses resumptive bound pronouns.

Contrast the syntax of the following cases, for example:

(1) *əlli a-y-uɣ-it*
Rel Irr-3MSG-take-3FSGAcc
the one who takes it
(El-Fogaha; Paradisi 1963: 95)

(2) *win ara ṭ y-aɣ-ən*
Rel.M.Sg Rel.Irr 3FSgAcc Pt-take-Pt
the one who takes it
(Kabyle)

The large-scale borrowing of numerals characteristic of most Berber varieties has had some interesting syntactic effects. It may have contributed to the simplification of the syntax of ordinary numeral phrases in some varieties, as suggested by Galand (2002: 215); what is certain is that, in almost all varieties, it has introduced entire paradigms of numeral+measure phrases directly taken from Arabic and contrary to the productive rules of Berber syntax. Thus in Kabyle, 'day' is *ass*, PL *ussan*, but 'five days' is *xəms iyyam* (Maghrebi *xəms iyyam* < *xams-at ʔayyām*); expected *xəmsa n wussan* is rarely used. In Siwi, the contrast can most elegantly be demonstrated with the Arabic loan *s-saʕ-ət* 'watch/hour': 'eleven watches' is *ħdaʕš n s-saʕ-iyyat* (eleven GEN N-watch-F.PL), formed regularly according to productive Siwi syntax, but 'eleven hours' is *əhdašəṛ saʕ-a* (eleven.Adnom hour-F.SG), a straightforward phrasal borrowing.

A considerable number of clause connectors have been borrowed from Arabic: for example, Chenoua *lukan* 'if (irrealis)' < *law kān* 'if it were,' *ɣir* 'when, as soon as' < *ɣayr* 'only' (Laoust 1912: 76). Some of these loans, such as *bəlli* 'that' or *u* 'and,' fill positions that were previously left empty in Berber, increasing the incidence of syntaxis at the expense of parataxis (Chaker 1989).

20.6 CONCLUSION

Arabic has had far-reaching impacts, even on the larger Berber languages: out of the World Loanword Database's forty-one-language sample, only Selice Romani had a higher percentage of loanwords than Rif Berber (Tadmor 2009). In the smaller Berber languages, the impact is often much greater. In Ghomara, complete paradigms of all major word classes including verbs have been borrowed, resulting in something that might not unreasonably be labeled as a mixed language. Much work remains to be done on the effects of contact on Berber; for example, the effects of sub-Saharan African languages in the Sahel have barely begun to be explored.

20.7 GLOSSED SIWI TEXT

The following text is extracted from a retelling of the story of how King Solomon met the Queen of Sheba. Arabic loans are in bold; simple Arabic calques are underlined; Punic loans are followed by an asterisk (*).

*yə-kkər a-**gə́nni**, i-ʕənʕín-a i **sayyídna slemán**, yə-ṃṃ-ás:*
3M.SG-arise M.SG-genie, 3M.SG-sit-PF to our.master Solomon, 3M.SG-say-3SGDat
The **genie** got up—he had been seated next to **our master Solomon**—and told him:

*"níš ga-ktər-y-ák-tət." yə-ṃṃ-ás **sayyídna slemán**:*
"I IRR-bring-1SG-2SGDat-3FSGAcc." 3M.SG-say-3SGDat our.master Solomon:
"I will bring her to you." **Our master Solomon** told him:

*"**qə́dṛ-aṭ** ga-kətr-at-tət fəlhal-fəlhál?" yə-ṃṃ-ás:*
"be.able-2SG IRR-bring-2SG-3FSGAcc quickly-quickly?" 3M.SG-say-3SGDat:
"Can you bring her quickly?" He told him:

"ga-kətr-áx-tət am šə́k ǵda." "ah, ṭáyyib."
"IRR-bring-1SG-3FSGAcc like you.M.SG here." "Yes, fine."
"I will bring her as you are here." "Yes—, fine."

díy ħə́dd srə́ʕ? yə́-kkər aggʷíd wən rə́ḅḅi y-uš-ásən,
EXISTanyonefaster? 3M-arise man REL God 3M.SG-give-3PLDat
"Is there **anyone faster?**" Someone got up whom **God** had given,

i-lə́md*-in-a a-yə́ṛṛa*, i-ħəfḍ-ín-a əddín,
3-learn-3PL-PF M.SG-to.read, 3-memorise-3PL-Pf religion,
who had learn*ed to read*, who had **memorized religion,**

yə-ṃṃ-ás: níš ga-ktər-y-ák-tət g tí-ṛawd-ət
3M.SG-say-3SGDat: I IRR-bring-1SG-2SGDat-3SGFAcc in FSG-glance-FSG
He told him: "I'll bring her to you at a **glance.**"

yə́-ʕmaṛ sayyídna sléman yə-stə́ʕjəb. mámək
3M.SG-do our.master Solomon 3M.SG-astonished. how
It **happened** that **our master Solomon** was **astonished.** How

di ə́jjən g əddə́nyət rə́bbi y-uš-ás
EXISTone in world God 3M.SG-give-3SGDat
can there be someone in the **world** to whom **God** has given

yə-qdáṛ ge-yə́-ktər əlkursí dílla mən ššárq ləlyárb g ti-ṛáwd-ət?
3M-be.able IRR-3M-bringthrone 3M.be.at from east to.west in FSG-glance-FSG
that he **can** bring a **throne** which is there **from east to west** at a **glance?**

af-ə́nni a-gə́nni yə́-ṃṃ-as ga-ktə́r-y-ak-tt
on-COMP M.SG-genie 3M.SG-say-3SGDat IRR-bring-1SG-2SGDat-3FAcc
When the **genie** told him "I will bring her to you

qbə́l ga-kkr-áṭ af a-mkan-ə́nnək am šə́kk gdá
before IRR-arise-2SG on M.SG-place-2M.SGGen like you.M.SG here
before you arise from your **place,**

niš ga-kətr-áx-tət," nə́šni nə́-jʕəl xlá́ṣ lá di
I IRR-bring-1SG-3FSGAcc" we 1PL-imagine that's.all NEG EXIST
as you are here I will bring her," we had **thought that's it,** there's **no** one

srə́ʕ n amsérwən. baʕdén nə-ssín-a anni i-gə́nn-an srí́ʕ-ən,
faster GEN thus. afterwards 1P-know-PF COMPMPL-genie-PL fast-MPL
faster than this. So we knew that genies are fast,

yer-ə́nni yə-ffáy di ħə́dd srə́ʕ-ənsən, d əlqúdṛət
but-COMP 3M-go.out EXIST someone faster-3PLGen,COM power
but it has emerged that there is **someone faster** than them, by **the power**

n ṛə́ḅḅi. ay wəḷḷáh. baʕd y-íf-a zdát-əs
GEN God oh by.God after 3M.SG-find-3MSGAccin.front.of-3SG,
of **God. Seriously! After** he found him in front of him

yə-ħmə́d ṛə́bbi, i-šə́kr-as i ṛə́bbi ənni yə-nʕə́m fə́ll-as
3M.SG-praise God, 3M.SG-thank-3SGDat to God COMP 3M-bestow on-3SG
he **praised God**, he **thanked God** that He had **bestow**ed upon him

nnʕáyəm i-zəwwár-ən da-wiyyé-rwən nnúba.
favours 3MPL-big-3MPL ADNOM-this.PL-2:PL all.
all these great **favors**.

REFERENCES

Baamrani, Jouhadi Lhocine. 2003. *Tarjamat maʕānī al-Qur'ān al-Karīm: Nūr ʕalā nūr / Tifawt f tifawt, bi-l-luġah al-'amāzīġiyyah.* Casablanca: Al-Najāḥ al-Jadīdah.

Boogert, Nico van den. 1997. *The Berber Literary Tradition of the Sous: With an Edition and Translation of "The Ocean of Tears" by Muhammad Awzal (d. 1749).* Leiden: Nederlands Institut voor het Nabije Osten.

Boogert, Nico van den, and Maarten Kossmann. 1997. Les premiers emprunts arabes en berbère. *Arabica: Journal of Arabic and Islamic Studies* 44: 317–322.

Boutkan, Dirk, and Maarten Kossmann. 1999. Some Berber parallels of European substratum words. *Journal of Indo-European studies* 27(1–2): 87–100.

Boutkan, Dirk, and Maarten Kossmann. 2001. On the etymology of "silver." *NOWELE: North-Western European Language Evolution* 38(1): 11–26.

Brugnatelli, Vermondo. Unpublished. Un témoin manuscrit de la "Mudawwan d'Abū Ghānim" en berbère. *Manuscrits Arabo-Berbères – Journée d'études* du 15 novembre 2011.

Chaker, Salem. 1984a. Les emprunts arabes dans quelques dialectes berbères: Kabyle - chleuh - touareg. In *Textes en linguistique berbère: Introduction au domaine berbère,* edited by Salem Chaker, 216–229. Paris: Editions du Centre national de la recherche scientifique.

Chaker, Salem. 1984b. Problèmes de phonologie et de notation du berbère (Kabyle). In *Textes en linguistique berbère: Introduction au domaine berbère,* edited by Salem Chaker, 77–120. Paris: Editions du Centre national de la recherche scientifique.

Chaker, Salem. 1989. Arabisation. *Encyclopédie berbère.* Aix-en-Provence: Edisud.

Cohen, David. 1972. Sur quelques mots berbères dans un écrit du IXe-Xe siècle. *Comptes rendus du Groupe Linguistique d'Etudes Chamito-Sémitiques* XVI: 121–127.

Colin, Georges Séraphin. 1926. Etymologies maġribines (I). *Hespéris* VI: 55–82.

Dallet, J. -M. 1982. *Dictionnaire kabyle-français: Parler des At Mangellat, Algérie.* Etudes Ethnolinguistiques Maghreb-Sahara 1. Paris: Société d'études linguistiques et anthropologiques de France.

Destaing, Edmond. 1914. *Dictionnaire Francais-Berbère: Dialecte des Beni-Snous.* Publications de la Faculté des Lettres d'Alger 49. Paris: Ernest Leroux.

Destaing, Edmond. 1920. *Etude sur la Tachelhît du Sous.* Vol. I: Vocabulaire français-berbère. Paris: Ernest Leroux.

El Hannouche, J. 2008. *Ghomara Berber: A Brief Grammatical Survey.* MA thesis, University of Leiden.

Galand, Lionel. 2002. *Études de linguistique berbère.* Leuven: Peeters.

Heath, Jeffrey. 2005. *A Grammar of Tamashek (Tuareg of Mali).* Mouton Grammar Library 35. Berlin: Mouton de Gruyter.

Heath, Jeffrey. 2006. *Dictionnaire Touareg du Mali: Tamachek-anglais-français*. Paris: Karthala.

Kahlouche, Rabah. 1999. Le berbère (kabyle) serait-il en train d'emprunter les marques du "nombre" du français? *Le Français en Afrique. Revue du Réseau des Observatoires du Français Contemporain en Afrique Noir* 13.

Kossmann, Maarten. 1997. *Grammaire du parler berbère de Figuig (Maroc oriental)*. Paris: Peeters.

Kossmann, Maarten. 1999. *Essai sur la phonologie du proto-berbère*. Köln: Rüdiger Köppe.

Kossmann, Maarten. 2002. Deux emprunts à l'égyptien ancien en berbère. In *Articles de linguistique berbère: Mémorial Werner Vycichl*, edited by Kamal Naït-Zerrad, 245–252. Paris: L'Harmattan.

Kossmann, Maarten. 2008. The collective in Berber and language contact. In *Berber in Contact: Linguistic and Sociolinguistic Perspectives*, Berber Studies Vol. 22, edited by Mena Lafkioui and Vermondo Brugnatelli, 231. Köln: Rüdiger Köppe.

Kossmann, Maarten. 2009. Loanwords in Tarifiyt. In *Loanwords in the World's Languages: A Comparative Handbook*, edited by Martin Haspemath and Uri Tadmor, 191–214. Berlin: de Gruyter.

Kossmann, Maarten. 2010. Parallel system borrowing: Parallel morphological systems due to the borrowing of paradigms. *Diachronica* 27(3): 459–487. doi:10.1075/dia.27.3.03kos.

Kossmann, Maarten. 2013. *The Arabic Influence on Northern Berber*. Leiden: Brill.

Laoust, Émile. 1912. *Etude sur le dialecte berbère du Chenoua, comparé avec ceux des Beni-Menacer et des Beni-Salah*. Publications de la Faculté des Lettres d'Alger r.50. Paris: Ernest Leroux.

Lewicki, Tadeusz. 1934. Quelques textes inedits en vieux berbere provenant d'une chronique ibadite anonyme. *Revue des Etudes Islamiques* 3: 275–305.

Lewicki, Tadeusz. 1958. Une langue romane oubliée de l'Afrique du Nord: Observations d'un arabisant. *Rocznik Orientalistyczny* 17: 415–480.

Lipinski, Edward. 1997. *Semitic Languages: Outline of a Comparative Grammar*. Orientalia Lovaniensia Analecta 80. Leuven: Peeters.

Lucas, Christopher. 2007. Jespersen's cycle in Arabic and Berber. *Transactions of the Philological Society* 105(3): 398–431. doi:10.1111/j.1467-968X.2007.00189.x.

Mammeri, Mouloud. 1976. *Tajerrumt n tmazight (tantala taqbaylit)*. Paris: Maspéro.

Mammeri, Mouloud. 1980. *Amawal Tamazight-Français et Français-Tamazight*. Paris: Imedyazen.

Millar, Fergus. 1968. Local cultures in the Roman Empire: Libyan, Punic and Latin in Roman Africa. *Journal of Roman Studies* 58(1–2): 126–134. doi:10.2307/299702.

Mitchell, Terence F. 2009. *Zuaran Berber (Libya): Grammar and Texts*, edited by Harry Stroomer and Stanly Oomen. Berber Studies Vol. 26. Köln: Rüdiger Köppe.

Múrcia Sánchez, Carles. 2010. *La llengua amaziga a l'antiguitat a partir de les fonts gregues i llatines*. Barcelona: Universitat de Barcelona. http://hdl.handle.net/10803/1724.

Olivier, P. 1878. *Dictionnaire français-kabyle*. Le Puy: Freydier.

Paradisi, Umberto. 1963. Il linguaggio berbero di El-Fogaha (Fezzân). *Istituto Orientale di Napoli* XIII: 93–126.

Schuchardt, Hugo. 1918. *Die romanischen Lehnwörter im Berberischen*. Wien.

Shaw, Thomas. 1758. *Travels or Observations Relating to Several Parts of Barbary and the Levant*. London: Millar.

Souag, Lameen. 2007. The typology of number borrowing in Berber. In *Proceedings for the Fifth Cambridge Postgraduate Conference in Linguistics*, edited by Naomi Hilton, Rachel Arscott, Katherine Barden, Sheena Shah, and Meg Zellers, 237–245. Cambridge: Cambridge Institute of Language Research. http://www.ling.cam.ac.uk/camling/.

Souag, Lameen. 2008. *Dictionary of the Tamasheq of North-East Burkina Faso*, by David Sudlow. *Afrika und Übersee* 90: 306–308.

Souag, Lameen. 2009. Siwa and its significance for Arabic dialectology. *Zeitschrift für Arabische Linguistik* 51: 51–75.

Souag, Lameen. 2010. *Grammatical Contact in the Sahara: Arabic, Berber, and Songhay in Tabelbala and Siwa.* School of Oriental and African Studies, University of London.

Souag, Lameen. 2013. Sub-Saharan lexical influence in North African Arabic and Berber. *African Arabic: Approaches to Dialectology*, edited by Mena Lafkioui, 211–236. Berlin: Mouton de Gruyter.

Sudlow, David. 2009. *Dictionary of the Tamasheq of North-East Burkina Faso.* Berber Studies Vol. 24. Köln: Rüdiger Köppe.

Tadmor, Uri. 2009. Loanwords in the world's languages: Findings and results. In *Loanwords in the World's Languages: A Comparative Handbook*, edited by Martin Haspelmath and Uri Tadmor, 55–75. Berlin: De Gruyter.

Taïfi, Miloud. 2008. L'emprunt au service de la poésie berbère. In *Berber in Contact: Linguistic and Sociolinguistic Perspectives*. Berber Studies Vol. 22, 101–112. Köln: Köppe.

Taine-Cheikh, Catherine. 2008. *Dictionnaire zénaga-francais: Le berbere de Mauritanie présenté par racines dans une perspective comparative.* Berber Studies Vol. 20. Köln: Rüdiger Köppe.

Vycichl, Werner. 1951. Eine vorhamitische Sprachschicht im Altägyptischen. *Zeitschrift der deutschen morgenländischen Gesellschaft* 26(101): 67–77.

Vycichl, Werner. 1952. Punischer Spracheinfluss im Berberischen. *Journal of Near Eastern Studies* 11(3): 198–204.

Vycichl, Werner. 2005. *Berberstudien; &, A Sketch of Siwi Berber (Egypt).* Berber Studies Vol. 10. Köln: Rüdiger Köppe.

CHAPTER 21

....

CONTACT INFLUENCES ON OSSETIC

....

OLEG BELYAEV

21.1 INTRODUCTION

....

IN this chapter, I will provide a review of the major contact-induced phenomena in Ossetic that have been proposed in the literature.[1] I will begin by briefly summarizing what is known on the history of the Ossetians inasmuch as it is relevant for the diachronic sociolinguistics of Ossetic (section 21.1.1). In section 21.2, I locate Ossetic in the wider context of the Caucasian linguistic area by specifying which of the common Caucasian properties identified by Chirikba (2008) it exhibits. In sections 21.3–21.6, I consider phonological, lexical, morphological, and syntactic contact phenomena in this consecutive order. Finally, in section 21.7, I summarize the external sources of different grammatical and lexical phenomena in Ossetic and attempt to provide preliminary generalizations on what sociolinguistic situation could have caused such a distribution.

21.1.1 A Historical and Sociolinguistic Overview of Ossetic

In this section, I will provide a general overview of what is known on the history and historical sociolinguistics of the Ossetic language. Before starting this account, a brief introduction to the history of Ossetia and the Ossetians is in order.

---

[1] I am grateful to Winfried Boeder, Alexei Kassian, Sergei Kullanda, Alexander Lubotsky, Alexander Rostovtsev-Popiel, and Arseniy Vydrin for their comments on earlier drafts of this paper. It goes without saying that all errors and misinterpretations remain my own.

The name "Ossetians," ("Ossetia") is an exonym (from Georgian *ovsi* 'Ossetian,' *ovs-eti* 'Ossetia'). Until recently, there was no term for Ossetians as a whole in Ossetic itself; the speakers identified themselves with their particular local societies or larger tribes, of which *iron* versus *digoron* (where *-on* is an adjectival suffix) was the main division, corresponding to the dialectal makeup of Ossetic. Afterward, *iron* came to be used as the name for Ossetians as a whole, as well as for Iron speakers, who constitute the majority of Ossetians; the term *dəguron/digoron* is still confined to speakers of the Digor dialect.[2]

In terms of language, Ossetians are descended from a medieval people called the Alans,[3] who, in turn, descended from one of the groups of the Sarmatian peoples populating the area around the northern Black Sea coast, roughly corresponding to modern southern Russia and eastern Ukraine (Miller 1887; Alemany 2000). The languages of the Sarmatians and Scythians are usually treated as a single "Scytho-Sarmatian" group of Iranian, but some scholars maintain that the two are quite distinct, with Scythian being a Southeast Iranian language, unlike the Northeast Sarmatian/ Alan/Ossetic (see Kullanda 2011, 2016 and references therein).

Originally a nomadic tribe, during the Early Middle Ages the Alans created a kingdom situated to the north of the Caucasian Mountains, which became an important regional power (Abaev and Bailey 1985). Their statehood suffered a devastating blow at the hands of the Mongols in the thirteenth century and was completely destroyed by the Timurids in the fourteenth century. The surviving population was mostly driven to the canyons of the Caucasus range, where it came into close contact with the native ethnic groups. Since the thirteenth century, many Ossetians have also been migrating beyond the Caucasus range, to the region now known as South Ossetia (Novosel'cev, ed. 1987: 155–157). By the end of the eighteenth century, when the first systematic descriptions of Ossetic and the Ossetians started to appear, the Ossetians were confined to mountainous areas of the North Caucasus and South Ossetia. The migration to the lowlands that now comprise most of North Ossetia has mostly occurred in the nineteenth and early twentieth centuries under Russian, and later Soviet, rule.

During the post-Alan period, various groups of Ossetians lived in close contact with, and sometimes under the domination of, Kabardian, South Caucasian (mainly Georgian), and Nakh peoples, which has naturally been accompanied by lexical and grammatical change. The connection of Ossetians and indigenous Caucasian peoples

---

[2] While Iron and Digor are both written and have their own literary standards, the official policy today is to treat them as dialects and not independent languages, which I find linguistically justified. In this chapter I will cite lexical material in both Iron and Digor forms, separated by a vertical line (*iron form | digor form*). Other data are mostly drawn from Iron as the more widespread variety; Digor data will be cited whenever the differences are significant for the discussion at hand.

[3] The term "Alan" has arguably survived in Ossetic fairy tales in the form *allon-billon* (Abaev 1958: 47–48).

has been perceived to be so great that many scholars have endorsed theories of a "mixed" nature of Ossetic. For instance, Abaev (1949) has developed a concept of a common substratum underlying Ossetic and other languages of the region, even up to Armenian (Abaev 1978), which determined their grammatical similarities. Axvlediani (1960b) has specifically stressed the importance of Ossetic-Georgian connections. While some of the ideas of these scholars were innovative for their time and certainly on the right track, in many cases the importance of Caucasian influence for Ossetic grammar has been overestimated. The plausibility of these claims will be discussed in the following.

21.1.1.1 *Sources on the History of Ossetic*

As Ossetic was an unwritten language until the end of the eighteenth century, there is very little data available on its earlier history. Two sources indicate that Proto-Ossetic/ Alan used to have a Greek-based writing system during the Middle Ages. The first is the so-called Zelenchuk inscription (dated tenth–twelfth centuries AD), a stone slab with an Alan epitaph written in Greek letters, discovered in 1888 at the shore of the river Zelenchuk near modern Arkhyz (Miller 1893; Kuznecov 1968). The second are the recently discovered marginal notes to a Greek liturgical manuscript (Engberg and Lubotsky 2003; Lubotsky 2015), which are dated to somewhere around the thirteenth or fourteenth centuries (Lubotsky 2015: 9). Turčaninov (1990) has presented a large number of other purported examples of Alan (and even earlier) inscriptions, but his decipherments have been utterly rejected by most scholars as pseudoscientific.

Highly interesting examples of the Alan language are provided in the poem "Theogonia" by Byzantine Greek poet John Tzetzes (ca. 1110–1180). In this poem, the author cites greeting formulae in a number of languages, including Alan (Moravcsik 1928–1929). The most up-to-date analysis is found in Lubotsky (2015).

Another valuable source on the hypothetical state of medieval Alan or Pre-Ossetic are the data of Jassic, a language closely related to Ossetic that was spoken in Hungary since the thirteenth century, when the Jassic people, chased by Mongols, were invited to Hungary by King Béla IV (Kambolov 2006: 208). In 1957, a list of words in an unknown language with Latin and Hungarian translations, dated 1422, was discovered in Hungarian state archives; due to the similarity of the terms to modern forms of Digor Ossetic, the language was soon established to be Jassic (Németh 1959).

21.1.1.2 *Sociolinguistics*

For the establishment of contact influence on grammar, it is important to consider the sociolinguistic situation under which transfer of features may have occured. Unfortunately, we do not have reliable data on the multilingualism of Ossetians before the Revolution of 1917. Today, the overwhelming majority of Ossetians living in North Ossetia are Ossetic–Russian bilinguals (Kambolov 2007), but this is clearly a very recent development. In the nineteenth century, Ossetians in the North could be expected to be bilingual in Kabardian, Karachay-Balkar, and/or Nakh, while in the

South, in Georgian. In particular, Kabardian was the major contact language in the western parts of North Ossetia, especially in the Digor area, while Georgian was dominant in South Ossetia.

When the ancestors of modern Ossetians migrated to their current location in the Caucasus, they certainly assimilated some indigenous groups that had previously inhabited the area. Unfortunately, there is not enough extra-linguistic evidence for a reliable conclusion with regard to the date of this migration and the genetic affinity of the language(s) that Ossetic displaced. Some scholars maintain that the Dualeti region of the North Ossetian highlands was inhabited by Nakh-speaking tribes until the Early Middle Ages (Gamrekeli 1968; Thordarson 1992). Volkova (1973: 116) argues that archaeological evidence indicates that the Alans could not have appeared in the alpine regions of North Ossetia earlier than in the seventh–eighth centuries AD. The existence of Nakh borrowings in Svan (Fähnrich 1988) shows that languages of this family used to extend far westward from where they are now spoken. Thus, with some reservations, we may assume that in the area where Ossetic is currently spoken it has supplanted an East Caucasian language, probably of the Nakh branch. However, since the evidence is scarce, this is but a plausible hypothesis (Kaloev 1967: 20). Genetic data actually suggest that Ossetians cluster with West Caucasian rather than East Caucasian populations (Balanovsky et al. 2011), but this may be due to later interference and does not necessarily imply that the language that Ossetic superseded belonged to this group.

21.2 OSSETIC AS A MEMBER OF THE CAUCASIAN LINGUISTIC AREA

The most recent examination of areal features in the Caucasus is Chirikba (2008), who heavily draws upon Klimov (1978). Chirikba provides a number of features that are characteristic of the Caucasus as a linguistic area. In Table 21.1, I give a brief characterization of Ossetic according to these features. However, it must be noted that not all of these traits are specific to the Caucasus: some, such as evidentiality, are wider areal features, some are cross-linguistically quite common (e.g., group inflection in noun phrases), and some are typical of both Caucasian and Indo-European languages (e.g., SOV word order, ablaut), and therefore cannot be used as evidence of Caucasian influence on Ossetic. Of course, one can never exclude areal influence as an important factor in the historical development of such features, but its reality cannot at present be conclusively proven.

Overall, since the features are so diverse, Table 21.1 has only an illustrative value and cannot serve as a basis for any definitive conclusions. I have marked those features that can be considered Caucasian "in the narrow sense," and some of which will be examined in more detail in the following, by italics.

Table 21.1 Caucasian Features in Ossetic According to Chirikba (2008)

Feature	Value	Comments
Phonology		See section 21.3
Rich consonantism	+/–	Richer than in some other languages, but not exceptional
Ternary contrast of stops and affricates	+	There is a four-level contrast if geminates are counted as a separate class.
Glottalization	+	
Rich sibilant systems	+/–	Relatively rich but fewer phonemes than in most languages of the indigenous Caucasian families
Rich postvelar (uvular, pharyngeal and laryngeal) systems	–	Only three uvular phonemes /χ/, /ʁ/ and /q/, no pharyngeal or laryngeal phonemes
Similarly built harmonic clusters	–	
Presence of schwa	+/–	Only in Iron
Lack of phonemic diphthongs	+	
Lack of vocalic clusters	+	
Ablaut	+	Mostly inherited from proto-Iranian
Morphology		
Agglutination	+/–	Only in noun morphology, verb is mostly synthetic, see section 21.5.1
Polysynthetism	–	
Predominance of prefixal conjugation	–	Only aspectual/spatial preverbs, see section 21.5.2.2
Predominance of postpositional constructions	+	See 21.6.2
Masdar (verbal noun)	+	See section
Morphological marking of causative	–/+	Causative formed analytically with *kənən* 'do,' but functions as a complex predicate (i.e., the preverbs are attached to the lexical verb)
Category of evidentiality	–	
Category of potential	–	
Attachment of coordination markers to each conjunct	–	Only as a marked option
A three-grade deictic distinction	–	Some traces in Digor
Vigesimal numeral system	+	Decimal also used, see section 21.4.2
Syntax		
Identical word order (SOV, Attr-N)	+	See sections 21.6.1–21.6.2
Ergative construction	–	
Inversive construction	–/+	A few verbs mark experiencer by genitive and stimulus by nominative.
The possessor constituent precedes the possessed one.	+	See section 21.6.2
Lexical semantics		
Stative vs. dynamic verbs	–	
Inversive verbs	–/+	See "inversive construction" in the preceding
Ambitransitive (labile) verbs	+	
Suppletive verbs for singular and plural arguments	–	

(continued)

Table 21.1 Continued

Feature	Value	Comments
Lexicon		See section 21.4
Common cultural terms not found outside the Caucasus	+	
Common phraseology specific to the area	+	
Common semantic patterns	+	

21.3 PHONOLOGY

In the area of phonology, all phenomena that one may suspect of being contact-induced are limited to the area of consonantism.[4]

There are two features that can be ascribed to Caucasian influence in the Ossetic consonantism. The first and the most undisputable one, noted at least since Abaev (1949: 112), is the presence of ejectives: /p'/, /t'/, /k'/, /c'/, /č'/ (the latter secondary, due to palatalization of /k'/ in Iron and palatalization of /c'/ in Digor). These mostly occur in words borrowed from languages of the Caucasus, for example c'ar | c'arɜ 'bark' (cf. Ingush č'or, čq'or 'peel, shell'; Nichols 2004: 184). Yet there are also cases where ejectives occur in native Iranian vocabulary: št'alə | ɜst'alu 'star' < PIr. *star-, (Abaev 1979: 160–162).

The second such feature is the separate series of tense (geminate) stops and affricates. While Dzaxova (2009) defends a biphonemic analysis of geminates such as /pp/ [p:], /tt/ [t:], other authors (Abaev 1949: 97–98; Sokolova 1953; Axvlediani 1960c) maintain that Ossetic has a special series of unvoiced unaspirated stops; such "deaspiration" occurs in various positions, but is only obligatory under gemination. Geminate stops are always phonetically unvoiced: this could be linked to progressive/regressive assimilation in cases like /bp/, /pb/ > [p:], but it is inexplicable for sequences of voiced stops

---

[4] It should be noted that the de facto standard pronunciation of the majority of Iron speakers does not correspond well to the orthography: in their speech, orthographic dental affricates are pronounced as fricatives (<з> /ʒ/ [d͡z] → /z/, <ц> /c/ [t͡s] → /s/), except, notably, for ejectives and geminates, which continue to be affricates; some speakers have also retained affricates after /n/, pronouncing e.g., <нц> as [nt͡sʰ]. At the same time, orthographic dental fricatives are post-alveolar in Iron (<з> /z/ → /ž/, <с> /s/ → /š/) in all positions. None of these changes has occurred in Digor.

like /bb/ > [pː]. The single phoneme analysis of geminates, if accepted, situates Ossetic in the wider context of neighboring languages where paradigmatic oppositions of voiced–unvoiced aspirated–tense (unvoiced unaspirated)–ejective (/b/–/pʰ/–/pː/–/p'/) are very widespread (Abaev 1949: 112).

To conclude, Ossetic consonantism shows clear signs of contact-induced change in the system of stops and affricates, which display the opposition of voiced, aspirated, tense, and ejective that is typical for the Caucasian linguistic area.

21.4 LEXICON

In this section, I will describe the main features of the Ossetic lexicon that may be the result of external influence. Apart from loanwords, these include a separate series of vigesimal numerals (untypical for Iranian languages) and certain lexical semantic features that are common to many languages of the Caucasus.

21.4.1 Loanwords

In the area of loanwords, it is useful to distinguish between borrowings in the basic lexicon (which can allow us to determine major sources of external influence, including substratum transfer) and borrowings in the cultural lexicon (which mostly reflect contact due to trade relationships and political dominance).

21.4.1.1 Basic Lexicon

The proportion of borrowings in the Ossetic basic lexicon is best illustrated by examining the 110-word Swadesh lists[5] for Iron and Digor published online in the Global Lexicostatistical database (Belyaev 2014b), collected using the method in Kassian et al. (2010).

As can be seen from the list, despite intensive contacts with non-Indo-European languages, the backbone of the basic vocabulary remains uncontestably Iranian: 81% (89 of 110) of all entries in both Iron and Digor have a clear Proto-Iranian etymology. Not all of the remaining 19% are borrowings: some of the items are onomatopoeic or have uncertain etymologies. The number of loanwords is 8–9 in Iron (7%–8%) and 10–11 in Digor (9%–10%). This is a relatively high number, comparable to the share of loanwords in such languages as English. Notably, some of the non-native vocabulary is among the meanings found out to be the least borrowable, according to the data of the World Loanword Database (WOLD; Haspelmath and Tadmor 2009a), that is, the "Leipzig-Jakarta list" (Tadmor 2009: 69–71): 'mouth' (rank 5), 'arm/hand' (rank 19), and possibly 'nose' (rank 2).

---

[5] I am grateful to Alexei Kassian for his help in annotating the lists.

It is remarkable that loans from indigenous North Caucasian language families far outnumber other sources (8 out of 9 probable borrowings in Iron, and 9 out of 11 in Digor), and that there are no borrowings from South Caucasian. Most of the North Caucasian loanwords look specifically East Caucasian. However, while it is commonly assumed that all or most of East Caucasian loanwords are from the neighboring Nakh languages (Chechen and Ingush), the actual situation seems to have been more complex.

Some of the words may have indeed been transferred through substratum influence from the language, or group of languages, that has been displaced by Ossetic in the area where it is currently spoken. As evident from the exposition in section 21.1, such a large-scale transfer must have happened only in the relatively recent period (i.e., after the thirteenth century AD). An example of this class may be $k'u\chi \mid k'o\chi$ 'hand,' for which Nikolayev and Starostin (1994: 706) have demonstrated that the source is an earlier (reconstructed) Chechen-Ingush form.

But other loanwords cannot be explained in this way. Some of them only have counterparts in East Caucasian languages that are quite remote from the areas where Ossetic was ever spoken, at least during the post-Alan period. A telling example is $c'3\chi$ 'blue, grey, green,' which apparently goes back to Proto-North Caucasian $*\underset{.}{c}V\chi V$ (Nikolayev and Starostin 1994: 370). This root is isolated in Avar-Andic and Lezgic (Nikolayev and Starostin 1994: 370), direct contact with which is historically improbable.

At this point, it is difficult to say under which historical and sociolinguistic circumstances these items were transferred into Ossetic. Some of them are clearly quite old. As Abaev (1960) has remarked, the fact that the Jassic glossary contains the words $b3\chi$ 'horse' (Jassic *bah*) and *gal* 'ox' (Jassic *gal*), most probably borrowed from East Caucasian (Abaev 1958: 255, 506), means that the Ossetic lexicon contained a substantial "Caucasian" component already by the fourteenth century. While these words are not in the Swadesh list, it seems reasonable to hypothesize that at least some of the borrowings in the core lexicon existed during that period. Similarly, the Zelenchuk inscription, dating to the early second millennium AD, includes the Caucasian (and Swadesh) term *l3g* 'man',[6] at least according to a probable reading (Thordarson 1992). Therefore, some of the Caucasian loanwords in the basic lexicon go back at least to the time of the Alanic kingdom, or even precede it. This puts the traditional concept of the Caucasian substratum into doubt: the Caucasian influence, whether substratal or otherwise, must have occurred much earlier than the Ossetians became isolated in the mountainous regions of the Caucasus. The historical and sociolinguistic implications of this conclusion remain to be explored.

21.4.1.2 *Cultural Lexicon*

Outside the core lexicon, we often encounter the same problems in attributing the source of borrowing. Apart from transparent, and relatively recent, borrowings from

---

[6] On the complicated history of this root in the Caucasian languages, see Trubetzkoy (1937) and Nikolayev and Starostin (1994: 749–750).

Nakh, such as *furd* | *ford* 'sea' (Nikolayev and Starostin 1994: 677), there is a large number of "Caucasian" words that are difficult to trace back to a specific source, but which seem to be East Caucasian (similarly to the examples in the preceding section).

Extensive data on Georgian loanwords is provided in Tedeevi (1983; also see Thordarson 1999). Tedeevi's survey shows that, while the overall number of such loanwords is large, most of them do not belong to the core lexicon and are phonetically (Tedeevi provides a system of mostly regular correspondences) and semantically transparent; some examples are *gagᵂə* | *gagu* 'pupil (of the eye)' ← G. *guga* 'id.,' *k'aba* 'dress' ← G. *k'aba* 'id.,' *qзdur* | *qзdorз* 'bean' ← G. *q'nduri* 'large beans.' An especially large share of Georgian loanwords is in the religious terminology, for example *zwar* | *ʒiwarз* 'cross, sanctuary, divinity' (← G. *ʒvari*), *čərəštə* | *kiriste* 'Christ' (← G. *krist'e*) (Thordarson 2009: 51–52). The Ossetic word for 'god,' *χᵂəsaw* | *χucaw*, has no acceptable Iranian etymology and is probably related to the Georgian root *xuc-* used in such words as *xuc-es-i* 'old man, priest,' *xuc-oba* 'priesthood,' *xuc-uri* 'ecclesiastical script' (Abaev 1989: 255). The number of Georgian loanwords is obviously higher in Ossetic varieties spoken in South Ossetia; these mostly include plant names and other terms referring to local conditions in Transcaucasia (Thordarson 1992).

West Caucasian loanwords are not always as transparent as Georgian ones, and some of them may be quite old, for example *šзn* | *sзnз* 'wine' (Nikolayev and Starostin 1994: 971; Kullanda 2016: 84). But the majority seem to be rather recent borrowings from the Circassian branch of this family; many of them are found only in Digor, whose contact with Circassian has been much more intense during the last centuries than that of Iron. The survey in Thordarson (2009: 38–42) shows that Circassian borrowings belong almost wholly to the cultural lexicon.

Apart from the indigenous Caucasian languages, by far the most significant lexical interference has apparently been from **Turkic**, although the paucity of Turkic loanwords in the basic lexicon does not support Thordarson's (2009: 64) assertion that "[t]he Turkic influence seems to have been stronger and more profound than that of the Caucasian languages." Still, some of the Turkic terms cover rather basic, if not the most stable, concepts, such as *birзʁ* | *berзʁ* 'wolf' (cf., e.g., Karachay *bürü*, etc.), *nзməg* 'grain, seed; berry' (Karachay *nanəq* 'berry'; Abaev 1973: 169). As Thordarson (1992) remarks, most of the alleged **Uralic** and non-Turkic Altaic loanwords have probably entered Ossetic through the medium of Turkic.

21.4.2 Vigesimal Number System

A clear case of Caucasian influence is in the domain of numerals. Today, many Ossetians use the decimal system, which is a fairly recent trend due to conscious language policy during the Soviet era. Before the creation of Iron and Digor literary standards and the Soviet period, the original Iranian decimal system only survived for the numbers 1–20, while all numbers starting from 20 were formed using the vigesimal system, with the exception of the professional sociolect of herdsmen, who preserved the decimal system for all numerals (Abaev 1949: 282, 399). While the independent development of such systems is attested elsewhere in Iranian (Thordarson 2009: 67), it is probably not an accident that Ossetic shares the vigesimal system with all neighboring indigenous Caucasian languages. Notably, the material used for the vigesimal system is native Iranian vocabulary. The only certain loanword in the numeral system (with the obvious exception of the words for 'million,' 'billion,' etc.) is *min* 'thousand,' from Turkic (Abaev 1973: 119).

21.4.3 Lexical Semantics

It has been claimed that an important pan-Caucasian areal feature is a distinction between two words for 'thick' and 'thin': for flat and roundish objects (Klimov 1978: 23–24; Chirikba 2008: 61–62). According to Klimov (1978: 23–24), this distinction is found throughout the Caucasus, but is most typical for South and West Caucasian (e.g., Georgian *txeli t'q'awi* 'thin hide' vs. *c'wrili titi* 'thin finger'; Kabardian *fe p'aśʼe* 'thin skin' vs. *baš psəǵʷe* 'thin stick'). Such a distinction is also attested in Ossetic: *štavd | (ӡ)stavd* 'thick' and *ləštɜg | listɜg* 'thin' are used for roundish or, rather, elongated objects (rope, thread), while *bɜžžən | bɜzgin* 'thick' and *tɜnɜg* 'thin' are used for flat objects (Abaev [1973] 1995: 505). Notably, here Ossetic also follows the typical Caucasian polysemy patterns 'thin (flat)' + 'watery' (Klimov 1978: 25). A similar semantic contrast which, according to Abaev (1989: 169–170), seems to be a specifically Ossetic–Georgian isogloss, is between two words for 'dry': Iron *χuš*, Digor *suχɜ* 'dry' are used for objects wet on the surface, while *umɜl | womɜl* 'wet' are used for objects that are dry or wet throughout.

While it may be possible that these semantic developments are contact-induced, we know too little of the structure of these semantic areas cross-linguistically and in Iranian in particular to make any definitive conclusions. At least the distinction between 'thin 1D' and 'thin 2D' seems to be a typologically frequent contrast, which is attested in such geographically and genetically remote languages as French and Chinese (Ryzhova et al. 2013; Kozlov et al. 2016). Thus, even if it is an areal feature, it may not be a narrowly "Caucasian" one. As usual, this does not by itself rule out contact influence, but makes it rather difficult to prove conclusively.

Abaev ([1973] 1995) has also noted parallelisms in the formation of phraseological expressions with various somatic terms between Georgian and Ossetic. For example, the word 'heart' is very widely used in both languages, for example Ossetic *šaw-žɜrdɜ, šav-gul-i* (black-heart) 'evil,' *iw-žɜrdɜg* (one-hearted), Georgian *ert-gul-i* (one-heart) 'devoted, faithful.' Other expressions common to Ossetic and Georgian include sayings with Ossetic *šɜr | sɜr* — Georgian *tav-i* 'head,' *quš | ʁos* — *qur-i* 'ear' (Abaev [1973] 1995). Similar expressions are found in other languages of the Caucasus, including Armenian (Chirikba 2008: 64) and Adyghe, as well as in neighboring linguistic areas, for example Persian: *del-siyâh* (heart-black) 'evil,' *del žostan* 'be pleasant,' lit. 'find heart,' and so on. However, there are fewer parallels in the exact form of expressions between Ossetic and Persian than between Ossetic and Georgian. Another interesting somatic-related isogloss is the use of the same word for 'mouth' and 'blade, edge': Ossetic *kom*, Georgian *p'iri*,[7] Armenian *beran* (Abaev [1973] 1995: 506–507).

21.5 Morphology

Contact-induced features in the area of morphology are quite different for nouns and verbs. The nominal paradigm in Ossetic is highly innovative and displays traits of external influence both in its structure and in the semantics of individual categories. The verb, in contrast, is overall rather archaic, and contact influence can be found mainly in the functions of preverbs.

21.5.1 Nominal inflection

Untypically for an Iranian language, Ossetic has a rich case system, with nine cases in Iron and eight in Digor. The system is agglutinative, and all nouns inflect according to the same pattern (there are only small differences between nouns ending with vowels and with consonants, and in Digor, the final *-ə* of nouns is deleted in most oblique cases). Only pronouns show irregularities in their inflection. The cases that are normally distinguished are as follows: nominative, genitive (*-ə* | *-i*), dative (*-ən*), allative (*-mə*), ablative (*-əj*), inessive (*-ə* | *-i*), superessive (*-əl* | *-bəl*), equative (*-aw*); an additional case, the comitative (*-imə*), is present in Iron. To this set one may add, following Belyaev (2010), two additional cases: directive (*-(ə)rdəm* | *-(ə)rdəmə*) 'in the direction of,' and recessive (*-(ə)rdəgəj* | *-(ə)rdigəj*) 'from the direction of,' grammaticalized from postpositions.[8]

While the exact origin of all Ossetic cases is not entirely clear, it is beyond any doubt that most of them are relatively late innovations. Only the genitive, inessive of pronouns, and, possibly, ablative can be traced back to Iranian case suffixes; the inessive of nouns and the equative go back to derivational suffixes; the rest of the cases are newly innovated from postpositions and other functional elements (Vogt 1944; Kim 2003; Cheung 2008; Belyaev 2010).

The development of an agglutinating system is due to two processes: (1) the generalization of the *a-inflection to all noun classes; (2) the innovation of the collective suffix *-tə* as a plural morpheme for all nouns (see Thordarson 2009: 117 and references

---

[7] This word actually means 'mouth' and 'edge,', ot 'blade' as such (Winfried Boeder, personal communication).

[8] This grammaticalization seems to have happened already in Proto-Ossetic, since the directive and recessive have the status of affixes in both Iron and Digor. Cf. also the form *ko-rdig-an* (which-side-ADJ) in Tzetzes (Lubotsky 2015: 55–57), derived by compounding the interrogative root with the same stem *ərd* (*əg*) | *ərd(ig)*.

therein). Both of these processes have probably already been underway during the Middle Iranian period. In particular, a marker cognate to Ossetic -*t(:)ʒ* was used in Sogdian, a closely related language. As seen from Yaghnobi, a "nephew" of Sogdian, this marker later displaced the Old Iranian plural (Sims-Williams 1979). Nor is Ossetic unique in its transition to agglutination among Indo-European languages. The same has happened in Tocharian (Carling 2012); Indo-Aryan languages, with different degrees of grammaticalization of the new cases (the two extremes are represented by clitics in Hindi and affixes in Romani; cf. Butt and King 2004); and Armenian (Kortlandt 2003: 45–51). Therefore, there are no particular reasons to attribute this development to external influence, although language contact may have played a role in reinforcing it (cf. Igartua 2015).

Overall, four features of the Ossetic nominal inflection show some evidence of contact influence: (1) the comitative case in Iron; (2) the equative case; (3) nominative/genitive DOM; (4) the overall structure of the case system.

21.5.1.1 *Comitative*

The comitative is without doubt an independent Iron innovation. None of the neighboring languages, and even none of the Caucasian languages in general, has a dedicated morphological comitative. The comitative affix -*imʒ* goes back to the allative form of the numeral *iw* | *jew* 'one,' used independently as an adverb *iwmʒ* | *jewmʒ* 'together' in both Iron and Digor (Abaev 1949: 101). As Thordarson (2009: 165) observes, this is similar to Modern Georgian -*(s)tan ertad*, which is the adverbial (originally lative) case of the numeral 'one' added to the adessive in -*(s)tan*. An even closer parallel is the Old Georgian comitative postposition -*urt*, which governs the instrumental case and is etymologically a variant of *ert*- 'one' (cf. *urti-ert*- 'one another'; Winfried Boeder, personal communication). We may thus be dealing with a similar pattern of semantic (but not morphological) development. At any rate, the fact that comitative only exists in Iron makes this a rather recent areal isogloss.

25.5.1.2 *Equative*

The core function of the Ossetic equative is comparison, for example *lʒg-aw* (man-EQU) 'like a man.' Cases that are explicitly labeled equative are extremely rare; however, so-called adverbial case endings are found in South and West Caucasian languages, also denoting comparison and related meanings. An even closer semantic counterpart to the Ossetic equative is the Old Georgian -*ebr* 'like.' Broadly similar affixes are found in other languages of the area as well, although they are not always viewed as case markers. In particular, Ingush has case-like adverbial forms in the singular, usually identical in form to one of the cases (Nichols 2011: 379). Turkic languages, including Karachay-Balkar, have the suffix -*ča* denoting comparison ('like'; Seegmiller 1996: 27) and other related meanings. It is thus possible that the influence of neighboring languages has played a role in the development of a full-fledged equative case (which ultimately goes back to an Old/Middle Iranian adverbial derivational marker; see Cheung 2008).

21.5.1.3 *Differential Object Marking*

Another parallel with the Turkic languages of the Caucasus is related to the system of direct object marking. In Ossetic, nominative and genitive compete for marking the direct object: generally, the nominative is used for inanimate arguments, while the genitive is used for animate ones. The same system seems to be found in Karachay and Kumyk: the so-called accusative case forms in these languages are always identical to the genitive forms (see Seegmiller 1996: 13ff. on Karachay; Dmitriev 1940 on Kumyk), due to the loss of the final -*ŋ* of the genitive suffix. Competition between nominative and genitive in object marking is not typical for Turkic, but is identical to the Ossetic system. At this stage, it is difficult to establish whether this similarity is accidental or due to earlier Ossetic or Alanic influence.

21.5.1.4 *The Case System*

The rest of the Ossetic case categories are cross-linguistically quite common, which makes it difficult to detect possible contact influences. The case system as a whole does not seem to share many similarities with neighboring systems either (for an overview, see Belyaev 2010). West Caucasian languages either lack case systems at all or possess two to three case forms; therefore, any kind of external influence in either direction is implausible. While the case systems of Nakh languages, Ingush in particular, have earlier been described as particularly influential (Abaev 1949), a detailed comparison shows that this similarity is largely superficial: the number of shared case values is about the same as the number of those that are unique to each language. Other East Caucasian systems are even less similar, as they involve a restricted number of grammatical cases and rich spatial systems organized into localization "series" (Creissels 2008). Ossetic, in contrast, has two neutral "directional" cases (allative and ablative), and two spatial cases combining essive and lative orientation (inessive and superessive). Turkic languages, similarly to Ingush, share only typologically trivial case values with Ossetic (such as genitive or dative), while lacking any of the less typical ones (superessive, allative, comitative). Superficially, South Caucasian systems are similar to Turkic: they share only basic grammatical cases (genitive, dative) and, possibly, the adverbial (see earlier discussion) with Ossetic. There are usually no specialized spatial cases, with the exception of Mingrelian and Laz, which have allative and ablative cases (Boeder 2004: 13), but this parallel is obviously too weak for a case of contact influence to be made.

However, in Modern Georgian, some of the Old Georgian postpositions have fused with the nominal stem to such an extent that some authors, such as Šaniʒe (1973), Vogt (1971), and Creissels (2008), treat them as case affixes (in the terminology of Vogt, *cas secondaires* 'secondary cases'). While some degree of morphologization is usually acknowledged, the status of these elements as case markers is controversial (Čikobava 1961; Boeder 2004: 14, 16; Slocum and Harris ms.). If "secondary cases" are included in the comparison, the set of spatial relations encoded by cases in Ossetic and Georgian becomes largely identical. Both languages possess dedicated cases for inessive (Oss. -*ə* | -*i*,

Georgian -*ši*) and superessive, as well as two localization-neutral directional cases, allative (Oss. -*mɜ*, Georgian -*mde*) and ablative (Oss. -*ɜj*, Georgian -*gan*, -*dan*). Remarkably, both additionally distinguish between allative and directive/approximative (Oss. -*(ə)rdɜm*, Georgian -*k'en*). Although many details concerning Georgian cases are still unclear, Georgian currently seems to be the best candidate for donor status with respect to Ossetic. Since both systems are innovations that happened around the same time, the contact situation that might underlie such an areal isogloss is also a topic for further research.

21.5.2 Verbs

As mentioned in the preceding, Ossetic verbal morphology is rather archaic. Two traits deserve particular attention: first, the use of converbs (which have been claimed by some authors to be contact-induced); second, the functions of preverbs.

21.5.2.1 *Converbs and Other Non-Finite Forms*

Ossetic possesses a number of non-finite verb forms, most of which are quite typical for Indo-European languages. Their use is rather limited. The infinitive, for example, is predominantly used in control constructions. Participles are usually either lexicalized or employed in periphrastic constructions (modality, passive voice, etc.). This is completely different from most neighboring languages (except South Caucasian), in which non-finite subordination is the main means of clause combining.

There is one non-finite form in Ossetic, though, that has been argued to have arisen due to external influence. It is the participle-converb in -*gɜ*, whose ablative form in -*gɜ-jɜ* serves as a converb proper: Ossetic National Corpus (ONC)

(1) quc:ə-t-ɜm   **kɜš-gɜ-jɜ**   ɜr-səd-əštə   ju   ɜrtɜ   uš-ə
     COW-PL-ALL   look-PCVB-ABL   PV-go-PST.3PL   one   three   woman-GEN
     '**Looking** at the cows, there came around three women.' (ONC: *Max dug* 8, 1999)

The form in -*gɜ* goes back to the instrumental form of a verbal derivate in *-*k*- (Thordarson 1986: 504). Apparently, a contamination of the nominative and this instrumental form has happened, which led to the participle-converb polyfunctionality: the converb use goes back to a kind of instrumental-marked absolute construction, typical for old Indo-European.

Thordarson (2009: 77) has argued that the development of converbs in Ossetic (see Belyaev and Vydrin 2011) may be due to the influence of North Caucasian and Turkic languages. These indeed utilize converbs extensively, but it is precisely this fact that makes it difficult to say that Ossetic has developed its forms due to their influence. In Turkic and North Caucasian, simple converbs function as the main narrative device, in a strategy that is called "clause chaining" in typological work (see, e.g., Givón 1987); nothing of the sort obtains in Ossetic. The main way of advancing the narrative is either by simply juxtaposing clauses or by using coordinating conjunctions *ɜmɜ* | *ɜma* 'and' and *fɜlɜ* | *fal* 'but.' Converbs are almost nonexistent in Ossetic spoken discourse, with only two examples being found among 346 randomly chosen clauses in the spoken corpus (http://ossetic-studies.org/texts/en); to compare, there are forty examples of correlative subordination (Belyaev 2014a). Since the converb in Ossetic is historically a direct continuation of the co-predicative participle, and this use of participles is typical for Indo-European in general, there seems to be no particularly strong evidence for contact influence in this case.

21.5.2.2 *Preverbs: Directionality and Perfectivization*

Ossetic has a rich and fairly regular system of preverbs, whose spatial meanings (in Iron) are summarized in the Table 21.2.

Table 21.2 Ossetic Preverbs

	Inside	Outside	Downward	Upwards
Toward speaker	*ɜrba-*	*ra-*	*ɜr-*	*š-*
From speaker	*ba-*	*a-*	*nɜ-*	

A peculiar feature of this system is that it encodes the direction of movement not only according to the agent, but also according to the speaker. That is, if someone enters a house, *χɜzar-mɜ ba-səd-i* (house-ALL PV-go-PST.INTR.3SG) 's/he **went into** the house' would be used if the speaker observes the action from outside the house, while *χɜzarmɜ* **ɜrba**-*sədi* 's/he **came into** the house' would be used if the situation is observed from the inside (this distinction is encoded by the opposition of *come* vs. *go* in English). Such an orientational system is unusual for Indo-European languages, and is also not typical for North Caucasian or Turkic languages. But, as Bielmeier (1981) and Tomelleri (2009) observe, it finds a direct counterpart in Georgian, where the system has the form shown in Table 21.3.

Table 21.3 Georgian Preverbs

	Inside	Outside	Downward	Upwards
Toward speaker	*še-mo-*	*ga-mo-*	*c'a-mo-*	*gad-mo-*
From speaker	*še-*	*ga-*	*c'a-*	*gada-*

In Georgian, the orientation toward the speaker is agglutinatively expressed by the prefix *mo-*, while in Ossetic, the preverbs are mostly morphologically primitive, which means that the language has rearranged existing Iranian material to construct the new system.

Another central function of preverbs in Ossetic is perfectivation. Ossetic possesses a "Slavic-style" (Bybee and Dahl 1981) aspectual system, where unprefixed verbs are imperfective, while prefixed verbs are perfective, for example *žawər walibɜχ χortːa*

'Zaur was eating a *walibakh*'[9] versus. *žawər walibʒχ ba-χortʲa* 'Zaur ate / has eaten a *walibakh*.' The similarity to Slavic is so striking that it has led Abaev (1964, 1965: 58–60) to claim a direct ancient areal isogloss between Slavic and Scythian/Sarmatian. However, as Tomelleri (2009) and Arkadiev (2014) rightly observe, such an idea is implausible: Slavic languages themselves have developed a regular preverbal perfective system in a fairly recent period (second millennium AD), when intense contacts with the Alans were out of the question.

Such an aspect system is an anomaly for Iranian languages (Èdel'man 1975: 381–382), but it is firmly established that Slavic-style aspect is a feature that is found not only in Georgian, but also in other South Caucasian languages and probably represents an internal South Caucasian development (Šanidze 1942). This has led some scholars to conclude that we deal with a case of Georgian influence on Ossetic (Tomelleri 2009). However, preverbal perfectivization is an innovation in both Ossetic and Georgian; thus, just as with case, we can speak of convergent development, but we can hardly prove influence in one direction or another.

21.6 SYNTAX

Contact-induced influence is plausible in three area of syntax: a salient preverbal position for interrogatives and other elements in the clause; the order of elements in noun phrases; and the marking of recipients in ditransitive constructions.

21.6.1 Clause-Level Word Order

Ossetic syntax is characterized by a mostly free word order; the basic order of the arguments is SOV, but all other permutations, especially SVO, are also encountered rather frequently. There is, however, an important constraint on word order that plays a central role in clause-level syntax: certain types of constituents, specifically interrogatives, most subordinators, and negative pronouns obligatorily occupy the preverbal area:

(2) ⟨*či⟩ zul   ⟨či⟩ ba-lχʒtʲ-a ⟨*či⟩?
    who bread   PV-buy-PST.3SG
    'Who bought bread?'

(3) ⟨*kʷə⟩ žawər-ə   ⟨kʷə⟩ fetʲ-on,   wʒd ba-sin   kotʲ-on
    when Zaur-GEN   see.PFV-PST.1SG then PV-happiness do-PST.1SG
    'When I saw Zaur, I became happy.'

---

[9] Ossetian specialty: a pie stuffed with cheese.

(4) ⟨*ni-či⟩   žawər-ə   ⟨ni-či⟩ žon-ə   ⟨*ni-či⟩
     NEG-who.NOM   Zaur-GEN   know-PRS.3SG
     'No one knows Zaur.'

Non-interrogative focus is also usually preverbal, although it may be postverbal. The relative order of the preverbal constituent types is rigidly fixed, and is "focus–interrogative/preverbal subordinator–negation or negative pronoun."

(5) a. ⟨3rm3št žawər-ə⟩ či   ⟨*3rm3št žawər-ə⟩ fet:-a⟨3rm3št žawər-ə⟩?
         only   Zaur-GEN who   see.PFV-PST.3SG
         'Who saw only Zaur?'

     b. ⟨*ni-sə⟩   či   ⟨ni-sə⟩ žon-ə?
         NEG-what   who   know-PRS.3SG
         'Who doesn't know anything?'

Preverbal focus and interrogative placement are typical for SOV languages, for example Hungarian (É. Kiss 2004: 77–105) and Turkish (Erguvanlı 1984). This phenomenon is found in many languages of the Caucasus as well (Testelec 1998; Forker and Belyaev 2015). Of the latter, Georgian is especially similar to Ossetic: focus, negative markers, and pronouns (Alxazišvili 1959: 384), interrogatives (Vogt 1971: 224), and, most importantly, certain subordinators (Vogt 1974; Boeder 2005; Kojima 2014) appear in the preverbal position. Erschler (2012) asserts that this particular constellation of items that occupy the area he calls "preverbal left periphery" is rather cross-linguistically rare. Since the "normal" position of subordinators in Indo-European languages is clause-initial, and this is also the usual reconstruction for Proto-Indo-European (see Kiparsky 1995), the natural conclusion is that the Ossetic pattern is a syntactic calque from Georgian.

   However, preverbal placement of foci, interrogatives, negation, and indefinites may not be that unusual for an Indo-European language. Especially relevant are the data of Hittite, where foci and interrogatives can alternatively be placed either clause-initially or preverbally (Goedegebuure 2009); indefinite pronouns (semantically not much different from Ossetic negative pronouns) and negation obligatorily occupy the immediately preverbal position (Hoffner and Melchert 2008: 286, 341–342); and certain subordinators, such as *kuit* 'because,' can be preverbal (see Sideltsev 2015 for a comprehensive overview). This similarity shows that a developed preverbal area is in fact typical for SOV languages, including Indo-European ones; its perceived exoticity may be merely due to a lack of sufficiently detailed descriptions. While Georgian influence cannot be ruled out, its role may have been relatively weak in comparison to general typological tendencies.

21.6.2 Noun Phrase structure

Ossetic possesses a noun phrase with very rigid head-final order of elements. Its structure is generally of the traditional dependent-marking, Indo-European type. Two features of Ossetic noun phrases, however, can be linked to areal influences.

The first such feature is the existence of possessive proclitics. Ossetic has a series of "short" possessive pronouns (*mɜ*= 'my,' *dɜ*= 'thy,' *jɜ*= 'his/her/its,' etc.), which, as Erschler (2009) has demonstrated, are proclitics (or, perhaps, even prefixes) that attach to the possessed noun phrase:

(6) *mɜ=*   [*mad*   *ɜmɜ*   *fəd*]   *χɜšt-ə*   *raž-mɜ*   *a-mard-əštə*
      my   mother   and   father   war-GEN   front-ALL   PV-die-PST.3PL
      '**My** mother and (**my**) father died before the war.'   (ONC: *Max dug* 1, 1999)

As Erschler shows, all of the other Iranian languages except Ossetic are characterized by the use of enclitics in the possessive function, which double as direct object markers. In Ossetic, as evidenced by the phonological similarity between possessive proclitics and direct object (genitive) enclitic pronouns, possessive proclitics must have originated from pronouns encliticized to the preceding constituent (amply attested in Old and Middle Iranian, as well as Pashto), which have apparently been reanalyzed as proclitics.

Erschler argues that this change must have happened as a result of the influence of West Caucasian languages, which use preposed possessive markers. This scenario appears plausible, given that no other Iranian language has undergone such a change, and in general a shift from enclisis to proclisis is not especially frequent. Notably, as with Caucasian influence in the lexicon, the shift of possessive markers to proclitic status must have happened at a relatively early stage, since we see the modern word order already in the Tzetzes fragments.

A few words must also be said about Abaev's often-repeated claim that the predominance of postpositions over prepositions in Ossetic is due to some Caucasian influence or substratum (Abaev 1949: 108; Abaev 1978). Indeed, there is only one productive preposition in Ossetic, *ɜnɜ* 'without.'[10] Yet using postpositions is typical for an SOV language (Greenberg 1963; Universal 4). There is no reason to suppose that Ossetic has acquired SOV order under contact influence, as the very same basic order was found in Old Iranian (Hale 1988), and is still found in all Iranian languages. Most postpositions in Ossetic have evolved from nouns with genitive dependents, and most of them still retain nominal properties. Other Iranian languages have undergone the same development, thus, as Thordarson (2009: 175) observes, the predominance of postpositions in Ossetic is explicable as an internal development. Specifically, Abaev's (1978) claim of an affinity between Ossetic and Armenian in their use of cases and postpositions appears to be entirely unmotivated: the few similarities in the system of cases and postpositions in these languages that can be observed are ascribable to universal typological tendencies, rather than areal isoglosses (Arkhangelskiy and Belyaev 2011).

At the same time, there is a curious similarity with Old Georgian, where, like in Ossetic, *twinier* 'except, without' is the only preposition: *twinier mam-isa tkuen-isa*

---

[10] *ɜd* 'with' is often regarded as a preposition in descriptive grammars, but it has limited productivity in the modern language, and it cannot attach to whole constituents. Perhaps it should be treated as a prefix rather than a preposition.

(except father-GEN your-GEN) 'except your father.' (Winfried Boeder, personal communication) There seems to be no formal or functional motivation for 'without' to be singled out as a preposition in a postpositional language; hence, some kind of areal interference in either direction is likely.

21.6.3 Recipient Marking

Unlike most Standard Average European languages, Ossetic allows coding Recipients in ditransitive constructions alternatively by dative or allative case:[11]

(7) ras-axšt-a   qašaj tɜrquš ɜmɜ =jɜ   **ɜldar-ɜn**   ratː-a
     PV-catch-PST.3SG Q.   hare   and   it.GEN lord-DAT   give.PFV-PST.3SG
     'Qasay caught a hare and gave it **to the lord** [dat.].'   (ONC: *Max dug* 7, 2002)

(8) čermen ra-jšt-a nomxɜʁd   xazɜmɜt-ə k'ux-ɜj   ɜmɜ =jɜ   **ɜxšar-mɜ**
     Ch.   PV-take-PST.3SG list Kh.-GEN hand-ABL and it.GEN A.-ALL
     ratː-a . . .
     give.PFV-PST.3SG
     'Chermen took the list from Khazimat's hand and gave it **to Akhsar** [all.].'
                                         (ONC: Qajttaty Sergej, *Fædisontæ*, 1984)

The contrast between these two examples is that (7) implies a more abstract transfer of property, while (8) conveys a sense of direct physical transfer of an object, with the intent of giving the list to be read rather than in permanent possession. Overall, the dative is the more general of the two cases, and can be used in any situation, while the allative cannot be used in more abstract contexts where there is no physical action involved, or in context where a permanent transfer is implied:

(9) nɜ= **adɜm-ɜn** / *adɜm-mɜ ratː-a   xɜrinag xʷɜsaw,
     our people-DAT people-ALL give.PFV-PST.3SG food   God
     xɜrinag-gɜn-ɜ̌-ətɜ   =ta   xɜjrɜg
     food-do-PTCP-PL   CONTR   devil
     'God gave **our people** [dat.] food, and the Devil, cooks.'
                                         (ONC: asoxty Muzafer, *Zond æmæ amond*, 2012)

(10) farašt ɜfšɜmɜr-ə   šɜ= xo-jə   **xɜmɜs-ɜn** / [??]xɜmɜs-mɜ ratː-oj
     nine brother-GEN their sister-GEN Kh.-DAT   Kh.-ALL   give.PFV-PST.3PL
     'Nine brothers gave their sister **to Khamits** [dat.] (in marriage).'
                                         (ONC: *Max dug* 2, 2006)

---

[11] The content of this section is based on joint work with Michael Daniel.

If the allative is used in (10), then, according to some native speakers, the only available interpretation is that the brothers gave ("lent") their sister to Khamits for a limited period of time, as opposed to giving her to him in marriage.

As demonstrated in Daniel et al. (2010), such an opposition between dative and allative in recipient marking is a typical trait of East Caucasian languages; see the following examples from Akhvakh:

(11) bešanoda ʁurušːi milica-sːʷ-a   o-xː-ada,   boqʼːeːdoda
      hundred   ruble   policeman-M-DAT   N-give-PFV.ASSINV forty
      ʁurušːi-la di   imo-Lːira   o-xː-ada   zikira   b-eL-uruLa
      ruble-and 1Sg.GEN father-AD.LAT   N-give-PFV.ASSINV zikr   N-lead-INF
      'I gave hundred rubles **to the policeman [dat.]** (as a bribe), and forty rubles **to my
      father [lat.]** to organize the *zikr* (a religious ritual).'   (Daniel et al. 2010, ex. 23)

(12) wašo-de ha-di miLʼaradi   ila-ɬːi-Lːira   e-xː-awi,
      boy.OBL-ERG   this-SAME.LEVEL fruit_stone.PL   mother-OBL-F-AD.LAT
      "ila,   "ila di-La   ha   miLʼaradi,
      NPL-give-EVID.NPL   mother 1Sg.OBL-DAT   this   fruit_stone.PL
      r-iqʼʷ-aj-a,   hani   qʼ-oːnuLa di-La   e-xː-a"
      NPL-crack-CAUS-IMP   kernel eat-INF   1Sg.OBL-DAT   N-give-IMP
      'The boy handed the fruit stones **to** (his) **mother [lat.]**, "Mother, crack these stones for me, and give them **to me [dat.]** for me to eat the kernel."'

                                                              (Daniel et al. 2010, ex. 31)

The money is permanently transferred to the policeman in (11), while the *zikr* in Daghestanian practice involves redistributing the money among the worshippers, thus the transfer is only temporary. In (12), both direct spatial transfer and the idea that this transfer is temporary are involved, while the return transfer from the mother to the boy is conceived of as permanent, for the reason that the kernel is to be eaten.

Hence, it appears likely that this phenomenon in Ossetic is due to influence from this group of languages, specifically from Nakh (or, alternatively, from the unknown substratum language that Ossetic displaced).

21.7 CONCLUSIONS

In this chapter, I have provided a brief overview of the major changes in the lexicon, phonology, and grammar of Ossetic that have come about as a result of external influence. The range of sources of such influence is quite diverse. Many features of Ossetic, such as the presence of ejectives or nominal agglutination, are characteristic of the Caucasus as a whole, or of even wider areas, and cannot be ascribed to a particular language or group of languages. When the source of influence can be reliably determined, the overall picture is not prone to easy generalization. On the one hand, the influence of East Caucasian appears to have been quite profound, with the majority of borrowings in the basic lexicon being clearly Nakh-Daghestanian, even though the particular language from which these words have been borrowed cannot be reliably identified. In contrast, there are no loanwords from South Caucasian, one reliable loanword from West Caucasian, and two loanwords from other sources. But the number of grammatical influences of East Caucasian on Ossetic is, in contrast, rather low, with only dative/allative recipient marking being a plausible candidate. On the other hand, West and South Caucasian have deeply influenced such fundamental areas of grammar as clause structure and possession marking, yet have left very few traces in the basic lexicon.

Unless Ossetic has other contact-induced features that we do not know about, which may change the general picture, this situation seems to confirm Ross's (2001: 152) observation that grammatical influence is possible in the absence of lexical borrowing. This suggests that contact situations with each of the neighboring languages were substantially different. The large number of East Caucasian words in the basic lexicon, accompanied by no significant grammatical influence, suggests an "aborted" language shift (Kassian 2014) from some unknown East Caucasian language to Alan/Proto-Ossetic. Contact with West Caucasian, South Caucasian, and Turkic, in contrast, was based on commercial, political, cultural, and religious relations, as well as on social institutions such as *Atalyk*, where a child was given away for upbringing by a different family (Thordarson 2009: 190–191). This means that the contact situation involved long-term bilingualism rather than language shift, which explains the high number of grammatical calquing (case system, clause structure) and the low number of loanwords in the basic lexicon. There have probably been several waves of influence in each case, corresponding to different donor language and different contact situations; a more fine-grained analysis of contact-induced change in Ossetic is a topic for further research.

REFERENCES

Abaev, Vasilij I. 1949. *Osetinskij jazyk i fol'klor* [Ossetian language and folklore]. Vol. 1. Moscow; Leningrad: Izdatel'stvo AN SSSR.

Abaev, Vasilij I. 1958–1989. *Istoriko-ètimologičeskij slovar' osetinskogo jazyka* [A historical and etymological dictionary of Ossetic]. Vol. 1: A–K', 1958; Vol. 2: L–R, 1973; Vol. 3: S–T', 1976; Vol. 4: U–Z. Moscow' Leningrad: Nauka.

Abaev, Vasilij I. 1959. *Grammatičeskij očerk osetinskogo jazyka* [A grammatical sketch of Ossetic]. Vladikavkaz: Severo-Osetinskoe knižnoe izdatel'stvo.

Abaev, Vasilij I. 1960. Comments on: Julius Nemet. *Spiskov slov na jazyke jasov, vengerskix alan* [A wordlist of Jassic, a language of Hungarian Alans]. Ordžonikidze: Severo-Osetinskij naučno-issledovatel'skij institut, 1960. Translation of Németh 1959 by Vasilij I. Abaev.

Abaev, Vasilij I. 1964. Preverby i perfektivnost': Ob odnoj skifo-slavjanskoj izoglosse [Preverbs and perfectivity: On one Scytho-Slavic isogloss]. In *Problemy indoevropejskogo jazykoznanija: ètjudy po sravnitel'no-istoričeskoj grammatike indoevropejskix jazykov,* edited by Vladimir N. Toporov, 90–99. [Problems of Indo-European linguistics: Studies on historical grammar of Indo-European languages]. Moscow: Nauka.

Abaev, Vasilij I. 1965. *Skifo-evropejskie izoglossy: na styke Vostoka i Zapada* [Scytho-European isoglosses: Between East and West]. Moscow: Nauka.

Abaev, Vasilij I. [1973] 1995. Nekotorye osetino-gruzinskie semantičeskie paralleli [Some Ossetic-Georgian semantic parallels]. *Iberijsko-kavkazskoe jazykoznanie* XVIII. Reprinted in Abaev (1995), *Izbrannye trudy* [Selected works], 502–509. Vladikavkaz: Ir.

Abaev, Vasilij I. 1978. Armeno-Ossetica. Tipologičeskie vstreči" [Armeno-Ossetica. Typological connections]. *Voprosy jazykoznanija* 6: 45–51. Reprinted in Abaev (1995), *Izbrannye trudy* [Selected works], 490–501. Vladikavkaz: Ir.

Abaev, Vasilij I. 1995. *Izbrannye trudy* [Selected works]. Vol. 2, *Obščee i sravnitel'noe jazykoznanie* [General and comparative linguistics]. Vladikavkaz: Ir.

Abaev, Vasilij I., and Harold W. Bailey. 1985. Alans. In *Encyclopædia Iranica*, edited by Ehsan Yarshater, 1(8): 801–803. London; Boston: Routledge & Kegan Paul.

Alemany, Agustí. 2000. *Sources on the Alans: A Critical Compilation*. Handbook of Oriental Studies. Section 8: Uralic and Central Asian Studies 5. Leiden: Brill.

Alxazišvili, Arcil. 1959. Porjadok slov i intonacija v prostom povestvovatel'nom predloženii gruzinskogo jazyka [Word-order and intonation of simple declarative sentence in Georgian]. In *Foneticeskij sbornik* 1, edited by Vladimir A. Artemov and Sergej M. Žgenti, 367–414. Tbilisi: Izdatel'stvo Tbilisskogo gosudarstvennogo universiteta.

Arkadiev, Peter. 2014. Towards an areal typology of prefixal perfectivization. *Scando-Slavica* 2: 384–405.

Arkhangelskiy, Timofey, and Oleg Belyaev. 2011. A comparison of Eastern Armenian and Iron Ossetic spatial systems. In *Languages and Cultures in the Caucasus: Papers from the International Conference "Current Advances in Caucasian Studies," Macerata, January 21–23, 2010* [Studies on Language and Culture in Central and Eastern Europe], edited by Vittorio S. Tomelleri, Manana Topadze, and Anna Lukianowicz, 285–299. München and Berlin: Verlag Otto Sagner.

Axvlediani, Georgij S. 1960a. *Sbornik izbrannyx rabot po osetinskomu jazyku* [Selected works on Ossetic]. Tbilisi: Izdatel'stvo Tbilisskogo gosudarstvennogo universiteta im. Stalina.

Axvlediani, Georgij S. 1960b. O nekotoryx voprosax alansko-(osetinsko)-gruzinskix jazykovyx vzaimootnošenij [On certain problems of the linguistic relations between Alans (Ossetians) and Georgians]. In Axvlediani (1960a), *Sbornik izbrannyx rabot po osetinskomu jazyku* [Selected works on Ossetic], 167–178. Tbilisi: Izdatel'stvo Tbilisskogo gosudarstvennogo universiteta im. Stalina.

Axvlediani, Georgij S. 1960c. K voprosu o geminacii i geminatax v osetinskom [On gemination and geminates in Ossetic]. In Axvlediani (1960a), *Sbornik izbrannyx rabot po osetinskomu jazyku* [Selected works on Ossetic], 117–121. Tbilisi: Izdatel'stvo Tbilisskogo gosudarstvennogo universiteta im. Stalina.

Balanovsky, Oleg, Khadizhat Dibirova, Anna Dybo, Oleg Mudrak, Svetlana Frolova, Elvira Pocheshkhova, Marc Haber, Daniel Platt, Theodore Schurr, Wolfgang Haak, Marina Kuznetsova, Magomed Radzhabov, Olga Balaganskaya, Alexey Romanov, Tatiana Zakharova, David F. Soria Hernanz, Pierre Zalloua, Sergey Koshel, Merritt Ruhlen, Colin Renfrew, R. Spencer Wells, Chris Tyler-Smith, Elena Balanovska, and The Genographic Consortium. 2011. Parallel evolution of genes and languages in the Caucasus region. *Molecular Biology and Evolution* 28(10): 2905–2920.

Belyaev, Oleg. 2010. Evolution of case in Ossetic. *Iran and the Caucasus* 14(2): 287–322.

Belyaev, Oleg I. 2014a. *Korreljativnaja konstrukcija v osetinskom jazyke v tipologičeskom osveščenii* [Ossetic correlatives in typological perspective]. Kandidat dissertation, Lomonosov Moscow State University. http://www.philol.msu.ru/~ref/dissertatsiya2014/d_belyaev.pdf (accessed April 20, 2014).

Belyaev, Oleg. 2014b. Ossetic wordlists in the Global Lexicostatistical Database. http://starling.rinet.ru/cgi-bin/response.cgi?root=new100&morpho=0&basename=new100\ier\irn (accessed January 6, 2016)

Belyaev, Oleg, and Michael Daniel. Forthcoming. Recipient marking in Ossetic: A case for contact influence. Submitted to *Folia Linguistica*.

Belyaev, Oleg, and Arseniy Vydrin. 2011. Participle-converbs in Iron Ossetic: Syntactic and semantic properties. In *Topics in Iranian Linguistics*, edited by Agnes Korn, Geoffrey Haig, Simin Karimi, and Pollet Samvelian, 117–134. Wiesbaden: Reichert.

Bielmeier, Ronald. 1981. Präverbien im Ossetischen. In *Monumentum Georg Morgenstierne*, Vol. 1 [Acta Iranica 21], 27–46. Leiden: Brill.

Boeder, Winfried. 2004. The South Caucasian languages. *Lingua* 115(1–2) (Special issue: Caucasian, edited by Helma van den Berg): 5–89.

Boeder, Winfried. 2005. Protasis and apodosis in the Kartvelian languages. *Sprachtypologie und Universalienforschung (STUF)* 58: 16–25.

Butt, Miriam, and Tracy Holloway King. 2004. The status of case. In *Clause Structure in South Asian Languages*, edited by Veneeta Dayal and Anoop Mahajan, 153–198. Dordrecht: Kluwer.

Bybee, Joan, and Östen Dahl. 1989. The creation of tense and aspect systems in the languages of the world. *Studies in Language* 13: 51–103.

Carling, Gerd. 2012. Development of form and function in a case system with layers: Tocharian and Romani compared. *Tocharian and Indo-European Studies* 13: 55–74.

Census 2002. *Vserossijska perepis' naselenija 2002 goda* [All-Russian census of 2002]. Vol. 4, table 4. *Rasprostranennost' vladenija jazykami (krome russkogo)* [Extent of command of languages (except Russian)]. http://www.perepis2002.ru/ct/doc/TOM_04_04.xls (accessed May 9, 2014).

Cheung, Johnny. 2008. The Ossetic case system revisited. In *Evidence and Counter-evidence: Essays in Honour of Frederik Kortlandt*, Vol. 1: *Balto-Slavic and Indo-European Linguistics*, edited by Alexander Lubotsky, Jos Schaeken, and Jeroen Wiedenhof, 87–105. Studies in Slavic and General Linguistics 32. Amsterdam; New York: Rodopi.

Chirikba, Viacheslav A. 2008. The problem of the Caucasian Sprachbund. In *From Linguistic Areas to Areal Linguistics*, edited by Pieter Muysken, 25–94. Studies in Language Companion Series 90. Amsterdam; Philadelphia: John Benjamins.

Čikobava, Arnold. 1961. Tandebulian brunvata sak'itxisatvis kartulši [On the question of adpositional cases in Georgian]. *Kartuli enis st'rukt'uris sak'itxebi* 2: 197–208.

Creissels, Denis. 2008. Spatial cases. In *The Oxford Handbook of Case*, edited by Andrej Malchukov and Andrew Spencer, 609–625. Oxford: Oxford University Press.

Daniel, Michael, Zarina Molochieva, and Zaira Khalilova. 2010. Ditransitive constructions in East Caucasian. In *Studies in Ditransitive Constructions: A Comparative Handbook*, edited by Andrej Malchukov, Martin Haspelmath, and Bernard Comrie, 277–317. Berlin: Walter de Gruyter.

Dmitriev, Nikolaj K. 1940. *Grammatika kumykskogo jazyka* [A grammar of Kumyk]. Moscow: Izdatel'stvo Akademii nauk SSSR.

Dzaxova, Veronika T. 2009. *Fonetičeskie xarakteristiki fonologičeskoj sistemy sovremennogo osetinskogo (ironskogo) literaturnogo jazyka* [The phonetic characteristics of modern Standard (Iron) Ossetic]. Vladikavkaz: Izdatel'stvo SOGPI, 2009.

Èdel'man, Džoj I. 1975. Kategorija vremeni i vida [Tense and aspect]. In *Opyt istoriko-tipologičeskogo issledovanija iranskix jazykov* [A historical typological study of Iranian languages], Vol. 2, *Èvoljucija grammatičeskix kategorij* [The evolution of grammatical categories], 337–411. Moscow: Nauka.

Engberg, Sysse, and Alexander Lubotsky. 2003. Alanic marginal notes in a Byzantine manuscript: A preliminary report. *Nartamongæ* 2(1–2): 41–46.

Erguvanlı, Eser E. 1984. *The Function of Word Order in Turkish Grammar*. Berkeley: University of California Press.

Erschler, David. 2009. Possession marking in Ossetic: Arguing for Caucasian influences. *Linguistic Typology* 13(3): 417–450.

Erschler, David. 2012. From preverbal focus to preverbal 'left periphery': The Ossetic clause architecture in areal and diachronic perspective. *Lingua* 122(6): 673–699.

Fähnrich, Heinz. 1988. Zu den nachisch-daghestanischen Lehnwörtern im Swanischen. *Wissenschaftlichen Zeitschrift der Friedrich-Schiller-Universität Jena* 37(2): 117–121.

Forker, Diana, and Oleg Belyaev. 2015. Word order and focus particles in Nakh-Daghestanian languages. In *Information structuring of spoken language from a cross-linguistic perspective*, edited by M. M. Jocelyne Fernandez-Vest and Robert D. Van Valin, Jr., 239–262. Trends in Linguistics. Studies and Monographs 283. Amsterdam: John Benjamins.

Gamrekeli, V. N. 1961. *Dvaly i Dvaletija v I–XV vv. n.è.* [Dvals and Dvaletia in the 1–15th cc. AD]. Tbilisi: Izdatel'stvo Akademii Nauk Gruzinskoj SSR.

Givón, Talmy. 1987. Beyond foreground and background. In *Coherence and Grounding in Discourse: Outcome of a Symposium, Eugene, Oregon, June 1984*, edited by Russell S. Tomlin, 175–188. Typological Studies in Language 11. Amsterdam; Philadelphia: John Benjamins.

Goedegebuure, Petra. 2009. Focus structure and Q-word questions in Hittite. *Linguistics* 47(4): 945–967.

Greenberg, Joseph H. 1963. Some universals of grammar with particular reference to the order of meaningful elements. In *Universals of Language*, edited by Joseph H. Greenberg, 73–113. Cambridge, MA: MIT Press.

Hale, Mark. 1988. Old Persian word order. *Indo-Iranian Journal* 31(1): 27–40.

Haspelmath, Martin, and Uri Tadmor (eds.). 2009a. *World Loanword Database*. Leipzig: Max Planck Institute for Evolutionary Anthropology, 1516 entries. http://wold.livingsources.org/vocabulary/13 (accessed March 3, 2014).

Haspelmath, Martin, and Uri Tadmor (eds.). 2009b. *Loanwords in the World's Languages: A Comparative Handbook*. Berlin: Mouton de Gruyter.

Hoffner, Harry A., and H. Craig Melchert. 2008. *A Grammar of the Hittite Language*. Languages of the Ancient Near East 1. Part 1, *Reference Grammar*. Winona Lake, IN: Eisenbrauns.

Kaloev, Boris A. 1967. *Osetiny: Istoriko-ètnografičeskoe issledovanie* [Ossetians: A historical and ethnographical study]. Moscow: Nauka (2nd edition: 1971).

Kambolov, Tamerlan T. 2006. *Očerk istorii osetinskogo jazyka* [A historical sketch of Ossetic]. Vladikavkaz: Ir.

Kambolov, Tamerlan T. 2007. *Jazykovaja situacija i jazykovaja politika v Severnoj Osetii: Istorija. Sovremennost'. Perspektivy* [Linguistic situation and language policy in North Ossetia: History. Modernity. Perspectives], 2nd edition. Vladikavkaz: Izdatel'stvo SOGU.

Kassian, Alexei, George Starostin, Anna Dybo, Vasiliy Chernov. 2010. The Swadesh wordlist. An attempt at semantic specification. *Journal of Language Relationship* 4: 46–89.

Kassian, Alexei. 2014. Lexical matches between Sumerian and Hurro-Urartian: Possible historical scenarios. *Cuneiform Digital Library Journal* 4. http://cdli.ucla.edu/pubs/cdlj/2014/cdlj2014_004.html (accessed December 22, 2015).

Kim, Ronald. 2003. On the historical phonology of Ossetic: The origin of the oblique case suffix. *Journal of the American Oriental Society* 123(1): 43–72.

Kiparsky, Paul. 1995. Indo-European origins of Germanic syntax. In *Clause Structure and Language Change*, edited by Ian Roberts and Adrian Battye, 140–167. Oxford Studies in Comparative Syntax. Oxford: Oxford University Press.

Kiss, Katalin. 2004. *The Syntax of Hungarian*. Cambridge Syntax Guides. Cambridge: Cambridge University Press.

Klimov, Georgij A. 1978. *Strukturnye obščnosti kavkazskix jazykov* [Structural similarities between Caucasian languages]. Moscow: Nauka.

Kojima, Yasuhiro. 2014. The position of *rom* and the pragmatics of subordinate clauses in Georgian. In *Advances in Kartvelian Morphology and Syntax*, edited by Nino Amiridze, Tamar Reseck, and Manana Topadze, 141–153. Bochum: Universitätsverlag Brockmeyer.

Kortlandt, Frederik H. H. 2003. *Armeniaca: Comparative notes*. Ann Arbor, MI: Caravan.

Kozlov, Alexey A., Anton V. Kukhto, Maria Ju. Privizentseva. 2016. O real'nosti semantičeskogo polja: leksiko-tipologičeskij podxod [On the reality of a semantic field: A lexical-typological approach]. *Acta Linguistica Petropolitana* 12(1): 522–533.

Kullanda, Sergej V. 2011. Uroki skifskogo [Lessons of Scythian]. *Voprosy jazykovogo rodstva* 5: 48–68.

Kullanda, Sergej V. 2016. *Skify: jazyk i ètnogenez* [The Scythians: Language and ethnic origins]. Moscow: Russkij fond sodejstvija obrazovaniju i nauke.

Kuznecov, Vladimir A. 1968. Novye dannye o Zelenčukskoj nadpisi X veka [New data on the 10th century Zelenchuk inscription]. *Izvestija Severo-Osetinskogo naučno-issledovatel'skogo instituta. Jazykoznanie* 27: 193–199.

Lubotsky, Alexander. 2015. *Alanic Marginal Notes in a Greek Liturgical Manuscript*. Vienna: Verlag der Österreichischen Akademie der Wissenschaften.

Miller, Vsevolod Th. 1887. *Osetinskie ètjudy* [Ossetic studies]. Part 3: *Izslědovanija* [Investigations]. [Učenyja zapiski Imperatorskago Moskovskago universiteta. Otděl″ istoriko-filologičeskìj 8]. Moscow: Tipografija V. G. Potapova.

Miller, Vsevolod Th. 1893. Drevneosetinskij pamjatnik iz Kubanskoj oblasti [An Old Ossetic monument from Kuban oblast]. *Materialy po arxeologii Kavkaza* 3: 103–118.

Moravcsik, Gyula. 1928–1929. Barbarische Sprachreste in der Theogonie des Johannes Tzetzes. *Byzantinisch-neugriechische Jahrbücher* 7: 352–365.

Németh, Gyula. 1959. *Eine Wörterliste der Jassen, der ungarländischen Alanen* [Abhandlungen der Deutschen Akademie der Wissenschaften zu Berlin. Klasse für Sprachen, Literatur und Kunst. Jahrgang 1958. Nr. 4]. Berlin: Akademie-Verlag.

Nichols, Johanna. 2004. *Ingush-English and English-Ingush dictionary*. London: Routledge-Curzon.

Nichols, Johanna. 2011. *Ingush Grammar*. Berkeley; Los Angeles; London: University of California Press.

Nikolayev, Sergei L., and Sergei A. Starostin. 1994. *A North Caucasian Etymological Dictionary*. Moscow: Asterisk. An updated version is available as a Starling database at: http://starling.rinet.ru/cgi-bin/response.cgi?basename=\data\cauc\caucet (accessed August 18, 2015).

Novosel'cev, Anatolij P. (ed.). 1987. *Istorija Severo-Osetinskoj ASSR* [The history of the North Ossetian Autonomous Soviet Socialist Republic], Vol. 1. Ordžonikidze: Ir.

Ross, Malcolm. 2001. Contact-induced change in Oceanic languages in North-West Melanesia. In *Areal Diffusion and Genetic Inheritance: Problems in Comparative Linguistics*, edited by Alexandra Y. Aikhenvald and R. M. W. Dixon, 134–166. Oxford: Oxford University Press.

Ryzhova, Daria, Alexey Kozlov, and Maria Privizentseva. 2013. Qualities of size: Towards a typology. Presentation at the 10th *Biennial Conference of the Association of Linguistic Typology*. Abstract: https://www.eva.mpg.de/lingua/conference/2013_ALT10/pdf/abstracts/Ryzhova_Kozlov_Privizentseva_130.pdf (accessed February 19, 2016).

Šanidze, Akakij. [= Šaniʒe, Ak'ak'i] 1942. Izmenenie sistemy vyraženija glagol'noj kategorii vida v gruzinskom i ego posledstvija [The change in the system of verbal aspect of Georgian and its consequences]. *Soobščenija Akademii nauk Gruzinskoj SSR* 3(9): 953–958.

Šaniʒe, Ak'ak'i. 1973. *Kartuli enis gramat'ik'is sapuʒvlebi* [Fundamentals of the grammar of the Georgian language]. Tbilisi: Universit'et'i.

Seegmiller, Steve. 1996. *Karachay*. Berlin: LINCOM EUROPA.

Sideltsev, Andrej. 2015. Hittite clause architecture. *Revue d'assyriologie et d'archéologie orientale* 109: 79–112.

Sims-Williams, Nicholas. 1979. On the plural and dual in Sogdian. *Bulletin of the School of Oriental and African Studies, University of London* 42(2): 337–346.

Slocum, Poppy, and Alice C. Harris. 'Clitics' and historical change in Georgian. Manuscript. https://linguistics.stonybrook.edu/sites/default/files/uploads/u26/publications/Postpositions%20in%20Georgian.pdf (accessed January 6, 2016).

Sokolova, Valentina S. 1953. *Očerki po fonetike iranskix jazykov* [Studies in the phonology of Iranian languages]. Vol. 2: *Osetinskij, jagnobskij i pamirskie jazyki* [Ossetic, Yaghnobi and Pamir languages]. Moscow; Leningrad: Izdatel'stvo AN SSSR.

Tadmor, Uri. 2009. Loanwords in the world's languages: Findings and results. In *Loanwords in the World's Languages: A Comparative Handbook*, edited by M. Haspelmath and U. Tadmor, 55–75. Berlin: Mouton de Gruyter.

Tedeevi, Olya. 1983. *Narḳvevebi Osur-Kartuli enobrivi urtiertobidan* [Studies on Ossetic-Georgian linguistic relations]. Tbilisi: Mecniereba. In Georgian.

Testelec, Yakov G. 1998. Word order in Daghestanian languages. In *Constituent Order in the Languages of Europe*, edited by Anna Siewerska, 257–280. Empirical Approaches to Language Typology 20-1. Berlin: Mouton de Gruyter, 1998.

Thordarson, Fridrik. 1986. Ossetisch *uæxsk* / *usqæ* 'Schulter'. Lexicalische Marginalien. In *Studia grammatica Iranica: Festschrift für Helmut Humbach*, edited by Rüdiger Schmitt and Prods Oktor Skjærvø, 499–511. München: R. Kitzinger.

Thordarson, Fridrik. 1992. Caucasus II: Language Contact. In *Encyclopædia Iranica*, edited by Ehsan Yarshater, 5:1: 92–95. Costa Mesa, CA: Mazda.

Thordarson, Fridrik. 1999. Linguistic contacts between the Ossetes and the Kartvelians: A few remarks. In *Studies in Caucasian Linguistics: Selected Papers from the Eighth Caucasian Colloquium*, edited by Helma van der Berg, 279–285. Leiden: Research School of Asian, African and Amerindian Studies.

Thordarson, Fridrik. 2009. *Ossetic Grammatical Studies* (Veröffentlichungen zur Iranistik 48). Vienna: Verlag der Österreichischen Akademie der Wissenschaften.

Tomelleri, Vittorio S. 2009. The category of aspect in Georgian, Ossetic and Russian. *Faits de langues* 1: 245–272.

Trubetzkoy, Nikolaï S. 1937. Zur Vorgeschichte der ostkaukasischen Sprachen. In *Mélanges de linguistique et de philologie offerts à Jacq. van Ginneken*, edited by Jan Wils, 171–178. Paris: Klincksieck.

Turčaninov, Georgij F. 1990. *Drevnie i srednevekovye pamjatniki osetinskogo pis'ma i jazyka.* Ordžonikidze: Ir.

Vogt, Hans. 1944. Le système de cas en ossète. *Acta Linguistica Hafniensia* 4: 17–41.

Vogt, Hans. 1971. *Grammaire de la langue géorgienne.* Oslo: Universitetsforlaget.

Vogt, Hans. 1974. L'ordre des mots en géorgien moderne. *Bedi Kartlisa* 32: 48–56.

Volkova, Natalija G. 1973. *Ètnonimy i plemennye nazvanija Severnogo Kavkaza* [Ethnic and tribal names of the North Caucasus]. Moscow: Nauka.

CHAPTER 22

....

NORTHEASTERN NEO-ARAMAIC AND LANGUAGE CONTACT

....

ELEANOR COGHILL

22.1 INTRODUCTION

....

NORTHEASTERN Neo-Aramaic is one of the modern branches of the Aramaic language family, which in turn belongs to the Semitic branch of Afro-Asiatic. The 3,000-year written history of Aramaic allows us to trace historical developments with more certainty than in most language families. This chapter will focus on the largest branch of modern Aramaic, Northeastern Neo-Aramaic (NENA), dialects of which are—or were—spoken by communities of Jews and Christians in a contiguous region in the borderlands of northern Iraq, southeastern Turkey, northwestern Iran, and northeastern Syria. Many of these communities were uprooted in the twentieth century, with some migrating within the region and others leaving for countries such as Israel, Sweden, Germany, the United States, Australia, and Britain. The Iraq war of 2003 and the subsequent instability, culminating in the conquest by ISIS (the Islamic State of Iraq and Syria) of Christian Aramaic-speaking villages in Iraq and Syria in 2014–2015, have led to further displacement. As a result, the dialects have become highly endangered.

The 'dialects' of NENA are highly diverse, with a very low degree of mutual comprehensibility in some cases. They are also diverse with regard to the degree and effects of language contact. Influence can be identified from several regional languages: most of all, Kurmanji and Sorani Kurdish (Iranian languages), but also Arabic (Semitic), both standard and vernacular, Iranian Azeri, and Turkish (both Turkic) and Persian (Iranian).[1] More recently, through missionaries and then colonial rulers, there has been

---

[1] At an earlier stage, Aramaic was in contact with Akkadian and Old Persian, and the influences from these live on in the modern dialects (for Akkadian, see Krotkoff 1985: 124–127; Khan 2008a: 1035), but will not form the focus here.

contact with European languages, predominantly English and French. In the diaspora the language has come under the influence of the languages of the new homelands, such as English, German, Swedish, and Modern Hebrew. Such influence deserves a study in itself and will not be covered here. The contact scenario for NENA is complicated somewhat by the fact that contact has taken place over the long term, in the case of Iranian languages going back thousands of years: thus it can sometimes be difficult to establish in which periods the influences first took root. Textual evidence can help here, as we have good records of earlier Aramaic varieties. In other cases, contact features are easy to date (English loanwords would most likely date to the British occupation of Iraq or later; Akkadian loanwords are clearly very ancient—and are often attested in earlier stages of Aramaic). Another complication is that some features, particularly loanwords, have been borrowed indirectly, via another language.

The current chapter deals with how NENA has been affected by language contact. Contact influence from Neo-Aramaic on the neighboring languages is much less apparent, although the Arabic vernaculars of Iraq show some similarities to Aramaic that could be due to the language shift from Aramaic (Aramaic was once far more widespread), for example differential object marking (Coghill 2014: 360–361). The primary contact language, Kurdish, has borrowed very little from NENA, by comparison with what NENA has borrowed from Kurdish. Some Neo-Aramaic borrowings can, however, be found in the area of the lexicon (Chyet 1997).

Contact influence on NENA seems to have arisen mainly through long-term bi- and multilingualism, rather than through language shift (i.e., speakers of other languages shifting to speaking Aramaic; see Thomason 2001: 74–76).[2] It cannot, however, be ruled out that some of the ancestors of modern-day Neo-Aramaic speakers spoke, for instance, Iranian languages (see Chyet 1995: 223), though it is perhaps less likely where it would have involved conversion from Islam.

22.2 INTERNAL CLASSIFICATION OF NENA

An internal genetic classification of NENA is not yet available: in fact, it is not certain that it is possible, there being to a large extent a dialect continuum (Kim 2008). The dialects will be grouped here by the religion of the speakers (Jewish or Christian), as these communities consistently spoke distinct dialects, even when in the same geographic location.

---

[2] If we take into consideration the ancient period, however, a language shift took place from Akkadian to Aramaic in the area where NENA is now spoken.

22.2.1 Jewish Dialects

The documented Jewish (J.) dialects are relatively clearly distinguishable on linguistic grounds, which also run along geographical lines. Mutzafi (2008b) distinguishes three groups. The first, **Lishana Deni** (lit. 'Our language'), comprises closely related dialects spoken mainly in northwestern Iraq (Sabar 2002), including the Jewish dialect of Zakho (Cohen 2012), Amadiya (Hoberman 1989; Greenblatt 2011), Betanure (Mutzafi 2008a), Challa (Fassberg 2010), Gzira/Cizre (Nakano 1973), and the dialect of the seventeenth-century manuscripts from Nerwa (Sabar 1976). The **Central Zab** group includes the Barzani dialect cluster (Mutzafi 2002). The **Trans-Zab** dialect group is more diverse. The northern branch comprises the Jewish dialects of Iranian **Azerbaijan** (Garbell 1965a), notably J. (Jewish) Urmi(a) (Khan 2008b). The southern branch comprises the **Southeastern (SE) Trans-Zab** dialects, of which the dialects of Sulemaniyya-Ḥalabja (Khan 2004) and Sanandaj (Khan 2009) are extensively documented. Between these two extremes we find the **Western Trans-Zab** dialects, such as Arbel (Khan 1999; the city is also known as Erbil or Hawler), Dobe, Ruwanduz, Rustaqa (Khan 2002b), and J. Koy Sanjaq (Mutzafi 2004a).

22.2.2 Christian Dialects

The Christian (C.) dialects are very diverse and have not yet been organized into genetic subgroups, if indeed this is possible. The geographical name given to each dialect or dialect group represents the situation prior to 1915, when most of the communities in Turkey were uprooted. Despite this and later upheavals, many dialects continued to be spoken and passed on. On the other hand, they have certainly been influenced by the dialects they have since come into contact with, and in some cases koines have developed.

On the outer northwestern fringe of NENA in Turkey, we find the dialects of **Hertevin** (Jastrow 1988), **Bohtan** (Fox 2009), and the **Cudi** dialects, including Bēṣpən (Sinha 2000) and Gaznax (Gutman 2015). Close by, in Iraq, we find the dialects of the **Zakho** region, including C. (Christian) Zakho itself and Peshabur (Coghill 2013). Near the border with Turkey is the dialect of **Barwar** (Khan 2008a) and the **Ṣapna** dialects, such as Aradhin (Krotkoff 1982). Further south, the **Nineveh Plain** dialects include Alqosh (Coghill 2004, 2005), Telkepe (Sabar 1978b, 1993; Coghill 2010, 2014, 2015) and Qaraqosh (Khan 2002a). To the east are the ʿ**Aqra** dialects, spoken in ʿAqra (Kurd. Akre) and neighboring villages. South and east are ʿ**Ankawa** (Borghero 2012, 2015), **C. Koy Sanjaq** (Mutzafi 2004b), and, in Iran, **C. Sanandaj** (*Senaya*) (Panoussi 1990; Heinrichs 2002).

In the Turkish **Hakkari** province there were many diverse dialects, too many to mention here. Grammars of individual dialects include Fox (1997) for Jilu and Borghero (2005) for Ashitha. Several of the Assyrian tribes of this province settled in

MAP 22.1 Map of Northeastern Neo-Aramaic dialects

NE Syria. Their dialects have been documented by Talay (2008). In Iranian Azerbaijan are the **C. Urmia** dialects, including Sardarid (Younansardaroud 2001) and Tazakand.

22.3 NOTES ON THE STRUCTURE OF NORTHEASTERN NEO-ARAMAIC

NENA lacks a canonical case system, although prepositions or particles sometimes play the role that case does in other languages (e.g., object or genitive marking). The dialects have prepositions rather than postpositions (with rare exceptions, due to language contact). The main genitive constructions have the dependent following the head, for example Telkepe *beθ-əd malkʋ* [house-CSTR king] 'the king's house.' The preceding typology was also valid for Late Aramaic (the last documented state of the language before Neo-Aramaic), even if the precise forms and structures have changed.

Like other Semitic languages, NENA has in its verbal morphology, and to a lesser extent in its nominal morphology, a non-concatenative root-and-pattern system, complemented by affixes. Thus, with the triradical root *šql*, we get such forms as *k-šāqəl* 'he takes,' *šqəl-lə* 'he took,' *šqālʋ* 'taking,' *šaqālʋ* 'taker,' *šqilʋ* 'taken,' and so on (Telkepe). When lexemes are borrowed, the questions arise as to what extent they are adapted to the native morphology and to what extent they have altered the morphological typology. These questions are of particular relevance to non-Semitic borrowings, such as those from Kurdish and Turkish, but also apply to borrowings from other Semitic languages, namely Arabic and Hebrew. These languages operate on the same general principles, but the precise morphology is different.

22.4 EXTENT OF BI- AND MULTILINGUALISM

Table 22.1 shows the languages that speakers of NENA dialects could have come into contact with, ordered according to region. Here the label Kurmanji encompasses the

Table 22.1 Contact Languages in the Neo-Aramaic-Speaking Region

Region	Christian NENA Dialects[a]	Jewish NENA Dialects	Local Vernaculars	Modern State Language
Şırnak, Siirt provinces, Turkey	Hertevin, Bohtan, Cudi dialects (Bēṣpən, Gaznax)	Lishana Deni (Gzira/ Cizre)	Kurmanji, Qəltu Arabic	Turkish
Hakkari province, Turkey	Hakkari dialects (Jilu, Ashitha)	Lishana Deni (Challa)	Kurmanji	Turkish
Zakho region, Iraq	C. Zakho, Peshabur	Lishana Deni (J. Zakho)	Kurmanji	Arabic
Dohuk-Amadiya region, Iraq	Barwar, Ṣapna dialects (Aradhin)	Lishana Deni (Amadiya, Betanure, Nerwa)	Kurmanji, Turkman[b]	Arabic
Plain north and east of Mosul, Iraq	Niniveh Plain dialects (Alqosh, Telkepe, Qaraqosh)	–	Kurmanji, Qəltu Arabic, Turkman	Arabic
Akre-Barzan region, Iraq	'Aqra dialects	Central Zab (Barzani)	Kurmanji, Jewish Qəltu Arabic	Arabic
NNE Iraq (Erbil/ Hawler/Arbel, Rewandiz region)	'Ankawa, C. Koy Sanjaq	Western Trans-Zab (Arbel, J. Koy Sanjaq)	Sorani, Jewish Qəltu Arabic, Turkman	Arabic
NE Iraq, NW Iran	C. Sulemaniyya, C. Sanandaj/Senaya	SE Trans-Zab (J. Sulemaniyya, J. Sanandaj)	Sorani, Turkman	Arabic; Persian
Iranian Azerbaijan	C. Urmia dialects	J. Azerbaijani (J. Urmi)	Azeri, Kurmanji, Sorani, Armenian	Persian

Notes: [a] The NENA varieties listed in the table are not exhaustive; [b] For the present-day distribution of Turkman dialects in Iraq, see Bulut (2007: 168).

Bahdini/Bahdinani dialects of northern Iraq, as well as the Kurmanji Kurdish dialects of Turkey.[3]

As can be seen, Kurdish dialects are spoken throughout the region, in particular the Kurmanji and Sorani varieties. Kurdish did not have any official status in the region until the 1990s, when Iraqi Kurdistan gained de facto autonomy within Iraq.

Iranian Azeri is a Turkic vernacular spoken in Iranian Azerbaijan, which has no official status. It is different from the Standard Azeri of Azerbaijan, and comprises many dialects. Foy (1903) and (1904) remain the most detailed sources on Iranian Azeri. Related Turkic dialects ("Turkman") are spoken in northern Iraq by the Turkman communities. Ottoman Turkish had an official status in the Ottoman Empire (i.e., in Turkey and Iraq but not Iran) until the empire's demise in 1918. After 1918, modern Turkish (reformed under Ataturk) became the official language of Turkey, while Arabic became the official language of Iraq.

Within the NENA-speaking area, Arabic is or was spoken as a vernacular only in pockets. Within Turkey these are found in Cizre, Siirt, and many villages around them (Jastrow 1978: 1–23). In Iraqi Kurdistan, Arabic was spoken by Jews in certain towns, such as ʿAqra/Akre and Erbil/Arbel/Hawler (Jastrow 1990). The Christian NENA-speaking villages of the Nineveh Plain border on the Arabic-speaking part of Iraq, beginning with the city of Mosul. The Arabic dialects spoken in or near the NENA area are all of the Mesopotamian 'Qəltu' type (see Jastrow 1978).

The actual occurrence of contact between speakers of the NENA dialects and speakers of these other languages is harder to establish. Proximity does not necessarily lead to actual regular interaction, let alone fluency in the other language. Sociological relationships between communities, as well as the relative prestige or political dominance of groups, and hence their languages, play an important role. Except in Iranian Azerbaijan, Kurds have long been the majority ethnic group in the region. Furthermore, Kurdish *aghas* wielded power in the region.

As for actual evidence of speakers knowing these languages, for the period before the twentieth century, we have brief statements from missionaries who resided in the region. Grant (1841: 47) noted that "many of the Nestorians [= Christians of the Church of the East] speak the Koordish language." Stoddard (1855: 3) stated, "In Persia, most of the Nestorians are indeed able to speak fluently the rude Tatar (Turkish) dialect [= Azeri] used by the Mohammedans of this province [= Iranian Azerbaijan], and those of the mountains are equally familiar with the language of the Koords."

For evidence of multilingualism in the twentieth century, we turn to grammatical descriptions of NENA dialects. Not all give information on the competence of the dialect speakers in other languages, but those that do indicate the following: that Jews and Christians across the Kurdish-speaking areas usually spoke the local Kurdish

---

[3] Note that the linguistic divide between Kurmanji and Sorani is not abrupt. Mackenzie (1961: 225), writing of the dialects of Iraq, gives a table of characteristics distinguishing the Sorani ("Group I") and Kurmanji ("Group II") dialects, which shows that the dialects of Arbil, Rewandiz, and Sūrči exhibit features typical of both groups.

dialect. Jews might additionally come into contact with vernacular Arabic, through commercial contacts. Mutzafi (2004a: 6) reports such contacts involving the Jewish men of Koy Sanjaq and the Arabic-speaking Jews of Kurdistan. In Iranian Azerbaijan, all the Jews spoke Azeri; Kurdish, on the other hand, seems to have been restricted to the southern areas (Garbell 1965a: 15; 1965b: 159).

Competence in the state languages, Standard Arabic, Turkish, and Persian, where these were not local vernaculars, was patchier and seems to be a relatively new phenomenon. From around the middle of the twentieth century, education in the state languages of Iraq, Syria, Iran, and Turkey (Arabic, Persian, and Turkish) became common, so that competence of NENA speakers in these languages has increased significantly.

For the Jews, until their emigration to Israel, Hebrew was important as the language of religion, but was not a language of everyday life. Mutzafi (2004a: 4) reports that Jewish men in Koy Sanjaq "were generally quite learned in Jewish religious matters and were literate in Hebrew."

22.5 OVERVIEW OF CONTACT INFLUENCES

By far the greatest amount of influence on NENA dialects comes from varieties of Kurdish. This is most evident in the Jewish dialects, and among the Jewish dialects it is more pervasive the farther east one goes: thus the Jewish dialect of Sanandaj shows strong influence in structure as well as lexicon and morphology. Most Christian dialects show less profound influence from Kurdish (although considerable lexical and some morphological borrowings), but a few of the more easterly dialects exhibit quite extensive contact influence, approaching that found in the Jewish dialects. For instance, the most easterly Christian dialect, that of C. Sanandaj (Senaya) shows SOV word order, under influence of (Sorani) Kurdish (see section 22.9).

Dialects in the Urmi(a) region of Iranian Azerbaijan, both Christian and Jewish, show considerable influence from Azeri Turkic. Dialects spoken in Iran, both in Iranian Azerbaijan and Kurdistan, show some lexical influence from the state language, Persian.

Arabic influence in NENA is considerable in the realm of the lexicon, but this has very often occurred via other contact languages, rather than directly. (All the contact languages show great influence from Arabic, at least in the lexicon.) Direct lexical borrowing and morphological and structural borrowing from Arabic are less common: they are, however, well attested in the Christian dialects of the Nineveh Plain, as well as some Jewish Lishana Deni dialects.

It is difficult to establish with any certainty which contact influences entered the dialects when. The earliest Christian and Jewish NENA texts (from the sixteenth and seventeenth centuries, some possibly composed earlier) already show considerable contact influence from Kurdish and Arabic. The extent of Arabic influence in the early Jewish Nerwa Texts (Sabar 1984) is quite surprising. The area in which these texts originate lies deep in Kurdistan, relatively far from the main Arabic-speaking part of

Iraq. It could be, however, that the Aramaic-speaking Jews were in close contact with those of their co-religionists who spoke Arabic as their mother tongue. Some contact influence in the NENA dialects is clearly of recent date, such as loanwords from English, which were probably borrowed during the British rule of Iraq (in the 1920s), or in the late twentieth century, due to globalization.

There are many features of the dialects that may be identified as resulting from contact, some of which seem well justified, while others are less certain. Many of these have been covered in existing literature, in particular Garbell (1965b), Sabar (1984), Pennacchietti (1988), Chyet (1995), Khan (2007b), and Kapeliuk (1996, 2002b, 2011).[4] It is not possible to cover all of them here: instead, a selection of those that are well established will be presented. They are divided into matter and pattern borrowings (see Sakel 2007). Under the former come lexicon, phonology, and morphology (see sections 22.6–22.8) and under the latter syntax and calqued idioms, which will be dealt with only briefly in section 22.9, and more comprehensively in a separate article. The two types of borrowing cannot be rigidly separated, however, as they often occur in conjunction.

22.6 Lexicon

All NENA dialects have adopted a large number of loanwords. Many of these are common to several languages of the region, especially words specific to local culture or to technologies.[5] While the ultimate source can usually be identified, it can sometimes

---

[4] Also Noorlander (2014), published after the submission of this chapter, which focuses on Kurdish influence on NENA.

[5] The main lexical sources used here for the less well-described contact languages are: for Kurmanji, Chyet (2003), for Sorani, Qazzaz (2000), for Iraqi Arabic, Woodhead and Beene (1967) and Clarity, Stowasser, and Wolfe (1964). The latter two are in fact for Baghdadi Arabic, a southern Mesopotamian "Gǝlǝt" dialect: unfortunately, a full dictionary for a Qǝltu dialect was not available. Nevertheless the two dialect groups share much lexicon and such forms will be labeled "I. Arabic." Where information was found specifically for a Qǝltu Arabic dialect, this will be labeled as such.

The transcription of NENA varies between authors in certain details: the system used by the present author follows the International Phonetic Alphabet, except for the following: (1) the use of macrons to indicate length, e.g., $\bar{a}$ for [aː] (for [eː] and [oː], however, length is not phonemic, and so these are written simply e and o); (2) ǝ = [ɪ~ə]; (3) č = [t͡ʃ], š = [ʃ], j = [d͡ʒ], ž = [ʒ], ḥ = [ħ], x = [x-χ], ġ = [ɣ-ʁ], ʾ = [ʔ], ʿ = [ʕ]; a subscript dot indicates "emphatic" (velarized/pharyngealized) pronunciation, e.g., ṭ = [tˤ]. Suprasegmental (whole-word) emphatic pronunciation may be marked with initial [+], e.g., [+]maɣara. Examples from the publications of other authors have not been adapted, so there will be small differences in transcription, e.g., /ə/ in a closed syllable written as 'i'.

The transcription system used here for Kurdish varieties generally follows the practice in Mackenzie (1961: 1), especially in the vowels, as it is similar to NENA conventions and thus aids comparison of the NENA loans with their forms in the donor language. To avoid confusion, long [eː] is transcribed with a macron: ē, as are the other long vowels (ā, ō, and ū). The consonants are transcribed as in IPA, except for š, č, ž, which have the same values as in NENA, and the following: ǰ [d͡ʒ], ḥ [ħ], ṱ [lˤ], r [ɾ] and r̄ [r]. Kurdish i is realized as [ɪ~ɨ], roughly equivalent to NENA ǝ. Kurmanji aspirated consonants are written with an acute accent, e.g., ṕ [pʰ].

Table 22.2 Proportion of Lexicon That Is Borrowed in Neo-Aramaic Varieties

	J. Sulemaniyya(Khan 2004: 443)	J. Azerbaijani(Garbell 1965b: 161–162)
Nouns	67%	69%
Adjectives	48%	24%
Verbs	15%	28% (root morphemes)
Particles	53%	54% (excluding prepositions)
		59% (prepositions)

be hard to determine the immediate donor of the loan. Nevertheless, there is sometimes evidence that can establish this. This is the case, for example, for Arabic words ending in the feminine suffix *tā' marbūṭa* (Classical Arabic *-a(t)*). The Arabic morpheme may be realized with or without the final *-t*, depending on various factors. Such Arabic words are borrowed into NENA sometimes with and sometimes without the /t/. Those with the /t/ have often been borrowed via Kurdish, in which such loans are also realized with final *-t*. Thus, for instance, J. Arbel *ḥājīta* 'tool' appears to have been borrowed from Arabic *ḥāja* 'need, necessity' via Sorani *ḥājat* 'tools'. Where singular nouns are taken from the Arabic plural form, this can also indicate Kurdish origin, for example, J. Arbel *tujār* 'merchant' (Sorani *tujār* 'merchant,' Arab. sg *tājir*, pl *tujjār*) (Khan 1999: 135). The gender in NENA can also suggest the immediate source. For instance *qalam* 'pen' in Arabic has masculine gender, but the loanword in Kurmanji may have feminine or masculine gender (Rizgar 1993: 322; Chyet 2003: 478). That *qalāma* 'pen' has feminine gender in certain NENA dialects (e.g., Alqosh, see Coghill 2004: 199) suggests that it was borrowed via Kurmanji.

For two Jewish dialects, statistics are available on the proportion of loans in different word classes (see Table 22.2). For J. Azerbaijani these statistics are also broken down between the (immediate) donor languages, whether Kurdish, Turkish, or indeterminate Kurdish/Turkish (the two languages share a great deal of lexicon). For each word class, a Kurdish origin is more commonly established than a Turkish one, although the large proportion of words that could be of either origin makes the true proportion uncertain. A predominance of Kurdish is slightly surprising, as Azeri is the majority language in the region. Perhaps this was not so in the past, or the Jews migrated from a Kurdish-dominant area.

Even in early sources of NENA, the proportion of lexemes that was borrowed was high: Sabar (1984: 208), looking at Arabic influence, found that in a typical Jewish Nerwa Text, 30% of lexemes are ultimately of Arabic origin (whether directly or via another language).

Loanwords are commonly found even in basic semantic fields, such as human body parts and family members, for example J. Sulemaniyya *pirča* 'strand of hair' (< Sor. *pirč* 'lock of woman's hair') and *da'aka* 'mother' (< Sor. *dāk* 'mother') (Khan 2004: 448–450). In these and other cases where a native word for the concept already existed, it is not obvious why the word was borrowed. Haspelmath (2009: 48–49) discusses possible motivations for such core borrowings. Prestige of the donor language may play a role, while in some cases the loanword does not precisely match the meaning of the native word. Thus in C. Alqosh *šəbbakiyə* (<Kurm.< Arab.) is used for a modern window, while the inherited lexeme *kāwə* is used for the traditional type of window.

In recent times European loanwords have entered the dialects. In some cases these seem to have entered via Arabic or Kurdish. Sabar (1990) gives many examples from the J. Zakho dialect, some of which are common in other NENA dialects: *pančar* 'puncture' (English), *lōri* 'lorry' (English), *+trambel* 'automobile,' *šamindarfmarbūṭar* 'train' (French *chemin de fer*). Sabar (1990: 57–58) finds that recent European loanwords belong to the following semantic fields: modern technology, modern culture in general, modern clothing, modern vegetables and food, and modern medicine.

22.6.1 Borrowed Nouns

Borrowed nouns may be integrated to varying extents. In many cases, the suffix -*a* is added, to conform with the majority of (masculine) nouns in NENA, for example C. Alqosh *barxa* 'lamb' (< Kurm. *barx*). There are also very many loanwords without the -*a*, for example Alqosh *mes* 'table' (< Kurm./I. Arab. *mēz* < Portugese). Loanwords sometimes bear the NENA feminine suffix -*ta/θa* (or its dialectal variants), for example Alqosh *dargušta* F 'cradle' (< Kurm. *dargūš* F). This could be simply to mark the gender explicitly as feminine, or it could be acting in its diminutive function. Feminine nouns ending with -*a* or no marking are also common, for example Alqosh *qalāma* F 'pen' (< Kurm. *qalam* F/M<Arab. *qalam* M.), *karwan* F 'caravan' (< Kurm. *kārvān* M [*sic*]/Arab. *karwan* M.). See Coghill (2004: 196–200) for further discussion. Although many Arabic nouns appear to be recent loans, some are already present in early NENA texts, such as the seventeenth-century texts in the J. Lishana Deni dialects, where they can be seen to be adapted in various ways (Sabar 1984: 205–206):

ʿāqɩl ~ ʿaqɩl	'mind, reason'	< Arab. *ʿaql* (Qəltu Arab. *ʿaqəl*)
qaṣr-a	'palace'	< Arab. *qaṣr*
qɩṣ-ta	'story'	< Arab. *qiṣṣa(t)*

Occasionally, borrowed nouns are adapted to the native root-and-pattern templates, following the selection of a root: this usually occurs when the root is also borrowed as a verb. Thus we find C. Qaraqosh *ʾəjbona* 'a will, wish' (Khan 2002a: 517), alongside the verb *ʾjb* I 'to please,' by analogy with native words on the pattern *CəCC-ona*, for example *yəqðona* 'a burn' (< *yqð* I 'to burn'). Likewise, J. Azer. *jəgra* 'anger' (*jgr* I 'to become angry') is built on the native *CəCCa* pattern (cf. *pəlga* 'half') (Garbell 1965b: 164; Khan 2008b). More often, however, loanwords are not adapted to native templates.

Borrowed nouns are quite commonly given Aramaic derivational suffixes. For instance, C. Alqosh *dəžmənūθa* 'enmity' is composed of *dəžmən* 'enemy,' borrowed from Kurm. *dižmin* 'enemy,' and the Aramaic abstract derivational suffix *-ūθa* (Coghill 2004: 247). See also Garbell (1965b: 165).

NENA dialects all have a variety of plural suffixes, the most common being perhaps *-e* (or its dialectal variant *-ə*). Loanwords, like inherited words, take a variety of native plural suffixes. In C. Alqosh, for instance, all inherited plurals are attested with loanwords, though certain suffixes are preferred or dispreferred for loanwords (Coghill 2005: 347).

22.6.2 Borrowed Adjectives

Occasionally, loan adjectives are adapted to the native root-and-pattern templates, after the selection of a consonantal root. For instance, Arabic *'azraq* 'blue' (√*zrq*) is borrowed by C. Alqosh as *zroqa* 'blue,' by analogy with certain inherited color adjectives of the form *CCoCa*, such as *smoqa* 'red.' More often, the stem of the loan adjective is borrowed more or less unchanged, e.g. Alqosh *faqira* 'poor' < Arab. *faqīr*.

Some borrowed adjectives in NENA take Aramaic inflection, for example C. Alqosh *kor-a* 'blind' (F *kor-ta*, PL *kor-ə*),[6] from Kurm. *kōr* 'blind.' Loan-adjectives of a certain group, including colors and bodily traits, behave in a special manner in some NENA dialects: they take Aramaic inflection for masculine and plural, but a special inflection *-ə* (identical to the plural ending) for the feminine. This occurs in C. Qaraqosh particularly with Arabic loan adjectives, for example *ṭarša* 'deaf' (F/PL *ṭaršə*, < Arab. M *'aṭraš*, F. *ṭaršā'*) and *zarqa* 'blue' (F/PL *zarqə*, < Arab. M *'azraq*, F *zarqā'*) (see Khan 2002a: 219). It appears to come from a dialectal reflex (*-ē*) of the Arab. *-ā'* F ending, found especially with adjectives of these semantic groups (Coghill 2004: 282). In Alqosh it has been extended to loanwords of Kurmanji origin, for example *kačal-a* 'bald' (F/PL *kačal-ə*). Other loan adjectives are inflected only for plural, not for feminine, for example C. Alqosh *brəndar* 'injured' (F *brəndar*, PL *brəndār-ə*, < Kurm. *birīndār* 'injured'). Still others are not inflected at all, for example C. Alqosh *tambal* 'lazy' (F/PL *tambal*, < Kurm. *tambal* 'lazy'). In other NENA dialects, such as J. Sulemaniyya and J. Urmi, loan adjectives that have not been adapted to Aramaic morphology are not inflected at all, or (in J. Urmi in some cases) only for number (Khan 2004: 200–201; 2008b: 181).

22.6.3 Borrowed Verbs

The borrowing of verbs is in many languages potentially more complex than the borrowing of other lexemes, due to their tendency to be morphologically complex (Matras 2009: 175). The borrowing of verbs in a Semitic language presents particular problems, due to the unusual root-and-pattern system. In Semitic languages verb

---

[6] The abbreviations F and M here are short for FSG and MSG (feminine and masculine singular). PL stands for CPL (common plural), as there is no gender distinction for adjectives in the plural.

lexemes are composed of a root (typically consisting of three—occasionally four—consonants or semi-vowels) and a derivation ('stem,' 'form,' 'binyan,' or 'theme'). For example, NENA dialects mostly have three triradical derivations (I, II, and III) and at least one quadriradical derivation (Q). A borrowed verb will usually be integrated into this system.[7] Two main strategies can be identified for the borrowing of verbs in NENA. One, common also in other Semitic languages (Wohlgemuth 2009: 173–180), is root-extraction, whereby from the phonological matter of the source verb a tri- or quadri-radical root is selected. This is usually then allocated to a verbal derivation. The other is the light verb strategy, whereby the loan verb consists of a light verb (with meanings such as *become* or *make*) and a (verbal) noun, the latter containing the main semantic content.

The root-extraction strategy is well attested across NENA dialects. It is particularly common with Arabic loan verbs: this is unsurprising, as these already have a root, which in many cases can simply be adopted as it is; for instance Arabic *ġlb* i 'to win' (*ġalaba* 'he won') is borrowed as C. Telkepe *ġlb* I 'to win.' Sometimes the root is adapted to conform to the rules of root-formation in NENA.

The root-extraction strategy is also perfectly possible with non-Semitic donor languages. In this case, typically the available consonants are extracted: very often these will be three or four in number, conforming to the NENA root-formation rules. Thus, English *to park* has been borrowed into the C. Telkepe spoken in America as *prk* II 'to park,' and *to cancel* as *knṣl* Q 'to cancel.'

The process of integration does not end with root-extraction, however. Every verb lexeme must have a derivation. Tendencies can also be identified for this: Arabic verbs are typically loaned into formally and functionally similar derivations (which are usually cognate; Coghill 2015); in some cases, however, derivational morphology itself is borrowed (see section 22.8.1).

Non-Semitic verbs do not come with a derivation. Those that are converted into triradical roots are commonly borrowed into the simplest derivation, I, or (where it exists) II. The use of II may be due to its function of deriving verbs from nominals (cf. Sabar 2002: 52).

The strategy of light verb plus noun[8] is itself a borrowing from Iranian and Turkic languages, which have a great number of such verbs. Such complex predicates are not part of the inherited structure of NENA. This strategy is particularly well attested in the Trans-Zab Jewish dialects, which have undergone intense contact with Kurdish, Turkish, and Persian. The complex predicates may be pure calques of the original lexemes, using only Aramaic lexical matter, or the noun itself may be borrowed. Example (1c) shows a pure calque:

---

[7] An exception can be found in Maltese, where a set of more recent loan verbs does not conform to the root-and-pattern system; see Hoberman and Aronoff (2003). Another exception is North-African Arabic; see Heath (1989: 104–112).

[8] See Wohlgemuth (2009: 102–113) for a survey of light verb strategies.

(1)   a. More conservative NENA (e.g. Telkepe) *gwr* I

b. Kurdish of Sulemaniyya   *šū*   *kirdin*
                                                   husband   make.INF

c. NENA of Jews of Sulemaniyya   *gora*   *'wl* I
                                                   husband   make
                                                   all: 'to marry'
                                   (own data; Qazzaz 2000: 378; Khan 2004: 141)

See Kapeliuk (2002a) for a detailed discussion of the light verb strategy in NENA, especially the Christian NENA of Iranian Azerbaijan (cf. also Younansardaroud 1999).

22.6.4 Grammatical Words and Closed Classes

NENA has freely borrowed grammatical words such as adpositions, conjunctions, and particles of various functions. Its inherited adpositions are prepositions, while both prepositions and postpositions are found in the contact languages: Arabic has prepositions, Turkish has postpositions, and Kurdish has both prepositions and circumpositions (i.e., preposition + postposition working in conjunction). The adpositions that have been borrowed by NENA dialects are almost exclusively prepositions (in both NENA and the donor language), suggesting that loans have been selected in harmony with the language's existing structure.[9] Some examples are as follows:

C. Alqosh: *ṣob* 'toward, near' (< Arab. *ṣawba* 'toward', cf. I. Arab. *ṣoob* 'direction'), *baḥás* 'about, concerning' (< Kurm. *baḥs* 'discussion (about)' < Arab. *baḥθ*),[10] *m-badal* 'instead of' (< I. Arab. *badaal*) (Coghill 2004: 300)

J. Arbel *gal* 'with' (< Sor. *lagał* 'with'), *ḍidd* 'against' (< Arab. *ḍidd* 'against') (Khan 1999: 188)

---

[9] Structural congruence or compatibility may be a factor in motivating borrowings (Haig 2001: 210–214), though it is not a prerequisite (Thomason and Kaufman 1988: 14–20). See also Moravcsik's (1978: 112) hypothesis that a lexical item of the 'grammatical' type (including adpositions) will not be borrowed unless "the rule that determines its linear order with respect to its head" is also borrowed, i.e., that a preposition will be borrowed as a preposition and an adposition as an adposition. A possible counterexample from NENA is the Jewish Azerbaijani preposition *qabaġ* 'before' (Garbell 1965b: 175), borrowed from Azeri, where it is a post-position. In both languages, however, the word is also a noun (meaning 'cover, lid'), and only functions as an adposition by means of a genitive construction. It is therefore not the clearest example of a borrowed adposition changing position. Otherwise, NENA appears to offer no counterexamples to these hypotheses.

[10] A reviewer suggested Arabic *bi-xuṣūṣ* 'concerning' as a preferable etymology. Direct Arabic borrowings, however, being more recent, tend to show less adaptation, and there is no reason to expect such shifts as *x>ḥ* or *ṣ>s*. While it may seem rather a jump from 'discussion' to 'concerning,' it is a smaller gap when one considers the Kurmanji compound verb *baḥs kirin* 'to discuss' (lit. 'to do discussion'). Any object of the compound verb will be in a genitive construction with *baḥs* (Thackston 2006: 35–37), making a reanalysis of *baḥs* as a preposition somewhat more plausible. The reanalysis may, however, have taken place in NENA (there is no entry for the word as a preposition in Chyet's 2003 dictionary of Kurmanji, only as an independent noun and as the nominal part of the

C. Bohtan has, however, developed a postposition of native origin -*ləl* (see Fox 2007: 74–75; 2009: 101). It may also occur with a preposition (e.g., *b*- 'in'), that is, as a circumposition. This seems be a pattern borrowing from Kurmanji. As for loan prepositions, they are not a new phenomenon, but are already attested in the J. Nerwa texts (Sabar 1984: 208).

Many NENA dialects, both Christian and Jewish, have borrowed a Kurdish enclitic meaning approximately 'also, even.' This has different forms in the different Kurdish dialects: *(ī)š* in Sorani and some Kurmanji, and *žī* in other Kurmanji dialects (Mackenzie 1961: 128–129, 201–202). As one might expect, the forms in NENA reflect this geographical distribution, although not precisely.

The Azeri adverbial participle marker -*ikän* '(while) being' has been borrowed into J. Azerbaijani NENA (Garbell 1965b: 167).

There are several borrowed particles functioning as adverbs, nominal modifiers, conjunctions, and so on, which are attested in many different dialects. Some of the most frequent include the following (found, e.g., in C. Barwar [see Khan 2008a: 446] and C. Alqosh [see Coghill 2004: 301–317]):

ham 'also' (e.g., C. Alqosh *hám=āna* 'I too') < Pers. *ham* 'also'/Sor. *ham* 'again; both, also'

ču ~ *hič* 'no, (not) any' (e.g., C. Alqosh *čú=dukθa* 'nowhere') < Kurm. *ču* ~ *tu*, Turk./Sor./Pers. *hič/hīč* 'no, any'

bəš 'more' (e.g. C. Alqosh *bə́š='atira* 'richer') < Pers. *biš* 'more'

bas 'only; but' < I. Arab. *bass* 'but; only' (see also Kurm. *bas* 'enough; but' < Arab.)

har 'just, still, always, again' < Kurm. *har* 'each, every; always' or Sor. *har* 'as soon as; only; to keep on; each, every' (see also Pers. and Turk. *har* 'each, every')

həš 'still, yet' < Kurm. *hē* ~ *hēž* 'still, yet' (see also Sor. *hēštā* 'still, yet')

yan 'or' < Kurm. *yān* 'or'

Certain verbal particles have been borrowed from Kurdish dialects. In SE Trans-Zab dialects, a particle expressing deontic modality has been borrowed from Sorani, namely *ba* (Khan 2004: 287; 2009: 83), from Sorani *bā* (Mackenzie 1961: 134).

22.7 PHONOLOGY

The phonology of NENA dialects has been significantly affected by contact influence. This is mostly through the acquisition of new phonemes (matter borrowings), but also through the borrowing of rules (pattern borrowings).

---

compound verb). According to Maclean's (1901: 26) dictionary of the Christian NENA dialects, the word functioned both as a noun, meaning 'report, fame' and, in a genitive construction, as a preposition, with optional *l-* 'on, about.' (It also functions as a noun in Lishana Deni; see Sabar 2002: 107). This is surely the missing link between noun and preposition. Note that Sabar (2002: 107), Maclean (1901: 26) and Mutzafi (2008a: 336) also derive this preposition ultimately from Arabic *baḥθ*.

22.7.1 New Phonemes

NENA dialects have gained new phonemes through language contact. These phonemes have entered the dialects via loanwords that were not fully adapted to Aramaic phonology. Some are restricted to loanwords, while others occur now also in native words, through internal processes such as assimilation. The following C. Alqosh phonemes can be attributed mainly to borrowing (Coghill 2004: 11–25). They are typical of many NENA dialects:

> From Kurdish: /v/, /ž/ [ʒ],
> From Arabic: /ḍ/ [dˤ], /ḏ̣/ [ðˤ], /f/,
> From Kurdish and Iraqi Arabic: /č/ [tʃ], /j/ [dʒ]
> From Classical Syriac and Arabic: /ʿ/ [ʕ], /ḥ/ [ħ], /ġ/ [ɣ-ʁ]

For comparison, J. Azerbaijani has gained the following phonemes through loanwords, according to Garbell (1965b: 161): /č/, /j/, /ž/. To these should be added /ġ/ and /f/, for example ⁺maγara 'cave' and kef 'well-being' (Garbell 1965a: 24, both ultimately < Arab.).

22.7.2 Sound Shifts

Khan (2007b: 198–200) presents some sound shifts in J. Sulemaniyya that find parallels in the Kurdish dialects of the region, such as the sound shift from */θ/ and */ð/ to /l/.

22.7.3 Synchronic Sound Alternations

Some NENA dialects, such as C. Alqosh (Coghill 2004: 27), exhibit final devoicing of voiced consonants. The voicing is realized when a suffix is added. There is also a strong tendency to devoicing in Kurdish (Mackenzie 1961: 49) and Qǝltu Arabic (Jastrow 1978: 98).

22.7.4 Stress Patterns

Most NENA dialects have predominantly penultimate word stress. The Jewish Trans-Zab dialects, however, have mostly word-final stress (see, e.g., Khan 1999: 70–74; Mutzafi 2008b: 415). This appears to be through influence from Kurdish and Turk-ish/Azeri, which also have predominantly word-final stress. Khan (2007b: 200) shows further that exceptions to word-final stress tend to be in the same contexts in J. Sulemaniyya NENA as in Sulemaniyya Sorani, for example the retracted stress found in vocatives and past tense verbs.

22.8 MORPHOLOGY

Both derivational and grammatical morphology has been borrowed into NENA dialects.

22.8.1 Derivational Morphology

A few nominal derivational affixes have been borrowed by NENA dialects. The Kurmanji diminutive suffix -*ik* (Mackenzie 1961: 145) has been borrowed into various NENA dialects, for example in C. Peshabur as -*əkk*-: *bays-a* 'house,' *bays-əkk-a* 'little house' (Coghill 2013: 40).

In southern J. Azerbaijani dialects, ordinal numbers are derived from the cardinals by means of the suffix -*min*, which is borrowed from Sorani -*(a)mīn*, for example *tre-min* 'second' (Garbell 1965b: 166); compare Sorani *ḥaftā-mīn* 'seventieth' (Mackenzie 1961: 72). In J. Urmi this is extended to -*mənji*, through the addition of the Turkish/Azeri ordinal marker -*nci*/-*nǰi* [ndʒi], for example *tre-mənji* (Khan 2008b: 186).

The Sorani verbal suffix -*awa* (Mackenzie 1961: 120–121) has been borrowed into the SE Trans-Zab dialects, J. Sulemaniyya and J. Sanandaj, as -*awa* and -*o*, respectively (Khan 2004: 329–331; 2007b: 206; 2009: 12, 313–317). It is also found in J. Barzani as -*hawa* (Mutzafi 2002: 64):

(2) a. J. Sulemaniyya
     híye-wa
     came.ABS.3MS-PRT
     'He came back.'   (Khan 2004: 329)

     b. Sorani
     gáyšt-m-awa
     arrived-ABS.1SG-PRT
     'I arrived back.'   (McCarus 1958: 34)

In NENA, as in Sorani, this typically expresses a sense of returning, repetition, or completion, but is also used in verbal idioms, with unpredictable meaning. It is frequently used with inherited Aramaic verbal lexemes.

NENA dialects of the Nineveh Plain and elsewhere have partially borrowed Arabic verbal derivations along with borrowed verb lexemes. The derivations, however, have not been extended to inherited roots, or used productively, unlike some Arabic derivations in Western Neo-Aramaic (see Coghill 2015 for full details).

22.8.2 Grammatical Morphology

In the Christian dialects of Iraq, it is common to use Arabic words with their original plural morphology, including the non-concatenative 'broken plurals.' Some dialects, such as C. Alqosh and C. Qaraqosh, have gone a step further and have borrowed one of the Arabic plural suffixes, namely -*ât* (normally used for feminine nouns). This was presumably borrowed via loanwords, rather than directly. It has now been formally integrated, in that it has lost its stress (both dialects have penultimate stress), and as a result the vowel has been shortened, resulting in *-at*, for example *maḥắllə* 'town quarter,' PL *maḥállat* (< Arab.). Its distribution has also been widened, so that it is not restricted to the Arabic words with which it was borrowed, but has been extended to loanwords from other languages and to a few inherited lexemes (Coghill 2005: 344). The *-at* plural suffix is also found in J. Lishana Deni dialects, with Arabic, Kurdish, European, and inherited lexemes (Sabar 1990: 57; 2002: 44–45).

Most NENA dialects do not consistently mark definiteness on a noun, although this function may be expressed by demonstratives (see Cohen 2012: 20–30), or (in the case of objects) by indexing on the verb (Coghill 2014). Some eastern Jewish dialects, including Arbel, Koy Sanjaq, and SE Trans-Zab dialects, have borrowed a suffix marking definiteness from Sorani, realized in NENA as *-ăke*, for example J. Sulemaniyya *baruxa* 'friend,' *barux-ăke* 'the friend' (Khan 2007b: 201–202).

Another grammatical morpheme that has been borrowed is the Iranian Ezafe marker *-ē/-ī*, which is used in genitive constructions. As this is associated with the borrowing of the Ezafe pattern as a whole, it is treated along with pattern borrowings, in section 22.9.

22.9 SYNTACTIC AND OTHER PATTERN BORROWINGS

For reasons of space, syntactic borrowings cannot be treated in any detail. The following are some examples:

i. **Ergativity**: Tense-conditioned ergativity (restricted to the past perfective) developed in Eastern Aramaic and to some extent is still found in the SE Trans-Zab dialects, albeit only in verbal inflection (see, e.g., Khan 2007a; Coghill 2016). Tense-conditioned ergativity developed in a similar manner in Iranian languages (see Haig 2008). That ergative alignment only developed in those Aramaic dialects which were most in contact with Iranian, namely in Eastern Aramaic, suggests that it emerged under Iranian influence (see, e.g., Kutscher 1969).

ii. **Word order**: Jewish Trans-Zab dialects, as well as C. Sanandaj, exhibit SOV as the most common word order of a clause, unlike most other NENA dialects, where SVO is the most common. The SOV order is most likely the result of contact with Iranian or, where appropriate, Turkic: Kurmanji, Sorani, Persian, Turkish, and Iranian Azeri all have verb-final word order.

iii. **Analytical passive construction**: Many northern NENA dialects, both Christian and Jewish, construct a passive using a verb 'to come' with a verbal noun (which may or may not be marked with *l-* 'to'). The *come*-passive is borrowed from Kurmanji (cf. Mackenzie 1961: 195); it is not found in Sorani dialects.

iv. **Genitive construction**: In Jewish Trans-Zab dialects, the *Ezafe* genitive construction has been borrowed from Iranian. In some dialects, such as the dialect of J. Sanandaj, the Ezafe particle itself (*//e//* or *//i//*) has been borrowed along with the structure (Khan 2009: 199). In J. Urmi the Ezafe particle *//ay//* has apparently been developed from NENA's own resources on the model of Iranian (Khan 2008b: 176). The distribution of the construction varies across dialects, for example whether it may also be used with adjectival modifiers, as in Iranian (see Gutman 2016 for further details).

v. **New tense**: Christian dialects of the Nineveh Plain possess a new future tense (more precisely prospective) which uses the verb *'zl* I 'to go' as an auxiliary. This construction appears to have developed on the model of the *rāyəḥ/raḥ-* future found in neighboring Arabic dialects, as it is only found in NENA dialects spoken close to the Arabic-speaking region (Coghill 2010, 2012).

vi. **Loss of gender distinction:** In the Jewish Trans-Zab dialects, the gender distinction in the third person personal pronouns has been lost, probably through influence from Kurdish, possible also Persian and Turkish, which also lack this distinction (see Khan 2007b: 200).

vii. **Idiomatic expressions (polylexemic matching)**: NENA shares many idiomatic expressions with neighboring languages. Garbell (1965b: 175–177) gives very many examples from J. Azerbaijani that are shared with Kurdish and Azeri. Among these are many formulae used regularly in specific contexts, such as telling a story or expressing thanks, congratulations, or condolences. Proverbs are another area where there are shared expressions (Segal 1955; Garbell 1965b: 175; Sabar 1978a; Chyet 1995: 234–236).

22.10 SUMMARY

Northeastern Neo-Aramaic dialects show a great deal of contact influence, not only in lexicon and phonology, but also in morphology and syntax. The precise borrowings and degree of influence vary from dialect to dialect. Contact influence from Kurdish is clear in all dialects, but is greater among eastern Jewish dialects such as Sanandaj, deep inside Kurdish-speaking territory, while influence from Arabic is most apparent among the Christian dialects of the Nineveh Plain, spoken in the closest proximity to the Arabic-speaking regions of Iraq. The precise forms of the borrowings, as well as their behavior, usually reflect the local dialects of the donor language (where data are available), showing how important fine-grained dialectal data are to a study of language contact. While some of the languages in contact, namely Kurdish, Turkish, and Persian, are structurally very different from NENA, structural congruence or compatibility plays at best a minor role in facilitating borrowings.

22.11 TEXT

The following text is from the Jewish dialect of Sanandaj, which is one of the dialects most strongly affected by language contact.

J. Sanandaj (text and translation from *The Tale of the Bald Boy*, Khan 2009: 480–481)[11]

(1) *xà| bronà| híye   ba-ʿolàm| kắčằl-yele.| məstá lìt-wa   ba-reš-éf.|*
    a   boy   came.ABS.3MS in-world bald-was.3MS hair   NEG.EXIST-ANT on-head-his
    'A boy came into the world who was bald. He did not have a hair on his head.'

xa	Indefinite (specific) markers such as this are common to the languages of the region, e.g. Sorani *-ēk* and Iraqi Arabic *fadd*.
bronà	Most non-verb words have stress on the final syllable, as in Kurdish, and unlike in most NENA dialects.
hiye	Verbs in the past perfective align largely ergatively in person indexing (§22.9).
ba	This preposition also has the variant *b-* (Khan 2009: 218), which is the form found in earlier Aramaic (and most of NENA). It is possible that the emergence of the *ba* variant has been influenced by the Kurdish preposition *ba*, which overlaps in meaning.
ʿolām	< Hebrew *ʿōlām*. Note the /ʿ/ (in NENA inherited words, */ʿ/> /ʾ/).
kắčăl	< Sorani *kačal* 'bald'

(2) *bár-d-o   xằrằe| ʾáy   bronà| bằruxá lìt-wa-le.|*
    after.that afterwards this boy   friend NEG.EXIST-ANT-to.him
    'Later this boy did not have a friend.'

băruxa   < Hebrew *bārūḵ* 'blessed' (with NENA nominal ending *-a* added; see section 22.6.1)

(3) *híč-kas   bằrux-èf   lá   xar-wá.| rə̀we,| rə̀we|*
    no-person friend-his not become.3MS-ANT grew.ABS.3MS grew.ABS.3MS
    'Nobody became his friend. He grew and grew'

híč-kas   < Sor. *hīč kas-ēk* [no person-INDF] 'no-one' (for *hič*, see §22.6.4)

(4) *tá-ʾinke xìr.| ba-xá bronà| taqribán ʾə̀srì   šə̀né.|*
    until   became.ABS.3MS in-a boy   about   twenty years
    'until he became a boy about twenty years old.'

ta-ʾinke	< Persian *ta inke* 'until'
taqriban	< Arabic *taqrīban*, possibly via Persian *taqriban* 'approximately'

---

[11] In this text the grave accent (ˋ) marks the nuclear accent of the intonation phrase, while the acute accent (ˊ) marks any other accents. The end of an intonation phrase is marked by '|'.

(5) 'áy   broná   be-čará   hìč-kas   lít-wa-le.|
     this   boy   without-solution   no-person   NEG.EXIST-ANT-to.him
     'This unfortunate boy had nobody.'

be-čara < Sorani *bē-čāra* 'without solution, helpless'. Note that *be* and *čara* are not only
       used in this loan-phrase, but also used independently in J. Sanandaj.

(6) xá-yoma   tíw   məntắke   daăk-èf| ḥqé-le   míre|
     one-day   sat.ABS.3MS   with   mother-his   spoke-ERG.3MS   said.ERG.3MS
     'One day he sat with his mother, spoke and said,'

daăka < Sorani *dāk, dāyik* 'mother'
ḥqy I < Qəltu Arabic *ḥky* **i** 'speak'

(7) dàyka| 'anà| hìč   băruxá   líti| wa-la   k-ắe-na   má   ho-nà.|
     mother   I   no   friend   EXIST.to.me and-not   IND-know-1MS   what do-1MS
     '"Mother, I do not have any friend and I do not know what to do."'

dayka   Stress is retracted in vocatives (see section 22.7.4)

(8) hàlax| tămắm 'áy   dawruwăr-àn| da'wàt   ho-nú|
     come.IMP.to.you.F   all   this   around-1PL   da'wat   do-1MS.OBJ.3PL
     'Come, let me invite everybody around us,'

tămām   < Persian *tamam* 'all' < Arab. *tamām* 'completeness, complete'
da'wat 'wl I   Complex predicate (noun + light verb): The structure/meaning, along with
             the nominal (but not the light verb), is borrowed from Persian *da'vat kardan*
             'to invite' (lit. 'to make an invitation,' Pers. *da'vat* < Arab. *da'wa(t)*). The
             borrowed nominal in J. Sanandaj seems to be restricted to this idiom.

(9) bašká   'ašná   xa-dána   mən-un-u| bəxlé   zəndəgì   hol-éxin.|
     perhaps   acquaintance   one-individual   with-3PL-and   together life   do-1PL
     'perhaps I shall become acquainted with one of them and we can spend time
     together.'

baška   < Sorani *baškā*
ašna   < Persian *'ašna* 'acquaintance'
zəndəgi < Persian *zendegi* 'life'

(10) xà-lele| rába   xàrj   wí-le| rába   xalà   trə̣ṣ-le.|
     a-night   much   xarj did-ERG.3MS much   food   made-ERG.3MS
     'One night he spent a lot of money and made a lot of food.'

rába xalà trə̣ṣle   Note here the typical OV word order, under influence of Iranian
                 (probably Sorani).
xarj 'wl I   Complex predicate (noun + light verb): The structure/meaning, along
                 with the nominal, is borrowed from Sorani *xarǰ kirdin*/Persian *xarj*
                 kardan 'to spend' (lit. 'to make expenditure,' Pers. *xarj* 'expenditure'
                 < Arab. *xarj* 'expenditure').

Acknowledgements

I am grateful to the editor and reviewers for their helpful comments on my chapter. I would like to acknowledge the German Research Council, which funded a large part of this research. I would like to thank the Neo-Aramaic speaking communities, without whose generosity and interest this research would be impossible. Thanks are also due to Yaron Matras, who guided my interest in language contact in this region at an early stage of my career.

References

Borghero, Roberta. 2005. *The Neo-Aramaic dialect of Ashitha*. PhD dissertation, University of Cambridge.

Borghero, Roberta. 2012. Some phonological and morphological features of the Christian Neo-Aramaic dialect of ʿAnkawa. *Aram Periodical* 24: 9–23.

Borghero, Roberta. 2015. The present continuous in the Neo Aramaic dialect of ʿAnkawa and its areal and typological parallels. In *Neo-Aramaic and Its Linguistic Context*, edited by Geoffrey Khan and Lidia Napiorkowska, 187–206. Gorgias Neo-Aramaic Studies 14. Piscataway: Gorgias Press.

Bulut, Christiane. 2007. Iraqi Turkman. In *Languages of Iraq, Ancient and Modern*, edited by J. N. Postgate, 159–187. Cambridge: British School of Archaeology in Iraq.

Chyet, Michael L. 1995. Neo-Aramaic and Kurdish: An interdisciplinary consideration of their influence on each other. In *Language and Culture in the Near East*, edited by Shlomo Izreʾel and Rina Drory, 219–252. Israel Oriental Studies 15. Leiden, New York and Cologne: Brill.

Chyet, Michael L. 1997. A preliminary list of Aramaic loanwords in Kurdish. In *Humanism, Culture and Language in the Near East: Studies in Honor of Georg Krotkoff*, edited by A. Afsaruddin and A. H. M. Zahniser, 283–300. Winona Lake, IN: Eisenbrauns.

Chyet, Michael L. 2003. *Kurdish-English Dictionary: Ferhenga Kurmancî-Inglîzî*. New Haven, CT; London: Yale University Press.

Clarity, Beverly E., Karl Stowasser, and Ronald G. Wolfe (eds.). 1964. *A Dictionary of Iraqi Arabic: English–Arabic*. The Richard Slade Harrell Arabic Series, no. 6. Washington, DC: Georgetown University Press.

Coghill, Eleanor. 2004. *The Neo-Aramaic Dialect of Alqosh*. PhD dissertation, Faculty of Oriental Studies, University of Cambridge.

Coghill, Eleanor. 2005. The morphology and distribution of noun plurals in the Neo-Aramaic dialect of Alqosh. In *Studi Afroasiatici. XI Incontro Italiano di Linguistica Camitosemitica*, edited by A. Mengozzi, 337–348. Milan: FrancoAngeli.

Coghill, Eleanor. 2010. The development of prospective aspect in a group of Neo-Aramaic dialects. *Diachronica* 27(3): 359–410.

Coghill, Eleanor. 2012. Parallels in the grammaticalisation of Neo-Aramaic *zil-* and Arabic *raḥ-* and a possible contact scenario. In *Grammaticalisation in Semitic*, edited by Domenyk Eades, 127–144. Journal of Semitic Studies Supplement Series. Oxford: Oxford University Press.

Coghill, Eleanor. 2013. The Neo-Aramaic dialect of Peshabur. In *Nicht nur mit Engelszungen: Beiträge zur semitischen Dialektologie. Festschrift für Werner Arnold zum 60. Geburtstag*, edited by R. Kuty, U. Seeger, and S. Talay, 37–48. Wiesbaden: Harrassowitz.

Coghill, Eleanor. 2014. Differential object marking in Neo-Aramaic. *Linguistics* 52(2) (special issue): 335–364.

Coghill, Eleanor. 2015. Borrowing of verbal derivational morphology between Semitic languages: the case of Arabic verb derivations in Neo-Aramaic. In *Borrowed Morphology*, edited by N. Amiridze, P. Arkadiev, and F. Gardani, 83–107. Language Contact and Bilingualism 8. Berlin; Boston: De Gruyter Mouton.

Coghill, Eleanor. 2016. *The Rise and Fall of Ergativity in Aramaic: Cycles of Alignment Change.* Oxford: Oxford University Press.

Cohen, Eran. 2012. *The Syntax of Neo-Aramaic: The Jewish Dialect of Zakho.* Piscataway, NJ: Gorgias Press.

Fassberg, Steven E. 2010. *The Jewish Neo-Aramaic Dialect of Challa.* Leiden: Brill.

Fox, Samuel E. 1997. *The Neo-Aramaic Dialect of Jilu.* Wiesbaden: Harrassowitz.

Fox, Samuel E. 2007. The story of *Mem u Zine* in the Neo-Aramaic Dialect of Bohtan. In *Studies in Semitic and Afroasiatic Linguistics Presented to Gene B. Gragg*, edited by Cynthia L. Miller, 69–80. Studies in Ancient Oriental Civilization 60. Chicago: Oriental Institute, University of Chicago.

Fox, Samuel E. 2009. *The Neo-Aramaic Dialect of Bohtan.* Piscataway, NJ: Gorgias Press.

Foy, Karl. 1903. Azerbajğanische Studien mit einer Charakteristik des Südtürkischen I. *Mitteilungen des Seminars für Orientalische Sprachen an der Friedrich Wilhelms-Universität zu Berlin* 6: 126–193.

Foy, Karl. 1904. Azerbajğanische Studien mit einer Charakteristik des Südtürkischen II. *Mitteilungen des Seminars für Orientalische Sprachen an der Friedrich Wilhelms-Universität zu Berlin* 7: 197–265.

Garbell, Irene. 1965a. *The Jewish Neo-Aramaic Dialect of Persian Azerbaijan: Linguistic Analysis and Folkloristic Texts.* Janua Linguarum Series Practica, 3. The Hague: Mouton de Gruyter.

Garbell, Irene. 1965b. The impact of Kurdish and Turkish on the Jewish neo-Aramaic dialect of Persian Azerbaijan and the adjoining regions. *Journal of the American Oriental Society* 85(2): 159–177.

Grant, Asahel. 1841. *The Nestorians: Or, The Lost Tribes: Containing Evidence of Their Identity; an Account of Their Manners, Customs, and Ceremonies; Together with Sketches of Travels in Ancient Assyria, Armenia, Media, and Mesopotamia; and Illustrations of Scripture Prophecy.* New York: Harper.

Greenblatt, Jared. 2011. *The Jewish Neo-Aramaic Dialect of Aməd̲ya.* Leiden: Brill.

Gutman, Ariel. 2015. Some features of the Gaznax dialect (South-East Turkey). In *Neo-Aramaic and Its Linguistic Context*, edited by Geoffrey Khan and Lidia Napiorkowska, 305–321. Gorgias Neo-Aramaic Studies 14. Piscataway, NJ: Gorgias Press.

Gutman, Ariel. 2016. *Attributive Constructions in North-Eastern Neo-Aramaic: Areal, Typological and Historical Perspectives.* PhD dissertation, University of Konstanz.

Haig, Geoffrey. 2001. Linguistic diffusion in present-day East Anatolia: From top to bottom. In *Areal Diffusion and Genetic Inheritance: Problems in Comparative Linguistics*, edited by Alexandra Y. Aikhenvald and R. M. W. Dixon, 195–224. Oxford: Oxford University Press.

Haig, Geoffrey L. J. 2008. *Alignment Change in Iranian Languages: A Construction Grammar Approach.* Berlin; New York: Mouton de Gruyter.

Haspelmath, Martin. 2009. Lexical borrowing: Concepts and issues. In *Loanwords in the World's Languages*, edited by Martin Haspelmath and Uri Tadmor, 35–54. Berlin: Mouton de Gruyter.

Heath, Jeffrey. 1989. *From Code-Switching to Borrowing: Foreign and Diglossic Mixing in Moroccan Arabic*. Library of Arabic Linguistics 9. London; New York: Kegan Paul International.

Heinrichs, Wolfhart. 2002. Peculiarities of the Verbal System of Senāya within the Framework of North Eastern Neo-Aramaic. In *Sprich doch mit deinen Knechten aramäisch, wir verstehen es! 60 Beiträge zur Semitistik. Festschrift für Otto Jastrow zum 60. Geburtstag*, edited by Werner Arnold and Hartmut Bobzin, 237–268. Wiesbaden: Harrassowitz.

Hoberman, Robert D. 1989. *The Syntax and Semantics of Verb Morphology in Modern Aramaic: A Jewish Dialect of Iraqi Kurdistan*. New Haven, CT: American Oriental Society.

Hoberman, Robert D., and Mark Aronoff. 2003. The verbal morphology of Maltese. *Language Acquisition and Language Disorders* 28: 61–78.

Jastrow, Otto. 1978. *Die mesopotamisch-arabischen qəltu-Dialekte*, Vol. I: *Phonologie und Morphologie*. Abhandlungen für die Kunde des Morgenlandes 43(4). Wiesbaden.

Jastrow, Otto. 1988. *Der neuaramäische Dialekt von Hertevin (Provinz Siirt)*. Semitica Viva 3. Wiesbaden: Harrassowitz.

Jastrow, Otto. 1990. *Der arabische Dialekt der Juden von ʿAqra und Arbîl*. Semitica Viva 5. Wiesbaden: Harrassowitz.

Kapeliuk, Olga. 1996. Is Modern Hebrew the only "Indo-Europeanized" Semitic language? And what about Neo-Aramaic? *Israel Oriental Studies* 19: 59–70.

Kapeliuk, Olga. 2002a. Compound verbs in Neo-Aramaic. In *Sprich doch mit deinen Knechten aramäisch, wir verstehen es!' 60 Beiträge zur Semitistik, Festschrift für Otto Jastrow zum 60. Geburtstag.* edited by Werner Arnold and Hartmut Bobzin, 361–377. Wiesbaden: Harrassowitz.

Kapeliuk, Olga. 2002b. Languages in Contact: The Contemporary World. In *Semitic Linguistics: The State of the Art at the Turn of the 21st Century*, edited by Shlomo Izre'el, 307–340. Israel Oriental Studies 20. Winona Lake: Eisenbrauns.

Kapeliuk, Olga. 2011. Language contact between Aramaic dialects and Iranian. In *The Semitic Languages*, edited by Stefan Weninger, Geoffrey Khan, Michael P. Streck, and Janet C. E. Watson, 739–747. Berlin and Boston: De Gruyter Mouton.

Khan, Geoffrey. 1999. *A Grammar of Neo-Aramaic: The Dialect of the Jews of Arbel*. Leiden: Brill.

Khan, Geoffrey. 2002a. *The Neo-Aramaic Dialect of Qaraqosh*. Leiden: Brill.

Khan, Geoffrey. 2002b. The Neo-Aramaic dialect of the Jews of Rustaqa. In *Sprich doch mit deinen Knechten aramäisch, wir verstehen es!' 60 Beiträge zur Semitistik, Festschrift für Otto Jastrow zum 60. Geburtstag*, edited by Werner Arnold and Hartmut Bobzin, 395–410. Wiesbaden: Harrassowitz.

Khan, Geoffrey. 2004. *The Jewish Neo-Aramaic Dialect of Sulemaniyya and Halabja*. Studies in Semitic Languages and Linguistics 44. Leiden: Brill.

Khan, Geoffrey. 2007a. Ergativity in the North Eastern Neo-Aramaic dialects, In *Studies in Semitic and General Linguistics in Honor of Gideon Goldenberg*, edited by T. Bar and E. Cohen, 147–157. Münster: Ugarit-Verlag.

Khan, Geoffrey. 2007b. North Eastern Neo-Aramaic. In *Grammatical Borrowing in Cross-Linguistic Perspective*, edited by Y. Matras and J. Sakel, 197–214. Berlin: Mouton de Gruyter.

Khan, Geoffrey. 2008a. *The Neo-Aramaic Dialect of Barwar*, Vol. 1: *Grammar*. Handbook of Oriental Studies Section 1: The Near and Middle East 96. Leiden: Brill.

Khan, Geoffrey. 2008b. *The Jewish Neo-Aramaic Dialect of Urmi*. Gorgias Neo-Aramaic Studies 2. Piscataway, NJ: Gorgias Press.

Khan, Geoffrey. 2009. *The Jewish Neo-Aramaic Dialect of Sanandaj*. Piscataway, NJ: Gorgias Press.

Kim, Ronald. 2008. "Stammbaum" or "Continuum"? The Subgrouping of Modern Aramaic Dialects Reconsidered. *Journal of the American Oriental Society* 128(3): 505–531.

Krotkoff, Georg. 1982. *A Neo-Aramaic Dialect of Kurdistan: Texts, Grammar, and Vocabulary.* American Oriental Series 64. New Haven, CT: American Oriental Society.

Krotkoff, Georg. 1985. Studies in Neo-Aramaic Lexicology. In *Biblical and Related Studies Presented to Samuel Iwry*, edited by Ann Kort and Scott Morschauser, 123–134. Winona Lake, IN: Eisenbrauns.

Kutscher, Edward Yechezkel. 1969. Two "passive" constructions in Aramaic in the light of Persian. *Proceedings of the International Conference on Semitic Studies*, Jerusalem: he Israel Academy of Sciences and Humanities, 132–151.

Mackenzie, David N. 1961. *Kurdish Dialect Studies I.* London: Oxford University Press.

Maclean, Arthur J. 1901. *A Dictionary of the Dialects of Vernacular Syriac as Spoken by the Eastern Syrians of Kurdistan, North-West Persia, and the Plain of Mosul.* Oxford: Clarendon Press.

Matras, Yaron. 2009. *Language Contact.* Cambridge: Cambridge University Press.

McCarus, Ernest N. 1958. *A Kurdish Grammar: descriptive analysis of the Kurdish of Sulaimaniya, Iraq.* No. 10. American Council of Learned Societies.

Moravcsik, Edith. 1978. Language Contact. In *Universals of Human Language: Method and Theory*, edited by Joseph Greenberg, Charles Ferguson, Edith Moravcsik, 93–122. Stanford, CA: Stanford University Press.

Mutzafi, Hezy. 2002. Barzani Jewish Neo-Aramaic and Its Dialects. *Mediterranean Language Review* 14: 41–70.

Mutzafi, Hezy. 2004a. *The Jewish Neo-Aramaic Dialect of Koy Sanjaq (Iraqi Kurdistan).* Wiesbaden: Harrassowitz.

Mutzafi, Hezy. 2004b. Features of the verbal system in the Christian Neo-Aramaic dialect of Koy Sanjaq and their areal parallels. *Journal of the American Oriental Society* 124(2): 249–264.

Mutzafi, Hezy. 2008a. *The Jewish Neo-Aramaic Dialect of Betanure (Province of Dihok).* Semitica Viva 43. Wiesbaden: Harrassowitz.

Mutzafi, Hezy. 2008b. Trans-Zab Jewish Neo-Aramaic. *Bulletin of the School of Oriental and African Studies* 71: 409–431.

Nakano, Aki'o. 1973. *Conversational Texts in Eastern Neo-Aramaic (Gzira Dialect).* Study of Languages and Cultures of Asia and Africa A4. Tokyo: Institute for the Study of Languages and Cultures of Asia and Africa.

Noorlander, Paul. 2014. Diversity in convergence: Kurdish and Aramaic variation entangled. *Kurdish Studies* 2(2): 201–224.

Panoussi, Estiphan. 1990. On the Senaya dialect. In *Studies in Neo-Aramaic*, edited by W. Heinrichs, 107–129. Harvard Semitic Studies. Atlanta, GA: Scholars Press.

Pennacchietti, Fabrizio A. 1988. Verbo neo-aramaico e verbo neo-iranico. In *Tipologie della convergenza linguistica: atti del convergno della Società italiana di glottologia*, edited by V. Orioles, 93–110. Pisa.

Qazzaz, Shafiq. 2000. *The Sharezoor Kurdish-English Dictionary.* Erbil: Aras Press.

Rizgar, Baran. 1993. *Kurdish-English, English-Kurdish Dictionary*, London: M. F. Onen.

Sabar, Yona (ed.). 1976. *Pəšaṭ Wayhi Bešallah, A Neo-Aramaic Midrash on Beshallah (Exodus): Introduction, Phonetic Transcription, Translation, Notes, and Glossary.* Wiesbaden: Harrassowitz.

Sabar, Yona. 1978a. Multilingual proverbs (Neo-Aramaic, Kurdish, Arabic) in the Neo- Aramaic dialect of the Jews of Zakho. *International Journal of Middle East Studies* 9: 215–235.

Sabar, Yona. 1978b. From Tel-Kepe (A Pile of Stones) in Iraqi Kurdistan to Providence, Rhode Island: The story of a Chaldean immigrant to the U.S.A in 1927. *Journal of the American Oriental Society* 98(4): 410–415.

Sabar, Yona. 1984. The Arabic elements in the Jewish Neo-Aramaic texts of Nerwa and 'Amadiya, Iraqi Kurdistan. *Journal of American Oriental Society* 104: 201–211.

Sabar, Yona. 1990. General European loanwords in the Jewish Neo-Aramaic dialect of Zakho, Iraqi Kurdistan. In *Studies in Neo-Aramaic*, edited by W. Heinrichs, 53–66. Harvard Semitic Studies. Atlanta, GA: Scholars Press.

Sabar, Yona. 1993. A folktale and folk songs in the Christian Neo-Aramaic dialect of Tel-Kēpe (Northern Iraq). In *Semitica: Serta philologica Constantino Tsereteli dicata*, edited by R. Contini, F. Pennacchietti and M. Tosco, 289–297. Turin: Silvio Zamorani.

Sabar, Yona. 2002. *A Jewish Neo-Aramaic dictionary: Dialects of Amidya, Dihok, Nerwa and Zakho, Northwestern Iraq: Based on Old and New Manuscripts, Oral and Written Bible Translations, Folkloric Texts, and Diverse Spoken Registers, with an Introduction to Grammar and Semantics, and an Index of Talmudic Words Which Have Reflexes in Jewish Neo-Aramaic.* Wiesbaden: Harrassowitz.

Sakel, Jeanette. 2007. Types of loan: Matter and pattern. In *Grammatical Borrowing in Cross-Linguistic Perspective*, edited by Yaron Matras and Jeanette Sakel, 15–29. Berlin: Mouton de Gruyter.

Segal, Judah B. 1955. Neo-Aramaic proverbs of the Jews of Zakho. *Journal of Near Eastern Studies* 14(4): 251–270.

Sinha, Jasmin. 2000. *Der neuostaramäische Dialekt von Bēṣpən (Provinz Mardin, Südosttürkei): Eine grammatische Darstellung.* Wiesbaden: Harrassowitz.

Stoddard, David Tappan. 1855. Grammar of the Modern Syriac language, as spoken in Oroomiah, Persiah and Koordistan. *Journal of the American Oriental Society* 5: 1–180.

Talay, Shabo. 2008. *Die neuaramäischen Dialekte der Khabur-Assyrer in Nordostsyrien.* Wiesbaden: Harrassowitz.

Thackston, Wheeler M. 2006. *Kurmanji Kurdish: A Reference Grammar with Selected Readings.* http://www.fas.harvard.edu/~iranian/Kurmanji/kurmanji_1_grammar.pdf (accessed January 4, 2013).

Thomason, Sarah G. 2001. *Language Contact: An Introduction.* Edinburgh: Edinburgh University Press.

Thomason, Sarah G., and Terrence Kaufman. 1988. *Language Contact, Creolization, and Genetic Linguistics.* Berkeley: University of California Press.

Wohlgemuth, Jan. 2009. *A Typology of Verbal Borrowings.* Berlin; New York: Mouton de Gruyter.

Woodhead, D. R., and W. Beene (eds.). 1967. *A Dictionary of Iraqi Arabic: Arabic-English.* The Richard Slade Harrell Arabic Series, no. 10. Washington, DC: Georgetown University Press.

Younansardaroud, Helen. 1999. The influence of Modern Persian on the Särdä:rïd dialect. *Journal of Assyrian Academic Studies* 13(1): 65–68.

Younansardaroud, Helen. 2001. *Der neuostaramäische Dialekt von Särdä:rïd.* Semitica Viva 26. Wiesbaden: Harrassowitz.

CHAPTER 23

CONTACT AND THE DEVELOPMENT OF MALAYALAM

P. SREEKUMAR

23.1 THE LANGUAGE AND ITS SPEAKERS

MALAYALAM (malayāḷam [mælə'jɑːləm], malayāḷa bhāśa) belongs to the South Dravidian I sub-branch of the Dravidian family and is spoken in the state of Kerala and the Laccadive (Lakshadweep) Islands of India. The geographical location of Kerala at the southwest tip of South Asia, facing the Arabian Sea with its large seashore, facilitated the reception, accommodation, and convergence of different streams of people, culture, and languages from different parts of the world. Subsequently, these contacts and convergences have resulted in the borrowing of phonological and grammatical features and many lexical items from different language families into Malayalam. Malayalam is the official language of Kerala state, spoken by 97% of the inhabitants. The 2011 Census reports that there are 36 million speakers. Full (100%) literacy is the significant sociolinguistic feature of Kerala. Therefore, the state is consistently placed at the top in the human development index of India and is on a par with the developed nations. Malayalam is used as a medium of instruction in school. However, for the last two decades there has been a high rate of choice of English against Malayalam as a medium of education. The high rate of literacy and mass education result in the emergence of a vibrant literary public sphere in Malayalam, with a greater number of Malayalam newspapers and magazines than any other languages in India. Since the formation of the state on linguistic grounds, the government of Kerala has been endeavoring to use Malayalam as a language of administration. In spite of these efforts, there has been limited success and slower progress than expected, mainly due to the linguistic attitude in favor of English. There exists a rich literary tradition in all genres of literature, with an exceptional presence of worldwide literary trends such as modernism, romanticism, existentialism, and postmodernism. It is the first language in South Asia into which almost all classical literary works from the major languages of the world have been translated, sold, and read at large. For more details of the people, language, and literature, see Madhavamenon (2002), Asher and Kumari (1997), and Krishna Chaithanya (1995), respectively.

MAP 23.1 Place of Malayalam Language, Kerala state in India.

23.1.1 Name and Classification

The name of the language Malayalam is a modern usage. Since medieval times, the language has been known as *kērala bhāśa* 'the speech of Kerala,' which is a compound of the palatalized form of *cēr-aḷam* into *kēr-aḷam* and the Sanskrit term *bhāśa* ('language'). The source word *cēr* means 'join,' or a name of the kingdom where the *cēra* dynasty ruled the land during 800–1122 CE. Otherwise, it indicates *kēra* 'coconut tree,' which grows in abundance in this region. The later name *malayāḷam* indicates 'hill' in the first part of the name *mala*; *āḷam* means closeness or edge. In short, it is a place name that indicates the geographical nature of the place. Later it was used to indicate the name of the language developed in the geographical area, which is common in the Indian linguistic area.

23.1.1.1 *Classification*

Based on written evidence, Malayalam is one of the later offshoots of the South Dravidian I sub-branch of Dravidian (see Figure 23.1) (Krishnamurti 2003: 19). The West-Coast dialect of the Proto-Tamil-Malayalam stage of South Dravidian spread around the West-Coast region of Southern India and has developed as Malayalam by early gradual contact with Prakrit and later by massive contact with Sanskrit (Govindankutty 1972: 52–60; Sankunni Nair 1995). Contact with Prakrit and Sanskrit languages belonging to Indo-Aryan acted as a superstratum impact for the emergence of Malayalam as an independent language, and the language was modernized by contact with European languages, especially English.

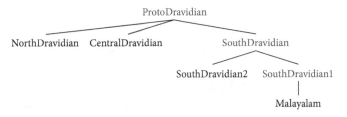

FIGURE 23.1 Genealogical tree of the Dravidian languages.

23.1.2 Sources of Data and Earlier Studies

In addition to the author's personal knowledge as a native speaker of the language, many published and unpublished dictionaries and other works have been consulted. The *Malayalam Lexicon*, published in a sequence of volumes by the University of Kerala (Kunjan Pillai 1965–), is the major source. It should be especially noted that loanword status and the donor language of entries are consistently mentioned in this lexicon. Monolingual dictionaries by Sreekanteswaram (2009 [1923]), Balakrishnan and Narayana Pillai (2006 [1991]), and a bilingual dictionary by Ramalingam Pillai

(2004 [1983] have been consulted. A pioneering series of studies by K. Godavarmma (1933–1934, 1946), Gopalakrishnan (1985: 31–54), and Joseph (1995 [1984]) about the Indo-Aryan loanwords in Malayalam and foreign words in Malayalam, respectively, track the sources and the linguistic features of almost all borrowed words in Malayalam until the date of publication. The later work by Joseph should be especially mentioned as a comprehensive study.

Asher and Kumari (1997: 250–251, 253, 418, 421–422) made a few occasional but substantial observations on loanwords in Malayalam. Narayanan's (2013) unpublished paper on the *Socio-Cultural Background of Genesis of Malayalam Language* is the recent advancement of the sociocultural aspects of the issues discussed in this chapter. In addition to the previously mentioned studies, thirteen items of published and unpublished studies are listed under the heading of borrowing and loanwords in the bibliography of *Malayalam Language and Linguistics* by Ramaiah and Rajasekharan (2001: 83).

23.2 CONTACT HISTORY

Contact with other languages, especially with Prakrit and Pali at the earlier stage and later with Sanskrit, is one of triggering factors of the development of Malayalam as an independent language from its status as a West Coast dialect of South Dravidian I. The history of this contact is parallel with the history of the development of Malayalam. This is detailed in Table 23.1.

23.2.1 Prakrit

Prakrit is a group of Middle Indo-Aryan languages developed from the scattered dialects of Old Indo-Aryan, spread throughout the Indian continent during the period 300 BCE to 1500 CE (Jamison 2008: 33–49). These languages had a superstratum impact on the vernaculars of India through the spread of the Buddhist and Jain religions. Buddhism and Jainism spread in Kerala from 300 BCE onward. Contact with Prakrit—especially the *Saurasīnī*, *Mahārāṣṭrī*, and *Apabhraṃśa* dialects of Prakrit—resulted in the first borrowings, which differentiated the phonology of Old Malayalam from its adjacent language Tamil. This process of contact with Prakrit especially started from the eighth century CE, and later Sanskrit replaced Prakrit and Pali.

Table 23.1 Periodization of Malayalam

Period	Development of Malayalam	Languages That Were in Contact
600 BCE–300 BCE	Proto-Tamil Malayalam dialect stage	No evidence of contact
300 BCE–700 CE	Proto-Malayalam	Prakrit dialects
800 CE–1400 CE	Old Malayalam	Prakrit and Sanskrit
1400 CE–1600 CE	Middle Malayalam	Sanskrit, Hindi, Marathi, Portuguese, Persian, Arabic, Latin, Hebrew, etc.
1600 CE–	Modern Malayalam	English and other languages

23.2.2 Sanskrit

Sanskrit influence on Malayalam was facilitated by the different streams of migration of the Brahmin community toward the southern part of the Indian subcontinent (Narayanan 2013). Members of this community used Sanskrit as their language of religion, ethics, and sciences. These communities, who were better organized than the natives of Kerala, exercised unprecedented hegemony over the latter through the Hindu religion, temple economy, and the introduction of the caste system in Kerala. This cultural hegemony has penetrated into the everyday world of the native people, and consequently led to the replacement of even names for basic body parts in the vocabulary of Malayalam by borrowed Sanskrit terms. Eventually, this contact situation of two languages from two families of languages resulted in the replacement of the old *vaṭṭezuththu* 'round shape writing system' of Dravidian by the *ārya-ezuththu* of Sanskrit to represent the integrated borrowed Sanskrit lexicon in Malayalam (see later discussion 23. 3.1.2.3). The emergence of the *Maṇipravāḷam* literary style by the harmonious blend of *Kēraḷabhāṣa* ('language spoken in Kerala region,' i.e., Old Malayalam) and Sanskrit is an aggregated result of this contact (Freeman 1998: 38–65). The impact of this contact still continues with the borrowing of Sanskrit words and the use of Sanskrit roots for loan creation from English. A typical example that is often cited is the borrowing of the Sanskrit word *āgōḷa* 'global' in the loan translation of the English word 'globalization' as *āgōḷavatkaraṇam*.

23.2.3 Hindi

Hindi is one of the major New Indo-Aryan languages with which Malayalam had been in contact from the medieval centuries and still continues in modern period. Hindi words are found in Malayalam literary works written in the fourteenth century. Contact with Hindi was not regular during medieval times. However, national movements, especially the freedom movement during the nineteenth and twentieth century, facilitated a social space where Hindi is learned as the language of nationalism and political movements. Therefore, most of the words like *lahaḷa* 'quarrel' < Hindi *jhagaḍa* 'quarrel,' *lātti* 'stick used by police' <Hindi *lāthī* 'stick' were borrowed during this period. After independence, contact of Malayalam with Hindi continued extensively by the teaching of Hindi in schools as a third language and the migration of Malayalam speakers to North India, where Hindi is spoken as the major language.

23.2.4 Marathi

Marathi occupies a significant position in the Indian linguistic area as a New Indo-Aryan language that developed with convergent features of Dravidian and Old Indo-Aryan (Southworth 2005: 288–321). There is no geographical continguity of Marathi with Malayalam, and no direct and intense contact has been reported thus far. However, Marathi-speakers had started to visit Kerala from the thirteenth century for trade, and people from Kerala started to migrate to Mumbai city from the eighteenth century for industrial jobs. The borrowing of words like *tapāl* 'post mail' < Marathi *ṭapāl* 'post, mail' in Malayalam is an indication of this. A good number of terms for food items that were not familiar to Kerala were introduced through this contact. The names of food items like *kiccaḍi* 'a type of curry' < Mar. *khicaḍī*, *jilēbi* 'a sweet dish' < Mar. *jilēbī*, *pūri* 'a deep-fried Indian bread' < Mar. *pūṛī*, *vaṭa* 'a snack' < Mar. *vaṭā* and *sāmpāṛ* 'a curry' < Mar. *sābāṛ* are instances of this.

23.2.5 Persian

The relationship of Persian with Malayalam is essentially related to trade and political governance. There exists evidence of Persian Christian missionary relations with Kerala from 300 CE. However, these pieces of evidence are not enough to assume a relationship in which Malayalam and Persian had been in intense contact. The influence of Persian in fact strengthened after the period of Tippu Sultan (1750–1799), a Mysore king who conquered the northern part of Kerala. From then onward, the northern part of Kerala was under the rule of Mysore kings. This resulted in the borrowing of a number of administrative words from Persian into Malayalam. The trade relations of Kerala with Persia contributed to the mercantilization of Kerala society to some extent. The borrowing of words like *basāṛ* 'market' < Per. *basāṛ*, *rasītə* 'receipt' < Per. *ṭasīd*, and *nirakkə* 'rate of product' < Per. *niṛnāma* are instances of this contact.

23.2.6 Hebrew

An inscription dated approximately 10 CE provides evidence of a royal sanction of trade rights to a Jewish merchant by Bhaskara Ravivarma, a king who ruled Kerala 962 CE–1021 CE (Narayanan 1996). Jewish contact with Kerala started mainly for trade. Later this trade contact was interrupted by the arrival of the Portuguese. It then resumed during the British period, and Hebrew was taught in the schools run by British missionaries. Then there was the case of Cochin, a seashore city in Kerala, where Jewish communities lived until they returned to Jerusalem in 1948. Their trade relations required them to be bilingual, so they used Hebrew at home and Malayalam for trade and social relations. This constant bilingualism among them and the healthy reception of the host in Kerala resulted in heavy borrowing from the religious lexicon of Hebrew into Malayalam and the emergence of a mixed language named Judeo-Malayalam. This is a blend of Hebrew, Malayalam, and Sanskrit (Gamliel 2013; Zacharia 2013). It is still spoken by a few families living in Cochin. It should be especially noted that a word related to everyday life, *metta* 'bed,' is borrowed from the Hebrew word *mitah* 'bed.' Almost all personal names used by the Christian community in Kerala were borrowed from Hebrew. There is nothing surprising in saying that the first wave of Christianity came into Malayalam through Hebrew.

23.2.7 Arabic

Malayalam had been historically in contact with Arabs by harmoniously hosting Arab merchants and Islam in Kerala. Nowadays a large majority of the labor force in Kerala heavily depends upon the Middle East for jobs, with the result that Arabic is again in contact with Malayalam. Malabar, another name of Kerala specifically representing the northern parts of Kerala, was given by Arab merchants who had been in contact with Kerala from the beginning of the Common Era. Even before the introduction of Islam in Kerala, Malayalam had been in an extensive mercantile contact with the Arab world. Later, since the arrival of Islam in Kerala, Arabic has been used as the language of Islam among the Muslim community in Kerala. The Muslim community in Kerala was antagonistic toward English-language education during the colonial period; therefore, they confined their education to Arabic-language schooling through the madrasa system. This resulted in a new blend of Arabic with Malayalam where the Arabic script was used to write Malayalam; eventually this constituted the emergence of a new form of Malayalam called Arabi-Malayalam with a new lexicon (Hassan 2009).

23.2.8 Syriac

Malayalam had been in contact with Syriac through Christianity. It is firmly believed that even as early as 52 CE, St. Thomas, the disciple, visited Kerala and started missionary activities there. The people who at first converted to Christianity may have been Brahmin or Buddhist people. For around seventeen centuries, Syriac has continued as the language of worship among the Christians in Kerala. The source of Syriac borrowing into Malayalam was from this Syriac, which had been highly localized by this long span of time. Due to the domain-specific contact, most of the lexical borrowing was in the parts of the lexicon related to religious worship and practices. The word for Jesus, *yēšu* in Malayalam, from Syriac *īšō* 'Jesus,' is an instance of this borrowing.

23.2.9 Portuguese

Portuguese had been in contact with Malayalam since 1498, and this contact continued until the end of the seventeenth century. The Portuguese came to Kerala as merchants in 1498. In addition to trade, they worked as missionaries and later became rulers. Therefore, they had a powerful influence on Kerala society, which resulted in immense borrowing of lexical items into Malayalam from Portuguese. Portuguese had been taught to the newly recruited native pastors by sending them to Portugal, and even the local rulers learned Portuguese to interact with the traders.

23.2.10 English

The contact of Malayalam with English started very late, at the end of the seventeenth century. However, later this contact turned out to be very intense, nearly equaling the influence of Sanskrit on Malayalam. In the beginning, before the British East India Company turned into rulers, English was one of the trade languages in Kerala. But after India became a colony of the British, the region in which Malayalam is spoken, namely Malabar, Cochin, and Travancore, came under the rule of the English under Madras Presidency. Consequently, the trade language changed into the language of rulers. Therefore, English gained prestige in society. On the other side, English missionaries started many schools in the different parts of Kerala where English was taught and used as a language of communication and as a medium of teaching. All this led to English becoming a language of social change and a language of the modernization of society from the age-old clutches of feudalism. During the national movement for freedom, English functioned as a language by which communication could be at a national level, in addition to Hindi. Above all, one peculiar feature of Kerala is the comparatively lesser prevalence of bi- and multilingualism, which necessitated the spread of English across the social spectrum as a language of social mobility and emancipation, too. Today, compared to all other states in India, English education is higher in Kerala both as content and medium in higher education. Therefore, the borrowing is heavier than from any other languages. The literary elite who had empathy for the mother tongue worried that English might replace Malayalam in the near future.

It should be noted that English contains a few dozen words of Dravidian origin, some of which are typically of Malayalam origin: *copra, jack*(fruit) < *koppa, cakka* (OED, accessed July 13, 2016).

23.2.11 Other Languages in Contact

Malayalam has been in contact with other languages, such as Tamil, Kannada, and other tribal languages. All belong to the Dravidian family of languages. Therefore, the impact of the contact is not discussed here.

23.3 RESULTS OF CONTACT

The contexts of the contact that I have discussed earlier resulted at different levels in the development of Malayalam. Heavy borrowing at the lexical level had direct impact on the phonological structure of the language. Morphology and syntax were least affected. Even then, there are a few grammatical features like reciprocals and postpositions borrowed from Sanskrit. Passive structure is observed as pedantic and unnatural in Malayalam (Asher and Kumari 1997: 268). The usage of passive constructions in academic prose and journalistic writing of Malayalam is ascribed to the impact of English at the syntactic level. This argument presupposes the absence of the passive voice in Malayalam, which is not linguistically proved. Therefore, this claim is ruled out. The widespread use of passive in today's Malayalam can be argued as being genre induced, rather than a result of the contact with English.

23.3.1 Lexicon

A considerable percentage of lexical items in Malayalam are loanwords. This borrowing is quite interestingly spread across different domains of vocabulary and from different languages, and it even affected the replacement of native terminology of body parts. A representative list of borrowed vocabulary from different languages is given in Table 23.2.

Table 23.2 Loanwords in Malayalam

From Prakrit	From Sanskrit
mōtiram 'ring' < *muddrā* 'sign'	*dandham* 'tooth' < *dantha*
cāram 'ash' < *chāra* 'ash'	*agni* 'fire' < *agnih*
achan 'father' < *ajja* 'gentile, father of '	*bālan* 'boy' < *bāla*
ottakam 'camel' < *usta* 'camel'	*tāti* 'jaw' < *dādhi*
āšān 'teacher' < *ācāriya* 'teacher'	*garbhini* 'pregnant' < *garbhavati*
canta 'market' < *šamdā* 'market'	*cēttanljyēstan* 'elder brother' < *jyestha*
canti 'buttock' < *šamdhī*	*ammāvan* 'uncle' < *māma*
pirikam 'eyebrow' < *buruga*	*kākka* 'crow' < *kāka*
ēni 'ladder' < *sēni*	*lōkam/ulakam* 'the world' < *lōkah*
caṇṇala 'chain' < *samkalā*	*manuṣyan* 'the man' < *manuṣhya*
tavi 'ladle' < *davvī*	*mukham* 'face' < *mukha*
muttə 'pearl'< *mutta*	
vaṭṭam 'circle' < *vaṭṭ*	

(continued)

Table 23.2 Continued

From Hindi	From Marathi
cāya 'tea' < cāy	tapāl 'post, mail' < ṭapāla
kūli 'wage' < kūli	katti 'knife' <katti
tampǝ 'tent' < tambu	sampāṛǝ 'a curry' < sābāṛ
toppi 'cap' <ṭōpī	vaṭ 'a snack item' <vṭā
aṇṭi 'nut' <amḍī	pūri 'a food item' <pūṛi
kūtti 'female dog' <kūtī	ḍambhǝ 'pride' < ḍambha
kañcāvǝ 'kanja' <gamjā	caṭṭini 'ground condiment' < caṭni
paṭakkam 'cracker' <paṭāka	paṇka 'fan'< pamghā
sāri 'sari' < sḍī	tōppǝ 'grove' <thōmbǝ
lahaḷa 'quarrel' <jhagaḍā	
pāṛāvǝ 'sentry' <pāṛā	
pōkkiri 'dissolute fellow' <pōkṛi	

From Persian	Hebrew
piññāṇam 'plate/brail' <finjān	anna 'a personal name' < anāh
accāṛ 'pickle'< acāṛ	tōmma 'a personal name' < tōma
kamāṇam 'arch' <kamāṇ	ṛāhēl 'a personal name'< ṛāhēl
uṣāṛ 'refresh' <ušāṛ	havva 'the first woman' <havvāv
bējāṛ 'worry'< bēsaṛ	ādam 'the first man' <ādām
sumāṛ 'about' <šumāṛ	īšō 'Christ' <īšō
šarāšari 'average' <sarāsaṛī	yahōva 'God' <yahōā
savāri 'riding' <savrī	āmēṇ 'let it be' < āmmēṇ
tamāš 'entertainment' <tamāšā	allēlūya 'thanks to God' < allēlūya
šikkāṛ 'hunting' < šikkāṛ	
saṛkkāṛ 'government' <sarkar	
kušāl 'happy, cheer' < xushal	
gumastaṇ 'writer' < gumastha	
kāṇēšumāri 'census' <khana-sumari	
maitāṇam 'open field' <maidan	
tayyāṛ 'ready' <tayyar	

Arabic	Syriac
kattǝ 'letter' < khatǝ	bāva 'the holy father' < bābā
kāli 'empty' < khāli	yavaṇakkāṛ 'people from Greece' < yavāṇ
kīl 'tar' < kīṛa	kabaṛ 'tomb' < kabaṛ
nakkal 'draft' < nkǝlǝ	kapyāṛ 'helper in a church' < kabāṛ
allāhu 'Allah' < allāhǝ	yēšu 'Jesus' < yēšū
ṛabbǝ 'God' < ṛabba	mālākha 'angel'< mālākā
sūphi 'Islamic saint' < sūphī	kuṛbāṇa 'sacrifice' < kuṛbāṇa
maulavi 'Islamic scholar' < maulǝvi	sāttāṇ 'devil' < sāttāṇā
cekuttāṇ 'devil' < šeittāṇ	
oppaṇa 'an Islamic dance form' < abbṇa	
sāyppǝ 'an Englishman' < sāhib	
īṇkyilābǝ 'social revolution' < ingkulābǝ	
takarāṛ 'problem' < takṛāṛ	
hājaṛ 'present' < hazir	
haṛji 'petition'< arz	
masāla 'spices' < masalih	
bākki 'balance' < baqi	

Portuguese	Greek
kappittāṇ 'captain of the ship' < *capitão*	*akkādami* 'academy' < *akadēmia*
paṭṭāḷam 'army' < *battellāo*	*metṟōpolītta* 'bishop' < *metro polites*
lēlam 'auction' < *leilāo*	*kṟəstu* 'Christ' < *khristos*
jaṇṇal 'window'< *jennella*	*baibiḷ* 'Bible' < *biblos*
cāvi 'key' < *chaveri*	*leksikkaṇ* 'lexicon' < *lexicon*
varānta 'terrace' < *veranda*	*ḍōḷphin* 'dolphin' < *dolphinos*
mēśa 'table < *mesa*	*āṟṟam* 'atom' < *atomos*
istiri 'iron box'< *estirar*	*kattolikkaṟ* 'Catholics' < *katholikos*
pātiri 'priest'< *padre*	
kuriśə 'cross' < *cruz*	
alamāra 'cupboard' < *almario*	
kōppa 'cup' < *copa*	
tuṟuŋku 'jail' < *tronco*	
vīppa 'cask' < *pipa*	
vīññə 'wine' < *vinho*	

Latin (largely via English)	English
pāppaṟ 'poor' < *pauper*	*kōṭati* 'court' < court
kōṭṭa 'share' < *quotus*	*billə* 'bill' < bill
bōṇas 'bonus' < *bonum*	*bāŋkə* 'bank' < bank
saṟkkass 'circus' < *circus*	*beñcə* 'bench' < bench
	kāppi 'coffee' < coffee
	saikkiḷ 'bicycle' < cycle
	ayirə 'ore' < ore

23.3.1.1 *Loan Translation*

Loan translation is another type of structural borrowing at the lexical level prevalent in Malayalam. English is the donor language of the source word structure. The source word is translated morpheme by morpheme, or word by word, into Malayalam.

Mal. *aṭi-kuṟippə* 'footnote' < Eng. 'footnote'
   footnote
Mal. *tūlika-nāmam* 'pen name' < Eng. 'pen name'
   pen name
Mal. *rejata- jūbili* 'silver jubilee' < Eng. 'silver jubilee'
   silver jubilee
Mal. *suvaṟaṇṇa avasaram* < Eng. 'golden opportunity'
   golden opportunity
Mal. *dūra daṟśaṇ* 'television' < Eng. 'television'
   distance-vision
Mal. *aṭi- poḷi* 'enough to be excited' < Eng. 'groundbreaking'
   groundbreaking
Mal. *kari chanta* 'black market' < Eng. 'black market'
   black market

Mal. *īšō mašiha* 'Jesus Christ' < Eng. 'Jesus Christ'
Jesus Christ
Mal. *ambara cumbi* 'sky-scraper' < Eng. 'skyscraper'
sky-kiss

Sanskrit words or stems are used even in loanword translation in Malayalam, unlike its related language Tamil, which often uses the native words in loan creation and neologism.

23.3.1.2 *Integration of Loanwords*

The previously mentioned loanwords are integrated into the linguistic structure of Malayalam at each level.

23.3.1.2.1 MORPHOLOGICAL INTEGRATION

All loanwords are integrated into the morphological structure of Malayalam irrespective of the class and sources of the words.

Table 23.3 Morphological Integration of Loanwords

Source of Loanword	Morphological Integration of the Loanwords	
Sanskrit	Inflects for number:	*stṛī-kaḷ* 'women' 'woman-PL
	Inflects for case:	*stṛī-kkə* 'to woman' woman-DAT
	Inflects for conjunct:	*stṛī-um* 'woman also' woman-CONJ
English	Inflects for number:	*ḍōkṭaṛ-māṛ* 'doctors' 'doctor-PL
	Inflects for case:	*ḍōkṭaṛ -kkə* 'to doctor' doctor-DAT
	Inflects for conjunct:	*ḍōkṭaṛ -um* 'doctor also' doctor-CONJ
Arabic	Inflects for number:	*kattu-kaḷ* 'letters' letter-PL
	Inflects for case:	*katti -ṇə* 'to the letter' letter-DAT
	Inflects for conjunct:	*katt -um* 'letter also' letter-CONJ

Generally, morphological features of the donor language are not retained in Malayalam. One exception is an instance of plural inflection of –s in English (Asher and Kumari 1999: 251).

entə	*āṇə*	*niṇṇaḷuṭe*	*prōblam-*	*s*
What	be-PRES	you-GEN	problem-	PL
			English inflection	

'What are your problems?'

ňaŋŋaḷ	klāsmēṟṟ-	s	āyiru-	nnu
We	classmate-	PL	be-	PST
	English inflection			

'We were classmates'

The nominalizing suffix *-am* is often suffixed to the Sanskrit loanwords ending with *-h*;

Sanskrit

Mal. *jala-am* 'water' < Skt. *jala*

Mal. *samudr-am* 'sea' < Skt. *samudra*

Mal. *van-am* 'forest' < Skt. *vana*

Mal. *vivāh-am* 'marriage' < Skt. *Vivāha*

The masculine gender suffix *-aṇ* is often suffixed to Sanskrit loanword:

Mal. *cātt-aṇ* 'a lord. masculine' < Skt. *śāstha*

Mal. *arac-aṇ* 'king. masculine' < Skt. *rāja*

Mal. *puruṣ-aṇ* 'mail' < Skt. *puruṣa*

Mal. *sahōdar-aṇ* 'brother' < Skt. *sahōdara*

23.3.1.2.2 PHONOLOGICAL

Borrowed lexical items in classical texts are classified into two types based on the phonological integration: *tadbhava-* (derived from Prakrit and not directly from Sanskrit; lit. 'derived from that') and *tatsama-* (unassimilated loanwords from Sanskrit; lit. 'same as that'). Most of the words borrowed from Prakrit belong to the first type. This classification is not enough to explain the phonological integration of loanwords from all the donor languages. Therefore, each language based on language families will be treated independently.

23.3.1.2.2.1 Integration of Indo-Aryan Loanwords: Loanwords from Indo-Aryan languages have integrated into Malayalam in several ways. Following are the prosodic phonological changes observed:

(i) De-aspiration of stop and loss of /h/ and replacement of /-h/ by *-am*:

Mal. *taṭākam* 'lake' < Skt. *taḍāgah*

Mal. *śāntam* 'calm' < Skt. *śāntah*

Mal. *sāgaram* 'sea' < Skt. *sāgarah*

Mal. *parvatam* 'mountain' < Skt. *parvatah*

Mal. *lōkam/ulakam* 'world' < Skt. *lōkah*

(ii) Addition of a prothetic vowel before word-initial *r* and *l*;

Mal. *ulakam* 'world' < Skt. *lōkah*

Mal. *uruvam* 'form' < Skt. *rūpa*

Mal. *aracan* 'king' < Skt. *rājaṇ*

(iii) −s/š > c
Mal. *cōdyam* 'question' <Skt: *šōdhya* 'problem'
Mal. *cārāuam* 'arrack' <Skt: *sāraka* 'essence'
Mal. *caŋkə* 'hart' <Skt. *šakha* '?'
Mal. *cāṇa* 'caana' <Skt. *šāṇa*

(iv) Shortening final vowel
Mal. *guha* 'cave' <Skt. *guhā*
Mal. *vaṇitā* 'female' <Skt. *vaṇitā*
Mal. *bhārya* 'wife' <Skt. *bhāryā*
Mal. *vivāhita* 'married woman' <Skt. *vivāhitā*
Mal. *putṛi* 'daughter' <Skt. *putṛī*
Mal. *sira* 'vain' <Skt. *siṛā*

(v) Change of *a* into *e* after initial consonants
Mal. *gendham* 'smell' <Skt. *gandha*
Mal. *jennam* 'people' <Skt. *janam*
Mal. *bendhu* 'relative' <Skt. *bandhu*
Mal. *deya* 'kindness' <Skt. *daya*

The preceding phonological changes are often prosodic. Words that are borrowed directly from Sanskrit frequently preserve the Sanskrit phonology. On the other hand, the Sanskrit word borrowed through any of the Prakrits is highly integrated at the level of phonology. Sanskrit loanwords were the indisputable triggering factor that changed the phonological structure of Malayalam. A snapshot review of the change of the segmental phonemes from Old Malayalam to Modern Malayalam shows this:

Proto-Dravidian consonants (Table 23.4): There are only seventeen consonants reconstructed for Proto-Dravidian (Krishnamurti 2003: 91).

Table 23.4 Proto-Dravidian Consonants

	Labial	Dental	Alveolar	Retroflex	Palatal	Velar	Glottal
Stops	p	t	ṯ	ṭ	c	k	
Nasal	m	n		ṇ	ñ		
Lateral			l	ḷ			
Flap/Approximate			r	ẓ			
Glides	w				y		H

Early Old Malayalam consonants (Table 23.5): There are only seventeen consonants reconstructed for early old Malayalam (until the twelfth century CE), which is a stage not much affected by Sanskrit contact (Sekhar 1953: 16).

Table 23.5 Early Old Malayalam Consonants

	Labial	Dental	Alveolar	Retroflex	Palatal	Velarr	Glottal
Stops	p	t		ṭ	c	k	
Nasal	m	n	ṉ	ṇ	ñ	ŋ	
Lateral			l	ḷ			
Flap/Approximate			r	ḻ			
Glides	v				y		

Source: Sekhar (1953: 16); table was prepared by this author.

Middle Malayalam (Table 23.6): During the medieval centuries (until the fifteenth century CE), the number of consonants significantly increased to thirty-seven, resulting from the contact with Sanskrit (Ramachandran 1973: 114). Voiced and aspirated features resulted in middle Malayalam due to the contact with Sanskrit.

Table 23.6 Middle Malayalam Consonants

		Labial		Dental		Alveolar		Retroflex		Palatal		Velar	
		vl	vd	vl	vd	vl	vd	vl	vd	vl	vd	vl	vd
Stops	Unaspirated	p	b	t	d	R		ṭ	ḍ	c	J	k	g
	Aspirated	ph	bh	th	dh			ṭh	ḍh	ch	jh	kh	gh
Nasal		m		n̪		n		ṇ		ñ		ṅ	
Lateral						l		ḷ					
Flap						r							
Continuants		v						ḻ		y			
Fricatives						s		ṣ		š		h	

Source: Ramachandran (1973: 114)

Modern Malayalam consonants (Table 23.7): The number of consonants is thirty-nine in Modern Malayalam (Asher and Kumara 1997: 406). In addition to the Sanskrit-contact-induced phonemes, the segments (f) that are bracketed in the Table 23.7 and an additional vowel ($æ$) are used to pronounce English loanwords.

Table 23.7 Modern Malayalam Consonants

	Labial	Dental	Alveolar	Retroflex	Palatal	Velar	Glottal
Stops vol.	p	t	ṯ	ṭ	c	k	
vol.asp	ph	th		ṭh	ch	kh	
vod.	b	d		ḍ	j	g	
vod.asp	bh	dh		ḍh	jh	gh	

(continued)

Table 23.7 Continued

	Labial	Dental	Alveolar	Retroflex	Palatal	Velar	Glottal
Fricatives	(f)		s	ṣ	š		h
Nasals	m	n	n̠	ṇ	ñ	ň	
Liquids							
Trill			r	ṛ			
Lateral			l	ḷ			
approximate				ḻ			
Glide	v					y	

Source: Asher and Kumari (1997: 406).

This shows that there was radical change in the phonology of Malayalam from Old Malayalam to Modern Malayalam, resulting from the contact with Sanskrit and English. Therefore, it can be safely argued that today's phonology of Malayalam is contact-induced.

23.3.1.2.2.2 Integration of Indo-European Loanwords: The increase in the number of phonological segments resulting from the contact with Sanskrit facilitated a diversified phonology in Malayalam. Therefore, the loanwords from Indo-European languages were integrated into Malayalam without much change. Even then, the following are the phonological strategies observed in Malayalam in the integration of English loanwords:

(i) Replacement of labiodentals with bilabial
Mal. *kāppi* 'coffee' <(American) Eng. *kafi*
Mal. *āppīsə* 'office' <Eng. *ɒfɪs*
Mal. *phān̠* 'fan' <Eng. *fæn*

(ii) Replacement of alveolar dental by retroflex
Mal. *ṭī* 'tea' <Eng. *ti*
Mal. *ṭippə* 'tip'<Eng. *tɪp*
Mal. *ṭāṛ* 'tar' <Eng. *tar*

(iii) Replacement of voiced sound with voiceless
Mal. *sū* 'zoo' <Eng. *zu*
Mal. *sībṛa* 'zebra' <Eng. *zibrə*

(iv) Addition of central vowel in final position
Mal. *kḻāssə* 'class' <Eng. *klæs*
Mal. *bessə* 'bus' <Eng. *bəs*
Mal. *bukkə* 'book' <Eng. *bʊk*
Mal. *ṭrakkə* 'truck' <Eng. *trək*

(v) Addition of full vowel at the final position
Mal. *pēn̠a* 'pen' < Eng. *pɛn*

These are the generally observed patterns of phonological integration of English loanwords into Malayalam. Due to the widespread practice of teaching through the medium of English and specialized training in English, the tendency to use English phonetic features is currently a developing feature.

23.3.1.2.3 IMPACT ON ORTHOGRAPHY

Change in the phonological structure of Malayalam induced by Sanskrit contact eventually resulted in the replacement of the orthographic system of Malayalam. Malayalam had been using a Dravidian system of writing named *vaṭṭeẓuttə* and *kōleẓuttə* in the earlier period. This orthography and the graphs were adequate to represent the Dravidian phonemes. The first inscription of Malayalam dating 830 CE was written in this script. Later, when Malayalam had started borrowing heavily from Sanskrit, the old writing system was replaced by the *grantha* script, which can represent both Dravidian and Sanskrit phonology. Therefore, it can be safely argued that the present-day orthography of Malayalam is a contact-induced one.

23.3.2 Grammatical Borrowing

Compared with lexical borrowing, grammatical borrowing is less prevalent in Malayalam. Many Sanskrit loanwords are grammaticalized in Malayalam. Postpositions and reciprocals are the two major forms that were created by the grammaticalization of borrowed Sanskrit lexical items in Malayalam.

23.3.2.1 *Postpositions*

Table 23.8 shows the postpositions created by the grammaticalization of borrowed Sanskrit lexicon in Malayalam.

Table 23.8 Grammatical Borrowing in Malayalam	
Grammatical Function	Borrowed from Sanskrit
Postpositions	Mal. *mukhāntiram* 'through' < Skt. *mukhēṇa* Mal. *mārggam* 'by' < Skt. *mārga* 'to seek, look for, to search' Mal. *sambadichu* 'about, on'< Skt. *sambadha* Mal. *śēṣam* 'after' < Skt. *śēṣa* 'remainder, residue' Mal. *kāraṇam* 'because of' < Skt. *kṛi* 'to do, perform, cause' Mal. *vaśam* 'with' < Skt. *vaś* 'to desire' Mal. *mūlam* 'because of, due to' < Skt. *mūl* 'to be rooted or from' Mal. *nimittam* 'because of, due to' < Skt. *nimitta* 'above, cause, motive, ground, reason'

23.3.2.2 *Reciprocals*

There are two pronominal reciprocals in Malayalam directly borrowed from Sanskrit. They are *parasaparam* and *aṉyōṉyam* 'each other.'

rāmaṉ-	um	ṛehim-	um	parasparam	picc-	i
Rama-	CONJ	Rahim-	CONJ	RECP	pinch-	PST

'Rama and Rehim pinched each other'

rāmaṉ-	um	ṛehim-	um	aṉyōṉyam	picc-	i
Rama-	CONJ	Rahim-	CONJ	RECP	pinch-	PST

'Rama and Rehim pinched each other'

23.3.3 Borrowing of Exclamations

It is interesting to see that Malayalam has borrowed exclamations from the various languages with which it has been in contact:

Mal. *jōṛ* ! 'very good!' <Per. *zōṛ* 'power'
Mal. *bhēṣə*! 'very good!' <Per. *beeṣə* 'very good'
Mal. *sabāṣə* !'good!' <Per. *šabaš* 'well done!'
Mal. *gabhīram* 'wonderful' <Skt. *gambhīṛ* 'marvelous'
Mal. *kaṣṭam* 'what a pity' <Skt. *kaṣṭa* 'difficulty'
Mal. *oh entu bhaŋŋi*! 'oh how beautiful' <Skt. *bhangi* 'shape'
Mal. *aṭi poḷi*! 'wonderful' <Eng. *groundbreaking* (calque)
Mal. *sūppeṛ* ! 'wonderful' <Eng. *super*

23.3.4 Borrowing of Greetings

Malayalam has borrowed greetings from the various languages with which it had been in contact.

Mal. *namsakāram*, 'I bow to you' < Skt. *namastē*
Mal. *salām* 'greeting' < Arb. *salāmat*
Mal. *assalāmum alēkum* 'Peace be upon you' < Arb. 'Peace be upon you'
Mal. *halō* 'vocative' <Eng. *hallo*
Mal. *kṣamikkaṇam* 'please forgive' <Skt. *kṣam* 'pardon'
Mal. *lāl salam* 'read salute' <Hindi *lāl salām*

23.3.5 Borrowing of Acronyms

Acronyms are directly borrowed from English and have been integrated and transliterated into Malayalam script.

Mal. *yuṇesko* <Eng. UNESCO
Mal. *ṉāsa* <Eng. NASA
Mal. *yūphō* <Eng. UFO

Mal. *eyiḍsǝ* <Eng. AIDS
Mal. *bibisi* <Eng. BBC

Borrowed acronyms are integrated into the morphology and are inflected for number and case; *yūphō-kaḷ* 'UFOs,' *yuṇeskō-yuṭe* 'UNESCO's,' and *bibisi-yil* 'in BBC,' and so on.

23.4 CONCLUSIONS

This chapter has given an account of the contact of Malayalam with twelve other languages and its impact at different levels of language from phonology to syntax. To sum up, the following conclusions can be drawn from the foregoing discussion. First of all, it can be safely argued that contact with other languages is the undeniable 'inter-linguistic trigger' in the development of Malayalam. Malayalam has developed as an independent language from its status as one of a group of West-Coast dialects of Proto-Tamil Malayalam due to the contact with Prakrit and Sanskrit.

Malayalam has been in contact with the major language family Indo-European and its subgroups like Indo-Iranian and Indo-Aryan. Indo-Aryan and Indo-European had a tremendous impact on Malayalam through the contact with Prakrit, Sanskrit, and English. There is no doubt that the geographical position of Kerala, projected to the Indian Ocean, facilitated this contact. Malayalam was more influenced by Sanskrit during the medieval period and later by English in the modern period. The former has in fact changed the segmental phonology of Malayalam, and both Sanskrit and English have enriched the vocabulary. Compared with other features, borrowing of grammatical features is less extensive, with the exception of the borrowing of reciprocals and postpositions from Sanskrit. Sanskrit impact on Malayalam is recognized with the general Sanskritization process observed in most of the vernaculars in India, and English influence is recognized in the modernization process. Phonology is the level of Malayalam that is more influenced by Sanskrit contact, followed by English. All the voiced and aspirated features of modern Malayalam have resulted from the contact of Sanskrit. Based on the preceding discussion, without any doubt it can be stated that Malayalam is one of the main Dravidian languages that have been shaped by contact and convergence.

ACKNOWLEDGMENTS

I am extremely grateful to Professor R. E. Asher (University of Edinburgh, UK) for helpful comments and suggestions for improvement on earlier versions of this chapter and to Professor Anthony Grant (Edge Hill University, UK) for his guidance and attention to detail throughout the process. Thanks to Mr. Ajayakumar A, Senior Project Fellow, IUCNRM, University of Kerala for drawing the map for this chapter. All remaining shortcomings are entirely my own.

APPENDIX

The text of a front-page news report from a leading Malayalam daily newspaper, *Mathrub-hūmi* (November 18, 2013, p. 1) substantiates the presence and integration of loanwords from different languages.

Note: Loanwords from Sanskrit, English, Hindi, Persian, and Arabic are distinguished by bold, italics, square brackets, underline, and asterisk, respectively.

Transliterated Text in Malayalam

innə [harthāl]. kaṛšaṇa surakṣa

svantam lēkhakaṇ

Thiruvananthapuram: kasṯūri regaṇ rippōrṯə naṭappākkunnatil **pratishēddiccə** iṭatu muṇ-ṇaṇi āhvāṇam ceyta [harttāl] tiŋkaḻāẕca naṭakkum. rāvile āṛu mutal vaikiṭṭə āṛu vare āṇə [harttāl]. palēṭattum vaṇ **pṛakṣōbhaŋŋaḷ** uṇṭāya sāhacaryattil pōlīsə kaṛšaṇa surakṣa ēṛppeṭutti kaẕiññu. kasṯūri regaṇ rippōrṯə **pṛābalyattilākkikoṇṭə kēndra** <u>saṛkkāriṇṛe</u> vijñā-**paṇam** puṛattiṛaŋŋiya **divasam** mutal **samsthāṇattiṇṛe** malayōra **mēkhalakaḷil** saŋkhaṛṣam tuṭarukayāṇə. cila **sthalaŋŋaḷil** pāṛa, **vaṇam** māphiyakkāṛ samarakkāṛkkiṭayil nuẕanju kayaṛi akṛamam pṛavaṛttaṇaŋŋaḷ naṭattukayum ceytu. ī sāhacaryattil vaṇ surakṣa **saṇṇāhamāṇə** pōlīsə orukkiyiṭṭuḷḷatə. iṭukki *jillayile malayōra **mēkhalakaḷil** ñāyaṛāẕca **rātṛi** taṇṇe **sāyudha** pōlīsiṇe ragattiṛakki.

English Translation

Hartal Today; tight security

by our own reporter

Thiruvananthapuram: The Hartal declared by the Left Front as a protest against the implementation of Kasturi Rangan Report will take place on Monday. A hartal will be held on Monday from six in the morning till six in the evening. In the situation of the mounting protests at many places, police have tightened the security. Violence has been continuing in the high-range areas of the state since the day of the declaration of the implementation of Kasturi Rangan Report by the Central Government. Rock and forest mafia people were infiltrated among the protesters and incited violence. In this context, police have taken heavy security measures. Armed police are already deployed in the high-range area of Idukki districts even in the night on Sunday.

(**Hartal,** from Gujarati *haDtaal,* means a strike or shutdown).

REFERENCES

Asher, R. E., and T. C. Kumari. 1997. *Malayalam*. London: Routledge.

Balakrishnan, B. C., and Pillai K. S Narayana. 2006 [1991]. *Sabdasāgaram: A Malayalam-Malayalam Dictionary*. Kottayam: DC Books.

Freeman, Rich. 1998. Rubies and coral: The lapidary crafting of language in Kerala. *The Journal of Asian Studies* 57(1): 38–65.

Gamliel, Ophira. 2013. Voices yet to be heard: On listening to the last speakers of Jewish Malayalam. *Journal of Jewish Languages* 1: 135–167.

Godavarma K. 1933–1934. *Indo-Aryan Loan Words in Malayalam with a study of some Dravidian Loans in Sanskrit.* Unpublished PhD dissertation, University of London.

Godavarma K. 1946. The change of /a/ to /e/ in the Indo-Aryan loan words of Malayalam. *Bulletin of the School of Oriental and African Studies* 8: 559–562.

Gopalakrishnan, Naduvattom. 1985. Sanskrit impact on Malayalam. In *History of Malayalam Language*, edited by Prabhakara Variar, 31–54. Madras: University of Madras.

Govindan, Kutty A. 1972. From Proto-Tamil Malayalam to West coast dialects. *Indo-Iranian Journal* 14(1–2): 52–60.

Hassan, Nediyanad. 2009. *Arabi Malayalam Padakosam.* Thrissur: Kerala Sahitya Akademi.

Jamison, Stephanie W. 2008. Middle Indic. In *The Ancient Languages of Asia and the Americas*, edited by Roger D. Woodard, 33–49. Cambridge: Cambridge University Press.

Joseph, P. M. 1984. *Malayalattile parakīya padaṅṅaḷ.* Thiruvananthapuram: Kerala Bhasha Institute.

Krishna, Chaitanya P. (ed.). 1995. *History of Malayalam Literature.* New Delhi: Orient Blackswan.

Krishnamurti, Bh. 2003. *Dravidian Languages.* Cambridge: Cambridge University Press.

Kunjan Pillai, Surnad (ed.). 1965–. *Malayalam Lexicon.* Thiruvananthapuram: University of Kerala.

Madhava, Menon T. 2002. *A Handbook of Kerala.* Thiruvananthapuram: International School of Dravidian Linguistics.

Narayana, M. G. S. 1996. *Perumals of Kerala: Political and Social Conditions of Kerala under the Cera Perumals of Makotai.* Calicut (a monograph under private circulation).

Narayana, M. G. S. *Socio-Cultural Background of Genesis of Malayalam Language* (an unpublished manuscript).

OED online. *Oxford English Dictionary.* https://www.eifl.net/e-resources/oxford-english-dictionary-online Accessed July 13, 2016.

Ramachandran, Puthusseri. 1970. *Language of Middle Malayalam.* Thiruvananthapuram: Dravidian Linguistic Association.

Ramaiah, L. S., and N. Rajasekharan Nair (eds.). 2001. *An International Bibliography of Dravidian Languages and Linguistics*, Vol. V: *Malayalam Language and Linguistics.* Chennai: T. R. Publications.

Ramalingam, Pillai T. 2004 [1983]. *English-English-Malayalam Dictionary.* Kottayam: DC Books.

Sankunni, Nair M. P. 1995. *Points of Contact between Prakrit and Malayalam.* Thiruvananthapuram: International School of Dravidian Linguistics.

Sekhar, A. C. 1953. *Evolution of Malayalam.* Pune: Deccan College.

Southworth, F. C. 2005. *Linguistic Archaeology of South Asia.* London; New York: Routledge Curzon.

Sreekanteswaram, Padmanabha Pillai G. 2009 [1923]. *Sabdatharavali: A Malayalam Dictionary.* Kottayam: National Book Stall.

Zacharia, Scaria. 2003. Jewish Malayalam. *Jewish Language Research Website*: http://www.jewish-languages.org/jewish-malayalam.html (accessed on July 20, 2013).

CHAPTER 24

LANGUAGE CONTACT IN KOREAN

HO-MIN SOHN

24.1 INTRODUCTION

KOREAN historians agree that it was during the period of Three Kingdoms—Koguryŏ (37 BC–AD 668), Paekche (18 BC–AD 660), and Silla (57 BC–AD 935)—that the first true, sophisticated states took shape on the Korean peninsula.[1] The Silla kingdom unified the three kingdoms in 668, although a greater portion of the Koguryŏ territory was lost, including the entire Manchurian region. Our information about the Three Kingdoms period come from Korea's oldest extant history, titled *Samguk sagi* 三國史記 (the Chronicle of the Three Kingdoms) compiled by Kim Pusik, a Koryŏ dynasty historian, in 1145.

Due to the dearth of reliable data, the nature of Korean prior to the period of the Three Kingdoms is difficult to access. Fragmentary linguistic reflexes of the Three Kingdoms are observed in *Samguk sagi* and other existing records written in the scripts (called *idu*, *kugyŏl*, and *hyangch'al*) that used Chinese characters as phonograms or semantograms to represent Korean words and suffixes. Compared to the scarcity of information about the Koguryŏ and Paekche languages, information about the Silla language is relatively abundant. A glimpse of the Silla language leads us to regard contemporary Korean as the descendant of the language of Unified Silla and the succeeding dynasties, Koryŏ (918–1392) and Chosŏn (1392–1910).

One remarkable cultural event in Korean history was the creation of the indigenous phonetic writing system by King Sejong of the Chosŏn dynasty and its promulgation in 1446. Owing to the invention of the alphabet (called *han'gŭl* 'the great writing'), detailed aspects of the Korean language were revealed for the first time.

---

[1] Korean expressions are Romanized following the McCune-Reischauer Romanization system.

Throughout the historic period, Korean, like other Altaic languages and Japanese but unlike Chinese or English, has evolved as a language of head-final and SOV-order syntax. All kinds of modifiers precede their heads. All particles are postpositional, while all inflectional affixes indicating tense, aspect, honorific, modality, and clause type are suffixed to the predicate that occurs at the end of a clause. It is an analytic language with a typical agglutinative morphology, in that a series of suffixes and particles are attached, respectively, to predicates and nominals in a fixed order with clear-cut meanings and functions. The Korean vocabulary has been enormously enriched, due mainly to constant language contact.

24.2 CONTACT WITH OTHER LANGUAGES

Koreans have had contact with surrounding countries, chiefly with China and Japan, and also with Western countries, notably the United States. The various historical, cultural, political, economic, social, and other relations between Korea and these countries have engendered enormous linguistic outcomes. The traditional pattern of linguistic contact was mainly with Chinese, whereas the modern pattern is predominantly with Japanese and Western languages, especially English. There have been other contacts, such as Sanskrit, Mongolian, and Manchu-Tungusic languages, but their linguistic impact has been minimal, except for a very small number of loanwords, such as Sanskrit *miruk posal* 'Maitreya,' *sŏkkamoni* 'Buddha,' and *namu amit'abul* 'save us, merciful Buddha'; Mongolian *sadon* 'relative by marriage,' *kara-mal* 'all-black horse,' *pora-mae* 'young hawk,' and *t'arak* 'cow's milk'; Manchu-Tungusic *sundae* 'a kind of sausage,' *pusŭkkae* 'furnace' (Hamgyŏng dialect), and *orangk'e* 'barbarian' (which originally meant a Jurchen tribe).

Contacts with Chinese, Japanese, and English have exerted the most powerful and extensive influences on the Korean language, as China, Japan, and the United States have been the world's leading powers, with technologically highly developed cultures. The most distinctive effect of these contacts has been on the Korean vocabulary; their influence on phonology, morpho-syntax, and discourse function has been minor.

The patterns of contact with the three languages are not the same. Chronologically, these contacts have been made with Chinese, Japanese, and English. In terms of the linguistic impact, Chinese is the strongest, followed by Japanese and English in that order.

24.2.1 Contact with Chinese

24.2.1.1 *Historical Overview*

The oldest and most powerful contact is with Chinese, as Korea has spent its entire history bordering China, a giant of world culture. Before the nineteenth century, when Western cultures began to penetrate East Asia, China had long been the center of

East Asian culture and civilization. Chinese culture and civilization were propagated to neighboring countries, mainly through written Chinese based on Chinese characters, a typical ideographical script. Thus, Korean borrowings from China are mostly written Chinese, including Buddhist texts, Confucian classics, historical and literary works, and various cultural and institutional terms, although there are a very small number of spoken words as well, as in *paech'u* 'Chinese cabbage,' *mŏk* 'black ink,' *put* 'brush,' *sal* 'arrow,' *toe* 'grain measure,' *sangt'u* 'topnot,' *mosi* 'ramie fabric,' *ryuwŏl* 'June,' and *siwŏl* 'October.' Koreans in general treat such fossilized borrowings from spoken Chinese as native words, while considering contemporary spoken Chinese as a foreign language.

It is not known exactly how and when Chinese and Chinese characters were first introduced into Korea. The only deduction we can make is that practical knowledge of Chinese and the Chinese script in Korea dates back to 194 BC, when Wiman, from Yen in China, founded a primitive Korean state in the northwestern part of the Korean peninsula. Subsequently, the establishment by China's Han dynasty of their four counties on the soil of Wiman's Ko-Josŏn (ancient Korea) in 108 BC must have familiarized the resident Koreans with Chinese and the Chinese script. According to *Samguk Sagi*, the Koguryŏ people had the Chinese script from the very beginning of their existence as a state in 37 BC. *Samguk Sagi* also records that history books written in Chinese characters were compiled in the Paekche dynasty in 375 and in the Silla dynasty in 545. One stele that was erected in 414 in honor of King Kwanggaet'o of Koguryŏ contains over 1,800 Chinese characters. All these suggest that Chinese culture and characters had achieved considerable popularity in Korea during the Three Kingdoms period.

During the reign of King Chijŭng (in 503) in the Silla dynasty, the native term for 'king' was changed to the Chinese word *wang* (王) and the name of the country to the Chinese-character word (or Sino-Korean word) *Silla* (新羅). Personal names of Silla male aristocrats were also changed following the Chinese pattern (consisting usually of a one-character family name followed by a two-character given name, as in Kim Yu-sin (金庾信), although commoners and women retained their native names.

With the unification of the Korean peninsula by the Silla dynasty in 677, the use of Sino-Korean (hereafter SK) words[2] in Korea gained even more popularity since Silla's unification was achieved with Tang China's military support. Subsequently, contact between the two countries increased. In the second year of King Sinmun (682) of Unified Silla, *Kukhak* 國學 (lit. 'national studies'), a government agency in charge of national education, was established, and many Chinese classics began to be taught. In the sixteenth year of King Kyŏngdŏk (in 757), native place names were Sinicized as two-Chinese-character words, and in his eighteenth year, all official titles were also made SK words.[3]

---

[2] All Koreanized words based on Chinese characters, whether they are ancient borrowings directly from China or re-borrowings indirectly from Sino-Japanese, or new coinages in Korea, are commonly called *hancha-ŏ* 'Chinese-character words' or Sino-Korean (SK) words.

[3] In 1946, one year after Korea was liberated from the thirty-five-year Japanese occupation, the former SK name of the capital city (Kyŏngsŏng) was changed to the native term, Sŏul (Seoul).

The number of SK words began to overtake that of native words in the Koryŏ dynasty (918–1392). The Koryŏ dynasty period may be characterized by, among other things, the influx of great numbers of SK words into the Korean vocabulary. This was particularly the case due to King Kwangjo's adoption, in 958, of the Chinese system of civil service examinations based on Chinese classics. Before the Koryŏ period, SK words were limited, in general, to the names of places, people, and government ranks. But starting with the Koryŏ dynasty, SK words pervaded the spoken language.

The Chosŏn dynasty (1392–1910) saw the all-out infiltration of SK words into every facet of Korean culture and society, chiefly because of the dynasty's adoption of Confucianism as a national ideology, and, as a result, the popular admiration of everything Chinese. Thus, the ruling classes of Korea devoted their entire lives to the study of Chinese classics, because it was the main goal of education, the official means of conducting government affairs and documenting public and private records, and the medium of civil service examinations.

The most prolific use of SK words took place during the eighteenth and early nineteenth centuries (e.g., I. Lee 2005: 245). In addition to words of daily use, a wide variety of items and concepts of Chinese and Western civilization were imported into early modern Korea, along with their SK names. Western terms were translated into Chinese in China before they were imported into Korea. Some examples are chó-myŏng-jong (self-ringing-bell) 'alarm clock,' ch'yŏl-li-gyŏng (1000-mile-mirror) 'telescopes,' chi-nam-ch'ŏl (point-south-iron) 'magnet,' hwa-yak (fire-medicine) 'gunpowder,' sŏng-gyŏng (holy-book) 'bible,' sin-bu (godfather) 'Catholic father,' and ch'ŏn-dang (sky-hall) 'heaven.'

Although direct borrowings from Chinese ceased toward the close of the Chosŏn dynasty when the Japanese annexed Korea, Chinese characters have continually been used by Koreans, as well as Japanese, to coin new SK words as needs arose.

24.2.1.2 *Sino-Korean Pronunciation*

The pronunciations of SK words are different from those of the corresponding Mandarin Chinese words and Sino-Japanese words. For instance, 學院 is pronounced as hag-wŏn 'institute' in SK, xué-yàn 'college' in Mandarin, and gaku-in 'institute' in Sino-Japanese. It is generally assumed that the pronunciations of Chinese used in the northern part of China during the eighth-century Tang dynasty constituted the basis of SK sounds. This was during the Unified Silla period, when a great many written materials about Chinese civilization, including those on Buddhist culture, were imported from China. Thus, pronunciations of contemporary SK words in Korean are similar to those of Late Middle Chinese (cf. Pulleyblank 1991).

SK words have followed the phonological patterns of Korean. Thus, tones were not distinguished. The rule changing n to l before or after l applied to both native and SK, as in native sŏl-lal (from sŏl + nal) 'New Year's Day' and SK sil-la (from sin + la) 'Silla dynasty.' Palatalization applied to both native and SK words, as in native chida (from tida) 'lose in a game' and SK ch'ŏn-ji (from t'yŏn-di) 'heaven and earth.' Both native and SK words contracted *ay* to *ae*, as in native *sae* (from *say*) 'bird' and SK *nae-il* (from *ray-il* 'come-day') 'tomorrow.'

24.2.1.3 *Formal and Semantic Changes in SK Words*

Many SK words from Chinese have undergone semantic and/or formal change in Korean. Examples with semantic change include *mi-ŭm* 'thin gruel' from 'rice-drink,' *nae-oe* 'husband and wife' from 'inside and outside,' and *sa-ch'on* 'cousin' from 'four nodes.' Examples of nativized words from SK are *amu* 'anyone' from SK *a-mo* 'anyone,' *kaji* 'eggplant' from SK *ka-ja* 'eggplant,' *sarang(-ha)* 'love' from SK *só-ryang(-hó)* 'think of,' *chirŏngi* 'earthworm' from SK *ti-rong-i* 'earthworm' (lit. 'earth dragon'), *sanyang* 'hunting' from SK *san-hóyng* 'mountain going,' *mŏngsŏk* 'straw mat' from SK *mang-sŏk* 'woven mat,' *kanan* 'poverty' from SK *kan-nan* 'difficulty,' *chimsŭng* 'animal' from SK *chyung-sóng* 'living things,' and *ssŏlmae* 'sled' from SK *sŏl-ma* 'snow horse,' *huch'u* 'black pepper' from SK *ho-ch'o* 'barbarian pepper,' *kage* 'store' from SK *ka-ga* 'false house,' *puch'ŏ* 'Buddha' from SK *pul-ch'e* 'Buddha's body,' and *ssŭ* 'write' (SK *sŏ* 'write,' ancient Chinese *siwo*).

24.2.1.4 *Native/SK Synonyms*

The influx of SK words has caused proliferation of SK-native synonyms. In general, two things have happened in synonymic clash. First, synonymous words are associated with different shades of meaning, stylistic nuances, or social values, enriching the Korean vocabulary. Native words usually represent unsophisticated traditional culture, both mental and physical, while SK words, conveying more formality, tend to denote higher quality objects, and more abstract and more socially prestigious concepts. For example, the native word *il-chari* (lit. 'workplace') usually refers to a low-paying and/or part-time job such as blue-collar work, whereas SK *chik-chang* (lit. 'job-place') generally implies a professional white-collar job. Native/SK pairs like *ch'an-mul/naeng-su* 'cold water,' *son-bal/su-jok* 'hands and feet,' *kap/ka-gyŏk* 'price,' *sum/ho-hŭp* 'breath,' *mok-sum/saeng-myŏng* 'life,' and *pilda/kidohada* 'pray' show similar connotations and differences. SK counterparts are used for relative honorification, as shown in *ne* (plain) versus *tangsin* (semi-formal) 'you,' *anae* (plain) versus *pu-in* (hon.) 'wife,' *nai* (plain) versus *yŏnse* (hon.) 'age,' *i* (plain) versus *ch'ia* (hon.) 'teeth,' *chip* (plain) versus *taek* (hon.) 'house,' and *irŭm* (plain) versus *sŏng-ham* (hon.) 'name.'

Second, in the synonymic battle between the native and SK stocks, the latter won out in many cases. Native words replaced by SK words (in parentheses) include *chat* (*sŏng*) 'castle,' *azóm* (*ch'inch'ŏk*) 'relatives,' *chŭmŭn* (*ch'ŏn*) 'one thousand' *hódaga* (*manil*) 'if,' *kóróm* (*kang, hosu*) 'river, lake,' *moy* (*san*) 'mountain,' *on* (*paek*) 'hundred,' *oray* (*mun*) 'gate,' *syurup* (*usan*) 'umbrella,' *hŭyn-soy* (*un*) 'silver,' *kilóma* (*anjang*) 'saddle,' *kip* (*pidan*) 'silk,' and *muruy* (*ubak*) 'hail.' Even native kinship terms have been replaced by SK counterparts since the eighteenth century. Thus, except for some native terms of the direct family line, which also had SK counterparts, most of the native terms were replaced by SK kinship terms.

24.2.2 Contact with Japanese

24.2.2.1 *Historical Background*

Korea, China, and Japan are geographically, historically, and culturally close to one another. While Koreans and the Japanese are considered to have descended from Altaic ancestors, they are not ethnically related to the mainstream Chinese. Korean (K) and Japanese (J) are the closest sister languages sharing the typology of agglutinative morphology and SOV syntax. Some three hundred basic vocabulary items are viewed as K-J cognates (e.g., K *pyel* vs. J *hosi* 'star'; K *sŏm* vs. J *sima* 'island'; K *kom* vs. J *kuma* 'bear'; K *tal* vs. J *tsuki* 'moon'). Chinese, on the other hand, is genetically Sino-Tibetan, with the typology of "isolating" morphology and SVO syntax. Yet, both Korean and Japanese have close linguistic relationships with Chinese in that they have borrowed a large number of Chinese words and characters throughout their long historical contacts with various Chinese dynasties.

Korea and Japan have long been in contact with each other. During the Three Kingdoms period, Korean states maintained diplomatic relations with Japan. In particular, Paekche's relationships with Japan were close. For instance, in the early fifth century, Paekche scholar Wang In took the text of *One Thousand-Characters* and *the Analects of Confucius* (10 volumes) to Japan at the invitation of the Japanese rulers. During the Chosŏn dynasty period, however, the relationships were not friendly. This was initiated by the Japanese invasion of Korea in 1592, popularly called *Imjin Waeran* (the 1592 Japanese invasion and the subsequent seven-year war). No record indicates, however, that there were any significant linguistic results in Korean during either the Three Kingdoms period or the Seven-Year War.

In 1876, Chosŏn Dynasty Korea was forced by Japan to agree to the "Japan-Korea Treaty of Amity." According to this treaty, Korea opened trade with Japan and began to import not only Japanese culture, but also Western civilization through Japan. In 1905, Japan deprived Korea of its diplomatic sovereignty and made Korea a protectorate of Japan through the "1905 Japan-Korea Protectorate Treaty." Japan finally annexed Korea in 1910 through the "Japan–Korea Annexation Treaty." The thirty-five-year colonial rule formally began on August 22, 1910, with the office of the Japanese Governor-General established in Seoul. Already by 1910, the number of Japanese settlers in Korea reached over 170,000. During the colonial period, millions of Japanese moved to and resided in Korea. When Japanese colonial rule was terminated at the end of World War II in 1945, almost all Japanese settlers in Korea returned to Japan, leaving behind a significant linguistic impact.

24.2.2.2 *Linguistic Results*

During the period from 1876 to 1945, the linguistic, as well as sociocultural, political, and economic impact of Japan on the Korean people was enormous. All levels of Korean students, as well as the educated public, became Korean-Japanese bilinguals. Korean was spoken mainly at home, while Japanese was a social and official language.

Use of Korean was banned in all levels of schools and government institutions. The Japanese influence on the Korean language may be summarized as follows.

First, Japanese words encroached into the Korean lexicon as loanwords in all walks of life, usually those words that did not have exact counterparts in Korean. Upon Korea's liberation from Japan in 1945, however, the nationwide movement to "eradicate Japanese remnants" put most native Japanese words into disuse, frequently replacing them with newly coined Korean words. Yet, quite a few Japanese words are still in use in colloquial speech, as in *kudu* 'leather shoes,' *kabang* 'bag,' *odeng* 'skewed fish cake,' *sasimi* 'sashimi,' *wasabi* 'wasabi,' *mocci* 'Japanese-style rice cake,' *tama* 'electric bulb,' *sibori* 'wet handkerchief,' *waribasi* 'splittable wooden chopsticks,' *mahobyŏng* 'thermos,' *ippai* 'fully,' *yudori* 'flexibility,' *ukki* 'float,' *eri* 'collar,' *pentto* 'box lunch,' *takkwang* 'pickled radish,' *yakki-mandu* 'fried dumplings,' *khado-chip* 'corner house,' *ssumekkiri* 'nail cutter,' *ssuri* 'pick-pocket,' *hiyasi* 'cooling,' *kisu* 'scar,' and *mudeppo* 'carelessly.' Japanese terms are still widely used in printing, sewing, construction, and artwork, as in *senaka* 'shelf-back of a book,' *kasane-nui* 'overlap sewing,' *kali-kumitate* 'temporary setup,' *ssumi* 'piling,' and *kakwubucci* 'frame.'

Second, Korea has imported thousands of Sino-Japanese (hereafter SJ) words that the Japanese created by translating all kinds of Western words representing neo-civilization and other modern concepts by means of Chinese characters (e.g., Kang 1995). A great many such SJ words were coined during the Meiji Restoration period in the nineteenth century. The SJ words imported as SK follow the SK pronunciation rules. Examples are SK *ŏn-ŏ-hak* (SJ *gen-go-gaku*) 'linguistics,' SK *pi-haeng-gi* (SJ *hi-koo-ki*) 'airplane,' *hak-kyo* (SJ *gak-koo*) 'school,' *an-nae* (SJ *an-nai*) 'guidance,' and *hyŏn-gŭm* (SJ *gen-kin*) 'cash.' The influx of SJ words of this kind continued even after 1945 and is still continuing. SK words like *naeng-jŏn* 'cold war,' *kong-hae* 'public pollution,' *misi-jŏk* 'microscopic,' and *kung-min-ch'ong-saeng-san* 'GNP' are borrowings from SJ after 1945.

SK words of Japanese origin range across all areas of Korean life, including government, politics, economy, society, education, academics, institutions, astronomy, geography, and all other up-to-date culture and civilization. When there were doublets between SJ words and Chinese words, Koreans have chosen SJ words, as in SJ *pang-mul-kwan* (Chinese *pang-mul-wŏn*) 'museum,' SJ *pyŏng-wŏn* (Chinese *yang-byŏng-wŏn*) 'hospital,' SJ *ch'ŏl-to* (Chinese *ch'ŏl-lo*) 'railroad,' SJ *hyŏn-gŭm* (Chinese *hyŏn-ŭn*) 'cash,' SJ *ki-ch'a* (Chinese *hwach'a* train), SJ *yŏng-hwa* (Chinese *chŏn-yŏng* movie), and SJ *chŭng-ga* (Chinese *ka-jŭng*) 'increase.'

Third, many native Japanese words written in Chinese characters as semantograms came into Korea, not as native Japanese loans but as disguised SJ loans. While such semantograms are pronounced as native words in Japanese, they are pronounced like any other SK words in Korea. For instance, the Japanese native word *iri-kuchi* (enter-mouth) 'entrance' is written as SJ 入口 and pronounced only as *iri-kuchi*. It was borrowed as SK *ip-ku*. Similar examples are *chul-gu* (J *te-kuchi*) 'exit,' *kyŏn-sŭp* (J *mi-narai*) 'intership,' *ip-chang* (J *tachi-ba*) 'situation,' *chŏk-cha* (J *aka-ji*) 'deficit,' *yŏk-hal* (J *yaku-wari*) 'role,' *ch'u-wŏl* (J *oi-kosi*) 'outrun,' *ch'wi-gŭp* (J *tori-atsukai*) 'handling,' *so-mae* (J *ko-uri*) 'retail,' *hal-in* (J *wari-biki*) 'discount,' and *yŏp-sŏ* (J *ha-gaki*) 'postcard.'[4] Such disguised Japanese loans couched in Chinese characters behave like any other SK words in Korean and are exempt from post-1945 expulsion.

Fourth, in the nineteenth century, Japan imported abundant foreign words as loanwords, together with the relevant cultural objects and concepts. These Japanized loanwords were re-borrowed as Korean loanwords during the colonial period. Examples include Chinese (e.g., *angkko* 'sweet red-bean paste,' *udon* 'needle,' *mandu* 'dumplings,' *raamen* 'noodle,' *tchang-kken-ppo* 'rock, paper, scissors'); Portuguese (e.g., *kasut'era* 'sponge cake,' *kappa* 'tent,' *tabako* 'tobacco,' *tempura* 'fried food,' *ppan* 'bread,' *birodo* 'velvet,' *potan* 'button'), Spanish (e.g., *meriyassu* 'knit undershirt'), Dutch (e.g., *inkki* 'ink,' *karasu* 'glass,' *gomu* 'rubber, eraser,' *sooda* 'soda,' *ppenkki* 'paint,' *ppomppu* 'pump,' *biiru* 'beer,' *madorosu* 'sailor'), English (e.g., *keekki* 'cake,' *kurakpu* 'club,' *kurisu* 'grease,' *sarada* 'salad,' *waisyassu* 'white shirt,' *seet'a* 'sweater,' *t'aia* 'tire,' *torakku* 'truck,' *dasu* 'dozen,' *ppada* 'butter,' *ppangkku* 'puncture,' *ppanssu* 'lower-underwear,' *bakessu* 'bucket,' *batteri* 'battery,' *gasu* 'gas,' *ppakku* 'moving backward'), German (e.g., *teema* 'theme,' *mensu* 'menses,' *gibusu* 'plastic cast,' *arubaito* 'part-time work'), and French (e.g., *ssubon* 'trousers,' *buraja* 'braziers,' *romansu* 'romance,' *debyuu* 'debut') (e.g., K. Song 1979; K. Kim 1995).

Fifth, there are morpho-syntactic influences. Complex phrasal constructions in Korean such as *–e iss-ŏsŏ* 'in regard to' (J *–ni oi-de*), *-e ŭiha-yŏ/ŭiha-myŏn* 'according to' (J *–ni yot-te/yor-eba*), *-e tae-ha-yŏ* 'regarding' (J *–ni tai-si-de*), *-ŭro-but'ŏ-ŭi* 'from' (J *–nohoo-kara-no*), *-esó-ŭi* 'at' (J *–te-no*), *-ŭn mullon* 'let alone' (J *–wa mochiron*), *ppunman anira* (J *nomi-narazu*) and *-e t'ŭllim ŏpsta* 'surely is' (J *–ni chigai nai*), have been modeled after the Japanese patterns. Similarly, a host of Korean idioms were coined modeling after similar Japanese expressions, as in *nun-ŭl ŭisimhada* (J *me-o utagau*) 'hard to believe' (lit. 'suspect one's eyes'), *sum-ŭl chugida* (J. *iki-o gorosu*) 'keep completely silent' (lit. 'kill the breath'), and *hŭimang-e pul t'ada* (J *giboo-ni moeru*) 'earnestly hope' (lit. 'burn with hope'). The most widely used SK adjectivizer suffix *–chŏk/-jŏk* '-tic, -al,' as in *minju-jŏk* 'democratic' and *nangman-jŏk* 'romantic,' came from SJ *–teki,* as in J *minshu-teki* and *roman-teki,* which was created in Japan in view of its phonetic similarity to English '-tic.'

During the colonial period, when use of Korean was discouraged, most Korean intellectuals read only Japanese written materials and wrote only in Japanese. Thus, upon liberation from Japan in 1945, they inevitably began writing Korean books, novels, and newspaper articles following Japanese styles. Such writing tradition still persists to a great extent, as observed in the following in the first few sentences of Kawabata Yasunari's Nobel Prize–winning novel *Yuki Kuni* (Snow Country) (1968) and the authentic translations in Korean and English:

---

[4] This is a major reason why Japanese retains many old native words, whereas, in Korean, many native words were replaced by equivalent SK words.

Japanese: "雪国" *Yuki-Kuni* 国境の長いトンネルを抜けると雪国であった。夜の底が白くなった。信号所に汽車が止まった。

*Kokkyo-no nagai **tonneru**-o nukeru-to yuki-kuni-deat-ta. Yoru-no soko-ga siroku-nat-ta. Singoosho-ni kisha-ga tomat-ta.*

Korean: "설국" *Sŏl-Guk*
국경의 긴 터널을 빠져나오자, 눈의 고장이었다. 밤의 밑바닥이 하얘졌다. 신호소에 기차가 멈춰 섰다.

*Kukkyŏng-ŭi kin **t'ŏnŏl**-ŭl ppajyŏnao-ja, nun-ŭi kojang-i-ŏt-ta. Pam-ŭi mitpadag-i hayae-jyŏ-t-ta. Sinhoso-e kich'a-ga mŏmch'wŏs-ŏt-ta.*   (translated by Yoo Sookja)

English: "Snow Country"
The train came out of the long tunnel into the snow country. The earth lay white under the night sky. The train pulled up at a signal stop.

(translated by E. G. Seidensticker)

Notice that the underlined SK and SJ words and a bold-faced loanword are shared. Among the Japanese semantograms, only the title of the book is rendered as SK *Sŏl-Guk*. All the other Japanese semantograms are translated in equivalent Korean native words. Given that Japanese and Korean are genetically related and typologically very similar, one may nevertheless be struck by the perfect match, word for word, in the written discourse style between the two languages.

24.2.3 Contact with English and Other Western Languages

24.2.3.1 *Overview*

Since the beginning of the twentieth century, Western words came into the Korean vocabulary as loanwords. As indicated in section 2.2, until 1945, loanwords were introduced into Korean almost exclusively through Japanese. Only some sporadic examples in novels and newspapers of the early 1900s were direct borrowings, for example, *t'ebŭl/t'eibŭl* 'table' (J *teeburu*), *ingk'ŭ* 'ink' (J *inkki*), *hot'el* 'hotel' (J *hoteru*), *kabi/k'ap'i/k'ŏp'i* 'coffee' (J *kohii*) (S. Kim 1998: 15).

Since the end of World War II, South Koreans have been in direct contact with many foreign languages, notably with English, through books, magazines, news media, movies, the Internet, language learning, the importation of new commodities and other cultural items, and interactions with native speakers. As a result, the Korean language has accommodated thousands of words as loanwords for both need- and prestige-based motivation.

Pae's loanword dictionary (1972) contains a total of 11,465 loanwords, of which English loanwords occupied 78.5% or 9,005, followed by Japanese (6.5% or 749), German (4.7% or 535), and French (3.2% or 363). Examples of German and French loanwords include German *hisŭt'eri* 'histeria,' *ideollogi* 'ideology,' *noiroje* 'neurosis,' *t'ema* 'theme'; and French *changrŭ* 'genre,' *ank'ol* 'encore,' *ellit'ŭ* 'elite,' *nyuangsŭ* 'nuance,' *pak'angsŭ* 'vacation,' *pet'erang* 'veteran,' *p'iangse* 'fiancé,' *p'ŭrop'il* 'profile,' and *tirŏksŭ* 'deluxe.'

The Korean government provided detailed regulations for spelling all loanwords regardless of whether they were borrowed before 1945 via Japanese or new incoming ones after 1945 (Sohn 1999: 116–117). Thus, Japanese-style loans (J) that were borrowed before 1945 were re-spelled and pronounced according to the government regulations, as, for example, in *k'ŏp* (J *koppu*) 'cup,' *k'eik'ŭ* (J *keekki*) 'cake,' *pŏt'ŭn* (J *botan*) 'button,' *pinil* (J *biniiru*) 'vinyl,' *p'ŏngk'ŭ* (J *ppangkku*) 'puncture,' *radio* (J *razio*) 'radio,' and *alba (it'ŭ)* (J *arubaito*) 'part-time work.'

24.2.3.2 *English Loanwords*

During the past forty-odd years since Pae's dictionary was published in 1972, a large number of additional English loanwords have been incorporated in the Korean lexicon. English words have constantly been introduced into South Korea, together with American sociocultural concepts, products, and institutions. Many existing loanwords from other languages, as well as some SK words, have been replaced by English loans. As a result, it is estimated that English comprises more than 90% of some 20,000 loanwords currently used in South Korea. In fact, most borrowings after 1945, especially in South Korea, are words from English, which range over all aspects of life including clothing, food and drink, electricity and electronics, automobiles, fashion, advertisements, sports, arts, social activities, politics, and economy, as well as in all areas of science and technology. Random examples are *aisŭ-k'ŭrim* 'ice-cream,' *allibai* 'alibi,' *hint'ŭ* 'hint,' *k'eibŭl-k'a* 'cable car,' *kolp'ŭ* 'golf,' *kurup* 'group,' *k'akt'eil* 'cocktail,' *k'allori* 'calorie,' *hom-shop'ing* 'home shopping,' *k'aemp'ŏsŭ* 'campus,' *k'ŏmp'yut'ŏ* 'computer,' *k'ŏp'i* 'coffee,' *k'ŭredit-k'adŭ* 'credit card,' *nyusŭ* 'news,' *p'at'i* 'party,' *pija* 'visa,' *pijŏn* 'vision,' *pŏsŭ* 'bus,' *pŭrip'ing* 'briefing,' *rip'ot'ŭ* 'report,' *semina* 'seminar,' *sŏbisŭ* 'service,' *t'erebijŏn* 'TV,' *s(y)up'ŏ* 'supermarket,' *sŭllip'ŏ* 'slippers,' *chin* 'blue jeans,' *p'ŭraip'en* 'frying pan,' *k'areraisŭ* 'curried rice,' *yunesŭk'o* 'UNESCO,' *pŭiaip'i* 'VIP,' *ap'at'ŭ* 'apartment,' *rŏksyŏri* 'luxurious,' *k'ombi* 'combination,' *p'aesyŏn* 'fashion,' *seksi-(hada)* 'be sexy,' *teit'ŭ-(hada)* 'to date,' and *syop'ing-(hada)* 'to shop.'

Even some compounds are coined in Korea based on English loanwords, as in *toŏ-p'on* 'door-phone,' *kasŭ-reinji* 'gas range,', *ai-syop'ing* 'window-shopping, literally: eye shopping,' *paek-miro* (back-mirror) 'rear-view mirror,' *obŏ-sensŭ* 'oversensitive,' *pihaindŭ-sŭt'ori* 'story behind the scene,' *paek-taensŏ* 'back(ground) dancer'; or on loan-native/SK words, as in *kasŭ-t'ong* 'gas container,' *tijit'ŏl-sigye* 'digital watch,' *pŏsŭ-p'yo* 'bus ticket,' *sinyong-k'adŭ* 'credit card,' and *anjŏn-belt'ŭ* 'safety belt.'

Indeed, Korean language, culture, and society are heavily influenced by American counterparts, in the same way that they were influenced by everything Chinese or Japanese in the past. For instance, C. Song (1998: 29) shows that 63.2% of all the titles of TV programs are wholly or partly in English loanwords; 47% of the menus of computer communication are wholly or partly in English loanwords; and 96% of the names of beauty shops are in English and other loanwords. Loanwords used in South Korea are not necessarily need-based, but also are prestige-based to a great extent.

On the other hand, North Korea, through its powerful language purification movement, has banned, as much as possible, the use of Western loanwords, including

English. T. Kim (2001: 93) states that North Korean residents are unaware of 8,284 loanwords commonly used in South Korea, including such simple terms as *nyusŭ* 'news.' This may be an inevitable consequence of globalization being strongly upheld in South Korea, while it is largely discouraged in North Korea.

New loanwords from English compete with existing native and SK words in many cases. Native words usually coexist with loanwords, as in *kul* 'tunnel, cave' versus loan *t'ŏnŏl* 'tunnel,' native *tanch'u* versus loan *pŏt'ŭn* 'buttons,' native *tŏhagi* versus loan *p'ŭllasŭ* 'addition,' and native *kit* versus loan *k'alla* 'collar.' The SK *sung-gang-gi* (move. up-move.down-machine) had long been used to denote an elevator, but has gradually been replaced by the English loanword *ellibeit'ŏ*. Similarly, the English loanword *k'ŏmp'yut'ŏ* 'computer' has replaced the SK word *chŏn-san-gi* (electronic-calculate-machine), although some SK compounds such as *chŏnsan-mang* 'computer network' and *chŏnsan hakkwa* 'department of computer science' are still in use. The loan *t'aip'ŭrait'ŏ* and the SK *t'a-ja-ki* (hit-letter-machine) for 'typewriter,' loan *p'ak'ing* and SK *chuch'a* for 'parking,' loan *t'aengk'ŭ* and SK *chŏnch'a* for 'tank,' and loan *k'amera* and SK *sajingi* for 'camera' are used interchangeably. A great many SK words for the items of daily use are still exclusively used, including *sŏnp'unggi* 'electric fan,' *naengjanggo* 'refrigerator,' *chadongch'a* 'car,' *chŏnhwa* 'telephone,' *ch'ong* 'gun,' *chajŏn'gŏ* 'bicycle,' *ch'aek* 'book,' *chihach'ŏl* 'subway,' *yŏnghwa* 'movie,' and *pihaenggi* 'airplane,' whereas quite a few loanwords such as *t'ŭrŏk* 'truck,' *pŏsŭ* 'passes,' *t'aeksi* 'taxi,' *ap'at'ŭ* 'apartment,' *hot'el* 'hotel,' *t'ŏminal* 'terminal,' and *ot'obai* 'auto-bicycle' are exclusively used.

When SK-loan doublets or native-SK-loan triplets exist, loanwords are, in general, associated with modern, stylish, and technological objects and concepts. For example, the native word *karak* 'rhythm' is usually used in reference to traditional Korean folk songs, the SK word *un-yul* (rhyme-law) in formal or academic situations, and the loanword *ridŭm* for some sort of Western flavor. *Ch'um* (native) connotes a traditional dance, *muyong* (SK) a formal or academic dance, and *taensŭ* (English loan) a social dance.

24.3 SUMMARY AND CONCLUSION

Contemporary Korean encompasses the results of the language contacts examined thus far. The following points may be made to summarize what has been discussed.

24.3.1 Lexicon

Both SK and loanwords are an integral part of the Korean vocabulary. Statistically, SK words occupy approximately 65% of the entire Korean vocabulary, as compared to the 30% native stock and the 5% loan stock (e.g., Sohn 1999: 87). In general, SK words are considered much more "native-like" than Japanese, English, and other loanwords, in that they have a much longer history, are more predominant and indispensable in use, and are much more integrative with Korean tradition, culture, and society.

There are three layers of SK words: (a) those introduced traditionally from China (e.g., *chayŏn* 'nature,' *ch'ŏnji* 'heaven and earth,' *haksaeng* 'student,' *pyŏnhwa* 'change,' *ŭibok* 'clothes,' *chilmun* 'question,' *hyoja* 'filial son'); (b) those introduced from SJ during the colonial period and thereafter (e.g., *ipku* 'entrance,' *ch'ulgu* 'exit,' *toro* 'road,' *kongjang* 'factory,' *pihaenggi* 'plane,' *yaksok* 'promise'); and (c) those coined in Korea (e.g., *p'yŏnji* 'letter,' *sosik* 'news,' *ch'onggak* 'bachelor,' *ilgi* 'weather,' *sikku* 'family,' and many contemporary institutional names). The first and second layers are much larger than the third. As indicated earlier, most loanwords are English ones.

24.3.2 Phonology

SK and loanwords have been adapted to the phonological patterns of native Korean. There are cases, however, where the native sound patterns themselves have been affected by non-native words. First, earlier Korean (before the sixteenth century) had—and the Kyŏngsang and Hamgyŏng dialects still have—lexical tones that are attributed to the prolonged influx of words from Chinese, a tone language.

Second, the massive influx of *r/l*-initial loanwords (e.g., *radio* 'radio,' *rait'ŏ* 'lighter,' *robi* 'lobby') in recent years has disrupted the original Altaic and Korean sound pattern in which no word allows a word-initial liquid.

Third, SK words where vowel harmony is not observed have partly contributed to the disruption of the long-sustained vowel harmony in native words. Vowel harmony is observable only in fossilized sound symbolic words and the infinitive suffix *–e/-a* in contemporary Korean.

24.3.3 Morphology

Non-native words have had certain effects on Korean morpho-syntax. First, SK compounds reflect Chinese verb-object order in transitivity, as in *sal-gyun* (kill-germs) 'sterilization' and *kŏ-du-jŏl-mi* (discard-head-cut-tail) 'giving the gist.' In the SK-native compound *sal-gyun-hada* 'kill germs,' SK *sal-gyun* follows the verb-object order, while native verb *hada* 'do' follows the Korean predicate-final order.

Second, Chinese and other foreign verbs and adjectives are introduced into Korean as verbal or adjectival nouns and never as independent predicates. To function as predicates, they must be compounded with a native predicate (most productively with *ha-* 'do, be,' but also with *toe-* 'become' and *i-* 'be'), as in SK *poksa-hada* and loan *k'op'i-hada* 'to copy,' SK *siwi-hada* and loan *temo-hada* 'do political demonstration,' SK *ch'ongmyŏng-hada* and loan *sŭmat'ŭ-hada* 'be smart,' SK *ch'wiso-doeda* and loan *k'aensŭl-doeda* 'be canceled,' and SK *kisulchŏk-ida* and loan *t'ek'ŭnik'ŏl-hada* 'be technical.'

Third, some SK morphemes function as derivational affixes, usually occurring with a SK stem (e.g., negative prefixes *pi-, mu-, mi-, mol-* and adjectival suffix –*chŏk/-jŏk,* as in *pi-inkan-jŏk* 'inhumane'). Fourth, SK elements have added a sizable number of function words. Examples are personal pronouns like *chagi* 'oneself, you (affectionate)' and *tangsin* 'you, him/herself,' adverbs like *cuk-si* 'immediately,' *chŏmjŏm* 'gradually,' *manil* 'if,' *simjiŏ* 'even,' *yŏhakan* 'in any case,' *pulgwa* 'no less than,' *muryŏ* 'as many as,' *panmyŏn* 'on the other hand,' and *kyŏlguk* 'after all,' and conjunctive endings like –*ch'a* 'for' and *mullon* 'let alone.' SK-native compounds include adverbs like *chŏn-hyŏ* '(not) at all,' *kyŏl-k'o* 'under any circumstances,' and conjunctives like *pulgu-hako, kosa-hako* 'despite' and *wi-hae* 'for.' Non-native words rarely function as particles or inflectional suffixes.

Finally, as indicated in section 2.2.2, a number of Korean idiomatic expressions are due to the equivalent Japanese constructions, as in –*e ŭiha-myŏn* 'according to' (J –*ni yor-eba*).

24.3.4 SK and Loans in Discourse

Contemporary Koreans are hardly able to manage daily lives without using SK words and loanwords. Observe the following random media excerpt, in which SK words are underlined and loanwords are boldfaced. The remainders (words, particles, and affixes) are native elements.

[KF갤러리] [*KF kaellŏri*] 'Korea Foundation Gallery'
<발레리오 로코 오를란도 '관계의 영역'>展, 문화가 있는 날 이벤트 안내
<*Pallerio Rok'o Olŭllando "kwankye ŭi yŏngyŏk"> chŏn, munhwa* ka in-nŭn nal **ibent'ŭ** annae
'Exhibition on **Valerio Rocco Orland**'s *Territory* of *Relations*', Guide to the cultural day **event**'

2월 5일부터 2월 26일, KF 문화센터 갤러리에서는 이탈리아 출신 미디어
2 wŏl 5 il put'ŏ 2 wŏl 26 il, KF munhwa **sent'ŏ kaellŏri** esŏ-nŭn It'allia ch'ulsin **midiŏ**
아티스트 발레리오 로코 오를란도의 개인전을 개최합니다.
at'isŭt'ŭ Pallerio Rok'o Olŭllando ŭi kaeinjŏn ŭl kaech'oe-ha-mnida.
'From February 5 to February 26, at the KF Culture **Center Gallery** will take place Italian media artist Valerio Rocco Orland's private exhibition.'

발레리오 로코 오를란도는 2002년부터 개인 및 집단 정체성 사이의
Pallerio Rok'o Olŭllando nŭn 2002 nyŏn put'ŏ kaein mit chiptan chŏngch'esŏng sai ŭi
관계에 초점을 맞춘 다양한 미디어 아트를 통해 공동체의
kwangye e ch'ochŏm ŭl match'u-n ta'yang-ha-n **midiŏ at'ŭ** rŭl t'ong-hae kongdongch'e ŭi
다양성을 다루는 프로젝트를 진행하고 있는 젊은 작가입니다.
Ta'yangsŏng ŭl taru-nŭn **p'ŭrojekt'ŭ** rŭl chinhaeng-ha-go in-nŭn chŏlm-ŭn chakka i-mnida.

'Valerio Rocco Orland is a young artist who has been working on a project, since 2002, in which he deals with a community's diversity through diverse media arts with the focus on the relations between individual identity and collective identity.'

Notice that native elements are limited to only some basic words and all grammatical particles and affixes, that only one SK word in the title is written in a Chinese character (展), that Koreans' daily communications would be virtually impossible without SK words; and, that loanwords are essential in the sociocultural life of contemporary Koreans.

To give another example, examine the titles of the SBS (Seoul Broadcasting System) TV program covering the twenty-four hours of March 20, 2015. Notice how deeply and extensively SK and English loan elements are integrated with native elements. Notice, in particular, that seventeen out of the total twenty-two titles contain at least one loanword and that eight titles consist entirely of English loanwords:

나이트 라인 *nait'ŭ lain* 'Night line'

풋볼 매거진 골! *p'utpol maegajin Gol!* 'Football magazine "Goal!"'

세상에서 가장 아름다운 여행 스페셜 *sesang esó kajang arŭmdaun yŏhaeng sŭp'esyŏl*
'World's best trips special'

SBS 뉴스 *SBS nyusŭ* 'SBS news'

굿모닝: 특별한 오늘 *kunmoning: t'ŭkpyŏlhan onŭl* 'Good morning: Special today'

모닝와이드 *moning waidŭ* 'Morning wide'

아침연속극 [황홀한 이웃] (55 회) *ach'im yŏnsok kŭk [hwangholhan iut]* (55 *hoe*)
'Morning drama series [Charming neighbours]
(episode 55)

좋은 아침 *chohŭn ach'im* 'Wonderful morning'

SBS 생활경제 *SBS saenghwal kyŏngje* 'SBS economy of daily life'

TV 동물농장 *TV tongmul nongjang* 'TV animal farm'

날씨와 생활 *nalssi wa saenghwal* 'Weather and life'

열린 TV 시청자 세상 *yŏllin TV sich'ŏngja saesang* 'World of open TV audience'

SBS 컬처클럽 *SBS k'ŏlch'ŏ k'ŭllŏp* 'SBS culture club'

SBS 애니갤러리 *SBS aeni kaellŏri* 'SBS Annie Gallery'

민영방송 공동기획 물은 생명이다 *minyŏng pangsong kongdong kihoek: mul ŭn
saengmyŏngida* 'Joint project of private broadcasting: [Water is life]'

SBS 뉴스퍼레이드 *SBS nyusŭ p'ŏreidŭ* 'SBS news parade'

우리 아이가 달라졌어요 *uri ai ka tallajy-ŏssŏyo* 'My child has changed.'

해피 투데이 *haep'i t'udei* 'Happy Today'

일일드라마 [달려라 장미] (68회) *iril tŭrama [tallyŏra changmi]* (68 *hoe*)
'Daily Drama: Run! Rose.' episode 68

궁금한 이야기 Y *kunggŭmhan iyagi Y* 'Curious story Y'

정글의 법칙 *chŏnggŭl ŭi pŏpch'ik* 'Rules of jungles'

웃음을 찾는 사람들 스페셜 핫 클립 *usŭm ŭl ch'annŭn saram tŭl sŭp'esyŏl hat k'ŭllip*
'Smile-seeking people's special hot clip'

24.3.5 Language Attitudes

Korea (together with China, Japan, Vietnam, etc.) has long been known as a country of the cultural sphere of Chinese characters. Yet, since 1945, both Koreas have attempted to eliminate Chinese characters from practical use, so that the Korean alphabet *han'gŭl* can be exclusively used. As a result, the use of Chinese characters is limited to a great extent in contemporary South Korea, despite the fact that 1,800 characters are taught in secondary schools. In North Korea, Chinese characters have been completely abolished from everyday use, but a limited number of characters are taught in schools for reading purposes only (e.g., Sohn 2004).

Due largely to the national feeling against Japanese colonial rule, native Japanese words have been almost completely eliminated from practical use in both Koreas since 1945. However, a huge quantity of SJ words, including both coined ones and the ones used as semantograms, have not been eliminated, as they are essentially need-based borrowings.

As the world's most powerful, prestigious, and widely used language, English is the first foreign language required to be taught at all secondary schools and universities in South Korea. Even many elementary schools have introduced English in their curriculum and instruction. Hundreds of native English speakers are employed to teach conversational English. In many universities, a number of courses are taught only in English. Even English-speaking villages have been established. Thousands of Korean students at all levels of schools go abroad to English-speaking countries, notably to the United States, not only to pursue regular academic programs, but also to receive English language training. Indeed, the fervor for English in South Korea is unprecedented. This is because fluency in English is an essential component in college entrance examinations and a prerequisite for employment in most government offices and corporations, as was the case with Chinese classics and Japanese in the past. As a result, all educated Koreans are bilingual in varying degrees of proficiency, from novice to superior. Many young speakers are multilinguals, with Chinese and/or Japanese as a third or fourth language.

24.3.6 Conclusion

The Korean language has been greatly enriched through contacts with the world's three most powerful languages. The abundant SK and loan items, most of them cultural borrowings, are of enormous benefit to the native speakers of Korean in many ways. They have enabled Koreans to absorb the world's advanced civilizations and cultures. They have provided linguistic foundations for Koreans to advance and refine their own tradition, culture, society, and technology. Extensively shared linguistic elements and features that resulted from language contact contribute to cultural and emotional affinity among the peoples involved and facilitate the learning of mutual languages and cultures. There have been no significant linguistic degeneration or displacement in the course of contacts, except for the replacement of numerous native words by SK words due to synonymic clash and the unsuccessful attempt by the Japanese to ban the use of Korean during the colonial period.

REFERENCES

Kang, Sin-hang. 1995. Sino-Japanese. *Saegugŏ Saenghwal* 5(2): 27–60.

Kim, Kwang-hae. 1995. Kugŏ-e taehan ilbonŏ-ŭi kansŏp (Intervention of Japanese in Korean). *Saegugŏ Saenghwal* 5(2): 3–26.

Kim, Sejung. 1998. Oeraeŏ-ŭi kaenyŏm-gwa pyŏnch'ŏn-sa (The concept and evolution of loanwords). *Saegugŏ Saenghwal* 8(2): 5–19.

Kim, Taesik. 2001. ŏllon ui nambukhan ŏnŏ tongjilsŏng hoebok pangan (A proposal to recover homogeneity in the two Koreas' mass media language). *Saegugŏ Saenghwal* 11(1).

Lee, In-ho. 2005. *Chosŏnmal Yŏksa 3* (A History of Korean 3). Pyongyang: Sahoegwahak ch'ulp'ansa.

Pae, Yang-seo. 1972. *Han'guk Oeraeŏ Sajŏn* (A Dictionary of Korean Loanwords). Seoul: Kugŏ-kungmun hakhoe.

Pulleyblank, E. 1991. *Lexicon of Reconstructed Pronunciation in Early Middle Chinese, Late Middle Chinese, and Early Mandarin*. Vancouver: University of British Columbia Press.

Sohn, Ho-min. 1999. *The Korean Language*. Cambridge, UK: Cambridge University Press.

Sohn, Ho-min. 2004. Language purification movements in North and South Korea. *Korean Linguistics* 12: 141–160.

Song, Cheol-ui. 1998. Oeraeŏ-ŭi sunhwa pangan-kwa suyong taech'aek (Purification and accommodation of loanwords). *Saegugŏ Saenghwal* 8(2): 21–40.

Song, Ki-joong. 1986. Remarks on modern Sino-Korean. *Language Research* 22(4): 469–501.

CHAPTER 25

....

LANGUAGE CONTACT
IN KHMER

....

JOHN HAIMAN

KHMER, the official language of Cambodia, is currently thought to be an isolated member of the Mon-Khmer family of languages (Headley 1976; Ferlus 1992), but over the last 1,500 years its speakers have been in different kinds of intimate contact with influential languages from two unrelated families: these are the Indic family, represented by Sanskrit and Pali, and the Tai family, represented by Thai and, to a much lesser extent, Lao.[1] Linguistic evidence of direct contact with other Mon-Khmer languages spoken within Cambodia, such as Stieng, is hard to confirm or refute on account of their great inherited similarity, though Khmer has certainly influenced them, and there may be Mon forms in Khmer. Contact with Austronesian languages such as Malay and Cham, the latter once spoken along the narrow coastal plains of south Vietnam (Thurgood 1999), while attested, is comparatively limited. Direct contact with the Vietnamese, speakers of another Austro-Asiatic language that displaced the Cham, goes back at least 500 years, and yet borrowings from that language seem to be conspicuously less frequent.[2] Recent borrowings from French (within the last 150 years)[3] and English (within the last fifty) are even more infrequent.

---

[1] I am very grateful to Frank Huffman (Khmer and Thai), Erik Davis (Khmer), Martha Ratliff (Hmong), and Anthony Diller (Thai) for many helpful leads, corrections, and suggestions. My continuing gratitude to Neurng Ourn and Veasna Keat for teaching me more and more about Khmer over the last 17 years. And I salute my wise mentor Philip Jenner, who passed away in January 2013, before I could run footnote 5 (Indic) and everything else in this essay past his eyes.

[2] Khmer people's historically motivated hatred of both the Vietnamese and the Thai as conquerors is well known, but Perez Pereiro (2012: 60–65) suggests that beyond that, the two kinds of xenophobia are altogether different. While Khmer may resent the modern Vietnamese as invaders, thieves, and parasites, they are not in any life-or-death competition with them as inheritors of the cultural legacy of India. With the Thai, they are. This common legacy is reflected in the current border dispute over the temple Preah Vihear, but it also pervades the vocabulary itself.

[3] Frank Huffman points out that French borrowing was much more extensive, even in colloquial discourse, before the civil war and the coming of the Khmer Rouge in 1975. He recalls a cyclo driver cursing out a passing jet plane in 1959 with the words *a:-reaksiyong* "damn jet!"

25.1 PALI CONTACT

Extensive borrowing from the Indic languages that were vehicles of Hinduism and Buddhism was already a fait accompli by the time of the pre-Angkorian Khmer inscriptions of the seventh century, although it continues today: there was, for example, a massive influx of over 3,000 neologisms in the 1950s, when technological calques comparable to our *telephone* and *oxygen* were created by a scholarly committee set up in 1947 (Jacob 1977). Indic borrowing was primarily accomplished via the highly restricted prestige medium of writing, a fact that is patently obvious from the orthography of Pali and Sanskrit transliterations, but two much more potentially egalitarian (spoken language, although not colloquial language) borrowing conduits are the following:

a) Theravada Buddhism, the state religion for centuries, and likely the dominant religion already by the fourteenth century. The Khmer share Theravada Buddhism today with people in Laos, Thailand, and Burma (Peang-Meth 1991; Harris 2006).
b) The Ramayana, the popular Indian epic, which exists not only in the written but also in the spoken traditions. Even oral redactions of this work (e.g., Ta: Saw:j 2000) show heavy lexical borrowing from Pali and Sanskrit. While modern Khmer speakers were until recently force-fed this classic text mainly in school, and are currently exposed to dubbed versions of current Indian productions on television, there were still bards whose memorized recitations were passed on as heard until apparently as recently as two generations ago (personal observation).[4]

25.1.1 Indices of Assimilation

Assimilation of loan elements has occurred at various levels in Khmer, and these are detailed in the following sections.

25.1.1.1 *Phonological Assimilation*

An Indic borrowing may be said to be assimilated phonologically, when it conforms to the canonical template of sesquisyllabicity: most Khmer words are either monosyllabic, or if polysyllabic, invariably iambic two syllable words with a sharply reduced initial syllable. (For example, Khmer has doublet borrowings from Indic *santih* 'peace.' The monosyllabic version in the compound *sok+san* 'peace and well-being' is more assimilated than the trochaic one in the derived nominal *sante'+ phiap* '(state of) peace'). Some totally assimilated borrowings are the following:

---

[4] Erik Davis notes that "one of the most exciting [recent] developments in Reamke (Ramayana) studies and vernacular traditional culture has been the digitization and release by the Buddhist Institute of enormous public performances of the Reamke by the great storyteller Ta Krut in the 1960s."

arawm	'feeling'[5]	from P. *a:rammana* 'sense object'
kru:	'teacher'	from S. *guru*
kba:l	'head'	from S. *ka:pala* 'skull'
muk	'face'	from P. *mukha*

25.1.1.2 *Morphological Assimilation*

A borrowing may be considered morphologically assimilated when it can be used as a base for native derivational morphological processes. For example, the word *ksawt* 'poor, wretched, miserable' comes from Sanskrit *kṣata* 'broken (down), torn,' but can be infixed to create a synonym *k-am-sawt*.

A borrowing may be also considered at least partially assimilated morphologically, when it is exploited as a companion for a near-synonym in order to satisfy the Khmer penchant for decorative symmetrical compounding (see section 25.5.3). Khmer accepts borrowings from both Indic and other languages for this purpose. The borrowings may be compounded with native words or—what is equally a sign of their assimilation—with other borrowings. Examples of possible assimilation from Thai are the following symmetrical compound expressions:

claeuj	*taw:p*	'answer'
'answer'	<T. *tɔ:b*	'answer'
tumniam	*tumloap*	'custom'
	?<T. *thamniam*	'habit'

Decorative symmetrical compounds that are put together with borrowings from Indic languages seem to be much more numerous. Some examples from Pali and Sanskrit are the following:

me:k	*sa:kha:*	'branches'	
'branch'	<P. *sa:kha:*	'branch'	
nivoat	*tralawp*	'return'	< P. *nivattana* 'return'
'returning'	return		
ni'jau:m	*co:l ceut*	'love'	
love	<P. *niyama*	love	

---

[5] A note on the alphabetization employed here: All symbols have their IPA values, except for:

Vowels:

Stressed monophthongs: aw= [ɑ]; au = [ɔ]; e = [ɛ] except before a palatal consonant or {v}, where it is equivalent to a sound between [i] and [ə]; ee = [e]; eu = [ɤ]; w = [ɯ];

Stressed diphthongs: the final {a} of {ia}, {ua}, {oa}, {wa} is equivalent to [ə];

Unstressed monophthongs: a = [ə].

Consonants:

b= [ɓ] syllable-initially

d= [ɗ] syllable-initially

nj= [ɲ]

v= [β]

'adhere to (custom)'

uba:j	*kawl*	'stratagem, ruse, trick'
trick	< P. *upa:ya*	trick
saw:m	*rum*	'agreeable' <P. *ramai:ya*
thae	*reaksa:*	'protect' <S.*raksha:*
saca'	*suca'reut*	'honest'
'truth'	'honest'	
<P.*sacca*	< S. *sucarita*	
pee:l	*vee:lia*	'time' <S.P. *ve:la:*'time'
poat	*poan*	'wrap around, entwine'
'snared'	'fetter (N)'	
<P. *baddha*	<P. *bandha*	
mun	*akum*	'spell, incantation'
'spell'	'religion'	
<.P.*manta*	< P. *a:gama*	

25.1.2 Borrowing from Indic into Written Khmer

This section discusses the various strata of borrowing from Indic languages in to Khmer over the past 1500 years.

25.1.2.1 *The Root Vocabulary*

Although there are hundreds of thoroughly assimilated Pali borrowings (e.g., *araw:m* 'feeling,' *kba:l* 'head,' *kru:* 'teacher,' *mnuh* 'person,' *muk* 'face,' *panjha:* 'problem,' *piak* 'word,' *phawl* 'fruit,' *phu:m* 'village,' *proat* 'thong,' *sat* 'animal,' *tnu:* 'bow; December') that occur in both spoken and written Khmer, the heavy use of phonetically unassimilated Pali vocabulary and formulaic expressions was and is primarily—if not always[6]—a feature of an elite literary register (Woznica), in not quite the same way, perhaps, as Norman French, Latinisms, and Greek borrowings are a feature of the literary register of English. Observe the following typical paragraph from a booklet about the Ramayana (Tha:n Sau:n:, nd, 15):

---

[6] The colloquial noun *pa:hi:* 'street vendor of quack medicines often accompanied by a trained begging monkey' denotes a common figure in modern Khmer life (cf. Cut Khaj 2010: 11–12). A *pa:hi: mwn si: luj* 'a vendor who doesn't take money' is one who gives away his medicines for free, and makes his living by begging through telling tales, and collecting from his audience by sending his monkey around. The word seems to have slipped unnoted through both the monolingual *Dictionnaire cambodgien* (1989, but most recently revised in 1967) and Headley et al. (1977). It probably derives from the Sanskrit *ba:hi: -ka* 'member of a despised people' (MacDonell 2004 [1924]). My thanks to Veasna Keat for translating the concept—the etymological guess is my own.

(1) *Lo:k*   *Saw:r Sa:run seuksa: sangkhee:p*   *rwang riam   kee:*
    Honorific   PN study   summarize   story Rama   heritage
    (Loans)   <S. loka   <S. siksa: <P. sankhepa   ?<Th.ryang   <S. ki:rti
    'world'   'study'   'synthesis'   'story'   'glory'

    ba:n tveu: *ka: -*   *viphiak*   *tev leu: ka:l*   *pa'ri'chaet*   *rwang daoj*
    past do   Nom.   analyze   go on time   division   story by
             <P. ka:ra <S. vibha:kara   <S.kala. P. paricheda ? <Th.ryang
             'matter' 'analyze'   'time'   'division'   'story'

    jo:ng ta:m   *vi:thi:*   *bej*   *ja:ng*   *kw:*   *vi:thi:*   *ti:*   *muaj*
    refer follow   method three   kind   ,viz.   method place   one
             <S. vidhi   < Ma. yang   <S. vidhi
             'form '   'form'   'form'

    priap   *thiap*   *piak*   *samdej*   *klia*   *prajo:k*   *dael praeu nev knong*
    compare   compare   word   speech   sentence   sentence   which use at in
             ?<Th. thiab   <P. va:kya   <S. prayoga
             'compare'   'speech'   'recitation'

    athabaw:t   *rwang*   *riam   kee:*   *tev nwng aksaw:*   *seul*
    text   story   Rama   heritage   go with   literature
    <P. atthapada   ?<Th.ryang   <S. aksara   <S. silpa
    'text'   'story'   'letter'   'art'

    sej'la: *ca:reuk nev*   *sa'maj*   *na: muaj*
    stone   inscribe at   era   any   one
    <P. sila: <S. samaya
    'rock'   'era'

"Professor Saw: Sa:run in his study and summary of the Ramayana analyzed the chronology of the story by relying on three methods: first, he compared the wording and the sentence structure which was used in the text of the Ramayana with the literary style of the inscriptions of the era."

This snippet also has borrowings from Malay and (possibly) Thai; moreover, a distinction may be drawn between the Indic borrowings that are thoroughly assimilated, and found in all levels of Khmer discourse, such as *ka:l* 'time' and *piak* 'word,' and the more arcane words, which betray their foreign origin and imperfect assimilation not only through their phonology, but through their infrequency and unfamiliarity.

By way of comparison, consider the following opening passage in "French Schoolboy," a popular personal memoir written by Cut Khaj in 2010, in which all borrowings may be considered to be thoroughly assimilated:

(2) *Khaet   kampaung ca:m kw: cia khaet muaj daw: samkhan nej prate:h kampucia*
      Province Kampong Cham :   be province one very important of nation   Cambodia
      (Loans)
      <S. kshetra   <Ma. kampong>   <S.pra-desa
      'province'   'port'   'region'

      dael   sambo: tev daoj sambat   thoamciat do:c cia prej cheu:
      which abundant go by   richness   natural   like be forest wood
      (Loans) <P. sampu:ra   <P. sampatti <P. dhamma+jati
               'richness'   'success'   'law'+'nature'

      camka: kaosu: vial srae daw: lveung lveu:j poan   heukta: daw: mian dej
              dej camka: roap ciat   <Th. phan <F. hectare.
      garden rubber field paddy very extensive   1,000   hectare very have earth
      earth garden count nature
      (Loans) <Fr. caoutchouc

      Ciat   nev   ta:m   moat   tunlee: prau:m   teang steung pre:k o:
      Nature be.at follow shore lake   together all   creek stream rivulet
      <P. jati

      nwng bwng bua dael   sambo: tev   daoj trej krup praphee:t
      and   lake   lake which   abundant go   by   fish   all   kind
                                                                   <S. prabheda

"Kampong Cham is a very important province of Cambodia, rich in natural resources such as forests, rubber plantations, extensive rice paddies and plantations of thousands of hectares of rich soil along the shores of the Tonlee Sap and its small tributary rivers which are rich in every variety of fish."

The etymology of *kampong* is uncertain as to whether it is an Austro-Asiatic loan into Malay or vice versa (Uri Tadmor, personal communication to Anthony Grant). It is the source of the English military noun *compound*.

What makes Pali unique are two facts. First, until very recently, every Khmer male was expected to spend at least one year of his life at a *voat* (pagoda school/ monastery). While there, much of his instruction consisted of learning to chant Pali texts. The second fact is that while he duly memorized these texts, he did so typically without knowing or in any significant way engaging with what they meant (Bilodeau 1955: 16; Harris 2006: 106, 118; Smith 2006: 327). To the extent that Pali consists of incantations, it is an "esoteric" language for Cambodian speakers in the narrowest sense of that word (Bernon 2006: 57). While due to the spelling system, all present-day literate speakers can identify phonetically and orthographically unassimilated Pali borrowings in their vocabulary (Haiman 2011: 34), there has never been any time when a significant number of Khmer speakers were truly bilingual in Pali. Rather than learning grammar, they learned to recite mantras (thus the vast majority of all males who were ex-monks), passages of the Ramayana (thus the bards), or they learned etymologies (thus, all speakers who are literate).

In addition to lexical borrowing, written Khmer has borrowed, to a limited extent, features of Indic word formation and syntax. From the same scholarly text that provides us with the first brief scholarly snippet we have just examined, we encounter also the following examples of structural borrowing.

25.1.2.2 *Word Formation*

Khmer is an almost exclusively prefixing language, but has borrowed a small number of derivational affixes from Indic as suffixes. The suffix *–phiap* 'state,' derived from Pali *bha:va* 'state,' appears as a suffix in the (doubly suffixed) word

pheak-	kdej-	phiap	'loyalty'
< P. *bhakti*	< S. *gati*	<P. *bha:va*	
'devoted'	'matter'	'state.'	

We encounter suffixation of this morpheme also in

reu'thia'nu-phiap   'power' (<S. *ṛtthia* 'powerful')
ku'ma:r –(a)phiap   'boyhood' (<P. *kuma:ra* 'boy').

It is most unusual to find this borrowed affix as a suffix on native roots, and usually, it appears on these words (or phrases) in the Khmer fashion as a prefix, thus:

phiap – lumba:k (state difficult) 'difficulty'
phiap – klaha:n (state brave) 'bravery'
phiap – meu:l mwn kheu:nj (state look not see) 'invisibility'
phiap – mwn a:c jaul ba:n (state not able understand succeed) 'incomprehensibility.'

There are a handful of other Indic morphemes that occur as either prefixes or suffixes: among them are *caun* 'person,' *tha:n* 'place,' *kec* 'matter, affair,' and one or two others. Whether they are actually now bound morphemes or separate words, if they occur in second position (that is, whether as phrase-final heads or as suffixes), this position reflects a persistence of Indic ordering.

The morpheme *tha:n* 'place' (< P. *ṭha:na* 'place') occurs as a suffix, as in

ka: - tha:n 'workplace' (< P. *ka:ra* 'work').

But it also occurs in the Khmer fashion as a prefix in (lexically) totally Indic compounds such as

tha:n – naurauk 'hell' (< P. *naraka* 'a hell').

The morpheme *kec* (<P. *kicca* 'affair') occurs as a suffix in words like

Phiarea'-kec   'duty' (<S.P. *bha:ra* 'charge, duty').

But it also occurs as a prefix in other words like

kec-ka: 'affair'
kec-sanja: 'contract.'

The morpheme *caun* 'person' (< P. *jana*) occurs as a suffix (or final head) in words like

pee:'kha'- caun   'candidate'
<P. *pekkha*
'intent upon'

But it occurs as a prefix (or initial head) in other words like

caun – a'na:tha: 'vagabond'
< P. *ana:tha*
'helpless.'

Other Indic derivational suffixes that remain exclusively suffixes include

–kaw: 'agent'(<S. *kara*) as in
ke'la:-kaw: 'athlete' (< P. *ki:la:* 'play, sport')
visva'-kaw: 'engineer' (S. *visvakara* 'engineer')
khiat(a)-kaw: 'murderer' (< P. *gha:ta* 'killing'),
–kam (< P. *kamma* 'action') as in
a'ni'ca –kam 'mortality, death' (< P. a+nicca' 'not + 'permanent')
pee:sa'ka' – kam   'mission' (<P. *pessa* 'servant' +? *kara* 'agent').

25.1.2.3 *Inflection*

Pali and Sanskrit are inflectional languages. Khmer is isolating. There are a handful of nominal borrowings from Indic that have preserved inflectional suffixes indicating gender, and, occasionally, number (see Table 25.1). (Compare *schemata, cherubim* in English.)

Table 25.1 Pali and Sanskrit Loans

Masculine	Feminine	Plural		
baksa: ~	baksej		'bird'	(<S. *paksha:* , *pakshi:*)
bot(ra)~	botrej		'(royal) offspring'	(<S. *putra, putri:*)
jo:thea' ~		jo:thia	'soldier'	(<P. *jodha, yodha:*)
ksat ~	ksatrej		'monarch'	(<S. *kshatra, kshatri:*)
kuma: ~	kuma:rej		'child'	(<S. *kuma:ra, kuma:ri:*)
mea'hengsa:~	mea'hengsej		'water buffalo'	(<P. *mahingsa*)
mea'ju:ra: ~	mea:ju:ri:		'oeacock'	(<P. *ma:yura, ma:yuri*)
mreuk ~	mreuki:	mreukia	'herd'	(<S. *mriga*),

25.1.2.4 *Syntax*

Pali and Sanskrit are modifier + head languages, and there are a handful of examples (all of them almost certainly borrowed as fixed phrases) in written Khmer only, which impose this word order on nominal expressions:

sante'	*vi:thi:*		'peaceful means; non-violence'
peace	method/way		
ree:	*paul*		'army, soldier'
invade	force		
riac	*sa:*		'royal letter'
king	letter		
put	*sa:h*	*bandwt*	'Buddhist institute'

Buddha religion learned (institute)

bo'pea' haet		'primal cause'
ancient cause		
sonta'rea'	*katha:*	'ceremonial speech'
eloquent	speech	
<P. *sundara*	< P. *katha:*	
a're'ja:	*thoa*	'national customs of the Aryans; civilization'
< P. *ariya*	< S. *dharma*	
'Aryan'	'way'	
sa'ca'	*thoa*	'the true path'
<P. *sacca*		'truth'

It is notable that all such modifier + head phrases are lexically 100% Indic, while many other phrases such as *kru: mha:* 'great teacher,' although they happen to be equally 100% Indic in their lexical content, observe head + modifier order. The presence of modifier + head phrases may be no more a sign of truly integrated head-final order in Khmer than the presence of expressions like *force majeure* signals head-initial order in English.

It is easy to dismiss both lexical and syntactic structures like these as totally superficial borrowings that are affectations of the written language, but they are more than that. It is notable, for example, that the spoken recension of the Ramayana by the totally illiterate bard Ta: Saw:j (2000) abounds in all of the types of lexical borrowing enumerated in the preceding. There is admittedly almost no evidence in that text of syntactic (word order) borrowing.

25.2 THAI (AND VIETNAMESE) CONTACT

Borrowing from Thai is a feature of the spoken language: Khmer has borrowed from Thai, and Thai from Khmer. Khmer-Thai contact can be dated to at least the high tide of Angkorian supremacy, a period of roughly 500 years when the empire extended over much of what is now Thailand and the lower Mekong Delta (Harris 2006: 30), and continued with the rise of Thai military power, when the political tables were turned. The beginning of this later development can be dated to 1220 CE with the Sukhotai uprising (Delvert 1983: 33), and continued with the Siamese sacking of Angkor in 1352, and the final abandonment of Angkor in 1432. After this major turning point, Thai armies invaded Cambodia on numerous occasions (1477, 1515, 1594, 1772, 1794, 1841), seizing territory (including Siem Reap, Sisophon, and Battambang provinces in 1794–1795) and capturing and forcibly removing thousands of craftsmen and intelligentsia as slaves. It can be said that Khmer was the politically prestigious language, that is,' the language with an army and a navy' for the first 500 years of contact at the very least, and continued to be the culturally prestigious language (much like Greek in the Roman Empire) for some time thereafter.

From early in the tenth century, the Vietnamese

> began the southward push, or the *nam tiến*, which would eventually extend the Vietnamese state to the Mekong Delta at the expense of the Cham and Khmer polities. Unlike other states in Southeast Asia at the time, Việt Nam struggled with overpopulation. While warfare in the region typically had as its goal either the extraction of tribute or the control over population centers and trade routes, the *nam tiến* was essentially a demographic push for Lebensraum, where landless Vietnamese peasant-soldiers would be granted paddy land at the conclusion of successful campaigns to settle with their families in fortified towns in a process similar to the colonization of the American West. (Perez Pereiro 2012: 28)

By 1698, the erstwhile Cambodian town of Prey Nokor in the Mekong Delta had become the Vietnamese capital Saigon.

Before the French established a rump Cambodian protectorate/colony in 1863, possibly thereby rescuing what was left of the nation-state from political extinction (Mabbett and Chandler 1995: 228), the Kingdom of Cambodia had been for at least 200 years the object of a territorial tug-of-war between Thailand and Vietnam.

Ratifying a status quo, the present-day Cambodian provinces of Siam Reap, Sisophon, and Battambang were officially ceded to Thailand by a Franco-Thai treaty in 1867, and only returned to (the still French colony of) Cambodia from Thailand in 1907—to be regained by Thailand, briefly in 1941–1945, and contested again in 1953 (Harris 2006: 139, 143). As for territory in the Mekong permanently lost to Vietnam, although there were nineteenth-century uprisings against Vietnamese overlordship in the Mekong Delta in 1831 and 1841, there has been no restoration of any Vietnamese acquisitions.

Partially as a result of these conquests, there are now large permanent Khmer-speaking populations in both Northeast Thailand (perhaps as many as 1.1 million speakers of Surin [Smalley 1994: 139], who have retained, among other inherited phonological features, the phonation contrast of clear versus breathy voice [Wayland and Jongman 2003]) and southern Vietnam (there are roughly 600,000 speakers of the

Kiengiang dialect in the Mekong Delta, who have acquired phonemic tone and have lost the disyllabic word structure that characterizes many Austro-Asiatic languages: both changes occurred under the influence of Vietnamese (Thach 1999). Given the aggressively nationalistic language policies of both Thailand and Vietnam, these currently "expatriate/irredentist" populations of Khmer speakers living outside of Cambodia can be certainly categorized as bilingual. Bilingualism in either Thai or Vietnamese seems to be infrequent, however, within present-day Cambodia, even in recently contested areas like Battambang and Siem Reap.

The true extent of Khmer-Thai bilingualism in Cambodia before the arrival of the French is a matter of conjecture. "Wilaiwan [suggests that] a large population of bilingual people arose as towns like Lopburi shifted from Khmer to Tai administration after about 1350.... This would help account for why really basic Khmer vocabulary came to be incorporated into Thai at that period, across the range of diglossic registers, from royal and bureaucratic vocabulary down to farmers' speech (nose, belly, walk, bridge, etc.)" (Anthony Diller, personal communication).

Khmer speakers are now a defeated and a subject "invisible minority" of Thailand (Vail 2003); over the previous 500 years, they were losers to the Thais in an almost unbroken series of military defeats. Given all this, it is remarkable that so much of the documented lexical and syntactic borrowing that resulted from the half-millenium of "virtual symbiosis" of Khmer and Thai between circa 1300 and circa 1900 (Pou 2004) should have been by bilingual Thai speakers borrowing from Khmer, rather than the other way around (Varasarin 1984; Khanittanan and Diller 2003). There is no question that during the preceding 500 years of the Pre-Angkorian and Angkorian periods, Khmer had immense prestige in Siam as the language of civilization: that is, it was the language of the court and aristocracy, of writing, the language of the producers of a fabulous architecture, and the language of religion (Delvert 1983: 34; Harris 2006: 31). The present-day Thai alphabet, traditionally ascribed to one inventor, a late thirteenth-century king of Siam, was directly modeled on that of Khmer (Iwasaki and Ingkaphirom 2001: 3); the very institution of ra:ca:sap, a royal register, used for speaking to and about royalty, and many of its words were borrowed in the same way from Khmer (Varasarin 1984: 247–252).

There are also, however, many Thai borrowings into Khmer, and it is also remarkable that borrowings from unrelated Thai into Khmer seem to greatly outnumber borrowings from the distantly related Vietnamese—a fact which may reflect either the much greater hostility that Khmer feel for the Vietnamese to this day as "the traditional enemy," or else simply the fact that Khmer-Thai contact goes back more than 1,000 years, compared with more recent Khmer-Vietnamese contact, which goes back only to the southward push into the Mekong Delta. (It is notable that in terms of shared phonetics and vocabulary, Khmer and Vietnamese are so distant that educated speakers of Khmer tend to express skepticism regarding the proven genetic relationship between their language and Vietnamese.)

25.2.1 Lexical Borrowing

This section examines lexical borrowings from a wide range of sources.

25.2.1.1 Common Borrowings from Indic

A number of words shared by Khmer and Thai are clearly common borrowings from Sanskrit or Pali (see Table 25.2).

Table 25.2 Indic Loans Common to Khmer and Thai

Khmer	Thai	Indic source	Current meaning
aci:p	'a:chî:b	<P. a:ci:va	career, livelihood
aha:	'a:hăn	<P. a:ha:ra	food
a:ju'	'a:j'	<P. a:yu	long time, age
ateut	'a:thîd	<S. a:ditya	week
cej	chaj	<P. jaya	victory
ciat	chă:d	<P. ja:ti	nation
cnea'	cháná'	<S. jina	'win'
dantrej	dontri	<S. tantri:	music
ka:	ka:n	<P. ka:ra	matter, work
kru:	khru:	<P. guru	teacher
niam	na:m	<P. na:ma	name
oka:h	'o:kà:d	<P. oka:sa	opportunity
phiasa:	pha:să:	<P. bha:sa:	language
phee:t	phê:d	<P. bheda	gender, sex, kind
prate:h	pràthê:d	<S. pra-deṣa	country
radev	radu:	<S. ṛtu	season
raut	rod	<P. ratha	vehicle
ru:p	ru:b	<P. ru:pa	image, picture
sa'mot	sàmùd	<S. samudra	sea
stha:ni:j	sàthă:ni	<S. stha:ni:ya	station
thu:li:	thúli:	<S. dhu:li	dust
tu:rasap	tho:rásăb	<P. du:ra + S. shabda	telephone

25.2.1.2 Clear Borrowings from Thai into Khmer

These include the decade numerals 30–90 (e.g., sa:m+swp 'three' + 'ten') *rau:j* '100' <*rɔ:j*; *poan* '1,000' < *phan*; *mweun* '10,000' < *my:n*; and *saen* '100,000' < *sɛ:n*. They also include most words featuring the diphthong {wa} [ɯə], among them words such as *krwang* 'machinery,' < *khryang*; *lwang* 'yellow' < *l̆yaŋ*; *nwaj* 'tired' < *nyaj*; *twan* 'remind, warn, harangue' < *tyan*.

25.2.1.3 *Clear Borrowings from Khmer into Thai*

Evidence for the direction of borrowing comes from both phonetics and morphology.

In modern Khmer, orthographic final {r} is silent and {l} is preserved. In Thai, all borrowings ending in either final {r} or [l] convert this final segment to [n]. All Khmer:Thai {r}/{l}:n correspondences may thus be confidently traced to an original Khmer source (Huffman 1976: 204), or possibly, a common earlier Indic source, as is the case for Khmer *aca:(r)* 'teacher,' Thai *'aca:n* 'professor,' both from S. *a:ca:rya*). Among them are Thai *phanan* 'wager' < Khmer *pnoal*, Thai *də:n* 'walk'< Khmer *daeu(r)*, Thai *nga:n* 'work' < Khmer *ngia(r)*, Thai *kràda:n* 'board' < Khmer *kda:r* 'board' (the last somewhat tentative on account of the extra [ra] in the Thai. Thai is not generally supposed to exhibit infixation. A mechanism exists for exactly this kind of meaningless/decorative infixation in both Thai and Khmer, however, as we will see later).

Huffman (1976: 200) argues that whereas derivation is reasonably widespread in Khmer, and is almost unknown in Thai, therefore, "it is a fairly safe assumption that whenever one finds a base and a derivative in Thai, it is of Khmer origin." Thus, where a pair *kaeut/kamnaeut* 'be born/birth' is matched by a Thai pair like *kəət/kamnəət*, it most likely Thai that has borrowed. As Huffman himself acknowledges, this criterion is not totally reliable—Khmer has assimilated borrowings at least from Indic by subjecting them to derivational changes (recall *ksawt~kamsawt* 'wretched'), and the pair *siang~samniang* 'sound' is "almost certainly a Thai loan" (1976: 201).

25.2.1.4 *Unclear Cases*

In some cases we cannot clearly tell whether the direction of borrowing was from or into Khmer. A number of these are given below.

25.2.1.4.1 PHONETICALLY INDETERMINATE CASES

There remain a fairly large number of cases where the direction of borrowing is difficult to determine on purely structural grounds. Very often there are near-regular correspondences:

- Where Thai has an aspirated initial consonant, Khmer will feature an unaspirated one;
- Where Khmer has a monosyllabic word, Thai will have a two-syllable word.

But it is impossible to say which language did the borrowing.

It may seem that the evidence from common borrowing may sometimes suggest an answer. For example, both Khmer and Thai retained Indic aspiration in examples like *tha:n/thă:ná* 'status.' But where both Khmer and Thai borrowed from an Indic source with an unaspirated consonant, then Thai aspiration is a fairly (but not entirely!) regular innovation in all cases like those shown in Table 25.3.

Table 25.3 Indic Loans in Thai and Khmer

Khmer	Thai	Indic	
ateut	'a:thíd	<S. a:ditya	week
cej	chaj	<P. jaya	victory
ciat	chă:d	<P. ja:ti	nation
kru:	khru:	<P. guru	teacher
niati:	na:thi:	<S. na:ɖi⁷	minute; rank, function
pe:t	phɛ:d	<S. vaidya	doctor
pise:h	phise:d	<P. visesa	special
tu:rasap	tho:rásàb	<S. dura +sabda	telephone

And so, we might ascribe to a Khmer source (which Thai modified by aspiration, as it did most of its common borrowings from Indic) correspondences like the ones in Table 25.4.

Table 25.4 Deaspirated Thai Loans in Khmer

Khmer	Thai	
anjceu:nj	chə:n	'invite'
baek	phɛ:k	'open, crack'
ciang	chaang	'skilful; artisan, craftsman'
cuaj	chûaj	'help'
kra:p	khráb	'prostrate oneself'
kiap	kha:p	'squeeze, pinch, crack, crush'
kaw:	khɔ:	'throat'
ku:	khû:	'couple'
kw:	khy	'viz., as follows'
kwt	khíd	'think'
paw:ng	phɔ:ng	'swell up'
pro:h	phrɔ'	'because of'
teang	thá:ng	'all'
tiahian	tháhă:n	'soldier'
ti:	thî:	'place'
toan	than	'be on time'
tumniam	thamniam	'custom'

Against this, there is the evidence offered by correspondences like

Khmer *cwa*   Thai *chya*   'believe'
Khmer *krwang*   Thai *khryang*: 'machinery,'

---

⁷ Generally I have relied on Headley et al. (1977) for all my initial etymological information. My thanks to Tony Diller for pointing out the common Indic source of both Khmer and Thai forms in this case.

where the nature of the nuclear diphthong strongly suggests that it is the Thai word that was borrowed into Khmer (Huffman 1976: 205 writes that "there is good evidence that most Khmer words having the diphthong {wa} . . . are of Thai origin").

There are a large number of corresponding words where neither the Khmer nor Thai forms exhibit aspiration, such as *ca:k/ca:k* 'move away, depart from,' *kaeut/kə:d* 'arise,' *to'/to'* 'table,' *kaev/kɛ:v* 'glass,' *kla:j/ kla:i* 'turn into,' *taong/ tɔng* 'must,' *ta:m/ta:m* 'follow,' *tae/tɛ:* 'but,' *taeng/tɛ:ng* 'adorn, compose,' *taw:p/tɔ:b* 'answer,' *trawng/trong* 'direct.'

Finally, there is a much smaller number of correspondences where both Khmer and Thai exhibit an aspirated consonant: *kha:ng/khâ:ng* 'side,' *thaem/thɛ:m* 'add.'

In another set of correspondences monosyllabic Khmer words correspond to Thai disyllables:

Khmer	Thai		
ktwm	*kàthiam*	'garlic'	
lkhaon	*lákhɔ:n*	'dramatic play'	?<Thai (Henderson 1952)
sbiang	*sabíang*	'food provision'	

The history of Khmer *cnea'* 'victory, win' suggests that it was borrowed by Khmer from a Thai source (compare also Champa *chanoh* and Old Mon *jnah*)—all of which borrowed ultimately from Sanskrit *jina*. But it would be dangerous to generalize from this that all the Khmer monosyllabics were equally borrowings. Henderson (1952) argued that 'play, theatre' was such an oddity within Khmer, with its initial triconsonantal cluster, that it was most likely borrowed from Thai. (But in that case, why exactly did Khmer innovate precisely in creating such a deviant cluster?)

25.2.1.4.2 MORPHOLOGICALLY INDETERMINATE CASES

Huffman (2006) suggests that shared sets of pairs which have a consistent derivational function in Khmer but not in Thai offer more reliable evidence for Khmer origin. "For example, the most common function of infixation in Khmer is the derivation of a bisyllabic noun from a monosyllabic verb, while in Thai the derivative is typically a stylistic variant of the base verb or a semantically specialized noun" (2006: 201–202). So to him it is clear that the correspondence *aoj/amnaoj* 'give/gift' (Khmer) *'uay/'amnuay* 'bestow/ bestow (elegant)' (Thai) is originally Khmer. Haiman (2011), however, argues that such purely decorative infixation is not unknown in Khmer (76–78), and may in fact have been the original basis for the infixation process of *–am(n)-* in Khmer as well (80–82). Until this issue is resolved, there is no strong argument that meaningless or stylistic infixation in Thai is necessarily a borrowing from Khmer, or vice versa.

Huffman also proposes that "the best evidence for identifying Khmer loans are Khmer derivational sets of which Thai has the derived form but not the base. For example *baek/pnaek* 'break/piece' Khmer correspond to only *phanɛ:k* 'section' (Thai) (Huffman 1976: 202). On the other hand, he acknowledges that "there are . . . some bases shared by both languages for which Khmer has a derivative and Thai does not, but these are less conclusive, . . . since in these cases Khmer could possibly have infixed a Thai loan" (1976: 203). Indeed, there are such cases, but again, until there is conclusive evidence that Thai infixation is totally and exclusively an imported phenomenon, this evidence is not totally convincing.

Finally, there is the historical record, but both actual attestations and reconstructions (Li 1977; Shorto 2006; Jenner 2009a, 2009b, 2011) must be taken with a grain of salt.

Regarding attestations in the written record: Khmer has been written since 612 CE, Thai since circa 1290. Borrowings from Indic are over 1,300 years old, those from Thai, comparatively recent. One might argue that a word that is current in present-day Khmer but was not attested in earlier (Pre-Angkorian, Angkorian, Middle) stages of the language is thus more likely to be a Thai or other borrowing than one which has been so attested. Accordingly, words designated with '?<Th.' in this chapter are those that are not attested in earlier recorded (epigraphic) stages of Khmer (Jenner 2009a, 2009b, 2011). However, the very restricted language of the inscriptions is scarcely representative of the everyday language spoken at the time, and absence of epigraphic evidence is very clearly not evidence of absence in this case.

Regarding comparative reconstructions: Li (1977) reconstructs a proto-Tai origin for a number of problematic words already listed, among them the (initially aspirated) Thai correspondences for *ciang* 'craftsman,' *cwa* 'believe,' *cuaj* 'help,' *kaw:* 'throat,' *kiap* 'pinch,' *ku:* 'couple,' *kla:j* 'turn into,' *kha:ng* 'side,' *pau:ng* 'swell up,' *ta:m* 'follow,' *taw:p* 'answer,' *thaem* 'add,' *teang* 'all,' and *ti:* 'place,' as well as the correspondences for *a:n* 'count, read,' *jiang* 'take a step,' *nih* 'this,' *ngau:* 'sesame,' *ruam* 'join,' *suan* 'garden.' Unfortunately, some words for which common Tai origins can be and were postulated are themselves demonstrably even more ancient common borrowings from Indic (thus *'un* 'warm') or Malay (thus *ja:ng* 'kind')—and the same common foreign (including possibly Mon-Khmer?) origin cannot be ruled out a priori for other etyma as well.

The case for a Tai origin for such words is, of course, strengthened if they are absent from other Mon-Khmer languages and the reconstructions based on them. Shorto provides Mon-Khmer reconstructions only for *kiap* 'pinch,' *nih* 'this,' *ngau:* 'sesame,' *pau:ng* 'swell up,' *ruam* 'join, assemble' for the Tai reconstructions in the preceding, so they must be reckoned as words that have been common to the area for millenia. The rest then may be tentatively identified as Thai borrowings.

25.3 GRAMMATICAL BORROWING

This section provides a brief account of the kinds of grammatical borrowings which Khmer has absorbed from a number of languages.

25.3.1 Basic Typology

The syntax of Khmer and Thai is so similar that it is difficult to be certain when or whether one language borrowed from the other (Huffman 1973). Both languages exhibit the following:

- SVO in clauses,
- head + modifier order in both nominal phrases and compounds,
- noun + numeral + classifier order within the NP, and
- a penchant for prefixing in their derivational morphology.
- Both mark possession in an NP with an optional particle (derived from 'thing') between possessum and possessor.
- Both distinguish between two copula verbs, one being used for nominal, and the other for adverbial, predicate complements.
- Both have serial verbs, which can function as directionals,
- and as quasi-perfective markers of successful achievement.

But two limits to this syntactic confluence can be observed.

25.3.1.1 *Classifiers*

While Khmer, particularly written Khmer, has a number of classifiers, and they occur in the same post-numeral position within the noun phrase (e.g., *cru:k pi: kba:l* 'pig two head/CL'), it is nowhere so categorical about their use as in Thai. In Khmer, moreover, classifiers never occur unless the noun phrase also includes a numeral or other quantifying expression (in one tentative analysis, both numeral and classifier belong to an entirely separate constituent called the measure phrase, rather than the NP (Haiman 2011: 140–174). In Thai, classifiers are obligatory with numerals, but may occur even in NP that have no numeral. Expressions like

> *mɛ:g kɔ:n*
> cloud CL
> 'clouds'
> *thànŏn   să:j   ní:*
> street   CL   this
> 'this street'
> *khly:n   lû:g   to:to*
> wave   CL   big
> 'big waves'
> *rôm   khan   nǎj*
> umbrella   CL   which
> 'which umbrella'

These do occur in Thai, but are impossible in Khmer, even in writing.

Thai has an exuberance of classifiers: there may be several hundred of them. Even so, it seems as if there are not quite enough to go around, so that for many nouns, among them *khon* 'person,' *sɔ:ng* 'envelope,' *tiang* 'bed,' the noun itself must serve as its own classifier:

> *tiang   sɔ:ng   tiang*
> bed   2   CL
> 'two beds'

This is almost never the case in Khmer (Haiman 2011: 146–147), where classifiers are overwhelmingly distinct from the nouns they classify. Moreover, with the exception of the human classifier *neak*, most classifiers simply do not occur in spoken Khmer.

25.3.2 Derivational Morphology

While Khmer has a fairly rich system of derivational morphology, almost none of this has been borrowed into Thai. The only likely exceptions are the decorative infix *–am-* , mentioned earlier, which just may be homegrown, and the agent prefix *nág-* '-er' (Haas and Subhanka 1945: 425), which is presumably borrowed from Khmer *neak* 'person; agent prefix,' and found in agentive nouns like

> *nág -*   *lên*   *lákhɔ:n*
> er   play   drama/theater
> 'actor'

Most derivational affixes (whether or not they are of Khmer origin), rather than signaling morphological functions such as nominalization, signal intensification instead (Varasarin 1984: 257–264), or are regarded as decorative or high-register embellishments that are added to roots for purely stylistic purposes, such as scansion in poetry (Varasarin 1984: 266). The somewhat dubious form *kràda:n* for 'plank, board,' cited earlier, may be an example of the decorative infixation of a syllabic [r]. Such purely decorative infixation is also attested in at least the Surin dialect of Khmer (Prakorb 1992: 255).

25.4 DEEPER DISCOURSE SYNTAX

Contact in Khmer has also affected syntax. Transferred elements at the level of syntax are discussed in this section, with sentential examples.

25.4.1 The Case of the Equative Particle *kw:* 'viz., to wit, colon; be'

Thai and Cambodian both have a grammatical particle (Cambodian *kw:*, Thai *khw:*) which can often be translated as 'viz., namely, that is' or simply as a colon. An example from the first sample text is repeated here:

(3) *jo:ng ta:m*   *vi:thi:*   *bej*   *ja:ng*   *kw:*   *vi:thi:*   *ti:*   *muaj*
    refer follow   method   three   kind   ,viz.   method   place   one
                       <S. vidhi   < Ma. yang   <S. vidhi
                       'form'   'form'   'form'
    'following three kinds of methods: to wit, the first method . . .'

Haiman (2011: 246) mistakenly suggested that the Thai word was the probable source of the Cambodian word. Comparative evidence makes it much more likely that the etymon was originally borrowed from Cambodian into Thai: on the one hand, it is amply attested as *gi~gi:~ giy~ gui~gui:~gu:i* from the earliest stages of Cambodian, where it is glossed as an "equative verb be(equal to); consist essentially of, be by nature; that is, as follows, namely" (Jenner 2009a: 96), and on the other hand, it is not found with the same meaning in other non-contact Thai languages, such as Lao. (Varasarin 1984: 288 notes the etymon does occur in Lao, but it is with other meanings: 'be (a)like,' 'match, be suitable'; cf. Enfield 2007: 97–98 et passim and Enfield personal communication). While the semantic transmission from 'be' to 'be the same as,' and thence to 'be like' is a plausible one, the syntax of Lao *khuu2* is currently not that of a copula or annunciatory (='Lo and behold!') focus particle, but rather that of a preposition or of a transitive verb. That is, while the etymon may have been borrowed from Khmer or Thai, with the same original meaning as in modern Khmer (Anthony Diller, personal communication), its syntax and semantic development have led to a different outcome. The following examples, juxtaposed from Haiman (2011) and Iwasaki and Ingkaphirom (2005), will make it clear just how closely they match each other in their syntax and their meaning.

In Cambodian, *kw:* may co-occur with and precede the normal copula verb *cia* in copula sentences with nominal predicate complements:

(4) *mnuh   tiap   dael   peak   vee:nta: nuh   kw: cia   aopuk   knjom*
    person   short   who   wear   glasses   that   that.is be   father I
    'The short man wearing glasses is my father.'

(5) *Kw: cia   krong   muaj   daw: praneut*
    that.is be   city   one   very   beautiful
    'It is a very beautiful city.'

In Thai, however, the two copula verbs *kw:* and *pen* are apparently in complementary distribution. While both occur in copular sentences of the form NP copula NP, *pen* occurs when the second NP denotes an attribute of the first, while *khw:* occurs when the second NP functions in a definition or designation (Iwasaki and Ingkapirom 2005: 223). From their examples, one could say that *pen* tends to occur when the second NP is non-referential (e.g., *Sam is a student*) and *khw:* when it is referential (e.g., *Sam is my brother*).

(6) *Prama:n   wa: pen   tamruat   sutcarit*
    approximate   say   be   police   honest
    'It seems like he is an honest police officer.'

(7) *Cut   thii   naam   dwat   khw: rau:j   ongsa:*
    point   which   water boil   be   100   degree
    'The boiling point of water is 100 degrees.'

But "another way to look at it is to consider it a focus" marker in Thai (Iwasaki and Ingkaphirom 2005: 224), that can best be translated as 'in other words, that is, namely, I mean' (225):

(8) *thii   sww: ne-ne: <u>khw:</u>   sabu: Imphiilian   Leethee na*
     which   buy   sure   namely soap   Imperial   Leather PP
     'What I will buy for sure is Imperial Leather soap'   (*sabu:* is from Portuguese)

(9) *may mii khay ruu   waa   khaw yuu thii-nay <u>khw:</u>   khaw pit   ma:k*
     not exist anyone know COMP 3   stay where I.mean 3   closed very
     'Nobody knows where she lives: I mean, she is very secretive.'

So, too, in Cambodian (Haiman 2011: 247–248), the same 'colon' or even 'lo and behold! 'reading is best in sentences like

(10) *mian   tun   vi'ni'jo:k robauh 4 pratee:h <u>kw:</u> awnglee:s, ba:rang, aleumawng,*
     exist capital investment of 4 country :   England, France, Germany,
     nwng   espanj
     and   Spain
     'Four countries have invested capital in this: England, France, Germany, and Spain.'

(11) *Alee:v mwn toan ceh nea'mo: (<u>kw:</u>   mwn ceh aksaw:)*
     Alee:v not yet know mumbo jumbo   (that is   not know letter)
     'A. did not yet know mumbo-jumbo: that is, he was not yet literate.'

(12) *Nev   kha:ng kraoj   suan   <u>kw:</u>   mha: vithej   muaj*
     Be.at side   behind garden behold great avenue   one
     'Behind the garden there was a great avenue.'

By another shift, Thai 'I mean' can come to serve as a hesitation marker (Haiman 2011: 247–248):

(13) *<u>khw:</u>   man   mwan   talok   a   man   mwan   kap   law len-tua*
     that.is 3   same.as funny PP   3   same   with play.hard
     'I mean, it's funny. It's like we're playing hard   (though we aren't).'

This may be paralleled by utterance-initial *kw:* in Khmer response utterances like:

(14) *Kw: peut   cia lumba:k smok   sma:nj   ciang   avej*
     ??? t rue   be   hard   complicated complex exceed what
     '(Ahem!) That is a really difficult (question).'

Thai then seems to have taken the meaning of this particle in at least one direction that is, to the best of the author's knowledge, not attested in Cambodian. By a small semantic shift, 'that is' can be extended to also mean 'because' (Iwasaki and Ingkapirom 2005: 226):

(15) *chau:p khotsana: chin ni: kau   khw: chau:p phlee:ng duay*
      like   commercial   CL   this LINK that.is like   song   also
      'I like this commercial that is (=because) I like the song too.'

25.5 THE CASE OF *KAW*: 'SO'

In his dictionary of pre-Angkorian Khmer, Jenner (2009: 1) identifies this "conjunctive marker of sequential or consecutive action" as a grammaticalized form of the verb 'build, construct, create, found, commence, start up, come into being,' via a conjectural 'it comes about as a consequence that . . .'. Again, its apparition in Thai and Lao (but not the other Tai languages) marks it as most likely a borrowing from Khmer (Varasarin 1984).

In both Khmer and Thai, the particle is found optionally conjoined with and following the completive aspect marker 'done' < coordinate conjunction 'and then' < 'finish' (Khmer *haeuj*, Thai *leew*) between clauses, and in both, the particle follows the subject of the second clause (if there is one expressed) (Iwasaki and Ingkaphirom 2005: 173–174; Haiman 2011: 328).

(16) *Cop eebek maa,   leew   kau: phakphaun   thii nwng*
      Finish PN ASP   and.then so   rest   a.little
      'I finished studying at the E. academy, and then rested a little.'   (Thai)

(17) *Tveu: anjceung cia craeun leu:k craeun   kria haeuj ko:n prasa:*
      Do thus be many time many time   and.then child son-in-law so
      kaw: reaksa: piak nuh   dadael dae
      care.for word that   same also
      'He did this many times, and his son-in-law kept saying the same words.'   (Khmer)

In Lao, the particle *kaø* can co-occur with, but, precede the perfective/completive conjunction *leej2* 'and then without ado' (Enfield 2007: 190).

In both Khmer and Thai, as in Lao, it precedes a foregrounded or highest (Enfield 2007: 195, 230, 350) narrative clause, and thus typically appears after an initial backgrounded or subordinate clause (Iwasaki and Ingkaphirom 2005: 174; Haiman 2011: 329), but cannot occur within such an embedded clause (Enfield 2007: 353).

(18) *Cop   mau: hok   kau: lian   laam*
      finish   middle.school six   so   study PN
      'After finishing middle school grade six, I began to study at Laam.'   (Thai)

(19) *Muaj srabawk   kraoj mau:k puak jeu:ng kaw: daeu tev   dawl camka:*
one   short.time after come group we   walk go   arrive garden
'After a break, we walked onward to the vegetable garden.'   (Khmer)

From marking consequentiality, it is a short conceptual step to marking inconsequentiality, and both Khmer and Thai seem to have taken this short step for the particle (Iwasaki and Inkaphirom 2005: 174; Haiman 2011: 330).

(20) *phuut   phuut   di-dii   <u>kau:</u>   may   fang*
speak   speak   nicely   so   not   listen
'Even if I speak nicely to him, he will not listen to me.'   (Thai)

(21) *rau:k   haeuj   rau:k   tiat   <u>kaw:</u>   mwn   kheu:nj*
seek   and.then   seek   more   so   not   see
'No matter how long I search for it, I cannot find it.'   (Khmer)

Again, Thai has taken this particle in directions that are peculiar to that language (Iwasaki and Ingkaphirom 2005: 175–176), and Khmer has done the same (Haiman 2011: 334–338). But the "core commonality" of meaning and syntax is probably due to language contact. It is important to emphasize that "core" here does not mean the ontologically original meanings, but the most entrenched and often repeated ones.

The chain of associations whereby one meaning suggests another is equally plausible in each language—but it is probably not the reason for the common meanings that these particles manifest. Rather, it seems most plausible that it is the most frequent meanings and constructions that are copied, irrespective of the chain of associations whereby they arose. For example, Khmer and Thai share one other meaning for this particle: I may mean 'also,' as in the following:

(22)   *khey pay lian khang nwng lew leu:k leu:y*
ASP go study tie one LINK quit PP
'I once studied (Japanese) but then I quit.'

(23)   *Poo-khaw <u>kau:</u> lian phasaa yiipun yuu*
PN so study language Japanese ASP
'PN is also studying Japanese.'   (Thai)

(24)   *Knjom <u>kaw:</u> anjceung dae*
I so thus also
'Me too.'   (Khmer)

Haiman (2011: 334–337) argued that this final meaning in Khmer arose via a series of associative changes or enchainment from a parallel construction (e.g., 'Both he and I are going' > 'He is going, and so am I'), and that the parallel construction arose via enchainment from the inconsequential (e.g., 'Whether you go or stay doesn't matter' > 'You can go; you can stay'). Now neither of these postulated intermediate links seems to be attested in Thai. Two conclusions are possible. First, the proposed model of enchainment was wrong. Or, second, that it is not the stages in the associative reasoning that are borrowed, but the most prominently exemplified links, irrespective of how they arose. While the first conclusion is certainly possible, the evidence from both Thai and Khmer seems to indicate that associative links leading to non-shared meanings are forged independently in each language.

25.6 THE WIDER VIEW

In a very important sense, talk of reciprocal borrowing between only Khmer and Thai misses a larger picture: that all of mainland eastern Southeast Asia is a linguistic alliance with morphosyntactic borrowing among not only Khmer and Thai, but also Lao, Hmong, Kmhmu, and Vietnamese. The remaining sections of the present chapter do no more than give a hint of this.

25.6.1 The Verb 'get'

An exhaustive investigation of the common syntactic behavior of the single polyfunctional verb 'get' (Khmer *ba:n*, Kmhmu *bwan*, Hmong *tau*, Vietnamese *được*, Lao *dâj*) in all of these languages, with forays into Sinitic and SW Tai, was undertaken in Enfield (2003). Any truly adequate characterization of interlanguage influence and borrowing would need to replicate Enfield's labors for the syntax of at least every polyfunctional word in the lexicon.

To very superficially recapitulate his main findings: Khmer has a main verb *ba:n* which can mean either 'get, acquire' or 'succeed, be OK, acceptable.' The corresponding etyma in each of the Southeast Asian languages in the preceding exhibit the same polysemy.[8] So, the Khmer verb may also function as a preverbal auxiliary meaning 'get to,' or 'past tense.' An example from one of our sample texts is repeated here:

(1) *ba:n* *tveu:* *ka: -* *viphiak* *tev* *leu:* *ka:l* *pa'ri'chaet* *rwang* *daoj*
      past do   Nom.   analyze   go   on   time   division   story   by
               <P. ka:ra <S. vibha:kara   <S. kala <P. paricheda ?<Th.ryang
               'matter'   'analyze'   'time'   'division'   'story'
      ' . . . has carried out an analysis following the divisions of the story . . . '

---

[8] With the possible exception of Hmong. Martha Ratliff (personal communication) points out that the main verb meaning 'succeed, be acceptable' in this language seems to be a Chinese borrowing *ying*.

The same is true for the corresponding verbs in the other languages. The Khmer verb may function as serial quasi-perfective 'success verb' meaning 'be able to, manage to, succeed in.' So may its congeners.[9] The Khmer verb may function as a complementizer, introducing expressions of extent or duration. So may its congeners.[10] Thus, each of the Khmer sentences with *ba:n* in the following may be translated, morpheme by morpheme, into each of the other languages noted in the preceding:

(25–26) Main verb: *mwn   deung   ba:n   ej   ho:p*
　　　　　　　　　　 not   know   get   anything eat
　　　　　　　　　　 '. . . couldn't know how to get anything to eat'

　　　　　　　　　　 Ja:ng   na: kaw: ba:n
　　　　　　　　　　 kind   any   also   OK
　　　　　　　　　　 'Any way will be OK.'

(27–28) Auxiliary verb: *via   mwn   ba:n   bamraeu   aopuk   mda:j   mkee:k*
　　　　　　　　　　　　 3   not   get.to serve   father   mother   in-law
　　　　　　　　　　　　 'He couldn't get to serve his in-laws.'

　　　　　　　　　　　　 teu:p   ba:n   dawl   pteah
　　　　　　　　　　　　 then   past   arrive house
　　　　　　　　　　　　 'Only then did he arrive home.'

(29) Serial verb: *rau:k   si: mian   (mwn)   ba:n*
　　　　　　　　　　 eat   seek   have   not   succeed
　　　　　　　　　　 '..(not) manage to get rich.'

(30) Introducing measure phrases: *kee: cap   kda:m   ba:n   muaj   lo:*
　　　　　　　　　　　　　　　　 3   catch   crab   amount   one   dozen
　　　　　　　　　　　　　　　　 'They caught a dozen crabs.'

25.6.2 The Verb 'give'

The Khmer verb *aoj* means 'give,' but it also has a number of other functions. Not surprisingly, given grammaticalization patterns in other languages (Heine and Kuteva 2002: 149–152), it may function as a benefactive or dative preposition meaning 'to/for,' and as a change-of-subject quasi-subjunctive complementizer meaning 'so that.' But it has another meaning that is shared (I believe) only within Southeast Asia, and even within this area only by Vietnamese *cho*, Thai *hâj*, and Kmhmu *an:* as a main verb

---

[9] Martha Ratliff (personal communication) points out that in Hmong, {tau} on low tone {taus} means 'have the ability to,' while on mid-tone {tau}, it means 'have permission.'

[10] Martha Ratliff notes (personal communication), "I had never thought that the verbal *tau* and the measurement word *tau* were the same. The latter is listed in Heimbach's dictionary as 'a unit of measurement representing the width of one fist.'"

(that is, not as an auxiliary or an affix), it may also mean 'cause/let.' This is not a typical grammaticalization change, whereby a major part of speech such as a main verb from an open-ended class gets 'demoted' and becomes a member of a minor part of speech or an affix. A main verb as 'give' or 'cause' is a rather unusual polysemy. Given that such polysemy exists in any one of the languages of the region, it could be generalized through other languages via polysemy-copying (Heine and Kuteva 2005). But the question still remains of how the polysemy could have arisen in the first place in any language.

A possible mechanism, dubbed "Cheshirization" by Matisoff (1973), works like this: a word may come to replace another (dropped) "higher-ranked" word with which it is frequently concatenated. (This happens in English with quondam adjectives like *commercial* that now stand as nouns.) It may have happened in Khmer with *aoj*, which, as a complementizer, so regularly appeared with a variety of higher verbs of causation, among them *tveu:* 'make,' that it allowed them to go unexpressed. The phenomenon is elsewhere attested in Khmer, where (for example) a complementizer associated with negative matrix verbs comes to function as one (Haiman 2011: 326–327) in their absence. If this speculation is correct, then the remarkable polysemy of complementizers like *aoj* 'so that' > 'cause' and *cia* 'that' > 'not' is something that can arise and be shared only in languages in which Cheshirization is a productive process, that is, languages that allow dropping of not just subject NP, but of all kinds of constituents, subject only to pragmatic recoverability. The Southeast Asian languages, including Chinese, seem to be eminently languages "without grammar" of this type, as has been recognized by every Western student since von Humboldt.

25.7 DECORATIVE SYMMETRICAL COMPOUNDING

Mention has already been made of the Khmer penchant for meaningless or non-iconic elaboration. In particular, this is a language that prefers to say, and ransacks its lexical resources to say, *last and final* rather than simply either *last* or *final*. Synonym compounds like the following examples:

baeu praseun	'if' + 'if' = 'if'
daeumbej aoj	'in order that' + 'so that' = 'so that'
s'awp kpeu:m	'hate' + 'loathe' = 'hate'
saw:p krup	'all' + 'all' = 'all'
raho:t dawl	'until' + 'until/arrive' = 'until'
phawp samna:ng	'luck' (<P.) + 'luck' = 'luck'

shade off, possibly via alliterating near synonyms like

bampleuh bamplaj	'exaggerate' + 'invent' = 'exaggerate'
khoat kheang	'arrest' + 'stop' = 'prevent'

ruap ruam	'join' + 'join' = 'join'
stiap steung	'feel' = 'probe' = 'assay, test'

(cf. our own *rough and ready*) and then phonetically conscripted non-synonyms like

lveung lveu:j	'vast' + 'weak' = 'vast'
lveung lviaj	'vast' + 'slow' = 'vast'
psah psa:	'heal' + 'market' = 'heal'
smok sma:nj	'box made of palm leaves[11] + 'intertwined' = 'complex, complicated'

(cf. our own *true blue*)

These can be turned into 'twin forms' (Marchand 1960) like

camrong camraeun	'?" + 'plenty'
don da:p	'?" + 'deteriorate'
mdec mda:	'how' + '?"
t'onj t'ae	'complain' + '?"

These are phrases of the *jibber jabber* type, where one (or sometimes both) alliterating members of the compound are entirely meaningless (cf. Chau:n Chiang 2002 for an explicit assertion by a native speaker linguist that the decorative words in such compounds are meaningless). The essential unity of all of these coordinate compounding processes from a typological perspective has been persuasively argued in Waelchli (2005).

While the "twin form" structure is not unknown in English, where it frequently (as in so-called Schmo reduplication, e.g., *justice-shmustice*) has pejorative connotations, it is fair to say that symmetrical nearly meaningless (hence, decorative) compounding is an obsession in Khmer (Haiman 2011: Chapter 4), and is explicitly and enthusiastically recognized by native Khmer grammarians, where the combination of alliterating words (or perhaps only the meaningless partner in each pair) is called *bo'riva: sap* 'entourage/ retinue word(s)' (<P. *pariva:ra* 'retinue' + *shabda* 'word'). Some examples of symmetrical compounds from our sample texts are repeated here for convenience:

(31–33) *priap*   *thiap*   piak samdej <u>klia</u>   *prajo:k* dael praeu nev knong
         compare compare word speech sentence sentence which use   be.at in
         ?<Th. thiab   <P. va:kya   <S. prayoga
         'compare'   'speech'   'recitation'
         'comparing the wording of sentences which are used . . .'

---

[11] This is the only present-day meaning of this etymon; but it exists in at least one other compound: *cak smok* 'messy, imprecise,' which may bear witness to an earlier, related meaning. In general, it may be that many of the apparently 'conscripted' retinue words, like the *kith* in our *kith and kin*, are relics of what were once synonyms.

> *camka: kaosu: vial srae   daw: <u>lveung lveu:j</u> dej   camka: roap poan*
> garden rubber field paddy very extensive   earth garden count 1000
> *heukta: daw: mian   dej   ciat*
> hectare   very   have   earth   nature
>   <Fr. Caotchouc   <Th.phan <F. hectare   <P.jati
> 'rubber plantations and extensive rice paddies, vegetable gardens of over 1,000
> hectares . . .'
>
> *nev   ta:m   moat   tunlee: prau:m   teang   <u>steung</u> <u>pre:k</u>   <u>o:</u>*
> be.at follow shore lake   together all   creek   stream   rivulet
> *nwng   <u>bwng</u>   <u>bua</u>   dael   sambo: tev   daoj   trej   krup praphee:t*
> and   lake   lake   which abundant go   by   fish   all   kind
> 'along the lakeshores, and creeks and lakes abundant in every kind of fish . . .'

The phenomenon is widespread in Southeast Asia, although the geographical limits of its distribution are unknown, and attention has been drawn to it in Miao (Ts'ao Tsui-yŭn 1961), Vietnamese (Nguyen 1965), Rengao (Gregerson 1984), Thai (Nacaskul 1976; Vongvipanand 1992), Lao (Roffe 1975; Compton 2007), Hmong (Ratliff 1992), and Sui (Stanford 2007). It is probably attested as well in Kmhmu (Svantesson 1983: 124–125), Minor Mlabri (Rischel 1995: 93–94) and Khasi (Weidert 1973: 141)—except that the Western scholars who reported the phenomenon were reluctant to admit the possibility of total meaninglessness for any morpheme.

The source of the meaningless partner in decorative symmetrical compounds is a matter of debate, and a number of mechanisms have been proposed. But while the exact etymologies of these pairs are unclear even in Khmer, the existence of such *bo'riva: sap* is not. They are simply another structural phenomenon, borrowed who knows how, or from which original group, and over how long a time, that defines the region.

REFERENCES

Bernon, O. D. 2006. The status of Pali in Cambodia: From canonical to esoteric. In *Buddhist Legacies in Mainland Southeast Asia*, edited by F. Laguarde and P. C. Koanantakool, 53–66. Paris: Ecole française d'extrême-Orient.

Bilodeau, C. 1955. Compulsory education in Cambodia. In *Compulsory Education in Cambodia, Laos, and Viet-Nam*, edited by C. Bilodeau, 11–67. Paris: UNESCO.

Chuon Nath et al. 1989 [1967]. *Dictionnaire cambodgien*. Cinquième édition. Phnom Penh: Institut Bouddhique.

Chiang, Cau:n. 2002. *Vee:jakaw: kma* [Khmer grammar]. Phnom Penh: Privately printed.

Compton, Carol. 2007. Four-word phrases in Lao discourse. In *SEALS 12: Papers from the 12th meeting of the Southeast Asian Linguistics Society 2002*, edited by R. Wayland, J. Hartmann, and P. Sidwell, 23–35. Canberra: Pacific Linguistics, Research School of Pacific Studies, Australian National University.

Cut Khaj. 2010. *Kmee:ng sa:la: ba:rang* [French schoolboy]. Phnom Penh: SIPAR.

Delvert, J. 1983. *Le cambodge*. (Que sais-je? 2080). Paris: Presses universitaires de France.

Diller, Anthony. 2003. Evidence for Austroasiatic strata in Thai. In *Language Contacts in Prehistory: Studies in Stratigraphy*, edited by Henning Andersen, 159–176. Current issues in Linguistic Theory, no. 239, Amsterdam Studies in the Theory and History of Linguistic Science. Amsterdam; Philadelphia: John Benjamins.

Enfield, Nicholas J. 2003. *Linguistic Epidemiology*. London: Routledge-Curzon.

Enfield, Nicholas J. 2007. *A Grammar of Lao*. Berlin: Mouton de Gruyter.

Ferlus, M. 1992. Essai de phonétique historique du khmer. *Mon-Khmer Studies* 21: 57–89.

Gregerson, Kenneth. 1984. Pharynx symbolism and Rengao phonology. *Lingua* 62: 209–238.

Haas, M., and H. Subhanka. 1945. *Spoken Thai*. New York: Holt.

Haiman, John. 2011. *Cambodian: Khmer*. Amsterdam: Benjamins.

Harris, Ian. 2006. *Cambodian Buddhism: History and Practice*. Honolulu: University of Hawai'i Press.

Headley, Robert K. 1976. Some considerations on the classification of Khmer. *Oceanic Linguistics, Special Publications* 13: 431–451.

Headley, Robert K, Kylin Chor, Lim Hak Keang, Lam Kheng Lim, and Chen Chun. 1977. *Cambodian-English Dictionary*. Washington, DC: Catholic University of America Press.

Heine, Benrd, and Tania Kuteva. 2002. *World Lexicon of Grammaticalization*. Cambridge: Cambridge University Press.

Heine, Bernd, and Tania Kuteva. 2005. *Language contact and grammaticalation*. Cambridge: Cambridge University Press.

Henderson, Eugenie. 1952. The main features of Cambodian pronunciation. *Bulletin of the School of Oriental and African Studies* 14: 149–174.

Huffman, Franklin. 1973. Thai and Cambodian: A case of syntactic borrowing? *Journal of the American Oriental Society* 93(4): 488–509.

Huffman, Franklin. 1976. Khmer loanwords in Thai. In *Papers from a Conference on Thai Studies in Honor of William J. Gedney*, edited by Robert Bickner. Michigan Papers on South and Southeast Asia Center for South and Southeast Asian Studies. The University of Michigan Number 25. Ann Arbor.

Iwasaki, Shoichi, and Preeya Ingkapirom. 2005. *A Reference Grammar of Thai*. Cambridge: Cambridge University Pres.

Jacob, Judith. 1977. Sanskrit loanwords in pre-Angkor Khmer. *MKS* VI: 151–168.

Jenner, Philip. 2009a, 2009b. *A Dictionary of pre-Angkorian Khmer*. Pacific Linguistics 597–598. Canberra: Research School of Pacific Studies, Australian National University.

Jenner, Philip. 2011. *A Dictionary of Middle Khmer*. Pacific Linguistics 633. Canberra: Research Scool of Pacific Studies, Australian National University.

Khanittanan, Wilaiwan. 2004. *Khmero-Thai: The Great Change in the History of the Thai Language of the Chao Phraya basin*. http://Sealang.net/sula/archives/pdf8/wiaiwan2004khmero.pdf

Khanittanan, Wilaiwan, and Anthony Diller, 2003. Bilingual mixing and diglossic differentiation: Thai and Khmer. In *Proceedings of the XVII International Congress of Linguists*, Prague, Czech Republic, July 2003. Issued as DVD.

Li, Fang Kuei. 1977. *A Handbook of Comparative Tai*. Oceanic Linguistics Special Publication 15. Honolulu: University of Hawai'i Press.

Mabbett, Ian, and David Chandler. 1995. *The Khmers*. Oxford: Blackwell.

MacDonell, Arthur. 2004 [1924]. *A practical dictionary of Sanskrit*. Delhi: Motilal Banarsidass.

Mahathera, A. P. Buddhadatta. 1994 [1957]. *Concise Pali-English Dictionary*. Delhi: Motilal Banarsidass.

Marchand, Hans. 1960. *The Categories and Types of English Word Formation*. Wiesbaden: Harrassowitz.

Matisoff, Jame. 1973. *The Grammar of Lahu*. Berkeley: University of California Press.

Nacaskul, Karnchana. 1976. Types of elaboration in some Southeast Asian languages. *Austroasiatic Studies*, Part 2, edited by P. Jenner et al., 873–890. Honolulu: University of Hawai'i Press.

Nguyen, Dinh-Hoa. 1965. Parallel constructions in Vietnamese. *Lingua* 15: 125–139.

Peang-Merth, Abdulgaffar. 1991. Understanding the Khmer: Sociological-Cultural observations. *Asian Survey* 31(5): 442–455.

Perez Pereiro, Alberto.2012. *Historical Imagination, Diasporic Identity, and Islamicity among the Cham Muslims of Cambodia*. Unpublished PhD thesis, Arizona State University.

Pou, Saveros. 2004 [1967]. Recherches sur la vocabulaire cambodgienne. In *Selected Papers on Khmerology*. Phnom Penh: Reyum. Originally in *Journal Asiatique* 1: 117–131.

Prakorb, Phon-Ngam. 1992. The problem of aspirates in Central Khmer and Northern Khmer. *Mon-Khmer Studies* 22: 251–256.

Ratliff, Martha. 1992. *Meaningful Tone: A Study of Tonal Morphology in Compounds, Form Classes, and Expressive Phrases in White Hmong*. Report 27. DeKalb: Northern Illinois Center for Southeast Asian Studies.

Rischel, Jørgen. 1995. *Minor Mlabri*. Copenhagen: Museum Tusculaneum.

Roffe, Edward. 1975. Rhyme, reduplication, etc. in Lao. In *Studies in Thai Linguistics in Honor of William Gedney*, edited by Robert Bickner, 285–317. Bangkok: Central Institute of English Language, Office of State Universities.

Shorto, Harry. 2006. *A Mon-Khmer Comparative Dictionary*, edited by Paul Sidwell, Doug Cooper, and Christian Bauer. Canberra: Pacific Linguistics, School of Pacific and Asian Studies.

Smalley, W. 1994. *Linguistic Diversity and National Unity: Language Ecology in Thailand*. Chicago: University of Chicago Press.

Smith, F. 2006. *Kamlang phiasa*: [The strength of the language]. A Khmer heritage language textbook for University level. Self-published.

Stanford, James. 2007. Sui adjective reduplication as poetic morpho-phonology. *Journal of East Asian Linguistics* 16(2): 87–111.

Svantesson, Jan-Olof. 1983. *Kammu Phonology and Morphology*. Malmo: CWK Gleerup.

Thach, N. M. 1999. Monosyllabization in Kiengiang Khmer. *Mon Khmer Studies* 29: 81–95.

Thurgood, Graham. 1999. *From Ancient Cham to Modern Dialects*. Oceanic Linguistics Special Publication 28. Honolulu: University of Hawai'i Press.

Ts'ao Ts'ui yŭn. 1961. A preliminary study of descriptive words in the Miao language of Eastern Kweischow. *Miao and Yao linguistic Studies: Selected Articles in Chinese*, translated by Chang Yŭ-hung and Chu Kwo-ray. Linguistic Series V, Data Paper 88. Ithaca, NY: Southeast Asia Program, Cornell University.

Twam Sophoan and Cian Sau:n. n.d. *The Study of Khmer Literature: Brahmanism (The Ramayana)*. [Seuksa: aksaw: seul kmae: Calna: Priam ni'jau:m (Rwang Riamkee:)]. Siam Reap.

Vail, Peter. 2010. *Thailand's Khmer as 'Invisible Minority': Language, Ethnicity, and Cultural Politics in North-Eastern Thailand*. http://Khamerlogue.wordpress.com/2010/01/15/thailand's-kmer-as-.

Varasarin, Uraisri. 1984. *Les éléments Khmers dans la formation de la langue Siamoise.* Paris: SELAF.

Vongvipanand, Peansiri. 1992. Lexicological significance of semantic doublets in Thai. In *Papers on Tai Languages, Linguistics, and Literatures in Honor of William J. Gedney on His 77th Birthday,* edited by C. Compton and J. Hartman. Ann Arbor, Michigan: University of Michigan Monographs on Southeast Asia, Occasional paper #16.

Wälchli, Bernard. 2005. *Co-compounds and Natural Coordination.* Oxford: Oxford University Press.

Wayland, Rattree, and Allard Jongman. 2003. Acoustic correlates of breathy and clear vowels: the case of Khmer. *Journal of Phonetics* 31: 181–201.

Weidert, Alfons. 1973. *I Tkong Amwi: Deskriptive Analyse eines Wardialekts des Khasi.* Wiesbaden: Otto Harrassowitz.

Woznica, Piotr. *Remarks on Sanskrit and Pali loanwords in Khmer.* http://www.inveling.amu.edu.pl/pdf/Wozica_20.pdf.

CHAPTER 26

....

LANGUAGE CONTACT IN WARLPIRI AND LIGHT WARLPIRI

....

CARMEL O'SHANNESSY

26.1 INTRODUCTION

....

AUSTRALIA is known to have been a site of extensive language contact for thousands of years (e.g., Dixon 1980, 2002; Koch 1997; McConvell and Bowern 2011). The Australian Pama-Nyungan language, Warlpiri, became well known in linguistics from the work of Ken Hale and colleagues (e.g., Hale 1973, 1982, 1983, 1992; Laughren 1984; Nash 1986; Hale, Laughren, and Simpson 1995; Simpson 1991), largely due to its non-configurational typology, although there had been documentation of aspects of Warlpiri since 1928 (Terry 1928, 1930). Yet there has also been considerable work on Warlpiri and its historical relationships to neighboring languages, which of necessity includes identification of effects of language contact (e.g., McConvell 1985; Koch 1997; Nash 1997, 2009; McConvell and Laughren 2004). More recently, dramatic contact effects have been seen in the emergence of a mixed language, Light Warlpiri (e.g., O'Shannessy 2005, 2009, 2012, 2013). This chapter reviews work on language contact with regard to Warlpiri from historical and contemporary perspectives.

The Warlpiri live in the Northern Territory of Australia, belonging to a large geographical area running about 700 kilometers from northwest of Alice Springs on the southern boundary, to the northern edge of the Tanami Desert on the northern boundary, and about 700 kilometers from east to west. The Warlpiri traditionally lived a hunter-gatherer lifestyle, and now most live in several small, remote communities in the Tanami Desert area, although there is a sizable diaspora (Burke 2013). See Map 26.1 for languages neighboring the Warlpiri area; see also Hoogenraad and Laughren (2012).

Before focusing on the Warlpiri language, it is important to note an interaction of work on language contact and on historical relationships between languages. The role of language contact in the formation of contemporary Australian languages has been

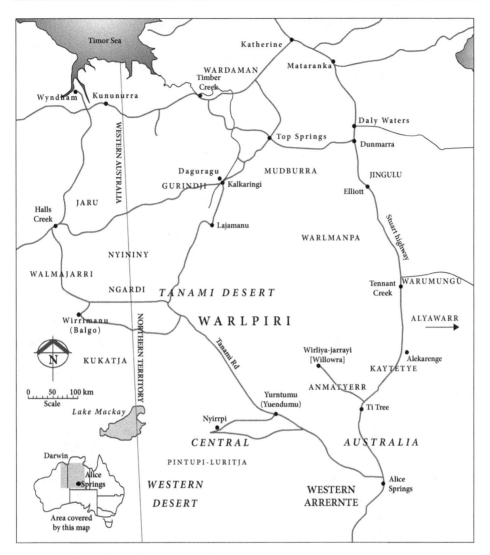

MAP 26.1 Area where Warlpiri is used.

an important issue for its own sake and in questions of genetic grouping. It can be difficult to identify whether some linguistic features are the result of language-contact processes or genetic inheritance, and this has been a major question in work on the prehistory of Australian languages. But there is an increasing amount of work success-fully disentangling the roles of the two types of process in the Australian context using historical-comparative methods (e.g., O'Grady 1966; Heath 1978; Hercus 1979; Evans 1988; Dixon 1997, 2002; Dench 2001; Alpher 2004; Bowern and Atkinson 2012).

In section 26.2 of the chapter, I situate the work on Warlpiri within a wider arena by reviewing work that distinguishes contact phenomena from genetic inheritance in

Australia more generally. In section 26.3 I discuss work on Warlpiri in contact with other languages in prehistory. Section 26.4 discusses Warlpiri in contact in contemporary times-first, mild contact effects on Warlpiri, followed by dramatic contact effects, specifically the development of a new mixed language, Light Warlpiri.

26.2 LANGUAGE CONTACT AND AUSTRALIAN LINGUISTIC PREHISTORY

The question of language contact in Australia's prehistory has been raised as a methodological issue with regard to the reconstruction of historical family groupings. It has been claimed that language contact effects are so extensive across Australia, and the time-depth involved is so great, that genetic relationships are not traceable (Dixon 2001: 88, 2002: 38). But a great deal of work using the historical-comparative method of analysis shows that historical relationships can be distinguished from contact effects (Koch 1997, 2004; McConvell and Laughren 2004; Nash 2009). In the historical-comparative method, synchronic data across languages are used to infer probable historical relationships. Words that are similar in form and meaning are collected from several languages that might have a genetic relationship. Sounds that occur in the same relative position (e.g., word initially) are compared, and hypotheses are formed as to what the original sound in that position may have been, and which processes may have taken place to result in the current sound in each language (Koch 1997). Sounds in languages in the same family may undergo different changes, and the changes are systematic, so once it has been established that a certain sound change occurred in a language, all inherited words will show the same pattern of change. Sound correspondences can be seen in different positions in words also.

Warlpiri is a member of the largest genetic group in Australia, Pama-Nyungan, a family that extends over approximately seven-eighths of the country. The name is from the words for 'person' in the extreme southwest and the northeast (Evans and McConvell 1998: 176; Alpher 2004). Evidence for the existence of Pama-Nyungan as a single family includes shared nominal case-marking forms, a new pronoun system, and some shared verbal inflections (Blake 1988; Evans 1988; Alpher 1990, 2004).

Based on lexico-statistical data, in which the number of words with similar forms are compared across languages, Warlpiri was first identified as belonging to a group called Ngarga (O'Grady, Voegelin, and Voegelin 1966), a member of the Nyungic or South-West subgroup within Pama-Nyungan. The group contained only Warlpiri and Warlmanpa. In recent historical-comparative work (McConvell and Laughren 2004) the Ngarga group is renamed Yapa (*yapa* is the word for 'person' in Warlpiri and Warlmanpa), and an intermediate-level group, Ngumpin-Yapa, is identified. Ngumpin-Yapa contains the Yapa and Ngumpin languages. Innovations in the

Ngumpin-Yapa group are several pronominal enclitic forms, some specific word forms, a sound change *rl < *r[1] and some verbal and reflexive morphology. Some of the innovations are similar to those found in a distantly related family, Warluwarric, spoken to the east of the Ngumpin-Yapa area, and it has been suggested that a few of the common features diffused through contact between proto-languages (McConvell and Laughren 2004: 165).

Running counter to the arguments for subgrouping due to inheritance, there is a claim that all Australian languages form one large linguistic area, created within a few thousand years of the first human habitation of the continent, approximately 40,000–50,000 years ago (Dixon 2001: 25, 39, 2002). A linguistic area is the result of the transfer of lexical and grammatical elements between many languages whose speakers interact. The outcome is that the languages in contact come to share lexical and grammatical items as a result of transfer. In Dixon's (2001: 48–54, 2002) view, similarities between Australian languages are due to diffusion through language contact, not genetic inheritance, and he discounts the existence of the Pama-Nyungan group. But evidence against the idea of Australia as a single large linguistic area is that the features chosen to exemplify this are from languages that are members of the Pama-Nyungan family (Koch 2004; Bowern and Atkinson 2012). However, researchers who provide evidence for genetic groupings also identify a prominent role for language contact. Smaller linguistic areas do exist in Australia; for example, one of the earliest identified is in southeast Arnhem Land (Heath 1978, 1981). It has been suggested that high rates of lexical borrowing between languages are due at least partially to a widespread Australian linguistic cultural practice in which the names of recently deceased persons are taboo, along with other words that begin with similar sounding syllables. Replacement words may be borrowed from other languages. This practice may lead to high levels of change in vocabulary (Dixon 1980: 28, 2002: 27), but not so much that genetic lines are obscured (Koch 1997: 41 and references therein). The practice does appear to have an effect on basic vocabulary (McConvell 2009: 30), which is thought to be less amenable to replacement than non-basic vocabulary (e.g., Thomason and Kaufman 1988).

The historical-comparative method can also be used to identify words that do not show patterns of genetic inheritance—loanwords. If a word does not contain a form that is the consequence of a sound change that occurred in the language, then it is likely that the word was transferred into the language from elsewhere after the sound change took place (Koch 1997, 2004; Nash 1997). In some cases, knowledge of the correspondences between words in related languages can allow the identification of the direction of borrowing, that is, which was the source language and which was the recipient language. Identifying loans when the languages are closely related is more difficult, but can be achieved in some instances (Koch 1997: 32).

Speakers of Australian languages in prehistoric times were hunter-gatherers, and many were multilingual (e.g., Evans 2010; McConvell and Bowern 2011). Meggitt (1962: 38)

---

[1] * denotes a reconstructed form posited as the proto-form

states that most adult Warlpiri men were bilingual or multilingual in the 1950s, although McConvell and Bowern (2011: 22) say that the Warlpiri were not typically multilingual. In many (or perhaps all) areas, when people traveled through lands belonging to speakers of other languages, they spoke the language belonging to the land they were on (e.g., Evans 2010). Some words have spread widely through long chains of contact, and it is now difficult to determine their source (McConvell 2009: 800). In some instances, exogamous marriages were the norm, men and women continued to maintain their own languages, and children grew up learning both, ensuring both multilingualism and constant language contact. In Warlpiri culture, most marriages are endogamous (Meggitt 1962), but marriages do take place between Warlpiri speakers and speakers of other languages. When a marriage is exogamous, the woman usually lives in the man's place of residence with his family and community, and adopts his language while she is there.

There has been a long-standing hypothesis that hunter-gatherer populations borrow proportionally more words than agriculturalist populations (Bowern et al. 2011 and references therein), and this claim has been made often for Australian languages (Koch 2004), but recent work by Bowern et al. (2011) shows that this is not the case. Bowern et al. (2011) surveyed 122 languages from hunter-gatherer and agriculturalist societies in Australia (31 from Australia, but Warlpiri was not included in the sample), and North and South America. They found that the mean proportion of borrowed words in basic vocabulary is 9.4%—far less than often supposed. The Australian languages sampled have more loans and show more variation than those on the other two continents. This is because some languages in the area of Australia to the north of the Warlpiri area have loan rates of up to 48% (e.g., for Gurindji, Warlpiri's neighbor to the north), but these are outliers, and are the results of specific population movements (e.g., McConvell 1996, 2009). When the outliers are removed, the mean proportion of loans is 6.6%. Languages with the highest rates of loans have one or more of the following properties: relatively fewer speakers; lower density of speakers in locations; speakers who practice linguistic exogamy; and speakers who are relatively mobile.

26.3 WARLPIRI AND LANGUAGE CONTACT IN PREHISTORY

Works in which Warlpiri language contact in prehistory has received specific attention include Koch (1997; loanwords to and from Kaytetye [Arandic]) and Nash (1997; loanwords for flora to and from many languages). Koch (1997: 32–34) gives clear examples of identification of words transferred between Warlpiri and Kaytetye in both directions, showing how they can be identified distinctly from inherited words. Kaytetye is an Arandic language, spoken to the east of Warlpiri country. All of the following examples are from Koch (1997: 32–34). A sound change took place in Kaytetye in which initial consonant sounds were dropped, but this change did not take place in Warlpiri. So, when a word is cognate in Warlpiri and Kaytetye, the Warlpiri word will have an initial consonant, but the Kaytetye word will not. For instance, *nyina-* 'sit' in Warlpiri corresponds with *ane-* 'sit' in Kaytetye. In contrast, the words for 'dingo' ('native dog') have an initial consonant in each language—in Warlpiri *wanapari* 'dingo,' and in Kaytetye *wanapare* 'dingo.' The lack of initial-dropping in the Kaytetye pronunciation indicates that the word was not inherited into both Warlpiri and Kaytetye—in which case it would have undergone the sound change—but must have been transferred into Kaytetye from Warlpiri after the Kaytetye sound change took place.

Another indicator is that if a word has alternative pronunciations, it is a candidate for having been transferred at different times and/or by different groups. For example, Warlpiri has two words for 'onion grass,' *yarlirlarlirlki* and *ngarlirlkarlirlki*. Based on this and other examples, the hypothesis is that word-initial nasals in Warlpiri were borrowed in from Kaytetye. The morphological structure of words can also be an indicator of borrowing. The word for 'father's father' is *warringiyi* in Warlpiri and *arrenge-ye* 'father's father–my' in Kaytetye. In Kaytetye the *–ye* morpheme means 'first person possessor,' but in the Warlpiri word it is not a separate morpheme, it is simply a syllable of the word. The word was probably borrowed from Kaytetye, but the morphological structure was not maintained, and the possessive morpheme was treated as part of the word stem. Another phenomenon is seen in words transferred from Warlpiri to Kaytetye but then integrated into Kaytetye such that they resemble cognates, called 'correspondence simultaneity' (deCourtenay 1972 [1885]: 187, in Nash 1997: 191), 'correspondence mimicry' (Alpher and Nash 1999) or 'loan adaptation' (Nash 1997: 191). Examples are *papirta* 'yam' in Warlpiri and *apetye* 'yam' in Kaytetye. The vowels in the word are almost identical in the two languages, suggesting that one of the words did not undergo a historical sound change (Koch 1997). Historically Warlpiri /a/ changed to /e/ in Kaytetye, so if a Kaytetye word now has /a/, it must have been borrowed after the sound change took place (Nash 1997). Additionally, if the direction of transfer was from Kaytetye, there is no explanation for why Warlpiri would have adopted initial consonants such as /p/. The probable explanation is that words such as 'yam' were transferred from Warlpiri to Kaytetye, then were adapted to Kaytetye phonotactic patterns, for instance by omitting the initial consonant.

A comparative study of flora terms aimed at identifying genetic links across languages in the Northern Territory provides some information on languages in contact with Warlpiri (Nash 1997). Plants provide sustenance for indigenous peoples and play a strong role in natural philosophy, including naming and describing tracts of land. The methodological criteria explained in the preceding (cf. Koch 1997) are used, along with information about where plant species grow. Difficulties in deciding between cognates and loanwords are discussed in detail.

Examples show transfer between Warlpiri and neighboring languages. For example, Warlpiri and Warlmanpa have several words for the 'bloodwood' tree (Latin: *Eucalyptus opaca*), *wurrkali*, *wirrkali*, and *yurrkali*, and Arandic languages have *urrkal*, suggesting that the words were borrowed from Arandic languages into Warlpiri and

Warlmanpa (and Gurindji and Wakaya). The Eastern Warlpiri word for the 'mulga' bush *wartiji* (Latin: *Acacia aneura*) was borrowed from Arandic *artetye*, and /w/ was added word-initially. In the other direction, the Warlpiri and Warlmanpa word for a fluff-bearing plant, *martukuru* (Latin: *Gomphrena brachystylis*), was transferred into Alywarra (Arandic) as *matekwer* and Kaytetye as *martekwer* after Arandic initial-dropping had taken place. There are also examples of indirect borrowing—a word is transferred into one language, then to another or others. The Alyawarra word for red-flowering kurrajong bush, *meyak* (Latin: *Brachychiton paradoxum*), was probably borrowed from Warlpiri and Wardaman *miyaka*. Additionally, a word may be trans-ferred into a language at some point in time, then later from that language back to the original source, in a different form. At some point in Warlpiri history—and in some other western Pama-Nyungan languages (Hale 1973)—consonant-final stems were augmented with *-pa* (this process also took place in some Western Desert dialects, but more recently). The presence of *-pa* in the Kaytetye word *merrernmerrernpe* (Latin: *Acacia hemignosta*) indicates that it was borrowed into Kaytetye after Warlpiri *-pa* augmentation took place.

Names for some plants that grow in the north of the Warlpiri area were borrowed from languages to the north, including Gurindji, Mudburra, Wardaman, and Jingulu. This is clear from systematic changes that took place once the word entered Warlpiri, such as replacement of a lateral-nasal cluster *lm* with a nasal-nasal cluster *nm*, addition of a vowel to a word-final consonant, or the presence of non-Warlpiri features, such as a syllable–final stop consonant. From these and other examples in Nash (1997), it is clear that there was extensive transfer of flora terms between neighboring languages at different points in time.

A dramatic example of the extent of language contact in Australia is the reconstruc-tion of the history of subsection terms. The reconstruction does not include details of movements of Warlpiri speakers specifically, but the history of the terms shows that the Warlpiri participated in their diffusion. Subsection terms, known colloquially as 'skin names,' are a set of eight forms that are used in parallel with individual personal names and kin terms—the three sets of terms coexist. These are widespread across Australia, and the terms have correspondences across languages. Examples from Warlpiri will illustrate the system. Society is divided into eight named groups, with corresponding names for each gender, as in Table 26.1.

Traditionally, marriages are preferred between particular subsections, for example, between Jungarrayi and Nangala, and the children of a marriage automatically take the appropriate subsection term. Biological sisters have the same subsection term, biological brothers the corresponding name, and so on. The names also represent Warlpiri relationships, for example, a person's mother's sisters are in a classificatory 'mother' relationship to the person, and they all have the same subsection term. A person's classificatory relationship to another is indicated by the subsection term—father to son, mother's brother, and so on, with differences in generations indicated within the system to a certain extent. Meggitt (1962: 167–187) provides details of the interactions between biological and classificatory relationships. The system plays

Table 26.1 Warlpiri Subsections

Woman	Man	Code*	Girl	Boy
Nakamarra	Jakamarra	D	Nakarra, Wajarla	Jakarra
Nungarrayi	Jungarrayi	A	Ngampukurlu	Jukurtayi, Jukurdayi
Nampijinpa	Jampijinpa	C	Ngampija, Ngampijakurdu	Jampirlka
Napanangka	Japanangka	B	Ngamana	Janama
Nangala	Jangala	C	Ngangkarla	Jangkarli
Napaljarri	Japaljarri	A	Ngalyirri, Ngamalyi	Japalyi
Napurrula	Jupurrula	D	Ngapurru, Ngampurla	Jurlama
Napangardi	Japangardi	B	Ngampayardi, Ngapayardi, Napangayi	Japayardi, Jangari, Japangayi

Notes: * code letters distinguish the semi-patrimoieties; AB vs. CD are the two patrimoieties. From: https://www.anu.edu.au/linguistics/nash/aust/wlp/skins.html.

an important role in all aspects of Warlpiri culture, including land ownership, ceremonial life, and traditional and contemporary social practices. People use the terms in addition to personal names, for instance, to address someone and to mention someone in conversation. I estimate that subsection terms are currently the most common form of naming and address used by the Warlpiri, followed by kin terms (e.g., 'mother,' 'older sister,' and so on). McConvell's (1985) reconstruction of the origin of Australian subsection systems suggests that earlier four-section systems were expanded into eight subsection systems through marriages between different language groups in the lower Victoria River Basin (to the north of the Warlpiri area). Four terms belonging to each of two language groups were merged, resulting in a system of eight terms. The subsection system then spread south and west through further language contact. Phonological correspondences indicate that the system diffused to Arandic languages via Warlpiri (Nash 1997: 201). Anthropological evidence supports this, as Spencer and Gillen (2010 [1899]: 90) reported that the subsection system being used by the Warlpiri at the time was "still in the process of acceptance by the southern Aranda" (Meggitt 1962: 168).

A question about the role of language contact versus genetic inheritance has been raised about the origin of Warlpiri verb roots, due to a typological difference in verb roots between Warlpiri and other members of the Ngumpin-Yapa subgroup. Warlpiri has over a hundred monomorphemic verb roots, in contrast to other languages in the Ngumpin-Yapa subgroup (cf. McConvell and Laughren 2004), which have between thirty and forty-four. One view is that Warlpiri previously had fewer verb roots, and much of the present verb inventory can be accounted for through transfer from Western Desert and Arandic languages (Dixon 2001: 74, 2002: 199). Comparative work by Nash (2009) offers a counter view. About half of Warlpiri verb roots occur with a coverb (also called a preverb) in a lexicalized combination of coverb-inflected verb, for example *kaarntarr-pardi* 'hiccup, belch'—the preverb *kaarntarr* only occurs in this inflecting verb, and *pardi* on its own means 'set off, leave.'

In these constructions the meaning is not the combined meaning of each of the items. Some verb roots may combine with a coverb productively, that is, the meaning is that of each of the items combined, for example *pina* 'return, back' combines with *ya-ni* 'go-PRES' to become *pina-ya-ni* 'return go-PRES.' About half of the verb roots have cognates in other Ngumpin-Yapa languages, and these mostly occur in Warlpiri in a lexicalized combination. Thirty-seven Warlpiri verb roots are inherited from proto-Ngumpin-Yapa, some of which occur uniquely in Warlpiri. Thirty-six verb roots are shared with a non-Ngumpin-Yapa neighboring language, and it is not clear whether the source is inheritance or borrowing. That they do not occur in other Ngumpin-Yapa languages suggests that they might be borrowings, but arguing against this is the occurrence of other verb roots that appear uniquely in Warlpiri, and some form or meaning changes that suggest inheritance. Six verbs are shared with Arrernte, twenty-five are shared with Pintupi/Luritja, and five have possible cognates in Pintupi/Luritja that are not verbs. Some verbs may be the result of reassignment of a cognate coverb to the inflecting verb category. The remaining thirty-four verb roots are posited as inherited from proto-Ngumpin-Yapa—they are unique to Warlpiri within this group, and do not have corresponding forms in neighboring languages. It is possible that some were borrowed from neighboring languages without contemporary sources.

This section has presented an overview of questions and data regarding the prehistory of Warlpiri, situated in the context of Australian languages more generally. In the following sections I move on to the effects of language contact since the colonization of Australia by the British. I first discuss mild effects, then more dramatic processes and outcomes.

26.4 WARLPIRI AND LANGUAGE CONTACT IN CONTEMPORARY TIMES: MILD CONTACT INFLUENCE

Contact between English and Warlpiri is relatively recent. Non-Indigenous people were exploring the central and northern areas of Australia from the 1850s (e.g., Meggitt 1962: 17), establishing cattle stations and gold mines in, and on the borders of, Warlpiri country from the 1880s (Meggitt 1962: 19). There were some violent clashes between the Warlpiri and the intruders. Over time, along with people from other language groups, the Warlpiri became unpaid or poorly paid, often involuntary, workers in the mines and on the cattle stations. Some of the older Warlpiri can remember when they first saw a non-Indigenous Australian, in the 1930s (Henry Cooke Jakamarra, Jerry Patrick Jangala, personal communication). From the 1940s, reserves for Indigenous people, including the Warlpiri, were established in Central Australia, managed by government or missionary organizations. These were not always on the traditional lands of the people who had to live in them (Meggitt 1962; Berndt and Berndt 1987; Rowse 1998). The reserves became self-administrating Indigenous communities within the structure of local government organization, but recently there has been a reduction in self-administration. Bilingual education programs in Warlpiri and English were established in Warlpiri communities from the 1970s, but their strength has varied in response to ever-changing government policies. A standard orthography for written Warlpiri has been in use since the 1970s, and the bilingual programs have produced a considerable amount of written and audiovisual texts, mostly used in schools and in higher education programs. The school programs are staffed by Warlpiri and visiting non-Indigenous teachers. Clearly, social and political domination by English speakers has had a major effect on all Australian languages, with many no longer spoken and those that are still spoken highly endangered. The work on prehistory in the previous section shows that interactions with speakers of other Australian languages have been occurring through a great time depth. Since colonization, non-Indigenous practices such as the establishment of mines for precious metals, cattle stations, and army camps (during World War II) have brought speakers of Australian languages together intensively for long periods. The Warlpiri are fairly mobile people, traveling hundreds or thousands of kilometers for family and ceremonial reasons (Meggitt 1962; Kuipers and Jangala 1977; Peterson 2000) into the country of speakers of other languages.

26.5 English Effects on Warlpiri

Warlpiri phonology differs from English in many ways, including that Warlpiri syllables have a CV or CVC pattern, words end in a vowel, there are only three vowels /a, ɪ, ʊ/ (which can be lengthened), there are no fricatives, and there is no voicing distinction in consonants.

The influence of English on Warlpiri in one Warlpiri community, Yuendumu, was documented in the 1980s (Bavin and Shopen 1985, 1991). Typical lexical influence is that English verbs are increasingly borrowed as coverbs combined with Warlpiri inflecting verbs, such as *sliipi-jarri-mi* 'sleep' (lit. 'sleep-INCHO-NPST') while Warlpiri also has *jarda-nguna-mi* 'sleep' (lit. 'sleep-LIE-NPST'). English terms are common for concepts that the Warlpiri encountered along with English speakers, but sometimes Warlpiri morphology is used to create a new word (a neologism, e.g., *kanja-kurlangu* 'drive-POSS' for 'steering wheel'). These may occur along with borrowings (Bavin and Shopen 1991: 105). These days English borrowings are much more common than neologisms, and the borrowed words are integrated phonologically into Warlpiri to varying degrees, for instance, *jijiji* 'scissors' and *warrki* 'work' (Bavin and Shopen 1985: 82). Children were observed using *na* or *nati*, from English 'no' and 'not,' as negative markers (Bavin 1989: 279; Bavin and Shopen 1991: 116). These days *nu*, from English 'no,' occurs commonly in alternation with the Warlpiri negator *kula* 'negative.'

Morphological changes have occurred in pronominal clitic forms in the auxiliary cluster. An inclusive-exclusive distinction is not always maintained, and a more transparent morphological structure is used by many speakers. The '1DU.INCL' form *-rli* and '1DU.EXCL' form *-rli-jarra* are being replaced by a more transparent first person dual form, *-rna-pala* '1SG-1DU' (Bavin and Shopen 1985, 1991: 108; Bavin 1989: 281).

The different auxiliary structure is probably not due to direct influence from English—Bavin and Shopen (1991: 108) see the changes as regular language change—but changes involving greater morphological transparency are common in situations of community language loss (Dorian 1978; Campbell and Muntzel 1989). Changes are occuring in Warlpiri phonotactics. Words are no longer always vowel-final, as in *wanti-m* 'fall-NPST' instead of *wanti-mi*. Some nominal case-marking forms are being simplified, mostly by reduction of the final vowel (O'Shannessy 2016). Some allomorphs of the ergative case-marker, *-ngku/-ngki*, are often pronounced *-ngu/-ngi* or *-ng*. The dative *-ku/-ki* is often *-k*, and the comitative *-kurlu/-kirli* is often *-kurl/-kirl*. The possessive marker *-kurlangu/-kirlangu* is often pronounced as *-kurlang/kirlang* or *-kang*. The shortened forms *-ng, -k* and *-kang* eliminate the need for vowel harmony between the suffix and the stem. These phonotactic changes are probably due at least partly to English influence because many words in English are consonant-final. It is possible, also, that contact with English has accelerated changes that may have otherwise taken place independently.

In terms of morphosyntax, data from the 1980–1990s show an increase in SVO word order in children's elicited narratives (Bavin and Shopen 1985, 1991). Warlpiri has pragmatically conditioned word order, with the most prominent information occurring first (Swartz 1991; Hale 1992; Simpson and Mushin 2005). Additionally, core arguments are omitted if they can be recovered anaphorically from the context. Swartz (1991: 32–36) documented word order patterns in traditional oral narratives in the Lajamanu community in the 1980s. Of 291 transitive and intransitive clauses, in 48% there was no overt subject or object. Of those with an overt transitive or intransitive subject, 84% had SV order (regardless of the occurrence or position of an overt object). In other words, the subject is elided almost half of the time, and when present, most often occurs before the verb. SV word order does not necessarily reflect pressure from English—if there is a switch of subject, the new subject should occur first, according to Warlpiri word order pragmatics.

The children Bavin and Shopen (1985, 1991) observed did use variable word order in informal speech to each other and in narratives with well-developed thematic structure. But older children used more subject-first order than younger children, suggesting an influence from English learned at school (Bavin and Shopen 1985: 87). In the children's narratives, subjects were overt more often than observed in adult oral narratives—as in English (Bavin and Shopen 1985: 91). Another observation was that ergative case-marking was not always applied by children in the elicited narratives (Bavin and Shopen 1985: 88). Influence from English is likely here, along with a functional explanation—because if SV word order can indicate subjecthood, then ergative case-marking is not needed for the same purpose.

26.5.1 Warlpiri Effects on Local Varieties of English

English is a second or subsequent language for Warlpiri speakers living in remote areas. The English of Warlpiri speakers may be, or may be very close to, Standard Australian English, or may show characteristics of Aboriginal English—English as spoken by Indigenous speakers, with influence from Kriol, Warlpiri, and second-language learning mechanisms. The following information is a combination of information in Nash (1983) and my observations, and is consistent with descriptions of Aboriginal English in Butcher (2008). As a consequence of the contrasts between English and Warlpiri phonological systems described earlier, English words may be pronounced with an additional final vowel, and with substitutions for fricatives and the vowels that do not occur in English. Consonant clusters may take an epenthetic vowel, may be simplified, or may be replaced, for example, 'baby' > /biːbi/, 'shower' > /awa/, 'blanket' > /bilankiti/. The default epenthetic vowel is /i/ (Harvey and Baker 2005: 1462). Where there is a voice distinction in standard varieties of English, consonants in Aboriginal English may be either aspirated or unaspirated. A glide or approximant is added to vowel-initial words, as in oval > /wupuu/. Warlpiri words have a minimum of two syllables, so single syllable English words are lengthened, as in 'one' > /wani/. Warlpiri words have the primary stress on the first syllable, so English words are sometimes pronounced with first-syllable stress also. Some of the properties of English words transferred into Warlpiri are retained in those words by some speakers when speaking English.

Effects on morphosyntax include many of those described for Aboriginal English by Butcher (2008). For example, word order is mainly SVO, but topicalization of complements through left dislocation is common, as in *Nother woman, e got* 'He's got another woman.' The verb 'to be' as a copula need not be present, verbs are usually not marked for tense, and past tense is indicated by preverbal *bin* (from earlier Australian Pidgin), as in *Where you bin go?* 'Where did you go?' Subordinate clauses may be adjoined and unmarked morphosyntactically, as they can be in Warlpiri. Nouns are often not marked for number, and number is often indicated elsewhere in the clause.

26.6 WARLPIRI AND LANGUAGE CONTACT IN CONTEMPORARY TIMES: DRAMATIC CONTACT INFLUENCE

The most dramatic result of contact between Warlpiri and English is the emergence of the new mixed language, Light Warlpiri. Before describing the essential properties of Light Warlpiri, I provide some sociolinguistic background. From the 1930s–1970s, many Warlpiri worked on cattle stations and as drovers, driving cattle for thousands of kilometers to the west and south (Meggitt 1962). On these trips, which lasted several months, and on the cattle stations, the Warlpiri would be in the company of speakers of other Australian languages, of Kriol, and of English. Workers on cattle stations typically spoke varieties of Kriol, an English-lexified creole, developed in the Northern Territory through interactions on cattle stations, in army camps, and in reserves set up for Indigenous people to avoid frontier violence (Sandefur 1986; Harris 1991, 1993). Kriol draws most lexicon from English, and grammar from English and local indigenous languages, with some elements the result of reanalysis through processes seen in second-language learning and language-contact situations. For descriptions of some varieties of Kriol and relevant discussions see, for example, Hudson (1983), Harris and Sandefur (1985), Sandefur (1991), Harris (1991, 1993), Munro (2004), and Nicholls (2009). In addition to Kriol, Indigenous speakers in the north of Australia may speak varieties of Aboriginal English (Malcolm and Kaldor 1991; Eades 1993; Butcher 2008). Most Warlpiri have added some elements of Kriol and/or Aboriginal English to their linguistic repertoire through interactions with non-Warlpiri speakers, Indigenous and non-Indigenous. People who lived in the northern-most Warlpiri community were more involved with cattle stations and more likely to speak Kriol, while those in communities in the south of the Warlpiri area were more likely to speak Aboriginal English rather than Kriol.

In the northernmost Warlpiri community, Lajamanu, in the 1970s–1980s, adults code-switched frequently between Warlpiri and Aboriginal English/Kriol. Warlpiri has a distinct baby talk register (Laughren 1984), and in the 1980s English elements were being used in this register. I hypothesize that when adults in this community were speaking to children in the 1970s–1980s, they used a particular pattern of code-switching as part of the baby talk register: they inserted a Kriol/Aboriginal English pronoun and verb into a string of Warlpiri, as in example (1).

(1) *yakarra nyanya* **wi hab-im** *nyanya wana ngalipa nganya*
     DIS food 1PL have-TR food DIS 1PL.INCL food
     'Gosh, we have food, food, you know, us, food.' (O'Shannessy 2012: 32)

That pattern was conventionalized by the children and ultimately became a new mixed language, called Light Warlpiri (O'Shannessy 2005, 2012, 2013). The emergence of a new conventionalized system is what I refer to as *dramatic contact influence*, and is the focus of this section. The new language is only spoken in the northern-most community. It is typologically a mixed language because it has more than one parent language (Thomason and Kaufman 1988), in this instance, Warlpiri and varieties of English and/or Kriol. Light Warlpiri has since become the primary language of speakers under about age forty in the community, and young children produce this language when they first begin to speak. The children also learn Warlpiri, which they also hear from birth, and as they grow up they add varieties of English and/or Kriol to their repertoire.

Light Warlpiri combines nominal case-marking from Warlpiri with verbal structure mostly from Aboriginal English/Kriol, but with striking innovations in the verbal auxiliary system. The auxiliary system comprises pronominal forms from English/ Kriol, reanalyzed and laid over structure from all of the sources, English/Kriol and

Warlpiri. Examples of Light Warlpiri are given in (2) and (3). Elements from Warlpiri are in italics, from English and/or Kriol in plain font, and the innovative auxiliary cluster is underlined.

(2) i-m jak-im *kanunju* dat *jurlpu-ng*
     3SG-NFUT throw-TRANS down that bird-ERG
     'The bird threw it down.' (LA21_Seal)

(3) *jalang* wi-m go krik-*kirra kurdu-kurdu-kurl*
     today 1PL-NFUT go creek-ALL child-REDUP-COM
     'Today we went to the creek with the children.' (LA21_2014)

In each example the verbs are derived from English (probably via Kriol), 'chuck' (meaning throw), and 'go.' In Light Warlpiri most—but not all—verbs are derived from English. Example (2) shows an ergative case suffix -*ng* 'ERGATIVE' on the lexical subject, *jurlpu* 'bird.' In (2) the transitive verb has a transitive suffix –*im* attached, which is derived ultimately from Australian Pidgin (Koch 2000) and came into Light Warlpiri via Kriol and/or Aboriginal English. Warlpiri suffixes occur on words from any source. In addition to the ergative suffix -*ng* 'ERGATIVE' on *jurlpu* 'bird' in (2), there is an allative suffix -*kirra* on the English-derived word *krik* 'creek' in (3). In (3) the innovative auxiliary cluster is seen clearly in *wi-m* '1PL-NONFUTURE,' in which a pronoun *wi* 'we' hosts a bound tense-mood morpheme, -*m* 'NONFUTURE.' Example (2) shows the same structure in *i-m* '3SG-NONFUTURE.' The structure in which –*m* indicates nonfuture time or realis mood is the result of reanalysis of components from all of the sources, none of which has a structural category of nonfuture or irrealis. The creation of this category is a striking innovation. The auxiliary paradigm of which it is a part is given in Table 26.2.

The last three rows of Table 26.2 show structures that are not unique to Light Warlpiri—they are attested in some Kriol-speaking communities and in another new mixed language, Gurindji Kriol (Meakins 2011). The irrealis structures, which include future and desiderative, are the result of the grammaticalization of forms in varieties of English and Kriol. The –*rra/da* forms are the result of reduction of *garra/gada* to –*rra/da*, with the same meaning of 'future' or 'have to,' and the –*na* form is the result of reduction of *wanna* 'want to' to –*na*. The shortened forms have been applied to single syllable pronouns from varieties of English and Kriol.

Table 26.2 Light Warlpiri Auxiliary Paradigms

Forms	1SG	1PL	2SG	3SG	3PL
Nonfuture	*a-m*	*wi-m*	*yu-m*	*i-m*	*de-m*
Future	*a-rra*	*a-l*	*wi-rra*	*wi-l*	*yu-rra*
i-rrai-l			*de-rra*		
Desiderative	*a-na*	*wi-na*	*yu-na*	*i-na*	*de-na*

Source: O'Shannessy (2013: 343)

The first row in Table 26.2 shows innovation through reanalysis of the meaning and distribution of a bilabial nasal, *-m*. The *-m* morpheme draws on standard English *I'm*, and Aboriginal English and Kriol *im* '3SG' and *dem* '3PL,' originally from English *him* and *them*. In Light Warlpiri the *-m* morpheme means nonfuture tense or realis mood. This is a reanalysis of the meaning of the morpheme from standard English, in which it means '1SG PRESENT,' and from Aboriginal English and Kriol, in which it is not a morpheme, but a phoneme. In Light Warlpiri the *–m* morpheme has taken on the meaning of past time in addition to present time, and is not restricted to 1SG. As shown in Table 26.2, the *-m* morpheme is applied to single syllable pronouns drawn from varieties of English and Kriol, with the reanalysis extending to *yu-m* '2SG NONFU-TURE,' and *wi-m* '1PL NONFUTURE.' Warlpiri influence is seen in the system in two ways. One is that in the Light Warlpiri system, pronominal elements host tense-mood elements. This is in contrast to varieties of English and Kriol, in which many of the tense-aspect-mood elements are separate words. The other influence is semantic: the distribution of Light Warlpiri auxiliary semantics maps onto that of Warlpiri auxiliary-verb semantics, in that there are three tense-mood categories, realis and irrealis, with irrealis divided into 'unactualized future' and 'unactualized irrealis' (Laughren 2012: 8). Note, though, that Warlpiri does not have one-to-one mapping of form to meaning in this area; the meanings are derived from combinations of Warlpiri auxiliary and verb forms. Warlpiri verbal semantic divisions are evident in the Light Warlpiri mapping of form and meaning.

Example (4) is an excerpt from a child's narrative in Light Warlpiri, told from picture stimulus (O'Shannessy 2004). It shows another interesting feature of Light Warlpiri, which is that not all verbs are derived from English. Some verbs are derived from Warlpiri, as in line (d). The Warlpiri verb *panti-rni* 'pierce-PRES' consists of a stem *panti-* and a present tense affix, *-rni*. But in Light Warlpiri the verb components have been reanalyzed so that there is a new stem, derived from the Warlpiri stem plus part of the present tense suffix, *panti-rn* 'pierce-PRES.' An Aboriginal English/Kriol transitive suffix is added, *-im*, and the resulting structure is *pantirn-im* 'pierce-TRANS.' Recall that in contemporary Warlpiri, final vowels are sometimes omitted from words, so that *panti-rni* 'pierce-PRES' could be pronounced *panti-rn* 'pierce-PRES.' This may have been part of the motivation for reanalyzing the stem as *pantirn*.

(4)   (a) *karnta-pawu-ng* i-m draiv-im *rarralykaj*
             woman-DIM-ERG 3SG-NONFUT drive-TRANS car
             'A woman drove the car.'

      (b) de-m look sun *warraja*
             3PL-NONFUT look sun visible
             'They saw that the sun was visible.'

      (c) *rarralykaj* i-m get flat tyre
             car 3SG-NONFUT get flat tyre
             'The car got a flat tire.'

(d) botul-*i-ng* i-m *pantirn*-im tyre
    bottle-EPEN-ERG 3SG-NONFUT pierce-TRANS tyre
    'A bottle pierced the tire.'

(e) boy-wan-*i-ng* i try fix-im tyre
    boy-one-EPEN-ERG 3SG try fix-TRANS tyre
    'The boy tried to fix the tire.'

(f) de-m sleep *watiya-nga*
    3PL-NONFUT sleep tree-LOC
    'They slept by the tree.'

(g) de-m mak-im *warlu*
    3PL-NONFUT make-TRANS fire
    'They lit a fire.'

Light Warlpiri appears to be stabilizing as a communication system, as it is currently being transmitted through generations. Children and young adults speak Light Warlpiri most of the time, but also learn and speak Warlpiri and varieties of English, code-switching between them.

26.7 Conclusion

This chapter has reviewed known language contact phenomena with regard to the Pama-Nyungan language, Warlpiri, situating the work within that about Australian languages more generally. There is clear evidence of the genetic position of Warlpiri, and also of transfer of lexical items between Warlpiri and neighboring languages, including diffusion of a subsection kinship system. Mild bidirectional contact effects between Warlpiri and English were reviewed, followed by the more radical effects resulting in a new mixed language, Light Warlpiri.

References

Alpher, Barry. 1990. Some Proto-Pama-Nyungan verb paradigms: A verb in the hand is worth two in the phylum. In *Studies in Comparative Pama-Nyungan*, edited by Geoffrey O'Grady and Darrell T. Tryon, 155–171. Canberra: Pacific Linguistics.

Alpher, Barry. 2004. Pama-Nyungan: Phonological reconstruction and status as a phylogenetic group. In *Australian Languages: Classification and the Comparative Method*, edited by Claire Bowern and Harold Koch, 93–126. Amsterdam: John Benjamins.

Alpher, Barry, and David Nash. 1999. Lexical replacement and cognate equilibrium in Australia. *Australian Journal of Linguistics* 19(1): 5–55.

Bavin, Edith L. 1989. Some lexical and morphological changes in Warlpiri. In *Investigating Obsolescence: Studies in Language Contraction and Death*, edited by Nancy C. Dorian, 267–286. Cambridge: Cambridge University Press.

Bavin, Edith L., and Tim Shopen. 1985. Warlpiri and English: Languages in contact. In *Australia, Meeting Place of Languages*, edited by Michael Clyne, 81–94. Canberra: Pacific Linguistics.

Bavin, Edith L., and Tim Shopen. 1991. Warlpiri in the 80s: An overview of research into language variation and child language. In *Language in Australia*, edited by Suzanne Romaine. Cambridge: Cambridge University Press, 104–117.

Berndt, Ronald Murray, and Catherine H. Berndt. 1987. *End of an Era: Aboriginal Labour in the Northern Territory*. Canberra: Australian Institute of Aboriginal Studies.

Blake, Barry. 1988. Redefining Pama-Nyungan: Towards the prehistory of Australian languages. *Aboriginal Linguistics* 1: 1–90.

Bowern, Claire, and Quentin Atkinson. 2012. Computational phylogenetics and the internal structure of Pama-Nyungan. *Language* 88(4): 817–845.

Bowern, Claire, Patience Epps, Russell D. Gray, Jane Hill, Keith Hunley, and Patrick McConvell. 2011. Does lateral transmission obscure inheritance in hunter-gatherer languages? *PloS One* 6(9): e25195.

Burke, Paul. 2013. Indigenous diaspora and the prospects for cosmopolitan 'orbiting': The Warlpiri case. *The Asia Pacific Journal of Anthropology* 14(4): 304–322.

Butcher, Andrew. 2008. Linguistic aspects of Australian Aboriginal English. *Clinical Linguistics and Phonetics* 22(8): 625–642.

Campbell, Lyle, and Martha C. Muntzel. 1989. The structural consequences of language death. In *Investigating Obsolescence: Studies in Language Contraction and Death*, edited by Nancy C. Dorian. Cambridge: Cambridge University Press, 181–196.

Dench, Alan. 2001. Descent and diffusion: The complexity of the Pilbara situation. In *Areal Diffusion and Genetic Inheritance: Problems in Comparative Linguistics*, edited by Alexandra Aikhenvald and R. M. W. Dixon, 105–133. Oxford: Oxford University Press.

Dixon, R. M. W. 1980. *The Languages of Australia*. Cambridge: Cambridge University Press.

Dixon, R. M. W. 1997. *The Rise and Fall of Languages*. Cambridge: Cambridge University Press.

Dixon, R. M. W. 2001. The Australian linguistic area. In *Areal Diffusion and Genetic Inheritance: Problems in Comparative Linguistics*, edited by Alexandra Aikhenvald and R. M. W. Dixon, 64–103. Oxford: Oxford University Press.

Dixon, R. M. W. 2002. *Australian Languages: Their Nature and Development*. Cambridge: Cambridge University Press.

Dorian, Nancy C. 1978. The fate of morphological complexity in language death: Evidence from East Sutherland Gaelic. *Language* 54(3): 590–609.

Eades, Diana. 1993. *Aboriginal ways of using English*. Melbourne: Primary English Teaching Association, 76.

Evans, Nicholas. 1988. Arguments for Pama-Nyungan as a genetic subgroup, with particular reference to initial laminalization. *Aboriginal Linguistics* 1: 91–110.

Evans, Nicholas. 2010. *Dying Words*. Malden; Oxford: Wiley-Blackwell.

Evans, Nicholas, and McConvell, Patrick. 1998. The enigma of Pama-Nyungan expansion in Australia. In *Archeology and Language*, Vol. II: *Correlating Archeological and Linguistic Hypotheses*, edited by Roger Blench and Matthew Spriggs, 174–191. London; New York: Routledge.

Hale, Kenneth. 1973. Person marking in Walbiri. In *A Festschrift for Morris Halle*, edited by Stephen Anderson and Paul Kiparsky, 308–344. New York: Rinehart and Winston.

Hale, Kenneth. 1982. Some essential features of Warlpiri verbal clauses. In *Papers in Warlpiri Grammar: In Memory of Lother Jagst*, edited by Stephen Swartz, 217–314. Darwin: Summer Institute of Linguistics-Australian Aborigines Branch.

Hale, Kenneth. 1983. Warlpiri and the grammar of non-configurational languages. *Natural Language and Linguistic Theory* 1(1): 5–47.

Hale, Kenneth. 1992. Basic word order in two 'free word order' languages. In *Pragmatics of Word Order Flexibility*, edited by Doris Payne, 63–82. Amsterdam; Philadelphia: John Benjamins.

Hale, Kenneth, Mary Laughren, and Jane Simpson. 1995. Warlpiri. In *An International Handbook of Contemporary Research*, edited by Joachim Jacobs, Arnim von Stechow, Wolfgang Sternefeld, and Theo Vennemann, 2: 1430–1449. Berlin: Walter de Gruyter.

Harris, John. 1991. Kriol: The creation of a new language. In *Language in Australia*, edited by Suzanne Romaine, 195–203. Cambridge: Cambridge University Press.

Harris, John. 1993. Losing and gaining a language: The story of Kriol in the Northern Territory. In *Language and Culture in Aboriginal Australia*, edited by Michael Walsh and Colin Yallop, 145–154. Canberra: Aboriginal Studies Press.

Harris, John, and John Sandefur. 1985. Kriol and multilingualism. In *Australia, Meeting Place of Languages*, edited by Michael Clyne, 257–264. Canberra: Pacific Linguistics.

Harvey, Mark, and Brett Baker. 2005. Vowel harmony, directionality and morpheme structure constraints in Warlpiri. *Lingua* 115: 1457–1474.

Heath, Jeffrey. 1978. *Linguistic Diffusion in Arnhem Land*. Canberra: Australian Institute of Aboriginal Studies.

Heath, Jeffrey. 1981. A case of intensive lexical diffusion: Arnhem Land, Australia. *Language* 57: 335–367.

Hercus, Luise Anna. 1979. In the margins of an Arabana-Wanganguru dictionary: The loss of initial consonants. In *Australian Linguistic Studies*, edited by Stephen A. Wurm, 621–651. Pacific Linguistics C-54. Canberra: Australian National University.

Hoogenraad, Robert, and Mary Laughren. 2012. *Warlpiri Picture Dictionary*. Alice Springs: Institute for Aboriginal Development Press.

Hudson, Joyce. 1983. *Grammatical and Semantic Aspects of Fitzroy Valley Kriol* (Vol. Series A, Volume 8). Darwin: Summer Institute of Linguistics, Australian Aborigines and Islanders Branch.

Koch, Harold. 1997. Comparative linguistics and Australian prehistory. In *Archaeology and Linguistics: Aboriginal Australia in Global Perspective*, edited by Patrick McConvell and Nicholas Evans, 27–43. Oxford: Oxford University Press.

Koch, Harold. 2000. The role of Australian Aboriginal languages in the formation of Australian Pidgin grammar: Transitive verbs and adjectives. In *Processes of Language Contact: Studies from Australia and the South Pacific*, edited by Jeff Siegel, 13–46. Montreal: Les Editions Fides (University of Montreal Press).

Koch, Harold. 2004. A methodological history of Australian linguistic classification. In *Australian Languages: Classification and the Comparative Method*, edited by Claire Bowern and Harold Koch, 17–66. Amsterdam: John Benjamins.

Kuipers, Ludo, and Abie Jangala (eds.). 1977. *Stories from Lajamanu*. Darwin, NT: Department of Education, Northern Territory Division.

Laughren, Mary. 1984. Warlpiri baby talk. *Australian Journal of Linguistics* 4: 73–88.

Laughren, Mary. 2012. A revised analysis of Warlpiri verb inflections plus auxiliary combinations: Their makeover in 'Light' Warlpiri. Paper presented at the Australian Linguistic Society Annual Canference, Perth.

Malcolm, I., and S. Kaldor. 1991. Aboriginal English: An overview. In *Language in Australia*, edited by Suzanne Romaine, 67–83. Cambridge: Cambridge University Press.

McConvell, Patrick. 1985. The origin of subsections in northern Australia. *Oceania* 56: 1–33.

McConvell, Patrick. 1996. Backtracking to Babel: The chronology of Pama-Nyungan expansion in Australia. *Archeology in Oceania* 31(3): 125–144.

McConvell, Patrick. 2009. Loanwords in Gurindji, a Pama-Nyungan language of Australia. In *Loanwords in the World's Languages: A Comparative Handbook*, edited by Martin Haspelmath and Uri Tadmor, 790–822. Berlin: Mouton de Gruyter.

McConvell, Patrick, and Claire Bowern. 2011. The Prehistory and internal relationships of Australian languages. *Language and Linguistics Compass* 5(1): 19–32.

McConvell, Patrick, and Mary Laughren. 2004. The Ngumpin-Yapa subgroup. In *Australian Languages: Classification and the Comparative Method*, edited by Claire Bowern and Harold Koch, 151–177. Amsterdam: Benjamins.

Meakins, Felicity. 2011. *Case-marking in Contact: The Development and Function of Case Morphology in Gurindji Kriol*. Amsterdam; Philadelphia: John Benjamins.

Meggitt, M. J. 1962. *Desert People*. London; Sydney; Singapore; Manila: Angus and Robertson.

Munro, Jennifer. 2004. *Substrate Language Influence in Kriol: The Application of Transfer Constraints to Language Contact in Northern Australia*. Dissertation, University of New England, Armidale, NSW.

Nash, David. 1983. TESL and Warlpiri children: Understanding Warlpiri children's problems in learning to speak English. *NT Bilingual Education Newsletter*, 6–24.

Nash, David. 1986. *Topics in Warlpiri Grammar*. New York; London: Garland.

Nash, David. 1997. Comparative flora terminology of the central Northern Territory. In *Archaeology and Linguistics: Aboriginal Australia in Global Perspective*, edited by Patrick McConvell and Nicholas Evans, 187–206. Oxford: Oxford University Press.

Nash, David. 2009. Warlpiri verb roots in comparative perspective. In *Morphology and Language History: In Honour of Harold Koch*, edited by Claire Bowern, Bethwyn Evans, and Luisa Miceli, 221–234. Amsterdam: John Benjamins.

Nicholls, Sophie. 2009. *Referring Expressions and Referential Practice in Roper Kriol (Northern Territory, Australia)*. Unpublished PhD dissertation, University of New England, Armidale.

O'Grady, Geoffrey. 1966. Proto-Ngayarda phonology. *Oceanic Linguistics* 5: 71–130.

O'Grady, Geoffrey, Charles F. Voegelin, and Florence M. Voegelin. 1966. Languages of the world: Indo-Pacific fascicle 6. *Anthropological Linguistics* 8(2): 1–199.

O'Shannessy, Carmel. 2004. *The Monster Stories: A Set of Picture Books to Elicit Overt Transitive Subjects in Oral Texts*. Unpublished series. Nijmegen, The Netherlands: Max Planck Institute for Psycholinguistics.

O'Shannessy, Carmel. 2005. Light Warlpiri: A new language. *Australian Journal of Linguistics* 25(1): 31–57.

O'Shannessy, Carmel. 2009. Language variation and change in a north Australian Indigenous community. In *Variationist Approaches to Indigenous Minority Languages*, edited by Dennis Preston and James Stanford, 419–439. Amsterdam: John Benjamins.

O'Shannessy, Carmel. 2012. The role of code-switched input to children in the origin of a new mixed language. *Linguistics* 50(2): 305–340.

O'Shannessy, Carmel. 2013. The role of multiple sources in the formation of an innovative auxiliary category in Light Warlpiri, a new Australian mixed language. *Language* 89(2): 328–354.

O'Shannessy, Carmel. 2016. Distributions of case allomorphy by multilingual children speaking Warlpiri and Light Warlpiri. *Linguistic Variation* 16(1): 68–102.

Peterson, Nicholas. 2000. An expanding Aboriginal domain: Mobility and the initiation journey. *Oceania* 70(3): 205–218.

Rowse, Tim. 1998. *White Flour, White Power*. Cambridge: Cambridge University Press.

Sandefur, John. 1986. *Kriol of North Australia: A Language Coming of Age* (Vol. Series A, Volume 10). Darwin: Summer Institute of Linguistics, Australian Aborigines and Islanders Branch.

Sandefur, John. 1991. A sketch of the structure of Kriol. In *Language in Australia*, edited by Suzanne Romaine, 204–212. Cambridge: Cambridge University Press.

Simpson, Jane. 1991. *Warlpiri Morpho-Syntax: A Lexicalist Approach* (Vol. 23). Dordrecht: Kluwer Academic.

Simpson, Jane, and Ilana Mushin. 2005. Clause initial position in four Australian languages. In *Discourse and Grammar in Australian Languages*, edited by Ilana Mushin and Brett Baker, 25–58. Amsterdam; Philadelphia: John Benjamins.

Spencer, Walter Baldwin, and Francis James Gillen. 2010 [1899]. *The Native Tribes of Central Australia*. Cambridge: Cambridge University Press.

Swartz, Stephen. 1991. *Constraints on Zero Anaphora and Word Order in Warlpiri Narrative Text*. Darwin: Summer Institute of Linguistics.

Terry, Michael. 1928. *Walmulla Language*. Notebook 2. Adelaide: South Australian Museum Archives.

Terry, Michael. 1930. *Hidden Wealth and Hiding People*. London; New York: Putnam.

Thomason, Sarah G., and Terrence Kaufman. 1988. *Language Contact, Creolization, and Genetic Linguistics*. Berkeley; Oxford: University of California Press.

CHAPTER 27

··

LANGUAGE CONTACT
AND TOK PISIN

··

ADAM A. H. BLAXTER PALIWALA

27.1 LANGUAGE CONTACT AND THE GRAMMAR OF TOK PISIN

THIS chapter focuses primarily on the grammar of the variety of Melanesian Pidgin English (MPE) I am most familiar with, Tok Pisin (TP), and highlights areas where ongoing contact with English is viewed to be leading to language change. In preparation for the final section on bilingual behaviors (CS "types") that lie behind apparently Anglicized or putatively "decreolized" varieties of MPE, the chapter concentrates on features and characteristics of most significance to that debate, found in the first-language "urban" TP learned and spoken alongside varieties of English taught in schools. It also draws attention to the character of Papua New Guinea English (PNGE) and its role in the language-contact dynamic.

Space does not permit a detailed analysis of the grammar of MPE, or a comparison across varieties. We are fortunate, however, that volumes of excellent research have already been published. The interested reader is encouraged to consider Hall's germinal grammar (Hall 1943), the papers in the outstanding collection of Wurm and Mühlhaüsler (1985) on Tok Pisin, and in particular Laycock (1985) on the influence of indigenous phonological systems on varieties of Tok Pisin, Wurm (1985) on the distinctively Melanesian intonation patterns in "pidgin English," Faraclas (1989) on substrate influence on prosody, and G. Smith (2002) in his discussion of the Highlands variety of Tok Pisin, all of which highlight the role and impact of indigenous languages on the phonology of MPE. Valuable contributions by Romaine (1992) and G. Smith (2002) provide detailed analyses of "creole Tok Pisin" in children's speech, while G. Sankoff and associates (G. Sankoff 1977; G. Sankoff and Brown 1980; G. Sankoff and Laberge (1980 [1973]); G. Sankoff and Mazzie 1991) have provided an outstanding record of the development of the expanded and creole morphosyntax. Crowley (1990) remains the authoritative source on Bislama, providing a vital sociocultural comparison with Tok Pisin (Crowley 1990b), and his various subsequent papers provide rich detail and analysis on the development of various aspects of the MPE grammar (Crowley 1990a, 2000, 2003). Jourdan is the outstanding contemporary researcher on Solomon Islands Pijin (Jourdan 1989; Jourdan and Keesing 1997; Jourdan 2008, 2009), while Keesing's (1988, 1991) contributions draw on his experience with Pijin to present essential reading on early MPE. On the lexicon of MPE, Mühlhaüsler (1979a) is the great resource, and Mihalic (1971) provides the standard reference for pre-Independence Tok Pisin. Schneider (2011) and Siegel and Smith (2013) provide accessible summaries of the distinctive features of MPE varieties. On PNGE, A. M. Smith (1986) is the germinal authority, while Platt et al. (1984) present an illuminating comparison of "Englishes" worldwide.

Our discussion serves to point out, in line with the view taken by Ochs and Schieffelin (2011) and Garrett (2011), that the implicit assumptions about the discreteness and boundedness of MPE and English varieties that lead to "decreolization" as being an expected outcome of continuing language contact between them are problematic. Some apparently new developments in MPE varieties are actually the consequence of code switching (CS).

27.2 PHONETICS AND PHONOLOGY

Tok Pisin (TP) has been spoken with a wider range of vowels than Mihalic's "core" set of five common vowels and three diphthongs since at least the 1940s. In addition to the influence of speakers' first languages on their TP, which leads to both variation and such characteristic features as allophonic p/f described in the literature, an expanded set of phonemes available has been consistently related by Hall (1943), Laycock (1985), Romaine (1992), and G. Smith (2002) to exposure to English. Alongside this, the local PNG dialect of English (PNGE), as described by A.-M. Smith (1978, 1986), has a similar vowel space to TP, indicating congruence between the vowel systems of these two languages.

In terms of consonants, my own data support a characterization of PNGE as featuring variation from "standard" English forms similar to those recorded by Laycock and others between TP and Australian English forms, in particular on words shared between TP and English, for some of my speakers. This also confirms an observed pattern of final consonant cluster simplification in PNGE.

27.2.1 Vowels

The standard "core" set (Laycock 1985: 297) of TP vowels is considered to be a set of five basic phonemes, /a/, /e/, /i/, /o/, and /u/, all with a short-mid length (Dutton and Thomas 1985), "fairly close to cardinal IPA values" (G. Smith 2004b: 719), and three diphthongs /ai/, /au/, and /oi/ (Mihalic 1971), common to all varieties of the language.

Hall's (1943) grammar actually allows for a much larger set of vowels than this, but it is significant that he is providing an account of TP as a regional lingua franca. As a consequence, his phonology for TP includes British and American pronunciations of certain words, and the influence of native English-language pronunciations is apparent. Observing changes that had taken place since the 1930s, Laycock (1970) described a ten-vowel set in coastal regions, and Mihalic (1971: 4) acknowledges this recent experience, recording nine of these in his dictionary, excluding the long [aː].

Taking the contemporary pronunciation of Melanesian speakers as a guide, we find numerous points of difference with the unofficial standard for written TP in Mihalic's orthography. This is because Mihalic makes no attempt to record the newer, variable distinctions, though he does acknowledge additional phones. Consequently, the simple five-vowel set of Mihalic's orthography represents an artificial standard, for it is clear from Hall, Laycock, and Mihalic's own revisions to "the sounds" of his orthography (Mihalic 1971: 4) that a larger set of vowel sounds continued to be available in the spoken TP varieties of Papua New Guineans.

Laycock (1985) allows twelve basic vowels for speakers whose dialect is not, as he says, entirely Anglicized. These include open-mid central [ɜ] and back [ɔ] vowels. In contrast, Verhaar categorically describes the "core" vowel set as reflecting the absence of distinctions between long/short, high/low vowels (Verhaar 1995: 9). This characteristic produces the TP *ken* [ken] from English *can* [kæn], *kantri* [kantri][1] from English *country* [kəntɹiː],[2] *gat* [gat] from *got* [gɒt], and *kot* [kot] from *court* [kɔt]. Verhaar's observation that diphthongs in borrowed words are reduced to simple vowels is reflected in TP *nem* [nem] from English *name* [neɪm] and *ston* [ston] from *stone* [stəʊn].

These transformations can be seen in the table that Laycock presents of vowels and vocalic nuclei showing the differences and similarities between English source vowels and TP pronunciations of equivalent words. These include eight diphthongs: /ia/, /ea/, /ai/, /oa/, /ua/, /ei/, /au/, and /oi/.

G. Smith's transcripts have the five basic vowels and include five diphthongs: /ai/, /au/, /ia/, /iu/, /oi/ (G. Smith 2002: 44). Though /ia/, in *hia* 'here,' is an addition to Mihalic's (1971) set, all of these except /iu/, in *niu* 'new,' are included in earlier descriptions of TP. This additional dipthong may be considered to have come along with the borrowing of *new* from English for the name of the independent country of Papua New Guinea: *Niugini* for many Tok Pisin speakers. G. Smith also gives examples of non-standard diphthongs /ai/, /ei/, and /ou/ found in his data, and ascribes them to the influence of the English pronunciation of words common to TP and English. Of these, only /ou/ is not found in Laycock's expanded inventory.

---

[1] Note that I am following standard British, American, and Australian dictionary usage here and indicating the alveolar approximant with the IPA character [r] rather than the formally correct [ɹ]. The use of [r] here should not be taken to indicate a trilled consonant, though trilled pronunciations are possible in PNGE.

[2] For English pronunciations in the body text, I use standard British English as a reference, except where otherwise noted.

A. M. Smith (1978, 1986, 1988) provided key accounts of PNGE that connected it convincingly with other World Englishes. She observed the influence of first languages on the phonology of Papua New Guinean speakers of English, but writing ten years after independence, noted that PNGE has a fairly consistent accent and form, with t/d deletion through word final CC deletion, and centralized vowels, when compared with Standard English.

In New/World Englishes in Africa, India, and Singapore, vowel transformations and a reduction in distinctions similar to those in PNGE have been observed (Platt, Weber, and Ho 1984: 31–37; A. M. Smith 1986: 116; Holzknecht 1989: 184). The fronting of central vowel [ɜ] to [ɛ] and of [ɑ] to 'front a' [a], the movement of [æ] to [a] or [e] and of [ɔ] to [ɒ] or [o], and the avoidance of a central mid vowel [ə] have also been observed. In addition, these indigenized Englishes, like PNGE, tend to reduce diphthongs to simple vowels, and have variable approaches to vowel length. Platt et al. note "the English of educated Papuans and New Guineans" alongside Indian and Philippine English as making occasional distinctions between some words on the basis of vowel length (Platt, Weber, and Ho 1984: 32).

Significantly, there is a general overlap between the phonology of PNGE and the expanded inventory of TP, and I have shown that similar transformations in vowels are present in both language varieties: the avoidance of central vowels such as [ɜ] and [ə]; the movement of near-open front [æ] to a fully open [a] or [ɑ] (ɑ); and the movement of [ʊ] to [u] at top/back. In both TP and PNGE, the English dipthong [ɪə] becomes [ɪa] (Weinreich 1963; Blaxter Paliwala 2012: 144–154).

27.2.2 Consonants

Accounts of substrate influences (Goulden 1987; Keesing 1988; Siegel 1999) in TP have shown variation in consonants. As discussed earlier, G. Smith (2002: 43), Laycock (1985), and Faraclas (1989) specifically address the impact of indigenous vernaculars on the way TP is spoken. While second-language varieties commonly see the impact of phonological and prosodic patterns from speakers' primary languages, G. Smith's study suggests that the single most common source for new phonemes in TP is English.

As with vowels, previous accounts of PNGE have focused on similarities between the consonants produced by different New/World Englishes and consistent differences between various indigenized varieties and inner circle "Standard" English pronunciations. However, we can see that these same differences between inner circle Englishes and outer circle "New'" Englishes are characteristic of TP pronunciations also.

The "core" consonants of Tok Pisin have been variously described as between fifteen (Hall 1943) and eighteen (Mihalic 1971; Laycock 1985) phonemes. This variation is partly due to the presence/absence of [j] and [dʒ], which only appear word-initially in TP, and to the exclusion of [h] from Hall's account (Hall 1943). G. Smith refers to Mihalic as the standard for comparison, but notes that those may not refer to the common spoken forms, especially in the case of rapid speech (G. Smith 2002: 44). However, where Mihalic includes [dʒ] in his inventory, as a word-initial option, G. Smith leaves it out of the core phonology of the creolized variety, and includes it under his list of new phonemes introduced from English in his data, where [ʤ] appears word-internally also.

Laycock's "core" phonemes list illustrates expected TP options replacing English phonemes /ʃ/, /ð/, /tʃ/, /ʒ/, /ʤ/, /θ/, and /z/. However, accounts from Hall (1943) onward have noted the presence of these phonemes in the Tok Pisin of some speakers. As is the case with vowels, these phonemes have commonly been ascribed either to foreign accents or to Anglicized Papua New Guinean accents. Mihalic leaves this set of "English" phonemes out of his standardizing orthography because it is based on a conservative variety.

Considering his corpus of creole speech, G. Smith found all of the "replaced'" English phonemes (G. Smith 2002). The extent to which such phonemes appear in TP as a result of an acquisition of English phonology by schoolchildren and adult bilinguals is something that G. Smith describes as an interference phenomenon, relating it to shared vocabulary items, and echoing the language of Haugen (1950) and Weinreich (1963). However, the longevity of such forms in TP, albeit limited to certain speakers and the "Urban" Anglicized variety, suggests that these pronunciations are not entirely novel borrowings from English. In fact, the adoption of new phonemes, reversing in some cases the standard transformations detailed by Laycock, again increases the congruence between Tok Pisin and English for some speakers, effectively blurring particular distinctions represented in the standard orthography of TP.

Hall's (1943) orthography of Tok Pisin includes a large set of viable consonant clusters, including those in the varieties spoken by American and British English speakers. Vowel epenthesis is common in Melanesians' TP, with insertion of unstressed vowels between consonants allowing for the maintenance of a regular consonant-verb (CV) syllable structure to be maintained in the pronunciation of those English-derived words where vowel diphthongs and consonant clusters occur. In a small study of a single TP speaker, Pawley (1974) successfully identified the relationship between vowel epenthesis and speed of delivery, uncovering a link between the rate of speech or degree of emphasis being placed on a word and the appearance of the epenthetic vowel.

In present-day TP, epenthesis appears more as an expressive strategy than an interference effect. Laycock (1985) gives a short list of phonemic consonant clusters in TP, for which vowel epenthesis is not a factor: in particular, homorganic nasal clusters appear in TP, when compared with their English counterparts, only when they fall across a syllable boundary.

Where the same consonant cluster occurs in the English word-finally, it is, in Laycock's examples, modified: in some cases the final consonant is omitted; in others, such as /nʃ/ or /nʒ/, vowel epenthesis occurs. These are the same techniques observed in PNGE and other New/World Englishes. In particular, word-final reduction in consonant clusters (t/d deletion) can result in the disappearance of tense markers on English words.

In addition to these, G. Smith identifies non-standard consonant clusters in established words in his data, indicating additional impact of English phonology on creole TP pronunciation (G. Smith 2002: 48). Non-standard consonant clusters appear in borrowings from English, as well as shared English words in TP.

27.2.3 Phonological Reduction

A final crucial aspect of contemporary MPE, recorded in the studies of G. Sankoff and Brown (1976), Romaine (1999), and G. Smith (2002) for TP, are clear tendencies toward the production of reduced phonological forms of many common words as a standard feature of creole Tok Pisin. The resulting speech is more rapid and fluid, and also produces surface forms that are phonologically distinct from their lexical roots: in TP, for example, the preposition *lo* is a reduced form quite distinct from its English root *belong*.

Phonologically reduced forms are as prevalent in my data as they are in earlier spoken corpora, and forms previously observed in children's creole speech can now be observed in the language of non-creole, adult speakers.

27.2.4 Summary

These findings have a significant impact on expectations of phonological congruence between some varieties of Tok Pisin and of English as it may be spoken in Papua New Guinea.

Just as TP pronunciations may be Anglicized, so too PNGE pronunciations are "Tok Pisin-ized." Some of the phonological changes result in the non-realization of grammatical morphemes, with consequences for the syntactic expression of tense. These changes result in distinctive variation within each language, and also in congruence between them.

My analysis of PNGE phonology (Blaxter Paliwala 2012: 141–170) shows that the PNGE "accent" is similar to TP pronunciations of shared lexical items, encouraging congruence between them and fluidity in speech. This is to be expected in the context of National Census data on multilingualism, which shows that English was the most prevalent language recorded in addition to TP by Papua New Guineans in 2000 (Paliwala 2012).

The observation that phonological variation is encouraged by exposure to English pronunciations means that, against the backdrop of widespread education in English, the way a word may be pronounced in TP can be very variable: more like English, less like English, and more like conservative TP, or less like English and conservative TP, especially when phonological reduction has taken place. Importantly, in PNGE this same variation is in evidence, with the result that when vocabulary is exchanged between TP and PNGE it can be unclear to which "inventory" a word belongs.

27.3 MORPHOSYNTAX

The origins and development of the morphosyntax of MPE have been considered from three directions: the perspective of the Oceanic Substrate (e.g., Keesing 1988, 1991) and other indigenous language influences reinforcing or eroding common patterns; from the perspective of proposed processes of pidginization and creolization, including hypothesized universal tendencies (e.g., Bickerton 1975, 1977); and from ongoing contact with English (e.g., Romaine 1989, 1992).

Features highlighted for a substrate source/reinforcement are the inclusive/exclusive distinction (*mipelai, yumipela*) and dual/trial pronouns (*yutupela, mitripela*) in the pronominal system, the marking of transitivity through a verbal suffix (*-im/-em*), the marking of adjectives or nominal modifiers with a suffix (*-pela/-fala*), and the use of a "subject referencing pronoun" (Keesing 1988) or "predicate marker" (Mühlhäusler 1985e) (*i*).

As discussed earlier, this section does not attempt a detailed account of the morphosyntax of different varieties of MPE, but focuses instead on some of the aspects of the language where language contact effects are most clearly expressed. These are the marking of plurality, where a general explanation on the basis of CS theory for "new" morphology found in Verhaar's (1995) corpus is presented, the system of pronouns, and in the set of conjunctions.

27.3.1 Plurals

Where English uses a nominal suffix to indicate plurality, TP uses the prenominal particle *ol*. As with many pidgin languages, early speakers of TP made no systematic distinction between singular and plural nouns, number being either inferred from context or explicitly defined through the use of a numeral. Plural marking developed in TP during the stabilization phase (Mühlhäusler 1985c: 113). Following a possibly universal tendency also observed in other creoles, the third person plural pronoun became grammaticalized as a marker of plurality, becoming obligatory for first-language speakers and also being applied redundantly in many cases (G. Smith 2004a).

Example (1) illustrates a developing tendency in TP that has previously been observed in creole speakers (Romaine 1992; G. Smith 2002) and in Anglicized varieties (Mühlhäusler 1985b). This is evidenced in my data: the most common pattern when English plural forms are used in TP is for double-marking with *ol* prenominally, even where plural is indicated on the English form with the *-s* suffix or even with a specific plural form of the noun, as in (2).

(1)   TiT#10b-07_L420
       <u>ol</u> ***problems*** yumi gat
       PL problem-PL 2PL.INCL have
       ol ***problems*** yumi gat
       'all (the) problems we have'

(2)   TiT#10b-07_L470
       <u>ol</u> ***pipol*** blong ol
       PL people PREP.POSS 3PL
       ol ***people*** bilong ol
       'their people'

Geoff Smith (2002: 75) predicts that double marking is an indication of competition between plural forms developed from internal resources, the *ol* marker adapted by universal inclinations to utilize pronouns as plural markers, and those borrowed from other languages, the English *-s* suffix. In pidginization, the borrowing of structural morphology is unlikely, and borrowing as a development process is not compatible with the monolingual comprehension of creole innovators. However, such structural borrowing is considered possible in later stages of development, and Thomason and Kaufman (1988) indicate that it is a phenomenon resulting from bilingualism.

CS models emphasize the role of bilingualism with English in the appearance of double marking, and encourages the re-evaluation of claims of structural borrowing of the English suffix morpheme. Irregularly applied and double marking with both TP and English morphemes indicates strong similarities between the use of *-s* suffixation in TP and other cases of interaction between language systems.

Verhaar's (1995) analysis of written TP expands the morphological inventory to include a significant number of English function (system) morphemes that appear in his corpus. The affixes he identifies appear in a modified form suggestive of TP pronunciations rather than English ones. Included in such 'new' morphology is a progressive suffix *-in* (English *-ing*), past tense *-d* English *-ed*, and agentive *-a* English *-er*.

As with plural marking, however, it is the case that the grammatical function of the English morphology appearing in the phonological form of some words used in TP is reduplicated by equivalent morphology in the TP sentence itself. As G. Smith notes in relation to his corpus of spoken TP, many such affixes remain unanalyzed for most speakers, and there is evidence of underlying tension between English and TP grammars in relation to the grammatical role of affixation (G. Smith 2002: 89–90).

In accounts of inter-sentential code-switching between languages, such as Myers-Scotton's Matrix Language Framework model (Myers-Scotton 1993a) and subsequent modifications, morphosyntactic integration is a particular focus. The System Morpheme Principle specifically prohibits the presence of certain types of functional morphology in mixed language, unless the items carrying this morphology are also grammatically well formed with reference to the language that structures the grammar of the speech. However, cases of double-marking, for example where grammatical morphemes from both languages are present to indicate plurality, are common in bilingual speech. Where the grammatical function is expressed in TP, the presence of English morphology marking the same grammatical relation is not, under the MLF, viewed as active. In fact, it can be present unanalyzed, considered as part of the phonological form of the inserted word, and consequently appearing as the standard form.

Where double-marking does take place, an appreciation of bilingual behaviors in other language communities indicates that the presence of inactive English morphology does not mean that a widespread change has taken place in TP.

27.3.2 Pronouns

Keesing's detailed discussion of competition between substrate forms in the early life of MPE (Keesing 1988) indicates how the present pronominal system might have evolved from indigenous language patterns.

Post-independence in 1975, Romaine (1992) and G. Smith (2002) have both discussed "anomalous" uses of the inclusive first person *yumi* in TP where the addressee was clearly not included. In my data, a politician provides a similar example:

(3)   TiT#35b-05_L57
       yu tok <u>yumi</u> no sanap
       2SG talk 2PL.incl NEG stand[3]
       yu tok <u>yumi</u> no sanap
       'you told us(inclusive) not (to) stand'

In (3) the speaker clearly did not include the addressee in the scope of *yumi*, yet the inclusive pronoun was used here and in several other similar utterances. This shows in adult speech the phenomena observed in children by Romaine and by G. Smith. Significantly, just as the lack of this distinction in Austronesian languages may undermine its use by TP speakers in communities of Austronesian language speakers, so too the lack of such a distinction in English provides an additional resistance to its use. For TP speakers with little exposure to traditional vernaculars, the influence of the English pronoun system could be responsible for the loss of this distinction.

In the pronoun system of PNGE there are no overt inclusive/exclusive or dual/plural distinctions to echo those found in TP. However, some speakers do use the TP first-person plural exclusive form *mipela* and the first singular *mi* as an object pronoun in PNGE:

(4)   TiT#24b-15_L682
       wi got trris we <u>mipla</u> li:vin
       1PL have trees LOC 1PL.EXCL live-CONT
       we got trees where/we[4] <u>mipela</u> living
       'we (have) got trees where we(exclusive) (are) living'

There may be some motivation for the transfer of inclusive/exclusive distinctions into PNG English for at least some speakers, as this has a significant cultural role. There is some

---

[3] This example is taken from a longer section: *yu tok yumi no sanap, mi nau mi rausim* 'you told us not to stand, I then I became angry.' The audio could be parsed as *yu tok yumi no sanap-0 mi, nau mi rausim* 'you told us not to stand me up, then I became angry,' with the verb *sanap* taken as transitive with the 1SG pronoun *mi* as its object, rather than (as given here) as the intransitive form. Clearly, the absence of the transitive suffix on *sanap* favors the analysis here, and is reflected in the division of the example as presented.

[4] I include both TP and standard English forms for homophones in the orthographic gloss of my examples where the word in question is significant. Such homophonous diamorphs are considered particularly significant under, e.g., Clyne's (1967) account of German/English CS.

precedent for culturally specific modifications to the pronominal paradigm of English in some dialects which retain a plural form of the second person pronoun such as *youse* 'you. pl.' However, given the observed variability in the maintenance of the inclusive/exclusive distinction in TP, it remains unclear at this stage what direction their development will take. Significantly, the removal of this grammatical distinction not found in English from some varieties of TP increases the congruence in their pronominal systems.

Some speakers also use the TP first person singular *mi* instead of standard English *I*:

(5)   TiT#08-507_L335
      ivan deːn *mi* stiːl kam wiv pis in mai hat
      even then 1SG still come-oPast CONJ peace PREP 1SG.POSS heart
      'even then *mi* still come with peace in my heart'
      'even then I still came with peace in my heart'

English pronouns are also sometimes used in TP. (6) includes the flagged use of forms intermediate between the TP third person singular (ungendered) *em* and the English third person singular (masculine) *him*:

(6)   mi ***thank*** yuː long ### ***im***
      1SG thank 2SG PREP 3SG.MASC
      mi tenk/***thank*** yu long, ***him***
      'I thank you for, him'

Though the form attested here [ɪm], without the continuant /h/, resembles the TP pronoun [em], the raising of [e] to [ɪ] has not been observed in TP phonology and reanalysis of the third person singular pronoun under influence from English is a more cogent explanation than phonological variation. This analysis is supported by this speaker's use of a standard [em] for *em* elsewhere, by the flagged hesitation before the English pronoun in (6), and by its repetition more fluidly a few lines later (7):

(7)   behain ***im*** bai maːkim yu l em
      after 2SG.MASC FUT mark-TR 2SG PREP 3SG
      behain ***him*** bai makim yu long em
      'after he will record you on it'

A further example can be seen at (8), where the English pronoun *they* is used in TP:

(8)   TiT#24b-15_L463
      dei guht ah- # wuhnpluh kain ***liːv*** ia
      3PL have ah- # one-ADJ type leaf LOC
      they got ah- , wanpela kain ***leaf*** ia
      'they have ah-, one type of leaf there'

Does the presence of these pronouns in these data suggest an extension to the TP paradigm through borrowing from English? A code-switching analysis allows us to view constructions such as those in the preceding without assuming a widespread change in the grammar of PNGE or of TP (Blaxter Paliwala 2012).

27.3.3 Conjunctions

As Mühlhäusler (1985e) notes, coordination is a development of the expansion of TP over time. Characteristically for a pidgin language, Hall (1943) describes TP as having only one 'true conjunction' *na*. However, Mühlhäusler (1985e) gives three: *na*, *tasol*, and *o*, and Romaine (1988) includes the conjunctive use of *orait*. Considering Mühlhäusler's 'true' conjunctions with additional items observed by Mihalic (1971: 40–41), Verhaar (1995: 421–499), and G. Smith (2002), it is clear that the latter's observation that the basic set of three conjunctions has been expanded is true of other data sets also. In addition, uniquely among the sources considered here, finding *bat* 'but' in his data, G. Smith notes in particular the presence of *bikos* as an alternative for causative *long wanem*, and this is also noted as an Anglicized alternative by Verhaar also. In fact, *bikos* is included in the TP section of Mihalic's dictionary (1971), indicating its use in at least some varieties of TP before Independence.

My data include *bikos* as a clear feature of the TP there, as in (9):

(9)   mi # ***putin*** se liklik **_bikoz_** ensidisi mas lulu lo disuhla
       1SG # put-CONT this little because NCDC must look PREP this
       mi, ***putting*** dispela liklik **_because_** NCDC must lukluk long dispela
       'I am saying this little thing because NCDC must look into this'

In addition, in the data, English *so* is used frequently in TP, primarily as a discourse connector, as in (10):

(10)   **_so_** duhsela em i: wanpela bigpela suhmthing
        DISC.CONJ this 3SG PM one-ADJ big-ADJ thing
        _so_ dispela em i wanpela bigpela samting
        'so this (is) a big issue'

English *and* is used in the form [æn] frequently in my data, as in (11):

(11)   nau disl ol ***sevis*** em i ***rrun daun*** ### **_an_** mi mi gat ***konsuhn*** tru lo displa .
        TIME DET PL service 3sg PM run down ### CONJ 1SG 1SG have concern EMP
        PREP DET(3sg)
        now dispela ol ***service*** em i ***run down,*** **_and_** mi mi gat ***concern*** tru long dispela
        'now this service is run down, and I I have serious concern about it'

Clearly, some 'English' conjunctions have a long history of use in TP: illustrating a continuous history of language contact. This runs somewhat counter to Siegel's (1997) claim that "innovations" from English are not found, except in loan phrases. However, a CS analysis such as that of Auer (1999) views conjunctions as peripheral elements under alternation, and therefore easily switched by bilinguals. As such, they can become salient indicators of new "mixed" varieties of speech innovated by bilinguals.

27.3.4 Conclusions

There remains a significant amount of work to be done on the morphosyntax of TP and PNGE, as with other varieties of MPE, and there are many more areas for investigation. While the use of the adjectival suffix *-pela* has not been reported in PNGE, there is evidence of the transitive suffix *-im* appearing on verbs in PNGE. There is also fascinating evidence of the apparent presence of a form of predicate marking in PNGE, using a reduplicated 3sg masculine pronoun, as well as the use of the English copula *is* in TP, where MPE traditionally has no copula. Likewise, changes in the VP of TP viewed as a "streamlining" effect of creolization (G. Sankoff 1991) also increase the congruence between it and English.

However, morphosyntactic accounts of CS, as we will see in the final section, can account for many aspects of Anglicized TP.

27.4 SOURCES OF THE MPE LEXICON

As a PC language, MPE has drawn both the content morphemes in its lexicon from various sources, and has developed its grammatical morphology from those same sources. Mühlhäusler (1979a, 1979b, 1985a, 1985d) provides excellent accounts of the lexicon of MPE, accounting for the variation in the amount of English, Tolai (the dominant language spoken in New Ireland, one of the key regions that workers on German plantations came from), other New Guinea languages, German, and Malay over the history of the language.

The topic of lexical borrowing from English in the present day is, however, crucial to our understanding of language contact between MPE and English. At times it seems that Anglicization of TP, for example, is defined almost transparently in terms of the replacement of core traditional TP vocabulary with new English loans, or in the "expansion" of the inventory through the addition of new words learned in school, or in the new urban environments of the last thirty-five years, which remain opaque to traditional speakers.

In CS theory, drawing a distinction between CS forms and true borrowings into a language has been proposed using a metric of phonological integration (Poplack 1980; D. Sankoff and Poplack 1981; D. Sankoff, Poplack, and Vanniarajan 1990; Myers-Scotton 1992). However, the similarities in accent between TP and PNGE discussed earlier make this distinction unworkable. Dictionaries of MPE are either older, and so fail to reflect common current usage, or entirely accepting of new vocabulary, and so these cannot necessarily be relied upon as authorities. In my own scholarship, I relied on Mihalic (1971) as a point of reference, concluding that all unlisted words in use in TP must have been borrowed into the language since it was published. However, the fundamental attitude of MPE speakers appears to be to accept new vocabulary with ease, and ongoing innovations in slang and semantics remain a vibrant source of word-play.

27.5 BILINGUAL BEHAVIOR AND "DECREOLIZATION"

Romaine (1992: 322) presented a set of utterances as evidence of "intermediate" varieties of speech emerging in PNG, and, in doing so, provided continuity to the theory of decreolization as an outcome for TP. In contrast, Siegel (1997: 251) asserted that the systems of TP and PNGE have retained their separate identities.

Mühlhaüsler (1985c: 148) had countered Bickerton's (1975) position that continuing contact between TP and English would inevitably lead to a creole continuum by asserting that while CS could be identified, it was clear that the systems remained distinct, and Siegel refined this by referring to "code alternation" and "insertion" as two types of CS.

Romaine's examples show some of the features continuing from Hall's early observations, and present problems for anyone trying to "pinpoint" code-switching, as Mühlhäusler indicates one can. While CS can be identified in many examples of Tok Pisin, to explain its variation in relationship to English entirely in terms of alternation or insertion appears inadequate, even on the basis of Romaine's examples alone. In particular, the casual omission of suffixes when a congruent English root is available and known to speakers and interchangeable pronouns lead to congruent structures where it is hard to tease "English" and "Tok Pisin" apart. The degree of bilingualism of speakers is very much a factor, as CS research has shown that extent of second-language knowledge has an impact on whether alternation is possible. The notion of Congruent Lexicalization (Muysken 1997, 2000) itself, however, indicates that speakers may have internalized a mixed grammar.

Blaxter Paliwala (2012) provided an analysis of naturally occurring language collected from Papua New Guinean speakers of Melanesian Pidgin English in terms of "normal" processes of bilingual behavior: if English was involved, it was involved as another language, not as a "target," just as if, for example, Buang was involved, it too would be involved as another language. It referred to work on traditional bi- and multilingualism both with indigenous languages and with TP, as recorded by Salisbury (1962), Sankoff (1980), Kulick (1992), and others. Bringing to bear contemporary models of bilingual behavior, it reanalyzed examples of Anglicized TP recorded by Mühlhäusler (1985f, 1985c), Romaine (1992), Siegel (1997), Nekitel (1998), and G. Smith (2002) and new data and showed that three different "types" of bilingual speech (Muysken 2000) created these new varieties.

This final section gives examples of different types of CS in MPE from PNG.

27.5.1 Alternation

On the one hand there is alternation, straightforward switching between languages, a common and often marked (Myers-Scotton 1993b) multilingual strategy with a range of pragmatic and metaphorical functions (Gumperz 1982; Auer 1984) from changing languages to address a particular person, to reiteration, interrogation, focus, and quotation, among others:

(12)   *okei* mipla kam daun lo # em tok *okei yu suhvaiv den*
      DISC 1PL.EXCL come down PREP # 3SG say okay 2SG survive ADV
      okay mipela kam daun long, em tok *okay you survive then*
      'Ok we (excl) came down to (them), they said "ok, you survive then"'

At the peripheries of such alternation, as in (4), discourse markers and conjunctions are easily introduced between languages.

27.5.2 Insertion

Another type of bilingual behavior is the insertion of material from one language into another, a process that is related, through consistent use of a new word, with borrowing. While single words and longer phrases may be inserted into a sentence unmarked and uncommented on by speakers, this type of behavior requires the grammar of the host or "matrix" language (Myers-Scotton 1993a) to remain intact and be responsible for the overall structure of the sentence:

(13)   olsem let uhs look nau ## seriuhsli long sitiuaishin # lo law an awda sitiuaishuhn
      # na reimprovais # improvais o ovahol olgeta disiplin fawses blo yumi
      same let 1PL look now ### seriously PREP situation # PREP law CONJ order
      situation # CONJ reimprovise # improvise CONJ overhaul all discipline-o force-
      PL PREP.POSS 1pl.INCL
      olsem let us look now/nau, seriously long situation, long law and order situation,
      na reimprovise, improvise o/or overhaul olgeta discipline forces bilong yumi
      'so let us look now, seriously at (the) situation, of law and order situation, and
      reimprovise [sic], improvise [sic] or overhaul all our discipline(d) forces'

While you may hear (as in this example) a large number of English words and phrases in a sentence, the grammatical structure—conveyed by the functional morphemes: the connectives, prepositions, conjunctions, quantifiers, possessives, and pronouns—can be clear Melanesian Pidgin.

27.5.3 Congruent Lexicalization

Where back-and-forth switching and an active role for grammatical morphology from both the languages involved make it difficult to identify which language, if either, is being "spoken". Muysken (1997, 2000) presents criteria for the presence of congruent lexicalization: the use of words from either language to fill a shared, congruent, grammatical structure. We can see this in examples of PNG speech:

(14)   ol *lida* bilo yumi i gat sambla kain *risuhn* # lo ol *pipol* bilong ol oa # ol i lai *tak*im samela kain *souht* o *souhtem mesuhs* lo # luki *veri kwik* # *thuh resals ova thuh neks faiv yias* taim ol i stap lo *palimant*

ol *leader* bilong yumi i gat sampela kain *reason*, long ol *people* bilong ol o, ol i laik *take*-im sampela kain *short* o *short-term measures* long, lukim *very quick, the results over the next five years' time*/taim ol i stap long *parliament*

'... our leaders have got some reason, from their people or, or electing in some short or short-term measures to, see very quick, the results over the next five years when they are in Parliament'

This third type of CS underlies cases where clearly English grammar is at work in people's TP sentences, as in (15), which shows the use of the English verbal copula *is*, a part of the grammar that has no equivalent in TP:

(15)   *klan* blo mi *is* tokim yu: longtaim
Clan PREP.POSS 1SG is talk-TR 2SG long-time
clan bilong mi *is* tokim yu longtaim
'my clan is telling you many times...'

It also structures PNGE sentences where the English third person masculine pronoun *he* is used in a role very similar to the TP verb marker *i*, a marker that Keesing (1988) identified as a subject referencing pronoun in line with his analysis of the Oceanic substrate grammar:

(16)   an den it wosn long aftuh dat <u>dat insiden hi hapen</u>
CONJ then 3SG was.NEG long after PRON DET incident 3SG.MASC/PM happen- Ø
and then it wasn't long after that that <u>incident he/i happened</u>
'and then it was not long after that that (this) incident happened'

Language like this is accounted for as bilingual behavior, the result of the living contact in people's lives between TP and PNGE.

27.6 CONCLUSION

Regional differences in varieties of MPE have been traced to different social histories, to differences in the language ecology of different regions in Melanesia, and to different educational and political statuses of MPE varieties in respect to English.

While English has influenced every aspect of the MPE grammar, both internal innovations and indigenous language behavior have also been influential. Appreciating the dynamics of contemporary MPE in PNG means accepting that TP is no more "decreolizing" or Anglicizing than PNGE is "re-pidginized" through substrate influence by Austronesian and Papuan language speakers, or is "Melanesianizing" in the direction of TP.

In fact, the only appropriate way to understand the language situation today is as a multilingual one, where multilingual people do what multilingual people do, just as they would have done in the contact situations on islands and sailing ships of the early nineteenth century. The significant difference today, however, is that these examples are recorded and occur in a mature language community. There is no question of transience or of small numbers: these behaviors occur as often and are as sophisticated in Melanesia as they are in Africa (Myers-Scotton 1993a), Europe (Auer 1998), or the Americas (Poplack 1980).

27.7 SAMPLE TEXT

The mixture of language in Papua New Guinea's Trilingual National Parliament is a well-known feature of speech in the House of Commons in Waigani, but has not been intensively studied (though see Nekitel 1998). Rhetorical style is at a premium in political speaking, and the TP of politicians is often noted as being the most influenced by English.

This short extract from a speech during Prime Minster's Question Time features many words recently borrowed from English specific to the new culture of the developing national culture: *ansa* 'answer,' *epot* 'airport,' *ofis* 'office,' *trening* 'training,' *minister* 'minister,' *distrik* 'district.' It also features longer noun phrases for new cultural referents, such as *foren afes* 'foreign affairs' and *trening program* 'training program.'

Illustrative of morphosyntactic code-switching are mixed constituents such as the English verb roots with TP transitive morphological suffixes: *direktim* 'to direct,' *eliftim* 'to airlift,' and *otoraiz-im* 'to authorize.'

Even more striking are the full constituent insertions from English of embedded language islands (Myers-Scotton 1993) such as *almost twelve thousand tons of materials*, and *up until now*.

Throughout, the TP morphosyntactic frame is maintained. Grammatically, this is fairly standard expanded TP. However, the combination of the borrowed English content, the embedded island phrases that characterize the discourse, and the use of temporal marker *wail* 'while' with that key NP 'twelve thousand tons of materials' being repeatedly expressed in English, the overall impression is of a new 'mixed' language.

However, as can be seen in the structure of the possessive phrases *minister blo foren afes* 'foreign affairs minister' and *ol disela metiriuhls bilo mipela* 'our materials,' with the latter double-marked for plurality both with the TP *ol* and the English plural *-s* suffix on the noun, this is Melanesian Pidgin English.

The code-switching here is frequent and rapid, but the language contact is evidenced by bilingual behavior, not decreolized speech.

1. na nau mi bin ra wanem raitim wanpla pas i kam long *ofis* blo yu *minista*
2. long *wail* ol wok g lon &tuh kerima(ut) disla *trening program* blong ol
3. mi gat *almost twelv tausen tans of meteriuhls* blong *distrik* blo mi
4. i stap lon *Vanimu epot* long *eliftim* i go antap.
5. na *ap antil nau* mi no kisi wanpla *ansa* blo yu
6. na *ofis* blo yu.
7. inap *ofis* blo yu i *direktim* ol lain
8. taim ol i laik go insaid lon *trenin*
9. inap ol i *eliftim* ol isela ol *twelv tausen tans of meteriels* blo mi
10. i wawk g long # *bara* blon *tanblo*
11. lon *Vanimo epot.*
12. &uh sapos nogat
13. inap yu *otoraizim* oa long *minista* blo *foren afes* i ken *otoraizim* mipla
14. long *askim* ol *Indonesien* long kam insaid lo *eliftim* ol disela *meteriuhls* blo mipla i go antap
15. suhpos yu n inap mekim.

1. 'So now I have wri- what written a letter to your office, minister
2. on while they are carrying out this training program of theirs
3. I have almost twelve thousand tons of materials for my district
4. stuck in Vanimo airport waiting for an airlift.'
5. 'And up until now I have not received any answer from you
6. and your office.'
7. 'Your office can direct those people
8. when they are doing training
9. then they should airlift all of my twelve thousand tons of materials
10. to the Tanblo barracks
11. from Vanimo Airport.'
12. 'Uh, if not
13. you can authorize or the foreign affairs minister can authorize us
14. to ask the Indonesian (government) to come in (to PNG) to airlift all our materials up the mountain,
15. if you are not able to do anything.'

REFERENCES

Auer, Peter. 1984. *Bilingual Conversation*. Amsterdam: John Benjamins.

Auer, P. (ed.). 1998. *Code-switching in Conversation: Language, Interaction and Identity*. London; New York: Routledge.

Auer, Peter. 1999. From codeswitching via language mixing to fused lects: Toward a dynamic typology of bilingual speech. *International Journal of Bilingualism* 3(4): 309–332.

Bickerton, D. 1975. Can English and Pidgin be kept apart? *Tok Pisin i go we?*, edited by Kenneth McElhanon, 21–27. Port Moresby: Linguistic Society of Papua New Guinea.

Bickerton, D. 1977. Pidginization and creolization: Language acquisition and language universals. In *Pidgin and Creole Linguistics*, edited by A. Valdman, 49–69. Bloomington: Indiana University Press.

Blaxter Paliwala, A. 2012. *Creole/Superstrate Code-switching: Analysing the Dynamic Relationship between Tok Pisin and English in Papua New Guinea*. PhD dissertation, University of Sydney.

Clyne, Michael 1967. *Transferrence and Triggering: Observations on the Language Assimilation of Postwar German Speaking Migrants in Australia*. The Hague: Nijhoff.

Crowley, Terry. 1990. *Beach-La-Mar to Bislama: The Emergence of a National Language in Vanuatu*. Oxford: Clarendon Press.

Crowley, T. 1990a. Serial verbs and prepositions in Bislama. In *Melanesian Pidgin and Tok Pisin*, edited by John Verhaar, 20. Amsterdam: John Benjamins.

Crowley, T. 1990b. The position of Melanesian Pidgin in Vanuatu and Papua New Guinea. In *Melanesian Pidgin and Tok Pisin*, edited by John Verhaar, 1–18. Amsterdam: John Benjamins.

Crowley, T. 2000. "Predicate Marking" in Bislama. In *Processes of Language Contact*, edited by Jeff Siegel, 47–74. Quebec: Fides.

Crowley, T. 2003. The emergence of transitive verbal morphology in Bislama. *Te Reo: Journal of the Linguistic Society of New Zealand* 46: 19–30.

Dutton, T., and D. R. Thomas 1985. *A New Course in Tok Pisin (New Guinea Pidgin)*. Canberra: Australian National University.

Faraclas, Nicholas. 1989. Prosody and creolization in Tok Pisin. *Journal of Pidgin and Creole Languages* 4(1): 132–139.

Garrett, P. B. 2011. Language socialization and language shift. In *The Handbook of Language Socialization*, edited by A. Duranti, E. Ochs, and B. B. Schieffelin, 515–535. Singapore: Blackwell.

Goulden, Rick J. 1987. *The Melanesian Content in Tok Pisin*. PhD dissertation, University of Toronto.

Gumperz, J. J. 1982. *Discourse Strategies*. Cambridge: Cambridge University Press.

Hall, R. A. 1943. *Melanesian Pidgin English, Grammar, Texts, Vocabulary*. Baltimore, MD: Linguistic Society of America.

Haugen, E. 1950. The analysis of linguistic borrowing. *Language* 26: 210–231.

Holzknecht, S. 1989. Sociolinguistic anaysis of a register: Birthday notices in Papua New Guinea *Post Courier*. *World Englishes* 8(2): 179–192.

Jourdan, C. 1989. Nativization and anglicization in Solomon Islands Pijin. *World Englishes* 8(1): 25–35.

Jourdan, C. 2008. Language repertoires and the middle class in urban Solomon Islands. In *Social Lives in Language*, edited by N. Nagy and M. Meyerhoff, 43–68. Amsterdam: John Benjamins.

Jourdan, C. 2009. Complexification or regularization of paradigms: The case of prepositional verbs in Solomon Islands Pijin. In *Complex Processes in New Languages*, edited by Enoch Aboh and Norbval Smith, 159–170. Amsterdam: John Benjamins.

Jourdan, C., and R. M. Keesing 1997. From Fisin to Pijin: Creolization in process in the Solomon Islands. *Language in Society* 26: 401–420.

Keesing, R. M. 1988. *Melanesian Pidgin and the Oceanic Substrate*. Stanford, CA: Stanford University Press.

Keesing, R. M. 1991. The expansion of Melanesian Pidgin: Further early evidence from the Solomons. *Journal of Pidgin and Creole Languages* 6(2): 215–229.

Kortmann, B., K. Burridge, R. Mesthrie, E. Schneider, and C. Upton. 2004. *Handbook of Varieties of English*, 2 Vols. Berlin: Mouton de Gruyter.

Kulick, D. 1992. *Language Shift and Cultural Reproduction: Socialization, Self, and Syncretism in a Papua New Guinean Village*. Cambridge; New York: Cambridge University Press.

Laycock, D. C. 1970. *Material in New Guinea Pidgin (Coastal and Lowlands)*. Canberra: Australian National University.

Laycock, D. C. 1985. Phonology: Substratum elements in Tok Pisin phonology. In *Handbook of Tok Pisin (New Guinea Pidgin)*, edited by Stephen A. Wurm and Peter Mühlhäusler, 295–307. Canberra: Dept. of Linguistics, Research School of Pacific Studies, Australian National University.

Mihalic, F. 1971. *The Jacaranda Dictionary and Grammar of Melanesian Pidgin*. Hong Kong: Jacaranda Press.

Mühlhäusler, P. 1979a. *Growth and Stucture of the Lexicon of New Guinea Pidgin*. Canberra: Australian National University.

Mühlhäusler, P. 1979b. Synonymy and communication across lectal boundaries in Tok Pisin. In *Papers in Pidgin and Creole Linguistics* No. 2, edited by S. A. Wurm, 57: 1–18. Canberra: Linguistic Circle of Canberra.

Mühlhäusler, P. 1985a. Etymologising and Tok Pisin. In *Handbook of Tok Pisin (New Guinea Pidgin)*, edited by Stephen A. Wurm and Peter Mühlhäusler, 177–219. Canberra: Dept. of Linguistics, Research School of Pacific Studies, Australian National University.

Mühlhäusler, P. 1985b. External history of Tok Pisin. In *Handbook of Tok Pisin (New Guinea Pidgin)*, edited by Stephen A. Wurm and Peter Mühlhäusler, 35–64. Canberra: Dept. of Linguistics, Research School of Pacific Studies, Australian National University.

Mühlhäusler, P. 1985c. Internal development of Tok Pisin. In *Handbook of Tok Pisin (New Guinea Pidgin)*, edited by Stephen A. Wurm and Peter Mühlhäusler, 75–166. Canberra: Dept. of Linguistics, Research School of Pacific Studies, Australian National University.

Mühlhäusler, P. 1985d. The lexical system of Tok Pisin. In *Handbook of Tok Pisin (New Guinea Pidgin)*, edited by Stephen A. Wurm and Peter Mühlhäusler, 423–440. Canberra: Dept. of Linguistics, Research School of Pacific Studies, Australian National University.

Mühlhäusler, P. 1985e. Syntax of Tok Pisin. In *Handbook of Tok Pisin (New Guinea Pidgin)*, edited by Stephen A. Wurm and Peter Mühlhäusler, 341–421. Canberra: Dept. of Linguistics, Research School of Pacific Studies, Australian National University.

Mühlhäusler, P. 1985f. Variation in Tok Pisin. In *Handbook of Tok Pisin (New Guinea Pidgin)*, edited by Stephen A. Wurm and Peter Mühlhäusler, 222–273. Canberra: Dept. of Linguistics, Research School of Pacific Studies, Australian National University.

Muysken, P. 1997. Alternation, insertion, congruent lexicalization. In *Language Choices: Conditions, Constraints and Consequences*, edited by M. Pütz, 361–380. Amsterdam: John Benjamins.

Muysken, P. 2000. *Bilingual Speech: A Typology of Code-mixing*. Cambridge: Cambridge University Press.

Myers-Scotton, C. 1992. Comparing codeswitching and borrowing. *Journal of Multilingual and Multicultural Development* 13(1–2): 19–40.

Myers-Scotton, C. 1993a. *Duelling Languages: Grammatical Structure in Codeswitching*. Oxford; New York: Clarendon Press; Oxford University Press.

Myers-Scotton, C. 1993b. *Social Motivations for codeswitching: Evidence from Africa*. Oxford: Clarendon Press.

Nekitel, O. 1998. *Voices of Yesterday, Today and Tomorrow, Language, Culture and Identity*. New Delhi: UBS Publishers' Distributors.

Ochs, E., and B. B. Schieffelin. 2011. The theory of language socialization. In *The Handbook of Language Socialization*, edited by A. Duranti, E. Ochs, and B. B. Schieffelin, 1–22. Singapore: Blackwell.

Paliwala, A. 2012. Language in Papua New Guinea: The value of census data. *Language & Linguistics in Melanesia* 30: 1–31.

Pawley, A. 1974. *On Epenthetic Vowels in New Guinea Pidgin*. Working Papers in Linguistics, held at Hawaii: University of the South Pacific, Hawaii.

Platt, J., H. Weber, et al. 1984. *The New Englishes*. London: Routledge & Kegan Paul.

Poplack, S. 1980. "Sometimes I'll start a sentence in Spanish y terminol Espanol": Toward a typology of code-switching. *Linguistics* 18: 581–618.

Romaine, S. 1988. *Pidgin and Creole Languages*. London; New York: Longman.

Romaine, S. 1989. English and Tok Pisin (New Guinea Pidgin English) in Papua New Guinea. *World Englishes* 8(1): 5–23.

Romaine, S. 1992. *Language, Education, and Development: Urban and Rural Tok Pisin in Papua New Guinea*. Oxford: Clarendon Press.

Romaine, S. 1999. Grammaticalization of the proximative in Tok Pisin. *Language* 75(2): 322–351.

Salisbury, R. F. 1962. Notes on bilingualism and linguistic change in New Guinea. *Anthropological Linguistics* 4(7): 1–13.

Sankoff, D., and S. Poplack 1981. A formal grammar for code-switching. *Papers in Linguistics: International Journal of Human Communication* 14(1): 3–46.

Sankoff, D., S. Poplack, et al. 1990. The case of the nonce loan in Tamil. *Language Variation and Change* 2: 71–101.

Sankoff, G. 1977. Creolization and syntactic change in New Guinea Tok Pisin. *Sociocultural Dimensions of Language Change*, edited by B. G. Blount and M. Sanches. New York: Academic Press.

Sankoff, G. (ed.). 1980. *The Social Life of Language*. Philadelphia: University of Pennsylvania Press.

Sankoff, G. 1991. Using the future to explain the past. In *Development and Structures of Creole Languages: Essays in Honor of Derek Bickerton*, edited by F. Byrne and T. Huebner, 61–74. Amsterdam; Philadelphia: John Benjamins.

Sankoff, G., and P. Brown. 1980. The origins of syntax in discourse: A case study of Tok Pisin relatives. In *The Social Life of Language*, edited by G. Sankoff, 211–256. Philadelphia: University of Pennsylvania Press.

Sankoff, G., and P. Brown. 1976. On the origins of syntax in discourse: A case study of Tok Pisin relatives. *Language* 52(3): 631–666.

Sankoff, G., and S. Laberge. 1980 [1973]. On the acquisition of native speakers by a language. In *The Social Life of Language*, edited by G. Sankoff, 195–210. Philadelphia: University of Pennsylvania Press.

Sankoff, G., and C. Mazzie. 1991. Determining noun phrases in Tok Pisin. *Journal of Pidgin and Creole Languages* 6(1): 1–24.

Schneider, E. W. 2011. *English around the World: An Introduction*. Cambridge: Cambridge University Press.

Siegel, J. 1997. Pidgin and English in Melanesia: Is there a continuum? *World Englishes* 16(2): 185–204.

Siegel, J. 1999. Transfer constraints and substrate influence in Melanesian Pidgin. *Journal of Pidgin and Creole Languages* 14(1): 1–44.

Siegel, Jeff, and Geoff Smith. 2013. Tok Pisin. In *Atlas of Pidgin and Creole Language Structures*, edited by S. M. Michaelis, P. Maurer, M. Haspelmath, and M. Huber, Vol. 1, 214–222. Oxford: Oxford University Press.

Smith, A.-M. 1978. *The Papua New Guinea Dialect of English*. Port Moresby: Educational Research Unit, University of Papua New Guinea, 43.

Smith, A.-M. 1986. *Papua New Guinea English*. PhD dissertation, University of Papua New Guinea.

Smith, A.-M. 1988. English in Papua New Guinea. *World Englishes* 7(3): 299–308.

Smith, Geoff. 2002. *Growing up with Tok Pisin: Contact, Creolization, and Change in Papua New Guinea's National Language*. London: Battlebridge.

Smith, Geoff. 2004a. Tok Pisin: morphology and syntax. In *Handbook of Varieties of English*, edited by B. Kortmann, K. Burridge, R. Mesthrie, E. Schneider, and C. Upton, Vol. 2, 720–741. Berlin: Mouton de Gruyter.

Smith, Geoff. 2004b. Tok Pisin: phonology. In *Handbook of Varieties of English*, edited by B. Kortmann, K. Burridge, R. Mesthrie, E. Schneider, and C. Upton, Vol. 2, 710–728. Berlin: Mouton de Gruyter.

Thomason, Sarah Grey, and Terrence Kaufman. 1988. *Language Contact, Creolization, and Genetic Linguistics*. Berkeley: University of California Press.

Verhaar, John W. M. 1995. *Toward a Reference Grammar of Tok Pisin: An Experiment in Corpus Linguistics*. Honolulu: University of Hawai'i Press.

Wurm, Stephen A., and Peter Mühlhäusler, eds. 1985. *Handbook of Tok Pisin (New Guinea Pidgin)*. Canberra: Dept. of Linguistics, Research School of Pacific Studies, Australian National University.

CHAPTER 28

BIDIRECTIONAL BORROWING OF STRUCTURE AND LEXICON

The Case of the Reef Islands

ÅSHILD NÆSS

28.1 INTRODUCTION

THE two languages of the Reef Islands, Äiwoo and Vaeakau-Taumako, present a scenario in which lexical items seem largely to have been borrowed in one direction, from Vaeakau-Taumako into Äiwoo, while grammatical structure appears to have been transferred in the opposite direction, from Äiwoo into Vaeakau-Taumako. Explaining this situation requires a careful analysis of the historical language situation in the area, and highlights the importance of teasing apart individual contributing factors that are often lumped together under headings such as "dominance" or "prestige." In the case of the Reef Islands, the interactions between socioeconomic and sociopolitical factors, on the one hand, and demographic factors, on the other, produced a situation where the numerically much smaller community was long socioeconomically dominant by force of their role in the trade network around which the traditional economy in the region was based. As a result, their language became the intergroup language used in trade and other interactions, meaning that this language acquired a much larger group of L2 speakers than it ever had L1 speakers. The unusual patterns of borrowing are an effect of this situation.

A related distinction is that between the factors that produce change in the linguistic patterns of a particular individual versus those that cause particular changes to spread through the language communities involved. Models of language contact tend to focus on one of these aspects (see, e.g., van Coetsem 1988, 2000, for an elaborated model of contact-induced change in individual speakers; and Milroy and Milroy 1985, Ross 1997, 2003 for accounts focusing on the spread of change through a community). What makes the Reefs–Santa Cruz case unusual is the interaction between the two: a change that arose in the community speaking Äiwoo as its L1 and Vaeakau-Taumako as its L2 subsequently spread to the community that spoke Vaeakau-Taumako as its L1, due to the numerical imbalance between the two communities.

28.2 THE LANGUAGE SITUATION IN THE REEF ISLANDS

28.2.1 The Languages and Their History

The Reef Islands are a small island group in Temotu Province, the easternmost province of Solomon Islands in the southwest Pacific. It is located about 70 kilometers northeast of Santa Cruz Island, the main island of Temotu, and consists of a series of small coral islands and atolls ranged around a large reef.

The two languages of the Reef Islands, Äiwoo and Vaeakau-Taumako, are related, but distantly so. Äiwoo belongs to the recently identified Temotu subgroup of Oceanic, in turn a subgroup of the Austronesian language family (Ross and Næss 2007). Vaeakau-Taumako is a so-called Polynesian Outlier; that is, it belongs to the Polynesian branch of the Central/Eastern Oceanic subgroup, but is spoken outside of the so-called Polynesian Triangle defined by the three corners of New Zealand, Hawai'i, and Easter Island.

These classifications have implications for the settlement history of the two groups in the area. The Äiwoo community is likely to descend from the original settlers of the area, who, based on archaeological evidence, arrived in the Reef Islands at least 3,200 years ago (Spriggs 1997: 97). As a Polynesian Outlier, on the other hand, Vaeakau-Taumako must have arrived in the area through back-migration from the core Polynesian areas after these were first settled from the west. No exact date can be posited for this arrival; however, signs of Polynesian settlement on nearby Tikopia island first appear in the archaeological record around 1200 AD (Kirch 2000: 144), and so it seems reasonable to assume an arrival date or around 800–1,000 years ago.

In other words, at the time of Polynesian arrival, the ancestors of today's Äiwoo speakers had already been present in the Reef Islands for upwards of 2,000 years. The geographical distribution of the two speech communities reflects this situation: while the Äiwoo speakers occupy the larger, more fertile Main Reef islands, Vaeakau-Taumako settlements in the Reefs are limited to the small and peripheral Outer Reef Islands. However, Vaeakau-Taumako is also spoken in the larger, though even more remote, Duff Islands (Taumako), some 100 kilometers northeast of the Reefs. Historically, this is probably the original Polynesian settlement in the area, and for a long time there was frequent contact between the Vaeakau-Taumako speakers in the two locations through the trade network described in section 28.2.2, though since the network ceased functioning about a century ago, the frequency of such contact has been considerably reduced.

28.2.2 The Contact Situation

At present, day-to-day contact between the two language communities in the Reef Islands is fairly sporadic. Vaeakau-Taumako speakers travel to the Main Reef Islands to visit the trade store there or to buy staple crops from the larger islands. However, it appears that Äiwoo speakers rarely visit the Outer Reefs, despite their proximity; several adult males of the author's acquaintance reported never having visited the Polynesian-speaking islands. Intermarriage does take place between the two communities; it is estimated that more Vaeakau-Taumako-speaking women marry into Äiwoo-speaking communities than vice versa, but no data are available on the frequency of intermarriage in either direction.

There is a marked demographic and economic inequality between the two communities. The Main Reef Islands, where the Äiwoo community resides, are both significantly larger than the Outer Reefs and considerably more fertile, supporting some 5,000–6,000 people as opposed to around 500–600 Vaeakau-Taumako speakers in the Outer Reefs (1999 census). The Outer Reef Islands are so small—the largest, Nifiloli, having a land area of only around 0.5 square kilometers, with the other islands being significantly smaller—that the crops that can be grown there are very limited, restricted largely to tree crops like coconuts and bananas. This means that the Vaeakau-Taumako community is dependent on food imports from the Main Reefs for their survival, and speakers often emphasize how difficult life is in the outer islands.

While the demographics are unlikely to have changed much over the history of the communities, it is clear that, up until a century or so ago, the socioeconomic relationships were very different. Far from being a marginalized community on the edges of the area, the Vaeakau-Taumako speakers were the key actors in a trade network that connected all the islands in the region: the Reef and Duff Islands, Santa Cruz, Utupua, and Vanikoro. Large ocean-going canoes were built in the Duff Islands and sailed to the Reef Islands, where they were sold to Reef Islanders, who in turn used them in trade voyages throughout the area. Such trade voyages were the main means of acquiring wealth and social prestige in the Reef and Duff Islands, and the political organization of the Duff Islands was built around an individual's ability to rally the support necessary to build and equip a sailing canoe for a trade voyage (Davenport 1968). After the British administration in the early twentieth century placed a ban on long inter-island voyages, as well as on the export of women as wives to other islands—a major component in the trade network but perceived by colonial administrators as a form of prostitution—the construction of sailing canoes ceased and the trade network stopped functioning, leaving the Vaeakau-Taumako community in the marginalized position in which they find themselves today.

It is difficult to reconstruct the historical language-contact situation with any certainty, as nearly all intergroup communication today takes place in the English-lexifier Solomon Islands Pijin. (Even in Pijin, though, the polite way of addressing a person from the other language community is with the word 'brother, friend' in the addressee's language, so that Äiwoo speakers address Vaeakau-Taumako speakers with the Vaeakau-Taumako term *thokana* 'same-sex sibling, friend,' while Vaeakau-Taumako speakers address Äiwoo speakers with the Äiwoo term *gisi* 'man's brother'[1]).

When asked about their ability to speak the other language, Äiwoo speakers readily claim to be able to speak at least some Vaeakau-Taumako, while Vaeakau-Taumako speakers typically deny any proficiency in Äiwoo, often adding statements to the effect that the language is far too difficult and impossible to understand. There is some linguistic reality to this, in the sense that Äiwoo has a highly complex verbal morphology that is in many ways atypical for an Oceanic language, and indeed for decades was thought not to be a member of the Austronesian family at all, largely on the basis of its structural complexity (e.g., Wurm 1978); whereas Vaeakau-Taumako is grammatically speaking a typical Polynesian language with very little bound morphology (cf. section 3.2.1).

It must be noted that no systematic survey of bilingualism patterns has been carried out in the Reef Islands. There is, however, some evidence suggesting that the present-day speakers' claims do line up with the historical situation in the area. Ivens (1918) briefly discusses the language situation in the Santa Cruz archipelago, noting that "[t]he peoples speaking Polynesian never learn the Melanesian tongues [i. e., Äiwoo and its relatives in Santa Cruz, Utupua and Vanikoro islands; author's note], whereas those who speak Melanesian are nearly always bilingual." Although the situation has changed today, with speakers of all languages now being bilingual in Solomon Islands Pijin and using this language in intergroup interaction, this statement largely agrees with the claims made about their language competence by Reef Islands people today.

28.3 CONTACT-INDUCED LANGUAGE CHANGE

There are two difficulties in assessing the effects of sustained language contact on the languages of the Reef Islands. The first is the state of documentation of the languages involved; while Vaeakau-Taumako is reasonably well described, with a reference grammar and a short dictionary published, descriptive work on Äiwoo is rather less advanced, and many aspects of the structure of the language are still poorly understood. Second, there is a long tradition of linguistic work on the Polynesian group of languages, to which Vaeakau-Taumako belongs, meaning that it is relatively easy to identify areas where Vaeakau-Taumako differs from its immediate relatives. By contrast, the Temotu subgroup to which Äiwoo belongs is extremely poorly described, as well as having much fewer members,[2]

---

[1] I have only observed such interactions between male speakers. The corresponding female term would be *sisi* 'woman's sister.'

[2] If the Temotu subgroup is indeed a single subgroup, it has ten members: Aba, Asuboa and Tanibili on Utupua, Teanu, Tanema and Lovono on Vanikoro, and Natügu, Nalögo, Engdewu, and Äiwoo in Santa Cruz and the Reef Islands; the latter four are classified as forming the Reefs–Santa Cruz subgroup

and so it is difficult to say to what extent the structural properties of Äiwoo are typical of the subgroup to which it belongs. Nevertheless, enough is known about Äiwoo to make it clear that it is very different from typical Polynesian languages at all levels of structure, making any parallels that do exist easier to identify.

An examination of the properties of the two languages that are likely to result from language contact yields a somewhat surprising result. There is clear evidence of both lexical items and grammatical structure having been transferred between the two languages. However, the two types of linguistic units seem largely to have moved in opposite directions: Äiwoo shows a large number of lexical borrowings from Vaeakau-Taumako, whereas Vaeakau-Taumako shows clear signs of structural influence from Äiwoo. Coupled with the historical distribution of bilingualism discussed earlier, and in particular the assumption that Vaeakau-Taumako speakers were never, as a group, bilingual in Äiwoo, this situation raises some interesting questions concerning the origin and spread of the contact-induced changes in the two communities.

28.3.1 Lexical Borrowing

28.3.1.1 *From Äiwoo to Vaeakau-Taumako*

There are certainly Äiwoo borrowings in Vaeakau-Taumako, though they are relatively scarce. A number of place names in the Polynesian-speaking islands appear from their phonological structure to be of Äiwoo origin, which is not surprising given that Äiwoo speakers probably resided in the Reef Islands for a couple of millennia before the arrival of the Polynesians. Notable is the name of the island Matemā, the most centrally located of the Polynesian-speaking Reef Islands. Though the Äiwoo name for this island is Noduwâ, the name Matemā most likely comes from Äiwoo *mwa-Temââ* 'Taumako Reef,' meaning a section of reef where people from Taumako have fishing rights; compare nearby *mwa-Tuwo*, the section of reef for which the fishing rights belong to the people of Tuwo village (Næss and Hovdhaugen 2007).

A few words are identifiable as being of Äiwoo origin from their structure: *niadoa*, *nienie* 'species of tree' (cf. Äiwoo *nya-* 'tree'), *nyänyie* 'casuarina (lit. fire-tree)'; *bekuma* 'type of basket' (cf. Äiwoo *be-* 'basket'). Other plausible borrowings include *uabelia* 'without purpose or system, all over the place' (Äiwoo *väbelia* 'scatter, move around aimlessly'), *melō* 'peace, peaceful' (Äiwoo *meloo*), *atanehi* 'orange (fruit)' (Äiwoo *vatinesi*), possibly *nabiola* 'huge,' a qualifier used only for lizards and pigs, (cf. Äiwoo *näbilou* 'lizard'). While this is not an exhaustive list, and while there are almost certainly further borrowings that have yet to be identified, this overview gives an idea of the very limited scale of Äiwoo borrowing into Vaeakau-Taumako, and of the scattered and fairly peripheral lexical domains to which such borrowings belong.

of Temotu by Ross and Næss (2007). However, François (2013) points out that the Utupua and Vanikoro languages differ greatly both in vocabulary and grammatical structure from the Reefs–Santa Cruz languages, and it is possible that further research will lead to this classification having to be revised.

28.3.1.2 *From Vaeakau-Taumako to Äiwoo*

The Äiwoo lexicon includes a significant portion of identifiably Polynesian borrowings, which must be assumed to stem from Vaeakau-Taumako. While there are other Polynesian languages spoken in Temotu Province, they are located on the extremely remote islands of Tikopia and Anuta, more than 300 kilometers distant from the Reef Islands; Vaeakau-Taumako is not only Äiwoo's closest neighbor, but also, as described earlier, the language of the shipbuilders and navigators who were in regular contact not just with Äiwoo, but with speakers of other languages throughout the region.

Äiwoo speakers are usually aware that a particular word is a Polynesian borrowing, and indeed the majority of loans include the accreted Polynesian specific article *te-*, assimilated to *to-* in some words. This is the case even for a number of borrowed verbs, which would not normally be expected to occur with an article, such as *temakona* 'strong' (Vaeakau-Taumako *makhona*), *tepeu* 'stupid' (Vaeakau-Taumako *peu*). It is tempting to deduce that the article functions as an overt marker of Polynesian origin on borrowings, though it must be noted that a few very common words, such as *kuli* 'dog', *kio* 'chicken,' lack the accreted article. There is also a small number of items where the accreted article takes the form *sa-*: *saliki* 'honor, honorable' (Vaeakau-Taumako *aliki* 'chief'), *sapolo* 'papaya' (Vaeakau-Taumako *napolo*), *sapulâu* 'single men's house' (Vaeakau-Taumako *holau*), *säkäi* 'coconut scraper' (Vaeaekau-Taumako *kai*). This may indicate that the items in *sa-* represent an earlier phase of borrowing, though no systematic research has so far been done on this point.

The Polynesian borrowings in Äiwoo range across a wide variety of semantic fields and include what must be considered basic vocabulary. Some examples are given in the following:

- Natural phenomena: *tewâ* 'rain' (VAT *ua*), *temotu* 'island' (VAT *motu*), *täpeo* 'storm, cyclone' (VAT *tapeo*), *tolokâ* 'swamp' (VAT *loka*)
- Fauna: *tepekâ* 'flying fox' (VAT *peka*), *toponu* 'turtle' (VAT *fonu*), *temaale* 'needlefish' (VAT *maile*), *tomoko* 'gecko' (VAT moko)
- Artifacts: *tekelebu* 'mortar' (VAT *kalebi, kelebi*), *telakâ* 'basket for food' (VAT *laka*), *teliki* 'armring' (VAT *liki*), *tematâu* 'fishhook' (VAT *matau*)
- Winds and sea travel: *tongâ, tetongâ* 'southeast wind' (VAT *tonga* 'east wind'), *teulu* 'south wind' (VAT *ulu*), *tekelâu* 'west wind' (VAT *tokelau* 'north/northeast wind'), *tepukei* 'sailing canoe' (VAT *puke*), *too* 'travel provisions' (VAT *oo*).

28.3.2 Structural Borrowing

28.3.2.1 *Structural Characteristics of Äiwoo and Vaeakau-Taumako*

Äiwoo and Vaeakau-Taumako are very different in their overall morphosyntactic typology. Vaeakau-Taumako is a typical Polynesian language in its very limited inventory of bound morphology, most grammatical categories being marked by particles or clitics. Äiwoo, by contrast, verges on the polysynthetic, with bound pronominal markers on the verb for subjects and (some) objects, obligatory aspect-mood inflection on verbs, and the possibility of including a wide array of morphemes into the verb word including directional affixes, serialized verb roots, and bound adverbs. Äiwoo retains some vestiges of the Proto Malayo-Polynesian symmetrical voice system and so shows OVA word order with 'object-oriented' transitive verbs (O-verbs) and AVO order with 'actor-oriented' verbs (A-verbs; Næss 2013, 2015, whereas Vaeakau-Taumako shows unmarked SV/AVO word order but marks postverbal transitive subjects with the preposition *e*, a reanalysis of the ergative case-marking system found in most Triangle Polynesian languages (Næss 2011, forthcoming).

(1) Vaeakau-Taumako:
     Ioko   te   ngata   ko-i   saki   ange   lhaua.
     CONJ   SG.SP   snake   INCP-3SG   leave   go.along   3DU
     'And the snake left them.'

(2) Äiwoo:
     Nepä   da-no   nä-ngäbe-eke-nyi-kä-mu.
     betel.mix   POSS:betel-1MIN   IRR-pound-fast-TR-DIR:3-2MIN.A
     'Pound my betel quickly.'

28.3.2.2 *From Vaeakau-Taumako to Äiwoo*

It is difficult to identify any aspects of Äiwoo grammatical structure that can plausibly be understood as resulting from Vaeakau-Taumako influence. One possible candidate is the structure of the pronominal paradigm, which shows an extra number category compared to those of Äiwoo's closest relatives, the languages of Santa Cruz.

All the Reefs–Santa Cruz languages have pronoun systems that follow what is known as a minimal-augmented pattern, meaning that the 'you and I' forms are treated as a distinct person category of the system, which accordingly has four persons: first person, second person, 'first+second' person and third person. The labels 'singular' and 'plural' are unsuitable for such a system since the first+second person does not have a singular, but refers minimally to two people; accordingly, the labels 'minimal' and 'augmented' are used instead. The system is illustrated by the Natügu paradigm in Table 28.1.

Table 28.1 Natügu Independent Pronouns

	Minimal	Augmented
1st	*ninge* 'I'	*nigö* 'I and others'
1st+2nd	*nigi* 'you and I'	*nigu* 'you and I and others'
2nd	*nim(ü)* 'you'	*nimu* 'you and others'
3rd	*nide* 's/he'	*nidö* 's/he and others'

Table 28.2 Äiwoo Independent Pronouns

	Minimal	Unit-Augmented	Augmented
1st	*iu* 'I'	*iungole* 'I and one other'	*iungo(pu)* 'I and others'
1st + 2nd	*iuji* 'you and I'	*iudele* 'you and I and one other'	*iude* 'you and I and others'
2nd	*iumu* 'you'	*imile* 'you and one other'	*imi* 'you and others'
3rd	*inâ* 's/he'	*ijiile* 's/he and one other'	*ijii* 's/he and others'

Table 28.3 Vaeakau-Taumako Independent Pronouns

	Singular	Dual	Plural
1st inclusive	*Iau*	*thaua*	*Thatou*
1st exclusive		*mhaua*	*Mhatou*
2nd	*Koe*	*khoulua*	*khoutou*
3rd	*Ia*	*Ihaua*	*Lhatou*

All the languages of Santa Cruz show similar paradigms, with the two number categories minimal and augmented. Äiwoo, however, has a third number category, 'unit-augmented,' referring to minimal number plus one. This is illustrated in Table 28.2.

Note that the unit-augmented is formed by suffixation of –*le* to the augmented forms. This is also the case for person marking on verbs, where there are no distinct unit-augmented forms of bound pronouns; instead, unit-augmented number of subject or object is marked by suffixation of –*le* to the augmented form of the verb. The fact that unit-augmented number is indicated in a formally different way from augmented number, as well as the fact that the category does not exist in any of the Santa Cruz languages, suggests that it is an innovation in Äiwoo. It may well have arisen under influence from Vaeakau-Taumako, which has a typically Polynesian pronominal paradigm with singular, dual, and plural number; the form of the unit-augmented suffix might be linked to the Äiwoo numeral *lilu* 'two.'

28.3.2.3 *From Äiwoo to Vaeakau-Taumako*

Vaeakau-Taumako show a number of grammatical features that are not generally known from other Polynesian languages, but that do occur in Äiwoo, making it a plausible inference that they result from language contact.

First, Vaeakau-Taumako has a set of subject proclitics that attach to the tense-aspect-mood (TAM) particle preceding the verb. Such proclitics are not attested in other Polynesian languages; some, like Samoan, do have preverbal subject pronouns, but these follow the TAM particle rather than preceding it. The subject clitics in Vaeakau-Taumako are not obligatory, but they are highly frequent, and function as the subject arguments of their verb, meaning that they may not co-occur with a co-referent argument NP within the same clause (Næss and Hovdhaugen 2011: 320–322).

(3) a. Ko=ko   hn-ange   ko=ko   kali   oho
         2SG=INCP   go-go.along   2SG=INCP   dig   go.down
         te   tahito   puka   na.
         SG.SP   root   tree.sp DEM:2
         'You go and dig up the root of that *puka* tree.'

     b. Kholu=no   fulo   ki   hea?
         2DU=IPFV   run.PL   to   where
         'Where are you (du.) going?'

Äiwoo marks subjects of intransitive verbs and transitive A-verbs by prefixes that precede the aspect-mood prefix on the verb. These function as arguments of the verb, and are normally omitted if there is an independent subject pronoun or NP in the clause:

(4) Äiwoo:
     a. **Me**-ku-mo   ba   nyopu-mä=gu   ngä ny-ee
         1AUG-IPFV-live   NEG   far-DIR:1=NEG   LOC place-DEM:PROX
         'We live not far from here.'

     b. Go   ku-mo   ngâ   nuumä=ke   **iumu.**
         because   IPFV-stay   LOC   village=DEIC:PROX   2MIN
         'Because you are the one who stays at home.'

The overall distribution of the Vaeakau-Taumako subject proclitics—preceding the TAM marker and functioning as an argument rather than an agreement marker—is very similar to that of the Äiwoo subject prefixes. The Vaeakau-Taumako forms are reduced, cliticized versions of the independent pronouns in the language, so it is not the prefixes as such that has been borrowed, just the grammatical pattern of bound pronominal subjects preceding the tense-aspect marking on the verb.

The second area where Vaeakau-Taumako appears to have adopted structural patterns from Äiwoo is in verb serialization. Within Oceanic, serialization constructions are mainly a property of Melanesian[3] languages, with Micronesian and Polynesian languages showing little evidence of serialization (Crowley 2002: 167).

Despite the scarcity of serial verb constructions in Polynesian languages in general, they are highly frequent in Vaeakau-Taumako, and both the types of serialization constructions found and their structural properties closely parallel those found in Äiwoo. Examples (5–6) show nuclear-layer serialization in Vaeakau-Taumako and

---

[3] "Melanesian" is a geographically rather than a genealogically based grouping, referring to the non-Polynesian Oceanic languages of New Guinea, Solomon Islands, Vanuatu, and New Caledonia.

Äiwoo (i.e., a construction where two verbs make up a single verb-phrase nucleus with a single set of grammatical markers):

(5)   Vaeakau-Taumako:
    No-i   motu~motu-ia pa-liki-ina   a   taveli.
    IPFV-3SG RED~cut-TR   PL-small-TR COLL banana
    'He is cutting the bananas into small pieces.'

(6)   Äiwoo:
    I-malei-päko-i-du-gu-i.
    PFV-care.for-good-TR-all- 3MIN.A-3AUG.O
    'She looked after all of them properly.'

Note that in both languages, when the first verb in the series is transitive,[4] the second verb receives a suffix glossed as 'transitive.' In Vaeakau-Taumako this suffix is –*ina*, the productive form of a suffix otherwise used to form transitive from intransitive verbs. In Äiwoo it is –*i* or –*nyi*, with the –*i* at least diachronically related to the –*i* seen at the end of the first verb of the series, *malei*, an O-verb; the corresponding A-verb is *malee*.

Examples (7–8) show a core-layer serialization construction in which the initial verb in both languages translates as 'take'; in this construction it contributes an emphasis on the volitional instigation of the action:

(7)   Vaeakau-Taumako:
    Ko   ia   ne   mohi~mohi oho   hua-lavoi   la
    TOP 3SG PFV RED~creep go.vertically CAUS-good DEM:3
    le~le~le-oho   na   ko-i   to-a
    RED~RED~go-go.vertically DEM:2 INCP-3SG take-TR
    ko-i   hua-pole-ngia   la   mha-la.
    INCP-3SG CAUS-jump-TR DEM:3 man-DEM:3
    'He crept up slowly, he came down and (intentionally) startled the man.'

(8)   Äiwoo:
    Lâto luwa-kä   toponu=kä,   ilâ   nyâ-nou
    then take-DIR:3 turtle=OBL.PRO DEIC:DIST tree-banana
    eângâ=kâ,   luwa-kä=nä
    DEM:DIST=DEIC:DIST take-DIR:3=OBL.PRO
    i-vägulo   go   nyimä
    PFV-hit.with.long.instrument with hand.3MIN
    'Then the turtle, that banana tree, he struck it with his hand.'

---

[4] For the purposes of this comparison, I am glossing over the problems inherent in applying the term *transitive* to verbs in Äiwoo; the set of verbs involved are those referred to earlier as O-verbs.

Finally, in narrative discourse, Vaeakau-Taumako shows a pattern known as tail-head linkage, in which the final element of a clause is repeated at the beginning of the following clause. While this is a common feature of narrative discourse in the Melanesian region (Crowley 2002: 69), it does not appear to be described for any other Polynesian language. In Vaeakau-Taumako it is highly frequent, and again structurally very similar to the tail-head linkage construction in Äiwoo. In both languages, the repeated sequence is usually a verb or verb plus postverbal elements, with the second occurrence marked by a deictic particle. In Äiwoo, which shows a two-term distance-based system of spatial deixis, this particle is the distal deictic clitic =Câ, whereas Vaeakau-Taumako, which has a three-term speaker-based system, uses the 'close to addressee' form *na*; it may be noted that the Vaeakau-Taumako system appears to be developing some characteristics of a distance-based system, with *na* functioning as a medial or neutral term (Næss and Hovdhaugen 2011: 122).

(9) a. Äiwoo:
    Ikâ   lâto   ki-dâ=to=wâ,   uule=kâ   mo
    heron then IPFV-float=PH=DEIC:DIST drift=DEIC:DIST and
    lâ   ki-dâ=kâ.   I-da=kâ,
    DEIC:DIST IPFV-float=DEIC:DIST PFV-float=DEIC:DIST
    lâ   i-de-to=to   ngä   nye-lägä=kâ.
    DEIC:DIST PFV-wash.up-go.in=CS LOC place-dry=DEIC:DIST
    'The heron started drifting, he drifted slowly. He drifted until he washed up in a dry place.'

   b. Vaeakau-Taumako:
    Thai langi na   ko   noho~noho na
    one   day   DEM:2 INCP RED~stay   DEM:2
    ko   **hano** **loa**   **ko**   **kaukau.**
    INCP   go.SG EMPH INCP bathe
    Ko   **hano** **ko**   **kaukau** **na,**   ioko   te   pakhola
    INCP   go.SG INCP bathe   DEM:2 CONJ SG.SP giant
    ko   ne-ho   ko-i   to-a.
    INCP go.SG-down INCP-3SG take-TR
    'One day she went to have a bath. She went to have a bath, and a giant came and took her.'

28.4 EXPLAINING THE PATTERNS

As noted in the introduction to this chapter, accounting for the patterns of contact-induced change described in section 28.3 requires a careful analysis of the interaction between two types of processes: that leading to the rise to new patterns of language use in individual speakers as a result of bilingualism in those individuals, and that leading to the spread of those patterns through the language communities. In order to understand the latter, it is further necessary to map out the individual factors that have shaped the relationships and interactions between the language communities, not just in terms of socioeconomic "prestige" but also in terms of the relative size of the communities involved; while these two factors are often linked, they are independent variables, which in this case need to be examined separately.

In terms of the origins of the transfer patterns observed, van Coetsem's (1998, 2000) model distinguishing between recipient-language agentivity and source-language agentivity provides a good explanation. It is clear that Vaeakau-Taumako is the source language for the lexical borrowing and the recipient language for the transfers of grammatical structure, whereas Äiwoo is the recipient language for lexical items and the source language for the grammatical structure. This is entirely as expected on the assumption laid out in section 2.2 that it was the Äiwoo L1 community that was historically bilingual; they would have borrowed vocabulary from Vaeakau-Taumako, their L2 (recipient-language agentivity), and would have imposed grammatical patterns from Äiwoo, their L1, onto their L2 version of Vaeakau-Taumako (source-language agentivity).

The challenge lies in explaining how the Äiwoo-influenced version of Vaeakau-Taumako came to spread to the L1 speakers, for whom there is no evidence of widespread bilingualism either historically or at present. A common explanation for structural interference from another language in an apparently monolingual community is language shift (e.g., Matras 2009: 68ff); after imperfectly acquiring an L2, onto which grammatical patterns from the L1 are imposed as part of the acquisition process, the community then abandons its original L1, leaving them with an altered version of the target language. But there is no evidence of a shift from Äiwoo to Vaeakau-Taumako having taken place at any point in the languages' history, and indeed such an explanation seems unlikely given what we know about the history of the region, with the Vaeakau-Taumako speakers being relatively recent arrivals who have maintained their Polynesian language at the margins of the larger Äiwoo-speaking community.

Rather, the key lies in the interaction between socioeconomic prestige and demographics. Although numerically the smaller community by a considerable factor, the Vaeakau-Taumako community traditionally derived considerable prestige and economic power from their role as shipbuilders, navigators, and traders throughout the region. The traditional trading relationship explains something that is otherwise difficult to account for, namely the fact that Äiwoo speakers appear to have been bilingual in Vaeakau-Taumako, rather than the other way around; on the basis of the present-day situation it would be very difficult to explain why the larger and economically more powerful group would have been bilingual in the language of the smaller and economically inferior group. However, we know that this relationship has shifted within the last century or so, making it likely that while the trading network was still operational, Vaeakau-Taumako was in fact the language of intergroup communication, despite being the L1 of the numerically smaller group.

The demographical imbalance in turn provides an explanation for the spread of the L2 variety of Vaeakau-Taumako into the community of L1 speakers. If today's population figures are taken as a heuristic, then the L2 speakers of Vaeakau-Taumako would have outnumbered the L1 speakers by a factor of probably between 5 and 10, depending on the proportion of the Äiwoo L1 community that was bilingual; judging from the pervasiveness of Vaeakau-Taumako loanwords in Äiwoo, this proportion is likely to have been considerable. With the L2 speakers numerically dominant, the L2 speakers' variety could gradually have become the norm, even among the largely monolingual L1 speakers. A factor in this development is likely to have been the trade relationship that was the basis for the interaction between the two groups; it is plausible that the Vaeakau-Taumako traders would have found it profitable to accommodate to the variety of their language spoken by their customers in the Main Reefs.

28.5 BIDIRECTIONAL BORROWING BEYOND THE REEF ISLANDS

While the pattern of bilingualism and L1-L2 interaction described in this chapter appears to be unusual, it is not unique. A similar situation is described by Næss and Jenny (2011) for southern Burma, where the Mon language, nationally a minority language but spoken by the majority in the region in question, has borrowed large amounts of vocabulary from Burmese, whereas the local variety of Burmese shows considerable grammatical influence from Mon. While the Mon speakers are typically bilingual, the Burmese speakers are not, raising the question of how the structural influence from Mon to Burmese has come about. Again, the key factor seems to be demographics: while Burmese speakers are the majority in the country as a whole, the Mon speakers predominate in at least some areas of southern Burma, where, as a result, L2 speakers speaking Mon-influenced versions of Burmese outnumber L1 speakers (Næss and Jenny 2011: 244).

Slater (2003: 8) proposes a similar process of imposition from local languages into the variety of Chinese spoken in China's Gansu Province: "it is likely that the non-native speakers of Chinese outnumbered the native speakers during much of this earlier period, since the Sinitic-speaking communities tended to be small, isolated settlements in river valleys, which certainly required significant economic interaction with their immediate neighbors. Since the Han had access to trade routes leading into the region, other local inhabitants would have had significant motivation to learn enough Chinese to carry out economic negotiations with them. As a result, the grammar of the non-native speakers' first languages gradually became the regional standard, even for Sinitic language varieties."

28.6 A Text Example: Äiwoo Structural Features in Vaeakau-Taumako

Excerpt from the story about the death of Bishop John Patteson, told by Henry Leni on Nukapu Island (Hovdhaugen and Næss 2010).

Italics: subject proclitics
<u>Underlined</u>: verb serialization
Bold: Tail-head linkage

A	ioko	i	a	hua-mna~mnatu-nga		na	iloa	loa
then	CONJ	LOC	COLL	CAUS-RED~think-NMLZ		DEM.2	know-TR	EMPH

po	te	tapena	phe-nā	po	mdea	po
COMP	SG.SP	prepare	like-DEM.2	COMP	maybe	COMP

mui	hinga	ala	ka	lau	ala	ite	ia.
small	thing	HYP	FUT	reach	HYP	LOC	3SG

'And maybe he thought such preparations could indicate that something would happen to him.'

A	*lhatu*=e	kav-atu	na,	**hua-tako~takoto-lia**	**loa**	**ia.**
then	3PL=GENR	carry-go.out	DEM.2	CAUS-RED~lie-TR	EMPH	3SG

'They brought him and put him to bed.'

Hua-takoto-lia	**ia**	*lhatu*=ko	<u>to-a</u>	<u>uhi-a</u>	<u>oho</u>
CAUS-lie-TR	3SG	3PL=INCP	take-TR	cover-TR	go.vertically

ona	mata	na	mui	vevei-kahu.
3SG.POSS	eye	DEM.2	small	scrap-cloth

'They put him to bed, and they covered his eyes with a piece of cloth.'

A-nā	e	**takoto**	**na**	i	te	holau	na.
then-DEM.2	GENR	lie	DEM.2	LOC	SG.SP	men's.house	DEM.2

'He lay there in the single men's house.'

Ko	**takoto**	**na**	ioko	thai	matua	ne	o	mua	ne,
INCP	lie	DEM.2	CONJ	one	man	DEM.1	POSS	place	DEM.1

na	ingoa	po	ko	Teatule.
3SG.POSS	name	COMP	TOP	Teatule.

'He lay there, and a man from here, his name was Teatule.'

Ko	mdea	e	ngakau	ange	po	ke-i	te-ia	a	ia.
TOP	maybe	GENR	guts	go.along	COMP	HORT-3SG	hit-TR	PERS	3SG

'I think he had decided to kill the bishop.'

A	ko-i	to-a	te	huasea,
then	INCP-3SG	take-TR	SG.SP	club

nekepō	e	lakau	no	ta-ia	ai	a	tai.
like	SG.NSP	tree	IPFV	hit-TR	OBL.PRO	COLL	person

'He took a club, that is, a stick to kill people with.'

A	ko-i	to-a	ko	mohi~mohi	ange	loa	ma	ia,
then	INCP-3SG	take-TR	INCP	RED~creep	go.along	EMPH	with	3SG

He took it and crept along with it,

ko	tolo	ange	mui	na	pihoulu	na,
INCP	crawl	go.along	place	3SG.POSS	head	DEM.2

'he crept along to where his [the bishop's] head was,'

tolo	ange	na	ko-i	to-a	ko-i	umai-a
crawl	go.along	DEM.2	INCP-3SG	take-TR	INCP-3SG	bring-TR

mui	ona	mata	na,
place	3SG.POSS	eye	DEM.2

'he crept up there and hit him on his face with it,'

ne-i	umai-a	ai	na	mate	loa.
PFV-3SG	bring-TR	OBL.PRO	DEM.2	die	EMPH

'he hit him with it and he died.'

Nā	e	takoto	loa.
DEM.2	GENR	lie	EMPH

'There where he was lying.'

REFERENCES

Crowley, Terry. 2002. *Serial Verbs in Oceanic: A Descriptive Typology.* Oxford: Oxford University Press.

Davenport, William. 1968. Social organization notes on the Northern Santa Cruz Islands: The Duff Islands (Taumako). Baessler-Archiv, Neue Folge, Band XVI, 137–205.

Hovdhaugen, Even, and Åshild Næss. 2006. *Stories from Vaeakau and Taumako/A lalakhai ma talanga o Vaeakau ma Taumako.* Oslo: The Kon-Tiki Museum.

Ivens, Walter G. 1918. *Dictionary and Grammar of the Language of Sa'a and Ulawa, Solomon Islands.* Washington, DC: Carnegie Institute.

Kirch, Patrick Vinton. 2002. *On the Road of the Winds: An Archaeological History of the Pacific Islands before European Contact.* Berkeley; Los Angeles: University of California Press.

Matras, Yaron. 2009. *Language Contact.* Cambridge: Cambridge University Press.

Milroy, James, and Lesley Milroy. 1985. Linguistic change, social network and speaker innovation. *Journal of Linguistics* 21(2): 339–384.

Næss, Åshild. 2011. Case on the margins: Pragmatics and case-marking in Vaeakau-Taumako and beyond. In *Case, Valency and Semantic Roles*, edited by Seppo Kittilä, Katja Västi, and Jussi Ylikoski, 305–328. Amsterdam: John Benjamins.

Næss, Åshild. 2013. From Austronesian voice to Oceanic transitivity: Äiwoo as the 'missing link.' *Oceanic Linguistics* 52(1): 106–124.

Næss, Åshild. 2015. The Äiwoo verb phrase: Syntactic ergativity without pivots. *Journal of Linguistics* 51: 75–106.

Næss, Åshild. forthcoming. Transitivity and argument marking in Vaeakau-Taumako: A comparative Polynesian perspective. In *Transitivity and Voice in Indo-European and Beyond: A Diachronic Typological Perspective*, edited by Ilja Serzant and Leonid Kulikov.

Næss, Åshild, and Even Hovdhaugen. 2011. *A Grammar of Vaeakau-Taumako*. Berlin: de Gruyter Mouton.

Næss, Åshild, and Mathias Jenny. 2011. Who changes language? Bilingualism and structural change in Burma and the Reef Islands. *Journal of Language Contact* 4: 217–249.

Ross, Malcolm. 1996. Contact induced change and the comparative method: Cases from Papua New Guinea. In *The Comparative Method Reviewed: Regularity and Irregularity in Language Change*, edited by Mark Durie and Malcolm Ross, 180–217. New York: Oxford University Press.

Ross, Malcolm. 1997. Social networks and kinds of speech-community event. In *Archaeology and Language I: Theoretical and Methodological Orientations*, edited by Roger Blench and Matthew Spriggs, 209–261. London: Routledge.

Ross, Malcolm. 2003. Diagnosing prehistoric language contact. In *Motives for Language Change*, edited by Raymond Hickey, 174–198. Cambridge: Cambridge University Press.

Slater, Keith W. 2003. *A Grammar of Mangghuer, a Mongolic language of China's Qinghai-Gansu Sprachbund*. London; New York: Routledge Curzon.

Spriggs, Matthew. 1997. *The Island Melanesians*. Oxford: Blackwell.

Thomason, Sarah Grey. 2001. *Language Contact: An Introduction*. Edinburgh: Edinburgh University Press.

van Coetsem, Frans. 1988. *Loan Phonology and the Two Transfer Types in Language Contact*. Dordrecht: Foris.

van Coetsem, Frans. 2000. *A General and Unified Theory of the Transmission Process in Language Contact*. Heidelberg: Universitätsverlag C. Winter.

Wurm, Stephen A. 1978. Reefs-Santa Cruz: Austronesian, but . . . ! In *Second International Conference on Austronesian Linguistics*, edited by Stephen A. Wurm and Lois Carrington, 969–1010. Canberra: Pacific Linguistics.

CHAPTER 29

LANGUAGE CONTACT IN UNANGAM TUNUU (ALEUT)

ANNA BERGE

29.1 INTRODUCTION

THE Aleut language, known preferentially as Unangam Tunuu in Alaska, and henceforth referred to as such, was traditionally spoken along the Aleutian Chain; the people are known as the Unangan (or Unangax̂ in the singular). It is the only language in its branch of the Eskimo-Aleut (EA) language family and comprises two dialects, Atkan and Eastern, with a third, Attuan, recently obsolete, and the mixed Russian-Attuan variety known as Copper Island Aleut (CIA). Unangam Tunuu (UT) is quite divergent from Eskimo languages and is traditionally considered to have developed in isolation from Eskimo and neighboring languages, until the Aleutians were colonized by Russians in the eighteenth century. To date, its primary contribution to studies of language contact has been the interest generated by CIA. However, recent advances in a number of fields are revising our understanding of the prehistory and history of language contact in the Aleutians. It is increasingly clear that the inhabitants of the Aleutians were never culturally isolated throughout their 9,000 years of recorded presence on the islands. There were several prehistoric periods of cultural contact in addition to the historic Russian period in the eighteenth and nineteenth centuries and the American period, from 1867 to the present, all of which have affected the language in different ways. In this chapter, I present an overview of the main periods of contact and the apparent linguistic effects of this contact on UT. I focus on the late prehistoric period, although the evidence is still speculative, as it has received the least attention but is of critical important in the divergence of UT within its language family. Prehistoric contact was extensive enough to result in deep structural changes; Russian and early American contact were primarily lexical and did not overwhelm UT; and the late American period is characterized by language shift.

29.2 THE PREHISTORIC PERIOD

The standard understanding of EA is that it developed on the Seward Peninsula 5,000–6,000 years ago; the two branches of EA have been diverging for approximately 4,000 years as a result of internal developments (Woodbury 1984; Bergsland 1986, 1989, 1997); they have developed in relative isolation from each other and from neighboring languages, with some admixture on border areas (Bergsland 1986, 1989, 1997; Krauss 1990;); and the sharp division between the branches of the language family is the result of a dialect continuum broken by the late intrusion of Alutiiq Eskimos in the boundary area (Krauss 1990):

> ... the relationship of Aleut and Eskimo may seem very distant, and the time of the "split" has been estimated to several millennia. The closer one looks into the linguistic facts, however, the closer the relationship appears, and there seems to be no reason to believe that the ancestors of the Aleuts and the Eskimos did ever "split" otherwise than fighting and trading with each other within a vast territory divided among numerous local groups ... there is no evidence for any foreign substratum in Aleut that could account for the differences from Eskimo. The differences must be regarded as the outcome of normal dialectal innovations.
>
> (Bergsland 1989: 73)

> The remarkable fact is rather the almost total absence of Amerindian (Athabaskan or Algonquian) loanwords in Eskimo and Aleut. . . . A . . . reasonable guess is that the actual Eskimo and Aleut languages are only remnants of a larger prehistoric continuum, and that the "split" may reflect nothing more than the loss of intermediate forms (Krauss 1980: 7–8; Woodbury 1984: 62).   (Bergsland 1986: 69)

Many features of UT, however, cannot easily be reconstructed to Proto-Eskimo-Aleut (PEA). The relationship between Eskimo and UT was first proposed in 1819, and phonological correlations and lexical cognates have been identified by Thalbitzer (1921), Marsh and Swadesh (1951), and Bergsland (1986; information on UT in Fortescue et al. 2011 is based on Bergsland 1986). Already in 1840, however, Veniaminov (1984: 294) remarked on UT's extreme lexical dissimilarity with Eskimo. Bergsland (1986: 129) estimated that only 15%–25% of UT morphemes and stems have cognates in Eskimo, although many proposed cognates are tentative. Grammatically, the most well-known development in UT was the loss of its nominal case endings, and the consequent reshuffling of its originally ergative case system to a typologically unusual anaphoric system, with far-reaching effects on its morphology and sentence structure (Bergsland 1997b; Fortescue 2002). Fortescue (1998, 2002) and Berge (2016) find internal motivation insufficient to account for all these effects.

Fortescue (1998, 2002) has advanced the possibility of language contact with an Athabaskan-speaking group because of a number of grammatically similar features between UT and Na-Dene languages (Leer 1991; Fortescue 1998, 2002).[1] It is difficult to find uncontroversial evidence of linguistic features shared as a result of contact, because rigorous reconstructions of some languages (including UT) remain to be done, the traits in questions have been unevenly covered in the literature of the various languages, and there is a strongly held belief that the typological distance between the language families is too great for features to be readily shared. Nevertheless, advances in our understanding of EA and Athabaskan-Eyak-Tlingit (AET), as well as in the prehistory of the people who presumably spoke those languages, strongly suggest that prehistoric language contact is an important factor in the development of UT.[2]

29.2.1 Archaeology, Genetics, and Ethnography

The archaeological, genetic, and historical evidence suggest a long history of shared culture between the Unangan people and the northern Northwest Pacific Coast, although the interpretation of the evidence is debated. The Eastern Aleutians were settled by 9000 BP, the Central Islands by 5000 BP, and the Near Islands by 2500 BP. Recent archaeological investigations show cultural continuity throughout the period and far less cultural isolation than previously assumed, including contact and cultural affinity with Kodiak Island and southeastern Alaska from the earliest period (Davis and Knecht 2010: 509, 521). The Arctic Small Tool tradition commonly associated with Eskimo culture was an intrusion into an already established culture and did not penetrate the Aleutians to any great degree (Dumond 2001: 300–301; Hatfield 2010: 527); thus, the ethnic Unangan may have already been well established in the Eastern Aleutians 4,000–2,000 years ago, when the Unangan and Eskimo cultures show the closest cultural affinity.

Genetic studies also give conflicting results. The Unangan have been a distinct genetic population for about 3,000 years. There are close relationships between the Eastern Unangan and the Chukchi and Siberian Eskimos, and between the western Unangan and the Alaskan Yupit; but there is a clear genetic break between the Central Alaskan Yupit and the Eastern Unangan, and a closer relationship between the Eastern Unangan and Na-Dene. This is possibly due to separate migrations of Eskimos and Unangan from Asia (Crawford 2011: 702), as well as to an influx of related people, perhaps related to the Thule migration, moving into the Eastern Aleutians about

---

[1] Menovshchikov also sees evidence for ancient foreign substrata, presumably Paleo-Asiatic, cf. Liapunova (1996: 14).

[2] Phylogenetic studies of highly divergent or isolated languages in a language family, including UT, support the idea of web-like rather than tree-like language development (Wichmann et al. 2011: 220; unfortunately, UT was not further examined for possible conflicts in phylogenetic signals, i.e., for the possibility of sociohistorical causes of reticulation, including language contact).

1,000 years ago and continuing westward throughout the immediate prehistoric period (Hatfield 2010: 545, 548).

There have been several periods of prehistoric contact between the Eastern and Central Aleutians and neighboring cultures, the first from 6,000 years ago with Kodiak Island, the second from 3,000 years ago with the Arctic Small Tool tradition, and the third from 1,000 years ago until the time of Russian contact. The latter is marked by increased social complexity and cultural interaction with non-Unangan peoples to the east, including the Pacific Eskimos from Kodiak and the Alaskan Peninsula, the Dena'ina and Eyak peoples of southeastern Alaska, and the Tlingit of the Pacific Northwest Coast (Dumond 2001).[3] The discussion here focuses on the last prehistoric period, in part because the diversification within UT suggests about 1,000 years of separation between the dialects, rather than the 4,000 years or more of language internal change since the split with Eskimo (Woodbury 1984), perhaps related to the recent westward expansion mentioned in the preceding.

The earliest historical records show that the Unangan and the Northwest Coast shared mythologies, cultural practices, and socioeconomic organization. The Unangan, like the Eyak, Tlingit, Haida, and Tsimshian, but unlike the Yupit, had a stratified society with up to five social classes, including slaves (Liapunova 1996: 138). The institution of slavery was well established, old, and most developed in the more densely populated eastern Aleutians. Both material goods and slaves, most often women and children, were acquired by frequent trade or war from the Kodiak Islanders, the Chugach, Tlingit, and Dena'ina communities to the east, and from neighboring Unangan communities on the chain (Veniaminov 1984). Some families may have had a slave for each member of the family, and as many as twenty slaves have been recorded in a family (Liapunova 1996: 138ff). The norm may have resembled the northern Northwest Coast, where despite considerable variability within and between communities, the number of slaves was enough to have a considerable socioeconomic and political impact on a community (Donald 1997: 197). Thus, at least in the Eastern Aleutians, Unangan speakers were in close contact with non-Unangan speakers for extended periods of time. Unangan men would have had had exposure to other languages during their travels, and women and children would have had exposure to other languages through slaves in their homes.

29.2.2 The Linguistic Evidence

Lexical evidence of prehistoric contact is informed by two sources: the distribution of cognates to non-cognates in certain semantic domains is suggestive of contact, and there are some identified loans and borrowings, mostly from UT into neighboring languages, although research is still incomplete. Of 199 words on the 200-word Swadesh list (the term 'woods' is not represented), there are 530 close equivalents, including dialectal

---

[3] There may have been occasional contact between the western Aleutians and Asia, although the nature of this contact is controversial (Black 1984; Liapunova 1996; Fortescue 1998).

variants and synonyms: 146 are cognate with Eskimo, 100 are questionably cognate, and 276 are clearly not cognate. Among the latter are 23 borrowings from Russian and one from English; no other languages have been identified as sources of borrowings, although a few of the possible cognates may be borrowings between Yupik and UT. Only the deictic and pronominal terms on the list are fully cognate with Eskimo; however, the deictic system has undergone a relatively recent prehistoric reorganization and regularization of the system from one more closely resembling that of Eskimo (Bergsland 1986: 113). Most inflectional morphemes on the list (and more generally) are cognate. Kinship terms and positional nouns are evenly divided into cognates and non-cognates on the list, but they have far more non-cognates in total. More than half of the verbs representing basic terms are non-cognate. Other groups of terms are mostly non-cognate, including color, body part, flora, fauna, geographical, temporal, and meteorological terms; these findings are true more generally as well, and the cognates are not necessarily the most basic terms (Menovshchikov also noted the lack of cognates among flora, fauna, and sea-hunting tools; cf. Liapunova, 1996: 14).

In the entire lexicon, Bergsland (1994: 654ff) identifies about 110 borrowings between Central Alaskan Yupik (CAY) or Alutiiq and (mostly Eastern) UT; almost 80 have been borrowed into the Yupik languages rather than vice versa, mostly terms for flora and fauna, with some body part and material culture terms. Some clearly predate Russian contact (e.g., UT *kudmachix̂* 'seine,' borrowed into or from Proto-Yupik before certain sound changes in either language; Bergsland 1986: 123); but most are not clearly datable. Bergsland identifies only two pre-contact loans into Eastern UT from Athabaskan, *nuunax̂* 'porcupine' and *qusx̂ix̂* 'marmot,' both also found in Alaskan Yupik. More UT words have made their way into Dena'ina, perhaps via Alutiiq or CAY (e.g., *kalagax̂* 'yellow sculpin,' Yupik *kalaaq*, Dena'ina *galaghaq*; Bergsland 1986: 120). Some are known throughout the region, as in UT *chaqalkan* 'kind of seaweed,' borrowed into or from Alutiiq *caqallqaq* 'algae, esp. dulse,' source of Dena'ina *jaqal'qa* 'dulse,' and also found in Eyak, Tlingit, Tsimshian, and Kwakiutl (Bergsland 1994: 132). Further investigation will probably turn up more such borrowings (as well as a potentially much older layer of shared terminology). Thus, UT was a regional influence at some point prehistorically, it was in contact with a number of neighboring languages, and this contact is evident in the lexica of those languages; the source(s) of the non-cognate forms in UT is still unknown.

Comparative studies of shared grammatical features may be more promising. Leer (1991) shows that a typologically unusual system of plural agreement is found in the UT, Eyak, Haida, and Tlingit languages, leading to his proposal for a northern Northwest Coast Sprachbund including UT, although the proposal is based on a single shared feature. Fortescue (1998: 216) lists some non-Eskimo features in UT indicative of a Na-Dene-related substratum. There are many more such features at all levels of grammatical structure, some of which are typologically unusual, and the similarities with known AET traits are indicative.[4]

---

[4] The designation "AET" should not be taken to mean that a given feature exists in all the languages. Nor should examples in this text be understood to suggest that one language is more likely to have been a source of borrowings into Aleut.

Phonologically, UT lacks initial nasals and the phoneme /p/ in native words (Fortescue 1998: 216). It also has a high degree of free variations in accepted vowel quality and length in various words, as in Pribilof Islands UT *ilaasix̂, ilaasax̂* 'friend, relative' (Berge fieldnotes), or as in Eastern *yax̂* and Atkan *yaax̂* 'cape, point of land' (Bergsland 1986: 6); this variability can sometimes be extreme, as in Eastern UT *uuĝ(u)mik(i)dax, uuĝ(u)mika(a)dax, uuĝamikadax, uumx̂ikaadax, uumĝika(a)dax̂, uunĝimkaadax̂, uuĝnimkaadax̂, aaĝumkidax* 'blowfly' (Bergsland 1994: 426). Likewise, uvulars and velars are often interchanged in UT, as in the final /x/ or /x̂/ *i*n the previous example. Eastern UT has some form of vowel harmony, involving raising of the back vowel /a/ (e.g., Eastern negative enclitic *−ulux* vs. Atkan and Attuan *−ulax*). All these features are lacking in Eskimo and are found to varying degrees in some Na-Dene languages (e.g., limited height harmony in Gwich'in and Navajo; Tuttle, personal communication, 2013; Eyak, Krauss 2010).

Morphologically, UT is assumed to be, like Eskimo, highly polysynthetic and exclusively agglutinating, with a [root-derivational affixes-inflectional affixes] word structure. However, polysynthesis is much reduced in UT (Fortescue 2002: 275), and it also has a number of non-Eskimo features, including stem=stem morphology arising from the merger of a lexical verb and an auxiliary, multiple slots for the same grammatical function, discontinuous dependencies, a number of zero morphemes, a large number of unproductive derivational morphemes, and different construction requirements of different moods (Berge 2016), all features of which are characteristic of AET languages (Rice 2000: 11; Vajda 2011: 39–40). The following examples (1–2) illustrate some of these points:

(1)   *waaĝa-l-niiĝ-na-x̂*
       arrive-CONJUNCTIVE-recently-PARTICIPIAL-3SINGULAR
       STEM-MOOD=STEM-MOOD-SUBJECT.PERSON/NUMBER
       'He came back here recently.' (St. Paul; Bergsland 1997a: 298)

(2)   *six̂i-laga-a-qa-an*
       break-NEGATIVE-OPTATIVE-ANAPHORA-2SINGULAR.ANAPHORA
       STEM-NEGATIVE-MOOD-ANAPHORA-SUBJECT.PERSON/NUMBER/ANAPHORA
       'Don't break it.' (Bergsland 1997a: 88)

Particular developments in UT noun phrase structure may be explained by language internal processes, such as syllable apocope leading to loss of oblique case marking, and consequently to the rise of postpositions (Bergsland 1986, 1997); but language contact is likely to have encouraged them (Fortescue 1998: 217; Berge 2016). Thus, noun phrases in UT are almost exclusively built on the model of the possessive phrase, cf. *kamgam ulaa* 'church (lit. house of feasting/prayer)' and *kamgam angunaa* 'a big feast.' The construction does not result in compounding, although it can be verbalized, as in *[kamgam ula]ĝilix* 'to have a church'; but it is the basis for designating a large number of concepts, including native flora, place, and personal names, and body parts (e.g., *aĝdiikam aahmaaĝii* 'dogwood (lit. ptarmigan's flower),' *agalum kitangis* 'roots (lit. feet) of the teeth'). The possessive phrase structure is from PEA and is identical in Eskimo, but lexicalized phrases are not typically traditional in Eskimo, and certainly not in personal names. And whereas Eskimo has seven nominal cases, UT nouns indicate absolutive and relative case, possession and, somewhat optionally, number; oblique case is marked on postpositions. In these respects, UT noun phrases resemble possessed noun phrases and noun compounds in AET. Likewise, noun phrases involving positional nouns are found in both Eskimo languages and UT (e.g., Greenlandic *illu-up ilu-ani* 'house-RELATIVE inside-3SINGULAR.POSSESSIVE.LOCATIVE' = 'in the inside of the house,' and UT *ula-m il-an* 'house-RELATIVE in.3SINGULAR.POSSESSIVE. LOCATIVE' = 'in the house'), although in Eskimo, case-marked nouns such as *illu-mi* 'house- LOCATIVE'= 'in the house' are more typical. There are seven cognate positional nouns between Eskimo and UT, but there are over fifty postpositions in UT. The same types of positional noun phrases are found in AET; they are structured similarly, consisting of a noun or pronoun and a postpositional element that may have been a positional noun in origin; and there are around thirty-five of them (Sapir 1915: 547). In both UT and AET, positional nouns are frequently used with unexpressed nouns; postpositions may head a nominalization or a relative clause (e.g., UT *ukux̂ta-gan il-an* 'look.at.NOMINALIZER-3SINGULAR.RELATIVE in.3singular.possessive.locative' = 'while he was looking at her' (Bergsland 1997a: 317; cf. Sapir 1915: 549); postpositions may be combined, even merging into compounds in UT (e.g., Eastern UT *qusamadaa* 'upward direction' from *qusam hadaa* 'above toward'; Bergsland 1997a: 69); and postpositions can take locational case marking (Sapir 1915: 547; Bergsland 1997a: 67). While UT does not incorporate postpositions, as AET languages do, it has an enclitic postposition.

Unlike Eskimo, both UT and AET languages have subordinating and negative clitics, a particle for yes-no questions (Atkan *ii?* Eastern *ee?*; cf. Leer 2000: 112) a particle for expressing hypothesis or irrealis (UT *kum*; Bergsland 1994: xxxvii attributes this to possible Russian influence from the analogous Russian particle *by*; cf. Leer 2000: 112), and a weak noun-verb distinction (Cook and Rice 1989: 23; Bergsland 1997a: 107). UT makes extensive use of passive constructions, including subjectless and intransitive passives (Berge 2012), it has a participial form unmarked morphologically, with general semantics, and its conditional mood is frequently used to refer to past events; all of these are features of Eyak (Krauss 2010), and none is characteristic of Eskimo languages. UT also has auxiliary constructions for specific tenses or moods, an independent copula in existential constructions, number marking of the subject or object on the verb rather than on the noun phrase, internally headed relative clauses, and relatively rigid SOV word order; most of these can be explained by language internal changes from PEA, but all are common of Na-Dene languages (Fortescue 1998: 216).

Semantic similarities between UT and AET need further analysis; however, the Eskimo verb *pi-* 'to do' is a semantically bleached or empty root; the direct cognate in UT is *hi-* 'to say,' although the functional equivalent of Eskimo *pi-* is UT *ma-* 'to do,' from *PEA *(u)ma-* 'to have been/done' (Fortescue et al. 2010: 453). In Athabaskan and Eyak, the use of the verb 'to say' is based on a verb meaning 'to have happen to one, to do' with a prefix indicating oral activity (Leer 2000: 118).

Finally, UT structures its discourse very differently from Eskimo languages (Berge 2009, 2010b), often introducing a new referent or context without naming it explicitly, and making extensive use of pre- and postposed noun phrases for focusing or topicalization; both characteristics have been noted for Koyukon (Axelrod 1993: 19), and research on this topic is in progress for a number of other languages (Krauss 2010; Tuttle, personal communication).

The pervasiveness of the differences with Eskimo and the similarities with AET throughout the grammar make language contact a viable interpretation of the linguistic facts. Prehistoric language contact, however, did not result in language replacement, but rather in change through meaning extension (i.e., convergence; Croft 2003: 51). What was borrowed was congruent with what already existed (Thomason and Kaufman 1988: 54). Despite many similarities with AET, UT retains cognate grammatical morphology and the basic structural framework of EA grammar. Although we have no way of knowing what pre-contact UT was like, PEA more likely resembled Eskimo than modern UT (cf. Bergsland 1997b; Fortescue 2002; Berge 2016). Many of the ways in which UT differs from Eskimo are in degree rather than in substance. Thus, both Eskimo and UT have positional noun phrases, but UT makes more abundant use of positional nouns, which have become postpositions; they have similar possessive noun phrase constructions, but these are more widely used in UT; UT has auxiliary constructions while Eskimo does not, but there is evidence for earlier auxiliation in PEA (Berge 2016). These may have been minor patterns in the language that expanded to become major patterns (Heine and Kuteva 2005: 45–46), perhaps through contact with neighboring languages with these features. Even modifications of grammatical structure have been readapted to the native structure; thus, words are understood as [root]-[derivational affixes]-[inflectional affixes] even if they are derived from merged stem=-stem structures.

The way in which the features are manifested in UT versus AET is sometimes quite different. For example, AET verbs are constructed as [loosely connected incorporated materials]-[derivational and inflectional affixes from a prehistoric auxiliary]-[lexical verb and associated affixes], and the merging of AET auxiliary and lexical verbs was lexicalized long ago (Vajda 2011). The UT merged verb, on the other hand, is a [lexical verb stem]-[auxiliary, now reinterpreted as an affix, with inflectional suffixes] and the process is still productive. Nevertheless, these differences may not be as significant as has been assumed. McDonough's (2000) perception studies of Navajo verb structure suggest that verbs are conceived of as bipartite, despite the time depth of grammaticization and lexicalization of the verb constructions; and as many of the components of AET verbs appear to be lexicalized, structural replication or borrowing probably happened at a higher than morphemic level. From this point of view, the UT and AET structures are not all that different. Analogous patterns existed in UT (and in PEA), so that adoption of a feature may have involved adaptation rather than innovation.

These observations suggest that speakers of an EA language probably had extensive contact with and influence from AET, although no single neighboring language with all of the similar features has been identified. From the lack of obvious borrowings into UT and the substantial numbers of loans from UT into neighboring languages (some, at least, predating Russian contact), it seems that a large population of AET speakers relative to the local EA-speaking population may have shifted languages, with marked features of AET carried over. Given the relative uniformity of the UT dialects, as well as some suspicious regularities in the grammar (e.g., in the deictic and nominal systems), this contact probably took place within the past 1,000 years, and was apparently more intense in the Eastern-speaking areas.

29.3 THE RUSSIAN PERIOD (1741–1867)

Although Russian explorers knew of land east of the Bering Strait in the seventeenth century (Black 2004: 19), and there are occasional speculations about Japanese landfalls on the Aleutians, there are neither sources describing contact with the Unangan nor established linguistic traces of late prehistoric contact between Unangan and Asians. The first intensive contact between Russians and the Unangan began with the rush to procure furs in the years after the official exploration of the Aleutians in 1741. The people involved in these activities consisted of a mixture of Russians, Pomor traders from the White Sea region, and indigenous peoples from the Kamchatkan and Chukchi peninsulas, particularly the Itel'men and Koryak. Most spoke distinct and non-standard varieties of Russian (Black 2004: 66), and many eventually established homes and families in the Aleutians. No comprehensive study has yet been done on the sources of the Russian borrowings into UT, which include dialectal, archaic, or now-obsolete Russian terms (Bergsland 1994: xv, xxxiii).

This period had a profound effect on the Unangax̂ population, lifestyle, culture, and language. Within a decade of contact, the Unangan were being relocated, concentrated into fewer settlements, and constrained to work for the Russians (Black 2004: 69). From an estimated pre-contact population of 12,000–20,000 people, the population was down to fewer than 3,000 people by the beginning of the nineteenth century as a result of warfare, disease, and the effects of relocation (Lantis 1984: 183). Some Unangan tribes had disappeared by the end of the eighteenth century, leaving only traces of their dialects in early records. New UT-speaking settlements were created along the Chain, on the Commander and Pribilof Islands, and briefly, on the Kurile Islands. In all areas, people from different dialectal and ethnic groups were thrown together, and a distinct class of Russian-Unangan Creoles soon developed (although dialect admixture occurred before Russian contact as well, with strong evidence for a westward expansion of the Eastern dialect; Veniaminov 1984: 495–496; Bergsland 1994: xxv; Berge 2010a: 566ff).

Russian influence along the Aleutian Chain was significant but not necessarily linguistically disruptive, contrary to common assumptions. The Russian language was taught to the Unangan from the beginning, and in some cases, children were removed from their families and taught Russian; but UT was taught as well, and by the nineteenth century, there were high levels of Unangax̂ literacy. Intermarriage was common, with Russian fathers and Unangan mothers (Reedy-Maschner 2010): when the Russian period officially ended with the sale of Alaska to the United States in 1867, 28% of the Easterners, 18% of Atkans, and 26% of Attuans were considered Creole. Russian influence continued to be felt into the twentieth century (Bergsland 1994: xxxiii) and appears to have been greatest in the Eastern dialect: Bergsland counts 640 Russian lexical loans in Eastern (with 300 more in the speech of the Pribilof Islanders; Philemonof, personal communication, 2004), or up to 20% of the recorded stems, 531 in Atkan (with 76 found only in one source from 1840), and 39 in Attuan (the latter reflecting lack of documentation rather than actual number of loans). Russian loans include religious and calendric terms, terms from material culture, names, and so forth. In some cases, Russian loans completely replaced native terminology; for example, by the end of the eighteenth century, all Unangan were baptized with Russian names, and Unangan naming practices were replaced by Russian Orthodox ones (Bergsland 1998). Likewise, contact affected the native conceptualization of the calendar year. Prior to contact, the Unangan distinguished twelve lunar months and six seasons, including terms for 'early spring' and 'early fall'; by the late eighteenth century, Russian names were borrowed for the days of the week, Russian terms replaced Unangan month names, and the seasons were reduced to four (Bergsland 1994: 572). In some domains, Russian loans were minimal, but native semantic relationships were replaced with Russian (and later English) ones. Thus, traditional kinship distinctions for age, sex, and consanguinity (*ludax̂* 'man's older brother/woman's older sister' and *huyux̂* 'woman's brother,' *hungix̂* 'man's sister,' *qitx̂ux̂* 'great-grandchild, great-great-grandparent,' etc.) were largely modified by the late nineteenth century to resemble the Russian (and American) system(s): the terms *braatax̂* 'brother' and *sistrax̂* 'sister' were borrowed from Russian (*brat* and *sistra*, respectively); and even when original native terms were used, they had broader applicability, as in 1870 Eastern *hungix̂* 'man's or woman's sister' (Bergsland 1994: 576–578). Color terminology underwent the same kind of modifications, with semantic rather than lexical borrowings, and Russian euphemisms and metaphors sometimes supplemented or replaced native ones (e.g., *sadalilix* 'to go outside,' = 'to go to the bathroom,' a calque from Russian *vychodit' na dvor'* 'to go outside, excrete'; Bergsland 1994: 343; Berge 2004).

The different dialects display variation in the nativization of borrowed terms, reflecting different varieties of Russian as their sources. For example, the standard Russian word *tombúy* 'float, buoy' became Atkan *tumbuuya-x̂*, whereas a possible source of the Eastern form *tuunpuya-x̂*, *tuumpaya-x̂* is the Siberian Russian variant *tómbuy* (Bergsland 1994: xxxiii). Early Russian loans were nativized, as in *xliima-x̂* 'bread' from Russian *khléb* 'bread.' In time, widespread knowledge of Russian resulted in the use of non-native sounds in borrowed words, as in the later variant of the same word *xliiba-x̂* (with the effect that the later adoption of English loans rarely involved the complete replacement of non-native sounds, even before the language endangerment of the second half of the twentieth century).

The degree of Russian influence on the lexicon is not necessarily reflected in the basic vocabulary. On the Swadesh 200-word list, 22 of the 530 words examined are Russian loans, most of which are secondary to the native term. For example, the native *anax̂* or *anaadax̂* 'mother' is more commonly used than *maamax̂* from Russian *mama*. Many have developed a specialized meaning (e.g., *suulix̂* 'salt' for 'table salt,' from Russian *solít'* 'to salt'). A few have replaced the native term, and in these cases, the latter is still used in a more restricted context; for example in Atkan, *guudax̂* 'year' from Russian *god* 'year' is used more generally than the native *qan'gix̂* 'winter, year.' One term, *fruuxtax̂* 'fruit' from Russian *frukt* 'fruit' never had a native equivalent, although there are post-contact coinages. Finally, although Eastern UT has many more Russian loans than Atkan overall, the distribution of loans on the Swadesh lists includes 22 in Eastern, versus 21 in Atkan (and 5 in Attuan).

There are few structural effects of Russian language contact on UT: Bergsland (1994: xxix) attributes the loss of dual forms, an expansion of the derivational morphology for the indication of tense, the use of equational sentences without a copula, the regularization of subject-verb agreement, and some word order changes in Eastern UT to Russian influence.

Russian was the greatest but not the only influence on UT during this period. Unangan were brought to the Kurile and Commander Islands, Kamchatka, various regions along the coast of southeastern Alaska, the Pacific Northwest Coast, and California in the service of the Russians. Although the majority of non-Russian loans come from neighboring Alutiiq and CAY, Bergsland (1994: 657) also identifies one or two Koryak loans (e.g., *kalikax̂* 'paper, document, book, letter' from Koryak *kalikal* 'book, letter'), one from Tlingit (*x̂aayax̂* 'steambath, bathhouse,' from Tlingit *x̂aay* 'steambath'), several Dena'ina loans into Eastern UT relating to a hand game, and several loans of unidentified origin. The Itel'men term *barabara* is in common use for the traditional semi-subterranean Unangax̂ house (Reedy-Maschner 2010: 590).

From 1826, several dozen Unangan and Creole families were moved to the Commander Islands from the Aleutians, predominantly from Atka and Attu, the Kurile Islands, where a small number of Attuans and Creoles had been resettled in 1800, and the Pribilof Islands; people of other ethnicities were also brought in, including Alutiiq Eskimos, Russians, and Itel'men (Golovko and Vakhtin 1990: 98). At some point, the mixed language known as CIA developed based on a mostly Attuan lexicon, derivational and nominal possessive morphology and Russian independent object pronouns, demonstratives, postpositions, some dependent verb forms, verbal inflectional endings, predicative negatives, auxiliary and complex sentence constructions, word order variation, and so on. Golovko and Vakhtin (1990: 115ff) suggest that CIA arose after the departure of the Russian American Company in 1867, leaving Russian-speaking Creoles and UT-speaking Unangan in a social and economic vacuum; or that it arose as a regional pidgin elsewhere. Thomason and Kaufman (1988: 237), following Menovshchikov, suggest that it arose from mixed marriages of Russian men and Unangan women. None of these proposals is wholly satisfactory: there are no traces of a regional pidgin elsewhere (Gray 1994: 111), Attuan speakers were never a clear majority on Copper Island (Golovko and Vakhtin 1990: 116), and although Unangan families may have been brought to the islands, it was especially the Unangan and Creole men who were sought for work (Reedy-Maschner 2010). CIA has been extensively used to illustrate the mixed language phenomenon (Thomason and Kaufman 1988; Matras and Bakker 2003).

29.4 THE AMERICAN PERIOD (1867–PRESENT)

The sale of Alaska to the United States had little immediate linguistic effect on UT. Most people continued to speak UT, and monolingual speakers of UT could be found in Atka as late as the 1950s. Most schoolchildren learned both UT and Russian; enforced schooling in English was not introduced until about 1910 (Bergsland 1979: 22), and it was unevenly enforced until just before World War II. While the western islands were still relatively isolated, the eastern islands including the Pribilofs saw an influx of English speakers, and a working knowledge of English was not uncommon before the war. Although no studies have been done on the scale of English influence during this period, English loans into UT included terms related to American culture, material culture, and the cash economy (e.g., *duulirax̂* 'dollar'; Bergsland 1994: 161), and one borrowed term, *tri* 'tree,' is on the Swadesh list (although it should be noted that the Aleutian Islands are largely treeless).

World War II brought the greatest recorded disruption and change to UT. All Unangan people from Unalaska and the Pribilofs to the west were displaced, or about half of all Unangan, the Attuans to Japan, and the rest to various camps on the Alaskan mainland. At the end of the war, Attu remained closed, and the little more than twenty remaining Attuans were resettled (mostly in Atka); today, Attuan is obsolete. Many small but viable settlements were never resettled after the war, for economic and logistical reasons, so that returning Unangan families found themselves either concentrated in larger towns, often with a large non-Unangax̂ population, or scattered among several towns, and participation in the cash economy increased, bringing long periods of work in non-UT speaking areas. English-only schooling and boarding-school education were more rigorously enforced. This all led to increased dialect mixing, especially of Eastern forms in Atkan, and to severe language endangerment. By 1971, most children in the Eastern region no longer spoke UT, and those in relatively isolated Atka were bilingual in English, with English replacing UT in certain domains (Bergsland 1979: 24ff). Speakers mixed English roots with UT derivational and inflectional morphology; the nominal inflectional system was partially reorganized (e.g., there were fewer case distinctions, dual number was gradually lost, but person marking became less ambiguous); and the use of aspirated consonants decreased (also as a result of Eastern influence). In Pribilof Islands UT (Berge fieldnotes), English loans show minimal phonological integration, code-switching is common, and alongside the native possessive phrase constructions (e.g., *braata-m kinguuĝi-i* 'brother-RELATIVE younger-3SINGULAR.POSSESSIVE.ABSOLUTIVE' = 'younger brother') are also constructions modeled on English phrases, with a great deal of variation in agreement patterns: *kinguuĝi-x̂ braata-x̂* 'younger-ABSOLUTIVE brother-ABSOLUTIVE' = 'younger brother'). There are also English-influenced extensions of native structures. For example, there is a very un-Eskimo-like UT construction involving the verb *liidalix* 'to be like; to look like' or as a noun 'some such' documented as early as 1791, with a range of possible uses: *amaagan kalikam liidanaan liidaa* 'whatever book, any book' (Bergsland 1994: 255). The use of *liidax̂* has been extended to English uses of the predicate 'be like,' for example *Alqutax̂ liidax̂ tutaltxin?* 'How do you feel?' (lit. 'What do you feel like?' Berge, field-notes). To a great extent, the latest period of contact is marked by language shift to English, although not all recent changes in the language are necessarily a result of shift.

29.5 CONCLUSION

Evidence from archaeological, biological, historical, and linguistic studies show language contact effects between UT and other languages throughout both the prehistoric and the historic periods, although rigorous comparative studies are needed to definitively establish the former. UT appears to have been a diffuse society, tolerant of contact and change. The three periods of contact reviewed here had very different effects on UT. Prehistoric contact may have involved some language shift by non-UT speakers and resulted in little obvious lexical borrowing but substantial grammatical changes within a basically EA framework. Russian (and English) influence resulted in heavy lexical borrowing, some phonological adaptations over the long term, and limited structural changes as a result of long-term bilingualism. The mixed language CIA aside, UT does not otherwise show extensive grammatical changes until the post–World War II language shift and language endangerment. This is evident in the following text, representing the state of the language after a century of American English influence; the Eastern speaker was already past middle age by the time language shift had started. It was recorded in 1982 by Knut Bergsland and Moses Dirks and was transcribed in 1982 and 2005. Here, she is describing traditional activities; the choice of a different topic would change the percentage of borrowings from either Russian or English. There are 96 words, with 61 unique lexical items. Among the latter are 3 Russian loans (underlined), 26 UT roots (bold), 26 EA roots (unmarked), and 6 questionable cognates (in square brackets); all but one inflectional ending is clearly EA, and most derivational morphemes are EA (non-initial bolded items are UT derivational or inflectional suffixes). Syntactically, the lack of extreme polysynthesis, rigid word order, preposed topic, use of auxiliaries and postpositions, use of the conditional mood for past tense, lack of specification of the object, and the frequently occurring subordinating enclitic are all in contrast to Eskimo word and clause structure, although the clause-chaining is like that of Eskimo.

29.6 TEXT

....

Underlined items are borrowings from Russian.

Saaqudig (i)m ilan <u>braatan</u>*ing* **awalix ulaĝilakan** *agung(in)*
'Some summers, my brothers, working, when they didn't stay home'

<u>braatan</u>*g kinguuĝii ama[yax]* <u>maaman</u>*g* **agachiidaa** *agiitalix* **ulaĝilix aguung**
'together with only my mother and my younger brother, I would stay home.'

[Qila]m **chaang** *ilan* **ax̂six aqad(a)guung**
'When I would get up at five in the morning,'

ting **chulilix** <u>bruudnik</u>*ing* **angasix chiĝanam**[5] *adan* **uya[d(a)]n(an)**
'I would get dressed, pull on my boots, and we would head to the creek.'

Uyaqad(a)guung chayalix, *aanun chayum ilaan* **qigdalix**
'When I got there, I would hook fish from the trap, pulling up red salmon from the trap';

[asx̂a]adgu **aqad(a)guung** *qamuusim* **daĝan aqad(a)gungin**
'when I would kill all of them, after they were on the string,'

qamulix **chiĝanam** *ilaan* **akaaĝaasalix**
'dragging it from the creek I would pull the fish up.'

<u>Maaman</u>*g,* **aan(un)** *ngaan* **udachx̂ilix aqalid(a)naq(ing)**
'My mother, I would start drying the red salmon for her.'

Lakaayax̂ liidanang **anuxtaasadanax̂ amustukuqing**
'I may have thought I was acting like a boy.'

Ataqasim <u>maaman</u>*g* **chamchugi[iĝan] anqaax̂tukux̂ anqakux̂**
'One day, when my mother went fishing,'

agiitalix anqanaqing inga
'I went with her.'

matalgakun **ukux̂tanang** *matalix*
'I was looking at what was being done to them'

Chamchuxsix alix̂takuqing(ng)aan, qax̂ **duxtang adĝakuĝaan** *ting* **amanilix**
'When I had been fishing for a while, a fish bit my hook and startled me,'

chamch(u)xing qangling *kangan* **ax̂six,** *nung* **idgi[x̂tusa]lix akuun(u)salix**
'putting my fish line on my shoulder, pulling it up to me, I took it up'

[chuguulĝu]n kungin **aĝaas(a)kuq(i)ngaan**
'when I placed it on the gravel/beach,'

<u>maaman</u>*g nung [tunu]k(u)ĝaan* **alanaqing**
'when mother spoke to me I turned around.'

---

[5] this root is probably related to others that are identified as cognate in Bergsland (1994), e.g. chiqa- 'to splash'

qang unugulux̂ txin qaqasaaĝan(ax̂) ax̂takuĝaan, qaqasaaĝan(ax̂) ax̂takuĝaan
'My fish will become food soon, it will become food.'

*gumax̂tanaqing gumax̂tanaqingaan, **taaĝatax** iisalix, qax̂ [asx̂a]six gumanaqing*
'That's what I did, I did it for the first time, I killed the fish, I did that.'

References

Axelrod, Melissa. 1993. *The Semantics of Time: Aspect Categorization in Koyukon Athabaskan.* Studies in the Anthropology of the North American Indians. Lincoln: University of Nebraska.

Berge, Anna. 2004. A preliminary look at Aleut Metaphor. Annual Meeting of the Society for the Study of the Indigenous Languages of America, Boston, MA, January 8–11, 2004.

Berge, Anna. 2009. Tracking topics: A comparison of "topic" in Aleut and Greenlandic discourse. In *Variations in Polysynthesis: The Eskaleut Languages*, edited by Marc-Antoine Mahieu and Nicole Tersis, 185–200. Typological Studies in Language 86. Amsterdam: John Benjamins.

Berge, Anna. 2010a. Unexpected non-anaphoric marking in Aleut. In *Rara & Rarissima: Documenting the Fringes of Linguistic Diversity*, edited by Jan Wohlgemuth and Michael Cysouw, Vol. II, 1–22. Empirical Approaches to Linguistic Typology (EALT) 46. Berlin; New York: Mouton de Gruyter.

Berge, Anna. 2010b. Origins of linguistic diversity in the Aleutian Islands. In *Human Biology* 82(5–6), *Special Issue on the Origins of the Populations of the Aleutian Islands.* edited by M. H. Crawford, Dixie L. West, and Dennis H. O'Rourke, 557–582. Detroit: Wayne State University.

Berge, Anna. 2012. Object reduction in Aleut. *Transitivity and Its Related Phenomena: Asian and African Languages and Linguistics* 7: 5–23.

Berge, Anna. 2016. Polysynthesis in Aleut (Unangam Tunuu). *Linguistic Typology of the North* 3, ed. by Tokusu Kurebito. Tokyo: ILCAA, 1-22.

Bergsland, Knut. 1979. Postwar vicissitudes of the Aleut language. In *Eskimo Languages: Their Present-Day Conditions*, edited by Bjarne Basse and Kirsten Jensen, 21–35. Aarhus: Arkona.

Bergsland, Knut. 1986. Comparative Eskimo-Aleut phonology and lexicon. *Journal de la Société Finno-ougrienne* 80: 63–137.

Bergsland, Knut. 1989. Comparative aspects of Aleut syntax. *Journal de la Société Finno-ougrienne* 82: 7–80.

Bergsland, Knut, compiler. 1994. *Aleut Dictionary: Unangam Tunudgusii.* Fairbanks: Alaska Native Language Center.

Bergsland, Knut. 1997a. *Aleut Grammar.* Fairbanks: Alaska Native Language Center.

Bergsland, Knut. 1997b. How did the Aleut language become different from the Eskimolanguages? In *Languages of the North Pacific Rim*, Vol. 2, edited by Osahito Miyaoka and Minoru Oshima, 1–17. Sakyo-ku: Kyoto University, Graduate School of Letters.

Bergsland, Knut. 1998. *Ancient Aleut Personal Names: Materials from the Billings Expedition 1790–1792.* Fairbanks: Alaska Native Language Center.

Black, Lydia. 1984. *Atka: An Ethnohistory of the Western Aleutians.* Alaska History 24. Kingston, ON: Limestone.

Black, Lydia. 2004. *Russians in America: 1732–1867.* Fairbanks: University of Alaska.

Cook, Eung-Do, and Keren Rice (eds.). 1989. Introduction. In *Athapaskan Linguistics: Current Perspectives on a Language Family*, 1–62. Trends in Linguistics State-of-the-Art Reports 15. Berlin: Mouton de Gruyter.

Crawford, M. H., Dixie L. West, and Dennis H. O'Rourke (eds.). 2010. *Human Biology* 82(5–6), *Special Issue on the Origins of the Populations of the Aleutian Islands*. Detroit: Wayne State University.

Crawford, Michael H., Rohina C. Rubicz, and Mark Zlojutro. 2010. Origins of Aleuts and the genetic structure of populations of the archipelago: Molecular and archaeological perspectives. In *Human Biology* 82(5–6), *Special Issue on the Origins of the Populations of the Aleutian Islands*. edited by M. H. Crawford, Dixie L. West, and Dennis H. O'Rourke, 695–717. Detroit: Wayne State University.

Croft, William. 2003. Mixed languages and acts of identity: An evolutionary approach. In *The Mixed Language Debate: Theoretical and Empirical Advances*, edited by Yaron Matras and Peter Bakker, 41–72. Trends in Linguistics: Studies and Monographs 145. New York: Mouton de Gruyter.

Davis, Richard S., and Richard A. Knecht. 2010. Continuity and change in the Eastern Aleutian archaeological sequence. In *Human Biology* 82(5–6), *Special Issue on the Origins of the Populations of the Aleutian Islands*, edited by M. H. Crawford, Dixie L. West, and Dennis H. O'Rourke, 507–524. Detroit: Wayne State University.

Donald, Leland. 1997. *Aboriginal Slavery on the Northwest Coast of North America*. Berkeley: University of California.

Dumond, Don. 2001. Toward a (yet) newer view of the (pre)history of the Aleutians. In *Archaeology in the Aleut Zone of Alaska, Some Recent Research*, edited by D. E. Dumond, 298–309. University of Oregon Anthropological Papers 58. Eugene: University of Oregon Press.

Fortescue, Michael. 1998. *Language Relations across the Bering Strait: Reappraising the Archaeological and Linguistic Evidence*. London: Cassell.

Fortescue, Michael. 2002. The rise and fall of Eskimo-Aleut polysynthesis. In *Problems of Polysynthesis*, edited by Nicholas Evans and Hans-Jürgen Sasse, 257–276. Berlin: Akademie Verlag.

Fortescue, Michael, Steven Jacobson, and Lawrence Kaplan. 1994. *Comparative Eskimo Dictionary with Aleut Cognates*. Fairbanks: Alaska Native Language Center.

Golovko, Evgeni V., and Nikolai B. Vakhtin. 1990. Aleut in contact: The CIA enigma. *Acta Linguistica Hafniensia* 22: 97–125.

Gray, Patty. 1994. Mednyj Aleut: Language contact in the North Pacific. *Journal of Pidgin and Creole Languages* 9(1): 109–113.

Hatfield, Virginia L. 2010. Material culture across the Aleutian Archipelago. In *Human Biology* 82(5–6), *Special Issue on the Origins of the Populations of the Aleutian Islands*, edited by M. H. Crawford, Dixie L. West, and Dennis H. O'Rourke, 525–556. Detroit: Wayne State University.

Heine, Bernd, and Tania Kuteva. 2005. *Language Contact and Grammatical Change*. Cambridge Approaches to Language Contact. Cambridge: Cambridge University.

IJAL, *International Journal of American Linguistics* (1917–).

Krauss, Michael. 1990. Typology and change in Alaskan languages. In *Language Typology 1987: Systematic Balance in Language, Papers from the Linguistic Typology Symposium, Berkeley, 1–3 December 1987. Current Issues in Linguistic Theory* 67, edited by Winfred P. Lehmann, 147–159. Amsterdam: John Benjamins.

Krauss, Michael. 2010. Eyak grammar draft. http://www.uafanlc.arsc.edu/data/Online/EY961K2009/Eyak_Grammar_Draft.pdf

Krauss, Michael. 2012. Eyak dictionary draft. http://www.uafanlc.arsc.edu/data/Online/EY961K2011/Eyak_Dictionary_2012-05-01.pdf

Lantis, Margaret. 1984. The Aleut social system, 1750–1810, from early historical sources. In *Ethnohistory in Southwestern Alaska and the Southern Yukon: Method and Content*, edited by Margaret Lantis, 131–303. Studies in Anthropology 7. Lexington: University Press of Kentucky.

Leer, Jeff. 1991. Evidence for a Northwest Coast language area: Promiscuous number marking and periphrastic possessive constructions in Haida, Eyak, and Aleut. *IJAL* 57(2): 158–193.

Leer, Jeff. 2000. The negative/irrealis category in Athabaskan-Eyak-Tlingit. In *The Athabaskan Languages: Perspectives on a Native American Language Family*, edited by Theodore B. Fernald and Paul R. Platero, 101–138. Oxford: Oxford University Press.

Liapunova, Roza G. 1996. *Essays on the Ethnography of the Aleuts: At the End of the Eighteenth and the First Half of the Nineteenth Century*, translated by Jerry Shelest, edited by William B. Workman and Lydia T. Black. Fairbanks: University of Alaska.

Marsh, Gordon, and Morris Swadesh. 1951. Kleinschmidt Centennial V: Eskimo Aleut Correspondences. *IJAL* 17(4): 209–216.

Matras, Yaron, and Peter Bakker (eds.). 2003. *The Mixed Language Debate: Theoretical and Empirical Advances*. Trends in Linguistics: Studies and Monographs 145. New York: Mouton de Gruyter.

McDonough, Joyce. 2000. On a bipartite model of the Athabaskan verb. In *The Athabaskan Languages: Perspectives on a Native American Language Family*, edited by T. Fernald and P. Platero, 139–166. Oxford: Oxford University Press.

Reedy-Maschner, Katherine. 2010. Where did all the Aleut men go? Aleut male attrition and related patterns in Aleutian historical demography and social organization. In *Human Biology* 82(5–6), *Special Issue on the Origins of the Populations of the Aleutian Islands*, edited by M. H. Crawford, Dixie L. West, and Dennis H. O'Rourke, 583–612. Detroit: Wayne State University.

Rice, Keren. 2000. *Morpheme Order and Semantic Scope: Word Formation in the Athabaskan Verb*. Cambridge: Cambridge University Press.

Sapir, Edward. 1915. The Na-Dene languages, a preliminary report. *American Anthropologist, N.S.* 17: 534–558.

Thalbitzer, William. 1921. The Aleutian language compared with Greenlandic: A manuscript by Rasmus Rask. *IJAL* 2: 40–57.

Thomason, Sarah Grey, and Terrence Kaufman. 1988. *Language Contact, Creolization, and Genetic Linguistics*. Berkeley: University of California.

Vajda, Edward J. 2011. A Siberian link with Na-Dene languages. In *The Dene-Yeniseian Connection*, edited by James Kari and Ben A. Potter, 33–99. *Anthropological Papers of the University of Alaska New Series* 5(1–2). Fairbanks: UAF Department of Anthropology and ANLC.

Wichmann, Søren, Eric W. Holman, Taraka Rama, and Robert S. Walker. 2011. Correlates of reticulation in linguistic phylogenies. *Language Dynamics and Change* 1: 205–240.

Woodbury, Anthony. 1984. Eskimo and Aleut languages. In *Handbook of North American Indians*, Vol. 5: *Arctic*, edited by David Damas, 49–63. Washington, DC: Smithsonian.

CHAPTER 30

THE LOWER MISSISSIPPI VALLEY AS A LINGUISTIC AREA

DAVID KAUFMAN

30.1 INTRODUCTION

THE Lower Mississippi Valley (LMV) (see Map 30.1) is postulated to be a linguistic area, or sprachbund (Kaufman 2014), 2019a) on par with other such areas around the world like the Balkans (Eastern Europe), South Asia (India), the Pacific Northwest, and the Vaupés region of the Amazon. The LMV displays many of the attributes of a linguistic area, including the convergence of language features. All of the LMV's languages, which are Atakapa, Biloxi, Chitimacha, Choctaw-Chickasaw,[1] Mobilian Trade Language (MTL; also called Mobilian Jargon), Natchez, Ofo, and Tunica, share certain phonetic and phonological, morphosyntactic, and lexical features. Biloxi and Ofo are members of the Siouan language family, Choctaw-Chickasaw is Muskogean, while the other languages (excluding MTL) are unaffiliated, or isolates.

There were other languages in the LMV, such as Koroa, Theloel, Taensa, and Avoyel, that went extinct with no known documentation, and some sprachbund features are shared with Dhegiha Siouan languages, especially Quapaw (Rankin 1988). The MTL, is a pidgin that derives from varieties of the Choctaw-Chickasaw complex, possibly from a Western Muskogean variety that was absorbed by other languages. MTL served as a trade language throughout the Southeast and lower Midwest of the United States, similar to Chinook Jargon in the Pacific Northwest and Delaware, or Unami, Jargon on the East Coast.

---

[1] Since Choctaw and Chickasaw are generally mutually comprehensible, for purposes of this chapter the two languages will be treated as a single unit.

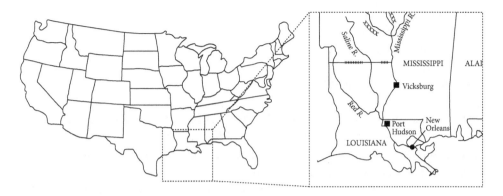

MAP 30.1 Map of the Lower Mississippi Valley.

Typologically, all LMV languages other than MTL are agglutinative, ranging from the mildly agglutinative Siouan languages to the heavily agglutinative Natchez and Tunica. LMV languages other than the pidgin have predominant subject-object-verb (SOV) word order and are postpositional with auxiliaries following the main verb. MTL has been analyzed as having largely object-subject-verb (OsV) word order (Drechsel 1997), which occasionally occurs in other LMV languages, such as Biloxi, perhaps under the influence of the pidgin. Natchez is the only LMV language that has four pitch contours: high, mid, rising, and falling (Kimball 2005: 396). MTL is largely isolating, having little morphosyntax other than a suffixed negative.

In all of the languages except MTL, verbs are the most highly inflected category, while nouns are relatively uninflected. Tunica is unique in the region in having all nouns, regardless of animacy, marked with masculine or feminine gender. Vowel nasality is prominent in Siouan and Western Muskogean. Atakapa and Tunica suffix subject (agentive) pronouns, while object (patientive) pronouns are prefixed. Biloxi and Choctaw-Chickasaw show heavily developed systems of subject reference tracking, while Natchez shows topic tracking. All of the languages show various degrees of discourse or pragmatic marking, such as focus markers. These discourse-centered features are especially important in a discussion of a linguistic area since borrowing of these more deeply embedded features is more difficult and of greater import than borrowing more surface-level features such as phonetic and lexical features. Borrowing of such deeply embedded features likely indicates a greater degree of intimate contact between languages and is thus more highly valued in assessing a sprachbund.

Features that define the LMV as a linguistic area include the following:

1. labiodental /f/ phoneme
2. retroflex /ṣ/ phoneme
3. lateral fricative /ɬ/ phoneme
4. predominant SOV basic word order
5. positional auxiliaries used as continuative aspectual markers
6. quinary number systems

7. evidentiality marking
8. emphatic marking
9. valence-reducing prefixation
10. alternation of /i/ and /u/
11. alternation of /h/ and Ø.

Due to space limitations, only those LMV features ranked highest in Kaufman (2014, 2019a) will be addressed, which are the /f/, /ṣ/, /ɬ/ phonemes, alternation of phonemes /i/ and /u/ and /h/ and Ø (zero-marking), emphatic marking, positional verb auxiliaries, and valence-reducing prefixation.

Certain features are widespread across LMV languages. For example, all LMV languages except Chitimacha and Tunica have nasalized vowels. Nasalized variants of *a*, *i*, and *o* occur in Biloxi and Ofo, as in most other Siouan languages. Nasalized variants of *a*, *e*, *i*, and *o* occur in Atakapa, and nasalized variants of all five vowels occur in Natchez, but only in word-final position and only as the result of phonological changes. Nasalized variants of *a*, *i*, and *o* occur in Choctaw-Chickasaw as well as in MTL. Muskogean and MTL have only a three-vowel system (*a*, *i*, *u*), while other LMV languages have at least a five-vowel system.

In my analysis of the LMV as a linguistic area, the LMV language with the most LMV features is Choctaw-Chickasaw (Kaufman 2014, 2019a). Natchez and Atakapa are next, followed by Biloxi, Tunica, Chitimacha, Ofo, and MTL. The latter, as to be expected, scores low in ranking of morphological features since there are almost no morphological features in the pidgin. Ofo ranks low, not necessarily because it shares fewer morphological features with the rest of the LMV, but more because data are simply indeterminate for several of the features since the language was little documented before it went dormant. The least LMV language in terms of feature ranking is Chitimacha. The reason for Chitimacha containing fewer features than other LMV languages is unclear, but there may be two possible reasons: either (1) Chitimachas were culturally or ideologically more resistant to borrowing, or (2) Chitimachas may have been more recent immigrants to the LMV and thus had less time for the sharing of features.

The fact that Natchez comes in a close second to Choctaw-Chickasaw in morphological ranking may indicate that Natchez and the Muskogean languages are indeed remotely genetically related. Or, since Natchez speakers were part of the Choctaw Confederacy after the French destroyed the Natchez homeland circa 1732, the many common features may be due to more intimate contact in post-European times.

30.2 PHONETIC AND PHONOLOGICAL FEATURES

The presence of four language isolates makes an analysis of phonetic and phonological copying in the LMV difficult, since we cannot determine if ancestral languages of the isolates contained certain features and thus involved internal change. Thus, by necessity, certain possible phonetic and phonological borrowings involving these languages must remain uncertain as there is no longer a means of determining internal (due to diachronic genetic changes within the language family) or external (due to language contact) origin.

The labiofricative /f/ occurs in Muskogean languages and in Ofo. The latter language likely borrowed this phoneme from the former, since this phoneme is not known in other Siouan languages.[2] All LMV languages except Biloxi and Chitimacha have the dental alveolar /l/. The voiceless lateral fricative /ɬ/ occurs in Atakapa, though rare, and in Muskogean languages, including MTL, though variations of this phoneme arose in MTL, usually with /š/ (Drechsel 1996: 282). The fact that the phoneme /ɬ/ is rare in Atakapa may indicate that it was not originally a feature of Atakapa and was likely borrowed, probably through contact with Tonkawa, Muskogean, or both. Devoicing of sonorants occurs in Chitimacha, Natchez, and Tunica. The retroflex phoneme /ʂ/ is a feature of Muskogean languages, and occurs in MTL, Natchez, and Tunica. The alternation of word initial /h/ ~ /Ø/ (zero marking) appears in Atakapa, Biloxi, and MTL, along with the alternation of /i/ and /u/ in Biloxi, Natchez, and Tunica.

Features that are weighted more highly (in Kaufman 2014, 2019) are nasalized vowels, voiceless labiodental fricative /f/, lateral fricative /ɬ/, retroflex sibilant /ʂ/, alternation of /i/ and /u/, alternation of word initial /h/ ~ /Ø/, and vowel harmony, all features that are relatively rare around the LMV periphery and are thus most representative of a an possible LMV sprachbund.

30.3 Morphological Features

As stated earlier, pragmatic features involving discourse-related phenomena are particularly important in a linguistic area since such features are embedded more deeply in a language and are not as easily accessible as phonetic, lexical, and certain other morphological features. I shall here address the closely linked discourse features of focus/topic and assertive marking, followed by valence-reducing prefixation, positional verb auxiliaries, and verb number suppletion.

30.3.1 Focus Markers

I use the term *focus* to refer to newly given information (what Prague school linguists call "rheme") (Payne 1997: 271). LMV focus-marking suffixes can occur on both nouns and verbs. On nouns, focus and topic marking can serve as a type of definiteness marking.

---

[2] There may have been a dialectal feature of Biloxi, however, in which /xw/ was pronounced, at least by some speakers, as /f/, judging by Emma Jackson's pronunciation of *nixuxwe* 'ear' as *nišofi* (Haas 1968).

Atakapa, Biloxi, Chitimacha, Choctaw-Chickasaw, and Natchez have focus-marking suffixation. In Atakapa and Chitimacha, the focus-marking suffix is *-š*, which also acts as a type of definite article:

Atakapa
(1)   *yul-š*
      writing-DEF
      'the letter'
      (Swanton 1932: 12)

(2)   Chitimacha
      ʔasi-š
      man-DEF
      'the man'
      (Hieber 2013, personal communication)

The Biloxi suffix *-di* is often adjoined to nouns in texts, particularly with nouns newly introduced into the narrative or discourse (Kaufman 2011). The suffix *-di* may descend directly from Proto-Siouan *-ri*, a focus marker also found in Hidatsa and Mandan (Boyle 2007, personal communication):

(3)   *Skakana-di*
      Ancient.of.Opposums-FOC
      'The Ancient of Opossums'
      (Dorsey and Swanton 1912: 26)

In Choctaw-Chickasaw, suffixes *-ooš* and *-ook* act as focus markers that can also be considered types of definite articles:

(4)   *hattak-ooš*
      man-FOC
      'the man (focus)'
      (Broadwell 2006: 77)

(5)   *ofi-hook-ano   isht-iya-l-aačį-h*
      dog-FOC-AC2   INST-go-1p-IRR-TNS
      'the dogs I'll take'
      (Broadwell 2006: 81)

Natchez also has a focus marker *o·k*, which could be due either to borrowing or to the possibility that Natchez is genetically distantly related to the Muskogean languages:

(6)   *toMičo·k*
      toM-ič-o·k
      person-ERG-FOC
      'As for the people . . . .'
      (Kimball 2005: 448)

30.3.2 Topic Markers

I use the term *topic* to refer to old, previously mentioned, or known information (what Prague school linguists call "theme") (Payne 1997: 271).

Biloxi *-yą* is a topic marker that also serves as a definite article occurring most frequently when the noun to which it is suffixed has already been introduced into a story, thus marking old or already given information, or *topic*. In the following example, 'child' was previously mentioned in the discourse:

(7) *ątatka-yą   khu-ni   ǫǫni   e-tu   xa.*
     child-TOP   3.give-NEG   PST   3.say-PL   always
     'always she did not give him the (previously mentioned) child'
     (Dorsey and Swanton 1912: 43)

The Choctaw-Chickasaw suffix *-aaš* fulfills the same role as Biloxi *-yą*:

(8) *Hattak-Ø-aaš-at   čaaha-h.*
     man-COP-PREV-NOM   tall-TNS
     'The (previously mentioned) man is tall.'
     (Broadwell 2006: 89)

30.3.3 Assertive Markers

Atakapa, Biloxi, Chitimacha, and Natchez have assertive markers, with which, as with emphatic focus- and topic-marking on nouns, speakers may choose to add particular emphasis to a verb. Atakapa and Biloxi call on their nominal focus suffixes, *-š* and *-di*, respectively, to do double duty as verbal focus, or assertive, markers. The following examples show the Atakapa assertive suffix *-š*:

(9) *šak-yon-š-ul-ăt*
     person-call-ASRT-3subj.PL-PERF
     'they called (him/them)'
     (Swanton 1932: 10)

Atakapa also has an emphatic suffix *-ne*:

(10) *n-yaw-ta   n-ok-ne*
      2s.obj-await-FUT (future)   2s.obj-come-EMPH
      'I will expect you to come!'
      (Swanton 1932: 12)

Chitimacha *ne* appears to correlate with Atakapa *-ne*. The Chitimacha particle *ne* is primarily used as the conjunction 'and' in Chitimacha (Hieber, 2013, personal communication), but it also occurs as an emphatic:

(11)   *susbink   pa·limičuy   ne′   himks   geti   ka·han*
       gun   shoot   even   3s   kill   unable
       'Even if you shot it with a gun, you could not kill it'
       (Swadesh 1939: 129)

The Chitimacha particle carries "emphatic reference 'just, precisely . . . [*sic*]'" (Swadesh 1939: 127).

Like the Atakapa and Chitimacha -*š*, the Biloxi focus marker -*di* attaches not only to nouns but also to verbs. With verbs, -*di* shows more emphasis or immediacy and has been glossed as an 'assertive' marker (Kaufman 2011), as the following example demonstrates:

(12)   *Sǫǫnitǫǫni-k   ǫha   ąyaa   ǫǫni   ustax   kanê-di*
       tar-ACC   with   man   make   stand.up   EVID2-ASRT
       'He made a tar baby [person] and stood it up there.'
       (Dorsey and Swanton 1912: 13)

Chitmacha has similar assertive marking:

(13)   *Kun   čuw-k-š   šeni-nk   hup   hi   ni-čw-iʔi.*
       indef   go-PRT-ASRT   pond-LOC   to   there   water-MOVE.UP-3s
       'Going and going some, he came there to a pond.'
       (Hieber 2012, personal communication)

Natchez has three marked degrees of emphasis: *ya·* 'that,' *ka·* 'this,' and *ma·* 'that there,' the latter appearing to be the least emphatic of the three (Kimball 2005: 422). These are based on the deictics *ya·na*, *ka·na*, and *ma·na* (Kimball 2005: 422). Kimball calls these "exclamatory postverbs" (2004: 422). Each of these is exemplified in the following:

(14)   *ʔeLhalawi.ta.N   tama.L   ʔawiti   kačassitanki   ma.na*
       ʔeLhalawi.ta.N   tama.L   ʔawiti-o   ka-čas-si-tan-ki   ma.na
       split-QT-AUX-MOD *woman* two-ABS PVB-*stand*-QT-DU-AUX- EMPH
       'two identical women stood there'
       (Kimball 2005: 423)

Tunica has an emphatic suffix -*pa(n)*, which, similar to the Chitimacha suffix, can be translated as 'too, also, even' (Haas 1946: 122):

(15)   *ta′-ya-ku-păn,*   *ʔun-ka′li-n*   *ʔun-ke′ni.*
       DEF-deer-MASC-EMPH   3S.MASC-STAND -create-?   3S.MASC-create
       'He created the deer, too.'
       (Haas 1946: 122)

Tunica -*pa* thus correlates with Atakapa -*ne* and Chitimacha *ne*.

All languages have operations that adjust the relationship of semantic roles and grammatical relations in languages, using a range of structures for accomplishing this (Payne 1997: 169). In the LMV, a preverb, or prefix, is used as a type of valence-reducing operation. Atakapa, Biloxi, Chitimacha, Choctaw-Chickasaw, Natchez, and Ofo all have valence-reducing prefixation. All of these languages, except Biloxi and Ofo, use a lexeme meaning 'thing, something' to accomplish such valence reduction. In the Siouan languages, Biloxi and Ofo, a special non-lexical prefix *(w)a-* is used.

30.3.4 Valence-Reducing Prefix for Indefinite Animate Subject or Object

A preverb, or prefix, meaning 'person' or 'people,' is used in Atakapa, Choctaw-Chickasaw, and Natchez as a type of indefinite person or animate subject or object marker.

In Atakapa, the prefix is *šak-*:

(16) *yul-š*   *šak-in*   *ok*
      letter-DEF   INDF.AN-ask   come
      'the letter of invitation'
      (Swanton 1932: 12)

The Choctaw word *oklah* 'people' is sometimes used for plural animate subjects:

(17) *Hitokooš*   *čokfi*   *oklah*   *falaama-tok*
      and:then   rabbit   INDF.PL   meet-PST
      'And then they met a rabbit.'
      (Broadwell 2006: 41)

The Natchez indefinite animate prefix is *tah-*:

(18) *tah-le·le·nal-ʔiš*
      INDF.AN-burn.repeatedly-INF
      'buckmoth caterpillar'
      (Kimball 2005: 434)

30.3.5 Valence-Reducing Prefix for Indefinite Inanimate Object

A different preverb, or prefix, is used for indefinite inanimate subject or object.

In Atakapa, the valence-reducing prefix is *šok-*:

(19) *šok-šil-kit*
      INDF.OBJ-sew-CONT
      'she was sewing (things)'
      (Swanton 1932: 15)

(20) *šok-koy*
      INDF.OBJ-speak
      'chief' ('speaking things')
      (Swanton 1932: 9)

The Chitimacha valence-reducing preverb is *ni:*[3]

(21) *ni   naki   dempi*[3]
      thing   chicken.hawk   killing
      'the story'
      (Hieber 2013: 6)

(22) *ni   katš   hamtši:k*
      thing   fortune   having
      'having (good) luck'
      (Hieber 2013: 10)

The Choctaw valence-reducing prefix is **naa-** or **nąn-**, likely deriving from *nanta* 'what, something, someone.'

(23) *nąn-óffo-ʹ*
      INDF.OBJ-plant-NZR
      'plant'
      (Broadwell 2006: 53)

(24) *naa-hóoyo-ʹ*
      INDF.OBJ (SUBJ)-hunt-NZR
      'hunter' or 'prey'
      (Broadwell 2006: 53)

Choctaw *nan-* or *naa-* can be ambivalent, since the prefix *naa-* can represent either the actor (hunter) or the patient (prey) (Broadwell 2006: 53).

The Natchez valence-reducing prefix is *kin-*:

(25) *nokkinhantawąą*
      nok-kin-han-ta-w-aa-n
      PVB-INDF.OBJ-make-1S-AUX-INC-PHR.TRM
      'I can work.'
      (Kimball 2005: 405)

Siouan languages have a valence-reducing prefix *wa-* (reduced to *a-* in Biloxi and Ofo), whose actual translation is murky, though it often can be translated as 'thing' or 'something' (i.e., an indefinite object prefix):

(26) *a-duska*
      something-bite
      'rat'
      (Dorsey and Swanton 1912: 186)

---

[3] 'To tell a story' is literally 'to kill chicken hawks' (Hieber 2013: 6).

30.3.6 Positional Verb Auxiliaries

Classificatory verbs of the LMV signal position classification of nouns: SIT, STAND, LIE, and sometimes MOVE. Positional verbs have been grammaticized in the Siouan languages as continuative aspect markers and proximal demonstrative determiners (Mithun 1999: 116), and they occur as markers of continuative aspect in most, if not all, of the Siouan languages (Rankin 2004: 203). Atakapa, Biloxi, Choctaw, Ofo, and Tunica all use positionals in a similar manner, indicating possible borrowing between them.

Following are examples of positional auxiliary verb usage in the LMV languages:[4]

(27) Atakapa
kew   kam-š-kin-tu
sit   protrusion-DEF-LOC-sit?
'I am (seated) paddling.'
(Gatschet and Swanton 1932: 61; Watkins 1976: 27)[4]

(28) Biloxi
Nihǫ   ani   dêxtowê   nê.
cup   water   full   STAND
'The cup is full of water.'
(Dorsey and Swanton 1912: 166)

(29) Chitimacha
wetk kas tuYti:k$^?$ pe$^?$anki
we-t-k   kas   tuYti-k$^?$ pe-$^?$e-nk-i
DEM-RFL-LOC   back(PREV)   stoop.down-   PRTP-be(horizontal)-3s-LOC-NZR
'when he had stooped down'
(Swadesh, unpublished notes)

(30) Choctaw-Chickasaw
Bill-at   ma   binįli
SUBJ   there   sit(ANIM)-n
'Bill is over there.'
(Watkins 1976: 21)

(31) Natchez
ya·   potkop   ka$^?$ašup   ka$^?$epe·nakiyaku·š
ya·   potkop   ka$^?$ašup-Ø   ka·$^?$epe··-na-ki-ya-ku·š
that   mountain   blue-ABS   PVB-lie-3P-AUX-ART-ALL
'(where) that blue mountain is (lying)'
(Kimball 2005: 438)

---

[4] Watkins (1976) identified *kamškintu* only as 'paddle.' I analyzed it into its component parts. Atakapa *kam* refers to a fish fin or apparently to any protrusion-like instrument used as a form of guidance.

(32)   Ofo
    b-ašě   *nǫki*
    1-sit   SIT
    'I am sitting down.'
    (Rankin 2002: 20)

(33)   Tunica
    t-uruna-tʔe-ku   *ʔuna*
    DEF-frog-large-MASC.SG   sit
    'There is the bullfrog.'
    (Watkins 1976: 26)

In many languages of the world, the same lexical item can express both actual physical stance and can be used as an auxiliary. In Biloxi, however, physical stance and locative-existential predicates/verbal auxiliaries generally form two different sets of lexemes. The stance verbs used as independent verbs in Biloxi are *toho* ('lie'), *xêhê* ('sit'), *sįhį* ('stand'), and *hine* and *ni* ('move'). Their grammaticized auxiliary counterparts are *mǫki* ('lie'), *nǫki* ('sit'), *nê* ('stand'), and *ǫde* and *hine* ('move'). The form *hine* is used for both singular and plural, while *ǫde* has a suppletive plural form, *yuke*. *ǫde* is used for general movement and running, while *hine* is for walking only. These auxiliary verbs SIT, STAND, LIE, and MOVE form a discrete set of auxiliary verbs that often no longer specify actual physical position or movement but, rather, are used to express nuanced aspectual meanings (Kaufman 2012). *Mǫki*, *nǫki*, and *nê* are used for both animates and inanimates, while *ǫde* and *hine* are confined to use only with animates. *Mǫki*, *nǫki*, and *nê* share a common plural form *(h)amǫki*, apparently a form of *mǫki*, 'lie.' The origin of these positionals is uncertain, but it appears that *mǫki* may be related to the word *(a)mǫ*, 'land' or 'earth,' and *ǫde* seems to incorporate the word for 'go' (*ǫ* ? + *de* [perhaps *dêê*] 'go') (Kaufman 2012).

The Chitimacha positional verbs are *hi(h)* 'neutral,' *ci(h)* 'standing,' and *pe(h)* 'lying.' What is unique about the Chitimacha positional system is that the connotation of a positional is more important than the denotation (Watkins 1976: 28). The horizontal positional *pe* connotes disrespect while *ci* connotes respect (Watkins 1976: 28).

In Tunica, nouns are also classified into three positions: standing (*kaʔtʔura* < *kaʔli* 'to stand' + *ʔura* 'lies' [lit. stand-lie]), sitting (*ʔuʹna*), and lying (*ʔuʹra*) (Haas 1946: 111). "Although the choice of auxiliary is in certain cases apparently arbitrary, it is found to depend in large part on a combination of the features of gender and position" (Haas 1946: 112). Human or non-human animate nouns can take any of these positions as their characteristic form of embodiment allows:

(34)   *t-oʹnĭ-ku,*   *ʔurá*
    DEF-man-MASC.SG   LIE
    'There is the man (in a lying position).'
    (Haas 1946: 110)

(35) *ta'-să-ku,*   ^ʔ*uná*
DEF-dog-MASC.SG   sit
'There is the dog (in a sitting position).'
(Haas 1946: 110)

Certain non-human elongated animates, as fish, snakes, and alligators, are always classified in the horizontal position:

(36) *ta'-nară-ku,*   ^ʔ*urá*
DEF-snake-MASC.SG   lie
'There is the (lying) snake.'
(Haas 1946: 110)

Certain other non-human animates, as frogs, birds, and insects, are always classified in sitting position:

(37) *t-e'hkuna-ku,*   ^ʔ*uná*
DEF-mosquito-MASC.SG   sit
'There is the (sitting) mosquito.'
(Haas 1946: 110)

Inanimate nouns that have a characteristic erect position use the 'standing' classifier:

(38) *ta'-hkă-ku,*   *ka'l^ʔurá*
DEF-corn.plant-MASC.SG   STAND.LIE
'There is the (standing) corn plant.'
(Haas 1946: 111)

Atakapa appears to have a correlation to the interesting Tunica STAND.LIE positional form, which may be due to contact:

(39) *yil   lat   himatol   u   ta-tixi   ăn   ta-ăt   ha   išat*
day three four   or STAND.LIE and stand-PERF his head
pam-lik-š   mon
beat-mash-ASRT   all
'For three or four days he lie there with his head all beaten and mashed in.'
(Gatschet and Swanton 1932: 10)

Tunica abstract nouns are classified as supine, or 'lying':

(40) *hi'nahkŭn,   la'hon   sa'hkŭn,   ^ʔará,   ha'tikàn*
now   morning   one   LIE   again
'Now there is one morning (left for you to do it) again.' ('Now one morning lies again.')
(Haas 1946: 111)

30.3.7 Verb Number Suppletion

The definition of suppletion includes cases that satisfy either of the following criteria: (1) exceptions to very productive derivational patterns, and (2) exceptions to established agreement patterns (Veselinova 2013). The verbal suppletion treated here relates to nominal arguments of the verb, and the verb agrees with its arguments. All languages of the LMV, except MTL and Natchez, have verbal number suppletion in relation to nominal arguments. This feature is further limited in the region by being primarily used in relation to the positional auxiliaries STAND, SIT, LIE, and MOVE. In Tunica, only these auxiliary verbs show suppletion, while other verbs in the language do not (Haas 1946: 40).

The Atakapa singular positional verb forms and their suppletive plural equivalents are as follows (Swanton 1932):

	singular	plural
STAND	*to* or *ta*	*tsot*
SIT	*kew*	*nul*
LIE	*tixt*	*yoxt*

The Biloxi forms are the following (Dorsey and Swanton 1912):

	singular	plural
STAND	*nê*	
SIT	*nąki*	*(h)amąki*
LIE	*mąki*	
MOVING	*ąde*	*yuke*

In Chitimacha, the conjugations of auxiliary (positional) verbs "are complicated and irregular, so that the simplest account is a list of the forms" (Swadesh 1939: 32). These forms are the following:

	singular	plural
STAND	*ci(h)*	
SIT	*hi(h)*	*na(h)*
LIE	*pe(h)*	

Chitimacha, like Biloxi, neutralizes the singular auxiliary forms to a single plural form, *na(h)*.

The Choctaw-Chickasaw forms include a dual as well as plural form and animate and inanimate forms of SIT:

	singular	dual	plural
STAND	*hikiya*	*hiili*	*(hi)yoh-*
SIT (anim.)	*binili*	*chiiya*	*binoh-*
SIT (inanim.)	*talaya*	*taloha*	*taloh-*
LIE	*ittola*	*kaha*	*kah-*

Perhaps telling as a case of contact, in Tunica suppletion is "a process not used by any other word-class of the language" other than positional auxiliaries (Haas 1946: 40). Tunica positional auxiliary forms are as follows:

	singular	dual	plural
STAND	*kali*	?	?
SIT	*ʔuna*	*ʔunana*	*ʔukʔɛra*
LIE	*ʔura*	*ʔurana*	*naʔara*

No such suppletion is evident in MTL. Verb number suppletion does not occur in Natchez, and, unfortunately, we have insufficient data to make any determination about verb number suppletion in Ofo.

30.4 LEXICAL FEATURES

Like other linguistic areas, and despite prior assertions to the contrary (e.g., Ballard 1985), the LMV shares a sizable number of lexical borrowings. Such lexical borrowing ranges from between only two languages, such as between Atakapa and Chitimacha, to several. The most lexical borrowings in the LMV occur in the semantic realms of zoology, then anatomy, or body parts, then agricultural and food terms.

The concept of basic vocabulary is important to the analysis of lexical borrowings in the LMV. Several lists have been created to reflect basic concepts that are considered to be universal and culturally independent, such as basic kinship (e.g., mother, father) and general animal terms (e.g., fish, bird), and basic verbs (e.g., make, go). The stability of the resulting list of "universal" vocabulary has been brought into question, however, and multiple lists of basic vocabulary have been published. The first was the Swadesh 100 basic word list, which was assembled by the linguist Morris Swadesh (1971). A newer list, the Leipzig-Jakarta (L-J) 100 basic word list (2009), is based on systematic empirical data from forty different languages, but such newer lists are not yet as widely known and used as the Swadesh list. Some sixty-two items overlap between the L-J and Swadesh lists (Tadmor et al. 2010: 242). However, "the major advantage of the Leipzig-Jakarta list is that it has a strong empirical foundation and is thus a more reliable tool for scientific purposes" (Tadmor et al. 2010: 242). For this reason, I have chosen the L-J list as the one most appropriate for this analysis (Table 30.1).

Atakapa, Chitimacha, and Biloxi have the largest number of apparently borrowed basic vocabulary items, followed by Tunica and Natchez. Ofo and Choctaw-Chickasaw rank the lowest in shared borrowed basic vocabulary items (Kaufman 2014, 2019).

Atakapa and Biloxi have sixteen lexical items copied between them (Kaufman 2014). Biloxi and Choctaw, however, share only six items (Kaufman 2014). Biloxis were found living in close proximity to Choctaws in 1699. Since the number of borrowed

Table 30.1 Some Leipzig–Jakarta List Items in Lower Mississippi Valley Languages

	Atakapa	Biloxi	Chitimacha	Choctaw-Chickasaw	MTL	Natchez	Ofo	Tunica
bird	šokšoš					šokoL		
blow	pun	po	puuh			puuh-hooiš		
breast	nik		mi					nič
cord		iką						yunka
cry		wahe						waha
earth	ne		ney					
fish				nani	nane			nini
hand	woš		waši					
hear	nak	naxe						
house	aŋ		hana					
knee	timak	cinąki						cina(hki)
laugh	hayu	xahaye						
mouth		ihi	i			ihi		
water	kaukau		ku			kų		
wind	howi	xux(w)e						huri
wood			šuš			šuu		

lexical terms is greater between Biloxi and Atakapa than between Biloxi and Choctaw, this would seem to indicate that Biloxis were in much closer contact with Atakapans and for perhaps a longer period of time than they were with Choctaws. This may indicate a fairly recent migration of Biloxis from perhaps a location west of the Mississippi River, thus placing them closer to Atakapas. Borrowing between Biloxi and Chitimacha, Choctaw, and Natchez was fairly equal, indicating little if any status differentiation between these groups. The much lesser rate of borrowing between Biloxi and Chitimacha than between Biloxi and Atakapa (six with Chitimacha, sixteen with Atakapa), would indicate a more intimate and frequent rate of contact between Biloxis and Atakapans. The relatively high number of borrowings between Chitimacha and Natchez (9) indicates a particularly high level of contact between these two groups.

Atakapa, Chitimacha, and Biloxi show the largest number of shared *basic* vocabulary followed by Tunica and Natchez. Ofo and Choctaw-Chickasaw rank the lowest in shared basic vocabulary. In addition, Atakapa and Chitimacha share basic words with languages on the periphery of the LMV: Comecrudo, Cotoname, Karankawa, and Tonkawa, possibly showing participation in another linguistic area along the Gulf Coast between the Atchafalaya River basin and the Rio Grande Valley.

Terms for bison/buffalo, bullfrog, cut, goose, metal, robin, split, town, turn, water, and woodpecker are well diffused in the LMV and, in some cases, into its periphery. The widespread copying of these terms across several languages of different genetic stocks may indicate that these items were particularly culturally relevant, perhaps in such intergroup activities as trade, hunting, sports competition, and feasting (see Table 30.2).

Table 30.2 Some Shared Lexical Features of Lower Mississippi Valley Languages

	Atakapa	Biloxi	Chitimacha	Choctaw-Chickasaw	MTL	Natchez	Ofo	Tunica
bison/buffalo		yinisa yanasa		yanaš	yanaš	yanašah	naf	yaniši
bullfrog	anenuy	koninuhi			hanono	hananai		uruna
cut	kets/ kuts	kutsi				keš		kušu
deer		(i)thaa				šaa		
goose				shilaklak		laalak		lalahki
metal		maasa maasi		malha 'tin pan'		nahlkw		
robin		sį kuki		biškoko	beškoko	miškokw		wiškohku
split	čal	ča	čap	ču'alli	čolate			čal
town		tą		tamaha	tamaha			
turn	miš	mixi	tamix					maxsi
water	kakaw		ku			kų		
woodpecker		pakpakhayi		bakbak		pukpuku		pahpahkana

The term for 'bison/buffalo' is particularly widespread in its diffusion, ranging from Caddoan in the western Plains to Catawba near the eastern seaboard. (The Ofo term *naf* 'cow' is likely also derived from this widespread bison term, minus the first and last syllables.) While the source of the borrowing is unknown, Taylor (1976: 166) suggested the possibility of its origin in an Athapascan language. However, I now doubt this origin and believe it most likely originated to the east, perhaps in the Cumberland Plateau region among speakers of Ohio Valley Siouan languages and Catawba, where several variants of the word exist. This, perhaps dialectal, variation implies a more likely point of origin.

Atakapa, Biloxi, Choctaw-Chickasaw, MTL, and Natchez have similar terms for 'bullfrog.' Other borrowed terms for animals include a broadly diffused word for 'goose,' which appears not only in the Southeast but also throughout the Southwest and West. Western and Eastern Muskogean languages, including MTL (Kaufman 2017), as well as Natchez and Tunica, share the similar 'goose' term. The term also occurs to the west in Karankawa and all the way into California, including Mutsun (Costanoan) *lalak*, Nisenan (Maiduan) *la·lak'*, Pomoan *lala*, Luiseño (Uto-Aztecan) *la?la*, and Southern Sierra Miwok (Miwokan) *laŋlaŋ* (Haas 1969: 82). This may support the idea of a Proto-Tunica migration from much farther west into the LMV, whence the term may have been borrowed into other LMV and Southeastern languages. Similar terms for 'robin' and 'woodpecker'[5] occur in the LMV in Biloxi, Choctaw-Chickasaw,

---

[5] While certain of the preceding terms, such as goose and woodpecker, may be due to onomatopoeia, or words mimicking the sounds of nature, "some resemblances are remarkably precise even if one allows for onomatopoeia" (Haas 1969: 82), and such resemblances warrant further exploration.

MTL, Natchez, and Tunica, extending into Eastern Muskogean languages. A similar term for 'deer' appears to have been borrowed in the LMV into the Plains. Such a borrowing may be related to the fact that deer were the most hunted animal in the LMV and the broader Southeast (Hudson 1976) as well as with the trade in deer hides.

A similar term for 'town' occurs in Western, but not Eastern, Muskogean and is widespread across Siouan languages. It is possible that the term was borrowed between the two families, though the direction of borrowing is uncertain. A similar term for 'turn' occurs in Atakapa, Biloxi, Chitimacha, and Tunica, and a similar term for 'water' occurs in Atakapa, Chitimacha, and Natchez, extending west into Caddoan, Karankawa, Tonkawa, and into Rio Grande Valley Coahuiltecan.

Certain semantic borrowings, or calques, are also evident in the LMV, such as 'sweet salt' for sugar (Atakapa, Biloxi, Choctaw-Chickasaw, MTL, Natchez), 'house mouth' for door (Atakapa, Chitimacha, Natchez), and 'sacred snake' or 'chief snake' for rattlesnake (Biloxi, Choctaw-Chickasaw, MTL). The latter two also extend into certain Mayan languages (Yukatek in the case of the last).

30.5 ATAKAPA TEXT

The following is a glossed version of an Atakapa text appearing in Gatschet and Swanton (1932: 17), exemplifying the use of certain LMV features here discussed. The text has been updated and revised to reflect current orthographical conventions as introduced in Kaufman (2019b).

Treatment of the Sick

1. ša   šok-heš   hiwew   ka-ul-ăn   takapo   išak
   someone   STG-pain   very   do-3s.PL-SUB   Atakapa   person
   Somebody   sick   very   when became   Atakapa   people

2. hat-wiw-ăt   ša-ik   šok-tey   hatseš miš-ul-ăt   iti   tanuk
   RFL-believe-PERF person-COM   STG-vine bad   give-3s.PL-PERF night   one
   believed   somebody   medicine bad   gave   night   one

3. ok-(k)in-ul-ul-ăt   ha   aŋ-kin   ina-ul-ăt
   come-LOC-3s.PL-3s.PL-PERF   his   house-LOC   enter-3s.PL-PERF
   they gathered   his   house-in   entered it

   šok-a(k)-ul-ăt   iti   maŋ
   STG-dance-3s.PL-PERF   night   long
   danced   night   long

4. maŋ šing-š-ne   šong-hia   ya   nak-š-ul-ăt   iŋš-waŋ-kin
   long rattle-DEF-NZR   rattle-?   and sound-ASRT-3s.PL-PERF   mourn-go-LOC
   long gourd-rattle   they rattled and played fiddle   they mourned
   yok
   sing
   singing

5. ya   yukiti ipšok   hal-kin   mok waŋ-kit   ok   hu ya
   and   Indian doctor behind-LOC   here go-CONT   come see and
   and   Indian conjurer afterwards   here was walking came saw and

6. pene-ăt   ya   yik-š-ăt   tanew   šak-inaw-š
   cure-PERF   and   pay-ASRT-PERF   other   PL-let.in-ASRT
   cured   and   he paid him   others to let in
   ko-ha-š-ul-ăt
   want-NEG-ASRT-3s.PL-PERF
   they would not

7. ikunyuts-ip inaw   šak-naw-š-ul   ha   išak   šok-heš   kaw-kin
   young-LOC   enter   PL-let-ASRT-3s.PL   NEG   person STG-pain   death-LOC
   young people go into they let in   not   of sick people after death

8. wiw-ul-ăt   šok   hatseš hiwew ka-ăt
   believe-3s.PL-PERF   thing   bad   very   do-PERF
   they believed   things wicked very had done

Translation:

When someone became very sick the Atakapa believed that he had been given bad medicine. One night they assembled at his house, entered it, and danced religious dances all night, shaking gourd rattles and playing fiddles. While they went along mourning they sang and afterward an Indian doctor [conjurer] came to see him and treated him and was paid for it. They would not let others go in. They would not let young people go in. If a sick person died, they believed that something wicked had caused it.

In the preceding Atakapa text, several examples of LMV features are evident. In lines 1–3 and 7, the prefix šok- 'thing, something' is evident in the examples šokheš 'sick' (literally 'thing-pain') and šok-tey 'medicine' (literally 'thing-vine'). The word šoka(k) is a bit less obvious, literally meaning 'thing-green,' but Swanton posited the idea that it may be related to the Green Corn Ceremony that was common in the LMV and Southeast when ritualistic and ceremonial dancing took place (1932: 23). In line 4, we see the -š nominal emphatic in siŋšne 'gourd rattle', in which -š- serves a type of definite article for siŋ 'gourd rattle' and -ne is a nominalizer for a thing or person that does something, similar to English -er, literally coming out as 'the rattle maker.' In lines 4 and 6–7 we see the -š- assertive marker with verbs. Also in lines 6–7 the prefix šak-, used for indefinite animate subjects or objects appears, refers to 'letting them in'—them in this case referring to other people who came to visit. (Note that the prefix šak- is based on the word išak 'person.')

REFERENCES

Ballard, W. L. 1985. sa/ša/la: Southeastern Shibboleth? *International Journal of American Linguistics* 51: 339–341.

Broadwell, George Aaron. 2006. *A Choctaw Reference Grammar*. Lincoln: University of Nebraska Press.

Dorsey, James, and John Swanton. 1912. *A Dictionary of the Biloxi and Ofo Languages.* Bureau of American Ethnology, Bulletin 47. Washington, DC: Government Printing Office.

Drechsel, Emanuel. 1996. An integrated vocabulary of Mobilian Jargon, a Native American Pidgin of the Mississippi Valley. *Anthropological Linguistics* 38: 248–354.

Gatschet, Albert, and John Swanton. 1932. *A Dictionary of the Atakapa Language: Accompanied by Text Material.* Washington, DC: Government Printing Office.

Haas, Mary. 1940. *Tunica.* Locust Valley: J. J. Augustin.

Haas, Mary. 1968. The last words of Biloxi. *International Journal of American Linguistics* 34: 77–84.

Haas, Mary. 1969. Swanton and the Biloxi and Ofo dictionaries. *International Journal of American Linguistics* 35(4): 286–290.

Hudson, Charles. 1976. *The Southeastern Indians.* Knoxville: University of Tennessee Press.

Kaufman, David. 2011. Biloxi realis and irrealis particles. *Kansas Working Papers in Linguistics* 32: 1–7.

Kaufman, David. 2013. Positional auxiliaries in Biloxi. *International Journal of American Linguistics* 79: 283–299.

Kaufman, David. 2014. *The Lower Mississippi Valley as a Language Area.* PhD dissertation. University of Kansas.

Kaufman, David. 2017. Mobilian Trade Language phrasebook and lexicon. Chicago: Exploration Press.

Kaufman, David. 2019a. Clues to Lower Mississippi Valley histories: language, archaeology, ethnography. Lincoln: University of Nebraska Press.

Kaufman, David. 2019b (forthcoming). Atakapa Išakkoy dictionary. Chicago: Exploration Press.

Kimball, Geoffrey. 2005. Natchez. In *Native Languages of the Southeastern United States*, edited by Heather K. Hardy and Janine Scancarelli, 385–453. Lincoln: University of Nebraska Press.

Payne, Thomas. 1997. *Describing Morphosyntax: A Guide for Field Linguists.* Cambridge: Cambridge University Press.

Rankin, Robert. 1988. Quapaw: Genetic and areal affiliations. In Honor of Mary Haas. *From the Haas Festival Conference on Native American Linguistics*, edited by William Shipley, 629–650. Berlin: Mouton de Gruyter

Rankin, Robert. 2002. *An Ofo Grammar Sketch and John R. Swanton's Ofo-English Dictionary.* Unpublished manuscript.

Swadesh, Morris. 1939. *Chitimacha Grammar, Texts, and Vocabulary.* Unpublished. In Franz Boas Collection of Materials for American Linguistics, Mss. 497.3. B63c. G6. 5. American Philosophical Society, Philadelphia, Pennsylvania.

Tadmor, Uri, Martin Haspelmath, and Bradley Taylor. 2010. Borrowability and the notion of basic vocabulary. *Diachronica* 27: 226–246.

Taylor, Allan R. 1976. Words for buffalo. *International Journal of American Linguistics* 42: 165–166.

Veselinova, Ljuba. 2013. Verbal number and suppletion. In *The World Atlas of Language Structures Online*, edited by Bernard Comrie, David Gil, Matthew Dryer, and Martin Haspelmath. Leipzig: Max Planck Institute for Evolutionary Anthropology. http://wals.info/chapter/80 (accessed on July 23, 2014).

Watkins, Laurel. 1976. Position in grammar: Sit, stand, lie. *Kansas Working Papers in Linguistics* 1: 16–41.

CHAPTER 31

LANGUAGE CONTACT CONSIDERING SIGNED LANGUAGE

DAVID QUINTO-POZOS
AND ROBERT ADAM

31.1 INTRODUCTION

DEAF communities around the world are fertile environments for the study of language contact, and this is most commonly true because signed languages exist within communities of spoken language users.[1] Whether or not Deaf people also use spoken language for communication, they typically have literacy skills in the written language of the ambient community, largely due to educational systems and the teaching of written/spoken language to deaf children. In short, Deaf people tend to be multilingual.

For example, signers of American Sign Language (ASL) or Australian Sign Language (Auslan) will generally also use English—in written and/or spoken form. This multilingualism means that aspects of the spoken and/or written languages of the larger communities are in everyday contact with the signed languages.[2] In some cases, this *bimodal contact* (i.e., contact of languages across signed, spoken, or written channels) has resulted in spoken or written language structures that have become incorporated into the signed languages— having been modified over time to conform to the linguistic processes of signed languages.

---

[1] We use the convention "Deaf" to refer to signed language users who are also part of a cultural minority. The non-capitalized "deaf" is used to refer to audiological status or in cases where linguistic and cultural status is not being highlighted.

[2] Following Wilcox and Wilcox (1997), we use the term "sign language" to refer to specific languages (e.g., Mexican Sign Language) and "signed language(s)" to refer more generally to visual-gestural language(s).

In addition, not only does contact take place between a spoken language and a signed language, it sometimes occurs between two signed languages, which can be described as *unimodal contact*, much like contact between two spoken languages. Contact between two signed languages occurs in countries where there exist more than one signed language community (e.g., Canada: *Langue de Signes Québécoise* and American Sign Language; or Thailand: Thai Sign Language and Ban Khor Sign Language; Nonaka 2004) or in transnational border areas where two national signed languages coexist (e.g., ASL and Mexican Sign Language [LSM] along the U.S.–Mexico border). Even in cases where unimodal contact occurs between two signed languages, bimodal or multimodal contact phenomena surface as well. Language contact thus plays a very important role in the creation and evolution of signed languages.

One additional and very important point is that signed languages are generally quite young—with slightly over 200 years of history for the oldest signed languages that we are aware of. This fact likely has an impact on the types of language-contact phenomena that appear in signed languages, though we set this discussion aside for the remainder of this work.

31.2 Language Modality and Language Contact

This chapter provides an overview of various commonly discussed language contact phenomena that characterize signing communities, and it also contains specific examples of evidence of contact in everyday language use.[3] For additional details and discussions, see Quinto-Pozos (2007), Quinto-Pozos and Adam (2012, 2013). The organization of the chapter highlights frequent outcomes of attested language contact between languages and across modalities by categorizing, to the extent that it is possible, contact that arises from the modalities of sign, speech, and writing. The categorizations we propose are intended to serve as a guide, rather than being mutually exclusive groupings. As such, one type of contact may apply to more than one category.

31.2.1 Sign-Speech Contact

Much research in the past has focused on sign-speech contact. In particular, many early works from Ceil Lucas and Clayton Valli (e.g., Lucas and Valli 1989, 1992) described, in detail, contact phenomena between ASL and English.

---

[3] Also see Quinto-Pozos (2007) and Adam (2012) for detailed accounts of linguistic loci for signed language contact.

31.2.1.1 *Influence from Spoken Language Grammar on the Signed Language*

In some cases, signed languages seem to take on characteristics of spoken language grammars. In the 1970s, some researchers argued for the existence of diglossia in the signed modality (Stokoe 1970; Woodward 1973), even though some (e.g., Tervoort 1973) countered that such an analysis is not appropriate since the signed and the spoken language are two different languages, as opposed to High and Low varieties of a single language.

In the case of ASL, a pidgin analysis was adopted by researchers (e.g., Woodward 1973) and many laypeople, which resulted in common use of the term Pidgin Signed English, or PSE. That label was used for years, even though the initial analysis was not without debate. In that early account, Woodward (1973: 40) suggested that PSE is characterized by "reduction and mixture of grammatical structures of both languages as well as some new structures that are common to neither of the languages." Among the structures referred to by Woodward were articles, plural markers, and the copula—none of which is common to both English and ASL.

However, over the years various authors have pointed out that, in several ways, PSE does not seem to resemble spoken-language pidgins. Fischer (1986) pointed out that the alleged pidgin, PSE, is the opposite of what is typically found in spoken-language pidgins since its vocabulary comes from the substrate (ASL), whereas its grammar comes from the superstrate (English). Additionally, Cokely (1983) argued in favor of an analysis that considered interactions between deaf and hearing signers as instances of *foreigner talk*, judgments of proficiency, and ASL learners' attempts to master the target language, rather than the creation of a pidgin.

At the time at which there was greatest interest in diglossia in signed languages, Tervoort (1973: 378) argued that for diglossia to be present, the High and Low forms had to be varieties of the same language. Since ASL and English were two different languages in a contact situation, the result was a form of bilingualism. Therefore if diglossia existed, it was not between signed language and English, but between signed language and a form of a manually coded English (MCE).

Later work suggested that a different analysis should characterize contact between English and ASL. In particular, Lucas and Valli (1992) proposed that the term *contact signing* was a more appropriate label for varieties of signed language that combine features of ASL and English and exhibit significant individual variation in terms of the occurrence of features. They also pointed out that, despite the individual variation, some linguistic features from ASL and English seldom occur in contact signing, such as ASL non-manual syntactic markers that occur with topicalization and various bound morphemes from English (e.g., plural -*s*, third-person singular -*s*, possessive *'s*, past tense -*ed*, or comparative -*er*).

31.2.1.2 *Influence from Spoken Words on the Signed Language: Mouthings*

Another characteristic of contact between a signed and a spoken language is the signer's voiceless articulation of spoken words while producing signs. In such cases, the signer articulates aspects of the *visual* signal that is perceived when looking at the mouth of the spoken language user.[4] Sometimes the visual signal seems to capture aspects of the entire spoken word, whereas other times there are only parts of that word visible (e.g., the onset of the word or certain syllables with other part of the spoken word not represented in the visual signal). Mouthings tend to occur most often when signers are manually articulating nouns, open-class items, and morphologically simpler signs (see Crasborn et al. 2008). These mouthings differ from *mouth gestures*, which are often used for adjectival or adverbial functions, are indigenous to a signed language, and do not usually reflect contact with a spoken language.

Several authors have described mouthings using data from various signed and spoken languages (ASL/English: Davis 1989; Swiss German Sign Language/German: Boyes Braem 2001; New Zealand Sign Language [NZSL] and Maori-influenced English: McKee et al. 2007; Chinese Sign Language/Chinese: Yang 2008; ASL/Spanish and Mexican Sign Language [LSM]/English: Quinto-Pozos, 2002, 2008; see Ann 2001 for other examples). For some authors, this type of contact reflects instances of borrowing, and the mouthings are often viewed as integrated into the morphosyntactic structures of signed languages (see Crasborn et al. 2008 for references); whereas another point of view is that the mouthings, while still coming about because of language contact, are examples of code-mixing and are not integrated into the linguistic structure of the signed language (e.g., see Ebbinghaus and Hessmann 2001; Hohenberger and Happ 2001).

31.2.1.3 *Vocabulary Creation through Contact*

Some vocabulary items in signed languages appear to be borrowed from spoken and written language words. Johnston and Schembri (2007) note that, in Auslan, compounds such as SPORT+CAR are created through contact with English. In some cases, the English-influenced compound coexists with a sign that is indigenous to the signed language, such as the loan translation BREAK DOWN and the native sign BREAK-DOWN, the latter of which was not borrowed from English. Generally, the semantics of the spoken language are used in the borrowed form. Brentari and Padden (2001) discuss similar examples in ASL, such as DEAD+LINE and BABY+SIT. Some compounds contain fingerspelled components such as SUGAR+F-R-E-E. In all of these cases, lexical items from the ambient spoken language have influenced the signs (and sign-fingerspelling combinations) that are used in the sign language.

31.2.1.4 *The Unique Mixing of Languages across Modalities: Code-Blending*

Various studies have reported on the use of features of a spoken and a signed language simultaneously. In most cases, the studies of this phenomenon have focused on the

---

[4] In many cases, deaf and hard-of-hearing people, like those with typical hearing, are also users of spoken language. This likely depends on various factors, such as the level of hearing that a deaf or hard-of-hearing person possesses, as well as whether or not he or she has participated in and benefited from speech-language therapy services.

language use of hearing individuals who are fluent in a signed and a spoken language, but the phenomenon could also appear in the language use of deaf individuals who choose to use speech in addition to sign—such as with their hearing children. The language users are often referred to as *bimodal bilinguals*[5] (Emmorey, Borinstein, and Thompson 2005; Bishop and Hicks 2008; Emmorey, Borinstein, Thompson, and Gollan 2008), and the language mixing has been termed *code-blending* because of the simultaneous expression of features of both languages. Various works have also considered children's code-blends (e.g., Dutch and Sign Language of the Netherlands [NGT]: van den Bogaerde and Baker 2005; Baker and van den Bogaerde 2008; Baker and van den Bogaerde 2014; English and ASL: Chen Pichler et al., 2014).

An example of ASL-English code-blending in childhood, taken from Chen Pichler et al. (2014), is shown in (1). In that example, the signs and English words are produced simultaneously, and the child demonstrates OV word order in the simultaneously produced English (note: (S)OV is common in ASL, though the basic word order is SVO). In the passage, "IX" represents a point to a location in space intended to serve as a third person reference.

(1)   Ben (age 2 years, 1 month)
       Eng: chocolate eat
       ASL: HOT CHOCOLATE IX EAT
       'He's eating hot chocolate.'

The word order of the signs/words in (1) follow ASL word order conventions.

31.2.2 Sign-Writing Contact

Signed languages contain many examples of contact with the written words of ambient spoken languages. Many people consider the contact to result in "borrowing," though the borrowing is characteristically different from spoken language borrowing. In particular, the proposed contact reflects influence from the orthography of spoken languages—the actual letters of the spoken language words.

31.2.2.1 *Fingerspelling*

Manual systems for representing entire words of written language are commonly known as *fingerspelling*, and it is the case that many (if not most) signed languages possess fingerspelling systems. Some of the systems are articulated with one hand (e.g., French Sign Language and Mexican Sign Language), and others require the use of two

[5] Although not generally the practice, the term *bimodal bilingual* could, in theory, also be used to refer to Deaf ASL signers who often engage in reading and writing English. However, many Deaf people use signed, written, and spoken language for communication, which would suggest that the term *multimodal* may also be appropriate.

hands for production (e.g., British Sign Language and Czech Sign Language; see Sutton-Spence 2003). In these systems, certain handshapes and movements (and locations, for two-handed fingerspelling) represent letters of the written alphabet.

Various researchers have highlighted ways in which fingerspelling can adapt to the natural processes of a signed language. Battison (1978) demonstrated that some fingerspelled words become lexicalized over time. For example, the fingerspelled letters B-A-N-K were the source material for a sign that developed in ASL (often transcribed as #BANK) with the same meaning and only some features of the original fingerspelled item. Only the handshapes that represent the first and last letters of the word are fully visible in the lexicalized form, and a downward movement of the hand, which hinges at the wrist joint, accompanies a transition from the B-handshape to the K-handshape that contains other hand-internal movement that depicts only some of the other letters of the fully fingerspelled word (-A-N-).

Similar types of lexicalization processes can occur in signed languages that utilize a two-handed system, such as British Sign Language (BSL). As with one-handed systems, BSL fingerspelling can demonstrate processes of nativization (Kyle and Woll 1985; Sutton-Spence 1994, 1998; Cormier et al. 2008) where a fingerspelled event is considered a lexical sign.

Fingerspelling has also been considered within a model that divides elements of signed languages into native and non-native items (Padden 1998; Brentari and Padden 2001). In that analysis, fingerspelling is viewed as a non-native subset of the lexicon, a part that is "borrowed" from English through contact, though the non-native items can undergo processes that allow them to appear more ASL-like (i.e., native-like), a suggestion that was also made years ago (Battison 1978). In some cases, the fingerspelled items can form compounds with ASL signs—as was mentioned earlier.

31.2.2.2 *Initialized Signs and Abbreviations as Examples of Borrowing*

Whereas fingerspelling is characteristically sequential (i.e., the letters of written words are depicted in a particular order, one after another), initialized signs are just like other signs of signed languages—with simultaneity being one of the primary forces driving linguistic structure.

In signed languages with one-handed fingerspelling systems, initialized signs are those whose handshape(s) correspond to the manual representations of letters of the written alphabet (see Padden 1998 for a discussion of such signs and various examples from ASL). For example, the ASL sign W̲ATER is articulated with an ASL W-handshape, and the LSM sign FAMILIA ('family') is produced with an LSM F-handshape. In some cases, there are initialized variants of a semantically related set of signs—such as T̲EAM, G̲ROUP, and C̲LASS in ASL, though there is a general sign for the concept of 'group' that is articulated with the ASL clawed-5 handshape. However, in the case of some initialized signs (e.g., ASL WINE; see Figure 31.1), there exist no non-initialized variants in current ASL.

Padden (1998) also writes about abbreviation signs in ASL, or those that also demonstrate some influence from letters of English words. Examples of such signs in

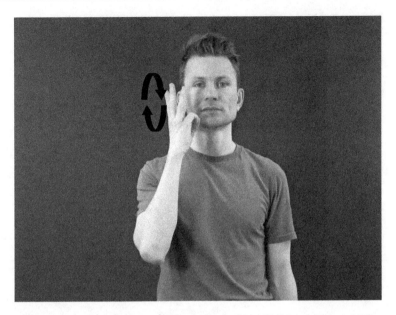

FIGURE 31.1 ASL WINE (handshape for fingerspelled letter 'W' in ASL).

ASL are WORKSHOP, FEEDBACK, and WITHDRAW. Such signs are like the initialized signs described in the preceding, yet they display the manual handshapes that correspond with two letters of the written word, rather than just the initial letter of the word. As such, for WORKSHOP, the letters 'W' and 'S' are found within the handshapes that comprise the sign, though the movement, place of articulation, and orientation values adhere to indigenous phonological constraints of word formation for the language.

Initialization of signs in languages with two-handed fingerspelling systems is also possible, but it is perhaps less common. The reason for this difference is that the one-handed systems usually support the identification of the alphabetic item with solely a handshape (in most cases), and that allows for the movement and place of articulation parameters to either mirror non-initialized variants, or else to engage in their own sanctioned combinations in order to create a sign. Since two-handed systems require place of articulation values (and also movements, in some cases), there are fewer parameters that are free for sign formation. Some authors (Sutton-Spence 1994; Sutton-Spence and Woll 1999; Cormier et al. 2008) have described this phenomenon using the label *single manual letter signs* (SMLS), which are signs that are produced by articulating the handshape and movement that corresponds with a letter from the ambient spoken language (usually the first, as in initialized signs in one-handed systems). See Figure 31.2 for an example of an SMLS with the BSL sign for GARAGE.

These signs generally allow for limited movements from the non-dominant hand and are usually articulated in neutral space (Cormier et al. 2008).

We have noted that initialized signs of signed languages represent contact between the signed and the written version of the spoken language. Certainly, initialized signs

FIGURE 31.2 BSL GARAGE (handshape for fingerspelled letter 'G' in BSL).

attest to long-standing contact between signed languages and the ambient spoken/ written languages of their communities. Much of this contact begins early in the history of a signed language, with the establishment of schools for deaf children and teaching methods that focus on the learning of spoken and/or written language.

Initialized signs exist in many signed languages. For example, they have been attested for Mexican Sign Language, which represents contact between LSM and Spanish (Guerra Currie 1999); Thai Sign Language, for contact with Thai (Nonaka 2004); and Quebec Sign Language, which reflects contact with French (Machabee 1995). Johnston and Schembri (2007) also report that some initialized signs in Australian Sign Language, a language with a two-handed fingerspelling system, are actually produced as one-handed signs because of contact with Irish Sign Language initialized signs.

31.3 Sign-Sign Contact and Other Forms of Visual-Gestural Communication

There are various possible outcomes of contact between two signed languages, as suggested by Lucas and Valli (1992) over twenty years ago. Among the possibilities they suggested are lexical borrowing, foreigner talk, interference, and the creation of pidgins, creoles, and mixed systems. Quinto-Pozos (2007) later suggested that language-contact phenomena are also influenced by various characteristics of signed languages. In particular, he suggested that visual iconicity and the utilization of gestural resources create language-contact phenomena that may be unique to signed language, and interlingual similarities between signed languages may also play a role in the results of contact between signed languages. One aspect of contact in the signed modality that can be readily compared to spoken-language contact is code-switching.

31.3.1 Code-Switching

Code-switching between two signed languages is one characteristic of contact. Quinto-Pozos (2002, 2007, 2008) provides evidence that U.S.–Mexico border signers of Mexican Sign Language (LSM) and ASL engage in *reiterative code-switching*, the sequential use of synonymous signs for the purposes of reiteration—much like certain switches described in spoken languages. In (2), ASL signs are represented by English glosses, LSM signs are represented by Spanish glosses, and similarly articulated signs are shown with a "/" between the two signs. Gestures are represented and described using lower case font, and a "+" refers to repetition of a sign.

(2)   EP3: NO ME NO++ ME gesture: "shake-finger" DEAF/SORDO
       gesture: "wave hand to negate" ME FAMILY **FAMILIA** MY/MI gesture: "well"
       'As for me, my family is not Deaf. Oh well.'

Adam (2012) describes other examples of reiterative code-switching for Deaf users of two sign languages, Australian Sign Language (Auslan) and Australian Irish Sign Language (AISL). In (3), (4), and (5) the items in bold represent AISL signs, whereas the non-bolded words represent Auslan signs (Adam 2012):

(3)   WITH ME LEARN SIGN MY MOTHER **MOTHER FATHER GONE**
       '. . . I learned to sign after my parents left'

(4)   IX ME THOUGHT ALL NUN **NUN** WAS MAN
       'I thought all nuns were men'

(5)   ME CAN TYPE **T-Y-P-E THERE SCHOOL** SCHOOL GOOD WHEN FINISH
       WORK NOTHING MACHINIST
       'I was able to type well at school but when I left school I became a machinist and never typed'

Example (5) illustrates a switch that would be unique to signed languages where the code-switching is reiterated through a different fingerspelling system, as opposed to a sign in the other signed language. This person signs TYPE in Auslan and then follows this sign with T-Y-P-E fingerspelled using the AISL fingerspelling system (a one-handed system that differs from the two-handed Auslan system), and then returns to signs of Auslan.

31.4 Linguistic Interference

Another possible outcome of contact between two signed languages is *interference*, and this can be described as the surfacing of the articulation of one signed language in the production of another—for example, in the phonological parameters of sign formation. Lucas and Valli (1992: 35) refer to this as follows: "It might be precisely the lack of phonological integration that might signal interference—for example, the involuntary use of a handshape, location, palm orientation, movement, or facial expression from one signed language in the discourse of the other." Interference may also be evident at other levels of language structure, such as the morphology or syntax of one or both of the signed languages.

Interference is also discussed in Quinto-Pozos (2002, 2008). The analyses focus primarily on the phonological parameter of handshape and the LSM and ASL non-manual signals that are used for *wh*-question formation. The data indicate that signers, like users of spoken language, exhibit features of interference when they articulate items from their non-native language. For example, a signer who grew up in Mexico signing LSM might sign ASL FAMILY with an LSM F handshape rather than an ASL F handshape. The two handshapes are similar, but they differ in the contact between thumb and index finger and also in the degree to which the non-selected fingers (i.e., the middle and ring fingers and the pinky) are spread apart (see Quinto-Pozos 2008).

31.4.1 Borrowing of Gestures from the Ambient Hearing Community

Signers take advantage of commonly used non-linguistic gestures from the ambient hearing communities. Some of those gestures may become part of the lexicon or grammar of the signed languages as evidenced, in part, by changes in their articulation vis-à-vis the manner in which hearing people use those gestures. However, Deaf signers also articulate gestures that, at least on the surface, do not appear to differ from some of those that hearing people use in conjunction with speech. As with iconic devices, such gestural resources—some of which may display language-like properties and others that seem to pattern in non-linguistic ways—present challenges for the researcher of signed language contact. For some analyses (e.g., a syntactic account of code-switching), it may be particularly difficult to determine whether a meaningful form is, in some cases, a sign or a non-linguistic gesture.

Various authors have suggested ways in which the gestures—both manual and non-manual—of hearing people can now be considered as part of a signed language. For example, Janzen and Shaffer (2002) maintain that some hand gestures have been grammaticalized as modals in ASL and that some facial gestures (specifically brow raise) have been incorporated as non-manual signals that provide syntactic information (e.g., topic markers). McClave (2001) has also proposed that non-manual signals (e.g., head shifts for direct quotes) in ASL have been influenced by the gestures of hearing people. Casey (2003) has shown that directional gestures and torso movements of non-signers are similar to verb directionality and torso movement for role shift in signed language. She suggests that directionality in ASL (and other signed languages) originated from non-linguistic gestures, but first- versus non-first-person distinctions have been grammaticized; thus not all of the directional gestures can be considered purely gestural.

31.5 CONCLUDING REMARKS

Most work on signed-language contact has focused on the interaction of signed and spoken and/or written languages. This multimodal contact may be due to the fact that signed languages most often exist within larger communities where spoken and written languages are used daily. These oral and written modalities of language exert much linguistic (and cultural) influence on signed languages. This has been true as long as deaf children have been educated and guided through the acquisition of literacy. This has also been true because of the interactions between deaf and hearing users of signed languages. Deaf people and signed languages do not exist in a vacuum; they are surrounded by many non-native signers and languages (both spoken and written) that are structured differently. We suggest that the fact that Deaf signers are multi-modal bilinguals/multilinguals creates a fertile landscape for the creation of contact phenomena.

There are also cases of signed languages coming into contact with each other—either in transnational border communities or through international travel experiences. Such cases of unimodal contact are particularly interesting because they allow the investigator of language contact an opportunity to examine how language contact may have unique characteristics if considered solely within the visual-gestural modality (see Quinto-Pozos 2007 for discussions of common characteristics of such contact).

It has been suggested that Deaf learners of a spoken/written language demonstrate learning strategies consistent with an L2 learner of a spoken/written language (Plaza-Pust 2008). Additionally, the multilingual development that most Deaf individuals experience likely leads to very specific language mixing. As Plaza-Pust (2008: 127) notes, "This is an important conclusion given the myths that surround the acquisition of a written language by deaf students." Language mixing and contact are the norm in Deaf communities.

The study of contact in the visual-gestural modality is fascinating. It can tell us much about natural language structure, the influence of society on language, and the role of modality on language. By considering the ways in which bimodal bilinguals/multilinguals shape their languages, the general study of the human language capacity is taken to another level.

ACKNOWLEDGMENTS

The support of the Economic and Social Research Council (ESRC) is gratefully acknowledged. Robert Adam was supported by the ESRC Deafness Cognition and Language Research Centre (DCAL) Grant RES-620-28-0002. We would also like to thank Jordan Fenlon for his assistance with the figures in this chapter.

REFERENCES

Adam, R. 2012. Language contact and borrowing. In *Sign Language: An International Handbook*, edited by R. Pfau, M. Steinbach, and B. Woll. 841–862 Berlin Mouton de Gruyter.

Adam, R. 2013. Ajello, R., L. Mazzoni, and F. Nicolai. 2001. Linguistic gestures: Mouthing in Italian Sign Language (LIS). In *The Hands Are the Head of the Mouth: The Mouth as Articulator in Sign Language*, edited by P. Boyes Braem and R. Sutton-Spence, 231–246. Hamburg: Signum.

Allsop, L., B. Woll, and J. M. Brauti. 1995. International sign: The creation of an international deaf community and sign language. In *Sign Language Research 1994: Proceedings of the Fourth European Congress on Sign Language Research, Munich, September 1–3, 1994. International Studies on Sign Language and Communication of the Deaf 29*, edited by H. F. Bos and G. M. Schermer. Hamburg: Signum.

Ann, J. 2001. Bilingualism and language contact. In *The Sociolinguistics of Sign Language*, edited by C. Lucas, 33–60. New York: Cambridge University Press.

Ann, J., W. H. Smith, and C. Yu. 2007. The sign language of Mainland China at the Ch'iying School in Taiwan. In *Sign Language Contact*, edited by D. Quinto-Pozos, 235–258. Washington, DC: Gallaudet University Press.

Baker, A. E., and B. van den Bogaerde. 2008. Codemixing in signs and words in input to and output from children. In *Sign Bilingualism: Language Development, Interaction, and Maintenance in Sign Language Contact Situations*, edited by C. Plaza-Pust and E. Morales-López, 1–27. Studies in Bilingualism 38. Amsterdam: John Benjamins.

Battison, R. 1978. *Lexical Borrowing in American Sign Language*. Silver Spring, MD: Linstok.

Bishop, M., and S. Hicks. 2008. Coda talk: Bimodal discourse among hearing, native signers. In *Hearing, Mother Father Deaf: Hearing People in Deaf Families*, edited by M. Bishop and S. Hicks. Washington, DC: Gallaudet University Press.

Brentari, D., and C. A. Padden. 2001. Native and foreign vocabulary in American Sign Language: A lexicon with multiple origins. In *Foreign Vocabulary in Sign Languages: A Cross-Linguistic Investigation of Word Formation*, edited by D. Brentari, 87–119. Mahwah, NJ: Lawrence Erlbaum.

Casey, S. 2003. *"Agreement" in Gestures and Signed Languages: The Use of Directionality to Indicate Referents Involved in Actions*. PhD dissertation, University of California–San Diego.

Chen Pichler, D., J. Lee, and D. Lillo-Martin. 2014. Language development in ASL-English bimodal bilinguals. In *Multilingual Aspects of Signed Language Communication and Disorder*, edited by D. Quinto, 235–260. Bristol, UK: Multilingual Matters.

Cokely, D. 1983. When is a pidgin not a pidgin? *Sign Language Studies* 38: 1–24.

Cormier, K., M. Tyrone, and A. Schembri. 2008. One hand or two? Nativisation of fingerspelling in ASL and BANZSL. *Sign Language and Linguistics* 11(1): 3–44.

Crasborn, O., E. van der Kooij, D. Waters, B. Woll, and J. Mesch. 2008. Frequency distribution and spreading of different types of mouth actions in three sign languages. *Sign Language and Linguistics* 11(1): 45–67.

Davis, J. 1989. Distinguishing language contact phenomena in ASL interpretation. In *The Sociolinguistics of the Deaf Community*, edited by Ceil Lucas, 85–102. San Diego, CA: Academic Press.

Ebbinghaus, H., and J. Hessmann 2001. Sign language as multidimensional communication: Why manual signs, mouthings, and mouth gestures are three different things. In *The Hands Are the Head of the Mouth: The Mouth as Articulator in Sign Language*, edited by P. Boyes Braem and Rachel Sutton-Spence, 133–151. Hamburg: Signum.

Emmorey, K., H. Borinstein, and R. Thompson. 2005. Bimodal bilingualism: Code-blending between spoken English and American Sign Language. In *ISB4: Proceedings of the 4th International Symposium on Bilingualism*, edited by J. Cohen, K. T. McAlister, K. Rolstad, and J. MacSwan, 663–673. Somerville, MA: Cascadilla Press.

Emmorey, K., H. Borinstein, R. Thompson, and T. Gollan. 2008. Bimodal bilingualism. *Bilingualism: Language and Cognition* 11(1): 43–61.

Fischer, S. 1996. By the numbers: Language-internal evidence for creolization. *International Review of Sign Linguistics* 1–22.

Groce, N. E. 1985. *Everyone Here Spoke Sign Language.* Cambridge, MA: Harvard University Press.

Guerra Currie, A.-M. 1999. *A Mexican Sign Language Lexicon: Internal and Cross-Linguistic Similarities and Variation.* Unpublished PhD dissertation, University of Texas, Austin.

Guerra Currie, A.-M. P., R. P. Meier, and K. Walters. 2002. A cross-linguistic examination of the lexicons of four sign languages. In *Modality and Structure in Signed and Spoken Languages*, edited by R. P. Meier, K. Cormier, and D. Quinto-Pozos, 224–236. New York: Cambridge University Press.

Hohenberger, A., and D. Happ. 2001. The linguistic primacy of signs and mouth gestures over mouthing: Evidence from language production in German Sign Language (DGS). In *The Hands Are the Head of the Mouth: The Mouth as Articulator in Sign Language*, edited by P. Boyes Braem and R. Sutton-Spence, 153–189. Hamburg: Signum.

Janzen, T., and B. Shaffer. 2002. Gesture as the substrate in the process of ASL grammaticization. In *Modality and Structure in Signed and Spoken Languages*, edited by R. P. Meier, K. Cormier, and D. Quinto-Pozos, 199–223. New York: Cambridge University Press.

Kyle, J., & Woll, B. 1985. Sign Language: The Study of Deaf People and Their Language. New York: Cambridge University Press.

Lucas, C., and C. Valli. 1992. *Language Contact in the American Deaf Community.* San Diego, CA: Academic Press.

McClave, E. Z. 2001. The relationship between spontaneous gestures of the hearing and American Sign Language. *Gesture* 11: 51–72.

McKee, R., D. McKee, K. Smiler, and K. Pointon. 2007. 'Maori Signs': The construction of indigenous Deaf identity in New Zealand Sign Language. In *Sign Languages in Contact*, edited by D. Quinto-Pozos, 31–81. Sociolinguistics in Deaf Communities Series 13. Washington, DC: Gallaudet University Press.

McNeill, D. 1992. *Hand and Mind.* Chicago: University of Chicago Press.

Murray, J. 2009. Sign languages. In *The Palgrave Dictionary of Transnational History*, edited by I. Iriye and P. Saunier. London: Palgrave Macmillan.

Nonaka, A. M. 2004. The forgotten endangered languages: Lessons on the importance of remembering from Thailand's Ban Khor Sign Language. *Language in Society* 33: 737–767.

Padden, C. 1998. The ASL lexicon. *Sign Language and Linguistics* 1: 39–60.

Pietrosemoli, L. 2001. Politeness in Venezuelan Sign Language. In *Signed Languages: Discoveries from International Research*, edited by V. Dively, M. Metzger, S. Taub, and A. M. Baer, 163–179. Washington, DC: Gallaudet University Press.

Plaza-Pust, C. 2008. Why variation matters. In *Sign Bilingualism: Language Development, Interaction, and Maintenance in Sign Language Contact Situations*, edited by C. Plaza-Pust and E. Morales-López, xvi. Studies in Bilingualism 38. Amsterdam: John Benjamins.

Quinto-Pozos, D. 2002. *Contact between Mexican Sign Language and American Sign Language in Two Texas Border Areas*. PhD dissertation, University of Texas, Austin.

Quinto-Pozos, D. 2007. Outlining considerations for the study of sign language contact. In *Sign Languages in Contact*, edited by D. Quinto-Pozos. Washington, DC: Gallaudet University Press.

Quinto-Pozos, D. 2008. Sign language contact and interference: ASL and LSM. *Language in Society* 37: 161–189.

Quinto-Pozos, D. 2009. Code-switching between sign languages. In *The Handbook of Code-Switching*, edited by B. Bullock and J. Toribio, 221–237. Cambridge: Cambridge University Press.

Quinto-Pozos, D., & Mehta, S. 2010. Register variation in mimetic gestural complements to signed language. Journal of Pragmatics, 42: 557–584.

Rosenstock, R. 2004. *An Investigation of International Sign: Analyzing Structure and Comprehension*. PhD dissertation, Gallaudet University, Washington, DC.

Sasaki, D. 2007. Comparing lexicons of Japanese Sign Language and Taiwan Sign Language: A preliminary study focusing on the differences in the handshape para- meter. In *Sign Languages in Contact*, edited by D. Quinto-Pozos, 123–150. Washington, DC: Gallaudet University Press.

Schmaling, C. 2001. ASL in northern Nigeria: Will Housa Sign Language survive? In *Signed Languages: Discoveries from International Research*, edited by V. Dively, M. Metzger, S. Taub, and A. M. Baer, 180–193. Washington, DC: Gallaudet University Press.

Stokoe, W. 1970. Sign language diglossia. *Studies in Linguistics* 21: 27–41.

Supalla, T., and R. Webb. 1995. The grammar of International Sign: A new look at pidgin languages. In *Language, Gesture, and Space*, edited by K. Emmorey and J. Reilly, 333–352. Mahwah, NJ: Lawrence Erlbaum.

Sutton-Spence, R. 1994. *The Role of the Manual Alphabet and Fingerspelling in British Sign Language*. PhD dissertation, University of Bristol.

Sutton-Spence, R. 1998. English verb loans in BSL. In *Pinky Extension and Eye Gaze: Language Use in Deaf Communities*, edited by C. Lucas. Washington, DC: Gallaudet University Press.

Sutton-Spence, R. 2003. British manual alphabets in the education of Deaf people since the 17th century. In *Many Ways to Be Deaf: International Variation in Deaf Communities*, edited by L. Monaghan, C. Schmaling, K. Nakamura, and G. T. Turner. Washington, DC: Gallaudet University Press.

Sutton-Spence, R., and Woll, B. 1999. *The Linguistics of British Sign Language: An Introduction*. Cambridge: Cambridge University Press.

Tervoort, B. 1973. Could there be a human sign language? *Semiotica* 9: 347–382.

van den Bogaerde, B., and Baker, A. 2005. Code mixing in mother-child interaction in deaf families. *Sign Language and Linguistics* 8(1–2): 155–178.

Wilcox, S., and P. Wilcox. 1997. *Learning to See: Teaching American Sign Language as a Second Language*. Washington, DC: Gallaudet University Press.

Woll, B. 1984. The comparative study of different sign languages: Preliminary analyses. In *Recent research on European Sign Languages*, edited by F. Loncke, P. Boyes Braem, and Y. Lebrun, 79–91. Lisse, The Netherlands: Swets and Zeitlinger.

Woll, B. 2010. *SLLING-L Digest: 18 Aug 2010 (#2010-41)*. [email] Message to Rannveig Sverris (rannsve@hi.is). Sent Thursday, July 18, 2010, 02:20. http://listserv.linguistlist.org/cgi-bin/wa?A0=SLLING-L (accessed August 29, 2010).

Woodward, J. 1973. *Implicational Lects on the Deaf Diglossic Continuum*. PhD dissertation, Georgetown University, Washington, DC.

Woodward, J. 2000. Sign languages and sign language families in Thailand and Viet Nam. In *The Signs of Language Revisited: An Anthology to Honor Ursula Bellugi and Edward Klima*, edited by K. Emmorey and H. Lane, 23–47. Mahwah, NJ: Lawrence Erlbaum.

Yang, Jun Hui. 2008. Sign language and oral/written language in deaf education in China. In *Sign Bilingualism: Language Development, Interaction, and Maintenance in Sign Language Contact Situations*, edited by C. Plaza-Pust and E. Morales-López, 297–331. Amsterdam; Philadelphia: John Benjamins.

Yoel, J. 2007. Evidence for first-language attrition of Russian Sign Language among immigrants to Israel. In *Sociolinguistics in Deaf Communities*, edited by D. Quinto-Pozos, Vol. 13. Washington, DC: Gallaudet University Press.

Yoel, J. 2009. *Canada's Maritime Sign Language*. Unpublished PhD dissertation, University of Manitoba, Winnipeg.

CHAPTER 32

LANGUAGE CONTACT IN PARAGUAYAN GUARANÍ

JORGE GÓMEZ RENDÓN

32.1 INTRODUCTION: THE LANGUAGE, THE NAMES, THE SPEAKERS

PARAGUAYAN Guaraní (henceforth PG) is a Tupian language spoken in Paraguay, the Argentinean province of Corrientes, and in several municipalities of the Brazilian state of Mato Grosso do Sul. PG has genealogical links to Jesuitical Guaraní (the language spoken by Indians living in the Jesuitical missions from 1610 to 1767) and contemporary indigenous Guaraní (the language spoken nowadays by ethnic groups such as Paí Tavytera, Mbya, Ava, and Ache), but is minimally intelligible with both, thus being considered a linguistically related but independent language. PG is an official language of Paraguay and was also declared official in Corrientes (2004) and the area of MERCOSUR (2006).[1]

PG is known in the literature also as Jopará Guaraní, Creole Guaraní, colloquial Guaraní, modern Guaraní, or simply Guaraní. While I restrict here the use of "traditional Guaraní" to the more conservative varieties of Paraguayan Guaraní, the other names deserve some comment. Both Jopará Guaraní and Creole Guaraní refer mainly to the Spanish-Guaraní mixture, which makes PG ostensibly different from Jesuitical and Indian varieties. Indeed, as I show in this chapter, Jopará, the most common name given to PG,[2] is characterized not only by the ubiquitous presence of Spanish lexical

---

[1] MERCOSUR or Mercado Común del Sur is an economic and political agreement among Argentina, Brazil, Paraguay, Uruguay, Venezuela, and more recently Bolivia, the purpose of which is to promote the fluid movement of goods, people, and currency among its member states.

[2] Jopará is often opposed to an ideally 'pure Guaraní' or Guaraníete. However, Guaraníete does not occur in spontaneous speech, neither in the cities nor in rural areas, but does so only in writing as a standardized norm. Still, Guaraníete might be used to refer to less Hispanicized varieties of Paraguayan

and grammatical borrowing, but also by the alternation of Guaraní and Spanish sentences, clauses, and phrases in discourse (code-switching). Even if Paraguayan (Jopará) Guaraní cannot be characterized as a Creole language or a bilingual mixed language similar to other varieties documented in the literature (cf. Bakker and Mous 1994; Thomason 1997; Gómez Rendón 2008), the generalized mixture shown by PG has led some authors to put PG as a "third language" linguistically distinct from Guaraní and Spanish (cf. Melià 1974).

However, recent studies have shown that Jopará Guaraní cannot be considered a third language, at least in strict structural terms (cf. Kalfell 2010). Jopará would be therefore a discursive and ultimately communicative strategy, depending "on the more or less extended knowledge the speakers have of the grammatical system and the lexicon of Guaraní and Spanish" (Dietrich 2010: 49). The status of Jopará in relation to code-switching will be discussed in the last section. For the purposes of this chapter, I reserve the label "(modern) Paraguayan Guaraní," as suggested by Dietrich (2010: 42) and Lustig (2006), to the Guaraní variety spoken nowadays in Paraguay, as distinct both from Jesuitical Guaraní and indigenous Guaraní, and showing different levels of mixing and switching with the official Spanish language, and to this extent I consider "(modern) Paraguayan Guaraní" and "Jopará Guaraní" to be synonyms.

According to the 1992 census, the percentage of Guaraní monolinguals in Paraguay was considerably higher than the percentage of Spanish monolinguals (39.30% > 6.40%). By the same year the percentage of bilinguals was scarcely less than half of the country's population (49%). In 2002 bilinguals increased to 59% while Guaraní monolinguals decreased to 27%. According to the last census (2012), Guarani monolinguals represent only 7.93% of the country's population whereas the number of bilinguals increased to 63.88%. All in all, the progressive decrease in the number of Guaraní monolinguals (39% > 27% > 7%) is accompanied by a sustained increase in the number of bilinguals (49% > 59%> 73%). The corollary is that societal bilingualism has never been the rule in Paraguay. However, it might be attainable in the next twenty years as the diatopic gap between PG (rural) and Spanish (urban) is gradually bridged, with bilingualism spreading nationwide. Notice, however, that societal bilingualism in Paraguay does not necessarily imply an absence of diglossia since Spanish and PG are not (yet) used on equal terms all over the country and throughout all communicative spaces. Yet major efforts have been made in this direction during recent years, particularly with the last education reform and the Ley de Lenguas passed in 2010.

To understand the profile of modern Guaraní as spoken in Paraguay and neighboring areas of Argentina and Brazil, the early history of contact must be considered.

Guaraní. Elsewhere (Gómez Rendón 2008: 195) I have identified Paraguayan Guaraní as composed of Guaraníete and Jopará without necessarily opposing one to the other. Since the topic of this chapter is to discuss the process and outcomes of contact between Spanish and Guaraní and not the status of a standardized variety, I will make use of Paraguayan Guaraní and Jopará as synonyms. Interestingly, the term *jopará* is formed by adding the reciprocal /-jo/ to the lexical root *para* 'multicolored.' In Paraguayan cuisine, *jopará* also refers to a typical dish made of maize and beans, which is served traditionally on the first day of October.

This is done in the following section (32.2). Sections 32.3 and 32.4 of this chapter will deal with lexical and grammatical borrowing on modern Guaraní, whereas Section 32.5 is devoted to providing an evaluation of code-switching in the shaping and nature of PG.

32.2 THE EARLY YEARS OF CONTACT AND THE SHAPING OF PARAGUAYAN GUARANÍ

The sociolinguistic status of Paraguay as the only Latin American country in which an originally indigenous language is spoken by the majority of the population is explained by its equally particular history of conquest and colonization. Unlike major cities in western South America, such as Bogotá, Quito, Lima, and Cuzco, some of them founded on the ruins of former Indian urban centers, Asunción, the capital city of Paraguay, was first established in 1537 as an outpost whose main goal was to support military expeditions in their way to the eastern Andes, an area well known for its precious metals. The search for a shorter route to the Andes had begun as early as 1516 with Alejo García's expedition and continued until the late 1560s, when it was finally acknowledged that no feasible route was to be found. These circumstances shaped the extent and pattern of early Spanish settlement in Paraguay and the sociolinguistic situation of the languages in contact.

It is difficult to determine with certainty the extent of the Guaraní-speaking population living in Eastern Paraguay by 1537,[3] but a conservative estimate gives a number around 300,000 souls, concentrated mainly along the basins of the upper and middle Parana and the middle Paraguay rivers (Kleinpenning 2011: 46). While this number is not particularly large if the area of settlement is considered—with a density of 33 per 100 square kilometers and 28 per 100 square kilometers in each basin, respectively[4]—it is certainly well beyond the number of Spanish conquerors who settled in Paraguay since 1537. Konetzke gives 3,087 as the total number of Spaniards who arrived in Paraguay between 1535 and 1600 (quoted in Kleinpenning 2011: 669). The bulk of Spanish migration arrived in the first three decades after 1535 and ended well before the turn of the seventeenth century. These numbers imply that Spaniards and Guaraní Indians were roughly in a ratio of one to 100 during most of the sixteenth century, which are the most decisive years for the emergence of PG. And yet, similar demographics have been attested for other Spanish colonies (cf. Newson 1995, for the northern Andes),

---

[3] Geographically Paraguay is divided into eastern and western parts by the vertical line of the Paraguay River. Western Paraguay, known as Chaco, remained well into the twentieth century inhabited only by non-Guaraní ethnic groups whose bellicose stand to any intruder made any permanent settlement unfeasible. For this reason, virtually all Spanish settlements were established only in eastern Paraguay.

[4] This estimate is provided by Steward (1949: 5, 659, 662) and endorsed first by Service (1954: 14) and more recently by Kleinpenning (2011: 46).

which prevents us from using them alone to explain the unique sociolinguistic situation of Paraguay. It is necessary, therefore, to include another sociodemographic factor so as to have a broader view of the early sociolinguistic developments. This factor is miscegenation and its related social, economic, and cultural aspects.

Spaniards who arrived in Paraguay during the sixteenth century included only a very small number of women. Service states that the first two decades (1536–1556) of Spanish colonization saw the coming of only twelve women among the immigrants (Service 1954: 32). This number increased to fifty for the rest of the sixteenth century (Velázquez 1977: 30). In these circumstances, the natural growth of early Paraguay's population can be explained only by an intense miscegenation between Spanish men and Indian women, a fact that is profusely attested in the chronicles. Indeed, miscegenation started very early and involved women from different Guaraní groups in the neighborhood of Asunción and beyond, including Carios, Tobatines, Guaranbaenses, and Paranaenses (Kleinpenning 2011: 672).

The process of miscegenation developed, first, through the practice of *kuñadazgo*, a form of concubinage based on amity relations between Spaniard conquerors and Indian men.[5] Later, a practice of serfdom known as *yanaconato* furthered the process of miscegenation.[6] Serfs were recruited from different Guaraní groups to attend to the households of Spaniards both in urban and rural areas and lived there on a permanent basis (Gómez Rendón 2017: 143, 145). According to Kleinpenning, *yanaconato* promoted miscegenation in two relevant ways: on the one hand, it led to a more frequent contact between Spaniards and Indians; on the other hand, Indian women preferred not to marry *yanacona* men as their offspring would continue to be serfs (Kleinpenning 2011: 672). This preference resulted not only in an increase in the number of mixed-blood children, but also in a corresponding decrease in the number of Indians.

Mixed-blood children usually grew up in the same households in which their mothers served and thus had the opportunity to learn Guaraní from their caregivers and Spanish from their fathers and other kin. This particular situation perhaps underlies the well-known fact that mestizos (mixed-blood individuals) were not considered as second-class citizens, as they were in other Spanish colonies, but earned early social acceptance. Moreover, mestizos were legally on equal terms with Spaniards provided a Spaniard considered them his offspring.

In general, the process of miscegenation was so rapid that there were already some 6,000 mixed-blood children in Paraguay by the end of the administration of Martínez de Irala (ca. 1556) (Kleinpenning 2011: 672). The dramatic mestizo growth was not only an urban development, but also took place in rural areas. By spreading all over the country and intensifying after the stop of Spanish immigration since the last quarter of the sixteenth century, miscegenation became the breeding ground for language mixing.

---

[5] The term *cuñadazgo* comes from Guaraní *kuña* 'woman.' While *kuña* may be used alone or in compounds such as *mitãkuña* 'girl' or even *kuña hekovai* 'prostitute,' its origin is traced back to Spanish *cuñada*, one of whose senses is 'the wife of one's brother.' The proper Guaraní name for 'wife' is *tembireko*.
[6] From Quechua *yana*, one of whose meanings is 'serf'.

By the first half of the eighteenth century, a highly mixed variety of Guaraní had long emerged in Paraguay, as attested by the witness of a missionary around 1758:

> El lenguaje o jerigonza que a los principios sabían no es otra cosa que un agregado de solecismos y barbarismos de la lengua guaraní y guaraní y castellano, como se usa en toda la gobernación del Paraguay y en la jurisdicción de las Corrientes. En una y otra ciudad, los más saben castellano, pero en las villas y en todas las poblaciones del campo, chacras y estancias no se habla ni se sabe por lo común, especialmente entre las mujeres, más que esta lengua tan corrupta [. . .] me fue necesario aprender esta tan adulterada lengua para darme a entender, porque la propia guaraní no la entendían, y menos el castellano; y así les predicaba en su desconcertado lenguaje.
>
> (quoted in Melià 1982: 146f)

Even if the first decades of contact were decisive for the emergence of PG as it is spoken today, the much less studied contribution of other Guaraní varieties cannot be overlooked. In fact, the participation of Indians from different Guaraní groups in the early process of miscegenation and language contact was crucial, but their presence in the mestizo society became significantly reduced over the years. After 1580 and throughout the seventeenth and eighteenth centuries, Guaraní Indians were concentrated in *pueblos de indios* (settlements specially intended for Indians) and in the Jesuitical missions, in which the contact with Spaniards and mestizos was reduced to the minimum, as were miscegenation and language contact (Gómez Rendón 2017: 147). Still, after the expel of the Jesuits in 1768, which led to the progressive abandonment of the former missions in the following decades, mission Indians integrated to the mainstream Paraguayan society, either settling down in towns and villages in central Paraguay or incorporating into already existing *pueblos de indios*. Thus, it is not far-fetched to assume that Jesuitical Guaraní[7] became somehow entangled not only with PG used in urban centers, but also with a non-standardized, perhaps more natural variety of indigenous Guaraní spoken in *pueblos de indios*. Eventually, the dissolution of the last *pueblos de indios* in 1848 and the moving of their population to urban and rural areas in the ensuing years led to another situation in which the language pool of PG became enriched by the contribution of indigenous Guaraní varieties.

32.3 LEXICAL OUTCOMES OF LANGUAGE CONTACT IN PARAGUAYAN GUARANÍ

The data presented in this and the following sections come from a corpus-based study of PG. The data were collected between 2004 and 2007 in urban and rural areas of Paraguay and include samples of spontaneous speech from thirty-eight speakers, as well as some

---

[7] Arguably, a process of dialect leveling took place during the 150 years of Jesuitical missionary administration and resulted in the creation of a *Guaraní koine* (Lustig 1996: 23).

samples extracted from newspapers and other periodicals of wide circulation in the country.[8] Following a description of overall borrowing percentages by parts of speech, I discuss their phonological and morphosyntactic assimilation to PG.

The influence of Spanish on PG is undoubtedly its most salient feature. The corpus included 17.4% of Spanish loanwords (tokens) and 23% of lemmatized items (types). These numbers do not include the numerous code-switches present in virtually any piece of natural speech. The specific contribution of code-switching will be dealt with in the last section of this chapter. Of the major parts of speech, nouns were by far the most frequently borrowed (37.2%), followed by verbs (18.3%), adjectives (7.4%), and manner adverbs (9.9%), which in general terms accords with borrowing tendencies and hierarchies put forward by several authors (cf. Moravcsik 1978; Muysken 1981; Gómez Rendón 2006, 2008b).

The process of phonological assimilation of Spanish loanwords in PG is determined by the levels of bilingualism of PG speakers, with coordinate bilinguals showing less phonological accommodation than subordinate and incipient bilinguals. A negative correlation between frequency and assimilation is attested, according to which speakers using larger numbers of Spanish loanwords show less assimilation than speakers whose speech is less Hispanicized. The phonological adaptation of Spanish loanwords in PG involves the following mechanisms:

1. Shift of stress to the last syllable, particularly in older loanwords and occasionally accompanied by other phonetic processes such as the drop of final consonants or post-tonic syllables: for example, Sp. *caballo* 'horse' [kabáʎo] > [kavayú]; Sp. *azúcar* 'sugar' [asúkar] > [asuká]; Sp. *almohada* 'pillow' [almoáda] > [armoxá]. However, a number of loanwords occur unassimilated and preserve primary stress in the same syllable as in the source language: for example, Spanish /késo/ 'cheese' occurs assimilated as [kesú] in traditional Guaraní but unassimilated as [késo] in PG.

2. Nasalization of vowels when preceded or followed by a nasal segment such as [n], [m] or [ñ]: for example Sp. *ajeno* 'another's' [axéno] > [axẽno]; Sp. *sábana* 'blanket' [sábana] > [savanã]; nasal codas in loanwords may be dropped with the resulting nasalization of the vocalic nucleus, as in Sp. *melon* 'melon' [melon] > [merõ]; *pelón* 'bald' [pelón] > [peɾõ].

3. Consonant changes represent the most frequent form of phonological assimilation of Spanish loanwords in PG. Such changes include the replacement of the voiced alveolar [d] with the flap [ɾ], as in Sp. *almidón* 'starch' [almiðón] > [aramiɾõ]; the replacement of the voiceless fricative labiodental /f/ with [p], as in Sp. *alfiler* 'pin' [alfilér] > [arapiɾé]; the replacement of voiced and voiceless velars [g] and [k] with the close central unrounded vowel [ɨ] in both homosyllabic and heterosyllabic clusters, as in Sp. *doctor* 'doctor' [doɨtor]; the replacement of the trill [r] with a flap, as in Sp. *corral* 'stockyard' [korál] > [koɾál]; the

---

[8] For a thorough description of the process of data collection and analysis, see Gómez Rendón (2008: I, 103–113).

replacement of the voiceless affricate alveopalatal [č] with the fricative [š] in all positions, as in Sp. *chica* 'girl' [čika] > [šika]; the simplification of consonant clusters, particularly in old loanwords, either by inserting an epenthetic vowel as in Sp. *cruz* 'cross' [krus] > [kurúsu] or by dropping one of the consonants as in Sp. *bolsa* 'sack' [bólsa] > [vosá]; and last by not least, the insertion of the glottal stop at the beginning of stressed mono-phonemic syllables in word-initial positions, as in Sp. *hora* 'hour' [óra] > [ʔóra].[9]

4. Vowel changes in assimilated Spanish loanwords include nasalization of vocalic nuclei after dropped nasal codas (cf. *supra*); the raising of /o/ to /u/ in old loanwords such as Sp. *zapato* 'shoe' [sapáto] > [sapatú]; and the de-diphthongi-zation of vowel sequences through the insertion of a glottal stop, as in *piola* 'cord' [pióla] >[piʔóla].[10]

The morpho-phonological assimilation of Spanish loanwords according to parts of speech is rather straightforward in PG. Spanish loanwords are inserted directly without any derivation. Verbs are inserted after dropping the final /-r/. The base form of irregular loan verbs (those with vowel alternation in the root, e.g., *sentir* 'to feel.INF' > /sient-/) is the verb root in infinitive form. Loan verbs that have dropped the infinitive ending receive the same verbal morphology as native verbs.[11] The loan verb *recoger* 'collect' in (1) receives the prefix of third person singular (*o-*) and the suffixes of emphasis (*-paité*) and obligation (*va'erã*).

(1) *ha'é-nte   o-rrekohe-paité-va'erã   mandyju*
     3-only   3-collect-EMPH-OBLG   cotton
     'She was the only one who had to collect cotton'

Adjectives and nouns are always borrowed with gender markers, if any. Similarly, loan manner adverbs usually occur with the Spanish adverbial marker /*-mente*/. In addition, an important number of nouns are borrowed with their plural endings (2) and some occur in Spanish noun phrases (3):

(2) *brasileros-kuéra   a-ñemongeta   hendi-kuéra   heta   vése*
     Brazilian-(sp)PL-PL   1SG-talk   3.COM-PL   many   time.PL
     'Brazilian people, I talk with them many times'

---

[9] Less noticeable than other phenomena involving consonants, this type of insertion is widespread not only in PG but also in the Spanish of subordinate bilingual speakers.

[10] De-diphthongization occurs across sociolects of PG and in the Spanish of PG-dominant bilinguals (Gregores & Suárez 1967: 90).

[11] Loan adjectives and nouns used as verbs in Guaraní do not undergo any morphological adaptation (cf. *infra*).

(3) *Oi-ko*   **alguno**   **líder**   *o-gusta-háicha*
     3-be   some   leader   3-like-so
     'There were some leaders who liked it that way'

(4) **Sanignacio**-*gua*   *no-ĩ-ri*   *ko*   *tembiapo*   *ndive*
     San.Ignacio-ABL   NEG-3.be-NEG   DEM   work   with
     'The people from San Ignacio do not work together'

Notice that the noun phrases are instances of code-switching. The reasons for treating them rather as complex lexical borrowings are various: (a) neither of their constituents can be individually modified nor otherwise dislocated inside or outside phrasal boundaries; (b) their intonation contours characterize them as single phonological words; (c) their occurrence is more frequent across speakers than ad hoc switched phrases; and (d) their semantic meaning is determined by physical, social, or other referents in the speaker's sociocultural space.

The syntactic assimilation of Spanish loanwords according to parts of speech was evaluated on the basis of the occurrence of nouns, verbs, adjectives, and manner adverbs in non-prototypical syntactic positions (cf. Hengeveld et al. 2004).[12] The analysis of the corpus showed that loan nouns and loan adjectives in particular were used in syntactic positions other than their prototypical ones.[13] Thus, for instance, 22.7% of loan adjectives were used not only as modifiers of referential phrases, but also as heads of same phrases (85.9%) or modifiers of predicate phrases (11.3%). These percentages suggest that major word classes may be syntactically assimilated to the parts-of-speech typology of the recipient language in the borrowing process (Bakker et al. 2008: 195, 228). The following are examples of a loan noun and a loan adjective used in non-prototypical syntactic positions:

(5) *la*   *che*   *gente-kuéra*   *che*   *rú-gui*   *o-lado*
     DEM   1.POS   people-PL   1.POS   father-ABL   3.side
     'My friends sided with my father'

(6) *I-**provechoso**-va'erã*   *pe*   *i-vida*   *diaria-pe*
     3-useful-FUT   DEM   3.POSS-life   daily-LOC
     'That will be useful in their daily life'

---

[12] Prototypical positions of nouns are heads of referential phrases; of verbs, heads of predicate phrases; of adjectives, modifiers of referential phrases; and of manner adverbs, modifiers of predicate phrases.

[13] For a discussion of lexical category in Tupi-Guaraní languages, see Dietrich (2001). Interestingly, Ciccone finds a similar non-prototypical use of loan nouns and adjectives from Spanish in Tapiete, a Tupi-Guaraní language spoken in northwestern Argentina, Bolivia, and Paraguay (Ciccone 2015: 214).

32.4 Grammatical Outcomes of Language Contact in Paraguayan Guaraní

Corresponding to a widespread influence of Spanish on the lexicon of PG is a similar influence on its grammar, activated mainly by the entrance of loanwords in the language. In fact, lexical borrowing has eventually affected not only phonology, but also morphology and syntax, thereby altering the original makeup of traditional Guaraní.

The phonological inventory of traditional Guaraní includes twenty-six sounds: fourteen consonants (/p/, /t/, /k/, /s/, /š/, /h/, /m/, /n/, /ŋ/, /v/, /y/, /ɣ/, /r/, /ʔ/) and twelve oral and nasal vowels (/a/, /ã/, /e/, /ẽ/ /i/ /ĩ/, /ɨ/, /ɨ̃/, /o/, /õ/, /u/, /ũ/). Another six have entered PG through loanwords: /ɸ/, /c/, /ð/, /r/, /l/ and /ʎ/. With the exception of /l/ and/ʎ/, the occurrence of these phonemes is limited to Spanish loanwords.[14] On occasion, these sounds occur in native items, too, especially in the speech of younger bilinguals. Segments /ɸ, c, r/ show the same primary articulation as native phonemes /p, š, r/ but differ from them in their secondary articulation. A significant degree of free variation is found across PG idiolects between /c/ ~ /š/ and /l/ ~ /r/. Unlike consonants, vowels in PG have remained virtually untouched by Spanish, except for the tendency observed in bilingual children and young adults to either relax the high central vowel /ɨ/ to produce [ɪ] or pronounce it like the fricative velar [ɣ].

Suprasegmental phonology shows the effects of contact in at least three aspects.[15] First, nasal harmony is not observed in the speech of bilingual children and young adults, who tend to not nasalize affixes attached to nasal roots (e.g., reciprocal *ñaño* pronounced as *jajo*). Second, spreading nasalization is not observed either in the speech of most PG urban speakers, who tend to de-nasalize originally nasal segments (e.g., [mitãgwera] 'children' pronounced as [mitangwera]). And last by not least, since a great number of Spanish loanwords are not assimilated in the speech of bilinguals, consonant clusters consisting of plosives and flaps (e.g., /tr/, /pr/), as well as sibilants in coda position, occur more often than not (e.g., *kosa-s-kuéra* 'things'), thus violating onset and coda restrictions of traditional Guaraní.[16]

In the following section, I discuss the results concerning grammatical borrowing. Loan items pertaining to grammar represent 36.1% of the corpus (tokens) and correspond to 19.3% of all lemmatized forms (types). This category includes articles, conjunctions, numerals, discourse markers, adpositions, and pronouns. The analysis

---

[14] Laterals /l/ and /ʎ/ have no native Guaraní counterparts in the place and manner of articulation and thus may be considered exclusive of PG. Still, some authors consider the possibility of an indigenous origin (cf. Gregores and Suarez 1967: 89).

[15] An experimental study of prosody of focus at the level of the utterance in Paraguayan Guaraní is Clopper and Tonhauser (2013).

[16] As a rule, onsets and codas are always monophonemic (Gregores and Suarez 1968: 61).

distinguishes articles and conjunctions as the most frequent classes of grammatical items borrowed from Spanish.

While the borrowing of connectives, including conjunctions and discourse markers, has been discussed somewhat extensively in the literature on language contact (e.g., Boas 1930; Muysken 1981; Brody 1987; Matras 1998; Stolz and Stolz 1996, 1997), article borrowing is a very uncommon phenomenon. Except for Muysken's continuum (1981: 130), scales of borrowability do not include articles. Notwithstanding, loan articles occur in contemporary Guaraní and do so in large numbers, even though their distribution is influenced by diatopic and diastratic factors. Articles represent 22.53% of the total borrowings in urban PG varieties, but only 11.25% in rural varieties. That a higher frequency of loan articles is associated with urban lects is not arbitrary but is motivated by the higher degree of urban bilingualism.

An explanation for the widespread presence of loan articles in PG may be found in the complex system of Guaraní deictics used to mark definiteness, spatial relations, and other referential functions (cf. Gregores and Suarez 1967: 141, 144), to which Spanish articles have been added as determiners and pro-forms (Lustig 1996: 10; Gómez Rendón 2007). The incorporation of Spanish articles to PG morphosyntactic structure suggests that traditional Guaraní had a structural slot for them. Of course, structure does not explain by itself why the language borrowed articles at all, especially if there is a complex system of native elements performing the same function satisfactorily. Typology is in this sense a promoting factor, but not a motivation, for borrowing. The motivation should be looked for in discourse strategies operative at the level of the bilingual speaker in multilingual contexts. The following is a summary of a broader description of loan articles in PG (Gómez Rendón 2007).

Loan articles in Guaraní can be cliticized to native and non-native nouns. Only two forms of the article have been borrowed in Paraguayan Guarani:[17] the feminine singular *la* and the plural masculine *lo(s)*–with the latter form being used in just one expression (7) and the former in all noun phrases involving both singular and plural referents (8).

(7) *che*   *a-segui*   *va'ekue*   *ko*   *edukasión*   *rehegua*
     1S   1S-follow   PST   DEM   education   concerning
     lo-mitã[18]   *apyté-pe*
     DET-people   middle-LOC
     'I continued to support people on educational issues'

---

[17] Notice, however, that Correntinean Guaraní, often classified as another variety of Paraguayan Guarani, is reported to have borrowed not only three different forms spoken of the Spanish article (*el*, *la*, and *lo*), but also two indefinite articles (*un*, *una*). An in-depth discussion of article borrowing can be found in Cerno (2011b). The most extensive phonological, morphological, and syntactic description of the Guaraní variety spoken in the Argentinean province of Corrientes is by the same author (Cerno 2011a).

[18] *Lo-mita* 'people' and *la-mita* 'children' are the only cases in which the loan article forms one phonological word with the noun.

(8) *Ha   umiva   piko   o-torva   **la**   mburuvicha-kuéra-pe*
     And   PRO.DIST EMPH   3-upset   DET   chief-PL-ACC
     'And that upset the chiefs!'

Both examples evidence that *la* is not borrowed with native categories proper of Spanish articles (number and gender), but rather has been fully assimilated to PG morphosyntax. Moreover, this assimilation confirms that composites of loan articles and loan nouns are not code-switches but two independent loans (cf. *supra*). Further proof of this is that possessive pronominal forms may be used between the article and the noun head (9) against Spanish syntactic rules. The resulting phrase (article-possessive-noun) is structurally motivated in traditional Guaraní inasmuch as possessives do not mark definiteness and require the use of determiners (10).

(9) *ij-apyte-pe-kuéra   o-u   **la**   che   tio*
     3.POSS-middle-LOC-PL   3S-come   DET   1.POSS   uncle

     *ha   o-henoi   **la**   iñ-ermano-kuéra*
     and   3-call   DET   3.POSS-sibling-PL
     'My uncle came with them and then called his brothers and sisters'

(10) *nd-ai-kuaá-i   **pe**   **nde**   róga*
     NEG-1S-know-NEG   DEM   2.POSS   house
     'I don't know your house' [lit. I don't know that your house]

Gregores and Suarez (1967: 128) group Spanish articles *la* and *lo* together with PG demonstrative *ku* because the three can make nominalized clauses of restrictive and non-restrictive scope. Indeed, the form *la* co-occurs with one of a set of tense-marked nominalizers (-*va* for present tense, -*va'ekue* for past tense, and -*va'erã* for future tense)[19] as illustrated in the following:

(11) ***la***   *o-ñe-mbo'é-va*   *nda-ha'e-i*
     DET   3-PAS-teach-NMLZ.PRS   NEG-3.be-NEG
     [*la misma cosa*]   ***la***   *o-ñe-ñe'ẽ-va*
     [the same thing]   DET   3-REFL-speak- NMLZ.PRS
     'What is taught is not the same as what is spoken

(12) *che   ru   **la**   o-mano-ma-va'ekue   o-japo   doce-año*
     1S   father   DET   3-die-already-NMLZ.PST   3-do   twelve-year
     'My father, who died twelve years ago'

---

[19] Tonhauser discusses the grammatical category of nominal tense in Guaraní, as well as the issue of Guaraní as a tenseless language (Tonhauser 2007, 2011).

(13) *nd-ai-kuaa-i*   *la*   *ha'e*   *va'erã*
     NEG-1S-know-NEG   DET   1S.say   NMLZ.FUT
     'I do not know what I would say'

Even if the preceding constructions are quite frequent in PG, they do not exhaust all the possible uses of loan articles. Other uses include pronominal roles in which *la* occurs as a freestanding form with co-referential functions, as illustrated in (14) to (16):

(14) *nda-che-tiempo-i*   *la*   *a-japo*   *hagua*   *otra*   *cosa*
     NEG-1S-time-NEG   PRO.DEM$_{(x)}$ 1S-do   PURP   (other   thing)$_{(x)}$
     'I don't have time to do other things'

(15) *alguno-ko*   *no-ñe'ẽ-i-ete*   *la*   *kastellano*,
     some-DEM   NEG-speak-NEG-very   DET   Spanish$_{(x)}$
     oi-ke-rõ   *eskuela-pe-nte*   *la*   *ña-aprende-pa*
     3-come-when   school-LOC-only   PRO.DEM$_{(x)}$ 1PL-learn-ALL
     'Some [of us] don't speak Spanish, only when we go to school, we learn it'

(16) *arema*   *rei-ko*   *nde*   *ko*   *Hernandarias-pe*
     long.time   2S-live   2S   (DEM   Hernandarias-LOC)$_{(x)}$
     arema   *ai-me-te*   *voi*   *la*   *a-nace*   *ko'ápe*
     long.time   1S-be-very   thus   PRO.DEM$_{(x)}$ 1S-be.born   here
     'Have you lived long here in Hernandarias? — I have long lived here where I was born'

In (14) *la* refers forward to the code-switch *otra cosa* 'something else' (cataphoric use) whereas the same form in (15) refers back to the noun phrase *la kastellano* 'the Spanish language' (anaphoric use). Finally, *la* in (16) refers back to the entire locative phrase *ko Hernandariaspe* 'here in Hernandarias' (elliptic use). The reference-tracking capability of the loan article in PG is further demonstrated in (17), where it refers back to *Brasil*.

(17) *che*   *nda-se-guasu-i*,   *Brasil-pe*   *la*   *a-ha*
     1S   NEG-leave-much-NEG   Brazil-LOC$_{(x)}$ PRO.DEM$_{(x)}$ 1S-go
     "I don't leave home too often, to Brazil (there) I have gone"

The productivity of the loan article in PG is amply demonstrated by its frequent occurrence in the corpus and the various functions it plays at phrasal, clausal, and sentential levels.[20] Yet, these uses are not contact-induced innovations since all of them existed in the language before contact. This means that the morphosyntactic structure

---

[20] Kalfell provides a similar explanation for the use of loan articles in his *Grammatik des Jopará* (2011: 33).

Table 32.1 Spanish Simple Connectors and Their PG Equivalents

	Coordination				Subordination		
G	Sp	PG		G	Sp	PG	
terã	o	o	'or'	-rõ	si	si	'if'
ha/katu	pero	pero	'but'	-re	porque	porke	'because'
ha	Y	y	'and'	-ramo	aunque	aunke	(al)though
				-ha	que	ke	'that,' 'which'

of traditional Guaraní enabled the borrowing and productive use of the Spanish article, although the borrowing itself was motivated by the restructuring of discourse strategies as a result of communicative pressures and the increasing bilingualism among the speech community.

As for conjunctions, the second most frequent class of grammatical items occurring in the corpus (7.5%), their occurrence does not depend on diastratic or diatopic factors. Table 32.1 shows loan connectives in PG with their equivalents in traditional Guaraní (G).

The corpus includes also some cases of phrasal connectors such as *a medida que* 'to the extent that.' Still, the majority are simple connectors either linking two main clauses (coordinators) or a subordinate clause to its main clause (subordinators), as illustrated in the following (18):

(18) *Ndo-ro-japó-i*   *mba'eve* *i-cóntra-pe*   **pero** *ro-torva*   *ichupe*
     NEG-2PL-do-NEG   nothing   3-against-LOC   but   1PL.EXC-annoy   3.ACC
     porke   *ha'é-nte*   *o-rrekohe-paité-va'erã*   *mandyju*
     because   3s-only   3-collect-ALL-OBL   cotton
     'We did nothing against her but annoy her because she was the only one who had cotton to collect in the area'

While *porke* and *pero* head the frequency list of loan conjunctions, coordinators *y* 'and' and *o* 'or' often occur linking code-switches. Their occurrence has not influenced Guaraní syntax, however. On the contrary, the incorporation of the subordinator *ke* 'that' has caused morphosyntactic changes at sentential, clausal, and phrasal levels (Gómez Rendón 2007). This becomes particularly evident from the use of the loan subordinator in comparative constructions, as shown in the following example (19).

(19) *i-kuenta-vé-ta*   *ña-ñe'ẽ*   *inglés*   *ke*   *la*   *Guaraní*
     3.be-count-more-FUT   1PL-speak   English   than   DET   Guaraní
     'Our speaking English will count more than our speaking Guaraní'

Loan subordinator *ke* has motivated two further changes: one is the drop of the comparative marker *-gui* on the reference of the comparison (in this case, the noun phrase *la Guaraní*); the other is the now obligatory position of the second term after the subordinator, whereas in traditional Guaraní the second term may be located before or after the element compared, provided it carries the comparative marker. As suggested by its co-occurrence also with code-switches, subordinator *ke* may have entered PG through intra-sentential code-switching. The relevance of this mixing strategy is discussed in the last section.

32.5 THE CONTRIBUTION OF CODE-SWITCHING TO THE EMERGENCE OF PARAGUAYAN GUARANÍ

A discussion has developed in the literature on mixed languages in relation to the relevance of code-switching in the emergence of a mixed language (cf. Backus 2003, 2005; McConvell and Meakins 2005). Several studies (cf. Dietrich 2010; Kalfell 2010) have insisted that Paraguayan (Jopará) Guaraní shows a high level of mixing but this feature does not qualify it as a mixed language, at least not as a mixed language such as Media Lengua. In the following, I add further support to this statement by comparing the different mixing strategies used by Media Lengua and Guaraní speakers on the basis of a statistic corpus-based study of both languages. A full description of the corpus and the detailed outcomes of the analysis are presented elsewhere (Gómez Rendón 2013).

The comparative study analyzed (a) the class and frequency of loanwords; (b) the sentential, clausal, and phrasal scope of code switches and their frequency; (c) the system morphemes and the language they come from; and (d) the order of constituents at the sentential, clausal, and phrasal level, including the order of inflectional and derivational morphemes, and the language they come from (cf. Myers-Scotton 2002).

The statistics show an important contribution of code-switching (30%) in PG with a prevalence of intra-sentential switches and a smaller percentage of loanwords (19%), resulting in an average ratio of 1.37 code-switches per loanword. Also, the analysis of the corpus led to the following conclusions: first, Guaraní is the language providing most system morphemes; second, word order at sentential and clausal levels comes from either Guaraní or Spanish, with a notable occurrence of syntactic calquing from Spanish constructions;[21] third, the order of constituents at the level of the noun phrase comes from Guaraní; and fourth, the order of inflectional and derivational morphology is Guaraní, too, although the level of polysynthesis in PG is lower than in traditional

[21] Several issues of Guaraní syntax are dealt with in depth by Colijn and Tonhauser (2010).

Guaraní. The analysis of Media Lengua, on the contrary, showed a different mixing strategy privileging lexical borrowing (59%) over code-switching (23%). The same analysis led us to conclude that the matrix language of Media Lengua is Kichwa—notwithstanding the copious amount of Spanish loanwords—insofar as Media Lengua preserves, from the latter language, early and late system morphemes, constituent order at sentential, clausal, and phrasal levels (including nominalization strategies), and the order of inflectional and derivational morphemes. We are, therefore, witnessing two different mixing strategies with discursively hybrid but not structurally similar outcomes.

32.6 CONCLUSION

From the preceding description, we are now in a position to better characterize Paraguayan (Jopará) Guaraní. The first remark in this respect is that PG seems to materialize in a series of mixed lects whose level and type of mixing is not characteristic of bilingual mixed languages as defined in the literature (Matras and Bakker 2003). This means that PG lacks a salient genealogical split between lexicon from one language and grammar from another. And yet, the contribution of Spanish lexical and grammatical borrowing is not unimportant. Moreover, considering the continuous varieties of Jopará ranging from more to less Hispanicized, it is wiser to characterize PG as a clearly differentiated though non-stable set of registers with different compositions of borrowing and code-switching according to the speaker's level of bilingualism, his or her identity affiliation, and other relevant factors, including gender, age, and education. That this set of mixed lects may evolve in the direction of a bilingual mixed language is unclear, but they need not to do so. From its mention in old historical records, Jopará seems to have long settled as a fruitful discursive strategy for the creation and negotiation of cross-linguistic and cross-cultural identities in Paraguay.

32.7 TEXT: PARAGUAYAN GUARANÍ SAMPLE

Name: Mirta[22]
Age: 30
Sex: Femenine
Education: Tertiary
Place: Tobatĩ

---

[22] Lexical and grammatical borrowings are in bold. Code switches are in square brackets.

Che-ngo   che-reñoi-va'ekue   táva   Atyra-pe,   táva   Atyrá-pe,
1S-EMPH   1S-be.born-PST   town   Atyra-LOC   lugar   Atyra-LOC
'Well, I was born in Atyra town, the town of Atyra'

*ha   upéi   a-ju-ma   a-ñe-**malcria**   **la**   táva   Tobatĩ-me,*
and   then   1S-come-already   1S-REFL-grow   DET   town   Tobatĩ-LOC
'and came to this town of Tobati to grow up'

*a-guereko   **trentitrés**   ary,   ha   upéi   a-**studia**   ñepyrũ-va'ekue*
1S-have   thirty-three   year   and   then   1S-study   begin-PST
'I am thirty-three years old, and I began to study'

***escuela**   P.J.C.-pe,   che   a-ju   **cinco**   **año**   a-guerekó-rõ-guare*
School   P.J.C.-LOC   1S   3-come   five   year   1S-have-COND-when
'in School P.J.C., I came (to Tobati) when I was five'

*a-juma-va'ekue   **la**   Tobatĩ-me,*
1S-come-already-PST   DET   Tobatĩ-LOC
'I came to Tobaty'

*ha   a-ñepyrũ-mba-ite   **la**   a-**studia***
and   1S-begin-CMP-SUP   DEM   1S-study
'and I begin to study'

ko   táva,   táva   Tobati-me   ha   uperire   a-ha   kuri   avei
DEM   town   town   Tobatĩ-LOC   and   after   1S-go   RECPST   also
'in this town and afterward I also went'

*mbo'ehaó   P.J.C-pe,   upéi   kuri   a-ha   a-je-tavy'o   **la**   ñane*
school   P.J.C-LOC   then   RECPST   1S-go   1S-REFL-learn   DET   1PL.POSS
'to P.J.C. high school, then I studied'

ñe'e   guaraní-me,   ajépa,   upérõ   a-je-abri   kuri
language   Guaraní-LOC   right:INT   then   1S-REFL-abrir   RECPST
'Guaraní, right? then it was the time'

***la**   [Ateneo de Lengua y Cultura Guaraní]   [Colegio Nacional D.M.]-pe*
DET   [Institute of Guaraní langauge and culture]   [National highschool D.M.]-LOC
'that Ateneo de Lengua y Cultura Guaraní opened the National High School D.M.'

*ha   upépe   oi-ko   raka'e   **la**   Ateneo   upépe   o-**funciona**   kuri*
and   there   3-ser   REMPST   DET   Ateneo   there   3-operate   RECPST
'Ateneo was there, and there it was open'

pyharekue,   ha   upépe   ore   ro-ho   kuri   [todos los días]
all.night.long   and   there   1PL.EXCL   1PL.EXCL-go   RECPST   [everyday]
'all the night long, and there we went everyday'

la   ro-*studia*   upé-pe,   ñane   ñe'e   *guaraní*
DET   1PL.EXCL-study there   1PL.POSS   language   Guaraní
'there we studied our Guaraní language'

[*por tres años*]
[for three years]
'for three years.'

REFERENCES

Backus, Alfred Marie. 2003. Can a mixed language be conventionalized alternational codeswitching? In *The Mixed Language Debate*, edited by Peter Bakker and Yaron Matras, 237–270. Berlin: Mouton de Gruyter,

Backus, Alfred Marie. 2005. Code-switching and language change: One thing leads to another? *International Journal of Bilingualism* 9(3–4): 307–340.

Bakker, Dik, Jorge Gómez Rendón, and E. Hekking. 2008. Spanish meets Guaraní, Quechua and Otomí. In *Proceedings of the Conference Romanicization Worldwide*, edited by Thomas Stolz and D. Bakker, 165–238. Bremen: Vervuert.

Bakker, Peter, and Marteen Mous (eds.). 1994. *Mixed Languages: 15 Case Studies in Language Intertwining*. Amsterdam: IFOTT.

Boas, Franz. 1930. Spanish elements in modern Nahuatl. In *Todd Memorial Volume*, edited by John D. FitzGerald and Pauline Taylor, 95–99. New York: Columbia University Press.

Brody, Jill. 1987. Particles borrowed from Spanish as discourse markers in Mayan languages. *Anthropological Linguistics* 29: 507–521.

Cerno, Leonardo. 2011a. *Descripción fonológica y morfosintáctica de una variedad de guaraní hablada en la provincia de Corrientes (Argentina)*. Tesis presentada en la Facultad de Humanidades y Artes de la Universidad Nacional de Rosario como requisito parcial para la obtención de Doctor en Lingüística. Rosario, Argentina.

Cerno, Leonardo. 2011b. Spanish articles in Correntinean Guarani: A comparison with Paraguayan Guaraní. *Sprachtypologie und Universalienforschung*, Akademie Verlag 63(1): 20–38.

Ciccone, Florencia. 2015. *Contacto, desplazamiento y cambio lingüístico en tapiete (tupi-guaraní)*. PhD Dissertation, Universidad de Buenos Aires.

Clopper, Cynthia G., and Judith Tonhauser, 2013. The prosody of focus in Paraguayan Guaraní. *International Journal of American Linguistics* 79(2): 219–251.

Colijn, Erika, and Judith Tonhauser. 2010. Word order in Paraguayan Guaraní. *International Journal of American Linguistics* 76(2): 255–288.

Dietrich, Wolf. 2010. Lexical evidence for a redefinition of Paraguayan Jopará. *Sprachtypologie und Universalienforschung* 63(1): 39–51.

Gómez Rendón, Jorge. 2006. Condicionamientos tipológicos en los préstamos léxicos del castellano: El caso del kichwa de Imbabura. In *Actas del XIV Congreso del ALFAL-2005*, 1–17. Monterrey: ALFAL.

Gómez Rendón, Jorge. 2007. Paraguayan Guaraní. In *Grammatical Borrowing: A Cross-Linguistic Survey*, edited by Yaron Matras and Jeanette Sakel, 523–550. Berlin: Mouton de Gruyter.

Gómez Rendón, Jorge. 2008a. *Una lengua mixta en los Andes: Génesis y estructura de la Media Lengua*. Quito: Editorial Abya Yala.

Gómez Rendón, Jorge. 2008b. *Linguistic and Social Constraints on Language Contact: Amerindian Languages in Contact with Spanish*. PhD dissertation, University of Amsterdam, 2 volumes.

Gómez Rendón, Jorge. 2013. Dos caminos del mestizaje lingüístico: El Jopará y la Media Lengua. In *Revista Letras*, Instituto Venezolano de Investigación Lingüísticas y Literarias, Vol. 54, No. 86.

Gómez Rendón, Jorge. 2017. The demographics of colonization and the emergence of Paraguayan Guarani. In Guarani Linguistics in the 21st century, edited by Bruno Estigarribia and Justin Pinta, 131–157. Leiden & Boston: Koninklijke Bril NV.

Gregores, Emma, and Jorge A. Suárez. 1967. *A Descriptive Grammar of Colloquial Guaraní*. La Haya: Mouton de Gruyter.

Hengeveld, Kees, Jan Rijkhoff, and Anna Siewierska. 2004. Parts of speech systems and word order. *Journal of Linguistics* 40(3): 527–570.

Kallfell, Guido. 2011. *Grammatik des Jopará: Gesprochenes Guaraní und Spanisch in Paraguay*. Frankfurt del Meno: Peter Lang.

Kleinpenning, Jan. 2011. *Paraguay 1515–1870: Una geografía temática de su desarrollo*. Traducción de Jorge Gómez Rendón. Asunción: Editorial Tiempos de Historia.

Lustig, Wolf. 1996. Mba'eichapa oiko la Guaraní? Guaraní y jopará en el Paraguay. *Papia* 4(2): 19–43.

Lustig, Wolf. 2006. La lengua del "Cacique Lambaré" (1867), primer modelo de un guaraní literario. In *Guaraní y "Mawetí-Tupí-Guaraní": Estudios históricos y descriptivos sobre una familia lingüística de América del Sur*, edited by Wolf Dietrich and Haralambos Symeonidis, 241–258. Münster: LIT-Verlag.

Matras, Yaron. 1998. Utterance modifiers and universals of grammatical borrowing. *Linguistics* 36(2): 281–331.

Matras, Yaron, and Peter Bakker (eds.). 2003. *The Mixed Language Debate*. Berlin: Mouton de Gruyter.

McConvell, Patrick, and Felicity Meakins. 2005. Gurindji Kriol: A mixed language emerges from code-switching. *Australian Journal of Linguistics* 25(1): 9–30.

Melià, Bartomeu. 1974. Hacia una tercera lengua en el Paraguay. *Estudios Paraguayos* (Revista de la Universidad Católica) 2: 31–71.

Melià, Bartomeu. 1982. Hacia una 'tercera lengua' en el Paraguay. In *Sociedad y Lengua: Bilingüismo en el Paraguay*, Vol. 1, edited by Grazziella Corvalán and Germán de Granda, 107–168. Asunción: Centro Paraguayo de Estudios Sociológicos

Moravscik, Edith. 1978. Universals of language contact. *Universals of Language*, Vol I: *Method and Theory*, edited by Joseph Greenberg and Charles Ferguson, 95–122. Stanford, CA: Stanford University Press.

Muysken, Pieter. 1981. Spaans en Quechua in Ecuador. *Teoretische Taalwetenschap Tijdschrift* 2: 124–138. Amsterdam: IFFOT.

Myers-Scotton, Carol. 2002. *Contact Linguistics: Bilingual Encounters and Grammatical Outcomes*. Oxford Linguistics. Oxford: Oxford University Press.

Newson, Linda A. 1995. *Life and Death in Early Colonial Ecuador*. The civilization of the American Indian Series, No. 214. Oklahoma: University of Oklahoma Press.

Service, Elman R. 1954. *Spanish-Guaraní Relations in Early Colonial Paraguay*. Ann Arbor: University of Michigan Press.

Shain, Cory, and Judith Tonhauser. 2010. The synchrony and diachrony of differential object marking in Paraguayan Guaraní. *Language Variation and Change* 22(3): 321–346.

Steward, Julian H. (ed.). 1949. *Handbook of South American Indians*, Vol. 5: *The Comparative Ethnology of South American Indians*. Washington, DC: US Government Printing Office.

Stolz, Christel, and Thomas Stolz. 1996. Funktionswortentlehnung in Mesoamerika: Spanish-amerinindischer Sprachkontakt. *Sprachtypologie und Universalienforschung* 49(1): 86–123.

Stolz, Christel, and Thomas Stolz. 1997. Universelle Hispanismen? Von Manila über Lima bis Mexiko und zurück: Muster bei der Entlehnung spanischer Funktionswörter in die indigenen Sprachen Amerikas und Austronesiens. *Orbis* 39: 1–77.

Thomason, Sarah Grey. 1997. *Contact Languages: A Wider Perspective*. Amsterdam: Benjamins.

Tonhauser, Judith. 2007. Nominal tense? The meaning of Guaraní nominal temporal markers. *Language* 83(4): 831–869.

Tonhauser, Judith. 2011. Temporal reference in Paraguayan Guaraní, a tenseless language. *Linguistics & Philosophy* 34(3): 257–303.

Velázquez, Rafael Eladio. 1977. Organización militar de la gobernación y capitanía general del Paraguay. *Estudios Paraguayos* 5(1): 25–69.

CHAPTER 33

LANGUAGE CONTACT IN CAPE VERDEAN CREOLE

A Study of Bidirectional Influences in Two Contact Settings

MARLYSE BAPTISTA, MANUEL VEIGA,
SÉRGIO SOARES DA COSTA, AND
LÍGIA MARIA HERBERT DUARTE LOPES ROBALO

33.1 INTRODUCTION

FOR the past 500 years, the Cape Verde Islands have been the locus of intense contact between the Portuguese language and Cape Verdean Creole (henceforth, CVC). In 1461, the first Portuguese settlers arrived on the island of Santiago. Shortly after, settlers and slave traders started to coexist with slaves brought in from the Senegambian coast (and beyond) in successive waves, throughout the nineteenth century. The intense contact between the Portuguese varieties spoken at the time and the African languages spoken by the slaves (Wolof, Temne, Mandinka, among many others) resulted in the emergence of CVC, presumably in the 1500s. With the emergence of this new code of communication, the African languages gradually subsided, but the Portuguese language remained, and although Cape Verde islands became independent from Portugal in 1975, Portuguese is to this day the only official language of the archipelago.

In spite of this intense, long-term, and continuous contact between Portuguese and CVC, the creole has survived and thrived along a continuum going from the most basilectal variety to an acrolectal variety imbued with Portuguese features. In the post-independence era, as schooling in Portuguese ceased to be the exclusive birthright of the Cape Verdean elite and became accessible to the other socioeconomical strata of the population, more speakers of the creole became bilingual. The more they become bilingual, the more contact effects can be observed in both languages. Indeed, contact effects are observable from Portuguese onto CVC and from CVC onto the spoken and written variety of Portuguese used in Cape Verde islands.

The study of such bidirectional influences is precisely the topic of this chapter. The objective of this work is threefold. Our first goal is to document the influences of Portuguese on CVC (based on Costa 2013; Veiga and Costa 2014) and the reverse effects of CVC onto written Portuguese (based on Herbert Robalo 2013).[1,2] Costa's study examines code-switching strategies that Cape Verdean deputies practice when delivering speeches in the Parliament. In contrast, Herbert Robalo's study considers how twelfth-grade high-school students' native language influences their written Portuguese. Our second goal is thus to analyze the code-switching strategies, as well as other contact mechanisms, such as transfer, that native speakers of CVC resort to in these two contact settings. A related third objective is to evaluate whether or not the contact mechanisms and outcomes are similar in the two settings.

The research questions driving this project are as follows: (1) What is the range and nature of contact phenomena that are observable in these two contact settings? (2) What are the types of code-switching strategies that speakers practice (Muysken 2000, 2013)? (3) With regard to code-switching specifically, is there a detectable pattern to when speakers are more inclined to code-switch?

These research questions guide the organization of this chapter. In the following section (33.2), we provide basic working definitions for the notions of code-switching, borrowing, and transfer, as they underlie our analyses of the data. We introduce Muysken's (2000, 2013) model of code-switching, as it will be instrumental to our account of the data, in section 33.3. In section 33.4, using Muysken's model, we examine patterns of code-switching and other contact phenomena in Veiga and Costa's (2014) study; using Muysken's notion of congruent lexicalization, we study the ways in which Portuguese influences CVC in the speech of Cape Verdean deputies at the Parliament. In section 33.5, we contrast the results of Veiga and Costa's study to the reverse effects that CVC may have on written Portuguese in the writings of twelfth-grade high-school students, as they are reported in Herbert Robalo's (2013) study. In the final section (33.5),

---

[1] All the data involving the influences of Portuguese on Cape Verdean Creole are drawn from a 2014 manuscript by Manuel Veiga and Sérgio Costa based on Costa's 2013 Master's thesis entitled "Interferénsias di purtugês na kriolu: Análizi di atas di seson plenáriu di mês di Abril, Maiu, Junhu y Julhu di 2011." This thesis was written in Cape Verdean Creole and supervised by Manuel Veiga. For ease of reference, we use Veiga and Costa (2014) when providing specific examples of speech excerpts, with the understanding that all of the data are drawn from Costa's (2013) Master's thesis.

The data illustrating how Cape Verdean Creole influences the written Portuguese of high-schoolers is taken from Lígia Herbert Robalo's Master's thesis entitled "Fenómenos de interferência linguística no português escrito de alunos do 12⁰ ano da Escola Secundária Cónego Jacinto Peregrino da Costa." Her thesis was written in Portuguese and was supervised by Marlyse Baptista. Both Costa and Herbert Robalo wrote their Master's theses in the context of the first Master's in Creolistics offered by the University of Cape Verde and for which Marlyse Baptista and Manuel Veiga were instructors. Both Costa and Herbert Robalo were part of the first graduating cohort for this particular Master's degree.

[2] We should make it clear from the onset that while we draw the empirical data from these two Master's theses (Costa, 2013; Herbert Robalo, 2013) and Veiga and Costa (2014), the research questions and analyses proposed in this chapter differ significantly from those found in the original works; such differences will be signaled explicitly, whenever they occur.

we reflect on the nature of the contact phenomena, patterns, and outcomes in the two modalities (oral and written) under study.

33.2 WORKING DEFINITIONS: ON THE CONCEPTS OF CODE-SWITCHING, BORROWING, AND TRANSFER

Given the vast literature and distinct approaches to contact phenomena such as code-switching, borrowing, and transfer, we provide in this section some basic definitions that will guide our analyses of the data at hand. We start by defining code-switching and distinguishing it from borrowing and transfer.

33.2.1 Teasing Apart Code-Switching from Borrowing

We contrast in this subsection the two notions of code-switching and borrowing, so that we may differentiate between the two in the data analysis we provide in the following.

Van Dulm (2007) and Grosjean (2010) are among two studies that succeed in teasing code-switching apart from borrowing in a fairly meaningful way. Referring to Hoffman's (1991: 110) definition, Van Dulm (2007: 9) refers to code-switching as "the alternate use of two [or more] languages within the same utterance or during the same conversation." Grosjean (2010) complements this definition by specifying the possible types of switches: "Code-switching is the alternate use of two languages, that is, the speaker makes a complete shift to another language for a *word*, a *phrase*, or *sentence* [my emphasis], and then reverts back to the base language. Hence, bilinguals who code-switch are speaking language X in a bilingual mode when they call upon language Y for a moment" (Grosjean 2010: 51–52).

Grosjean (2010) draws a useful distinction between code-switching and borrowing by characterizing a borrowing as a word or short expression whose phonology and morphology have been adapted to the base language with the result that it blends in. As he puts it, "Unlike code-switching, which is the alternate use of two languages, borrowing is the integration of one language into another" (Grosjean 2010: 58). Figure 33.1, taken from Grosjean (2010: 58), illustrates the point.

Grosjean also distinguishes between code-switching and borrowing by presenting code-switching as involving two grammars (an alternation between language A and language B), whereas borrowing only involves one.

In spite of the useful distinctions based on morpho-phonological adaptation and two grammars versus one, it remains at times challenging to distinguish a single-word switch from a borrowing. This may be in part due to the way a code-switch may gradually evolve into a borrowing. On this matter, Muysken (1995: 189, quoted in Van Dulm 2007: 9) assumes three main stages that a code-switch may go through before

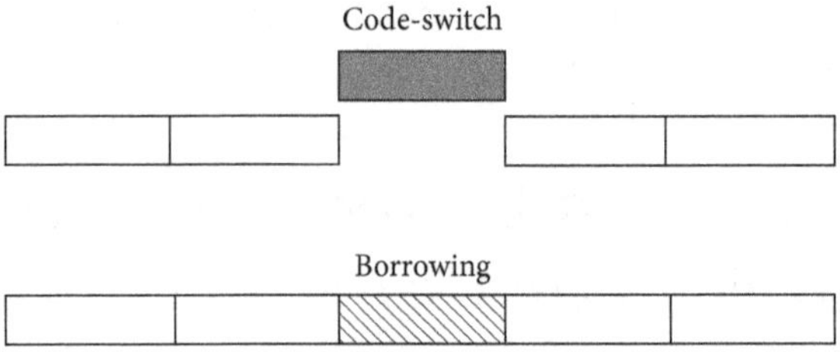

FIGURE 33.1 Code-switching as alternation between language A and language B; borrowing as integration of language A into language B.

turning into a borrowing. In stage 1, Muysken proposes that a fluent bilingual speaker may insert a lexical item from language A into a sentence of language B. The speaker's fluency allows her to insert this item as a code-switched element from language A into language B. Over time, this lexical item is used with a higher degree of frequency and spreads to the entire community, a phenomenon Muysken labels "conventionalized code-switching." Finally, in the last stages of the word's integration into the lexicon of language B, it becomes phonologically, morphologically, and syntactically integrated into the grammatical structure of language B. This is the stage when the word becomes a borrowing (Muysken 1995 in Van Dulm 2007: 9), familiar and identified by monolingual speakers as being part of their own language.

In the domain of borrowings, Poplack, Sankoff, and Miller (1988: 93) (quoted in Van Dulm 2007: 9 and Grosjean 2010) distinguish two types of borrowings: nonce loans and established loans. Nonce loans are typically used by a single speaker in a given situational setting and are not recognizable by monolingual speakers. In contrast, established loans are used by a speech community and are highly recognizable. Both types of borrowings undergo phonological, morphological, and syntactic adaptation to language B. We will retain from all these studies that a basic distinction between a code-switch and a borrowing is that a code-switch involves two grammars (language A and language B), whereas a borrowing only involves one. This basic difference will guide our exploration of the data in the following, when teasing apart code-switching from mere borrowings. In the next section, we introduce Muysken's model of code-switching, as it is instrumental to our analyses of the data presented in Veiga and Costa (2014).

33.3 Muysken's Model
of Code-Switching

33.3.1 Identifying Code-Switching Strategies

In our view, Muysken's (2000, 2013) model of code-switching captures well the various code-switching patterns found in bilingual speakers' discourse, including those in our corpus. He acknowledges that the different code-switching strategies are not always clearly separable from each other, but he manages to reduce them to three main patterns: insertional, alternational, and congruent lexicalization.

He provides the following definitions and illustrative examples for the various strategies. Insertional code-switching refers to the insertion of well-defined chunks of language B into a sentence that otherwise belongs to language A (Muysken 2013: 712). A typical example of insertion in Bolivian Spanish is provided in (1), followed by a commentary from Muysken:

(1) *Q'aya suya-wa-nki*   *[las cuatro-ta].*
     tomorrow wait-1OB-2sg   at four-AC
     Qo-yku-sqa-sun-ña   *[bukis]*
     give-ASP-ASP1PL.FUT.con   box
     'Tomorrow you wait for me at four. We'll have a go at boxing.'
     (Quechua/Spanish; Urioste 1966: 7, quoted in Muysken 2013: 712)

In the Bolivian example (1), the Spanish expression *las cuatro* 'at four' is modified by the Quechua accusative marker *–ta* and is inserted into a Quechua clause. The lexical item *bukis* 'box' is taken from Spanish and appears without the accusative case marker. Muysken notes that the SVO order of the second clause, used instead of the canonical SOV word order, could be occurring under the influence of Spanish, though one cannot be directly speaking of code-switching in such cases (Muysken 2013: 712).

Alternational code-switching in Muysken's framework refers to the alternating sequence of expressions from language A and B, making it difficult to assert whether a sentence belongs to language A or B (Muysken 2013: 713). Consider (2):

(2) *Andale pues, and do come again.*
     'That's all right then, and do come again.'
     (Spanish/English; Poplack 1980: 589, cited in Muysken 2013: 713)

In example (2), representative of Mexican-American speech, the Spanish expression *ándale pues* is juxtaposed to the English expression 'do come again,' such juxtaposition impeding the subordination of a language to the other.

In contrast to insertion and alternation, congruent lexicalization refers to the structural properties that two languages in contact may have in common, facilitating the integration of words from either language into the shared structure.

Example (3) exemplifies congruent lexicalization:

(3) *Això   a   él   a   ell   no   li   i(m)porta.*
     this   to   him   to   him   not   3sg.   matters
     'This he, he doesn't care.'
     (Catalan/Spanish; Vila i Moreno 1996: 393, in Muysken 2013: 713)

In the sentence in (3) (produced by a Spanish speaker who is non-fluent in Catalan), the Spanish preposition and pronoun cluster *a él* 'to him' is naturally integrated into the

---

Table 33.1 Muysken's Model

Insertion: Use the L1 (i.e., the grammatical and lexical properties of the first language) as the matrix or base language.
Alternation: Use universal combinatory principles, procedures by which fragments from different languages can be combined independently of the grammars involved.
Congruent lexicalization: Produce structures and words that share properties of L1 and L2.

Source: Muysken (2013: 714).

Catalan sentence, due to the structural and morpho-lexical parallels between these two languages (Muysken 2013: 713).

Table 33.1 provides a succinct summary of each of the strategies laid out in Muysken's model.

33.3.2 The Predictions of Muysken's Model

In terms of when these strategies are implemented by speakers, Muysken isolates several social, cognitive, and linguistic factors that may promote the use of one of these strategies over others; social factors involve (a) power relations, (b) normativity, (c) political competition, and (d) network memberships/generation and duration of language contact. Cognitive factors involve bilingual speakers' varying degrees of proficiency in the two languages they use. Linguistic factors involve typological and lexical distances between the two languages.

Regarding (a), Muysken's predictions are that in situations of uneven power relationships between the languages, insertional patterns of code-switching are preferred, whereas in cases of more even power relations, other strategies may be implemented. With regard to (b), his model also makes the prediction that a high degree of normativity in the two languages tends to inhibit congruent lexicalization, whereas the reverse obtains (congruent lexicalization is favored) in contexts where the norms are looser. As for (c), strong political competition between the two languages favors alternational code-switching, whereas when speakers do not perceive as much contrast between languages, congruent lexicalization is favored. With regard to (d), Muysken argues that congruent lexicalization occurs in close-knit communities. In immigrant communities, the first generation uses insertional code-switching, whereas the second generation uses the other strategies including backflagging, which consists in inserting heritage language items in L2 discourse. The longer the two languages are in contact, the more often congruent lexicalization is used. At the cognitive level, this correlates with speakers' degree of proficiency in the two languages; Muysken proposes that high proficiency leads to a higher rate of congruent lexicalization, whereas lower proficiency favors insertion.

Finally, as far as the linguistic factors are concerned, typological and lexical distance seem to play a role in the type of code-switching that is adopted. According to

Muysken, the more typologically distant languages favor the use of insertion and alternation, whereas the more typologically close languages privilege congruent lexicalization. The same goes for lexical distance whereby congruent lexicalization occurs when there is little distance between the languages in presence (Muysken 2013: 714).

We show in the following that some of these predictions carry through in our analyses of the data, whereas others do not, and we provide an alternative analysis to account for the observable patterns.

Before delving into the data, we briefly survey the range of motivations that may lead speakers to code-switch, as we are able to identify some of these motivations for the speakers under study.

33.3.3 Motivations for Code-Switching

Grosjean (2010) lays out several key motivations for code-switching. A speaker may code-switch when he realizes that a particular concept is better expressed in another language. For instance, a bilingual speaker of English and Portuguese may code-switch from English to Portuguese when referring to the notion of *saudade*, which carries the meaning of nostalgia, homesickness, sadness, and deep longing for one's loved ones. All of these emotions are encapsulated in the one term, *saudade*, and for that reason, may trigger the switch. A second motivation is to fill in a lexical gap when a given word does not exist in a given language. For instance, a bilingual French-English speaker may switch from French to English when referring to a culturally based concept such as 'brunch' or 'pot-luck.' A third motivation Grosjean identifies is that of group identity. A speaker may code-switch with an interlocutor when wishing to express a particular bond, a particular connection with members of the same community. A fourth motivation is to raise one's status, show expertise, or exclude outsiders by code-switching. A speaker may code-switch with the deliberate intent to ostracize and alienate. We will see in the following that a subset of such motivations apply to the speakers that we examine in this chapter.

We end this section by introducing a working definition of the term *transfer*, as we resort to this concept in our analysis of our data, particularly Herbert Robalo's corpus.

33.3.4 On Transfer

Weinreich's (1953) pioneering work in interference studies (a.k.a effects of language contact) could easily earn him the title of one of the modern founders of contact linguistics. To him, the notion of interference has the broader meaning of transfer, but he cautions that the very nature of this transfer and its outcome vary dramatically, depending on the social context in which it takes place. Hence, early on, Weinreich's objective was to draw a strong connection between contact effects in bilingual speech and the social factors underlying such effects. Not surprisingly, the notion of transfer has also been critical to studies of second-language acquisition. In these studies, the notion of transfer often takes on the label of substratum transfer and refers to the ways in which a source language, generally a speaker's native language, affects his acquisition of a second language. As a result, the notion of transfer is relevant and inextricably linked to the fields of both contact linguistics and second language acquisition.

For the purpose of this chapter, we use Odlin's (1989: 27) definition of transfer, which states that "transfer is the influence resulting from similarities and differences between the target language and any other language that has been previously (and perhaps imperfectly) acquired." While we could view transfer as being typically an imposition of a feature from L1 onto a second language, we should keep in mind that transfer may also occur in the opposite direction (from L2 onto L1), particularly when a speaker attains a high degree of proficiency in the two languages.

Two types of transfer have been identified in the literature: positive transfer and negative transfer. One of the best characterizations of the differences between the two can be found in Windford (2003). According to this author, "in cases where L1 and L2 match each other closely, L1 retentions may result in relatively close approximations to the target element or structure, leading to positive transfer. In cases of mismatch, such retentions often lead to 'imperfect learning' and represent forms of 'negative transfer'" (Windford 2003: 210). The term *interference* can be equated to negative transfer, meaning that a feature from L1 is transferred to L2 but when no counterpart exists in L2, the transfer results in (and stands out as) an error. This is in contrast to positive transfer, which is "the facilitating influence of cognate vocabulary or any other similarities between the native and target languages" (Odlin 1989: 26). This distinction will come in handy in section 33.5, when we observe that the majority of students' "errors" in Herbert Robalo's study are actual cases of positive transfer, attesting to students' sensitivity to the similarities between CVC and Portuguese.

Returning to the pivotal role of transfer in both contact linguistics and the field of second language acquisition, as Odlin (1989) points out, Schuchardt ([1891] 1980) was the first to comment on the role of transfer and other contact effects on the languages of nineteenth- century Europe and to draw a connection between the linguistic features that emerged in such contact situations and those found in pidgins and creoles. Over time, he noted that a common feature among the various contact situations he examined is that they all involved various degrees and types of simplification. Children simplify grammatical features of their native language in the initial stages of language development; some adults simplify their language when addressing children; and foreigners simplify the grammar of the second language they learn. Similar strategies could be found in the grammars of some pidgins and creoles (Odlin 1989: 11). As a result, one of Schuchardt's key findings was the realization that there exist universal tendencies toward simplicity in most, if not all, situations involving language contact and language acquisition (Odlin 1989: 11). On this issue, we concur with Mühlhäusler (1986) and Odlin (1989) and take the position that explanations based on transfer and those based on universal tendencies are entirely compatible and actually reinforce each other, often leading to a multicausal account of a given phenomenon.[3] We wish to emphasize this point here, as we will return to it when analyzing the written production of Herbert Robalo's students' writing samples in section 33.5. We will capitalize on Schuchardt's original point that a tendency toward simplicity[4] is observable in both situations of language contact and language acquisition.

Having presented in this section the working definitions of code-switching, borrowing, and transfer—all contact phenomena at the heart of our data—we now turn to the linguistic analyses of the two corpora that were the bases of Costa's and Herbert Robalo's theses.

33.4 LANGUAGE CONTACT IN CAPE VERDEAN CREOLE

33.4.1 Contact effects from Portuguese onto Cape Verdean Creole

The following examples, drawn from Veiga and Costa (2014) and all based on Costa's (2013) original thesis, show different ways in which the Portuguese spoken in Cape Verde islands influences the creole spoken in public arenas such as the Parliament. In this section, we bring new analyses to the corpus data that Costa collected, in addition to his own interpretation of the data. As will be discussed, such influences include transfer (both positive and negative transfer), borrowing, and code-switching. Our study has two main components. On the one hand, we report on some of Veiga's and Costa's findings and examine contact effects from Portuguese onto CVC in the areas of gender agreement, number agreement, verb morphology, and complementizer phrases. As we show, these are mostly cases of transfer (positive and negative) and lexical borrowing of single words and idiomatic expressions. On the other, we examine code-switching strategies used by some of the speakers and analyze the trigger points for the switches.

---

[3] We wish to emphasize that the field is far from having reached a consensus on this matter. Not all scholars attribute a pivotal role to transfer. Some errors like article and copula deletion, in addition to reduction in inflectional complexity, are often viewed as involving simplification instead of transfer (Odlin 1989: 18). Speakers with very distinct linguistic backgrounds have been observed to make errors that are very similar to those involved in the acquisition of a first or second language, meaning that the same kind of errors appear, irrespective of the speaker's linguistic background. This has led some to believe that the two processes are very similar, hence casting doubt on the value and reality of transfer.

[4] In order to avoid any misunderstanding of the sense in which we use the notion of 'simplicity,' we wish to clarify that we do not ascribe to the position that situations of language contact and language acquisition lead to the emergence of "simpler" linguistic systems. We use the term only to address the lack of inflectional morphology and agreement in the data that we analyze in Costa's and Herbert Robalo's works.

Let us start by examining the cases of transfer and borrowing in the domains of gender agreement, number agreement, verb morphology, and complementizer phrases.

33.4.1.1 *Contact Effects on Gender Marking*

In the domain of gender agreement, gender marking may occur in CVC on both nouns and adjectives but in restricted contexts (Pires 1995; Quint 2000; Veiga 2000; Baptista 2002). Baptista (2002) noted that animacy and the [+ human] feature in particular play an important role in determining whether a noun expresses a morphological distinction between masculine and feminine. Pires (1995) was one of the first studies to discuss at length this trait, following Portuguese patterns. The examples in (4) show that kinship terms can express gender distinction (–*u* standing for masculine and –*a* for feminine). The examples in (5) describe various human attributes. The set in (6) exemplifies honorary, aristocratic titles.

(4)   a. *fidju-fidja*   (Pires 1995: 76)
        son-daughter

    b. *noibu-noiba*
        groom-bride

(5)   a. *ladron-ladrona*   (Pires 1995: 77)
        thief (m.)-thief (f.)

    b. *trabadjador-trabadjadera*
        hard-worker (m.)/hard-worker (f.)

    c. *papiador-papiadera*
        talker (m.)/talker (f.)

(6)   a. *duki-dukeza*   (Pires 1995: 77)
        duke-duchess

    b. *prispi-prinseza*
        prince-princess

    c. *kondi-kondesa*
        count-countess

Gender marking is one of the areas where the factor of animacy plays a major role in the grammar of the language. In contrast, for inanimate entities, it is customary in CVC for them to be neutralized to a default masculine ending. In (7), for instance, the noun *menza* from the feminine Portuguese word *mesa* 'table' is modified by an adjective that has been neutralized to a masculine ending.

(7)   *un   menza   redondu*
       a   table   round
       'a round table'

The distinctive behavior of gender agreement with respect to animate and inanimate entities in the CVC grammar is, however, not attested in many of the deputies' speech excerpts that Veiga and Costa (2014) documented; in their speeches, gender agreement with inanimate entities is rampant, following the Portuguese model. The example in (8a) illustrates the agreement reflecting the Portuguese pattern, instead of the proto-typical CVC expression in (8b):

(8)   a. *língua caboverdiana*   (Portuguese)
         language Capeverdean+FEM
         'Cape Verdean language'

      b. *língua kabuverdianu*   (Cape Verdean Creole)
         language Capeverdean+MAS
         'Cape Verdean language' (Veiga and Costa 2014: 6)

Veiga and Costa (2014) rightfully refer to such examples as cases of code-switching marked not only by gender agreement, but also by the adoption of the Portuguese stress patterns and phonology.

33.4.1.2 *Contact Effects on Number Agreement*

In the area of number agreement, as discussed in Veiga (2000), Quint (2000) and Baptista (2002), one of the standard strategies in marking number in CVC is via determiners (9b), deictics (10b), possessives (10c), numerals (11) and floating quantifiers (12), while the nominal stem, as a rule, remains bare, making plural marking generally economical. The following examples are drawn from Baptista (2002).

      Indefinite determiner
(9)   a. *un rapariga*
         'a young woman'

      b. *uns rapariga*
         'some young women'

      Demonstrative/definite determiner
(10) a. *kel rapariga*
         'that/the young woman'

      b. *kes rapariga*
         'those/the young women'
         possessive

      c. *Nhas fidju*   (MR-FO)
         'my children/my sons'

      Numerals
(11) N *pari*   *oitu*   *fidju* (C-ST)
      I   deliver eight   children
      'I had eight children.'

Quantifier

(12) **Tudu**   rapariga   staba ta   txora.
      all   young women   were TMA   crying
      'All the young women were crying.'

However, in the deputies' speech excerpts, number agreement between quantifiers/possessives and nouns takes place repeatedly:

(13)   a. *txeu   kabras*
          a lot of   goat+PL
          'a lot of goats'

       b. *txeu   mudjeris*
          a lot of   woman+PL
          'a lot of women'

       c. *nhas   amigus*
          my+PL   friend+PL
          'my friends' (Veiga and Costa 2014: 6)

The basilectal counterparts to the examples in (13) are in (14), where number marking on the head noun is optional:

(14)   a. *txeu kabra*
          lot of goat
          'a lot of goats'

       b. *txeu mudjer*
          a lot of woman
          'a lot of women'

       c. *nhas amigu*
          my friend
          'my friends'

Note that examples such as those in (13) may be interpreted in two ways. The head noun *kabras* 'goats' in (13a) and *amigus* 'friends' in (13c) have their exact counterparts *cabras* and *amigos* in Portuguese and could, as a result, be viewed as examples of insertional code-switching; this interpretation is the one that Veiga and Costa (2014) provide, which seems valid. Such examples could, however, also be interpreted as illustrating the transfer (see definition in section 33.3.4) of a major use pattern of overt plural agreement inherited from Portuguese.

33.4.1.3 *Verb Morphology*

In the domain of verb morphology, Veiga and Costa (2014) note the use of Portuguese verb forms in the speech of deputies and interprets these forms as code-switches. It is indeed the case that in the particular example in (15a), the form *seria* is from Portuguese, but it is important to note that the entire expression in (15a) is code-switched, not just the verb form. According to Muysken's model, laid out in section 33.3.1, the expression in (15a) could be viewed both as a case of alternational code-switching, denoting a switch at the clausal level, and a case of congruent lexicalization, given the word-to-word mapping between the Portuguese expression in (15a) and its CVC counterpart in (15b).

(15) a. *Isso   seria   bom*   (Portuguese)
         this   would be   good
         'This would be good'

      b. *kel-li   ta   sérba   bon*   (CVC)
         this   would   be   good
         'This would be good' (Veiga and Costa 2014: 7)

In (15), Portuguese *seria* (15a) and CVC *sérba* (15b) clearly belong to distinct languages. One should note, however, that there are other verb forms in CVC that may be more accurately viewed as competing with each other; some of the competing forms are clearly Portuguese, others are phonologically adapted from Portuguese, whereas others are genuine creole innovations. Such competing forms have been present in the CVC language for some time and attest to the enduring, ongoing, and intense contact between Portuguese and CVC. For instance, the cluster *tinha* (Portuguese), *tenha* (phonologically adapted), and *tenba* (creole), semantically equivalent and translatable as 'had,' reflects such a competition. The Portuguese verb form *tinha* 'had or used to have' in (16) can be found in fieldwork data Baptista collected in 2007 on the island of Santiago, and seems to occur in free variation with *tenha* (17) and *tenba* (18). *Tenha* was found in the corpus Baptista collected in Santiago and Fogo and *tenba* in the data she collected on the island of Brava. All forms seem to be present across the Southern varieties of the language.

(16) *Nu   ka   tinha   kulpa*   (Santiago)
      we   NEG   had   guilt
      'It was not our fault'

(17) *Kaba   e   ba   na   un   pilon   ki   tenha   midju   la*   (Fogo)
      finish he   go   to   a   mortar   that had   corn   there
      'At the end, he went to a mortar that had corn in it'

      Nu   atxa fomi   li,   kenhi ka   tenha un tiston, e   ka   tenba pasadiu,
      we   find hunger here who   NEG   had   a cent   he NEG   had   ration to eat
      'We found hunger here, those who didn't have one cent, they didn't have anything to eat' (Fogo)

(18) *N   ka   tenba   dinheru   na   kel   tenpu*   (Brava)
      I   NEG   had   money   at   that   time
      'I had no money in those days'

The creole continuum mentioned in the introduction and encompassing the basilectal, mesolectal, and acrolectal varieties of the language may account for the healthy competition between these forms, resulting in basilectal speakers preferring *tenba* whereas their acrolectal peers may use the Portuguese form *tinha*.

Veiga and Costa (2014) observe the same competition between passive structures (19a) that are more Portuguese-like in nature whereas their active voice counterparts (19b) are more felicitous in the Cape Verdean language.

(19)   a. *Livru   foi   kunpradu   pa   mi*   (CVC)
           book   was   bought   by   me
           'The book was bought by me.'

        b. *Livru   ki   mi   ki   kunpra*   (CVC)
           book   that   me   that   bought
           'The book that I bought' (Veiga and Costa 2014: 7)

Note that (19a) can only be viewed as a case of structural transfer and not alternational code-switching (per the definition provided in section 33.3.4), as the Portuguese counterpart in (20) would involve the use of the overt definite determiner *o*, a distinct preposition *por*, a distinct pronoun *mim*, and past-participle *comprado*.

(20)   *O   livro   foi   comprado   por   mim*   (Portuguese)
        the   book   was   bought   by   me
        'The book was bought by me.'

33.4.1.4 *A Focus on Code-Switching Strategies*

In the next examples, we examine cases of code-switching (both insertional and alternational), involving prepositional phrases. Veiga and Costa (2014) focus on prepositions as single points of code-switching (akin to insertional code-switching), but we modify their analysis by proposing instead that prepositions act as trigger sites, typically giving way to alternational code-switching.

In the following examples, the trigger lexical head for alternational code-switching is the Portuguese preposition *em* 'in,' which is used in place of its CVC counterpart *na*. The (a) examples (taken from Costa's corpus) illustrate utterances that are code-switched to Portuguese but which Veiga and Costa chose to transcribe in the ALUPEC orthography.[5] The choice of orthographic convention masks that these are instances of alternational code-switching to Portuguese. In order to capture the switches, we provide the Portuguese examples (b), using the Portuguese orthographic convention. The (c) examples are the CVC counterparts, clearly distinct from the (a) examples. For instance, comparing (21a) taken from Costa's speech excerpts to its Portuguese

[5] The ALUPEC for Alfabeto Unificado Para a Escrita do Caboverdiano 'Unified Alphabet for the Writing of Cape Verdean.' This orthographic convention became the official alphabet of Cape Verdean Creole in 2009. It is a compromise between the Portuguese etymological script and a phonemic spelling.

counterpart in (21b) clearly shows that the code-switching affects the entire expression *em diferentes pontos* (not just the preposition *em*), hence involving the preposition, adjective, and noun in addition to marking number agreement between the adjective and the noun. In (21a), the speaker reverses to CVC at the boundary of the constituent *di ilha* 'of the island.' In sum, out of the two Prepositional Phrases *en diferentis pontus* and *di ilha* involved in this expression, code-switching only affects the first Prepositional Phrase.

(21)   a. *en diferentis pontus di ilha* (transcribed in the ALUPEC)
     b. *em diferentes pontos da ilha* (transcribed in Portuguese)
     c. *na diferenti pontu di ilha* (CVC)
       'in different sites of the island' (Veiga and Costa 2014: 8)

In (22b), the Portuguese orthographic convention disguises the fact that the head noun *ritmo* is pronounced in the same way as it is transcribed in CVC ((22a) and (22c)). As a result, the entire expression in (22) is an alternational code-switch from CVC to Portuguese.

(22)   a. *en bon rítimu* (transcribed in the ALUPEC)
     b. *em bom ritmo* (transcribed in Portuguese)
     c. *na bon rítimu* (CVC)
       'in good rhythm' (Veiga and Costa 2014: 8)

In (23a), the entire expression also seems to be a code-switch from CVC to Portuguese with the caution that the spelling of *primeru* 'first' does not reflect the diphthong present in the Portuguese adjective in (23b). It remains unclear whether a genuine switch occurred or whether phonological adaptation took place instead.

(23)   a. *en primeru lugar* (transcribed in the ALUPEC)
     b. *em primeiro lugar* (transcribed in Portuguese)
     c. *na purmeru lugar* (CVC)
       'in the first place' (Veiga and Costa 2014: 8)

The same code-switching patterns are detectable with the Portuguese preposition *para* 'for/to' that is used instead of the CVC preposition *pa*. In the following excerpts, the preposition *para* seems to operate as a trigger for alternational or insertional code-switching. The (a) examples illustrate the code-switched sentences in Portuguese and the (b) examples, their CVC counterparts. In (24a), the Portuguese code-switch in this sentence, uttered in the variety spoken in São Vicente, affects the entire PP and features plural agreement between the adjective *prósimes* and the noun *anus*. The CVC counterpart in (24b) features the CVC preposition *pa* and lacks number agreement on the head noun.[6]

---

[6] We revisit these examples in light of congruent lexicalization in the following, in support of Muysken's observation (mentioned earlier) that the different code-switching strategies are not always clearly separable.

(24) a. *y   é   pur   ise   ke   no   ta   kestiona-l   sê   kontinuidade*
     and this for this that we ASP question-it its continuity
     para prósimes -anus
     for next+PL year-PL

    b. *y é pur ise ke no ta kestiona-l sê kontinuidade **pa prosimes óne***
     and this for this that we ASP question-it its continuity   for next+PL year
     'and this is the reason why we question its continuation for the next years'
     (Veiga and Costa 2014: 8)

In (25a) and (26a), the code-switch only affects the prepositional head and possibly the following adverbs *kuandu* and *alén* in (25) and (26), respectively, but one cannot be categorical on this point due to the homophony of these lexemes in the two languages.

(25) a. ***para** kuandu ki Guvérnu ta pensa inísia es konstruson*
    b. pa   kuandu ki Guvérnu ta pensa inísia es konstruson
     'for when the government thinks in starting this construction'
     (Veiga and Costa 2014: 8)

(26) a. *Kulunatu é un perímitru irigadu ki **para** alén di stóriku, ten sidu fonti di rendimentu pa sentenas di famílias di Chãu Bon y di Mangi*

    b. *pa alén di storiku*
     'Kulunatu is a surface irrigated beyond the historical, it has been the source of livelihood for hundreds of families from Chãu Bon and Mangi'
     (Veiga and Costa 2014: 8)

The examples in (21) through (26) illustrate how prepositions can operate as trigger switches for both alternational and insertional code-switching; in so doing, they also seem to be prime candidates for congruent lexicalization, per Muysken's definition in section 33.3.1 Indeed, we observe that even if only insertional code-switching takes place (meaning that the switch only involves the Portuguese prepositional head), the switch is licensed only in cases where the following constituent or clause is structurally isomorphic in both languages. We do not claim that this is a fool-proof hypothesis, but the empirical evidence attests to such patterns and supports congruent lexicalization; this observation also supports Muysken's point (reported in section 33.3) that the code-switching strategies that speakers implement are not always clearly separable from each other: they can overlap. Hence, insertional code-switching, for instance, may overlap with congruent lexicalization, as insertion may be facilitated by structural isomorphy between the two languages.

    The same patterns may be observed with respect to two other prepositions in Costa's original corpus: the Portuguese preposition *por* 'for' is used instead of CVC *pa*, and whenever it is used, it gives way to congruent lexicalization. As we noted earlier with the preposition *em* 'in,' the (a) example in (27) shows the code-switched prepositional head in the original speech excerpt, transcribed in the ALUPEC. The (b) example shows the Portuguese equivalent (transcribed in Portuguese), and the (c) example its

CVC counterpart when no code-switching has occurred. The juxtaposed set of examples clearly illustrates the structural mapping between Portuguese and CVC, facilitating the observed code-switching pattern. As in example (23), in which the lack of diphthong in *primeru* 'first' may have betrayed phonological adaptation rather than a genuine code-switch, there is no diphthong in 'respetu' in the (a) example, but again, it may be simply that the phoneme was not adequately reported in the original transcript. Other than this slight discrepancy, (27) seems to illustrate alternational code-switching.

(27) a. *N ta gostaba di rifiriba un bokadinhu a es metudulujia ki, **pur falta di respetu**,*
      I ASP like+PAST to refer+PAST a little to this methodology that, for lack of respect
      ka foi ditu li kual ki el é
      NEG was say here what that it is
      'I would like to refer a little to this methodology that, for lack of respect, was not elaborated upon what it is.' (transcribed in the ALUPEC)

   b. ***por falta de respeito*** ... (transcribed in Portuguese)

   c. ***pa falta di ruspetu*** ... (CVC)
      'for lack of respect' (Veiga and Costa 2014: 8)

In contrast to (27), which can reasonably be viewed as a case of alternational code-switching, the examples in (28) and (29) are cases of insertional code-switching, where only the prepositional head (and possibly the head noun in (28a)) carries the switch.

(28) a. ***pur** respetu a es povu* (transcribed in the ALUPEC)
      b. por respeito a este povo (transcribed in Portuguese)
      c. pa *ruspetu pa es povu* (CVC)
      'out of respect for this people' (Veiga and Costa 2014: 8)

(29) a. ***pur más ki Opozison fla*** (transcribed in the ALUPEC)
      b. *por mais que a Oposição diga* (transcribed in Portuguese)
      c. *pa más ki Opozison fla* (CVC) (Veiga and Costa 2014: 8)
      'for more than what the Opposition may say ... '

We would like to propose, though, that this switch is facilitated by the near-perfect structural mapping of the following lexical items in the two languages. We suggest that all the examples in (21) through (29) show congruent lexicalization at work; we elaborate on this observation with the following examples.

In the following excerpt presented in (30), the Portuguese preposition *com* 'with,' transcribed as [kon], was originally analyzed in Veiga and Costa (2014) as the site of insertional code-switching. Based on the strategies introduced thus far, we analyze instead the entire utterance as participating in alternational code-switching in (30). (30a) and (30b) show the correspondence in every respect between the sentence transcribed in the ALUPEC and the one transcribed in Portuguese. (30c) shows that the CVC counterpart is isomorphic with Portuguese in the first part of the sentence, but is otherwise distinctive elsewhere by making use of the CVC preposition *ku* and the CVC quantifier *txeu*, the counterparts to Portuguese *com* and *muita*, respectively.

(30) a. *un prugrama ton konpléksu, ben konsebidu, kon muita transparênsia*
     a   program so complex well conceived with much transparency
     (transcribed in the ALUPEC)

    b. *um programa tão complexo, bem concebido, com muita transparênsia*
       (transcribed in Portuguese)

    c. un programa tan konpleksu, ben konsebidu, ku txeu transparénsia (CVC)
      'a program so complex, well conceived with a lot of transparency'
      (Veiga and Costa 2014: 8)

The excerpt in (31) shows the same parallel properties as the one in (30), except that the site of the alternational code-switching occurs after the preposition *na* 'in.' The site of the switch is clear in this case, as the CVC preposition does not vary for gender, whereas its Portuguese counterpart agrees in gender and number (*nos* [MASC. PL], *nas* [FEM. PL]) with the following noun. The preposition *no* [MASC. SG] in (31b) shows such agreement, in contrast to *na* in (31a).

(31) a. *na planu ki   foi   aprizentadu juntamenti kon   orsamentu*
     in plan that was presented   together   with budget

     ta   parse un vérba   pa   konstruson di skóla   sikundária
     ASP appear a   deposit for construction of school secondary

     di Santa Maria, di seis mil   kontu...
     of Santa Maria of six thousand contos... (transcribed in the ALUPEC)

    b. *no plano que foi aprizentado juntamente com o orçamento* (Portuguese)

    c. *na planu ki foi prezentadu juntu ku orsamentu ... (CVC)*
      'in the plan that was presented together with the budget, appears a money deposit for the construction of the secondary school of Santa Maria, for six thousand contos [former Portuguese currency].'
      (Veiga and Costa 2014: 8)

The code-switching patterns witnessed thus far attest to insertional, alternational code-switching and congruent lexicalization. We note that prepositions act as a privileged site for congruent lexicalization, either by single-handedly participating in the switch, as witnessed in example (29), or as a trigger (the starting point of the switch), as in (24). The generalization we would like to propose regarding the data at hand is that both insertional and alternational code-switching could be viewed in this case as integral to the overall strategy of congruent lexicalization; by this, we mean that code-switching, under all its forms and with respect to the examples examined in Costa's corpus, occurs when there is a similar mapping in the grammatical structure of the two languages, making the switch between them fairly seamless. We propose that congruent lexicalization is the dominant pattern and the engine behind speakers' choices of code-switching sites in Costa's corpus. In other words, whether speakers practice insertional or alternational code-switches, they tend to perform the switches whenever the structures between the two languages are congruent.

In the next set of examples, we shift our focus from the analysis of code-switching patterns to language change in CVC. We will argue that such a change may have been contact-induced at first, under the influence of Portuguese, but eventually became a case of language-internal development due to analogy; we elaborate on this point later in the chapter. The next examples concern complementizer phrases and display the consistent use of the Portuguese complementizer *que*, which appears in the form of *ki* in CVC.

In order to justify our interpretation of this feature as undergoing *change*, a brief background to the behavior of complementizers in CVC is necessary. In Baptista and Obata (2015), it is observed that CVC illocutionary verbs select the complementizer *ma*, as shown in (32a) and (32b), whereas non-illocutionary verbs typically select the complementizer *ki*, as seen in (33).

(32) a. *Kuze   ki   João   fra   ma   Maria   odja?*
        what   COMP   João   say   COMP   Maria   see
        'What did João say that Maria saw?

    b. *Undi   ki   bu   ta   pensa   ma   João   kunpra   libru?*
        where   COMP   you   ASP   think   COMP   João   buy   book
        'Where do you think that João bought the book?'

(33) *João   odja   ki   Maria   staba   xatiada.*
      João   see   that   Maria   was   upset
      'João saw that Maria was upset.'

However, Baptista (2002) observed that such a division of labor is becoming less clear-cut in CVC, even in monolingual speech. She noted in her corpus that verbs like *sabe* 'to know,' which is expected to occur with *ma* as an illocutionary verb (34), may also occur with *ki* (35):

(34) *Bu   ka   sabe   ma   nu   fronta?*   (RS-ST)   (Baptista 2002: 179)
      CL   NEG   know   COMP   we   insulted
      'Do you know that we were insulted?'

(35) *Nu   sabe   ki   nos pai   e   Sinhor Deus.* (RS-ST) (Baptista 2002: 179)
      we   know   COMP   our father   COP   Lord   God
      'We know that our Father is the Lord.'

Corroborating this observation, Veiga and Costa (2014) report on a number of verbs that select *ki* rather than *ma* in the deputies' speech excerpts. These authors present the use of *ki* as a case of code-switching (insertional), but closer examination may suggest instead two other possible scenarios. *Ki* may be viewed as a case of transfer from Portuguese, a change that has permeated both the speech of monolinguals and bilinguals alike. All the verbs listed in (36), (37), and (38) take *que* in Portuguese, shown in the (b) examples, whereas *ma* would be expected in CVC, as shown in the (c) examples. This would point to a case of contact-induced change. Another possibility could be a language internal development in which, through analogy, the subset of illocutionary verbs is starting to conform to the behavior of all the other verbs in the language by selecting *ki*. The examples (36), (37), and (38) found in Costa's corpus attest to the widespread change regarding the use of the complementizer in the language of bilingual speakers.

(36) a. *intende ki* (speech excerpt)
      b. *entender que* (Portuguese)
      c. *ntende ma* (CVC)
         'to understand that . . .' (Veiga and Costa 2014: 10)

(37) a. *garanti ki* (speech excerpt)
      b. *garantir que* (Portuguese)
      c. *garanti ma* (CVC)
         'to warrant that . . .' (Veiga and Costa 2014: 10)

(38) a. *atxa ki* (speech excerpt)
      b. *achar que* (Portuguese)
      c. *atxa ma* (CVC)
         'to find that . . .' (Veiga and Costa 2014: 10)

In addition to code-switching and transfer, we also found cases of borrowings in Costa's corpus. These could be interpreted as insertional code-switching (an analysis Veiga and Costa propose in their paper), but using the working definition we provide in section 33.2.1, whereby code-switching involves two grammars and borrowings only one, we choose instead to analyze them here as borrowings. These expressions may involve some degree of phonological adaptation; the fact that there is no indication from the corpus that the individuals who produced such utterances were fluent in the other language (French in (39), Latin in (40), and English in (41)) reinforces this point.

(39) *Na kumunikason   jurídiku, nu debe ten   sénpri preokupason di enprega*
      in   communication judicial   we must have always preoccupation of employment
      konseitu   própriu   y   adekuadu, kér-dizer: **le mot uste**
      concept   proper   and adequate, meaning: le mot juste
      'In judicial communication, we must always be concerned with employment, a
      proper and adequate concept, meaning: le mot juste.' (Veiga and Costa 2014: 4)

(40) *Konstituison   di   República   é   nos   Lei-Mãi,   nos* **Carta   Magna**[7]
      Constitution of   Republic   is our   law-mother   our   Carta   Magna
      'The Constitution of the Republic is our main law, our Carta Magna.'
      (Veiga and Costa 2014: 4)

---

[7] Note that the speaker has inverted the noun-adjective word order from the original Latin expression Magna Carta; the cause of the inversion is unclear.

(41) *Oji   N   ka   sta   ku   dispozison,   N   ka   sta   ku   **feeling**.*
      today I   NEG   be   with disposition,   I   NEG   be   with feeling
      'Today I am not well disposed, I don't have the feeling.'
      (Veiga and Costa 2014: 4)

Veiga and Costa argue in their paper that this type of code-switching/borrowing has an upgrading function, in that it brings CVC to the same level as the other languages. Referring back to the motivations for code-switching, discussed in section 33.3.3, we could identify various motivations for each of the preceding examples. Examples (39) and (40) could be responding to a lexical gap given that there are no direct equivalents to 'le mot juste' and 'Carta Magna' in CVC. In contrast, *feeling* in (41) has a CVC counterpart, *sentidu*, so it is plausible that the speaker may have used the English word to raise his or her status (the fourth motivation in section 33.3.3) by showing expertise in the English language.

In summary, the discussed examples of code-switching and transfer seem to reflect contact effects between CVC and Portuguese. Some of these contact effects could be interpreted as contact-induced change currently taking place in CVC under the influence of Portuguese. For instance, with respect to complementizers, one could propose that the change from *ma* to *ki* may be triggered by Portuguese, but this could also be interpreted as an instance of analogical change, due to speakers gradually neglecting to select *ma* with illocutionary verbs to generalize instead the use of *ki* to all verbs. There may also be a frequency effect at work in this particular situation: given that the majority of verbs in the language select *ki*, we could assume that it was only a matter of time before illocutionary verbs chose that path as well. However, as this is not a quantitative study, we cannot be too categorical on this point. In brief, complementizers could be interpreted as a domain where contact-induced change and language-internal change would conflate, hence illustrating a case of multiple causation (Thomason 2001).

One of our core findings is that the various code-switching strategies we identified all seem to be contributing to a general pattern of congruent lexicalization, in the sense that code-switching seems to occur when enabled (if not triggered) by isomorphic parallel structures in the two languages.

In the next section, we supplement this study of oral contact effects from Portuguese onto CVC by examining the effects of contact in the reverse direction, meaning from CVC onto Portuguese, but with two major differences. The first is that we examine reverse-contact effects from CVC onto Portuguese using a different modality, the writing of high schoolers. The second difference is that we document the process of transfer of L1 features onto L2, but transfer in this case may not reflect change in progress, in contrast to the previous section.

In sum, the next section is meant to document how contact effects can be observed in the writing of Portuguese by high-school students who are native speakers of CVC. These are errors reflecting transfer of L1 to L2 that are unlikely to trigger changes (for the time being at least) in the Portuguese variety spoken in Cape Verde islands. There are studies focusing on the Portuguese variety spoken in the archipelago, but we make no claim here that the transfer errors we document are participating in changes that are originating from CVC and impacting the local Portuguese variety. We reserve such study for further research.

33.5 Transfer from L1 to L2 or Simply L2 Acquisition Strategies?

In this section, we briefly examine how CVC may be influencing the Portuguese used in the classroom. We draw our data from Herbert Robalo's (2013) thesis, which specifically considers how twelfth-grade high-school students' native language influences their written Portuguese. We will see that it is not always very clear whether an error in the written Portuguese is the genuine result of transfer from CVC or whether it is the result of second-language strategies. In this section, as mentioned earlier, it is important to emphasize that the "errors" under consideration are not viewed as instantiating change in the Portuguese spoken in Cape Verde, but rather illustrate how CVC features may surface (via transfer) in the written Portuguese of high-school students. Such a broad view of contact has the advantage of bringing to light the bidirectional effects the two languages have on each other, albeit in different modalities.

The domains we focus on in Herbert Robalo's data are those of the verb infinitival forms and lack of agreement between nouns and adjectives specifically. We privilege these two domains in her data not only because they are an inherent part of the CVC grammar, but also because they instantiate strategies of second-language learning, making the identification of the source of students' errors more uncertain. This allows us to entertain the possibility of a possible convergence between these particular features of CVC grammar and strategies of L2 acquisition accounting for the pervasiveness of these features in high schoolers' written Portuguese. This is in keeping with Schuchardt's early observation (discussed in section 33.3.4) that outcomes of language contact and language acquisition are similar in nature. It also supports Mühlhäusler's (1986) and Odlin's (1989) position that explanations based on transfer and those based on universal tendencies are compatible and often lead to a rather robust multicausal account for the emergence of a given feature.

The examples we introduce in the following are meant to have an illustrative purpose and are representative of the great majority of the sample students' "errors" that Herbert Robalo reports in her thesis.

The following examples reflect the use of infinitival forms in some of the texts that the students were analyzing. In the annotation, the students' production is flagged by HS (high schooler), whereas the correct European Portuguese counterpart is flagged by EP (European Portuguese).

In (42a), the past tense of the matrix verb *dizer* 'to say,' which is *dizia* 'said,' should have triggered the use of past tense of the verb *conseguir* 'to succeed' in the embedded clause, which should have been *conseguia* in Portuguese, as in (42b). Instead, the student uses the uninflected verb form of the non-stative CVC verb *konsigi* (spelled here *consigui*) to convey past tense. As in most creole languages, the bare stems of stative verbs convey the present tense in CVC, whereas the bare stems of non-stative verbs convey anteriority (past tense reading). The student's use of the bare stem form of *konsigi* could be viewed as supporting the idea that transfer of the CVC verb, in form (uninflected) and in meaning (past tense interpretation), has occurred. In other words, the student's error can be accounted for by assuming that she or he has transferred this L1 feature onto the L2, the verb form carrying abstract features for anteriority and abstract number agreement. This is in contrast to the Portuguese example in (42b), in which overt agreement between the subject and the verb takes place in person, number, and tense.

(42) a. *Rousseau* **dizia** *que* *o* *homem* *não* **consigui** *resolver* *todos*
Rousseau said that the man NEG succeed solve all
os *problemas* (HS)
the problems

b. *Rousseau* *dizia* *que* *o* *homem* *não* **conseguia** *resolver* *todos*
Rousseau said that the man NEG succeed solve all
os *problemas* (EP)
the problems
'Rousseau said that man did not succeed to resolve all problems.'

In the example in (43), a clear infinitival form (and the same form that would be used in a CVC sentence) is used, instead of the Portuguese past subjunctive.

(43) *É* *preciso* **comunicar-lhes** *para* *o* *ser* *conhecidas* (HS)
is necessary communicate-to them for the be known

É *preciso* **comunicá-las** *para* *que* **sejam** *conhecidas* (EP)
is necessary communicate-them for be+ SUBJ known
'It is necessary to communicate to them [these issues] so that they be known.'

Herbert Robalo notes three issues with the HS sentence in (43). The first is that the student starts the sentence with the wrong verb form, ignoring the phonological rule according to which when a Portuguese verb ends in [r], [s], or [z], even if the following pronoun is dative, it takes on the accusative form of *lo* [MASC. SG], *la* [FEM. SG], *los* [MASC. PL], or *las* [FEM. PL], while the verb loses the infinitival ending 'r.' Instead of following this rule, the student leaves as is the overt infinitival marker on the verb and uses the dative form of the pronoun, rather than the accusative form. Finally, the student also uses the infinitival form of the verb *ser* 'to be' instead of the Portuguese subjunctive form.

We could add to Herbert Robalo's descriptive analysis that each of these features could be viewed as cases of transfer from CVC grammar. Indeed, the CVC equivalent to (43), which is (44), would require the infinitival form of both to 'communicate' *communicar* and 'be' *ser*. Given that the Portuguese phonological rule is absent from the CVC grammar, the student's error could be viewed as a case of negative transfer. The student is ignoring the Portuguese phonological rule that is absent in his or her language and chooses instead to transfer the dative form of the CVC pronoun, which is homophonous with the accusative form in the creole, but which is expected given that the verb 'communicate' involves in this case an indirect object.

(44) *É   presizu   komunika-s   pe's   ser   konhesidu* (CVC)
Is   necessary communicate-them[DAT] for+them be   known
'It is necessary to communicate them so that they be known.'

Sentences (42) and (43) reflect speakers' tendency to prefer bare verb forms or infinitival forms to conjugated forms. This could possibly point to the transfer of a general L1 feature to L2 in that CVC does not mark overtly agreement for person, number, or gender between subjects and verbs.

The following set of examples from Herbert Robalo's corpus further illustrates a general lack of agreement within the verbal domain, which also extends to the nominal domain.

To be more precise, the example in (45a), found in Herbert Robalo's corpus, reflects lack of agreement between the plural subject *as pessoas* 'the people' and the bare form of the verb *consigui* 'succeed.' Recall that in their bare forms, non-stative verbs in CVC carry the meaning of anteriority. However, *consigui* in (45) does not carry that meaning and looks more like an infinitival form. As such, one could argue that it reflects an L2 acquisition strategy; in such cases, learners tend to make abstraction of verb inflectional paradigms and rely instead on the infinitive forms of verbs. Note that the use of *consigui* in (45) contrasts from its use in (42), in which we argued that it reflected transfer (of meaning) due to its past tense interpretation.

(45) a. *A   pessoas   não consigui   fazer higiene em condições* (HSS)
the[SG] people[PL] NEG succeed[-AGR] make hygiene in conditions
'The people do not succeed in making conditions for hygiene.'

b. *As   pessoas   não conseguem   fazer higiene em condições* (EP)
the[PL] people[PL] NEG succeed[AGR] make hygiene in conditions
'The people do not succeed in making conditions for hygiene.'

The contrast between examples (42) and (45) shows that in some cases, one can argue for transfer (transfer of form and meaning), as in (42), whereas in others, learners are simply resorting to some basic L2 acquisition strategy, as in (45). In sum, when meaning is passed on, as in (42), one could reasonably argue for transfer, but in other cases, conclusions must remain tentative.

The contrast between examples (42) and (45) is a good illustration of Schuchardt's original point that outcomes of language contact and of language acquisition can be similar; this, in turn, can create a blurry line between effects of language contact and universal tendencies of language acquisition (Odlin 1989), as discussed in section 33.3.4.

The lack of verbal agreement between subjects and verbs, documented earlier, also affects the nominal domain. In that domain, as already discussed in section 33.4.1.2, determiners and nouns do not agree in number and, not surprisingly, adjectives do not agree with nouns. Lack of agreement in number between the (pro)noun and the adjective can be observed in example (46), produced in one of the students' writings in Herbert Robalo's corpus.

(46) a. *Eu   exigo   que   elas   sejam   respeitado.*   (HSS)
       I   demand   that   they   be[SUBJ]   respected[-PL]
       'I demand that they be respected.'

   b. *Eu   exijo   que   eles   sejam   respeitados*   (EP)
       I   demand   that   they   be[SUBJ]   respected[+PL]
       'I demand that they be respected.'

Absence of agreement is a common feature of CVC grammar; such absence of agreement is rampant in Herbert Robalo's corpus and could be interpreted in two ways. It could be analyzed as a case of negative transfer, in that students are transferring the lack of number agreement in their L1 grammar onto Portuguese, leading to the observed error. It could also be interpreted an L2 acquisition strategy whereby learners make abstraction of inflectional morphology on nouns, verbs, and in this case, adjectives.

The same lack of agreement that is observable between subjects and verbs, determiners and nouns, and nouns and adjectives can be observed between prepositions and the nouns they modify, in contrast to Portuguese, where such agreement takes place:

(47) a. *muito   obrigado   por   sua   compreensão.*   (HSS)
         very   thankful   for[-AGR]   your   understanding

   b. *muito   obrigado   pela   sua   compreensão.*   (EP)
         very   thankful   for[+FEM-SG]   your   understanding

   c. *mutu   obrigada   pa   bu   konpreenson.*   (CVC)
         very   thankful   for[-AGR]   your   understanding
         'I am very grateful for your understanding.'

This could be interpreted again in two ways: it could be viewed as a case of transfer, as prepositions in the CVC grammar do not agree with the nouns they modify, or as an L2 acquisition strategy, doing away with agreement requirements.

So far, all cases documented in Herbert Robalo's corpus point to transfer or L2 acquisition strategy, but one can also find illustrations of code-switching, attesting that code-switching is not exclusive to the realm of orality but can also be found in the written domain.

Consider a clear example of code-switching in the writing of one of the high-school students (48):

(48) a. ***Por   isso   es   decide   forma   um   contrato   social***   (HS)
          for   this   they   decide   form   a   contract   social

   b. ***Por   isu,   es   desidi   forma   un   kontratu   sosial***   (CVC)
          for   this   they   decide   form   a   contract   social

   c. *Por   isso   eles   decidiram   firmar   um   contrato   social*   (EP)
          for   this   they   decided to   form   a   social   contract
          'For this reason, they decided to form a social contract.'

The comparison between (48a) and (48b) shows the exact correspondence between the produced utterance and CVC, pointing to a clear case of code-switching, notwithstanding the different spelling. Interestingly for our purpose, the code-switching seems to have been favored by the isomorphic structure of this particular utterance in CVC and Portuguese. Congruent lexicalization seems to be the code-switching strategy of choice in both the oral and written modes.

33.6 SUMMARY

The research questions underlying this project are threefold. The focus of this chapter being the comparison of two contact settings in two different modes (oral and written) and involving bidirectional influences (Portuguese onto CVC, and CVC onto Portuguese), our main concerns were as follows: (1) What is the range and nature of contact phenomena that are observable in these two contact settings? (2) What are the types of code-switching strategies that speakers practice? (3) With regard to code-switching specifically, is there a detectable pattern to when speakers are more inclined to code-switch?

In response to the first question, we showed in Costa's study that the deputies' speech production in CVC is imbued with Portuguese features. Such features involve primarily code-switching from CVC into Portuguese, borrowings and transfer of Portuguese grammatical properties (mostly agreement patterns) onto CVC. In contrast, Herbert Robalo's study revealed that in the written mode, transfer was the dominant type of contact effect, this time from CVC onto Portuguese. With respect to code-switching strategies, we observed that while bilingual speakers in Costa's study practiced insertional, alternational code-switching and congruent lexicalization, a general pattern emerged from the examples under study: we propose that congruent lexicalization is the dominant pattern and the keystone behind speakers' choices of code-switching sites in Costa's corpus. We observe that whether speakers practice insertional or alternational code-switches, they tend to perform the switches whenever the structures between the two languages are congruent.

In Herbert Robalo's corpus, we noted that many of her examples illustrated transfer from CVC to Portuguese. The use of infinitival verb forms and lack of agreement in both the verbal and nominal domain were diagnosed at times as transfer (whenever the meaning of the form was clearly transferred) and at other times as an L2 acquisition strategy, but the distinction between the two was not clear in all cases.

In the next phase of this research, we will consider whether factors such as proficiency level and age would influence contact outcomes in the two modalities under consideration.

REFERENCES

Baptista, Marlyse. 2002. *The Syntax of Cape Verdean Creole*. Philadelphia; Amsterdam: John Benjamins.

Baptista, Marlyse, and Miki Obata 2015. Complementizer-alternation in creole languages: New evidence for spec-head agreement. *PAPIA: Revista Brasileira de Estudos Crioulos e Similares* 25(2): 155–176.

Costa, Sérgio. 2013. *Interferénsias di purtugês na kriolu: Análizi di atas di seson plenáriu di mês di Abril, Maiu, Junhu y Julhu di 2011*. Master's thesis, University of Cape Verde.

Grosjean, François. 2010. *Bilingual: Life and Reality*. Cambridge, MA: Harvard University Press.

Herbert Robalo, Lígia. 2013. *Fenómenos de interferência linguística no português escrito de alunos do 12⁰ ano da escola secundária cónego Jacinto Peregrino da Costa*. Master's thesis, University of Cape Verde.

Hoffmann, Charlotte. 1991. *Introduction to Linguistics*. New York: Routledge.

Muysken, Pieter. 1995. Code-switching and grammatical theory. In *One Speaker, Two Languages*, edited by Lesley Milroy and Pieter Muysken, 177–198. Cambridge: Cambridge University Press.

Muysken, Pieter. 2000. *Bilingual Speech: A Typology of Code-Mixing*. Cambridge: Cambridge University Press.

Muysken, Pieter. 2013. Language contact outcomes as the result of bilingual optimization strategies. *Bilingualism: Language and Cognition* 16: 709–730.

Odlin, Terence. 1989. *Language Transfer*. Cambridge: Cambridge University Press.

Mühlhäusler, Peter. 1986. *Pidgin and Creole Linguistics*. Oxford: Basil Blackwell.

Pires, H. 1995. Analyse contrastive de la flexion nominale du créole de Santiago (Cap-Vert). *Etudes Créoles* 18(1): 74–83.

Poplack, Shana, David Sankoff, and Chris Miller. 1988. The social correlates and linguistic processes of lexical borrowing and assimilation. *Linguistics* 26(1): 47–104.

Quint, Nicolas. 2000. *Grammaire de la Langue Cap-Verdienne, Etude Descriptive et Compréhensive du Créole Afro-Portugais des Iles du Cap-Vert*. Paris: L'Harmattan.

Schuchardt, Hugo. [1891] 1980. Indo-English. In *Pidgin and Creole Languages: Selected Essays by Hugo Schuchardt*, edited by Glenn G. Gilbert, 38–64. London: Cambridge University Press.

Thomason, Sarah. 2001. *Language Contact: An Introduction*. Washington, DC: Georgetown University Press.

Van Dulm, Ondeen. 2007. *The Grammar of English-Afrikaans Code-Switching: A Feature Checking Account*. CLS. Netherlands: LOT.

Veiga, Manuel. 2000. *Le Créole du Cap-Vert: Etude Grammaticale, Descriptive et Contrastive*. Paris: Karthala.

Veiga, Manuel, and Sérgio Costa. 2014. Code-switching no Crioulo Caboverdiano- CCV: O positivo e o Negativo). Manuscript.

Weinreich, Uriel. 1953. *Languages in Contact: Findings and Problems*. New York: Mouton.

Winford, Donald. 2003. *An Introduction to Contact Linguistics*. Malden: Blackwell.

INDEX

·················

Note: Page numbers in *italic* denote tables

'L1' and 'L2' are used to indicate references to 'first language' and 'second language' respectively

'NENA' denotes 'Northeastern Neo-Aramaic'

A

Abaev, Vasilij 469, 474, 476, 482, 484
abbreviations and initialized signs 684–6
Aboriginal English 597, 598–600
accommodation
   endangered languages 250–1
   grammatical 360–5
Acehnese 77–8, 80, 81
acronyms, borrowed 536–7
adaptation 62, 75, 87, 88
adoption 56, 60, 79, 144, 356, 543, 610, 723
adult L2 acquisition 174; *see also* language
   shift
African languages 83, 713
   and English 125, 288, 298
   and Spanish 399
   see also Arabic; mixed languages; North
     African languages; West Africa(n)
Afrikaans 16, 285
Afro-Asiatic hypothesis 339–40; *see also*
   Uralic
Aikhenvald, Alexandra Y. 6, 15, 56, 126
Aitchison, Jean 215, 217, 234
Äiwoo 627–42
Akhvakh 486
Akkadian 21–2, 311, 495
Alan 469
Alaskan Yupik 647
Albanian 112–13, 125, 146
Aleut, *see* Unangam Tunuu (Aleut)
Algonquian 3, 9, 18
Alleyne, Mervyn 289, 298
allophones 76

Alqosh 503–4, 506, 507–8
Alsea 10
alternation 619
American Norwegian 250
American Signed Language (ASL) 5, 679–89
Amerindian languages 63, 313, 314–16,
   398–9, 644
   Algonquian 3, 9, 18
   see also Mexico/Mexican
Andalusian Arabic 391–3
Andamanese 10
Anderson, Gregory D. S. 5, 234
Angas-Goemai, *see* Goemai
Anglicisms 198, 200
Anglo-American culture, influence of 168, 549
Anglo-Norman 342–5, 383
Angloromani 312, 313–14, 316–17
Anglo-Saxon 166
Angolar 311
Ansaldo, Umberto 186–7
Arabic 4, 6, 14, 22–5, 76, 106, 143, 391–2
   code-switching 63
   creoles and pidgins 268, 269, 284
   influence on Berber 451–62
   Maghrebi 452, 455–6, 460
   and Malayalam 525
   morphology and syntax 456–62
   and NENA 494, 495, 498–513
   phonology 454–6
   Qur'an 22
   sound loans 79, 80–1
   Standard 453–4
Aragonese 167